PSYCHWARE

PSYCHWARE: A Reference Guide to Computer-Based Products for Behavioral Assessment in Psychology, Education, and Business

COMPILED AND EDITED BY

Samuel E. Krug, Ph.D.

TEST CORPORATION OF AMERICA • KANSAS CITY, MISSOURI
Distributed exclusively to libraries in North America by the Gale Research
Company, Book Tower, Detroit, Michigan 48226

COPYRIGHT/TRADEMARK ACKNOWLEDGEMENTS

The sample reports are reprinted here by kind permission of the copyright holders. For details, please see the individual product samples.
APPLE is a registered trademark of APPLE COMPUTER, INC. IBM-PC is a registered trademark of IBM Corp. Minnesota Multiphasic Personality Inventory, MMPI, and the Minnesota Report are trademarks of the University of Minnesota Press. Timeline is a trademark of the Institute for Personality and Ability Testing, Inc. Adult Personality Inventory is a trademark of MetriTech, Inc. TRS-80 is a registered trademark of Radio Shack, Inc. CP/M is a registered trademark of Digital Research Corporation. ASSIST is a trademark of American Guidance Service. MMPI: Computer Version 2.0 and 16 Personality Factor Test: Computer Version are trademarks of Psychological Assessment Resources. MICROTEST, Sentry Plus, and Sentry 3000 are trademarks of National Computer System.

NOTICE

Every effort has been made to ensure the accuracy of the contents of this book. If any errors are detected, please notify the publisher so that the information can be corrected in future editions.

LIBRARY OF CONGRESS CATALOGING IN PUBLICATION DATA

Krug, Samuel E.
   Psychware: a reference guide to computer-based products for behavioral assessment in psychology, education, and business.

   Includes indexes.
   1. Behavioral assessment—Data processing—Catalogs. 2. Psychodiagnostics—Data Processing—Catalogs. 3. Educational tests and measurements—Data processing—Catalogs. 4. Vocational guidance—Data processing—Catalogs. 5. Personnel management—Data processing—Catalogs.
I. Title.
BF39.5.K78   1984   155.2′8   84-16461
ISBN 0-9611286-5-8

Printed in the United States of America

CONTENTS

ACKNOWLEDGEMENTS

I wish to thank Raymond W. Kulhavy who assisted greatly in the early stages of this project. I am grateful for my wife Mimi's help as she read more about computer-based products than she ever intended in the course of working on this book. The staff members of Test Corporation of America were uniformly helpful, stimulating, and professional. I appreciate the consideration they showed me while we worked on this project.

INTRODUCTION

SOLID STATE PSYCHOLOGY

The introduction of radiographic techniques at the turn of the century led to exciting and rapid developments in both the science and practice of medicine. Suddenly, physicians were able to analyze problems with greater sophistication and in a way that greatly improved their diagnostic accuracy and treatment effectiveness. Medical progress accelerated dramatically.

Psychology now seems to be experiencing a similar phenomenon. For many years, behavioral science was identified with the technology of animal and physics laboratories. This isn't at all surprising, since scientific psychology emerged from these very laboratories in the late 19th century. But, in the last few decades there has been a major shift in technology and APPLES are now nearly as common as activity cages.

In the area of human assessment, computers have played a particularly significant role. Most modern test construction would not have been possible without the help of computers. The management of massive volumes of normative data for the Strong-Campbell Interest Inventory, the analysis and reduction of a 3000-item source pool for the Personality Research Form, the development of the mathematically sophisticated personality model underlying Cattell's 16 Personality Factor Questionnaire—none of these would be possible without computers.

Perhaps because computers were first introduced as *number crunchers*, there is a tendency on the part of many people to think of their contribution to contemporary assessment solely in terms of convenience, economy, or speed. Like Sherlock Holmes' faithful assistant, Dr. Watson, the computer is perceived as a patient, perhaps naive, but always loyal second to the more insightful, penetrating clinician. The computer is only a *scoring machine*, simply doing clerical tasks more quickly than could be done by hand.

The fact is that at the present time an increasingly large number of assessment devices are not really hand scorable any more, at least not in any practical sense. For example, how long would it take to score the hundreds of scales known to exist in the Minnesota Multiphasic Personality Inventory (MMPI) item pool or even the 60-70 typically calculated in a computer-based MMPI interpretation? The Executive Profile Survey employs a scoring method that requires test users to multiply 94 item responses by each of 11 separate arrays of decimal weights to produce the test profile. The Jenkins Activity Survey uses a highly complex set of weights developed by discriminant function methodology to maximize the differences between coronary prone and non-coronary prone individuals.

Data Base Management

It is not only in the efficient execution of complex scoring algorithms that the computer makes its contribution to assessment. In slightly more than a century since research on tests began in earnest, that research has led to a knowledge explosion. The eight Mental Measurements Yearbooks now published catalogue approximately 60,000 research references involving more than 1,000 different tests (Buros, 1978). It is increasingly difficult for the unassisted test user to access even a small portion of this accumulation of information reliably and consistently. Like the sorcerer's apprentice the test user faces an ever-increasing, uncontrollable, and bewildering array of information.

But, the indexing, storage, and a retrieval task is easy for the computer. Consequently, it is a relatively trivial matter, for example, to score and report 100 to 200 MMPI scales beyond the basic clinical and validity scales. A vast number of empirically tested decision rules can be evaluated in microseconds. Extensive statement libraries can be developed, maintained, and reviewed. In short, professionally developed software can add significantly to the amount of useful information derived from a single test protocol.

Still, the computer is not valuable in the area of assessment simply because it adds powerful data management capabilities to an otherwise efficient scoring unit. It has been 30 years since Paul Meehl (1954) first assembled evidence to suggest that actuarial or statistical prediction, like that done by computer interpretive programs, is frequently superior to clinical prediction. The simple fact is that computers are more consistent than humans in following well-defined decision rules. Kleinmuntz (1963) showed that a computer program written to categorize people as well-adjusted or poorly-adjusted on the basis of test scores outperformed all ten clinicians against which it was compared—even the one on whose performance the program was modeled. Goldberg (1970) has also shown that statistical models of clinicians generally outperform the clinicians themselves.

To summarize, the tests currently available to us represent increasingly sophisticated products of assessment and computer technology. They are complex analog-to-digital converters—instruments that take people and convert them into arrays of numbers. They require correspondingly sophisticated technologies to handle the reciprocal conversion process that transforms the number arrays back into a format—usually that of a verbal report—that directly communicates information to a clinician, counselor, or interviewer.

Computer-Based Interpretation—Past, Present, and Future

The first instruments to become targets for computer-based interpretations appear to have been personality tests. Among the earliest attempts to generate electronic reports were those carried out by Swenson and Pierson (1964) with the MMPI. The actual program appeared to have been in use for five years at the time of their publication. That would make the first computer-based interpretations operational about a decade after computer hardware began to appear in the marketplace and only a few years after software—especially programming languages—developed beyond relatively primitive assemblers.

At roughly the same point in time, parallel work was being done with the 16 Personality Factor Questionnaire by Eber (1964), the Weschler Adult Intelligence Scale by Kleinmuntz (1982), and the Rorschach by Piotrowski (1964). Campbell's research with Strong's Vocational Interest Blanks led to the development of an instrument that could only be scored by computer.

During the last decade, measurement experts have begun to develop the test administration potential of the computer (Johnson & Johnson, 1981) in addition to the scoring and interpretation capabilities. The benefits of on-line testing at first appeared to be simply greater control of reaction time and immediate availability of scored output. But, within a very short time new and perhaps unintended benefits began to appear. For example, the computer may be a particularly powerful administrator of tests for neurological deficits that require shape or symbol manipulation. Measurement error arising from administration procedures in the case of tests that require complex presentation of stimuli, tightly controlled time limits, etc., can be dramatically reduced. Electronic capabilities open up an entire new horizon with respect to the assessment dimensions that can be explored and the measurement process itself.

Although the shift to computer applications in assessment began less than a quarter century ago, developments have been rapid and dynamic. This first attempt to compile a directory of relevant products resulted in the identification of more than 190 products. This number is impressive considering that we are only in the second generation of a technology that did not even exist 20 years ago. The variety and scope of products available within the next few years seems almost certain to be even more dramatic.

USING THIS DIRECTORY

This directory is designed to identify and describe computer-based products that have applications for assessing or modifying human behavior. To be included, a particular application generally has to go beyond simple test scoring. Consequently, most of the products included here would most appropriately be described as *computer-based interpretations*. A large number involve computer testing as well, presenting test items or stimulus material via the console.

Product listings are presented in alphabetic order by product title. Each listing is divided into seven parts: name, supplier, product category, applications, sale restrictions, type/cost of service provided, and product description. Most of the information was obtained in response to a questionnaire sent to service providers. Only minor editorial changes were made to the material submitted. In a few instances the descriptions needed to be shortened because of space limitations. In other cases, some additional comment was necessary to explain unusual price structures or special sale restrictions.

The remainder of this Section further explains the seven parts which produce a typical product listing and provides definitions of terms used throughout these listings and additional information that will be helpful in using the directory most effectively.

Name

A number of product titles appear at first glance to be identical. *Minnesota Multiphasic Personality Inventory,* for example, appears at least eight times. But each listing corresponds to one product offering by one supplier. In a very few cases, these are identical products available from more than one supplier and the only real choice is between location, or perhaps reputation, of the suppliers. More often, the product is different in some important way, even if the name is the same. For example, a number of products that are built on the same test differ in the style of report offered, in the type of service provided, in cost, in terms of whether the test is administered on line or not, etc.

Product Category

Up to five classifications may be reported for a single product. When more than one category is indicated, the order of presentation is the order of rated importance by the supplier. In most cases, however, only a single classification was selected. The list of possible categories is as follows:

Career/Vocational. This is used principally to describe products that emphasize career choice or that deal with concepts that have special relevance for selection or promotion decisions in the industrial context. This is the primary designation for 15% of the products listed. An additional 6% give this as one of two or more applicable designations.

Cognitive/Ability. This category is used to describe products that emphasize dimensions of intelligence, abilities, or aptitudes. In a few instances, the products consider achievement variables—scholastic or linguistic. But, most products falling within this category would more correctly be described as aptitude measures. This is the primary designation for 19% of the products listed. An additional 3% give this as one of two or more applicable designations.

Interest/Attitudes. There is some overlap between this category and the Career/Vocational area, but products with this designation tend to deal with a broader range of interests than just vocational interests such as lifestyle concerns and personal belief systems. This is the primary category for 6% of the products listed and an additional 7% give this as one of two or more applicable designations.

Motivation/Needs. Most of the products which use this designation emphasize dynamic variables, such as Murray's list of manifest needs. Very few entries (2%) listed this as the primary designation, but approximately 8% selected this as one applicable category.

Personality. Products in this category emphasize trait or temperament concepts, and this is by far the most frequently selected product category. Almost half (49%) of the entries use this as the primary designation and an additional 3% as one applicable category.

Structured Interview. The products which receive this designation (8%) are often described as *intake interviews*. The questions used are not necessarily thought to assess personality characteristics as much as background variables: age, education, work history, etc. Although called an interview, the products in this category are almost always self-administered by the examinee.

Utility. Products in this category (1%) are intended to assist in assessment activity, but are not thought of primarily as assessment devices. The most typical product in this category is a report writer that integrates information from other sources into a verbal report.

Applications.

Up to five applications, from a list of seven, may be employed to describe the kinds of uses for which the product was developed or to which it may be put. The rank of presentation is usually the order of importance as determined by the supplier. The categories used are as follows:

Behavioral Medicine. This category is used to describe products which emphasize physical health issues. Presumably any instrument which considers psychological adjustment could be construed to have medical implications, but this category has been reserved for those products which deal more directly with health characteristics, such as Type A behavior, physical symptoms, etc. This is the primary application area for 5% of all products listed and one of several application areas for another 1%.

Clinical Assessment/Diagnosis. This is the primary application area for 47% of all products listed and one of several application areas for another 17%. The typical product in this category emphasizes dimensions of psychological characteristics—especially aberrant characteristics—and psychodiagnostic concepts.

Educational Evaluation/Planning. This title is used to describe applications in the school setting that have to do with assessing educational outcomes and projecting educational needs. With regard to the latter issue there is some overlap with career planning and vocational guidance applications since career choice and educational needs are necessarily closely connected. This is the primary application area for 8% of all products listed and one of several application areas for another 18%.

Personal/Marriage/Family Counseling. This category overlaps substantially with the Clinical Assessment area. One difference between those that list this rather than Clinical Assessment as the primary application area appears to be a greater emphasis on less aberrant assessment dimensions. This is the primary application area for 9% of all products listed and one of several application areas for another 38%.

Personnel Selection/Evaluation. This application area includes products that have immediate relevance for screening of potential employees or placement of employed personnel. This is the primary application area for 8% of all products listed and one of several applications for another 21%.

Training/Development. This area emphasizes training or instructional technology (e.g., behavior change) rather than assessment technology. This is the primary area for 4% of all products listed and one of several application areas for another 4%.

Vocational Guidance/Counseling. Products listed in this area emphasize assessment dimensions especially relevant to career choice and vocational success. This is the primary application area for 19% of all products listed and one of several application areas for another 16%.

Sale Restrictions

Four categories are listed to provide some indication as to whether the sale of a product is restricted in any way by the supplier. Restrictions are usually based on the educational, training, or other professional qualifications of the purchaser.

American Psychological Association guidelines. Although the guidelines do not address computer-based products in detail, the presumption is that products so classified would not normally be sold to individuals who do not have formal training and experience in the assessment area. A higher level of training (e.g., a Ph.D., M.D., or M.S.W., for example) would be expected for an instrument used for clinical diagnosis.

Qualified Professional. In most cases it would appear to have approximately the same meaning as the American Psychological Association guidelines. However, it seems to be used by suppliers to suggest that the principal product user is in some profession other than psychology (e.g., psychiatry, social work, etc.).

Authorized/Certified Representatives. Some suppliers have selected this category to indicate that this product is only available through certain individuals or agencies. Whenever possible, details of the restrictions are provided in the Product Description area.

None. Products so designated are presumably available to anyone without regard to training or experience.

Service Type/Cost

Three types of service are classfied here. For each category, there is a statement of availability, the unit cost, and an indication of whether discounts are provided for quantity purchases.

Cost figures are given for single purchases. In a number of cases, particularly when mail-in service is provided, minimum order charges make this figure substantially higher than the *average* price at which the service is usually provided. Discounts of 40 to 50% are available from many suppliers. However, this kind of discount is usually obtained only by an advance purchase of prepaid coupons in the amount of $100 or more or some similar purchase guarantee. Complete price schedules are available from the suppliers.

Mail-In. This category is used to describe the kind of service in which answer sheets or some other response document must be sent to a remote data processing center which, in turn, returns reports to service users. Some suppliers offer alternatives to the U.S. Postal System (e.g., United Parcel Service, Air Express services, etc.) at somewhat higher prices for quicker turnaround. Mail-in service is provided for 42% of products listed.

Teleprocessing. This category is used to describe the kind of service in which responses are transmitted electronically to a remote processing facility. Return is virtually instantaneous. This kind of service usually requires some kind of user investment in terminal and/or data transmission equipment. Teleprocessing support is provided for 15% of products listed.

Local. This category is used to describe products that operate on user-owned (or user-leased) equipment without the necessity of transmitting data to and from a remote data processing facility. Most of the products included in this category are designed to operate on microcomputers. Local service is provided for 71% of the products listed.

Product Description

Each entry concludes with a brief description of the product. Information was provided by the supplier, catalogs, and other promotional literature. Some editing was done because of space limitations.

The descriptions are intended to provide a summary of the main features of each product. In addition, this space is used to provide, when necessary, clarification of specific issues with regard to product availability or pricing.

Product Samples

Reproductions of actual samples in reduced format are provided for most products described in *Psychware*. A few products were so long that only selected pages could be included and that fact is noted in the instances where this has occurred. Occasionally, a product is available from more than one source in identical or essentially identical form. To conserve space, only one sample is shown of a given product.

REFERENCES

Buros, O.K. (Ed.). (1978). *The eighth mental measurements yearbook.* Highland Park, NJ: The Gryphon Press.

Eber, H.W. (1964). Computer interpretation of the 16 PF test. Paper presented to the American Psychological Association, Los Angeles.

Goldberg, L.R. (1970). Man vs. model of man: A rationale, plus some evidence for a method of improving on clinical inference. *Psychological Bulletin, 73,* 422-432.

Johnson, J.H., & Johnson, K.N. (1981). Psychological consideration related to the development of computerized testing stations. *Behavior Research Methods and Instrumentation, 13,* 421-424.

Kleinmuntz, B. (1963). MMPI decision rules for the identification of college maladjustment: A digital computer approach. *Psychological Monographs, 77.*

Kleinmuntz, B. (1982). *Personality and psychological assessment.* New York: St. Martin's Press.

Meehl, P.E. (1954). *Clinical versus statistical prediction.* Minneapolis: University of Minnesota Press.

Piotrowski, Z. (1964). Digital computer interpretation of ink-blot test data. *Psychiatric Quarterly, 38,* 1-26.

Swenson, W.M. & Pearson, J.S. (1964). Automation techniques in personality assessment: A frontier in behavioral science and medicine. *Methods of Information in Medicine, 3,* 34-36.

PRODUCT LISTINGS

NAME: Adjective Check List

SUPPLIER: NCS/Professional Assessment Services
P.O. Box 1416
Minneapolis, MN 55440
(800) 328-6759

PRODUCT CATEGORY

Personality

PRIMARY APPLICATIONS

Clinical Assessment/Diagnosis
Personal/Marriage/Family Counseling

SALE RESTRICTIONS American Psychological Association Guidelines

SERVICE TYPE/COST	Type	Available	Cost	Discount
	Mail-In	Yes	$3.25	Yes
	Teleprocessing	Yes	$3.25	Yes
	Local	No		

PRODUCT DESCRIPTION

The ADJECTIVE CHECK LIST is a standard method for assessing the personal attributes of clients or research subjects. It has its primary applications in personality assessment and psychometric research. The 300 adjectives require an 8th-grade reading level and about 15-20 minutes to complete. The items are scored on 37 scales (personality dimensions) including four Method of Response scales, 15 Need scales, nine Topical scales, five Transactional scales, and four Origence-Intelligence scales. The single page report records and plots all scores on clearly defined scales for easy interpretation.

THE ADJECTIVE CHECK LIST

by Harrison G. Gough, Ph.D. and Alfred B. Heilbrun, Jr., Ph.D.

ID= 22222222   SEX= FEMALE   DATE= 13-APR-84   NCS CODE= 736-0004

Standard Scores

	Raw Score	Std Score	0	10	20	30	40	50	60	70	80	90	100
Modus Operandi scales													
1. NO. CKD (no. of adj. checked)	91	44						X					
2. FAV (no. of favorable adjective)	39	40					X						
3. UNFAV (no. of unfavorable adj.)	6	48						X					
4. COM (communality)	14	48						X					
Need scales													
5. ACH (achievement)	9	46						X					
6. DOM (dominance)	2	45						X					
7. END (endurance)	7	48						X					
8. ORD (order)	2	42					X						
9. INT (intraception)	13	48						X					
10. NUR (nurturance)	11	44					X						
11. AFF (affiliation)	15	38					X						
12. HET (heterosexuality)	4	38					X						
13. EXH (exhibition)	-3	43					X						
14. AUT (autonomy)	-1	45					X						
15. AGG (aggression)	-4	50						X					
16. CHA (change)	7	55							X				
17. SUC (succorance)	-1	44					X						
18. ABA (abasement)	-1	46					X						
19. DEF (deference)	2	48						X					
Topical scales													
20. CRS (counseling readiness)	4	52							X				
21. S-CN (self-control)	-1	48						X					
22. S-CFD (self-confidence)	1	35				X							
23. P-ADJ (personal adjustment)	2	32				X							
24. ISS (ideal self)	9	58							X				
25. CPS (creative personality)	1	44					X						
26. MLS (military leadership)	-1	24			X								
27. MAS (masculine attributes)	11	66								X			
28. FEM (feminine attributes)	6	24			X								
Transactional Analysis scales													
29. CP (critical parent)	9	56							X				
30. NP (nurturing parent)	5	43					X						
31. A (adult)	5	47						X					
32. FC (free child)	5	53						X					
33. AC (adapted child)	0	60							X				
Origence-Intellectence scales													
34. A-1 (high O, low I)	-7	-2	X										
35. A-2 (high O, high I)	7	52						X					
36. A-3 (low O, low I)	4	29				X							
37. A-4 (low O, high I)	7	39					X						

0   10   20   30   40   50   60   70   80   90   100

Standard Scores

Scored by NATIONAL COMPUTER SYSTEMS, P.O. Box 1294, Minneapolis, Minnesota 55440

4 *psychware*

BASIC SOURCES

Complete information about the 37 standard scales of the Adjective Check List (ACL), normative data for nearly 10,000 subjects, and summaries of the significant research and interpretational findings may be found in:

H.G. Gough & F. Gendre (1982). Manuel de la liste d'adjectifs - Adjective Check List - (A.C.L). Paris: Les Editions du Centre de Psychologie Appliquée.

H.G. Gough & A.B. Heilbrun, Jr. (1980). The Adjective Check List bibliography. Palo Alto, California: Consulting Psychologists Press.

H.G. Gough & A.B. Heilbrun, Jr. (1983). The Adjective Check List manual - 1983 edition. Palo Alto, California: Consulting Psychologists Press.

H.G. Gough, A.B. Heilbrun, Jr., & M. Fioravanti (1980). Manuale della versione italiana dell'Adjective Check List. Firenze: Organizzazioni Speciali.

USEFUL REFERENCES

E. Costantini & K.H. Craik (1980). Personality and politicians: California party leaders, 1960-1976. Journal of Personality and Social Psychology, 38, 641-661.

F. Gendre, M. Lavoëgie, & H.G. Gough (1982). Validité conceptuelle de l'Adjective Check List (ACL): Une étude factorielle interdomaine de l'Adjective Check List et de l'inventaire psychologique de californie (CPI). Le Travail Humain, 45, 223-240.

H.G. Gough (1960). The Adjective Check List as a personality assessment research technique. Psychological Reports, 6, 107-122.

H.G. Gough (1979). A creative personality scale for the Adjective Check List. Journal of Personality and Social Psychology, 37, 1398-1405.

H.G. Gough, M. Fioravanti, & R. Lazzari (1983). Some implications of self versus ideal-self congruence on the revised Adjective Check List. Journal of Personality and Social Psychology, 44, 1214-1220.

A.B. Heilbrun, Jr. (1959). Validation of a need scaling technique for the Adjective Check List. Journal of Consulting Psychology, 23, 347-351.

A.B. Heilbrun, Jr. (1968). Counseling readiness and the problem-solving behavior of clients. Journal of Consulting and Clinical Psychology, 32, 131-136.

A.B. Heilbrun, Jr. (1982). Psychological scaling of defensive cognitive styles on the Adjective Check List. Journal of Personality Assessment, 46, 495-505.

E.E. Jones & C.L. Zoppel (1979). Personality differences among Blacks in Jamaica and the United States. Journal of Cross-Cultural Psychology, 10, 435-456.

G.S. Welsh (1975). Creativity and intelligence: A personality approach. Chapel Hill: University of North Carolina Institute for Research in Social Science.

J.E. Williams & D.L. Best (1982). Measuring sex stereotypes. Beverly Hills, California: Sage Publications.

K.B. Williams & J.E. Williams (1980). The assessment of transactional analysis ego states via the Adjective Check List. Journal of Personality Assessment, 4, 120-129.

Scored by NATIONAL COMPUTER SYSTEMS, P.O. Box 1294, Minneapolis, Minnesota 55440

NAME: Adjective Check List

SUPPLIER: PSYCH Systems, Inc.
600 Reisterstown Road
Baltimore, MD 21208
(800) 368-3366

PRODUCT CATEGORY	PRIMARY APPLICATIONS
Personality	Clinical Assessment/Diagnosis Personal/Marriage/Family Counseling

SALE RESTRICTIONS   Qualified Professional

SERVICE TYPE/COST	Type	Available	Cost	Discount
	Mail-In	No		
	Teleprocessing	No		
	Local	Yes	See Below	

PRODUCT DESCRIPTION

The ADJECTIVE CHECK LIST was developed as a rapid means of describing an individual in terms of words and ideas commonly used in everyday life. People taking the ACL select from the list of adjectives those which best describe themselves.

The Psych Systems ACL program administers, scores, and provides a printout of test results. In the report, the adjectives selected as self descriptive are grouped into five categories: Personal Effectiveness, Assertiveness, Sociability, Personal Adjustment, and Individuality. Within each category the trait is defined, followed by a list of the individual's self-descriptive adjectives which are positively associated with the trait and those which are negatively associated with the trait.

A variety of instructional formats can be followed. Clients may be asked to complete an ACL as they would like to be. In relationship counseling couples may be asked to describe both themselves and each other.

Psych Systems programs operate on the IBM PC-XT, COMPAQ Plus, Dec Professional 350, and most DEC PDP-11 systems. Various hardware/ software configurations are available directly from Psych Systems, with single-user systems starting at approximately $12,000. A per test fee also applies.

```
-----------------------------------
|         |                       |
|  ACL    |   Adjective Check List |
|         |                       |
-----------------------------------
```

The Adjective Check List consists of 300 adjectives which may be
used to describe a person's characteristics or attributes. It may be
used by an individual as a self-evaluation.

The report which follows is a summary of the adjectives selected by this
person as self-descriptive. The adjectives are grouped according to
relevant personality dimensions. It should be kept in mind that the
adjectives represent the individual's self-description and not an external
assessment. The use of this computerized report should be restricted to
qualified professionals in conjunction with a clinical evaluation. No
decisions should be based solely upon the contents of this report.

The computer program generating this report was designed by Psych
Systems, Inc., Baltimore, Maryland 21208. Copyright (C) 1984 by
Psych Systems, Inc. The Adjective Check List is reproduced by
permission. Copyright (C) 1952, 1965, 1980, 1983 by Consulting
Psychologists Press, Incorporated, 577 College Avenue, Palo Alto,
California 94306. No portion of the ACL may be reproduced by any
process without prior written permission of the publisher. All
rights reserved.

The adjectives selected as self-descriptive by this individual are grouped into five categories: Personal Effectiveness, Assertiveness, Sociability, Individuality and Personality Adjustment.

Within each category, the trait is defined, followed by a list of this individual's self-descriptive adjectives which are positively associated with the trait and those which are negatively associated with the trait.

PERSONAL EFFECTIVENESS

Definition: People high on Personal Effectiveness are resourceful, resolute and conscientious. They tend to be productive, work-oriented people who set goals for themselves and persist until they are attained. They value intellect, rational thinking, and self discipline. Personal Effectiveness is associated with three item clusters: Achievement, Endurance, and Order.

The following adjectives checked by this person are positively associated with Personal Effectiveness :

ambitious	deliberate	dependable	enterprising
enthusiastic	independent	industrious	intelligent
organized	perservering	stable	steady

The following adjectives checked by this person are negatively associated with Personal Effectiveness :

hurried	indifferent	reckless	shiftless

ASSERTIVENESS

Definition: People high on Assertiveness are ascendant, demanding and strong willed. They tend to be ambitious, determined and forceful people who seek positions of leadership and compete vigorously. Assertiveness is associated with three item clusters: Dominance, Exhibition, and Aggression.

The following adjectives checked by this person are positively associated with Assertiveness :

aggressive	ambitious	arrogant	clever
demanding	dominant	enterprising	excitable
opinionated	outspoken	sarcastic	

The following adjectives checked by this person are negatively associated with Assertiveness :

calm	discreet	indifferent	reflective
reserved	submissive	withdrawn	

SOCIABILITY

Definition: People high on Sociability are gregarious and compassionate with a capacity for close relationships. They tend to be cheerful, cooperative and adaptable, and they are comfortable in social situations. Sociability is associated with two item clusters: Nurturance and Affiliation.

The following adjectives checked by this person are positively associated with Sociability :

appreciative	attractive	cheerful	considerate
contented	cooperative	dependable	friendly
helpful	loyal	optimistic	trusting
warm			

The following adjectives checked by this person are negatively associated with Sociability :

arrogant	indifferent	sarcastic

INDIVIDUALITY

Definition: Persons high on Individuality tend to be imaginative, ingenious and unconventional. They are autonomous self-starters who sometimes act independently of social expectations. They tend to be spontaneous and to take pleasure in change, variety and new experiences. Individuality is associated with three item clusters: Autonomy, Change and Introspection (Need to understand self and others).

The following adjectives checked by this person are positively associated with Individuality :

adventurous	aggressive	calm	considerate
daring	enthusiastic	frank	independent
individualistic	intelligent	interests wide	opinionated
outspoken	reflective		

The following adjectives checked by this person are negatively associated with Individuality :

cautious	contented	dependable	indifferent
steady	submissive	withdrawn	

ADJUSTMENT

Definition: People high on Adjustment have a positive attitude toward life, enjoy being with others, and are able to establish meaningful relationships. They feel capable and self confident about their ability to achieve their goals. Adjustment is associated with three item clusters: Ideal Self, Self-Confidence, and Personal Adjustment.

The following adjectives checked by this person are positively associated with Adjustment :

artistic	attractive	calm	clever
considerate	enterprising	enthusiastic	good-looking
handsome	healthy	industrious	intelligent
perservering	trusting	warm	

The following adjectives checked by this person are negatively associated with Adjustment :

arrogant	commonplace	excitable	moody
reserved	stubborn	submissive	withdrawn

The categories listed in the report are made up of specific item clusters or scales. The definition of each category and scale follows.

  I. Personal Effectiveness: Resourceful, Resolute, and Goal Oriented

      A. Achievement - striving to be outstanding in worthwhile activities
      B. Endurance - persisting in any task
      C. Order - being organized and thinking ahead

 II. Assertiveness: Ascendent, Demanding, and Strong Willed

      A. Dominance - seeking leadership, influence and control
      B. Exhibition - seeking attention from others
      C. Aggression - attacking, overwhelming or harming others

III. Sociability: Compassionate, Optimistic, and Attentive to others

      A. Nurturance - providing sympathy, support or benefits to others
      B. Affiliation - seeking to maintain close personal relationships

 IV. Individuality: Imaginative, Ingenious, and Unconventional

      A. Intraception - attempting to understand one's self or others
      B. Autonomy - acting independently of others and social expectations
      C. Change - seeking new experiences and avoiding routine

  V. Personal Adjustment

      A. Self-Confidence - feeling able to achieve goals
      B. Ideal Self - feeling satisfied with one's self
      C. Personal Adjustment - enjoying one's life, work and personal
                              relationships

NAME: Adult Diagnostic Screening Battery

SUPPLIER: Joseph M. Eisenberg, Ph.D.
204 E. Joppa Road Suite #10
Towson, MD 21204
(301) 321-9101

PRODUCT CATEGORY

Structured Interview

PRIMARY APPLICATIONS

Clinical Assessment/Diagnosis

SALE RESTRICTIONS American Psychological Association Guidelines

SERVICE TYPE/COST	Type	Available	Cost	Discount
	Mail-In	No		
	Teleprocessing	No		
	Local	Yes	$100.00	

PRODUCT DESCRIPTION

The ADULT DIAGNOSTIC SCREENING BATTERY is designed to help the clinician identify diagnostic possibilities among those listed in DSM-III. The program provides a questionnaire for the patient and a questionnaire for the clinician. Each questionnaire can be completed in as little as 15 minutes and entered into the computer in less than five minutes. Responses are structured in such a way as to be compared to all possible diagnoses listed in the manual. The configural pattern of answers provided in both questionnaires are matched according to suggested diagnostic possibilties and those that are compatible are selected. Printouts provide a list of responses made by both patient and clinician so that specific areas of difficulty can be noted. The program is designed to operate on Apple or Apple-compatible microcomputer systems with 64K of memory and an 80-column card. Only one disk drive is required for program execution, but two disk drives are strongly recommended in order to minimize swapping and speed up program execution. A manual is provided that describes use and application of the program as well as how to use printouts generated by the program.

NAME: Adult Personality Inventory

SUPPLIER: Institute for Personality and Ability Testing, Inc.
P.O. Box 188
Champaign, IL 61820
(217) 352-4739

PRODUCT CATEGORY	PRIMARY APPLICATIONS
Personality	Clinical Assessment/Diagnosis
	Personnel Selection/Evaluation
	Vocational Guidance/Counseling

SALE RESTRICTIONS American Psychological Association Guidelines

SERVICE TYPE/COST Type	Available	Cost	Discount
Mail-In	Yes	$16.00	Yes
Teleprocessing	No		
Local	No		

PRODUCT DESCRIPTION

The ADULT PERSONALITY INVENTORY is a tool for analyzing and reporting individual differences in personality, interpersonal style, and career/life-style preferences. The ADULT PERSONALITY INVENTORY consists of a self-report Questionnaire and a computer-generated Individual Assessment Report. The Questionnaire contains 324 items and requires one hour to complete. It was designed to measure 16 personality traits that form the basis of a widely researched, extensively validated, and well-documented theory of behavior. The Report, on the other hand, addresses user concerns rather than measurement constructs. It was designed to transform the psychometric profile into answers to the kinds of questions most frequently asked by personality test users: What is the person like? How does the person relate to others? What implications do these data hold for career decisions and life planning?

The ADULT PERSONALITY INVENTORY is intended to facilitate selection and placement decisions in industry. Six Career/Life-Style scales (Practical, Scientific, Aesthetic, Social, Competitive, Structured) have implications for the kinds of occupational roles that the individual will enjoy and grow in. The test also has applications in individual counseling. Seven scales (Extraverted, Adjusted, Tough-Minded, Independent, Disciplined, Creative, Enterprising) reflect major personality dimensions and provide awareness of underlying dynamics. Eight Interpersonal scales (Caring, Adapting, Withdrawn, Submissive, Hostile, Rebellious, Sociable, Assertive) provide a simple, understandable model for explaining how the individual relates to others and how relationships between people are affected by differences in primary styles.

ADULT PERSONALITY INVENTORY

by

Samuel E Krug, PhD

Name...............................Evelyn C Sample
Sex..Female
Age..23
Date..............................May 1, 1984

The Adult Personality Inventory measures a variety of relatively stable characteristics that help to understand present behavior patterns and to predict future performance. This Report describes individual strengths, interpersonal style, and considers implications for career choice and life style programming.

The Report contains personal information about the individual that should be treated confidentially and responsibly. Consider it in the context of what else is known about the person, including interests and goals, skills and aptitudes, past achievements, and current options open to the individual.

This part of the Report deals with patterns that characterize broad segments of behavior, including overall adjustment, cognitive style, and achievement orientation.

Ms Sample describes herself as extraverted and outgoing. She prefers the outside world of people and events to the inner world of thoughts and feelings. Consequently, it's very difficult for her to be by herself or work alone for any extended period.

Ms Sample is a person who looks at problem situations very rationally and objectively. Her solutions consider only the facts that are present. She isn't at all sensitive to other people's feelings and entirely ignores that dimension in the solutions she reaches.

She is strongly self-directed, independent, and self-sufficient. She likes to do things her own way and make her own decisions. Ms Sample relies on herself, rather than others, and finds it very difficult to accept direction from other people.

Her overall level of emotional maturity and adjustment is much higher than most people report. Ms Sample approaches situations calmly and matter-of-factly. She isn't easily upset by changing circumstances and she generally reacts well to stress.

Ms Sample is reasonably flexible and spontaneous. She doesn't follow established patterns rigidly and may sometimes lack the persistence to finish things she's started.

With respect to achievement motivation, the pattern of boldness and determination that typifies success-oriented people is not absent from her profile, but neither is it a very strong element.

Ms Sample is above average in creativity. She is flexible in her thinking and, on occasion, she can be counted on to generate novel solutions to problems.

This section of the Report focuses on how Ms Sample relates to other people. The Adult Personality Inventory evaluates eight different styles, as the chart below shows. Most people's results show high scores in two or three related areas and this leads to fairly consistent predictions about how they interact with others. A verbal summary of the chart follows on the next page.

```
      0   10  20  30  40  50  60  70  80  90  100  %


CARING
      ▨▨▨▨▨▨▨▨▨▨▨▨▨▨▨▨▨▨▨▨▨▨▨▨▨▨▨▨▨▨▨▨▨

ADAPTING
      ▨

WITHDRAWN
      ▨

SUBMISSIVE
      ▨▨▨

HOSTILE
      ▨▨▨▨▨▨▨▨▨▨▨▨▨▨▨▨▨▨▨▨▨▨▨▨▨▨

REBELLIOUS
      ▨▨▨▨▨▨▨▨▨▨▨▨▨▨▨▨▨▨▨▨▨▨▨▨▨▨▨▨▨▨▨▨▨▨▨▨▨▨

SOCIABLE
      ▨▨▨▨▨▨▨▨▨▨▨▨▨▨▨▨▨▨▨▨▨▨▨▨▨▨▨▨▨▨▨▨▨▨▨▨▨▨▨▨▨

ASSERTIVE
      ▨▨▨▨▨▨▨▨▨▨▨▨▨▨▨▨▨▨▨▨▨▨▨▨▨▨▨▨▨▨▨▨▨▨▨▨▨▨▨▨▨


      0   10  20  30  40  50  60  70  80  90  100  %
```

Summary

Her relationships with other people are primarily characterized by deep involvement in social activities. She enjoys other people. Most people probably find her fun, but from time to time she may come on too strong and leave some with an impression of being immature or, perhaps, unstable.

She has far more leadership skills than most people and usually exercises these skills tactfully.

Relationships with others are least likely to be characterized by withdrawal or insecurity. She likes to be the one in charge.

PART 3 . . . . CAREER/LIFE STYLE FACTORS

Occupational and life style preferences can be considered from the perspective of six different orientations that are each present to some extent in all of us. Of course, they usually aren't equally strong. Consequently, career choices and job satisfaction are most likely to be influenced by the stronger orientations. The following pattern is that reported by Ms Sample.

PRACTICAL

This component reflects a preference for dealing with problems that require concrete solutions. High-scoring people are strongly oriented to practical realities.

```
0   10   20   30   40   50   60   70   80   90  100  %
```

SCIENTIFIC

This component reflects the extent to which the person is drawn to explore problems analytically. High-scoring people are stimulated by oppportunities to use their investigative and deductive skills to find new solutions.

```
0   10   20   30   40   50   60   70   80   90  100  %
```

AESTHETIC

This component blends artistic sensitivity and intellectual resources. Such a combination usually leads people who score high on this scale to be most comfortable in work settings that allow them to express their imagination and creativity.

```
 0   10   20   30   40   50   60   70   80   90   100  %
```

SOCIAL

This component reflects degree of involvement with other people. Higher-scoring people are more comfortable in work settings that allow them to interact with other people, often in roles in which they can take care of other people.

```
 0   10   20   30   40   50   60   70   80   90   100  %
```

COMPETITIVE

People who score high on this component are very likely to be described as ambitious and goal-directed. They are oriented toward business. They have the intellectual skills and practical determination to take on difficult tasks despite obstacles they may encounter along the way.

```
 0   10   20   30   40   50   60   70   80   90   100  %
```

STRUCTURED

Scores on this scale reflect preferences for well-defined activities and unambiguous job requirements. High-scoring people value steady, even progress toward goals.

```
 0   10   20   30   40   50   60   70   80   90   100  %
```

```
Name..............................Evelyn C Sample
Sex......................................Female
Age..........................................23
Date............................May 1, 1984
```

Note

The material in this Appendix requires some technical knowledge and a thorough familiarity with the test Manual to be
interpreted properly. It is not intended to be shared directly with the client.

Profile Pattern Code

The code that corresponds to Ms Sample's score pattern
is 3133. This pattern occurs with average frequency.
For additional interpretive hypotheses regarding this Report, see
Interpreting 16 PF Profile Patterns," which is available from IPAT.

Stylistic Factors

Four response style scales are scored in the Adult Personality Inventory to check how different test-taking attitudes
may have operated to produce the score profile. In this case,
all indicators are within normal limits. The Report results
can be accepted as accurate and reliable, as the chart below shows.

```
  0   10   20   30   40   50   60   70   80   90  100  %



Good Impression
 ▨▨▨▨▨▨▨▨▨▨


Bad Impression
 ▨▨▨▨▨▨▨▨▨▨▨▨▨▨▨▨▨▨▨▨


 Infrequency
  ▨▨▨


Uncertainty
  ▨
  0   10   20   30   40   50   60   70   80   90  100  %
```

PERSONAL CHARACTERISTICS

```
      low        a v e r a g e       high
  1   2   3   4   5   6   7   8   9   10
-------------------------------------------
          :               :           X   Extraverted........10.0
          :               :   X           Adjusted........... 8.4
          :               :       X       Tough-Minded....... 9.3
          :               :   X           Independent........ 8.8
      X:              :               Disciplined........ 3.8
          :       X       :           Creative........... 5.9
          :           X:              Enterprising....... 6.9

-------------------------------------------
```

INTERPERSONAL STYLE

```
      low        a v e r a g e       high
  1   2   3   4   5   6   7   8   9   10
-------------------------------------------
          :           X:              Caring............. 6.8
  X       :               :           Adapting........... 1.4
  X       :               :           Withdrawn.......... 1.2
      X   :               :           Submissive......... 2.9
          :       X       :           Hostile............ 5.9
          :               :   X       Rebellious......... 8.8
          :               :       X   Sociable...........10.0
          :               :   X       Assertive.......... 9.6

-------------------------------------------
```

CAREER/LIFE STYLE FACTORS

```
      low        a v e r a g e       high
  1   2   3   4   5   6   7   8   9   10
-------------------------------------------
          :       X   :               Practical.......... 6.4
          :           :       X       Scientific......... 9.7
          :       X   :               Aesthetic.......... 6.7
          :           :   X           Social............. 8.1
          :           :       X       Competitive........10.0
      X   :           :               Structured......... 3.1

-------------------------------------------
```

Item Summary

This page provides a record of individual item responses. Items marked "True" are represented by "T," those marked "False" by "F." Middle or uncertain responses are indicated by a question mark. Responses to the intelligence items are represented by "a," "b," or "c," as appropriate. The column heading shows the last digit of the item number. The row heading shows the first digit(s). Item 197, for example, will be found in row 19 and column 7.

	0	1	2	3	4	5	6	7	8	9
0		F	T	F	T	F	F	T	F	T
1	T	T	T	F	F	?	F	F	T	F
2	T	F	F	F	F	F	F	T	T	T
3	T	T	T	F	T	T	F	F	T	F
4	T	T	F	F	T	F	T	T	F	T
5	F	T	T	?	F	T	T	T	T	F
6	F	F	F	T	T	T	T	F	F	?
7	F	F	F	F	F	T	T	T	F	T
8	F	T	T	F	F	T	T	T	T	T
9	T	F	T	F	F	F	T	F	T	F
10	T	T	F	?	F	T	F	T	T	F
11	F	T	T	?	T	F	F	F	T	T
12	F	T	F	T	F	F	F	F	F	F
13	T	T	F	F	F	F	c	b	c	a
14	a	a	a	c	c	c	b	b	b	a
15	a	b	c	c	c	a	a	c	a	a
16	b	c	b	b	b	c	F	T	F	T
17	T	F	T	F	F	F	T	T	F	T
18	T	T	F	T	T	?	F	F	F	T
19	F	F	T	F	T	T	T	F	F	F
20	T	F	F	F	F	F	T	T	F	T
21	F	F	T	F	?	T	T	F	F	T
22	?	T	T	F	F	T	F	T	T	T
23	T	T	T	F	T	F	F	T	F	?
24	T	T	T	T	F	T	T	F	T	T
25	T	F	F	T	T	T	T	T	F	T
26	T	F	T	T	T	T	?	T	F	F
27	T	T	T	T	F	F	F	T	T	T
28	F	T	F	T	T	T	T	T	F	F
29	F	F	T	T	F	F	F	T	T	T
30	T	F	F	F	F	T	T	F	T	?
31	T	F	?	T	F	T	T	T	F	T
32	T	F	F	F	F					

NAME: AIM

SUPPLIER: Intran Corporation
4555 West 77th Street
Minneapolis, MN 55435
(800) 328-7930

PRODUCT CATEGORY	PRIMARY APPLICATIONS
Career/Vocational	Vocational Guidance/Counseling
Interest/Attitudes	Personal/Marriage/Family Counseling
Cognitive/Ability	

SALE RESTRICTIONS Authorized/Certified Representatives

SERVICE TYPE/COST	Type	Available	Cost	Discount
	Mail-In	Yes	NA	
	Teleprocessing	No		
	Local	No		

PRODUCT DESCRIPTION

This interpretive report integrates information from the USES Interest Inventory and the General Aptitude Test Battery. Results from these two inventories help in exploring career opportunities by matching special abilities with interests.

Scores in 12 interest areas are related to aptitude scores by reference to 66 Work Groups. The 13-page report includes both graphical and verbal analyses of the test scores and provides specific suggestions for additional readings about job descriptions and educational/training requirements.

A two-page counselor's report is also provided that summarizes the basic score data.

AIM is available only to the various state employment services and other organizations which have permission to use the General Aptitude Test Battery.

INTERPRETIVE REPORT FOR:

SAMPLE JOHN A

Recently you completed two inventories developed by the U.S. Employment Services: (1) the General Aptitude Test Battery (GATB), and (2)
an Interest Inventory. Results from these two inventories are designed to help you in your exploration of career opportunities that
match your special abilities and interests. Each person is unique and
has abilities and interests that are important in deciding on a career
in the world of work.

The GATB is a highly developed measure of your abilities that are related to jobs and activities; these results indicate how your aptitudes
match with those of workers in 66 specific Work Groups. The Interest
Inventory was developed to measure your liking and disliking for various jobs and activities in the world of work; these results indicate
the strength of your preferences in 12 broad Interest Areas.

Since each person is unique, no inventory can measure perfectly all
the differences among individuals. However, the results from these
inventories have been well researched and can be considered as good
indicators of your interests and aptitudes. They should be used as a
guide and starting point for further thinking, discussion, and exploration with a vocational professional. During this career exploration
process, other factors also should be considered by you such as past
life experiences, past and future educational training, previous job
experiences, and personal values.

Prepared by:
Intran Corporation
4555 West 77th Street
Minneapolis, MN 55435

07/29/83

INTEREST AREAS

Your results on the Interest Inventory will provide you with a guide and frame-work for understanding your preferences for activities and jobs in the world of work. Brief descriptions for each of the 12 interest areas are given below. These interest areas represent broad areas in the occupational world and a good understanding of each will help you during the interpretation and discussion of your results.

 01 ARTISTIC: Interest in creative expression of feelings or ideas, such as the performing arts of drama, music or dance, the visual arts of painting or sculpturing, or literary arts of writing and editing.

 02 SCIENTIFIC: Interest in discovering, collecting, and analyzing infor-mation about the natural world and applying scientific research findings to problems in medicine, and life or natural sciences.

 03 PLANTS & ANIMALS: Interest in activities involving plants and ani-mals, usually in outdoor settings, such as farming, taking care of or training animals, of forestry types of endeavors.

 04 PROTECTIVE: Interest in the use of authority to protect people and property, such as the fields of fire fighting, law enforcement, or security services.

 05 MECHANICAL: Interest in applying mechanical principles to practical solutions, using machines, handtools, or techniques, such as skilled trades, engineering, construction, mining, or operating vehicles.

 06 INDUSTRIAL: Interest in repetitive, concrete, or organized activities in a factory setting, such as setting up machines, or using handtools or your hands to manufacture things.

 07 BUSINESS DETAIL: Interest in organized, clearly defined activities requiring accuracy and attention to detail, usually in an office setting, such as keeping records or typing.

 08 SELLING: Interest in bringing others to a point of view through per-sonal persuasion, using sales and promotion techniques in fields that deal directly on a one-to-one basis with others.

 09 ACCOMMODATING: Interest in catering to the wishes of others, usually by providing services for the convenience of them, such as hospi-tality services or personal services.

 10 HUMANITARIAN: Interest in helping others with their mental, social, spiritual, physical, or vocational needs, such as the counseling, welfare, therapy, and rehabilitation fields.

 11 LEADING-INFLUENCING: Interest in leading and influencing of others through activities involving high-level verbal or numerical abil-ities, such as law, education, management, or social research.

 12 PHYSICAL PERFORMING: Interest in physical activities that are per-formed before an audience, such as sports or other areas like at a circus, carnival, theater, or amusement park.

YOUR INTERESTS

The following results are based on responses to the USES Interest Inventory. The score for each of the 12 interest areas is indicated in the Standard Score (Std. Score) column. For each scale, the population average is 50. Most people have scores between 43 and 57 and thus, this range is labeled AVERAGE INTEREST. Scores higher than 57 indicate more interest for activities and jobs in that area, while scores lower than 43 indicate less interest. Since females and males respond somewhat differently for some areas, additional information is provided by indicating the percentile corresponding to the gender of the individual. If gender was not indicated on the inventory, then data for both females and males are provided on the right of the graph.

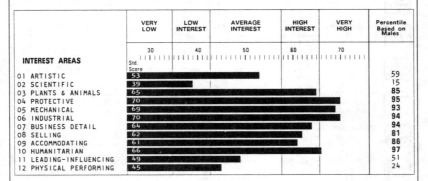

INTEREST AREAS	Std. Score	Percentile Based on Males
01 ARTISTIC	53	59
02 SCIENTIFIC	39	15
03 PLANTS & ANIMALS	65	85
04 PROTECTIVE	70	95
05 MECHANICAL	69	93
06 INDUSTRIAL	70	94
07 BUSINESS DETAIL	64	94
08 SELLING	62	81
09 ACCOMMODATING	61	86
10 HUMANITARIAN	66	97
11 LEADING-INFLUENCING	49	51
12 PHYSICAL PERFORMING	45	24

Many people have high or very high scores in two, three, or even four different areas; these strong interest areas should be indications of starting points for further career exploration and discussions. Sometimes, high scores will be apparent for more than four areas indicating a broad liking for a wide range of items on the inventory. In these instances, consideration should be given to the two or three highest scores as starting points for further exploration and discussions.

If all scores are in the average range or lower, this indicates indifference, uncertainy, or even a strong disliking for the activities on the inventory. This may be the result of unfamiliarity or inexperience with the activities, especially with young individuals, or there may be narrow occupational areas not specifically covered by the inventory that may represent positive areas for further discussion. As a starting point consider those areas that show the strongest interests currently.

Added consideration also should be given to those interest areas where the percentile based on the individual's gender is 75 or higher, even if the standard score does not reach the "high" category. Remember, all jobs are open to everyone regardless of gender and further discussions should not be limited to current stereotypes.

APTITUDE-INTEREST COMBINATIONS

Your aptitude test results from the GATB are shown on the next page with your interest inventory results.

First, your interest inventory results on each of the twelve interest areas are presented from highest to lowest interest. Next, within each of these twelve broad interest areas are listed specific Work Groups that share similar interests. For example, the 01 ARTISTIC interest area can be divided into eight different but related Work Groups, such as 0101 Literary Arts, 0102 Visual Arts, 0103 Performing Arts-Dance, and so forth.

Following each Work Group are two columns of numbers that are important for you and your vocational counselor. The first column lists appropriate page numbers in the *Guide for Occupational Exploration* (GOE). The GOE was produced by the U.S. Employment Service and provides extensive information on each Work Group, describing the types of work involved, skills and abilities that are needed, examples of occupations, and how to prepare for that type of work. The next column lists Occupational Aptitude Pattern (OAP) numbers which are used in interpreting aptitude scores on the GATB, and which are described in other publications used by your vocational counselor.

Finally, a graph indicates your Aptitude Level for doing the work required for each specific Work Group. Aptitude Levels in the high range indicate you have similar abilities to workers performing satisfactorily in their jobs. Aptitude Levels in the moderate range indicate your abilities are close to those performing satisfactorily, but somewhat lower than those in the high level. Aptitude Levels in the low range indicate that the probability of performing satisfactorily in an occupation for that Work Group is low. For some Work Groups, asterisks appear which mean that the aptitude levels have not been developed yet for that area or that specific information was not available from the GATB.

When exploring various jobs and career options, a good starting point are the interest areas for which you scored "Very High" or "High." Within these strong interest areas, you should consider those Work Groups where your Aptitude Levels are the strongest. By focusing on those areas where your interests and aptitudes are the highest, you will be identifying occupations and careers for which you have the best chance of being satisfied and performing satisfactorily.

For some people, interests and aptitudes, as indicated by Interest Inventory and GATB results, do not match up very well. That is, the occupational areas where interests are strongest may not be the strongest from the point of view of aptitude for performing in the occupation satisfactorily. Or you may not have any particularly strong interests at all. In such cases it may be helpful to explore first those Work Groups for which there is strong aptitude regardless of the Interest Inventory results. You may find that you would be interested in some of the specific occupations in these Work Groups.

DISCUSSION OF YOUR APTITUDE

AND INTEREST RESULTS

Your aptitudes and interests are important when related to occupational groups and specific occupations within these groups. Thus, your results are discussed below in terms of occupational possibilities that would utilize your strongest interests and strongest aptitudes. The Interest Areas and the Work Groups referred to in the discussion are those used to classify all occupations in the *Guide for Occupational Exploration*, developed by the U.S. Department of Labor.

YOUR VERY HIGH AND HIGH INTERESTS

A discussion of the Interest Areas for which you have high or very high interests follows. Even though your strongest interest areas are good starting points in thinking about careers, you also should consider your aptitude for doing the tasks involved in each job. Thus, the discussion focuses on your aptitude for performing tasks in specific Work Groups within Interest Areas.

--INTEREST AREA 04: PROTECTIVE

Your interest level indicates your preference for using authority to protect people and property. This area includes two different Work Groups: (1) safety and law enforcement; and (2) security services.

While you have strong interest in this general area, your aptitude for doing the tasks required of the following Work Groups is in the low range. This indicates that you would have a low probability of performing the work satisfactorily. If you feel very strongly about pursuing careers in those areas where you have low aptitude, you should discuss the possibilities with a vocational counselor. This will help you to evaluate your interest in these Work Groups and to determine whether it is of sufficient strength to overcome some deficiency in aptitude for these jobs.

    WORK GROUPS:
    04:01 Safety & Law Enforcement   04:02 Security Services

--INTEREST AREA 06: INDUSTRIAL

Your interest level indicates your preference for the industrial area. This area includes four different Work Groups: (1) production technology, such as inspecting and supervising others; (2) production work, such as making a product; (3) quality control, such as checking products; and (4) elemental work, such as tending machines and equipment.

The following are those Work Groups where you have a moderate aptitude.
Your interest score indicates that you have a strong liking for doing the
activities in this general area and your aptitude score indicates that you
are close to those who are performing satisfactorily in their job, but
your chances are somewhat less of being successful than those whose aptitude is in the high range.

> Work Group 06:01 Production Technology
> Sample Occupations: Assembler, Inspector, Machine Operator,
> Optical Instrument Assembler, Solderer, Bench Hand, Calibrator

While you have strong interest in this general area, your aptitude for
doing the tasks required of the following Work Groups is in the low range.
This indicates that you would have a low probability of performing the
work satisfactorily. If you feel very strongly about pursuing careers
in those areas where you have low aptitude, you should discuss the possibilities with a vocational counselor. This will help you to evaluate
your interest in these Work Groups and to determine whether it is of sufficient strength to overcome some deficiency in aptitude for these jobs.

> WORK GROUPS:
> 06:02 Production Work   06:03 Quality Control
> 06:04 Elemental Work - Industrial

--INTEREST AREA 05: MECHANICAL

Your interest level indicates your preference for the mechanical area. This
area includes twelve different Work Groups: (1) engineering; (2) managerial
work; (3) engineering technology; (4) air and water vehicle operation; (5)
craft technology; (6) systems operation; (7) quality control; (8) land and
water vehicle operation; (9) materials control; (10) crafts; (11) equipment
operation; and (12) elemental work which include a variety of unskilled tasks.

The following are those Work Groups where you have a moderate aptitude.
Your interest score indicates that you have a strong liking for doing the
activities in this general area and your aptitude score indicates that you
are close to those who are performing satisfactorily in their job, but
your chances are somewhat less of being successful than those whose aptitude is in the high range.

> Work Group 05:08 Land & Water Vehicle Operation
> Sample Occupations: Ambulance Driver, Deckhand, Truck Driver,
> Tow Truck Operator, Locomotive Engineer, Motor Operator

> Work Group 05:10 Crafts
> Sample Occupations: Baker, Cook, Drapery Hanger, Painter, Lather,
> Roofer, Television Installer, Floor Layer, House Repairer,
> Electrical Repairer, Carpet Layer, Service Station Attendant

> Work Group 05:11 Equipment Operation
> Sample Occupations: Concrete Paving Machine Operator, Truck-
> Crane Operator, Drilling Machine Operator, Sanitary Landfill
> Operator, Miner, Well Driller Operator, Bulldozer Operator

YOUR APTITUDES-INTERESTS

		GOE	OAP	APTITUDE LEVELS LOW < MODERATE < HIGH

VERY HIGH INTERESTS 66+

		GOE	OAP
04 PROTEC-TIVE SS=70 Per=95	0401 Safety & Enforcement	66	15
	0402 Security Services	68	16
06 INDUSTRIAL SS=70 Per=94	0601 Production Technology	138	31
	0601 Production Technology	138	30
	0602 Production Work	147	32
	0603 Quality Control	172	33
	0604 Elemental Work: Industrial	180	34
05 MECHANICAL SS=69 Per=93	0508 Land & Water Vehicle Operation	108	23
	0510 Crafts	115	26
	0511 Equipment Operation	123	28
	0501 Engineering	72	17
	0502 Managerial Work: Mechanical	77	18
	0503 Engineering Technology	81	19
	0504 Air & Water Vehicle Operation	85	20
	0505 Craft Technology	88	21
	0507 Quality Control	104	22
	0509 Materials Control	110	24
	0509 Materials Control	110	25
	0510 Crafts	115	27
	0512 Elemental Work: Mechanical	127	29
	0506 Systems Operation	101	**
10 HUMANITARIAN SS=66 Per=97	1001 Social Services	276	49
	1002 Nursing Therapy & Special. Teach.	278	50
	1003 Child & Adult Care	281	51

HIGH INTERESTS 58-65

		GOE	OAP
03 PLANTS & ANIMALS SS=65 Per=85	0301 Mgr. Work: Plants & Animals	51	11
	0303 Animal Training & Service	57	12
	0303 Animal Training & Service	57	13
	0304 Elemental Work: Plants & Animals	59	14
	0302 General Supv.: Plants & Animals	54	**
07 BUSINESS DETAIL SS=64 Per=94	0701 Administrative Detail	229	35
	0702 Mathematical Detail	232	36
	0703 Financial Detail	235	37
	0704 Oral Communications	237	38
	0705 Records Processing	241	39
	0706 Clerical Machine Operation	245	40
	0707 Clerical Handling	247	41
08 SELLING SS=62 Per=81	0801 Sales Technology	251	42
	0802 General Sales	255	43
	0803 Vending	259	44
09 ACCOMMODATING SS=61 Per=88	0903 Passenger Services	266	47
	0901 Hospitality Services	262	45
	0902 Barber & Beauty Services	264	46
	0905 Attendant Services	271	48
	0904 Customer Services	269	**

AVERAGE INTERESTS 43-57

		GOE	OAP
01 ARTISTIC SS=53 Per=59	0101 Literary Arts	16	1
	0102 Visual Arts	18	2
	0103 Performing Arts, Drama	21	3
	0104 Performing Arts, Music	23	4
	0105 Performing Arts, Dance	26	5
	0106 Craft Arts	28	6
	0107 Elemental Arts	32	**
	0108 Modeling	34	**
11 LEADING-INFLUENCING SS=49 Per=51	1101 Mathematics & Statistics	285	52
	1102 Education & Library Services	287	53
	1102 Education & Library Services	287	54
	1103 Social Research	290	55
	1103 Social Research	290	56
	1104 Law	292	57
	1104 Law	292	58
	1105 Business Administration	294	59
	1106 Finance	298	60
	1107 Services Administration	301	61
	1108 Communications	304	62
	1109 Promotion	306	63
	1110 Regulations Enforcement	308	64
	1111 Business Management	310	65
	1112 Contracts & Claims	314	66
12 PHYSICAL PERFORMING SS=45 Per=24	1201 Sports	318	**
	1202 Physical Feats	321	**

LOW INTERESTS 35-42

		GOE	OAP
02 SCIENTIFIC SS=39 Per=15	0201 Physical Sciences	38	7
	0202 Life Sciences	41	8
	0203 Medical Sciences	43	9
	0204 Laboratory Technology	46	10

VERY LOW INTERESTS -34

None

The following lists those Work Groups for which specific aptitude measures
were not available. Since your interest is strong for this general area,
you may want to explore further the aptitudes needed to be successful
in the specific jobs and with the aid of a vocational counselor decide
whether or not you have the abilities needed.

> Work Group 05:06 Systems Operation
> Sample Occupations: Water Treatment Plant Operator, Turbine
> Operator, Hydroelectric Station Operator, Power Plant Operator,
> Heating Plant Operator, Substation Operator, Stationary Engineer

While you have strong interest in this general area, your aptitude for
doing the tasks required of the following Work Groups is in the low range.
This indicates that you would have a low probability of performing the
work satisfactorily. If you feel very strongly about pursuing careers
in those areas where you have low aptitude, you should discuss the possibilities with a vocational counselor. This will help you to evaluate
your interest in these Work Groups and to determine whether it is of sufficient strength to overcome some deficiency in aptitude for these jobs.

> WORK GROUPS:
> 05:01 Engineering   05:02 Managerial Work- Mechanical
> 05:03 Engineering Technology   05:04 Air & Water Vehicle Oper.
> 05:05 Craft Technology   05:07 Quality Control
> 05:09 Materials Control   05:12 Elemental Work - Mechanical

--INTEREST AREA 10: HUMANITARIAN

Your interest level indicates your preference for helping individuals and
caring for them. This area includes three different Work Groups: (1) social
services; (2) nursing therapy and specialized teaching; and (3) child and
adult care.

While you have strong interest in this general area, your aptitude for
doing the tasks required of the following Work Groups is in the low range.
This indicates that you would have a low probability of performing the
work satisfactorily. If you feel very strongly about pursuing careers
in those areas where you have low aptitude, you should discuss the possibilities with a vocational counselor. This will help you to evaluate
your interest in these Work Groups and to determine whether it is of sufficient strength to overcome some deficiency in aptitude for these jobs.

> WORK GROUPS:
> 10:01 Social Services   10:02 Nursing Ther. & Sp. Teach.
> 10:03 Child & Adult Care

--INTEREST AREA 03: PLANTS & ANIMALS

Your interest level indicates your preference for working with plants and
animals, usually in an outdoor setting. This area includes four different
Work Groups: (1) managerial work; (2) general supervision where you supervise others; (3) animal training and service; and (4) elemental work, such
as using your hands or equipment or machinery in an outdoor setting.

The following lists those Work Groups for which specific aptitude measures
were not available. Since your interest is strong for this general area,
you may want to explore further the aptitudes needed to be successful
in the specific jobs and with the aid of a vocational counselor decide
whether or not you have the abilities needed.

> Work Group 03:02 General Supervision - Plants & Animals
> Sample Occupations: Field Supervisor, Dairy Farm Supervisor,
> Lawn and Tree Service Supervisor, Artificial-Breeding Technician,
> Logging Supervisor, Forest Nursery Supervisor

While you have strong interest in this general area, your aptitude for
doing the tasks required of the following Work Groups is in the low range.
This indicates that you would have a low probability of performing the
work satisfactorily. If you feel very strongly about pursuing careers
in those areas where you have low aptitude, you should discuss the possibilities with a vocational counselor. This will help you to evaluate
your interest in these Work Groups and to determine whether it is of sufficient strength to overcome some deficiency in aptitude for these jobs.

> WORK GROUPS:
> 03:01 Mgr. Work- Plants & Animals　　　03:03 Animal Training & Service
> 03:04 Element. Work- Plants & An.

--INTEREST AREA 07: BUSINESS DETAIL

Your interest level indicates your preference for working with details.
This area includes seven different Work Groups: (1) administrative detail; (2) mathematical detail; (3) financial detail; (4) oral communications; (5) records processing; (6) clerical machine operation; and (7)
clerical handling.

While you have strong interest in this general area, your aptitude for
doing the tasks required of the following Work Groups is in the low range.
This indicates that you would have a low probability of performing the
work satisfactorily. If you feel very strongly about pursuing careers
in those areas where you have low aptitude, you should discuss the possibilities with a vocational counselor. This will help you to evaluate
your interest in these Work Groups and to determine whether it is of sufficient strength to overcome some deficiency in aptitude for these jobs.

> WORK GROUPS:
> 07:01 Administrative Detail　　　07:02 Mathematical Detail
> 07:03 Financial Detail　　　　　07:04 Oral Communication
> 07:05 Records Processing　　　　07:06 Clerical Machine Operation
> 07:07 Clerical Handling

--INTEREST AREA 08: SELLING

Your interest level indicates your preference for convincing and persuading
others. This area includes three different Work Groups: (1) sales technology, which usually is an advising type of sales; (2) general sales, which
usually involves retail sales; and (3) vending, which usually involves
selling small inexpensive items.

While you have strong interest in this general area, your aptitude for
doing the tasks required of the following Work Groups is in the low range.
This indicates that you would have a low probability of performing the
work satisfactorily. If you feel very strongly about pursuing careers
in those areas where you have low aptitude, you should discuss the possibilities with a vocational counselor. This will help you to evaluate
your interest in these Work Groups and to determine whether it is of sufficient strength to overcome some deficiency in aptitude for these jobs.

> WORK GROUPS:
> 08:01 Sales Technology   08:02 General Sales
> 08:03 Vending

--INTEREST AREA 09: ACCOMMODATING

Your interest level indicates your preference for catering to the wishes
of others. This area includes five different Work Groups: (1) hospi-
tality services; (2) barber and beauty services; (3) passenger services;
(4) customer services; and (5) attendant services.

The following are those Work Groups where you have a moderate aptitude.
Your interest score indicates that you have a strong liking for doing the
activities in this general area and your aptitude score indicates that you
are close to those who are performing satisfactorily in their job, but
your chances are somewhat less of being successful than those whose aptitude is in the high range.

> Work Group 09:03 Passenger Services
> Sample Occupations: Bus Driver, Chauffeur, Taxi Driver,
> Driving Instructor

The following lists those Work Groups for which specific aptitude measures
were not available. Since your interest is strong for this general area,
you may want to explore further the aptitudes needed to be successful
in the specific jobs and with the aid of a vocational counselor decide
whether or not you have the abilities needed.

> Work Group 09:04 Customer Services
> Sample Occupations: Waiter/Waitress, Car Wash Attendant,
> Newspaper Carrier, Bartender, Gambling Dealer, Sales Clerk,
> Customer Service Clerk, Food Concession Manager, Car Hop

While you have strong interest in this general area, your aptitude for
doing the tasks required of the following Work Groups is in the low range.
This indicates that you would have a low probability of performing the
work satisfactorily. If you feel very strongly about pursuing careers
in those areas where you have low aptitude, you should discuss the possibilities with a vocational counselor. This will help you to evaluate
your interest in these Work Groups and to determine whether it is of sufficient strength to overcome some deficiency in aptitude for these jobs.

> WORK GROUPS:
> 09:01 Hospitality Services   09:02 Barber & Beauty Services
> 09:05 Attendant Services

psychware **31**

YOUR AVERAGE INTERESTS

A discussion follows of the Interest Areas where you had scores in the average range. Since the Interest Inventory covers a broad range of activities, you may find that you really like some of the activities in the area, but not all of the activities, or you may be uncertain whether or not you like the activities. These situations would tend to result in scores in the average range. You should think more about the tasks done by people in jobs for these areas and particularly where your aptitudes are the strongest.

--INTEREST AREA 01:　ARTISTIC

Your interest level indicates your preference for the creative and performing arts fields. This area includes eight different Work Groups: (1) literary arts, such as writing and editing; (2) visual arts, such as painting and designing; (3) drama; (4) music; (5) dance; (6) craft arts, such as making things like ceramics; (7) elemental arts, such as working at a carnival; and (8) modeling.

The following lists those Work Groups for which specific aptitude measures were not available. Since your interest for this general area was in the average range, all of the career examples probably would not be appealing to you, but you may find some specific occupations that would be satisfying. Before deciding on a specific occupation, you should explore further with the aid of a vocational counselor as to whether or not you have the ability needed to be successful.

　　　Work Group 01:07 Elemental Arts
　　　Sample Occupations:　Graphologist, Impersonator, Ring Conductor,
　　　Amusement Park Entertainer, Carnival Barker or Announcer
　　　Work Group 01:08 Modeling
　　　Sample Occupations:　Show Girl, Artist's Model, TV Stand-in or
　　　Double, Modeling Instructor, Fashion Model

Your aptitude for doing the tasks required of the following Work Groups is in the low range indicating that you would have a low probability of performing the work satisfactorily. Since your overall interest for this area is in the average range, there may be some specific careers in this area that would be appealing to you but probably not all the careers. If you feel very strongly about pursuing a career in an area that is appealing to you, even though you have a low aptitude, you should discuss your plans carefully with a vocational counselor so as to be informed about the various possibilities and requirements needed for the job.

　　　WORK GROUPS:
　　　01:01 Literary Arts　　　　　　　01:02 Visual Arts
　　　01:03 Performing Arts - Drama　　01:04 Performing Arts - Music
　　　01:05 Performing Arts - Dance　　01:06 Craft Arts

--INTEREST AREA 11:　LEADING-INFLUENCING

Your interest level indicates your preference for leading and influencing others through high-level verbal or numerical abilities. This area includes 12 different Work Groups: (1) mathematics and statistics; (2) education and library services; (3) social research; (4) law; (5) business administration; (6) finance; (7) services administration; (8) communications; (9) promotion; (10) regulations enforcement; (11) business management; and (12) contracts and deeds.

32　*psychware*

Your aptitude for doing the tasks required of the following Work Groups
is in the low range indicating that you would have a low probability of
performing the work satisfactorily. Since your overall interest for this
area is in the average range, there may be some specific careers in this
area that would be appealing to you but probably not all the careers. If
you feel very strongly about pursuing a career in an area that is appealing to you, even though you have a low aptitude, you should discuss your
plans carefully with a vocational counselor so as to be informed about
the various possibilities and requirements needed for the job.

        WORK GROUPS:
        11:01 Mathematics & Statistics   11:02 Education & Library Service
        11:03 Social Research   11:04 Law
        11:05 Business Administration   11:06 Finance
        11:07 Services Administration   11:08 Communications
        11:09 Promotion   11:10 Regulations Enforcement
        11:11 Business Management   11:12 Contracts & Claims

--INTEREST AREA: 12 PHYSICAL PERFORMING

Your interest level indicates your preference for performing physical activity before an audience. This area includes two different Work Groups:
(1) sports, such as a professional athlete; and (2) physical feats, such
as doing daring acts to entertain people.

The following lists those Work Groups for which specific aptitude measures
were not available. Since your interest for this general area was in the
average range, all of the career examples probably would not be appealing
to you, but you may find some specific occupations that would be satisfying. Before deciding on a specific occupation, you should explore further with the aid of a vocational counselor as to whether or not you have
the ability needed to be successful.

        Work Group 12:01 Sports
        Sample Occupations: Sports Instructor, Professional Athlete,
        Coach, Automobile Racer, Professional Sports Scout
        Work Group 12:02 Physical Feats
        Sample Occupations: Acrobat, Rodeo Performer, Juggler, Aerialist,
        Show Horse Driver, Stunt Performer, Aquatic Performer

LOW AND VERY LOW INTERESTS

A discussion follows of the Interest Areas where you had scores in the low or
very low ranges. Even though you had a low score, you may find some specific
activities very appealing to you as you explore various careers in these areas.
Further exploration and thinking about the world of work may be necessary to
help you decide on areas that would be of interest to you.

--INTEREST AREA 02: SCIENTIFIC

Your interest level indicates your preference for scientific endeavors. This
area includes four different Work Groups: (1) physical sciences; (2) life
sciences; (3) medical sciences; and (4) laboratory technology.

psychware **33**

The following are those Work Groups for which you do not have a strong
aptitude or strong interest. Before you explore these areas further,
you should discuss the requirements of these jobs with a vocational
counselor to help you further determine if these Work Groups offer possibilities for you. You should first consider any other area where you
have a higher aptitude or higher interest level.

WORK GROUPS:
02:01 Physical Sciences   02:02 Life Sciences
02:03 Medical Sciences   02:04 Laboratory Technology

The preceding has provided you with an analysis of your strongest interests and aptitudes. To provide you with additional information or help
in your occupational and career search, the following sources are recommended:

--A vocational counselor is an excellent source of information about occupations and how to prepare for them. Vocational counselors are located in Job Service Offices, high schools, community colleges and
  universities.

--The following publications, developed by the U.S. Department of Labor,
  are excellent resources and are available in Job Service Offices, in
  schools, and in the reference sections of many libraries.

  --The *Guide for Occupational Exploration* provides information about
    requirements for almost all occupations. It groups these occupa-
    tions according to aptitudes, skills, and interests involved in the
    performing of the job duties.

  --The *Occupational Outlook Handbook* provides basic information about
    most of the important occupations, training needed, salary levels,
    and prospects for employment in these occupations.

COUNSELOR REPORT FOR AIM

Prepared by
Intran Corporation - 4555 West 77th St. - Minneapolis, MN 55435
07/29/83

SAMPLE JOHN A   Male Age: 45 Yrs. 7 Mos. Educ.: 10 Yrs.

The following results are based on responses to the Occupational AIM (Aptitude-Interest Measurement) System. First, the scores for each of the 12 interest areas are indicated below in the Standard Score (Std. Score) column. For each scale, the population average is 50; most people have scores between 43 and 57 and thus, this range is labeled AVERAGE INTEREST. Scores higher than 57 indicate more interest for activities and jobs in that area, while scores lower than 43 indicate less interest. Since females and males respond somewhat differently for some areas, additional information is provided by indicating the percentile corresponding to the gender of the individual. If gender was not indicated, then data for both females and males are provided on the right of the graph.

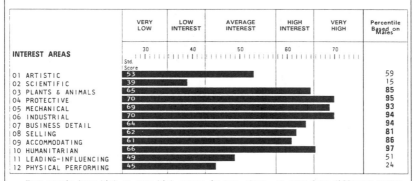

INTEREST AREAS	VERY LOW	LOW INTEREST	AVERAGE INTEREST	HIGH INTEREST	VERY HIGH	Percentile Based on Males
01 ARTISTIC	53					59
02 SCIENTIFIC	39					15
03 PLANTS & ANIMALS	65					85
04 PROTECTIVE	70					95
05 MECHANICAL	69					93
06 INDUSTRIAL	70					94
07 BUSINESS DETAIL	64					94
08 SELLING	62					81
09 ACCOMMODATING	61					86
10 HUMANITARIAN	66					97
11 LEADING-INFLUENCING	49					51
12 PHYSICAL PERFORMING	45					24

Many people have high or very high scores in two, three, or even four different areas; these strong interest areas should be indications of starting points for further career exploration and discussions. Sometimes, high scores will be apparent for more than four areas indicating a broad liking for a wide range of items on the inventory. In these instances, consideration should be given to the two or three highest scores as starting points for further exploration and discussions.

If all scores are in the average range or lower, this indicates indifference, uncertainty, or even a strong disliking for the activities on the inventory. This may be the result of unfamiliarity or inexperience with the activities, especially with young individuals, or there may be narrow occupational areas not specifically covered by the inventory that may represent positive areas for further discussion. As starting point, consider those areas that show the strongest interests currently.

Added consideration also should be given to those interest areas where the percentile based on the individual's gender is 75 or higher, even if the standard score does not reach the "high" category. Remember, all jobs are open to everyone regardless of gender and further discussions should not be limited to current stereotypes.

Further information is provided on the reverse side for OAP aptitude levels from the General Aptitude Test Battery and appropriate references to the *Guide for Occupational Exploration* for discussion and exploration of Work Groups and specific occupations.

YOUR APTITUDES-INTERESTS

			GOE	DAP	LOW	APTITUDE LEVELS < MODERATE < HIGH

VERY HIGH INTERESTS 66+

04 PROTEC-TIVE	SS=70 Per=95	0401 Safety & Enforcement	66	15		
		0402 Security Services	68	16		
06 INDUSTRIAL	SS=70 Per=94	0601 Production Technology	138	31		
		0602 Production Work	147	32		
		0603 Quality Control	172	33		
		0604 Elemental Work: Industrial	180	34		
05 MECHANICAL	SS=69 Per=93	0508 Land & Water Vehicle Operation	108	23		
		0510 Crafts	115	26		
		0511 Equipment Operation	123	28		
		0501 Engineering	72	17		
		0502 Managerial Work: Mechanical	77	18		
		0503 Engineering Technology	81	19		
		0504 Air & Water Vehicle Operation	85	20		
		0505 Craft Technology	88	21		
		0507 Quality Control	104	22		
		0509 Materials Control	110	24		
		0509 Materials Control	110	25		
		0510 Crafts	115	27		
		0512 Elemental Work: Mechanical	127	29		
		0506 Systems Operation	101	**	**	
10 HUMANITARIAN	SS=66 Per=97	1001 Social Services	276	49		
		1002 Nursing Therapy & Special. Teach.	278	50		
		1003 Child & Adult Care	281	51		

HIGH INTERESTS 58-65

03 PLANTS & ANIMALS	SS=65 Per=85	0301 Mgr. Work: Plants & Animals	51	11		
		0303 Animal Training & Service	57	12		
		0303 Animal Training & Service	57	13		
		0304 Elemental Work: Plants & Animals	59	14		
		0302 General Supv.: Plants & Animals	54	**	**	
07 BUSINESS DETAIL	SS=64 Per=94	0701 Administrative Detail	229	35		
		0702 Mathematical Detail	232	36		
		0703 Financial Detail	235	37		
		0704 Oral Communications	237	38		
		0705 Records Processing	241	39		
		0706 Clerical Machine Operation	245	40		
		0707 Clerical Handling	247	41		
08 SELLING	SS=62 Per=81	0801 Sales Technology	251	42		
		0802 General Sales	255	43		
		0803 Vending	258	44		
09 ACCOMMODATING	SS=61 Per=86	0903 Passenger Services	266	47		
		0901 Hospitality Services	262	45		
		0902 Barber & Beauty Services	264	46		
		0905 Attendant Services	271	48		
		0904 Customer Services	269	**	**	

AVERAGE INTERESTS 43-57

01 ARTISTIC	SS=53 Per=59	0101 Literary Arts	16	1		
		0102 Visual Arts	18	2		
		0103 Performing Arts, Drama	21	3		
		0104 Performing Arts, Music	23	4		
		0105 Performing Arts, Dance	26	5		
		0106 Craft Arts	28	6		
		0107 Elemental Arts	32	**	**	
		0108 Modeling	34	**	**	
11 LEADING-INFLUENCING	SS=49 Per=51	1101 Mathematics & Statistics	285	52		
		1102 Education & Library Services	287	53		
		1102 Education & Library Services	287	54		
		1103 Social Research	290	55		
		1103 Social Research	290	56		
		1104 Law	292	57		
		1104 Law	292	58		
		1105 Business Administration	294	59		
		1106 Finance	298	60		
		1107 Services Administration	301	61		
		1108 Communications	304	62		
		1109 Promotion	306	63		
		1110 Regulations Enforcement	308	64		
		1111 Business Management	310	65		
		1112 Contracts & Claims	314	66		
12 PHYSICAL PERFORMING	SS=45 Per=24	1201 Sports	318	**	**	
		1202 Physical Feats	321	**	**	

LOW INTERESTS 35-42

02 SCIENTIFIC	SS=39 Per=15	0201 Physical Sciences	38	7		
		0202 Life Sciences	41	8		
		0203 Medical Sciences	43	9		
		0204 Laboratory Technology	46	10		

VERY LOW INTERESTS –34

None

36 *psychware*

NAME: Alcohol Troubled Person Questionnaire

SUPPLIER: Applied Innovations, Inc.
South Kingstown Office Park, Suite A-1
Wakefield, RI 02879
(800) 272-2250

PRODUCT CATEGORY	PRIMARY APPLICATIONS
Structured Interview	Clinical Assessment/Diagnosis

SALE RESTRICTIONS American Psychological Association Guidelines

SERVICE TYPE/COST	Type	Available	Cost	Discount
	Mail-In	No		
	Teleprocessing	No		
	Local	Yes	$275.00	

PRODUCT DESCRIPTION

The ALCOHOL TROUBLED PERSON QUESTIONNAIRE approaches the problem of alcohol risk assessment according to the model of the Alcohol Troubled Person as developed and presented by Alan Willoughby, Ph.D. The Alcohol Troubled Person is defined as someone whose drinking reduces the quality of the person's life in one or more of the following areas: emotional and cognitive, social, financial, and physical. Scores are provided in each of these four areas in the form of a single page report. The program is designed for easy use by the client with minimal guidance from the professional or para-professional.

This software operates on most available personal computers including IBM, Apple, Digital, and Kaypro.

LICENSED TO APPLIED INNOVATIONS
NETWORKER SCREENER RESULTS
ATP SCALE

ATP 1

03/13/1984
HARRY S. CLARK
MALE
IDENTIFICATION #: 222222222

This evaluation is based on the ALCOHOL TROUBLED PERSON MODEL AS DEVELOPED
AND PRESENTED BY ALAN WILLOUGHBY, Ph.D. Elaboration of this concept
can be found in THE ALCOHOL TROUBLED PERSON: KNOWN AND UNKNOWN.

HARRY stated that there are NO alcohol related problems in
      part of his life.

Social Scale Total: 17   Indicating   Moderate trouble
Financial Scale Total: 6   Indicating   Minimal trouble
Physical Scale Total: 15   Indicating   Moderate trouble
Emotional Scale Total: 22   Indicating   Severe trouble

After answering the screening questions
HARRY stated that there are NO alcohol related problems
in part of his life.

NAME: Alcohol Use Inventory

SUPPLIER: PSYCH Systems, Inc.
600 Reisterstown Road
Baltimore, MD 21208
(800) 368-3366

PRODUCT CATEGORY

Personality

PRIMARY APPLICATIONS

Clinical Assessment/Diagnosis
Personal/Marriage/Family Counseling

SALE RESTRICTIONS   Qualified Professional

SERVICE TYPE/COST	Type	Available	Cost	Discount
	Mail-In	No		
	Teleprocessing	No		
	Local	Yes	See Below	

PRODUCT DESCRIPTION

The ALCOHOL USE INVENTORY provides a means for understanding how and why a person uses and abuses alcohol. The test yields a profile on 15 primary factors: Daily Quantity When Drinking, Social Role Maladaptation, Psychoperceptual Withdrawal, Psychophysical Withdrawal, Loss of Behavior Control, Obsessive Compulsive Drunk, Sustained vs. Periodic Drinking, Guilt, Prior Use of Help, Drink to Change Mood, Social Benefit Drinking, Drink to Improve Mental Condition, Gregarious vs. Solo Drinking, Drinking Causes Marital Problems, and Drinking Follows Marital Problems.

This Psych Systems product administers, scores, and provides a 9-page printout of results. Information about symptoms, styles, and phases of drinking is provided by the test. The information can be used in the planning and execution of programs to help many different kinds of problem drinkers.

Psych Systems programs operate on the IBM PC-XT, COMPAQ Plus, Dec Professional 350, and most DEC PDP-11 systems. Various hardware/ software configurations are available directly from Psych Systems, with single-user systems starting at approximately $12,000. A per test fee also applies.

222-22-2222   Jane Doe   32 yr old white female   16-Feb-84

```
      ------------------------------------
                   |
           AUI     |  Alcohol Use Inventory
                   |
      ------------------------------------
```

This clinical report is designed to assist in psychodiagnostic
evaluation. It is available only to qualified professionals and
should be used in conjunction with professional evaluation. No
decision should be based solely upon the contents of this report.

The computer program generating this report was designed by Psych
Systems, Inc., Baltimore, Maryland 21208. Copyright (C) 1984 by
Psych Systems, Inc. The Alcohol Use Inventory is reproduced by
permission under exclusive license with author. Copyright (C) 1974,
1983, John L. Horn. The interpretive logic utilized in the
generation of the report was designed by John L. Horn, Ph.D., Kenneth
W. Wanberg, Ph.D., F. Mark Foster, Ph.D. Copyright (C) 1984, John L.
Horn, Kenneth W. Wanberg, F. Mark Foster. All rights reserved.

Alcohol Use Inventory (AUI)*

The scales of the (AUI) provide a means for understanding how and why a person uses and abuses alcohol. The basis for this understanding are fifteen primary factors that resolve into five second-level factors. These factors yield profiles and derived scores that can indicate various kinds of alcohol-use problems; the factors also indicate difficulties one can encounter in efforts to treat maladaptive use of alcohol. Information about symptoms, benefits, styles, and phases of drinking is provided. Such information can be used in the planning and execution of programs to help problem drinkers of several kinds. Programs can be tailored to fit particular individuals and particular configurations of problems.

The AUI provides a foundation of operational definitions for multiple-pattern, multiple-syndrome, multiple-condition theories and treatment philosophies. It allows one to expand beyond the narrow idea that alcoholism is a singular, unitary condition. The scales, and the research on which the scales are based, point to the complex, multidimensional nature of problems people can have when they use alcohol improperly.

Description of High Scores on
Primary Scales

Daily Quantity When Drinking

Estimates derived from reported amount of beer, wine, or distilled spirits consumed in a "typical" day.

Raw Score: 6   Range: High Medium

Social Role Maladaptation

These individuals have been jailed for public drunkeness or charged with driving under the influence of alcohol, unemployed for one to three months, and separated from spouse for at least six months due to drinking.

Raw Score: 7   Range: High Medium

Psychoperceptual Withdrawal

The perceptual abilities of these individuals have been distorted
during or after drinking. They may report weird and frightening
experiences when drinking or sobering up. Symptoms such as delirium
tremens are common.

Raw Score: 8   Range: High

Psychophysical Withdrawal

As a result of drinking, these individuals become physically sick.
During the sobering up period, they may experience convulsions,
shakes, heart palpitation, and excessive perspiration.

Raw Score: 7   Range: High

Loss of Behavior Control

Loss of behavior control results from the excessive consumption of
alcohol. These individuals drink until their motor coordination is
impaired. The impairment of motor activity may be accompanied by
amnesic periods or blackouts. Belligerent acts toward others and
physical harm to themselves may also occur.

Raw Score: 10 .   Range: High Medium

Obsessive Compulsive Drunk

These individuals experience persistent thoughts about drinking.
They often fear that they will not have a drink available when they
need it. To avoid confrontation with others, these individuals sneak
drinks and hide their bottles.

Raw Score: 7   Range: High

Sustained vs. Periodic

These individuals report daily drinking for at least six months.
They generally remain intoxicated throughout the day. Low scores on
this scale do not necessarily represent absence of a drinking
problem; such scores may represent a binge type of drinker.

Raw Score: 7   Range: High Medium

42 *psychware*

Post-Drink, Fear, Guilt, Worry

These indivduals worry about their drinking behavior and feel guilty
about the hardships it causes family and friends. Attempts to cover
up the frequency of drinking leads to lying and making excuses.
These individuals experience guilt for drinking and are fearful of
their inability to control it.

Raw Score: 9   Range: High

Prior Use of Help

In the past, these individuals have taken steps to stop drinking.
These steps may include the use of tranquilizers and other medicines
to calm themselves. Hospitalization, involvement in self-help
groups, and religion are other help seeking behaviors common to these
people.

Raw Score: 7   Range: High

Drink to Change Mood

These individuals drink to forget unpleasant thoughts and
difficulties. By drinking, they gain relief from tension and
anxiety. Their drinking may prompt distinct mood swings.

Raw Score: 7   Range: High

Social Benefit Drinking

These individuals drink to make themselves feel important. In social
setting, drinking helps them to overcome shyness and to relax. When
drinking, they are able to make friends and get along with others.
Drinking assists these individuals in relating to the opposite sex
and in experiencing their thoughts and emotions more freely.

Raw Score: 9   Range: High

Drink to Improve Mental Condition

These individuals feel drinking improves their general state of mind.
Drinking makes them feel mentally alert and it increases their work
productivity and creativity.

Raw Score: 5   Range: High

Gregarious vs. Solo Drinking

These individuals drink to maintain social contacts. Drinking occurs outside the home and is used to achieve and maintain conviviality.

Raw Score: 7   Range: High

Drinking Causes Marital Problems

In the past, the drinking behavior of these individuals has provoked marital discord. They link the use of alcohol to their spouse who they describe as constantly badgering and finding fault in them. When drinking, these users of alcohol may become physically abusive with spouse. Elevated scale scores suggest drinking problem occurred prior to marital difficulties.

Raw Score: 6   Range: High

Drinking Follows Marital Problems

These individuals blame their drinking problem on marital difficulties. These users of alcohol suspect the fidelity of their spouses. They view their spouse as too friendly with the opposite sex. Elevated scale scores indicate marital difficulties occurred prior to drinking problem.

Raw Score: 6   Range: High

Description of High Scores on General Scales

Uncontrolled Disruptive Drinking

These individuals are unable to stop drinking after one or two drinks. They experience blackouts and uncontrollable staggering, stumbling, and weaving when drinking. They generally live alone and have a poor work record due to drinking. They often have delirium tremens, and distorted auditory, perceptual or tactile sensations as a result of drinking. They scarcely eat and require minimal sleep during a drinking binge. Drinking often starts in the morning to

relieve a hangover. These individuals may experience a "dry drunk"
(when you act or feel drunk but have had nothing alocholic).

Raw Score: 27   Range: High

Anxious Concern About Drinking

These individuals are concerned about their drinking and usually
resent others comments about it. They drink to relieve tension,
forget unpleasant things, and to overcome depression. They make
excuses to cover up their drinking and often avoid talking to others
about it. Belligerent behavior when drinking is common. Such
inappropriate behavior may lead to guilt and remorse. These
individuals worry about the hardships their drinking causes friends
and family, and fear that it is getting out of their control.

Raw Score: 20   Range: High

Obsessed with Drinking

These individuals are intoxicated daily. They report little or no
time between drinking periods. They may carry a bottle close at hand
for fear of not having a drink when they need it. They drink
throughout the day, including workdays and weekends. They believe
drinking helps them to feel important, overcome shyness, relax
socially, and make friends. They also feel drinking assists them in
expressing ideas and opinions, and in relating their feelings and
thoughts to others.

Raw Score: 13   Range: High

Self-Enhanced Commitment to Drinking

These individuals drink to enhance their lives and to have fun. They
drink because they feel that their social life requires it. Drinking
helps them to express themselves to the opposite sex and it also
helps them to work better and think more freely. They are generally
happy and interpersonally friendly when drinking.

Raw Score: 16   Range: High

General Alcoholism

This scale is comprised of items that make up the basic categories of
alcohol use and misuse. Most of the scale items are found in the

second-order dimensions of UNCONDIS and ANXCONCS. Scores on this
scale can be used to gain a general indication of whether a person is
reporting a substantial number of the symptoms that are commonly said
to indicate alcoholism.

Raw Score: 45   Range: High

222-22-2222   Jane Doe   32 yr old white female   16-Feb-84

Alcohol Use Profile

Scale	Description	R	Decile Score (1–10)
			1 2 3 4 5 6 7 8 9 10

First Order

Scale	Description	R	Decile (asterisk position)
QUANTITY	Daily Average Quantity of Alcohol	6	7
ROLEMALA	Social Role Maladaption	7	6
DELIRIUM	Perceptual Withdrawal Symptoms	8	9
HANGOVER	Psychophysiological Withdrawal	7	8
LCONTROL	Loss of Control Drinking	10	7
COMPULSV	Compulsive Drinking	7	10
SUSTAIND	Daily, Habitual, Sustained Drinking	7	7
GUILTWOR	Drinking, Guilt, and Worry	9	10
HELPBEFR	Sought External Help	7	10
MOODCHNG	Drink to Change Mood	7	9
SOCIALMP	Drink to Improve Sociability	9	10
MENTALMP	Drink to Improve Mental Condition	5	10
GREGARDK	Gregarious Drinking	7	9

Marital Problems

Scale	Description	R	Decile
MARIPROB	Drinking Provokes Marital Problems	6	10
MARICOPE	Drink to Cope With Marital Problem	6	10

Second Order

Scale	Description	R	Decile
UNCONDIS	Uncontrolled Disruptive Drinking	27	8
ANXCONCN	Anxious Concern About Drinking	20	9
OBSESSED	Obsessed About Drinking	13	8
ENHANCED	Drinking Enhancements	16	10

General Factor

Scale	Description	R	Decile
GENALCOH	General Alcoholism	45	8

Decile Ranges for the AUI Profile

Each of the 10 scores represents a 10 percent grouping of the raw
scores. A decile score of 1, for example, represents the scores of
that 10 percent of the norm sample for which the scores were lowest.
A decile score of 10 indicates that a raw score is among the 10
percent of scores that were largest in the norm sample.

Decile

8 - 10   High scores on the scales indicate severe condition of
          maladaption and maladjustment coupled with much use of
          alcohol.

6 - 7   High medium scores on the scales indicate significant
          prevalence of alcohol misuse.

3 - 5   Low medium scores on the scales indicate no significant
          factors indicative of alcohol misuse.

1 - 2   Low scores on the scales reveal little to no significant
          indicators of alcohol overuse. Alcohol use appears
          controlled and problems resulting from alcohol misuse
          are minimal or non-existent.

*   Information contained in this report has been derived from
    the Guidelines for Understanding Alcohol Use and Abuse:
    The Alcohol Use Inventory. Horn, J.L., Wanberg, K.W., and
    Foster, M.F., (1983).

46 *psychware*

NAME: Alcohol Use Questionnaire

SUPPLIER: Applied Innovations, Inc.
South Kingstown Office Park, Suite A-1
Wakefield, RI 02879
(800) 272-2250

PRODUCT CATEGORY	PRIMARY APPLICATIONS
Structured Interview	Clinical Assessment/Diagnosis

SALE RESTRICTIONS   American Psychological Association Guidelines

SERVICE TYPE/COST	Type	Available	Cost	Discount
	Mail-In	No		
	Teleprocessing	No		
	Local	Yes	$125.00	

PRODUCT DESCRIPTION

The ALCOHOL USE QUESTIONNAIRE consists of 40 questions which assess the extent and nature of an individual's use of alcohol, including medical and personal history related to alcohol use, attitudes toward the use of alcohol, and current alcohol consumption. The program is designed for easy use by the client with minimal guidance from the professional or para-professional. The client's answers to questions determine the subsequent questions that are asked. Thus, only questions relevant to the client's circumstances are presented. This questionnaire may be presented as often as needed. Each presentation is recorded in the client's file and may be displayed and printed.

The software operates on most available personal computers including IBM, Apple, Digital, and Kaypro.

03/13/1984
HARRY S. CLARK

The following are HARRY's responses to the ALCOHOL USE QUESTIONNAIRE.

 1. What was your Father's ATTITUDE toward alcohol?
                Light to moderate drinker.

 2. What was your Mother's ATTITUDE toward alcohol?
                Light to moderate drinker.

 3. What was your age when you first drank?
                17 to 20

 4. When drinking over the past year, how many drinks
    did you usually have in 24 hours?
                NONE

 5. What type of alcohol do you drink most often?
                VODKA

 6. When you get drunk, how bad is your hangover?
                NOT BAD.

HARRY WAS ASKED TO INDICATE HOW OFTEN THE FOLLOWING SITUATIONS
HAVE OCCURRED AS A RESULT OF THE USE OF ALCOHOL.

            NEVER
            ONCE
            TWICE
            THREE TIMES
            FOUR OR MORE TIMES

7.	SHAKES THE MORNING AFTER..?	NEVER
8.	HALLUCINATIONS..?	NEVER
9.	CONVULSIONS..?	NEVER
10.	DT'S..?	NEVER
11.	VOMITING BLOOD..?	NEVER
12.	BLACKOUTS (IN PART OR TOTAL)..?	NEVER
13.	DEPRESSION OR LONELINESS..?	ONCE
14.	DOCTOR SAID YOU HAD PANCREATITIS..?	NEVER
15.	DOCTOR SAID YOU HAD LIVER PROBLEM.?	NEVER
16.	DOCTOR SAID YOU SHOULD CUT DOWN ON OR QUIT YOUR DRINKING..?	NEVER
17.	FRIENDS/FAMILY SAID YOU SHOULD CUT CUT DOWN OR QUIT YOUR DRINKING..?	ONCE
18.	HAVE YOU THOUGHT YOU MIGHT BE DRINKING TOO MUCH..?	ONCE
19.	SOUGHT HELP BECAUSE OF YOUR DRINKING..?	NEVER
20.	MISSED TIME ON THE JOB/SCHOOL..?	NEVER

21. DEMOTED OR FIRED FROM WORK..?   NEVER
22. LEFT WORK/SCHOOL EARLY..?   ONCE
23. HAD AN AUTO/VEHICLE ACCIDENT..?   NEVER
24. HAD A MOVING VIOLATION..?   NEVER
25. PICKED UP FOR DRUNK DRIVING..?   NEVER
26. WORK/SCHOOL DISCIPLINARY ACTION..?   NEVER
27. MEDICAL INJURY..?   NEVER
28. HOSPITALIZED..?   NEVER
29. PHYSICAL FIGHTS..?   NEVER
30. VERBAL FIGHTS..?   NEVER
31. ARRESTED..?   NEVER
32. MADE A BAD BUSINESS DECISION..?   NEVER
33. MADE A BAD SOCIAL DECISION..?   NEVER
34. LOST FRIENDSHIPS..?   NEVER
35. GOT SEPARATED/DIVORCED..?   NEVER

36. Do You think that alcohol May be affecting
    YOUR MEDICAL HEALTH OR SOCIAL LIFE (Y/N/?)? N

38. Have you ever tried to cut dowm or
    change your drinking pattern..?   Y

39. In the past 6 months, What is the longest
    TIME WITHOUT ANY USE OF ALCOHOL?   A WEEK OR TWO

40. Do you think you can improve your life
    WITHOUT CHANGING YOUR DRINKING PATTERN..(Y/N/?)? Y

psychware **49**

NAME: Athletic Motivation Program

SUPPLIER: Winslow Research Institute
951 Mariners Island Blvd.
San Mateo, CA 94404
(415) 571-1100

PRODUCT CATEGORY	PRIMARY APPLICATIONS
Motivation/Needs	Training/Development

SALE RESTRICTIONS   None

SERVICE TYPE/COST	Type	Available	Cost	Discount
	Mail-In	Yes	$20.00	Yes
	Teleprocessing	No		
	Local	No		

PRODUCT DESCRIPTION

The ATHLETIC MOTIVATION PROGRAM is a scientific method of identifying the mental attitude and winning motivation of high school, college, and professional athletes quickly and accurately. Used for 14 years by coaches in football, baseball, ice hockey, and soccer, as well as many Olympic teams, it is an effective and respected technique for helping athletes reach maximum potential.

The Coach's Report is a four-page report prepared on each athlete. It contains a profile chart that visually illustrates how the athlete compares to other athletes in the same sport, at the same competitive level, and of the same sex. The Athlete's Report provides objective feedback on athletic attitudes and tells athletes what they can do, on their own, to improve performance.

NAME: Barclay Classroom Assessment System

SUPPLIER: Western Psychological Services
12031 Wilshire Blvd.
Los Angeles, CA 90025
(213) 478-2061

PRODUCT CATEGORY	PRIMARY APPLICATIONS
Interest/Attitudes	Educational Evaluation/Planning
Motivation/Needs	

SALE RESTRICTIONS American Psychological Association Guidelines

SERVICE TYPE/COST Type	Available	Cost	Discount
Mail-In	Yes	$3.60	Yes
Teleprocessing	No		
Local	No		

PRODUCT DESCRIPTION

The BARCLAY CLASSROOM ASSESSMENT SYSTEM assesses individual, social, and affective interactions of students in grades 3-6. It has been standardized on nearly 10,000 children and is the result of more than 20 years of research and field testing.

The computer report generated for each classroom identifies possible gifted students, underachievers, learning-handicapped, or students in need of referral. Individual reports for each student provide summaries of peer, teacher, and self ratings (and their comparisons) on six, major factor dimensions: Task-Order Achievement, Control-Predictability, Reserved-Internal, Physical-Activity, Sociability-Affiliation, and Enterprising- Dominance. Recommendations for remediation or preferred teaching and counseling strategies are included for each child.

The instrument provides valuable information about the non- cognitive functioning of students in contrast with their classroom achievement. Problems of the disruptive or isolated student can be documented. The BARCLAY CLASSROOM ASSESSMENT SYSTEM has been widely used in program evaluation, in developing Individualized Education Plans, and in complying with P.L. 94-142.

BARCLAY CLASSROOM ASSESSMENT SYSTEM (BCAS)

by James R. Barclay, Ph.D.

Published by

Western Psychological Services

Western Psychological Services • 12031 Wilshire Boulevard • Los Angeles, California 90025

CLASSROOM AND INDIVIDUAL REPORTS

Classroom Number: 11   Grade: 2   Date of Report: APR 2, 1984

Total Number of Students Processed: 20   Boys: 9   Girls: 11

CONTENTS OF THIS REPORT: 1 Classroom Summary
                         20 Individual Reports
                          6 Group Data Tables

```
**********************IMPORTANT INFORMATION FOR THE READER**********************
*                                                                            *
*     This report provides a description of each student in this classroom   *
* and information about the ways the teacher and peer group describe each     *
* student.  The Barclay Classroom Assessment System (BCAS) is a highly       *
* sophisticated and complex assessment procedure designed to aid in the early*
* detection of suspected problems of individual students.  It presents some  *
* general suggestions for working with specific children or groups.  However,*
* the BCAS is no substitute for careful and thorough analysis.  Although it   *
* is based on more than 20 years of research on tens of thousands of         *
* students, it relies completely on the responses given by each student and  *
* the teacher to each part of the instrument.  Thus, it indicates how things *
* were perceived at the time the inventory was administered.                  *
*                                                                            *
******************************************************************************
```

HOW TO USE THE REPORTS ON THE FOLLOWING PAGES

CLASSROOM SUMMARY: The student numbers of specific children who may need
special attention are listed for each of several suspected problem areas.
Note the student numbers of children you would like to study further and
then find their reports in the Individual Reports section of this printout.
In cases of possible referral, multiple problems, or suspected gifted or
learning-disabled status, relay this report to school psychologists or other
resource people who may wish to provide help with these particular children.

INDIVIDUAL REPORTS: A more detailed report is provided for each student.
Profiles of scores, summary interpretations, and suggested interventions
are provided to assist you in designing individual programs for students.

GROUP DATA: Tables summarizing student scores and classroom average scores
are provided for in-depth analysis of students or the classroom as a whole.

SEE THE BCAS MANUAL FOR FURTHER INFORMATION

WPS TEST REPORT

52 *psychware*

Suspected Problem Areas and Referral Recommendations
for Individual Children

1. GENERAL REFERRALS

These children had four or more suspected problem areas that were considered serious enough to suggest a referral. A conference with parents and/or referral to professionals who can help is suggested.

No students identified.

2. POSSIBLE LEARNING HANDICAPPED

These children show a pattern of ratings by peers, teacher, and self that is similar to that of learning-disabled or handicapped students. Referral for individual diagnostic testing or review of the child's individualized program is recommended.

Student(s): 13, 15
The possible accuracy in identifying these students is somewhat reduced because some or all of the achievement test scores were not provided.

3. POSSIBLE GIFTED STUDENTS

These children show a pattern of BCAS ratings and achievement scores like those of gifted students. Special programs or further testing is suggested.

Student(s): 1, 6, 8, 9, 10, 14, 16, 20
The possible accuracy in identifying these students is somewhat reduced because some or all of the achievement test scores were not provided.

4. OTHER PROBLEM AREAS

Some children need an increase in attention and concern in the following areas which were judged to be at a level serious enough to deserve review.

Self-Confidence and Feelings of Being Skillful

Student(s): 2, 9, 17

Peer Support and Group Recognition

Student(s): 14, 17

Self-Control and Social Responsibility

Student(s): 4, 6, 7, 21

Verbal Skills and Willingness to Speak Out

Student(s): 4, 13, 21

Physical Skills

Student(s): 14

Teacher Support and Recognition

Student(s): 5, 13, 14, 18

Attitudes Toward School

Western Psychological Services • 12031 Wilshire Boulevard • Los Angeles, California 90025

WPS TEST REPORT

psychware **53**

5. PROBLEM AREAS OF GREATEST CONCERN IN THIS CLASSROOM

       A comparison of the number of problems in this classroom to a large
sample of classrooms suggests that the following areas are of greatest
concern:

       For boys in this classroom, the most frequent problem is in the
area of self-control. The ratings of peers and teacher suggest that
some of the boys have problems with inappropriate behavior and self-
management.

       For girls in this classroom, the most frequent problem is in the
area of verbal-skill deficits, shyness, or reticent behavior, according
to ratings of peers and teacher.

6. VOCATIONAL AWARENESS

       These children show some lack of awareness or interest in alternative
vocational activities. Sometimes this is due to a lack of information about
careers, and sometimes to concentration on one specific vocational area.

       Student(s): 10

7. PEER TUTORS

       Sometimes children can be helpful in tutoring their peers. Some or
all of the following might be used in this manner provided they are willing
and you can train them in methods of tutoring.

       Student(s): 1, 10, 15

8. SPECIAL LEARNING CONSIDERATIONS

       Some children may benefit from a contracting procedure where you
indicate very clearly what the assignment is and monitor their progress.
When they complete the work well, they can earn privileges such as library
time, supplementary reading, work on a project, or free time.

       Student(s): 17

       Some children may benefit from being able to organize their own learning
experiences, doing special projects, and working with one or two others
like themselves.

       No students identified.

9. TEMPERAMENT PATTERNS OF CHILDREN IN THIS CLASSROOM

       On the basis of overall characteristics measured by self, peer, and
teacher ratings, children in this classroom can be described in terms of
six temperament patterns. These patterns have been identified by research
on children of this age, and they provide descriptions of enduring,
consistent traits of the behavior of children. (See next page.)

DO NOT GROUP CHILDREN ACCORDING TO THESE PATTERNS, but rather, attempt to intermix children from each pattern in work groups so that they can learn from each other. The BCAS manual provides more detailed information about these temperament patterns.

PATTERN 1: Children who show this pattern of temperament tend to be controlled, responsible, internally motivated, and persistent. They are average in peer support, above average in achievement, may be in need of an increase in self-competency and self-esteem, and may need help in over-coming shyness. They typically do well in structured learning situations.

Student(s): 9, 16, 20

PATTERN 2: Children with this temperament pattern tend to be seen as leaders, have high social ratings, have high aspirations, and seldom overestimate their ability. They may show some tendency to problems in self-control but show superior achievement. They learn well under any type of instructional strategy.

Student(s): 1, 4, 10, 15, 21

PATTERN 3: These children often need an increase in peer or teacher support, feel isolated, and have multiple problems including underachievement or poor achievement. They may be helped by positive attention from the teacher to improve their social interaction. After an adequate diagnosis of cognitive learning problems, these children may benefit from tutorial help and considerable practice. Learning experiences need to be carefully sequenced and taught one step at a time.

Student(s): 2, 3, 5, 12, 18, 19

PATTERN 4: These children often possess some leadership characteristics but may be achieving below their potential. They tend to underestimate their own skills and show the highest frequency of group interaction and self-control problems. They may need help in changing their tendency to attribute failure to the fault of others rather than to their own deficient effort. The use of clear instructions, behavioral reinforcement, and careful monitoring of their learning may be beneficial.

Student(s): 7, 17

PATTERN 5: This is a blend of Patterns 1 and 2. These children tend to be somewhat overestimating of their ability, but show some interest in leadership activities. They tend to be average to above average in achievement. Some problems may be observed in shyness and self-control although the occurrence of problems is low. They can generally adapt to alternative methods of instruction.

Student(s): 6, 8, 14

PATTERN 6: This is a blend of Patterns 3 and 4. These children tend to be the average students in the class both academically and socially. They sometimes feel that they have not received enough recognition, and may show some problems in self-competency or attitude. Using them as leaders in small-group activities may help. Small-group activities would also be suggested for any cognitive or achievement problems in these children.

Student(s): 13

Comprehensive Achievement Analysis Omitted Because Achievement Test Scores Were Not Reported.

Western Psychological Services • 12031 Wilshire Boulevard • Los Angeles, California 90025

WPS TEST REPORT

Student 5, Female   Classroom 11, Grade 2   BCAS Code B-5-G--64
         Age 8   Date of Report APR 2, 1984

Summary_Based_On_Factor_Scores_

```
-------------Percentile____1_____5_____25_____50____75_____95_____99_
1. Task-Order Achievement    *********************42
2. Control-Predictability    ****************************69
3. Reserved-Internal         *********************42
4. Physical-Activity         ****** 4
5. Sociability-Affiliation   ***********12
6. Enterprising-Dominance___*****************27_____
```

SUMMARY: This student is seen as having an adequate thrust for
achievement, and is viewed as being generally persistent. She demonstrates a
consistent level of predictable and stable behavior. She has an adequate level
of verbal expressiveness. In physical activities or working with her hands,
she is seen as being consistently changeable and possessing a fluctuating
energy level. She exhibits considerable remoteness and the inability to relate
to other people and interact with them. Finally, she tends to be a follower
and is viewed as somewhat nonassertive.

-----★★★-----

Comparison_Of_Total_Ratings_By_Self,_Peers_And_Teacher

```
-------------Percentile____1_____5_____25_____50____75_____95_____99_
1. Total Self Ratings        ***************21
2. Total Peer Ratings        ****************25
3. Teacher_Positive_Ratings_*************11_____
```

SUMMARY: This student has a very low estimate of personal and social
skills, and this same judgment is given by the peer group. Perhaps this is a
somewhat isolated child in this classroom. She is in serious need of more
support and recognition from the teacher. May be a rejected or new student in
the classroom.

Description_of_Self_Ratings

Overall this student maintains a low estimate of self skills.
Indications are that her estimates are high in the Artistic-Intellectual skills
area and low in the Outdoor-Mechanical and Social-Cooperative skills areas.
Generally, this student exhibits a wide range of vocational interests. In
particular she has high vocational interest in intellectual-scientific and
clerical occupational areas. In addition, her self ratings indicate a usually
favorable attitude towards school.

Description_of_Student_by_Peers

Perceived overall by peers as possessing a limited number of personal and
social skills. Estimates of her skills by peers are low in the Outdoor-
Mechanical skills areas.

Western Psychological Services • 12031 Wilshire Boulevard • Los Angeles, California 90025

WPS TEST REPORT

Personal adjustment for this student is seen by the teacher as occasionally poor. In the areas of social interaction, responsiveness, and cooperation, the teacher feels that this child is showing occasionally poor adjustment. The work habits and attitudes of this student are described as being at a level that does not cause any particular concern.

-----***-----

Achievement_Summary_And_Recommendations

An important section of individual evaluation is missing due to absent achievement scores.

Item responses for class number 11 Student number 05 Page 18

TEACHER CHECKLIST
2   17

PART A

1(N)	11(Y)	21(Y)	31(N)	41(Y)	51(Y)	61(Y)	71(N)
2(Y)	12(N)	22(N)	32(Y)	42(Y)	52(N)	62(Y)	72(Y)
3(N)	13(Y)	23(N)	33(N)	43(Y)	53(N)	63(N)	
4(Y)	14(Y)	24(Y)	34(N)	44(N)	54(Y)	64(Y)	
5(N)	15(N)	25(N)	35(N)	45(N)	55(N)	65(N)	
6(Y)	16(Y)	26(N)	36(Y)	46(Y)	56(Y)	66(N)	
7(N)	17(Y)	27(Y)	37( )	47(N)	57(Y)	67(Y)	
8(Y)	18(N)	28(Y)	38(N)	48(N)	58(Y)	68(N)	
9(N)	19(Y)	29(Y)	39(Y)	49(N)	59(N)	69(Y)	
10(Y)	20(N)	30(Y)	40(N)	50(Y)	60(N)	70(Y)	

PART B

1(Y)	11(Y)	21(Y)	31(Y)
2(N)	12(Y)	22(N)	32(N)
3(Y)	13(N)	23(N)	33(Y)
4(N)	14(Y)	24(N)	34(N)
5(N)	15(Y)	25(N)	35(N)
6(N)	16(N)	26(Y)	36(Y)
7(N)	17(N)	27(Y)	37(Y)
8(Y)	18(Y)	28(N)	38(Y)
9(Y)	19(Y)	29(Y)	39(Y)
10(Y)	20(N)	30(Y)	40(Y)

PART C

1(X)	11(0)	21(0)	31(1)	41(0)	51(2)
2(0)	12(1)	22(0)	32(2)	42(2)	52(1)
3(1)	13(0)	23(2)	33(0)	43(1)	
4(0)	14(0)	24(2)	34(0)	44(0)	
5(2)	15(1)	25(1)	35(1)	45(2)	
6(1)	16(2)	26(2)	36(0)	46(0)	
7(2)	17(2)	27(2)	37(2)	47(0)	
8(0)	18(1)	28(2)	38(2)	48(2)	
9(2)	19(2)	29(1)	39(0)	49(1)	
10(2)	20(2)	30(0)	40(2)	50(2)	

PART D

1(06)	11(04)	21(21)
2(03)	12(14)	22(15)
3(15)	13(17)	23(04)
4(20)	14(10)	24(17)
5(16)	15(04)	25(03)
6(05)	16(15)	26(21)
7(15)	17(04)	27(18)
8(05)	18(15)	28(11)
9(03)	19(07)	
10(15)	20(15)	

NOTE: No. 1 of Part C has been eliminated from BCAS scoring

[* indicates a double response]
[( ) indicates a blank or 'light mark]

Western Psychological Services • 12031 Wilshire Boulevard • Los Angeles, California 90025

WPS TEST REPORT

Student 15, Female   Classroom 11, Grade 2   BCAS Code C-3-J--25
          Age 8   Date of Report APR 2, 1984

Summary_Based_On_Factor_Scores

Percentile	1	5	25	50	75	95	99
1. Task-Order Achievement	************************50						
2. Control-Predictability	****************************73						
3. Reserved-Internal	******************31						
4. Physical-Activity	**************************54						
5. Sociability-Affiliation	****************************62						
6. Enterprising-Dominance	**************************58						

SUMMARY: This student is seen as having an adequate thrust for
achievement, and is viewed as being generally persistent. She demonstrates a
consistent level of predictable and stable behavior. She appears to be
generally open and verbally expressive. In physical activities or working with
her hands, she is viewed as having a normally adequate level of effort and
perseverance. She exhibits adequate ability to relate to other people and
interact with them. Finally, she is viewed as occasionally having the need for
leadership roles.

-----***-----

Comparison_Of_Total_Ratings_By_Self,_Peers_And_Teacher

Percentile	1	5	25	50	75	95	99
1. Total Self Ratings	**************************59						
2. Total Peer Ratings	********************************80						
3. Teacher Positive Ratings	********7						

SUMMARY: This student has given a reasonably positive rating to her
personal and social skills and this is somewhat of an underestimate in
comparison to the judgment of peers. She is not receiving a very high level of
recognition from the teacher and is missing a needed source of support.
Perhaps this is a student who has done something controversial or is a student
unfamiliar to the teacher.

Description_of_Self_Ratings

The overall self skills estimate that this student maintains is of an
adequate range. Indications are that her estimates are high in the Artistic-
Intellectual skills area. Generally, this student chooses a great number of
vocational interests. This may reflect either a wide variety of interests or a
failure to make distinctions. In particular she has high vocational interest
in intellectual-scientific, social, clerical and art-music occupational areas.
She has also indicated that she has high interest in activities that deal with
school-oriented tasks, family orientation, traditionally female peer group
orientation and low interest in activities that deal with primary reinforcers
(such as money, food, candy, etc.). In addition, her self ratings indicate a
usually favorable attitude towards school.

Perceived overall by peers as possessing definite personal and social skills. Estimates of her skills by peers are high in the Social-Cooperative skills areas.

Description_of_Student_by_Teacher

Personal adjustment for this student is seen by the teacher as inconsistent, with few positive or negative ratings. In the areas of social interaction, responsiveness, and cooperation, the teacher feels that this child is showing occasionally poor adjustment. The work habits and attitudes of this student are described as usually responsible and dependable.

Achievement_Summary_And_Recommendations

An important section of individual evaluation is missing due to absent achievement scores.

Item responses for class number 11 Student number 15   Page 45

TEACHER CHECKLIST
6 18 22 58

PART A
1(N)	11(Y)	21(Y)	31(Y)	41(Y)	51(Y)	61(N)	71(Y)
2(Y)	12(Y)	22(Y)	32(N)	42(Y)	52(N)	62(Y)	72(Y)
3(Y)	13(N)	23(N)	33(Y)	43(Y)	53(N)	63(N)	
4(Y)	14(Y)	24(N)	34(N)	44(Y)	54(Y)	64(N)	
5(Y)	15(N)	25(N)	35(N)	45(N)	55(N)	65(N)	
6(Y)	16(Y)	26(N)	36(Y)	46(Y)	56(Y)	66(Y)	
7(N)	17(Y)	27(N)	37( )	47(N)	57(N)	67(Y)	
8(Y)	18(N)	28(Y)	38(N)	48(Y)	58(N)	68(Y)	
9(N)	19(Y)	29(Y)	39(N)	49(Y)	59(Y)	69(Y)	
10(Y)	20(Y)	30(Y)	40(Y)	50(Y)	60(Y)	70(Y)	

PART B
1(Y)	11(Y)	21(Y)	31(Y)
2(Y)	12(Y)	22(Y)	32(N)
3(Y)	13(N)	23(Y)	33(Y)
4(N)	14(Y)	24(N)	34(N)
5(N)	15(Y)	25(N)	35(N)
6(N)	16(N)	26(Y)	36(Y)
7(Y)	17(N)	27(Y)	37(Y)
8(Y)	18(Y)	28(N)	38(Y)
9(Y)	19(Y)	29(N)	39(Y)
10(N)	20(Y)	30(Y)	40(Y)

PART C
1(X)	11(1)	21(2)	31(2)	41(1)	51(2)
2(2)	12(0)	22(1)	32(2)	42(2)	52(2)
3(2)	13(2)	23(2)	33(0)	43(2)	
4(2)	14(2)	24(2)	34(0)	44(1)	
5(2)	15(2)	25(2)	35(0)	45(0)	
6(2)	16(2)	26(2)	36(1)	46(2)	
7(2)	17(1)	27(2)	37(1)	47(1)	
8(0)	18(2)	28(1)	38(2)	48(2)	
9(2)	19(1)	29(2)	39(2)	49(0)	
10(2)	20(0)	30(2)	40(0)	50(1)	

PART D
1(01)	11(06)	21(04)
2(12)	12(03)	22(01)
3(05)	13(10)	23(05)
4(17)	14(17)	24(21)
5(16)	15(01)	25(07)
6(09)	16(16)	26(08)
7(16)	17(17)	27(20)
8(18)	18(09)	28(10)
9(21)	19(16)	
10(01)	20(20)	

NOTE: No. 1 of Part C has been eliminated from BCAS scoring

[* indicates a double response]
[( ) indicates a blank or 'light mark]

Western Psychological Services • 12031 Wilshire Boulevard • Los Angeles, California 90025

WPS TEST REPORT

Student 20, Male   Classroom 11, Grade 2   BCAS Code C-5-H--30
          Age 7   Date of Report APR 2, 1984

Summary Based On Factor Scores

```
---------------Percentile----1------5--------25-----50----75---------95-----99-
1. Task-Order Achievement     ***********************54
2. Control-Predictability     ******************************73
3. Reserved-Internal          **********************46
4. Physical-Activity          *****************27
5. Sociability-Affiliation    **************************58
6. Enterprising-Dominance     ********************42
```

SUMMARY: This student is seen as having an adequate thrust for
achievement, and is viewed as being generally persistent. He demonstrates a
consistent level of predictable and stable behavior. He has an adequate level
of verbal expressiveness. In physical activities or working with his hands, he
is viewed as being changeable and possessing a fluctuating energy level. He
exhibits adequate ability to relate to other people and interact with them.
Finally, he is viewed as occasionally having the need for leadership roles.

-----***-----

Comparison Of Total Ratings By Self, Peers And Teacher

```
---------------Percentile----1------5--------25-----50----75---------95-----99-
1. Total Self Ratings         **************************59
2. Total Peer Ratings         ***********************49
3. Teacher Positive Ratings   *******************35
```

SUMMARY: This student has given a reasonably positive rating to his
personal and social skills and this is similar to the judgment given by the
peer group. He is receiving an adequate amount of support from the teacher.

Description of Self Ratings

The overall self skills estimate that this student maintains is of an
adequate range. Indications are that his estimates are high in the Artistic-
Intellectual skills area. Generally, this student exhibits a wide range of
vocational interests. In particular he has high vocational interest in
intellectual-scientific and prestige occupational areas. He has also indicated
that he has high interest in activities that deal with school-oriented tasks
and family orientation. In addition, his self ratings indicate a usually
favorable attitude towards school.

Description of Student by Peers

Perceived overall by peers as possessing a number of personal and social
skills.

Description of Student by Teacher

Personal adjustment for this student is seen by the teacher as generally
good. In the areas of social interaction, responsiveness, and cooperation, the
teacher feels that this child is showing a reasonable level of adjustment. The
work habits and attitudes of this student are described as being at a level
that does not cause any particular concern.

-----***-----

Achievement Summary And Recommendations

An important section of individual evaluation is missing due to
absent achievement scores.

TEACHER CHECKLIST
1   5   16   17

PART A

1(N)	11(Y)	21(N)	31(N)	41(N)	51(Y)	61(N)	71(Y)
2(N)	12(N)	22(N)	32(Y)	42(Y)	52(Y)	62(Y)	72(N)
3(Y)	13(Y)	23(N)	33(N)	43(Y)	53(N)	63(Y)	
4(Y)	14(Y)	24(Y)	34(Y)	44(N)	54(Y)	64(Y)	
5(N)	15(N)	25(Y)	35(Y)	45(Y)	55(Y)	65(N)	
6(N)	16(Y)	26(N)	36(N)	46(N)	56(Y)	66(N)	
7(Y)	17(Y)	27(Y)	37( )	47(Y)	57(Y)	67(N)	
8(N)	18(Y)	28(N)	38(N)	48(Y)	58(N)	68(Y)	
9(Y)	19(Y)	29(N)	39(Y)	49(N)	59(N)	69(N)	
10(Y)	20(N)	30(N)	40(N)	50(N)	60(N)	70(Y)	

PART B

1(N)	11(Y)	21(Y)	31(Y)
2(N)	12(Y)	22(N)	32(Y)
3(Y)	13(N)	23(Y)	33(N)
4(N)	14(Y)	24(N)	34(N)
5(Y)	15(Y)	25(Y)	35(Y)
6(Y)	16(Y)	26(Y)	36(Y)
7(N)	17(Y)	27(N)	37(Y)
8(Y)	18(N)	28(Y)	38(Y)
9(Y)	19(Y)	29(Y)	39(N)
10(Y)	20(N)	30(N)	40(Y)

PART C

1(X)	11(2)	21(1)	31(1)	41(2)	51(2)
2(0)	12(2)	22(2)	32(2)	42(2)	52(2)
3(2)	13(2)	23(2)	33(2)	43(2)	
4(2)	14(2)	24(2)	34(2)	44(0)	
5(2)	15(2)	25(2)	35(2)	45(0)	
6(2)	16(2)	26(2)	36(2)	46(0)	
7(0)	17(2)	27(2)	37(1)	47(2)	
8(2)	18(0)	28(2)	38(2)	48(2)	
9(2)	19(2)	29(1)	39(2)	49(2)	
10(2)	20(2)	30(1)	40(2)	50(2)	

PART D

1(10)	11(04)	21(21)
2(20)	12(20)	22(20)
3(13)	13(08)	23(21)
4(03)	14(21)	24(04)
5(20)	15(20)	25(20)
6(01)	16(03)	26(03)
7(10)	17(21)	27(16)
8(08)	18(20)	28(20)
9(09)	19(20)	
10(03)	20(20)	

NOTE: No. 1 of Part C has been eliminated from BCAS scoring

[* indicates a double response]
[( ) indicates a blank or "light mark"]

Western Psychological Services • 12031 Wilshire Boulevard • Los Angeles, California 90025

WPS TEST REPORT

NAME: Basic Inventory of Natural Language Software

SUPPLIER: Publishers Test Service
2500 Garden Road
Monterey, CA 93940
(800) 538-9547

PRODUCT CATEGORY

Cognitive/Ability

PRIMARY APPLICATIONS

Educational Evaluation/Planning
Clinical Assessment/Diagnosis

SALE RESTRICTIONS American Psychological Association Guidelines

SERVICE TYPE/COST	Type	Available	Cost	Discount
	Mail-In	No		
	Teleprocessing	No		
	Local	Yes	NA	

PRODUCT DESCRIPTION

This program, designed for operation on an Apple computer, allows the user to analyze the naturally-produced language of children in grades K-12. Photographs are used to elicit an unstructured sample of language which is tape recorded and transcribed for computer scoring. The BASIC INVENTORY OF NATURAL LANGUAGE yields three scores which provide a profile of the child's language proficiency: Fluency, Complexity, and Average Sentence Length. The test has been found to be particularly useful in bilingual, English as a Second Language, and language development programs and is used in speech and language remediation programs by therapists and language specialists.

The program may also be used to score written language samples and to analyze the complexity of reading materials. Thirty-two languages (including English and Spanish) may be evaluated.

NAME: Basic Personality Inventory

SUPPLIER: PSYCH Systems, Inc.
600 Reisterstown Road
Baltimore, MD 21208
(800) 368-3366

PRODUCT CATEGORY

Personality

PRIMARY APPLICATIONS

Clinical Assessment/Diagnosis
Personal/Marriage/Family Counseling

SALE RESTRICTIONS   Qualified Professional

SERVICE TYPE/COST	Type	Available	Cost	Discount
	Mail-In	No		
	Teleprocessing	No		
	Local	Yes	See Below	

PRODUCT DESCRIPTION

The BASIC PERSONALITY INVENTORY is a multi-trait, objective, personality inventory designed to assess eleven areas of functioning. This 240-item instrument consists of eleven clinical scales and one critical item scale. It was developed primarily to indicate areas of personal maladjustment or psychopathology. Given the bipolar nature of the scale definitions, it is possible for the inventory to indicate areas of personal strength and normal personality functioning also.

This Psych Systems program administers, scores, and provides a printout of test results. The clinical scales measure dimensions associated with antisocial behavior, rebellious attitudes, impulsivity, and neurotic tendencies. Other traits measured by the instrument are relevant to both adjusted and maladjusted behavior patterns, such as Social Introversion, Anxiety, and Self-Confidence/Self-Deprecation.

Psych Systems programs operate on the IBM PC-XT, COMPAQ Plus, Dec Professional 350, and most DEC PDP-11 systems. Various hardware/software configurations are available directly from Psych Systems, with single-user systems starting at approximately $12,000. A per test fee also applies.

```
-------------------------------------------
|          |                               |
|   BPI    |   Basic Personality Inventory |
|          |                               |
-------------------------------------------
```

The Basic Personality Inventory (BPI) was added to FASTTEST for Research Purposes. The BPI does possess impressive psychometric features, however, additional research is required before an interpretive system can be developed. It is therefore strongly recommended that the BPI be used in conjuction with the MMPI and the Adjective Checklist (ACL). This proposed battery will provide the empirical rationale for constructing a detailed BPI interpretive system.

The computer program generating this report was designed by Psych Systems, Inc., Baltimore, Maryland 21208. Copyright (C) 1984 by Psych Systems, Inc. The Basic Personality Inventory is reproduced by permission. Copyright (C) 1983 by Douglas N. Jackson. Reproduced under license from Research Psychologists Press, Inc., Port Huron, Michigan 48060. All rights reserved.

The BPI inventory contains 11 bipolar personality trait scales and 1 critical item scale (Deviation). In this report the scale descriptions are based on HIGH scorers (T 60+). In reviewing the BPI profile, it is recommended that the professional consults the HIGH score descriptions, and psychological and psychometric scale clusters. Although this information will assist the professional in understanding the BPI protocol, the BPI does not currently have a completed test manual. This means that the BPI results should be used with extreme care.

BPI TRAIT DESCRIPTIONS FOR HIGH SCORERS

Hypochondriasis (HYP)

People HIGH on HYP report a variety of somatic symptoms. They are preoccupied with health and physical functioning. They complain of chronic fatigue, pain, and weakness.

Depression (DEP)

People HIGH on DEP are pessimistic about the future. They feel depressed, unhappy, and dysphoric. They suffer from a lack of self confidence.

Denial (DEN)

People HIGH on DEN lack insight into their own behavior. They avoid excitement and are emotionally unresponsive people.

Interpersonal Problems (IPS)

People HIGH on IPS react poorly to criticism from others. They seldom involve themselves in social interactions or groups. These uncooperative people may resist rules and regulations.

Social Deviation (SOD)

People HIGH on SOD act contrary to social norms and mores. They harbor little, if any, guilt for their actions. They frequently depart from the truth.

Persecutory Ideas (PID)

People HIGH on PID blame others for problems and short comings. They feel misunderstood and are inclined to brood.

Anxiety (AXY)

People HIGH on AXY express fear and apprehension when placed in unfamiliar surroundings. They worry excessively. Although they are hyperattentive, they are easily distracted.

Thinking Disorder (THD)

People HIGH on THD show confusion in thought. They feel misunderstood and mistreated. They usually report living in a dreamlike world.

Impulse Expression (IME)

People HIGH on IME fail to consider the consequences of their actions. They behave in a risky and irresponsible manner. Because they are doers rather than thinkers, they lack impulse control.

222-22-2222 Jonathan Doe   32 yr old white male   16-Feb-84

Social Introversion (SOI)

People HIGH on SOI feel uncomfortable with others. They lack
interpersonal skills. They are overcontrolled and unable to enjoy
interactions with others.

Social Depreciation (SDP)

People HIGH on SDP are self-effacing. They lack self-confidence and
typically refuse credit for accomplishments.

Deviation (DEV)

People HIGH on DEV display behavior patterns very different from most
people. They admit to unusual and pathological characteristics.

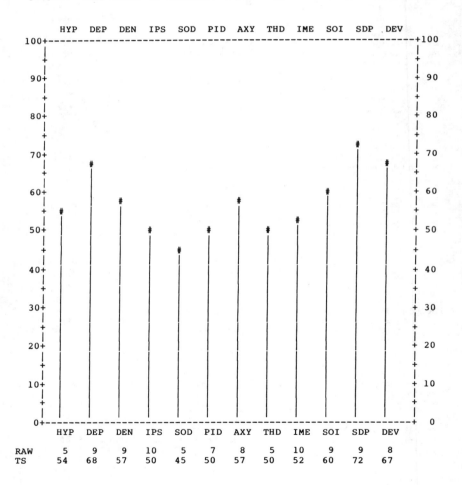

	HYP	DEP	DEN	IPS	SOD	PID	AXY	THD	IME	SOI	SDP	DEV
RAW	5	9	9	10	5	7	8	5	10	9	9	8
TS	54	68	57	50	45	50	57	50	52	60	72	67

66 *psychware*

BASIC PERSONALITY INVENTORY SCALE CLUSTERS
----- ----------- --------- ----- --------

    A. Cognitive Style and Infrequency

       1. Denial
       2. Deviation

    B. Personal Cognitive Adjustment

       1. Persecutory Ideation
       2. Thinking Disorder

    C. Personal Emotional Adjustment

       1. Depression
       2. Anxiety
       3. Hypochondriasis

    D. Social and Self-Perception

       1. Self-Depreciation
       2. Social Introversion

    E. Antisocial Orientation

       1. Interpersonal problems
       2. Social Deviation
       3. Impulse Expression

222-22-2222 Jonathan Doe   32 yr old white male   16-Feb-84

CRITICAL ITEMS
-------- -----

T - I have strange fears of places and things.
T - I frequently experience terrible headaches.
T - I have often used dangerous drugs and chemicals.
T - I would enjoy watching someone suffer great pain.
T - I am very much attracted to members of my own sex.
T - I have been in serious trouble with the law.
T - I do not care for anyone very much.
T - I always have difficulty sleeping.

NAME: Beck Depression Inventory

SUPPLIER: NCS/Professional Assessment Services
P.O. Box 1416
Minneapolis, MN 55440
(800) 328-6759

PRODUCT CATEGORY

Personality

PRIMARY APPLICATIONS

Clinical Assessment/Diagnosis

SALE RESTRICTIONS American Psychological Association Guidelines

SERVICE TYPE/COST	Type	Available	Cost	Discount
	Mail-In	No		
	Teleprocessing	No		
	Local	Yes	$5.50	Yes

PRODUCT DESCRIPTION

The BECK DEPRESSION INVENTORY serves as a clinical tool for assessing the severity of depressive symptoms. The 22 items measure complaints, symptoms, and attitudes related to depression. Assessments are made in the following areas: sadness, pessimism, sense of failure, lack of satisfaction, guilty feelings, sense of being punished, self-dislike, self-accusations, suicidal wishes, crying spells, irritability, withdrawal, and indecisiveness. The report indicates severity of depressed mood, lists major complaints, and provides treatment recommendations.

MICROTEST Assessment Software from National Computer Systems, used with a microcomputer system ($2000-$3000 purchase price), automatically administers test items, scores test results, and generates complete test reports. The cost for local scoring refers to the cost-per-test when diskettes are purchased in units of 20 administrations (minimum purchase).

CLINICAL INTERPRETIVE ANALYSIS

OF THE

BECK DEPRESSION INVENTORY

CASE NO. DEMO12

TEST DATE: 3/17/83

This computer-generated report is based on the result of the
Beck Depression Inventory. Its purpose is to assist qualified
professionals in clinical assessment and should be used in
conjunction with the clinician's professional experience.

_____
Reviewing Professional

CASE NO. DEMO12   DATE: 3/17/83
                    BECK DEPRESSION INVENTORY

    Results of this inventory indicate severity of depressed mood.
Each of the 21 items assesses a symptom level usually associated
with depression. Symptoms are self-evaluated on a 3-point scale.
Maximum score is 63.

            Mild   Moderate   Severe

****

            BECK DEPRESSION INVENTORY SCORE: 13
                    (MAXIMUM = 63)

    This individual's BECK DEPRESSION INVENTORY score is considered
to be in the mildly depressed range.

    The major symptom-attitude complaints endorsed by this person
include the following: sadness, pessimism, sense of failure,
lack of satisfaction, guilty feeling, sense of being punished,
self-dislike, self accusations, suicidal wishes, crying spells,
irritability, withdrawal, indecisiveness.

    The individual also indicates purposely trying to lose weight
by eating less.

                    TABLE OF RESPONSES
            (SCORES REPRESENTED ON A 0-3 SCALE)

1. 1   2. 1   3. 1   4. 1   5. 1   6. 1   7. 1   8. 1

9. 1   10. 1   11. 1   12. 1   13. 1   14. 0   15. 0   16. 0

17. 0   18. 0   19. 0   20. 0   21. 0   22. T

NAME: Beck Depression Inventory Report

SUPPLIER: Psychologistics, Inc.
P.O. Box 3896
Indialantic, FL 32903
(305) 727-7900

PRODUCT CATEGORY

Personality
Motivation/Needs

PRIMARY APPLICATIONS

Clinical Assessment/Diagnosis
Personal/Marriage/Family Counseling

SALE RESTRICTIONS American Psychological Association Guidelines

SERVICE TYPE/COST	Type	Available	Cost	Discount
	Mail-In	No		
	Teleprocessing	No		
	Local	Yes	$1.90	

PRODUCT DESCRIPTION

The BECK DEPRESSION INVENTORY REPORT is designed to facilitate administration and scoring of the Beck Depression Inventory.

The program introduces the user to the computer, administers test items, and prints a narrative summary. Test answers may be input directly by the client or by the clinician. No computer experience is needed to use the program, which provides continuous prompts to guide the user. All calculations and scoring are accomplished by the program.

A one-page narrative report is automatically generated, including a listing of the client's item selections. The report contains interpretive statements indicating nature and degree of depressive symptoms, probable degree of life impairment, intervention recommendations, and cautions.

The price shown above is the cost-per-test when diskettes are purchased in units of 50 administrations (minimum purchase). The program is compatible with Apple II + , IIe, and IBM PC microcomputer systems.

PSYCHOLOGISTICS INC.

BECK DEPRESSION INVENTORY REPORT

NAME: JOHN X. DOE
AGE: 25
SEX: MALE
DATE OF TEST: FEBRUARY 27, 1984

***   TOTAL SCORE = 34   SEVERE DEPRESSION   **

    This score suggests the presence of a broad range of depressive
symptoms. Individuals with similar scores report experiencing severe
dysphoria, self-depreciation, withdrawal, and apathy. Decision
making may be impaired. Notable impairments in work, leisure
activities, and/or family life are typical. Close supervision, and
possibly hospitalization, should be considered at this time.
Suicidal ideation and tendencies should be carefully evaluated.

THE CLIENT'S ITEM SELECTIONS WERE AS FOLLOWS:

3 = I used to be able to cry, but now I can't cry even though I want to.
    I don't get irritated at all by the things that used to irritate me.
    I have lost all of my interest in other people.
    I can't make decisions at all anymore.
    I can't do any work at all.
    I have lost interest in sex completely.

2 = I feel I have nothing to look forward to.
    I don't get real satisfaction out of anything anymore.
    I blame myself all the time for my faults.
    I feel that there are permanent changes in my appearance that make me
       look unattractive.
    My appetite is much worse now.

1 = I feel sad.
    I feel I have failed more than the average person.
    I am disappointed in myself.
    I have thoughts of killing myself, but I would not carry them out.
    I don't sleep as well as I used to.
    I get tired more easily than I used to.

0 = I don't feel particularly guilty.
    I don't feel I am being punished.
    I haven't lost much weight, if any, lately.
    I am no more worried about my health than usual.

                        EXAMINER

            COPYRIGHT (C) 1982   THOMAS H. HARRELL, PHD

psychware **71**

NAME: Beck Depression and Hopelessness Scale

SUPPLIER: PSYCH Systems, Inc.
600 Reisterstown Road
Baltimore, MD 21208
(800) 368-3366

PRODUCT CATEGORY

Personality

PRIMARY APPLICATIONS

Clinical Assessment/Diagnosis

SALE RESTRICTIONS Qualified Professional

SERVICE TYPE/COST	Type	Available	Cost	Discount
	Mail-In	No		
	Teleprocessing	No		
	Local	Yes	See Below	

PRODUCT DESCRIPTION

Rationally developed as an instrument to measure the level of severity of a dysphoric mood, the BECK DEPRESSION SCALE is useful for obtaining screening information. From the results of this test the clinician can learn the current state of the individual's mood.

The BECK HOPELESSNESS SCALE was developed on a large sample of patients who had attempted suicide. When used in combination with the Depression Scale, the clinician receives a strong indication of the level of depression and the possibility of suicide.

This Psych Systems program administers, scores, and provides an interpretive printout of the test.

Psych Systems programs operate on the IBM PC-XT, COMPAQ Plus, Dec Professional 350, and most DEC PDP-11 systems. Various hardware/ software configurations are available directly from Psych Systems, with single-user systems starting at approximately $12,000. A per test fee also applies.

222-22-2222 Jane Doe   6 yr old white female 16-Feb-84

```
-----------------------------------------------------
              |
    BECK      | Beck Depression/Hopelessness Survey
              |
-----------------------------------------------------
```

The Beck Depression/Hopelessness Survey is made up of two scales:
the Depression Inventory and the Hopelessness Scale.

The Depression Inventory was developed to measure the severity of
depression mood. It was not designed to provide an independent
diagnosis of depression or to distinguish among the various types
of depression.

The Hopelessness Scale was developed to measure pessimism and
hopelessness.

The computer program generating this report was designed by Psych
Systems, Inc., Baltimore, Maryland 21208. Copyright (C) 1984 by
Psych Systems, Inc. The Beck Depression Inventory is reproduced
by permission. Copyright (C) 1972, Aaron T. Beck, M.D.,
Philadelphia, Pennsylvania. All rights reserved.

222-22-2222   Jane Doe   6 yr old white female   16-Feb-84

I. Depression Inventory

    A. Score: 24

    B. Interpretation: This score suggests that the respondent
        is experiencing a moderately depressed mood. The individual's
        score equals or exceeds 69% of those evaluated in this
        clinician's population.

```
0        10        20        30        40        50        60
************************----------------------------------!
!          !  Mild  ! Moderate !           Severe         !
```

    c. Critical Items
        - I am so concerned with how I feel or what I feel that it is
           hard to think of much else

II. Hopelessness Scale

    A. Score: 8

    B. Interpretation: This score suggests that the respondent
        is mildly pessimistic about the future. The individual's
        score equals or exceeds 55% of those evaluated in this
        clinician's population.

```
0         5          10           15           20
*************************----------------------------------!
!               !  Mild   !  Moderate   !  Severe   !
```

    c. Critical Items
        - I might as well give up because I can't make things better for
           myself (TRUE)

NAME: Bender Report

SUPPLIER: Psychologistics, Inc.
P.O. Box 3896
Indialantic, FL 32903
(305) 727-7900

PRODUCT CATEGORY

Cognitive/Ability
Personality

PRIMARY APPLICATIONS

Clinical Assessment/Diagnosis
Educational Evaluation/Planning

SALE RESTRICTIONS American Psychological Association Guidelines

SERVICE TYPE/COST	Type	Available	Cost	Discount
	Mail-In	No		
	Teleprocessing	No		
	Local	Yes	$149.00	

PRODUCT DESCRIPTION

The BENDER REPORT is designed to facilitate scoring and furnish a detailed interpretation of the Bender Gestalt test. The program provides for scoring and interpretation of child and adult protocols. The logic suggested by Koppitz is used for children and the logic suggested by Hutt is used for adults.

Factor definitions and scoring criteria are provided by the program. Minimal computer experience is needed to use the program, which provides continuous memory prompts to supplement the manual. All calculations and scoring are accomplished by the program.

A one- to two-page narrative report is automatically generated. For adults, the report contains interpretive statements based on the 26 specific factors and the Psychopathology Scale developed by Hutt. The child report addresses developmental level and emotional factors as conceptualized by Koppitz.

Software versions are available for the Apple II + , IIe, III and IBM PC computer systems. The price shown includes a manual and unlimited usage of the program.

BENDER-REPORT
CHILD VERSION

CLIENT: JOHN X. DOE, JR.
DATE OF BIRTH: 11-01-75
DATE OF TEST: 02-27-84
AGE: 8 YEARS, 3 MONTHS
EXAMINER: JOHN Q. SMITH, PH.D.

ON THIS ADMINISTRATION OF THE BENDER-GESTALT-VISUAL-MOTOR-TEST, 11 ERRORS IN REPRODUCTION ARE PRESENT WHICH CORRESPONDS TO A PERCEPTUAL-MOTOR DEVELOPMENTAL AGE THAT FALLS BETWEEN 5 YEARS, 4 MONTHS AND 5 YEARS, 5 MONTHS. THIS SCORE SUGGESTS THAT MATURATION OF VISUO-GRAPHIC SKILLS IS SUBSTANTIALLY BELOW THAT EXPECTED OF CHILDREN THE SAME AGE.

TOTAL TIME TO COMPLETION OF ALL FIGURES WAS 7 MINUTES AND 43 SECONDS. THIS TIME IS WITHIN THE RANGE SHOWN BY OTHER CHILDREN THE SAME AGE.

THE CHILD'S PERFORMANCE SHOWS 7 ERRORS WHICH HAVE BEEN ASSOCIATED WITH NEUROLOGICAL IMPAIRMENT IN CHILDREN OF SIMILAR AGE. THERE ARE 6 REPRODUCTION ERRORS EXHIBITED WHICH HAVE BEEN SHOWN TO OCCUR MORE OFTEN, BUT NOT EXCLUSIVELY IN NEUROLOGICALLY IMPAIRED CHILDREN. THERE ARE 1 ERRORS PRESENT WHICH HAVE BEEN SHOWN TO BE PRODUCED ALMOST EXCLUSIVELY BY CHILDREN WHO SHOW SOME DEGREE OF ORGANIC IMPAIRMENT.

EXAMINATION OF OVERALL PERFORMANCE INDICATES THAT 2 EMOTIONAL INDICATORS ARE PRESENT, WHICH SUGGESTS (BUT DOES NOT RULE OUT) THAT EMOTIONAL FACTORS DID NOT SIGNIFICANTLY INTERFERE WITH PERFORMANCE. IF THERE IS BEHAVIORAL EVIDENCE OR SUSPICION THAT EMOTIONAL DYSFUNCTIONS ARE PRESENT FURTHER PSYCHOLOGICAL EVALUATION IS RECOMMENDED.

THE ORDER OF THE FIGURES APPEARS SOMEWHAT CONFUSED. THIS IS SOMETIMES ASSOCIATED WITH POOR PLANNING AND DIFFICULTY ORGANIZING MATERIAL. THE POSSIBILITY OF MENTAL CONFUSION SHOULD BE RULED OUT PARTICULARLY IF INTELLECTUAL FUNCTIONING IS ABOVE AVERAGE.

THE CHILD'S REPRODUCTIONS SHOW AN INCREASE IN SIZE ON AT LEAST ONE OF THE FIGURES. THIS IS SOMETIMES ASSOCIATED WITH EXPLOSIVENESS AND/OR LOW FRUSTRATION TOLERANCE.

JOHN Q. SMITH, PH.D.
EXAMINER

CLIENT: JOHN X. DOE
AGE: 25
DATE OF TEST: FEBRUARY 27, 1984   PAGE 1
EXAMINER: JOHN Q. SMITH, PH.D.

     The following statements should be considered as interpretive
hypotheses. They suggest possible areas of difficulty and behavior
disposition. These hypotheses are based on empirical findings and
clinical experience. Caution should be used in applying these
interpretive statements to a specific individual. Areas of possible
difficulty and personality disposition suggested in this report need
to be validated before they are accepted.

     Scorable deviations occurred on three factors related to
organization of the figures. The overly methodical sequence suggests
compulsive tendencies. The abnormal position of the first drawing
indicates possible adjustment difficulties. Similar abnormal use of
the margin may be related to covert anxiety and/or attempts to
maintain control through the use of external support.

     One factor had a deviation regarding size of the figures.
Isolated changes in size occurred and this may have idiosyncratic
meaning related to the figure on which it occurred.

     Two factors had abnormalities regarding changes in the gestalt.
Psychological blocking, indecisiveness, compulsive doubting, and
phobias tend to be associated with similar mild crossing difficulty.
The moderate curvature difficulty is thought to be indicative of
emotional disturbance. This may take the form of over emotionality
or depression.

     One deviation was scored regarding distortion of the gestalt.
Difficulty in adaptability is indicated by the mild perseveration.

     One deviation occurred on a factor related to movement/drawing.
Internalized anxiety may be indicated by the presence of faint lines.

     The Psychopathology Score of 39.25 suggests limited
psychological problems.

     JOHN Q. SMITH, PH.D.
            EXAMINER

NAME: Bexley-Maudsley Automated Psychological Screening

SUPPLIER: NFER-Nelson Publishing Company Ltd
2 Oxford Road East
Windsor, Berks., SL4 1DF
ENGLAND

PRODUCT CATEGORY

Cognitive/Ability

PRIMARY APPLICATIONS

Clinical Assessment/Diagnosis

SALE RESTRICTIONS   Qualified Professional

SERVICE TYPE/COST	Type	Available	Cost	Discount
	Mail-In	No		
	Teleprocessing	No		
	Local	Yes	$285.00	

PRODUCT DESCRIPTION

The BEXLEY-MAUDSLEY test battery is designed to screen patients for psychological deficits resulting from organic brain damage. Developed and standardized during work with detoxified alcoholics, it is especially suited for screening chronic alcoholic patients. The battery consists of six tests: Visual Spatial Ability, Perceptual Motor Speed, Visual Perceptual Analysis, Verbal Recognition Memory, Visual Spatial Recognition Memory, and Abstract Problem Solving.

The tests are administered to the subject via the computer screen. A specially designed patient keyboard includes nine response keys. Since some tests use less than nine keys, three masks are provided so that the patient is always presented with the exact number of alternatives for each test. The keyboard fits over keyboards on Commodore Pet and Apple II computers. Manuals for both versions give clear details of administration, scoring, and theoretical background.

Raw scores and standardized scores are available immediately after the tests are completed, either on the screen or by hard-copy printout from the computer. The price shown here includes the cost of the keyboard. However, the program may be purchased separately.

NAME: Bipolar Psychological Inventory

SUPPLIER: Precision People, Inc.
3452 North Ride Circle. S.
Jacksonville, FL 32217
(904) 262-1096

PRODUCT CATEGORY	PRIMARY APPLICATIONS
Personality	Clinical Assessment/Diagnosis

SALE RESTRICTIONS American Psychological Association Guidelines

SERVICE TYPE/COST Type	Available	Cost	Discount
Mail-In	No		
Teleprocessing	No		
Local	Yes	$250.00	

PRODUCT DESCRIPTION

This program provides for completely computerized administration, scoring, and interpretation of a 300-item psychological inventory. Affect and behavior are assessed with respect to 15 scales: Invalid, Lie, Defensive, Psychic Pain, Depression, Self-Degradation, Dependence, Unmotivated, Social Withdrawal, Family Discord, Sexual Immaturity or Problem Index, Social Deviancy, Impulsiveness, Hostility, and Insensitivity. The narrative report includes separate male/female formats, a personal profile of the individual, normative information based on normal populations, and printouts of significant items as well as the responses entered for all items.

The inventory takes only about 30 minutes to complete, items are easily read on an 8th-grade level, and dimensions are relevant to the client population.

The software is compatible with the Apple microcomputer. A manual and sample printout are available for $34.00.

NAME: Brief Intelligence Test

SUPPLIER: PSYCH Systems, Inc.
600 Reisterstown Road
Baltimore, MD 21208
(800) 368-3366

PRODUCT CATEGORY

Cognitive/Ability

PRIMARY APPLICATIONS

Clinical Assessment/Diagnosis
Personnel Selection/Evaluation
Personal/Marriage/Family Counseling
Vocational Guidance/Counseling

SALE RESTRICTIONS   Qualified Professional

SERVICE TYPE/COST	Type	Available	Cost	Discount
	Mail-In	No		
	Teleprocessing	No		
	Local	Yes	See Below	

PRODUCT DESCRIPTION

The BRIEF INTELLIGENCE TEST measures verbal competence and mathematical reasoning. The 60 item-test takes 20 minutes to complete. When used in a clinical setting it provides a gross measure of cognitive functioning. Deviations between vocabulary and arithmetic reasoning may indicate neurological impairment or serious psychotic thinking disturbance. Scores obtained on the vocabulary sub-section serve as reasonable measures of overall intelligence. Scores obtained on numerical reasoning reflect abilities necessary in certain job functions.

This Psych Systems program administers, scores, and provides an interpretive printout of the test.

Psych Systems programs operate on the IBM PC-XT, COMPAQ Plus, Dec Professional 350, and most DEC PDP-11 systems. Various hardware/ software configurations are available directly from Psych Systems, with single-user systems starting at approximately $12,000. A per test fee also applies.

222-22-2222 Jonathan Doe   32 yr old white male   16-Feb-84

```
-------------------------------------
|        |                           |
|  BIT   |  Brief Intelligence Test  |
|        |                           |
-------------------------------------
```

I. Intelligence

		General Normed Percentile	Age-Normed Percentile	Age-Normed Estimated IQ
Section	Raw Score			
Numerical	2	5%	3%	70
Verbal	37	90%	83%	115

PSYCH SYSTEMS®

NAME: Caldwell Report for the MMPI

SUPPLIER: Caldwell Report
3122 Santa Monica Blvd.
Santa Monica, CA 90404
(213) 829-3644

PRODUCT CATEGORY	PRIMARY APPLICATIONS
Personality	Clinical Assessment/Diagnosis

SALE RESTRICTIONS American Psychological Association Guidelines

SERVICE TYPE/COST	Type	Available	Cost	Discount
	Mail-In	Yes	$40.00	
	Teleprocessing	Yes	$40.00	
	Local	No		

PRODUCT DESCRIPTION

The CALDWELL REPORT for MMPI interpretation is among the most sophisticated programs available. Its statement library contains more than 25,000 entries. The report is written in narrative style and incorporates sections dealing with test-taking attitude, symptoms and personality characteristics, diagnostic impression, and treatment considerations. Well-established two-point code correlates are presented. However, the program logic also considers primary and secondary scale elevations, age, sex, education, and marital status. Among the specific treatment considerations evaluated are suicide risk factors, which medication (or none), transference problems, and points for interview focus.

NAME: California Psychological Inventory

SUPPLIER: NCS/Professional Assessment Services
P.O. Box 1416
Minneapolis, MN 55440
(800) 328-6759

PRODUCT CATEGORY	PRIMARY APPLICATIONS
Personality	Vocational Guidance/Counseling
Career/Vocational	Personnel Selection/Evaluation

SALE RESTRICTIONS American Psychological Association Guidelines

SERVICE TYPE/COST	Type	Available	Cost	Discount
	Mail-In	Yes	$4.00	Yes
	Teleprocessing	Yes	$4.00	Yes
	Local	No		

PRODUCT DESCRIPTION

The CALIFORNIA PSYCHOLOGICAL INVENTORY is designed to measure adult and adolescent personality characteristics significant in the daily living and social interactions of normal persons. The 480 true-false items require a 6th-grade reading level and 45 minutes for completion. The test measures 18 characteristics: Dominance, Capacity for Status, Sociability, Social Presence, Self-Acceptance, Sense of Wellbeing, Responsibility, Socialization, Self-control, Tolerance, Good Impression, Communality, Achievement via Conformance, Achievement via Independence, Intellectual Efficiency, Psychological-mindedness, Flexibility, and Femininity.

The single page report records and plots all scores on clearly defined scales for easy interpretation.

CALIFORNIA PSYCHOLOGICAL INVENTORY

by Harrison G. Gough

ID-   SEX- **FEMALE**   DATE- **13-FEB-84**   NCS CODE- **395-0007**

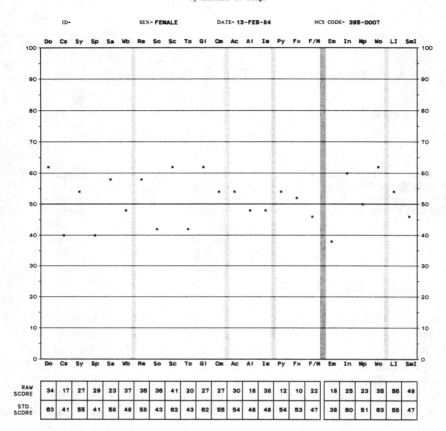

	Do	Cs	Sy	Sp	Sa	Wb	Re	So	Sc	To	Gi	Cm	Ac	Ai	Ie	Py	Fx	F/M	Em	In	Mp	Wo	LI	SmI
RAW SCORE	34	17	27	29	23	37	36	36	41	20	27	27	30	18	38	12	10	22	18	25	23	35	58	49
STD. SCORE	63	41	55	41	58	49	58	43	62	43	62	55	54	48	48	54	53	47	38	60	51	63	55	47

84 *psychware*

SPECIAL SCALES AND INDICES

Empathy (Em). This scale was developed by Robert Hogan, Ph.D., to assess the capacity to think intuitively about people and to understand their feelings and attitudes. The CPI version of the scale contains 39 items. High-scorers are often described as friendly, versatile, and outgoing. Low-scorers are often described as withdrawn, shy, and rather hard to please. For more information see: E. B. Greif & R. T. Hogan, The theory and measurement of empathy. Journal of Counseling Psychology, 1973, 20, 280-284.

Independence (In). The purpose of this scale is to identify individuals who are independent, confident, and resourceful, but not necessarily affiliative. High-scorers are often described as strong, determined, and resourceful. Low-scorers are often described as absent-minded, lacking in confidence, and easily discouraged. In is similar in intended meaning to the Autonomy scale developed by William Kurtines, Ph.D. (See: W. Kurtines, Autonomy: A concept reconsidered. Journal of Personality Assessment, 1974, 38, 243-246.)

Managerial Potential (Mp). This is a research scale, intended to identify persons who have a talent for supervisory and managerial roles, and who tend to seek out such positions. High-scorers are often described as ambitious, well-organized, and clear-thinking. Low-scorers are often described as dissatisfied, impatient with convention, and inconstant in the pursuit of long-range goals.

Work Orientation (Wo). This is a research scale, intended to identify persons imbued with a strong work ethic, who are likely to perform well even in routine work and subordinate positions. High-scorers are often described as reliable, reasonable, dependable and moderate. Low-scorers are often described as distractible, strong-willed and self-centered.

Leadership Index (LI). This index is scored on a cluster of five scales from the inventory. Its purpose is to assess factors of leadership potential, foresight, and decision-making ability. For information on the index see: H. G. Gough, A leadership index on the California Psychological Inventory. Journal of Counseling Psychology 1969, 16, 283-289; and J. C. Hogan, Personological dynamics of leadership. Journal of Research in Personality, 1978, 12, 390-395.

Social Maturity Index (SmI). This index is scored on a cluster of six scales from the inventory. Its purpose is to assess factors of self-discipline, good judgment, and sensitivity to ethical and moral issues. For information on the index see: H. G. Gough, Appraisal of social maturity by means of the CPI. Journal of Abnormal Psychology, 1966, 71, 189-195; and H. G. Gough, Scoring high on an index of social maturity. Journal of Abnormal Psychology, 1971, 77, 236-241.

NAME: California Psychological Inventory

SUPPLIER: Behaviordyne, Inc.
599 College Ave. Suite 1
Palo Alto, CA 94306
(415) 857-0111

PRODUCT CATEGORY

Personality
Career/Vocational

PRIMARY APPLICATIONS

Personal/Marriage/Family Counseling
Educational Evaluation/Planning
Vocational Guidance/Counseling

SALE RESTRICTIONS American Psychological Association Guidelines

SERVICE TYPE/COST	Type	Available	Cost	Discount
	Mail-In	Yes	See Below	
	Teleprocessing	No		
	Local	No		

PRODUCT DESCRIPTION

Behaviordyne's computer reports for the CALIFORNIA PSYCHOLOGI-
CAL INVENTORY provide a variety of options to the test user. Specific
report types include a comprehensive clinical, diagnostic, physician's, correctional, counseling, personnel, and profile report. Each report can also be
obtained in a brief form.

The test itself is a 480-item instrument that measures normal adult and
adolescent personality. Scores are derived for 18 scales of socially desirable
behavior tendencies: Dominance, Capacity for Status, Sociability, Social
Presence, Self-Acceptance, Sense of Well-being, Responsibility, Socialization, Self-Control, Tolerance, Good Impression, Communality, Achievement
via Conformance, Achievement via Independence, Intellectual Efficiency,
Psychological-Mindedness, Flexibility, and Femininity. This test assists
counselors of non-psychiatrically disturbed clients by measuring personality
characteristics important for social living and social interaction.

Prices for reports range from $40.00 for the comprehensive clinical report
to $8.00 for the profile report, with most other reports at $16.00. Brief reports
range in price from $10.00 to $18.00.

BEHAVIORDYNE PSYCHODIAGNOSTIC

LABORATORY REPORT

SEX: MALE
AGE: 36

ACCOUNT: 100
SUBJECT: 10491
DATE: 26 APR 84

REPORT: 7
OPTIONS: (NONE)
INVENTORY: MMPI

SAMPLE

THIS IS A DETAILED CLINICAL REPORT FOR PSYCHODIAGNOSIS. IT IS SENT ONLY TO PROFESSIONALS WHO
ARE LICENSED FOR THE INDEPENDENT PRACTICE OF PSYCHODIAGNOSIS AND PSYCHOTHERAPY.

THIS IS A BEHAVIORDYNE, INCORPORATED REPORT. IT IS A PROFESSIONAL CONSULTATION COMPOSED BY
COMPUTER, FOLLOWING A METHOD DESIGNED BY A PSYCHIATRIST AND A CLINICAL PSYCHOLOGIST. LIKE ANY
REPORT BASED ON AN INVENTORY, THIS IS SUBJECT TO ERROR. NO DECISION SHOULD BE MADE FROM THIS REPORT
ALONE, BUT ONLY FROM CONSIDERATION OF THE CASE HISTORY AND ALL THE AVAILABLE EVIDENCE.

ANALYSIS OF THIS KIND CAN BE DONE FROM ANY OF SEVERAL PSYCHOLOGICAL INVENTORIES. IN THIS CASE,
THE INVENTORY COMPLETED AND SUBMITTED FOR ANALYSIS WAS THE MINNESOTA MULTIPHASIC PERSONALITY
INVENTORY.

TELEPHONE: (415) 857-0111

BEHAVIORDYNE   994 SAN ANTONIO ROAD □ PALO ALTO, CALIFORNIA 94303-4951

PROFILE   ACCOUNT: 100   SUBJECT: 10491   (MALE,36)   PAGE 2

TFAT:"T" SCALE	L	F	K	HSK	D	HY	PDK	MF	PA	PTK	SCK	MAK
SCORE	38.5	59.3	38.2	33.5	38.8	21.6	49.5	22.1	67.1	51.4	51.8	63.5

SCALE SCORE												
+++ 105												
100												
95												
90												
85												M
80												
75												
70	M								M			
65										M	M	
60							M					
55	T								T	T	T	T
50							T					
45					M							
40	M		M		T							
35	T		T	M		M		M				
30				T		T						
25								T				
20												

THE "T" POINTS ON THIS GRAPH ARE TRUE T-SCORES NORMALIZED TO THE FINNEY SAMPLE OF 2000 NORMAL MEN AND WOMEN. THEY ARE CORRECTED TO REDUCE THE FACTOR OF SOCIAL DESIRABILITY,ANXIETY AND THE EFFECTS OF RESPONSE SET FOR ANY RARE (POSSIBLY RANDOM) ANSWERS.

THE "M" POINTS ON THIS GRAPH ARE THE MINNESOTA STANDARD SCORES. THEY ARE NOT TRUE T-SCORES, BUT ARE THE REGULAR,NON-NORMALIZED M.M.P.I. SCORES.

ANY "X" POINTS ON THIS GRAPH ARE THERE TO REPRESENT BOTH AN "M" AND A "T" IN THE SAME LOCATION.

THE MF SCORE IS BASED ON SCORES BY SUBJECTS OF THE SAME SEX AS THIS SUBJECT.

MS: "M" SCORE	39.7	70.0	40.1	42.7	48.5	34.5	59.7	33.5	79.2	66.5	66.8	81.8
SCALE	L	F	K	HSK	D	HY	PDK	MF	PA	PTK	SCK	MAK

BEHAVIORDYNE   994 SAN ANTONIO ROAD □ PALO ALTO, CALIFORNIA 94303-4951

------------ VALIDITY AND RESPONSE ATTITUDE ------------

HE GIVES SOME RARE ANSWERS, EITHER BECAUSE OF SOME RANDOM ERROR, OR BECAUSE HE MAY BE SOMEWHAT RESTLESS OR UNSTABLE.

HE DOES NOT GIVE A CONSISTENTLY FAVORABLE NOR A CONSISTENTLY UNFAVORABLE PICTURE OF HIMSELF. HE TELLS US SOME GOOD THINGS AND SOME BAD THINGS ABOUT HIMSELF. HE IS REALISTIC ENOUGH TO LOOK AT HIMSELF CRITICALLY. HE ADMITS MANY SMALL FLAWS OR IMPERFECTIONS IN HIMSELF. WHEN HE COMES ON NEUROTIC-SOUNDING STATEMENTS EXPRESSING FEAR AND ANGER HE TENDS TO MARK THEM TRUE. HE CLAIMS TO BE ADVENTUROUS AND YET VIRTUOUS. HE DENIES WORRIES. HE DENIES ANY EVIL IMPULSES OR ANY BAD BEHAVIOR. HE SEEMS SOMEWHAT DEFENSIVE. HE DENIES ANY FAULTS. HE LIKES TO PICTURE HIMSELF AS WELL BEHAVED AND DEVOTED TO DUTY.

SOME OF HIS ANSWERS ARE WORTH NOTING. HERE IS WHAT HE SAID:

66.   TRUE.   I SEE THINGS OR ANIMALS OR PEOPLE AROUND ME THAT OTHERS DO NOT SEE.

121. TRUE.   I BELIEVE I AM BEING PLOTTED AGAINST.

123. TRUE.   I BELIEVE I AM BEING FOLLOWED.

179. TRUE.   I AM WORRIED ABOUT SEX MATTERS.

197. TRUE.   SOMEONE HAS BEEN TRYING TO ROB ME.

200. TRUE.   THERE ARE PERSONS WHO ARE TRYING TO STEAL MY THOUGHTS AND IDEAS.

202. TRUE.   I BELIEVE I AM A CONDEMNED PERSON.

205. TRUE.   AT TIMES IT HAS BEEN IMPOSSIBLE FOR ME TO KEEP FROM STEALING OR SHOPLIFTING SOMETHING.

323. TRUE.   I HAVE HAD VERY PECULIAR AND STRANGE EXPERIENCES.

334. TRUE.   PECULIAR ODORS COME TO ME AT TIMES.

350. TRUE.   I HEAR STRANGE THINGS WHEN I AM ALONE.

358. TRUE.   BAD WORDS, OFTEN TERRIBLE WORDS, COME INTO MY MIND AND I CANNOT GET RID OF THEM.

360. TRUE.   ALMOST EVERY DAY SOMETHING HAPPENS TO FRIGHTEN ME.

BEHAVIORDYNE 994 SAN ANTONIO ROAD □ PALO ALTO, CALIFORNIA 94303-4951

476. TRUE. I AM A SPECIAL AGENT OF GOD.

IT MAY BE WORTHWHILE TO DISCUSS THOSE ANSWERS WITH HIM TO FIND OUT WHAT HE MEANT BY THEM.

HIS PERSONALITY MAKEUP IS ONE THAT IS NOT AT ALL TYPICAL OF PATIENTS SEEN BY PSYCHIATRISTS AND BY CLINICAL PSYCHOLOGISTS. HE DOESN'T TAKE THINGS OUT ON HIMSELF AS MUCH AS MOST PATIENTS. HE IS BETTER ORGANIZED, MORE SELF-CONTROLLED, AND MORE SYSTEMATIC THAN ARE MOST PATIENTS. HE IS BOLDER AND MORE AGGRESSIVE THAN ARE MOST PATIENTS. HE SEEMS TO DO MORE HARM TO PEOPLE THAN MOST PATIENTS.

EVEN THOUGH HE HAS SOME PSYCHOTIC TENDENCIES, HIS OVERALL BALANCE OF FORCES FOR HIS MENTAL HEALTH IS GOOD. THE LONG-TERM OUTLOOK FOR HIM IS FAVORABLE.

HE IS A TENSE AND RIGID PERSON WHO WORRIES ABOUT THINGS. THE BEST THAT CAN BE SAID OF HIM IS THAT HE IS STRONG-WILLED AND ENERGETIC, AND THAT HE KEEPS TRYING HARD. BEING WELL ORGANIZED IS IMPORTANT TO HIM, AND HE KEEPS FEELING FRUSTRATED THAT HE IS NOT SO WELL ORGANIZED AS HE TRIES TO BE. THE EFFORT LEAVES HIM STIFF, TENSE, AND UP TIGHT.

HE CONSISTENTLY DOES THINGS THE HARD WAY. HE IS FULL OF NERVOUS ENERGY, AND HE CAN'T RELAX AND TAKE THINGS EASY. HE CAN'T STAND TO WASTE MONEY, AND HE CAN'T STAND TO WASTE TIME. HE BELIEVES THAT DUTY COMES BEFORE PLEASURE. HE FEELS A STRONG NEED TO BE IN CONTROL OF A SITUATION, OR TO BE IN CONTROL OVER PEOPLE. HE GETS TENSE WHEN HE FINDS THAT HE CAN'T CONTROL THINGS AROUND HIM.

WHEN HE IS THE BOSS, HE IS STRICT AND RIGID IN A NERVOUS SORT OF WAY, SO THAT HE SEEMS BOSSY AND ARBITRARY TO WHOSO WORKS UNDER HIM. HE KEEPS STUBBORNLY TRYING TO MAKE PEOPLE FOLLOW THE RULES THAT HE SETS, BUT HE DOESN'T ALWAYS SUCCEED. HE DOESN'T ALWAYS PLEASE HIS SUPERIORS, EITHER, BECAUSE HE OFTEN SEEMS TO BE TRYING TO FOLLOW ANOTHER SET OF RULES THAT BELONG TO SOME OTHER JOB. HE KEEPS TRYING TO MAKE THINGS RUN THE WAY HE THINKS THEY OUGHT TO, AND WHEN THEY DON'T, HE FEELS FRUSTRATED AND THWARTED.

HE IS A RATHER STIFF, RIGID, STINGY, AND UNSOCIABLE PERSON. HE IS ONE OF THOSE UNFRIENDLY PEOPLE WHO SEEM TO TAKE A DISLIKE TO MANY OTHER PEOPLE RATHER EASILY, AND VIEW THEM AS FOES. THINGS THAT PEOPLE DO SEEM TO IRRITATE HIM, AROUSE HIS RESENTMENT, OR MAKE HIM ANGRY. HE MAY FEEL THAT THE OTHER PARTY IS DOING WRONG TO HIM, TREATING HIM UNJUSTLY OR UNFAIRLY. SO HE SEES THE OTHER PARTY AS AN ENEMY.

HE IS CONVINCED THAT HIS PRINCIPLES ARE THE RIGHT WAY OF LIFE. HE BECOMES ANNOYED WHEN PEOPLE DON'T DO THINGS THE WAY HE BELIEVES THEY SHOULD. HE IS SLOW TO MAKE HIS MIND UP OR TO FORM AN OPINION; AND ONCE IT IS MADE UP, HE IS SLOW TO CHANGE IT. HE RESENTS PEOPLE TRYING TO MAKE HIM DO THINGS IN WAYS OTHER THAN WHAT HE BELIEVES IS THE RIGHT WAY. HE HATES TO WASTE MONEY, AND HE HATES TO WASTE TIME. HE IS ANNOYED BY PEOPLE BEING SLOPPY OR DISORDERLY. HE IS NOT VERY ADAPTABLE.

HE IS A VERY UNRELIABLE PERSON. HE IS NOT VERY ABLE OR CAPABLE OF DOING GOOD WORK, AND HE DOESN'T SEEM TO CARE WHETHER HE DOES GOOD WORK OR NOT. HIS THINKING IS NOT WELL ORGANIZED. HE

BEHAVIORDYNE   994 SAN ANTONIO ROAD □ PALO ALTO, CALIFORNIA 94303-4951

DOESN'T SEEM ABLE TO ANALYZE A COMPLEX SITUATION AND GRASP THE KEY POINTS. HE IS NOT GOOD AT MAKING PLANS TO GET SOMETHING DONE; AND HE DOESN'T REALLY CARE IF THE JOB IS DONE WELL OR NOT. SO LONG AS IT IS OTHER PEOPLE WHO SUFFER AND NOT HIMSELF. HE DOESN'T CARE ABOUT BEING FAIR TO PEOPLE. DUTIES AND OBLIGATIONS DON'T SEEM TO MATTER TO HIM. HE IS NOT GOOD AT STAYING WITH A PLAN AND FOLLOWING IT THROUGH. HIS WORK IS NOT THOROUGH, AND HIS FELLOW WORKERS SEE HIM AS DULL AND LAZY. HE IS OPINIONATED, AND WILL NOT LISTEN TO OTHER PEOPLE'S JUDGMENT. HE CANNOT BE RELIED ON OR DEPENDED ON. HE MAKES RASH AND IMPULSIVE DECISIONS. HE IS CLUMSY AND AWKWARD WITH PEOPLE. HE HAS A CYNICAL ATTITUDE TOWARD PEOPLE: HE DOESN'T TRUST PEOPLE OR BELIEVE THEM. MUCH OF THE TIME HE FEELS DISSATISFIED.

AT HIS BEST HE IS SOFT-HEARTED, GENEROUS, AFFECTIONATE, AND SENTIMENTAL. HE IS ALSO ENERGETIC. BRAVE, BOLD, AND FRANK.

BUT HE HAS STRONG FEELINGS ABOUT THINGS. HE IS SENSITIVE TO SLIGHTS AND GETS HIS FEELINGS HURT EASILY. HE HATES TO ADMIT BEING WRONG. WHEN A SITUATION PUTS PRESSURE ON HIM. HE IS LIKELY TO LASH OUT FORCEFULLY AGAINST HIS ENEMIES.

HE IS NOT AT ALL THE SORT OF PERSON THAT GETS BODILY SYMPTOMS TO SYMBOLIZE HIS EMOTIONAL CONFLICTS WITHOUT ORGANIC CAUSE.

------------------------ EVIDENCE FOR PSYCHOSIS OR MENTAL ILLNESS ------------------------

HIS JUDGMENT IS OFTEN IMPAIRED BY HIS PERSONAL FEELINGS. THIS IS A TENDENCY TOWARD MENTAL ILLNESS; THAT IS, PSYCHOSIS. HE PROBABLY HAS BEEN OR WILL BE OVERTLY PSYCHOTIC AT SOME TIME IN HIS LIFE, AND HE MAY BE SO NOW. HE TENDS TO GET EMOTIONALLY INVOLVED IN ISSUES AND HIS THINKING IS NOT ALWAYS REALISTIC. HE EXPRESSES MANY UNREALISTIC OR OBVIOUSLY DELUSIONAL THOUGHTS.

THE PATTERN OF SCORES SUGGESTS A POSSIBILITY THAT HE MAY NEED TO BE TREATED IN A HOSPITAL BY A PSYCHIATRIST, USING PSYCHIATRIC MEDICINES AND OTHER PSYCHIATRIC TREATMENTS. FOR THAT REASON, HE SHOULD BE SEEN BY AN EXPERT, FULLY TRAINED SPECIALIST IN PSYCHIATRY, WHO CAN DO A THOROUGH CLINICAL EXAMINATION, INCLUDING MENTAL STATUS, HISTORY, PHYSICAL AND LABORATORY EXAMINATIONS AS NEEDED. ASSESS THE PATIENT'S NEEDS, AND, IF NECESSARY, PROVIDE PSYCHIATRIC TREATMENT IN A HOSPITAL.

------------------------ BASIC TRUST, CONFIDENCE, AND SELF-ESTEEM ------------------------

HIS ATTITUDE IS RATHER PESSIMISTIC. HE DOESN'T HAVE MUCH CONFIDENCE IN HIMSELF TO MAKE A SUCCESS, NOR CONFIDENCE IN OTHERS TO DO WELL BY HIM. HE EXPECTS POORLY OF THE FUTURE. HE IS FREE OF BODILY PREOCCUPATIONS. HE SEEMS ALERT ENOUGH AND SELF-RELIANT ENOUGH.

THE IMPRESSION THAT PEOPLE GET FROM OBSERVING HIM IS THAT HE HAS EVEN LESS FEELING OF GUILT, EMBARRASSMENT, FEAR, AND WORRY THAN WHAT HE SAYS. IN GENERAL, HE APPEARS TO HAVE LESS THAN THE AVERAGE AMOUNT OF SUCH FEELINGS. HE TELLS OF MODERATE FEELINGS OF GUILT. HE SEEMS VERY LITTLE CONCERNED BY WHAT PEOPLE THINK OF HIM. HE TELLS OF SOME FEARS AND PHOBIAS. HE SEEMS NOT TO BE

BEHAVIORDYNE   994 SAN ANTONIO ROAD □ PALO ALTO, CALIFORNIA 94303-4951

```
NARRATIVE REPORT          ACCOUNT:  100    SUBJECT:    10491            (MALE,36)           PAGE   6

WORRYING.

------------------------------- DEPENDENCY PROBLEMS ----------------------------------

    HE IS NOT A DEPENDENT PERSON.  HE WILL NOT LEAN ON YOU FOR EMOTIONAL SUPPORT.   COMPARISON OF
HIS DEPENDENCY IN ACTION WITH HIS DEPENDENCY URGE SHOWS THAT HE DOES NOT MAKE MUCH USE OF THE
DEFENSE OF REACTION FORMATION AGAINST DEPENDENCY.

---------------------------- DEMANDINGNESS OR ORAL AGGRESSION ------------------------

    HE IS A RATHER DEMANDING PERSON.  IF YOU KEEP SEEING HIM HE WILL PUT YOU ON THE SPOT WITH
DEMANDS THAT ARE HARD TO SATISFY.  HE IS NOT EASY TO PLEASE.

    FROM ANOTHER POINT OF VIEW, HE IS RATHER HEADSTRONG AND SOMEWHAT OPINIONATED.  HE CAN BE ALMOST
STUBBORNLY DEMANDING.  HE IS NOT KNOWN FOR SELF-DENIAL.

----------------------- MASOCHISTIC DEPENDENCY AND BITTERNESS -------------------------

    HE DOES NOT SEEM ESPECIALLY BITTER.  IF IT IS SO, IT IS VERY SLIGHTLY SO.  HE DOES NOT SEEM TO
FEEL ESPECIALLY SORRY FOR HIMSELF.  TO SOME DEGREE, HE DOES THINGS SO AS TO GET INTO TROUBLE OR TO
GET PEOPLE TO PUNISH HIM.  IS THIS PERSON DRIVEN BY A TRUE SELF-PUNISHING NEED?  DOES HE GET A
NEUROTIC SATISFACTION FROM GETTING INTO TROUBLE AND BEING PUNISHED?  MOST LIKELY NOT.  INSTEAD, THE
SOURCE OF THE TROUBLE IS THAT HE TRAMPLES ON HIS SELF-CONTROLS SO THAT THEY DON'T KEEP HIM FROM
PUTTING HIS IMPULSES INTO ACTION.  SO HE DOES THINGS THAT PROVOKE OTHER PEOPLE INTO A BELATED
CONTROL THAT TAKES THE FORM OF PUNISHMENT.  BUT THE EXPECTATION OF PUNISHMENT DOES NOT SEEM TO BE
THE MOTIVE FOR HIS BEHAVIOR.  WITHIN THE AVERAGE OR NORMAL RANGE, THERE IS NO EVIDENCE OF DEPENDENT
MASOCHISM.

------------------------------- HOSTILITY AND COPING ---------------------------------

    HE IS A SOMEWHAT HOSTILE PERSON.  HE BUILDS SOME RESENTMENT UP WITHIN HIMSELF, AND SOME URGE TO
LASH OUT.  NOW LET US SEE WHAT HE DOES WITH THAT URGE.

    IN GENERAL, HE IS A PERSON WHO DOES NOT TAKE THINGS OUT ON HIMSELF.  IN THIS CASE, HOWEVER,
THERE MIGHT BE OTHER CONSIDERATIONS.  HE LOOKS AFTER HIS OWN WELFARE MUCH MORE THAN HE LOOKS AFTER
OTHER PEOPLE'S.

    HE TENDS TO BLAME OTHER PEOPLE.  HE TENDS TO BE CYNICAL, AND PERHAPS DISTRUSTFUL OR INTOLERANT
OF PEOPLE.  HE EXPRESSES SOME CYNICAL OPINIONS.  HE FEELS THAT PEOPLE TAKE ADVANTAGE OF HIM, AND
DON'T DO RIGHT TO HIM.

    HE DOESN'T TURN HOSTILITY AGAINST HIMSELF.  HE THINKS WELL OF HIMSELF.  HE IS CHEERFUL, AND HE
HAS CONFIDENCE IN HIMSELF.  HE FEELS THAT HE IS ADEQUATE AS A PERSON.  HE DOES NOT APPEAR TO BE
```

BEHAVIORDYNE 994 SAN ANTONIO ROAD □ PALO ALTO, CALIFORNIA 94303-4951

DISCOURAGED. HE IS PRONE TO PUTTING HIS IMPULSES INTO ACTION. HE IS ENERGETIC, ACTIVE, AND EXCITABLE. HE IS CHEERFUL AND CONFIDENT, ON THE WHOLE. HE IS LIKELY TO DO WHAT HE FEELS LIKE.

------------------- RESPONSE TO AUTHORITIES -------------------

HE SHOWS SOME TENDENCY TO GET PEOPLE TO TELL HIM WHAT TO DO AND THEN RESIST THEM. HE EXPRESSES MOSTLY REBELLIOUS FEELINGS.

------------------- COMPULSIVE CHARACTER FEATURES -------------------

HE IS A SYSTEMATIC AND METHODICAL PERSON. USING THE DEFENSE MECHANISM OF REACTION FORMATION, HE DELAYS HIS GRATIFICATIONS, TAKING THEM ONLY AT A SET TIME AND IN A SET WAY. HE LIKES TO DO THINGS IN A WELL ORGANIZED, ORDERLY, AND CONSISTENT WAY. HE SEEMS TO LIKE TO CONTROL PEOPLE.

------------------- HYSTERICAL PERSONALITY FEATURES -------------------

HE TENDS TO MAKE THE WORST OF HIS TROUBLES AND EMPHASIZES HIS DISTRESS. BUT OTHERWISE, HE SHOWS NO SIGN OF HYSTERICAL PROCESSES. HE DOESN'T HAVE CONVERSION REACTIONS. HIS SEXUAL FUNCTIONING SEEMS TO BE GOOD, IN COMPARISON WITH OTHERS OF HIS AGE AND BACKGROUND. HE MAY OVEREMPHASIZE SEXUAL ABILITY FOR SOME REASON OR ANOTHER.

------------------- IDENTIFICATIONS, IDEALS, AND RESPONSIBILITIES -------------------

THE ANSWERS THAT HE GIVES TO QUESTIONS ARE MORE TYPICALLY GIVEN BY MEN THAN BY WOMEN. HE IS A SIMPLE AND UNAFFECTED PERSON: AT HIS BEST, CHEERFUL, CONTENTED, AND JOLLY; AND OFTEN EARTHY, COARSE, OR RECKLESS. HIS INTERESTS ARE NARROW. HE IS WANTING IN ORIGINALITY AND IN INSIGHT. HE PREFERS DIRECT ACTION, NOT THOUGHT. HE IS NOT A CULTURED PERSON. HE IS ROUGH AND MASCULINE.

THERE ARE SIGNS THAT HE MAY BE SOMEWHAT LACKING IN A SENSE OF RESPONSIBILITY AND OF FAIR PLAY. HE DOESN'T ALWAYS DEAL FAIRLY WITH PEOPLE. HE DOESN'T ALWAYS RESPECT PEOPLE'S RIGHTS. HIS CONSCIENCE IS SOMEWHAT WEAK. HE SOMETIMES DOES WRONG TO PEOPLE, AND HIS CONSCIENCE DOESN'T BOTHER HIM MUCH. HE IS SOMETHING OF AN OPPORTUNIST. HE TENDS TO BE GUIDED BY EXPEDIENCY. HE TENDS TO BE A RATHER HEADSTRONG PERSON AT TIMES. HE IS NOT KNOWN FOR SELF-DENIAL. HE WANTS TO GRATIFY HIS OWN NEEDS, AND HE DOESN'T ALWAYS STOP TO THINK OF THE OTHER PERSON'S RIGHTS. HE IS NOT ALWAYS COMPLETELY HONEST WITH PEOPLE.

ALL TOGETHER, THOUGH HIS CONSCIENCE, HIS IDEALS, AND HIS SENSE OF GOAL IN LIFE, ARE WEAK, HIS IMPULSES MAY NOT BE VERY STRONG, OR HE MAY HAVE SOME WAY OF CONTROLLING OR INHIBITING THEM. OTHER THAN TRUE CONSCIENCE OR EGO IDEAL: PERHAPS REACTION FORMATION. SO HIS CONDUCT FOR THE MOST PART IS WITHIN NORMAL LIMITS. HE SUFFERS ONLY AN AVERAGE AMOUNT OF GUILT. THE SITUATION DOES NOT SEEM TO CALL FOR ANY TREATMENT.

IT IS NOT EASY FOR HIM TO GIVE WARMTH AND AFFECTION TO PEOPLE. HE DOESN'T RESPOND WITH MUCH

BEHAVIORDYNE   994 SAN ANTONIO ROAD □ PALO ALTO,CALIFORNIA 94303-4951

SYMPATHY. BUT HE IS PERCEPTIVE. HE OBSERVES PEOPLE SHARPLY. HE IS ALERT IN GAUGING WHAT PEOPLE ARE THINKING AND FEELING, AND WHAT THEY REALLY WANT.

-------- WORLD OF WORK --------

LET'S CONSIDER HOW HE FITS IN WITH VARIOUS KINDS OF WORK.

HE IS SORELY LACKING IN WHAT IT TAKES TO DO MOST KINDS OF WORK. AS HE STANDS TODAY, HE HAS SOME WEAK POINTS THAT CAN HAMPER HIM SERIOUSLY AND HOLD HIM BACK FROM DOING WELL IN THE WORLD OF WORK. SOME KINDS OF WORKING SITUATIONS FIT HIM BETTER THAN OTHERS.

HIS STRONGEST POINT, THE ONE THAT CAN HELP HIM THE MOST TO SUCCEED IN HIS WORK, IS HIS CAREFULNESS, ACCURACY, AND SELF-CONTROL. HE IS AT LEAST AVERAGE IN ACCURACY, SELF-CONTROL, AND CAREFULNESS IN HIS WORK. HE CAN DO WELL ENOUGH IN A JOB THAT CALLS ON HIM TO DO PRECISE, ACCURATE, WELL CONTROLLED WORK WITH CAREFUL ATTENTION TO THE DETAILS.

ANOTHER STRONG POINT THAT CAN HELP HIM IN HIS WORK IS HIS ABILITY TO KEEP HIS EMOTIONS FROM INTERFERING WITH THE TEAMWORK THAT IS NEEDED IN A COMPETITIVE JOB. HE IS NOT AT ALL STRONG IN THAT QUALITY. BUT IT IS STRONGER THAN SOME OF HIS OTHER POINTS.

YOU WILL BE WISE TO HELP HIM CHOOSE A LINE OF WORK THAT CALLS ON HIS STRONG POINTS. IN THE RIGHT LINE OF WORK, AND IN THE RIGHT WORKING CONDITIONS AND SETTING, PEOPLE WILL APPRECIATE HIM FOR HIS BEST QUALITIES.

ONE OF HIS WEAK POINTS, SOMETHING THAT MAY HANDICAP HIM IN HIS WORK, IS SOME LACK OF WILLINGNESS TO CONFORM TO THE CUSTOMS AND EXPECTATIONS OF SOCIETY. HE IS SOMETHING OF AN INDIVIDUALIST. HE HAS HIS OWN OPINIONS, AND HE MAY NOT ALWAYS BE POLITE TO PEOPLE THAT DISAGREE WITH HIM. HE WILL NOT DO WELL IN A JOB IN WHICH HE NEEDS TO KEEP PLEASING THE PUBLIC. HE MAY DO WELL EITHER IN A JOB IN WHICH HE DOES NOT MEET THE PUBLIC, OR IN ONE IN WHICH HE MEETS PEOPLE IN UNCONVENTIONAL WAYS, OR ON HIS OWN TERMS. IF ONE OF THE MAIN REQUIREMENTS IN HIS WORK IS TO OBEY THE RULES PATIENTLY, LIVE BY THE CUSTOMS AND CONVENTIONS, AND AVOID OFFENDING PEOPLE, IT MAY BE HARD FOR HIM.

ANOTHER POSSIBLE DRAWBACK, A POINT THAT MAY HAMPER HIM IN HIS WORK, IS SOME LACK OF AMBITION AND URGE FOR ACHIEVEMENT. HE SEEMS SOMEWHAT LACKING IN THE DRIVE FOR ACHIEVEMENT. IF, IN HIS WORK, HE NEEDS TO SHOW AMBITION AND DRIVE FOR ACHIEVEMENT, HE MAY HAVE SOME TROUBLE WITH IT.

STILL ANOTHER POINT MAY HOLD HIM BACK IN HIS WORK. HE DOESN'T FIND IT EASY TO TAKE RESPONSIBILITY FOR GOING AHEAD WITH THE WORK AND SOLVING PROBLEMS FOR HIMSELF. KEEP WORKING CONSTRUCTIVELY WITHOUT BEING SUPERVISED, AND USE SOUND JUDGMENT IN MAKING DECISIONS ABOUT THE WORK.

YOU WILL BE WISE TO HELP HIM CHOOSE A LINE OF WORK THAT DOESN'T DEMAND SO MUCH ALONG THOSE LINES.

BEHAVIORDYNE 994 SAN ANTONIO ROAD □ PALO ALTO, CALIFORNIA 94303-4951

YOU MAY DISCUSS HIS WEAK POINTS WITH HIM, SEE IF HE RECOGNIZES THEM, AND SEE WHETHER HE FEELS WILLING AND ABLE TO CHANGE IN THIS REGARD OR NOT.

BECAUSE HIS WAY OF THINKING IS RATHER RIGID AND INFLEXIBLE, HE IS UNLIKELY TO DO ANYTHING VERY CREATIVE OR ORIGINAL IN HIS WORK. BUT, OF COURSE, THAT WON'T KEEP HIM FROM DOING GOOD WORK IN A JOB THAT DOESN'T REQUIRE ORIGINALITY.

WITH HIS SOMEWHAT CYNICAL VIEW OF PEOPLE IN GENERAL, HE MAY TEND TO ACHIEVE LESS THAN HE WOULD OTHERWISE BE CAPABLE OF.

WHENEVER EMOTIONAL PROBLEMS ARISE IN HIM, THEY CAN LOOM OVER HIS VIEW OF THE WORLD. AT SUCH TIMES HIS ABILITY TO THINK THINGS THROUGH BECOMES IMPAIRED. HE TENDS TO WITHDRAW INTO HIMSELF, AND HE LOSES INTEREST IN OTHER PEOPLE AND HIS WORK. THIS PUTS A LIMITATION ON HIS ABILITY TO BE SUCCESSFUL IN HIS WORK AND TO DEAL WITH THE PROBLEMS OF LIVING.

HIS EMOTIONAL PROBLEMS HAVE AFFECTED HIM SO MUCH THAT HIS THINKING HAS BECOME DISTORTED ON SOME TOPICS.

———————————— DIAGNOSTIC IMPRESSION ————————————

CATEGORIZING A PATIENT WITH A DIAGNOSTIC JUDGMENT MUST NEVER BE DONE FROM THE RESULTS OF PSYCHOLOGICAL TESTING ALONE, NOR FROM THE REPORTS OF OTHER LABORATORY TESTS ALONE. IN MAKING YOUR DIAGNOSTIC ASSESSMENT OF THIS PATIENT, YOU WILL RELY UPON THE CAREFUL HISTORY THAT YOU HAVE TAKEN, AND UPON THE SHREWD OBSERVATIONS THAT YOU HAVE MADE OF THE PATIENT'S BEHAVIOR IN THE INTERVIEW AS WELL AS THE LABORATORY RESULTS. THE DIAGNOSES LISTED BELOW ARE BASED ON DSM II.

INSOFAR AS WE CAN JUDGE FROM THE ANALYSIS OF THE PSYCHOLOGICAL TESTING ALONE, THE DIAGNOSTIC LABEL MOST LIKELY TO FIT THE PATIENT BEST IS:

295.3 PSYCHOSIS, SCHIZOPHRENIA, PARANOID TYPE. THE PARANOID ELEMENTS ARE STRONGER THAN THE SCHIZOPHRENIC ONES, AND THE CASE COULD ALSO BE CALLED 297.0 PSYCHOSIS, PARANOID STATE. ANOTHER POSSIBLE CLASSIFICATION IS 295.73 PSYCHOSIS, SCHIZOPHRENIA, SCHIZO-AFFECTIVE TYPE, EXCITED, WITH PARANOID AND MANIC FEATURES. IN SOME CASES THIS DISORDER OF THINKING MAY BE A 293.9 PSYCHOSIS FROM ACUTE OR CHRONIC BRAIN SYNDROME.

OTHER DIAGNOSTIC LABELS WHICH MAY BE WORTH CONSIDERING ARE AS FOLLOWS; THEY ARE ORDERED ACCORDING TO THE PROBABILITY OF APPLICATION TO THIS PATIENT:

301.0 PERSONALITY PATTERN DISORDER, PARANOID PERSONALITY, WITH AGGRESSIVE HOSTILE BEHAVIOR.

319.0 QUESTIONABLE VALIDITY OF TEST. IN SPITE OF ANYTHING ELSE THAT MAY SHOW UP, THERE ARE SOME SIGNS THAT IN CERTAIN WAYS HE MAY HAVE TWISTED HIS ANSWERS IN THE DIRECTION OF LOOKING GOOD. FOR THIS REASON, WE CANNOT PUT THE USUAL DEGREE OF CONFIDENCE IN THE FINDINGS.

BEHAVIORDYNE 994 SAN ANTONIO ROAD □ PALO ALTO, CALIFORNIA 94303-4951

NARRATIVE REPORT   ACCOUNT: 100   SUBJECT: 10491   (MALE,36)   PAGE 10

301.7 ANTISOCIAL PERSONALITY, RESENTFUL AND IRRESPONSIBLE TYPE.

----------------------- POTENTIAL FOR PSYCHOTHERAPY -----------------------

HE IS NOT A CANDIDATE FOR INTENSIVE PSYCHOTHERAPY OF THE KIND THAT AIMS AT SELF-UNDERSTANDING.

HE IS IN ENOUGH DISTRESS, BUT HE DOESN'T HAVE THE KIND OF CHARACTER TO MAKE GOOD USE OF
INTENSIVE PSYCHOTHERAPY, AND TO LEARN TO BECOME AWARE OF HIS MOTIVES, AND TO THINK REFLECTIVELY
ABOUT THE WAYS IN WHICH HE DEALS WITH PEOPLE.

ANOTHER SIDE OF HIS CHARACTER IS A PROBLEM. HE WARDS SELF-CRITICISM AWAY AND CASTS THE BLAME
ON OTHER PEOPLE. CRITICISM OF HIMSELF IS TOO PAINFUL TO BEAR.

HE IS IN DISTRESS, AND HE CAN USE SUPPORTIVE PSYCHOTHERAPY OR SOCIAL CASEWORK.

HE MAY BE HELPED BY ANTIPSYCHOTIC MEDICINES.

HE MAY NOT BE THE EASIEST PERSON TO TREAT, BECAUSE RESPONSIBILITY IS NOT ONE OF HIS STRONG
POINTS. HE MAY FAIL TO FOLLOW THROUGH. YOU MAY WISH TO ENCOURAGE HIM TO PAY SOME HEED TO THIS
POINT, IF PSYCHOTHERAPY WERE UNDERTAKEN. ONE GOAL WOULD BE TO WORK TOWARD MORE RESPONSIBLE
BEHAVIOR. MAYBE YOU CAN HELP HIM DECIDE WHAT HE WANTS OUT OF LIFE, AND BEGIN TO FIND A REALISTIC
WAY OF GOING AFTER IT.

----------------------- SUMMARY -----------------------
THE STATEMENTS THAT CAN BE MADE MOST CLEARLY ABOUT THIS PERSON ARE AS FOLLOWS; THESE STATEMENTS ARE
GENERATED FROM THE SCALE SCORES WHICH ARE MOST DEVIANT FROM 50.0:

ON A CORRECTION SCALE, HE SHOWS PSYCHOTIC TRENDS. THIS DOESN'T MEAN ANYTHING UNLESS OTHER
SIGNS OF PSYCHOSIS ARE FOUND.

HE DENIES AESTHETIC INTERESTS.

HE IS DIRECT AND MATTER-OF-FACT, AND NOT AT ALL AFFECTED. HE DENIES ANY BODILY SYMPTOMS. HE
SEEMS NOT TO USE THE DEFENSES OF REPRESSION AND CONVERSION.

HE IS A SIMPLE AND UNAFFECTED PERSON: AT HIS BEST, CHEERFUL, CONTENTED, AND JOLLY; AND OFTEN
EARTHY, COARSE, OR RECKLESS. HIS INTERESTS ARE NARROW. HE IS WANTING IN ORIGINALITY AND IN
INSIGHT. HE PREFERS DIRECT ACTION, NOT THOUGHT. HE IS NOT A CULTURED PERSON. HE IS ROUGH AND
MASCULINE.

THE ANSWERS THAT HE GIVES TO QUESTIONS ARE MORE TYPICALLY GIVEN BY MEN THAN BY WOMEN.

BEHAVIORDYNE 994 SAN ANTONIO ROAD □ PALO ALTO, CALIFORNIA 94303-4951

NARRATIVE REPORT   ACCOUNT: 100   SUBJECT: 10491   (MALE,36)   PAGE 11

HE EXPRESSES MANY UNREALISTIC OR OBVIOUSLY DELUSIONAL THOUGHTS.

HE SEEMS VERY LITTLE CONCERNED FOR WHAT PEOPLE THINK OF HIM.

THERE MAY BE SOME PROBLEM IN THE WAY HE HANDLES HIS HOSTILITY.   THE NATURE OF THE PROBLEM IS
NOT CLEAR.

BEHAVIORDYNE 994 SAN ANTONIO ROAD □ PALO ALTO, CALIFORNIA 94303-4951

DATA   ACCOUNT: 100   SUBJECT: 10491   (MALE,36)   PAGE 12

THE FOLLOWING ARE MINNESOTA STANDARD SCORES (NOT "T" SCORES) FOR THE SCALES INDICATED:

L= 39.7   F= 70.0   K= 40.1   HSK= 42.7   D= 48.5   HY= 34.5   PDK= 59.7
MF= 33.5   PA= 79.2   PTK= 66.5   SCK= 66.8   MAK= 81.8   SI= 59.7   ?= 41.0

TESTS FOR PSYCHOSIS:

CRITERION:	PSYCHOTIC	INDETERMINATE	NONPSYCHOTIC
MEEHL-DAHLSTROM	*		
TAULBEE-SISSON	*		
SCK-PTK METHOD		*	
ELEVATION OF SX	*	*	
TWO POINT CODE		*	
ELEVATION OF SCK	*		*
GOLDBERG METHOD		*	
ELEVATION OF PA		*	
FINNEY METHOD			
	---	---	---
	4	4	1

PSYCHOTIC POINT COUNT = 12
(9+P) - N

RANKINGS OF THE EIGHT MMPI CLINICAL SCALES - WITH THE FORMULA CORRECTION:

	TFAT	AT	FAT	T
HIGHEST:	PA (6) = 67.1	PA (6) = 66.1	PA (6) = 65.1	PA (6) = 69.1
SECOND:	MAK (9) = 63.5	MAK (9) = 62.6	MAK (9) = 61.4	MAK (9) = 65.6
THIRD:	SCK (8) = 51.8	SCK (8) = 50.3	PTK (7) = 47.6	SCK (8) = 56.3
FOURTH:	PTK (7) = 51.4	PDK (4) = 48.8	SCK (8) = 47.3	PTK (7) = 55.2
FIFTH:	PDK (4) = 49.5	PTK (7) = 47.7	PDK (4) = 46.7	PDK (4) = 52.4
SIXTH:	D (2) = 38.8	D (2) = 34.9	D (2) = 35.1	D (2) = 42.4
SEVENTH:	HSK (1) = 33.5	HSK (1) = 32.5	HSK (1) = 31.8	HSK (1) = 35.3
LOWEST:	HY (3) = 21.6	HY (3) = 21.1	HY (3) = 20.7	HY (3) = 22.4
TWO PT. CODES:	(6,9)	(6,9)	(6,9)	(6,9)

THE MIS-MARK AND/OR BLANK COUNT FOR THIS TEST IS: 0

ADDICTION BAND NUMBER=2 (HIGH=5;LOW=1)   ALCOHOLISM BAND NUMBER=1 (HIGH=5;LOW=1)

BEHAVIORDYNE 994 SAN ANTONIO ROAD □ PALO ALTO, CALIFORNIA 94303-4951

FACTOR SCORES: A=60.68 B=63.13 C=66.84 D=51.27 E=71.19 Z=57.01 Y=32.66 X=29.05
STRENGTH FACTOR=71.2 SPEED FACTOR=47.4 PUNITIVE FACTOR=42.8 COMPARATIVE INTRAPUNITIVE FACTOR=32.9

MEEHL-DAHLSTROM:
BETA = 42.09
DELTA = 61.62
WELSH = 0.90
BAND NUMBER= 5
SELECTION RULE= 2

TAULBEE-SISSON:
13 N   17 P   26 P   39 P
14 P   18 P   34 P   75 N
15 N   19 P   35 N   76 P
16 P   24 P   36 P   78 P
CLASSIFICATION COUNT= 4

NEUROTIC INDEX: 1
AVERAGE DEPENDENCY SCORE: 40.8
ORAL AGGRESSION AVERAGE: 59.1
BITTERNESS INDEX: 53.96
GENERAL HOSTILITY AVERAGE: 55.6
A. C. G. CODES: 1 0 1 2
AVERAGE CREATIVITY SCORE: 34.1
COUNSELING PREDICTION SCORE: 99.
MASOCHISTIC ELEMENT: 52.0
RESILIENCY ELEMENT: 49.1
LISTENING ELEMENT: 54.5
NP ELEMENT: 0.0
SEVEN ELEMENT TOTAL: 309.4
SUCCESSFUL SOCIOPATH BAND: 1

HYSTERIA SCORE: 40.1
HYSTERICAL INDEX: 0
DENIAL INDEX: 18 (RANGE 3-24)
MASCULINITY SCORE: 66.8
RESPONSIBILITY AVERAGE: 41.0
JOB SUCCESS CODES: 1 1 0 4
RIGID COMPULSIVE CHARACTER AVERAGE: 51.7
FUTILE ACTIVITY ELEMENT: 29.2
CREATIVITY ELEMENT: 14.2
PSYCHOLOGICAL MINDEDNESS ELEMENT: 62.4
AMBITION ELEMENT: 48.2
PSYCHOTHERAPY CHARACTER SCORE: 38.7
EIGHT ELEMENT TOTAL: 309.4
POLICE EFFECTIVENESS: 41.4

BEHAVIORDYNE 994 SAN ANTONIO ROAD □ PALO ALTO, CALIFORNIA 94303-4951

SCALE	RAW	T	AT	FAT	TFAT	DEFINITION
1 DU	26	52.4	35.4	36.8	44.6	AMOUNT OF DEPENDENCY URGE: MANIFESTED OR NOT.
2 DA	26	60.3	52.5	53.9	57.1	DEPENDENCY IN ACTION. LOW T FOR REACTION FORMATION.
3 RD	8	56.6	53.2	53.4	55.0	REPRESSION OF DEPENDENCY.
4 TCO	22	38.1	44.9	42.7	40.4	BASIC TRUST, CONFIDENCE, AND OPTIMISM.
5 DI	18	49.8	29.1	30.0	39.9	DISCOURAGEMENT.
6 RDI	20	40.8	48.4	48.4	44.6	REPRESSION OF DISCOURAGEMENT.
7 ANX	32	58.0	46.7	48.4	53.2	ANXIETY.
8 BIT	26	56.8	43.8	44.7	50.7	BITTERNESS.
9 DMD	28	62.1	56.8	55.6	58.9	DEMANDINGNESS.
10 ORD	22	50.5	51.7	52.0	51.3	ORDERLINESS.
11 SBT	24	55.3	46.0	48.0	51.7	SEEKING BEING TOLD WHAT TO DO.
12 RBT	22	62.6	57.9	56.6	59.6	RESISTING BEING TOLD WHAT TO DO.
13 ARH	28	58.6	47.9	48.8	53.7	AMOUNT OF RESENTMENT/HOSTILITY: MANIFESTED OR NOT.
14 BS	16	49.9	32.3	33.3	41.6	BLAMING SELF.
15 BO	16	63.5	58.4	57.1	60.3	BLAMING OTHERS.
16 TS	30	55.0	39.9	41.6	48.3	TAKING THINGS OUT ON SELF.
17 TTO	24	59.3	53.4	52.1	55.7	TAKING THINGS OUT ON OTHERS.
18 RFA	22	58.8	53.6	54.2	56.5	REACTION FORMATION AGAINST AGGRESSION.
19 POH	18	63.4	58.6	57.3	60.4	PROJECTION OF HOSTILITY.
20 SOH	24	55.4	45.1	46.4	50.9	SUPPRESSION AND OUTBURSTS OF HOSTILITY.
21 UAH	6	33.3	22.8	23.6	28.4	UNCONSCIOUS ACTING-OUT OF HOSTILITY.
22 CAS	44	58.6	64.6	64.4	61.5	CONTROLLINGNESS AND SADISM.
23 UAS	12	55.8	50.4	51.2	53.5	UNCONSCIOUS ACTING-OUT OF SEX.
24 IAF	14	41.4	29.1	30.0	35.7	IMPOTENCE AND FRIGIDITY.
25 PRO	26	62.5	57.1	56.1	59.3	PROMISCUITY.
26 DTH	12	53.9	43.0	44.2	49.0	DOING THINGS THE HARD WAY.
27 CWO	16	29.5	25.8	26.7	28.1	CONCERN WITH WHAT PEOPLE THINK.
28 PM	32	63.6	58.6	57.9	60.8	PSYCHOPATHIC MANIPULATION.
29 GF	18	51.8	36.6	37.8	44.8	GUILT FEELINGS.
30 CONS	16	36.7	41.9	43.2	40.0	CONSCIENCE.
31 WI	16	33.6	36.8	37.5	35.6	WARMTH.
32 AMB	12	31.4	32.8	32.0	31.7	AMBITION.
33 SS	34	59.3	48.7	50.8	55.0	FEELING SORRY FOR SELF.
34 DPM	30	58.1	46.3	47.9	53.0	DEPENDENT MASOCHISM, GETTING REJECTED.
35 BTP	34	67.5	65.0	64.0	65.8	BEHAVING TO GET PUNISHED.
36 REP	10	35.8	37.5	38.6	37.2	REPRESSION.
37 DEN	18	52.4	64.0	63.2	57.8	DENIAL.
38 PJT	10	61.9	56.2	54.8	58.3	PROJECTION.
39 RF	24	59.5	57.3	57.7	58.6	REACTION FORMATION.
40 CONV	12	45.6	30.1	30.8	38.2	CONVERSION.
41 PPR	14	44.6	28.5	29.5	37.0	PSYCHOPHYSIOLOGIC REACTION.

SCALE INFORMATION ACCOUNT: 100 SUBJECT: 10491 (MALE,36)

SCALE	RAW	T	AT	FAT	TFAT	DEFINITION
42 PAF	20	50.6	30.2	31.2	40.9	PHOBIA AND FEAR.
43 COM	12	56.0	48.0	48.8	52.4	COMPULSION.
44 WAO	20	47.6	25.1	25.9	36.8	WORRY AND OBSESSION.
45 PSY	20	58.1	47.0	46.3	52.2	PSYCHOSIS.
46 L	2	37.8	40.8	39.2	38.5	LIE.
47 F	24	61.9	56.6	56.5	59.3	VALIDITY.
48 K	14	36.4	41.6	40.1	38.2	CORRECTION.
49 HS	10	46.6	36.8	36.5	41.6	HYPOCHONDRIASIS.
50 HSK	17	35.3	32.5	31.8	33.5	HYPOCHONDRIASIS WITH K CORRECTION.
51 DO	16	47.1	33.1	33.2	40.2	DEPRESSION, OBVIOUS.
52 DS	16	42.9	47.6	47.8	45.4	DEPRESSION, SUBTLE.
53 D	32	42.4	34.9	35.1	38.8	DEPRESSION.
54 HYAD	6	37.6	21.3	21.3	29.4	HYSTERIA ADMISSION.
55 HYDN	10	31.8	35.1	34.4	33.1	HYSTERIA DENIAL.
56 HY	16	22.4	21.1	20.7	21.6	HYSTERIA.
57 PD	40	57.3	51.3	49.3	53.3	PSYCHOPATHIC DEVIATE.
58 PDK	46	52.4	48.8	46.7	49.5	PSYCHOPATHIC DEVIATE WITH K CORRECTION.
59 MFM	24	22.9	20.5	21.2	22.1	MASCULINITY-FEMININITY, MALE.
60 PAO	28	74.5	74.0	74.0	74.2	PARANOIA, OBVIOUS.
61 PAS	8	38.6	40.3	40.1	39.4	PARANOIA, SUBTLE.
62 PA	36	69.1	66.1	65.1	67.1	PARANOIA.
63 PT	48	59.9	49.9	51.3	55.6	PSYCHASTHENIA.
64 PTK	62	55.2	47.7	47.6	51.4	PSYCHASTHENIA WITH K CORRECTION.
65 SC	48	60.0	51.3	48.1	54.1	SCHIZOPHRENIA.
66 SCK	62	56.3	50.3	47.3	51.8	SCHIZOPHRENIA WITH K CORRECTION.
67 MA	56	67.0	63.6	62.5	64.8	HYPOMANIA.
68 MAK	59	65.6	62.6	61.4	63.5	HYPOMANIA WITH K CORRECTION.
69 SI	68	56.6	50.8	51.6	54.1	SOCIAL INTROVERSION.
70 A	48	59.0	47.6	49.5	54.3	1-ST FACTOR (ANXIETY).
71 R	26	45.0	47.3	47.4	46.2	2-ND FACTOR (REPRESSION).
72 SD	16	23.2	21.9	22.7	22.9	SEX DIFFERENCE.
73 ES	78	42.7	49.8	49.1	45.9	EGO STRENGTH.
74 FM	32	50.1	42.7	43.6	46.9	FEMALE MASOCHISM.
75 UL	86	46.5	59.9	60.2	53.4	ULCER PERSONALITY.
76 BA	82	44.4	52.4	55.2	49.8	SUCCESS IN BASEBALL (TEAMWORK IN COMPETITION).
77 CR	82	38.8	46.4	46.1	42.5	CONVERSION REACTION AND DENIAL.
78 SX	30	83.1	91.8	91.3	87.2	CORRECTION FOR SCHIZOPHRENIA SCALE.
79 PAV	26	56.9	48.5	47.2	52.1	PAROLE VIOLATION.
80 EC	44	64.8	60.3	59.0	61.9	ESCAPE FROM PRISON.
81 C	42	58.5	53.8	53.3	55.9	3-RD FACTOR (CONTROL).
82 B	88	68.7	65.5	65.7	67.2	RESPONSE BIAS (TENDENCY TO SAY "TRUE").

BEHAVIORDYNE 994 SAN ANTONIO ROAD □ PALO ALTO, CALIFORNIA 94303-4951

psychware **101**

SCALE	RAW	T	AT	FAT	TFAT	DEFINITION
83 PH	16	62.2	57.4	58.2	60.2	PHOBIA (CONTENT).
84 AL	84	52.6	50.2	49.6	51.1	ALCOHOLISM (FINNEY).
85 TO	20	32.7	36.0	36.9	34.8	TOLERANCE.
86 MP	34	60.6	66.3	65.1	62.8	POSITIVE MALINGERING (FAKE-GOOD).
87 RBW	34	58.0	55.7	55.9	56.9	RESPONSE BIAS.
88 SDW	48	66.5	67.8	67.1	66.8	SOCIAL DESIRABILITY.
89 EM	10	50.6	44.0	45.7	48.2	EMBARRASSMENT (CONTENT).
90 GU	10	67.5	64.0	64.9	66.2	GUILT (CONTENT).
91 REB	24	68.3	65.4	64.8	66.5	REBELLION (CONTENT).
92 SUB	10	33.9	36.4	37.3	35.6	SUBMISSION (CONTENT).
93 AC	18	37.4	43.2	44.6	41.0	ACHIEVEMENT BY CONFORMITY.
94 AI	10	31.2	34.5	35.5	33.3	ACHIEVEMENT BY INDEPENDENCE.
95 CS	16	37.9	42.4	42.4	40.1	CAPACITY FOR STATUS.
96 DOM	16	42.9	48.8	48.6	45.8	DOMINANCE.
97 IE	58	32.9	36.1	37.1	35.0	INTELLECTUAL EFFICIENCY (IQ).
98 RE	22	39.2	43.9	45.6	42.4	RESPONSIBILITY.
99 SO	12	29.2	31.9	33.1	31.1	SOCIALIZATION.
100 SY	28	41.3	45.4	45.0	43.2	SOCIABILITY.
101 WB	52	37.9	44.3	45.5	41.7	WELL BEING (NOT FAKING BAD).
102 SP	24	39.6	45.0	44.4	42.0	SOCIAL PRESENCE.
103 SA	16	51.5	55.5	55.3	53.4	SELF ACCEPTANCE.
104 SCN	24	45.8	56.3	56.7	51.3	SELF CONTROL.
105 PY	10	58.2	66.7	66.5	62.4	PSYCHOLOGICAL MINDEDNESS.
106 GI	2	39.6	42.4	42.3	41.0	GOOD IMPRESSION (FAKING GOOD).
108 FE	12	43.6	41.6	43.2	43.4	FEMININITY.
109 CM	2	51.1	54.8	54.8	53.0	COMMONALITY (ABSENCE OF RARE ANSWERS).
110 OB	16	59.9	52.3	54.0	56.9	OBSESSIVE WORRY (CONTENT).
111 N	6	50.0	45.8	46.2	48.1	NARCISSISM.
112 W2	66	62.0	57.9	58.3	60.2	WARMTH.
113 DEM	0	44.4	38.5	38.8	41.6	DEMANDINGNESS (CONTENT).
114 ID	10	55.5	61.8	60.8	58.2	INNER DIRECTION.
115 STB	10	59.3	57.9	57.5	58.4	STUBBORNNESS (CONTENT).
116 AN	10	63.5	63.0	62.6	63.0	ANAL PERSONALITY.
119 SAD	2	53.4	49.4	48.0	50.7	SADISTIC.
120 OR	2	53.1	53.0	53.4	53.3	ORDERLINESS.
122 REPX	4	62.2	59.6	58.7	60.4	HYSTERICAL CHARACTER.
123 H	62	39.4	41.5	40.7	40.1	HOSTILITY, UNCONSCIOUS.
124 ODY	4	42.0	42.8	43.4	42.7	OPTIMISTIC DEPENDENCY.
125 PVI	64	61.8	55.6	57.4	59.6	PHARISAICAL VIRTUE.
126 AP	38	41.6	41.5	43.1	42.4	ACCEPTANCE OF PASSIVITY.
127 EF1	28	55.4	45.8	47.7	51.6	EICHMAN FACTOR 1 (ANXIETY).

SCALE INFORMATION ACCOUNT: 100 SUBJECT: 10491 (MALE,36)

SCALE	RAW	T	AT	FAT	TFAT	DEFINITION
128 EF2	18	45.9	46.0	45.7	45.8	EICHMAN FACTOR 2 (REPRESSION).
129 EF3	4	38.3	29.3	28.6	33.4	EICHMAN FACTOR 3 (SOMATIC PREOCCUPATION).
130 EF4	26	65.6	61.5	59.6	62.6	EICHMAN FACTOR 4 (ACTING-OUT OF IMPULSES).
131 RDC	14	35.5	40.1	38.9	37.2	REPRESSION DISSOCIATION CHARACTER.
132 MFEM	22	20.3	18.8	19.4	19.8	FEMININITY (MF* + MF1).
133 MHOM	2	49.3	44.2	43.1	46.2	IDENTIFICATION PROBLEM (MF2).
134 DY	30	54.4	44.7	46.3	50.4	DEPENDENCY.
136 CTO	2	53.4	49.4	49.4	51.4	CONTROL OF OTHERS.
137 MFF	30	95.2	94.7	98.7	96.9	MASCULINITY-FEMININITY, FEMALE.
138 SU	24	53.1	32.1	31.7	42.4	SUICIDE.
139 AD	54	63.1	58.1	57.1	60.1	ADDICTION.
140 WM	54	69.9	70.9	70.4	70.2	WARMTH.
141 SHX	46	60.0	54.8	53.6	56.8	SHOWOFF, EXHIBITIONIST.
142 DM	52	46.0	45.9	46.9	46.4	DOMINATES.
143 RBL	52	58.4	53.6	53.2	55.8	REBELLIOUS.
144 QS	30	31.5	31.2	31.7	31.6	QUIET STUBBORN.
145 EV	28	58.8	67.0	66.0	62.4	EVADES.
146 SHM	32	55.3	49.4	50.1	52.7	SHAME.
147 FRM	52	36.7	42.1	43.1	39.9	FIRM.
148 SSO	56	45.3	62.1	62.8	54.1	STINGY WITH SELF AND OTHERS.
149 NCS	38	53.0	45.3	44.9	49.0	NARCISSISM, SELF-CENTERED.
150 UMM	56	64.8	60.2	60.0	62.4	UNSCRUPULOUS, MANIPULATES, MANOEUVERS.
151 WDN	42	64.0	60.5	60.3	62.1	WITHDRAWN.
152 RGD	54	45.8	50.2	52.2	49.0	RIGIDITY.
153 CUS	42	60.8	52.8	53.1	57.0	CRUEL, UNKIND, SADISTIC.
154 SPR	12	38.9	41.1	41.6	40.2	SULLEN, PASSIVELY RESENTFUL.
155 HFS	30	54.8	41.5	42.2	48.5	HURT FEELINGS, SENSITIVE.
156 IMP	50	68.8	69.7	68.6	68.7	IMPULSIVE.
157 RIH	20	60.7	54.8	52.5	58.6	RAMBLING, INCOHERENT.
158 RTS	34	63.8	58.9	57.5	60.6	REALITY TESTING SHAKY.
159 OSM	42	37.4	43.1	44.1	40.8	ORDERLY AND SYSTEMATIC.
160 IBO	42	64.6	60.7	60.3	62.5	INFLUENCED BY OTHERS.
161 AMA	54	58.7	56.7	55.4	57.0	ALCOHOLISM (MACANDREWS).
162 AVA	82	55.9	54.3	55.6	55.7	ALCOHOLIC VERSUS ADDICT.
163 AHS	54	29.6	32.6	32.3	31.0	ALCOHOLIC DIFFERENTIATION.
164 AHP	136	62.3	56.0	57.7	60.0	ALCOHOLISM (HAMPTON).
165 AHM	44	36.9	35.6	35.2	36.0	ALCOHOLISM (HOLMES).
166 ANT	36	67.3	66.3	65.6	66.4	ANTISOCIAL.

1-T	2-T	3-F	4-F	5-T	6-T	7-T	8-T	9-T	10-F	11-F	12-T	13-T	14-F
15-F	16-F	17-T	18-T	19-T	20-T	21-T	22-T	23-F	24-T	25-F	26-T	27-F	28-F
29-F	30-T	31-F	32-F	33-F	34-F	35-F	36-T	37-T	38-T	39-T	40-F	41-T	42-T
43-F	44-F	45-T	46-F	47-F	48-F	49-F	50-F	51-T	52-T	53-F	54-T	55-T	56-F
57-T	58-F	59-T	60-T	61-F	62-F	63-F	64-F	65-T	66-T	67-T	68-T	69-F	70-F
71-T	72-F	73-T	74-F	75-T	76-F	77-F	78-F	79-F	80-T	81-T	82-T	83-T	84-T
85-T	86-F	87-F	88-T	89-T	90-T	91-F	92-F	93-T	94-T	95-F	96-T	97-F	98-T
99-F	100-T	101-T	102-T	103-F	104-F	105-F	106-T	107-T	108-F	109-T	110-T	111-T	112-T
113-T	114-T	115-T	116-T	117-T	118-T	119-T	120-T	121-T	122-T	123-T	124-T	125-T	126-F
127-T	128-T	129-T	130-T	131-F	132-F	133-T	134-T	135-T	136-T	137-T	138-F	139-F	140-F
141-T	142-T	143-T	144-T	145-T	146-T	147-T	148-T	149-F	150-F	151-F	152-T	153-F	154-F
155-T	156-T	157-T	158-T	159-F	160-F	161-F	162-F	163-T	164-T	165-T	166-T	167-T	168-F
169-T	170-T	171-T	172-F	173-T	174-T	175-T	176-T	177-T	178-T	179-T	180-T	181-F	182-F
183-T	184-F	185-T	186-T	187-T	188-T	189-F	190-F	191-F	192-T	193-T	194-T	195-T	196-T
197-T	198-T	199-T	200-T	201-T	202-T	203-F	204-F	205-T	206-F	207-T	208-T	209-F	210-F
211-F	212-T	213-T	214-T	215-F	216-T	217-F	218-F	219-T	220-T	221-T	222-T	223-T	224-T
225-T	226-T	227-T	228-T	229-T	230-F	231-T	232-F	233-T	234-T	235-T	236-F	237-T	238-F
239-F	240-F	241-T	242-T	243-T	244-T	245-F	246-F	247-T	248-T	249-T	250-T	251-T	252-T
253-T	254-F	255-T	256-T	257-T	258-T	259-F	260-T	261-T	262-T	263-F	264-T	265-T	266-T
267-T	268-T	269-F	270-T	271-F	272-F	273-T	274-T	275-F	276-T	277-T	278-T	279-T	280-T
281-F	282-F	283-T	284-T	285-T	286-T	287-T	288-F	289-T	290-T	291-F	292-T	293-F	294-F
295-F	296-T	297-F	298-F	299-F	300-T	301-F	302-T	303-T	304-T	305-T	306-T	307-T	308-T
309-T	310-T	311-T	312-T	313-T	314-T	315-F	316-T	317-T	318-T	319-T	320-T	321-F	322-T
323-T	324-T	325-T	326-T	327-T	328-T	329-F	330-T	331-T	332-F	333-T	334-T	335-F	336-F
337-T	338-T	339-T	340-T	341-T	342-T	343-F	344-T	345-T	346-T	347-T	348-T	349-T	350-F
351-T	352-T	353-T	354-T	355-F	356-F	357-F	358-T	359-T	360-T	361-T	362-T	363-F	364-T
365-T	366-T	367-T	368-F	369-F	370-T	371-T	372-T	373-T	374-F	375-F	376-T	377-T	378-T
379-T	380-T	381-T	382-T	383-T	384-T	385-T	386-F	387-F	388-F	389-T	390-T	391-F	392-T
393-F	394-T	395-T	396-T	397-T	398-T	399-T	400-T	401-T	402-F	403-T	404-T	405-F	406-T
407-T	408-T	409-T	410-T	411-T	412-T	413-F	414-F	415-T	416-F	417-T	418-T	419-T	420-T
421-T	422-T	423-T	424-T	425-T	426-T	427-T	428-T	429-F	430-T	431-T	432-F	433-T	434-T
435-F	436-T	437-F	438-T	439-T	440-T	441-T	442-F	443-F	444-T	445-T	446-T	447-T	448-T
449-T	450-T	451-T	452-F	453-T	454-T	455-T	456-F	457-T	458-T	459-T	460-T	461-T	462-T
463-T	464-F	465-T	466-T	467-T	468-T	469-T	470-T	471-F	472-F	473-T	474-T	475-T	476-T
477-F	478-F	479-T	480-T	481-T	482-F	483-F	484-T	485-T	486-F	487-T	488-F	489-F	490-F
491-T	492-T	493-T	494-T	495-T	496-T	497-T	498-T	499-T	500-T	501-T	502-T	503-T	504-T
505-T	506-T	507-T	508-T	509-F	510-T	511-F	512-T	513-F	514-T	515-T	516-T	517-F	518-T
519-T	520-T	521-T	522-F	523-T	524-T	525-T	526-F	527-T	528-T	529-T	530-T	531-T	532-T
533-T	534-T	535-T	536-T	537-T	538-F	539-T	540-T	541-T	542-T	543-F	544-T	545-T	546-T
547-F	548-T	549-F	550-F	551-T	552-T	553-F	554-T	555-T	556-T	557-F	558-T	559-F	560-F
561-T	562-T	563-T	564-T	565-F	566-F								

BEHAVIORDYNE 994 SAN ANTONIO ROAD □ PALO ALTO, CALIFORNIA 94303-4951

104 *psychware*

NAME: California Psychological Inventory

SUPPLIER: Applied Innovations, Inc.
South Kingstown Office Park, Suite A-1
Wakefield, RI 02879
(800) 272-2250

PRODUCT CATEGORY

Personality
Career/Vocational

PRIMARY APPLICATIONS

Personal/Marriage/Family Counseling
Educational Evaluation/Planning
Vocational Guidance/Counseling

SALE RESTRICTIONS American Psychological Association Guidelines

SERVICE TYPE/COST	Type	Available	Cost	Discount
	Mail-In	No		
	Teleprocessing	No		
	Local	Yes	$375.00	

PRODUCT DESCRIPTION

This program scores, profiles, and interprets the CALIFORNIA PSYCHO-LOGICAL INVENTORY (CPI) and a CPI-derived MMPI. It provides both normal and clinical narrative interpretations. The software operates on most available personal computers including IBM, Apple, Digital, and Kaypro.

The test itself is a 480-item measure containing 18 basic scales. It was designed for those 13 years of age and older who are not psychiatrically disturbed. Scales included in the test are: Dominance, Capacity for Status, Sociability, Social Presence, Self-Acceptance, Sense of Well-being, Responsibility, Socialization, Self-Control, Tolerance, Good Impression, Commu-nality, Achievement via Conformance, Achievement via Independence, Intellectual Efficiency, Psychological-Mindedness, Flexibility, and Femininity.

Name—SAMPLE CLIENT   Date—
Sex—MALE   Age—22

Validity

   This type of individual likes to create favorable
impressions and is very concerned about what others think
of him/her. This type of person presents themself as
virtuous and deny any unfavorable traits. Somewhat modest,
this type of individual may have taken this test in such a
way as to present himself/herself in a highly favorable
light.

Personal Traits

Individuals with this profile type generally exhibit good
judgement and are socially conforming. It is important to
them to make a good impression. They generally are not
impulsive, demonstrate good emotional stability, and are
usually not mentally disturbed. They value personal
relationships and work at being personable. These
individuals view themselves as reasonable. They are firm
believers in thinking and letting their minds rule their
hearts.

These individuals are socially poised, self-assured, and
interpersonally adequate. They tend to come from families
of higher than average socioeconomic status, and often
have high verbal intelligence.They are upwardly mobile,
ascendant, and verbally fluent. In general they are well
adjusted, extraverted, outgoing, and rarely become
depressed and do not usually have conflicts or anxieties.
These individuals often do well in occupations requiring
leading and managing people. Occupations such as army
officer, police officer, administrator or school
superintendent are congruent with their interest patterns.
They generally seek occupations where they are in
authority, but do not necessarily demand social status.
They may do less well at jobs requiring artistic talent.

These individuals think independently and often reject
authoritarian attitudes. They are often original and
creative. They are interested in intellectual matters and
likely have liberal moral values. Artists, architects,
psychologists, musicians, and authors often have profiles
similar to this one.

These individuals are generally poised and
self-confident. They have a strong sense of duty and are
extremely persistent and committed to tasks they embark
upon. They are reality oriented. These individuals think
independently. They have a high sense of personal worth
and accept themselves for what they are. They have
positive self-concepts and are high in ego-strength. They
can realistically appraise the positive and negative
qualities in themselves and others. This individual tends
to be responsible, dependable and conscientious. They
tend to govern their life based on reason rather than
emotion. They are emotionally stable and generally are
not impulsive or rebellious. They are open, honest, and
flexible. An interest in esthetic, artistic and
intellectual pursuits is suggested. This individual has a
strong need to achieve. Performance and structured
academic environments is likely to be good if adequate
intellectual endowment is evident. These individuals tend
to be diligent, planful people. They think ahead and are
performance oriented. They tend to be even tempered.
Individuals with this profile type tend to achieve in
environments where independence, creativity and self
actualization are rewarded. These individuals tend to
tolerate ambiguity and do not express or value
authoritarian attitudes. They tend to be self actualized
to such an extent that they are unpopular. They tend to
be well adjusted and have a well developed moral, value
and ethical system.

106 *psychware*

Socialization

These people like to be leaders and generally aspire to
leadership positions. They enjoy having authority over
others. They seek social status and are upwardly mobile.
They often belong to clubs, organizations, and enjoy
social activities. They are generally tolerant of others
who do not have similar values or standards. They tend to
engage in clever, witty, and sometimes, sarcastic
conversation. They are often argumentative. These
individuals may be somewhat over controlled and tend to
be socially inhibited and modest.

Self Description

Adventurous	Capable
Confident	Dominant
Efficient	Forceful
Forgetful	Independent
Intelligent	Logical
Outgoing	Pleasure seeking
Poised	Rational
Responsible	Self-controlled
Sociable	Witty

Name: SAMPLE CLIENT   Sex: MALE
Date: Age: 22

	DO	CS	SY	SP	SA	WB	RE	SO	SC	TO	GI	CM	AC	AI	IE	PY	FX	FE
R	35	26	30	41	22	44	31	36	40	30	33	23	35	27	45	18	18	13
T	66	67	61	63	58	66	50	49	62	65	72	40	66	70	62	75	76	42

psychware **107**

NAME: California Psychological Inventory

SUPPLIER: PSYCH Systems, Inc.
600 Reisterstown Road
Baltimore, MD 21208
(800) 368-3366

PRODUCT CATEGORY

Personality
Career/Vocational

PRIMARY APPLICATIONS

Personal/Marriage/Family Counseling
Educational Evaluation/Planning
Vocational Guidance/Counseling

SALE RESTRICTIONS Qualified Professional

SERVICE TYPE/COST	Type	Available	Cost	Discount
	Mail-In	No		
	Teleprocessing	No		
	Local	Yes	See Below	

PRODUCT DESCRIPTION

This PSYCH Systems program administers and scores the CALIFORNIA PSYCHOLOGICAL INVENTORY, then provides an interpretive report based on the test results. The main body of the report contains predictive and descriptive statements based on the test scales. The test itself is a 480-item instrument containing 18 basic scales that measure socially desirable behavioral tendencies: Dominance, Capacity for Status, Sociability, Social Presence, Self-Acceptance, Sense of Well-Being, Responsibility, Socialization, Self-Control, Tolerance, Good Impression, Communality, Achievement via Conformance, Achievement via Independence, Intellectual Efficiency, and Femininity. It was designed for those 13 years of age and older who were not psychiatrically disturbed. The characteristics it measures are important for social living and social interactions and have wide applicability to human behavior.

Psych Systems programs operate on the IBM PC-XT, COMPAQ Plus, Dec Professional 350, and most DEC PDP-11 systems. Various hardware/ software configurations are available directly from Psych Systems, with single-user systems starting at approximately $12,000. A per test fee also applies.

```
--------------------------------------------------------
|           |                                            |
|   CPI     |   California Psychological Inventory        |
|           |                                            |
--------------------------------------------------------
```

This clinical report is designed to assist in psychodiagnostic
evaluation. It is available to qualified professionals. This
report was produced by a computerized analysis of the data given
by the client listed above, and is to be used in conjunction with
professional evaluation. No decision should be based solely upon
the contents of this report.

The computer program generating this report was designed by Psych
Systems, Inc., Baltimore, Maryland 21208. Copyright (C) 1984 by
Psych Systems, Inc. The interpretive logic utilized in the
generation of the report was designed by Duke E. Ellis, Ph. D. and
James T. Webb, Ph. D. Copyright (C) 1982 Duke E. Ellis and James T.
Webb. Reproduced under license from UPSA Inc. Psychometric Laboratory.
The California Psychological Inventory is reproduced by permission.
Copyright (C) 1956, 1957, 1975 by Consulting Psychologists Press
Incorporated, 577 College Avenue, Palo Alto, California 94306. No
portion of the CPI may be reproduced by any process without prior
written permission of the publisher. All rights reserved.

This person gave a large number of highly unusual answers during this testing to such a degree that the validity of the test results must be considered questionable pending further study. Consideration should be given to the possibility that he answered carelessly or in some other fashion did not take the test seriously. Alternatively, the possibility exists that he had extreme difficulty in following the directions or in comprehending the test items.

This person presented himself as one who lacks good emotional self-control. The possibility exists that he may be attempting to present himself in an unfavorable light for some reason. If this can be ruled out the results suggest that he is impulsive, often acts without sufficient forethought and is likely to be seen by others as headstrong, excitable, temperamental, and even aggressive. He responds quickly to frustration or annoyance, and may even react aggressively to threat or interference. He has difficulty in giving up short-term gratification in order to achieve long-term goals.

He reports that he is not overly preoccupied with the impression his behavior creates in others, and does not particularly care what others think of him. This may be because he is currently depressed. If this is not the case, then he is generally not sensitive to criticism, and may even be somewhat insensitive to appropriate criticism because he judges his own behaviors independently of the attitudes of others.

Although he can assume leadership roles, he generally would prefer not to. Leadership roles are not greatly important to him, and he is not likely to seek them out. Although he may be effective at exercising control over limited groups, he will tend to delegate responsibility for direct leadership. He would rather participate in a group or committee than lead or organize it.

Socioeconomic symbols of status or achievement are not important to him at this time, and he is not willing to endure personal discomfort in order to achieve in such areas as education, prestige or income. He likely will be acquiescent, non-assertive, or even apathetic, and may be quite restricted in his outlook and interests, perhaps reflecting rather non-traditional values.

He appears to be somewhat uncomfortable socially, and probably is not very outgoing interpersonally. He may even be retiring and shy, particularly in situations where he is the center of attention.

Behavior patterns that differ from his own may be difficult to accept fully. He may have a somewhat restricted view of what behaviors are proper, and he will tend to be critical of others who do not adhere

to "proper" behaviors. He may often be concerned that his own behavior is within accepted norms, and is not unconventional. Others may see him as cautious, serious and conforming.

He indicates that he is reasonably self-confident and comfortable with himself at this time. He will likely be seen by others as outgoing, assured, self-reliant, and perhaps even adventurous.

He appears to rely heavily on his own views, opinions and judgments. However this may stem more from a sense of distrust of others or alienation from them, rather than from any great sense of self-confidence.

Civic responsibility, in the usual sense, does not appear to be important to him; he is not likely to be concerned about the "general good" of society. Generally such persons are unwilling to make personal sacrifices for the benefit of "future generations" or other similar abstract others. He may even be uncomfortable in assuming responsibility for persons related to him, such as spouse or children. Others are likely to see him as preoccupied with himself, lacking in self-discipline, or even irresponsible.

Society's norms appear to be unimportant to him. He apparently has rejected such standards, and feels alienated from and distrustful of society generally. He likely feels that most social, governmental or other organized institutions exploit people, rather than serving them. He may be overtly rebellious or defiant toward these norms and conventions. He will have difficulty in relations with others, including his own family, and has numerous interpersonal conflicts and problems. Others will see him as alienated, irresponsible, impulsive, unconventional, rash, foolish, and even as deceitful.

Although he is aware of expectations regarding family, social, or civic responsibilities, he is not likely to see them as important. Others may see him as careless or irresponsible about his duties, and perhaps as preoccupied with himself. He is unlikely to make personal sacrifices for the benefit of future generations or for established civic institutions.

He appears to have little concern with achievement at this time. He is likely to be an underachiever. He may generally distrust the opinions of others and feels rather alienated from conventional authority. One subgroup of these persons is clinically depressed, or has a history of generalized inadequacy in coping, particularly intellectually. Others are likely to see him as lazy, careless, shallow, unrealistic, immature, and perhaps as irresponsible, self-centered, or even unstable.

222-22-2222   Jonathan Doe   32 yr old white male   16-Feb-84

He appears to be quite doubtful and even critical of his intellectual abilities, and may in fact be unskilled in intellectual endeavors. However his self-doubt may also stem from current personal distress such as anxiety, depression, or other emotional problems, particularly if these difficulties are accompanied by problems in concentrating or remembering.

New ideas and experiences appear to cause him noteable discomfort, and he finds it difficult to seriously contemplate or to try new approaches to problems. He appears to be cautious, conservative, worrying, and intellectually rigid and tradition-bound. He is lacking in general overall adaptive flexibility.

```
         Do Cs Sy Sp Sa Wb Re So Sc To Gi Cm Ac Ai Ie Py Fx Fe
         --------------------------------------------------------
 100+                      +             +             +          +100
    ¶                      +             +             ¶          ¶
  95+                      +             +             +          + 95
    ¶                      ¶             ¶             ¶          ¶
  90+                      +             +             +          + 90
    ¶                      ¶             ¶             ¶          ¶
  85+                      +             +             +          + 85
    ¶                      ¶             ¶             ¶          ¶
  80+                      +             +             +          + 80
    ¶                      ¶             ¶             ¶          ¶
  75+                      +             +             +          + 75
    ¶                      ¶             ¶             ¶          ¶
  70+                      +             +             +          + 70
    ¶                      ¶             ¶             ¶          ¶
  65+                      +             +             +          + 65
    ¶                      ¶             ¶             ¶          ¶
  60+                      +             +             +          + 60
    ¶                      ¶             ¶             ¶          ¶
  55+                      +             +             +*      *  + 55
    ¶                      ¶             ¶             ¶          ¶
  50+--------------------------+-------------+----------+---------+ 50
    ¶  *                   ¶             ¶             ¶          ¶
  45+                   *  +             +             +          + 45
    ¶        *  *          ¶             ¶             ¶          ¶
  40+                      +             +             +          + 40
    ¶                      ¶             ¶             ¶          ¶
  35+                      +         *   +             +          + 35
    ¶                      ¶             ¶             ¶          ¶
  30+                      +             +             +          + 30
    ¶                      ¶*            ¶             ¶          ¶
  25+     *                +       *   * +     *       + *        + 25
    ¶                      ¶             ¶             ¶          ¶
  20+                      +             +*            +          + 20
    ¶                    * ¶             ¶             ¶          ¶
  15+                      +             +             +          + 15
    ¶                      ¶             ¶             ¶          ¶
  10+                      +             +          *  +          + 10
    ¶                      ¶             ¶             ¶          ¶
   5+                      +             +             +          + 5
    ¶                      ¶          *  ¶             ¶          ¶
   0+                    * +             +             +          + 0
         --------------------------------------------------------
         Do Cs Sy Sp Sa Wb Re So Sc To Gi Cm Ac Ai Ie Py Fx Fe
RS:      26 10 21 30 18 11 20 19 15 11 12 12 15  8 21 13  1 19
SS:      48 26 43 43 47  1 28 19 28 25 37  4 22 25 10 57 27 57
```

222-22-2222 Jonathan Doe   32 yr old white male   16-Feb-84

Police Effectiveness Index =   43

Raw Data

```
         1234567890 1234567890 1234567890

  1- 30  TTTTTTTTTF FTFFFFTFTT TTTFTFTTTT
 31- 60  FTFTTTTFFT TFTFFTTTTF TTTTTTFFFF
 61- 90  FFFFFTTTTF FFFTTTTTTT TTTTFFFFFF
 91-120  FTTTTTTFFT TTFFFFFFTT TTTFFFFFFF
121-150  FFFFTTTFTT FFFFFFFFFF FFFFTTTTTT
151-180  TTTTTTTTTT TTTTTTTTTT TTFFFTTTTT
181-210  TTTTTTTTTT TTTTTTTTTT TTTTTTTTTT
211-240  TTTTTTTTTT TTTTTTTTTT TTTTTTTTTT
241-270  TTTTTTTTTT TTTTTTTTTT TTTTTTTTTT
271-300  TTTTTTTTTT TTTTTTTTTT TTTTTTTTTT
301-330  TTTTTTTTTT TTTTTTTTTT TTTTTTTTTT
331-360  TTTTTTTTTT TTTTTTTTTT TTTTTTTTTT
361-390  TTTTTTTTTT TTTTTTTTTT TTTTTTTTTF
391-420  FFFFFFTTTT TTTTTTTTTT TTTTTTTTTT
421-450  TTTFFFFFFF TTTTTTTTTT TTTTTTTTTT
451-480  TTTTTTTTTT TTTTFFFFFF FFFFFFFFFF
```

NAME: Career Assessment Inventory

SUPPLIER: NCS/Professional Assessment Services
P.O. Box 1416
Minneapolis, MN 55440
(800) 328-6759

PRODUCT CATEGORY	PRIMARY APPLICATIONS
Career/Vocational	Vocational Guidance/Counseling
Interest/Attitudes	Personnel Selection/Evaluation

SALE RESTRICTIONS   None

SERVICE TYPE/COST	Type	Available	Cost	Discount
Mail-In	Yes	$10.00	Yes
Teleprocessing	Yes	$10.00	Yes
Local	Yes	$6.00	Yes

PRODUCT DESCRIPTION

This individualized, 16-19 page narrative contains scale descriptions, score interpretation and comparisons, plus additional reference information followed by a four-page detachable summary. The test itself has 305 items with five response choices. It requires a 6th-grade reading level and takes 20-35 minutes to complete. The CAREER ASSESSMENT INVENTORY was designed to aid in career development by assessing vocational interests of individuals who do not plan to obtain a four-year college education. The test includes 91 Occupational Scales, 22 Basic Interest Scales, 6 General Occupational Themes (corresponding to Holland's RIASEC scheme), four non-occupational scales, and two administrative indexes. The CAREER ASSESSMENT INVENTORY items (but not the interpretive report) are also available in Spanish and French.

A scores only report (Profile Report) is also available at approximately 40% of costs shown here for the complete report.

Two systems are available for local processing of test results. MICRO-TEST Assessment Software from National Computer Systems, used with a Sentry 3000 tabletop scanner (purchase price approximately $4000) and microcomputer system ($2000-$3000 purchase price), allows tests to be administered off-line. Answer sheets are then scanned and scored automatically, one at a time or in a batch. The software also permits on-line administration of the test via microcomputer. In either case, the same report is provided. The cost for local scoring refers to the cost-per-test when diskettes are purchased in units of 20 administrations (minimum purchase).

PREPARED BY--
NCS INTERPRETIVE SCORING SYSTEMS
P.O. BOX 1294
MINNEAPOLIS, MN 55440
29-SEP-83

001 0028

CAREER ASSESSMENT INVENTORY

****
SAMPLE   B   FEMALE
****

INTERPRETIVE REPORT FOR

THE IMPORTANT PROCESS OF CHOOSING A CAREER REQUIRES THAT SEVERAL THINGS BE CONSIDERED. YOUR ABILITIES ARE VERY IMPORTANT IN DECIDING UPON A JOB, BUT YOUR INTERESTS, PERSONAL PREFERENCES, AND LIFE EXPERIENCES ALSO PLAY AN IMPORTANT PART IN HELPING YOU DECIDE ON AN OCCUPATION WHERE YOU WILL BE SATISFIED. RESEARCH HAS SHOWN THAT INDIVIDUALS HAVE A BETTER CHANCE OF BEING SATIS-FIED IN AN OCCUPATION IF THEIR INTERESTS ARE SIMILAR TO THOSE OF PEOPLE ALREADY EMPLOYED IN THAT OCCUPATION. THE RESULTS BELOW ARE BASED ON YOUR LIKE AND DISLIKE ANSWERS TO THE ITEMS ON THE CAREER ASSESSMENT INVENTORY. THESE RESULTS WILL POINT OUT AREAS WHERE YOUR INTERESTS DO AND DO NOT MATCH THOSE OF PEOPLE WHO ARE WORKING IN DIFFERENT OCCUPATIONS. THE RESULTS CAN HELP YOU UNDERSTAND BETTER HOW YOUR PREFERENCES FIT INTO THE WORLD OF WORK.

IMPORTANTLY, THESE RESULTS ARE MEASURES OF ONLY YOUR INTERESTS AND NOT OF YOUR ABILITIES OR APTITUDES. FOR EXAMPLE, YOUR RESULTS MAY INDICATE THAT YOU WOULD LIKE THE DAILY ROUTINE OF ART-ISTS AND THAT YOU LIKE ARTISTIC ACTIVITIES, BUT THE RESULTS WILL NOT TELL YOU IF YOU HAVE THE TALENT TO BE AN ARTIST.

THESE RESULTS CAN GIVE YOU SOME USEFUL INFORMATION ABOUT YOURSELF, BUT DO NOT EXPECT MIRA-CLES. WHILE YOU MAY FEEL THAT THE SCORES TELL YOU NOTHING MORE THAN YOU ALREADY KNOW ABOUT YOURSELF, THEY WILL PERMIT YOU TO SEE HOW THE STRENGTHS OF YOUR INTERESTS COMPARE TO THE AVERAGE INTERESTS OF OTHER PEOPLE. THESE RESULTS ARE DESIGNED TO BE AN AID TO HELP YOU REACH A CAREER DECISION THAT WILL BE MOST SATISFYING TO YOU.

* * * * * * * * * * * * * * * * * * * *

* * * * * * * * * * * * * * * * * * * *

THREE MAIN SETS OF SCORES ARE PRESENTED ON THE FOLLOWING PAGES. FIRST ARE YOUR RESULTS ON SIX GENERAL OCCUPATIONAL THEMES--THEY GIVE YOU A GENERAL OVERALL VIEW OF YOUR INTERESTS. SECOND ARE YOUR RESULTS ON THE BASIC INTEREST SCALES--THESE SCORES TELL YOU ABOUT THE STRENGTH OF YOUR INTERESTS IN MORE SPECIFIC AREAS SUCH AS SALES, WRITING, AND MECHANICAL ACTIVITIES. THIRD ARE THE OCCUPATIONAL SCALES--THEY TELL YOU HOW SIMILAR OR DISSIMILAR YOUR INTERESTS ARE TO PEOPLE IN DIFFERENT OCCUPATIONS SUCH AS POLICE OFFICER, INTERIOR DESIGNER, SECRETARY, AND SO FORTH.

```
* * * * * * * * * * * *
*  *  *  *
*  *  *  *  GENERAL  THEMES  *  *  *  *
*  *  *  *
* * * * * * * * * * * *
```

RESEARCH HAS SHOWN THAT INTERESTS CAN BE GROUPED INTO SIX CATEGORIES AND THAT EACH OF THESE
GROUPINGS CAN BE DESCRIBED BY A GENERAL THEME. BELOW ARE YOUR SCORES ON THE SIX GENERAL THEME
SCALES AND A GRAPH TO VIEW YOUR RESULTS BETTER. THE ABBREVIATED THEME NAMES ARE LISTED IN THE
SCALE COLUMN WITH THE COMPLETE NAMES LISTED TO THE RIGHT OF THE GRAPH. MOST PEOPLE HAVE SCORES
BETWEEN 43 AND 57 ON THESE SCALES, SO THIS RANGE, 43-57, IS CALLED THE AVERAGE RANGE OF SCORES.
SCORES BELOW 43 GENERALLY ARE CONSIDERED AS LOW INTEREST IN THAT THEME. SCORES ABOVE 57 GENER-
ALLY ARE CONSIDERED AS HIGH INTEREST IN THAT THEME. IF YOU INDICATED YOUR SEX ON THE INVENTORY,
THERE IS A RANGE OF DOTS FOR EACH SCALE SHOWING THE AVERAGE SCORE RANGE FOR YOUR SEX. ALSO, THE
AVERAGE RANGES FOR FEMALES AND MALES ARE LISTED TO THE RIGHT.

```
                                                        AVERAGE RANGES
         YOUR                                           FEMALE   MALE
SCALE    SCORE   ....0.........0.........0.........0.........0.........0.........0.....
                    3         4         5         6         7

A-THEME    61                                            *          (ARTISTIC)        46-59    41-54
E-THEME    59                                        *              (ENTERPRISING)    43-56    44-57
C-THEME    48                              .*.                      (CONVENTIONAL)    46-60    41-53
S-THEME    41                  *                                    (SOCIAL)          46-59    41-54
I-THEME    39                *                                      (INVESTIGATIVE)   42-56    45-58
R-THEME    27       *                                              (REALISTIC)       40-52    48-60
```

DESCRIPTIONS ARE GIVEN BELOW FOR EACH OF THE THEMES. THESE ARE IDEAL DESCRIPTIONS OF THE
INTERESTS AND CHARACTERISTICS RELATED TO EACH THEME, SO ALL THE DESCRIPTIONS MAY NOT FIT EXACTLY
ANY ONE PERSON. FEW PEOPLE HAVE HIGH SCORES ON JUST ONE THEME AND LOW SCORES ON THE OTHERS.
MOST PEOPLE SCORE HIGH ON TWO OR EVEN THREE THEMES AND THUS THEY SHARE SOME OF THE DESCRIPTIONS
WITH MORE THAN ONE THEME. SOME PEOPLE SCORE LOW ON ALL THEMES WHICH WOULD INDICATE THAT STRONG
PATTERNS OF INTERESTS, AS MEASURED BY THESE THEMES, HAVE NOT BEEN FORMED YET--THIS IS PARTICU-
LARLY TRUE FOR YOUNG PEOPLE. GENERALLY, THE HIGHER YOUR SCORE, THE MORE CHARACTERISTICS YOU
SHARE WITH THAT PARTICULAR THEME.

A   A-THEME---PEOPLE WHO SCORE HIGH ON A-THEME HAVE AN ARTISTIC BENT TO THEIR NATURE AND LIKE
A   TO WORK IN JOBS WITH MANY POSSIBILITIES FOR EXPRESSING THEMSELVES BY MAKING AND CREATING WORKS
A   OF ART. THEY USUALLY LIKE TO WORK ALONE AND TO WRAP THEMSELVES UP IN WHAT THEY ARE DOING. OC-
A   CUPATIONS SUCH AS ARTIST, AUTHOR, CARTOONIST, SINGER, POET, AND INTERIOR DESIGNER REFLECT THIS
A   THEME. THE WORD USED TO DESCRIBE THIS AREA IS ARTISTIC, THUS A-THEME.
A   YOUR SCORE OF 61 ON THE A-THEME SCALE INDICATES THAT MANY OF THE ABOVE DESCRIPTIONS ARE
A   MOST LIKELY TRUE FOR YOU AND YOU MIGHT FIND ARTS AND CRAFTS TYPES OF ACTIVITIES REWARDING.

116 *psychware*

E-THEME---PEOPLE WHO HAVE HIGH SCORES ON E-THEME ARE GOOD AT TALKING AND USING WORDS TO PERSUADE PEOPLE. OFTEN THEY ARE IN SALES WORK AND THEY ARE GOOD AT THINKING UP NEW WAYS OF DOING THINGS TO LEAD AND CONVINCE PEOPLE. THEY SEE THEMSELVES AS FULL OF ENERGY, ENTHUSIASTIC, LIKING ADVENTURE, AND CONFIDENT. MANY TIMES THEY ARE IN OCCUPATIONS SUCH AS SALES, MANAGERS, BUYER, MERCHANDISING, AND BUSINESS. ENTERPRISING DESCRIBES THESE INTERESTS, THUS, E-THEME.
YOUR SCORE OF 59 ON THE E-THEME SCALE INDICATES THAT MANY OF THE ABOVE DESCRIPTIONS ARE TRUE FOR YOU. YOU POSSIBLY WOULD ENJOY BUSINESS TYPES OF ACTIVITIES OR SELLING.

C-THEME---THIS TYPE PREFERS ACTIVITIES AND JOBS WHERE THEY KNOW EXACTLY WHAT IS EXPECTED OF THEM AND WHAT THEY ARE SUPPOSED TO DO. THEY WORK WELL IN LARGE OFFICES, BUT USUALLY DO NOT SEEK LEADERSHIP JOBS. THEY DESCRIBE THEMSELVES AS CONVENTIONAL, STABLE, WELL-CONTROLLED, AND DEPENDABLE. THEY PREFER MANY TYPES OF JOBS IN THE BUSINESS WORLD SUCH AS BANK TELLER, BOOKKEEPER, ACCOUNTANT, COMPUTER OPERATOR, AND SECRETARY. CONVENTIONAL DESCRIBES THIS AREA, THUS C-THEME.
YOUR SCORE OF 48 ON C-THEME INDICATES THAT SOME OF THE ABOVE DESCRIPTIONS MAY BE MORE TRUE FOR YOU THAN OTHER DESCRIPTIONS.

S-THEME---PEOPLE WHO HAVE HIGH SCORES ON S-THEME TEND TO HAVE A STRONG CONCERN FOR OTHERS AND LIKE TO HELP THEM SOLVE PERSONAL PROBLEMS. THEY SEE THEMSELVES AS CHEERFUL, POPULAR, AND ARE GOOD LEADERS. THEY PREFER TO SOLVE PROBLEMS BY TALKING THINGS OUT AND THEY GET ALONG WELL WITH MANY TYPES OF PEOPLE. SOME OCCUPATIONS PREFERRED BY THESE PEOPLE ARE SOCIAL WORKER, NURSE, RECREATION LEADER, CAMP COUNSELOR, AND TEACHER. THIS IS THE SOCIAL OR S-THEME.
YOUR SCORE OF 41 ON S-THEME INDICATES THAT PROBABLY VERY FEW OF THE ABOVE DESCRIPTIONS ARE TRUE FOR YOU. YOU MAY NOT ENJOY WORKING WITH PEOPLE OR HELPING THEM WITH THEIR PROBLEMS.

I-THEME---THIS THEME TENDS TO CENTER AROUND SCIENCE AND SCIENTIFIC ACTIVITIES. PEOPLE WHO HAVE HIGH SCORES TEND TO ENJOY WORKING WITH WORDS AND IDEAS TO FIND THEIR OWN ANSWERS AND SOLUTIONS TO PROBLEMS. THEY PREFER WORKING ALONE AND FREQUENTLY ARE ORIGINAL AND CREATIVE. THEY ENTER OCCUPATIONS SUCH AS LABORATORY RESEARCH WORKER, MEDICAL TECHNICIAN, COMPUTER PROGRAMMER, AND OTHER SCIENTIFIC JOBS. INVESTIGATIVE IS USED TO DESCRIBE THIS THEME, THUS I-THEME.
YOUR SCORE OF 39 ON THE I-THEME SCALE INDICATES THAT MOST LIKELY VERY FEW OF THE ABOVE DESCRIPTIONS ARE TRUE FOR YOU AND YOU MIGHT NOT ENJOY ACTIVITIES THAT INVOLVE SCIENTIFIC PROBLEMS.

R-THEME---PEOPLE WHO HAVE HIGH R-THEME SCORES LIKE TO WORK WITH THEIR HANDS AND TOOLS TO REPAIR THINGS OR BUILD THINGS. GENERALLY, THEY LIKE TO BE OUTSIDE WORKING RATHER THAN AT A DESK IN AN OFFICE. THEY HAVE GOOD PHYSICAL SKILLS, ARE PRACTICAL, RUGGED, AND GENERALLY PREFER TO WORK WITH THINGS RATHER THAN PEOPLE. THEY PREFER OCCUPATIONS SUCH AS MECHANIC, SKILLED TRADES, FORESTER, AND FARMER. THE WORD REALISTIC HAS BEEN USED TO DESCRIBE THIS AREA, THUS R-THEME.
YOUR SCORE OF 27 ON THE R-THEME SCALE INDICATES THAT MOST LIKELY NONE OF THE ABOVE DESCRIPTIONS ARE TRUE OF YOU AND YOU WOULD NOT ENJOY ACTIVITIES WHERE YOU WORK WITH YOUR HANDS.

* * * * * * * * * * * * *

THE ABOVE SIX THEME SCORES PROVIDED YOU WITH A BROAD, GENERAL, OVER-VIEW OF YOUR INTERESTS. THE NEXT SECTION PRESENTS YOUR RESULTS ON THE MORE SPECIFIC BASIC INTEREST AREA SCALES. THESE SCALES GIVE YOU MORE INFORMATION ON YOUR INTERESTS IN PURE TYPES OF ACTIVITIES SUCH AS SALES, TEACHING, MECHANICAL ACTIVITIES, AND OFFICE PRACTICES.

```
* * * * * * * * * * * * * * * *
* * * *  BASIC INTEREST AREAS  * * * *
* * * * * * * * * * * * * * * *
```

BELOW ARE YOUR RESULTS ON 22 BASIC INTEREST SCALES. THEY SHOW THE STRENGTH OF YOUR INTEREST IN A VARIETY OF PURE TYPES OF AREAS. THESE SCORES WILL SHOW AREAS WHERE YOU WILL FIND SATISFACTION OR DISSATISFACTION. THEY CAN BE IMPORTANT IN MAKING CAREER CHOICES OR IN DECIDING ON LEISURE-TIME ACTIVITIES. AN AVERAGE INTEREST FALLS BETWEEN 43 AND 57 ON EACH SCALE. ON SOME OF THE SCALES, FEMALES AND MALES RESPOND SOMEWHAT DIFFERENTLY AND, IF YOU INDICATED YOUR SEX ON THE INVENTORY, A SERIES OF DOTS APPEARS FOR EACH SCALE SHOWING THE AVERAGE RANGE OF SCORES FOR YOUR SEX. ALSO, THE AVERAGE RANGES FOR FEMALES AND MALES ARE LISTED TO THE RIGHT.

BASIC INTEREST AREAS	YOUR SCORE	AVERAGE RANGES FEMALE	MALE
VERY HIGH INTEREST (66+)			
WRITING	70	46-59	41-54
HIGH INTEREST (65-58)***			
OFFICE PRACTICES	61	47-61	41-51
PERFORMING/ENTERTAINING	59	45-58	41-55
AVERAGE INTEREST (57-43)			
BUSINESS	54	44-57	43-56
CLERICAL/CLERKING	49	46-60	41-53
SOCIAL SERVICE	47	46-58	41-55
SALES	44	43-56	43-58
ARTS/CRAFTS	43	48-60	39-52
LOW INTEREST (42-35)****			
FOOD SERVICE	42	48-60	39-52
RELIGIOUS ACTIVITIES	41	44-58	42-56
SCIENCE	41	42-56	45-58
TEACHING	40	45-58	42-55
NUMBERS	39	43-57	44-57
MANUAL/SKILLED TRADES	37	40-51	48-61
CHILD CARE	36	47-60	41-53
AGRICULTURE	35	40-53	47-60
VERY LOW INTEREST (34-)*			
NATURE/OUTDOORS	34	44-57	43-56
MEDICAL SERVICE	34	45-59	41-54
ELECTRONICS	34	40-50	49-61
ANIMAL SERVICE	34	43-57	44-56
MECHANICAL/FIXING	31	39-51	49-61
CARPENTRY	29	40-53	47-60

YOUR HIGHEST SCORES IN THE BASIC INTEREST AREAS ARE LISTED BELOW WITH A DESCRIPTION OF THE KINDS OF ACTIVITIES AND OCCUPATIONS RELATED TO EACH OF THE AREAS. THE HIGHER YOUR SCORE, THE MORE YOU LIKE THE ACTIVITIES THAT ARE A PART OF THAT SCALE. IN GENERAL, THESE AREAS PROBABLY CAN BE SOURCES OF SATISFACTION IN YOUR LIFE. ALTHOUGH THEY MAY OR MAY NOT BE PART OF THE OCCU-PATION THAT YOU CHOOSE, THEY WILL BE AREAS OF LEISURE-TIME SATISFACTION. IF YOU CAN CHOOSE A CAREER THAT IS RELATED TO YOUR HIGHEST SCORES, YOU PROBABLY WILL FIND IT MORE REWARDING.

ALSO LISTED ARE PAGE REFERENCES FOR THE OCCUPATIONAL OUTLOOK HANDBOOK (OOH), BULLETIN NO. 2075. THIS BOOK CAN BE FOUND IN YOUR LOCAL LIBRARY AND PROVIDES INFORMATION ABOUT RECENT TRENDS IN EMPLOYMENT OPPORTUNITIES AND EDUCATIONAL REQUIREMENTS FOR VARIOUS OCCUPATIONS THAT ARE RE-LATED DIRECTLY TO YOUR HIGHEST INTEREST AREAS.

70 WRITING------------YOUR SCORE INDICATES THE DEGREE THAT YOU WOULD ENJOY EXPRESSING YOURSELF BY WRITING. PEOPLE WHO SCORE HIGH ON THIS SCALE SHOW A LIKING FOR DOING THINGS SUCH AS WRITING POETRY, NEWSPAPER REPORTING, CREATIVE WRITING, AND WRITING STORIES FOR MAGAZINES. WRITERS, REPORTERS, AND JOURNALISTS ARE EXAMPLES.

   OOH 193-200

61 OFFICE PRACTICES---TYPING LETTERS, OPERATING OFFICE MACHINES SUCH AS TYPEWRITERS OR COPYING MACHINES OR ADDING MACHINES, AND WORKING AT A DESK ARE MEASURED BY THIS SCALE. OCCUPATIONS SUCH AS SECRETARY, STENOGRAPHER, AND RECEPTIONIST ARE RELATED TO THIS INTEREST AREA.

   OOH 269-272

59 PERFORM/ENTERTAIN.--BEING IN FRONT OF A GROUP OF PEOPLE AND ENTERTAINING OR PERFORMING IS INDI-CATED BY THIS AREA. ACTING IN A PLAY, DIRECTING A PLAY, STUDYING MUSIC, PLAYING A MUSICAL INSTRUMENT, BEING IN A BAND, BEING AN ACTRESS OR ACTOR, AND SO FORTH ARE PART OF THIS GENERAL INTEREST AREA.

   OOH 212-218

THE PRECEDING TWO SECTIONS HAVE ANALYZED YOUR RESULTS IN TERMS OF GENERAL THEME SCALES AND THE MORE SPECIFIC BASIC INTEREST SCALES. AGAIN, YOU SHOULD TRY TO LOCATE THE OCCUPATIONAL OUT-LOOK HANDBOOK IN YOUR LOCAL LIBRARY OR COUNSELING CENTER AND READ FURTHER ABOUT THE VARIOUS CAREERS THAT ARE RELATED TO YOUR HIGH INTERESTS.

* * * * * * * * * * * * * * * * * * * *

THE FOLLOWING STARTS THE NEXT SECTION OF ANALYSIS, THE OCCUPATIONAL SCALES. THESE RESULTS ARE STILL MORE SPECIFIC. THEY COMPARE YOUR ANSWERS TO THOSE OF PEOPLE IN A VARIETY OF OCCUPA-TIONS. YOU SHOULD NOT ASSUME THAT BECAUSE YOU HAVE A HIGH SCORE ON A SCALE, THAT YOU WILL BE GOOD IN THAT OCCUPATION. OTHER FACTORS, SUCH AS ABILITY, PAST LIFE EXPERIENCES, AND EDUCATIONAL TRAINING ARE ALSO IMPORTANT CONSIDERATIONS. HOWEVER, YOU CAN INTERPRET HIGH SCORES AS INDICA-TING THAT YOU HAVE SIMILAR INTERESTS WITH PEOPLE ACTUALLY IN THAT OCCUPATION.

```
* * * * * * * * * * * * * * * * * *
* * * *                     * * * *
* * * *  OCCUPATIONAL SCALES  * * * *
* * * *                     * * * *
* * * * * * * * * * * * * * * * * *
```

THE OCCUPATIONAL SCALES INDICATE THE DEGREE OF SIMILARITY BETWEEN YOUR INTERESTS AND THOSE OF EMPLOYED PEOPLE IN VARIOUS OCCUPATIONS. ABOUT 2/3 OF THE WORKERS IN AN OCCUPATION HAVE SCORES 45 AND HIGHER ON THEIR OWN OCCUPATIONAL SCALE. MOST PEOPLE NOT IN THE OCCUPATION HAVE SCORES IN THE MID-RANGE, 26-44. SCORES OF 25 AND LOWER INDICATE THAT YOUR INTERESTS DO NOT MATCH THOSE OF WORKERS IN THE OCCUPATION, WHILE SCORES OF 45 AND HIGHER INDICATE SIMILARITY OF YOUR INTERESTS WITH THOSE EMPLOYED IN THE OCCUPATION. IF YOU INDICATED YOUR SEX ON THE INVENTORY, A SERIES OF DOTS APPEARS FOR EACH SCALE SHOWING THE AVERAGE RANGE OF SCORES FOR EMPLOYED PEOPLE OF YOUR SEX WHO ARE NOT IN THE OCCUPATION. TO THE RIGHT ARE THE AVERAGE RANGES FOR MALES AND FEMALES NOT IN THE OCCUPATION. TO THE LEFT OF EACH SCALE IS A ONE-THREE LETTER THEME CODE INDICATING THE IMPORTANT THEME INTEREST CHARACTERISTICS FOR THAT SCALE. THE FIRST LETTER INDICATES THE STRONGEST RELATIONSHIP AND ANY ADDITIONAL LETTERS INDICATE LESSER IMPORTANT INTEREST CHARACTERISTICS.

RESEARCH HAS INDICATED THAT PEOPLE WHO ENTER AN OCCUPATION WHERE THEY HAVE SIMILAR SCORES TEND TO REMAIN IN THAT OCCUPATION AND ARE MORE SATISFIED THAN IF THEY ENTER AN OCCUPATION WHERE THEY HAVE DISSIMILAR SCORES. FURTHERMORE, THESE SCORES MAY INDICATE INTEREST IN AN OCCUPATION THAT YOU MAY NOT HAVE CONSIDERED BEFORE AND THEY CAN HELP YOU THINK ABOUT VARIOUS CAREERS. YOU ALSO ARE ENCOURAGED TO CONSIDER OCCUPATIONS WHERE YOUR SCORE IS CONSIDERABLY HIGHER THAN THE AVERAGE FOR YOUR SEX EVEN IF YOUR SCORE IS NOT IN THE VERY SIMILAR OR SIMILAR RANGE.

THEME CODE	OCCUPATIONAL SCALES	YOUR SCORE	VERY DISS. -15	DIS-SIMILAR 16-25	MID-RANGE 26-44	SIMILAR 45-54	VERY SIMILAR 55+	AVERAGE RANGES FEMALE	MALE
RI	AIRCRAFT MECHANIC	3	*					12-24	20-33
R	AUTO MECHANIC	4	*					12-22	19-32
R	BUS DRIVER	4	*					18-28	26-37
RI	CAMERA REPAIR TECH.	11	*					10-22	18-31
R	CARPENTER	5	*					16-27	21-32
RI	CONSERVATION OFFICER	1	*					9-24	14-27
RI	DENTAL LAB. TECH.	17		*				25-35	29-39
RI	DRAFTER	12		*				14-26	20-32
R	ELECTRICIAN	6	*					12-22	19-32
RS	EMERGENCY MED. TECH.	7	*					21-33	22-34
R	FARMER/RANCHER	21			*			23-31	27-36
R	FIREFIGHTER	1	*					16-29	22-35
RI	FOREST RANGER	1	*					0-17	2-19
RC	HARDWARE STORE MGR.	2	*					8-19	15-28
R	JANITOR/JANITRESS	12		*				22-31	26-37
R	MACHINIST	1	*					6-18	15-29
RC	MAIL CARRIER	4	*					17-28	20-32

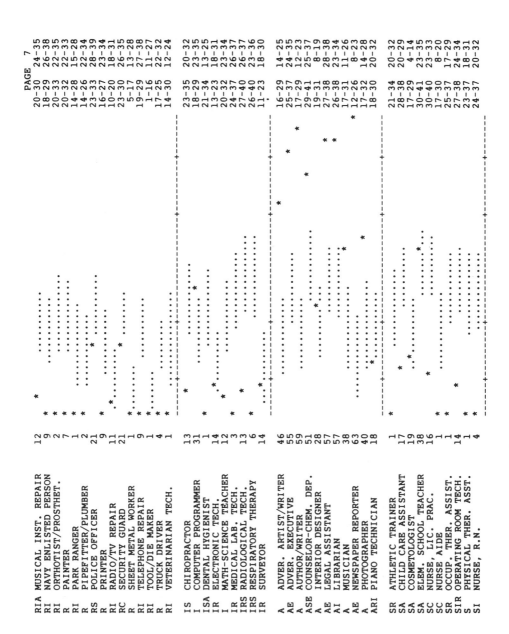

Code	Occupation	N	Range 1	Range 2
RIA	MUSICAL INST. REPAIR	12	20-30	24-35
RI	NAVY ENLISTED PERSON	9	18-29	26-38
RI	ORTHOTIST/PROSTHET.	2	20-33	22-35
R	PAINTER	7	20-32	22-33
RI	PARK RANGER	1	14-28	15-28
R	PIPEFITTER/PLUMBER	2	14-26	22-34
RS	POLICE OFFICER	21	23-33	28-39
R	PRINTER	9	16-27	23-34
RI	RADIO/TV REPAIR	11	10-20	18-31
RC	SECURITY GUARD	21	23-30	26-35
R	SHEET METAL WORKER	1	5-17	13-28
RI	TELEPHONE REPAIR	9	19-29	27-38
RI	TOOL/DIE MAKER	1	1-16	11-27
R	TRUCK DRIVER	4	17-25	22-32
RI	VETERINARIAN TECH.	1	14-30	12-24
IS	CHIROPRACTOR	13	23-35	20-32
I	COMPUTER PROGRAMMER	31	18-29	23-35
ISA	DENTAL HYGIENIST	4	21-34	13-25
IR	ELECTRONIC TECH.	14	13-23	18-31
I	MATH-SCIENCE TEACHER	12	20-32	23-34
IR	MEDICAL LAB. TECH.	3	24-37	26-37
IRS	RADIOLOGICAL TECH.	13	27-40	26-37
IRS	RESPIRATORY THERAPY	6	26-40	23-36
IR	SURVEYOR	14	11-23	18-30
A	ADVER. ARTIST/WRITER	46	16-29	14-25
AE	ADVER. EXECUTIVE	55	25-37	24-35
A	AUTHOR/WRITER	59	17-29	12-23
ASE	COUNSELOR-CHEM. DEP.	51	29-41	25-37
A	INTERIOR DESIGNER	28	19-31	8-19
AE	LEGAL ASSISTANT	57	27-38	28-38
AI	LIBRARIAN	57	26-38	23-34
A	MUSICIAN	38	17-31	11-26
AE	NEWSPAPER REPORTER	63	12-26	8-23
A	PHOTOGRAPHER	40	17-32	14-28
ARI	PIANO TECHNICIAN	18	18-30	20-32
SR	ATHLETIC TRAINER	1	21-34	20-32
SA	CHILD CARE ASSISTANT	17	28-38	20-29
SA	COSMETOLOGIST	19	17-29	4-14
SA	ELEM. SCHOOL TEACHER	38	30-41	23-35
SC	NURSE, LIC. PRAC.	16	30-40	23-33
SC	NURSE AIDE	1	17-30	8-20
SR	OCCUP. THER. ASSIST.	1	25-37	17-29
SIR	OPERATING ROOM TECH.	14	27-38	24-34
S	PHYSICAL THER. ASST.	1	23-37	18-31
SI	NURSE, R.N.	4	24-37	20-32

Code	Occupation	Score	OOH Ref.	DOT Ref.
ER	BARBER/HAIRSTYLIST	7	11-23	7-16
EAS	BUYER/MERCHANDISER	52	27-38	22-32
E	CARD/GIFT SHOP MGR.	52	28-39	26-37
ES	CATERER	30	27-36	18-29
E	FLORIST	34	26-36	19-28
ECS	FOOD SERVICE MANAGER	23	26-36	21-30
ECS	HOTEL/MOTEL MANAGER	41	26-38	25-36
ESC	INSURANCE AGENT	37	22-33	22-33
E	MANUFACTURING REP.	26	16-27	20-30
EAS	PERSONNEL MANAGER	54	25-37	28-39
EA	PRIVATE INVESTIGATOR	52	25-36	25-36
EC	PURCHASING AGENT	20	23-33	30-40
E	REAL ESTATE AGENT	40	17-30	20-31
ESA	RESERVATION AGENT	35	28-40	25-35
ECS	RESTAURANT MANAGER	31	28-37	23-32
EC	TRAVEL AGENT	49	26-37	22-32
CE	ACCOUNTANT	40	20-32	25-36
CE	BANK TELLER	34	25-38	17-27
C	BOOKKEEPER	39	26-38	25-35
C	CAFETERIA WORKER	8	19-30	13-21
CE	COURT REPORTER	58	26-37	24-32
CE	DATA ENTRY OPERATOR	42	29-40	25-35
CS	DENTAL ASSISTANT	19	28-39	22-31
CSE	EXECUTIVE HOUSEKEEP.	27	26-35	23-32
CS	MEDICAL ASSISTANT	29	22-35	13-24
CS	PHARMACY TECHNICIAN	29	31-41	25-33
CS	SECRETARY	42	27-37	23-30
C	TEACHER AIDE	35	23-36	15-25
CSE	WAITER/WAITRESS	23	30-39	22-30

```
VERY . + DIS-  . +       . +      . + VERY .
DISS. + SIMILAR + MID-RANGE + SIMILAR +SIMILAR
```

YOUR HIGHEST SCORES APPEARED ON THE FOLLOWING SCALES AND INDICATE THE GREATEST DEGREE OF SIMILARITY BETWEEN YOUR ANSWERS AND THOSE OF WORKERS IN THESE CAREERS. AS BEFORE, REFERENCES ARE GIVEN FOR THE OCCUPATIONAL OUTLOOK HANDBOOK (OOH) WHICH GIVES ADDITIONAL INFORMATION ON EMPLOYMENT OPPORTUNITIES AND RELEVANT WORK SITUATIONS. ALSO, REFERENCES ARE LISTED FOR THE DICTIONARY OF OCCUPATIONAL TITLES (DOT), FOURTH EDITION. THE DOT GIVES DETAILED JOB DESCRIPTIONS OF THE DUTIES AND FUNCTIONS OF EACH OCCUPATION AND SHOULD BE AVAILABLE IN YOUR LOCAL LIBRARY OR LOCAL COUNSELING OFFICE. THE FIRST DOT REFERENCE IS FOR PAGE NUMBER AND THE SECOND DOT REFERENCE IS FOR THE DOT CODE FOR THAT OCCUPATION.

63 NEWSPAPER REPORTER——REPORTERS GATHER NEWS ON CURRENT EVENTS AND WRITE IT DOWN FOR PUBLICATION IN DAILY OR WEEKLY NEWSPAPERS. SOMETIMES THEY ARE ASSIGNED TO COVER A CERTAIN KIND OF NEWS, SUCH AS STATE GOVERNMENT OR POLICE ACTIVITIES. A FOUR-YEAR COLLEGE DEGREE, PREFERABLY IN JOURNALISM, IS NECESSARY FOR JOB ENTRY. COMPETITION FOR JOBS IS EXPECTED TO CONTINUE, WITH POSITIONS IN SMALL TOWNS OR SUBURBS MOST PLENTIFUL FOR BEGINNERS.

OOH 196-199
DOT 78
DOT 131.267

59 AUTHOR/WRITER——AUTHORS PLAN AND WRITE ORIGINAL FICTION OR NON-FICTION STORIES FOR PUBLICATION AS BOOKS, PLAYS, OR MAGAZINE ARTICLES. THEY CHOOSE A SUBJECT, CHART THE PLOT, AND REWRITE THE STORY UNTIL IT IS IN ITS BEST FORM. A GOOD BACKGROUND IN ENGLISH COMPOSITION, STYLE, AND GRAMMAR IS HELPFUL FOR SUCCESS IN THIS OCCUPATION, BUT COMPETITION FOR STEADY EMPLOYMENT IN THIS FIELD IS VERY KEEN.

OOH 192
DOT 78
DOT 131.067

58 COURT REPORTER——COURT REPORTERS USE A SPECIAL MACHINE CALLED A STENOGRAPH TO RECORD IN SHORTHAND FORM EVERY WORD SPOKEN DURING A COURT CASE. THEN THEY TYPE AND SUBMIT THIS RECORD AS AN OFFICIAL TRANSCRIPT OF THE PROCEEDINGS. BEING ABLE TO LISTEN CAREFULLY, TYPE RAPIDLY, AND WORK IRREGULAR HOURS ARE ESSENTIAL FOR THIS JOB. THE TRAINING PROGRAM TO BECOME A COURT REPORTER LASTS TWO YEARS, AND THE JOB OUTLOOK FOR THIS OCCUPATION IS VERY GOOD.

OOH 270-273
DOT 154
DOT 202.362

57 LIBRARIAN——LIBRARIANS SELECT, ORGANIZE, AND MAINTAIN THE COLLECTION OF BOOKS AND OTHER MATERIALS IN A LIBRARY. A FOUR-YEAR COLLEGE DEGREE PLUS COMPLETION OF A ONE-YEAR MASTERS DEGREE PROGRAM IN LIBRARY SCIENCE IS NECESSARY FOR JOB ENTRANCE. LIBRARIANS MUST BE INTELLECTUALLY CURIOUS AND ADEPT AT VERBAL EXPRESSION. WHILE EMPLOYMENT IS EXPECTED TO GROW SLOWLY THROUGH THE 1980S, THE SUPPLY OF QUALIFIED PEOPLE WILL EXCEED THE DEMAND.

OOH 138-140
DOT 72
DOT 100.127

57 LEGAL ASSISTANT——LEGAL ASSISTANTS (OR PARALEGAL ASSISTANTS) DO RESEARCH AND INVESTIGATION INTO RECORDS AND FACTS. WHILE THEY ARE NOT LICENSED TO PRACTICE LAW, THEY FREQUENTLY WORK FOR LAWYERS, ATTORNEYS, OR LAW FIRMS IN HELPING PREPARE NECESSARY BACKGROUND MATERIAL THAT IS NEEDED FOR VARIOUS CASES. AN INTEREST IN LAW IS IMPORTANT AS IS AN ABILITY TO DO DETAILED WORK. COLLEGES AND UNIVERSITIES OFFER COURSES IN LAW THAT ARE VERY HELPFUL. EMPLOYMENT SHOULD INCREASE AS THE NEED FOR MORE LAWYERS INCREASES.

OOH 227-229
DOT 76
DOT 119.267

55 ADVERTISING EXECUTIVE——THIS OCCUPATION IS MANY-SIDED. PEOPLE IN THIS PROFESSION MAY BE IN CHARGE OF THE BUDGET FOR THE ADVERTISING AGENCY, BE A POLICY PLANNER, OR SUPERVISE OTHER ARTISTS AND COPYWRITERS. A GOOD KNOWLEDGE OF ART AND WRITING, PLUS THE ABILITY TO SELL IDEAS TO CLIENTS, AND THE ABILITY TO MANAGE PEOPLE ARE NECESSARY TO BECOME SUCCESSFUL IN THIS FIELD. IF AVAILABLE, SEE 1982 OOH FOR DISCUSSION.

OOH 235-236
DOT 97
DOT 164.117-.167

* * * * * * * * * *

THE U.S. GOVERNMENT PRINTING OFFICE ALSO HAS A REPRINT SERIES THAT WILL PROVIDE YOU WITH ADDITIONAL INFORMATION ON EMPLOYMENT, WORKING CONDITIONS, AND THE SALARY FOR MANY JOBS. THESE REPRINT BULLETINS ARE SECTIONS OF THE OOH IN PAMPHLET FORM. LISTED BELOW IS THE BULLETIN NUMBER AND COST FOR EACH REPRINT THAT WOULD BE IMPORTANT FOR YOU IF THE OOH IS NOT READILY AVAILABLE. THESE PAMPHLETS CAN BE ORDERED FROM THE GOVERNMENT PRINTING OFFICE.

BULLETIN NO.	COST	TITLE
2075- 35	$1.25	COMMUNICATIONS-RELATED OCCUPATIONS
2075- 5	$1.25	CLERICAL OCCUPATIONS
2075- 12	$1.25	EDUCATION AND RELATED OCCUPATIONS
2075- 30	$1.25	LAWYERS, CITY MGRS., AND SOCIAL SERVICE
2075- 8	$1.25	BUSINESS OCCUPATIONS

TO LEARN MORE ABOUT THE DAILY ROUTINE OF PEOPLE IN OCCUPATIONS WHERE YOU HAVE HIGH SCORES, YOU MAY WISH TO CONSIDER READING THE FOLLOWING--

--NEWSGATHERING. BY DANIEL R. WILLIAMSON. HASTINGS, 1979.
--MAKE EVERY WORD COUNT. BY GARY PROVOST. WRITERS DIGEST, 1980.
--LAW AND COURT STENOGRAPHER, 3RD. ED. BY DAVID R. TURNER. ARCO, 1978.
--OPPORTUNITIES IN LIBRARY AND INFORMATION SCIENCE. BY PEGGY SULLIVAN. NATIONAL TEXTBOOK, 1977.
--THE PARALEGAL--A NEW CAREER. BY RICHARD DEMING. ELSEVIER-NELSON, 1979.
--ADVERTISING MANAGEMENT. BY R.L. ANDERSON AND T.E. BARRY. MERRILL, 1979.

* * * * * * * * * *

YOU SHOULD PAY PARTICULAR ATTENTION TO THOSE OCCUPATIONS WHERE YOUR SCORES INDICATE THAT YOU HAVE THE MOST SIMILAR INTERESTS. YOU WILL HAVE THE BEST CHANCE OF FINDING SATISFACTION IF YOU DECIDE ON AN OCCUPATION WHERE YOUR INTERESTS ARE SIMILAR WITH YOUR CO-WORKERS AND LESS OF A CHANCE WHERE YOUR INTERESTS ARE DISSIMILAR. IF YOU RECORDED THE SAME LIKES AND DISLIKES AS THE WORKERS, YOUR SCORE WILL BE HIGH FOR THAT OCCUPATION. IF YOUR LIKE AND DISLIKE RESPONSES WERE DIFFERENT FROM THOSE IN THE OCCUPATION, YOUR SCORE WILL BE LOW AND YOU WOULD NOT LIKELY BE SATISFIED.

* * * * * * * * * *

YOU SHOULD PAY ATTENTION TO YOUR HIGH AND LOW SCORES ON ALL THREE SETS OF SCALES THAT HAVE BEEN PROVIDED --- THE 6 GENERAL THEME SCALES, THE 22 BASIC INTEREST AREAS, AND THE OCCUPATIONAL SCALES. YOU MAY FIND THAT EVEN THOUGH YOU HAVE A HIGH SCORE IN ONE OF THE BASIC AREAS, SUCH AS SALES, YOUR RESPONSES MAY HAVE INDICATED THAT YOU WOULD NOT LIKE THE ROUTINE AND LIFE SITUATIONS OF AN INSURANCE AGENT AND YOU HAD A LOW SCORE ON THE INSURANCE AGENT SCALE. SUCH COMPARISONS CAN HELP YOU BETTER EVALUATE THE TYPES OF WORK SITUATIONS THAT MATCH YOUR INTERESTS.

SUMMARIZED BELOW ARE YOUR SCORES ON EACH THEME SCALE, RELATED BASIC INTEREST AREA SCALES, AND OCCUPATIONAL SCALES WITHIN EACH THEME AREA. IN THE GENERAL POPULATION THE AVERAGE SCORES FOR ADULTS ARE IN THE 43-57 RANGE ON EACH OF THE 6 THEME SCALES AND EACH OF THE 22 BASIC INTEREST AREA SCALES. HOWEVER, FOR THE OCCUPATIONAL SCALES, SCORES OF 45 AND HIGHER INDICATE SIMILARITY WITH WORKERS IN THE OCCUPATION AND LOWER SCORES INDICATE MORE DISSIMILARITY.

I. 61 A-THEME ----- (ARTISTIC) -------

BASIC AREA SCALES	OCCUPATIONAL SCALES	CODE
70 WRITING	63 NEWSPAPER REPORTER	AE
59 PERFORM./ENTER.	59 AUTHOR/WRITER	A
43 ARTS/CRAFTS	57 LIBRARIAN	AI
	57 LEGAL ASSISTANT	AE
	55 ADVER. EXECUTIVE	AE
	51 COUNSELOR-CHEM. DEP.	ASE
	46 ADVER. ARTIST/WRITER	A
	40 PHOTOGRAPHER	A
	38 MUSICIAN	A
	28 INTERIOR DESIGNER	A
	18 PIANO TECHNICIAN	ARI

II. 59 E-THEME ----- (ENTERPRISING) -------

BASIC AREA SCALES	OCCUPATIONAL SCALES	CODE
54 BUSINESS	54 PERSONNEL MANAGER	EAS
44 SALES	52 PRIVATE INVESTIGATOR	EA
	52 BUYER/MERCHANDISER	EAS
	52 CARD/GIFT SHOP MGR.	E
	49 TRAVEL AGENT	EC
	41 HOTEL/MOTEL MANAGER	ECS
	40 REAL ESTATE AGENT	ECS
	37 INSURANCE AGENT	ESC
	35 RESERVATION AGENT	ESA
	34 FLORIST	E
	31 RESTAURANT MANAGER	ECS
	30 CATERER	ES
	26 MANUFACTURING REP.	E
	23 FOOD SERVICE MANAGER	ECS
	20 PURCHASING AGENT	EC
	7 BARBER/HAIRSTYLIST	ER

III. 48 C-THEME ----- (CONVENTIONAL) -------

BASIC AREA SCALES	OCCUPATIONAL SCALES	CODE
61 OFFICE PRACTICES	58 COURT REPORTER	CE
49 CLERICAL/CLERK.	42 SECRETARY	C
42 FOOD SERVICE	42 DATA ENTRY OPERATOR	CE
	40 ACCOUNTANT	CE
	39 BOOKKEEPER	C
	35 TEACHER AIDE	CS
	34 BANK TELLER	CE
	29 PHARMACY TECHNICIAN	CS
	29 MEDICAL ASSISTANT	CS

IV. 41 S-THEME ----- (SOCIAL) -------

BASIC AREA SCALES	OCCUPATIONAL SCALES	CODE
47 SOCIAL SERVICE	38 ELEM. SCHOOL TEACHER	SA
41 RELIGIOUS ACTVS.	19 COSMETOLOGIST	SA
40 TEACHING	17 CHILD CARE ASSISTANT	SA
36 CHILD CARE	16 NURSE, LIC. PRAC.	SC
34 MEDICAL SERVICE	14 OPERATING ROOM TECH.	SIR
	4 NURSE, R.N.	SI
	1 NURSE AIDE	SC
	1 OCCUP. THER. ASSIST.	SR
	1 ATHLETIC TRAINER	SR

1 PHYSICAL THER. ASST. S

27 EXECUTIVE HOUSEKEEP. CSE
23 WAITER/WAITRESS CSE
19 DENTAL ASSISTANT CS
8 CAFETERIA WORKER C

V. 39 I-THEME ----- (INVESTIGATIVE) -------

BASIC AREA SCALES	OCCUPATIONAL SCALES	CODE
41 SCIENCE	31 COMPUTER PROGRAMMER	I
39 NUMBERS	14 SURVEYOR	IR
	14 ELECTRONIC TECH.	IR
	13 CHIROPRACTOR	IS
	13 RADIOLOGICAL TECH.	IRS
	12 MATH-SCIENCE TEACHER	I
	6 RESPIRATORY THERAPY	IRS
	3 MEDICAL LAB. TECH.	IR
	1 DENTAL HYGIENIST	ISA

VI. 27 R-THEME ----- (REALISTIC) -------

BASIC AREA SCALES	OCCUPATIONAL SCALES	CODE
37 MANUAL/SKILL. T.	21 SECURITY GUARD	RC
35 AGRICULTURE	21 POLICE OFFICER	RS
34 ANIMAL SERVICE	21 FARMER/RANCHER	R
34 NATURE/OUTDOORS	17 DENTAL LAB. TECH.	RI
34 ELECTRONICS	12 MUSICAL INST. REPAIR	RIA
31 MECHANICAL/FIX.	12 JANITOR/JANITRESS	R
29 CARPENTRY	12 DRAFTER	RI
	11 RADIO/TV REPAIR	RI
	11 CAMERA REPAIR TECH.	RI
	9 TELEPHONE REPAIR	RI
	9 PRINTER	R
	9 NAVY ENLISTED PERSON	RI
	7 EMERGENCY MED. TECH.	RS
	7 PAINTER	R
	6 ELECTRICIAN	R
	5 CARPENTER	R
	4 TRUCK DRIVER	R
	4 MAIL CARRIER	RC
	4 BUS DRIVER	R
	4 AUTO MECHANIC	R
	3 AIRCRAFT MECHANIC	RI
	2 HARDWARE STORE MGR.	RC
	2 ORTHOTIST/PROSTHET.	RI
	2 PIPEFITTER/PLUMBER	R
	1 VETERINARIAN TECH.	RI
	1 FIREFIGHTER	R
	1 CONSERVATION OFFICER	RI
	1 PARK RANGER	RI
	1 SHEET METAL WORKER	RI
	1 FOREST RANGER	RI
	1 TOOL/DIE MAKER	RI
	1 MACHINIST	R

```
* * * * * * * * * * * * * * * * * * * *
*  *  *                                *  *  *
*  *  *    ADMINISTRATIVE  INDICES     *  *  *
*  *  *                                *  *  *
* * * * * * * * * * * * * * * * * * * *
```

THE FOLLOWING ARE THE ADMINISTRATIVE INDICES AND SPECIAL SCALES. DATA FOR I-III INDICATE YOUR RESPONSE PERCENTAGES -- LIKE VERY MUCH (LL), LIKE SOMEWHAT (L), INDIFFERENT (I), DISLIKE SOMEWHAT (D), AND DISLIKE VERY MUCH (DD) -- TO THE THREE SECTIONS OF THE INVENTORY. TOTAL RESPONSES INDICATE THE NUMBER OF ITEMS YOU ANSWERED ON THE INVENTORY. DESCRIPTIONS OF THE OTHER SCORES ARE GIVEN BELOW.

RESPONSE PERCENTAGES

	LL	L	I	D	DD
I. ACTIVITIES	17	12	15	21	36
II. SCHOOL SUBJECTS	33	7	16	5	40
III. OCCUPATIONS	10	11	17	20	42

TOTAL RESPONSES	=	305
FINE ARTS-MECHANICAL	=	39
OCC. EXTRO-INTROVERSION	=	52
EDUCATIONAL ORIENTATION	=	46
VARIABILITY OF INTERESTS	=	35

YOUR SCORE ON THE FINE ARTS-MECHANICAL SCALE INDICATES A STRONG LIKING FOR MANY FINE ARTS AND AESTHETIC TYPES OF ACTIVITIES AND A GENERAL INDIFFERENCE OR DISLIKING FOR MANY MECHANICAL ACTIVITIES AND OCCUPATIONS. GENERALLY, PEOPLE IN CREATIVE AND SOCIAL-SERVICE OCCUPATIONS HAVE SCORES SIMILAR TO YOURS AND SKILLED TRADES AND TECHNICAL PEOPLE TEND TO HAVE MUCH HIGHER SCORES.

YOUR SCORE ON THE OCCUPATIONAL EXTROVERSION-INTROVERSION SCALE IS IN THE AVERAGE RANGE. SCORES GREATER THAN 50 INDICATE A MILD PREFERENCE FOR WORKING ALONE, WHILE SCORES LESS THAN 50 INDICATE MORE OF A LIKING FOR WORKING WITH PEOPLE.

YOUR SCORE ON THE EDUCATIONAL ORIENTATION SCALE INDICATES THAT YOUR INTEREST PREFERENCES ARE SIMILAR TO STUDENTS ENROLLED IN COLLEGE AND TO ADULTS WHO HAVE OBTAINED A TWO-YEAR OR FOUR-YEAR DEGREE AT A COMMUNITY COLLEGE OR UNIVERSITY. THESE INDIVIDUALS PREFER MANY FINE ARTS AND SCIENTIFIC ACTIVITIES AND LIKE THE COURSE WORK INVOLVED IN THEIR STUDIES.

YOUR SCORE ON THE VARIABILITY OF INTERESTS SCALE INDICATES THAT OVERALL YOU PROBABLY FIND ONE OR TWO INTEREST AREAS VERY REWARDING TO YOU AND YOU PROBABLY ARE INDIFFERENT OR DISLIKE THE REST OF THE ACTIVITIES SUGGESTED BY THIS INVENTORY.

```
*   *   *   *   *   *   *   *   *   *   *   *   *   *   *
*   *   *   *   *   *   *   *
*   *   *   *      CLOSING    COMMENTS      *   *   *   *
*   *   *   *   *   *   *   *
*   *   *   *   *   *   *   *   *   *   *   *   *   *   *
```

YOUR ANSWERS TO THE CAREER ASSESSMENT INVENTORY HAVE PRODUCED YOUR INTEREST SCORES ON A
WIDE RANGE OF GENERAL INTERESTS AND SPECIFIC OCCUPATIONAL SCALES. YOU SHOULD NOT BE TOTALLY SET
ON A SINGLE OCCUPATION WHERE YOUR SCORE IS HIGH, AT LEAST NOT AT AN EARLY AGE. IN THE WORLD OF
WORK THERE ARE HUNDREDS OF SPECIALTIES AND RELATED CAREERS, AND YOU SHOULD USE THIS INFORMATION
AS A GUIDE FOR FURTHER CAREER EXPLORATION AND THINKING.

RESEARCH WITH INTEREST INVENTORIES SUCH AS THE CAREER ASSESSMENT INVENTORY HAS SHOWN THAT
THESE TYPES OF SCORES ARE VERY STABLE. ADULTS WILL SHOW VERY LITTLE CHANGE IN THEIR SCORES OVER
THE YEARS. HIGH SCHOOL STUDENTS AND YOUNG ADULTS WILL SHOW SOME CHANGE AFTER TWO OR THREE YEARS
AND MORE CHANGE AFTER TEN OR FIFTEEN YEARS. GENERALLY, SCORES ON INTEREST INVENTORIES ARE VERY
STABLE, AND OVERALL, YOU WOULD FIND YOUR SCORES TO BE VERY SIMILAR IF YOU ANSWERED THE INVENTORY
AGAIN DURING THE NEXT SIX MONTHS TO A YEAR.

EACH PERSON IS UNIQUE AND NO INVENTORY CAN PREDICT WITH PERFECT ACCURACY ALL THE DIVERSITY
AMONG VARIOUS INDIVIDUALS. THUS, THE RESULTS PRESENTED TO YOU SHOULD BE USED AS GUIDELINES IN
HELPING YOU TO UNDERSTAND BETTER YOUR CAREER AND VOCATIONAL INTERESTS AND SHOULD BE CONSIDERED
TOGETHER WITH OTHER RELEVANT INFORMATION IN MAKING ANY CAREER DECISION.

FOR ADDITIONAL INFORMATION, THE FOLLOWING SOURCES ARE RECOMMENDED--
--CONSULT A PROFESSIONALLY TRAINED GUIDANCE COUNSELOR.
--THE MANUAL FOR THE CAREER ASSESSMENT INVENTORY ($9.00).   WRITE NCS/INTERPRETIVE SCORING
  SYSTEMS, P.O. BOX 1416, MINNEAPOLIS, MINNESOTA 55440.
--WHAT COLOR IS YOUR PARACHUTE -- BY RICHARD BOLES ($7.95).   WRITE NCS/INTERPRETIVE SCORING
  SYSTEMS.
--THE DICTIONARY OF OCCUPATIONAL TITLES (DOT) FOURTH EDITION, 1977, WRITE US GOV. PRINTING
  OFFICE, WASHINGTON D.C.
--THE OCCUPATIONAL OUTLOOK HANDBOOK (OOH), BULLETIN NO. 2075 WRITE US GOV. PRINTING OFFICE,
  WASHINGTON D.C.
--THE CAREER INFORMATION CENTER AT YOUR LOCAL LIBRARY. MANY LIBRARIES HAVE AN EXCELLENT SET OF
  BOOKS BY VISUAL EDUCATION CORPORATION (BUTTERICK PUBLISHING, 1979) THAT PROFILES VARIOUS JOB
  REQUIREMENTS, TRAINING NEEDED, AND SO FORTH.
--IF YOU DO NOT KNOW WHERE YOU ARE GOING YOU WILL PROBABLY END UP SOMEWHERE ELSE--BY DR. DAVID
  P. CAMPBELL ($3.50).   WRITE NCS/INTERPRETIVE SCORING SYSTEMS.

**PLEASE INCLUDE $2.50 SHIPPING AND HANDLING WITH EACH ORDER.

END OF REPORT FOR   SAMPLE   B   FEMALE   29-SEP-83   001 0028

********* SUMMARY COPY OF RESULTS **********

PREPARED BY--
NCS/INTERPRETIVE SCORING SYSTEMS
P.O. BOX 1294
MINNEAPOLIS, MN 55440
29-SEP-83

REPORT FOR SAMPLE   B   FEMALE

SECTION A. ADMINISTRATIVE INDICES AND SPECIAL SCALES

THE FOLLOWING ARE THE ADMINISTRATIVE INDICES AND SPECIAL SCALES.
DATA FOR I-III INDICATE THE RESPONSE PERCENTAGES -- LIKE VERY MUCH - LIKE
SOMEWHAT - INDIFFERENT - DISLIKE SOMEWHAT - DISLIKE VERY MUCH -- TO THE
THREE SECTIONS OF THE INVENTORY. DATA FOR THE OTHER SCALES CAN BE FOUND
IN THE MANUAL FOR THE CAREER ASSESSMENT INVENTORY.

RESPONSE PERCENTAGES

		LL	L	I	D	DD
I.	ACTIVITIES	17	12	15	21	36
II.	SCHOOL SUBJECTS	33	7	16	5	40
III.	OCCUPATIONS	10	11	17	20	42

TOTAL RESPONSES	= 305
FINE ARTS-MECHANICAL	= 39
OCC. EXTRO-INTROVERSION	= 52
EDUCATIONAL ORIENTATION	= 46
VARIABILITY OF INTERESTS	= 35

SECTION B. GENERAL THEME SCALES AND PROFILE

IF SEX OF THE INDIVIDUAL WAS INDICATED ON THE INVENTORY, THEN THE
PROFILE CONTAINS A SERIES OF DOTS INDICATING THE AVERAGE RANGE OF SCORES
RELATIVE TO THE SEX OF THE INDIVIDUAL. TO THE RIGHT ARE THE AVERAGE RANGES
FOR FEMALES AND MALES IN THE GENERAL POPULATION.

										AVERAGE RANGES	
SCALE	SCORE	3	4	5	6	7				FEMALE	MALE
A-THEME	61					*			(ARTISTIC)	46-59	41-54
E-THEME	59				*				(ENTERPRISING)	43-56	44-57
C-THEME	48			*					(CONVENTIONAL)	46-60	41-53
S-THEME	41		*						(SOCIAL)	46-59	41-54
I-THEME	39		*						(INVESTIGATIVE)	42-56	45-58
R-THEME	27	*							(REALISTIC)	40-52	48-60

psychware **129**

SECTION C. BASIC INTEREST AREA SCALES AND PROFILE

IF SEX OF THE INDIVIDUAL WAS INDICATED ON THE INVENTORY, THEN THE PROFILE CONTAINS A SERIES OF DOTS INDICATING THE AVERAGE RANGE OF SCORES RELATIVE TO THE SEX OF THE INDIVIDUAL. TO THE RIGHT ARE THE AVERAGE RANGES FOR FEMALES AND MALES IN THE GENERAL POPULATION.

BASIC INTEREST AREAS	SCORE	AVERAGE RANGES FEMALE	MALE
VERY HIGH INTEREST (66+)			
WRITING	70	46-59	41-54
HIGH INTEREST (65-58)***			
OFFICE PRACTICES	61	47-61	41-51
PERFORMING/ENTERTAINING	59	45-58	41-55
AVERAGE INTEREST (57-43)			
BUSINESS	54	44-57	43-56
CLERICAL/CLERKING	49	46-60	41-53
SOCIAL SERVICE	47	46-58	41-55
SALES	44	43-56	43-58
ARTS/CRAFTS	43	48-60	39-52
LOW INTEREST (42-35)****			
FOOD SERVICE	42	48-60	39-52
RELIGIOUS ACTIVITIES	41	44-58	42-56
SCIENCE	41	42-56	45-58
TEACHING	40	45-58	42-55
NUMBERS	39	43-57	44-57
MANUAL/SKILLED TRADES	37	40-51	48-61
CHILD CARE	36	47-60	41-53
AGRICULTURE	35	40-53	47-60
VERY LOW INTEREST (34-)*			
NATURE/OUTDOORS	34	44-57	43-56
MEDICAL SERVICE	34	45-59	41-54
ELECTRONICS	34	40-50	49-61
ANIMAL SERVICE	34	43-57	44-56
MECHANICAL/FIXING	31	39-51	49-61
CARPENTRY	29	40-53	47-60

SECTION D. OCCUPATIONAL SCALES AND BASIC INTEREST
AREA SCALES WITHIN EACH THEME AREA

SUMMARIZED BELOW ARE YOUR SCORES ON EACH THEME SCALE, RELATED BASIC INTEREST AREA SCALES,
AND OCCUPATIONAL SCALES WITHIN EACH THEME AREA. IN THE GENERAL POPULATION THE AVERAGE SCORES
FOR ADULTS ARE IN THE 43-57 RANGE ON EACH OF THE 6 THEME SCALES AND EACH OF THE 22 BASIC INTER-
EST AREA SCALES. HOWEVER, FOR THE OCCUPATIONAL SCALES, SCORES OF 45 AND HIGHER INDICATE SIMI-
LARITY WITH WORKERS IN THE OCCUPATION AND LOWER SCORES INDICATE MORE DISSIMILARITY.

I.   61 A-THEME ----- (ARTISTIC)   -------

BASIC AREA SCALES		OCCUPATIONAL SCALES	CODE
70	WRITING	63 NEWSPAPER REPORTER	AE
59	PERFORM./ENTER.	59 AUTHOR/WRITER	A
43	ARTS/CRAFTS	57 LIBRARIAN	AI
		57 LEGAL ASSISTANT	AE
		55 ADVER. EXECUTIVE	AE
		51 COUNSELOR-CHEM. DEP.	ASE
		46 ADVER. ARTIST/WRITER	A
		40 PHOTOGRAPHER	A
		38 MUSICIAN	A
		28 INTERIOR DESIGNER	A
		18 PIANO TECHNICIAN	ARI

II.   59 E-THEME ----- (ENTERPRISING)   -------

BASIC AREA SCALES		OCCUPATIONAL SCALES	CODE
54	BUSINESS	54 PERSONNEL MANAGER	EAS
44	SALES	52 PRIVATE INVESTIGATOR	EA
		52 BUYER/MERCHANDISER	EAS
		52 CARD/GIFT SHOP MGR.	E
		49 TRAVEL AGENT	EC
		41 HOTEL/MOTEL MANAGER	ECS
		40 REAL ESTATE AGENT	E
		37 INSURANCE AGENT	ESC
		35 RESERVATION AGENT	ESA
		34 FLORIST	E
		31 RESTAURANT MANAGER	ECS
		30 CATERER	ES
		26 MANUFACTURING REP.	E
		23 FOOD SERVICE MANAGER	ECS
		20 PURCHASING AGENT	EC
		7 BARBER/HAIRSTYLIST	ER

III.   48 C-THEME ----- (CONVENTIONAL)   -------

BASIC AREA SCALES		OCCUPATIONAL SCALES	CODE
61	OFFICE PRACTICES	58 COURT REPORTER	CE
49	CLERICAL/CLERK.	42 SECRETARY	C
42	FOOD SERVICE	42 DATA ENTRY OPERATOR	CE
		40 ACCOUNTANT	C
		39 BOOKKEEPER	CS
		35 TEACHER AIDE	CS
		34 BANK TELLER	CS
		29 PHARMACY TECHNICIAN	CS
		29 MEDICAL ASSISTANT	CS
		27 EXECUTIVE HOUSEKEEP.	CSE
		23 WAITER/WAITRESS	CSE

IV.   41 S-THEME ----- (SOCIAL)   -------

BASIC AREA SCALES		OCCUPATIONAL SCALES	CODE
47	SOCIAL SERVICE	38 ELEM. SCHOOL TEACHER	SA
41	RELIGIOUS ACTVS.	19 COSMETOLOGIST	SA
40	TEACHING	17 CHILD CARE ASSISTANT	SA
36	CHILD CARE	16 NURSE, LIC. PRAC.	SC
34	MEDICAL SERVICE	14 OPERATING ROOM TECH.	SIR
		4 NURSE, R.N.	SI
		1 NURSE AIDE	SC
		1 OCCUP. THER. ASSIST.	SR
		1 ATHLETIC TRAINER	SR
		1 PHYSICAL THER. ASST.	S

19 DENTAL ASSISTANT CS
8 CAFETERIA WORKER C

V. 39 I-THEME ----- (INVESTIGATIVE) -----

BASIC AREA SCALES	OCCUPATIONAL SCALES	CODE
41 SCIENCE	31 COMPUTER PROGRAMMER	I
39 NUMBERS	14 SURVEYOR	IR
	14 ELECTRONIC TECH.	IR
	13 CHIROPRACTOR	IS
	13 RADIOLOGICAL TECH.	IRS
	12 MATH-SCIENCE TEACHER	I
	6 RESPIRATORY THERAPY	IRS
	3 MEDICAL LAB. TECH.	IR
	1 DENTAL HYGIENIST	ISA

VI. 27 R-THEME ----- (REALISTIC) -----

BASIC AREA SCALES	OCCUPATIONAL SCALES	CODE
37 MANUAL/SKILL. T.	21 SECURITY GUARD	RC
35 AGRICULTURE	21 POLICE OFFICER	RS
34 ANIMAL SERVICE	21 FARMER/RANCHER	R
34 NATURE/OUTDOORS	17 DENTAL LAB. TECH.	RI
31 ELECTRONICS	12 MUSICAL INST. REPAIR	RIA
31 MECHANICAL/FIX.	12 JANITOR/JANITRESS	R
29 CARPENTRY	12 DRAFTER	RI
	11 RADIO/TV REPAIR	RI
	11 CAMERA REPAIR TECH.	RI
	9 TELEPHONE REPAIR	RI
	9 PRINTER	R
	9 NAVY ENLISTED PERSON	RI
	7 EMERGENCY MED. TECH.	RS
	7 PAINTER	R
	6 ELECTRICIAN	R
	5 CARPENTER	R
	4 TRUCK DRIVER	R
	4 MAIL CARRIER	RC
	4 BUS DRIVER	R
	4 AUTO MECHANIC	R
	3 AIRCRAFT MECHANIC	RI
	2 HARDWARE STORE MGR.	RC
	2 ORTHOTIST/PROSTHET.	RI
	1 PIPEFITTER/PLUMBER	R
	1 VETERINARIAN TECH.	RI
	1 FIREFIGHTER	R
	1 CONSERVATION OFFICER	RI
	1 PARK RANGER	RI
	1 SHEET METAL WORKER	R
	1 FOREST RANGER	RI
	1 TOOL/DIE MAKER	RI
	1 MACHINIST	R

001 0028

**** END OF SUMMARY REPORT FOR SAMPLE   B   FEMALE

NAME: Career Assessment System

SUPPLIER: PSYCH Systems, Inc.
600 Reisterstown Road
Baltimore, MD 21208
(800) 368-3366

PRODUCT CATEGORY	PRIMARY APPLICATIONS
Career/Vocational	Vocational Guidance/Counseling Personal/Marriage/Family Counseling Educational Evaluation/Planning

SALE RESTRICTIONS Qualified Professional

SERVICE TYPE/COST	Type	Available	Cost	Discount
	Mail-In	No		
	Teleprocessing	No		
	Local	Yes	See Below	

PRODUCT DESCRIPTION

This comprehensive career inventory provides the clinician with an indication of the client's vocational preferences, verbal aptitude, numeric aptitude, and personality as they relate to the attainment of that person's life goals. Three separate instruments---the Brief Intelligence Test, the Johns Hopkins Personality Inventory, and the Self-Directed Search---are used in combination to evaluate 13 aspects of human performance.

This Psych Systems program administers and scores the three components together. About one hour of testing is required. The final output is an integrated, narrative report that includes a plotted profile of score results.

Psych Systems programs operate on the IBM PC-XT, COMPAQ Plus, Dec Professional 350, and most DEC PDP-11 systems. Various hardware/ software configurations are available directly from Psych Systems, with single-user systems starting at approximately $12,000. A per test fee also applies.

```
-------------------------------------
|        |                          |
|  CAS   |  Career Assessment System |
|        |                          |
-------------------------------------
```

This clinical report is designed to assist in psychodiagnostic
evaluation. It is available to qualified professionals. This
report was produced by a computerized analysis of the data given
by the client listed above, and is to be used in conjunction
with professional evaluation. No decision should be based solely
upon the contents of this report.

The computer program generating this report was designed by Psych
Systems, Inc., Baltimore, Maryland 21208. Copyright (C) 1984 by
Psych Systems, Inc. The interpretive logic utilized in the
generation of the report was designed by Robert Hogan. Copyright
(C) 1981. Reproduced under license from ESES, Baltimore,
Maryland 21208. The Self-Directed Search is reproduced by permis-
sion. Copyright (C) 1974, 1979, 1982 by Consulting Psychologists Pres
Incorporated, 577 College Avenue, Palo Alto, California 94306. No
portion of the CAS may be reproduced by any process without prior
written permission of the publisher. All rights reserved.

REASON FOR REFERRAL
Jonathan Doe was referred for problems handling reality by Dr. Williams.

BEHAVIORAL OBSERVATIONS
The testing supervisor reported that the individual arrived for his appointment early. Upon entering the office, he seemed uncomfortable. He spoke readily, but his voice was shaky. He appeared nervous. Eye contact with the testing supervisor was fair. In the testing situation, the respondent was cooperative. Motivation for completing the testing process was fair and attention span appeared to be sufficient to complete the task. He appeared to be able to comprehend the process with little or no difficulty.

SUMMARY
Jonathan Doe is an energetic but practical person of the type that does well in business. He has social skills and the ability to create a favorable impression on others, which is especially important in business, banking, and finance. Among Jonathan Doe's most important personal characteristics is his originality; he is an imaginative and unconventional person. He also has leadership potential. His scores are at the 43rd percentile on our measure of intellectance.

VOCATIONAL INTERESTS
On our vocational preference measure, Jonathan Doe received his highest scores for conventional and enterprising interests. Jonathan Doe is a sociable and socially correct person, poised, mannerly, and pleasant. Such persons tend to be well-controlled, socially skilled, ambitious, and upwardly mobile. Persuasive and extraverted, they value economic and political success; they tend not to value scholarly achievement. They see themselves as persistent, self-confident, neat, and conservative. Others describe them as well-adjusted, polite, conservative, and charming. They do particularly well in business, sales, and finance, and they should consider the following occupations: stockbroker, financial expert, postman, market analyst, personal secretary, real estate salesperson, CPA, hotel manager, life insurance salesman, and banker.

INTELLECTANCE
Jonathan Doe's scores on our measures of intellectance show that he is a normally intelligent person. His scores are at the 43rd percentile compared to a national sample of persons his age. Overall, he seems likely to have enough talent to complete a college curriculum. These scores are not in the range to suggest post-graduate training as well. Jonathan Doe's score on the verbal portion of our test is higher than the numerical portion. This suggests that he will tend to do better in courses in the humanities and social sciences than he will do in courses in the physical and biological sciences. Such persons are aesthetically oriented, intuitive, imaginative, and articulate.

Intellectance measures are primarily designed to predict people's success in schooling. Some occupations require more schooling than others. Persons aspiring to careers in medicine, science, or college teaching, all of which require extensive post-graduate education, should score at least at the 80th percentile for Intellectance. Persons desiring degrees in law or other professions requiring the equivalent of a Master's degree (CPA,MBA), should score at least at the 60th percentile for Intellectance. Persons who score at the 50th percentile can expect to complete a college degree at an appropriate institution. It should be noted that there is no necessary relationship between the number of years of education after high school and occupational success defined in terms of income.

PERSONAL CHARACTERISTICS

A. ORIGINALITY

Jonathan Doe's score on our measure of originality puts him at
the 81st percentile for his age range. He has a normal or
average degree of originality, as indicated by our tests. He
can work by himself without supervision, or in the company of
others with supervision.

The trait of originality is important for some occupations but
less adaptive for others. Originality will be important for
persons who are interested in careers typified by the following
two letter codes: ES or SE, SA or AS, AE or EA, SI or IS, IE or
EI, and especially AI or IA. Originality will be less
important, and possibly even maladaptive, for persons interested
in careers designated by the following codes: EC or CE, RS or
SR, and especially RC or CR. Originality will be essentially
irrelevant to success for the remaining occupational types: RI
or IR, RE or ER.

B. ADJUSTMENT

Jonathan Doe's score on our measure of adjustment puts him at
the 17th percentile for his norm group. Such persons are
normally adjusted. They are reasonably calm, stable,
self-accepting, and even-tempered, and they experience a normal
amount of illness and physical complaints.

Generally speaking, it is useful to be well-adjusted.
Nonetheless, adjustment is more important for success in some
vocations than others. Specifically, persons in sales,
supervisory, and managerial jobs (E and S occupations) will be
handicapped by low scores for adjustment. Conversely, artists,
musicians, and scientists (persons in I and A occupations) tend
to receive below average scores for adjustment and it doesn't
seem to matter very much.

C. INTERPERSONAL EFFECTIVENESS

Jonathan Doe's score on our measure of interpersonal
effectiveness indicates that he has an average degree of
self-confidence and sociability. Neither an extravert nor an
introvert, he is a normally competent and socially effective
person.

Interpersonal effectiveness is like adjustment in that some
occupations require it more than others. Specifically, it is
very important for persons in enterprising (E) and conventional
(C) occupations. Conversely, persons in Investigative (I) and
Artistic (A) occupations score lower than the average adult on
interpersonal effectiveness, and this seems to be no handicap.

D. DEPENDABILITY

Jonathan Doe's score on our measure of dependabilty suggests
that he is a normally responsible and reliable person. He has
no problems with authority, responds to supervision, and will be
conscientious in carrying out assigned tasks and duties.

The importance of dependability also depends on a person's
career choice. For those planning careers in business, finance,
and sales (Enterprising and Conventional occupations), low
scores for dependability will be disadvantageous. For those
planning careers in science, art, music, or journalism
(Investigitive and Artistic occupations), high scores for
dependability seem less important.

E. AMBITION

On our measure of ambition, Jonathan Doe's score suggests that
he has normal aspirations and standards of achievement. He is
reasonably hard working, but knows how to relax. Neither an
over- nor an under-achiever, he has developed a balance between
his talents and career expectations.

Ambition is associated with achievement in every occupation.
Although luck plays a role in the development of everyone's
career, ambitious people often have a knack for being lucky.

136 *psychware*

```
     222-22-2222  Jonathan Doe    32 yr old white male  16-Feb-84
                     Career Assessment System Profile
         IC-V IC-N         AD  DE  AM  IE  OR      R  I  A  S  E  C
    100-             ¶100-                     ¶50-                    -
      -              ¶   -                     ¶  -                    -
      -              ¶   -                     ¶  -                    -
      -              ¶   -                     ¶  -                    -
      -              ¶   -                     ¶  -                    -
     90-             ¶ 90-                     ¶45-                    -
      -              ¶   -                     ¶  -                    -
      -       *      ¶   -                     ¶  -                    -
      -       .      ¶   -                     ¶  -                    -
     80-      .      ¶ 80-                     ¶40-                    -
      -       .      ¶   -                     ¶  -                    -
      -       .      ¶   -                     ¶  -                    -
      -       .      ¶   -                     ¶  -                    -
     70-      .      ¶ 70-                     ¶35-                    -
      -       .      ¶   -                     ¶  -                  * -
      -       .      ¶   -                     ¶  -                .   -
      -       .      ¶   -                     ¶  -              *  . -
     60-      .      ¶ 60-                    * ¶30- *           .  . -
      -       .      ¶   -                   . ¶  -        *     .  . -
      -       .      ¶   -                   . ¶  -        .  *  .  . -
      -       .      ¶   -                   . ¶  -        .  .  .  . -
     50-----------+ 50--------------------+25--------------------------
      -       .      ¶   -                   . ¶  -        .  .  .  . -
      -       .      ¶   -               *   . ¶  -        *  .  .  . -
      -       .      ¶   -           *   .   . ¶  -        .  .  .  . -
     40-      .      ¶ 40- *     .   .   . ¶20-        .  .  .  . -
      -       .      ¶   -       .   .   . ¶  -        .  .  .  . -
      -       .      ¶   -       .   .   . ¶  -        .  .  .  . -
      -       .      ¶   -       .   .   . ¶  -        .  .  .  . -
     30-      .      ¶ 30- .     .   .   . ¶15-        .  .  .  . -
      -       .      ¶   - .     .   .   . ¶  -        .  .  .  . -
      -       .      ¶   - .     .   .   . ¶  -        .  .  .  . -
      -       .      ¶   - .     .   .   . ¶  -        .  .  .  . -
     20-      .      ¶ 20- .     .   .   . ¶10-        .  .  .  . -
      -       .      ¶   - .     .   .   . ¶  -        .  .  .  . -
      -       .      ¶   - .     .   .   . ¶  -        .  .  .  . -
     10-      .      ¶ 10- .     .   .   . ¶ 5-        .  .  .  . -
      -       .      ¶   - .     .   .   . ¶  -        .  .  .  . -
      -       .    * ¶   - .     .   .   . ¶  -        .  .  .  . -
      -       .    . ¶   - .     .   .   . ¶  -        .  .  .  . -
      0-      .    . ¶  0- .     .   .   . ¶ 0-        .  .  .  . -
         IC-V IC-N         AD  DE  AM  IE  OR      R  I  A  S  E  C
    P%   83    3    T:  40  41  43  46  59  R: 30 22 29 28 31 33
```

222-22-2222 Jonathan Doe   32 yr old white male   16-Feb-84

Table of abbreviations used in Profile
Intellectance (percentile scores)

    IC-V   Verbal
    IC-N   Numerical
Hopkins Personality Inventory (T-scores)

    AD   Adjustment
    DE   Dependability
    AM   Ambition
    IE   Interpersonal Effectiveness
    OR   Originality

Self Directed Search (Raw-scores)

    R   Realistic
    I   Investigative
    A   Artistic
    S   Social
    E   Enterprising
    C   Conventional

psychware **137**

NAME: Career Decision Making Interpretive Report

SUPPLIER: American Guidance Service
Publisher's Building
Circle Pines, MN 55014
(800) 328-2560

PRODUCT CATEGORY	PRIMARY APPLICATIONS
Career/Vocational	Vocational Guidance/Counseling

SALE RESTRICTIONS None

SERVICE TYPE/COST

Type	Available	Cost	Discount
Mail-In	Yes	$7.50	Yes
Teleprocessing	No		
Local	Yes	$165.00	

PRODUCT DESCRIPTION

The HARRINGTON-O'SHEA CAREER DECISION-MAKING SYS-TEM is a systematized approach to career decision making that integrates five major dimensions in choosing a career—abilities, job values, future plans, subject preferences, and interests. Based on a sound theoretical foundation, the SYSTEM provides individuals with a wealth of information to help in choosing a career and selecting a course of study or a job. The SYSTEM is widely used by guidance and career education counselors in junior and senior high and vocational-technical schools, colleges, and for adult job placement programs in the social services, business, and industry.

The report includes a separate page to aid counselors in interpreting results. The 12-page, personalized computer print-out points out the consistencies and inconsistencies in the survey results and presents extensive career planning information.

```
****************************
*******   CAREER PLANNING FOR   *******
*******                         *******
*******      TERRY JOHNSON      *******
*******                         *******
****************************
```

THE HARRINGTON/O'SHEA CAREER DECISION-MAKING SYSTEM (R)

TERRY, A SHORT TIME AGO YOU FILLED OUT A SURVEY THAT ASKED YOU A LOT ABOUT YOURSELF AND YOUR REACTIONS TO A WIDE VARIETY CF WORK SITUATIONS. YOUR ANSWERS WERE FED INTO THE COMPUTER TO ORGANIZE THEM AND SUGGEST WHAT THEY MIGHT MEAN. BEFORE GOING ON, HOWEVER, LET'S LOOK AT WHAT WE ARE DOING.

YOU ARE INVOLVED IN A PROCESS OF CAREER DECISION MAKING. YOU ARE EXAMINING YOURSELF AND THE WORLD OF WORK MORE CLOSELY THAN YOU PROBABLY HAVE IN THE PAST. YOU ARE TRYING TO FIND OUT HOW YOU CAN FIT INTO THAT WORLD IN THE MOST SATISFYING WAY POSSIBLE.

FIRST, YOU EXPRESSED YOUR LIKES AND DISLIKES FOR MANY JOB ACTIVITIES. THE OCCUPATIONS SUGGESTED FOR YOUR CONSIDERATION ARE BASED ON THESE INTERESTS OF YOURS. INTERESTS, THEN, ARE ONE OF THE THINGS WHICH YOU MUST THINK ABOUT IN CAREER DECISION MAKING. A WORD OF CAUTION: INTERESTS SUGGEST JOBS THAT YOU MIGHT FIND SATISFYING. THEY DO NOT MEASURE ABILITY - WHAT YOU CAN DO WELL. ABILITY, THEN, IS A SECOND CONSIDERATION IN CAREER DECISION MAKING.

THERE ARE OTHER MATTERS YOU MUST TAKE INTO CONSIDERATION. THERE ARE VALUES, WHAT YOU BELIEVE MOST IMPORTANT TO YOU IN A JOB CHOICE, FOR EXAMPLE, SECURITY, SERVICE TO OTHERS, OR MONEY. IN ADDITION, THERE ARE PHYSICAL AND PERSONALITY CHARACTERISTICS AND LEVEL AND LENGTH OF TRAINING REQUIRED. WE ARE GOING TO LOOK AT ALL OF THESE.

A FEW MORE CAUTIONS: CAREER DECISION-MAKING IS A LONG PROCESS. DON'T EXPECT TO MAKE AN INSTANT FINAL DECISION. YOU MAY CHANGE YOUR MIND OFTEN. YOU WILL LEARN FROM THE EXPERIENCES THAT RESULT FROM YOUR CHOICES. WHAT WE ARE TRYING TO DO IS ORGANIZE YOUR THINKING AS OF NOW AND TO COME UP WITH A LIST OF CAREER POSSIBILITIES YOU WILL WANT TO EXPLORE AS PROMISING CHOICES FOR YOU.

THIS COMPUTER PRINTOUT WILL NOT TELL YOU EXACTLY WHICH CAREER YOU SHOULD PURSUE. IT WILL SUGGEST CAREERS FOR YOUR EXPLORATION. IT WILL TEACH YOU HOW TO GO ABOUT YOUR CAREER DECISION MAKING. YOU WILL HAVE TO WORK YOUR WAY THROUGH THE PRINTOUT WITH CARE AND EFFORT. YOU WILL HAVE TO RE-STUDY THE INFORMATION TO GET THE BEST RESULTS.

```
************************
******** YOUR INTEREST SCORES ********
************************
```

YOUR LIKES AND DISLIKES FOR A LONG LIST OF JOB ACTIVITIES WERE SCORED AGAINST SIX MAJOR
WORK SETTINGS - THE ARTS, CLERICAL, CRAFTS, BUSINESS, SOCIAL, SCIENTIFIC. YOUR SCORES ARE
GIVEN BELOW. PEOPLE TOO CAN BE DESCRIBED ACCORDING TO THESE SAME SIX CATEGORIES. PSYCHOLOGICAL
RESEARCH, ESPECIALLY THAT OF DR. JOHN HOLLAND, HAS SHOWN THAT PEOPLE TEND TO SEARCH OUT AND FIND
SATISFACTION IN A WORK SETTING THAT IS IN AGREEMENT WITH THEIR PERSONALITY TYPE. THUS, FOR
EXAMPLE, SCIENTIFIC TYPES WILL FIND THEIR GREATEST SATISFACTION IN A SCIENTIFIC WORK SETTING.

THE HIGHEST POSSIBLE SCORE ON A SCALE IS 40, THE LOWEST 0. IF ALL OF YOUR SCORES ARE BELOW
10, YOU MAY NOT YET HAVE DEVELOPED A DEFINITE PATTERN OF INTERESTS. SUCH SCORES, THOUGH THEY
ARE OFTEN MEANINGFUL, SHOULD BE TREATED WITH CAUTION. IN GENERAL, YOUR HIGHER SCORES POINT
TO WORK SETTINGS THAT YOU ARE LIKELY TO FIND ENJOYABLE AND REWARDING. LOW SCORES ARE VERY
IMPORTANT IN IDENTIFYING ENVIRONMENTS THAT YOU WOULD PROBABLY FIND DISTASTEFUL.

```
SCALE          YOUR SCORE       1    1    2    2    3    3    4
*****          **********    1....5....0....5....0....5....0....5....0

SCIENTIFIC        28          XXXXXXXXXXXXXXXXXXXXXXXXXXXX
SOCIAL            26          XXXXXXXXXXXXXXXXXXXXXXXXXX
THE ARTS          21          XXXXXXXXXXXXXXXXXXXXX
CRAFTS            17          XXXXXXXXXXXXXXXXX
BUSINESS          16          XXXXXXXXXXXXXXXX
CLERICAL           7          XXXXXXX
```

****SCALE DESCRIPTIONS****

SCIENTIFIC: VALUE MATH AND SCIENCE HIGHLY; TEND TO BE CURIOUS, CREATIVE, THEORETICAL, STUDIOUS;
**********   OFTEN PREFER TO WORK ALONE; EXAMPLES: CHEMIST, ENGINEER, MATHEMATICIAN, PHYSICIST.

SOCIAL: INTERESTED IN THE WELFARE OF OTHERS; GENERALLY GET ALONG WELL WITH OTHERS; HAVE STRONG
******   VERBAL SKILLS; EXAMPLES: COUNSELOR, SOCIAL WORKER, NURSE, TEACHER, PHYSICAL THERAPIST.

THE ARTS: EAGER TO BE CREATIVE AND SELF-EXPRESSIVE; OFTEN PREFER A NON-CONFORMING, INDEPENDENT
********   LIFE STYLE; EXAMPLES: MUSICIAN, WRITER, ARTIST, INTERIOR DECORATOR, PERFORMER.

CRAFTS: INTERESTED IN PRACTICAL, MECHANICAL ACTIVITIES; PREFER WORKING WITH TOOLS AND OBJECTS
******   RATHER THAN WORDS AND PEOPLE; EXAMPLES: FARMER, CARPENTER, DENTAL TECHNICIAN, WELDER.

BUSINESS: SKILLED WITH WORDS; PREFER CAREERS WHERE THEY CAN LEAD OTHERS AND CONVINCE OTHERS TO
********   THINK THE WAY THEY DO OR BUY THEIR PRODUCTS; EXAMPLES: SALES, BANKER, EXECUTIVE.

CLERICAL: PREFER ROUTINE, CLEARLY DEFINED DUTIES; ENJOY VERBAL AND NUMERICAL TASKS; ORDERLY AND
********   CONFORMING; VALUE FINANCIAL SUCCESS; EXAMPLES: SECRETARY, ACCOUNTANT, BANK TELLER.

```
**********************************************
*********   INTERPRETING YOUR SCORES   *********
*********                               *********
**********************************************
```

YOU SHOULD BE AWARE THAT MOST PEOPLE DO NOT FALL INTO ONLY ONE AREA. INSTEAD, COMBINA-
TIONS OF A PERSON'S HIGHEST TWO OR THREE SCORES ARE MOST USEFUL IN SUGGESTING APPROPRIATE
OCCUPATIONS FOR EXPLORING. WE HAVE DIVIDED UP THE WORLD OF WORK INTO 18 CAREER AREAS. EACH
AREA CONTAINS JOBS THAT ARE VERY SIMILAR IN THAT ALL THE JOBS IN THE AREA INVOLVE THE SAME
COMBINATION OF OCCUPATIONAL INTERESTS. FOR EXAMPLE, MEDICAL-DENTAL JOBS HAVE BEEN GROUPED
TOGETHER BECAUSE THEY CALL FOR SCIENTIFIC AND SOCIAL SERVICE ACTIVITIES AND INTERESTS. THUS,
A PERSON WHOSE HIGHEST SCORES ON THIS SURVEY ARE SCIENTIFIC AND SOCIAL SERVICE WILL HAVE THE
MEDICAL-DENTAL FIELD SUGGESTED AS ONE AREA FOR CLOSE STUDY.

```
**********************************************************************************
* CAREER AREAS AND TYPICAL JOBS THAT YOUR RESPONSES SUGGEST FCR CAREFUL EXPLORATION:  *
*                                                                                *
* MEDICAL-DENTAL    DENTIST, DOCTOR, VETERINARIAN, OPTOMETRIST, PSYCHIATRIST, SPEECH *
*                   PATHOLOGIST, ORTHODONTIST, CHIROPRACTOR                        *
*                                                                                *
* MATH-SCIENCE      METEOROLOGIST, PHYSICIST, MATHEMATICIAN, COMPUTER PROGRAMMER, ARCHITECT, *
*                   ENGINEER, BIOLOGIST, CHEMIST, ANIMAL SCIENTIST, SURGEON, LAB TECHNICIAN *
*                                                                                *
* FURTHER EXAMINATION OF YOUR SURVEY RESPONSES WOULD SUGGEST THAT YOU ALSO EXPLORE: *
*                                                                                *
* TECHNICAL WORK    DRAFTER, AIRPLANE PILOT, ELECTRONIC TECHNICIAN, QUALITY-CONTROL TECHNICIAN, *
*                   SURVEYOR, TECHNICAL ILLUSTRATOR, FORESTER AIDE, SCIENTIFIC HELPER *
*                                                                                *
* EDUCATION WORK    TEACHER, COLLEGE PROFESSOR, SPECIAL NEEDS TEACHER, LIBRARIAN, SCHOOL *
*                   PRINCIPAL, NURSERY SCHOOL TEACHER, HOME ECONOMIST             *
*                                                                                *
**********************************************************************************
```

REGARDLESS OF YOUR SEX, YOU ARE ENCOURAGED TO LOOK AT ALL THE CAREER OPTIONS SUGGESTED TO
YOU, NOT JUST THOSE YOU MAY ASSOCIATE WITH YOUR OWN SEX GROUP. THERE IS NO ACTIVITY OR
OCCUPATION THAT IS EXCLUSIVELY MALE OR FEMALE.

WE ARE NOW GOING TO LOOK CLOSELY AT EACH OF THESE CAREER AREAS TO LEARN AS MUCH AS POSSIBLE
ABOUT IT AND TO SEE HOW IT FITS INTO THE PICTURE YOU GAVE OF YOURSELF IN THE SURVEY WHEN YOU IN-
DICATED YOUR CAREER PLANS AND RATED YOUR ABILITIES, VALUES, AND PREFERENCES FOR SCHOOL SUBJECTS.

```
************************
*****      MEDICAL-DENTAL      *****
************************
```

MEDICAL-DENTAL IS THE CAREER AREA THAT YOUR SCALE SCORES WOULD SUGGEST FOR PRIMARY CON-
SIDERATION. BELOW ARE LISTED SOME TYPICAL JOBS IN THIS AREA WITH SOME INFORMATION ABOUT THEM.

```
**************************************************
*                                                                              *
*  USING THE JOB LISTS                                                         *
*  ------------------                                                          *
*                                                                              *
*  1.  THE 02.03 AFTER THE JOB GROUP TITLE, MEDICAL SCIENCES, IS THE NUMBER OF A RELATED WORK  *
*      GROUP IN THE GUIDE FOR OCCUPATIONAL EXPLORATION, PUBLISHED BY THE DEPARTMENT OF LABOR   *
*      AND USEFUL FOR LEARNING MORE ABOUT JOBS.  SEE YOUR COUNSELOR OR LIBRARIAN FOR A COPY.   *
*                                                                              *
*  2.  THE 376 IN FRONT OF ANESTHESIOLOGIST IS THE PAGE NUMBER IN THE OCCUPATIONAL OUTLOOK    *
*      HANDBOOK, ANOTHER DEPARTMENT OF LABOR PUBLICATION, WHERE YOU CAN FIND OUT WHAT         *
*      ANESTHESIOLOGISTS DO; THEIR SALARIES, WORK CONDITIONS, REQUIREMENTS AND TRAINING.       *
*                                                                              *
*  3.  THE LETTER -E- BEFORE ANESTHESIOLOGIST MEANS THAT JOB PROSPECTS ARE EXCELLENT THROUGH   *
*      1990 ACCORDING TO LABOR DEPARTMENT FORECASTS.  CONDITIONS MAY VARY FROM PLACE TO PLACE. *
*                                                                              *
*         E = EXCELLENT    G = GOOD    F = FAIR    P = POOR    NA = ESTIMATE NOT AVAILABLE      *
*                                                                              *
*  4.  THE DESCRIPTIONS OF DUTIES AND REQUIREMENTS ARE BRIEF AND GENERAL DUE TO SPACE LIMITA-  *
*      TIONS. EVERY STATEMENT WILL NOT NECESSARILY APPLY TO EVERY JOB.  FOR MORE SPECIFIC IN-  *
*      FORMATION USE THE OCCUPATIONAL OUTLOOK HANDBOOK AND GUIDE FOR OCCUPATIONAL EXPLORATION. *
*                                                                              *
**************************************************
```

JOBS IN THE MEDICAL SCIENCES - 02.03
****

376-E	ANESTHESIOLOGIST	376-E	PEDIATRICIAN
405-G	AUDIOLOGIST	376-E	PHYSICIAN
372-F	CHIROPRACTOR	378-G	PODIATRIST
365-E	DENTIST	376-E	PSYCHIATRIST
376-E	OBSTETRICIAN	376-E	RADIOLOGIST
365-E	ORTHODONTIST	405-G	SPEECH
373-G	OPTOMETRIST		PATHOLOGIST
374-G	OSTEOPATHIC	379-G	VETERINARIAN
	PHYSICIAN		

**DUTIES: APPLY MEDICAL OR DENTAL SCIENCE TO
DIAGNOSIS, PREVENTION, AND TREATMENT OF HUMAN
AND ANIMAL HEALTH PROBLEMS

**REQUIREMENTS: 8 TO 9 YEARS COLLEGE AND MEDI-
CAL OR DENTAL SCHOOL; 3-6 YEARS MORE FOR SPE-
CIALISTS; STATE LICENSE; SUPERIOR INTELLIGENCE AND
SCHOOL GRADES; ANALYTICAL ABILITY IN DIAGNOSIS;
VERBAL ABILITY; MANUAL AND FINGER DEXTERITY;
MOTOR COORDINATION; NUMERICAL AND SCIENTIFIC
ABILITY; WORK WELL UNDER STRESS FOR LONG PERIODS

```
*******************************************
******   NARROWING DOWN YOUR CHOICES   ******
*******************************************
```

AS YOU WILL SEE, THERE ARE MANY JOBS IN EACH CAREER CLUSTER. WE WILL TRY TO NARROW DOWN THE
NUMBER YOU WILL WANT TO STUDY IN DEPTH. WE WILL MOVE STEP BY STEP THROUGH THE CAREER DECISION-
MAKING PROCESS GUIDED BY YOUR ANSWERS ON THE SURVEY AS TO YOUR FUTURE PLANS, EDUCATIONAL PREFER-
ENCES, ABILITIES, AND VALUES. IN EACH CASE YOU SHOULD TRY TO SEE WHETHER THE WAY YOU DESCRIBED
YOURSELF ON THE SURVEY IS IN GENERAL AGREEMENT WITH THE CAREER CLUSTER YOU ARE EXAMINING. THE
GREATER THE AGREEMENT, THE GREATER THE CHANCE YOU WOULD FIND SATISFACTION IN THAT CAREER CLUSTER

IMPORTANT: YOU WILL FIND A NUMBER OF SCHOOL SUBJECTS, VALUES, AND ABILITIES LISTED FOR EACH
---------   CAREER CLUSTER. EACH SUBJECT, VALUE, AND ABILITY MAY NOT BE RELATED TO EVERY JOB IN
            THE CLUSTER, BUT MOST WILL BE.

YOUR STATED CAREER CHOICES
****

        YOU WILL REMEMBER THAT YOU WERE ASKED TO CHOOSE FROM 18 CAREER AREAS THE TWO YOU PREFERRED
MOST. YOU CHOSE TECHNICAL WORK AND EDUCATION WORK. IT IS IMPORTANT TO COMPARE THESE
CHOICES TO THE CAREER CLUSTERS SUGGESTED BY YOUR HIGH SCORES ON THE SURVEY TO SEE IF THEY AGREE.

        IN THIS CASE THEY DO NOT AGREE BECAUSE   MEDICAL-DENTAL   WAS NOT ONE OF YOUR CHOICES. THIS
MEANS THAT THE SURVEY HAS OPENED UP A NEW CAREER AREA THAT YOU SHOULD CAREFULLY EXPLORE BEFORE
MAKING A FINAL DECISION.

EDUCATIONAL PREFERENCES
****

        HELPFUL CLUES TO A SATISFYING CAREER CHOICE CAN OFTEN BE FOUND IN THE SCHOOL SUBJECTS AND
RELATED ACTIVITIES IN WHICH A PERSON HAS ACHIEVED SUCCESS AND ENJOYMENT. THE GREATER THE AGREE-
MENT BETWEEN THE SCHOOL SUBJECTS YOU HAVE LIKED AND THOSE RELATED TO THIS CAREER CLUSTER, THE
MORE LIKELY IT IS THAT YOU WOULD FIND SATISFACTION IN THE JOBS IN THIS CLUSTER.

SUBJECT AREAS YOU CHECKED   SUBJECT AREAS RELATED TO MEDICAL-DENTAL
-------------------------   --------------------------------------
  SCIENCE   MATHEMATICS   AGRICULTURE
  SOCIAL STUDIES   SCIENCE   ENGLISH

psychware **143**

ABILITIES
****

TO BE SUCCESSFUL IN A JOB, IT IS, OF COURSE, NECESSARY TO HAVE THE ABILITIES REQUIRED TO DO THE JOB WELL. INTEREST ALONE IS NOT ENOUGH. IF YOU JUDGE THAT YOU DO NOT HAVE ABILITY FOR AN AREA THAT STRONGLY INTERESTS YOU, IT WOULD BE WISE TO DISCUSS THIS CONFLICT WITH A COUNSELOR.

ABILITIES YOU RATED YOUR STRONGEST   ABILITIES REQUIRED IN MEDICAL-DENTAL JOBS
--------------------------------   ---

MATH   SCIENTIFIC   SCIENTIFIC   MATH   SPATIAL
MECHANICAL   SOCIAL   SOCIAL   LANGUAGE   MANUAL

JOB VALUES
****

REMEMBER THAT VALUES ARE HIGHLY PERSONAL, THAT DIFFERENT PERSONS WILL ACHIEVE DIFFERENT VALUES DOING THE SAME JOB. HOWEVER, CERTAIN VALUES ARE COMMONLY ASSOCIATED WITH PARTICULAR JOB CLUSTERS. IF YOUR VALUES ARE TOTALLY DIFFERENT FROM THOSE THAT ARE MOST OFTEN GAINED IN A CAREER CLUSTER, YOU MIGHT NOT FIND SATISFACTION IN IT.

JOB VALUES YOU SELECTED   VALUES OFTEN ASSOCIATED WITH MEDICAL-DENTAL WORK
----------------------   --

PRESTIGE-STATUS   WORK WITH MIND   PRESTIGE   HIGH ACHIEVEMENT   WORKING WITH MIND
WORK WITH PEOPLE   LEADERSHIP   LEADERSHIP   WORKING WITH PEOPLE GOOD SALARY
                                            CREATIVITY   VARIETY

TRAINING
****

THE TYPE OF PREPARATORY TRAINING REQUIRED FOR MEDICAL AND DENTAL CAREERS IS A COLLEGE PRE-MEDICAL OR PREDENTAL PROGRAM FOLLOWED BY MEDICAL OR DENTAL SCHOOL AND SPECIALIZED TRAINING.

YOUR PLAN TO ATTEND A FOUR-YEAR COLLEGE OR UNIVERSITY IS APPROPRIATE PROVIDED THE INSTI-TUTION OFFERS A SUITABLE PREMEDICAL OR PREDENTAL PROGRAM.

```
************************************
******        MATH-SCIENCE        ******
************************************
```

MATH-SCIENCE IS ANOTHER CAREER AREA THAT YOUR SCALE SCORES WOULD SUGGEST FOR CON-
SIDERATION. BELOW ARE LISTED SOME TYPICAL JOBS IN THIS AREA WITH SOME INFORMATION ABOUT THEM.

JOBS IN ENGINEERING - 05.01
****
284-G	AEROSPACE ENGINEER
463-F	ARCHITECT
544-G	AUTOMOTIVE ENGINEER
286-G	CHEMICAL ENGINEER
287-G	CIVIL ENGINEER
288-G	ELECTRICAL ENGINEER
NA	MARINE ENGINEER
289-G	MECHANICAL ENGINEER
290-E	MINING ENGINEER
543-G	NUCLEAR ENGINEER
291-E	PETROLEUM ENGINEER

JOBS IN THE PHYSICAL SCIENCES - 02.01
****
309-P	ASTRONOMER	293-E	GEOLOGIST
310-G	CHEMIST	305-P	MATHEMATICIAN
293-G	ENVIRONMENTAL	312-G	PHYSICIST
	SCIENTIST	296-G	METEOROLOGIST
421-G	GEOGRAPHER	297-F	OCEANOGRAPHER

*DUTIES: PLAN, DESIGN, DIRECT THE CONSTRUC-
TION OF BUILDINGS, BRIDGES, ROADS, AIRPORTS,
CARS, AND OTHER EQUIPMENT AND STRUCTURES;
TEST MATERIALS AND PARTS; PREPARE REPORTS;
DEVELOP WAYS OF GENERATING POWER; MANUFACTUR-
ING CHEMICALS; AND EXTRACTING METAL FROM ORE

**REQUIREMENTS: MINIMUM IS BACHELOR'S DEGREE;
LICENSE IN SOME STATES; SUPERIOR MATH-SCIENCE
ABILITY; PROBLEM SOLVING SKILL; ADAPTABILITY
TO CHANGE; LOGICAL THINKING; ABILITY TO
VISUALIZE SPATIAL RELATIONSHIPS; ORGANIZA-
TIONAL ABILITY

*DUTIES: INVESTIGATE, DISCOVER, TEST NEW
THEORIES OR NEW MATERIALS OR PROCESSES; WORK
OFTEN ABSTRACT, CREATIVE, AND PRECISE

**REQUIREMENTS: BACHELOR'S DEGREE IN SPECIAL-
TY MINIMUM REQUIREMENT; ADVANCED DEGREE FOR
MOST BASIC MATH RESEARCH AND COLLEGE TEACH-
ING; HIGH MATH-SCIENCE ABILITY; THOROUGHNESS;
CURIOSITY; LOGICAL, CREATIVE THINKING

JOBS IN MATHEMATICS AND STATISTICS - 11.01
****
107-F ACTUARY
98 -E COMPUTER
       PROGRAMER
307-E STATISTICIAN
100-E SYSTEMS ANALYST

**DUTIES: USE ADVANCED MATH AND STATISTICS TO ANALYZE AND INTERPRET NUMERICAL DATA FOR PROBLEM SOLVING AND PLANNING

**REQUIREMENTS: USUALLY FOUR OR MORE YEARS CCLLEGE MATH AND STATISTICS; EXPERIENCE IN BANKING, ACCOUNTING, OR A RELATED FIELD FOR SOME JOBS; ACCURACY IN SPEAKING AND WRITING; ABILITY TO USE ADVANCED LOGIC AND SCIENTIFIC THINKING; EXCELLENT MATH AND COMPUTER SKILLS

JOBS IN LABORATORY TECHNOLOGY - 02.04
****
NA   CRIMINALIST
386-E LABORATORY TECHNICIAN
386-E MEDICAL TECHNOLOGIST
413-F PHARMACIST

**DUTIES: PERFORM LABORATORY TESTS AND OTHER RESEARCH FOR DOCTORS, CHEMISTS, PHYSICISTS, BIOLOGISTS, AND ENGINEERS; RECORD RESULTS
**REQUIREMENTS: 2- OR 4-YEAR COLLEGE DEGREE FCR MOST; STATE LICENSE FOR SOME; SOMETIMES ON-THE-JOB TRAINING FOR THOSE WITH APPROPRIATE SKILLS OR EXPERIENCE; SUCCESS IN MATH AND LAB COURSES; SKILLED USE OF EYES, HANDS, FINGERS TO OPERATE DELICATE EQUIPMENT; PRECISION

JOBS IN LIFE SCIENCES - 02.02
****
301-G ANATOMIST   301-G HORTICULTURIST
301-G ANIMAL   297-F MARINE BIOLOGIST
       SCIENTIST   301-E PATHOLOGIST
300-G BIOCHEMIST   301-G PHARMACOLOGIST
301-G BIOLOGIST   301-G PHYSIOLOGIST
301-G BOTANIST   279-F SOIL CONSERVATIONIST
275-F FORESTER   376-E SURGEON
MA   GENETICIST   301-G ZOOLOGIST

**DUTIES: RESEARCH LIVING THINGS; SOME STUDY ENVIRONMENTAL EFFECTS ON PLANTS AND ANIMALS; OTHERS STUDY CAUSES AND CONTROL OF DISEASE

**REQUIREMENTS: USUALLY A BACHELOR'S DEGREE WITH A LIFE SCIENCE MAJOR; GRADUATE DEGREES FOR MOST RESEARCH AND COLLEGE TEACHING; LOGICAL THINKING; SKILL IN USING EYES, HANDS, FINGERS FOR PRECISE LAB WORK; GOOD DECISION-MAKING SKILLS; SUCCESS IN LAB COURSES

YOUR STATED CAREER CHOICES
****

YOU WILL REMEMBER THAT YOU WERE ASKED TO CHOOSE FROM 18 CAREER AREAS THE TWO YOU PREFERRED
MOST. YOU CHOSE TECHNICAL WORK AND EDUCATION WORK. IT IS IMPORTANT TO COMPARE THESE
CHOICES TO THE CAREER CLUSTERS SUGGESTED BY YOUR HIGH SCORES ON THE SURVEY TO SEE IF THEY AGREE.

IN THIS CASE THEY DO NOT AGREE BECAUSE MATH-SCIENCE WAS NOT ONE OF YOUR CHOICES. THIS
MEANS THAT THE SURVEY HAS OPENED UP A NEW CAREER AREA THAT YOU SHOULD CAREFULLY EXPLORE BEFORE
MAKING A FINAL DECISION.

EDUCATIONAL PREFERENCES
****

SUBJECT AREAS YOU CHECKED

      SCIENCE
      SOCIAL STUDIES

SUBJECT AREAS RELATED TO MATH-SCIENCE

MATHEMATICS   AGRICULTURE   ENGLISH
SCIENCE   TECHNICAL STUDIES

ABILITIES
****

ABILITIES YOU RATED YOUR STRONGEST

MATH   SCIENTIFIC
MECHANICAL   SOCIAL

ABILITIES REQUIRED IN MATH-SCIENCE JOBS

SCIENTIFIC   MATH   MECHANICAL
COMPUTATIONAL LANGUAGE   SPATIAL

JOB VALUES
****

JOB VALUES YOU SELECTED

PRESTIGE-STATUS   WORK WITH MIND
WORK WITH PEOPLE   LEADERSHIP

VALUES OFTEN ASSOCIATED WITH MATH-SCIENCE

LEADERSHIP   HIGH ACHIEVEMENT   SALARY
CREATIVITY   WORK WITH MIND   VARIETY
PRESTIGE   INDEPENDENCE

TRAINING
****

THE PREPARATORY TRAINING REQUIRED FOR THE GREAT MAJORITY OF MATH-SCIENCE CAREERS IS A
COLLEGE DEGREE WITH A MAJOR IN THE APPROPRIATE FIELD. IN ADDITION, MANY SUCH CAREERS DEMAND AN
ADVANCED DEGREE.

THUS YOUR PLAN TO ATTEND A FOUR-YEAR COLLEGE OR UNIVERSITY IS APPROPRIATE FOR MATH-SCIENCE
CAREERS. SOME WILL REQUIRE THAT YOU GO ON TO GRADUATE SCHOOL.

```
**************************************
******    TECHNICAL WORK    ******
******                      ******
**************************************
```

TECHNICAL WORK WAS NOT A CAREER AREA THAT YOUR SCALE SCORES WOULD SUGGEST FOR PRIMARY CON-
SIDERATION. HOWEVER, IT WAS YOUR FIRST CHOICE WHEN YOU WERE ASKED ON A SURVEY TO CHOOSE FROM
18 CAREER AREAS THE TWO YOU PREFERRED MOST. AND WHAT PEOPLE SAY THEY WANT FOR A CAREER IS OFTEN
A VERY IMPORTANT CLUE TO WHAT THEIR FUTURE WORK WILL BE. THEREFORE, WE ARE GOING TO DO AN IN-
DEPTH STUDY OF TECHNICAL WORK. YOU SHOULD, HOWEVER, BE AWARE THAT SUCH WORK INVOLVES ACTIV-
ITIES THAT YOU RATED LESS HIGHLY THAN OTHERS IN YOUR INTEREST SURVEY RESPONSES. THUS YOU SHOULD
APPROACH THIS CAREER CLUSTER WITH SOME CAUTION.

JOBS IN AIR/WATER VEHICLE OPERATION - 05.04
****
243-P AIRPLANE PILOT
NA   FLYING INSTRUCTOR
NA   HELICOPTER PILOT
249-G SHIP CAPTAIN
249-G SHIP MATE

**DUTIES: PILOT PLANES OR SHIPS OR SUPERVISE
THOSE WHO DO

**REQUIREMENTS: FOR AIRPLANES AT LEAST HIGH
SCHOOL DIPLOMA; COLLEGE DEGREE PREFERRED; FLIGHT
TRAINING IN MILITARY CR IN FAA APPROVED SCHOOLS;
FOR SHIP CAPTAINS TRAINING AT A MARINE ACADEMY
IS USUAL; QUICK REACTION IN EMERGENCY; GOOD
HEARING , VISION, COORDINATION; LEADERSHIP SKILL

JOBS IN ENGINEERING TECHNOLOGY - 05.01
********************************05.03
240-P AIR TRAFFIC CONTROLLER
315-G DRAFTER
316-G ELECTRICAL TECHNICIAN
316-G ELECTRONICS TECHNICIAN
NA   ESTIMATOR
243-P FLIGHT ENGINEER
276-P FORESTRY TECHNICIAN
316-G MECHANICAL ENGINEERING TECHNICIAN
NA   NAVIGATOR
321-G SURVEYOR
504-G TECHNICAL ILLUSTRATOR

**DUTIES: COLLECT AND COORDINATE TECHNICAL IN-
FORMATION IN SURVEYING, DRAFTING, PETROLEUM PRO-
DUCTION, COMMUNICATIONS CONTROL, ETC.; TECH-
NICIANS APPLY THEORETICAL KNOWLEDGE DEVELOPED BY
ENGINEERS AND SCIENTISTS TO REAL SITUATIONS

**REQUIREMENTS: COURSEWORK IN TECHNICAL-VOCA-
TIONAL SCHOOLS AND 2-YEAR COLLEGES OR ON-THE-
JOB TRAINING OR WORK EXPERIENCE; SUPERIOR MATH
SKILLS; WORK UNDER STRESS; WRITE CLEAR TECHNICAL
REPORTS; DRAWING ABILITY; EYE-HAND COORDINATION
IN SKETCHING, OPERATING EQUIPMENT, AND MAKING
PRECISE MEASUREMENTS

JOBS IN LABORATORY TECHNOLOGY - 02.04
****
316-G BIOLOGICAL TECHNICIAN
316-G QUALITY CONTROL TECHNICIAN
316-G RESEARCH ASSISTANT
316-G WEATHER OBSERVER

**DUTIES: PERFORM LAB TESTS FOR CHEMISTS, BIOL-
OGISTS, PHYSICISTS, DOCTORS, AND ENGINEERS

**REQUIREMENTS: SCIENCE OR TECHNICAL COURSES IN
HIGH SCHOOL OR BEYOND; ON-THE-JOB TRAINING AT
TIMES; SOME MOVE UP FROM PROTECTION JOBS; MATH
SKILL; ABILITY TO USE SCIENTIFIC LANGUAGE; EYE-
HAND COORDINATION FOR USING PRECISION EQUIPMENT

148 *psychware*

EDUCATIONAL PREFERENCES
****

SUBJECT AREAS YOU CHECKED

SCIENCE
SOCIAL STUDIES

SUBJECT AREAS RELATED TO TECHNICAL WORK

MATHEMATICS   ART   SHOP-CRAFTS
AGRICULTURE   SCIENCE   TECHNICAL STUDIES

ABILITIES
****

ABILITIES YOU RATED YOUR STRONGEST

MATH   SCIENTIFIC
MECHANICAL ABILITY SOCIAL ABILITY

ABILITIES REQUIRED IN TECHNICAL WORK

MATH   COMPUTATIONAL   ARTISTIC   SPATIAL
MANUAL   MECHANICAL   SCIENTIFIC

JOB VALUES
****

JOB VALUES YOU SELECTED

PRESTIGE-STATUS   WORK WITH MIND
WORK WITH PEOPLE   LEADERSHIP

VALUES OFTEN ASSOCIATED WITH TECHNICAL WORK

PHYSICAL ACTIVITY   WORK WITH MIND
WORK WITH HANDS   ROUTINE ACTIVITY
SUPERVISED WORK

TRAINING
****

THE TYPE OF PREPARATORY TRAINING REQUIRED FOR TECHNICAL OCCUPATIONS VARIES RATHER WIDELY
BUT USUALLY INCLUDES COURSEWORK IN MATH AND SCIENCE. FOR MANY OF THE JOBS, SPECIALIZED TECHNICAL
TRAINING IN HIGH SCHOOL, TECHNICAL INSTITUTE, OR COLLEGE IS REQUIRED OR HIGHLY PREFERRED.

THUS YOUR PLAN TO ATTEND A FOUR-YEAR COLLEGE OR UNIVERSITY IS SUITABLE FOR MANY TECHNICAL
JOBS PROVIDED YOU COMPLETE A PROGRAM APPROPRIATE TO YOUR FIELD OF INTEREST. HOWEVER, MOST
TECHNICAL JOBS DO NOT DEMAND A COLLEGE DEGREE.

CONTINUING YOUR CAREER EXPLORATION

1. STUDY THOSE CAREERS THAT ESPECIALLY INTEREST YOU:

   **TALK WITH PEOPLE WORKING IN THE CAREERS.
   **WHEN POSSIBLE, VISIT THEM AT THEIR PLACE OF WORK.
   **SEEK THE ADVICE OF CAREER COUSELORS.
   **READ AS MUCH AS POSSIBLE ABOUT THE CAREERS.
   **TRY TO FIND RELATED PART-TIME JOBS OR VOLUNTEER EXPERIENCES.

2. FROM TIME TO TIME REVIEW THIS REPORT; LOOK FOR CHANGES IN YOUR CAREER THINKING.

3. THIS REPORT MAY HAVE SUGGESTED TO YOU THE SAME CAREERS YOU HAD ALREADY JUST ABOUT DECIDED ON. IF IT HAS, YOU HAVE FURTHER EVIDENCE TO INCREASE CONFIDENCE IN YOUR CURRENT CHOICES.

4. FINAL CAREER CHOICE IS YOUR RESPONSIBILITY. OTHERS CAN ONLY SUGGEST REASONABLE OPTIONS.

5. THE TABLE BELOW IS TO HELP YOU FURTHER CHECK OUT YOUR CURRENT PLANS. WE SUGGEST THAT IN THE LEFT-HAND COLUMN YOU LIST THOSE JOBS THAT APPEAL TO YOU, EITHER FROM THOSE DESCRIBED IN THIS REPORT OR ANY OTHERS THAT HAVE OCCURRED TO YOU SINCE YOU BEGAN YOUR EXPLORATION. USE THE CHART TO ORGANIZE WHAT YOU HAVE LEARNED ABOUT YOURSELF AND THE WORLD OF WORK.

JOB	REQUIRED EDUCA- TIONAL LEVEL	AGREES WITH MY FUTURE PLANS YES/NO	REQUIRED SKILLS AND ABILITIES	AGREES WITH MY ABILITY RATINGS YES/NO	JOB PROSPECTS -EXCELLENT- -GOOD- -FAIR- -POOR-	THIS JOB SATISFIES MY VALUES YES/NO

```
******************************************************
* CAREER DECISION-MAKING PROFILE FOR TERRY JOHNSON    *
*                                                      *
*   GRADE: 11      DATE: 02/19/82    SCHOOL: JOHN DOE HIGH  *
******************************************************

1. SCALE           SCORE
   *****           *****                 1    1    2    2    3    3    4
                                    1....5...0....5....0....5....0....5....0
   SCIENTIFIC       28              XXXXXXXXXXXXXXXXXXXXXXXXXXXX
   SOCIAL           26              XXXXXXXXXXXXXXXXXXXXXXXXXX
   THE ARTS         21              XXXXXXXXXXXXXXXXXXXXX
   CRAFTS           17              XXXXXXXXXXXXXXXXX
   BUSINESS         16              XXXXXXXXXXXXXXXX
   CLERICAL          7              XXXXXXX

******************************************************
* 2. CAREER AREAS AND TYPICAL JOBS THAT THIS COMBINATION SUGGESTS FCR CAREFUL EXPLORATION:   *
*                                                                                            *
* MEDICAL-DENTAL    DENTIST, DOCTOR, VETERINARIAN, OPTOMETRIST, PSYCHIATRIST, SPEECH         *
*                   PATHOLOGIST, ORTHODONTIST, CHIROPRACTOR                                  *
*                                                                                            *
* MATH-SCIENCE      METEOROLOGIST, PHYSICIST, MATHEMATICIAN, COMPUTER PROGRAMMER, ARCHITECT, *
*                   ENGINEER, BIOLOGIST, CHEMIST, ANIMAL SCIENTIST, SURGEON, LAB TECHNICIAN  *
*                                                                                            *
* FURTHER EXAMINATION OF YOUR SURVEY RESPONSES WOULD SUGGEST THAT YOU ALSO EXPLORE:          *
*                                                                                            *
* TECHNICAL WORK    DRAFTER, AIRPLANE PILOT, ELECTRONIC TECHNICIAN, QUALITY-CONTROL TECHNICIAN/ *
*                   SURVEYOR, TECHNICAL ILLUSTRATOR, FORESTER AIDE, SCIENTIFIC HELPER        *
*                                                                                            *
* EDUCATION WORK    TEACHER, COLLEGE PROFESSOR, SPECIAL NEEDS TEACHER, LIBRARIAN, SCHOOL     *
*                   PRINCIPAL, NURSERY SCHOOL TEACHER, HOME ECONOMIST                        *
*                                                                                            *
******************************************************

3. STATED OCCUPATIONAL PREFERENCES:          6. JOB VALUES

   FIRST CHOICE:    TECHNICAL WORK              PRESTIGE-STATUS
   SECOND CHOICE:   EDUCATION WORK              WORKING WITH MIND
                                                WORK WITH PEOPLE
4. SCHOOL SUBJECT PREFERENCES:                 LEADERSHIP

   FIRST CHOICE:    SCIENCE STUDY            7. ABILITIES
   SECOND CHOICE:   SOCIAL STUDIES
                                                MATH ABILITY
5. FUTURE PLANS:                                SCIENTIFIC ABILITY
                                                MECHANICAL ABILITY
   FOUR-YEAR COLLEGE OR UNIVERSITY              SOCIAL ABILITY

COPYRIGHT CAREER PLANNING ASSOCIATES, INC., 1974, 1977, 1980, 1981
```

NAME: Career Directions Inventory

SUPPLIER: Research Psychologists Press
P.O. Box 984
Port Huron, MI 48061
(800) 265-1285

PRODUCT CATEGORY	PRIMARY APPLICATIONS
Career/Vocational	Vocational Guidance/Counseling Educational Evaluation/Planning

SALE RESTRICTIONS   American Psychological Association Guidelines

SERVICE TYPE/COST	Type	Available	Cost	Discount
	Mail-In	Yes	$3.25	Yes
	Teleprocessing	No		
	Local	No		

PRODUCT DESCRIPTION

The CAREER DIRECTIONS INVENTORY was developed to assist high school and college students in educational and career planning. The test contains a total of 100 triads of statements describing job related activities. For each triad, the respondent is asked to mark his/her most preferred and least preferred activity.

The report yields a profile of 16 basic interest scales. The pattern of these interests is compared to the pattern of interests shown by individuals in a wide variety of occupations. The occupational groups to whom the respondent is most similar are described in a narrative summary, which also lists sample occupations and their D.O.T. codes. The report, which includes a counselor summary page, has been designed in a format to facilitate use by clients.

NAME: Career and Vocational Interest Inventory

SUPPLIER: Integrated Professional Systems
5211 Mahoning Avenue Suite 135
Youngstown, OH 44515
(216) 799-3282

PRODUCT CATEGORY

Career/Vocational
Interest/Attitudes

PRIMARY APPLICATIONS

Vocational Guidance/Counseling
Educational Evaluation/Planning
Personnel Selection/Evaluation

SALE RESTRICTIONS Qualified Professional

SERVICE TYPE/COST	Type	Available	Cost	Discount
	Mail-In	No		
	Teleprocessing	No		
	Local	Yes	See Below	

PRODUCT DESCRIPTION

The CAREER AND VOCATIONAL INTEREST INVENTORY is an educational and career guidance instrument designed to assist high school students and adults in making educational and/or career decisions. Scores on the six Holland theme scales and over 30 basic interest scales are provided. Narrative statements as well as a list of occupations that match the subject's interests are presented.

An operating software package, priced from $200-$850 depending on the complexity of the package, is required for program use, plus an additional fee of $3.00 per use.

NAME: Career-Wise

SUPPLIER: NCS/Professional Assessment Services
P.O. Box 1416
Minneapolis, MN 55440
(800) 328-6759

PRODUCT CATEGORY	PRIMARY APPLICATIONS
Interest/Attitudes	Vocational Guidance/Counseling

SALE RESTRICTIONS None

SERVICE TYPE/COST	Type	Available	Cost	Discount
	Mail-In	Yes	$7.75	Yes
	Teleprocessing	No		
	Local	No		

PRODUCT DESCRIPTION

CAREER-WISE is a career planning program for use with high school students in career decision-making courses and job training partnership programs. The program consists of three assessment components: interests, personality, and work values and aptitudes. CAREER-WISE components can be customized to a particular setting to include: the STRONG-CAMPBELL INTEREST INVENTORY for careers requiring college or graduate school training; the CAREER ASSESSMENT INVENTORY for students planning to enter the workforce immediately after high school graduation or for careers requiring minimal post secondary training; the TEMPERAMENT AND VALUES INVENTORY to help the student understand the full range of job-related personal values and needs; and the WORD AND NUMBER ASSESS-MENT INVENTORY to match verbal and numerical skills to appropriate career areas.

Students use the results of these assessments in a workbook in which they plot inventory scores and integrate additional self-assessments in a single profile format to develop a more comprehensive picture of future career potential. A CAREER-WISE Counselor's Guide is included with each CAREER-WISE order.

For additional information on this product, see that provided under STRONG-CAMPBELL INTEREST INVENTORY (Profile Report), CAREER ASSESSMENT INVENTORY (Profile Report), TEMPERA-MENT AND VALUES INVENTORY (Profile Report), and WORD AND NUMBER ASSESSMENT INVENTORY.

NAME: Child Diagnostic Screening Battery

SUPPLIER: Joseph M. Eisenberg, Ph.D.
204 E. Joppa Road Suite #10
Towson, MD 21204
(301) 321-9101

PRODUCT CATEGORY

Structured Interview

PRIMARY APPLICATIONS

Clinical Assessment/Diagnosis

SALE RESTRICTIONS American Psychological Association Guidelines

SERVICE TYPE/COST	Type	Available	Cost	Discount
	Mail-In	No		
	Teleprocessing	No		
	Local	Yes	$100.00	

PRODUCT DESCRIPTION

The CHILD DIAGNOSTIC SCREENING BATTERY is designed to help the clinician identify diagnostic possibilities among those listed in DSM-III. The program provides a questionnaire for the patient and/or parent or guardian and a questionnaire for the clinician. Each questionnaire can be completed in as little as 15 minutes and entered into the computer in less than five minutes. Responses are structured in such a way as to be compared to all possible diagnoses listed in the manual. The configural pattern of answers provided in both questionnaires are matched according to suggested diagnostic possibilties and those that are compatible are selected. Printouts provide a list of responses made by both patient and clinician so that specific areas of difficulty can be noted. The program is designed to operate on Apple or Apple-compatible microcomputer systems with 64K of memory and an 80-column card. Only one disk drive is required for program execution, but two disk drives are strongly recommended in order to minimize swapping and speed up program execution. A manual is provided that describes use and application of the program as well as how to use printouts generated by the program.

NAME: Children's Personality Questionnaire Narrative Report

SUPPLIER: Institute for Personality and Ability Testing, Inc.
P.O. Box 188
Champaign, IL 61820
(217) 352-4739

PRODUCT CATEGORY	PRIMARY APPLICATIONS
Personality	Personal/Marriage/Family Counseling Clinical Assessment/Diagnosis Educational Evaluation/Planning

SALE RESTRICTIONS American Psychological Association Guidelines

SERVICE TYPE/COST	Type	Available	Cost	Discount
	Mail-In	Yes	$16.00	Yes
	Teleprocessing	Yes	$17.00	Yes
	Local	No		

PRODUCT DESCRIPTION

This program provides a complete narrative report for each child assessed with the CHILDREN'S PERSONALITY QUESTIONNAIRE. This report includes descriptions of all personality characteristics of significance, as well as the individual's projected levels of creativity and anticipated achievement in 10 school-related areas.

The CHILDREN'S PERSONALITY QUESTIONNAIRE itself is a broad-range normal personality test useful in predicting and evaluating personal, social, and academic development for children 8-11 years old (3rd-grade reading level required). The 140 forced-choice items require 30-60 minutes to complete. Fourteen primary personality traits measured by the test include Emotional Stability, Self-Concept, Excitability, and Self-Assurance. Scores for Extraversion, Anxiety, and other broad trait patterns are calculated and reported by the program. Test applications include assessing the normal strengths and weaknesses in a child's personality development, diagnosis and treatment of children, planning appropriate educational or rehabilitation programs, and facilitating cooperation among parents, teachers, and others working with the child.

THE INSTITUTE FOR PERSONALITY AND ABILITY TESTING
P. O. BOX 188   CHAMPAIGN, ILLINOIS 61820
CPQ PROFILE

SCORE		TRAIT		1 2 3 4 5 6 7 8 9 10		PERCENTILE
RAW	STEN					
9	7	A	COOL, RESERVED	*	WARM, EASYGOING	77
10	8	B	DULL	*	BRIGHT	89
6	5	C	EASILY UPSET	*	CALM, STABLE	40
4	4	D	STOIC, LISTLESS	*	EXCITABLE	23
6	7	E	NOT ASSERTIVE	*	DOMINANT	77
3	3	F	SOBER, SERIOUS	*	HAPPY-GO-LUCKY	11
10	8	G	EXPEDIENT	*	CONSCIENTIOUS	89
2	2	H	SHY, TIMID	*	VENTURESOME	4
7	6	I	TOUGH-MINDED	*	TENDER-MINDED	60
7	8	J	PARTICIPATING	*	INTROSPECTIVE	89
3	4	N	FORTHRIGHT	*	SHREWD	23
2	4	O	SELF-ASSURED	*	APPREHENSIVE	23
10	9	Q3	UNDISCIPLINED	*	SELF-DISCIPLINED	96
5	5	Q4	RELAXED	*	TENSE, DRIVEN	40

PRIMARY PERSONALITY CHARACTERISTICS OF SIGNIFICANCE
CAPACITY FOR ABSTRACT VERBAL SKILLS IS ABOVE AVERAGE.
HIS REACTION TO SITUATIONS IS SOBER, SERIOUS, AND CAUTIOUS.
REGARD FOR STRICT MORAL STANDARDS, DUTY, AND CONSCIENTIOUS PERSEVERANCE
    IS HIGH.
HE IS SHY, THREAT-SENSITIVE, AND RETIRING.
AT SCHOOL AND ELSEWHERE, HE IS SOMEWHAT OF A LONER, DOES NOT ENJOY
    PARTICIPATION, AND TENDS TO BE OBSTRUCTIVE.
A DEFINITE SELF-CONCEPT AND DETERMINATION TO CONTROL ONESELF TO FIT A
    PERSONAL AND SOCIAL IMAGE CHARACTERIZES THIS PERSON.
BROAD INFLUENCE PATTERNS

THE PERSONALITY ORIENTATION IS NEITHER EXTRAVERTED NOR INTRAVERTED. HIS
    ATTENTION IS BALANCED EQUALLY BETWEEN THE OUTER ENVIRONMENT AND INNER
    THOUGHTS AND FEELINGS.
HIS APPROACH TO TASKS AND PROBLEMS PLACES EQUAL EMPHASIS UPON GETTING
    THINGS DONE AND UPON EMOTIONAL RELATIONSHIPS.
HIS LIFE STYLE IS BALANCED BETWEEN NEED TO CONTROL THE ENVIRONMENT AND
    WILLINGNESS TO ADAPT TO WHAT IS AVAILABLE.
AT THE PRESENT TIME, HIS GENERAL LEVEL OF ANXIETY IS NO HIGHER NOR LOWER
    THAN WHAT WOULD NORMALLY BE EXPECTED.
HIS GENERAL CAPACITY TO WORK CREATIVELY, TO TRANSCEND CUSTOM, AND TO
    GENERATE NEW IDEAS IS ABOVE AVERAGE.
ANTICIPATED ACHIEVEMENT IN VARIOUS SCHOOL SUBJECTS

THE CALCULATIONS IN THIS SECTION OF THE REPORT ARE BASED ON THE EQUATIONS
IN TABLE 12 OF THE CPQ HANDBOOK.   DETAILS OF THE STUDY FROM WHICH THEY
WERE DERIVED ARE PROVIDED IN THE HANDBOOK.

SUBJECT	EXPECTED ACHIEVEMENT LEVEL
VOCABULARY	ABOVE AVERAGE
WRITING	HIGH
SPELLING	HIGH
LANGUAGE ARTS	HIGH
ARITHMETIC	HIGH
SOCIAL STUDIES	HIGH
HEALTH/PHYSICAL ED	ABOVE AVERAGE
SCIENCE	ABOVE AVERAGE
MUSIC	ABOVE AVERAGE
ART	BELOW AVERAGE

NAME: Clinical Analysis Questionnaire

SUPPLIER: NCS/Professional Assessment Services
P.O. Box 1416
Minneapolis, MN 55440
(800) 328-6759

PRODUCT CATEGORY	PRIMARY APPLICATIONS
Personality	Clinical Assessment/Diagnosis Personal/Marriage/Family Counseling Personnel Selection/Evaluation Vocational Guidance/Counseling

SALE RESTRICTIONS American Psychological Association Guidelines

SERVICE TYPE/COST	Type	Available	Cost	Discount
	Mail-In	Yes	$16.25	Yes
	Teleprocessing	Yes	$16.25	Yes
	Local	Yes	$8.70	Yes

PRODUCT DESCRIPTION

This report presents a narrative discussing normal personality characteristics and psychopathological symptoms, as well as a vocational section projecting occupational fitness patterns. The report includes a plotted score profile.

The test itself has 272 trichotomous items. It can be completed in one to two hours by individuals with a 6th-grade reading level. The test measures the same 16 normal personality traits as the 16 PF along with 12 psychopathological dimensions (e.g., Paranoia).

Two systems are available for local processing of test results. MICRO-TEST Assessment Software from National Computer Systems, used with a Sentry 3000 tabletop scanner (purchase price approximately $4000) and microcomputer system ($2000-$3000 purchase price), allows tests to be administered off-line. Answer sheets are then scanned and scored automatically, one at a time or in a batch. The software also permits on-line administration of the test via microcomputer. In either case, the same report is provided. The cost for local scoring refers to the cost-per-test when diskettes are purchased in units of 20 administrations (minimum purchase).

For a sample printout of this product, see the one shown under CLINICAL ANALYSIS QUESTIONNAIRE INTERPRETIVE REPORT.

NAME: Clinical Analysis Questionnaire Interpretive Report

SUPPLIER: Institute for Personality and Ability Testing, Inc.
P.O. Box 188
Champaign, IL 61820
(217) 352-4739

PRODUCT CATEGORY

Personality

PRIMARY APPLICATIONS

Clinical Assessment/Diagnosis
Personal/Marriage/Family Counseling
Personnel Selection/Evaluation
Vocational Guidance/Counseling
Educational Evaluation/Planning

SALE RESTRICTIONS American Psychological Association Guidelines

SERVICE TYPE/COST	Type	Available	Cost	Discount
	Mail-In	Yes	$16.00	Yes
	Teleprocessing	Yes	$17.00	Yes
	Local	No		

PRODUCT DESCRIPTION

Intended for general clinical diagnosis and evaluating therapeutic progress, the CLINICAL ANALYSIS QUESTIONNAIRE was developed to meet the need of clinical psychologists for objective measurement of primary behavioral dimensions. A special feature of the test is that it measures 16 normal personality dimensions (the 16 PF scales) as well as Hypochondriasis, Agitated Depression, Suicidal Depression, Anxious Depression, Guilt, Energy Level, Boredom, and five other dimensions in the pathology domain. The report provides a graphical presentation of test scores, narrative regarding personality characteristics of significance, psychopathological considerations, and a series of occupational projections.

THE INSTITUTE FOR PERSONALITY AND ABILITY TESTING
P.O. BOX 188   CHAMPAIGN, ILLINOIS 61820

This computer interpretation is intended only for properly qualified
professionals and should be treated as a confidential report.

4/20/1984
NAME-John   Sample   AGE-29
                            SEX-M

```
* * * * * * * * *   V A L I D I T Y    S C A L E S   * * * * * * * * * *
*                                                                      *
*   Validity indicators are within acceptable ranges.                  *
*      Faking good/MD (sten) score is very low (2.0).                  *
*      Faking bad (sten) score is extremely low (1.0).                 *
*                                                                      *
* * * * * * * * * * * * * * * * * * * * * * * * * * * * * * * * * * * * *
```

CAQ PROFILE---PART I

	SCORES		LOW MEANING	1 2 3 4 5 6 7 8 9 10	HIGH MEANING
RAW	STEN				
6	3	A	RESERVED, DETACHED	<-----	WARM, EASYGOING
8	6	B	CONCRETE THINKING	->	ABSTRACT THINKING
3	1	C	EASILY UPSET	<---------	CALM, STABLE
8	3	E	SUBMISSIVE	<-----	DOMINANT
10	4	F	SERIOUS, PRUDENT	<---	IMPULSIVE
11	4	G	EXPEDIENT	<---	CONSCIENTIOUS
4	2	H	SHY, TIMID	<-------	VENTURESOME
14	8	I	TOUGH-MINDED	----->	SENSITIVE
8	6	L	TRUSTING	->	SUSPICIOUS
12	5	M	PRACTICAL	<-	IMAGINATIVE
7	4	N	FORTHRIGHT	<---	SHREWD
10	6	O	CONFIDENT	->	INSECURE, APPREHENSIVE
13	8	Q1	CONSERVATIVE	----->	EXPERIMENTING
10	6	Q2	GROUP-ADHERENT	->	SELF-SUFFICIENT
6	1	Q3	UNDISCIPLINED	<---------	SELF-DISCIPLINED
12	6	Q4	RELAXED	->	TENSE, FRUSTRATED

CAQ PROFILE--PART II

	SCORES		LOW MEANING	1 2 3 4 5 6 7 8 9 10	HIGH MEANING
RAW	STEN				
15	9	D1	HEALTHY	------->	HYPOCHONDRIACAL
9	8	D2	CONTENTED, ZESTFUL	----->	DESPONDENT, SUICIDAL
12	5	D3	RESTRAINED	<-	AGITATED, HYPOMANIC
7	6	D4	COMPOSED	->	SHAKY, FRIGHTENED
17	8	D5	ENERGETIC	----->	FATIGUED, WORN OUT
18	10	D6	UNTROUBLED	--------->	RESENTFUL
10	8	D7	PARTICIPATIVE	----->	BORED, SECLUSIVE
2	4	PA	REASONABLE	<---	PARANOID
9	2	PP	INHIBITED	<-------	UNINHIBITED
8	7	SC	REALITY-ORIENTED	--->	SCHIZOPHRENIC
10	7	AS	NON-OBSESSIVE	--->	OBSESSIVE, COMPULSIVE
13	8	PS	ADEQUATE	----->	INADEQUATE

PRIMARY PERSONALITY CHARACTERISTICS OF SIGNIFICANCE

Mr Sample is generally reserved and withdrawn. He tends to prefer activities which do not involve others. In fact, he may have a history of unsatisfactory interpersonal relationships.

Mr Sample's capacity for abstract skills is average. He can comfortably deal with practical problems, but may encounter more difficulty in understanding subtle, abstract relationships.

He is easily affected by his feelings. Involvement in problems may evoke emotional upset and instability. This, in turn, could interfere with his ability to respond to daily challenges successfully.

Mr Sample is not aggressive. Rather, he tends to be mild, conforming, and submissive. In interpersonal relationships, he would be more likely to accommodate others than to impose his will upon them.

He is shy and timid. He is not socially bold. Instead, he tends to be threat sensitive.

He is emotionally sensitive and tender-minded. He is attentive to his emotions and feelings. He may encounter some difficulty in coping with stress.

Mr Sample is experimenting and has an inquiring mind. He likes new ideas and tends to be critical of traditions. He may be critical of those in authority, perhaps to the point of being rebellious.

Mr Sample tends to be undisciplined and to lack self control. He tends to follow his own urges and desires rather than following "shoulds." He appears to permit a considerable amount of disorder and ambiguity in his life.

BROAD INFLUENCE PATTERNS

Mr Sample is introverted. He directs his attention inward to thoughts and feelings and tends to prefer solitary activities to social activities. This tendency is very high.

At the present time, Mr Sample describes himself as more anxious than most people. He is rather tense and frustrated. As a result, he may have difficulty coping with everyday stresses. His anxiety level is high.

Mr Sample tends to approach problems and situations with an emphasis upon emotional considerations. This may, at times, interfere with his ability to make decisions as objectively as some situations could require. This tendency is above average.

He attempts both to adapt himself to conditions in which he finds himself as well as to exert influence so as to change those conditions. Thus, he is neither overly accommodating nor overly inflexible. His level of independence is average.

He tends to be very expedient and to pursue his own wishes rather than the expectations of others. Thus, he may lack restraint and may fail at times to meet his responsibilities. This tendency is very high.

DEPRESSION

He tends to be distinctly sad and melancholic. He has great difficulty handling interpersonal contact and this probably leads to feelings of hopelessness and inadequacy. His overall depression level is very high.

He reports a high number of nonspecific somatic complaints. This may reflect pathological overconcern with bodily functions.

Mr Sample reports strong feelings of disgust for himself. He feels that his life is empty and meaningless. He has few hopes for the future and he may harbor thoughts of self-destruction.

He is not very energetic and is rarely likely to wake up full of energy. Mr Sample's experience significantly involves feelings of weariness. It may be the case that he has difficulty generating the energy to cope.

Mr Sample reports a high number of somatic complaints, coupled with a severe lack of energy. It may be the case that he is suffering from an as-yet undiagnosed physical illness which is medically treatable. Referral for a complete medical evaluation should be considered.

psychware **161**

Mr Sample is very self-critical. He tends to blame himself for everything that goes wrong. He experiences guilt feelings. This guilt is probably coupled with feelings of resentment and hosility, as well.

He tends to be uncomfortable with people and frequently avoids interpersonal contact. His tendency to withdraw may be accompanied by a general feeling that relationships are too pointless to care about at all.

OTHER CLINICAL INDICATORS

Mr Sample's responses do not indicate that he has difficulty evaluating reality accurately. He reports no withdrawal from others or from reality. His degree of disorientation does not differ significantly from that of most people.

Mr Sample's responses indicate that he is not anxious or self-deprecating. He is probably not overly dependent upon the approval of others for his sense of self worth. His level of neurotic maladjustment, by itself, gives no cause for alarm.

Mr Sample describes himself as feeling worthless and helpless. He may distort reality in the area of self worth. He may be unable to muster the resources to cope effectively with many situations which confront him.

Specific intervention suggestions that might be productively explored include—

----A graded series of success experiences to improve self-confidence.

----Emphasis upon plans and their execution to develop self-discipline.

----A structured, active stress management program to reduce anxiety.

VOCATIONAL OBSERVATIONS

At Mr Sample's own ability level, the potential for creative functioning is high.

In a group of peers, potential for leadership is very low.

Potential for benefit from formal academic training, at Mr Sample's own level of ability, is below average.

The need for interpersonal isolation at work is above average.

Habits are suitable either for work that requires dependability or for a job that permits inconsistency. However, extremes should be avoided.

Considering his psychological makeup, Mr Sample's potential to grow and meet increasing job demands is below average.

The extent to which Mr Sample is accident prone is above average.

OCCUPATIONAL FITNESS PROJECTIONS

In this segment of the report, his results are compared with various occupational profiles. All projections should be considered with respect to other information about him, particularly his interests and abilities.

```
              Accountant.....................below average (4.4)
              Airline Flight Attendant......below average (3.8)
              Airline pilot.................low (3.0)
              Artist........................very low (2.4)

              Bank Manager..................average (6.5)
              Biologist.....................average (5.1)
              Business Executive............low (2.6)

              Chemist.......................average (5.1)
              Computer Programmer...........average (5.6)
              Credit Union Manager..........average (5.0)
              Editorial Worker..............extremely low (1.0)
              Electrician...................low (2.7)
              Employment Counselor..........above average (7.1)
              Engineer......................low (3.3)
```

```
Firefighter................extremely low (1.0)

Geologist..................above average (7.3)

Janitor....................extremely low (1.0)

Kitchen Worker.............below average (4.2)

Machine Operator...........below average (3.7)
Mechanic...................extremely low (1.2)
Middle Level Manager.......low (3.4)
Musician...................very high (9.0)

Nurse......................low (3.1)

Personnel Manager..........above average (6.6)
Physician..................above average (6.8)
Physicist..................average (4.9)
Plant Foreman..............high (8.3)
Police Officer.............extremely low (1.0)
Priest (RC)................extremely high (10.0)
Production Manager.........average (6.4)
Psychiatric technician.....low (2.7)
Psychologist...............average (5.4)

Real Estate Agent..........average (4.9)
Retail Counter Clerk.......average (4.6)

Sales Supervisor...........very low (2.4)
Salesperson---Retail.......low (2.5)
Salesperson---Wholesale....very low (2.5)
School Counselor...........above average (6.6)
School Superintendent......low (3.0)
Secretary-Clerk............above average (7.4)
Service Station Dealer.....average (5.3)
Social Worker..............average (5.4)

Store Manager..............average (5.8)

Teacher---Elementary Level...below average (3.6)
Teacher---Junior High Level...very high (9.1)
Teacher---Senior High Level...extremely high (10.0)
Time/Motion Study Analyst.....average (4.5)
Truck Driver..............below average (3.8)

University Administrator......below average (4.2)
University Professor.........very high (8.6)
Writer......................very low (1.9)
```

SECOND-ORDER SCORE SUMMARY

```
Extraversion...............very low (2.4)
Anxiety....................high (8.4)
Tough Poise................low (3.2)
Independence...............average (4.9)
Superego Strength..........very low (2.5)
Socialization..............average (6.0)
Depression.................very high (8.7)
Psychoticism...............average (5.8)
Neuroticism................above average (7.1)
```

NAME: Complex-Attention Rehabilitation

SUPPLIER: Robert J. Sbordone, Ph.D., Inc.
8840 Warner Ave. Suite 301
Fountain Valley, CA 92708
(714) 841-6293

PRODUCT CATEGORY	PRIMARY APPLICATIONS
Cognitive/Ability	Training/Development

SALE RESTRICTIONS American Psychological Association Guidelines

SERVICE TYPE/COST	Type	Available	Cost	Discount
	Mail-In	No		
	Teleprocessing	No		
	Local	Yes	$150.00	

PRODUCT DESCRIPTION

The COMPLEX-ATTENTION REHABILITATION program provides computer-based training in attentional tasks using visual tracking of single or multiple stimuli for patients with impaired cognitive functioning. The program carefully monitors the patient's behavior and automatically determines when rest periods are needed. It increases the complexity of the task as the patient's performance improves and offers a wide variety of tasks. A speech synthesizer option (which requires an Echo Speech Synthesizer in addition to the basic computer hardware) produces a voice accompaniment to the program's visual display to utilize language-mediated complex attentional skills.

The program also maintains patient performance data over training sessions and provides a comprehensive analysis of these data.

The program operates on the Apple II + , IIe, III, or Apple-compatible hardware and on the IBM PC-100 microcomputer system. No special computer knowledge is needed. The software comes with an instruction manual.

NAME: Comprehensive Client History

SUPPLIER: Applied Innovations, Inc.
South Kingstown Office Park, Suite A-1
Wakefield, RI 02879
(800) 272-2250

PRODUCT CATEGORY	PRIMARY APPLICATIONS
Structured Interview	Clinical Assessment/Diagnosis Personal/Marriage/Family Counseling

SALE RESTRICTIONS American Psychological Association Guidelines

SERVICE TYPE/COST Type	Available	Cost	Discount
Mail-In	No		
Teleprocessing	No		
Local	Yes	$375.00	

PRODUCT DESCRIPTION

This program is designed to operate in conjunction with the INITIAL SCREENER program available from the same supplier. A comprehensive client history is compiled through a series of questions that are interactive with the client's responses. A branching logic is used to determine which items are presented. Information is obtained regarding education, employment, family, social/psychological history, substance abuse, and community involvement. The program is designed for easy use by the client with minimal guidance from the professional or para-professional. After the items have been completed, the program displays and prints the client's responses.

This software operates on most available personal computers including IBM, Apple, Digital, and Kaypro.

10/30/1983
HARRIET BERTHA SMITH
SSN: 333333333
F 30

PREVIOUS TREATMENT: Y
FIRST SEEN AT THE AGE OF: 27
PAST TREAMENT WAS FAMILY
TREATED AS AN: OUTPATIENT
FIRST HOSPITALIZED:

PRIMARY DIAGNOSIS: ALCOHOL PROBLEM
CURRENTLY IN SCHOOL:

GRADUATED H.S.:   Y
   MILITARY HISTORY: N

   WORK HISTORY
LAST TIME WORKED: OVER 5 YEARS AGO
AT THAT JOB: OVER 1 YEAR AGO
LONGEST JOB HELD: OVER 1 YEAR
EVER BANKRUPT: N
RECEIVING FINANCIAL HELP: N

   SOCIAL HISTORY
SOCIAL ACTIVITY: SAME
CHURCH/CHURCH FUNCTIONS: Y
ATTEND: MONTHLY
COMPETITIVE SPORT ACTIVITY: N

SMOKE CIGARETTES?   Y
10-15

   MEDICATIONS/DRUGS
ALLERGIC TO MEDS?   Y
TAKING PRESCRIBED MEDS?   N
NON-PRESCRIBED MEDS?   N
ALCOHOLIC BEVERAGES?   Y
TIME BETWEEN DRINKS? MONTHS
PERIODIC DRINKING?   N
PAST USE OF ALCOHOL?
USE SEDATIVES?   N
USE NARCOTICS?   N
USE STIMULANTS?   N
USE HALLUCINOGENS?   N

PHYSICAL ATTRIBUTES
LAST FELT WELL: OVER 5 YEARS AGO
DECREASE ENERGY/INTEREST?   Y
MORE
INCREASE ENERGY/INTEREST?   Y
LESS
WHEN WELL, SLEEP IS: GOOD
HOURS PER DAY: 8
NOW GET: 8
DREAM: SAME
DREAMS ARE: PLEASANT
DREAM IN COLOR?   Y
REFRESHED AFTER SLEEPING?   Y
WHEN WELL, APPETITE IS: GOOD
RECENT APPETITIE CHANGE?   N
RECENT WEIGHT CHANGE?   N
CERTAIN FOODS AVOIDED?   N

FORCE VOMIT?   N
   SEX HISTORY
SEXUAL PREFERENCE: HETERO
SEXUAL INTEREST: SAME
SEXUAL INTERCOURSE: SAME
TWICE A MONTH
SEXUAL MEDICAL CONDITIONS?   N
CONTRACEPTION: CONDOMS
INTERFERE WITH SEX ENJOYMENT?   N

   FOR THE FOLLOWING QUESTIONS
A=HISTORY OF; B=RECENTLY; C=NEVER
DIFFICULTY GETTING EXCITED?   C
DIFFICULTY MAINTAINING EXCITEMENT? C
REACHING ORGASM TOO QUICKLY?   C
DIFFICULTY IN REACHING ORGASM?   C
INABILITY TO HAVE ORGASM?   C
INCONVENIENT TIMING?   C
INABILITY TO RELAX?   C
ATTRACTION TO OTHERS, OPPOSITE SEX? C
DISINTEREST?   C
ATTRACTION TO OTHERS, SAME SEX?   C
DIFFERENT SEXUAL HABITS?   C
'TURNED OFF'?   C
TOO LITTLE FOREPLAY?   C
TOO LITTLE TENDERNESS?   B
OTHER SEX DIFFICULTIES?   Y

166 *psychware*

LIFE HISTORY QUESTIONNAIRE

DEVELOPE STRONG LIKING TO PERSON, EVEN AFTER SHORT CONTACT?	Y
GET VERY UPSET WHEN SEPARATED FROM PEOPLE YOU LIKE?	N
HAVE TROUBLE KNOWING WHAT TIME IT IS?	N
WORRY ABOUT YOUR HEALTH?	N
HAVE A FEELING THAT SOMEONE IS CONTROLLING YOU?	Y
TEND TO BE VERY MOODY?	N
ACT AS IF NOTHING HAPPENED EVEN WHEN A FAMILY MEMBER OR A CLOSE FRIEND IS SERIOUSLY HURT?	N
MAKE MANY PROMISES, BUT NOT KEEP THEM?	N
TRY TO AVOID WORK OR OTHER RESPONSIBILITIES?	N
EAT EXCESSIVELY?	N
TEND TO BE BOSSED AROUND BY EVERYONE?	Y
HEAR VOICES THAT TELL YOU WHAT TO DO?	N
PREFER INDOOR TO OUTDOOR ACTIVITIES?	N
OFTEN ARGUE WITH FAMILY MEMBERS?	N
TEND TO FALL ASLEEP DURING THE TIME YOU SHOULD BE WORKING?	N
COMPLAIN OF BEING MISTREATED BY FAMILY MEMBERS?	N
HAVE FRIENDS WHO ARE ALWAYS IN TROUBLE WITH THE LAW?	N
BECOME FEARFUL WITHOUT ANY REASON?	N
NOTICE A CHANGE IN YOUR HANDWRITING?	N
THINK THAT EVEN YOUR SECRET THOUGHTS CAN BE PICKED UP BY OTHER PEOPLE?	N
ARE YOU CURRENTLY SUING ANYONE?	N
ARE YOU CURRENTLY BEING SUED?	N
HAVE YOU EVER HAD AN AUTOMOBILE/VEHICLE ACCIDENT?	Y
HOW MANY ACCIDENTS HAVE YOU HAD?	2
HAVE ANY OF THESE ACCIDENTS RESULTED IN INJURIES?	N
WHAT IS THE DATE OF YOUR LAST ACCIDENT?	1980
WERE YOU UNDER THE INFLUENCE OF DRUGS/MEDICATIONS?	N
HAS ANY ACCIDENT RESULTED IN POLICE/LEGAL ACTION?	N
HAVE ANY ACCIDENTS THAT DID NOT INVOLVE MOTOR VEHICLES?	N
HAVE YOU EVER THOUGHT YOU WERE BETTER OFF DEAD?	N
HAVE YOU EVER THOUGHT ABOUT SUICIDE?	Y
HAVE YOU EVER THREATENED TO TAKE YOUR OWN LIFE?	N
HAVE YOU EVER ATTEMPTED TO TAKE YOUR OWN LIFE?	N
WHEN SOMETHING UNPLEASANT HAPPENS, HOW DO YOU REACT?	CAREFULLY

GYNECOLOGICAL HISTORY

FIRST MENSTRUAL PERIOD AT THE AGE OF 10
HARRIET IS STILL HAVING HER PERIODS
MENSTRUAL CYCLE IS REGULAR
SHE IS NOT MENSTRUATING TODAY
HARRIET EXPECTS NEXT PERIOD IN 14
SYMPTOMS EXPERIENCED BEFORE PERIOD:IRRITABLE
HARRIET HAS HAD 9 PREGNANCIES,
THE YOUNGEST CHILD IS 1
PREGNANCY AND DELIVERY PROBLEMS: Y
HARRIET IS NOT CURRENTLY PREGNANT
CHILDREN: 4
PREGNANCIES OUR OF WEDLOCK: NONE
CHILDREN GIVEN UP FOR ADOPTION: NONE
THERE ARE NO OTHER CHILDREN LIVING IN THE HOME.
THERE HAS BEEN ABORTIONS OR MISCARRIAGES

DID YOU BETWEEN THE AGES OF 6 TO 16.........

OFTEN FALL OR GET INTO ACCIDENTS?	N
HAVE TICS?	N
HAVE POOR EYESIGHT?	N
HAVE STRABISMUS (CROSS EYED)?	N
FEAR GOING TO SCHOOL?	N
HAVE DIFFICULTY WITH READING?	Y
HAVE DIFFICULTY WITH WRITING?	N
FEAR THE DARK?	N
HAVE DIFFICULTY WITH ADDITION, MULTIPLICATION AND OTHER TASKS INVOLVING NUMBERS?	N
TEND TO USE LEFT HAND FOR THROWING, USING TOOLS, ETC?	N
TEND TO MISPRONOUNCE CETAIN WORDS OR LETTERS.... LIKE S, L, R, TH.....ETC?	N
STUTTER OR STAMMER?	N
LISP OR HAVE SLURRED SPEECH?	N
FEEL AWKWARD AT GAMES?	N
STAY AWAY FROM SCHOOL WITHOUT PERMISSION?	N
RUN AWAY FROM HOME?	N
STEAL THINGS FROM HOME?	N
STEAL THINGS FROM OTHER PEOPLE?	N
TELL LIES TO FAMILY MEMBERS?	N
TELL LIES TO OTHER PEOPLE?	N
WET THE BED?	N
HAVE NIGHTMARES?	N
SLEEPWALK?	N
SLEEP POORLY?	N
SLEEP EXCESSIVELY?	N
DID YOU EVER FAIL ANY SUBJECTS IN SCHOOL?	N
DID YOU EVER REPEAT ANY GRADES?	Y
WERE YOU EVER IN ANY REMEDIAL CLASSES?	Y
WERE YOU EVER IN ANY ADVANCED CLASSES?	Y
DID YOU EVER SKIP ANY GRADES?	N

                    PARENTS, GUARDIANS, ETC......
RAISED BY NATURAL PARENT(S)
MOTHER: IRISH
FATHER: IRISH
MOTHER: CATHOLIC
FATHER: CATHOLIC
MOTHER ED: 15
FATHER ED: 17
MOTHER ALIVE
FATHER ALIVE
MOTHER: REGISTERED NURSE
FATHER: ENGINEER

168 *psychware*

FAMILY MEDICAL/ILLNESS/PROBLEMS

```
HEART DISEASE:          N
HIGH BLOOD PRESSURE     MOTHER
STROKE:                 N
DIABETES:               BOTH PARENTS
ATTEMPTED SUICIDE:      N
COMMITTED SUICIDE:      N
DRIKING PROBLEM:        HUSBAND & DAD
DELINQUENCY:            SISTER, JANIE
MENTAL RETARDATION:     N
MENTAL ILLNESS:         N
EPILIPSY:               N
MOOD SWINGS:            M
PECULIAR BEHAVIOR:      N
COLOR BLINDNESS:        N
OTHER: ASTMA, ALL KIDS
FINANCIAL: N
```

MILITARY ELABORATION
NONE

ALLERGIC TO MEDICATIONS
DEMEROL CAUSES ME TO VOMIT
X

PRESCRIBED MEDICATIONS
NONE

NON-PRESCRIBED MEDICATIONS
NONE

SEDATIVES, SLEEPING PILLS AND ANTI-ANXIETY DRUGS
NONE

NARCOTICS OR PAIN KILLERS
NONE

STIMULANTS
NONE

HALLUCINOGENS
NONE

OPERATIONS EFFECTING SEX LIFE
NONE

CONTRACEPTIVE INTERFERENCE WITH SEX LIFE
NONE
OTHER SEXUAL DIFFICULTIES
MY HUSBAND IS NOT KIND TO ME. WE DON'T
MAKE LOVE OFTEN ENOUGH BECAUSE WE DO NOT
SEE EACH OTHER OFTEN ENOUGH. HE IS OFTEN
UNDER THE INFLUENCE OF ALCOHOL. HE READS
PROBLEMS WITH PREGNANCY/DELIVERY
MISCARRIED FOUR TIMES IN ONE YEAR. TWO
WERE BREACH, AND I BLED ALOT WITH ALL
OF THEM. SUZAN WAS A C SECTION.
X
ELABORATION OF ACCIDENTS
NONE
SUICIDE THOUGHTS AND/OR ATTEMPTS
I ONLY THOUGT ABOUT IT. I WAS DEPRESSED
A FEW YEARS AGO. NOTHING TO IT REALLY.
X
ELABORATION ON EARLY CHILDHOOD REARING
NONE
INDIVIDUALS INPORTANT TO CLIENT
MY MOTHER AND FATHER
JANIE, MY OLDER SISTER
ANN, MY YOUNGER SISTER
SUZAN, A CLOSE FRIEND
MY HUSBAND AND CHILDREN
X
SIBLING INFORMATION
JANIE 37, MARRIED WITH 3 KIDS
ANN 26, MARRIED WITH 2 KIDS
OTHERS ARE DEAD
X
ELABORATION OF SCHOOL HISTORY
HAD STREP WHEN I WAS IN FIRST GRADE.
HOSPITALIZED FOR NEPHRITIS SO I MISSED
LAST HALF AND STAYED BACK THAT YEAR.
I HAD BOTH REMEDIAL HELP AND WAS ALSO
IN ADVANCED SUBJECTS.

ADDITIONAL RELEVANT INFORMATION
HAROLD AND I HAVE HAD DISAGREEMENTS ON
HIS MOTHER INTERFERENCE IN OUR
MARRIAGE. SHE HAS NEVER LIKED ME.
I AM ALSO LONELY, HAROLD GOES OUT
DRINKING EVERY NIGHT AFTER WORK. HE
THEN ACTS LIKE I AM HIS ENEMY. I CAN'T
SEEM TO CONTROL THE KIDS. THEY GO TO
THEIR FATHER IF THERE IS A PROBLEM.
I JUST DON'T KNOW WHAT TO DO.
X

NAME: Computer Career Planning Series

SUPPLIER: Publishers Test Service
2500 Garden Road
Monterey, CA 93940
(800) 538-9547

PRODUCT CATEGORY	PRIMARY APPLICATIONS
Career/Vocational	Vocational Guidance/Counseling

SALE RESTRICTIONS American Psychological Association Guidelines

SERVICE TYPE/COST	Type	Available	Cost	Discount
	Mail-In	No		
	Teleprocessing	No		
	Local	Yes	$349.95	

PRODUCT DESCRIPTION

The COMPUTER CAREER PLANNING SERIES consists of three widely used self-assessing career interest inventories (JOB-O, MAJOR-MINOR FINDER, CAREER EXPLORATION SERIES) that feature quick scoring and data-search for use in career centers, counseling offices, and classrooms. JOB-O, based on student responses to general assessment questions, selects up to 10 of the 120 most popular and traditional jobs and displays the list on the screen. The MAJOR-MINOR FINDER elicits students responses to questions about college and work interests. Based on the responses, a list of 10 most appropriate (from a pool of 99 most popular) college majors is displayed. The CAREER EXPLORATION SERIES allows focused exploration of careers in the areas of agriculture, business, consumer and scientific professions, economics, design, art, and communication.

Software is available for use with Apple, TRS-80 and Commodore PET computers.

NAME: Computerized Rorschach System

SUPPLIER: Applied Innovations, Inc.
South Kingstown Office Park, Suite A-1
Wakefield, RI 02879
(800) 272-2250

PRODUCT CATEGORY	PRIMARY APPLICATIONS
Personality	Clinical Assessment/Diagnosis

SALE RESTRICTIONS American Psychological Association Guidelines

SERVICE TYPE/COST	Type	Available	Cost	Discount
	Mail-In	No		
	Teleprocessing	No		
	Local	Yes	$125.00	

PRODUCT DESCRIPTION

The COMPUTERIZED RORSCHACH SYSTEM is a computer program that generates descriptive statements for the Rorschach based on 10 universal Rorschach scores (M, FM, C, CF, FC, A%, F + %, W, S, and P). It is compatible with all the popular Rorschach systems. Descriptive statements output by the program are based on all significant T-scores (35-T and below; 65-T and above). The program also calculates a validity index which helps the clinician determine the relative significance of each statement generated. A brief, two-page report is generated.

The SYSTEM comes with a special scoring form that allows the Rorschach to be scored during the inquiry. This SYSTEM saves valuable clinical time. The software operates on most available personal computers including IBM, Apple, Digital, and Kaypro.

RORSCHACH INTERPRETATION

Bruce Duthie, Ph.D

&

Ernest G. Allen

APPLIED INNOVATIONS, INC.
SOUTH KINGSTOWN OFFICE PARK, SUITE A-1
WAKEFIELD, RHODE ISLAND 02879
(800) 272-2250

MicroBlot-RD is an aid for generating interpretive hypotheses from Rorschach
determinant scores. The determinants analyzed are in general scored similarly
in all the major Rorschach systems. All hypotheses generated should be
validated by an appropriately qualified psychologist.

		20	25	30	35	40	45	50	55	60	65	70	75	80
Human Movement	(M)					I**				I				
Animal Movement	(FM)					I				I		**		
Color/Color Naming	(C)					I				I		**		
Color Form	(CF)					I		**	I					
Form Color	(FC)					I				**I				
Good Form %	(F+)**					I				I				
Popular	(P)				**	I				I				
Animal %	(A)					I				I				**
White Space	(S)					I				I				**
Whole	(W)					I		**		I				

Experience actual = 9.5
Erlebistypus = .266667
FC / CF + C = 4.5
W / M = 4

M = 2 FM = 5 C = 2 CF = 2 FC = 5 F+% = 44 P = 2 A% = 80 S = 5 W = 8

Name: Harry S. Clark   Age: 33   Sex: Male   Date: 3/24/84

* * NORMAL TRAITS * *
2 Below average intellectual functioning
2 Aggressive and assertive

* * NEUROTIC INDICATIONS * *
3 Free-floating anxiety
2 Marked anxiety
2 Neurotic inhibition
2 Feels tense
4 S U I C I D E   P O T E N T I A L   with ideation

* * INDICATIONS OF PERSONALITY OR CONDUCT DISORDER * *
2 Rebellious
3 Has potential to act-out; impulsivity
2 Emotionally labile
2 Cannot delay gratification
2 Immaturity
2 Excited or potentially agitated
3 Hostile or assaultive

* * PSYCHOTIC SYMPTOMS * *
2 Impulsive, bizarre,psychotic behavior
4 Psychosis with propensity to act-out
2 Inappropriate affect
3 Tends toward hypomanic episodes

* * DEFENSE MECHANISMS * *
2 Repression

* * DIAGNOSTIC SUGGESTIONS * *
3 Anxiety
2 Somatization
3 Narcissistic personality
2 Immature personality
2 Sociopathic personality
2 Borderline personality
2 Paranoia
2 Disorganized schizophrenia
3 Paranoid schizophrenia
3 Schizophrenia
2 Depressive psychosis
4 Organicity
2 Senility
3 Mental retardation

* * TREATMENT CONSIDERATIONS * *
2 Prognosis poor or guarded

174 *psychware*

NAME: Computerized Stress Inventory

SUPPLIER: Preventive Measures, Inc.
1115 West Campus Road
Lawrence, KS 66044
(913) 842-5078

PRODUCT CATEGORY

Personality

PRIMARY APPLICATIONS

Behavioral Medicine
Clinical Assessment/Diagnosis

SALE RESTRICTIONS   Qualified Professional

SERVICE TYPE/COST	Type	Available	Cost	Discount
	Mail-In	No		
	Teleprocessing	No		
	Local	Yes	$490.00	

PRODUCT DESCRIPTION

The COMPUTERIZED STRESS INVENTORY, a computer-administered series of questions and scales, is designed to be a stress and coping 'check-up.' Respondents receive a 12-16 page stress profile detailing particular strengths and weaknesses, as well as a graphic summary of their sources and symptoms of stress. The profile covers more than 25 areas of the person's life, including such areas as work or primary activity, lifestyle, family relationships, life changes, eating habits, time management, worrying, frustrations, and joys.

The focus of the report is on prevention of illness and enhancement of the quality of life. It is based on the premise that everyone expriences excess stress in some areas of their lives at some times and that personal information about one's own sources and symptoms of stress is the first step toward positive change.

The COMPUTERIZED STRESS INVENTORY is available on most major microcomputers, including IBM, Zenith, Compaq, Apple II series, Kaypro, and Osborne.

NAME: Computerized Visual Searching Task

SUPPLIER: PSYCH Systems, Inc.
600 Reisterstown Road
Baltimore, MD 21208
(800) 368-3366

PRODUCT CATEGORY	PRIMARY APPLICATIONS
Cognitive/Ability	Clinical Assessment/Diagnosis Personal/Marriage/Family Counseling

SALE RESTRICTIONS   Qualified Professional

SERVICE TYPE/COST	Type	Available	Cost	Discount
	Mail-In	No		
	Teleprocessing	No		
	Local	Yes	See Below	

PRODUCT DESCRIPTION

The COMPUTERIZED VISUAL SEARCHING TASK is a 27-item test which serves as a preliminary screening device for determining the possibility of neurological impairment in adults up to 65 years of age. The test items are based on 20 grids which present the various visual searching tasks. Results of studies show that the COMPUTERIZED VISUAL SEARCHING TASK is a good discriminator of brain-damaged and non-brain-damaged individuals. Reaction time is also totalled and used to determine further need for neurological testing. This Psych Systems program administers, scores, and provides a printout of the test.

Psych Systems programs operate on the IBM PC-XT, COMPAQ Plus, Dec Professional 350, and most DEC PDP-11 systems. Various hardware/software configurations are available directly from Psych Systems, with single-user systems starting at approximately $12,000. A per test fee also applies.

222-22-2222 Jonathan Doe   32 yr old white male   16-Feb-84

```
-------------------------------------
|        |                            |
|  VST   |   Visual Searching Task    |
|        |                            |
-------------------------------------
```

I. Total Performance Time: 7

II. Total Errors: 3

III. Individual Target Times: Mean =   0.3500 SD =   0.7452

Target	Elapsed Time	Target	Elapsed Time
1	3	11	1
2	1	12	1
3	1	13	1
4	1	14	1
5	1	15	1
6	1	16	1
7	1	17	1
8	1	18	1
9	1	19	1
10	1	20	1

IV. Interpretation:

The subject has not exceeded the cutoff score of 453 seconds on
the CVST. The scores suggest that the individual does not have
cognitive dysfunction. No definitive diagnoses should be
made based on these results alone.

psychware **177**

NAME: Coronary Risk Report

SUPPLIER: Institute for Personality and Ability Testing, Inc.
P.O. Box 188
Champaign, IL 61820
(217) 352-4739

PRODUCT CATEGORY	PRIMARY APPLICATIONS
Personality	Behavioral Medicine Personal/Marriage/Family Counseling Clinical Assessment/Diagnosis Personnel Selection/Evaluation

SALE RESTRICTIONS   American Psychological Association Guidelines

SERVICE TYPE/COST	Type	Available	Cost	Discount
	Mail-In	Yes	$16.00	Yes
	Teleprocessing	No		
	Local	No		

PRODUCT DESCRIPTION

This 3-4 page report considers coping behaviors, attitudes, and personality traits as they relate to one's physical and emotional health. It assists the health professional in identifying what is popularly referred to, today, as the Type A behavior pattern.

The report is comprised of three sections. The first is titled Health Risk Patterns and focuses on those personality traits that are known to relate to diminished physical functioning/ performance, such as stress, anxiety, and tension. Also provided are suggestions for the alleviation of debilitating behaviors. Section 2, titled Life Style Patterns, describes how the person typically responds to other people and situations. The third section, titled Cognitive Factors, describes one's approach to problem-solving situations.

A final section, titled Health Maintenance Summary, provides an overall statement regarding health maintenance and, as appropriate, additional suggestions for behavior change. Also included with the report is a profile of 16 PF and related scores for use by the professional.

CORONARY RISK REPORT

NAME... John Sample
SEX.... M
AGE.... 30
DATE... 4/20/1984

INTRODUCTION

In reviewing this confidential report, keep in mind this only
considers coping behaviors, attitudes, preferences, and other
personality characteristics, as they relate to physical and emotional
health. As such, it represents one component of what should be a
more comprehensive evaluation.

RESPONSE PATTERNS

It appears that Mr Sample answered the 16PF questionnaire in a
natural and truthful way. As a result, this report gives an honest
picture of his personality. Even so, the material that follows will
be most useful when it is considered along with other available
information.

HEALTH RISK PATTERNS

There does not appear to be a consistent CAD risk pattern evident
in Mr Sample's reported attitudes or behavior. There are some
indicators that could be at more optimum levels, but these are not
yet serious enough to cause great concern. From a health maintenance
point of view, though, there are some early warning signs which, if
remain unaltered, may contribute to diminishing health.

Mr Sample is experiencing a great deal of tension and anxiety.
His level of stress-coping skills, however, is average. This would
indicate that normal stressors are adequately handled by him.
However, extreme or prolonged stress is likely to lead to stress-
related disorders. Steps should be taken to identify and alleviate
the sources of his anxiety.

From a psychiatric risk point of view, evidence regarding unusual
behaviors or thoughts is inconclusive. Mr Sample tends to be sad and
melancholic. He has difficulty in handling interpersonal contact and
this probably leads to feelings of hopelessness and inadequacy. His
overall depression level is very high. Mr Sample's clinical signs
indicate the presence of increased likelihood for psychiatric
dysfunction. In order to make this determination more conclusive, an
in-depth interview and additional testing may be required.

On occasion, he will project inner tension by blaming others and
will become jealous or suspicious easily.

Mr Sample should consider certain modifications in order that he
maintains a balance in his behaviors, attitudes, and life style.
Specifically, he should consider the following areas.

He becomes upset when things go wrong. He needs to become more
realistic in setting goals and in his expectations of others.
Mr Sample is a very shy and timid person. It would be helpful for
him to become more bold during social engagements. Perhaps among
friends he can come forward and occasionally become the focus of
attention.

psychware **179**

He is inclined to become irritated and stubborn when others do
things that he doesn't like. He needs to learn constructive ways of
dealing with unsatisfactory situations that will help in bringing
about positive change. He should not dwell on vague feelings of
uneasiness, dread, or worthlessness. He needs to practice greater
self-control, rather than leaving too many things to chance. He
possesses excess energy which is not ordinarily discharged and
results in increased frustration, tension, and agitation. He should
learn appropriate ways to "let off steam."

As far as accident proneness is concerned he is no more
susceptible than the average person.

LIFE STYLE PATTERNS

In general, Mr Sample shows about equal preference for situations
that involve working alone and those that involve working with
others. He is shy and tends to be inhibited in the presence of
others. He is very sensitive to threat. Mr Sample is self-
sufficient and generally able to function autonomously.

He does not try to maintain strict control over his behavior.
However, he is not so impulsive or irresponsible that this will
present major problems. Overall, his life style is subdued and
accepting of the environment in which he finds himself. He usually
adapts to circumstances.

COGNITIVE FACTORS

Mr Sample tends to allow his emotions and emotional factors to
play a major role in influencing his actions. As a consequence, he
is frequently less objective than he should be in arriving at
solutions to problems. It would be helpful if he could learn to deal
more objectively with situations. Otherwise, the continual wear and
tear on his emotions are likely to become unbearable for him. In
general, his capacity for abstract verbal skills as well as his level
of creativity are both expected to be very high. He is an
intelligent and innovative problem-solver. His solutions are often
unique and insightful.

HEALTH MAINTENANCE SUMMARY

In this report, areas of concern have been noted that will help
Mr Sample achieve and maintain a healthy balance in his self beliefs,
interests, and life style. Specifically, Mr Sample should begin by
working on the modifications introduced in the HEALTH RISK PATTERNS
section.

PHYSICIAN'S SUMMARY

CHART 1: HEALTH RISK PATTERNS

```
         LOW      A V E R A G E      HIGH
         1   2   3   4   5   6   7   8   9  10
         ----------------------------------------
C AD                 :           X:                  CAD Risk................  7. 0
SCS              X   :           :                   Stress Coping Skills....  3. 6
ANX                  :           :           X       Anxiety................. 10. 0
PRS                  :       X   :                   Psychiatric Risk Status.  5. 6
DEP                  :           :       X           Depression Tendency.....  9. 5
ACP                  :       X   :                   Accident Proneness......  6. 0
         ----------------------------------------
```

CHART 2: LIFE STYLE PATTERNS

```
         LOW      A V E R A G E      HIGH
         1   2   3   4   5   6   7   8   9  10
         ----------------------------------------
IC                   : X         :                   Extraversion...........  4. 5
LD               X   :           :                   Leadership.............  3. 3
IN                   :X          :               .   Independence...........  4. 4
EM                   :           :   X               Emotionality...........  7. 1
         ----------------------------------------
```

CHART 3: PERSONALITY ORIENTATION

```
         LOW      A V E R A G E      HIGH
         1   2   3   4   5   6   7   8   9  10
         ----------------------------------------
A                    :           X                   Warmth.................  7. 0
B                    :           :       X           Intelligence...........  9. 0
C                X   :           :                   Stability..............  3. 0
E                    :   X       :                   Dominance..............  5. 0
F                    :           X                   Impulsivity............  7. 0
G                    :           :       X           Conformity.............  9. 0
H            X       :           :                   Boldness...............  2. 0
I                    :           X                   Tender-Mindedness......  7. 0
L                    :           :   X               Suspiciousness.........  8. 0
M                X   :           :                   Imagination............  4. 0
N                    :       X   :                   Shrewdness.............  6. 0
O                    :           :           X       Guilt Proneness........ 10. 0
Q1                   :           X                   Criticalness...........  7. 0
Q2                   :           :       X           Self-sufficiency.......  9. 0
Q3       X           :           :                   Compulsivity...........  1. 0
Q4                   :           :           X       Tension................ 10. 0
         ----------------------------------------
```

psychware **181**

NAME: Counselaid

SUPPLIER: Ontometrics Corporation
6476 Adobe Road
29 Palms, CA 92277
(619) 367-6193

PRODUCT CATEGORY	PRIMARY APPLICATIONS
Personality	Personal/Marriage/Family Counseling Clinical Assessment/Diagnosis

SALE RESTRICTIONS Qualified Professional

SERVICE TYPE/COST	Type	Available	Cost	Discount
	Mail-In	Yes	$35.00	Yes
	Teleprocessing	No		
	Local	No		

PRODUCT DESCRIPTION

Counselaid is a system for pastoral counseling designed for qualified professionals and clergy. The Couselaid system encompasses: (1) a computer-interpreted psychological report of the personality and pathology of an individual or couple; (2) a set of questionnaires for Marriage Readiness or Marriage Interaction information; and (3) a continuing series of bulletins on the use of these materials. Psychological reports are based on responses to the 16 Personality Factor Questionnaire and the Clinical Analysis Questionnaire.

There is an initial enrollment fee of $25 for materials used in the Counselaid system.

```
COUNSELAID FOR                    THIS SAMPLE COUNSELAID PRINTOUT WAS CHOSEN
MATTHEW (NAME WITHHELD)           BECAUSE IT DEMONSTRATES MOST OF THE
SARAH (NAME WITHHELD)             FEATURES OF THE COUNSELAID SERVICE.
(DATE)
```

DEAR REV. (COUNSELOR'S NAME)

PART I

ESPECIALLY FOR YOU

It is important for you to know if your client is willing and able to benefit from testing and counseling, so this part of the report is especially important for your own information; and may be shared with your clients at your discretion.

MATTHEW (NAME WITHHELD)

He has probably tried to be truthful about himself, and has avoided putting himself in a good light.   *THE 'FAKING SCALES' HELP DETERMINE IF THIS PERSON'S TEST RESPONSES ARE RELIABLE.*

SARAH (NAME WITHHELD)

Her answers suggest that there may be some resistance to self insight or self analysis, and that your client has been somewhat inclined to answer questions in a socially desirable direction.

PART II

DESCRIPTION AND COMPARISON OF OUTSTANDING PERSONALITY FACTORS

The following is a description of some of the outstanding factors in the personalities of your clients as suggested by the tests. For the sake of brevity, the personality factors that are average are not listed below.

For the complete list of personality factors, see the sheet that came with your packet.

This description is not intended to replace your judgement but to give you additional information to help in your counseling.

Measures such as these are not infallible, and they are sometimes difficult to interpret even though they are accurate. So the best procedure is do discuss them with your clients rather than just report what is written here. Some personality variables appear more important to a person than others, and are therefore more likely to determine how the person feels about things, or what he does.   *MALE AND FEMALE SCORES ON THE PROFILE FOR EASY COMPARISON*

MATTHEW (NAME WITHHELD)

E   Assertiveness, independence, aggressiveness, competitiveness, and even stubbornness, seem to be very characteristic of this person. He probably appears very self-assured and authoritarian.

F   He is very sober, prudent, serious and deliberate. He may sometimes be dour, pessimistic and overly sober.

Q1   Very conservative respect of established ideas is characteristic of him. He is tolerant of traditional difficulties, confident of what he has been taught to believe, and accepts the ''tried and true''. He tends to oppose and postpone change, and is inclined to go along with tradition.

Q4   Because he is very tense, frustrated, driven, and overwrought, this person is going to be excitable, restless, fretful, and impatient. He may indeed be tired but unable to stop.

SARAH (NAME WITHHELD)

C   Your client seems to be so extremely affected by feelings and so emotionally unstable and easily upset that she probably is unable to tolerate any kind of unsatisfactory condition, probably evades all the necessary reality demands, and may have many neurotic symptoms--which she probably blames on everything but herself.

psychware   **183**

M   This is a very practical, careful, conventional person, regulated by external forces and proprieties. She tends to be anxious to do the right things and
to be dictated by what is obviously possible. This may sometimes help her to
keep her head in emergencies but it may also make her rather unimaginative.

N   She is very forthright, natural, artless and unsophisticated. She may sometimes appear to be a bit crude and awkward but is easily pleased and content
with what comes. She is very natural and spontaneous.

O   She is very inclined to feel guilty. This guiltiness is then expressed in
worry, depressiveness, moodiness, and apprehension.

Q1   Very conservative respect of established ideas is characteristic of her.
She is tolerant of traditional difficulties, confident of what she has been
taught to believe, and accepts the ''tried and true''. She tends to oppose and
postpone change, and is inclined to go along with tradition.

Q4 Because she is extremely tense, frustrated, driven, and overwrought, this
person is very excitable, restless, fretful and impatient. She may be so driven
that she has to remain active even when she is very tired. All this activity
probably does not diminish the need for continued more activity. It is an
important component in much mental illness.

*EACH OF THESE IS CALCULATED
WITH THE USE OF A
SPECIFICATION EQUATION THAT
COMBINES A NUMBER OF THE
PRIMARY 16
PERSONALITY
FACTORS
ABOVE*

THIS IS HOW THEY ARE LIKELY TO FUNCTION
IN VARIOUS LIFE SITUATIONS

. INTROVERSION	.	.	M	.	F	.	.	.	.	EXTROVERSION
. DEPENDENCE	.	.	F	.	.	.	.	M	INDEPENDENCE
. FEELING	.	.	.	.	M	.	.	F	.	THINKING
. EXPEDIENT	.	.	.	.	M	.	.	.	CONSCIENTIOUS
. NOT A LEADER	.	.	F	M	.	.	.	.	LIKELY A LEADER
. UNCREATIVE	.	.	.	F	.	.	M	.	.	CREATIVE
LIKELY UNHAPPY	.	.	.	.	M	.	F	.	.	LIKELY HAPPY IN MARRIAGE
LIKELY UNHAPPY	.	.	.	.	.	.	.	M	.	LIKELY HAPPY--COMBINED
NOT PRONE	.	.	.	M	.	.	F	.	ALCOHOL ADDICTION PRONE
NOT PRONT	M	.	.	F	.	.	.	.	DRUG ADDICTION PRONE

```
------1-------1-----------------1-------1------
EXTREME1 VERY  1    AVERAGE     1 VERY 1EXTREME
       1 MUCH  1                1 MUCH 1
```

THE FOLLOWING OCCUPATIONS HAVE CHARACTERISTIC PERSONALITY PROFILES LIKE HIS

B UNIVERSITY ADMINISTRATOR
B AIRCRAFT ENGINEER APPRENTICE
B AIRLINE PILOT
B ARTIST
B CHEMIST
B EDITORIAL WORKER
B GEOLOGIST
B PLANT FOREMAN
B GARAGE MECHANIC
B NURSE
B UNIVERSITY PROFESSOR
B RETAIL SALESMAN

*M,F AND B INDICATE THE POPULATION
ON WHICH THE ORIGINAL OCCUPATION
PROFILES WERE OBTAINED....
M = MALES, F = FEMALES, B = BOTH*

THE FOLLOWING OCCUPATIONS HAVE CHARACTERISTIC PROFILES SOMEWHAT SIMILAR TO HIS

B ELECTRICIAN
F EMPLOYMENT COUNSELOR
M ENGINEER
B PHYSICIST
B PSYCHIATRIC TECHNICIAN
B SALES MANAGER
B WHOLESALE SALESMAN
B SCHOOL COUNSELOR
B SCHOOL SUPERINTENDENT

THE FOLLOWING OCCUPATIONS HAVE CHARACTERISTIC PERSONALITY PROFILES LIKE HERS

B COOK
B RESEARCH SCIENTIST

THE FOLLOWING OCCUPATIONS HAVE CHARACTERISTIC PERSONALITY PROFILES SOMEWHAT
SIMILAR TO HERS

B UNIVERSITY ADMINISTRATOR
B BIOLOGIST
F EMPLOYMENT COUNSELOR
F ENGINEER
M ENGINEER
B GEOLOGIST
B PLANT FOREMAN
B JANITOR
B NURSE

B PHYSICIAN
B POLICEMAN
B WHOLESALE SALESMAN
F ELEMENTARY SCHOOL TEACHER

MARRIAGE STABILITY INDEXES

Research in the field of marriage stability tells us to what extent one may
expect persons with the above kinds of personalities to say their marriage is
satisfying. This is an important factor in marriage stability. The indicators
are not always the same for each partner, and the index for the two partners
together may vary considerably from their index as individuals.

Recent statistics show that about 40% of marriages that begin now end in failure. Keep this in mind when interpreting these indexes, because it could mean
that a person with ''average'' marriage stability has a 10% chance of staying
married.

COMPATIBLE AND INCOMPATIBLE CHARACTERISTICS

Counselaid helps you make the best use of interviews with prospective marriage
partners, or couples with marital problems, by highlighting areas in which their
personality factors appear to be either compatible or incompatible.

The following paragraphs call attention to some of these personality factors.
Discuss them with your clients. Whether these will indeed be strengths or
weaknesses in their marriage sometimes depends a good deal on their own special
circumstances, and on the total pattern of their way of life. Many combinations
of personality factors may be important in their particular situation. The
following seem to stand out rather readily from the above materials.

The following could be strengths.

Both are about the same in their degree of reservedness or outgoingness.

They have approximately the same degree of intelligence.

They seem to be about equally conscientious, so that one will not be conscious-
stricken about the behavior of the other.

They share about the same amount of trustingness versus suspicion.

Their relatively similar nature with respect to conservatism vs. experimentalism
is probably compatible.

Since they are quite similar in their degree of need for group adherence versus
self-sufficiency, it is likely that they will be able to agree quite well about
whether they should do things that get them social approval or whether they
should make their own decisions and go their own way.

COULD BE INCOMPATIBLE

The following combinations of personality characteristics sometimes cause
problems in marriage. Discuss them.

There are one or more ''extreme'' scores in their 16 PF profiles. Look carefully at them. Such extreme personality characteristics (except factor B)
stand the possibility of being disruptive to the marriage relationship. The
16 PF portion does not measure specific pathology (that is reported below under
the ''Clinical Pathological States''), but extreme scores suggest at least that
this factor is very far from average, and should therefore be carefully studied.
The couple needs to be aware of them, and take them into account.

When there is the great difference in practicalness and imaginativeness that
there is between these two, one might well discuss with them whether they will
experience difficulty about whether to do things in the careful conventional
manner, or to do them in an unconventional, creative way.

They differ considerably in the extent to which they are calculating and shrewd
or natural and forthright. Does this create problems in which one seems to be
too blunt and the other too cynical?

There is considerable difference between them in the degree of confidence vs.
worry. Does this mean that one of them will seem quite worried or guilty while
the other remains untroubled? This could lead to accusations of ''You don't
care about how I feel!'' and ''You make mountains out of molehills''.

When either or both of your clients is as tense, frustrated and driven as we
have noted above, does it not seem that there will be introduced into the
marriage a considerable amount of tension? Also, parental tension is
destructive to children's development. The frequently heard statement, ''I've
always been nervous,'' is much like the statement, ''I've always been sick''.

Most mental and physical sickness can be overcome with the proper professional
help. Your clients deserve to know that psychotherapy is designed to eliminate
''nervousness''.

psychware **185**

THE FOLLOWING MATERIALS SHOW CLINICAL PATHOLOGICAL STATES

OUT OF 12 SPECIFIC PATHOLOGICAL STATES WHICH THE CAQ MEASURES, YOUR CLIENTS
RESPONSES INDICATE THE FOLLOWING DIFFICULTIES, EACH OF WHICH IS SUFFICIENTLY
SEVERE TO DESERVE THE HELP OF A CLINCIAL PSYCHOLOGIST OR A PSYCHIATRIST.

MATTHEW (NAME WITHHELD)

Very strong inclination to be unhappy, alone and withdraw from people.

Very disturbing and confusing tendencies are reported by your client,
which may include lapses of memory, strange impulses or much difficulty getting
ideas into words.

Very strong feelings of insignificance or inadequacy such as your client
reports are unrealistic and seldom improved by facts or reassurance from others.

SARAH (NAME WITHHELD)

Very much troubled by feelings that life is so empty and meaningless
that suicide may seem an acceptable alternative.

Very much gloom, listlessness and low energy are reported by your
client. Since many physical ailments have these same symptoms, it would be
wise to get a check-up by a physician.

Very much guilt and resentement are reported by your client. This is an
even more dangerous symptom than O+ on the 16 PF factors above.

Very disturbing and confusing tendencies are reported by your client,
which may include lapses of memory, strange impulses or much difficulty getting
ideas into words.

Very strong feeling of being helpless to stop doing or thinking things
that are pointless or troublesome. Nail biting, persistent unpleasant thoughts,
or overcompulsive cleanliness are common

    CLIENTS WHO ANSWER AS SHE HAS DONE SHOULD BE CONSIDERED
    SERIOUSLY;AS POSSIBLE SUICIDE RISKS

*THESE INDICATORS OF OVERALL MENTALLY ILL WAYS OF TRYING TO COPE WITH LIFE
ARE CALCULATED WITH SPECIFICATION EQUATIONS THAT INCLUDE BOTH THE 16 PRIMARY
FACTORS AND THE 12 PATHOLOGY FACTORS GIVEN ABOVE. THEY THEREFORE REPRESENT
A BROAD VIEW OF THE PERSONALITY AS A WHOLE AND SHOULD BE TAKEN SERIOUSLY.*

THE COMBINED PERSONALITY PROFILE FOR
MATTHEW (NAME WITHHELD)
SHOWS A PATHOLOGICAL PROFILE OF INABILITY TO COPE WITH LIFE BECAUSE OF---

    * * very strong tendency in the direction of psychosis.

THE COMBINED PERSONALITY PROFILE FOR
SARAH (NAME WITHHELD)
SHOWS A PATHOLOGICAL PROFILE OF INABILITY TO COPE WITH LIFE BECAUSE OF...

    * * very high neurosis.

    * * extremely high anxiety.

    * * very strong depression.

Thank you for using Counselaid. We hope this report has enriched your understanding of your clients and will help in your further counseling with them.

186 *psychware*

NAME: Detroit-80 Diagnostic Report

SUPPLIER: Precision People, Inc.
3452 North Ride Circle. S.
Jacksonville, FL 32217
(904) 262-1096

PRODUCT CATEGORY	PRIMARY APPLICATIONS
Cognitive/Ability	Educational Evaluation/Planning Clinical Assessment/Diagnosis

SALE RESTRICTIONS American Psychological Association Guidelines

SERVICE TYPE/COST	Type	Available	Cost	Discount
	Mail-In	No		
	Teleprocessing	No		
	Local	Yes	$299.00	

PRODUCT DESCRIPTION

DETROIT-80 is a diagnostic program for the Detroit Tests of Learning Aptitude. Basic demographic data is input from the keyboard along with raw scores on each of the 27 subtests actually completed by the examinee. The program then prints out mental ages on each of the subtests as well as an overall IQ score. The next 3-4 pages of the report provide a narrative analysis of performance by area: comprehension and reasoning analysis, practical judgment, verbal ability, time and space relationships, number ability, auditory attentive ability, visual attentive ability, and motor ability/precision. This is followed by a modality analysis of all subtests which indicates subtests falling within expectancy based on overall performance in the area and subtests falling below expectancy. The program concludes with a one-page diagnostic summary that includes suggestions for remediation.

The software is compatible with IBM PC, Apple and TRS-80 (Models I, II, and III) microcomputers. A manual and sample printout are available for $34.00.

```
                DETROIT - 80

     A  DIAGNOSTIC  PROGRAM  FOR  THE

     DETROIT  TESTS  OF  LEARNING  APTITUDE


          JOHN J. TRIFILETTI, PH.D.

          DIANE A. TRIFILETTI, PH.D.

          ALFRED H. TRACY III


     COPYRIGHT (C) 1983:

     PRECISION PEOPLE, INC.
     3452 NORTH RIDE CIRCLE S.
     JACKSONVILLE, FL.  32217

         DETROIT - 80  DEMOGRAPHIC  DATA

     NAME         (1)   PETER JONES
     AGE          (2)   10
     SEX          (3)   MALE
     PARENT       (4)   GLORIA JONES
     SCHOOL       (5)   CLEARWATER ELEM
     GRADE        (6)   FIFTH
     REFERRED BY (7)   ESE TEAM
     REASON FOR REFERRAL      (8)   SLD

     OTHER TESTS ADMINISTERED (9)   BENDER


     EXAM DATE MM/DD/YY       (10)   10/10/82

     BIRTH DATE MM/DD/YY      (11)   10/10/72



         DETROIT - 80   INPUT RAW SCORES

     PICTORAL ABSURDITIES            (1) 15
     VERBAL ABSURDITIES              (2) 15
     PICTORIAL OPPOSITES             (3) 15
     VERBAL OPPOSITES                (4) 15
     2 MIN. MOTOR SPEED (CUMULATIVE) (5) 15
     3 MIN. MOTOR SPEED (CUMULATIVE) (6) 155
     4 MIN. MOTOR SPEED (CUMULATIVE) (7) 155
     AUD. ATTN. SPAN WORDS (SIMPLE)  (8)
     AUD. ATTN. SPAN WORDS (WEIGHT)  (9)
     ORAL COMMISSIONS                (10) 15
     SOCIAL ADJUSTMENT A             (11) 15
     VIS. ATTN. SPAN OBJ. (SIMPLE)   (12)
     VIS. ATTN. SPAN OBJ. (WEIGHT)   (13)
     ORIENTATION                     (14) 15
```

```
        DETROIT - 80 INPUT RAW SCORES
FREE ASSOC. 1 MIN (CUMULATIVE) (15) 155
FREE ASSOC. 2 MIN (CUMULATIVE) (16) 5
FREE ASSOC. 3 MIN (CUMULATIVE) (17) 15
FREE ASSOC. 4 MIN (CUMULATIVE) (18) 15
FREE ASSOC. 5 MIN (CUMULATIVE) (19) 51
MEMORY FOR DESIGNS             (20) 15
AUD. ATTN. SPAN FOR SYLLABLES  (21) 15
NUMBER ABILITY                 (22)
SOCIAL ADJUSTMENT B            (23)
VISUAL ATTN. SPAN FOR LETTERS  (24) 15
DISARRANGED PICTURES           (25) 15
ORAL DIRECTIONS                (26) 15
LIKENESSES AND DIFFERENCES     (27) 15

   SUBTEST MENTAL AGES - RANK ORDERED

ORAL DIRECTIONS 13 -0       CA = 10 -0
FREE ASSOC      10 -11
MOTOR SPEED     10 -5 MED. MA = 8 -9
VERBAL ABS       9 -9
LIKENESS & DIFF  9 -9       IQ = 88
PICTORAL ABS     9 -0
PICTORAL OPP     8 -9
DISARRANGE PICT  8 -9
MEMORY DESIGNS   7 -6
ORAL COM         7 -0
VERBAL OPP       6 -9
VISUAL ATTN LET  5 -9
SOCIAL ADJUST A  5 -3
ORIENTATION      4 -9
AUD ATTN SYL     3 -0
AUD ATTN WORDS  -----
VISUAL ATTN OBJ -----
NUMBER ABILITY  -----
SOCIAL ADJUST B -----
```

COMPREHENSION AND REASONING ANALYSIS
THE CLIENT RECEIVED 5 REASONING
AND COMPREHENSION SUBTEST(S).
2 SUBTESTS SIGNIFICANTLY BELOW MEDIAN.
0 SUBTESTS SIGNIFICANTLY ABOVE MEDIAN.
COMPREHENSION AND REASONING ARE COMPLEX
ABILITIES REQUIRING AN UNDERSTANDING OF
THE PROBLEM, AS WELL AS ANALYZING AND
SYNTHESIZING ABILITIES. THE FINAL SOLU-
TION REQUIRES THAT ALL ELEMENTS FALL
INTO PLACE. WEAKNESSES ON SUBTESTS MAY
BE AN INDICATION OF LEARNING DIFFICUL-
TIES IN GRASPING RELATIONSHIPS IN
ARITHMETIC PROBLEMS, READING COMPREHEN-
SION, HISTORY AND GEOGRAPHY.

PRACTICAL JUDGEMENT
THE CLIENT RECEIVED 4 PRACTICAL
JUDGEMENT SUBTEST(S).
1 SUBTEST SIGNIFICANTLY BELOW MEDIAN.
4 SUBTESTS SIGNIFICANTLY ABOVE MEDIAN.

PRACTICAL JUDGEMENT IS REQUIRED IN A
NUMBER OF LEARNING SITUATIONS. WEAK-
NESSES ON THESE SUBTESTS MAY INDICATE
DIFFICULTY IN VOCATIONAL SUBJECTS,
PHYSICAL TRAINING, AND SCHOOL PROJECTS
IN THE ARTS. PRACTICAL JUDGEMENT IS A
COMPLEX BEHAVIOR REQUIRING EXPERIENCE,
APPROPRIATE MODELING OF THE BEHAVIOR,
AND AN ATMOSPHERE WHERE EXPERIMENTATION
IN MAKING DECISIONS IS ENCOURAGED.
COMPUTER SIMULATIONS SUCH AS OREGON
TRAIL, LUNAR SURVIVAL, THREE MILE ISLAND
AND LEMONAID STAND ARE RECOMMENDED.

VERBAL ABILITY
THE CLIENT RECEIVED 4 VERBAL
ABILITY SUBTEST(S).
1 SUBTEST SIGNIFICANTLY BELOW MEDIAN.
1 SUBTEST SIGNIFICANTLY ABOVE MEDIAN.
VERBAL ABILITY IS AN IMPORTANT ELEMENT
IN INTELLIGENCE. VERBAL ABILITY IS
NECESSARY FOR READING COMPREHENSION
WHICH IS REQUIRED IN ALMOST EVERY
SCHOOL SUBJECT.
A PLANNED PROGRAM OF VOCABULARY DEVELOP-
MENT IS RECOMMENDED FOR STUDENTS WEAK
IN THIS ABILITY. COMPUTERIZED VOCAB-
ULARY BUILDERS WHICH ARE INTERACTIVE
AND REINFORCING ARE RECOMMENDED.
THE STUDENT SHOULD BE ENCOURAGED TO USE
NEW VOCABULARY IN SCHOOL AND AT HOME.

TIME AND SPACE RELATIONSHIPS
THE CLIENT RECEIVED 3 TIME AND
SPACE RELATIONSHIP SUBTEST(S).
1 SUBTEST SIGNIFICANTLY BELOW MEDIAN.
0 SUBTESTS SIGNIFICANTLY ABOVE MEDIAN.
TIME AND SPACE RELATIONSHIPS REFLECT
ONE'S PERCEPTION OR AWARENESS OF WHERE
THEY ARE. WEAKNESSES ON THESE SUBTESTS
MAY INDICATE DIFFICULTIES IN ART, MAP
DRAWING, GEOMETRY, AND HANDWRITING.
REMEDIATION STRATEGIES INCLUDE BODY
AWARENESS EXERCISES AND NON-COMPETITIVE
PHYSICAL FITNESS PROGRAMS. TRACING,
COPYING, DOT-TO-DOT DRAWING, AND PAINT-
BY-NUMBER EXERCISES ARE RECOMMENDED.
THESE CHILDREN SHOULD WEAR A DIGITAL
WATCH AND FREQUENTLY ASKED FOR THE TIME.

NUMBER ABILITY
THE CLIENT RECEIVED 1 NUMBER
ABILITY SUBTEST(S).
0 SUBTESTS SIGNIFICANTLY BELOW MEDIAN.
0 SUBTESTS SIGNIFICANTLY ABOVE MEDIAN.
SIMPLE NUMBER CONCEPTS SUCH AS COUNTING,
IDENTIFYING NUMBERS, AND SEQUENCING ARE
MEASURED BY THESE SUBTESTS. CHILDREN
WEAK IN THIS ABILITY CAN BE STRENGTHENED
BY INSTRUCTION WITH MANIPULATIVE MATER-
IALS WHICH BUILD NUMBER CONCEPTS. USE

OF DOMINOES, COUNTING RODS, NUMBERED
STICKS, AND REAL COINS IS RECOMMENDED.
COUNTING BY 2'S, 3'S, 4'S, ETC., WILL
ASSIST ACQUISITION OF MULTIPLICATION
AND DIVISION BASIC FACTS.
AUDITORY ATTENTIVE ABILITY
THE CLIENT RECEIVED 3 AUDITORY
ATTENTIVE ABILITY SUBTEST(S).
1 SUBTEST SIGNIFICANTLY BELOW MEDIAN.
1 SUBTEST SIGNIFICANTLY ABOVE MEDIAN.
LEARNING IS GREATLY DEPENDENT UPON
LISTENING FOR DIRECTIONS. WEAKNESS IN
THIS ABILITY MAY AFFECT SPELLING WHICH
IS DICTATED. CALLING OUT THE STUDENT'S
NAME PRIOR TO GIVING DIRECTIONS IS
HELPFUL. FREQUENTLY AND RANDOMLY ASKING
THE STUDENT TO REPEAT WHAT WAS HEARD
WILL BUILD AUDITORY ATTENTION. TRY TO
REDUCE AUDITORY DISTRACTIONS AND DELIVER
DIRECTIONS VISUALLY AND AUDITORILY.
SEAT THE STUDENT AWAY FROM NOISE CENTERS
AND IN CLOSE PROXIMITY TO THE EDUCATOR.
INFORCE ONE PERSON TALKING AT A TIME.
VISUAL ATTENTIVE ABILITY
THE CLIENT RECEIVED 6 VISUAL
ATTENTIVE ABILITY SUBTEST(S).
1 SUBTEST SIGNIFICANTLY BELOW MEDIAN.
1 SUBTEST SIGNIFICANTLY ABOVE MEDIAN.

VISUAL ATTENTION CAN BE INCREASED BY
LIMITING VISUAL DISTRACTIONS AND HIGH-
LIGHTING THE STIMULUS MATERIAL. STUDY
CARRELS ARE USUALLY EFFECTIVE.
COMPUTERIZED INSTRUCTION IS PARTICULARLY
EFFECTIVE FOR STUDENTS WITH WEAKNESS IN
THIS ABILITY. PROGRAMMING IN COMPUTER
LANGUAGES SUCH AS LOGO, BASIC, OR PASCAL
IS RECOMMENDED FOR BUILDING THE ABILITY.

MOTOR ABILITY AND PRECISION
THE CLIENT RECEIVED 4 MOTOR
ABILITY SUBTEST(S).
0 SUBTESTS SIGNIFICANTLY BELOW MEDIAN.
1 SUBTEST SIGNIFICANTLY ABOVE MEDIAN.
MOTOR SPEED AND PRECISION DIRECTLY
DIRECTLY AFFECT PERFORMANCE ON TIMED
TESTS AND MANY STANDARDIZED ACHIEVEMENT
MEASURES. WEAKNESS IN THIS ABILITY MAY
HAVE UNFORTUNATE SOCIAL AND EMOTIONAL
EFFECTS. 'WEAKNESS CAN BE CONFIRMED BY
MEASUREMENT OF HANDWRITING RATES. NORMAL
RATE FOR PRINTING LETTERS A-Z IS 80 TO
100 CORRECT LETTERS PER MINUTE IN GRADES
3 - 6. NORMAL WRITING DIGITS 1-10 RATE
IS 100-120 CORRECT DIGITS PER MINUTE IN
GRADES 3 - 6. ACCELERATE HANDWRITING
UNLESS ANXIETY IS EXCESSIVE.

```
                DETROIT-80 MODALITY ANALYSIS
                ANALYSIS OF ALL SUBTESTS
                MEDIAN MENTAL AGE = 8 -9
        WITHIN EXPECTANCY          BELOW EXPECTANCY
        -----------------          ----------------
        18 AUD-MOT 13 -0           12 VIS-MOT 7 -6
        11 AUD-VOC 10 -11          7 AUD-MOT 7 -0
        5 VIS-MOT 10 -5            4 AUD-VOC 6 -9
        2 AUD-VOC 9 -9             16 VIS-VOC 5 -9
        19 AUD-VOC 9 -9            8 AUD-VOC 5 -3
        1 VIS-VOC 9 -0             10 AUD-VOC 4 -9
        3 VIS-MOT 8 -9             13 AUD-VOC 3 -0
        17 VIS-MOT 8 -9

                DETROIT-80 MODALITY ANALYSIS
                AUDITORY SUBTESTS
                MEDIAN AUDITORY MENTAL AGE = 7 -0
        WITHIN EXPECTANCY          BELOW EXPECTANCY
        -----------------          ----------------
        18 AUD-MOT 13 -0           4 AUD-VOC 6 -9
        11 AUD-VOC 10 -11          8 AUD-VOC 5 -3
        2 AUD-VOC 9 -9             10 AUD-VOC 4 -9
        19 AUD-VOC 9 -9            13 AUD-VOC 3 -0
        7 AUD-MOT 7 -0
                VISUAL SUBTESTS
                MEDIAN VISUAL MENTAL AGE = 8 -9
        WITHIN EXPECTANCY          BELOW EXPECTANCY
        -----------------          ----------------
        5 VIS-MOT 10 -5            12 VIS-MOT 7 -6
        1 VIS-VOC 9 -0             16 VIS-VOC 5 -9
        3 VIS-MOT 8 -9
        17 VIS-MOT 8 -9
```

DETROIT-80 DIAGNOSTIC SUMMARY

```
                LONG TERM MEMORY MAY BE DEFICIENT.
                REMEDIATION SHOULD ATTEMPT TO INCREASE
                ATTENTION AND CONCENTRATION BY IDENTIFY-
                ING AND RELIEVING CAUSATIVE FACTORS.
                THE CLIENT'S ATTENTION TO AUDITORY
                STIMULI IS INCREASED WITH SIMULTANEOUS
                VIEWING OR HANDLING OF MATERIAL BEING
                DISCUSSED.  PICTORIAL CUES WILL INCREASE
                RECALL OF SYMBOLIC MATERIAL.:CT=CT+5
                THE CLIENT SHOULD HAVE EXCELLENT MEMOR-
                IZATION SKILLS FOR POETRY, SPEECHES,
                LECTURES, ETC.
                ABILITY TO FILLOW FAMILIAR ORAL DIREC-
                TIONS SHOULD BE INTACT.
                VISUAL INPUT WILL INCREASE THE CLIENT'S
                ABILITY TO REMEMBER AND INTERPRET ORAL
                DIRECTIONS.
                VISUAL MEMORY IS DEFICIENT.  CHECK
                VISUAL FUNCTION AND VISUAL PERCEPTION.
                CHECK FOR EXCESSIVE ANXIETY INTERFEERING
                WITHVISUAL MEMORY.
                MEANINGFUL CONTENT IS NEEDED FOR RECALL
                AND COMPREHENSION.
                THE CLIENT MAY BE WITHDRAWN OR EXPER-
                IENCE POOR CONTACT WITH SURROUNDINGS.
                QUANTITATIVE SUBJECT MATERIAL SHOULD BE
                MORE DIFFICULT THAN LANGUAGE MATERIAL.
                POOR BODY AWARENESS, PROBLEMS IN DIREC-
                TIONALITY, AND POOR ATTENTION TO DETAIL
                MAY BE PRESENT.
```

NAME: Developmental History Report

SUPPLIER: Psychologistics, Inc.
P.O. Box 3896
Indialantic, FL 32903
(305) 727-7900

PRODUCT CATEGORY

Personality

PRIMARY APPLICATIONS

Clinical Assessment/Diagnosis
Educational Evaluation/Planning

SALE RESTRICTIONS American Psychological Association Guidelines

SERVICE TYPE/COST	Type	Available	Cost	Discount
	Mail-In	No		
	Teleprocessing	No		
	Local	Yes	$195.00	

PRODUCT DESCRIPTION

The DEVELOPMENTAL HISTORY REPORT presents an automated structured interview which gathers basic developmental information and generates a written narrative. Information is obtained about areas relevant for a developmental assessment. These areas are as follows: Pregnancy, Birth, Development, Health, Family, Education, and Behavior.

In addition to the narrative report, a section is printed which highlights important responses. Two categories of answers and their corresponding questions are printed in one list. One category consists of clinically significant answers. The second category consists of answers that the respondent indicated a desire to discuss in more detail.

The DEVELOPMENTAL HISTORY REPORT can be administered on the computer or by using a paper-and-pencil format and takes about 30-45 minutes to complete. The respondent is the one who knows the most about the child being evaluated. Software versions are available for the Apple II + , IIe, III and IBM PC computer systems. The price shown is for unlimited usage of the program. This program allows the user to store the report in a text file for additional word processing.

DEVELOPMENTAL HISTORY REPORT

JOHN X. DOE, JR.
Birthdate: 11-01-74
Date of Report: 2-27-84
Age: 10

INTRODUCTION This developmental history was given by Jane R. doe.
Jane R. doe is the natural mother of John. John is a Caucasian boy.
John currently lives with his natural mother and stepfather. He has
2 brothers and 1 sister. John's biological parents were married 1 to
3 years at conception. The natural father does not live with John
now because of divorce. There is a current custody dispute about
John.

PREGNANCY John was his mother's second pregnancy. The pregnancy was
not planned. A miscarriage had occurred before this pregnancy. At
the time of conception, his mother was 20 years of age. His natural
father was 22 years of age. During the pregnancy, the mother had
bleeding, had mild morning nausea and did have major medical
problems. The following occurred during the pregnancy: poor
emotional health. While pregnant, the mother smoked less than 1 pack
of cigarettes a day and drank alcohol on an infrequent social basis.
It was reported that the mother and father used hard drugs before the
pregnancy. The father used drugs during the gestation. The mother
was exposed to radiation before or during gestation. The father was
exposed to neither chemicals nor radiation before the pregnancy.

BIRTH Labor was described as hard. The baby was delivered breech.
The baby's oxygen supply was not endangered during delivery. Forceps
were used. Trouble breathing occurred. The baby was not blue at
birth. John did not have any birth defect. Special medical
attention was necessary. The mother did not have post-natal
complications. The baby was in the hospital for five days. He
weighed about five pounds at birth.

DEVELOPMENT The baby ate well in the first few months. During this
period sleep was a problem. Breathing problems did not occur during
the first few months of life. The mother was the main caretaker
during infancy. Additional caretaking help was available. The baby
did have medical problems at birth that continued. The baby was
described as cranky and hard to please. He cried a lot and seemed
slow to develop. The baby was late for most of the developmental
milestones. He walked alone when older than 15 months. Language
seemed to develop late. Toilet training began later than 3 years of
age. It was a battle. The child had frequent toilet accidents after
3 years of age. He is dry during the day. During the night John
does stay dry. Soiling does not occur during the day. At night
soiling does not occur.

HEALTH With respect to physical injuries, John has never had a
significant head injury. John has had a broken bone. Ingestion of a
poison or medicine has not been a problem. John has had a major
illness. He has never been hospitalized. Ear infections at an early

age did not occur. No problem exists regarding hearing. Vision is not a problem.

FAMILY John's parents had problems in their relationship during the pregnancy, during the child's infancy, and during the child's early childhood. Conflict has taken the form of constant arguing, constant shouting, and threatening to leave. They have been separated. They have been divorced. The mother has remarried. The father has remarried. A brief biological family history revealed a postive history of emotional problems and alcoholism. During John's development, at least one parent took medication for nerves. The child's caretakers reportedly have been accused of abuse or neglect. With respect to separation, the longest John was separated was more than 14 days.

EDUCATION When asked if John had attended Day Care before age three, Jane R. doe reported he had. He did not go to nursery school. John did go to kindergarten. The following discribes John during the early grades: sad. During the first few years of school he had problems with teachers. Currently he does have behavior problems in school. Learning has been a problem. Reading is a problem. He has had special testing for school problems. John has never been placed in an Exceptional Education Program. The child has never been in counseling.

BEHAVIOR John has no trouble with friendships. Setting fires has been a problem in the past. He reportedly does not hallucinate. John has hurt pets or small children. At no time in the past has the child wished to die or inflict self-injury. He has been in trouble because of running away.

EXAMINER

EAR-MARKED AND CLINICALLY SIGNIFICANT ANSWERS
(EAR-MARK = EM & CLINICALLY SIGNIFICANT = CS)

CS 3. THE PEOPLE WHO LIVE IN THE CHILD'S HOME NOW INCLUDE:
natural mother and stepfather
CS 7. HOW LONG WERE THE CHILD'S NATURAL PARENTS MARRIED UNTIL THE
PREGNANCY?
married 1 to 3 years
CS 9. THE NATURAL FATHER DOES NOT LIVE WITH THE CHILD NOW BECAUSE OF

divorce
CS 10. ARE THERE CURRENTLY ANY CUSTODY DISPUTES ABOUT THIS CHILD?
is
CS 11. WAS THIS A PLANNED PREGNANCY?
was not
CS 13. DID ANY OF THE MOTHER'S PREGNANCIES BEFORE THIS ONE END IN
MISCARRIAGE?
A
CS 17. DID THE MOTHER HAVE BLEEDING DURING THE PREGNANCY?
had
CS 19. DURING PREGNANCY DID THE MOTHER HAVE ANY ILLNESSES OR MEDICAL
PROBLEMS?
did
CS 20. WHILE PREGNANT, WHICH OF THESE MEDICATIONS DID THE MOTHER
TAKE?
medicine for nerves
CS 21. WHILE PREGNANT, THE MOTHER SMOKED
less than 1 pack of cigarettes a day
CS 23. DID THE MOTHER OR FATHER USE ANY HARD DRUGS BEFORE THIS
PREGNANCY?
the mother and father
CS 24. DID THE MOTHER OR FATHER USE ANY HARD DRUGS WHILE PREGNANT?
The father
CS 25. COMPLICATIONS OF THIS PREGNANCY INCLUDED:
poor emotional health
CS 26. WAS THE MOTHER EXPOSED TO CHEMICALS OR RADIATION BEFORE OR
DURING PREGNANCY?
radiation
CS 28. LABOR WAS
hard
CS 29. THE BABY WAS BORN
breech
CS 31. WERE FORCEPS USED?
were
CS 32. DID THE BABY HAVE TROUBLE BREATHING AT BIRTH?
Trouble
CS 35. DID THE BABY NEED SPECIAL MEDICAL HELP AT BIRTH?
s
CS 38. BABY WEIGHED HOW MANY POUNDS AT BIRTH?
five pounds
CS 40. IN THE FIRST FEW MONTHS DID THE BABY SLEEP WELL?
was
CS 44. DID THE BABY HAVE MEDICAL PROBLEMS AT BIRTH THAT CONTINUED?
did
CS 45. THE BABY WAS:
cranky and hard to please
CS 46. THE BABY:
cried a lot and seemed slow to develop
CS 47. MOST OF THE BABY'S DEVELOPMENTAL MILESTONES SEEMED TO BE
late
CS 48. THE BABY WALKED ALONE WHEN
walked alone when older than 15 months

196 *psychware*

CS 49. THE BABY'S STARTED TO TALK
late
CS 50. THE BABY'S TOILET TRAINING BEGAN
later than 3 years of age
CS 51. WAS TOILET TRAINING A BATTLE?
was
CS 52. THE CHILD
had frequent toilet accidents after 3 years of age
CS 58. DID THE CHILD EVER HAVE A BROKEN BONE?
has
CS 60. WHAT IS THE LONGEST THE CHILD WAS SEPARATED FROM BOTH PARENTS
AT ONE TIME?
more than 14 days
CS 61. THE PARENTS (CARETAKERS) HAD PROBLEMS IN THEIR RELATIONSHIP
during the pregnancy, during the child's infancy, and during the
child's early childhood
CS 62. THE PARENTS (CARETAKERS) HAD PROBLEMS SUCH AS
constant arguing, constant shouting, and threatening to leave
CS 63. HAVE THE CARETAKERS BEEN LEGALLY SEPARATED DURING THE CHILD'S
LIFE?
have
CS 64. DURING THE CHILD'S LIFE HAVE THE PARENTS (CARETAKERS) BEEN
DIVORCED?
have
CS 65. HAS THE CHILD'S MOTHER BEEN REMARRIED?
has
CS 66. HAS THE CHILD'S FATHER BEEN REMARRIED?
has
CS 68. HAS THE CHILD HAD ANY MAJOR ILLNESSES?
has
CS 71. DID THE CHILD ATTEND DAY CARE BEFORE AGE 3 YEARS
had
CS 74. WHICH OF THE FOLLOWING DESCRIBES THE CHILD IN THE EARLY
GRADES?
sad
CS 75. WHICH OF THE FOLLOWING DESCRIBES THE CHILD IN THE EARLY
GRADES?
had problems with teachers
CS 76. DOES THE CHILD HAVE BEHAVIOR PROBLEMS IN SCHOOL NOW?
does
CS 77. DOES THE CHILD HAVE LEARNING PROBLEMS IN SCHOOL NOW?
has
CS 78. HAS THE CHILD HAD TROUBLE LEARNING TO READ?
is
CS 79. HAS THE CHILD HAD SPECIAL TESTING FOR SCHOOL PROBLEMS?
has
CS 84. DID THE CHILD EVER SET A FIRE?
been a problem in the past
CS 86. DOES THE CHILD HURT PETS OR SMALL CHILDREN?
has
CS 92. BLOOD KINFOLKS HAVE HAD THE FOLLOWING
emotional problems and alcoholism
CS 94. HAS THE CHILD HAD TROUBLE BECAUSE OF
running away
CS 95. DURING THE CHILD'S DEVELOPMENT, A PARENT (CARETAKER) HAS TAKEN
medication for nerves
CS 96. IS THERE ANYTHING THAT HAS NOT BEEN ASKED THAT SHOULD BE
KNOWN?
needs
CS 97. HAVE ANY OF THE CHILD'S CARETAKERS BEEN ACCUSED OF CHILD
NEGLECT OR ABUSE?
have

psychware **197**

NAME: Developmental Profile II

SUPPLIER: Psychological Assessment Resources
P.O. Box 98
Odessa, FL 33556
(813) 977-3395

PRODUCT CATEGORY	PRIMARY APPLICATIONS
Personality	Clinical Assessment/Diagnosis
Cognitive/Ability	Educational Evaluation/Planning

SALE RESTRICTIONS American Psychological Association Guidelines

SERVICE TYPE/COST	Type	Available	Cost	Discount
	Mail-In	No		
	Teleprocessing	No		
	Local	Yes	$180.00	

PRODUCT DESCRIPTION

This program scores the results and generates reports based on the DEVELOPMENTAL PROFILE II. The test is an updated and revised version of the Alpern-Boll Developmental Profile for assessing child development from birth to nine years of age. Five key areas of development are assessed: physical, self-help, socialization, academic, and communication. After the data from the DEVELOPMENTAL PROFILE II scoring form is entered into the computer, the user has the option of printing one of three interpretive reports: the Adaptive Age Report, the Teacher's Report, or the Parent's Report. Results of this test serve as a measure of the child's existing skills and development with minimal bias arising as a function of sex, race, and socioeconomic status. The profile can also be used to establish a child's eligibility for special programs, to develop Individual Education Plans, and to identify children experiencing developmental lags, as part of the requirements specified in P.L. 94-142.

Software is available for the Apple II + and IIe microcomputer sytems. The program requires 32K and a 132-column printer for execution.

PAR software

P.O. Box 98 / Odessa, Florida 33556

Telephone: (813) 977-3395

Apple   569-CP

DEVELOPMENTAL PROFILE II MICROCOMPUTER SYSTEM

CLIENT: TYLER ALLEN   SCHOOL: ASPEN ELEMENTARY

BIRTHDATE: JANUARY 15 1978   AGE AT TIME OF INTERVIEW: 5-2

GRADE: KINDERGARDEN   INTERVIEWER: GERALD ALPERN

DATE OF INTERVIEW: MARCH 24 1983   INTERVIEWEE: SHIRLEY ALLEN

                                       RELATIONSHIP TO CHILD: MOTHER

SUMMARY OF PURPOSE

THE DEVELOPMENTAL PROFILE II (ALPERN, BOLL, & SHEARER; PSYCHOLOGICAL DEVELOPMENT
PUBLICATIONS, 1980) IS 'AN INVENTORY OF SKILLS DESIGNED TO ASSESS A CHILD'S
DEVELOPMENT FROM BIRTH THROUGH AGE NINE'. IT IS PARTICULARLY SUITED FOR MEASUR-
ING THOSE BEHAVIORS THAT ARE TYPICALLY LEARNED BY THE CHILD BEFORE HE/SHE ENTERS
SCHOOL AND/OR THOSE BEHAVIORS THAT ARE USUALLY LEARNED OUTSIDE OF THE SCHOOL
SETTING (I.E., SO-CALLED 'ADAPTIVE' BEHAVIORS). THE ITEMS REFLECT DEVELOPMENT
IN FIVE AREAS: PHYSICAL, SELF-HELP, SOCIAL, ACADEMIC, AND COMMUNICATION.

FOR EACH AREA ADMINISTERED, TYLER'S OBTAINED DEVELOPMENTAL AGE IS
GIVEN IN MONTHS AS WELL AS IN YEARS AND MONTHS. FURTHER, THE DIFFERENCE BETWEEN
HIS CHRONOLOGICAL AGE AND OBTAINED DEVELOPMENTAL AGE IS LISTED ALONG WITH THE
PERCENTAGE OF DEVELOPMENT REFLECTED BY THIS DISCREPENCY. FOR INSTANCE, IF
HIS CHRONOLOGICAL AGE WERE 98 MONTHS (8 YEARS - 2 MONTHS) AND HE OBTAINED
A DEVELOPMENTAL AGE ON THE PHYSICAL SCALE OF 77 MONTHS, THEN THE DISCREPANCY
WOULD BE -21 MONTHS (1 YEAR - 9 MONTHS) OR ROUGHLY 21% (21 DIVIDED BY 98) BELOW
AGE EXPECTANCY FOR PHYSICAL DEVELOPMENT.

TO AID IN THE IDENTIFICATION OF POSSIBLE DEFICITS IN ADAPTIVE BEHAVIOR, THE
REFERRAL GUIDELINE CATEGORY PROVIDES A RULE OF THUMB ESTIMATE OF THE DEGREE
(I.E., NORMAL DEVELOPMENT, BORDERLINE, SIGNIFICANT DELAY) OR ANY CHRONOLOGICAL
AGE - DEVELOPMENTAL AGE DISCREPENCIES. (NOTE: THESE CLINICAL IMPRESSIONS ARE
CALCULATED AND REPORTED IN ACCORDANCE WITH THE GUIDELINES DESCRIBED IN THE
DPII MANUAL).

IT IS EMPHASIZED THAT THE INFORMATION PRESENTED HERE ON TYLER IS
DEPENDANT UPON THE ACCURACY OF THE INFORMATION OBTAINED IN THE ADAPTIVE INTER-
VIEW AND, AS SUCH, SHOULD BE CONSIDERED AS ONLY ESTIMATES AND NOT AS ABSOLUTE
DETERMINATIONS OF ADAPTIVE BEHAVIOR.

TYLER'S OBTAINED ADAPTIVE AGES AND RELATED INFORMATION PER AREA
IS PRESENTED BELOW:

AREA	DEVELOPMENTAL AGE (MONTHS)	DEVELOPMENTAL AGE (YEARS-MONTHS)	CHRONOLOGICAL AGE-DEVELOPMENTAL AGE DISCREPANCY	PERCENT OF DEVELOPMENT REFLECTED	REFERRAL GUIDE LINES
PHYSICAL	54	4-6	-8 MO(0-8)	-10%	BORDERLINE
SELF-HELP	46	3-10	-16 MO(1-4)	-20%	SIGNIFICANT DELAY
SOCIAL	64	5-4	+2 MO(0-2)	+2%	NORMAL OR ABOVE
ACADEMIC	40	3-4	-22 MO(1-10)	-28%	SIGNIFICANT DELAY
COMMUNICATION	50	4-2	-12 MO(1-0)	-15%	BORDERLINE

AVERAGE OF SCALES	50	4-2	-12 MO(1-0)	-15%	SEE NOTE 3 BELOW

NOTE 3: THE DPII TABLES DO NOT ALLOW FOR THE DETERMINATION OF A REFERRAL GUIDELINE FOR OVERALL ADAPTIVE DEVELOPMENT.
AN ESTIMATE OF OVERALL ADAPTIVE SKILLS MAY BE OBTAINED BY REFERRING TO THE PERCENTAGE OF DEVELOPMENT REFLECTED.

THIS IS AN OPTIONAL LETTER WHICH MAY OR MAY NOT BE PRINTED OUT TO ACCOMPANY THE PARENT REPORT

MARCH 24, 1983

MS SHIRLEY ALLEN
118 EAST LUPINE DR.
ASPEN, COLORADO 81611

DEAR MS ALLEN,

ENCLOSED IS A LIST OF SOME OF THE THINGS YOU CAN WORK ON AT HOME WITH TYLER.
IF YOU CAN TEACH HIM JUST A FEW OF THESE THINGS, IT WOULD HELP HIM A GREAT
DEAL IN SCHOOL.

THE ITEMS LISTED ARE THINGS YOU DO AROUND THE HOUSE ALL OF THE TIME. YOU DO
NOT HAVE TO BUY ANYTHING OR MAKE ANY SPECIAL TRIPS. ALL YOU NEED IS TO SPEND
SOME TIME WITH TYLER TO MAKE SURE HE LEARNS THE THINGS HE NEEDS TO.

PLEASE CALL ME IF YOU HAVE ANY QUESTIONS ABOUT THIS LIST OR HOW YOU CAN GO
ABOUT TEACHING TYLER THESE THINGS.

SINCERELY,

GERALD ALPERN

PSYCHOLOGIST

200 *psychware*

PARENT REPORT PRINTOUT

PHYSICAL DEVELOPMENT

PHYSICAL DEVELOPMENT DEALS WITH HOW THE BODY GROWS AND HOW WELL COORDINATED A CHILD IS.

THINGS THAT TYLER COULD USE SOME HELP ON:

1. CAN HOP FORWARD ON ONE FOOT FOR A DISTANCE OF AT LEAST 10 FEET WITHOUT HAVING TO STOP AND START AGAIN.
2. CAN MAKE A SNOW OR MUDBALL WHICH WILL STAY TOGETHER AND WHICH THE CHILD CAN THROW AT LEAST 8 FEET.
3. CAN PLAY HOPSCOTHCH OR A SIMILAR GAME WHICH REQUIRES SKILLED HOPPING.
4. CAN ROLLER SKATE; SKATEBOARD; OR ICE SKATE FOR AT LEAST 10 FEET WITHOUT FALLING.
5. CAN CUT OUT A 4-INCH PICTURE OF AN ANIMAL OR HUMAN WITHOUT BEING MORE THAN 1/4 INCH OFF ANYWHERE.
6. CAN SKIP ROPE AT LEAST FOUR TIMES WHILE HOLDING BOTH ENDS OF THE ROPE.

SELF-HELP DEVELOPMENT

SELF-HELP DEVELOPMENT DEALS WITH HOW WELL A CHILD CAN TAKE CARE OF HIM/HERSELF IN SUCH THINGS AS DRESSING, FEEDING, AND WASHING.

THINGS THAT TYLER COULD USE SOME HELP ON:

1. PUTS TOYS AWAY NEATLY WHEN ASKED TO DO SO.
2. FIXES A BOWL OF DRY CEREAL WITHOUT HELP.
3. USUALLY USES A TABLE KNIFE FOR SPREADING BUTTER OR JAM ON BREAD OR CRACKERS.
4. ANSWERS THE TELEPHONE AND TEL... THE PERSON CALLED THE RIGHT MESSAGE.
5. IS ABLE TO FIX A SANDWICH (INCLUDES GETTING RIGHT FOODS AND PUTTING THEM TOGETHER).
6. USES A KNIFE CORRECTLY FOR CUTTING FOODS (SOME HELP MAY BE NEEDED FOR UNGROUND MEATS SUCH AS STEAK).
7. BRUSHES OR COMBS HAIR WELL ENOUGH THAT ADULT HELP IS NOT USUALLY NEEDED.
8. DOES HOUSEHOLD CHORES AT LEAST ONCE A WEEK WHICH DO NOT REQUIRE REDOING BY AN ADULT.

SOCIAL DEVELOPMENT

SOCIAL DEVELOPMENT DEALS WITH HOW THE CHILD GETS ALONG WITH OTHER PEOPLE.

THINGS THAT TYLER COULD USE SOME HELP ON:

1. SHOWS AWARENESS OF HOW OTHER FEEL BY SAYING THINGS LIKE 'HE IS MAD'; 'SHE IS ANGRY'; 'HE IS AFRAID' OR 'YOU ARE CRANKY'.
2. PLAYS TABLE GAMES SUCH AS CHECKERS; OLD MAID; CANDYLAND OR LOTTO WITH A FRIEND OF ABOUT THE SAME AGE.
3. HAS AT LEAST ONE REAL CHORE (LIKE RAKING LEAVES; MAKING A BED; CLEANING OR DUSTING) WHICH IS DONE AT LEAST WEEKLY.
4. KNOWS THAT VOTING IS A WAY OF DECIDING SOMETHING.

ACADEMIC DEVELOPMENT

ACADEMIC DEVELOPMENT DEALS WITH A LOT OF THOSE THINGS A CHILD NEEDS TO BE ABLE TO DO SO THAT THEY CAN DO A GOOD JOB IN SCHOOL.

THINGS THAT TYLER COULD USE SOME HELP ON:

1. CAN COUNT SIX THINGS CORRECTLY.
2. KNOWS THAT DIFFERENT ACTIVITIES OCCUR AT DIFFERENT TIMES OF THE DAY (LIKE BREAKFAST IS IN THE MORNING).
3. DRAWS A CROSS AFTER AN ADULT MAKES ONE.
4. WHEN ASKED TO DRAW A PERSON; DRAWS A HEAD THAT LOOKS LIKE A HEAD AND AT LEAST ONE OTHER BODY PART.
5. TELLS A PENNY FROM A NICKLE AND A DIME BY NAMING OR POINTING TO THE PENNY WHEN IT IS NAMED.
6. OFFERS REAL WORD RHYMES TO SIMPLE WORDS SUCH AS 'TREE' OR 'CAP'.
7. DRAWS A PICTURE OF A PERSON THAT LOOKS LIKE A PERSON (INCLUDING A TRUNK; ARMS AND LEGS).
8. COPIES OR DRAWS A TRIANGLE.
9. TAKES OUT 13 OBJECTS FROM A GROUP OF 20 WHEN ASKED.
10. GIVES HER/HIS ADDRESS WHEN ASKED (INCLUDING ALL NECESSARY MAILING INFORMATION).
11. CAN ANSWER SIMPLE QUESTIONS ABOUT THE MAIN FACTS (LIKE NAMES OR EVENTS) OF A 10 SENTENCE STORY TOLD TO HIM/HER.

COMMUNICATION DEVELOPMENT

COMMUNICATION DEVELOPMENT DEALS WITH HOW WELL A CHILD CAN UNDERSTAND OTHER PEOPLE AND HOW WELL OTHER PEOPLE CAN UNDERSTAND THE CHILD. THE USE AND UNDERSTANDING OF SPOKEN, WRITTEN, AND GESTURE LANGUAGE.

THINGS THAT TYLER COULD USE SOME HELP ON:

1. TELLS PEOPLE (BY SPEAKING OR HOLDING UP FINGERS) HIS/HER AGE THIS YEAR; AGE LAST YEAR; AND AGE NEXT YEAR.
2. SOMETIMES ASKS THE MEANING OF A WORD AND THEN USES THAT WORD IN HER/HIS OWN SPEECH.
3. TELLS (WITHOUT USING PICTURES FOR HELP) A STORY SUCH AS 'LITTLE RED RIDING HOOD' OR 'THE THREE BEARS'.
4. SOMETIMES USES LOGIC ABOUT CAUSE AND EFFECT (WORDS LIKE 'BECAUSE' OR 'SINCE' MAY BE USED).
5. RECOGNIZES AT LEAST FIVE WRITTEN WORDS AND SHOWS UNDERSTANDING OF WHAT THEY MEAN.
6. DIALS A TELEPHONE NUMBER OR ASKS THE OPERATOR FOR A NUMBER CORRECTLY WHEN WANTING TO CALL SOMEONE.
7. RECITES THE ENTIRE 'PLEDGE OF ALLEGIANCE' OR SOMETHING LIKE IT (LIKE A POEM OR FORMAL PRAYER OF AT LEAST 25 WORDS).

THIS IS
AN EXAMPLE
OF THE TEACHER REPORT
PRINTOUT

ITEM LISTING FOR

DEVELOPMENTAL PROFILE II

CLIENT: TYLER ALLEN

BIRTHDATE: JANUARY 15 1978

GRADE: KINDERGARDEN

DATE OF INTERVIEW: MARCH 24 1983

SCHOOL: ASPEN ELEMENTARY

AGE AT TIME OF INTERVIEW: 5-2

INTERVIEWER: GERALD ALPERN

INTERVIEWEE: SHIRLEY ALLEN

RELATIONSHIP TO CHILD: MOTHER

SUMMARY OF PURPOSE

THE DEVELOPMENTAL PROFILE II (ALPERN, BOLL, & SHEARER; PSYCHOLOGICAL DEVELOPMENT
PUBLICATIONS, 1980) IS 'AN INVENTORY OF SKILLS DESIGNED TO ASSESS A CHILD'S
DEVELOPMENT FROM BIRTH THROUGH AGE NINE'. IT IS PARTICULARLY SUITED FOR MEASUR-
ING THOSE BEHAVIORS THAT ARE TYPICALLY LEARNED BY THE CHILD BEFORE HE/SHE ENTERS
SCHOOL AND/OR THOSE BEHAVIORS THAT ARE USUALLY LEARNED OUTSIDE OF THE SCHOOL
SETTING (I.E., SO-CALLED 'ADAPTIVE' BEHAVIORS). THE ITEMS REFLECT DEVELOPMENT
IN FIVE AREAS: PHYSICAL, SELF-HELP, SOCIAL, ACADEMIC, AND COMMUNICATION.

A LISTING OF THE ITEMS FOR WHICH THE CHILD HAS REPORTEDLY DEMONSTRATED MASTERY
AND NON-MASTERY IS PRESENTED PER EACH DEVELOPMENTAL AREA BELOW:

PHYSICAL DEVELOPMENT

PHYSICAL DEVELOPMENT INVOLVES THOSE ABILITIES REQUIRING LARGE AND SMALL MUSCLE
COORDINATION, STRENGTH, STAMINA, FLEXIBILITY, AND SEQUENTIAL CONTROL SKILLS.

BEHAVIORS WHICH TYLER HAS REPORTEDLY MASTERED:

1. USES SCISSORS WITH ONE HAND TO CUT (NOT TEAR) PAPER OR CLOTH (OTHER HAND MAY BE USED TO HOLD MATERIAL).(P-16)
2. CAN HOP FORWARD ON ONE FOOT WITHOUT SUPPORT FOR AT LEAST FIVE FEET.(P-17)
3. USUALLY WALKS UPSTAIRS AND DOWNSTAIRS BY PLACING ONLY ONE FOOT ON EACH STAIR (RAILING OR WALL MAY BE USED).(P-18)
4. CAN ACCURATELY THROW ANY SIZE BALL TO AN ADULT STANDING FIVE FEET AWAY.(P-19)
5. CAN RELEASE LATCH AND OPEN AN INSIDE DOOR.(P-20)
6. CAN USE SCISSORS TO CUT OUT A PRINTED CIRCLE (SILVER DOLLAR SIZE) WITHOUT BEING MORE THAN 1/4 INCH OFF ANYWHERE.(P-21)
7. CAN CATCH A BALL (ANY SIZE) THROWN BY AN ADULT WHO IS STANDING FIVE FEET AWAY AT LEAST 50% OF THE TIME.(P-22)
8. CAN JUMP ROPE AT LEAST TWICE OR CAN JUMP OVER SEVERAL 8 INCH HIGH OBJECTS WITHOUT STOPPING.(P-24)
9. CAN USE A KEY TO OPEN AND UNLOCK A SMALL PADLOCK.(P-25)

BEHAVIORS WHICH TYLER REPORTEDLY HAS NOT MASTERED:

1. CAN HOP FORWARD ON ONE FOOT FOR A DISTANCE OF AT LEAST 10 FEET WITHOUT HAVING TO STOP AND START AGAIN.(P-23)
2. CAN MAKE A SNOW OR MUDBALL WHICH WILL STAY TOGETHER AND WHICH THE CHILD CAN THROW AT LEAST 8 FEET.(P-26)
3. CAN PLAY HOPSCOTHCH OR A SIMILAR GAME WHICH REQUIRES SKILLED HOPPING.(P-27)
4. CAN ROLLER SKATE; SKATEBOARD; OR ICE SKATE FOR AT LEAST 10 FEET WITHOUT FALLING.(P-28)
5. CAN CUT OUT A 4-INCH PICTURE OF AN ANIMAL OR HUMAN WITHOUT BEING MORE THAN 1/4 INCH OFF ANYWHERE.(P-29)
6. CAN SKIP ROPE AT LEAST FOUR TIMES WHILE HOLDING BOTH ENDS OF THE ROPE.(P-30)

SELF-HELP DEVELOPMENT

SELF-HELP DEVELOPMENT REFLECTS THE ABILITY TO COPE INDEPENDENTLY WITH THE
ENVIRONMENT WITH SUCH TASKS AS EATING, DRESSING, AND WORKING. IN OTHER WORDS,
SELF-HELP INVOLVES MANY OF THOSE BEHAVIORS WHICH ARE NECESSARY IN ORDER FOR AN
INDIVIDUAL TO CARE FOR HIM/HERSELF AND OTHERS.

BEHAVIORS WHICH TYLER REPORTEDLY HAS MASTERED:

1. PUTS ON HIS/HER OWN COAT WITHOUT HELP (BUTTONING NOT REQUIRED).(SH-16)
2. UNDOES LARGE BUTTONS; SNAPS; SHOELACES; AND ZIPPERS.(SH-17)
3. PUTS ON HIS/HER SHOES (TYING OR FASTENING NOT REQUIRED;DO NOT HAVE TO BE ON CORRECT FEET).(SH-18)
4. CARES FOR HIS/HER OWN TOILETING NEEDS WITHOUT HELP (INCLUDES UNDRESSING; WIPING; AND DRESSING).(SH-19)
5. HAS NO MORE THAN ONE TOILETING ACCIDENT PER MONTH (INCLUDES WAKING AND SLEEPING).(SH-20)
6. USUALLY WASHES AND DRIES FACE AND HANDS WITHOUT HELP.(SH-21)
7. COMPLETELY DRESSES EXCEPT FOR SHOELACE TYING AND DIFFICULT FASTENINGS.(SH-22)

BEHAVIORS WHICH TYLER REPORTEDLY HAS NOT MASTERED:

1. PUTS TOYS AWAY NEATLY WHEN ASKED TO DO SO.(SH-23)
2. FIXES A BOWL OF DRY CEREAL WITHOUT HELP.(SH-24)
3. USUALLY USES A TABLE KNIFE FOR SPREADING BUTTER OR JAM ON BREAD OR CRACKERS.(SH-25)
4. ANSWERS THE TELEPHONE AND TELLS THE PERSON CALLED THE RIGHT MESSAGE.(SH-26)
5. IS ABLE TO FIX A SANDWICH (INCLUDES GETTING RIGHT FOODS AND PUTTING THEM TOGETHER).(SH-27)
6. USES A KNIFE CORRECTLY FOR CUTTING FOODS (SOME HELP MAY BE NEEDED FOR UNGROUND MEATS SUCH AS STEAK).(SH-28)
7. BRUSHES OR COMBS HAIR WELL ENOUGH THAT ADULT HELP IS NOT USUALLY NEEDED.(SH-29)
8. DOES HOUSEHOLD CHORES AT LEAST ONCE A WEEK WHICH DO NOT REQUIRE REDOING BY AN ADULT.(SH-30)

SOCIAL DEVELOPMENT

SOCIAL DEVELOPMENT RELATES TO INTERPERSONAL RELATIONSHIP ABILITIES. THE
CHILD'S EMOTIONAL NEEDS FOR PEOPLE, AS WELL AS THE MANNER IN WHICH THE CHILD
RELATES TO FRIENDS, RELATIVES, AND VARIOUS ADULTS EXEMPLIFY THE SKILLS WHICH
PROMOTE ADEQUATE INTERPERSONAL RELATIONS.

BEHAVIORS WHICH TYLER REPORTEDLY HAS MASTERED

1. FOLLOWS THE RULES AND DIRECTIONS IN A GAME RUN BY AN ADULT.(S-16)
2. IS ABLE TO TAKE TURNS AND WILL ALLOW SOMEONE ELSE TO GO FIRST AT LEAST 75% OF THE TIME.(S-17)
3. KNOWS WHAT A TOY CAN AND CANNOT AND USES THEM IN THE RIGHT WAY (LIKE HE/SHE DOES NOT USE A DOLL FOR HAMMERING).(S-18)
4. PLAYS GAMES (LIKE TAG; HOPSCOTCH; HIDE-AND-SEEK) WITHOUT NEEDING CONSTANT ATTENTION BY AN ADULT.(S-19)
5. IS ABLE TO KEEP WORKING FOR AT LEAST 30 MINUTES WITH A SIMILAR-AGE CHILD ON A SINGLE TASK (LIKE BLOCK BUILDING).(S-20)
6. ASKS PERMISSION TO USE OTHER PEOPLE'S THINGS INSTEAD OF JUST TAKING THEM AND KNOWS THAT THE OWNER HAS FIRST CHOICE.(S-21)
7. DRAWS A PERSON (INCLUDING A HEAD AND A BODY OR A HEAD AND EYES; NOSE OR MOUTH) SO THAT AN ADULT CAN TELL WHAT WAS DRAWN.(S-22)
8. IS ALLOWED TO PLAY IN NEIGHBORHOOD WITHOUT BEING WATCHED BY AN ADULT (DOES NOT INCLUDE CROSSING THE STREET).(S-23)
9. KNOWS AND USES (ALTHOUGH NOT ALWAYS) THE TERMS 'THANK YOU'; 'PLEASE' AND YOU'RE WELCOME' AT THE RIGHT TIMES.(S-24)
10. HAS ASKED QUESTIONS ABOUT HIS/HER OWN BODY; HEARTBEAT; WHERE FOOD GOES OR SEXUAL DIFFERENCES.(S-25)
11. VISITS AND PLAYS AT A SIMILAR-AGED FRIEND'S HOUSE WITHOUT NEED TO BE WATCHED BY AN ADULT (EXCEPT FOR AN HOURLY CHECK).(S-28)

BEHAVIORS WHICH TYLER REPORTEDLY HAS NOT MASTERED:

1. SHOWS AWARENESS OF HOW OTHER FEEL BY SAYING THINGS LIKE 'HE IS MAD'; 'SHE IS ANGRY'; 'HE IS AFRAID' OR 'YOU ARE CRANKY'.(S-26)
2. TELLS SECRETS TO A FRIEND AND DOES NOT TELL THEM TO PARENTS OR OTHER ADULTS.(S-27)
3. PLAYS TABLE GAMES SUCH AS CHECKERS; OLD MAID; CANDYLAND OR LOTTO WITH A FRIEND OF ABOUT THE SAME AGE.(S-29)
4. HAS AT LEAST ONE REAL CHORE (LIKE RAKING LEAVES; MAKING A BED; CLEANING OR DUSTING) WHICH IS DONE AT LEAST WEEKLY.(S-30)
5. KNOWS THAT VOTING IS A WAY OF DECIDING SOMETHING.(S-31)

ACADEMIC DEVELOPMENT

ACADEMIC DEVELOPMENT REFLECTS INTELLECTUAL ABILITIES BY ASSESSING, AT THE YOUNGER PRE-SCHOOL LEVEL, THE DEVELOPMENT OF SKILLS PREREQUISITE TO SCHOLASTIC FUNCTIONING AND, AT OLDER PRE-SCHOOL AND SCHOOL AGE LEVELS, ACTUAL ACADEMIC FUNCTIONING.

BEHAVIORS WHICH TYLER REPORTEDLY HAS MASTERED:

1. UNDERSTANDS THE CONCEPT OF THREE SO THAT WHEN ASKED; WILL HAND YOU THREE PIECES FROM A BOWL OF CANDY. (A-13)
2. COPIES A CIRCULAR FORM WITH A PENCIL. (A-14)
3. POINTS CORRECTLY TO AT LEAST TWO COLORS WHEN ASKED. (A-15)
4. DRAWS OR COPIES A SQUARE. (A-21)

BEHAVIORS WHICH TYLER REPORTEDLY HAS NOT MASTERED:

1. CAN COUNT SIX THINGS CORRECTLY. (A-16)
2. KNOWS THAT DIFFERENT ACTIVITIES OCCUR AT DIFFERENT TIMES OF THE DAY (LIKE BREAKFAST IS IN THE MORNING). (A-17)
3. DRAWS A CROSS AFTER AN ADULT MAKES ONE. (A-18)
4. WHEN ASKED TO DRAW A PERSON; DRAWS A HEAD THAT LOOKS LIKE A HEAD AND AT LEAST ONE OTHER BODY PART. (A-19)
5. TELLS A PENNY FROM A NICKLE AND A DIME BY NAMING OR POINTING TO THE PENNY WHEN IT IS NAMED. (A-20)
6. OFFERS REAL WORD RHYMES TO SIMPLE WORDS SUCH AS 'TREE' OR 'CAP'. (A-22)
7. DRAWS A PICTURE OF A PERSON THAT LOOKS LIKE A PERSON (INCLUDING A TRUNK; ARMS AND LEGS). (A-23)
8. COPIES OR DRAWS A TRIANGLE. (A-24)
9. TAKES OUT 13 OBJECTS FROM A GROUP OF 20 WHEN ASKED. (A-25)
10. GIVES HER/HIS ADDRESS WHEN ASKED (INCLUDING ALL NECESSARY MAILING INFORMATION). (A-26)
11. CAN ANSWER SIMPLE QUESTIONS ABOUT THE MAIN FACTS (LIKE NAMES OR EVENTS) OF A 10 SENTENCE STORY TOLD TO HIM/HER. (A-27)

COMMUNICATION DEVELOPMENT

COMMUNICATION DEVELOPMENT REFLECTS EXPRESSIVE AND RECEPTIVE COMMUNICATION SKILLS WITH BOTH VERBAL AND NONVERBAL LANGUAGE. IN OTHER WORDS, IT RELFECTS THE USE AND UNDERSTANDING OF SPOKEN, WRITTEN, AND GESTURE LANGUAGE.

BEHAVIORS WHICH TYLER REPORTEDLY HAS MASTERED:

1. USUALLY OFFERS BOTH FIRST AND LAST NAMES WHEN ADULTS ASK FOR HIS/HER WHOLE NAME. (C-19)
2. TELLS AN APPROPRIATE STORY BY LOOKING AT PICTURES IN A BOOK. (C-20)
3. HAS TALKED APPROPRIATELY WITH SOMEONE ON THE TELEPHONE. (C-21)
4. HAS SUNG A SONG OF AT LEAST 30 WORDS WITHOUT HELP. (C-22)
5. IS ABLE TO BUY SOMETHING IN A STORE WITHOUT HELP. (C-23)

BEHAVIORS WHICH TYLER REPORTEDLY HAS NOT MASTERED:

1. TELLS PEOPLE (BY SPEAKING OR HOLDING UP FINGERS) HIS/HER AGE THIS YEAR; AGE LAST YEAR; AND AGE NEXT YEAR. (C-24)
2. SOMETIMES ASKS THE MEANING OF A WORD AND THEN USES THAT WORD IN HER/HIS OWN SPEECH. (C-25)
3. TELLS (WITHOUT USING PICTURES FOR HELP) A STORY SUCH AS 'LITTLE RED RIDING HOOD' OR 'THE THREE BEARS'. (C-26)
4. SOMETIMES USES LOGIC ABOUT CAUSE AND EFFECT (WORDS LIKE 'BECAUSE' OR 'SINCE' MAY BE USED). (C-27)
5. RECOGNIZES AT LEAST FIVE WRITTEN WORDS AND SHOWS UNDERSTANDING OF WHAT THEY MEAN. (C-28)
6. DIALS A TELEPHONE NUMBER OR ASKS THE OPERATOR FOR A NUMBER CORRECTLY WHEN WANTING TO CALL SOMEONE. (C-29)
7. RECITES THE ENTIRE 'PLEDGE OF ALLEGIANCE' OR SOMETHING LIKE IT (LIKE A POEM OR FORMAL PRAYER OF AT LEAST 25 WORDS). (C-30)

THIS CONCLUDES THE TEACHER REPORT ·

NAME: Digit-Digit Attention Test

SUPPLIER: Robert J. Sbordone, Ph.D., Inc.
8840 Warner Ave. Suite 301
Fountain Valley, CA 92708
(714) 841-6293

PRODUCT CATEGORY

Cognitive/Ability

PRIMARY APPLICATIONS

Behavioral Medicine
Clinical Assessment/Diagnosis

SALE RESTRICTIONS American Psychological Association Guidelines

SERVICE TYPE/COST	Type	Available	Cost	Discount
	Mail-In	No		
	Teleprocessing	No		
	Local	Yes	$125.00	

PRODUCT DESCRIPTION

The DIGIT-DIGIT ATTENTION TEST provides fully automatic serial testing of complex attention skills utilizing randomly generated test stimuli. It is intended to be used with normal, brain-injured, and cognitively-impaired patients.

The program provides user-friendly, on-line testing that is understandable by all levels of users with little or no supervision required. Instructions for taking the test are provided on-line by the program to simplify administration and insure that the examinee understands the test procedure.

Examinee records (including biographic data and test scores) are automatically maintained for up to 900 examinees. The program also generates various statistical and trend analyses.

The program operates on the Apple II + , IIe, III or Apple-compatible hardware and on the IBM PC-100 microcomputer system. No special computer knowledge is needed. The software comes with an instruction manual.

NAME: Dissimulation Index

SUPPLIER: PSYCH Systems, Inc.
600 Reisterstown Road
Baltimore, MD 21208
(800) 368-3366

PRODUCT CATEGORY

Interest/Attitudes
Personality

PRIMARY APPLICATIONS

Clinical Assessment/Diagnosis

SALE RESTRICTIONS Qualified Professional

SERVICE TYPE/COST	Type	Available	Cost	Discount
	Mail-In	No		
	Teleprocessing	No		
	Local	Yes	See Below	

PRODUCT DESCRIPTION

The DISSUMULATION INDEX assesses a person's ability to undergo on-line testing and determines the likelihood that the test results will be valid. The 21-item test is designed for use with individuals 16 years of age and older and requires approximately five minutes to administer. This screening tool has items from the MMPI validity scales as well as newly constructed items.

Psych Systems programs operate on the IBM PC-XT, COMPAQ Plus, Dec Professional 350, and most DEC PDP-11 systems. Various hardware/software configurations are available directly from Psych Systems, with single-user systems starting at approximately $12,000. A per test fee also applies.

222-22-2222 Jonathan Doe   32 yr old white male   16-Feb-84

```
---------------------------------
|        |                       |
|   Q1   |  Dissimulation Index  |
|        |                       |
---------------------------------
```

The subject has not exceeded the cutoff score on the dissimulation
index.

                        Critical Items

(T) Everybody lies--The only difference is that some
    don't get caught.
(T) When these tests get too long, I sometimes just go down
    the rows marking answers randomly.

Score: 2

The computer program generating this report was designed by Psych
Systems, Inc., Baltimore, Maryland 21208. Copyright (C) 1984 by
Psych Systems, Inc. All rights reserved.

NAME: Dyadic Adjustment Scale: Computer Version

SUPPLIER: Psychological Assessment Resources
P.O. Box 98
Odessa, FL 33556
(813) 977-3395

PRODUCT CATEGORY	PRIMARY APPLICATIONS
Personality	Personal/Marriage/Family Counseling

SALE RESTRICTIONS American Psychological Association Guidelines

SERVICE TYPE/COST	Type	Available	Cost	Discount
	Mail-In	No		
	Teleprocessing	No		
	Local	Yes	$3.00	

PRODUCT DESCRIPTION

The DYADIC ADJUSTMENT SCALE is a self-report measure of relationship adjustment. Extensive research has supported the use of this measure in determining the degree of relationship dissatisfaction couples are experiencing. Many of the potentially sexist items from the Lock-Wallace Marital Adjustment Scale were avoided in the development of this test.

This computer program allows the direct administration of the test by computer to each partner or responses can be directly entered from the keyboard. Four factored sub-scales are then scored: (1) Dyadic Satisfaction, (2) Dyadic Cohesion, (3) Dyadic Consensus, and (4) Affective Expression. Scores below 100 are indicative of relationship distress. Additional interpretive information is also provided. The program allows data to be saved for further reference or for research purposes.

The software is intended for use on the Apple II + and IIe microcomputer systems. The price shown above is the cost-per-test when diskettes are purchased in quantities of 50 administrations (minimum purchase).

PARsoftware

P.O. Box 98 / Odessa, Florida 33556

Telephone: (813) 977-3395

```
****************
*              *
*  DAS SUMMARY  *
*              *
****************
```

NAME: REICH   FILE #: 1001

BIRTHDATE: 01/07/50   AGE: 34

SEX: F   EDUCATION: 16

THERAPIST: DR.   DATE: 05/01/84

```
DYADIC CONSENSUS          47
--------------------------------
DYADIC SATISFACTION       41
--------------------------------
AFFECTIONAL EXPRESSION    10
--------------------------------
DYADIC COHESION           15
================================
DYADIC ADJUSTMENT        113
--------------------------------
```

```
                        ITEMS LISTING
                        =============


        DYADIC CONSENSUS:

                        FAMILY FINANCES    (3)
                        MATTERS OF RECREATION    (3)
                        RELIGIOUS MATTERS    (5)
                        FRIENDS    (4)
                        PROPER BEHAVIOR    (3)
                        PHILOSOPHY OF LIFE    (4)
                        PARENTS OR IN-LAWS    (4)
                        GOALS    (4)
                        TIME TOGETHER    (3)
                        MAKING DECISIONS    (4)
                        HOUSEHOLD TASKS    (3)
                        LEISURE ACTIVITIES    (3)
                        CAREER DECISIONS    (4)


        DYADIC SATISFACTION:

                        TALK OF ENDING RELATIONSHIP    (5)
                        LEAVING AFTER A FIGHT    (5)
                        THINGS GOING WELL    (4)
                        CONFIDING IN MATE    (4)
                        REGRET BEING TOGETHER    (5)
                        QUARREL    (3)
                        ON EACH OTHER'S NERVES    (3)
                        KISS MATE    (4)
                        DEGREE OF HAPPINESS    (4)
                        FUTURE OF RELATIONSHIP    (4)


        AFFECTIONAL EXPRESSION:

                        SHOWING AFFECTION    (4)
                        SEX RELATIONS    (4)
                        TOO TIRED FOR SEX    (1)
                        NOT SHOWING LOVE    (1)


        DYADIC COHESION:

                        OUTSIDE INTERESTS    (2)
                        EXCHANGE OF IDEAS    (3)
                        LAUGH TOGETHER    (3)
                        CALMLY DISCUSSING    (4)
                        WORK TOGETHER    (3)
```

OVERALL, THIS INDIVIDUAL IS REPORTING AN AVERAGE LEVEL OF DYADIC
ADJUSTMENT IN COMPARISON TO MARRIED PEOPLE.

THE DYADIC CONSENSUS SCORE, REPRESENTING AMOUNT OF AGREEMENT WITH
PARTNER, IS IN THE AVERAGE RANGE FOR THIS INDIVIDUAL WHEN COMPARED
TO MARRIED PEOPLE. INDIVIDUALS WITH HIGH DYADIC ADJUSTMENT SHOULD
GENERALLY AGREE ON MATTERS OF IMPORTANCE TO THE RELATIONSHIP.

DYADIC SATISFACTION MEASURES THE INDIVIDUAL'S OVERALL AMOUNT OF POSITIVE
FEELING IN THE RELATIONSHIP. INDIVIDUALS WHO ARE SATISFIED WITH THE
RELATIONSHIP HAVE FEW COMPLAINTS ABOUT THEIR RELATIONS AND FEW DOUBTS
ABOUT THE CERTAINTY OF THE MARRIAGE'S CHANCES OF SUCCEEDING. IT CAN
BE AN INDICATION OF DIVORCE POTENTIAL, COMMITMENT, AND HOPE FOR THE
FUTURE OF THE RELATIONSHIP. THIS INDIVIDUAL REPORTS AN AVERAGE SCORE
IN DYADIC SATISFACTION.

THE AFFECTIONAL EXPRESSION SCALE, INDICATING SATISFACTION WITH SEX,
AFFECTION AND CONSIDERATIONAL ASPECTS OF THE RELATIONSHIP, IS IN THE
AVERAGE RANGE FOR THIS INDIVIDUAL WHEN COMPARED TO MARRIED PEOPLE.

THE DYADIC COHESION SCALE, REPRESENTING THE AMOUNT OF INVOLVEMENT
TOGETHER IN MUTUALLY ENJOYABLE ACTIVITIES AND INTERESTS, IS AT AN
AVERAGE LEVEL FOR THIS INDIVIDUAL WHEN COMPARED TO MARRIED PEOPLE.

NOTE: THESE RESULTS SHOULD BE INTERPRETED WITH CAUTION AS THIS IS
ONLY ONE ELEMENT OF A COMPLETE DYADIC ASSESSMENT. THE NORMS USED FOR
THIS REPORT ARE FROM: SPANIER, G.B. (1976) MEASURING DYADIC ADJUSTMENT:
NEW SCALES FOR ASSESSING THE QUALITY OF MARRIAGE AND SIMILAR DYADS.
JOURNAL OF MARRIAGE AND THE FAMILY, 38, 15-28.

RAW DATA
========

1.	3	17.	5
2.	3	18.	4
3.	5	19.	4
4.	4	20.	5
5.	4	21.	3
6.	4	22.	3
7.	3	23.	4
8.	4	24.	2
9.	4	25.	3
10.	4	26.	3
11.	3	27.	4
12.	4	28.	3
13.	3	29.	1
14.	3	30.	1
15.	4	31.	4
16.	5	32.	4

NAME: Early School Personality Questionnaire Narrative Report

SUPPLIER: Institute for Personality and Ability Testing, Inc.
P.O. Box 188
Champaign, IL 61820
(217) 352-4739

PRODUCT CATEGORY	PRIMARY APPLICATIONS
Personality	Personal/Marriage/Family Counseling

SALE RESTRICTIONS American Psychological Association Guidelines

SERVICE TYPE/COST	Type	Available	Cost	Discount
	Mail-In	Yes	$16.00	Yes
	Teleprocessing	No		
	Local	No		

PRODUCT DESCRIPTION

The EARLY SCHOOL PERSONALITY QUESTIONNAIRE NAR-RATIVE REPORT provides a complete report for each individual's primary personality characteristics and the most important broad influence patterns affecting early-school-age children.

The format of the Early School Personality Questionnaire makes objective personality measurement possible as children begin their school years. Questions are read aloud by the teacher or an audio cassette tape, which is available, may be used. Answers are marked on a pictorial answer sheet. To use the answer sheet, the child need only be able to discriminate the letter A from the letter B and to recognize pictures of a bird, cat, tree, flower, and other common objects.

THE INSTITUTE FOR PERSONALITY AND ABILITY TESTING
P. O. BOX 188   CHAMPAIGN, ILLINOIS 61820

ESPQ
PERSONALITY PROFILE

SCORE RAW STEN	TRAIT	LOW MEANING	1 2 3 4 5 6 7 8 9 10	HIGH MEANING	PER- CENTILE
6 5	A	COOL, RESERVED	*	WARM, EASYGOING	40
15 7	B	DULL	*	BRIGHT	77
8 6	C	EASILY UPSET	*	CALM, STABLE	60
5 4	D	STOIC, LISTLESS	*	EXCITABLE	23
7 4	E	NOT ASSERTIVE	*	DOMINANT	23
9 8	F	SOBER, SERIOUS	*	HAPPY-GO LUCKY	89
6 4	G	EXPEDIENT	*	CONSCIENTIOUS	23
8 7	H	SHY, TIMID	*	VENTURESOME	77
10 10	I	TOUGH-MINDED	*	TENDER-MINDED	99
7 8	J	PARTICIPATING	*	INTROSPECTIVE	89
4 4	N	FORTHRIGHT	*	SHREWD	23
2 4	O	SELF-ASSURED	*	APPREHENSIVE	23
5 5	Q4	RELAXED	*	TENSE, DRIVEN	40

PRIMARY PERSONALITY CHARACTERISTICS OF SIGNIFICANCE

HIS STYLE OF EXPRESSION IS OFTEN LIVELY, OPTIMISTIC, AND ENTHUSIASTIC.

AS A PERSON, HE IS TENDERMINDED AND SENSITIVELY IMAGINATIVE, AS
    FROM A SHELTERED LIFE.

AT SCHOOL AND ELSEWHERE, HE IS SOMEWHAT OF A LONER, DOES NOT ENJOY
    PARTICIPATION, AND TENDS TO BE OBSTRUCTIVE.

BROAD INFLUENCE PATTERNS

THE PERSONALITY ORIENTATION IS NEITHER EXTRAVERTED NOR INTROVERTED.
    ATTENTION IS DIRECTED ABOUT EQUALLY TOWARD THE OUTER ENVIRONMENT
    AND TOWARD INNER THOUGHTS AND FEELINGS. THIS CHILD'S SCORE MAY BE
    DESCRIBED AS AVERAGE (5.6).

THE CHILD'S LEVEL OF ANXIETY MAY BE CONSIDERED TO BE HIGH (8.1).

TASKS AND PROBLEMS ARE APPROACHED WITH EMPHASIS UPON EMOTIONAL RELATION-
    SHIPS RATHER THAN RATIONAL AND OBJECTIVE CONSIDERATIONS. THIS TENDENCY
    IS ABOVE AVERAGE (7.4).

THE LIFE STYLE IS BALANCED BETWEEN NEED TO CONTROL THE ENVIRONMENT AND
    WILLINGNESS TO ADAPT TO WHAT IS AVAILABLE. IN THIS RESPECT, THE
    CHILD'S SCORE IS AVERAGE (6.0).

NAME: Eating Disorder Inventory: Computer Version

SUPPLIER: Psychological Assessment Resources
P.O. Box 98
Odessa, FL 33556
(813) 977-3395

PRODUCT CATEGORY	PRIMARY APPLICATIONS
Personality	Behavioral Medicine Clinical Assessment/Diagnosis Personal/Marriage/Family Counseling

SALE RESTRICTIONS American Psychological Association Guidelines

SERVICE TYPE/COST	Type	Available	Cost	Discount
	Mail-In	No		
	Teleprocessing	No		
	Local	Yes	$3.20	

PRODUCT DESCRIPTION

The EATING DISORDER INVENTORY: COMPUTER VERSION is an administration, scoring and interpretive program. The program produces a profile of the individual's test results either on the display or in printed form that compares the test results to both normal and patient normative groups. In addition, the program provides interpretive statements for each scale. Both operator and patient entry are permitted. The program also allows the user to save data on a diskette for future reference or for research purposes.

The Eating Disorder Inventory is a 64-item self-report inventory assessing a broad range of psychological and behavioral traits common in eating disorders. Scores are obtained for eight separate scales. The test can be used to measure specific cognitive and behavioral dimensions that may differentiate sub-groups of individuals with eating disorders, to distinguish those individuals with serious psychopathology from normal dieters, and to help in the understanding and treatment of individuals with eating disorders.

The software is compatible with the Apple II + and IIe computer systems. The price shown above is the cost-per-test when diskettes are purchased in quantities of 50 uses (minimum purchase).

NAME: Edwards Personal Preference Schedule

SUPPLIER: NCS/Professional Assessment Services
P.O. Box 1416
Minneapolis, MN 55440
(800) 328-6759

PRODUCT CATEGORY

Personality
Motivation/Needs

PRIMARY APPLICATIONS

Personal/Marriage/Family Counseling
Clinical Assessment/Diagnosis

SALE RESTRICTIONS American Psychological Association Guidelines

SERVICE TYPE/COST	Type	Available	Cost	Discount
	Mail-In	Yes	$4.55	Yes
	Teleprocessing	No		
	Local	No		

PRODUCT DESCRIPTION

The EDWARDS PERSONAL PREFERENCE SCHEDULE is a 210-item device for measuring personality in adults 18 years of age and older. The forced-choice format is designed to measure the relative importance of 15 needs and motivations defined by Henry Murray. Scores in this report are provided for the following scales: Achievement, Deference, Order, Exhibition, Autonomy, Affiliation, Intraception, Succorance, Dominance, Abasement, Nurturance, Change, Endurance, Heterosexuality, and Aggression. The test has enjoyed wide use, especially in college counseling applications.

CLINICAL INTERPRETIVE ANALYSIS

OF THE

EDWARDS PERSONAL PREFERENCE SCHEDULE

TEST NO. 006

CASE NO. DEMO12

TEST DATE   10/ 19/ 81

This computer generated report is based on the Edwards
Personal Preference Schedule. Its purpose is to assist
qualified professionals in the evaluation of personality
variables and should be used in conjunction with the
clinician's professional experience.

_____
Reviewing Professional

EDWARDS PERSONAL PREFERENCE SCHEDULE

The Edwards Personal Preference Schedule provides measures
of 15 personality variables. The names of these variables
are as follows :

		Raw Score	Percent
ACH	ACHIEVEMENT............	16	65
DEF	DEFERENCE..............	7	4
ORD	ORDER..................	9	15
EXH	EXHIBITION.............	15	75
AUT	AUTONOMY...............	17	77
AFF	AFFILIATION............	17	75
INT	INTRACEPTION...........	12	36
SUC	SUCCORANCE.............	10	50
DOM	DOMINANCE..............	13	44
ABA	ABASEMENT..............	9	17
NUR	NURTURANCE.............	18	70
CHG	CHANGE.................	25	99
END	ENDURANCE..............	13	23
HET	HETEROSEXUALITY........	23	91
AGG	AGGRESSION.............	6	8

Additional Measure

CON	CONSISTENCY............	13	87

psychware **217**

PERCENTILE SCORE

SCORE	1	25	50	75	99

```
65.0 ACH                              ***********
 4.0 DEF  *********************************
15.0 ORD     **************************
75.0 EXH                      ******************
77.0 AUT                      *******************
75.0 AFF                      ******************
36.0 INT               ***********
50.0 SUC                         *
44.0 DOM                    ******
17.0 ABA      ***********************
70.0 NUR                      *************
99.0 CHG                      ***********************************
23.0 END         *******************
91.0 HET                      ******************************
 8.0 AGG    *****************************
```

	1	25	50	75	99

218 *psychware*

EDWARDS PERSONAL PREFERENCE SCHEDULE

In the following analysis, each of the 15 variables are defined by test statements that characterize each variable, and which were endorsed by the subject. Thus it is possible to specify more exactly what the variable means for each subject. Statements which characterize the variable most are listed first, with the number of endorsements in parenthesis ( ) .

CHANGE

To move about the country and live in different places(4)
To experience novelty and change in daily routine(3)
To experiment and try new things(3)
To try new and different jobs(3)
To meet new people(3)
To participate in new fads and fashions(3)
To travel(2)
To do new and different things(2)
To eat in new and different places(2)

HETEROSEXUALITY

To go out with members of the opposite sex(3)
To engage in social activities with the opposite sex(3)
To be in love with someone of the opposite sex(3)
To be regarded as physically attractive by those of the
    opposite sex(3)
To listen to or to tell jokes involving sex(3)
To become sexually excited(3)
To participate in discussions about sex(2)
To read books and plays involving sex(2)
To kiss those of the opposite sex(1)

AUTONOMY

To be independent of others in making decisions(3)
To avoid situations where one is expected to conform(3)
To do things without regard to what others may think(3)
To avoid responsibilities and obligations(3)
To feel free to do what one wants(2)
To say what one thinks about things(2)
To be able to come and go as desired(1)

EDWARDS PERSONAL PREFERENCE SCHEDULE

EXHIBITION

To be the center of attention(3)
To use words that others do not know the meaning of(3)
To ask questions others cannot answer(3)
To talk about personal achievements(2)
To talk about personal adventures and experiences(2)
To tell amusing jokes and stories(1)
To have others notice and comment upon one's appearance(1)

AFFILIATION

To participate in friendly groups(3)
To share things with friends(3)
To form strong attachments(3)
To do things for friends(2)
To write letters to friends(2)
To be loyal to friends(1)
To do things with friends rather than alone(1)
To form new friendships(1)
To make as many friends as possible(1)

NURTURANCE

To show a great deal of affection toward others(4)
To be generous with others(3)
To treat others with kindness and sympathy(2)
To sympathize with others who are hurt or sick(2)
To forgive others(2)
To have others confide in one about personal problems(2)
To assist others less fortunate(1)
To do small favors for others(1)
To help friends when they are in trouble(1)

ACHIEVEMENT

To solve difficult problems and puzzles(3)
To be able to do things better than others(3)
To write a great novel or play(3)
To be successful(2)
To do one's best(2)
To accomplish tasks requiring skill and effort(1)
To accomplish something of great significance(1)
To do a difficult job well(1)

EDWARDS PERSONAL PREFERENCE SCHEDULE

SUCCORANCE

To have others be kindly(3)
To have others do favors cheerfully(2)
To have others be sympathetic and understanding about personal
   problems(1)
To receive a great deal of affection from others(1)
To seek encouragement from others(1)
To be helped by others when depressed(1)
To have a fuss made over one when hurt(1)

DOMINANCE

To be regarded by others as a leader(2)
To make group decisions(2)
To settle arguments and disputes between others(2)
To tell others how to do their jobs(2)
To be a leader in groups to which one belongs(1)
To argue for one's point of view(1)
To persuade and influence others to do what one wants(1)
To supervise and direct the actions of others(1)
To be elected or appointed chairman of committees(1)

INTRACEPTION

To analyze the behavior of others(4)
To put one's self in another's place(2)
To understand how others feel about problems(2)
To predict how others will act(2)
To analyze the motives of others(1)
To analyze one's motives and feelings(1)

ENDURANCE

To stick at a problem even though it may seem as if no
   progress is being made(4)
To complete any job undertaken(3)
To work hard at a task(2)
To work at a single job before taking on others(1)
To put in long hours of work without distraction(1)
To keep at a job until it is finished(1)
To avoid being interrupted while at work(1)

EDWARDS PERSONAL PREFERENCE SCHEDULE

ABASEMENT

To feel better when giving in and avoiding a fight than
   when having one's own way(2)
To feel the need for confession of errors(2)
To feel that personal pain and misery suffered does more good
   than harm(1)
To feel guilty when one does something wrong(1)
To accept blame when things do not go right(1)
To feel depressed by inability to handle situations(1)
To feel timid in the presence of superiors(1)

ORDER

To make advance plans when taking a trip(3)
To have things arranged so that they run smoothly without
   change(3)
To have written work neat and organized(1)
To organize details of work(1)
To have things organized(1)

AGGRESSION

To tell others what one thinks about them(3)
To criticize others publicly(1)
To tell others off when disagreeing with them(1)
To blame others when things go wrong(1)

DEFERENCE

To praise others(2)
To let others make decisions(2)
To accept the leadership of others(1)
To conform to custom and avoid the unconventional(1)
To get suggestions from others(1)

CASE NO. DEMO12   DATE 10/ 19/ 81

EDWARDS PERSONAL PREFERENCE SCHEDULE

RESPONSES

	1	2	3	4	5	6	7	8	9	10
	1	2	1	2	1	1	1	1	1	1
11	2	2	1	1	1	1	2	1	1	2
21	1	1	2	1	2	1	2	2	1	2
31	1	2	2	2	1	2	2	1	1	1
41	2	1	2	1	2	2	2	2	1	2
51	1	2	2	1	2	1	2	2	2	1
61	2	2	1	2	2	2	2	2	2	1
71	1	1	1	2	1	2	2	2	2	2
81	1	1	1	1	2	1	2	1	1	1
91	1	1	2	2	2	2	1	2	2	2
101	1	1	2	1	2	1	2	1	1	1
111	1	2	1	1	1	1	1	1	1	2
121	1	2	2	1	1	1	2	2	2	2
131	2	2	2	2	2	2	1	1	1	2
141	2	2	2	2	2	1	1	1	1	2
151	1	1	1	1	2	2	1	2	1	2
161	1	1	1	1	1	1	1	1	2	2
171	2	1	2	2	2	2	1	2	1	2
181	1	1	2	1	2	1	1	2	1	1
191	1	1	1	1	2	1	1	1	1	1
201	1	1	2	1	2	1	2	2	2	2
211	2	1	1	1	1	2	1	2	2	2
221	1	1	1	1	1	1				

THIS CONCLUDES THE SCORING OF TEST #006

NAME: Edwards Personal Preference Schedule

SUPPLIER: Applied Innovations, Inc.
South Kingstown Office Park, Suite A-1
Wakefield, RI 02879
(800) 272-2250

PRODUCT CATEGORY

Personality
Motivation/Needs

PRIMARY APPLICATIONS

Personal/Marriage/Family Counseling
Clinical Assessment/Diagnosis

SALE RESTRICTIONS American Psychological Association Guidelines

SERVICE TYPE/COST	Type	Available	Cost	Discount
	Mail-In	No		
	Teleprocessing	No		
	Local	Yes	$175.00	

PRODUCT DESCRIPTION

The EDWARDS PERSONAL PREFERENCE SCHEDULE is a 210-item test that measures personality in adults 18 years of age and older. The forced-choice format is designed to measure the relative importance of 15 need patterns originally described by Henry Murray: Achievement, Deference, Order, Exhibition, Autonomy, Affiliation, Intraception, Succorance, Dominance, Abasement, Nurturance, Change, Endurance, Heterosexuality, and Aggression. The test has been widely used, especially in college counseling applications.

This program provides a two-part report based on the percentile scores of the test. In the first part, percentile scores are graphed. The second part includes the following sections: personal traits, social functioning, and vocational interests. The report is 1-2 pages in length.

The software operates on most available personal computers, including IBM, Apple, Digital, and Kaypro.

EPPS COMPUTER REPORT

by

APPLIED INNOVATIONS INC.
SOUTH KINGSTOWN OFFICE PARK, SUITE A-1
WAKEFIELD, RHODE ISLAND 02879
(800) 272-2250

This is a computer-generated psychological interpretation of the Edwards
Personal Preference Schedule. The results are confidential and should be considered as working hypotheses to be further investigated by a qualified mental
health professional.

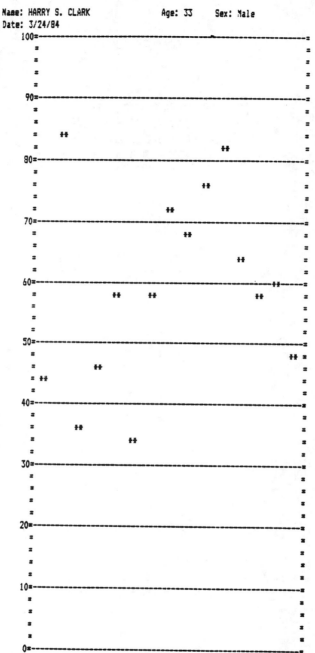

Name: HARRY S. CLARK   Age: 33   Sex: Male
Date: 3/24/84

Percent: 45 85 37 47 58 34 58 73 68 76 82 64 59 60 49
Scales: ACH DEF ORD EXH AUT AFF INT SUC DOM ABA NUR CHA END HET AGG

These individuals tend to be conventional and conforming.
They are concerned about staying in control, and usually are
not impulsive. These individuals like to be leaders. They
tend to be ambitious, reasonable, outgoing, and sociable.
They are often involved in helping others, and often
identify with the social groups they belong to. These
people tend to be critical of themselves. These individuals
may lack self-confidence and therefore need emotional
support and reassurance from others. They tend to be
somewhat inhibited and temperamental.

These individuals tended not to date much in high school.
They often engaged in intellectual pursuits such as reading.

These individuals tend to have anxious temperament and
probably have a low tolerance to environmental stress.
These individuals tend to have low self-esteem and a poor
self-concept. These individuals tend to be tense and
nervous, and are prone to develop anxiety in times of stress.
These individuals have a higher proneness toward
hypertension than individuals with other profile types.

These individuals tend to like to work with ideas in stable
situations. They do not do well in conflictual work
situations. They tend to be attracted to occupations such
as those found in social service, biological science, and
medicine. These individuals prefer stable work situations
with a minimum of interpersonal conflict. They tend to like
'realistic' occupations such as farming, aviation and
carpentry. Other types of jobs congruent with their
interest needs are school superintendent, personnel director,
youth camp director, social science teacher, social worker
and minister.

NAME: Evaluacion de las Caracteristicas en Hacer Cumplir la Ley

SUPPLIER: Jeseg, S.A.
Apartado 291
Caracas 1010, VENEZUELA
(011-58-2) 571 18 91

PRODUCT CATEGORY

Career/Vocational

PRIMARY APPLICATIONS

Personnel Selection/Evaluation

SALE RESTRICTIONS Qualified Professional

SERVICE TYPE/COST	Type	Available	Cost	Discount
	Mail-In	Yes	$20.00	Yes
	Teleprocessing	No		
	Local	No		

PRODUCT DESCRIPTION

This report is a translation into Spanish and adaptation of the Law Enforcement Assessment and Development Report. It identifies individuals who are the most likely to become successful law enforcement officers. It allows comparisons of applicants in terms of predicted overall performance as well as in four job-related areas: Emotional Maturity, Integrity/Control, Intellectual Efficiency, and Interpersonal Relationships.

For a sample printout of this product (in English), see the one shown under the LAW ENFORCEMENT ASSESSMENT AND DEVELOPMENT REPORT.

NAME: Executive Profile Survey

SUPPLIER: NCS/Professional Assessment Services
P.O. Box 1416
Minneapolis, MN 55440
(800) 328-6759

PRODUCT CATEGORY	PRIMARY APPLICATIONS
Personality	Personnel Selection/Evaluation
Career/Vocational	Vocational Guidance/Counseling

SALE RESTRICTIONS None

SERVICE TYPE/COST Type	Available	Cost	Discount
Mail-In	Yes	$20.00	Yes
Teleprocessing	Yes	$20.00	Yes
Local	Yes	$20.00	Yes

PRODUCT DESCRIPTION

The EXECUTIVE PROFILE SURVEY is designed to measure self-attitudes, values, and beliefs of individuals in comparison with over 2,000 top-level executives. The 94 multiple-choice test items were developed from a 10-year study of the executive personality. Scores are obtained for 11 profile dimensions: Ambitious, Assertive, Enthusiastic, Creative, Spontaneous, Self-focused, Considerate, Open-minded, Relaxed, Practical, and Systematic. The Survey also incorporates two validity scales. The test requires a 12th-grade reading level and one hour for administration.

This 5-page report defines 11 profile dimensions, reports and plots the individual's score on each dimension, and compares the scores with the norm group. The data base covers bankers, businessmen, and intellectuals, including groups ranging from the largest to the smallest organizations and educational institutions. For a sample printout of this product, see the one shown under EXECUTIVE PROFILE SURVEY provided by the Institute for Personality and Ability Testing.

Two systems are available for local processing of test results. MICRO-TEST Assessment Software from National Computer Systems, used with a Sentry 3000 tabletop scanner (purchase price approximately $4000) and microcomputer system ($2000-$3000 purchase price), allows tests to be administered off-line. Answer sheets are then scanned and scored automatically, one at a time or in a batch. The software also permits on-line administration of the test via microcomputer. In either case, the same report is provided. The cost for local scoring refers to the cost-per-test when diskettes are purchased in units of 20 administrations (minimum purchase).

psychware **229**

NAME: Executive Profile Survey

SUPPLIER: Institute for Personality and Ability Testing, Inc.
P.O. Box 188
Champaign, IL 61820
(217) 352-4739

PRODUCT CATEGORY

Personality
Career/Vocational

PRIMARY APPLICATIONS

Personnel Selection/Evaluation
Vocational Guidance/Counseling

SALE RESTRICTIONS   None

SERVICE TYPE/COST	Type	Available	Cost	Discount
	Mail-In	Yes	$20.00	
	Teleprocessing	No		
	Local	No		

PRODUCT DESCRIPTION

The EXECUTIVE PROFILE SURVEY is designed to measure self-attitudes, values, and beliefs of individuals in comparison with over 2,000 top-level executives. The 94 multiple-choice test items were developed from a 10-year study of the executive personality. The 11 profile dimensions assess the Ambitious, Assertive, Enthusiastic, Creative, Spontaneous, Self-Focused, Considerate, Open-Minded, Relaxed, Practical, and Systematic traits of the individual. The SURVEY also incorporates two validity scales. It requires a 12th-grade reading level and one hour for administration.

The report provides a clear, concise, non-technical description of those dimensions most important in business, management, and executive settings. The data base covers bankers, businessmen, and intellectuals, including groups ranging from the largest to the smallest businesses and educational institutions. A detailed manual provides comprehensive data on norms, reliability, and validity.

```
* * * * * * * * * * * * * * * * * * * * * * * * * * * * * * * * * *
*                                                                 *
*                                                                 *
*                                                                 *
*         E X E C U T I V E   P R O F I L E   S U R V E Y         *
*                                                                 *
*                                                                 *
*                                                                 *
*                                                                 *
*                              BY                                 *
*                                                                 *
*                     Virgil R Lang, PhD                          *
*                                                                 *
*                                                                 *
* * * * * * * * * * * * * * * * * * * * * * * * * * * * * * * * * *
```

Name: John Smith
Date: April 20, 1984
Sex: Male
Age: 34

The following report assesses how this individual stands with
respect to 11 important dimensions that have been identified in
studies of the self-concept of top executives and managers.

Like any personal data it should be treated confidentially.
Because it reflects attitudes and perspectives that change over
time, the date of the report should be carefully noted when
examining this document. Outdated information may be of
little positive value in making decisions about people. The
report should be available only to individuals who are
qualified to interpret and act on the information it contains.
It is intended to supplement, not replace, other valid data
about this individual that may be available.

The norms for the Executive Profile Survey are based on results
from 2000 executives, including presidents of banks ranging in
deposit size from $5,000,000 to more than a billion dollars,
presidents of Fortune 500 companies, certified public accountants,
executives who earned a Harvard MBA degree, presidents of
advertising agencies, presidents of colleges, universities,
and religious insititutes, deans of business schools, and
newspaper editors.

For full details of the 10-year study on which this report is
based, please refer to "Perspectives on the Executive Personality:
a Manual for the Executive Profile Survey."

VALIDITY INDICATORS

The Executive Profile Survey incorporates two scales to measure
Mr Smith's attitude toward the questionnaire itself. The first
measures his tendency to "fake good" or to give socially desirable
answers rather than answers that are really true for him. On this
scale Mr Smith scores within normal limits. The second scale
reflects the carefulness with which he has approached the
questionnaire and the degree of consistency in his answers. In his
case this index is acceptable. Since both scales are within normal
limits the scores on the 11 profile dimensions can be considered to
reflect Mr Smith's self-attitudes, self-values, and self-beliefs with
reasonable accuracy.

PROFILE DIMENSION 1: AMBITIOUS

This dimension identifies a cluster of characteristics associated
with resourcefulness, forcefulness, ambition, and drive. People who
are high on this dimension describe themselves as purposeful and
forward-looking. They feel that they are able to take the initiative
and move steadily toward goals. On this dimension Mr Smith is
below average with respect to top executives and managers.

```
          10   20   30   40   50   60   70   80   90        %
RANK      *******************                                37
```

PROFILE DIMENSION 2: ASSERTIVE

People who score high on this dimension tend to be dominant
individuals who prefer to "take charge" rather than wait for things
to happen. They value activity rather than passivity. Low-scoring
individuals, on the other hand, stress the value of quiet
contemplation and frequent self-examination before reaching decisions
and acting within the framework of their occupational role. In this
respect Mr Smith is very high.

```
          10   20   30   40   50   60   70   80   90        %
RANK      *********************************************      88
```

PROFILE DIMENSION 3: ENTHUSIASTIC

This dimension revolves around a cluster of characteristics related
to extraversion, poise, and exuberance. It reflects the individual's
belief that he can do and say the correct thing in social situations
with a quality admired by others. Mr Smith is high.

```
          10   20   30   40   50   60   70   80   90        %
RANK      *****************************************          77
```

232 *psychware*

PROFILE DIMENSION 4: CREATIVE

This dimension reflects Mr Smith's preference for generating new ideas and for seeking out novel solutions to problems. In comparison with top executives on this characteristic, Mr Smith is low.

```
        10   20   30   40   50   60   70   80   90        %
RANK    ***************                                   29
```

PROFILE DIMENSION 5: SPONTANEOUS

People who score high on this dimension tend to value departures from established patterns of doing things and break with precedent. On occasion they may act too rashly without having given the proper thought and consideration to their behavior. Mr Smith is low in this regard.

```
        10   20   30   40   50   60   70   80   90        %
RANK    *************                                     26
```

PROFILE DIMENSION 6: SELF-FOCUSED

People who score high on this dimension describe themselves as determined, self-reliant people who want to reach decisions and act on their own. They may be viewed by others as somewhat self-centered, perhaps, narcisstic, and may act in ways that show little concern for others. With respect to this dimension of self-motivated, autonomous behavior, Mr Smith is extremely high.

```
        10   20   30   40   50   60   70   80   90        %
RANK    *************************************************  97
```

PROFILE DIMENSION 7: CONSIDERATE

This dimension highlights a basic concern for people in the nature of trust and approachableness in interpersonal relations. It reflects consideration for others. Individuals who score high on this dimension tend to describe themselves as loyal, trusting, generous, and devoted. Mr Smith is average on this dimension.

```
        10   20   30   40   50   60   70   80   90        %
RANK    ************************                          48
```

psychware **233**

PROFILE DIMENSION 8: OPEN-MINDED

This dimension underscores the active ability to change and remain adaptable to life events without being excessively pliable or "bending with the wind," it also reflects the less obvious attitudinal flexibility of undogmatic people. Mr Smith is average on this dimension.

```
        10   20   30   40   50   60   70   80   90        %
RANK    *********************                             41
```

PROFILE DIMENSION 9: RELAXED

In this dimension, even-temperedness and calmness emerge as major indicators of the degree of emotional control he has in stressful, as well as non-stressful, situations. It further reflects a measure of maturity that is related not particularly to age but to the ability to exercise patience and firmness in a wide variety of situations. Mr Smith is extremely low on this characteristic.

```
        10   20   30   40   50   60   70   80   90        %
RANK    *****                                             9
```

PROFILE DIMENSION 10: PRACTICAL

People who score high on this dimension tend to describe themselves as fairly realistic, problem-oriented, tough-minded individuals. They tend to focus on the "here-and-now" and do not think of themselves as particularly idealistic, curious, or sensitive. Mr Smith is high in this respect.

```
        10   20   30   40   50   60   70   80   90        %
RANK    *****************************************          78
```

PROFILE DIMENSION 11: SYSTEMATIC

What the last of these eleven dimensions captures is the degree to which Mr Smith considers himself to be efficient in daily practices by using an orderly and methodical approach to business affairs. The need for structure---the importance of method, rather than what is done---combined with some degree of meticulousness, is involved as well. Mr Smith is average on this dimension.

```
        10   20   30   40   50   60   70   80   90        %
RANK    *****************************                      59
```

234 *psychware*

In summary, Mr Smith's scores show the following general pattern with regard to the executives who have been studied during the development of the Executive Profile Survey. For easy reference they are repeated here, not in their usual order, but this time in order ranging from the strongest characteristic to those of less prominence.

In reviewing the profile, keep in mind that percentile scores between 40 and 60 are usually interpreted as the average range. Scores from 60 to 70 are considered above average, scores from 70 to 80, high, scores of 80 to 90, very high, and scores above 90, extremely high. Similarly, scores from 30 to 40 are below average, scores between 20 and 30 are low, scores between 10 and 20 are very low, and scores below 10 are extremely low.

EXECUTIVE PROFILE SURVEY
CAPSULE SUMMARY

	DIMENSION	10	20	30	40	50	60	70	80	90	%
6	SELF-FOCUSED	**									97
2	ASSERTIVE	***									88
10	PRACTICAL	**************************************									78
3	ENTHUSIASTIC	**************************************									77
11	SYSTEMATIC	*****************************									59
7	CONSIDERATE	************************									48
8	OPEN-MINDED	*********************									41
1	AMBITIOUS	*******************									37
4	CREATIVE	***************									29
5	SPONTANEOUS	*************									26
9	RELAXED	*****									9

NAME: Explorer

SUPPLIER: Publishers Test Service
2500 Garden Road
Monterey, CA 93940
(800) 538-9547

PRODUCT CATEGORY

Cognitive/Ability

PRIMARY APPLICATIONS

Clinical Assessment/Diagnosis
Educational Evaluation/Planning

SALE RESTRICTIONS American Psychological Association Guidelines

SERVICE TYPE/COST	Type	Available	Cost	Discount
	Mail-In	No		
	Teleprocessing	No		
	Local	Yes	$50.00	

PRODUCT DESCRIPTION

The EXPLORER is used for interpreting results from the Weschler Intelligence Scale for Children-Revised. It is designed to aid in generating some predictable statements about a child's or youth's general level of intellectual functioning and specific strengths and weaknesses. The program, along with the training and insight of the clinician, can provide flexible and efficient individualization of reports for up to 50 students.

EXPLORER provides a description and performance summary of each of the 12 subtests and of the three IQ scores obtained. It also provides a set of hypotheses as to why an individual scored high or low on each subtest. An option is the inclusion of factor scores that provide hypotheses about the student for factors such as successive versus simultaneous brain functioning, field independence versus field dependence, Bannatyne's categorization of WISC-R subtest scores, and other meaningful profiles based on various combinations of the subtests.

NAME: Eysenck Personality Questionnaire

SUPPLIER: PSYCH Systems, Inc.
600 Reisterstown Road
Baltimore, MD 21208
(800) 368-3366

PRODUCT CATEGORY

Personality

PRIMARY APPLICATIONS

Clinical Assessment/Diagnosis

SALE RESTRICTIONS Qualified Professional

SERVICE TYPE/COST	Type	Available	Cost	Discount
	Mail-In	No		
	Teleprocessing	No		
	Local	Yes	See Below	

PRODUCT DESCRIPTION

Aimed at measuring personality aspects related to vocational and interpersonal settings, this questionnaire has properties that make it ideal for normal personality evaluation on an individual case basis. Scales scored from the 90 items in the test are Toughmindedness, Extroversion, Neuroticism, and Lie. The EYSENCK PERSONALITY QUESTIONNAIRE has its most appropriate use in settings where brief evaluation of normal personality functioning is required.

This Psych Systems program administers and scores the test. The interpretive report it provides is brief and aims specifically at characteristics related to vocational and interpersonal performance. In addition, appropriate methods of motivation for the individual are also discussed.

Psych Systems programs operate on the IBM PC-XT, COMPAQ Plus, Dec Professional 350, and most DEC PDP-11 systems. Various hardware/software configurations are available directly from Psych Systems, with single-user systems starting at approximately $12,000. A per test fee also applies.

```
---------------------------------------------------
|         |                                         |
|   EPQ   |  Eysenck Personality Questionnaire      |
|         |                                         |
---------------------------------------------------
```

The computer program generating this report was designed by Psych
Systems, Inc., Baltimore, Maryland 21208. Copyright (C) 1984 by
Psych Systems, Inc. The Eysenck Personality Questionnaire is
reproduced by permission. Copyright (C) 1975 by Edits, San Diego,
California 92107. All rights reserved.

Test responses show a pattern that is indicative of a valid protocol.
Therefore, the following interpretation is likely a non-biased
picture of the individual's personality functioning. People such as
this are somewhat cynical individuals who enjoy being by themselves
and who rather like a degree of danger in the situation surrounding
them.

They are sometimes viewed as eccentric and socially withdrawn. Their
behavior is likely to be unpredictable (sometimes overly impulsive
and sometimes overly cautious) and somewhat unusual. Often they seem
to have a seething sense of anger toward others around them. While
seldom expressed openly and directly, this hostility may take the
form of litigious behavior or vandalism and stealing. They are
socially cold people who tend to lack empathy. They are much more
interested in things than they are in people. As a result, few of
these individuals ever have truly good long-term relationships with
others.

They are likely to perform best in vocational settings where they can
work alone, where fearlessness is required, and where a mistrusting
attitude toward others is precautionary. Examples of appropriate
jobs include roofers, iron workers involved in the construction of
skyscrapers and bridges, securities officers, military personnel, and
surgeons.

                    Summary of Scores

           Scale   Raw   Tscore

             L   9   53
             P   12   81
             E   9   41
             N   10   51

                    Raw Data

           1234567890 1234567890 1234567890

    1- 30 YYYYNYNYNN YNYNNYNYNY NYNNYYYYNY
   31- 60 NNNYYYYYYY YYYYYNYYNY YNNNNNNNNN
   61- 90 NNNYNNYYNN NNYNNNYYYY YYNNNNNYNY

                                          psychware **239**

NAME: Eysenck Personality Questionnaire (Adult)

SUPPLIER: EdITS
P.O. Box 7234
San Diego, CA 92107
(619) 222-1666

PRODUCT CATEGORY	PRIMARY APPLICATIONS
Personality	Clinical Assessment/Diagnosis Personal/Marriage/Family Counseling

SALE RESTRICTIONS American Psychological Association Guidelines

SERVICE TYPE/COST	Type	Available	Cost	Discount
	Mail-In	No		
	Teleprocessing	No		
	Local	Yes	$0.30	Yes

PRODUCT DESCRIPTION

This program presents the Eysenck Personality Questionnaire (Adult) via the computer console. The test provides scores on three personality dimensions (Extraversion, Neuroticism, and Psychoticism) and on a lie scale. The complex scoring procedure is handled by the computer, which presents results immediately on the screen. Scores can be printed out and recorded on disk, thereby permitting the development of a local databank. The program also measures response time latencies, an assessment not available in printed paper administration.

The questionnaire is completed using a light pen to touch the screen, so that the examinee never needs to use the keyboard. The program is designed for use with a Commodore PET 4000 or 8000 Series microcomputer, with 32KB memory and a 4040 dual disk drive. An Alphatronic 200 Series light pen is also required. The price shown is the cost-per-test when diskettes are purchased in units of 250 administrations (minimum purchase). Release codes are available that allow an additional 250 administrations for $.12 per administration.

NAME: Eysenck Personality Questionnaire (Junior)

SUPPLIER: EdITS
P.O. Box 7234
San Diego, CA 92107
(619) 222-1666

PRODUCT CATEGORY	PRIMARY APPLICATIONS
Personality	Clinical Assessment/Diagnosis Personal/Marriage/Family Counseling

SALE RESTRICTIONS American Psychological Association Guidelines

SERVICE TYPE/COST	Type	Available	Cost	Discount
	Mail-In	No		
	Teleprocessing	No		
	Local	Yes	$0.30	Yes

PRODUCT DESCRIPTION

This program presents the Eysenck Personality Questionnaire (Junior) via the computer console. The test provides scores on three personality dimensions (Extraversion, Neuroticism, and Psychoticism) and on a lie scale. The complex scoring procedure is handled by the computer and the results presented on the screen immediately. Scores can be printed out and recorded on disk. The latter feature allows the development of a local databank. The program also measures response time latencies, an assessment not available in printed paper administration.

The questionnaire is completed using a light pen to touch the screen, so that the examinee never needs to use the keyboard. The program is designed for use with a Commodore PET 4000 or 8000 Series microcomputer, with 32KB memory and a 4040 dual disk drive. An Alphatronic 200 Series light pen is also required. The price shown is the cost-per-test when diskettes are purchased in units of 250 administrations (minimum purchase). Release codes are available that allow an additional 250 administrations for $.12 per administration.

NAME: Eysenck Personality Questionnaire Junior

SUPPLIER: PSYCH Systems, Inc.
600 Reisterstown Road
Baltimore, MD 21208
(800) 368-3366

PRODUCT CATEGORY

Personality

PRIMARY APPLICATIONS

Personal/Marriage/Family Counseling
Clinical Assessment/Diagnosis

SALE RESTRICTIONS Qualified Professional

SERVICE TYPE/COST	Type	Available	Cost	Discount
	Mail-In	No		
	Teleprocessing	No		
	Local	Yes	See Below	

PRODUCT DESCRIPTION

The EYSENCK PERSONALITY QUESTIONNAIRE JUNIOR is a brief, self-report measure appropriate for boys and girls between the ages of seven and fifteen. The four scales included are Toughmindedness, Extroversion, Neuroticism, and Lie.

This Psych Systems program administers and scores the test. The interpretive report it provides focuses on motivating, managing, and stimulating children in school situations and at home. Information is reported about general personality characteristics and specific recommendations for child management are given. The reports are prescriptive and focus on positive personality aspects.

Psych Systems programs operate on the IBM PC-XT, COMPAQ Plus, Dec Professional 350, and most DEC PDP-11 systems. Various hardware/ software configurations are available directly from Psych Systems, with single-user systems starting at approximately $12,000. A per test fee also applies.

222-22-2222 Jonathan Doe Jr.   10 yr old white male 16-Feb-84

```
    ----------------------------------------------------------
    |                 |                                       |
    |     EPQJR       |   Eysenck Personality Questionnaire Junior   |
    |                 |                                       |
    ----------------------------------------------------------
```

The computer program generating this report was designed by Psych
Systems, Inc., Baltimore, Maryland 21208. Copyright (C) 1984 by
Psych Systems, Inc. The interpretive logic utilized in the
generation of the report was designed by James A. Wakefield, Jr.,
Ph.D. Copyright (C) 1982, James A. Wakefield, Jr. The Eysenck
Personality Questionnaire Junior is reproduced by permission.
Copyright (C) 1975 by Edits, San Diego, California 92107. All
rights reserved.

Jonathan Doe Jr. is likely to show behavior problems, disrupt class,
and try to dominate his peers through aggressions. He is likely to
be difficult to control with either praise or punishment, but clear
rules enforced consistently by a vigilant and strict teacher produce
the best results. Clear negative consequences, such as time out or a
reduction in privleges, carried out with a minimum of emotional
display should be instituted. He tends to seek stimulation. If
rewards are to be used, material rewards (e.g. toys, candy, etc.)
will be more effective than social rewards and praise. He is likely
to be withdrawn and hostile. His misbehavior is more likely to be
vandalism against property than direct aggression against others.
Continuous monitoring for this possibility is necessary. He should
be allowed to work alone as much as possible. The opportunity to
work alone may be tried as a reward for appropriate social
interactions.

He is not likely to plan ahead and will often forget or lose interest
in goals or objectives he has undertaken. He should be encouraged to
plan ahead and follow these plans in an orderly fashion. The teacher
will need to monitor his performance continuously, remind him about
assignments, and avoid allowing him to be distracted.

Evaluation of his cognitive abilities is recommended, if it has not
already be done. High abilities for him suggest creative tendencies
which should be encouraged. Low abilities place him at risk for
serious psychological disturbances.

Summary of Scores

Scale	Raw	Z-Score
P	10	2.12
E	10	-2.52
N	13	0.65
L	9	-0.12

Individual Item Responses

```
    1234567890 1234567890 1234567890
 0: YYYYYYYYYY YYYYYYYYYY YYYYYYYYNN
30: NNNNNNNNNN YNYNYNYYYN NNYYNNYNNY
60: NYNNYYNNYN NYNYNYNYNY N
```

NAME: FIRO-B: Computer Version

SUPPLIER: Psychological Assessment Resources
P.O. Box 98
Odessa, FL 33556
(813) 977-3395

PRODUCT CATEGORY	PRIMARY APPLICATIONS
Personality	Personal/Marriage/Family Counseling Training/Development

SALE RESTRICTIONS American Psychological Association Guidelines

SERVICE TYPE/COST	Type	Available	Cost	Discount
	Mail-In	No		
	Teleprocessing	No		
	Local	Yes	NA	

PRODUCT DESCRIPTION

The program for this fully-computerized version of the Fundamental Interpersonal Relations Orientation-Behavior administers the test items, calculates all scores, and provides a four-part interpretive report based upon the client's responses. The interpretive report was designed and written by Dr. Leo R. Ryan, one of the leading experts on clinical interpretation of this test. Either client or clinician response entry is permitted and a summary of the client's responses to test items is provided.

The test measures characteristic behavior toward other people. Fifty-four test items measure the following six dimensions of interpersonal relations: Expressed Inclusion, Expressed Control, Expressed Affection, Wanted Inclusion, Wanted Control, and Wanted Affection. The test is used in individual and group psychotherapy, executive development programs, and as a measure of compatibility in relations.

The software is compatible with the Apple II + , IIe, and IBM PC microcomputers systems.

NAME: General Aptitude Test Battery

SUPPLIER: NCS/Professional Assessment Services
P.O. Box 1416
Minneapolis, MN 55440
(800) 328-6759

PRODUCT CATEGORY

Cognitive/Ability
Career/Vocational

PRIMARY APPLICATIONS

Vocational Guidance/Counseling
Personnel Selection/Evaluation
Educational Evaluation/Planning

SALE RESTRICTIONS Authorized/Certified Representatives

SERVICE TYPE/COST	Type	Available	Cost	Discount
	Mail-In	Yes	$0.75	Yes
	Teleprocessing	No		
	Local	Yes	See Below	

PRODUCT DESCRIPTION

The GENERAL APTITUDE TEST BATTERY, developed by the United States Employment Service, measures 9 major aptitudes required for occupational success. The battery is extensively normed on employed workers in over 460 occupations. Total testing time is 2.5 hours. Aptitudes assessed are General Learning Ability, Verbal, Numerical, Spatial, Form Perception, Clerical Perception, Motor Coordination, Finger Dexterity, and Manual Dexterity. Reports include raw and standard scores and 66 occupational aptitude patterns as well as up to 10 specific occcupations.

Local service: MICROTEST Assessment Software from National Computer Systems, used with a Sentry 3000 tabletop scanner (purchase price approximately $4000) and microcomputer system ($2000-$3000 purchase price), allows tests to be administered off-line. Answer sheets are then scanned and scored automatically, one at a time or in a batch. Complete test reports are then automatically generated and printed. Software purchase price for local service is $1500 plus an annual fee of $100.

Use of this service is restricted to those agencies and organizations authorized to use the test by the United States Employment Service. First-time requests for test materials will not be processed without authorization from the appropriate employment service agency.

FORM B SAMPLE	F	03	24	84	11	23	00	UNIV OF VIRGINIA	VA	B	AD
NAME	SEX	MO.	DAY	YR.	EDUC. LEVEL	YRS.	MOS.	TEST CENTER		FORM	NORM
			TEST DATE			AGE					

ADDRESS:

SOCIAL SECURITY NUMBER
(OR OTHER IDENTIFYING NO.) YRS. MOS. JOB EXP.

COMMENTS:

THE 1979 EDITION OF THE OAP PATTERNS WAS USED.

OCCUPATIONAL APTITUDE PATTERNS

1	2	3	4	5	6	7	8	9	10	11	12	13	14	15	16	17	18	19	20
L	L	L	L	L	L	L	L	L	L	L	L	H	H	H	L	L	L	L	L

21	22	23	24	25	26	27	28	29	30	31	32	33	34	35	36	37	38	39
L	L	L	L	L	L	L	L	H	H	L	L	L	H	L	L	L	L	L

40	41	42	43	44	45	46	47	48	49	50	51	52	53	54	55	56	57	58	59	60	61	62	63	64	65	66	67	68	69	70
L	H	L	L	H	H	L	L	H	H	L	L	L	L	L	L	L	L	L	L	L	L	L	L	L	L	L	L	X	X	X

71	72	73	74	75	76	77	78
X	X	X	X	X	X	X	X

GATB INDIVIDUAL APTITUDE PROFILE

	G	V	N	S	P	Q	K	F	M
APTITUDE SCORE	64	76	57	74	56	150	159	80	118
APTITUDE SCORE + 1SEm	70	82	63	82	65	159	166	92	129

*APTITUDE SCORE INVALID DUE TO "0" RAW SCORE

REPORTED BY
NATIONAL COMPUTER SYSTEMS
P.O. BOX 1294
MPLS., MN. 55440
PROCESS NUMBER
116-0005

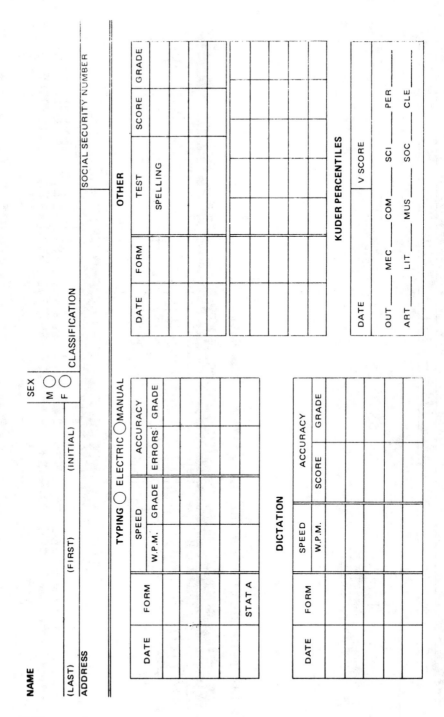

NAME

(LAST)   (FIRST)   (INITIAL)

ADDRESS

SEX   M ◯   F ◯

CLASSIFICATION

SOCIAL SECURITY NUMBER

OTHER

DATE	FORM	TEST	SCORE	GRADE
		SPELLING		

KUDER PERCENTILES

DATE		V SCORE	

OUT ____ MEC ____ COM ____ SCI ____ PER ____

ART ____ LIT ____ MUS ____ SOC ____ CLE ____

TYPING ◯ ELECTRIC ◯ MANUAL

DATE	FORM	SPEED		ACCURACY	
		W.P.M.	GRADE	ERRORS	GRADE
	STAT A				

DICTATION

DATE	FORM	SPEED	ACCURACY	
		W.P.M.	SCORE	GRADE

248 *psychware*

NAME: Giannetti On-Line Psychosocial History

SUPPLIER: NCS/Professional Assessment Services
P.O. Box 1416
Minneapolis, MN 55440
(800) 328-6759

PRODUCT CATEGORY	PRIMARY APPLICATIONS
Structured Interview	Clinical Assessment/Diagnosis Personal/Marriage/Family Counseling Personnel Selection/Evaluation

SALE RESTRICTIONS   American Psychological Association Guidelines

SERVICE TYPE/COST	Type	Available	Cost	Discount
	Mail-In	No		
	Teleprocessing	No		
	Local	Yes	$6.50	Yes

PRODUCT DESCRIPTION

This report provides, in a narrative format, a comprehensive psychosocial history. Sophisticated branching ensures that only relevant questions are presented. The GIANETTI ON-LINE PSYCHOSOCIAL HISTORY can be used to gather information about 10 different facets of the client's background and current life circumstances: Current Living Situation, Family of Origin, Client Development, Educational History, Marital History/Present Family, Occupational History/Current Finances, Legal History, Symptom Screening-Physical, Symptom Screening-Psychological, Military History. The 3-12 page report presents the client's responses in a narrative fashion.

MICROTEST Assessment Software from National Computer Systems, used with a microcomputer system ($2000-$3000 purchase price), automatically administers test items, scores test results, and generates complete test reports. The cost for local scoring refers to the cost-per-test when diskettes are purchaed in units of 20 administrations (minimum purchase).

NAME: GuidePak

SUPPLIER: Behaviordyne, Inc.
599 College Ave. Suite 1
Palo Alto, CA 94306
(415) 857-0111

PRODUCT CATEGORY

Career/Vocational
Interest/Attitudes
Motivation/Needs

PRIMARY APPLICATIONS

Vocational Guidance/Counseling
Personnel Selection/Evaluation
Educational Evaluation/Planning

SALE RESTRICTIONS   None

SERVICE TYPE/COST	Type	Available	Cost	Discount
	Mail-In	Yes	See Below	
	Teleprocessing	No		
	Local	No		

PRODUCT DESCRIPTION

GUIDEPAK is a vocational planning package that includes a California Psychological Inventory, a Strong Campbell Interest Inventory, and a planning workbook.

GUIDEPAK is available at $25.00 to individuals and $20.00 to institutional customers.

SCII Profile for ▓▓▓▓▓▓▓ ▓▓▓▓▓▓▓

00	001	926641 Sheet ID

Sex	Age	Date Scored	Date Administered
F	25	02/15/84	02/10/84

CONSULTING PSYCHOLOGISTS PRESS

Counselor's Copy

Administrative Indexes

	L%	I%	D%
Occupations	17	26	57
School Subjects	8	36	56
Activities	31	37	31
Amusements	15	23	62

	L%	I%	D%
Types of People	21	29	50
Preferences	23	37	40
Characteristics	43	21	36
All Parts	20	30	50

Total Responses	325
Infrequent Responses	4

Special Scales

Academic Comfort	22
Introversion-Extroversion	61

Occupational Scales

Code	Scale	Std Score M	Std Score F
RC	Air Force Officer	10	39
RC	Army Officer	13	36
RC	Navy Officer	6	
RC	Farmer		40
RCE	Voc. Agriculture Teacher	8	
RE	Police Officer	31	47
R	Navy Officer		36
R	Farmer	36	
R	Forester	24	
R	Skilled Craftsperson	24	
R	Radiologic Technologist		51
R	Radiologic Technologist	39	
RI	Forester		26
RI	Engineer	15	26
RI	Veterinarian	17	
RIC	Licensed Practical Nurse		13
RAS	Occupational Therapist	29	39
IR	Veterinarian		29
IR	Chemist	5	20
IR	Physicist	5	10
IR	Geologist	26	34
IR	Medical Technologist	7	25
IR	Dental Hygienist		32
IR	Dentist	21	27
IR	Optometrist	11	35
IR	Physical Therapist	17	33
IR	Physician	10	24
IRS	Registered Nurse	15	
IRS	Math-Science Teacher	18	
IRC	Math-Science Teacher		32
IRC	Systems Analyst	19	39
IRC	Computer Programmer	32	35
IRE	Chiropractor	31	15
IE	Pharmacist	27	
I	Pharmacist		43
I	Biologist	19	17
I	Geographer	27	41
I	Mathematician	26	12
IA	College Professor	34	33
IA	Sociologist	19	23
IAS	Psychologist	29	32
AIR	Architect	30	28
AI	Lawyer	20	34
AE	Public Relations Director	18	25
AE	Advertising Executive	37	41
AE	Interior Decorator	40	21
A	Musician	43	35
A	Commercial Artist	33	37
A	Fine Artist	33	41
A	Art Teacher	22	12
A	Photographer	43	45

Occupational Scales

Code	Scale	Std Score M	Std Score F
A	Librarian	31	27
A	Foreign Language Teacher	24	9
A	Reporter	25	30
A	English Teacher		6
AS	English Teacher	23	
SA	Speech Pathologist	20	31
SA	Social Worker	31	35
SA	Minister		6
SIE	Minister	4	
SI	Registered Nurse		24
S	Licensed Practical Nurse	36	
S	Special Ed. Teacher	27	38
S	Elementary Teacher	19	27
SR	Physical Ed. Teacher	20	31
SRE	Recreation Leader	28	34
SE	YMCA/YWCA Director	21	26
SE	School Administrator	22	28
SCE	Guidance Counselor	27	
SEC	Guidance Counselor		19
SEC	Social Science Teacher	26	17
EA	Flight Attendant	38	47
EA	Beautician	47	
E	Beautician		49
E	Department Store Manager	36	39
E	Realtor	29	18
E	Life Insurance Agent	10	22
E	Elected Public Offical	21	23
E	Public Administrator		30
EI	Investment Fund Manager	35	
EI	Marketing Executive	40	41
E	Personnel Director	24	36
E	Chamber of Comm. Exec.	13	
E	Restaurant Manager	30	
EC	Restaurant Manager		31
EC	Chamber of Comm. Exec.		22
EC	Buyer	25	33
EC	Purchasing Agent	22	33
ERC	Agribusiness Manager	25	
ES	Home Economics Teacher		22
ECS	Nursing Home Admin.	22	
EC	Nursing Home Admin.		23
EC	Dietitian		25
ECR	Dietitian	19	
CER	Executive Housekeeper	27	20
CES	Business Ed. Teacher	16	12
CE	Banker	21	25
CE	Credit Manager	16	24
CE	IRS Agent	30	31
CA	Public Administrator	11	
C	Accountant	18	30
C	Secretary		28
C	Dental Assistant		46

psychware **251**

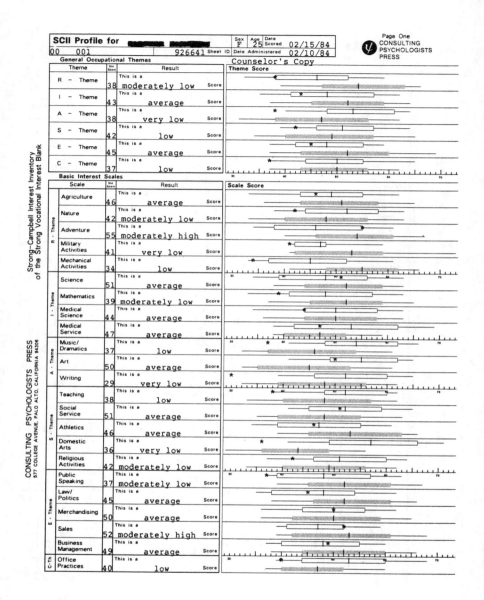

NAME: Guilford-Zimmerman Temperament Survey

SUPPLIER: NCS/Professional Assessment Services
P.O. Box 1416
Minneapolis, MN 55440
(800) 328-6759

PRODUCT CATEGORY

Personality

PRIMARY APPLICATIONS

Clinical Assessment/Diagnosis
Personal/Marriage/Family Counseling

SALE RESTRICTIONS American Psychological Association Guidelines

SERVICE TYPE/COST	Type	Available	Cost	Discount
	Mail-In	Yes	$7.70	Yes
	Teleprocessing	Yes	$7.70	Yes
	Local	Yes	$6.25	Yes

PRODUCT DESCRIPTION

The GUILFORD-ZIMMERMAN TEMPERAMENT SURVEY yields scores on 10 important dimensions of normal adult personality: Activity, Restraint, Ascendance, Sociability, Stability, Objectivity, Friendliness, Thoughtfulness, Personal Relations, and Masculinity. Test applications include personnel selection, vocational guidance, and clinical evaluation. This report is a comprehensive numerical, graphical, and interpretive analysis of these 10 dimensions.

Two systems are available for local processing of test results. MICRO-TEST Assessment Software from National Computer Systems, used with a Sentry 3000 tabletop scanner (purchase price approximately $4000) and microcomputer system ($2000-$3000 purchase price), allows tests to be administered off-line. Answer sheets are then scanned and scored automatically, one at a time or in a batch. The software also permits on-line administration of the test via microcomputer. In either case, the same report is provided. The cost for local scoring refers to the cost-per-test when diskettes are purchased in units of 20 administrations (minimum purchase).

CLINICAL INTERPRETIVE ANALYSIS

OF THE

GUILFORD - ZIMMERMAN TEMPERAMENT SURVEY

(MALE)

TEST NO. 019

CASE NO. DEMO12

TEST DATE   8/ 24/ 1982

This computer generated report of the Guilford-Zimmerman
Temperament Survey is based on information and logic provided
by Sheridan Psychological Services. Its purpose is to assist
qualified professionals in psychodiagnosis and should be used
in conjunction with the clinician's professional experience.

_____

Reviewing Professional

GUILFORD - ZIMMERMAN TEMPERAMENT SURVEY

Definitions

Scale	Low C score description	High C score description
G	Inactivity, slowness - Procrastination, avoiding any great output of energy at any cost.	General activity energy - A tendency to do everything at a rapid rate of speed and to use a large amount of metabolic energy.
R	Impulsiveness - Very spontaneous, Emotionally immature, flexible.	Restraint, seriousness - Very regimented, responsible, lacks flexibility, self-disciplined.
A	Submissiveness - Follower, refuses responsibility, insecure, likely to have difficulty obtaining the respect or attention of others.	Ascendance, social boldness - A need to maintain tight control, manipulative, anxious.
S	Shyness, seclusiveness - Unsociable, can't tolerate much interaction with others.	Social interest, sociability - The need to do almost everything in a social framework, dependent on others.
E	Emotional instability, depression - Less stable, moody, possibly neurotic, doesn't react well to emotional stress.	Emotional stability - A tendency to react the same in most conditions most of the time. Not extremely flexible. Will not fall apart in stress.
O	Subjectivity, hypersensitiveness - Thin skinned, likely to respond intensely to rejection.	Objectivity - Low interaction between exterior events and interior feelings, insensitive.
F	Hostility - Belligerent, trusts no one, always on the alert.	Friendliness, agreeableness - Congenial, trusting, likeable.
T	Unreflectiveness - Not interested in why.	Thoughtful, reflective - Has to know why, obsessed at times, inflexible.

P	Criticalness, intolerance - Intolerant of other's beliefs, fundamentally strong convictions.	Personal relations, cooperativeness - Accepting of others without evaluation, respectful, tolerant.
M	Male - More feminine characteristics than traditional male stereotype.	Female - Traditional feminine stereotype.
	Female - More masculine characteristics than traditional female stereotype.	Male - Traditional male stereotype.

GUILFORD - ZIMMERMAN TEMPERAMENT SURVEY
SCORE SUMMARY TABLE

CATEGORY	RAW SCORE	NEAREST TSCORE	CENTILE RANK	CSCORE
G	30	75	99	10
R	18	55	60	6
A	26	70	95	9
S	24	55	70	6
E	17	50	50	5
O	19	50	60	5
F	10	45	30	4
T	20	55	70	6
P	22	55	70	6
M	26	65	95	8

CSCORE GRAPH BY TRAIT

LOW SCORE DESCRIPTION		CSCORE 0 1 2 3 4 5 6 7 8 9 10	HIGH SCORE DESCRIPTION
INACTIVITY	G	*********************	ENERGETIC
IMPULSIVENESS	R	*************	RESTRAINT
SUBMISSIVENESS	A	*******************	BOLDNESS
SHYNESS	S	*************	SOCIABILITY
INSTABILITY	E	***********	STABILITY
SUBJECTIVITY	O	***********	OBJECTIVITY
HOSTILITY	F	*********	FRIENDLINESS
UNREFLECTIVE	T	*************	THOUGHTFULNESS
CRITICALNESS	P	*************	COOPERATIVE
FEMININITY	M	*****************	MASCULINITY

FACTOR	G	R	A	S	E	O	F	T	P	M	FACTOR
CSCORE	10	6	9	6	5	5	4	6	6	8	CSCORE
TSCORE	75	55	70	55	50	50	45	55	55	65	TSCORE
NEAREST PERCENT	99	60	95	70	50	60	30	70	70	95	NEAREST PERCENT

GUILFORD - ZIMMERMAN TEMPERAMENT SURVEY

SUMMARY

In self-restraint, scores are slightly above average. He takes things rather seriously and is not too likely to act impulsively. When it comes to assuming responsibility, he probably should be trusted with slightly more than the average person. Most of the time, he probably acts relatively inhibited.

He scores slightly above average in sociability, and sometimes enjoys being surrounded by other people, and will more often than not initiate conversations with strangers. There is some need for friends and acquaintances. He is not usually inclined to keep to himself.

In emotional stability, he scores slightly above average and is fairly happy most of the time. In situations that involve prolonged tension or stress, he ought to be able to cope. He could probably be described as an even-tempered person and is slightly more of an optimist than a pessimist.

In the ability to view things objectively, he scores average. He does not often take things too personally and has an average tendency to be suspicious of the motives of other people. It is moderately easy to hurt his feelings. When criticized, he usually tends to react normally.

In friendliness, he scores slightly below average. He may not put up with belligerence from other people. He feels hostile toward others slightly more often than most people do and is slightly inclined to get into arguments or fights. It is not likely that others will take advantage of him.

He is slightly above average in the extent to which he engages in introvertive thinking. He would probably like assignments that required the application of intensive thinking, planning, or analysis. He probably spends slightly more time than average in observation and analysis of himself and others.

He probably has less than average difficulty in getting along well with other people and is generally fairly easy to live and work with. His faith in mankind and his institutions is higher than average. He tends to be slightly less critical and intolerant than most people.

He has an unusually high energy level, is rarely idle or motionless, and would find sedentary work extremely difficult since he has trouble sitting still. His very high energy level will tend to exaggerate his other characteristics.

GUILFORD - ZIMMERMAN TEMPERAMENT SURVEY

He is extremely dominant in interpersonal relations and never hesitates to stand up for his rights. If called upon to exercise authority or leadership, he would be very aggressive in dealing with subordinates. He probably could not adjust to a job (position) in which he was expected to be subservient to someone else.

It is likely that he will appear to others to be very domineering and bossy.

This individual is quite high in the extent to which his interests and attitudes parallel those of the stereotyped "male" in this society. Compared to most men, he is considerably less sensitive and sympathetic. He would have difficulty in accepting a woman who did not play what he considered to be the stereotyped "feminine" role. It is likely that this person will find it very difficult to accept sympathy and nurturance from others. It is very possible that he may be denying or compensating for feminine tendencies although without additional information, no inference may be drawn. He should probably not be put into a position where he would be required to supervise or to take orders from women, particularly aggressive women. His masculinity score is very dissimilar from those generally obtained by men in such occupations as the arts, literature, counseling, the clergy, or any job in which sensitivity is essential to success. His masculinity score is similar to those generally obtained by men in such occupations as police work, engineering, forestry, manual labor, and both skilled and semiskilled trades.

GUILFORD - ZIMMERMAN TEMPERAMENT SURVEY

RESPONSES

	1	2	3	4	5	6	7	8	9	10	11	12	13	14	15	16	17	18	19	20
	T	F	T	T	T	F	F	T	T	F	T	T	F	T	F	T	T	T	F	F
21	F	T	F	F	T	T	T	F	T	F	F	F	F	T	T	F	T	T	T	F
41	T	T	F	T	T	T	T	T	T	T	T	T	T	F	F	T	F	T	T	F
61	F	T	F	F	T	F	T	T	F	F	T	T	T	F	F	F	F	T	F	T
81	F	F	F	F	F	T	T	T	F	F	F	T	T	F	F	T	F	F	F	T
101	T	F	F	F	T	F	T	F	T	T	T	F	F	F	F	T	T	T	T	T
121	T	T	T	T	T	T	F	T	F	F	T	F	F	F	T	T	T	T	T	T
141	T	F	F	T	F	T	F	T	F	F	T	T	F	T	T	T	T	T	F	F
161	F	F	T	F	T	F	T	T	T	T	T	T	T	T	F	F	F	F	F	F
181	T	F	F	F	T	F	T	T	F	F	T	T	T	T	F	F	T	T	T	F
201	F	T	F	T	T	T	F	F	F	F	T	T	F	T	T	T	F	T	T	F
221	F	T	T	T	F	T	F	T	T	T	T	F	T	F	F	T	F	T	F	T
241	F	T	T	F	T	F	T	F	T	F	F	F	F	F	F	F	F	T	F	T
261	T	T	T	T	F	F	T	F	T	T	T	T	F	T	F	F	T	F	T	T
281	F	F	T	T	F	F	F	F	F	F	F	T	T	F	T	F	T	T	T	T

THIS CONCLUDES THE SCORING OF TEST NO. 019

NAME: Halstead-Reitan Neuropsychological Battery

SUPPLIER: Integrated Professional Systems
5211 Mahoning Avenue Suite 135
Youngstown, OH 44515
(216) 799-3282

PRODUCT CATEGORY

Cognitive/Ability

PRIMARY APPLICATIONS

Behavioral Medicine
Clinical Assessment/Diagnosis

SALE RESTRICTIONS American Psychological Association Guidelines

SERVICE TYPE/COST	Type	Available	Cost	Discount
	Mail-In	No		
	Teleprocessing	No		
	Local	Yes	See Below	

PRODUCT DESCRIPTION

This program assists in the use and interpretation of the HALSTEAD-REITAN BATTERY. The battery itself is a series of tests which is intended to assist in the clinical neuropsychological analysis of organic brain disfunction. The tests used in this evaluation are the Halstead Neuropsychological Test Battery, the Wechsler Adult Intelligence Scale, the Trail Making Test, the Reitan-Indiana Aphasia Screening Test, various tests of sensory-perceptual functions, and the Minnesota Multiphasic Personality Inventory.

The report developed by this program presents findings with respect to intellectual performance, speech, auditory, memory, and motor functioning. Results help to verify the existence and location of cortical damage. Statements in the program are based on analyses which should be considered as hypotheses for further consideration in light of other clinical factors.

An operating software package, priced from $200-$850 depending on the complexity of the package, is required for program use, plus an additional fee per administration.

```
    ****  THE HALSTEAD - REITAN NEUROPSYCHOLOGICAL BATTERY  ****

  ***********************************************************************
  *            Copyright 1983 By  ESDATA & Associates                  *
  *       Distributed By INTEGRATED PROFESSIONAL SYSTEMS, INC.          *
  *    5211 Mahoning Avenue - Suite 135      Youngstown, Ohio  44515    *
  *                     ALL RIGHTS RESERVED                             *
  ***********************************************************************


                  Reproduced by permission granted to


                       IPS Scoring Services
                  5211 Mahoning Avenue, Suite 135
                       Youngstown, OH 44515
                       Phone (216) 799-3282
```

JOHN SAMPLE is a 56 year old male with 12 years of education. He was
examined on March 1, 1984.

This is a confidential report for use by professional staff only. The
words used in the interpretation are technically defined and have
specific meaning for clinical patients. The program which generates this
report considers many decision rules and the results need to be
interpreted in light of the limitations of the test battery. Statements
are based on analyses which should be considered as hypotheses for
further consideration in combination with the patient's verbal
admissions and other clinical factors.

```
                          ------------------------   ------------
                          REVIEWING PROFESSIONAL        DATE
```

260 *psychware*

THE   HALSTED - REITAN   NEUROPSYCHOLOGICAL   PROFILE

TEST	Rating	Normal 0	1	2	3	4	Impaired 5
Halstead Category	4.77	.				+	.
TPT - Total Time	5.00	.					+
- Memory	4.50	.				+	
- Location	4.30	.				+	.
Speech Perception	4.58	.				+	.
Seashore Rhythm	3.70	.			+		.
Finger Tapping - D	4.14	.				+	.
- N	3.68	.			+		.
Trail Making - A	5.00	.					+
- B	5.00	.					+
Aphasia	0.83	.	+				.
Spatial Relations	5.00	.					+
Perceptual Disorders	5.00	.					+
Digit Symbol	5.00	.					+

TEST	Rating	0	1	2	3	4	5
		Normal					Impaired

D : Dominant Hand   N : Non-Dominant Hand   - : Test Not Given

Average Impairment Rating = 4.32

Modified Impairment Index = 0.92

The Average Impairment Rating and the Modified Impairment Index are based
on results of the following tests :

    Halstead Category Test
    Halstead Tactual Performance Test - Total Time
    Halstead Tactual Performance Test - Memory
    Halstead Tactual Performance Test - Location
    Halstead Speech Perception Test
    Seashore Rhythm Test
    Halstead Finger Tapping Test - Dominant Hand
    Halstead Finger Tapping Test - Non-Dominant Hand
    Trail Making A
    Trail Making B
    Aphasia Examination
    Spatial Relations Examination
    Perceptual Disorders Examination
    Digit Symbol Test from WAIS

```
                SUMMARY    OF    TEST    SCORES

Test                                                         Score
------------------------------------------------------------------

WAIS Subtests (Scaled Score)

        Information    ......................................   13
        Comprehension  ......................................   10
        Arithmetic     ......................................    7
        Similarities   ......................................    9
        Digit Span     ......................................   10
        Vocabulary     ......................................   11
        Digit Symbol   ......................................    0
        Picture Completion  .................................    7
        Block Design   ......................................    0
        Picture Arrangement  ...............................     2
        Object Assembly  ....................................    4

WAIS Verbal IQ  .................................................  100
WAIS Performance IQ  ............................................   68
WAIS Full Scale IQ  .............................................   86

Halstead Category Test - # of errors  .................  136

Halstead Tactual Performance Test
        Dominant Hand      - Speed in minutes  ..........   10.0
                           - # of blocks inserted  ......    0
        Non-Dominant Hand  - Speed in minutes  ..........   10.0
                           - # of blocks inserted  ......    0
        Both Hands         - Speed in minutes  ..........   10.0
                           - # of blocks inserted  ......    0
        Total Time in Minutes  .........................   30.0
        Memory  - # correct  ...........................    1
        Location - # correct  ..........................    0

Halstead Speech Perception Test - # of errors  .......   31

Seashore Rhythm Test - # of errors  ..................   16

Halstead Finger Tapping Test
        Dominant Hand  ...............................   25
        Non-Dominant Hand  ...........................   25

Trail Making A in seconds  ........................  172
Trail Making B in seconds  ........................  300

Aphasia Examination - # of errors  ..................    4

Spatial Relations Examination
        Total Scores for 2 Crosses  ..................   10
        Modified Score  ..............................   12
```

262 *psychware*

```
++++++++++++++++++++++++
++++++++++++++++++++++++
++   TEST  FINDINGS   ++
++++++++++++++++++++++++
++++++++++++++++++++++++
```

The subject is RIGHT-HANDED; is RIGHT-EYED; and does NOT
have CROSSED EYE-HAND DOMINANCE.

He has DULL NORMAL intelligence with test performance that
falls into the VERY SEVERELY IMPAIRED range of higher mental
funtions.

The test findings are CONSISTENT with the presence of brain
dysfunction.

With regard to differential functioning of the cerebral
hemispheres, cortical damage is STRONGLY LATERALIZED to the
RIGHT.

The nature of the dysfunction is an ACUTE LESION.

```
+++++++++++++++++++++++++++
+ SUMMARY OF TEST SCORES +
+++++++++++++++++++++++++++
```

Perceptual Disorders Examination

	Right	Left
Finger Agnosia	17	14
Finger Tip Writing	15	15
Tactile Hypesthesia	—	—
Tactile Suppressions (total)	6	6
Auditory Suppressions	0	0
Visual Suppressions	2	6
Homonymous Hemianopia (1=yes, 2=no)	—	—

— : Test not given.

psychware **263**

NAME: High School Personality Questionnaire Narrative Report

SUPPLIER: Institute for Personality and Ability Testing, Inc.
P.O. Box 188
Champaign, IL 61820
(217) 352-4739

PRODUCT CATEGORY	PRIMARY APPLICATIONS
Personality	Educational Evaluation/Planning
Cognitive/Ability	Personal/Marriage/Family Counseling
	Vocational Guidance/Counseling

SALE RESTRICTIONS American Psychological Association Guidelines

SERVICE TYPE/COST	Type	Available	Cost	Discount
	Mail-In	Yes	$16.00	Yes
	Teleprocessing	Yes	$17.00	Yes
	Local	No		

PRODUCT DESCRIPTION

The HIGH SCHOOL PERSONALITY QUESTIONNAIRE NAR-RATIVE REPORT is intended to guide institutional personnel, counselors, and school psychologists in working with all students. The report is built around 14 primary personality dimensions that include Stability, Tension, Warmth, Enthusiasm, and 10 others. Scores for Anxiety, Extraversion, Creativity, Leadership, and other broad trait patterns are also calculated and reported.

The test and report are useful in helping to spot the potential dropout, the drug user, or the low achiever, for example. The test is often used in correctional settings with delinquents, drug users, behavior problems, etc., to facilitate parent-teacher, parent-officer, and parent-clinic cooperation.

THIS COMPUTER ANALYSIS OF THE HIGH SCHOOL PERSONALITY QUESTIONNAIRE
IS INTENDED ONLY FOR PROPERLY QUALIFIED PROFESSIONALS AND SHOULD BE
TREATED IN THE SAME MANNER AS ANY CONFIDENTIAL REPORT.

NAME.... MALE SAMPLE
ID......
AGE..... 13
SEX..... M
DATE.... 4/20/1984

STEN SCORES ON THE PRIMARY-FACTOR TRAITS OF THE HSPQ

AVERAGE

FACTOR	SCORE RAW	STEN	LOW MEANING	1 2 3 4 5 6 7 8 9 10	HIGH MEANING	CENTILE
A	11	6	RESERVED		OUTGOING	60
B	06	5	DULL		BRIGHT	40
C	08	5	EASILY UPSET		CALM, STABLE	40
D	08	4	STOIC, LISTLESS		EXCITABLE	23
E	10	5	SUBMISSIVE		DOMINANT	40
F	13	7	SOBER, SERIOUS		LIVELY	77
G	06	3	EXPEDIENT		CONSCIENTIOUS	11
H	08	4	SHY, TIMID		VENTURESOME	23
I	07	6	TOUGH-MINDED		TENDER-MINDED	60
J	05	3	PARTICIPATING		INTROSPECTIVE	11
O	12	7	SECURE, PLACID		APPREHENSIVE	77
Q2	05	3	GROUP-ORIENTED		SELF-SUFFICIENT	11
Q3	11	6	UNDISCIPLINED		SELF-DISCIPLINED	60
Q4	11	6	RELAXED		TENSE, DRIVEN	60

PRIMARY PERSONALITY CHARACTERISTICS OF SPECIAL INTEREST
REGARD FOR RULES AND RESPECT FOR FINE MORAL OBLIGATIONS IS NOT HIGH.

AT SCHOOL AND ELSEWHERE, HE IS A SOLID MEMBER OF A GROUP, ZESTFULLY
    PLAYING HIS PART AND SHARING THE EXPERIENCES OF HIS GROUP
    THIS CHARACTERISTIC IS HIGH.

HE HAS SOME LACK OF SELF-SUFFICIENCY AND PREFERS TO BE A JOINER AND DEPEND
    ON GOING ALONG WITH THE GROUP.

EVALUATION OF SECOND-STRATUM TRAITS AND CRITERIA OF GENERAL IMPORTANCE

THIS PERSON IS NEITHER EXTRAVERTED NOR INTROVERTED BUT IS APPROXIMATELY
    AVERAGE WITH A SCORE OF 6.4.

THIS INDIVIDUAL'S ANXIETY SCORE OF 6.4 IS AVERAGE.

HIS PROPENSITY TOWARDS ALERT AND DECISIVE RESPONSES, REFLECTED IN A
    SCORE OF 6.1, MAY BE CONSIDERED AVERAGE.
THE TENDENCY OF THIS INDIVIDUAL TOWARDS INDEPENDENT AND SELF-DIRECTED
    BEHAVIOR IS EXPRESSED BY A SCORE OF 2.6, WHICH CAN BE THOUGHT OF AS
    LOW.
THE DEGREE OF SOCIAL RESPONSIBILITY AND CONTROL HE HAS ACHIEVED IS
    REFLECTED IN A SCORE OF 4.1 THAT MAY BE CONSIDERED BELOW AVERAGE.
A SCORE OF 6.9 INDICATES THAT HIS ACCIDENT PRONENESS IS ABOVE AVERAGE.

HIS GENERAL CAPACITY TO WORK CREATIVELY, TO TRANSCEND CUSTOM, AND TO
GENERATE NEW IDEAS, INDICATED BY A SCORE OF 4.0, IS BELOW AVERAGE.
A SCORE OF 3.4 ON LEADERSHIP POTENTIAL SUGGESTS THAT THE PROBABILITY
OF HIS EFFECTIVELY ACCEPTING A ROLE OF CENTRAL AUTHORITY AND
DIRECTION IN ANY GROUP SITUATION IS LOW.

ESTIMATING THIS INDIVIDUAL'S SCORE OF 3.4 FROM KNOWN RELATIONSHIPS
BETWEEN PERSONALITY AND SCHOLASTIC PERFORMANCE INDICATES THAT HIS
LEVEL OF ACHIEVEMENT IN MAIN SCHOOL SUBJECTS WILL BE LOW.

THE CAPACITY OF THIS INDIVIDUAL TO ADJUST TO THE DEMANDS OF A SKILLED
OCCUPATION AND TO GROW INTO A JOB IS EXPRESSED IN A SCORE OF 3.6,
THAT MAY BE REGARDED AS BELOW AVERAGE.

A SCORE OF 4.6 SUGGESTS THAT HIS ABILITY TO PERFORM DEPENDABLY IN
A JOB OR TASK WHICH IS REPETITIVE OR TEDIOUS IS AVERAGE.

psychware **265**

NAME: Hogan Personality Inventory

SUPPLIER: NCS/Professional Assessment Services
P.O. Box 1416
Minneapolis, MN 55440
(800) 328-6759

PRODUCT CATEGORY	PRIMARY APPLICATIONS
Personality	Personal/Marriage/Family Counseling Personnel Selection/Evaluation

SALE RESTRICTIONS   American Psychological Association Guidelines

SERVICE TYPE/COST Type	Available	Cost	Discount
Mail-In	Yes	$4.50	Yes
Teleprocessing	Yes	$4.50	Yes
Local	Yes	$2.60	Yes

PRODUCT DESCRIPTION

The HOGAN PERSONALITY INVENTORY is a theory-based inventory designed to assess the entire range of normal personality characteristics. The 300 true-false items require an 8th-grade reading level and 30-40 minutes for completion. The instrument measures six primary traits: Intellectance, Adjustment, Prudence, Ambition, Sociability, and Likeability. In addition to one validity scale, the test also includes six occupational scales: Service Orientation, Clerical Performance, Sales Performance, Managerial Performance, Stress Tolerance, and Reliability. Each of the scales is composed of 4-10 homogeneous item composites from a total of 45. Applications of the HOGAN PERSONALITY INVENTORY include counseling, employment decisions, research, and self-development.

The two-page profile report presents raw and percentile scores for the primary scales along with a listing of the 45 homogeneous item composites.

Two systems are available for local processing of test results. MICRO-TEST Assessment Software from National Computer Systems, used with a Sentry 3000 tabletop scanner (purchase price approximately $4000) and microcomputer system ($2000-$3000 purchase price), allows tests to be administered off-line. Answer sheets are then scanned and scored automatically, one at a time or in a batch. The software also permits on-line administration of the test via microcomputer. In either case, the same report is provided. The cost for local scoring refers to the cost-per-test when diskettes are purchased in units of 20 administrations (minimum purchase).

NAME: Holland Occupational System

SUPPLIER: Publishers Test Service
2500 Garden Road
Monterey, CA 93940
(800) 538-9547

PRODUCT CATEGORY	PRIMARY APPLICATIONS
Career/Vocational	Vocational Guidance/Counseling

SALE RESTRICTIONS American Psychological Association Guidelines

SERVICE TYPE/COST	Type	Available	Cost	Discount
	Mail-In	No		
	Teleprocessing	No		
	Local	Yes	$165.00	

PRODUCT DESCRIPTION

This program has been developed to automate the use of Holland occupational codes and DOT entries that have been linked to those codes.

Clients may enter their Holland codes and receive a listing or printout of all relevant DOT occupational titles. Over 2,200 DOT occupations are present in the data base. To assist the student in learning more about the occupations that match his or her Holland code, the program provides both the DOT number and the occupational group code. An easy-to-follow User's Guide explains the purpose of the program, how to use it, how to maintain it, and what to do if any problems occur.

NAME: Human Resource Development Report

SUPPLIER: Institute for Personality and Ability Testing, Inc.
P.O. Box 188
Champaign, IL 61820
(217) 352-4739

PRODUCT CATEGORY	PRIMARY APPLICATIONS
Personality	Personnel Selection/Evaluation
Motivation/Needs	Training/Development

SALE RESTRICTIONS American Psychological Association Guidelines

SERVICE TYPE/COST	Type	Available	Cost	Discount
	Mail-In	Yes	$30.00	Yes
	Teleprocessing	Yes	$31.00	Yes
	Local	No		

PRODUCT DESCRIPTION

The HUMAN RESOURCE DEVELOPMENT REPORT is a computer-generated narrative report that assesses an individual's management style by looking at his/her personality characteristics. Three main management skills are addressed in the report: (1) Motivating Others, which includes leading, evaluating subordinates, and acting with others; (2) Organizing, which includes controlling people and events, dealing with demands, and using resources; (3) Taking Action, which includes using power, making decisions, and handling tension/stress. The report also addresses whether the person was distorting his/her responses.

The HUMAN RESOURCE DEVELOPMENT REPORT is one part of a total selection/promotion system. It should be used in conjunction with interview data, supervisor ratings, employment history, and reference checks, as well as other suitable measures of ability. It describes a test taker's personal style and probable behavior.

HUMAN RESOURCE DEVELOPMENT REPORT

NAME...John   Sample
SEX....M
AGE....42
DATE... 4/20/1984

VALIDITY INDICATORS

Indications are that Mr Sample's answers to the surveys used were made without excessive attention paid to the "social desirability" of the various alternatives. As a consequence, the following report is likely to represent a fair analysis of his attitudes, interests, and personality makeup. While there is no reason to doubt the accuracy of the report it must be integrated with other information that is known about him. In this respect, the report will be most useful as a tool to suggest areas for further exploration and inquiry.

LEADING OTHERS

Mr Sample displays a combination of personality traits that indicates he has a definite preference for functioning in a leadership capacity. He demonstrates an awareness of the interpersonal dynamics involved in the leader-follower relationship and is sensitive to the needs of others. He likes to be the one in charge and expects others to act promptly on his ideas and suggestions. Mr Sample is likely to challenge any oppostition with assertiveness and direction. In general, his interpersonal skills, in combination with his assertive, almost forceful nature, allow him to get his points across without appearing too unreasonalbe.

EVALUATING SUBORDINATES

This section is concerned with Mr Sample's attitudes toward evaluating the performance of his personnel. He views evaluation sessions as a time when he can sit down with each employee and together they can evaluate the employee's performance. He weighs his employees' opinions with his own ideas and then proceeds to generate new goals for the employees to reach. The sessions are not one sided, however, and employees are free to speak their concerns. Mr Sample uses this information along with his own feelings of what each employee is capable of doing to set goals for each employee to reach. Mr Sample is likely to conduct individual assessments of employee performance in addition to those sessions already scheduled. he is confident of his social skills and his ability to get along with others. Therefore, he is likely to talk with personnel about their performance whenever he or they deem it appropriate.

INTERACTING WITH OTHERS

Mr Sample shows an equally high preference for situations involving group endeavors or individual efforts. He is typically good-natured and considerate. He is socially bold, is generally well liked, and enjoys talking. He views his ability to work well with others as an important managerial tool in getting others to do what he wants. Although outwardly warm and friendly, he will not hesitate to exploit others and his relationships with them in order to gain his own ends. On the other hand, he realizes that some situations will demand his individual attention. In this event, he would be expected to function more than adequately. He is independent and autonomous, but also assertive and self-willed. He enjoys opportunities to work alone and usually accomplishes a great deal. Also, working on his own gives him a chance to make full use of the talent and expertise that he has acquired through his years of management experience.

psychware **269**

CONTROLLING PEOPLE AND EVENTS

Mr Sample is results oriented and motivated toward goal accomplishment and task completion. He likes to have the lines of authority clearly defined and specific objectives for each employee clearly delineated. He apparently believes that managerial guidance is best provided through establishing realistic goals for people to meet, which will, hopefully, serve a motivational function as well. Mr Sample seems to be concerned with helping subordinates attain their goals by building up their self-confidence and serving as a resource in areas in which they have little expertise. He indicates that it is important to structure the work situation in a way that meets both the demands of the company and the individual needs of the employee. At the same time, he realizes the adverse effects that too much structure can create, such as reduced production and decreased employee satisfaction. Consequently, he probably attempts to achieve a balanced work environment, providing enough structure and task identity so that the work gets done, yet providing employees with enough autonomy and skill variety so they won't get bored.

USING HUMAN RESOURCES

Mr Sample is a forceful, strong-willed, and persevering individual. He is poised, productive, and optimistic about the future. He is confident of his ability to do what he wishes and is shrewd and calculating in his behavior. He faces up to tough situations and is able to maintain his cool under the pressure of impending deadlines. He is well versed in the managerial art of juggling multiple contingencies and attempting to simultaneously solve many problems. Mr Sample is not the type of person to let incomplete tasks go unfinished. If he sees a job that needs to be done, he tries to take care of it as soon as possible. He is typically perceptive and alert and able to comprehend problems and situations rapidly and incisively. If he does have a problem, it is that he can't leave well enough alone. hE is eager for action and will frequently change the way of doing things when there is no need to. This may irritate superiors and confuse subordinates whom are both accustomed to the old procedures. He enjoys experiencing novelty and change in his daily routine. He prefers variety and dislikes delay. He is quick in temperament and reaction and might even be called impulsive. Mr Sample is impatient and intolerant of unproductive effort or attention. In his hurry to get things done, he may frequently overlook critical details. It's not quality that interests him, but quantity.

He usually has a very clear idea about how things should be done. Therefore, in group problem-solving situations, he would probably attempt to take command and control the direction of the group.

DEALING WITH DEMANDS

The effectiveness of his behavior controls is average. Mr Sample needs, at times, to guard against acting irresponsibly on impulses and inner conflicts. Coupled with this is the fact that his reported regard for rules and group standards is below average. As far as accidents and errors are concerned, he is no more susceptible than the average person. Overall, his life style is independent and self-directed, leading to active attempts to achieve freedom of choice and control of his environment.

USING POWER

Mr Sample possesses a pattern of personality characteristics that suggests an extremely high preference for controlling others. He enjoys being in a management position, finding it rewarding as well as challenging. He believes that having the authority to direct others is a valuable tool and, because of his rather bold and assertive nature, one that he probably uses without hesitation. However, he feels that skilled and experienced managers should be able to direct others toward organizational accomplishments without subordinates' feeling controlled. He is diplomatic under pressure and is able to criticize coworkers tactfully, so that they do not take offense. He seems to possess the ability to calculate the reactions of his subordinates to his authority and, in general, knows how to use people and manage groups to reach company objectives. He maintains a calm, relaxed atmosphere that employees probably find enjoyable to work in. Mr Sample is aware of the demand for bottom-line results, but keeps in mind the attitudes and opinions of employees. Thus, he would be expected to use his authority in a subtle and tactful fashion, but with just enough force to nudge subordinates in the direction most beneficial to the organization.

MAKING DECISIONS

The ability to make decisions is one of Mr Sample's strengths. He is decisive and action oriented. He is tough-minded and practical, and his approach to most problems and situations is cool and objective. He is more concerned about getting things done than with how they are done. He appears to be alert and well informed, and probably places a high value on cognitive and intellectual matters. In general, he is very adept in the areas of verbal skills and abstract thought, but his level of creativity is considered to be only average.

HANDLING TENSION AND STRESS

At the present time Mr Sample sees himself as less anxious than most people. He is self-assured and seems to possess the emotional reserve to deal with conflicts and problems in an effective manner. He responds in a controlled fashion and probably doesn't get upset easily. He is likely to take risks in order to achieve both personal and organizational goals. He is trusting and accepting of people and his environment. He approaches problems with calm emotional stability and realism.

NAME: IDEAS

SUPPLIER: NCS/Professional Assessment Services
P.O. Box 1416
Minneapolis, MN 55440
(800) 328-6759

PRODUCT CATEGORY	PRIMARY APPLICATIONS
Interest/Attitudes	Vocational Guidance/Counseling

SALE RESTRICTIONS None

SERVICE TYPE/COST	Type	Available	Cost	Discount
	Mail-In	No		
	Teleprocessing	No		
	Local	Yes	$4.50	Yes

PRODUCT DESCRIPTION

This interest inventory serves as an introduction to career planning and occupational exploration at the junior high and high school level. The inventory consists of 112 items with five response choices. It requires a 6th-grade reading level and about 30-40 minutes for completion.

The report graphically presents scores on the following scales: Mechanical/Fixing, Electronics, Nature/Outdoors, Science/ Numbers, Writing, Arts/Crafts, Social Service, Child Care, Medical Service, Business, Sales, Office Practices, and Food Service.

MICROTEST Assessment Software from National Computer Systems, used with a microcomputer system ($2000-$3000 purchase price), automatically administers test items, scores test results, and generates complete test reports. The cost for local scoring refers to the cost-per-test when diskettes are purchased in units of 20 administrations (minimum purchase).

NAME: Index of Somatic Problems

SUPPLIER: PSYCH Systems, Inc.
600 Reisterstown Road
Baltimore, MD 21208
(800) 368-3366

PRODUCT CATEGORY	PRIMARY APPLICATIONS
Structured Interview	Clinical Assessment/Diagnosis Personal/Marriage/Family Counseling

SALE RESTRICTIONS Qualified Professional

SERVICE TYPE/COST	Type	Available	Cost	Discount
	Mail-In	No		
	Teleprocessing	No		
	Local	Yes	See Below	

PRODUCT DESCRIPTION

This instrument uses a true/false format to summarize troublesome somatic problems most frequently found among psychiatric patients. Test administration uses a branching logic in item presentation. The total number of items varies from 14-60 items.

The INDEX OF SOMATIC PROBLEMS is most appropriately used to determine which psychosomatic problems a patient is using as a way of coping with emotional difficulties. Its purpose is to delineate visible complaints with distinct psychogenic characteristics.

This Psych Systems program administers and scores the test, then provides a brief printout of test results.

Psych Systems programs operate on the IBM PC-XT, COMPAQ Plus, Dec Professional 350, and most DEC PDP-11 systems. Various hardware/ software configurations are available directly from Psych Systems, with single-user systems starting at approximately $12,000. A per test fee also applies.

222-22-2222 Jonathan Doe   32 yr old white male 16-Feb-84

```
------------------------------------------
|       |                                  |
|  ISP  |   INDEX OF SOMATIC PROBLEMS      |
|       |                                  |
------------------------------------------
```

The respondent reports no problems with sex organs,
muscle pains and nausea. However the respondent reports specific
problems as follows:

abdominal pains   -sudden onset
                         -lasting longer than 30 minutes
                         -located in lower middle area

abdominal swelling   -located in upper middle area
                         -located in upper part
                         -located in upper left area
                         -located in upper right area

chest pains   -sudden onset
                         -causes sweating
                         -several attacks
                         -constricting

headaches   -steady, long-lasting
                         -caused by tension

thyroid   -recent operation

seizures

coughing

nervous complaints   -tremor
                         -fainting
                         -light-headed dizziness
                         -room-spinning dizziness

The computer program generating this report was designed by Psych
Systems, Inc., Baltimore, Maryland 21208. Copyright (C) 1984 by
Psych Systems, Inc. All rights reserved.

274 *psychware*

NAME: Individualized Stress Management Program

SUPPLIER: Institute for Personality and Ability Testing, Inc.
P.O. Box 188
Champaign, IL 61820
(217) 352-4739

PRODUCT CATEGORY	PRIMARY APPLICATIONS
Personality	Personnel Selection/Evaluation Clinical Assessment/Diagnosis Training/Development

SALE RESTRICTIONS   Authorized/Certified Representatives

SERVICE TYPE/COST	Type	Available	Cost	Discount
	Mail-In	Yes	$30.00	
	Teleprocessing	No		
	Local	No		

PRODUCT DESCRIPTION

The INDIVIDUALIZED STRESS MANAGEMENT PROGRAM is a complete assessment and training package designed for those who conduct stress management in business, health care, education, government, and private counseling settings. The leader can administer the program to individuals or groups who want to learn how to handle stress.

Using their own customized book, individuals learn how to understand the stress they experience, recognize its sources, and develop ways to control or prevent it.

Diagnostic data from the 16 PF and Stress Evaluation Inventory yield personality and lifestyle information which forms the basis for a personalized prescription plan for each individual. This self-paced, self-help approach easily fits into a seminar, course, or individual consultation setting. Statistical data are documented in the administrator's manual.

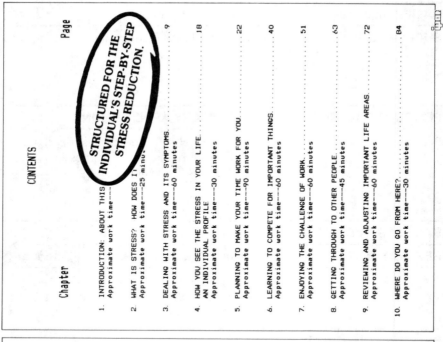

CONTENTS

Chapter

Page

STRUCTURED FOR THE INDIVIDUAL'S STEP-BY-STEP STRESS REDUCTION.

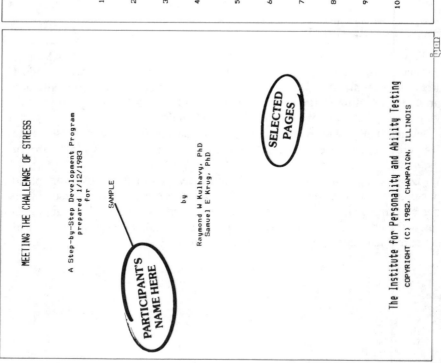

MEETING THE CHALLENGE OF STRESS

A Step-by-Step Development Program
prepared 1/12/1983
for

SAMPLE

PARTICIPANT'S NAME HERE

by

Raymond W Kulhavy, PhD
Samuel E Krug, PhD

SELECTED PAGES

The Institute for Personality and Ability Testing

sources of stress in your own life in comparison with people just like you throughout the country.

Chapters 5 through 8 were uniquely selected and written for you to provide you with specialized techniques for meeting your personal needs and using your own personal resources best. With practice you can develop more effective ways to cope with the challenges that confront you in your work, home, and personal life.

Because this book has been specifically published for you, and because the exercises take more time than just reading, we've given you some rough guidelines as to how much time you might expect to spend on each chapter, reading the material and working through the specially-selected exercises. These are just estimates to help you plan your path through the book. You might actually spend a little more or a little less time on a particular chapter. Our estimates are based on the average time other people have taken to complete the material.

The more time you have to spend, the more you'll get out of the information and exercises provided. But whatever you do, don't try to complete a chapter we estimate might take you 60 minutes in a 15-minute time slot. In the long run, the only one you're hurting is you.

SUMMARIZES CHAPTER CONTENT.

1. INTRODUCTION: ABOUT THIS BOOK

This book is unlike any you've ever read before. It was written for you from information you alone provided. The different chapters, the order of those chapters, and even the content of those chapters have been individually selected to create a unique workbook, one that will work best for you.

This book is about stress and how you can best deal with it. By best, we mean the best way for YOU! We have taken what you've said about stress and yourself when you answered the questionnaires earlier.

----In Chapter 2, you'll learn more about just what stress does to you and how it affects your life each day.

----In Chapter 3, you'll discover some simple, but effective, general techniques you can use every day to reduce stress and live more comfortably.

----In Chapter 4, you'll see how high you rank various

Your answers were grouped together under three headings——JOB, FAMILY, and PERSONAL——in terms of the degree of stress you reported for each of these target areas. The chart below shows how much of the overall score comes from each area.

Relative Degree of Stress Reported
In Three Areas

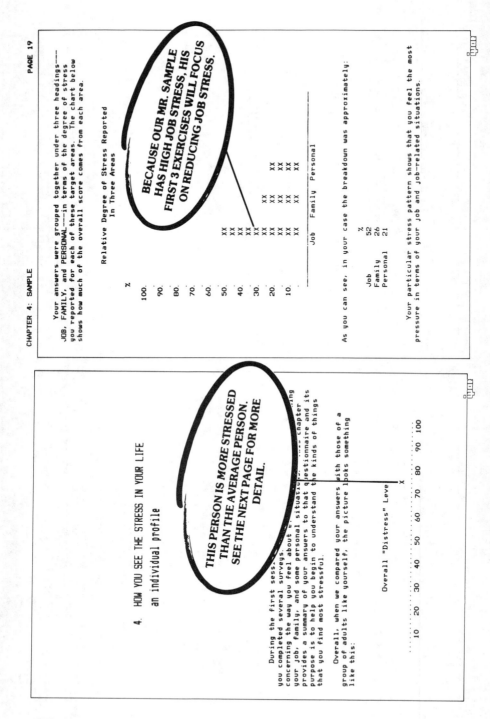

BECAUSE OUR MR. SAMPLE HAS HIGH JOB STRESS, HIS FIRST 3 EXERCISES WILL FOCUS ON REDUCING JOB STRESS.

As you can see, in your case the breakdown was approximately:

	%
Job	52
Family	26
Personal	21

Your particular stress pattern shows that you feel the most pressure in terms of your job and job-related situations.

---

4. HOW YOU SEE THE STRESS IN YOUR LIFE
   an individual profile

THIS PERSON IS MORE STRESSED THAN THE AVERAGE PERSON. SEE THE NEXT PAGE FOR MORE DETAIL.

During the first sess... you completed several surveys. concerning the way you feel about ...ing your job, family, and some personal situation... ...chapter provides a summary of your answers to that questionnaire and its purpose is to help you begin to understand the kinds of things that you find most stressful.

Overall, when we compared your answers with those of a group of adults like yourself, the picture looks something like this:

Overall "Distress" Leve...

10 20 30 40 50 60 70 80 90 100

278 *psychware*

Based on this information we have chosen three Exercises especially aimed at helping with stress sources of the kind you have expressed most concern about. The next three chapters of this book contain these exercises, which are titled:

CHAPTER 5. PLANNING TO MAKE YOUR TIME WORK FOR YOU
CHAPTER 6. LEARNING TO COMPETE FOR IMPORTANT THINGS
CHAPTER 7. ENJOYING THE CHALLENGE OF WORK

Your second highest area invo... situations. Although you don't... area, it is still important to b... it in order to cut down your ove...

We have selected one Exercis... to help you in this area of stress.

CHAPTERS 5-9 CONTAIN PERSONAL BEHAVIORAL GOALS TO MANAGE STRESSFUL EVENTS.

CHAPTER 8. GETTING THROUGH TO OTHER PEOPLE

Your area of lowest stress potential lies in matters related to family and family-related situations. Again, we have selected one Exercise which should help you in maintaining good stress-man-agement skills overall. It is titled:

CHAPTER 9. REVIEWING AND ADJUSTING IMPORTANT LIFE AREAS

Certain of your answers on the questionnaire may supply a clue to specific situations that are most stressful for you. Before going on to the rest of the book, take a moment to review the following items which you said applied to you a lot of the time.

* I wish that I could change my personal relationship with a member of my family.

* Because I am so busy, I prefer to keep my social
  contacts to a minimum.

* Lately, I have been losing my temper more often
  than usual.

5. PLANNING TO MAKE YOUR TIME WORK FOR YOU

1 OF 4 POSSIBLE EXERCISES FOR REDUCING JOB STRESS.

This chapter has been selected for you to help you learn to better manage your time at work and, by doing so, reduce some of the stress that you reported to be comparatively strong in that area.

We estimate that it will take you about 90 minutes to read through the material presented here and to work through the exercises. It will be more effective to complete the entire chapter at a single sitting, so don't begin unless you have an hour and a half available now.

One of the most common sources of stress for busy people is a constant feeling of being overcommitted and not having enough time to complete all required tasks. At one point or another, everyone has the experience of too much to do and not enough time in which to do it. Over a long period, these feelings lead to tension and anxiety and act as a continuous source of stress on the system. In the exercise that follows, we call this particular state of affairs TIME-REFERENCED STRESS.

Time-Referenced Stress often occurs because we:

* commit ourselves to more activities than we can realistically handle and tend to take on even more responsibilities as the pressure to produce increases;

* fail to establish personal priorities based on the importance of individual tasks to our life plan;

* have no overall plan for organizing and using the productive time that we do have available.

Any one of the three time-stress activities just covered can result in feelings of rushing, no time available for work that needs to be done, worry over jobs not completed, and missing important deadlines. The time-stress pattern affects us in many ways and off___ ___nt feelings of anxiety and panic. Time-Re____ ___ated, but the same feeling of los___ ___ social activities and family r___

BACKGROUND INFORMATION
MR. SAMPLE WILL USE IN
THE FOLLOWING EXERCISES.

_ of Time-Referenced Stress, ___stionnaire that you should ___ chapter. The score that you ___ help to determine to what extent ___seful to you.

follow___ ___structions on the page after the questionnaire.

___ next page, complete the questionnaire, and

Before we begin this chapter, it will be helpful to consider certain PERSONAL BEHAVIOR GOALS. These goals are suggestions for making changes in the way you react to people, situations, and events. The suggestions are based on an analysis of the answers you gave to the questionnaires and take into account your unique personal characteristics.

You'll find it easier to learn effective time-management skills if you work at becoming more self-sufficient and less dependent upon the input of other people. Whenever possible, try to schedule your day around events that you personally feel are important and pay less attention to the priorities of other people.

No matter how self-sufficient you are, there will still be times when your consistency and self-discipline will be challenged by the changing nature of assignments. In your case this could be especially troublesome. You may well find yourself, on occasion, shifting aimlessly from one job to another without really accomplishing anything. You'll be in a better position to manage stress effectively if you make an extra effort to stay on course and stick to the time management plan you set for yourself.

You tend to blame yourself and worry when things don't go as planned. Try instead to approach challenges with confidence. ___ ___rust in your ability to follow ___ ___ns that you develop. In ___ up. In ___ plan consis___ another par___ that you c___ step at a ti___

You have an ___ tend, quite ___ traditional soluti___ spend too much time ___ to problems. However, ___ pressures by recognizing that ___ requires a novel solution.

1 TO 4 PERSONAL BEHAVIOR
GOALS STATE BOTH TYPE AND
DIRECTION OF NEEDED BEHAVIOR
CHANGES. SCORE INTERPRETATION
IS DONE FOR YOU!

TIME ORGANIZATION QUESTIONNAIRE

0 . . . . 1 . . . . 2 . . . . 3 4
Does Not   Somewhat   Very
Apply to Me   Descriptive   Descriptive

There are ten Time-Organization statements given
below. Write the number from the scale above
which best describes how you see yourself in
terms of each statement.

Rating

_____ A.   Busy from d...
             feeling of com...

_____ B.   Cluttered, unorgani...
             tasks seem to get lost ...

_____ C.   Frequently missing deadlines, even though they
             were established well ahead of time.

_____ D.   Often being in the position of having to choose
             which of two or more tasks will actually get
             completed.

_____ E.   A chronic feeling of being under great pressure
             with too much to do.

_____ F.   Days so full and busy that you frequently miss
             lunch or important appointments.

_____ G.   Often having to spend long hours at work that
             seems to have low priority.

_____ H.   Never having enough time to pursue recreation
             activities or interpersonal relationships.

_____ I.   A feeling of being constantly overwhelmed by
             details and trivia, to the extent that critical
             tasks don't get finished.

_____ J.   Using weekends and holidays to "catch up" on
             work not completed on time.

STEP-BY-STEP EXERCISES HELP MR. SAMPLE ANALYZE AND DEVELOP WAYS TO CONTROL HIS STRESS.

psychware **281**

NAME: Initial Screener

SUPPLIER: Applied Innovations, Inc.
South Kingstown Office Park, Suite A-1
Wakefield, RI 02879
(800) 272-2250

PRODUCT CATEGORY	PRIMARY APPLICATIONS
Structured Interview	Clinical Assessment/Diagnosis Personal/Marriage/Family Counseling

SALE RESTRICTIONS American Psychological Association Guidelines

SERVICE TYPE/COST Type	Available	Cost	Discount
Mail-In	No		
Teleprocessing	No		
Local	Yes	$425.00	

PRODUCT DESCRIPTION

This program systematically obtains information from clients in less than 45 minutes. It is designed for easy use by the client with minimal guidance from the professional or para-professional. It presents questions consistent with gender and lifestyle in four topic categories: Background Information, Request for Services, Significant Life Events, and Basic Health.

The program also displays and prints a summary of the data collected and highlights the client's need for additional supportive services. It prepares the client and practitioner for the first appointment. This program comes in three versions: teen (13-17), adult (18 years of age and older) and third party (including pre-school, school-age, and teen-age). The price shown is per version.

This software operates on most available personal computers including IBM, Apple, Digital, and Kaypro.

APPLIED INNOVATIONS

Applied Innovations, Inc.
IN-SITE SCREENING RESULTS
for
HARRY S. CLARK

222222222

03/12/1984

03/12/1984
HARRY S. CLARK
M 33 YEARS OLD

FURTHER ATTENTION AREAS
(ELABORATION: SLE & BHQ PG 1)

MEDICAL EXAM INDICATED

CLIENT SPECIFIED SERVICE NEEDS:
  (ELABORATION: RFS PG 1)

  CLARIFICATION

  ADVICE

  SOCIAL INTERVENTION

THIS IS A SELF REFERRAL

PROBLEM/SITUATION: I HAVE JUST RETURNED TO SCHOOL AND THERE
IS ALOT OF TENSION IN MY FAMILY. MY
WIFE TRIES TO BE UNDERSTANDING, BUT SHE
CONTINUES TO NAG ME ABOUT HOUSEHOLD
CHORES. I TRY TO MAKE HER UNDERSTAND
THAT I NEED TIME TO STUDY, BUT SHE
CONTINUES TO COMPLAIN. SINCE I LEFT MY
JOB TO RETURN TO SCHOOL WE HAVE BEEN
REAL SHORT ON CASH. I THINK MY WIFE
RESENTS MY RETUNING TO SCHOOL.

ON AN URGENCY SCALE (LEAST [1] TO MOST [10]),
  HARRY REPORTS THAT IS IS A: 6

PRIOR TREATMENT EXPERIENCE (ELABORATION: CB PG 1): N

RELEVANT SUPPORT SERVICES/AGENCIES

HEALTH CENTERS
FINANCIAL ASSISTANCE/INCOME MAINENANCE

LICENSED TO APPLIED INNOVATIONS
NETWORKER SCREENER RESULTS   CB   1
CLIENT BACKGROUND

03/12/1984
HARRY S. CLARK
M 33 YEARS OLD

BUS/SCHOOL PH:(401)277-3800
UNIVERSITY OF RHODE ISLAND
PROMENADE ST.
PROVIDENCE RI
02908

SSN: 222222222
23 WATERMAN STREET
PROVIDENCE, RI
02908
(401)232-4579

HARRY DOES NOT HAVE HEALTH INSURANCE

THIS IS A SELF REFERRAL

THE PROBLEM/SITUATION IS A FAMILY SITUATION

PROBLEM/SITUATION: I HAVE JUST RETURNED TO SCHOOL AND THERE
IS ALOT OF TENSION IN MY FAMILY. MY
WIFE TRIES TO BE UNDERSTANDING, BUT SHE
CONTINUES TO NAG ME ABOUT HOUSEHOLD
CHORES. I TRY TO MAKE HER UNDERSTAND
THAT I NEED TIME TO STUDY, BUT SHE
CONTINUES TO COMPLAIN. SINCE I LEFT MY
JOB TO RETURN TO SCHOOL WE HAVE BEEN
REAL SHORT ON CASH. I THINK MY WIFE
RESENTS MY RETUNING TO SCHOOL.

ON A URGENCY SCALE (1-10), HARRY REPORTS THAT IT IS A: 6

PRIOR TREATMENT/EXPERIENCE: N

ELABORATION:

                                        MARRIED TO: JANET V. CLARK
                                        DATE: 02/15/1980

HARRY S. CLARK
SSN: 222222222

                                        HOUSEWIFE
                                        PRESENTLY EMPLOYED
                                        SATISFACTORY CONDITIONS AT WORK

                                        AGE-30 BIRTHDAY 02/11/1953
                                        12 YEARS OF EDUCATION
                                        WHITE CATHOLIC

                    INFORMATION ON CHILDREN

JOHN A. CLARK;MALE;06/05/1982;AT HOME
                    OTHER RELEVANT INFORMATION

I WANT HELP TO KEEP MY FAMILY
TOGETHER. I DON'T KNOW WHAT TO DO.
I DON'T WANT TO QUIT SCHOOL, BUT
I WILL IF OUR PROBLEMS CAN'T BE RESOLVED
X

GROSS INCOME IS $8000.00

TOTAL INCOME IS NOT SUFFICIENT FOR NEEDS

                    RELEVANT SUPPORT SERVICES/AGENCIES

FINANCIAL ASSISTANCE/INCOME MAINENANCE   INFORMATION AND REFERRAL

03/12/1984
HARRY S.   CLARK

HARRY was presented with 70 questions that reflect 14
categories of services. His responses indicate the categories
he perceives as desirable.

SERVICE NEEDS AS SPECIFIED BY THE CLIENT

	LOW NEED			UNDECIDED			HIGH NEED			RAW SCORE
	5	8	10	12	14	16	18	20	22	24	25	
CLARIFICATION							X					19
VENTILATION						X						17
PSYCHODYNAMIC INSIGHT				X								13
REALITY CONTACT		X										8
ADVICE								X				20
SUCCORANCE					X							14
CONTROL		X										8
CONFESSION					X							14
PSYCHOLOGICAL EXPERTISE				X								13
COMMUNITY TRIAGE			X									9
MEDICAL	X											7
SOCIAL INTERVENTION									X			22
ADMINISTRATIVE REQUESTS					X							12
NO SERVICE DESIRED			X									10

	5	8	10	12	14	16	18	20	22	24	25	RAW SCORE

286 *psychware*

BRIEF ELABORATION OF INDIVIDUAL 'NEED CATEGORIES'.

CLARIFICATION NEEDS: (HARRY has a score of 19)
   Client wants help to put feelings, thoughts, or behaviors in some
   perspective. Wants to be active in the therapeutic process.
ADVICE NEEDS: (HARRY has a score of 20)
   Client wants guidance about what to do in personal/ social matters.
SOCIAL INTERVENTION NEEDS: (HARRY has a score of 22)
   Client sees the problem in the people or situations around him/her.
   Asking for the clinician's 'social influence'.

HARRY was presented with a comprehensive medical history questionnaire
and requested to indicate any/all conditions that apply.

NUMBER OF POSITIVE RESPONSES: 14

HIGHLIGHT #1 : MEDICAL EXAM INDICATED
                    POSITIVE QUESTION RESPONSES:
DROWSINESS:
BLEEDING GUMS:
TREMORS OR 'SHAKES':
RESTLESSNESS, INABILITY TO BE STILL:
HEADACHES:
NERVOUSNESS:
NAUSEA OR VOMITING:
CONSTIPATION:
CHILLS:
IRREGULAR HEART BEAT:
COUGH:
LACK OF ENERGY:
INCREASED SWEATING:
INCREASED THIRST:
                    RELEVANT SUPPORT SERVICES/AGENCIES

HEALTH CENTERS

HARRY was presented with a list of 44 Significant Life Events and was
requested to identify any/all that have occurred in the past 6 months.
HARRY was also presented with several options as to the impact of any
event that did occur in the past six months.
                    POSITIVE QUESTION RESPONSES:

EVENT:	EFFECT: THE STESS IN MY LIFE ...
MAJOR CHANGE IN SLEEPING HABITS:	MODERATELY INCREASES
MAJOR CHANGE IN EATING HABITS:	MODERATELY INCREASES
A CHANGE IN PERSONAL HABITS:	GREATLY INCREASES
OUTSTANDING PERSONAL ACHIEVEMENT:	GREATLY REDUCES
SEXUAL DIFFICULTIES:	GREATLY INCREASES
MAJOR CHANGE IN FINANCIAL STATUS:	MODERATELY INCREASES
INCREASE/DECREASE OF ARGUMENTS WITH SPOUSE:	GREATLY INCREASES
MAJOR CHANGE IN USUAL TYPE AND/OR AMOUNT RECREATION:	MODERATELY INCREASES
MAJOR CHANGE IN SOCIAL ACTIVITIES:	MODERATELY INCREASES
MAJOR CHANGE IN LIVING CONDITIONS:	MODERATELY INCREASES
CHANGING TO A NEW SCHOOL:	MODERATELY INCREASES
BEGINNING OR CEASING FORMAL SCHOOLING:	MODERATELY INCREASES

NAME: Intake Narrative Report Writer

SUPPLIER: Applied Innovations, Inc.
South Kingstown Office Park, Suite A-1
Wakefield, RI 02879
(800) 272-2250

PRODUCT CATEGORY

Utility

PRIMARY APPLICATIONS

Clinical Assessment/Diagnosis

SALE RESTRICTIONS American Psychological Association Guidelines

SERVICE TYPE/COST	Type	Available	Cost	Discount
	Mail-In	No		
	Teleprocessing	No		
	Local	Yes	$275.00	

PRODUCT DESCRIPTION

INTAKE NARRATIVE REPORT WRITER is designed to work in conjunction with the INITIAL SCREENER available from the same supplier. The INTAKE NARRATIVE REPORT WRITER receives the information gathered from the INITIAL SCREENER and combines it with additional comments from the practitioner to produce a summary narrative report. The narrative summary provides a common mental health format for the report.

This software operates on most available personal computers including IBM, Apple, Digital, and Kaypro.

NAME: HARRY S. CLARK   CLIENT ADDRESS:
DATE OF BIRTH: 06/12/1950   23 WATERMAN STREET
AGE: 33   PROVIDENCE RI 02908
DATE OF REPORT: 03/22/1984   CLIENT PHONE: (401)232-4579
PERSON GENERATING REPORT: DR. MICHAEL NOVER   CLIENT SS#: 222222222

REASON FOR REFERRAL:

    HARRY referred himself to this agency. HARRY notes that his family
is presently experiencing difficulty. He described his present problem as
follows: "I HAVE JUST RETURNED TO SCHOOL AND THERE IS ALOT OF TENSION IN
MY FAMILY. MY WIFE TRIES TO BE UNDERSTANDING, BUT SHE CONTINUES TO NAG ME
ABOUT HOUSEHOLD CHORES. I TRY TO MAKE HER UNDERSTAND THAT I NEED TIME TO
STUDY, BUT SHE CONTINUES TO COMPLAIN. SINCE I LEFT MY JOB TO RETURN TO
SCHOOL WE HAVE BEEN REAL SHORT ON CASH. I THINK MY WIFE RESENTS MY
RETUNING TO SCHOOL. " HARRY has had no prior contact with a mental health
professional.

BACKROUND:

    HARRY has 12 years of education, when asked to describe his
occupation he indicated: "STUDENT". He is presently unemployed. HARRY
notes that he is presently in school/training instead of work. He
indicated that his present unemployment was creating problems in his
relationships and family life. HARRY noted that his total family income
is 8000.00, which is not sufficient for the family's needs. HARRY is a 33
year old male reporting his enthnic/religious backround as WHITE CATHOLIC.
He is presently married to JANET V. CLARK. They have been together for 4
years. JANET V. CLARK has 12 years of education, when asked to describe
her occupation she indicated: "HOUSEWIFE". JANET V. CLARK is presently
employed.

    HARRY indicated that they have children and provided the following
information on each child:
    JOHN A. CLARK;MALE;BORN 06/05/1982;LIVING AT HOME

ADDITIONAL INFORMATION:

    HARRY provided the following additional information for consideration
during intake procedures: "I WANT HELP TO KEEP MY FAMILY TOGETHER. I
DON'T KNOW WHAT TO DO. I DON'T WANT TO QUIT SCHOOL, BUT I WILL IF OUR
PROBLEMS CAN'T BE RESOLVED "

CLIENT REQUEST FOR SERVICES

    HARRY was presented with 70 questions which review his perception of
needs for service. HARRY indicated that he wants help to put feelings,
thoughts,or behaviors in some perspective. Wants to be active in the
therapeutic process. He wants guidance about what to do in
personal/social matters. He sees the problem in the people or situations
around himself. Asking for the clinician's "social influence".

psychware   **289**

SIGNIFICANT LIFE EVENTS

HARRY was presented with a list of 44 Significant Life Events and was requested to identify any/all that have occurred in the past 6 months. He also specified the impact of these events. The events which recently occurred in HARRY'S life and their impact include:

MAJOR CHANGE IN SLEEPING HABITS: MODERATELY INCREASES THE STRESS IN MY LIFE

MAJOR CHANGE IN EATING HABITS: MODERATELY INCREASES THE STRESS IN MY LIFE

A CHANGE IN PERSONAL HABITS: GREATLY INCREASES THE STRESS IN MY LIFE

OUTSTANDING PERSONAL ACHIEVEMENT: GREATLY REDUCES THE STRESS IN MY LIFE

SEXUAL DIFFICULTIES: GREATLY INCREASES THE STRESS IN MY LIFE

MAJOR CHANGE IN FINANCIAL STATUS: MODERATELY INCREASES THE STRESS IN MY LIFE

INCREASE/DECREASE OF ARGUMENTS WITH SPOUSE: GREATLY INCREASES THE STRESS IN MY LIFE

MAJOR CHANGE IN USUAL TYPE AND/OR AMOUNT RECREATION: MODERATELY INCREASES THE STRESS IN MY LIFE

MAJOR CHANGE IN SOCIAL ACTIVITIES: MODERATELY INCREASES THE STRESS IN MY LIFE

MAJOR CHANGE IN LIVING CONDITIONS: MODERATELY INCREASES THE STRESS IN MY LIFE

CHANGING TO A NEW SCHOOL: MODERATELY INCREASES THE STRESS IN MY LIFE

BEGINNING OR CEASING FORMAL SCHOOLING: MODERATELY INCREASES THE STRESS IN MY LIFE

HEALTH STATUS

HARRY completed a comprehensive health questionnaire and noted health conditions which he is currently experiencing or has recently experienced. These included:

DROWSINESS
BLEEDING GUMS
TREMORS OR 'SHAKES'
RESTLESSNESS, INABILITY TO BE STILL
HEADACHES
NERVOUSNESS
NAUSEA OR VOMITING
CONSTIPATION
CHILLS
IRREGULAR HEART BEAT
COUGH
LACK OF ENERGY
INCREASED SWEATING
INCREASED THIRST

HIGHLIGHTS:

Several support agencies may provide additional services which are relevant for HARRY. These may include:
HEALTH CENTERS

CLINICIAN'S SUMMARY:

Further clinical assessment, including psychological testing is indicated.   Need to investigate apparent conflict with wife and the potential suitability of Marital Therapy. Detailed report will folllow after further assessment.

290 *psychware*

NAME: Integrated Report Writer

SUPPLIER: PSYCH Systems, Inc.
600 Reisterstown Road
Baltimore, MD 21208
(800) 368-3366

PRODUCT CATEGORY	PRIMARY APPLICATIONS
Utility	Clinical Assessment/Diagnosis

SALE RESTRICTIONS Qualified Professional

SERVICE TYPE/COST	Type	Available	Cost	Discount
	Mail-In	No		
	Teleprocessing	No		
	Local	Yes	See Below	

PRODUCT DESCRIPTION

A unique feature of Psych Systems approach to on-line testing is the capability to combine results from several different instruments into a coordinated patient report. Through the INTEGRATED REPORT WRITER documents can be produced that approximate those written by the individual clinician. Through a link to word processing software the clinician has the capability of inserting additional, individual comments and observations to further personalize the report.

Psych Systems programs operate on the IBM PC-XT, COMPAQ Plus, Dec Professional 350, and most DEC PDP-11 systems. Various hardware/ software configurations are available directly from Psych Systems, with single-user systems starting at approximately $12,000. A per test fee also applies.

222-22-2222   Jonathan Doe   32 yr old white male   29-Feb-84

```
-------------------------------
|        |                      |
|  IRW   |  EVALUATION REPORT   |
|        |                      |
-------------------------------
```

This clinical report is designed to assist in psychodiagnostic evaluation. It is available to qualified professionals. This report was produced by a computerized analysis of the data given by the client listed above, and is to be used in conjunction with professional evaluation. No decision should be based solely upon the contents of this report.

Jonathan Doe is a 32 year old white divorced father of 1 child.
He attended business school or partial college. Currently he is a
part-time student and employed full time in sales. Monthly income
for his household is $1000-$2000 derived primarily from his job. He
has no trouble with the law. He has had no psychiatric hospitalization but
has had outpatient therapy. He currently resides in a house which is
owned. He lives alone.

REASON FOR REFERRAL

Jonathan Doe was referred for problems handling reality by Dr.
Williams.

BEHAVIORAL OBSERVATIONS

The testing supervisor reported that the individual arrived for his
appointment early. Upon entering the office, he seemed
uncomfortable. He spoke readily, but his voice was shaky. He
appeared nervous. Eye contact with the testing supervisor was fair.
In the testing situation, the respondent was cooperative. Motivation
for completing the testing process was fair and attention span
appeared to be sufficient to complete the task. He appeared to be
able to comprehend the process with little or no difficulty.

TESTS ADMINISTERED

Beck Depression & Hopelessness   Multidimensional Aptitude Battery
MMPI   Social History
Index of Somatic Problems   Visual Searching Task

FAMILY HISTORY

The respondent was raised primarily by both natural parents. He has 3
siblings. His natural mother has died from an illness. The
respondent reports the presence of obvious psychopathology and
physical health problems in immediate blood relatives as follows:

father : severe nervous troubles, alcohol problems, stomach trouble,
severe headaches and numerous physical complaints before age 40.

mother : nervous breakdown, psychiatric hospitalization, suicidal
behavior, alcohol problems, extreme moodiness and numerous physical
complaints before age 40.

siblings: severe nervous troubles, severe depression, suicidal
behavior, stomach trouble, severe headaches and numerous physical
complaints before age 40.

He reports that his mother and father would physically attack each
other and would frequently lose their tempers. His mother is viewed
as having been domineering and cruel. His father is seen as having
been brutal and unfaithful. He complains of generally impaired
relationships with them manifested by exclusion from conversation,
frequent disagreements, running away from home and severe restrictions.

CHILDHOOD AND ADOLESCENCE

He admits to childhood difficulties with overt aggression (temper
tantrums and quick to anger), hyperactivity (always on the go) and
emotional lability (frequent crying). He reports engaging in lying,
thievery and fire-setting at an early age. In school he was slow in
learning to read. He received failing grades and was not promoted
normally. He admits to having trouble with school authorities. As an
adolescent he states that he was generally happy. He had friends but
did not date.

psychware **293**

LIFE STRESS AND ROLE IMPAIRMENT

He reports experiencing several stressful events during the past year. These were in the area of social participation (church activities family get-togethers) and work situation (change in working conditions, change in responsibilities and being fired). He indicated some financial difficulties. His financial problems include a poor credit rating. He reports problems with his child. These include getting easily frustrated, feeling his care is inadequate and noticing the child seems to be having more problems. At work, he indicates that he has been increasingly absent. The respondent admits to having used narcotics but not marijuana, amphetamines, cocaine, barbiturates and hallucinogens.

INTELLECTUAL FUNCTIONING

Results from the Multidimensional Aptitude Battery indicate that this individual is functioning in the borderline range, based on Verbal scores. Estimated Verbal IQ is 97 and Performance IQ is 52. The results of the Visual Searching Task suggest a normal level of cognitive functioning.

PERSONALITY FUNCTIONING: CURRENT STATE INFORMATION

This profile type is more frequently found in a correctional rather than psychiatric population. Presentation in a psychiatric setting is often associated with or secondary to legal difficulties. The profile suggests a classic sociopathic orientation, as described by Cleckly.

These individuals are energetic, active, and outgoing. They become restless and easily bored with the routine or mundane pursuits of everyday life. Such persons appear to have a strong need to program stimulation and excitement in their lives, and choice of friends and activities are often based on these needs. Being impulsive and risk-taking, they are accident prone. Alcohol/Drug abuse is one method commonly used by such persons to meet their needs for stimulus change.

Individuals like this are egocentric, selfish and demanding of others in a narcissistic manner. However, they lack empathy and concern for the rights and needs of others. There is a lack of adequate conscience development and these persons are free of inhibiting guilt, anxiety, or remorse. Thus, they can violate social norms with relative personal impunity. Non-conforming, antisocial, and illegal behavior is common. However, having good social skills and being able to "read" people well, such persons are often able to impress others, at least on initial meeting. Relationships are maintained at a superficial level and often with manipulative intent. Longer term observation will reveal a pattern of behavior reflecting impulsivity, irresponsibility, and untrustworthiness.

Judgement is typically poor. These individuals do not seem to learn from past experience and repeatedly make the same mistakes. Their inability to postpone gratification, low frustration tolerance, and poor planning ability lead to difficulty in any enterprise requiring sustained effort. A high percentage of these individuals have extremely poor marital adjustments. They do not maintain personal loyalty, become bored, and often seek extra-marital involvement.

This pattern of behavior often diminishes with increasing age. As they approach middle age, these persons may reflect upon lost relationships and opportunities, and realize that their lives are not going well. Concomitantly, they may experience increased emotional distress. However, these persons often are unable to translate this into positive life changes.

Treatment considerations: Most persons with this profile have an extremely poor prognosis for change with any type of psychotherapy. Their motivation is poor and they tend to discontinue therapy impulsively. Often therapeutic involvement is under duress, for example, spouse or the courts. If in legal difficulty, correctional supervision can have a salutory impact. These persons seem to respond best to the presence of clearcut guidelines and immediate consequences.

DIAGNOSTIC IMPRESSION

Although a formal diagnosis must be based on demographic, interview and case history data, psychological test results can sometimes be of assistance to the clinician in making the diagnostic decision. The DSM-III diagnostic categories most frequently associated with various MMPI profile types were identified and subsequently confirmed by a panel of experienced clinicians. The following, while not presented as a diagnosis, is a diagnostic possibility based on that consensus.

Impression: Axis I   V71.09   None

                Axis II   301.70   Antisocial Personality Disorder

The results from the Beck Depression Inventory indicate that this individual is currently experiencing a moderate amount of depression. In comparison with the MMPI, this indicates that he is more willing to talk openly of depressive issues. The results from the Beck Hopelessness Scale suggest that he is mildly pessimistic about his future.

PERSONALITY FUNCTIONING: TRAIT INFORMATION

This person tends to be impulsive, self-indulgent, poorly controlled, and easily frustrated. He is willing to manipulate others to gratify his needs, perhaps to the point of conscious deceit. His behavior tends to be unpredictable, and his mood is prone to rapid fluctuations.

This person is likely to be verbally fluent and relatively at ease in social interactions. Others see him as usually cheerful, good-humored, and not overly difficult to approach. He is able to deal with adverse circumstances without exaggerated discomfort.

Whatever problems this person is currently experiencing, he is generally not overly pessimistic about life. His self-esteem is relatively intact and he is not overly apprehensive about the long term future. Depending on his current situation, this may be inappropriate. He portrays himself as self-confident and competent and not easily influenced by the opinions of others.

He is basically mistrustful of people and feels they are motivated primarily by relentless self-interest. He tends to view an interpersonal relationship as a condition of mutual exploitation.

He has an adequate reservoir of energy and can mobilize his resources to meet everyday problems.

He suffers from tendencies toward excessive demandingness, cynicism and resentment for real or imagined harms. Preferred defense mechanisms are intellectualization, projection and regression.

MEDICAL CONCERNS AND SOMATIZATION

Results suggest that this individual is not excessively concerned about health and physical functioning. He may be prone to substance abuse and addictive behavior. He is likely to show faster recovery from physical illness, injury or surgery than most people.

The respondent reported no problems with muscle pains and nausea. However, he acknowledged problems with abdominal pain, abdominal swelling, chest pains, headaches, seizures, fainting and coughing.

NAME: IQ Test Interpretation-Adult

SUPPLIER: Precision People, Inc.
3452 North Ride Circle. S.
Jacksonville, FL 32217
(904) 262-1096

PRODUCT CATEGORY	PRIMARY APPLICATIONS
Cognitive/Ability	Clinical Assessment/Diagnosis
	Personal/Marriage/Family Counseling
	Personnel Selection/Evaluation

SALE RESTRICTIONS American Psychological Association Guidelines

SERVICE TYPE/COST	Type	Available	Cost	Discount
	Mail-In	No		
	Teleprocessing	No		
	Local	Yes	$475.00	

PRODUCT DESCRIPTION

The IQ TEST INTERPRETATION-ADULT translates results on the Weschler Adult Intelligence Scale-Revised into meaningful interpretations and recommendations. There is an interpretation section listing many ratios and scores and brief interpretations of these. Recommendations have three sections: educational, vocational, and clinical. The user has a choice of any combination of the three.

The WAIS-R is a widely-used test for assessing intelligence in adolescents and adults. Eleven subtests are divided into two major divisions yielding a verbal IQ, a performance (non-verbal) IQ, and a full scale IQ. The verbal section includes the following subtests: information comprehension, arithmetic, similarities, digit span, and vocabulary. The performance section includes digit symbol, picture completion, block design, picture arrangement, and object assembly. This program provides a means for analyzing the scores from these various tests.

The software is compatible with IBM PC, Apple, and TRS-80 (Models I, II, and III) microcomputers. A manual and sample printout are available for $34.00.

NAME: IQ Test Interpretation-Clinical

SUPPLIER: Precision People, Inc.
3452 North Ride Circle. S.
Jacksonville, FL 32217
(904) 262-1096

PRODUCT CATEGORY	PRIMARY APPLICATIONS
Cognitive/Ability	Clinical Assessment/Diagnosis Educational Evaluation/Planning

SALE RESTRICTIONS   American Psychological Association Guidelines

SERVICE TYPE/COST	Type	Available	Cost	Discount
	Mail-In	No		
	Teleprocessing	No		
	Local	Yes	$495.00	

PRODUCT DESCRIPTION

The IQ TEST INTERPRETATION-CLINICAL translates results on the Weschler Intelligence Scale for Children-Revised into meaningful educational interpretations and recommendations. This report is detailed and comprehensive and recommendations are both clinical and educational. Statements are backed by research.

The WISC-R is a widely-used intelligence test for children ages 6-16 years. Twelve subtests are divided into two major divisions yielding a verbal IQ, a performance (non-verbal) IQ, and a full scale IQ. The verbal section includes the following subtests: general information, general comprehension, arithmetic, similarities, vocabulary, and digit span. The performance section includes picture completion, picture arrangement, block design, object assembly, coding, and mazes. This program provides a means for analyzing the scores from these various tests.

The report provide a list of the client's strengths and weaknesses compared to the general population, the client's expected level of ability, and interpretation of the three major statistically derived WISC-R factors (Verbal Comprehension, Freedom from Anxiety, and Perceptual Organization). Clinical and educational recommendations are also provided.

The software is compatible with IBM PC, Apple, and TRS-80 (Models I, II, and III) microcomputers. A manual and sample printout are available for $34.00.

W I S C R - 9 0
A CLINICAL PROGRAM FOR THE
WECHSLER INTELLIGENCE SCALE FOR CHILDREN REVISED.
JOHN J. TRIFILETTI, PH.D.

RICHARD M. TRIFILETTI, M.A.

ROBERT J. TRIFILETTI, MS.C.

COPYRIGHT (C) 1983 PRECISION PEOPLE INC.

```
NAME           (1)   ARTHUR SOMMES
AGE            (2)   10-0
SEX            (3)   MALE
PARENT         (4)   GLADYS SOMMES
SCHOOL         (5)   CLEARWATER ELEMENTARY
GRADE          (6)   SIX
REFERRED BY    (7)   DR. HOLMES
```

REASON FOR REFERRAL   (8)   SHORT
ATTENTION SPAN   IMPULSIVITY

OTHER TESTS ADMINISTERED (9)   BENDER
DRAW-A-MAN   DETROIT

EXAM DATE (MM/DD/YY)   (19)   10/15/82

BIRTH DATE (MM/DD/YY)   (11)   10/10/72

W I S C R - 9 0

I N P U T   R A W   S C O R E S

```
INFORMATION           (1)   15
SIMILARITIES          (2)   12
ARITHMETIC            (3)   13
VOCABULARY            (4)   40
COMPREHENSION         (5)   18
DIGIT SPAN            (6)   07
PICTURE COMPLETION    (7)   20
PICTURE ARRANGEMENT   (8)   30
BLOCK DESIGN          (9)   22
OBJECT ASSEMBLY      (10)   20
CODING               (11)   20
MAZES                (12)   22
```

```
        W I S C R - 9 0      P R O F I L E
     1  2  3  4  5  6  7  8  9  1  1  1  1  1  1  1  1  1  1
                                0  1  2  3  4  5  6  7  8  9
 I  .  .  .  .  .  .  .  .  .  .  *  .  .  .  .  .  .  .  .
 S  .  .  .  .  .  .  .  .  .  *  .  .  .  .  .  .  .  .  .
 A  .  .  .  .  .  .  .  .  .  .  *  .  .  .  .  .  .  .  .
 V  .  .  .  .  .  .  .  .  .  .  .  .  .  .  *  .  .  .  .
 C  .  .  .  .  .  .  .  .  .  .  *  .  .  .  .  .  .  .  .
DS. .  .  .  *  .  .  .  .  .  .  .  .  .  .  .  .  .  .  .

PC. .  .  .  .  .  .  .  .  .  .  .  *  .  .  .  .  .  .  .
PA. .  .  .  .  .  .  .  .  .  .  .  *  .  .  .  .  .  .  .
BD. .  .  .  .  .  .  .  .  *  .  .  .  .  .  .  .  .  .  .
OA. .  .  .  .  .  .  .  .  *  .  .  .  .  .  .  .  .  .  .
 C  .  .  *  .  .  .  .  .  .  .  .  .  .  .  .  .  .  .  .
 M  .  .  .  .  .  .  .  .  .  .  *  .  .  .  .  .  .  .  .
       W I S C R - 9 0        S C O R E S
            RAW   STD.   SCALE
 SUBTEST   SCORE  DEV.   SCORE   M.A.   %TILE
   INF.     15    .33     11    10-10    63
   SIM.     12    0       10     9-10    50
   ARI.     13    .67     12    11-6     75
 + VOC.     40    1.67    15    13-10    95
   COM,     18    .33     11    10-10    63
 - D.S.     07   -1.67     5     6-6      5
   P.C.     20    .67     12    12-6     75
   P.A.     30    .67     12    12-10    75
   B.D.     22   -.33      9     9-6     37
   O.A.     20    0       10     9-10    50
 - COD.     20   -2.33     3    <8-2      1
   MAZ.     22    .33     11    11-2     63
         WISCR-90 SCORE SUMMARY
 V  I.Q.  = 111         MAE     = 10 -1
 P  I.Q.  = 93          (2 MA + CA / 3)
FS  I.Q.  = 102

                       85% MAE = 8 -7
                       80% MAE = 8 -1
MEAN MA   = **         75% MAE = 7 -7
C.A.      = 10 -0      70% MAE = 7 -1
CALC. MA  = 10 -2      65% MAE = 6 -7
SIGNIFICANT DIFFERENCE BETWEEN VERBAL
AND PERFORMANCE I.Q. SCORES
(95% CONFIDENCE LEVEL)
```

```
W  I  S  C  R  -  9  0      I.Q.      C  U  R  V  E
                        *******
                  ***   :   ***
                ***     :     ***
               **       :       **
             **         :         **
            **          :          **
           **:          :          :**
          *** :         :         : ***
         ***  :         :         :  ***
      ****  :     :     :     :     : ****
        :     :     :         :     :     :  :
     -:---:----:--------:--------:----:---:-
     55    70    85        100       115   130 145
```

SCALES	I.Q.	S.S.	SD	IQ RANGE
VIQ	111	59	.73	HIGH AVERAGE
PIQ	93	46	-.47	AVERAGE
FSIQ	102	105	.13	AVERAGE

W I S C R - 9 0
CLINICAL INTERPRETATIONS

THE FOLLOWING CLINICAL INTERPRETATIONS
ARE BASED ON SIGNIFICANT DIFFERENCES IN
SUBTEST SCORES. RELATIVE STRENGTHS AND
WEAKNESSES ARE BASED UPON A DIFFERENCE
OF THREE (3) SCALED SCORES FROM THE
CLIENT'S OWN MEAN ON VERBAL AND PERFOR-
MANCE SCALES. ABSOLUTE STRENGTHS AND
WEAKNESSES ARE BASED ON A DIFFERENCE OF
THREE (3) SCALED SCORES FROM THE MEAN OF
10. THE STATEMENTS THAT FOLLOW ARE
PROVIDED TO THE PSYCHOLOGIST AS SUGGES-
TIONS OF INTERPRETIVE HYPOTHESIS TO BE
CONFIRMED BY CLINICAL JUDGEMENT. AS
SUCH THEY MAY OR MAY NOT BE INCLUDED
WITH THE PSYCHOLOGIST'S FINAL REPORT.
THE CURRENT SCORES CAN BE TAKEN AS AN
ACCURATE ASSESSMENT OF THE CLIENT'S
CURRENT LEVEL OF FUNCTIONING.
VERBAL SCORES ARE SIGNIFICANTLY HIGHER
THAN PERFORMANCE SCORES. THIS PATTERN

MAY INDICATE GOOD ACADEMIC ACHIEVEMENT
OR OVERACHIEVING TENDENCIES. PATIENTS
WHO TEND TO REMAIN IN THERAPY DEMON-
STRATE THIS PATTERN, AS DO NORMAL OLDER
INDIVIDUALS. THIS PATTERN HAS BEEN
ASSOCIATED WITH:

1. MOST NEUROSES, ESPECIALLY ANXIETY
   AND TENSION STATES, SOMATIZATION
   DISORDERS AND OBSESSIVE COMPULSIVE
   DISORDERS.
2. MOST PSYCHOSES, ESPECIALLY SCHIZO-
   PHRENIA, CHRONIC TYPES.
3. ORGANIC AND APHASIC CONDITIONS,
   PARTICULARLY WITH RIGHT HEMISPHERE
   DYSFUNCTIONING.
4. DEPRESSIVE OR DYSTHYMIC DISORDERS.

BANNATYNE ANALYSIS OF WISC-R

THE BANNATYNE ANALYSIS COMBINES
WISC-R SUBTESTS INTO FOUR CATEGORIES:
1. VERBAL CONCEPTUALIZING FACTOR
   (COM., SIM., VOC.)
2. SPATIAL FACTOR
   (P.C., B.D., O.A.)
3. ACQUIRED KNOWLEDGE FACTOR
   (VOC., INF., ARI.)
4. SEQUENCING FACTOR
   (D.S., ARI., CODING)

EACH OF THE ABOVE CATEGORIES HAS AN
EXPECTED MEAN OF 30. A SCORE OF 21 OR
LESS IS CONSIDERED SIGNIFICANTLY LOW.
37 OR MORE IS SIGNIFICANTLY HIGH.

VERBAL CONCEPTUALIZING SCORE = 36

THE SUBTESTS THAT MAKE UP THIS SCORE
MEASURE COMMON SENSE, JUDGEMENT, AND
REASONING: ABSTRACT AND CONCRETE REASON-
ING ABILITIES, VERBAL CONCEPT FORMATION
AND CAPACITY FOR ASSOCIATIVE THINKING,
AND THE ABILITY TO UNDERSTAND WORDS.
ALSO REFLECTED ARE QUALITY AND LEVEL OF
EDUCATION AND ENVIRONMENTS.

SPATIAL SCORE = 31

THIS SCORE IS COMPOSED OF PERFORMANCE
SUBTESTS WHICH DON'T INVOLVE SEQUENCING.
THEY MEASURE THE ABILITY TO VISUALIZE
ESSENTIAL FROM NON-ESSENTIAL DETAIL AND
TO IDENTIFY FAMILIAR STIMULI IN THE
ENVIRONMENT; THE ABILITY TO SYNTHESIZE
CONCRETE PARTS INTO MEANINGFUL WHOLES
AND THE ABILITY TO PERCEIVE, ANALYZE
SYNTHESIZE AND REPRODUCE ABSTRACT
DESIGNS.
ACQUIRED KNOWLEDGE SCORE = 38

THE SUBTESTS WHICH MAKE UP THIS SCORE
MEASURE ASSOCIATIVE THINKING AND GENERAL
COMPREHENSION OF FACTS ACQUIRED AT HOME
AND IN SCHOOL. THE ACQUISITION OF THESE
FACTS IS BASED ON INTEREST, BACKGROUND,
ALERTNESS TO SURROUNDINGS AND OVERALL
URGE TO COLLECT KNOWLEDGE. THE ABILITY
TO UNDERSTAND WORDS, VERBAL LEARNING
ABILITY, RANGE OF IDEAS, AND FUND OF
INFORMATION IS REFLECTED. ARITHMETIC
PROCESSES AND PROBLEM SOLVING SKILLS ARE
MEASURED, AS WELL AS THE ABILITY TO
UTILIZE ABSTRACT CONCEPTS OF NUMBER AND
NUMERICAL OPERATIONS.

SEQUENCING SCORE = 20

THE SUBTESTS WHICH COMPOSE SEQUENCING
SCORE MEASURE THE ABILITY TO RECALL AUD-
ITORY INFORMATION IN PROPER SEQUENCE AND
DETAIL, THE ABILITY TO HOLD ATTENTION,
AND THE ABILITY TO SYNTHESIZE AND
ORGANIZE IN A STRUCTURED SITUATION.
ALSO MEASURED IS THE ABILITY TO SEE A
TOTAL SITUATION BASED ON VISUAL COMPRE-
HENSION, ORGANIZATION AND ENVIRONMENTAL
EXPERIENCES; FLEXIBILITY IN NEW LEARNING
SITUATIONS, ABILITY TO ABSORB NEW
MATERIAL IN AN ASSOCIATIVE CONTEXT, AND
OVERALL PSYCHO-MOTOR ABILITY.

RELATIVE HIGH SC.: VOCABULARY
ABSOLUTE HIGH SC.: VOCABULARY
SCALE SCORE= 15, MEAN VERBAL= 10.67

HIGH SCORES REFLECT GOOD CULTURAL AND
EDUCATIONAL OPPORTUNITIES, VERBAL COM-
PREHENSION AND MEMORY, AND A BETTER THAN
AVERAGE FUND OF INFORMATION. ABILITY TO
CONCEPTUALIZE AND STRIVE INTELLECTUALLY
AS WELL AS GOOD PERSCHOOL EXPERIENCES
ARE INDICATED. CLINICAL FACTORS INCLUDE
INTELLECTUALIZING, OBSESSIVE-COMPULSIVE
TENDENCIES, SCHIZOPHRENIC, OR OVER IDEA-
TIONAL PRESCHIZOPHRENIC CONDITIONS.

RELATIVE LOW SC.: DIGIT SPAN
ABSOLUTE LOW SC.: DIGIT SPAN
SCALE SCORE= 5, MEAN VERBAL= 10.67
LOW SCORES REFLECT POOR ATTENTION AND
DISTRACTIBILITY. POOR AUDITORY SEQUENC-
ING AND LEARNING PROBLEMS ARE POSSIBLE.
CLINICAL FACTORS INCLUDE ANXIETY AND
TENSION. THIS PATTERN HAS BEEN FOUND
WITH MANIC-DEPRESSIVE CONDITIONS,
EPILEPTIC CONDITIONS, AND PSYCHOSOMATIC
MIGRAINE CONDITIONS. HEARING IMPAIRMENT
IS POSSIBLE.
CHECK FOR ANXIETY OF THE KIND FOUND IN
NEUROTIC, DEPRESSED, & PRESCHIZOPHRENIC
PATIENTS.
CHECK FOR ORGANIC CONDITIONS.

RELATIVE LOW SC.: CODING
ABSOLUTE LOW SC.: CODING
SCALE SCORE= 3, MEAN PERFORMANCE= 9.5

SCORES MAY REFLECT DISTRACTIBILITY,
PROBLEMS WITH VISUAL MOTOR COORDINATION,
AND POOR MOTOR SPEED. ROTE LEARNING
ABILITY, CONCENTRATION, AND ATTENTION
MAY BE DEFICIENT. CLINICAL FACTORS

MAY INCLUDE READING DISABILITY. THIS
PATTERN HAS BEEN ASSOCIATED WITH BRAIN
DAMAGE, DEPRESSION, ANXIETY, FEELINGS OF
FRUSTRATION AND TENSION, NEUROTIC OR IN-
ADEQUATE PERSONALITY, DISSOCIATIVE OR
SCHIZOID PROCESSES, HYPERACTIVE OR MANIC
TENDENCIES, AND EPILEPTIC CONDITIONS.

****

EDUCATIONAL OBJECTIVES FOR DIGIT SPAN
CHRONOLOGICAL AGE = 10-0

GIVEN A SEQUENCE OF NUMBERS, REPEAT THE
SEQUENCE FORWORD AND BACKWARD.
SEE AND WRITE TELEPHONE NUMBER AND
ADDRESS FROM MEMORY.
REPEAT SENTENCES OF VARYING LENGTH.
REPEAT A SERIES OF LETTERS, NUMBERS,
WORDS, SENTENCES, OR EVENTS.
REPEAT WORDS TO POPULAR SONGS.
READ AND RETELL STORIES.
REPEAT AND PERFORM SEQUENTIAL
DIRECTIONS.
REPEAT LISTS OF SHOPPING ITEMS.
PARTICIPATE IN MEMORY GAMES.
REVIEW WHAT HAS BEEN LEARNED AFTER A
DAILY LESSON OR CLASS.
FOLLOW DIRECTIONS FOR PAPER FOLDING
ACTIVITIES.
NAME IN CORRECT SEQUENCE THE MUSICAL
INSTRUMENTS IN A RECORDING.
LIST THE CLUES IN A MYSTERY STORY.
MAKE A LIST OF DIRECTIONS FOR FINDING
HIDDEN TREASURE.
LIST THE STEPS INVOLVED IN A SCIENCE
EXPERIMENT.

****

EDUCATIONAL OBJECTIVES FOR CODING
CHRONOLOGICAL AGE = 10 -0

MAKE JEWELRY FROM BEADS, MACARONI
PIECES, SHELLS, ETC.
COMPLETE PAINT-BY-NUMBER PICTURES.
COMPLETE HANDWRITING ASSIGNMENTS WITH
COPYING LETTERS, WORDS, AND NUMBERS IN
SPECIFIED TIME LIMITS.
MATCH LETTERS, NUMBERS, AND WORDS.
MEMORIZE POEMS, SONGS, RIDDLES, AND
PROVERBS.
PARTICIPATE IN MEMORY GAMES SUCH AS
'CONCENTRATION'.
CONSTRUCT PICTURE STORIES WITH EACH
PICTURE REPRESENTING A WORD OR THOUGHT
OR ACTION.
GIVEN A BRIEF PRESENTATION OF LETTERS,
WORDS, OR DESIGNS, REPRODUCE THEM.
PARTICIPATE IN 'SIMON SAYS' GAMES.
EXPLAIN MAP SYMBOLS AND PLAN A TRIP
USING A MAP ROUTE.
COPY EXERCISES, DIRECTIONS, OR
ASSIGNMENTS FROM THE CHALK BOARD IN
SPECIFIED TIME LIMITS.
COMPLETE PUZZLES IN TIMED FORMAT.
PARTICIPATE IN VISUAL TRACKING
EXERCISES.
REPRODUCE DESIGNS, DIAGRAMS, & PICTURES
FROM MEMORY.
USE THE TYPEWRITER OR WORD PROCESSOR
TO COPY LETTERS, WORDS, AND SENTENCES.

THANK YOU FOR USING WISCR-90.

NAME: IQ Test Interpretation-Educational

SUPPLIER: Precision People, Inc.
3452 North Ride Circle. S.
Jacksonville, FL 32217
(904) 262-1096

PRODUCT CATEGORY	PRIMARY APPLICATIONS
Cognitive/Ability	Clinical Assessment/Diagnosis Educational Evaluation/Planning

SALE RESTRICTIONS American Psychological Association Guidelines

SERVICE TYPE/COST	Type	Available	Cost	Discount
	Mail-In	No		
	Teleprocessing	No		
	Local	Yes	$299.00	

PRODUCT DESCRIPTION

The IQ TEST INTERPRETATION-EDUCATIONAL is a computerized diagnostic program for the Wechsler Intelligence Scale for Children-Revised. The program translates WISC-R results into meaningful clinical interpretations. IQ TEST INTERPRETATION- EDUCATIONAL inputs raw scores from an administration of the WISC-R. Output includes scaled scores, mental IQ's, intelligence ranges, graphic display of the scaled score profile, standard deviations, and clinical impressions for significantly low or high subtests.

The WISC-R is a widely-used intelligence test for children ages 6-16 years. Twelve subtests are divided into two major divisions yielding a verbal IQ, a performance (non-verbal) IQ, and a full scale IQ. The verbal section includes the following subtests: general information, general comprehension, arithmetic, similarities, vocabulary, and digit span. The performance section includes picture completion, picture arrangement, block design, object assembly, coding, and mazes. This program provides a means for analyzing the scores from these various tests.

The software is compatible with IBM PC, Apple, and TRS-80 (Models I, II, and III) microcomputers. A manual and sample printout are available for $34.00.

```
                    W I S C R - 8 0


            A DIAGNOSTIC PROGRAM FOR THE


    WECHSLER INTELLIGENCE SCALE FOR CHILDREN


                    REVISED.

          DIANE T. TRIFILETTI, PH.D.

          RICHARD M. TRIFILETTI, M.A.

          ROBERT J. TRIFILETTI, MS.C.

    COPYRIGHT (C) 1982 PRECISION PEOPLE INC.


    NAME          (1)   ALICE SOMMES
    AGE           (2)   10-0
    SEX           (3)   FEMALE
    PARENT        (4)   GLADYS SOMMES
    SCHOOL        (5)   CLEARWATER ELEMENTARY
    GRADE         (6)   SIX
    REFERRED BY   (7)   DR. HOLMES


    REASON FOR REFERRAL       (8)   SHORT
       ATTENTION SPAN     IMPULSIVITY


    OTHER TESTS ADMINISTERED (9)   BENDER
       DRAW-A-MAN      DETROIT


    EXAM DATE (MM/DD/YY)      (19)   10/15/81

    BIRTH DATE (MM/DD/YY)     (11)   10/10/71

                W I S C R - 8 0

          I N P U T   R A W   S C O R E S
    INFORMATION           (1)    15
    SIMILARITIES          (2)    12
    ARITHMETIC            (3)    13
    VOCABULARY            (4)    40
    COMPREHENSION         (5)    18
    DIGIT SPAN            (6)    07
    PICTURE COMPLETION    (7)    20
    PICTURE ARRANGEMENT   (8)    30
    BLOCK DESIGN          (9)    22
    OBJECT ASSEMBLY       (10)   20
    CODING                (11)   20
    MAZES                 (12)   22
```

```
           W I S C R - 8 0    P R O F I L E


       1 2 3 4 5 6 7 8 9 1 1 1 1 1 1 1 1 1 1
                         0 1 2 3 4 5 6 7 8 9

  I  . . . . . . . . . . * . . . . . . . . .
  S  . . . . . . . . . * . . . . . . . . . .
  A  . . . . . . . . . . * . . . . . . . . .
  V  . . . . . . . . . . . . . . * . . . . .
  C  . . . . . . . . . * . . . . . . . . . .
  DS . . . . * . . . . . . . . . . . . . . .

  PC . . . . . . . . . . * . . . . . . . . .
  PA . . . . . . . . . . * . . . . . . . . .
  BD . . . . . . . . * . . . . . . . . . . .
  OA . . . . . . . . . . * . . . . . . . . .
  C  . . * . . . . . . . . . . . . . . . . .
  M  . . . . . . . . . . * . . . . . . . . .

        W I S C R - 8 0    S C O R E S
               RAW   STD.   SCALE
       SUBTEST SCORE DEV.   SCORE  M.A.   %TILE

         INF.    15   .33     11   10-10   63
         SIM.    12   0       10    9-10   50
         ARI.    13   .67     12   11-6    75
       + VOC.    40  1.67     15   13-10   95
         COM.    18   .33     11   10-10   63
       - D.S.    07 -1.67      5    6-6     5
         P.C.    20   .67     12   12-6    75
         P.A.    30   .67     12   12-10   75
         B.D.    22  -.33      9    9-6    37
         O.A.    20   0       10    9-10   50
       - COD.    20 -2.33      3   <8-2     1
         MAZ.    22   .33     11   11-2    63

              WISCR-80 SCORE SUMMARY
   V  I.Q.  = 111        MAE      = 10 -1
   P  I.Q.  = 93         (2 MA + CA / 3)
   FS I.Q.  = 102
                         85% MAE = 8 -7
                         80% MAE = 8 -1
   MEAN MA  = **         75% MAE = 7 -7
   C.A.     = 10 -0      70% MAE = 7 -1
   CALC. MA = 10 -2      65% MAE = 6 -7


   SIGNIFICANT DIFFERENCE BETWEEN VERBAL
   AND PERFORMANCE I.Q. SCORES
   (95% CONFIDENCE LEVEL)
```

```
   W  I  S  C  R  -  8  0.     I.Q.       C  U  R  V  E
                         ********
                     ***          ***
                   ***:          :***
                  **    :         :  **
                **     :          :   **
                **     :          :   **
              **:      :          :   :**
             *** :     :          :   : ***
           *** :     :          :   :   ***
        **** :     :     :          :     :   : ****
          :    :     :     :          :     :   :    :
       -:--:----:----:---------:----:----:---:-
        60   70   80    90        110  120  130 140

   SCALES   S.S.   IQ    SD      IQ RANGE
   ------------------------------------------------
   VIQ      59     111   .73     HIGH AVERAGE
   PIQ      46     93    -.47    AVERAGE
   FSIQ     105    102   .13     AVERAGE
```

                    W I S C R - 8 0

                 CLINICAL INTERPRETATIONS

THE FOLLOWING INTERPRETATIONS ARE BASED
ON SIGNIFICANT DIFFERENCES IN SUBTEST
SCORES FROM THE CLIENT'S OWN MEAN.
A DIFFERENCE OF THREE (3) SCALED SCORES
IS REQUIRED TO CALL THE FOLLOWING INTER-
PRETATIONS.

THE STATEMENTS THAT FOLLOW ARE PROVIDED
TO THE PSYCHOLOGIST AS SUGGESTIONS OF
INTERPRETIVE HYPOTHESES TO BE CONFIRMED
BY CLINICAL JUDGEMENT BASED UPON INTER-
VIEWING, HISTORY AND OTHER CLINICAL
PROCEDURES. AS SUCH, THEY MAY OR MAY
NOT BE INCLUDED WITH THE PSYCHOLOGIST'S
FINAL REPORT.

THE CURRENT SCORES CAN BE TAKEN AS AN
ACCURATE ASSESSMENT OF THE CLIENT'S
CURRENT LEVEL OF FUNCTIONING.

VERBAL SCORES ARE SIGNIFICANTLY HIGHER
THAN PERFORMANCE SCORES.

SCORES MAY REFLECT POOR VISUAL LEARNING,
SLOW PSYCHOMOTOR SPEED, POOR VISUAL
ORGANIZATION, POOR SPATIAL ABILITIES,
LOW MOTIVATION, ANXIETY, POOR VISUAL
ACUITY, OR POOR MOTOR ABILITY.

+ VOCABULARY
SCALE SCORE = 15

MEAN SCALED SCORE = 10.08

UNUSUALLY HIGH SCORES ON THE VOCABULARY
SUBTEST ARE REFLECTIVE OF GOOD CULTURAL
AND EDUCATIONAL OPPORTUNITIES, GOOD
VERBAL COMPREHENSION AND MEMORY, AND A
BETTER THAN AVERAGE FUND OF INFORMATION.
THIS SUBTEST HAS BEEN CONSIDERED THE
BEST SINGLE MEASURE OF INTELLIGENCE.
HIGH VOCABULARY SCORES REFLECT THE
ABILITY TO CONCEPTUALIZE AND STRIVE
INTELLECTUALLY. THEY MAY ALSO REFLECT
GOOD PRE-SCHOOL EXPERIENCES.
- DIGIT SPAN
SCALE SCORE = 5

MEAN SCALED SCORE = 10.08

LOW DIGIT SPAN SCORES MAY REFLECT POOR
ATTENTION AND DISTRACTABILITY, POOR
AUDITORY SEQUENCING, AND POSSIBLE LEARN-
ING DIFFICULTIES.
- CODING
SCALE SCORE = 3

MEAN SCALED SCORE = 10.08

LOW SCORES ON THE CODING SUBTEST REFLECT
DISTRACTIBILITY, VISUAL-MOTOR COORDINA-
TION, POOR MOTOR SPEED, AND POSSIBLY
POOR ROTE LEARNING ABILITY. POOR CON-
CENTRATION AND ATTENTION ARE INDICATED.
LOW SCORES MAY ALSO REFLECT LOW
MOTIVATION.

****

EDUCATIONAL OBJECTIVES FOR DIGIT SPAN
CHRONOLOGICAL AGE = 10-0

****

GIVEN A SEQUENCE OF NUMBERS, REPEAT THE

SEQUENCE FORWORD AND BACKWARD.

SEE AND WRITE TELEPHONE NUMBER AND

ADDRESS FROM MEMORY.

REPEAT SENTENCES OF VARYING LENGTH.

REPEAT A SERIES OF LETTERS, NUMBERS,

WORDS, SENTENCES, OR EVENTS.

REPEAT WORDS TO POPULAR SONGS.

READ AND RETELL STORIES.

REPEAT AND PERFORM SEQUENTIAL

DIRECTIONS.

REPEAT LISTS OF SHOPPING ITEMS.

PARTICIPATE IN MEMORY GAMES.

REVIEW WHAT HAS BEEN LEARNED AFTER A

DAILY LESSON OR CLASS.

FOLLOW DIRECTIONS FOR PAPER FOLDING

ACTIVITIES.

NAME IN CORRECT SEQUENCE THE MUSICAL

INSTRUMENTS IN A RECORDING.

LIST THE CLUES IN A MYSTERY STORY.

MAKE A LIST OF DIRECTIONS FOR FINDING

HIDDEN TREASURE.

LIST THE STEPS INVOLVED IN A SCIENCE

EXPERIMENT.
****

EDUCATIONAL OBJECTIVES FOR CODING
CHRONOLOGICAL AGE = 10 -0

****

MAKE JEWELRY FROM BEADS, MACARONI

PIECES, SHELLS, ETC.

COMPLETE PAINT-BY-NUMBER PICTURES.

COMPLETE HANDWRITING ASSIGNMENTS WITH

COPYING LETTERS, WORDS, AND NUMBERS IN
SPECIFIED TIME LIMITS.
MATCH LETTERS, NUMBERS, AND WORDS.
MEMORIZE POEMS, SONGS, RIDDLES, AND
PROVERBS.
PARTICIPATE IN MEMORY GAMES SUCH AS
 CONCENTRATION'.
CONSTRUCT PICTURE STORIES WITH EACH
PICTURE REPRESENTING A WORD OR THOUGHT
OR ACTION.
GIVEN A BRIEF PRESENTATION OF LETTERS,
WORDS, OR DESIGNS, REPRODUCE THEM.
PARTICIPATE IN 'SIMON SAYS' GAMES.
EXPLAIN MAP SYMBOLS AND PLAN A TRIP
USING A MAP ROUTE.
COPY EXERCISES, DIRECTIONS, OR
ASSIGNMENTS FROM THE CHALK BOARD IN
SPECIFIED TIME LIMITS.
COMPLETE PUZZLES IN TIMED FORMAT.
PARTICIPATE IN VISUAL TRACKING
EXERCISES.
REPRODUCE DESIGNS, DIAGRAMS, & PICTURES
FROM MEMORY.
USE THE TYPEWRITER OR WORD PROCESSOR
TO COPY LETTERS, WORDS, AND SENTENCES.

THANK YOU FOR USING WISCR-80.

NAME: Irrational Beliefs Report

SUPPLIER: Test Systems International
P.O. Box 18347
Wichita, KS 67218

PRODUCT CATEGORY

Personality
Interest/Attitudes

PRIMARY APPLICATIONS

Clinical Assessment/Diagnosis
Personal/Marriage/Family Counseling

SALE RESTRICTIONS Qualified Professional

SERVICE TYPE/COST	Type	Available	Cost	Discount
	Mail-In	Yes	$12.00	Yes
	Teleprocessing	No		
	Local	No		

PRODUCT DESCRIPTION

This report provides scores and a narrative report based upon a factor-analytic model and three broad dimensions derived from Ellis' Rational Emotive Therapy. The scales have proven their stability over fifteen years of use. The report unobstrusively incorporates empirical relationships between scales and other conditions such as stress, pathology, personality, motivation, organization roles, and decision styles. It serves as a tool for diagnosis, treatment, and industrial or personal counseling.

NAME: Jackson Vocational Interest Survey

SUPPLIER: Research Psychologists Press
P.O. Box 984
Port Huron, MI 48061
(800) 265-1285

PRODUCT CATEGORY

Career/Vocational

PRIMARY APPLICATIONS

Vocational Guidance/Counseling

SALE RESTRICTIONS American Psychological Association Guidelines

SERVICE TYPE/COST	Type	Available	Cost	Discount
	Mail-In	Yes	$7.00	Yes
	Teleprocessing	No		
	Local	No		

PRODUCT DESCRIPTION

The JACKSON VOCATIONAL INTEREST SURVEY was developed to assist high school, college, and general adult populations with career planning and educational guidance. This 289-item inventory consists of paired statements covering 10 occupational themes: Expressive, Logical, Inquiring, Practical, Assertive, Socialized, Helping, Conventional, Enterprising, and Communicative. Individuals mark one of two response choices. Scoring yields a sex-fair profile of 34 basic interest scales and 32 occupational clusters. A 7th-grade reading level is required.

The Basic Report graphically portrays 34 scores from interest scales. The Extended Report includes additional information and text for interpretation. Price information given here is for the Extended Report.

```
        CASE, M.                      RESPONDENT NO. 123456789    SEX FEMALE
        DATE OF REPORT   29-JUN-83
```

THIS PROFILE AND REPORT ARE BASED UPON YOUR ANSWERS TO THE JACKSON VOCA-
TIONAL INTEREST SURVEY (JVIS). YOUR STATED PREFERENCES TO WORK-RELATED
ACTIVITIES FORM THE BASIS FOR YOUR SCORES. THESE SCORES INDICATE YOUR
AREAS OF HIGH AND LOW INTEREST, AND HOW THESE INTERESTS COMPARE WITH
THOSE OF PEOPLE ENROLLED IN DIFFERENT EDUCATIONAL PROGRAMS AND EMPLOYED
IN A RANGE OF OCCUPATIONS.

IT IS EXTREMELY IMPORTANT TO RECOGNIZE THAT INTERESTS ARE DIFFERENT FROM
ABILITIES. THESE RESULTS TELL YOU ABOUT YOUR INTERESTS. THEY DO NOT IN-
DICATE WHETHER OR NOT YOU HAVE THE ABILITY, SKILL, OR EDUCATIONAL BACK-
GROUND NECESSARY FOR A PARTICULAR KIND OF WORK. THUS, A HIGH SCORE ON THE
MATHEMATICS SCALE WOULD INDICATE AN INTEREST IN USING MATHEMATICAL REASON-
ING IN SOLVING PROBLEMS, BUT WOULD NOT MEAN THAT YOU NECESSARILY HAVE THE
ABILITY TO BECOME A MATHEMATICIAN. IN ADDITION TO INTEREST TEST RESULTS,
OTHER SOURCES OF INFORMATION, AS WELL AS YOUR PAST RECORD OF PERFORMANCE,
SHOULD BE CONSIDERED IN EDUCATIONAL AND CAREER PLANNING.

MOST PEOPLE FIND THAT THEIR RESULTS FROM VOCATIONAL INTEREST TESTING ARE
VERY USEFUL, BUT YOU SHOULD NOT EXPECT THESE RESULTS TO CHOOSE A CAREER
FOR YOU WITHOUT SOME CAREFUL THINKING ON YOUR PART. QUITE OFTEN RESULTS
TURN OUT TO BE WHAT YOU EXPECTED. IF SO, IT IS OF SOME BENEFIT TO KNOW
THAT AN OBJECTIVE COMPARISON OF YOUR INTEREST TEST SCORES IN RELATION TO
THOSE OF OTHERS CONFIRMS THE DIRECTION OF YOUR PRESENT PLANNING. IF YOUR
MEASURED INTERESTS INDICATE CAREER DIRECTIONS VERY DIFFERENT FROM YOUR
PRESENT PLANS, YOU SHOULD CAREFULLY REVIEW THESE PLANS AND YOUR REASONS
FOR MAKING THEM. GENERALLY, PEOPLE ARE MORE LIKELY TO BE SATISFIED IN AN
OCCUPATIONAL AREA TO WHICH THEIR INTERESTS ARE SIMILAR RATHER THAN DIS-
SIMILAR.

YOU ARE ALSO ENCOURAGED TO FIND OUT MORE ABOUT SPECIFIC OCCUPATIONS IN THE
AREAS TO WHICH YOUR INTERESTS ARE SIMILAR. TO DO SO, CONSULT CAREER IN-
FORMATION FILES AND REFERENCE BOOKS AT A LIBRARY OR IN A CAREER COUNSEL-
ING OFFICE.

PAGE THREE CONTAINS RESULTS FOR 10 GENERAL OCCUPATIONAL THEMES FOLLOWED
BY SCORES FOR ADMINISTRATIVE INDICES AND A SCORE FOR ACADEMIC ORIENTATION.
PAGE FOUR CONTAINS SCORES INDICATING THE SIMILARITY OF YOUR INTEREST
PROFILE TO THOSE OF A VARIETY OF DIFFERENT KINDS OF COLLEGE STUDENTS
AND TO PERSONS IN EACH OF 32 OCCUPATIONAL CLUSTERS. THE LAST FOUR PAGES
PROVIDE MORE DETAILED INFORMATION ABOUT YOUR THREE HIGHEST-RANKED OCCUPA-
TIONAL CLUSTERS AND SUGGESTED READINGS TO ASSIST YOUR EXPLORATION OF YOUR
INTERESTS IN THESE AREAS.

```
        ************************************************
        *****   JVIS BASIC INTEREST SCALE PROFILE    *****
        ************************************************
```

YOUR PROFILE ON PAGE TWO GIVES RESULTS FOR THE 34 BASIC INTEREST
SCALES. A HIGH SCORE INDICATES THAT YOU SHOW A PREFERENCE FOR WORKING IN
SETTINGS INVOLVING ACTIVITIES DESCRIBED BY THE SCALE NAMES. A LOW SCORE
INDICATES THAT YOU WOULD PREFER NOT TO WORK IN SUCH SETTINGS AND WOULD
PROBABLY FIND SUCH WORK UNSATISFYING. THUS, IF YOUR PROFILE INDICATES
A HIGH SCORE FOR LAW AND A LOW SCORE FOR PLANFULNESS, IT MEANS THAT YOU
WOULD PREFER TO WORK AT ACTIVITIES LIKE THOSE PERFORMED BY LAWYERS, BUT
NOT AT THOSE REQUIRING A HIGH DEGREE OF PLANFULNESS. THESE SCORES WOULD
NOT NECESSARILY MEAN THAT YOU WOULD MAKE A GOOD LAWYER, OR THAT YOU LACK
THE TRAIT OF PLANFULNESS.

psychware **315**

```
                                    VERY                 STANDARD SCORE              VERY
                              P/C-  LOW          LOW        AVERAGE       HIGH        HIGH
                              TILE  10    15    20    25    30    35    40    45    50    55
                        SCORE  F  M  .     .     .     .     .     .     .     .     .     .
 ••••••••••••••••••••••••••••••••••••••••••••••••••••••••••••••••••••••••••••••••••••••••••
 CREATIVE ARTS            7  18 30  XXXXXXXXXXXXXX
 PERFORMING ARTS          7  36 41  XXXXXXXXXXXXXXXXXX
 
 MATHEMATICS              2  13  5  XXXXXXXXX
 PHYSICAL SCIENCE         2  10  3  XXXXXXXX
 ENGINEERING              4  30  5  XXXXXXXXXXX
 LIFE SCIENCE             3  10  8  XXXXXXXX
 SOCIAL SCIENCE          13  74 82  XXXXXXXXXXXXXXXXXXXXXXXXXXXXXXXXXX
 
 ADVENTURE                2   3  1  X
 NATURE-AGRICULTURE       8  46 43  XXXXXXXXXXXXXXXXXXXXXX
 SKILLED TRADES           3  36 26  XXXXXXXXXXXXXXX
 
 PERSONAL SERVICE         5   9 24  XXXXXXXXXXXX
 FAMILY ACTIVITY          8  22 41  XXXXXXXXXXXXXXXXXX
 MEDICAL SERVICE          3  21 17  XXXXXXXXXXXX
 
 DOMINANT LEADERSHIP      1   5  1  XXXXXXX
 JOB SECURITY             0   0  0  X
 STAMINA                 11  70 57  XXXXXXXXXXXXXXXXXXXXXXXXXXXX
 ACCOUNTABILITY          12  57 49  XXXXXXXXXXXXXXXXXXXXXXXXXX
 
 TEACHING                13  77 89  XXXXXXXXXXXXXXXXXXXXXXXXXXXXXXXXXXXXXX
 SOCIAL SERVICE          12  43 79  XXXXXXXXXXXXXXXXXXXXXXXXXXXXX
 ELEMENTARY EDUCATION     9  30 70  XXXXXXXXXXXXXXXXXXXXXXXXX
 
 FINANCE                  9  73 53  XXXXXXXXXXXXXXXXXXXXXXXXXXXX
 BUSINESS                13  91 88  XXXXXXXXXXXXXXXXXXXXXXXXXXXXXXXXXXXXXXXXXX
 OFFICE WORK              8  60 70  XXXXXXXXXXXXXXXXXXXXXXXXXX
 SALES                    9  62 67  XXXXXXXXXXXXXXXXXXXXXXXXXX
 
 SUPERVISION             14  96 91  XXXXXXXXXXXXXXXXXXXXXXXXXXXXXXXXXXXXXXXXXXXXX
 HUMAN RELATIONS MGT      13  81 79  XXXXXXXXXXXXXXXXXXXXXXXXXXXXXXXXX
 LAW                     12  75 72  XXXXXXXXXXXXXXXXXXXXXXXXXXXXXX
 PROFESSIONL ADVISING    13  91 89  XXXXXXXXXXXXXXXXXXXXXXXXXXXXXXXXXXXXXX
 
 AUTHOR-JOURNALISM       11  58 75  XXXXXXXXXXXXXXXXXXXXXXXXX
 ACADEMIC ACHIEVEMENT     9  36 37  XXXXXXXXXXXXXXXXXXX
 TECHNICAL WRITING       13  93 95  XXXXXXXXXXXXXXXXXXXXXXXXXXXXXXXXXXXXXX
 
 INDEPENDENCE            13  81 79  XXXXXXXXXXXXXXXXXXXXXXXXXXXXXXXXX
 PLANFULNESS             13  84 86  XXXXXXXXXXXXXXXXXXXXXXXXXXXXXXXXXX
 INTERPERSONAL
   CONFIDENCE            14  64 76  XXXXXXXXXXXXXXXXXXXXXXXXXXXXXXXX
 ••••••••••••••••••••••••••••••••••••••••••••••••••••••••••••••••••••••••••••••••••••••••••
```

THE BAR GRAPH PRINTED NEXT TO EACH SCALE NAME INDICATES HOW YOUR STANDARD
SCORES COMPARE WITH THOSE OF A LARGE GROUP OF MALE AND FEMALE STUDENTS
AND YOUNG ADULTS. AVERAGE SIMILARITY TO THIS GROUP IS A STANDARD SCORE
OF 30 ON THIS PROFILE. A HIGHER SCORE INDICATES GREATER RELATIVE INTEREST.
THE COLUMN LABELED "SCORE" TO THE LEFT INDICATES THE NUMBER OF ACTIVITIES
RELATED TO THAT AREA FOR WHICH YOU HAVE INDICATED A PREFERENCE.
THE PERCENTILE (P/C-TILE) INDICATES THE NUMBER OF FEMALES (F) AND MALES (M)
OUT OF 100 WHO WOULD RECEIVE A SCORE LOWER THAN YOUR SCORE. A HIGHER SCORE
INDICATES GREATER RELATIVE INTEREST.

RESPONDENT CASE, M.   123456789   FEMALE   29-JUN-83   PAGE 3

```
                    **********************************************
                    *****   GENERAL OCCUPATIONAL THEMES    *****
                    **********************************************
```

STUDIES WITH THE JVIS HAVE REVEALED 10 GENERAL PATTERNS OF INTERESTS.
THESE REFLECT GENERAL ORIENTATIONS TO THE WORLD OF WORK, RATHER THAN SPE-
CIFIC INTERESTS IN PARTICULAR AREAS. BELOW IS A PROFILE OF YOUR GENERAL
OCCUPATIONAL THEMES. YOUR PERCENTILE IS PLOTTED IN TERMS OF YOUR OWN SEX,
WITH PERCENTILES FOR BOTH SEXES APPEARING TO THE LEFT.

DESCRIPTIONS OF EACH OF THE 10 THEMES ARE PRESENTED FOLLOWING YOUR PROFILE.
YOU SHOULD NOT EXPECT THAT ALL OF THE CHARACTERISTICS DESCRIBING A PARTI-
CULAR THEME, EVEN THOSE THAT YOU RECEIVE HIGH SCORES ON, WILL FIT YOU PER-
FECTLY. MOST OFTEN A PERSON IS SIMILAR TO SOME ELEMENTS OF THE DESCRIP-
TIONS GIVEN FOR HIS OR HER TWO OR THREE HIGHEST SCORES.

```
                P/C-  VERY LOW                PERCENTILE              VERY HIGH
                TILE  0    10    20    30    40    50    60    70    80    90    99
                 F  M  .     .     .     .     .     .     .     .     .     .     .
 ••••••••••••••••••••••••••••••••••••••••••••••••••••••••••••••••••••••••••••••••••••••••••
 EXPRESSIVE       35 53  XXXXXXXXXXXXXXXXXXX
 LOGICAL          15  3  XXXXXXXXX
 INQUIRING        22 23  XXXXXXXXXXXX
 PRACTICAL        20 32  XXXXXXXXXXX
 ASSERTIVE        57 52  XXXXXXXXXXXXXXXXXXXXXXXXXXXXXXXX
 
 SOCIALIZED       52 39  XXXXXXXXXXXXXXXXXXXXXXXXXXXX
 HELPING          53 87  XXXXXXXXXXXXXXXXXXXXXXXXXXXXX
 CONVENTIONAL     88 88  XXXXXXXXXXXXXXXXXXXXXXXXXXXXXXXXXXXXXXXXXXXXXX
 ENTERPRISING     93 87  XXXXXXXXXXXXXXXXXXXXXXXXXXXXXXXXXXXXXXXXXXXXXXXX
 COMMUNICATIVE    76 84  XXXXXXXXXXXXXXXXXXXXXXXXXXXXXXXXXXXXXX
 ••••••••••••••••••••••••••••••••••••••••••••••••••••••••••••••••••••••••••••••••••••••••••
```

EXPLANATION OF P/C-TILE (PERCENTILE) -- THE PERCENTAGE OF FEMALES (F) AND
MALES (M) RECEIVING A SCORE LOWER THAN YOUR SCORE.

EXPRESSIVE--PEOPLE SCORING HIGH ON THIS THEME ARE LIKELY TO BE CONSIDERED
ARTISTIC BY OTHERS, REGARDLESS OF WHETHER OR NOT THEY ARE ACTUALLY PRE-
SENTLY ENGAGED IN ANY ARTISTIC WORK. THEY ENJOY CREATIVE ACTIVITIES, WHICH
MIGHT TAKE A WIDE VARIETY OF FORMS, INCLUDING ANY OF THE APPLIED OR FINE
ARTS, DRAMA, MUSIC, WRITING, VISUAL ART, OR IN THE WORLD OF IDEAS.
SUCH PEOPLE ARE ALSO MORE LIKELY TO ENJOY THE CREATIVE WORK OF OTHERS.
THESE INDIVIDUALS TEND TO CONSIDER THEMSELVES PERCEPTIVE, INVENTIVE,
SENSITIVE, IMAGINATIVE, AND AWARE OF THEIR ENVIRONMENTS. PEOPLE IN THE
ARTS RECEIVE HIGH SCORES ON THIS THEME, BUT MANY OTHERS COMBINE THIS THEME
WITH OTHERS IN FINDING EXPRESSION FOR THEIR INTERESTS.

LOGICAL--HIGH SCORERS ENJOY RATIONAL, ABSTRACT THOUGHT THAT IS CHARACTER-
IZED BY TESTABLE GENERALIZATIONS, DEDUCTIVE REASONING, AND PRECISION.
THEY ENJOY THE CHALLENGE OF DIFFICULT INTELLECTUAL WORK, PARTICULARLY IN
THE AREAS OF MATHEMATICS AND THE PHYSICAL SCIENCES, BUT ALSO IN APPLICA-
TIONS SUCH AS IN ENGINEERING AND TECHNOLOGY, WORK WITH COMPUTERS, AND,
INDEED, IN A VARIETY OF OTHER AREAS WHERE QUANTITATIVE AND EXACTING WORK
MAY BE REQUIRED. A PREFERENCE FOR WORKING WITH THE PHYSICAL WORLD OR
WITH ABSTRACT IDEAS OVER WORKING PRIMARILY WITH PEOPLE FREQUENTLY CHARAC-
TERIZES HIGH SCORERS.

INQUIRING--HIGH SCORERS ON THIS THEME SHOW A GREAT DEAL OF CURIOSITY ABOUT
THEIR ENVIRONMENTS, PARTICULARLY ABOUT LIVING THINGS, OTHER PEOPLE, AND
SOCIAL INSTITUTIONS. THEY HAVE A DESIRE TO LEARN ABOUT MANY AREAS OF
KNOWLEDGE, AND ARE DESCRIBED AS INVESTIGATIVE, INTELLECTUALLY PROBING,
AND REFLECTIVE. SUCH PEOPLE SOMETIMES ENTER ONE OF THE SOCIAL OR BIO-
LOGICAL SCIENCES, OR ONE OF THE PROFESSIONS, OR, JUST AS OFTEN, COMBINE
THIS THEME WITH OTHERS IN CHOOSING A CAREER.

PRACTICAL--HIGH SCORERS ENJOY ACTIVITIES REQUIRING PHYSICAL OR MECHANI-
CAL SKILL, SEEKING SATISFACTION FROM THE QUALITY OF THEIR WORK, RATHER
THAN IN EXERCISING INFLUENCE OR POWER OVER OTHERS. THEY ENJOY OUTDOOR
WORK AND ARE NOT OVERLY CONCERNED ABOUT PHYSICAL RISKS. THEY TEND TO
AVOID ACTIVITIES REQUIRING THEM TO BE THE CENTER OF ATTENTION AND PREFER
PRACTICAL ARTS TO THE WORLD OF ABSTRACT IDEAS. THEY ENJOY CLOSE FAMILY
TIES AND ARE SOMETIMES CONCERNED WITH ARRANGING FOR THE COMFORT AND WELL-
BEING OF OTHERS. SUCH PERSONS ARE FOUND IN A WIDE VARIETY OF ACTIVITIES--
AGRICULTURE, SKILLED TRADES, SERVICE ACTIVITIES, AND OTHERS.

ASSERTIVE--HIGH SCORES ON THIS THEME INDICATE A PREFERENCE FOR WORKING
IN SITUATIONS IN WHICH ONE CAN EXERCISE CONTROL AND WHERE ONE'S AUTHORITY
IS CLEARLY DEFINED. SUCH PEOPLE ENJOY EXERCISING AUTHORITY OVER OTHERS,
AND DO SO SELF-CONFIDENTLY, WITHOUT THE NEED TO SEEK ADVICE OR ASSISTANCE.
SOMETIMES SEEN AS OUTSPOKEN AND DIRECT WITH OTHERS, THESE PEOPLE ENJOY
WORKING WITH OTHER PEOPLE, ESPECIALLY IN A DOMINANT ROLE. PERSONS WORKING
IN ENVIRONMENTS IN WHICH THIS STYLE OF LEADERSHIP IS APPROPRIATE, SUCH AS
THE MILITARY, FREQUENTLY RECEIVE HIGH SCORES ON THIS THEME.

SOCIALIZED--PEOPLE OBTAINING HIGH SCORES ON THIS THEME ARE USUALLY REGARD-
ED AS RESPONSIBLE, STABLE WORKERS, DISCIPLINED, PROMPT, SYSTEMATIC, AND
DELIBERATE, BUT NOT USUALLY CREATIVE. THEY WOULD RATHER BE CONFIDENT
ABOUT A RELATIVELY CERTAIN FUTURE AT A PREDICTABLE SALARY, THAN ACCEPT
THE UNCERTAINTY OF A RISKIER BUT POSSIBLY MORE REWARDING PROSPECT.
OCCUPATIONS WHICH OFFER SUCH STABILITY AND REWARD THESE TRADITIONAL
VIRTUES ARE LIKELY TO BE FAVORED BY HIGH SCORERS.

HELPING--PEOPLE SCORING HIGH EXPRESS A GENUINE CONCERN FOR OTHER PEOPLE,
PARTICULARLY THOSE WITH PROBLEMS OR DIFFICULTIES OR WHO REQUIRE ASSIS-
TANCE, OR EDUCATION. HIGH SCORERS ARE CHARACTERIZED AS BENEVOLENT,
COMFORTING, SYMPATHETIC, SUPPORTING, CHARITABLE, ASSISTING,
COOPERATIVE, AND AS ENJOYING SOCIAL INTERACTION AND GIVING ADVICE.
OCCUPATIONS IN WHICH THEY MAY TAKE A DIRECT ROLE IN HELPING, SERVING,
OR TEACHING OTHERS ARE DISTINCTLY PREFERRED.

CONVENTIONAL--HIGH SCORERS ON THIS THEME PREFER WELL-DEFINED WORK ROLES
WITHIN A BUSINESS OR OTHER LARGE ORGANIZATION. THEY ENJOY THE DAY-TO-DAY
OPERATIONS OF BUSINESS, WHETHER INVOLVING THE DETAILED OPERATION OF A BUS-
INESS OFFICE, SALES, MAKING BUSINESS DECISIONS, OR SUPERVISING OTHERS IN
THESE CAPACITIES. THEY SHOW A PREFERENCE FOR WORKING WITH OTHERS IN
SMOOTHLY RUNNING ORGANIZATIONS, RATHER THAN IN HIGHLY-CHARGED OR HIGHLY
VARIABLE ENVIRONMENTS. THEY THRIVE ON DETAIL, BUT PREFER NOT TO BE RE-
QUIRED TO BE HIGHLY CREATIVE, NOR TO WORK AT TASKS INVOLVING PHYSICAL OR
MECHANICAL SKILL, DISCOMFORT, OR PHYSICAL RISK.

ENTERPRISING--PERSONS RECEIVING HIGH SCORES ON THIS THEME ENJOY WORK IN-
VOLVING TALKING WITH OTHER PEOPLE, PARTICULARLY IF THE PURPOSE OF THE DIS-
CUSSION IS TO PERSUADE OR INFLUENCE. SELF CONFIDENT, RARELY
SHY ABOUT ENTERING DIFFICULT SITUATIONS, DOMINANT, AND FORCEFUL, THESE
PEOPLE ARE USUALLY INTERESTED IN MARKETING OR MANAGEMENT ASPECTS OF BUSI-
NESS, RATHER THAN IN THE DETAILS OF DAY-TO-DAY OPERATION OR IN PARTICULAR
SPECIALTIES. THEY ARE OFTEN MOTIVATED BY THE CONVENTIONAL SYMBOLS OF
SOCIAL STATUS--MONEY, INFLUENCE, AND PRESTIGE--RATHER THAN IN OTHER FORMS
OF RECOGNITION. IN ADDITION TO BUSINESS, PEOPLE REPRESENTED PRIMARILY BY
THIS THEME MAY BE FOUND IN THE LEGAL PROFESSION, ADMINISTRATION, PUBLIC
RELATIONS, DIPLOMACY AND RELATED AREAS.

COMMUNICATIVE--HIGH SCORERS ARE INTERESTED IN IDEAS AND IN PARTICULAR IN
COMMUNICATING THESE IDEAS TO OTHERS IN WRITING. THEY ENJOY ANY SERIOUS
EXPRESSION OF THOUGHTS, ATTENDING LECTURES, READING, STUDYING, TAKING
NOTES, VISITING A LIBRARY, OR ENGAGING IN DEBATE OR INTELLECTUAL
DISCUSSIONS. THEIR ENJOYMENT OF WRITING IS MORE HIGHLY FOCUSED UPON
EXPRESSING OR FORMULATING CONCEPTS, RATHER THAN UPON ENTERTAINING OTHERS,
ALTHOUGH THEY MIGHT ENJOY THAT AS WELL. SUCH PEOPLE TEND TO BE DESCRIBED
AS INTELLECTUAL, ARTICULATE, WELL-INFORMED, AND AS HAVING A BROAD RANGE OF
INTERESTS. PROFESSIONAL WRITERS, OF COURSE, SCORE HIGHLY ON THIS THEME,
BUT SINCE WRITTEN EXPRESSION IS IMPORTANT IN A WIDE RANGE OF OCCUPATIONS,
MANY OTHERS SCORE HIGHLY AS WELL.

```
                          *****ADMINISTRATIVE INDICES*****

NUMBER OF *A* RESPONSES = 91    NUMBER OF DOUBLE RESPONSES      =    0
NUMBER OF *B* RESPONSES = 198   PERCENTAGE SCORABLE RESPONSES  =  100
NUMBER OF OMITS         =  0    RELIABILITY INDEX *            = +0.85

 * THE RELIABILITY INDEX INDICATES THE CONSISTENCY WITH WHICH YOU COMPLETED
   THE JVIS.  SCORES MAY RANGE FROM 1.00 TO BELOW 0.00.  A HIGH SCORE
   INDICATES THAT YOU RESPONDED PURPOSEFULLY AND CAREFULLY, WHILE LOW SCORES
   INDICATE SOME LACK OF STABILITY IN INTERESTS OR POSSIBLE CARELESSNESS IN
   COMPLETING THE JVIS.

                          *****ACADEMIC ORIENTATION*****

ACADEMIC ORIENTATION STANDARD SCORE          436

THE AVERAGE STANDARD SCORE IS 500.  APPROXIMATELY TWO THIRDS OF HIGH
SCHOOL AND COLLEGE STUDENTS HAVE SCORES BETWEEN 400 AND 600.

THIS ACADEMIC ORIENTATION SCORE INDICATES THE DEGREE OF SIMILARITY OF YOUR
PROFILE TO THOSE OF THE AVERAGE ACADEMIC UNIVERSITY STUDENT.  IT DOES NOT
REFLECT YOUR ABILITY NOR YOUR PROBABLE SUCCESS AS A UNIVERSITY STUDENT.
RATHER, IT MIGHT INDICATE YOUR ENJOYMENT OF PURSUING A TRADITIONAL ACADEMIC
AND/OR SCIENTIFIC COURSE OF STUDY.

      **************************************************************************
      *****   SIMILARITY TO COLLEGE AND UNIVERSITY STUDENT GROUPS   *****
      **************************************************************************

                                            FEMALES               MALES

AGRICULTURE                                -0.58 (VERY LOW)       -0.56
ARTS & ARCHITECTURE                        -0.16 (VERY LOW)       -0.09
BUSINESS                                   +0.64 (VERY HIGH)      +0.69
EARTH & MINERAL SCIENCE                                           -0.50
EDUCATION                                  +0.44 (HIGH)           +0.50
ENGINEERING                                -0.26 (VERY LOW)       -0.37
HEALTH, PHYSICAL EDUC. & RECREATION        -0.50 (VERY LOW)
HUMAN DEVELOPMENT                          +0.32 (MODERATE)       +0.61
LIBERAL ARTS                               +0.72 (VERY HIGH)      +0.72
SCIENCE                                    -0.51 (VERY LOW)       -0.47
NURSES                                     -0.04 (VERY LOW)
MEDICAL STUDENTS                           +0.04 (LOW)            -0.06
TECHNICAL COLLEGE                                                 -0.19
      **************************************************************************
      *****   SIMILARITY TO OCCUPATIONAL CLASSIFICATIONS   *****
      **************************************************************************

BELOW ARE RANKED THE OCCUPATIONAL CLASSIFICATIONS FOUND TO BE SIMILAR
TO YOUR INTEREST PROFILE.  A POSITIVE SCORE INDICATES THAT YOUR PROFILE
SHOWS SOME DEGREE OF SIMILARITY TO THOSE ALREADY WORKING IN THE
OCCUPATIONAL CLUSTER, WHILE A NEGATIVE SCORE INDICATES DISSIMILARITY.

SCORE   SIMILARITY                 OCCUPATIONAL CLASSIFICATION
-----   ----------                 ---------------------------
+0.72 VERY SIMILAR             OCCUPATIONS IN LAW AND POLITICS
+0.71 VERY SIMILAR             COUNSELORS / STUDENT PERSONNEL WORKERS
+0.69 VERY SIMILAR             ADMINISTRATIVE AND RELATED OCCUPATIONS
+0.64 VERY SIMILAR             PERSONNEL / HUMAN MANAGEMENT
+0.57 SIMILAR                  TEACHING AND RELATED OCCUPATIONS
+0.55 SIMILAR                  SALES OCCUPATIONS
+0.54 SIMILAR                  OCCUPATIONS IN MERCHANDISING
+0.54 SIMILAR                  OCCUPATIONS IN RELIGION
+0.53 SIMILAR                  OCCUPATIONS IN ACCOUNTING, BANKING AND FINANCE
+0.50 SIMILAR                  CLERICAL SERVICES
+0.48 SIMILAR                  OCCUPATIONS IN SOCIAL SCIENCE
+0.47 SIMILAR                  OCCUPATIONS IN SOCIAL WELFARE
+0.34 MODERATELY SIMILAR       OCCUPATIONS IN WRITING
+0.33 MODERATELY SIMILAR       MILITARY OFFICERS
+0.29 MODERATELY SIMILAR       OCCUPATIONS IN PRE-SCHOOL AND ELEMENTARY TEACHING
-0.03 NEUTRAL                  ASSEMBLY OCCUPATIONS-INSTRUMENTS & SMALL PRODUCTS
-0.04 NEUTRAL                  SERVICE OCCUPATIONS
-0.17 NEUTRAL                  OCCUPATIONS IN MUSIC
-0.20 NEUTRAL                  OCCUPATIONS IN ENTERTAINMENT
-0.25 DISSIMILAR               PROTECTIVE SERVICES OCCUPATIONS
-0.29 DISSIMILAR               OCCUPATIONS IN COMMERCIAL ART
-0.36 DISSIMILAR               AGRICULTURALISTS
-0.45 DISSIMILAR               ENGINEERING AND TECHNICAL SUPPORT WORKERS
-0.48 DISSIMILAR               MACHINING / MECHANICAL AND RELATED OCCUPATIONS
-0.48 DISSIMILAR               MATHEMATICAL AND RELATED OCCUPATIONS
-0.50 DISSIMILAR               OCCUPATIONS IN FINE ART
-0.54 DISSIMILAR               CONSTRUCTION / SKILLED TRADES
-0.58 DISSIMILAR               OCCUPATIONS IN THE PHYSICAL SCIENCES
-0.61 VERY DISSIMILAR          HEALTH SERVICE WORKERS
-0.64 VERY DISSIMILAR          MEDICAL DIAGNOSIS AND TREATMENT OCCUPATIONS
-0.65 VERY DISSIMILAR          SPORT AND RECREATION OCCUPATIONS
-0.69 VERY DISSIMILAR          LIFE SCIENCES

            *****DESCRIPTIONS OF OCCUPATIONAL CLASSIFICATIONS*****

     DISCUSSIONS AND JOB TITLES CHARACTERISTIC OF EACH OF YOUR THREE
HIGHEST RANKED OCCUPATIONAL CLASSIFICATIONS ARE PRESENTED ON THIS AND
THE NEXT PAGE.  REMEMBER, THE RANKING OF THESE OCCUPATIONAL CLUSTERS
REFLECTS HOW SIMILAR YOUR MEASURED INTERESTS ARE TO PEOPLE EMPLOYED IN
THESE CLUSTERS.  IT IS NOT A REFLECTION OF YOUR ABILITY TO PERFORM
REQUIRED DUTIES NOR TO BENEFIT FROM TRAINING IN THESE AREAS.  YOU MAY
FIND THIS INFORMATION USEFUL IN PLANNING YOUR EDUCATION AND DECIDING
WHERE AND HOW TO GET IT, AS WELL AS IN CAREER PLANNING.  YOUR
COUNSELOR OR ADVISER CAN BE OF HELP TO YOU IN THIS PROCESS.
```

318 *psychware*

IN THE DISCUSSIONS BELOW, DOT CODE NUMBERS ARE LISTED NEXT TO JOB TITLES. DOT STANDS FOR THE DICTIONARY OF OCCUPATIONAL TITLES, FOURTH EDITION, 1977.

TO USE THE IDENTIFIED DOT CODE NUMBERS AND JOB TITLES, LOCATE 'THE DICTIONARY OF OCCUPATIONAL TITLES, FOURTH EDITION, 1977. THIS BOOK MAY LIKELY BE FOUND IN A LIBRARY OR A COUNSELOR'S OFFICE. THE DOT CLUSTERS JOBS INTO CATEGORIES, DIVISIONS AND GROUPS ON THE BASIS OF SIMILAR OCCUPATIONAL, INDUSTRIAL AND WORKER CHARACTERISTICS. OCCUPATIONS ARE LISTED BY DOT CODE NUMBER, AND EACH JOB IS DESCRIBED. ANOTHER SECTION OF THE DOT LISTS OCCUPATIONS ALPHABETICALLY BY JOB TITLE. BY USING THE DOT CODE NUMBERS AND JOB TITLES IDENTIFIED IN THIS REPORT, YOU WILL MORE EASILY LOCATE SPECIFIC INFORMATION IN THIS REFERENCE BOOK.

THE SPECIFIC OCCUPATIONS LISTED IN THIS REPORT ARE ONLY A SAMPLE OF POSSIBLE CAREERS. YOU ARE ENCOURAGED TO EXPLORE OTHER RELATED OCCUPA- TIONAL AREAS BY LOOKING AT DESCRIPTIONS OF OTHER OCCUPATIONS IN THE DOT DIVISIONS AND GROUPS SUGGESTED IN THE DISCUSSIONS BELOW.

PAGES NINE AND TEN OF THIS REPORT CONTAIN ADDITIONAL INFORMATION TO ASSIST YOUR CAREER EXPLORATION. THIS INFORMATION INCLUDES A LIST OF PAM- PHLETS AND BOOKS RELATED TO CAREERS IN YOUR THREE HIGHEST RANKED OCCUPA- TIONAL CLUSTERS.

OCCUPATIONS IN LAW AND POLITICS

INDIVIDUALS IN THIS AREA ARE CONCERNED WITH THE APPLICATION OF PRINCIPLES RELATING TO STATUTE LAW AND ITS ADMINISTRATION. THESE OCCUPATIONS INCLUDE LEGAL REPRESENTATION OF INDIVIDUALS, ORGANIZATIONS OR GOVERNMENT, PREPARATION OF LEGAL DOCUMENTS, PRESIDING OVER LEGAL GATHERINGS AND OTHER LAW-RELATED TASKS. LISTED BELOW ARE SOME OCCUPATIONS REPRESENTATIVE OF THE LEGAL/POLITICAL FIELD. FOR OTHER OCCUPATIONS EXAMINE DOT OCCUPATIONAL DIVISION 11 (LAW AND JURISPRUDENCE). THIS IS NOT A COMPLETE LIST, AS MANY COMPANIES AND PRIVATE ORGANIZATIONS SEEK DIFFERENT LEVELS AND KINDS OF LEGAL ADVICE. PEOPLE IN THESE AREAS TEND TO SHOW HIGH INTERESTS ON THE JVIS IN LAW, HUMAN RELATIONS MANAGEMENT, FINANCE, TECHNICAL WRITING, SUPERVISION AND INTERPERSONAL CONFIDENCE. THEY ARE OFTEN INTERESTED IN POLITICS AND GOVERNMENT SERVICE, BUT, OF COURSE, ONE CAN ENTER POLITICS FROM OTHER FIELDS, AS WELL AS FROM LAW.

OCCUPATION	DOT NO.	OCCUPATION	DOT NO.
LAWYER	110.107-010	PARALEGAL ASSISTANT	119.267-026
PATENT AGENT	119.167-014	ABSTRACTOR	119.267-101
LAWYER, CORPORATION	110.117-022	BAR EXAMINER	110.167-010
MAGISTRATE	111.107-014	APPEALS REFEREE	119.267-014
JUDGE	111.107-010	TITLE EXAMINER	119.287-010
LAWYER, CRIMINAL	110.107-014	DISTRICT ATTORNEY	110.117-010

COUNSELORS / STUDENT PERSONNEL WORKERS

PEOPLE IN THESE OCCUPATIONS ASSIST OTHERS IN UNDERSTANDING AND OVERCOMING INDIVIDUAL AND SOCIAL PROBLEMS. THEY ORGANIZE INFORMATION ABOUT SUCH THINGS AS CAREERS AND STUDY SKILLS, AND SHARE THIS INFORMATION WITH OTHERS IN SUCH A WAY THAT IT IS MEANINGFUL AND HELPFUL TO THE PERSON SEEKING ASSISTANCE. THEY ALSO CONDUCT RESEARCH TO EVALUATE TECHNIQUES AND NEW METHODS IN THE COUNSELING AREA. DOT OCCUPATIONAL GROUP 045 DEALS WITH OCCUPATIONS IN PSYCHOLOGY WHILE GROUP 090 INCLUDES JOBS WITH A COUNSELING FOCUS IN EDUCATION. INDIVIDUALS IN THESE AREAS TEND TO SCORE HIGH IN TEACHING, SOCIAL SERVICE, HUMAN RELATIONS MANAGEMENT, AND PROFESSIONAL ADVISING. SOME REPRESENTATIVE JOBS ARE LISTED BELOW AS A SAMPLE OF CAREERS IN THIS AREA.

OCCUPATION	DOT NO.	OCCUPATION	DOT NO.
COUNSELOR, CAMP	159.124-010	DIRECTOR OF GUIDANCE	045.117-010
COUNSELOR	045.107-010	RESIDENCE COUNSELOR	045.107-038
EMPLOYMENT INTERVIEWER	166.267-010	PSYCHOMETRIST	045.067-018
PSYCHOLOGIST, COUNSELING	045.107-026	PSYCHOLOGIST, SCHOOL	045.107-034
DIRECTOR OF COUNSELING	045.107-018	VOCATIONAL REHABILITATION	
FOREIGN STUDENT ADVISOR	090.107-010	COUNSELOR	045.107-042
CAREER GUIDANCE		DEAN OF STUDENTS	090.117-018
TECHNICIAN	249.367-014	DIRECTOR OF PLACEMENT	166.167-014
DIRECTOR OF STUDENT		FINANCIAL-AID COUNSELOR	169.267-018
AFFAIRS	090.167-022	DIRECTOR, EMPLOYMENT	
		SERVICES	188.117-078

ADMINISTRATIVE AND RELATED OCCUPATIONS

THIS OCCUPATIONAL CLUSTER INVOLVES PLANNING AND CONTROLLING ACTIVITIES WITHIN VARIOUS ORGANIZATIONS AS WELL AS OVERSEEING AND ANALYZING INFORMATION RELATING TO THEIR WORKING POLICIES. PEOPLE IN THIS CATEGORY TEND TO SHOW HIGH INTERESTS IN LAW, SUPERVISION, HUMAN RELATIONS MANAGEMENT AND PROFESSIONAL ADVISING. THEY ALSO TEND TO RECEIVE HIGH SCORES ON INTERPERSONAL CONFIDENCE AND PLANFULNESS. SEE PARTICULARLY DOT OCCUPATIONAL DIVISION 16 FOR ADMINISTRATIVE SPECIALIZATIONS, 18 FOR MANAGERS AND OFFICIALS AND 19 FOR SOME OTHER MANAGERIAL JOBS. YOU WILL FIND A SAMPLE OF CAREERS IN THIS AREA LISTED BELOW. IT IS NOT A COMPLETE LIST, BUT WILL GIVE YOU SOME IDEA OF THE RANGE OF JOBS AVAILABLE.

OCCUPATION	DOT NO.	OCCUPATION	DOT NO.
MANAGER, TRAFFIC	184.167-094	MANAGER, CITY	188.117-114
ADMINISTRATOR, SOCIAL		DIRECTOR, RESEARCH AND	
WELFARE	195.117-010	DEVELOPMENT	189.117-014
CONSTRUCTION INSPECTOR	182.267-010	CONTRACT ADMINISTRATOR	162.117-014
MANAGER, OFFICE	169.167-034	DIRECTOR, INSTITUTION	187.117-018
DIRECTOR, UTILITY		MANAGER, ADVERTISING	
ACCOUNTS	160.267-014	AGENCY	164.117-014

psychware **319**

```
**************************************************
*****   OCCUPATIONAL EXPLORATION INFORMATION   *****
**************************************************
```

SOME OCCUPATIONAL INFORMATION DESIGNED ESPECIALLY FOR WOMEN IS AVAILABLE
FROM THE WOMENS BUREAU, U.S. DEPARTMENT OF LABOR, WASHINGTON, D.C. 20210

SOME BOOKS OF PARTICULAR INTEREST TO WOMEN INCLUDE,
SPLAVER, SARAH. NONTRADITIONAL CAREERS FOR WOMEN. JULIAN MESSNER, 1973.
YOUR FUTURE AS A WORKING WOMAN. RICHARDS ROSEN, 1975.

OCCUPATIONAL INFORMATION AND OUTLOOK

THE *OCCUPATIONAL OUTLOOK HANDBOOK* (OOH) PREPARED BY THE BUREAU OF LABOR
STATISTICS OF THE U.S. DEPARMENT OF LABOR PROVIDES AN ENCYCLOPEDIA OF
CAREER INFORMATION, WITH 850 OCCUPATIONS AND OVER 30 MAJOR INDUSTRIES.
EACH JOB IS DESCRIBED, AND INFORMATION IS PROVIDED ON JOB PROSPECTS,
TRAINING AND EDUCATIONAL REQUIREMENTS, WORKING CONDITIONS, EARNINGS,
AND CHANCES FOR ADVANCEMENT. IT IS AVAILABLE FOR $7.00 FROM THE
SUPERINTENDENT OF DOCUMENTS, U.S. GOVERNMENT PRINTING OFFICE,
OR LIBRARIAN. A SERIES OF REPRINTS FROM THE OCCUPATIONAL OUTLOOK
HANDBOOK MAY BE ORDERED FOR 35 CENTS EACH FROM THE SUPERINTENDENT OF
DOCUMENTS. BELOW ARE LISTED SOME OF THESE REPRINTS SELECTED TO BE
COMPATIBLE WITH YOUR INTERESTS. ALSO LISTED ARE SOME BOOKS WHICH
PROVIDE MORE CAREER INFORMATION. YOU MIGHT ASK YOUR COUNSELOR OR
LIBRARIAN FOR FURTHER INFORMATION ABOUT OCCUPATIONS IN THE AREAS OF
YOUR INTEREST. ADDITIONAL WAYS OF FINDING OUT ABOUT OCCUPATIONS IS TO
TALK TO PEOPLE ALREADY WORKING IN THE FIELD AND TRY TO SPEND SOME TIME
WITH THEM ON THE JOB.

OCCUPATIONS IN LAW AND POLITICS

OCCUPATIONAL OUTLOOK REPRINTS

1875-32   LAWYERS

BOOKS

WHAT LAWYERS REALLY DO. ASBELL, BERNARD. WYDEN, INC., 1970.
CAREERS IN THE LEGAL PROFESSION. SARNOFF, PAUL. JULIAN MESSNER, 1970.

COUNSELORS / STUDENT PERSONNEL WORKERS

OCCUPATIONAL OUTLOOK REPRINTS

1875-115   COUNSELING OCCUPATIONS
1875-33   PERSONNEL AND LABOR RELATIONS WORKERS, COLLEGE STUDENT
            PERSONNEL WORKERS

BOOKS

OPPORTUNITIES IN PSYCHOLOGY CAREERS TODAY. SUPER, DONALD E. AND SUPER,
  CHARLES M. VOCATIONAL GUIDANCE MANUALS, 1976.
YOUR FUTURE IN PERSONNEL WORK. POND, JOHN H. RICHARDS ROSEN, 1971.

ADMINISTRATIVE AND RELATED OCCUPATIONS

OCCUPATIONAL OUTLOOK REPRINTS

1875-29   CITY MANAGERS
1875-31   INDUSTRIAL TRAFFIC MANAGER, PURCHASING AGENTS
1875-155   GOVERNMENT OCCUPATIONS, FEDERAL CIVILIAN EMPLOYMENT, STATE AND
            LOCAL GOVERNMENT, ARMED FORCES (45 CENTS).
1875-110   HEALTH SERVICE ADMINISTRATORS

BOOKS

CAREERS IN CORPORATE MANAGEMENT. 1975. B'NAI B'RITH, CAREER AND
  COUNSELING SERVICES, 1640 RHODE ISLAND AVE. NW, WASHINGTON,
  D.C. 20036 (21 PP., $1.50).
CAREERS IN CITY MANAGEMENT. 1976. (SAME AS ABOVE) (14 PP., $1.50).
EXPLORING CAREERS IN HOSPITAL AND HEALTH ADMINISTRATION. 1976.
  ASSOC. OF UNIVERSITY PROGRAMS IN HOSPITAL ADMINISTRATION,
  1755 MASSACHUSETTS AVE. N.W., WASHINGTON, D. C. 20036 (FREE, 16 PP.).
MANAGEMENT CAREERS FOR WOMEN. PLACE, IRENE AND ARMSTRONG, ALICE.
  VOCATIONAL GUIDANCE MANUALS, 1975.
YOUR FUTURE IN HOSPITAL AND HEALTH SERVICES ADMINISTRATION.
  KIRK, RICHARD W. RICHARDS ROSEN, 1976.
YOUR FUTURE IN HOTEL MANAGEMENT. SONNABEND, ROGER P.
  RICHARDS ROSEN, 1975.

```
**********************************************************************
*****   SUMMARY OF JACKSON VOCATIONAL INTEREST SURVEY RESULTS   *****
**********************************************************************
```

```
        CASE, M.               RESPONDENT NO. 123456789   SEX FEMALE
        DATE OF REPORT  29-JUN-83
```

```
            **********************************************************
            *****   JVIS BASIC INTEREST SCALE PROFILE   *****
            **********************************************************
```

	SCORE	P/C-TILE F	P/C-TILE M	VERY LOW 10	15	LOW 20	25	STANDARD SCORE AVERAGE 30	35	HIGH 40	45	VERY HIGH 50	55
CREATIVE ARTS	7	18	30	XXXXXXXXXXXXXXX									
PERFORMING ARTS	7	36	41	XXXXXXXXXXXXXXXXXXX									
MATHEMATICS	2	13	5	XXXXXXXXXX									
PHYSICAL SCIENCE	2	10	3	XXXXXXXX									
ENGINEERING	4	30	5	XXXXXXXXXXXX									
LIFE SCIENCE	3	10	8	XXXXXXXX									
SOCIAL SCIENCE	13	74	82	XXXXXXXXXXXXXXXXXXXXXXXXXXXXXXXXXXXX									
ADVENTURE	2	3	1	X									
NATURE-AGRICULTURE	8	46	43	XXXXXXXXXXXXXXXXXXXXXXX									
SKILLED TRADES	3	36	26	XXXXXXXXXXXXXXXX									
PERSONAL SERVICE	5	9	24	XXXXXXXXXXXX									
FAMILY ACTIVITY	8	22	41	XXXXXXXXXXXXXXXXXXXX									
MEDICAL SERVICE	3	21	17	XXXXXXXXXXXX									
DOMINANT LEADERSHIP	1	5	1	XXXXXXX									
JOB SECURITY	0	0	0	X									
STAMINA	11	70	57	XXXXXXXXXXXXXXXXXXXXXXXXXXXXX									
ACCOUNTABILITY	12	57	49	XXXXXXXXXXXXXXXXXXXXXXXXXXXX									
TEACHING	13	77	89	XXXXXXXXXXXXXXXXXXXXXXXXXXXXXXXXXXXXXXX									
SOCIAL SERVICE	12	43	79	XXXXXXXXXXXXXXXXXXXXXXXXXXXXXXX									
ELEMENTARY EDUCATION	9	30	70	XXXXXXXXXXXXXXXXXXXXXXXX									
FINANCE	9	73	53	XXXXXXXXXXXXXXXXXXXXXXXXXX									
BUSINESS	13	91	88	XXXXXXXXXXXXXXXXXXXXXXXXXXXXXXXXXXXXXXXXXXXX									
OFFICE WORK	8	60	70	XXXXXXXXXXXXXXXXXXXXXXXXXXX									
SALES	9	62	67	XXXXXXXXXXXXXXXXXXXXXXXXXX									
SUPERVISION	14	96	91	XXXXXXXXXXXXXXXXXXXXXXXXXXXXXXXXXXXXXXXXXXXXXX									
HUMAN RELATIONS MGT	13	81	79	XXXXXXXXXXXXXXXXXXXXXXXXXXXXXXXXXXXXXXX									
LAW	12	75	72	XXXXXXXXXXXXXXXXXXXXXXXXXXXXXXXXXXXX									
PROFESSIONL ADVISING	13	91	89	XXXXXXXXXXXXXXXXXXXXXXXXXXXXXXXXXXXXXXXX									
AUTHOR-JOURNALISM	11	58	75	XXXXXXXXXXXXXXXXXXXXXXXXXXXXXX									
ACADEMIC ACHIEVEMENT	9	36	37	XXXXXXXXXXXXXXXXXXXX									
TECHNICAL WRITING	13	93	95	XXXXXXXXXXXXXXXXXXXXXXXXXXXXXXXXXXXXXXXXXXXX									
INDEPENDENCE	13	81	79	XXXXXXXXXXXXXXXXXXXXXXXXXXXXXXXXXXXXX									
PLANFULNESS	13	84	86	XXXXXXXXXXXXXXXXXXXXXXXXXXXXXXXXXXXXXX									
INTERPERSONAL CONFIDENCE	14	64	76	XXXXXXXXXXXXXXXXXXXXXXXXXXXXXX									

psychware **321**

```
*************************************************
*****     GENERAL OCCUPATIONAL THEMES     *****
*************************************************
```

```
                P/C- VERY LOW                PERCENTILE                      VERY HIGH
                TILE 0   10   20   30   40   50   60   70   80   90   99
                F  M  .    .    .    .    .    .    .    .    .    .    .
.............................................................................
EXPRESSIVE      35 53 XXXXXXXXXXXXXXXXXXXX
LOGICAL         15  3 XXXXXXXXX
INQUIRING       22 23 XXXXXXXXXXXX
PRACTICAL       20 32 XXXXXXXXXXX
ASSERTIVE       57 52 XXXXXXXXXXXXXXXXXXXXXXXXXXXXXXXX

SOCIALIZED      52 39 XXXXXXXXXXXXXXXXXXXXXXXXXXXXX
HELPING         53 87 XXXXXXXXXXXXXXXXXXXXXXXXXXXXX
CONVENTIONAL    88 88 XXXXXXXXXXXXXXXXXXXXXXXXXXXXXXXXXXXXXXXXXXXXXXXXXX
ENTERPRISING    93 87 XXXXXXXXXXXXXXXXXXXXXXXXXXXXXXXXXXXXXXXXXXXXXXXXXXXXXXXXXX
COMMUNICATIVE   76 84 XXXXXXXXXXXXXXXXXXXXXXXXXXXXXXXXXXXXXXXXXX
.............................................................................
```

```
*****ADMINISTRATIVE INDICES*****
```

```
NUMBER OF 'A' RESPONSES =  91   NUMBER OF DOUBLE RESPONSES   =    0
NUMBER OF 'B' RESPONSES = 198   PERCENTAGE SCORABLE RESPONSES =  100
NUMBER OF OMITS         =   0   RELIABILITY INDEX *           = +0.85
```

```
*****NON-OCCUPATIONAL SCALES*****
```

ACADEMIC ORIENTATION STANDARD SCORE   436

```
*******************************************************************
*****   SIMILARITY TO COLLEGE AND UNIVERSITY STUDENT GROUPS   *****
*******************************************************************
```

	FEMALES		MALES
AGRICULTURE	-0.58	(VERY LOW)	-0.56
ARTS & ARCHITECTURE	-0.16	(VERY LOW)	-0.09
BUSINESS	+0.64	(VERY HIGH)	+0.69
EARTH & MINERAL SCIENCE			-0.50
EDUCATION	+0.44	(HIGH)	+0.50
ENGINEERING	-0.26	(VERY LOW)	-0.37
HEALTH, PHYSICAL EDUC. & RECREATION	-0.50	(VERY LOW)	
HUMAN DEVELOPMENT	+0.32	(MODERATE)	+0.61
LIBERAL ARTS	+0.72	(VERY HIGH)	+0.72
SCIENCE	-0.51	(VERY LOW)	-0.47
NURSES	-0.04	(VERY LOW)	
MEDICAL STUDENTS	+0.04	(LOW)	-0.06
TECHNICAL COLLEGE			-0.19

```
*******************************************************************
*****   SIMILARITY TO OCCUPATIONAL CLASSIFICATIONS   *****
*******************************************************************
```

SCORE	SIMILARITY	OCCUPATIONAL CLASSIFICATION
+0.72	VERY SIMILAR	OCCUPATIONS IN LAW AND POLITICS
+0.71	VERY SIMILAR	COUNSELORS / STUDENT PERSONNEL WORKERS
+0.59	VERY SIMILAR	ADMINISTRATIVE AND RELATED OCCUPATIONS
+0.64	VERY SIMILAR	PERSONNEL / HUMAN MANAGEMENT
+0.57	SIMILAR	TEACHING AND RELATED OCCUPATIONS
+0.55	SIMILAR	SALES OCCUPATIONS
+0.54	SIMILAR	OCCUPATIONS IN MERCHANDISING
+0.54	SIMILAR	OCCUPATIONS IN RELIGION
+0.53	SIMILAR	OCCUPATIONS IN ACCOUNTING, BANKING AND FINANCE
+0.50	SIMILAR	CLERICAL SERVICES
+0.48	SIMILAR	OCCUPATIONS IN SOCIAL SCIENCE
+0.47	SIMILAR	OCCUPATIONS IN SOCIAL WELFARE
+0.34	MODERATELY SIMILAR	OCCUPATIONS IN WRITING
+0.33	MODERATELY SIMILAR	MILITARY OFFICERS
+0.29	MODERATELY SIMILAR	OCCUPATIONS IN PRE-SCHOOL AND ELEMENTARY TEACHING
-0.03	NEUTRAL	ASSEMBLY OCCUPATIONS-INSTRUMENTS & SMALL PRODUCTS
-0.04	NEUTRAL	SERVICE OCCUPATIONS
-0.17	NEUTRAL	OCCUPATIONS IN MUSIC
-0.20	NEUTRAL	OCCUPATIONS IN ENTERTAINMENT
-0.25	DISSIMILAR	PROTECTIVE SERVICES OCCUPATIONS
-0.29	DISSIMILAR	OCCUPATIONS IN COMMERCIAL ART
-0.35	DISSIMILAR	AGRICULTURALISTS
-0.46	DISSIMILAR	ENGINEERING AND TECHNICAL SUPPORT WORKERS
-0.48	DISSIMILAR	MACHINING / MECHANICAL AND RELATED OCCUPATIONS
-0.48	DISSIMILAR	MATHEMATICAL AND RELATED OCCUPATIONS
-0.50	DISSIMILAR	OCCUPATIONS IN FINE ART
-0.54	DISSIMILAR	CONSTRUCTION / SKILLED TRADES
-0.58	DISSIMILAR	OCCUPATIONS IN THE PHYSICAL SCIENCES
-0.61	VERY DISSIMILAR	HEALTH SERVICE WORKERS
-0.64	VERY DISSIMILAR	MEDICAL DIAGNOSIS AND TREATMENT OCCUPATIONS
-0.65	VERY DISSIMILAR	SPORT AND RECREATION OCCUPATIONS
-0.69	VERY DISSIMILAR	LIFE SCIENCES

NAME: Jenkins Activity Survey

SUPPLIER: Psychological Corporation
7500 Old Oak Blvd.
Cleveland, OH 44130
(216) 234-5300

PRODUCT CATEGORY	PRIMARY APPLICATIONS
Personality	Behavioral Medicine Clinical Assessment/Diagnosis

SALE RESTRICTIONS American Psychological Association Guidelines

SERVICE TYPE/COST	Type	Available	Cost	Discount
	Mail-In	Yes	$10.40	Yes
	Teleprocessing	No		
	Local	No		

PRODUCT DESCRIPTION

The JENKINS ACTIVITY SURVEY is a self-report measure of the intensity and breadth of the Type A behavior pattern that has been associated with the furture risk of coronary heart disease. The test is intended for use with medical patients and individuals in stressful situations when evaluating the future risk and stress factors associated with coronary heart disease. The 52-item multiple-choice questionnaire requires 20 minutes to complete. Four scales are measured—the overall Type A score and three component scales: Speed and Impatience, Job-Involvement, and Hard-Driving and Competitive.

The computer-generated individual report form presents a raw score, a standard score, and a percentile rank for each of four scales measured by the JENKINS ACTIVITY SURVEY.

INTERPRETATION OF SCORES FROM THE JENKINS ACTIVITY SURVEY

Scores on the *Jenkins Activity Survey (JAS)* are estimates of the intensity and breadth of the Type A behavior pattern, found in several studies to be associated with future risk of coronary heart disease (CHD). The *JAS* is also used in social psychological and physiological research.

Four scores are presented: the Type A score and three additional scores representing the independent factors that identify the specific aspects of behavior contributing most strongly to the Type A pattern.

The **Type A score** is an overall estimate of the coronary-prone behavior pattern — a style of living characterized by extremes of competitiveness, striving for achievement, aggressiveness, haste, impatience, restlessness, commitment to vocation, and being under the pressure of time and responsibilities.

The **Speed and Impatience factor** deals with the time urgency revealed in the style of behavior of some Type A persons. High scorers tend to be impatient with others, speak up frankly when they feel irritated, and admit to having strong tempers.

The **Job Involvement factor** reflects the degree of dedication to occupational activity. High scorers report having high pressure jobs that challenge them and make mental and emotional demands. They work overtime and confront important deadlines. They are committed to their career and receive personal rewards, such as promotions, from it.

The **Hard-Driving and Competitive factor** involves the perception of oneself as being more hard-driving, competitive, and conscientious than other people. In addition, high scorers are achievement-oriented, responsible, serious, and energetic.

Three kinds of scores are presented for the four scales. The **raw score** is based on a sum of individual item response weights. This score is not directly interpretable. The **standard score** is a score with a mean of 0 and a standard deviation of 10 points. Positive scores indicate a tendency toward Type A behavior; negative scores indicate the absence of the Type A behavior pattern, i.e., Type B behavior. In general, a difference of about 5 standard points between scores can be taken as an indication that the difference is not a chance fluctuation. The **percentile score** indicates the percent of persons in the reference population who score below an examinee, i.e., more in the Type B direction.

The reference population for both the standard and percentile scores is a group of 2,588 men, aged 48 to 65, employed in middle and higher level occupations.

Published data indicate that men with high Type A scores have a higher risk of developing CHD as well as a higher risk of recurrent myocardial infarction if they have already had previous infarctions.

When the *JAS* is used in medical settings, its scores should be considered together with information on other risk factors to generate a more broadly based estimate of overall CHD risk. Space is provided for indicating key medical risk factors.

Most of the research data on the association between risk factors and the incidence of heart attacks have been based on studies of males over the age of 40.

Users of the *Jenkins Activity Survey* are referred to the Manual for instructions on the correct administration and interpretation of the test. In **no instance** should scores from the *JAS* or any other CHD risk factor be represented to an individual as a prediction that he or she will or might have a heart attack.

Jenkins Activity Survey

C. David Jenkins, Ph.D.   Stephen J. Zyzanski, Ph.D.   Ray H. Rosenman, M.D.

FORM C

APPLY ROBERT C

Sex   M   Age   43   Date   01/18/84

	Raw Score	Standard Score	Percentile Rank*	Type B Low Risk		Type A High Risk
Type A Behavior	244		57			
Factor S (Speed and Impatience)	124		23			
Factor J (Job Involvement)	276		83			
Factor H (Hard-Driving and Competitive)	138		67			

Standard Score†

−30   −20   −10   0   +10   +20   +30

*Percentile ranks are based on scores of 2,588 men, 48 to 65 years of age, employed in middle and higher level occupations.

†Standard scores below − 30 are plotted as − 30; scores above + 30 are plotted as + 30.

Additional Information:

Blood pressure _____

Serum cholesterol _____

Cigarettes per day _____

Pounds overweight _____

Prior history of CHD _____

Diabetes _____

Family history of CHD _____

Robert Smith, Ph.D.

See explanation on back.

The Psychological Corporation
A Subsidiary of Harcourt Brace Jovanovich, Inc.

78-117T

1/1

NAME: Jenkins Activity Survey

SUPPLIER: PSYCH Systems, Inc.
600 Reisterstown Road
Baltimore, MD 21208
(800) 368-3366

PRODUCT CATEGORY	PRIMARY APPLICATIONS
Personality	Behavioral Medicine
	Clinical Assessment/Diagnosis

SALE RESTRICTIONS   Qualified Professional

SERVICE TYPE/COST	Type	Available	Cost	Discount
	Mail-In	No		
	Teleprocessing	No		
	Local	Yes	See Below	

PRODUCT DESCRIPTION

The JENKINS ACTIVITY SURVEY was developed to duplicate the clinical assessment of Type A behavior by a standardized, psychometric procedure. The JENKINS ACTIVITY SURVEY is used to measure the intensity of impatience, irritability, sense of time urgency, competitiveness, striving for achievement, and dedication to career. This instrument measures behavioral/ psychological contributions to the risk of coronary heart disease. Thus, the JENKINS ACTIVITY SURVEY has applicability in business and industry and can be incorporated into assessment of stress and/or seminars on stress management.

This Psych Systems program administers and scores the JENKINS ACTIVITY SURVEY. It then provides a narrative interpretation of test results.

Psych Systems programs operate on the IBM PC-XT, COMPAQ Plus, Dec Professional 350, and most DEC PDP-11 systems. Various hardware/ software configurations are available directly from Psych Systems, with single-user systems starting at approximately $12,000. A per test fee also applies.

NAME: JOB-O

SUPPLIER: Publishers Test Service
2500 Garden Road
Monterey, CA 93940
(800) 538-9547

PRODUCT CATEGORY	PRIMARY APPLICATIONS
Career/Vocational	Vocational Guidance/Counseling

SALE RESTRICTIONS American Psychological Association Guidelines

SERVICE TYPE/COST	Type	Available	Cost	Discount
	Mail-In	No		
	Teleprocessing	No		
	Local	Yes	$59.95	

PRODUCT DESCRIPTION

JOB-O is a self-administering career exploration instrument that has been used by over three million students in its printed form. In this computer form, students enter responses to general assessment questions. The computer selects up to 10 of the 120 most popular and traditional jobs and displays the list on the screen. Software that can also provide descriptive information about all job titles is available.

The Dictionary of Occupational Titles, the Occupational Outlook Handbook, and Schutz's FIRO-B provide the theoretical base for JOB-O. Assessment takes into account nine variables related to educational aspirations, occupational interests, and interpersonal and physical characteristics of occupations. JOB-O is tied to current labor statistics, trends, and predictions. Information on the 120 job titles selected for JOB-O is updated every two years to include the latest national job trends as presented in the Occupational Outlook Handbook. This interactive program is extremely useful in the school career center or library.

Software is available for use with Apple, TRS-80, and Commodore PET computers.

NAME: Karson Clinical Report

SUPPLIER: Institute for Personality and Ability Testing, Inc.
P.O. Box 188
Champaign, IL 61820
(217) 352-4739

PRODUCT CATEGORY

Personality

PRIMARY APPLICATIONS

Clinical Assessment/Diagnosis
Personal/Marriage/Family Counseling

SALE RESTRICTIONS American Psychological Association Guidelines

SERVICE TYPE/COST	Type	Available	Cost	Discount
	Mail-In	Yes	$16.00	Yes
	Teleprocessing	No		
	Local	No		

PRODUCT DESCRIPTION

The KARSON CLINICAL REPORT gives the psychologist, the psychiatrist, the psychiatric social worker, and the physician a report that features an in-depth analysis of underlying personality dynamics in the language of the clinician. This four-page report includes a concise narrative that provides a complete overview of personality and clinical patterns. Additional charts give a visual display of the scores in five significant areas: primary personality characteristics, clinical signs and syndromes, interpersonal patterns, cognitive factors, and need patterns.

```
* * * * * * * * * * * * * * * * * * * * * * * * * * * * * * * * *
*                                                               *
*                                                               *
*                                                               *
*        1 6 P F   C L I N I C A L   R E P O R T                *
*                                                               *
*                                                               *
*                                                               *
*                            BY                                 *
*                                                               *
*                    SAMUEL KARSON, PHD                         *
*                                                               *
*                                                               *
* * * * * * * * * * * * * * * * * * * * * * * * * * * * * * * * *
```

Name: Mr   Sample
Date: April 20, 1984
  Id:
 Sex: Male
 Age: 25

This confidential report is designed for use by appropriately
qualified professionals. The presentation of information is
compact and the language of the Report is technical. It was
not intended to be used for patient feedback.

For additional information about the Report and its contents,
please refer to the "Manual for the Karson Clinical Report",
available through IPAT.

TEST-TAKING ATTITUDE

Faking good attempts are slightly higher than normal. There
is little or no evidence of a response set to look bad or to
exaggerate anxiety symptoms deliberately. Indications are
that he read the items carefully and clearly understood what
was required. The random index is within normal limits.

PERSONALITY CAPSULE DESCRIPTION

A strong need for dominance and marked evidence of
assertiveness are clear in his personality makeup. He is not
a particularly sophisticated or shrewd person, but instead he
tends to be direct and forthright in his interpersonal
relationships. This suggests a lack of experience in social
situations. His obsessive-compulsive defense mechanisms are
not currently operating satisfactorily. This suggests that
he has not satisfactorily resolved his own identity problems.
A history of conflicting family relationships is suggested
that has probably succeeded in interfering with his ability
to empathize with other people, and which makes him tend to
move away from them. His capacity for abstract verbal skills
appears to be high. He is a cool, tough-minded, realistic
person who is not apt to lose control of himself in
emergencies. He may resort to fantasy activity or
daydreaming at a time when he ought to be responding to the
exigencies of the stimulus situation confronting him.
Consequently, attending to routine details is probably not
his strong suit.

He is basically a shy, timid, restrained person who finds it
difficult to handle threats of any kind successfully. He is
seen as someone who tends to be suspicious of other people's
motives and who displaces and projects his angry feelings.
Superego introjection is somewhat below average, but not
seriously so. He probably has little problem with depression
originating in conflict with his superego. He tends to be an
accepting person who is respectful of traditions and of the
'establishment'. He does not adopt a critical and radical
approach to authority. Much dependency gratification is
required from the people he encounters in his life and in his
job in particular. His free-floating anxiety is above
average and suggests higher than average feelings of tension
and frustration.

PRIMARY PERSONALITY TRAITS

```
          LOW       A V E R A G E        HIGH
          1   2   3   4   5   6   7   8   9   10
       --------------------------------------------

   A          X   :                   :
   B              :       X           :         X
   C              :   X               :
   E              :               :           X
   F              :           X   :
   G              :           X   :
   H              :   X           :
   I          X   :               :
   L              :           X   :
   M              :               X
   N          X   :               :
   O              :   X           :
  Q1              :   X           :
  Q2              :   X           :
  Q3          X   :               :
  Q4              :           X   :

       --------------------------------------------
```

Trait	Score
Warmth	3
Intelligence	8
Ego Strength	5
Dominance	9
Impulsivity	6
Group Conformity	6
Boldness	4
Tender-Mindedness	3
Suspiciousness	7
Imagination	8
Shrewdness	2
Guilt Proneness	4
Rebelliousness	4
Self-Sufficiency	4
Compulsivity	2
Free-Floating Anxiety	7

CLINICAL SIGNS AND SYNDROMES

```
          LOW     A V E R A G E      HIGH
          1   2   3   4   5   6   7   8   9   10
-----------------------------------------------------
ANX                   :       X   :              Anxiety................. 6.3
NEU               : X                            Neuroticism............. 4.2
PSY               :               : X            Psychoticism............ 7.3
SOC               :           X:                 Sociopathy.............. 6.8
BC            X:           :                      Behavior Control........ 3.9
-----------------------------------------------------
```

INTERPERSONAL PATTERNS

```
          LOW     A V E R A G E      HIGH
          1   2   3   4   5   6   7   8   9   10
-----------------------------------------------------
EX                    :       X   :              Extraversion............ 6.7
LD                :       X   :                  Leadership.............. 5.0
IN                :               :   X          Independence............ 7.6
-----------------------------------------------------
```

COGNITIVE FACTORS

```
          LOW     A V E R A G E      HIGH
          1   2   3   4   5   6   7   8   9   10
-----------------------------------------------------
CORT                  :               :       X  Tough Poise.............10.0
CR                    :           X   :          Creativity.............. 6.7
AC                    :           X:             Academic Achievement.... 6.9
-----------------------------------------------------
```

NEED PATTERNS

```
          LOW     A V E R A G E      HIGH
          1   2   3   4   5   6   7   8   9   10
-----------------------------------------------------
ABA                   :   X           :          Abasement............... 4.5
ACH                   :               :   X      Achievement............. 8.2
AFF               X   :               :          Affiliation............. 2.6
AGG                   :               :   X      Aggression.............. 7.5
AUT                   :           X:             Autonomy................ 6.8
CHG                   :           X   :          Change.................. 6.2
DEF               X   :               :          Deference............... 2.4
DOM                   :   X       :              Dominance............... 5.1
END                   : X             :          Endurance............... 4.3
EXH                   :           X:             Exhibition.............. 6.9
HET                   :       X   :              Heterosexuality......... 6.1
INT                   :       X   :              Intraception............ 5.2
NUR               X   :               :          Nurturance.............. 2.3
ORD                 X :               :          Order................... 3.3
SUC                   :       X   :              Succorance.............. 5.2
-----------------------------------------------------
```

RAW SCORES *

A: 6   B: 10   C: 18   E: 20   F: 14   G: 15   H: 10   I: 5
L: 9   M: 18   N: 4   O: 5   Q1: 6   Q2: 7   Q3: 8   Q4: 12

Faking Good: 8   Faking Bad: 0   Random: 3

* BEFORE CORRECTION FOR FAKING GOOD/FAKING BAD (IF APPROPRIATE)

NAME: Kaufman Assessment Battery for Children-ASSIST

SUPPLIER: American Guidance Service
Publisher's Building
Circle Pines, MN 55014
(800) 328-2560

PRODUCT CATEGORY	PRIMARY APPLICATIONS
Cognitive/Ability	Educational Evaluation/Planning Clinical Assessment/Diagnosis

SALE RESTRICTIONS American Psychological Association Guidelines

SERVICE TYPE/COST	Type	Available	Cost	Discount
	Mail-In	No		
	Teleprocessing	No		
	Local	Yes	$103.50	

PRODUCT DESCRIPTION

The KAUFMAN ASSESSMENT BATTERY FOR CHILDREN is a clinical instrument for measuring the intelligence and achievement of preschool children, learning disabled and mentally retarded children, and minority group children. Sixteen subtests of mental processing skills and achievement include three subtests of sequential processing, seven subtests of simultaneous processing, and six subtests of achievement (acquired knowledge, reading, and arithmetic). The Battery yields four major scores: Sequential Processing, Simultaneous Processing, Mental Processing Composite, and Achievement. All subtests are individually administered.

ASSIST (Automated System for Scoring and Interpreting Standardized Tests) software for this instrument obtains derived scores and generates profiles showing an individual's strengths and weaknesses. The software is compatible with Apple II + and IIe, DOS 3.3 microcomputers. The program reduces by two thirds the time that otherwise would be spent in clerical tasks. It provides interpretation data including standard scores, confidence intervals on standard scores, national and/or sociocultural percentile ranks, percentile intervals corresponding to the confidence intervals, age equivalents, descriptive classifications, and global scale comparisons.

K - A B C

KAUFMAN ASSESSMENT BATTERY

FOR CHILDREN

A S S I S T

ANALYSIS RESULTS

COPYRIGHT 1983 AGS

AMERICAN GUIDANCE SERVICE
CIRCLE PINES MN 55014

VERSION 1.1

NAME MARY B   SEX FEMALE

PARENTS' NAMES
RITA AND JAMES

HOME ADDRESS 807 S LINCOLN

GRADE 4   SCHOOL CENTRAL ELEMENTARY

EXAMINER NORMA EHRHARDT

	YEAR	MONTH	DAY
TEST DATE	83	5	15
BIRTH DATE	72	8	11
CHRONOLOGICAL AGE	10	9	4

ANALYSIS DECISIONS

	YES	NO
SOCIOCULTURAL PERCENTILES ETHNIC GROUP (BLACK)	X	
EDUCATIONAL ATTAINMENT HIGHEST GRADE (6) YEARS	X	
NONVERBAL SCALE		X
OUT-OF-LEVEL NORMS		X
AGE EQUIVALENTS	X	
GRADE EQUIVALENTS	X	
CONFIDENCE LEVEL (90%)		

CASE NOTES:

psychware **333**

G L O B A L   S C A L E   C O M P A R I S O N S

	SIGNIFICANCE LEVEL
SEQUENTIAL = SIMULTANEOUS	NS
SEQUENTIAL = ACHIEVEMENT	NS
SIMULTANEOUS > ACHIEVEMENT	01
MPC > ACHIEVEMENT	01

FOR MOST ASSESSMENT PURPOSES, 95 PERCENT CONFIDENCE (P<.05) IS AMPLE, ALTHOUGH EXAMINERS MAY WISH TO USE THE MORE CONSERVATIVE 99 PERCENT LEVEL (P<.01) WHEN IMPORTANT DECISIONS RELY ON THE DISCREPANCY.

G L O B A L   S C A L E   D E R I V E D   S C O R E S

	SUM OF SUBTEST SCORES	STANDARD SCORE	ERROR BAND	CONFID. INTERVAL 90%	NATIONAL %ILE RANK	NATIONAL %ILE RANK INTERVAL 90%
SEQUENTIAL PROCESSING	27	93	8	85-101	32	16 - 53
SIMULTANEOUS PROCESSING	47	95	6	89-101	37	23 - 53
MENTAL PROCESSING COMPOSITE	74	93	6	87- 99	32	19 - 47
ACHIEVEMENT	418	81	4	77- 85	10	6 - 16

	SOCIOCULTURAL %ILE RANK	SOCIOCULTURAL %ILE INTERVAL 90%	AGE EQUIVALENT	DESCRIPTIVE CATEGORY
SEQUENTIAL PROCESSING	50	30-75	11- 9	BELOW AVERAGE/ AVERAGE
SIMULTANEOUS PROCESSING	80	60-90	9- 9	BELOW AVERAGE/ AVERAGE
MENTAL PROCESSING COMPOSITE	70	50-90	9- 9	BELOW AVERAGE/ AVERAGE
ACHIEVEMENT	30	20-40	8- 9	WELL BELOW AVERAGE/ BELOW AVERAGE

M E N T A L   P R O C E S S I N G   S C A L E
S U B T E S T   D E R I V E D   S C O R E S

	RAW SCORE	SCALED SCORE SEQ	SCALED SCORE SIM	STRENGTH/ WEAKNESS (.05)	NATIONAL %ILE RANK	AGE EQUIVALENT
3. HAND MOVEMENTS	14	10			50	11- 9
4. GESTALT CLOSURE	22		14	S	91	>12- 6
5. NUMBER RECALL	12	11			63	>12- 6
6. TRIANGLES	12		8		25	8- 0
7. WORD ORDER	10	6		W	9	6- 6
8. MATRIX ANALOGIES	13		9		37	9- 9
9. SPATIAL MEMORY	13		7		16	8- 3
10. PHOTO SERIES	12		9		37	9- 9

NOTE: THIS CHILD'S MENTAL PROCESSING COMPOSITE MEAN IS 9.

ACHIEVEMENT SCALE
SUBTEST DERIVED SCORES

	RAW SCORE	STANDARD SCORE	ERROR BAND	CONFIDENCE INTERVAL 90%	STRENGTH/ WEAKNESS
12. FACES & PLACES	15	87	8	79- 95	
13. ARITHMETIC	28	92	8	84-100	
14. RIDDLES	23	99	9	90-108	S
15. READING/DECODING	22	73	8	65- 81	W
16. READING/UNDERSTANDING	6	67	8	59- 75	W

	NATIONAL %ILE RANK	NATIONAL %ILE RANK INTERVAL 90%	SOCIOCULTURAL %ILE RANK	SOCIOCULTURAL %ILE RANK INTERVAL 90%	AGE GRADE EQUIVALENTS	
12. FACES & PLACES	19	8 - 37	35	15-60	8- 9	
13. ARITHMETIC	30	14 - 50	70	45-85	9- 6	4.3
14. RIDDLES	47	25 - 70	90	70-98	10- 6	
15. READING/DECODING	4	1 - 10	10	5-20	7- 6	2.4
16. READING/UNDERSTANDING	1	0.3- 5	5	2-15	7- 3	1.9

NOTE: THIS CHILD'S ACHIEVEMENT SCALE MEAN IS 84.

SHARED ABILITIES

POSSIBLE STRENGTHS

ATTENTION TO VISUAL DETAIL
    4. GESTALT CLOSURE
    8. MATRIX ANALOGIES
   10. PHOTO SERIES

POSSIBLE WEAKNESSES

READING ABILITY
   15. READING/DECODING
   16. READING/UNDERSTANDING

NOTE: ALL OF THE ABOVE INFLUENCES ARE BIPOLAR. ONE END OF EACH CONTINUUM
ENHANCES PERFORMANCE ON THE K-ABC, WHILE THE OPPOSITE END SERVES TO DEPRESS
A CHILD'S SCORES. (SEE THE K-ABC ASSIST USER'S MANUAL, APPENDIX F, FOR MORE
INFORMATION.)

UNIQUE ABILITIES

POSSIBLE STRENGTHS

GESTALT CLOSURE
   PERCEPTUAL CLOSURE
   PERCEPTUAL INFERENCE
   CONVERSION OF ABSTRACT STIMULI
   INTO A CONCRETE OBJECT

POSSIBLE WEAKNESSES

WORD ORDER
   AUDITORY-VISUAL INTEGRATION
   AUDITORY-MOTOR MEMORY
   RETENTION WITHOUT REHEARSAL
   UNDERSTANDING AND FOLLOWING
   DIRECTIONS

READING/DECODING
   LETTER NAMING
   WORD ATTACK STRATEGIES
   WORD RECOGNITION
   PRONUNCIATION

READING/UNDERSTANDING
   READING COMPREHENSION
   GESTURAL COMMUNICATION

NOTE: HYPOTHESES BASED UPON INDIVIDUAL SUBTESTS ARE LESS ROBUST
THAN THOSE BASED UPON GLOBAL SCALES AND SHARED ABILITIES.

NAME: Law Enforcement Assessment and Development Report

SUPPLIER: Institute for Personality and Ability Testing, Inc.
P.O. Box 188
Champaign, IL 61820
(217) 352-4739

PRODUCT CATEGORY

Career/Vocational

PRIMARY APPLICATIONS

Personnel Selection/Evaluation

SALE RESTRICTIONS American Psychological Association Guidelines

SERVICE TYPE/COST	Type	Available	Cost	Discount
	Mail-In	Yes	$25.00	Yes
	Teleprocessing	Yes	$26.00	Yes
	Local	No		

PRODUCT DESCRIPTION

The LAW ENFORCEMENT ASSESSMENT AND DEVELOPMENT REPORT is a four-page computer-based report that identifies individuals who are most likely to become successful law enforcement officers. This report allows comparisons of applicants in terms of predicted overall performance as well as in four job-related areas: Emotional Maturity, Integrity/Control, Intellectual Efficiency, and Interpersonal Relationships. The Manual which accompanies the report documents the basic research on which the report was developed and validated.

LAW ENFORCEMENT ASSESSMENT AND DEVELOPMENT REPORT

NAME... John   Sample
SEX... M
AGE... 25
DATE... 04/20/1984

INTRODUCTION

In reviewing this report, keep in mind that it considers only the
results of personality analysis. As such, it represents only one
component of a comprehensive candidate evaluation.

The paragraphs that accompany each LEADR dimension score graph
are individually tailored. Even when someone shows overall high
performance in an area, some cautionary statements may still appear
in order to present a more balanced portrait of the candidate.
Similarly, some positive-sounding statements can appear even when the
individual obtains a low score in an area. This is done to highlight
personal strenghts toward which training efforts can be directed most
effectively.

RESPONSE PATTERNS

It appears that Mr Sample answered the LEADR survey in a natural
and truthful way. As a result, this report gives an honest picture
of the candidate's personality. Even so, the material that follows
will be most useful when it is considered along with other available
information, such as his background and physical ability.

DIMENSION 1: PERFORMANCE

A study of Mr Sample's personality characteristics suggests that
his chances of successful law enforcement performance would be above
average.

```
          10   20   30   40   50   60   70   80   90       %
  RANK    *********************************************    89
```
Research shows that certain personal qualities help a person
succeed as a law enforcement officer. In Mr Sample's case, the
following are particularly noteworthy characteristics. (*)
Mr Sample is shrewd and insightful. He seems to be very conscious of
his public image and tries to present himself as emotionally
detached and in command. (*) Mr Sample is very sure of himself. He
is not easily bothered by doubts or feelings of uncertainty.

DIMENSION 2: EMOTIONAL MATURITY

This section of the report analyzes the way a person handles his
feelings. Qualities, such as the ability to act calmly and suitably
in uncertain or stressful situations are noted. Given what is known
about Mr Sample's personality, he ranks above average in this area.

```
          10   20   30   40   50   60   70   80   90       %
  RANK    ****************************************          78
```
At the present time, Mr Sample feels he worries less than most
people. He is self-assured and seems to have the emotional reserves
to deal with conflicts and problems in an effective manner. He
responds in a controlled fashion and probably doesn't get upset
easily. He is relaxed, composed and experiencing few feelings of
frustration. He usually feels secure, self-assured and in no need of
any self-justification.

DIMENSION 3: INTEGRITY/CONTROL

This section of the report describes the candidate's ability to
act in a dependable, conscientiously controlled manner. Given what
is known about Mr Sample's personality, he ranks above average in
this area.

```
          10   20   30   40   50   60   70   80   90       %
  RANK    ***************************************           78
```

psychware   **337**

Mr Sample's ability to control his behavior and act responsibly is above average. His profile suggests that his regard for rules and group standards is average. Mr Sample makes no more mistakes and has no more accidents than the average person.

DIMENSION 4: INTELLECTUAL EFFICIENCY

This section of the report analyzes the candidate's ability to reason and solve problems. Given what is known about Mr Sample's personality, he ranks above average in this area.

```
          10    20    30    40    50    60    70    80    90        %
RANK      ******************************************              77
```

With regard to intellectual— especially verbal —functioning, he is on a par with the rest of the population. Although Mr Sample appears to be well organized, he may occasionally display poor judgment and be sidetracked, pursuing alternatives that are unrelated in a clear way to planned objectives. It would help if he could become more aware of the realities surrounding a given situation.

DIMENSION 5: INTERPERSONAL RELATIONS

This section of the report describes the candidate's ability to get along with others. Given what is known about Mr Sample's profile, he ranks average in this area.

```
          10    20    30    40    50    60    70    80    90        %
RANK      ********************                                    38
```

In general, Mr Sample is as much at home when he works alone as he is when he works with others. He does like to work with others. But, he balances this with an ability to do things on his own. He has a positive, considerate nature.

Mr Sample thinks it's important to be independent and to direct his own life. He doesn't like others to decide for him. Therefore, he probably works hard to gain control of his life and work.

PERSONALITY ORIENTATION

	LOW		A V E R A G E				HIGH				
	1	2	3	4	5	6	7	8	9	10		
A				:			X				Warmth	7.0
B				:	X						Intelligence	6.0
C				:			X				Stability	7.0
E				:	X						Dominance	6.0
F			X								Impulsivity	3.0
G				:	X						Conformity	5.0
H				:		X					Boldness	6.0
I				:		X					Sensitivity	6.0
L				X							Suspiciousness	5.0
M			X								Imagination	4.0
N				:			X				Shrewdness	7.0
O		X		:							Apprehensiveness	2.0
Q1				:					X		Experimenting	9.0
Q2				X							Self-sufficiency	5.0
Q3				:			X				Self-Disciplined	8.0
Q4		X		:							Tension	3.0

LEADR DIMENSIONS

	LOW		A V E R A G E				HIGH				
	1	2	3	4	5	6	7	8	9	10		
PER				:			:	X			Performance	8.1
EM				:			X				Emotional Maturity	7.1
IC				:			X				Integrity/Control	7.1
IE				:			X				Intellectual Efficiency	7.0
IR			X	:							Interpersonal Relations	4.9

ADDITIONAL SCALES

	LOW		A V E R A G E				HIGH				
	1	2	3	4	5	6	7	8	9	10		
AX		X	:								Anxiety	2.6
TP		X	:								Tough Poise	3.3
IN			:			X:					Independence	6.8
LD			:			X					Leadership	7.1
AP		:	X	:							Accident Proneness	4.4

NAME: Louisville Behavior Checklist

SUPPLIER: Western Psychological Services
12031 Wilshire Blvd.
Los Angeles, CA 90025
(213) 478-2061

PRODUCT CATEGORY

Personality

PRIMARY APPLICATIONS

Clinical Assessment/Diagnosis
Personal/Marriage/Family Counseling
Educational Evaluation/Planning

SALE RESTRICTIONS American Psychological Association Guidelines

SERVICE TYPE/COST	Type	Available	Cost	Discount
	Mail-In	Yes	$5.95	Yes
	Teleprocessing	No		
	Local	No		

PRODUCT DESCRIPTION

This inventory covers the entire range of social and emotional behaviors indicative of psychopathological disorders in children and adolescents. Parents provide answers to 164 true-false questions which provide a wealth of information for mental health workers on a number of interpretive scales. Three different forms are designed for various age groups beginning with children 4 years old and ending with 17-year-old adolescents.

There are six parts to the computer-generated report: (1) a profile of scores; (2) validity considerations, (3) a description of elevated scales; (4) a statistical analysis of deviant scores; (5) critical items; and (6) a listing of all background information and item responses for archival purposes. Scales analyzed in the report include Aggression, Inhibition, Learning Disability, Infantile Aggression, Hyperactivity, Antisocial Behavior, Sensitivity, Fear, Academic Disability, Immaturity, Normal Irritability, Prosocial Deficit, Severity Level, Rare Deviance, Neurotic Behavior, Psychotic Behavior, Somatic Behavior, and Sexual Behavior.

LOUISVILLE BEHAVIOR CHECKLIST (LBC)
Form E2

A WPS TEST REPORT by Western Psychological Services
12031 Wilshire Boulevard
Los Angeles, California 90025
Copyright (c) 1983 by Western Psychological Services
Version HPIII.340122.01.001

Western Psychological Services • 12031 Wilshire Boulevard • Los Angeles, California 90025

Client ID: 8430275
Sex: MALE   Age: 11
Grade: SPECIAL EDUCATION   Ethnic Background: WHITE
Report Date: APR 2, 1984   Relationship to Child: MOTHER

***** LBC TEST REPORT *****

     This summary is based on an analysis of the Mother's description of
the child using the 164-item Louisville Behavior Checklist, a standardized
and widely used measure of the behavior and functioning of children ages 7
to 12 [Form E2].

     There are six major parts of this summary:

     1. PROFILE OF SCORES. A profile of T-scores for this child is drawn
using norms from the general population. Scale abbreviations and raw
scores, enclosed in parentheses ( ), are provided to aid in interpretation.
A key to the abbreviations is provided at the bottom of the profile.

     2. VALIDITY OF RESPONSES. Responses and profile scores are inspected
to see if an overly positive or unusually negative view of the child has
been given by the respondent.

     3. DESCRIPTION OF ELEVATED SCALES. If the child shows one or more
scales above 65T on the profile, the meaning and content of these
significantly elevated scales are described.

     4. HIGH OR LOW SCORES. Profile scores are tested for statistical
significance against the mean score for all profile scales. This section
of the report should help suggest areas of greatest clinical concern, or
show the areas where the child has a relative absence of problems.

     5. SCAN AND PROSOCIAL ITEMS. Individual items that are indicators
of clinical significance are listed in this section of the report.

     6. BACKGROUND SUMMARY. A listing of all background information and
item responses is provided for archival purposes.

     The listing of scan items or profile elevations is intended as a
guide to the formation of clinical hypotheses that should be verified by
additional information such as behavioral observations, clinical
interviews, and other measures. The reader should be thoroughly familiar
with the test manual for the LBC, published by Western Psychological
Services (WPS Catalog No. W-145D). The test manual should be used for
detailed information about definitions of scales, characteristics of
standardization samples, and interpretive guidelines.

Page 1

340   *psychware*

LOUISVILLE BEHAVIOR CHECKLIST PROFILE
Form E2
(Based on General Population Norms)

Western Psychological Services • 12031 Wilshire Boulevard • Los Angeles, California 90025

```
                                              T SCORES
       SCALES      SCORES    20   30   40   50   60   70   80   90  100  110  120
                   RAW   T   I++++I++++I++++I++++I++++I++++I++++I++++I++++I++++I
                             I              :         :                         I
         AG        (34)  95  ]]]]]]]]]]]]]]]]]]]]]]]]]]]]]]]]]]]]]]]]            I
                             I              :         :                         I
         IN        (20)  72  ]]]]]]]]]]]]]]]]]]]]]]]]]]]]]]]                    I
                             I              :         :                         I
         LD        (19)  85  ]]]]]]]]]]]]]]]]]]]]]]]]]]]]]]]]]]]]]               I
                             I------------------------------------------------I
         Ia        (21)  96  ]]]]]]]]]]]]]]]]]]]]]]]]]]]]]]]]]]]]]]]]]]]        I
                             I              :         :                         I
         Ha        (9)   69  ]]]]]]]]]]]]]]]]]]]]]]]]]]]]]]                     I
                             I              :         :                         I
         As        (10) 125  ]]]]]]]]]]]]]]]]]]]]]]]]]]]]]]]]]]]]]]]]]]]]]]]]]]]]
                             I              :         :                         I
         Sw        (6)   61  ]]]]]]]]]]]]]]]]]]]]]]]]] :                        I
                             I              :         :                         I
         Sn        (6)   66  ]]]]]]]]]]]]]]]]]]]]]]]]]]]                        I
                             I              :         :                         I
         Fr        (9)   85  ]]]]]]]]]]]]]]]]]]]]]]]]]]]]]]]]]]]]                I
                             I              :         :                         I
         Ad        (13)  82  ]]]]]]]]]]]]]]]]]]]]]]]]]]]]]]]]]]]]                I
                             I              :         :                         I
         Im        (6)   76  ]]]]]]]]]]]]]]]]]]]]]]]]]]]]]]]]]]                  I
                             I              :         :                         I
         Ni        (3)   58  ]]]]]]]]]]]]]]]]]]]]]]]] :                         I
                             I              :         :                         I
         Pd        (9)   88  ]]]]]]]]]]]]]]]]]]]]]]]]]]]]]]]]]]]]]]]]            I
                             I              :         :                         I
         SL        (67)  91  ]]]]]]]]]]]]]]]]]]]]]]]]]]]]]]]]]]]]]]]]]]          I
                             I              :         :                         I
                   RAW   T   I++++I++++I++++I++++I++++I++++I++++I++++I++++I++++I
       SCALES      SCORES    20   30   40   50   60   70   80   90  100  110  120
```

NOTE. The display of T-scores less than 20 or greater than 120 is truncated.

ADDITIONAL SCALES

	Rd	Neu	Psy	Som	Sex
RAW	3	6	2	3	1
T-SCORE	110	76	60	58	49

NOTE. Scores greater than 65T are considered elevated and clinically important signs.

AG -- Aggression	Im -- Immaturity	
IN -- Inhibition	Ni -- Normal Irritability	
LD -- Learning Disability	Pd -- Prosocial Deficit	
Ia -- Infantile Aggression	SL -- Severity Level	
Ha -- Hyperactivity	Rd -- Rare Deviance	
As -- Antisocial Behavior	Neu -- Neurotic Behavior	
Sw -- Social Withdrawal	Psy -- Psychotic Behavior	
Sn -- Sensitivity	Som -- Somatic Behavior	
Fr -- Fear	Sex -- Sexual Behavior	
Ad -- Academic Disability		

WPS TEST REPORT

LOUISVILLE BEHAVIOR CHECKLIST (LBC)
Form E2

NOTE. The broad-band factors of Aggression, Inhibition, and Learning Disability are separated from the other profile scales in order to provide an overview of the child's behavior. These factors represent the common dimensions of child behavior -- externalizing, internalizing, and cognitive-developmental problems. A fourth dimension that provides an overview is "extreme behavior" reflected in the Rare Deviance, Psychotic, and Sexual Behavior scales. See the test manual for more details about the composition of the broad-band factors.

VALIDITY CONSIDERATIONS

The pattern of scores obtained is highly unusual, with high scores in all three areas of major clinical concern: Aggression (AG) (externalizing), Inhibition (In) (internalizing) and Learning Disability (LD) (developmental delay). Further investigation should be made of the possibility that the informant is overpathologizing or overreacting to the child.

ELEVATED SCALES

The following is a list of profile scales that were found to be clinically significant for this child (elevated above 65T). A brief description of the content of each elevated scale, explaining what each was intended to measure, is provided.

AG   Aggression, the broad-band factor composed of infantile aggression, hyperactivity, and antisocial behavior.

IN   Inhibition, a broad-band factor including failure to master age-specific cognitive tasks, and physical and social immaturity.

LD   Learning Disability, a broad-band factor including specific deficits in academic skill and abilities, and social and physical immaturity.

Ia   Infantile Aggression, which describes egocentric, emotionally demanding, and interpersonally belligerent behavior.

Ha   Hyperactivity, referring to impulsive and constant motion involving both large and small muscles.

As   Antisocial Behavior, including illegal and destructive behavior in which the main thrust is against property and person, self and others.

Sn   Sensitivity, characterized by a subjective sense of "unlikableness," combined with a tendency to cope with stress through a combination of somatizing, impulsive, immature, and rivalrous behavior.

Western Psychological Services • 12031 Wilshire Boulevard • Los Angeles, California 90025

WPS TEST REPORT

ELEVATED SCALES (Continued)

Fr   Fear, referring to manifest anxiety focusing around multiple objects
      with special concern over sleep, death, and assuring availability of
      a companion.

Ad   Academic Disability, reflecting specific deficits in academic skill
      and abilities commonly associated with learning failures.

Im   Immaturity, referring to both social and physical processes, including
      babyishness, dependency, whining, slow physical growth, and clumsy,
      poor coordination.

Pd   Prosocial Deficit, measuring the lack of behaviors highly valued by
      society, such as "relaxed and able to concentrate" and "has a good
      sense of right and wrong."

SL   Severity Level, a broad-band scale composed of all noxious and
      pathogenic behaviors on the inventory minus the Normal Irritability
      items (except for an item concerning feelings of guilt or shame
      after being caught misbehaving) and a few physical and mild disability
      items.

Rd   Rare Deviance, describing highly unusual and noxious behaviors reported
      to occur in less than 1% of the general population.

Neu   Neurotic Behavior, containing items traditionally assumed to indicate
      a psychoneurotic process, such as phobias, obsessions, compulsions,
      and depression.

psychware **343**

LOUISVILLE BEHAVIOR CHECKLIST (LBC)
Form E2

DEVIATION OF SCALES FROM THE MEAN T-SCORE
(Based on General Population Norms)

MEAN OF ALL PROFILE T-SCORES: 82.07

SCALES	DIFFERENCE FROM MEAN	SEM	DIFFERENCES FROM MEAN T-SCORE
			-20 -15 -10 -5 0 5 10 15 20
AG	12.93**	3.37	----X----
IN	-10.07**	3.32	---X---
LD	2.93	3.61	----X----
Ia	13.93**	4.56	----X----
Ha	-13.07**	4.12	----X----
As	42.93***	5.20	-- -- -- -- ->>
Sw	-21.07***	4.47	<<- -- -- -- --
Sn	-16.07***	4.47	----X----
Fr	2.93	3.61	----X----
Ad	-.07	3.32	---X---
Im	-6.07	5.33	------X------
Ni	-24.07***	4.90	<<- -- -- -- --.
Pd	5.93	6.63	-------X-------
SL	8.93	3.46	---X---

-20 -15 -10 -5   0   5   10 15 20

* p<.10   ** p<.05   *** p<.01

NOTE. The significance of the deviation of a T-score for a particular
scale from an individual's mean T-score across all profile scales is given
by p, the probability that a deviation of this size could have occurred by
chance. All significance tests are corrected for multiple comparisons
using Bonferonni's t' (see manual).
     Approximately 68% of individuals with a true score equal to X would
be expected to fall in the interval bounded by plus or minus one standard
error of measurement (SEM) if retested again within six weeks. The SEM
interval is marked by dashes (-) on either side of the observed T-score, X.
Differences from the mean greater than plus or minus 20 are indicated by a
row of double dashes (--) ending with symbols >> or <<.

LOUISVILLE BEHAVIOR CHECKLIST (LBC)
Form E2

SCAN ITEMS

Thirty items from the checklist have been recommended as significant
indicators of more extreme behavior that may be of particular clinical
importance. Listed below, if any, are the items from this set that were
found in this child's protocol.

NUMBER   ITEM

10   Wets the bed at night at least once a month.

14   Afraid of school; has to be forced to attend.

38   Sets fires.

60   Behind in school at least two grades.

65   Steals outside the home.

90   Has been taken to a probation officer or accused by the police
     of committing a crime.

110 Steals at home.

130 Soils underpants or bedclothing.

139 Physically abusive, assaultive; hurts other children.

160 Is disobedient; out of control of adults.

164 Has been hospitalized or placed in a special school for a
     mental or emotional disorder.

PROSOCIAL ITEMS

Thirteen items from the checklist were designed to measure
characteristics that are highly valued by society. These prosocial items
show the positive and adaptive skills of the child. Listed below, if any,
are the items from this set that were found in the protocol.

NUMBER   ITEM

65   Enjoys being with children own age.

105 Sexual interest and awareness normal for age.

135 Generally healthy.

psychware **345**

LOUISVILLE BEHAVIOR CHECKLIST (LBC)
Form E2

PROSOCIAL ITEMS (Continued)

NUMBER   ITEM

145 Expresses delight over the happiness of others.

LOUISVILLE BEHAVIOR CHECKLIST (LBC)
Form E2

BACKGROUND INFORMATION

Child

Sex: MALE
Age: 11
Ethnic Background: WHITE
Grade: SPECIAL EDUCATION

Respondent

Relationship to child: MOTHER
Marital Status: DIVORCED / SEPARATED
Education (in years): 12
Occupation: UNSKILLED
Referral source: NOT PROVIDED

Western Psychological Services • 12031 Wilshire Boulevard • Los Angeles, California 90025

ITEM RESPONSES

    1(F)   11(T)   21(F)   31(F)   41(T)   51(T)   61(T)   71(T)   81(T)   91(F) 101(T)
    2(T)   12(T)   22(F)   32(T)   42(T)   52(F)   62(T)   72(F)   82(F)   92(T) 102(F)
    3(F)   13(T)   23(T)   33(T)   43(F)   53(T)   63(T)   73(F)   83(F)   93(F) 103(F)
    4(F)   14(T)   24(F)   34(F)   44(T)   54(F)   64(F)   74(F)   84(F)   94(T) 104(T)
    5(F)   15(F)   25(F)   35(F)   45(F)   55(F)   65(T)   75(F)   85(T)   95(F) 105(T)
    6(T)   16(F)   26(F)   36(T)   46(T)   56(F)   66(F)   76(F)   86(F)   96(T) 106(T)
    7(F)   17(F)   27(T)   37(F)   47(T)   57(F)   67(T)   77(F)   87(F)   97(F) 107(T)
    8(T)   18(T)   28(T)   38(T)   48(F)   58(T)   68(F)   78(F)   88(F)   98(F) 108(T)
    9(T)   19(T)   29(F)   39(T)   49(F)   59(F)   69(F)   79(F)   89(F)   99(F) 109(F)
   10(T)   20(F)   30(F)   40(F)   50(F)   60(T)   70(F)   80(F)   90(T) 100(F) 110(T)

  111(T) 121(T) 131(T) 141(T) 151(T) 161(F)
  112(F) 122(T) 132(F) 142(F) 152(F) 162(T)
  113(F) 123(F) 133(T) 143(T) 153(F) 163(F)
  114(F) 124(F) 134(T) 144(T) 154(T) 164(T)
  115(F) 125(F) 135(T) 145(T) 155(F)
  116(F) 126(F) 136(T) 146(F) 156(F)
  117(F) 127(F) 137(F) 147(T) 157(F)
  118(T) 128(T) 138(F) 148(T) 158(T)
  119(F) 129(F) 139(T) 149(T) 159(T)
  120(F) 130(T) 140(F) 150(F) 160(T)

WPS TEST REPORT

NAME: Luria-Nebraska Neuropsychological Battery

SUPPLIER: Western Psychological Services
12031 Wilshire Blvd.
Los Angeles, CA 90025
(213) 478-2061

PRODUCT CATEGORY	PRIMARY APPLICATIONS
Cognitive/Ability	Clinical Assessment/Diagnosis Behavioral Medicine

SALE RESTRICTIONS American Psychological Association Guidelines

SERVICE TYPE/COST	Type	Available	Cost	Discount
	Mail-In	Yes	$7.90	Yes
	Teleprocessing	No		
	Local	No		

PRODUCT DESCRIPTION

The LURIA-NEBRASKA battery is designed to assess a broad range of neuropsychological functions. It consists of 269 discrete, scored items which produce a profile for 14 scales: Motor, Rhythm, Tactile, Visual, Receptive Speech, Expresive Speech, Writing, Reading, Arithmetic, Memory, Intellectual, Pathognomonic, Left Hemisphere, and Right Hemisphere. It is designed for persons 15 years of age or older, but has been used successfully with 12-year-olds.

The 11-page TEST REPORT is designed as a scoring and interpretive aid for users who have an advanced background in neuropsychology and in the use of the Battery. In addition to automatically computing and profiling T-scores for each of the four major groups of scales, the program also calculates estimated IQ scores and produces tables showing significant deviations of individual scale scores from the overall scale means. These tables will be helpful in attempting to localize organic brain impairment.

LURIA-NEBRASKA NEUROPSYCHOLOGICAL BATTERY (LNNB)
FORM II

A WPS TEST REPORT by Western Psychological Services
12031 Wilshire Boulevard
Los Angeles, California 90025
Copyright (c) 1983 by Western Psychological Services
Version 1.2

Answer Sheet: 00000379   Client ID: 26802
Sex: FEMALE   Age: 42
Education (in years): 4   Ethnic Background: WHITE
Test Date: 04/04/84   User: SAMPLE

***** LNNB TEST REPORT *****

     This summary is based on a systematic comparison of the client's
scores with data obtained from the evaluation of individuals with suspected
or documented neurological difficulties. These results may be useful in
forming clinical hypotheses about the nature and extent of disruption in
various functional systems and possible localization of brain damage.
However, the relative elevations of the various summary scores are only
one factor in interpreting the LNNB. They need to be integrated with
scores across the different types of scales and with individual item
responses. In addition, the LNNB should never be used simplistically or
in isolation. The hypotheses suggested by the test should be corroborated
by other methods, including clinical interviews, behavioral observations,
detailed clinical history, and other neurodiagnostic procedures.

     The LNNB TEST REPORT is designed as a scoring and interpretive aid
for users who have an advanced background in neuropsychology and in the use
of the LNNB. In addition to automatically computing and profiling T-scores
for each of the four major groups of scales, the program also calculates
estimated IQ scores and produces ipsative tables showing significant deviations
of individual scale scores from the overall scale means. These tables may be
especially useful in assessing clients' individual patterns of strengths
and weaknesses given their general level of functioning, as suggested by
Reynolds (Journal of Consulting and Clinical Psychology, 1982, 50(4),
525-529). The key to the labeling of the various scales is presented on
the last page of this report, and may be torn off and used in interpreting
the individual tables. However, users should bear in mind that these
labels are intended solely as convenient mnemonic devices. Appropriate
interpretation of the scales assumes a thorough familiarity with the
content and psychometric properties of the individual scales, as presented
in the Manual.

     Studies underlying the LNNB TEST REPORT are discussed in the
"Luria-Nebraska Neuropsychological Battery, Forms I and II: Manual"
(WPS Catalog Number W-168) published by Western Psychological Services.
Other important references include "Diagnosis and Rehabilitation in Clinical
Neuropsychology" (WPS Catalog Number T-50), "Item Interpretation of the
Luria-Nebraska Neuropsychological Battery" (WPS Catalog Number UN-2), and
"Interpretation of the Luria-Nebraska Neuropsychological Battery: Volumes
1 & 2" (WPS Catalog Number G-110).

LURIA-NEBRASKA CLINICAL AND SUMMARY SCALES

Critical level: 72
Clinical and summary scales above critical level: 11

```
                                        T SCORES
              SCORES   20   30   40   50   60   70   80   90  100  110  120
SCALES      RAW    T   I++++I++++I++++I++++I++++I++++I++++I++++I++++I++++I
                       I              :         *                         I
  C1        (39)  67   ]]]]]]]]]]]]]]]]]]]]]]]]] *                        I
                       I              :         *                         I
  C2        (16)  86   ]]]]]]]]]]]]]]]]]]]]]]]]]]]]]]]]]                  I
                       I              :         *                         I
  C3        (19)  66   ]]]]]]]]]]]]]]]]]]]]]]]]] *                        I
                       I              :         *                         I
  C4        (18)  69   ]]]]]]]]]]]]]]]]]]]]]]]]]]]*                       I
                       I              :         *                         I
  C5        (16)  59   ]]]]]]]]]]]]]]]]]]]]]]     *                       I
                       I              :         *                         I
  C6        (49)  97   ]]]]]]]]]]]]]]]]]]]]]]]]]]]]]]]]]]]]]]]]           I
                       I              :         *                         I
  C7        (22)  85   ]]]]]]]]]]]]]]]]]]]]]]]]]]]]]]]]]]]                I
                       I              :         *                         I
  C8        (19)  81   ]]]]]]]]]]]]]]]]]]]]]]]]]]]]]]]]]                  I
                       I              :         *                         I
  C9        (34) 123   ]]]]]]]]]]]]]]]]]]]]]]]]]]]]]]]]]]]]]]]]]]]]]]]]]]]
                       I              :         *                         I
  C10       (24)  79   ]]]]]]]]]]]]]]]]]]]]]]]]]]]]]]]]]]                 I
                       I              :         *                         I
  C11       (53)  96   ]]]]]]]]]]]]]]]]]]]]]]]]]]]]]]]]]]]]]]]]            I
                       I              :         *                         I
  C12       (19) 103   ]]]]]]]]]]]]]]]]]]]]]]]]]]]]]]]]]]]]]]]]]]]]]      I
                       I----------------------------------------------------I
  S1        (31)  74   ]]]]]]]]]]]]]]]]]]]]]]]]]]]]]                       I
                       I              :         *                         I
  S2        (16)  66   ]]]]]]]]]]]]]]]]]]]]]]]] * *                       I
                       I              :         *                         I
  S3        (15)  65   ]]]]]]]]]]]]]]]]]]]]]]]  *                         I
                       I              :         *                         I
  S4        (40) 121   ]]]]]]]]]]]]]]]]]]]]]]]]]]]]]]]]]]]]]]]]]]]]]]]]]]]
                       I              :         *                         I
  S5        (40)  87   ]]]]]]]]]]]]]]]]]]]]]]]]]]]]]]]]]]]]                I
                       I              :         *                         I
SCALES      RAW    T   I++++I++++I++++I++++I++++I++++I++++I++++I++++I++++I
            SCORES     20   30   40   50   60   70   80   90  100  110  120
                                        T SCORES
```

NOTE. The critical level, which corrects for differences in age and
educational level, is indicated by the vertical row of asterisks (*)
on the profile. T-scores above 120 are truncated.

psychware **349**

ESTIMATED IQ SCORES

Verbal: 62 (+or- 7)   Performance: 69 (+or- 9)   Full Scale: 61 (+or- 8)

These IQ scores are estimates of Verbal, Performance, and Full Scale IQ
scores for the Wechsler Adult Intelligence Scale (WAIS) derived by McKay,
Golden, Moses, Fishburne, and Wisniewski (Journal of Consulting and Clinical
Psychology, 1981, 49(o), 940-946) on a sample of psychiatric, neurologically
impaired, and normal adults. These estimated scores were obtained by applying
a regression equation using selected scales of the LNNB (Form I). The
multiple correlations of these selected scales with the WAIS IQ scores were
.88 with Verbal IQ, .50 with Performance IQ, and .87 with Full Scale IQ.
In interpreting these scores, the user should keep in mind that WAIS Full
Scale IQ scores average about 7.5 points higher than the equivalent WAIS-R
IQ scores.

LURIA-NEBRASKA LOCALIZATION SCALES

Critical level: 72
Localization scales above critical level: 6

```
                                            T SCORES
            SCORES   20   30   40   50   60   70   80   90  100  110 .120
SCALES      RAW  T   I+++++I++++I++++I++++I++++I++++I++++I++++I++++I++++I
                     I            :         *                           I
  L1        (49) 98  ]]]]]]]]]]]]]]]]]]]]]]]]]]]]]]]]]]]]]]]]]]]]       I
                     I            :         *                           I
  L2        (36) 74  ]]]]]]]]]]]]]]]]]]]]]]]]]]]]]]]]                   I
                     I            :         *                           I
  L3        (34) 87  ]]]]]]]]]]]]]]]]]]]]]]]]]]]]]]]]]]]]]]              I
                     I            :         *                           I
  L4        (22) 65  ]]]]]]]]]]]]]]]]]]]]]]]]]]]]  *                     I
                     I-------------------------------------------------I
  L5        (22) 77  ]]]]]]]]]]]]]]]]]]]]]]]]]]]]]]]]]]                  I
                     I            :         *                           I
  L6        (16) 63  ]]]]]]]]]]]]]]]]]]]]]]]]]  *                        I
                     I            :         *                           I
  L7        (31) 83  ]]]]]]]]]]]]]]]]]]]]]]]]]]]]]]]]]]]]]]              I
                     I            :         *                           I
  L8        (39) 87  ]]]]]]]]]]]]]]]]]]]]]]]]]]]]]]]]]]]]]]              I
                     I            :         *                           I
SCALES      RAW  T   I+++++I++++I++++I++++I++++I++++I++++I++++I++++I++++I
            SCORES   20   30   40   50   60   70   80   90  100  110  120
                                            T SCORES
```

NOTE. The critical level, which corrects for differences in age and
educational level, is indicated by the vertical row of asterisks (*)
on the profile. T-scores above 120 are truncated.

350 *psychware*

LURIA-NEBRASKA FACTOR SCALES

Critical level: 72
Factor scales above critical level: 12

```
                                              T SCORES
                    SCORES    20   30   40   50   60   70   80   90  100  110  120
SCALES         RAW    T    I++++I++++I++++I++++I++++I++++I++++I++++I++++I++++I
                           I                   :              *                I
  M1           (3)   58    ]]]]]]]]]]]]]]]]]]]]]                               I
                           I                   :              *                I
  M2           (5)   51    ]]]]]]]]]]]]]]]]]                  *                I
                           I                   :              *                I
  M3          (12)   75    ]]]]]]]]]]]]]]]]]]]]]]]]]]]]]]]]                    I
                           I                   :              *                I
  M4           (0)   48    ]]]]]]]]]]]]]]]]:                  *                I
                           I                   :              *                I
  M5           (2)   59    ]]]]]]]]]]]]]]]]]]]]]             *                 I
                           I                   :              *                I
  RH1         (16)   89    ]]]]]]]]]]]]]]]]]]]]]]]]]]]]]]]]]]]]]]]]]]          I
                           I                   :              *                I
  T1           (9)   80    ]]]]]]]]]]]]]]]]]]]]]]]]]]]]]]]]]]]]]               I
                           I                   :              *                I
  T2           (1)   43    ]]]]]]]]]]]]]]   :                 *                I
                           I                   :              *                I
  V1           (4)   55    ]]]]]]]]]]]]]]]]]]]]               *                I
                           I                   :              *                I
  V2           (6)   68    ]]]]]]]]]]]]]]]]]]]]]]]]]]]]]] *                    I
                           I                   :              *                I
  R1           (0)   40    ]]]]]]]]]]]      :                 *                I
                           I                   :              *                I
  R2          (12)   79    ]]]]]]]]]]]]]]]]]]]]]]]]]]]]]]]]]]]]                I
                           I                   :              *                I
  R3           (0)   48    ]]]]]]]]]]]]]]]]:                  *                I
                           I                   :              *                I
  R4           (0)   49    ]]]]]]]]]]]]]]]]]                  *                I
                           I                   :              *                I
SCALES         RAW    T    I++++I++++I++++I++++I++++I++++I++++I++++I++++I++++I
               SCORES     20   30   40   50   60   70   80   90  100  110  120
                                               T SCORES
```

NOTE. The critical level, which corrects for differences in age and
educational level, is indicated by the vertical row of asterisks (*)
on the profile. T-scores above 120 are truncated.

psychware **351**

LURIA-NEBRASKA FACTOR SCALES (Continued)

Critical level: 72

```
                                            T SCORES
              SCORES    20   30   40   50   60   70   80   90  100  110  120
SCALES   RAW    T    I++++I++++I++++I++++I++++I++++I++++I++++I++++I++++I
                     I              :              *                        I
E1       (12)   94   ]]]]]]]]]]]]]]]]]]]]]]]]]]]]]]]]]]]]]]]                I
                     I              :              *                        I
E2        (7)   76   ]]]]]]]]]]]]]]]]]]]]]]]]]]]]]]]                        I
                     I              :              *                        I
E3        (6)   62   ]]]]]]]]]]]]]]]]]]]]]]]]]]  *                          I
                     I              :              *                        I
RE1      (12)   64   ]]]]]]]]]]]]]]]]]]]]]]]]]]]]]]]]]]]                    I
                     I              :              *                        I
RE2       (5)   70   ]]]]]]]]]]]]]]]]]]]]]]]]]]]]]]*                        I
                     I              :              *                        I
W1       (18)   79   ]]]]]]]]]]]]]]]]]]]]]]]]]]]]]]]]]]                     I
                     I              :              *                        I
W2        (4)  102   ]]]]]]]]]]]]]]]]]]]]]]]]]]]]]]]]]]]]]]]]]]]]]          I
                     I              :              *                        I
A1       (24)   95   ]]]]]]]]]]]]]]]]]]]]]]]]]]]]]]]]]]]]]]]]]              I
                     I              :              *                        I
A2       (10)  176   ]]]]]]]]]]]]]]]]]]]]]]]]]]]]]]]]]]]]]]]]]]]]]]]]]]]]]]]I
                     I              :              *                        I
ME1       (3)   71   ]]]]]]]]]]]]]]]]]]]]]]]]]]]]]]]]]                      I
                     I              :              *                        I
ME2       (8)   68   ]]]]]]]]]]]]]]]]]]]]]]]]]]]]]] *                       I
                     I              :              *                        I
I1       (22)   71   ]]]]]]]]]]]]]]]]]]]]]]]]]]]]]]]]]                      I
                     I              :              *                        I
I2       (11)   64   ]]]]]]]]]]]]]]]]]]]]]]]]]]]]  *                        I
                     I              :              *                        I
I3       (12)   91   ]]]]]]]]]]]]]]]]]]]]]]]]]]]]]]]]]]]]]]                 I
                     I              :              *                        I
SCALES   RAW    T    I++++I++++I++++I++++I++++I++++I++++I++++I++++I++++I
              SCORES    20   30   40   50   60   70   80   90  100  110  120
                                            T SCORES
```

NOTE. The critical level, which corrects for differences in age and
educational level, is indicated by the vertical row of asterisks (*)
on the profile. T-scores above 120 are truncated.

Western Psychological Services • 12031 Wilshire Boulevard • Los Angeles, California 90025

WPS TEST REPORT

RELATIVE STRENGTHS AND WEAKNESSES: CLINICAL AND SUMMARY SCALES

Mean T-score for clinical and summary scales: 83.74

```
                                 STRENGTH ---------------------- WEAKNESS

         DIFFERENCE                    DIFFERENCES FROM MEAN T-SCORE
         FROM                 -20  -15  -10  -5    0    5   10   15   20
SCALES   MEAN       SEest     I++++I++++I++++I++++I++++I++++I++++I++++I
                              I                    :                    I
  C1     -16.42***   4.80     ----x-----           :                    I
                              I                    :                    I
  C2       2.35      6.40     I             ------x-----:-              I
                              I                    :                    I
  C3     -17.77**    5.66     --x------            :                    I
                              I                    :                    I
  C4     -14.55      5.92     -----x------         :                    I
                              I                    :                    I
  C5     -24.66***   5.00     <<-  --  --  --  -- :                    I
                              I                    :                    I
  C6      13.47      5.20     I                    :         -----x----- I
                              I                    :                    I
  C7       1.16      5.66     I             ------x------                I
                              I                    :                    I
  C8      -3.23      5.20     I           -----x-----                   I
                              I                    :                    I
  C9      39.15***   4.12     I                    : --  --  --  -- ->> I
                              I                    :                    I
  C10     -4.98      6.03     I          ------x------                  I
                              I                    :                    I
  C11     12.66*     4.58     I                    :        -----x----- I
                              I                    :                    I
  C12     19.02***   3.16     I                    :             ---x-  I
                              I-------------------------------------------I
  S1      -9.57      5.00     I       -----x-----  :                    I
                              I                    :                    I
  S2     -18.19***   5.39     --x-----             :                    I
                              I                    :                    I
  S3     -18.63***   5.39     -x-----              :                    I
                              I                    :                    I
  S4      37.33***   4.90     I                    : --  --  --  -- ->> I
                              I                    :                    I
  S5       2.86      5.00     I            -----x-----                  I
                              I                    :                    I
                             I++++I++++I++++I++++I++++I++++I++++I++++I
                             -20  -15  -10  -5    0    5   10   15   20
*p<.10.    **p<.05.    ***p<.01.       DIFFERENCES FROM MEAN T-SCORE
```

NOTE. The significance of the deviation of a T-score for a particular scale
from an individual's mean T-score across all profile scales is given by p,
the probability that a deviation of this size could have occurred by chance.
All significance tests are two tailed and corrected for multiple comparisons
using Bonferonni's t (see Manual). Approximately 68% of the individuals
with the "true" score, X, would be expected to score in the interval bounded
by plus or minus one standard error of estimate (SEest). Differences from
the mean greater than plus or minus 20 are indicated by a row of double
dashes (--) ending with the symbols << or >>.

Western Psychological Services • 12031 Wilshire Boulevard • Los Angeles, California 90025

WPS TEST REPORT

RELATIVE STRENGTHS AND WEAKNESSES: FACTOR SCALES

Mean T-score for factor scales: 73.00

```
                                    STRENGTH ----------------------- WEAKNESS
              DIFFERENCE                    DIFFERENCES FROM MEAN T-SCORE
                FROM                  -20  -15  -10  -5    0    5    10   15   20
  SCALES        MEAN      SEest       I++++I++++I++++I++++I++++I++++I++++I++++I
                                      I                      :                 I
   M1          -14.55     7.55        -----X--------         :                 I
                                      I                      :                 I
   M2          -21.70*    7.45        <<-----  --   --   --  :                 I
                                      I                      :                 I
   M3            1.55     5.55        I          -------X-------                I
                                      I                      :                 I
   M4          -23.59*    6.77        <<-----  --   --   --  :                 I
                                      I                      :                 I
   M5          -13.52     9.11        ------X---------       :                 I
                                      I                      :                 I
   RH1          15.74     5.55        I                      :        ------X----
                                      I                      :                 I
   T1            0.66     6.55        I                      :  -------X-------  I
                                      I                      :                 I
   T2          -30.41***  6.35        <<-  --   --   --   -- :                 I
                                      I                      :                 I
   V1          -13.32     7.55        --X--------            :                 I
                                      I                      :                 I
   V2           -5.25     8.12        I      --------X--------                  I
                                      I                      :                 I
   R1          -32.52***  5.59        <<-  --   --   --   -- :                 I
                                      I                      :                 I
   R2            5.37     7.75        I                      :  -------X--------  I
                                      I                      :                 I
   R3          -24.62     9.94        <<-----  --   --   --  :                 I
                                      I                      :                 I
   R4          -23.95*    9.05        <<-----  --   --   --  :                 I
                                      I                      :                 I
                                      I++++I++++I++++I++++I++++I++++I++++I++++I
                                      -20  -15  -10  -5    0    5    10   15   20
*p<.10.   **p<.05.   ***p<.01.             DIFFERENCES FROM MEAN T-SCORE
```

NOTE. The significance of the deviation of a T-score for a particular scale
from an individual's mean T-score across all profile scales is given by p,
the probability that a deviation of this size could have occurred by chance.
All significance tests are two tailed and corrected for multiple comparisons
using Bonferonni's t (see Manual). Approximately 68% of the individuals
with the "true" score, X, would be expected to score in the interval bounded
by plus or minus one standard error of estimate (SEest). Differences from
the mean greater than plus or minus 20 are indicated by a row of double
dashes (--) ending with the symbols << or >>.

Mean T-score for factor scales: 73.00

```
                                       STRENGTH --------------------- WEAKNESS
                     DIFFERENCE                DIFFERENCES FROM MEAN T-SCORE
                     FROM              -20  -15  -10  -5   0    5    10   15   20
 SCALES              MEAN     SEest    I++++I++++I++++I++++I++++I++++I++++I++++I
                                       I                   :                    I
 E1                  21.42    5.43     I                   :  --   --   -- ---->>
                                       I                   :                    I
 E2                   3.15    7.31     I              --------X--------          I
                                       I                   :                    I
 E3                 -11.37    5.48     I     ------X------  :                    I
                                       I                   :                    I
 RE1                 11.03    6.15     I                   :   ------X------     I
                                       I                   :                    I
 RE2                 -3.10    7.37     I          -------X-------                I
                                       I                   :                    I
 W1                   0.27    6.40     I              ------X------              I
                                       I                   :                    I
 W2                 27.31***   7.00    I                   :  --   --   --   -->>
                                       I                   :                    I
 A1                 21.69***   4.00    I                   :  --   --   --  -->>
                                       I                   :                    I
 A2                102.72***   5.00    I                   :  --   --   --  ->>
                                       I                   :                    I
 ME1                 -2.41    7.43     I         -------X-------                 I
                                       I                   :                    I
 ME2                 -5.41    6.80     I       -------X-------                   I
                                       I                   :                    I
 I1                  -1.77    6.08     I         ------X------                   I
                                       I                   :                    I
 I2                  -5.71    7.55     I     --------X--------:                  I
                                       I                   :                    I
 I3                  17.53    7.42     I                   :       -------X--    I
                                       I                   :                    I
                                       I++++I++++I++++I++++I++++I++++I++++I++++I
                                      -20  -15  -10  -5   0    5    10   15   20
 *p<.10.    **p<.05.    ***p<.01.        DIFFERENCES FROM MEAN T-SCORE
```

NOTE. The significance of the deviation of a T-score for a particular scale from an individual's mean T-score across all profile scales is given by p, the probability that a deviation of this size could have occurred by chance. All significance tests are two tailed and corrected for multiple comparisons using Bonferonni's t (see Manual). Approximately 68% of the individuals with the "true" score, X, would be expected to score in the interval bounded by plus or minus one standard error of estimate (SEest). Differences from the mean greater than plus or minus 20 are indicated by a row of double dashes (--) ending with the symbols << or >>.

RELATIVE STRENGTHS AND WEAKNESSES: LOCALIZATION SCALES

Mean T-score for localization scales: 79.21

```
                                       STRENGTH ---------------------- WEAKNESS

              DIFFERENCE                      DIFFERENCES FROM MEAN T-SCORE
                 FROM               -20  -15  -10   -5    0    5    10   15   20
   SCALES        MEAN      SEest     I++++I++++I++++I++++I++++I++++I++++I++++I
                                     I                   :                     I
     L1       19.12***     4.58      I                   :                -----X-
                                     I                   :                     I
     L2        -5.39       5.92      I         ------X------                   I
                                     I                   :                     I
     L3         7.42       4.24      I                   :  ----X----          I
                                     I                   :                     I
     L4       -14.10**     4.90      I-----X-----        :                     I
                                     I------------------------------------------I
     L5        -2.25       6.08      I           ------X------                  I
                                     I                   :                     I
     L6       -10.26**     5.48      ----X-----          :                     I
                                     I                   :                     I
     L7         3.77       5.66      I              ------X------              I
                                     I                   :                     I
     L8         7.91       5.20      I                   :  -----X-----         I
                                     I                   :                     I
                                     I++++I++++I++++I++++I++++I++++I++++I++++I
                                    -20  -15  -10   -5    0    5    10   15   20
   *p<.10.   **p<.05.   ***p<.01.                   DIFFERENCES FROM MEAN T-SCORE
```

NOTE. The significance of the deviation of a T-score for a particular scale
from an individual's mean T-score across all profile scales is given by p,
the probability that a deviation of this size could have occurred by chance.
All significance tests are two tailed and corrected for multiple comparisons
using Bonferonni's t (see Manual). Approximately 68% of the individuals
with the "true" score, X, would be expected to score in the interval bounded
by plus or minus one standard error of estimate (SEest).

WPS TEST REPORT Western Psychological Services • 12031 Wilshire Boulevard • Los Angeles, California 90025

BACKGROUND INFORMATION

Sex: FEMALE
Age: 42
Education (in years): 4
Ethnic Background: WHITE
Occupation: NOT EMPLOYED OUTSIDE THE HOME
Dominant Hand: RIGHT
Age of Onset (in years): 30
Reason for evaluation: DIFFERENTIAL WITH PSYCHIATRIC
User: SAMPLE

RESULTS OF NEUROLOGICAL PROCEDURES

Neurological Exam:	UNKNOWN	Postsurgical Lesion:	UNKNOWN
Angiogram:	UNKNOWN	Brain Scan:	UNKNOWN
EEG:	UNKNOWN	Myelogram:	UNKNOWN
CAT Scan:	UNKNOWN	X-Ray:	UNKNOWN
Pneumoencephalogram:	UNKNOWN	Cerebral Blood Flow:	UNKNOWN

LURIA-NEBRASKA ITEM RESPONSES FOR FORM II

1(2)	11(0)	21(2)	31(0)	41(2)	51(0)	61(2)	71(0)	81(2)	91(0)	101(0)
2(2)	12(0)	22(2)	32(2)	42(1)	52(2)	62(2)	72(0)	82(0)	92(2)	102(0)
3(1)	13(2)	23(2)	33(2)	43(0)	53(1)	63(2)	73(0)	83(0)	93(2)	103(0)
4(1)	14(0)	24(2)	34(0)	44(1)	54(1)	64(0)	74(1)	84(0)	94(2)	104(0)
5(0)	15(0)	25(0)	35(0)	45(1)	55(2)	65(0)	75(2)	85(0)	95(2)	105(0)
6(0)	16(0)	26(0)	36(0)	46(1)	56(0)	66(1)	76(2)	86(0)	96(2)	106(2)
7(0)	17(2)	27(0)	37(1)	47(1)	57(0)	67(1)	77(2)	87(0)	97(2)	107(2)
8(0)	18(2)	28(0)	38(0)	48(2)	58(2)	68(1)	78(2)	88(0)	98(2)	108(0)
9(0)	19(0)	29(0)	39(0)	49(0)	59(2)	69(1)	79(2)	89(1)	99(2)	109(2)
10(0)	20(0)	30(2)	40(2)	50(1)	60(2)	70(0)	80(2)	90(1)	100(0)	110(0)

111(0)	121(0)	131(0)	141(0)	151(2)	161(0)	171(2)	131(0)	191(0)	201(0)	211(0)
112(0)	122(0)	132(2)	142(0)	152(2)	162(2)	172(2)	182(2)	192(2)	202(2)	212(2)
113(0)	123(2)	133(0)	143(2)	153(2)	163(2)	173(2)	183(2)	193(2)	203(1)	213(2)
114(0)	124(0)	134(0)	144(2)	154(0)	164(1)	174(2)	184(2)	194(0)	204(2)	214(2)
115(0)	125(2)	135(1)	145(2)	155(0)	165(1)	175(2)	185(2)	195(2)	205(2)	215(2)
116(0)	126(0)	136(0)	146(0)	156(0)	166(1)	176(2)	186(2)	196(2)	206(0)	216(2)
117(0)	127(0)	137(2)	147(2)	157(0)	167(2)	177(2)	187(2)	197(1)	207(2)	217(2)
118(0)	128(0)	138(2)	148(0)	158(1)	168(0)	178(2)	188(2)	198(2)	208(2)	218(2)
119(0)	129(0)	139(0)	149(2)	159(0)	169(2)	179(2)	189(2)	199(2)	209(1)	219(2)
120(0)	130(2)	140(2)	150(0)	160(0)	170(2)	130(0)	190(0)	200(2)	210(0)	220(2)

221(2)	231(2)	241(2)	251(2)	261(2)	271(2)
222(2)	232(2)	242(0)	252(2)	262(2)	272(2)
223(2)	233(0)	243(0)	253(0)	263(2)	273(1)
224(2)	234(2)	244(1)	254(2)	264(2)	274(2)
225(2)	235(2)	245(2)	255(0)	265(2)	275(2)
226(2)	236(0)	246(2)	255(2)	266(2)	276(2)
227(2)	237(1)	247(2)	257(2)	267(2)	277(2)
228(2)	238(2)	248(0)	258(2)	268(2)	278(2)
229(2)	239(2)	249(2)	259(2)	269(1)	279(2)
230(2)	240(2)	250(2)	260(2)	270(2)	

psychware **357**

KEY TO THE LABELING OF THE LURIA-NEBRASKA SCALES

CLINICAL SCALES

C1 -- Motor Functions
C2 -- Rhythm
C3 -- Tactile Functions
C4 -- Visual Functions
C5 -- Receptive Speech
C6 -- Expressive Speech

C7 -- Writing
C8 -- Reading
C9 -- Arithmetic
C10 -- Memory
C11 -- Intellectual Processes
C12 -- Intermediate-Term Memory

SUMMARY SCALES

S1 -- Patnognomonic
S2 -- Left Hemisphere
S3 -- Right Hemisphere

S4 -- Profile Elevation
S5 -- Impairment

LOCALIZATION SCALES

L1 -- Left Frontal
L2 -- Left Sensorimotor
L3 -- Left Parietal-Occipital
L4 -- Left Temporal

L5 -- Right Frontal
L6 -- Right Sensorimotor
L7 -- Right Parietal-Occipital
L8 -- Right Temporal

FACTOR SCALES

M1 -- Kinesthesis-Based Movement
M2 -- Drawing Speed
M3 -- Fine Motor Speed
M4 -- Spatial-Based Movement
M5 -- Oral Motor Skills
RH1 -- Rhythm & Pitch Perception
T1 -- Simple Tactile Sensation
T2 -- Stereognosis
V1 -- Visual Acuity & Naming
V2 -- Visual-Spatial Organization
R1 -- Phonemic Discrimination
R2 -- Relational Concepts
R3 -- Concept Recognition
R4 -- Verbal-Spatial Relationships

E1 -- Simple Phonetic Reading
E2 -- Word Repetition
E3 -- Reading Polysyllabic Words
RE1 -- Reading Complex Material
RE2 -- Reading Simple Material
W1 -- Spelling
W2 -- Motor Writing Skill
A1 -- Arithmetic Calculations
A2 -- Number Reading
ME1 -- Verbal Memory
ME2 -- Visual & Complex Memory
I1 -- General Verbal Intelligence
I2 -- Complex Verbal Arithmetic
I3 -- Simple Verbal Arithmetic

Western Psychological Services • 12031 Wilshire Boulevard • Los Angeles, California 90025

WPS TEST REPORT

358 *psychware*

NAME: Luria-Nebraska Scoring

SUPPLIER: Precision People, Inc.
3452 North Ride Circle. S.
Jacksonville, FL 32217
(904) 262-1096

PRODUCT CATEGORY	PRIMARY APPLICATIONS
Cognitive/Ability	Clinical Assessment/Diagnosis Behavioral Medicine

SALE RESTRICTIONS American Psychological Association Guidelines

SERVICE TYPE/COST	Type	Available	Cost	Discount
	Mail-In	No		
	Teleprocessing	No		
	Local	Yes	$199.00	

PRODUCT DESCRIPTION

LURIA-NEBRASKA is is program for organizing and reporting scores on the Luria-Nebraska Neuropsychological Battery. Raw and T scores are provided for 14 Profile scales, 10 Localization scales, and 30 Experimental/Factor-Derived scales (raw scores only). T-scores that exceed critical levels are indicated as such. A four-page detailed report follows that lists item responses for each of the scored scales.

The software is compatible with Apple microcomputers. A manual and sample printout are available for $34.00.

LURIA-NEBRASKA NEUROPSYCHOLOGICAL BATTERY

SCORING SUMMARY

CLIENT NAME---JOHN   AGE---34   EDUCATION---15

TESTING DATE---07/15/83   CRITICAL LEVEL = 54.026

PROFILE SCALES

```
MOTOR SCALE..................42          T-SCORE =  76.07***
RHYTHM SCALE.................17          T-SCORE =  92.08***
TACTILE SCALE................28          T-SCORE =  88.57***
VISUAL SCALE.................12          T-SCORE =  57.98***
RECEPTIVE SPEECH SCALE.......30          T-SCORE =  90.31***
EXPRESSIVE SPEECH SCALE......40          T-SCORE =  85.82***
WRITING SCALE................10          T-SCORE =  62.03***
READING SCALE.................8          T-SCORE =  57.22**
ARITHMETIC SCALE.............26          T-SCORE = 107.24***
MEMORY SCALE.................13          T-SCORE =  62.45***
INTELLECTUAL PROCESSES SCALE..37         T-SCORE =  72.52***
PATHOGNOMONIC SCALE..........33          T-SCORE =  76.98***
LEFT HEMISPHERE SCALE........21          T-SCORE =  80.88***
RIGHT HEMISPHERE SCALE.......23          T-SCORE =  86.21***
```

LOCALIZATION SCALES

```
EXPANDED LEFT HEMISPHERE SCALE..36       T-SCORE =  72.75***
EXPANDED RIGHT HEMISPHERE SCALE.39       T-SCORE =  69.61***
LEFT FRONTAL.................37           T-SCORE =  79.75***
LEFT SENSORIMOTOR............33           T-SCORE =  71.71***
LEFT PARIETAL-OCCIPITAL......16           T-SCORE =  60.16***
LEFT TEMPORAL................27           T-SCORE =  74.29***
RIGHT FRONTAL................14           T-SCORE =  61.9***
RIGHT SENSORIMOTOR...........17           T-SCORE =  67.05***
RIGHT PARIETAL-OCCIPITAL.....30           T-SCORE =  83.16***
RIGHT TEMPORAL...............27           T-SCORE =  68.13***
```

EXPERIMENTAL FACTOR-DERIVED SCALES

```
KINESTHESIS-BASED FACTOR......2     LOGICAL GRAMMATICAL RELATIONS.3
DRAWING SPEED FACTOR..........3     SIMPLE PHONETIC READING.......11
FINE MOTOR SPEED FACTOR.......2     WORD REPETITION FACTOR........7
SPATIAL-BASED MOVEMENT FACTOR.6     READING POLY-SYLLABIC WORDS...2
ORAL MOTOR SKILLS FACTOR......2     READING COMPLEX MATERIAL......3
RHYTHM AND PITCH PERCEPTION...14     READING SIMPLE MATERIAL.......3
SIMPLE TACTILE SENSATION......14     SPELLING FACTOR...............6
STEREOGNOSIS FACTOR..........11     MOTOR WRITING SKILL FACTOR....4
VISUAL ACUITY & NAMING FACTOR.7     ARITHMETIC CALCULATIONS.......14
VISUAL-SPATIAL ORGANIZATION...0     NUMBER READING FACTOR.........12
PHONEMIC DISCRIMINATION.......7     VERBAL MEMORY FACTOR..........5
RELATIONAL CONCEPTS FACTOR....9     VISUAL & COMPLEX MEMORY.......2
CONCEPT RECOGNITION FACTOR....2     GENERAL VERBAL INTELLIGENCE...25
VERBAL-SPATIAL RELATIONSHIPS..1     COMPLEX VERBAL ARITHMETIC.....4
WORD COMPREHENSION FACTOR.....1     SIMPLE VERBAL ARITHMETIC......5
```

*** INDICATES T-SCORE EXCEEDS CRITICAL LEVEL

LURIA-NEBRASKA NEUROPSYCHOLOGICAL BATTERY
SCORING DETAIL: PATHOGNOMIC & LATERALIZATION

CLIENT NAME---JOHN AGE---34 EDUCATION---15
TESTING DATE---07/15/83 CRITICAL LEVEL = 54.026

PATHOGNOMIC SCALE ITEM	SCORE	LEFT HEMISPHERE SCALE ITEM	SCORE	RIGHT HEMISPHERE SCALE ITEM	SCORE	EXPANDED LEFT HEMISPHERE ITEM	SCORE	EXPANDED RIGHT HEMISPHERE ITEM	SCORE
(8)	0	(1)	0	(2)	0	(1)	0	(2)	1
(9)	2	(3)	1	(4)	0	(3)	1	(6)	0
(19)	1	(5)	0	(6)	0	(5)	1	(10)	0
(37)	0	(7)	0	(8)	2	(7)	0	(18)	1
(39)	2	(11)	2	(10)	1	(11)	2	(23)	0
(42)	2	(13)	2	(12)	2	(17)	2	(33)	2
(43)	0	(15)	1	(14)	2	(27)	1	(51)	1
(45)	1	(17)	0	(16)	1	(44)	0	(57)	2
(64)	1	(19)	2	(18)	0	(62)	2	(63)	0
(77)	2	(64)	1	(65)	2	(86)	0	(65)	2
(79)	2	(68)	0	(69)	2	(105)	1	(71)	2
(82)	1	(70)	1	(71)	2	(117)	1	(75)	0
(85)	2	(72)	2	(73)	2	(134)	0	(77)	2
(89)	0	(74)	2	(77)	2	(144)	0	(79)	2
(101)	0	(76)	1	(79)	2	(176)	1	(81)	2
(102)	2	(78)	0	(81)	2	(182)	0	(85)	2
(103)	0	(80)	1	(84)	2	(185)	0	(89)	1
(108)	1	(82)	2	(85)	2	(187)	2	(92)	0
(109)	0	(83)	1			(202)	0	(94)	1
(157)	2					(208)	1	(122)	2
(162)	2					(210)	2	(146)	0
(166)	1					(214)	1	(157)	1
(175)	2					(219)	2	(169)	2
(178)	1					(223)	2	(171)	0
(184)	0					(225)	0	(172)	1
(185)	0					(240)	1	(173)	2
(187)	2					(249)	2	(217)	2
(196)	2					(258)	2	(227)	2
(221)	2					(261)	1	(236)	1
(227)	2					(268)	0	(239)	2
(241)	0					(269)	0	(265)	2
(267)	0							(266)	1
TOTAL =33		TOTAL =21		TOTAL =23		TOTAL =36		TOTAL =39	
T = 76.98		T = 80.98		T = 86.21		T = 72.75		T = 69.61	

LURIA-NEBRASKA NEUROPSYCHOLOGICAL BATTERY
SCORING DETAIL: LOCALIZATION

CLIENT NAME---JOHN AGE---34 EDUCATION---15
TESTING DATE---07/15/83 CRITICAL LEVEL = 54.026

LEFT FRONTAL ITEM	SCORE	LEFT SENSORI MOTOR ITEM	SCORE	L. PARIETAL-OCCIPITAL ITEM	SCORE	LEFT TEMPORAL ITEM	SCORE	R.PARIETAL-OCCIPITAL ITEM	SCORE	RIGHT TEMPORAL ITEM	SCORE
(1)	0	(5)	1	(5)	1	(31)	2	(10)	0	(29)	0
(59)	2	(11)	2	(7)	0	(63)	2	(24)	1	(42)	2
(62)	2	(17)	2	(8)	0	(100)	2	(39)	2	(66)	0
(104)	2	(21)	0	(90)	0	(101)	2	(53)	0	(49)	1
(105)	0	(38)	0	(95)	1	(102)	2	(59)	0	(95)	0
(123)	2	(40)	0	(96)	0	(103)	2	(60)	0	(98)	2
(125)	0	(41)	0	(149)	0	(109)	2	(65)	0	(117)	1
(134)	1	(44)	2	(151)	0	(120)	1	(75)	0	(127)	2
(138)	0	(46)	1	(175)	2	(121)	1	(77)	0	(157)	2
(140)	1	(52)	2	(179)	0	(122)	2	(79)	2	(172)	0
(143)	0	(56)	0	(187)	1	(126)	1	(81)	2	(173)	0
(144)	2	(61)	2	(191)	0	(129)	2	(83)	2	(174)	2
(157)	2	(70)	1	(195)	0	(130)	1	(84)	2	(184)	0
(161)	0	(71)	1	(199)	2	(131)	0	(85)	2	(195)	0
(162)	2	(78)	1	(203)	2	(155)	1	(87)	1	(217)	2
(166)	2	(82)	1	(204)	2	(156)	1	(90)	1	(227)	2
(168)	0	(86)	0	(207)	0	(174)	1	(91)	2	(233)	0
(192)	2	(87)	1	(215)	2	(183)	0	(94)	2	(235)	0
(196)	2	(99)	2	(221)	0	(186)	1	(97)	2	(237)	2
(202)	2	(145)	0	(222)	1	(199)	2	(103)	2	(239)	2
(207)	0	(150)	2	(233)	1	(214)	2	(158)	2	(247)	2
(208)	2	(221)	0	(243)	0	(232)	2	(215)	2	(254)	2
(219)	0	(223)	2	(251)	1	(238)	0	(225)	2	(256)	2
(225)	0	(229)	0	(255)	0	(239)	2	(236)	2	(262)	2
(230)	2	(240)	2	(263)	0			(239)	2	(264)	1
(237)	1	(242)	1					(257)	0		
(248)	1	(249)	2					(265)	2		
(250)	2	(253)	2								
(257)	0										
(259)	2										
(261)	1										
TOTAL =37		TOTAL =33		TOTAL =16		TOTAL =27		TOTAL =30		TOTAL =27	
T = 79.75		T = 71.71		T = 60.16		T = 74.29		T = 83.16		T = 68.13	

RIGHT FRONTAL ITEM	SCORE	RIGHT SENSORI MOTOR ITEM	SCORE
(6)	0	(4)	0
(7)	0	(10)	2
(13)	2	(36)	2
(33)	2	(46)	2
(39)	2	(51)	2
(40)	1		
(44)	0	(54)	1
(45)	1	(56)	2
(47)	1	(84)	2
(53)	2	(89)	0
(63)	2	(92)	1
(93)	1	(172)	0
(94)	0	(175)	1
(117)	1	(179)	2
(125)	2	(202)	2
(169)	0	(219)	2
TOTAL =14		TOTAL =17	
T = 61.9		T = 67.05	

psychware **361**

LURIA-NEBRASKA NEUROPSYCHOLOGICAL BATTERY
SCORING DETAIL: EXPERIMENTAL FACTORS

CLIENT NAME---JOHN   AGE---34   EDUCATION---15   CRITICAL LEVEL = 54.026
TESTING DATE---07/15/83

KINESTHESIS-BASED MOVEMENT (M1)

ITEM	SCORE
(5)	1
(6)	0
(7)	0
(8)	0
(48)	0
(50)	1
TOTAL = 2	

DRAWING SPEED (M2)

ITEM	SCORE
(37)	1
(39)	0
(41)	0
(43)	0
(45)	1
(47)	1
TOTAL = 3	

FINE MOTOR SPEED (M3)

ITEM	SCORE
(1)	0
(2)	1
(3)	1
(4)	0
(21)	0
(22)	0
(23)	0
TOTAL = 2	

SPATIAL-BASED MOVEMENT (M4)

ITEM	SCORE
(9)	2
(10)	0
(11)	2
(12)	1
(15)	0
(16)	1
TOTAL = 6	

ORAL MOTOR SKILLS (M5)

ITEM	SCORE
(29)	0
(32)	0
(35)	2
TOTAL = 2	

RHYTHM & PITCH PERCEPTION (RH1)

ITEM	SCORE
(52)	2
(53)	2
(54)	1
(55)	2
(58)	1
(59)	0
(60)	2
(62)	2
(63)	2
TOTAL = 14	

SIMPLE TACTILE SENSATION (T1)

ITEM	SCORE
(64)	2
(65)	0
(68)	1
(69)	1
(72)	2
(73)	2
(74)	2
(75)	1
(76)	1
(79)	2
TOTAL = 14	

VISUAL STEREOGNOSIS (T2)

ITEM	SCORE
(67)	2
(70)	1
(71)	1
(82)	1
(83)	2
(84)	2
(85)	2
TOTAL = 11	

VISUAL ACUITY AND NAMING (V1)

ITEM	SCORE
(87)	2
(88)	1
(89)	1
(90)	1
(91)	0
(99)	2
TOTAL = 7	

VISUAL-SPATIAL ORGANIZATION (V2)

ITEM	SCORE
(94)	0
(95)	0
(97)	0
TOTAL = 0	

PHONEMIC DISCRIMINATION (RC1)

ITEM	SCORE
(100)	2
(101)	2
(102)	2
(103)	0
(104)	2
(105)	1
TOTAL = 7	

RELATIONAL CONCEPTS (RC2)

ITEM	SCORE
(106)	0
(117)	2
(123)	2
(125)	2
(129)	2
(130)	2
(132)	1
TOTAL = 9	

SIMPLE PHONETIC READING (E1)

ITEM	SCORE
(145)	2
(146)	2
(147)	1
(150)	2
(152)	2
(153)	2
(163)	2
TOTAL = 11	

CONCEPT RECOGNITION (RC3)

ITEM	SCORE
(110)	2
(113)	0
(116)	0
TOTAL = 2	

VERBAL-SPATIAL RELATIONS (RC4)

ITEM	SCORE
(118)	0
(119)	0
(120)	0
TOTAL = 1	

WORD COMPREHENSION (RC5)

ITEM	SCORE
(108)	1
(111)	0
(114)	0
TOTAL = 1	

LOGICAL GRAMMATICAL RELATIONS (RC6)

ITEM	SCORE
(124)	0
(125)	2
(126)	1
TOTAL = 3	

LURIA-NEBRASKA NEUROPSYCHOLOGICAL BATTERY
SCORING DETAIL: EXPERIMENTAL FACTORS

CLIENT NAME---JOHN   AGE---34   EDUCATION---15   CRITICAL LEVEL = 54.026
TESTING DATE---07/15/83

WORD REPETITION (E2)

ITEM	SCORE
(133)	0
(134)	0
(135)	1
(137)	1
(138)	2
(140)	1
(141)	1
(142)	0
TOTAL = 7	

READING POLY-SYLLABIC WORDS (E3)

ITEM	SCORE
(144)	1
(148)	1
(149)	0
(151)	0
(155)	1
TOTAL = 2	

READING COMPLEX MATERIAL (RG1)

ITEM	SCORE
(189)	0
(192)	0
(195)	1
(196)	2
(199)	0
(200)	0
TOTAL = 3	

READING SIMPLE MATERIAL (RG2)

ITEM	SCORE
(190)	0
(193)	1
(194)	0
(197)	2
TOTAL = 3	

SPELLING (W1)

ITEM	SCORE
(175)	2
(176)	1
(179)	1
(182)	0
(183)	2
(184)	0
(185)	0
(186)	0
(187)	0
TOTAL = 6	

MOTOR WRITING SKILL (W2)

ITEM	SCORE
(177)	0
(178)	1
(180)	1
(181)	2
TOTAL = 4	

ARITHMETIC CALCULATIONS (A1)

ITEM	SCORE
(202)	0
(207)	0
(212)	2
(213)	2
(215)	2
(216)	2
(217)	2
(218)	1
(219)	2
(220)	0
(221)	0
(222)	0
TOTAL = 14	

NUMBER READING (A2)

ITEM	SCORE
(201)	0
(203)	2
(204)	2
(205)	1
(206)	0
(208)	2
(210)	1
(211)	2
(214)	2
TOTAL = 12	

VERBAL MEMORY (ME1)

ITEM	SCORE
(223)	2
(225)	2
(230)	1
(232)	0
(233)	0
TOTAL = 5	

VISUAL & COMPLEX MEMORY (ME2)

ITEM	SCORE
(227)	2
(229)	0
(234)	0
(235)	0
TOTAL = 2	

GENERAL VERBAL INTELLIGENCE (I1)

ITEM	SCORE
(236)	2
(237)	1
(242)	2
(243)	1
(244)	2
(245)	2
(246)	2
(247)	1
(248)	2
(249)	2
(250)	2
(251)	0
TOTAL = 25	

SIMPLE VERBAL ARITHMETIC

ITEM	SCORE
(252)	0
(255)	0
(258)	2

VERBAL ARITHMETIC (I3)

ITEM	SCORE
(259)	2
(260)	0
(261)	1
(263)	0
TOTAL = 5	

COMPLEX VERBAL ARITHMETIC (I2)

ITEM	SCORE
(264)	1
(265)	2
(266)	2
TOTAL = 4	

NAME: Major-Minor Finder

SUPPLIER: Publishers Test Service
2500 Garden Road
Monterey, CA 93940
(800) 538-9547

PRODUCT CATEGORY	PRIMARY APPLICATIONS
Career/Vocational	Vocational Guidance/Counseling

SALE RESTRICTIONS American Psychological Association Guidelines

SERVICE TYPE/COST	Type	Available	Cost	Discount
	Mail-In	No		
	Teleprocessing	No		
	Local	Yes	$59.95	

PRODUCT DESCRIPTION

The MAJOR-MINOR FINDER is designed to help students select a college major that matches aptitudes and interests. It also presents job outlook predictions and numbers of colleges offering various majors. Based on student responses to questions about college and work interests, a list of 10 of the 99 most popular college majors is displayed.

Software is available for use with Apple, TRS-80, and Commodore PET computers.

NAME: Management Edge

SUPPLIER: Human Edge Software, Inc.
2445 Faber Pl.
Palo Alto, CA 94303
(415) 493-1593

PRODUCT CATEGORY	PRIMARY APPLICATIONS
Interest/Attitudes	Training/Development

SALE RESTRICTIONS None

SERVICE TYPE/COST	Type	Available	Cost	Discount
	Mail-In	No		
	Teleprocessing	No		
	Local	Yes	$250.00	

PRODUCT DESCRIPTION

The MANAGEMENT EDGE is designed to aid managers improve their supervisory skills. The user enters self-descriptive information by answering screen prompts. Also entered are data on the nature of the problem and profiles of other people involved. The program uses this data to help the user resolve conflicts with personnel, improve communication within an organization, identify the proper position for an employee, determine compatibility between the user and the organization, and develop an employee career plan.

This program uses artificial intelligence techniques that allow the user to communicate in English with the computer and reach solutions to business problems.

The software is designed for use on IBM PC and PC-compatible microcomputer systems.

NAME: Marriage Counseling Report

SUPPLIER: Institute for Personality and Ability Testing, Inc.
P.O. Box 188
Champaign, IL 61820
(217) 352-4739

PRODUCT CATEGORY	PRIMARY APPLICATIONS
Personality	Personal/Marriage/Family Counseling

SALE RESTRICTIONS American Psychological Association Guidelines

SERVICE TYPE/COST	Type	Available	Cost	Discount
	Mail-In	Yes	$16.00	Yes
	Teleprocessing	Yes	$17.00	Yes
	Local	No		

PRODUCT DESCRIPTION

The MARRIAGE COUNSELING REPORT is a seven-page computer interpreted report of paired 16 PF profiles that examines individual and joint strengths and weaknesses in the personality organization of the two individuals. Interpersonal patterns and differences that represent potential sources of conflict or rapport in the relationship are identified.

Valuable in both premarital and troubled marriage situations, the recently reorganized format provides the interviewer with a step-by-step procedure for in-depth counseling.

Developed for psychologists, counselors, ministers, and other professionals as an accurate and time-saving instrument, the MCR is a dynamically expanding tool that augments the counseling skills of the professional.

THE INSTITUTE FOR PERSONALITY AND ABILITY TESTING
P.O. BOX 188   CHAMPAIGN, ILLINOIS 61820

THIS COMPUTER INTERPRETATION OF THE 16 PF IS INTENDED ONLY FOR PROPERLY
QUALIFIED PROFESSIONALS AND SHOULD BE TREATED AS A CONFIDENTIAL REPORT.
MARRIAGE COUNSELING REPORT—R7.01
SECTION 1
4/20/1984

```
NAME—JOHN SMITH                                          AGE—31
ID NUMBER—IPAT   83                                      SEX—M
```

```
* * * * * * * * * *  V A L I D I T Y   S C A L E S  * * * * * * * * * *
*                                                                      *
*  VALIDITY INDICATIONS ARE WITHIN ACCEPTABLE RANGES.                  *
*    FAKING GOOD/MD (STEN) SCORE IS LOW (3.0).                         *
*    FAKING BAD (STEN) SCORE IS AVERAGE (5.0).                         *
*                                                                      *
* * * * * * * * * * * * * * * * * * * * * * * * * * * * * * * * * * * *
```

16 PF
PERSONALITY PROFILE

SCORES				LEFT MEANING	1 2 3 4 5 6 7 8 9 10	RIGHT MEANING	%
R	U	C					
7	4	4	A	COOL, RESERVED	<---	WARM, EASYGOING	23
11	9	9	B	CONCRETE THINKING	------->	ABSTRACT THINKING	96
19	7	7	C	EASILY UPSET	--->	CALM, STABLE	77
18	8	8	E	NOT ASSERTIVE	----->	DOMINANT	89
12	5	5	F	SOBER, SERIOUS	<-	ENTHUSIASTIC	40
10	4	4	G	EXPEDIENT	<---	CONSCIENTIOUS	23
14	5	5	H	SHY, TIMID	<-	VENTURESOME	40
7	5	5	I	TOUGH-MINDED	<-	SENSITIVE	40
7	5	5	L	TRUSTING	<-	SUSPICIOUS	40
7	2	2	M	PRACTICAL	<-------	IMAGINATIVE	4
9	6	6	N	FORTHRIGHT	->	SHREWD	60
9	5	5	O	SELF-ASSURED	<-	SELF-DOUBTING	40
9	6	6	Q1	CONSERVATIVE	->	EXPERIMENTING	60
9	5	5	Q2	GROUP-ORIENTED	<-	SELF-SUFFICIENT	40
13	5	5	Q3	UNDISCIPLINED	<-	SELF-DISCIPLINED	40
10	5	5	Q4	RELAXED	<-	TENSE, DRIVEN	40

NOTE: "R" DESIGNATES RAW SCORES, "U" DESIGNATES (UNCORRECTED) STEN SCORES,
AND "C" DESIGNATES STEN SCORES CORRECTED FOR DISTORTION (IF APPROP-
RIATE).   THE INTERPRETATION WILL PROCEED ON THE BASIS OF CORRECTED
SCORES.

THE INFORMATION THAT FOLLOWS IS BASED UPON THE RESPONSES GIVEN FOR
THE QUESTIONNAIRE ITEMS.   THE REPORTED SCORE ON A GIVEN PERSONALITY
FACTOR INDICATES THAT THE PERSON WILL USUALLY BEHAVE IN A WAY THAT
REFLECTS THAT PERSONALITY TRAIT.   IN INTERPRETING THE STATEMENTS,
ASSESSING THE IMPACT OF ACTUAL BEHAVIORS WILL BE MOST USEFUL.

1.   PRIMARY PERSONALITY CHARACTERISTICS OF SIGNIFICANCE

CAPACITY FOR ABSTRACT SKILLS IS VERY HIGH.
IN INTERPERSONAL RELATIONSHIPS HE LEADS, DOMINATES, OR IS STUBBORN.
HE   IS PRACTICAL AND ALERT TO EVERYDAY REQUIREMENTS.

BROAD INFLUENCE PATTERNS

HIS PERSONALITY ORIENTATION IS NEITHER EXTRAVERTED NOR INTROVERTED.
ATTENTION IS DIRECTED ABOUT EQUALLY TOWARD THE OUTER ENVIRONMENT AND
TOWARD INNER THOUGHTS AND FEELINGS (5.5).
AT THE PRESENT TIME, HE SEES HIMSELF AS NO MORE OR LESS ANXIOUS
THAN MOST PEOPLE (4.8).
HE   TENDS TO BE RULED BY HIS INTELLECT AND TO KEEP HIS FEELINGS IN CHECK.
TASKS AND PROBLEMS ARE APPROACHED WITH EMPHASIS UPON RATIONALITY AND
GETTING THINGS DONE. LESS ATTENTION IS PAID TO EMOTIONAL RELATIONSHIPS.
THIS TENDENCY IS ABOVE AVERAGE (7.1).
HIS LIFE STYLE IS BALANCED BETWEEN NEED TO CONTROL THE ENVIRONMENT AND
WILLINGNESS TO ADAPT TO WHAT IS AVAILABLE (6.0).
AT HIS OWN ABILITY LEVEL, POTENTIAL FOR CREATIVE FUNCTIONING IS
ABOVE AVERAGE (6.8).
IN A GROUP OF PEERS, THE LIKELIHOOD THAT THIS PERSON WILL ASSUME A
LEADERSHIP ROLE IS AVERAGE (6.2).

SECTION 2

4/20/1984

NAME-JANE SMITH   AGE-30
ID NUMBER-IPAT   83   SEX-F
* * * * * * * * *   V A L I D I T Y   S C A L E S   * * * * * * * * * * *
*   *
*   VALIDITY INDICATIONS ARE WITHIN ACCEPTABLE RANGES.   *
*   FAKING GOOD/MD (STEN) SCORE IS AVERAGE (5.0).   *
*   FAKING BAD (STEN) SCORE IS AVERAGE (6.0).   *
*   *
* *

16 PF
PERSONALITY PROFILE

SCORES				LEFT MEANING	1 2 3 4 5 6 7 8 9 10	RIGHT MEANING	%
R	U	C					
8	4	4	A	COOL, RESERVED	<---	WARM, EASYGOING	23
9	7	7	B	CONCRETE THINKING	--->	ABSTRACT THINKING	77
19	7	7	C	EASILY UPSET	--->	CALM, STABLE	77
6	3	3	E	NOT ASSERTIVE	<-----	DOMINANT	11
14	6	6	F	SOBER, SERIOUS	->	ENTHUSIASTIC	60
13	6	6	G	EXPEDIENT	->	CONSCIENTIOUS	60
12	5	5	H	SHY, TIMID	<-	VENTURESOME	40
7	2	2	I	TOUGH-MINDED	<-------	SENSITIVE	4
4	4	4	L	TRUSTING	<---	SUSPICIOUS	23
12	5	5	M	PRACTICAL	<-	IMAGINATIVE	40
15	9	9	N	FORTHRIGHT	------->	SHREWD	96
15	8	8	O	SELF-ASSURED	----->	SELF-DOUBTING	89
4	3	3	Q1	CONSERVATIVE	<-----	EXPERIMENTING	11
19	10	10	Q2	GROUP-ORIENTED	-------->	SELF-SUFFICIENT	99
14	6	6	Q3	UNDISCIPLINED	->	SELF-DISCIPLINED	60
9	4	4	Q4	RELAXED	<---	TENSE, DRIVEN	23

NOTE: "R" DESIGNATES RAW SCORES, "U" DESIGNATES (UNCORRECTED) STEN SCORES,
       AND "C" DESIGNATES STEN SCORES CORRECTED FOR DISTORTION (IF APPROP-
       RIATE). THE INTERPRETATION WILL PROCEED ON THE BASIS OF CORRECTED
       SCORES.
    REPORT PROCESSED USING MALE, ADULT (GP) NORMS FOR FORM A, 67-68 EDITION.
    THE PERSONALITY PROFILE PATTERN CODE IS 2232.

JANE SMITH   PAGE-2   4/20/1984
    THE INFORMATION THAT FOLLOWS IS BASED UPON THE RESPONSES GIVEN FOR
    THE QUESTIONNAIRE ITEMS. THE REPORTED SCORE ON A GIVEN PERSONALITY
    FACTOR INDICATES THAT THE PERSON WILL USUALLY BEHAVE IN A WAY THAT
    REFLECTS THAT PERSONALITY TRAIT. IN INTERPRETING THE STATEMENTS,
    ASSESSING THE IMPACT OF ACTUAL BEHAVIORS WILL BE MOST USEFUL.
            1. PRIMARY PERSONALITY CHARACTERISTICS OF SIGNIFICANCE
CAPACITY FOR ABSTRACT SKILLS IS ABOVE AVERAGE.
IN INTERPERSONAL RELATIONSHIPS SHE TENDS TO BE MILD, HUMBLE, AND
    SUBMISSIVE.
AS A PERSON, SHE IS REALISTIC, TOUGH-MINDED, AND UNSENTIMENTAL.
IN HER DEALINGS WITH OTHERS, SHE IS SHREWD AND CALCULATING. HER MOTIVES
    FREQUENTLY TEND TO BE DISGUISED.
SHE SOMETIMES SUFFERS FROM WORRY, GUILT, AND A FEELING OF
    BEING WORTHLESS AND INADEQUATE.
SHE TENDS TO BE CONSERVATIVE AND TO DISLIKE CHANGE.
BEING SELF-SUFFICIENT, SHE PREFERS TACKLING THINGS RESOURCEFULLY, ALONE.
                    BROAD INFLUENCE PATTERNS
HER PERSONALITY ORIENTATION IS INTROVERTED. THAT IS, HER ATTENTION IS
    DIRECTED INWARD TO THOUGHTS AND FEELINGS. THIS TENDENCY IS
    HIGH (8.1).
AT THE PRESENT TIME, SHE SEES HERSELF AS NO MORE OR LESS ANXIOUS
    THAN MOST PEOPLE (5.0).
TASKS AND PROBLEMS ARE APPROACHED WITH EMPHASIS EQUALLY UPON GETTING
    THINGS DONE AND UPON EMOTIONAL RELATIONSHIPS (5.2).
HER LIFE STYLE IS SUBDUED AND ACCEPTING OF THE GIVEN ENVIRONMENT AND SHE
    ADAPTS TO CIRCUMSTANCES. THIS TENDENCY IS HIGH (8.1).
AT HER OWN ABILITY LEVEL, POTENTIAL FOR CREATIVE FUNCTIONING IS
    AVERAGE (5.1).
IN A GROUP OF PEERS, THE LIKELIHOOD THAT THIS PERSON WILL ASSUME A
    LEADERSHIP ROLE IS AVERAGE (6.2).

psychware **367**

REPORT PROCESSED USING FEMALE, ADULT (GP) NORMS FOR FORM A, 67-68 EDITION.
THE PERSONALITY PROFILE PATTERN CODE IS 1221.

                                    SECTION 3.
                          COMBINED 16PF PERSONALITY PROFILE
        SCORE   TRAIT   LEFT MEANING   RIGHT MEANING
      HIS HER   1 2 3 4 5 6 7 8 9 10
        4   4   A   COOL, RESERVED   B   WARM, EASYGOING
        9   7   B   CONCRETE THINKING   F---M   ABSTRACT THINKING
        7   7   C   EASILY UPSET   B   CALM, STABLE
        8   3   E   NOT ASSERTIVE   F---------M   DOMINANT
        5   6   F   SOBER, SERIOUS   M-F   ENTHUSIASTIC
        4   6   G   EXPEDIENT   M---F   CONSCIENTIOUS
        5   5   H   SHY, TIMID   B   VENTURESOME
        5   2   I   TOUGH-MINDED   F-----M   SENSITIVE
        5   4   L   TRUSTING   F-M   SUSPICIOUS
        2   5   M   PRACTICAL   M-----F   IMAGINATIVE
        6   9   N   FORTHRIGHT   M-----F   SHREWD
        5   8   O   SELF-ASSURED   M-----F   SELF-DOUBTING
        6   3   Q1   CONSERVATIVE   F-----M   EXPERIMENTING
        5   10   Q2   GROUP-ORIENTED   M---------F   SELF-SUFFICIENT
        5   6   Q3   UNDISCIPLINED   M-F   SELF-DISCIPLINED
        5   4   Q4   RELAXED   F-M   TENSE, DRIVEN
                                    SECOND ORDER SCORES
      5.5 2.9   EX   INTROVERTED   F---M   EXTRAVERTED
      4.8 5.0   AX   COMPOSED   B   TENSE
      7.1 5.2   TP   EMOTION-ORIENTED   F---M   REASON-ORIENTED
      6.0 2.9   IN   ADAPTING STYLE   F-----M   INDEPENDENT STYLE

THE DEGREE OF PERSONALITY SIMILARITY BETWEEN THESE TWO INDIVIDUALS MAY
   BE CONSIDERED AVERAGE (6.0).

                    SUMMARY OF SALIENT PERSONALITY CHARACTERISTICS
                   HE IS   SHE IS
                   -----   ------
ABSTRACT THINKING
ASSERTIVE/COMPETITIVE/DOMINANT <-NOTE-> CONSIDERATE/SUBMISSIVE/HUMBLE
          ----------   TOUGH MINDED/UNSENTIMENTAL
CONVENTIONAL/PRACTICAL   ----------
          ----------   SHREWD/POLISHED/CALCULATING
          ----------   APPREHENSIVE/SELF-DOUBTING
          ----------   CONSERVATIVE/TRADITIONAL
          ----------   *-NOTE-* SELF-SUFFICIENT
                        SECOND-ORDER SCORES
          ----------   INTROVERTED
          ----------   ACCOMMODATING STYLE

   NOTE: -------- SHOWS THAT THE PERSON'S SCORE IS ABOUT AVERAGE.
          <-NOTE-> SHOWS THAT THE TWO ARE AT OPPOSITE ENDS OF THE TRAIT.
          -NOTE- SHOWS THAT THE TWO ARE VERY DIFFERENT, BUT NOT OPPOSITE,
                   ON THE TRAIT.

4. POTENTIAL FOR MARRIAGE ADJUSTMENT

THE MARITAL ADJUSTMENT PREDICTION IS BASED UPON RESEARCH
IDENTIFYING PERSONALITY TRAITS RELATED TO MARITAL ADJUSTMENT.
EACH PERSON WAS COMPARED TO OTHER INDIVIDUALS OF THE SAME SEX.
SINCE THE COMPARISON IS TO PERSONS INVOLVED IN TRADITIONAL
SEX-ROLE MARRIAGES IT WOULD BE GOOD TO EXPLORE THIS PARTICULAR
COUPLE'S ROLE ADOPTIONS.   THIS IS ESPECIALLY TRUE IF EITHER
OBTAINS A LOW MARITAL ADJUSTMENT PREDICTION.

COMPARING HIS PROFILE TO OTHER INDIVIDUALS OF HIS OWN SEX, THE OUTLOOK
FOR SUCCESSFUL MARITAL ADJUSTMENT APPEARS TO BE BELOW AVERAGE (4.4).
HIS PERSONALITY TRAITS THAT ARE RELATED TO THIS PREDICTION ARE:

HIS DOMINANCE LEVEL IS HIGHER THAN HAS BEEN SHOWN TO BE DESIRABLE
IN MANY RELATIONSHIPS.   SHE IS MUCH DIFFERENT FROM HIM IN THIS
RESPECT.   IT COULD HAVE A DAMAGING EFFECT ON HER SELF-ESTEEM UNLESS
SHE PREFERS OR HAS ADAPTED TO A NON-ASSERTIVE ROLE.

COMPARING HER PROFILE TO OTHER INDIVIDUALS OF HER OWN SEX, THE OUTLOOK
FOR SUCCESSFUL MARITAL ADJUSTMENT APPEARS TO BE HIGH (8.1).
HER PERSONALITY TRAITS THAT ARE RELATED TO THIS PREDICTION ARE:

HER GREAT TENDENCY TO WORRY ABOUT TRIVIAL MATTERS AND HER LACK
OF SELF-ASSURANCE MIGHT WELL PLACE TEDIOUS AND UNREALISTIC
DEMANDS ON HIM.

5. MARRIAGE COUNSELING DATA

THE FOLLOWING SECTION CAPSULIZES INFORMATION ESPECIALLY RELEVANT
TO COUNSELING CONCERNS:

SHE DESCRIBES HERSELF AS SHREWD AND CALCULATING.   BECAUSE SHE TENDS
TO BE INDIRECT AND MANIPULATIVE, HER MOTIVES FOR GOING INTO
COUNSELING MAY BE HIDDEN.

BOTH HAVE AN ABOVE AVERAGE ABILITY TO DEAL WITH ABSTRACT CONCEPTS.
THEY BOTH ARE LIKELY TO EXPRESS THEMSELVES WELL VERBALLY.   THIS
SHOULD ENHANCE THE THERAPY.

BOTH INDIVIDUALS POSSESS AN ABOVE AVERAGE DEGREE OF EGO STRENGTH.
THAT IS, BOTH ARE EMOTIONALLY MATURE AND ABLE TO DEAL WITH
PROBLEMS.   THIS DEGREE OF STABILITY HAS GOOD IMPLICATIONS FOR
THERAPY.

THEY BOTH TEND TO BALANCE EMOTIONAL CONCERNS WITH FACTUAL ONES.
THUS, BOTH SHOULD BE ABLE TO RECOGNIZE THE IMPACT OF THEIR
ACTIONS UPON THEIR PARTNER'S FEELINGS.   ALSO, BOTH WILL
PROBABLY BE ABLE TO ACT UPON THEIR OWN FEELINGS.

NAME: McDermott Multidimensional Assessment of Children

SUPPLIER: Psychological Corporation
7500 Old Oak Blvd.
Cleveland, OH 44130
(216) 234-5300

PRODUCT CATEGORY	PRIMARY APPLICATIONS
Career/Vocational	Clinical Assessment/Diagnosis
	Educational Evaluation/Planning

SALE RESTRICTIONS American Psychological Association Guidelines

SERVICE TYPE/COST	Type	Available	Cost	Discount
	Mail-In	No		
	Teleprocessing	No		
	Local	Yes	NA	

PRODUCT DESCRIPTION

MCDERMOTT MULTIDIMENSIONAL ASSESSMENT OF CHILDREN is a comprehensive system of over 100 integrated computer programs for psychologists, educational diagnosticians, teachers, and administrators. It is the most comprehensive computer system for analyzing and interpreting psychological and educational evaluations of children 2 to 18 years of age. The system uses test results, behavioral data, and demographic variables to produce objective classifications of childhood normality and exceptionality. It can also assist in the development of Individual Educational Programs based on achievement test and behavioral data in fundamental skill areas.

The program has two levels of operation. Within the Classification level, it uses information from one or more of 22 highly-regarded scales to provide reliable and defensible differential diagnosis of mental retardation or giftedness, learning disabilities, including such things as developmental reading and math disorders, and problems in communication and perceptual motor functioning. It also interprets data regarding attention deficit, anxiety-withdrawal, and conduct disorders. Following input of classification data, the program prepares a 6-18 page report that provides integrated interpretation of test data and systematic classification decisions consistent with AAMD and PL 94-142 guidelines.

Within the Program Design level, the program uses criterion-referenced information to specify important behavioral objectives for IEP planning and/or clinical remediation in the areas of reading, mathematics, general learning style, and adaptive functioning. For each of these areas, the program provides sets of behavioral objectives based on demonstrated skills. Information from any of nine criterion-referenced instruments can be used in designing IEPs.

NAME: Medical History Survey

SUPPLIER: PSYCH Systems, Inc.
600 Reisterstown Road
Baltimore, MD 21208
(800) 368-3366

PRODUCT CATEGORY	PRIMARY APPLICATIONS
Structured Interview	Behavioral Medicine Clinical Assessment/Diagnosis Personal/Marriage/Family Counseling

SALE RESTRICTIONS Qualified Professional

SERVICE TYPE/COST	Type	Available	Cost	Discount
	Mail-In	No		
	Teleprocessing	No		
	Local	Yes	See Below	

PRODUCT DESCRIPTION

The MEDICAL HISTORY SURVEY is designed to obtain a detailed medical history directly from the patient, print a summary of the patient's response for use by the physician, and store the responses for future reference. The computer communicates with the patient with instructions that are geared to anyone with an elementary school education. A branching strategy is used to select questions for presentation to the patient. Average length of time for completion is about 45 minutes.

Psych Systems programs operate on the IBM PC-XT, COMPAQ Plus, Dec Professional 350, and most DEC PDP-11 systems. Various hardware/ software configurations are available directly from Psych Systems, with single-user systems starting at approximately $12,000. A per test fee also applies.

222-22-2222 Jonathan Doe   32 yr old white male   16-Feb-84


```
----------------------------------------
|          |                            |
|   MHS    |   Medical History Survey   |
|          |                            |
----------------------------------------
```


Patient: Jonathan Doe   (male, age 32)

This report is designed to assist in medical evaluation. It is
available only to qualified professionals. This report was produced
by a computerized analysis of the data given by the patient listed
above. This report is designed to be used in conjunction with
professional evaluation. No decision should be based solely upon
the contents of this report.

The computer program generating this report was designed by Psych
Systems, Inc., Baltimore, Maryland 21208. Copyright (C) 1984 by
Psych Systems, Inc. The techniques utilized in the analysis of the
information and in the generation of the report were designed by
Warner Slack, M.D. and Richard Pope, M.D. of Harvard Medical School
and Beth Israel Hospital. The Medical History Survey is reproduced
by permission under license from Beth Israel Hospital, Boston,
Massachusetts 02215. All rights reserved.

I. REASON FOR APPOINTMENT

-- Help with a medical problem --
Most important problem: 'Lack of appetite'; Present for weeks

Last check-up was 1-2 years ago.

Appointment was made by the patient.

II. PROBLEM LIST   (See Review Of Systems For Details)

Most Important:

Important:

cold intolerance

sore throat
skin rash
poor appetite
slightly overweight

Not Important:

tremulousness
hematuria (bloody urine)
productive cough (cough producing sputum)
hemoptysis (coughed up blood)
problems with teeth or gums

III. PATIENT REQUESTS

Help with stopping smoking

IV. MEDICAL HISTORY

A. GENERAL HEALTH: NOT GOOD

B. CURRENT MEDICATIONS:
eyedrops
  'Digel'
medication for sleep

Hx neg for drug allergies

C. DIAGNOSTIC TESTS AND PROCEDURES:

TB Skin Test: negative
Chest X-ray (within the past year): results unknown
Barium Enema (twice, the most recent within the past month): results
unknown
Sigmoidoscopy (once, within the past month): results unknown
Cystoscopy (over a year ago)

D. HOSPITALIZATIONS AND OPERATIONS:

1983,   'Undiagnosed problems involving headaches'
  '1983,pneumonia'

  '1982,pneumonia'

E. INJURIES: NONE

F. REVIEW OF SYSTEMS
CONSTITUTIONAL
Hx neg for feverish feelings
Ideal Weight: 170; presently slightly overweight
LYMPH NODES
Hx negative for cervical, axillary and inguinal adenopathies.
ALLERGY

Hx NEG for asthma and hay fever

psychware **373**

IV. MEDICAL HISTORY

F. REVIEW OF SYSTEMS   (continued)

DERMATOLOGY
Rash (appeared over a month ago, getting worse, pruretic)
Nevus Undergoing Changes (noticed within the past year)
Sore (that does not heal)
Hx NEG for eczema and psoriasis.

EYES, EARS, NOSE AND THROAT
Dental Care: (problems with teeth or gums) dentist seen for this problem
Blurred Vision With Glasses
Glaucoma (diagnosed by a physician) uses eyedrops daily
Sore Throat (began in the past month, staying about the same)
Hx NEG for hoarseness.
UNCERTAINTY regarding hearing difficulty.

RESPIRATORY
Cough (for 1 - 2 months, staying about the same, productive) hemoptysis
indicated
Pneumonia (diagnosed within the past year)
Tuberculosis Skin Test (negative)
Chest X-ray (most recent within the past year, results unknown)
Hx NEG for TB.

CARDIOVASCULAR
History of Rheumatic Fever (twice, first occurrence at age 16; never told
of a murmur)
Hx NEG for chest pain, ankle edema, hypertension, EKG, tachycardia and
palpitations.

GASTROENTEROLOGY
Heartburn; treated with unknown medication:
Hemorrhoids (previously diagnosed)
Barium Enema (twice, the most recent within the past month):   results
unknown
Sigmoidoscopy (once, within the past month):   results unknown
Hx NEG for poor appetite, recent nausea, recent vomiting, recent
abdominal pain, black stools, ulcers, recent diarrhea, frequent
use of laxatives, blood in stools, rectal pain, jaundice and hepatitis.
UNCERTAINTY regarding weight loss.

GENITO-URINARY
Frequency: for 6 weeks; no change since onset;
Urgency: for 6 days; staying about the same
Cystoscopy (more than a year ago)
Hematuria
Hx NEG for dysuria, urinary tract infections, renal calculi,
IVP's, catheterization, proteinuria, hospitalization for renal
problems, testicular lump or swelling and discharge from penis.

NEUROLOGIC
Headaches: (migraine diagnosed) bilateral; several times a week; staying
about the same; described as intolerable, sharp, heavy, splitting, aching,
pounding, shooting; lasting several days; interferes with usual activities;
preceded by vision and mood changes; treated with; some relief from medication;
Hx NEG for vertigo, focal weakness, seizure and loss of consciousness
for no apparent reason.

374 *psychware*

HEMATOLOGY
Hx NEG for anemia, sickle cell test and bleeding disorder.

ENDOCRINE/METABOLIC
Recent Tremulousness
Cold Intolerance
Hx NEG for diabetes, diagnosed thyroid problem, heat intolerance and
sweats.

RHEUMATOLOGY
Hx NEG for joint pain and neck or back pain

V.   PERSONAL HABITS

SMOKING: Smokes less than a pack of cigarettes a day; does not inhale;
has been smoking for 12 years; is interested in stopping
COFFEE: drinks 1-2 cups a day
ALCOHOL: drinks beer or ale; several times a week (usually 3 or
4 drinks each time) has not tried to cut down;

EXERCISE: None Reported
DIETARY PREFERENCES: does not usually eat breakfast, lunch or dinner;
does not eat fruit, vegetables, fish or other seafood, chicken or poultry,
beef, pork or other meat, eggs, milk, cheese or other dairy products,
candy, pastries or other sweet food, unspecified food

VI.   FAMILY HISTORY

POSITIVE for hypertension and cancer .
Hx NEG for heart disease and a hereditary illness.
UNCERTAINTY regarding diabetes and heart attacks before age 45.

VII.   PREVENTIVE HEALTH REMINDERS

NOTE: Smokes cigarettes
May not eat 3 regular meals
May not get regular exercise
May use medication for sleep

VIII.   CLINICIAN'S COMMENTS

NAME: Millon Adolescent Personality Inventory: Clinical Report

SUPPLIER: NCS/Professional Assessment Services
P.O. Box 1416
Minneapolis, MN 55440
(800) 328-6759

PRODUCT CATEGORY

Personality

PRIMARY APPLICATIONS

Clinical Assessment/Diagnosis
Personal/Marriage/Family Counseling

SALE RESTRICTIONS American Psychological Association Guidelines

SERVICE TYPE/COST

Type	Available	Cost	Discount
Mail-In	Yes	$16.50	Yes
Teleprocessing	Yes	$16.50	Yes
Local	Yes	$11.30	Yes

PRODUCT DESCRIPTION

The MILLON ADOLESCENT PERSONALITY INVENTORY: CLINICAL REPORT presents a detailed narrative interpretation that aids in the identification of adolescent problems arising from emotional difficulties and behavioral disorders. The 4-5 page report includes a plotted score profile.

The test itself is comprised of 150 true-false items that take 20-30 minutes and a 6th-grade reading level to complete. Eight Personality Style scales (e.g., Forceful, Sensitive), six Expressed Concerns scales (e.g., Peer Security), four Behavioral Correlates scales (e.g., Impulse Control), and two reliability and validity indicators are included in the report.

Two systems are available for local processing of test results. MICRO-TEST Assessment Software from National Computer Systems, used with a Sentry 3000 tabletop scanner (purchase price approximately $4000) and microcomputer system ($2000-$3000 purchase price), allows tests to be administered off-line. Answer sheets are then scanned and scored automatically, one at a time or in a batch. The software also permits on-line administration of the test via microcomputer. In either case, the same report is provided. The cost for local scoring refers to the cost-per-test when diskettes are purchased in units of 20 administrations (minimum purchase).

MILLON ADOLESCENT PERSONALITY INVENTORY
CLINICAL REPORT
CONFIDENTIAL INFORMATION FOR PROFESSIONAL USE ONLY

REPORT FOR: 0123456789   SEX: MALE   AGE: 13

ID NUMBER: UNIT G   QUESTIONABLE RELIABILITY DATE: 23-FEB-84

CODE:

8 2 **- * - + 3 6 " 1 4 5 7 //A H B E G **D C F * - + - " - //WWSSUUTT**- *
                             ------   ----
//

```
********************************************************************************
SCALES   * SCORE *       PROFILE OF BR SCORES       *
         *RAW  BR*    35  60       75        85      100 DIMENSIONS
*********+**+***+***+--------+---+--------+---------+--------+*******************
     1    9   15 XXX                                         INTROVERSIVE
   +--+--+--+---+---+--------+---+--------+---------+--------+-----------------
     2   28  109 XXXXXXXXXXXXXXXXXXXXXXXXXXXXXXXXXXXXXXXXXXX INHIBITED
   +--+--+--+---+---+--------+---+--------+---------+--------+-----------------
     3   18   50 XXXXXXXXX                                   COOPERATIVE
   +--+--+--+---+---+--------+---+--------+---------+--------+-----------------
PERSNLTY 4 10 13 XXX                                         SOCIABLE
   +--+--+--+---+---+--------+---+--------+---------+--------+-----------------
STYLES  5  9    3 X                                          CONFIDENT
   +--+--+--+---+---+--------+---+--------+---------+--------+-----------------
     6   13   35 XXXXXX                                      FORCEFUL
   +--+--+--+---+---+--------+---+--------+---------+--------+-----------------
     7    6    1 X                                           RESPECTFUL
   +--+--+--+---+---+--------+---+--------+---------+--------+-----------------
     8   33  111 XXXXXXXXXXXXXXXXXXXXXXXXXXXXXXXXXXXXXXXXXXX SENSITIVE
*********+**+***+***+--------+---+--------+---------+--------+*******************
     A   30  112 XXXXXXXXXXXXXXXXXXXXXXXXXXXXXXXXXXXXXXXXXXX SELF-CONCEPT
   +--+--+--+---+---+--------+---+--------+---------+--------+-----------------
     B   27   99 XXXXXXXXXXXXXXXXXXXXXXXXXXXXXXXXXXXXXXXXXX  PERSONAL ESTEEM
   +--+--+--+---+---+--------+---+--------+---------+--------+-----------------
     C   14   75 XXXXXXXXXXXXXXXXXXXXXX                      BODY COMFORT
   +--+--+--+---+---+--------+---+--------+---------+--------+-----------------
EXPRESSD D 16 76 XXXXXXXXXXXXXXXXXXXXXX                      SEXUAL ACCEPTNCE
   +--+--+--+---+---+--------+---+--------+---------+--------+-----------------
CONCERNS E 17 97 XXXXXXXXXXXXXXXXXXXXXXXXXXXXXXXXXXXXXXXX    PEER SECURITY
   +--+--+--+---+---+--------+---+--------+---------+--------+-----------------
     F   12   75 XXXXXXXXXXXXXXXXXXXXXX                      SOCIAL TOLERANCE
   +--+--+--+---+---+--------+---+--------+---------+--------+-----------------
     G   16   95 XXXXXXXXXXXXXXXXXXXXXXXXXXXXXXXXXXXXXXX     FAMILY RAPPORT
   +--+--+--+---+---+--------+---+--------+---------+--------+-----------------
     H   21  101 XXXXXXXXXXXXXXXXXXXXXXXXXXXXXXXXXXXXXXXXXXX ACADEMIC CONFDNCE
*********+**+***+***+--------+---+--------+---------+--------+*******************
    SS   23   99 XXXXXXXXXXXXXXXXXXXXXXXXXXXXXXXXXXXXXXXXXX  IMPULSE CONTROL
BEHAVIOR TT 23 85 XXXXXXXXXXXXXXXXXXXXXXXXXXXXXXXX           SOCIAL CONFORMITY
   +--+--+--+---+---+--------+---+--------+---------+--------+-----------------
CORRE-  UU  28 98 XXXXXXXXXXXXXXXXXXXXXXXXXXXXXXXXXXXXXXXX   SCHOLAST ACHVMNT
   +--+--+--+---+---+--------+---+--------+---------+--------+-----------------
LATES   WW  28 101 XXXXXXXXXXXXXXXXXXXXXXXXXXXXXXXXXXXXXXXXXX ATTNDNCE CNSTNCY
*********+**+***+***+--------+---+--------+---------+--------+*******************
```

MAPI CLINICAL REPORT NARRATIVES HAVE BEEN NORMED ON ADOLESCENT
PATIENTS SEEN IN PROFESSIONAL TREATMENT SETTINGS FOR EITHER GENUINE
EMOTIONAL DISCOMFORTS OR SOCIAL DIFFICULTIES AND ARE APPLICABLE
PRIMARILY DURING THE EARLY PHASES OF ASSESSMENT OR PSYCHOTHERAPY.
DISTORTIONS SUCH AS GREATER SEVERITY MAY OCCUR AMONG RESPONDENTS WHO
HAVE INAPPROPRIATELY TAKEN THE MAPI FOR ESSENTIALLY EDUCATIONAL OR
SELF-EXPLORATORY PURPOSES; IN AN ACADEMIC COUNSELING SETTING, THE
MAPI GUIDANCE REPORT IS LIKELY TO BE MORE RELEVANT AND PROVIDE A MORE
SUITABLE PICTURE OF THE PSYCHOLOGICAL AND VOCATIONAL TRAITS OF THIS
TEENAGER. INFERENTIAL AND PROBABILISTIC, THIS REPORT MUST BE VIEWED AS
ONLY ONE ASPECT OF A THOROUGH DIAGNOSTIC STUDY. MOREOVER, THESE
INFERENCES SHOULD BE REEVALUATED PERIODICALLY IN LIGHT OF THE PATTERN
OF ATTITUDE CHANGE AND EMOTIONAL GROWTH THAT TYPIFIES THE ADOLESCENT
PERIOD. FOR THESE REASONS, IT SHOULD NOT BE SHOWN TO PATIENTS OR THEIR
RELATIVES.

THE RESPONSES OF THIS ADOLESCENT TO THE MAPI ITEMS INDICATE A
TENDENCY TO BE UNUSUALLY SELF-DEPRECIATING, EXCESSIVELY COMPLAINING, OR
EXTREMELY VULNERABLE AND FEELING DEFENSELESS. THIS MAY SIGNIFY AN
ANXIOUS PLEA FOR HELP AS A CONSEQUENCE OF AN INABILITY TO COPE WITH
CURRENT LIFE STRESSES. THOUGHTFUL, PROFESSIONAL JUDGMENT IS WARRANTED.

PERSONALITY PATTERNS

THE FOLLOWING PERTAINS TO THOSE ENDURING AND PERVASIVE CHARACTERO-
LOGICAL TRAITS THAT UNDERLIE THE PERSONAL AND INTERPERSONAL DIFFICULTIES
OF THIS YOUNGSTER. RATHER THAN FOCUS ON SPECIFIC PROBLEM AREAS AND
COMPLAINTS, TO BE DISCUSSED IN LATER PARAGRAPHS, THIS SECTION CONCENTRATES
ON THE MORE HABITUAL, MALADAPTIVE METHODS OF RELATING, BEHAVING, THINKING
AND FEELING.

THE BEHAVIOR OF THIS YOUNGSTER IS TYPIFIED BY HIS EMOTIONALITY, HIS
SHAKY SELF-CONCEPT, FEELINGS OF HOPELESSNESS AND THE PRESENCE OF MULTIPLE
SO-CALLED NEUROTIC SYMPTOMS. THERE IS A HIGH DEGREE OF LABILITY, PERIODS
OF IMPULSIVE ACTING-OUT, DEPRESSIVE COMPLAINTS, EXCESSIVE FANTASY AND SULKING
BEHAVIORS. NOTABLE IS HIS HYPERSENSITIVITY TO CRITICISM, LOW FRUSTRATION
TOLERANCE, RESTLESSNESS, PERIODIC SELF-ACCUSATIONS AND GUILT. UNMODERATED
EMOTIONS SURGE READILY TO THE SURFACE, CHARACTERIZING HIS BEHAVIOR AS DIS-
TRACTIBLE AND ERRATIC.
THE MOODS OF THIS YOUNGSTER TEND TO BE VARIABLE, WITH PERIODS OF HIGH
EXCITEMENT ALTERNATING WITH LETHARGY, FATIGUE, OVERSLEEPING, AND THE POSSIBLE
OVERUSE OF DRUGS OR ALCOHOL. HIS FEELINGS MAY SWING FROM QUIET WORRYING TO
EXCITED DESPERATION, AND TEND TO BE EXPRESSED MORE INTENSELY THAN JUSTIFIED
BY THE SITUATION. IN A SELF-FULFILLING PROPHECY, HE OFTEN ANTICIPATES WRANGLES
WITH FAMILY MEMBERS AND WILL ACT IN A MANNER THAT PROMOTES THEIR OCCURRENCE.
IF CUT OFF FROM NEEDED SUPPORT AND NURTURANCE, HE WILL BECOME EITHER TESTY
AND CONTENTIOUS OR DEJECTED AND FORLORN.
THIS YOUNG MAN FEELS MISUNDERSTOOD AND IS DISAPPOINTED WITH BOTH WHO HE IS
AND WITH HIS MATURATION AND LOOKS. HE IS OFTEN CRITICAL AND ENVIOUS OF THE
GOOD FORTUNES OF OTHERS, GRUDGES THEIR GOOD LUCK, AND REACTS IRRITABLY TO
ANY SLIGHT THAT OTHERS COMMUNICATE. HE MAY EXHIBIT UNUSUAL PREOCCUPATIONS
WITH BODILY FUNCTIONS AND HEALTH, OVERREACT TO ILLNESS, AND MAKE UNREASONABLE
COMPLAINTS ABOUT THE INJUSTICES IN HIS LIFE. COMPLAINTS AND PHYSICAL SYMPTOMS
MAY BE DISPLAYED PROMINENTLY SO AS TO GAIN THE ATTENTION AND SUPPORT HE FEELS
HE CANNOT OTHERWISE ELICIT. PARTICULARLY PAINFUL ARE THE DIFFICULTIES HE FEELS
WITHIN HIS FAMILY RELATIONSHIPS AND THE LACK OF ACCEPTANCE HE SENSES FROM HIS
PEERS.

EXPRESSED CONCERNS

THE SCALES COMPRISING THIS SECTION PERTAIN TO THE PERSONAL PERCEPTIONS
OF THIS YOUNGSTER CONCERNING SEVERAL ISSUES OF PSYCHOLOGICAL DEVELOPMENT,
ACTUALIZATION AND CONCERN. BECAUSE EXPERIENCES DURING THIS AGE PERIOD
ARE NOTABLY SUBJECTIVE, IT IS IMPORTANT TO RECORD HOW THIS TEENAGER SEES
EVENTS AND REPORTS FEELINGS, AND NOT ONLY HOW OTHERS MAY OBJECTIVELY
REPORT THEM TO BE. FOR COMPARATIVE PURPOSES, THESE SELF-ATTITUDES REGARDING
A WIDE RANGE OF PERSONAL, SOCIAL, FAMILIAL AND SCHOLASTIC MATTERS ARE
CONTRASTED WITH THOSE EXPRESSED BY A BROAD CROSS-SECTION OF TEENAGERS
OF THE SAME SEX AND AGE.

THIS YOUNGSTER EXPRESSES CONSIDERABLE CONCERN OVER FEELING CONFUSED
IF NOT LOST IN LIFE. HE DOES NOT HAVE A CLEAR SENSE OF HIS IDENTITY AND
SEEMS NOTABLY UNFOCUSED AS TO HIS FUTURE GOALS AND VALUES. HE IS TROUBLED
BY HIS INABILITY TO WORK TOWARD A CLEARER SENSE OF SELF AND A MEANS
OF FINDING A DIRECTION FOR HIS FUTURE.

378 *psychware*

THIS TROUBLED YOUNGSTER REPORTS EXPERIENCING GLOBAL DISSATISFACTION. HE FEELS NOT ONLY CONSIDERABLE DISTRESS WHEN VIEWING HIMSELF, BUT FINDS MINIMAL ACCEPTANCE FROM OTHERS AS WELL. FALLING FAR SHORT OF WHAT HE ASPIRES TO BE, HIS LOW PERSONAL ESTEEM AND LACK OF FULFILLMENT INTRUDES PAINFULLY INTO ALL ASPECTS OF FUNCTIONING.

THIS YOUNGSTER REPORTS DISSAPPOINTMENT WITH REGARD TO HIS PHYSICAL MATURATION AND APPEARANCE. ALTHOUGH A COMMON CONCERN, HE EXPRESSES A GREATER THAN AVERAGE DEGREE OF DISCONTENT WHICH, IN TURN, MAY LEAD TO BOTH REAL AND PERCEIVED DIFFICULTIES ASSOCIATED WITH PEER GROUP ACCEPTANCE.

THIS YOUNGSTER APPEARS MORE DISTRESSED CONCERNING SEXUALITY THAN IS TYPICAL, REPORTING PERIODIC FEELINGS OF CONFUSION OR UNHAPPINESS WITH HIS IMPULSES OR THE ROLES THEY MAY REQUIRE OF HIM.

PEER RELATIONSHIPS ARE A MAJOR ELEMENT IN THE TROUBLES OF THIS YOUNGSTER. HE SADLY REPORTS STRONG FEELINGS OF PEER REJECTION AND SEES HIMSELF AS UNSUCCESSFUL IN OBTAINING THEIR APPROVAL. ALTHOUGH REJECTION SEEMS PROBABLE AGAIN, HE LONGS FOR PEER ACCEPTANCE AND MAY CONTINUE TO STRIVE DESPITE REPEATED REBUFF.

THIS YOUNGSTER TAKES A TOUGH STANCE IN RELATION TO THE WEAKNESSES OF OTHERS. HAVING LITTLE SYMPATHY FOR THEM OR THEIR PROBLEMS, HE APPEARS COOLY INDIFFERENT TO THEIR WELFARE. JUDGING SUCH PERSONS AS LACKING, HE DEMONSTRATES LITTLE WILLINGNESS TO BE OF HELP.

THE NORMAL TURBULENCE OF FAMILY RELATIONSHIPS IN EARLY ADOLESCENCE IS GREATLY MAGNIFIED IN THE CASE OF THIS YOUTH. HE FINDS HIS FAMILY BOTH A SOURCE AND A FOCUS OF TENSION AND CONFLICT. FEW ELEMENTS OF RECIPROCAL SUPPORT ARE REPORTED AND THERE IS A GENERAL FEELING OF ESTRANGEMENT AND LACK OF UNDERSTANDING. CONFLICTS WITHIN THE HOME APPEAR TO TAKE UP MUCH OF THE EMOTIONAL ENERGY OF THIS YOUNGSTER AND ARE LIKELY TO BE A CENTRAL FOCUS OF HIS EXPRESSED DIFFICULTIES.

THIS YOUNGSTER REPORTS SERIOUS CONCERNS ABOUT SCHOLASTIC PERFORMANCE, SEEING HIS ACTUAL PERFORMANCE AS FALLING FAR BELOW ACCEPTABLE LEVELS. LITTLE SATISFACTION APPEARS TO BE GAINED IN EITHER ACADEMIC OR EXTRA-CURRICULAR ACTIVITIES. SOMEWHAT DEMORALIZED AND DISMAYED, HE MAY ALREADY BE ENTRENCHED IN BOTH THE BELIEFS AND HABIT SYSTEMS THAT WILL MAKE FUTURE ACADEMIC SUCCESS DIFFICULT.

BEHAVIORAL CORRELATES

THE SCALES COMPRISING THIS SECTION FOCUS ON PROBLEMS THAT FREQUENTLY COME TO THE ATTENTION OF SCHOOL COUNSELORS, FAMILY AND OTHER AGENCIES, AS WELL AS THERAPEUTIC CLINICIANS. IT SHOULD BE NOTED THAT THESE SCALES DO NOT PROVIDE DIRECT EVIDENCE THAT THE YOUNGSTER HAS OR IS LIKELY TO EXHIBIT THE DIFFICULTIES REFERRED TO. RATHER, THEY GAUGE THE EXTENT TO WHICH THE RESPONSES OF THIS TEENAGER ARE SIMILAR TO THOSE WHO HAVE BEEN IDENTIFIED BY COUNSELORS AND CLINICIANS AS EVIDENCING TROUBLESOME BEHAVIORS SUCH AS IMPULSIVITY, SOCIAL NONCOMPLIANCE, UNDERACHIEVEMENT AND NONATTENDANCE.

QUICKLY REACTIVE, THIS YOUNG TEEN ANSWERED THE MAPI IN A MANNER THAT STRONGLY INDICATES THAT HE RESPONDS IMPULSIVELY AND SOMEWHAT THOUGHTLESSLY TO EVENTS IN HIS LIFE. THIS MAY BE FOLLOWED WITH VOICED REGRETS. HOWEVER, A PATTERN SUCH AS THIS MAY LEAD TO EVER-WORSENING RELATIONSHIPS WITH BOTH FAMILY AND SOCIAL AUTHORITIES.

YOUNGSTERS WHO HAVE COMPLETED THE MAPI IN THE SAME MANNER AS THIS TEEN ARE OFTEN FOUND TO BE DIFFICULT AND UNMANAGEABLE IN BOTH SCHOOL AND OTHER SOCIAL SETTINGS. ANGRILY RESPONDING TO THE IMPOSITION OF RESTRAINTS AND REGULATIONS, HE MAY HAVE PERIODIC PROBLEMS WITH LAW ENFORCEMENT AGENCIES.

MARKED SCHOLASTIC UNDERACHIEVEMENT CAN BE NOTED IN THE RESPONSES OF THIS YOUNGSTER. OFTEN THE PATTERN DEMONSTRATED SHOWS A HISTORY OF REPEATED FAILURES THAT BUILD TO SUCH A LEVEL WHERE THE YOUTH DISENGAGES AND DROPS OUT OF SCHOOL. STEPS ARE NECESSARY TO AVOID A SPIRAL OF LATER VOCATIONAL DIFFICULTIES.

THE MAPI STRONGLY SUGGESTS A POOR ATTENDANCE RECORD ON THE PART OF THIS STUDENT, PERHAPS OWING TO TRUANCY OR OTHER PSYCHOSOCIAL PROBLEMS. REPEATED ABSENCES MAY LEAD TO SERIOUS SCHOLASTIC AND VOCATIONAL DIFFICULTIES IN THE FUTURE.

NOTEWORTHY RESPONSES

THE FOLLOWING STATEMENTS WERE ANSWERED BY THIS YOUNGSTER IN THE DIRECTION NOTED IN THE PARENTHESES. THESE ITEMS SUGGEST SPECIFIC PROBLEM AREAS THAT MAY DESERVE FURTHER INQUIRY ON THE PART OF THE CLINICIAN.

SOCIAL ALIENATION:

37.   MY SOCIAL LIFE IS VERY SATISFYING TO ME.   (F)
44.   I HAVE ALMOST NO CLOSE TIES WITH OTHERS MY AGE.   (T)
59.   I OFTEN DOUBT WHETHER PEOPLE ARE REALLY INTERESTED IN WHAT I AM SAYING TO THEM.   (T)
62.   I SEEM TO HAVE A PROBLEM GETTING ALONG WITH OTHER TEENAGERS.   (T)
72.   IT IS NOT UNUSUAL TO FEEL LONELY AND UNWANTED.   (T)
83.   LOTS OF KIDS SEEM TO HAVE IT IN FOR ME.   (T)
88.   I VERY OFTEN THINK I AM NOT WANTED BY OTHERS IN A GROUP.   (T)
97.   I FEEL LEFT OUT OF THINGS SOCIALLY.   (T)
104. OTHERS MY AGE NEVER SEEM TO CALL ME TO GET TOGETHER WITH THEM.   (T)
143. MOST OTHER TEENAGERS DO NOT SEEM TO LIKE ME.   (T)
147. I OFTEN FEEL THAT OTHERS DO NOT WANT TO BE FRIENDLY WITH ME.   (T)

BEHAVIORAL PROBLEMS:

20.   I LIKE TO FOLLOW INSTRUCTIONS AND DO WHAT OTHERS EXPECT OF ME.   (F)
33.   IT IS EASY FOR ME TO TAKE ADVANTAGE OF PEOPLE.   (T)
76.   MY PARENTS OFTEN TELL ME I AM NO GOOD.   (T)
82.   I WOULD RATHER JUST LIE AROUND DOING NOTHING THAN WORK OR GO TO SCHOOL.   (T)
87.   PUNISHMENT NEVER STOPPED ME FROM DOING WHATEVER I WANTED.   (T)

135. I MAKE NASTY REMARKS TO PEOPLE IF THEY DESERVE IT.   (T)

EMOTIONAL DIFFICULTIES:

16.   I BECOME VERY EXCITED OR UPSET ONCE A WEEK OR MORE.   (T)
55.   I DO NOT SEEM TO KNOW WHAT I WANT OUT OF LIFE.   (T)
89.   OTHERS MY AGE SEEM TO HAVE THINGS TOGETHER BETTER THAN I DO.   (T)
91.   I OFTEN FEEL SO ANGRY I WANT TO THROW AND BREAK THINGS.   (T)
113. I AM JEALOUS OF THE SPECIAL ATTENTION THAT THE OTHER CHILDREN IN THE FAMILY GET.   (T)
133. SO LITTLE OF WHAT I HAVE DONE HAS BEEN APPRECIATED BY OTHERS.   (T)
148. IT IS VERY DIFFICULT FOR ME TO STOP FEELINGS FROM COMING OUT.   (T)
150. I CAN CONTROL MY FEELINGS EASILY.   (F)

THERAPEUTIC IMPLICATIONS

THE FOLLOWING CONSIDERATIONS ARE LIKELY TO BE OF GREATER UTILITY AND ACCURACY DURING EARLY TREATMENT PLANNING THAN IN LATER MANAGEMENT PHASES.

IT IS PROBABLE THAT THIS YOUNGSTER WILL ACTIVELY SOLICIT AND DEMAND MORE ATTENTION AND NURTURANCE THAN MAY BE CALLED FOR. SHOULD THESE MANIPULATIONS FAIL TO GAIN SPECIAL CONSIDERATIONS, THE PATIENT MAY RESPOND WITH GREAT MOODINESS AND VOICED DISAPPOINTMENT IN THE CARE SHOWN BY BOTH FAMILY AND CLINICIAN. THE FRAGILE TRUST THAT THIS YOUNGSTER FEELS IN OTHERS IS READILY SHAKEN, LEADING TO DEMANDS, FEELING SORRY FOR ONESELF, AND SO ON. THIS LONG-STANDING PATTERN IS LIKELY TO BE DISPLAYED NUMEROUS TIMES. THERE MAY BE A LONG HISTORY OF PRIOR THERAPEUTIC EXPERIENCES, ALL OF WHICH HAVE FAILED, SO TO SPEAK, TO PROVIDE THE ATTENTIONS SOUGHT. PROBLEMS OF COMPLIANCE ARE LIKELY TO ARISE WITH THIS YOUNGSTER. ALTHOUGH COOPERATIVE AT FIRST, THERE MAY BE LITTLE SUSTAINING POWER. THERE IS A HIGH PROBABILITY THAT THE PATIENT WILL BE ERRATIC IN ADHERING TO ANY RECOMMENDED BEHAVIORAL REGIMEN, DISPLAYING A FAILURE TO PERSEVERE OVER THE LONG HAUL OR SLIPPING BACK AFTER EARLY PROGRESS. FREQUENT CONTACT IS STRONGLY RECOMMENDED SINCE IT CANNOT BE ASSUMED THAT PROGRESS WILL BE MAINTAINED WITHOUT CLOSE SUPERVISION. IT IS IMPORTANT TO RESPOND TO ANGRY OUTBURSTS, PASSIVE-RESISTANT BEHAVIORS, OR THE REPEATED SEEKING OF REASSURANCE WITHOUT EXASPERATION OR THE APPLYING OF DIRECT PRESSURE FOR CHANGE. SYMPATHETIC EXPRESSIONS OF CONCERN, CONVEYED WITH AN ATTITUDE OF INTEREST AND COMPETENCE, ARE LIKELY TO COUNTERACT AND ABATE SOME OF THESE ACTIONS. ALSO, A FIRM AND AUTHORITATIVE MANNER WILL WORK BEST IN CONSTRAINING THE ERRATIC AND NEGATIVE PATTERN. A GOOD POLICY TO EMPLOY IS A DEFINITE SET OF RULES, FOLLOWED WITH FREQUENT CONTACTS THAT ARE SEEN AS GENUINE AND CARING.

PUBLISHED BY INTERPRETIVE SCORING SYSTEMS,
A DIVISION OF NATIONAL COMPUTER SYSTEMS INC.
P.O. BOX 1294, MINNEAPOLIS, MN 55440

NAME: Millon Adolescent Personality Inventory: Guidance Report

SUPPLIER: NCS/Professional Assessment Services
P.O. Box 1416
Minneapolis, MN 55440
(800) 328-6759

PRODUCT CATEGORY

Personality

PRIMARY APPLICATIONS

Personal/Marriage/Family Counseling
Vocational Guidance/Counseling

SALE RESTRICTIONS Qualified Professional

SERVICE TYPE/COST	Type	Available	Cost	Discount
	Mail-In	Yes	$10.50	Yes
	Teleprocessing	Yes	$10.50	Yes
	Local	Yes	$6.20	Yes

PRODUCT DESCRIPTION

The MILLON ADOLESCENT PERSONALITY INVENTORY: GUID-ANCE REPORT presents a detailed narrative interpretation that discusses the major features of the adolescent's personality style (e.g., self-expression and scholastic behavior) and also flags potential problem areas. The 4-5 page report includes a plotted profile. The test contains 150 true-false items that take 20-30 minutes and a 6th-grade reading level to complete. Eight Personality Style scales (e.g., Forceful, Sensitive), six Expressed Concerns scales (e.g., Peer Security), four Behavioral Correlates scales (e.g., Impulse Control), and two reliability and validity indicators are included in the report.

Two systems are available for local processing of test results. MICRO-TEST Assessment Software from National Computer Systems, used with a Sentry 3000 tabletop scanner (purchase price approximately $4000) and microcomputer system ($2000-$3000 purchase price), allows tests to be administered off-line. Answer sheets are then scanned and scored automatically, one at a time or in a batch. The software also permits on-line administration of the test via microcomputer. In either case, the same report is provided. The cost for local scoring refers to the cost-per-test when diskettes are purchased in units of 20 administrations (minimum purchase).

```
                    MILLON ADOLESCENT PERSONALITY INVENTORY
                               GUIDANCE REPORT
                 CONFIDENTIAL INFORMATION FOR PROFESSIONAL USE ONLY

                REPORT FOR:                    SEX: FEMALE    AGE: 14

       ID NUMBER:  102013202      VALID AND RELIABLE REPORT  DATE: 22-SEP-83


       CODE:

       6 **8 2 * 1 + 3 5 " 4 7   //G F H B D **- * E A C + - " -   //- **TT* //
```

```
***************************************************************************************
SCALES      * SCORE *        PROFILE OF BR SCORES            *
            *RAW  BR*    35  60        75        85        100 DIMENSIONS
*********+**+***+***+------+---+---------+---------+---------+***************************
         1   16  67 XXXXXXXXXXXXXX                              INTROVERSIVE
         +--+---+---+------+---+---------+---------+---------+-----------------
         2   19  75 XXXXXXXXXXXXXXXXXXX                         INHIBITED
         +--+---+---+------+---+---------+---------+---------+-----------------
         3   20  46 XXXXXXXX                                    COOPERATIVE
         +--+---+---+------+---+---------+---------+---------+-----------------
PERSNLTY 4   12  29 XXXXX                                       SOCIABLE
         +--+---+---+------+---+---------+---------+---------+-----------------
 STYLES  5   21  41 XXXXXXX                                     CONFIDENT
         +--+---+---+------+---+---------+---------+---------+-----------------
         6   19  85 XXXXXXXXXXXXXXXXXXXXXXXXXXXXXX              FORCEFUL
         +--+---+---+------+---+---------+---------+---------+-----------------
         7   12  27 XXXXX                                       RESPECTFUL
         +--+---+---+------+---+---------+---------+---------+-----------------
         8   23  81 XXXXXXXXXXXXXXXXXXXXXXXXXXXX               SENSITIVE
*********+**+***+***+------+---+---------+---------+---------+***************************
         A   14  68 XXXXXXXXXXXXXXX                             SELF-CONCEPT
         +--+---+---+------+---+---------+---------+---------+-----------------
         B   16  87 XXXXXXXXXXXXXXXXXXXXXXXXXXXXXX             PERSONAL ESTEEM
         +--+---+---+------+---+---------+---------+---------+-----------------
         C   12  66 XXXXXXXXXXXXXX                              BODY COMFORT
         +--+---+---+------+---+---------+---------+---------+-----------------
EXPRESSD D   17  85 XXXXXXXXXXXXXXXXXXXXXXXXXXXXXX             SEXUAL ACCEPTNCE
         +--+---+---+------+---+---------+---------+---------+-----------------
CONCERNS E   11  71 XXXXXXXXXXXXXXXXX                           PEER SECURITY
         +--+---+---+------+---+---------+---------+---------+-----------------
         F   11  92 XXXXXXXXXXXXXXXXXXXXXXXXXXXXXXXXXX        SOCIAL TOLERANCE
         +--+---+---+------+---+---------+---------+---------+-----------------
         G   16 110 XXXXXXXXXXXXXXXXXXXXXXXXXXXXXXXXXXXXXXXXXXX FAMILY RAPPORT
         +--+---+---+------+---+---------+---------+---------+-----------------
         H   14  89 XXXXXXXXXXXXXXXXXXXXXXXXXXXXXX            ACADEMIC CONFDNCE
*********+**+***+***+------+---+---------+---------+---------+***************************
         SS  19  65 XXXXXXXXXXXXX                              IMPULSE CONTROL
         +--+---+---+------+---+---------+---------+---------+-----------------
BEHAVIOR TT  22  79 XXXXXXXXXXXXXXXXXXXXXX                     SOCIAL CONFORMITY
         +--+---+---+------+---+---------+---------+---------+-----------------
 CORRE-  UU  21  71 XXXXXXXXXXXXXXXXX                          SCHOLAST ACHVMNT
         +--+---+---+------+---+---------+---------+---------+-----------------
 LATES   WW  15  65 XXXXXXXXXXXXX                              ATTNDNCE CNSTNCY
*********+**+***+***+------+---+---------+---------+---------+***************************
```

382 *psychware*

THIS GUIDANCE REPORT ASSUMES THAT THE MAPI ANSWER FORM WAS COMPLETED
BY A YOUNG PERSON AT THE LATER JUNIOR HIGH SCHOOL, SENIOR HIGH SCHOOL OR BEGIN-
NING COLLEGE LEVEL. IT SHOULD BE NOTED THAT THIS REPORT HAS BEEN WRITTEN WITHIN
THE FRAMEWORK OF SCHOOL COUNSELING OR GUIDANCE SERVICES. IT IS DESIGNED AS AN
AID IN IDENTIFYING, UNDERSTANDING AND PREDICTING STYLES OF SELF-EXPRESSION AND
SCHOLASTIC BEHAVIOR CHARACTERISTIC OF ADOLESCENTS, AS WELL AS PROBLEM AREAS THAT
TYPIFY THIS AGE GROUP. THE SPECIFIC DESCRIPTIONS THAT COMPRISE THIS INDIVIDUAL
REPORT DERIVE FROM BOTH RESEARCH AND THEORY. AS SUCH, THEY ARE PROBABILITY
INFERENCES RATHER THAN DEFINITIVE STATEMENTS, AND SHOULD BE EVALUATED WITHIN THE
CONTEXT OF THE DEVELOPMENTAL, SOCIAL AND ACADEMIC BACKGROUND OF THE STUDENT.
MOREOVER, THESE INFERENCES SHOULD BE REEVALUATED PERIODICALLY IN LIGHT OF THE
PATTERN OF ATTITUDE CHANGE AND EMOTIONAL GROWTH THAT TYPIFIES THE ADOLESCENT
PERIOD. THE FACT THAT THE REPORT IS OF A PERSONAL NATURE REQUIRES THAT IT BE
HANDLED WITH THE HIGHEST LEVEL OF DISCRETION AND CONFIDENTIALITY THAT CAN BE
GIVEN ASPECTS OF THE COUNSELING RELATIONSHIP.

THIS YOUNGSTER SHOWED NO UNUSUAL CHARACTEROLOGICAL OR TEST-TAKING
ATTITUDES THAT MAY HAVE DISTORTED THE MAPI RESULTS.

PERSONALITY PATTERNS

THE FOLLOWING PERTAINS TO THE MORE ENDURING AND PERVASIVE TRAITS THAT
CHARACTERIZE HOW THIS YOUNGSTER IS SEEN BY AND RELATES TO OTHERS. RATHER THAN
FOCUS ON SPECIFIC AREAS OF CONCERN, TO BE DISCUSSED IN LATER PARAGRAPHS, THIS
SECTION CONCENTRATES ON THE BROAD AND HABITUAL WAYS OF BEHAVING AND FEELING.

THIS YOUNG WOMAN IS QUITE DIRECT AND OUTSPOKEN, EXPRESSING HER FEELINGS
AND THOUGHTS WITH MINIMAL RESTRAINT OR REFLECTION. STRUGGLING BETWEEN HER
DEPENDENCY NEEDS AND HER DESIRE TO REBEL AND ASSERT HERSELF, SHE IS LIKELY
TO EXHIBIT A WIDE RANGE OF DIFFERENT MOODS AND EMOTIONS. NOT DISPOSED TO
TOLERATE FRUSTRATIONS EASILY, NOR INCLINED TO INHIBIT HER IMPULSES, SHE IS
LIKELY TO BE RESTLESS AND CONTRARY, READILY OFFENDED BY THE MILDEST OF
RESTRICTIONS AND CRITICISM. HENCE, SHE MAY FEEL MISUNDERSTOOD AND UNAPPRECI-
ATED, BECOME MOODY AND WITHDRAWN, OR CONTENTIOUS AND DIFFICULT. VACILLATING
BETWEEN WANTING RESPECT AND ATTENTION, AND REJECTING OVERTURES OF KINDNESS
AND CONSIDERATION, SHE MAY GET INTO FREQUENT WRANGLES WITH OTHERS.
HER RELATIONSHIPS WITH PEERS ARE LIKELY TO BE VARIABLE AND ERRATIC, SOME
GOING WELL FOR A WHILE, BUT MOST BECOMING PROBLEMATIC AND SHORT-LIVED. SHE
IS NOT LIKELY TO COMFORTABLY ASSUME A LEADERSHIP ROLE, NOR IS SHE SELECTED
FOR SUCH PURPOSES BY OTHERS. EXTRACURRICULAR ACTIVITIES ARE ALSO LIKELY TO
BE MINIMAL. HER CLASSROOM BEHAVIOR AND ACTIVITIES MAY BE TROUBLESOME,
ESPECIALLY IF SHE IS NOT A GOOD ACADEMIC STUDENT. ACTING OUT IS A DISTINCT
POSSIBILITY, THOUGH NOT A HIGH PROBABILITY. SHOULD HER BEHAVIOR BRING HER INTO
A COUNSELING OR GUIDANCE SITUATION, SHE IS NOT LIKELY TO BE ESPECIALLY COOPER-
ATIVE OR COMFORTABLE EXPLORING HER MORE TROUBLESOME ACTIONS.

EXPRESSED CONCERNS

THE SCALES COMPRISING THIS SECTION PERTAIN TO THE PERSONAL PERCEPTION
OF THIS YOUNGSTER CONCERNING SEVERAL ISSUES OF PSYCHOLOGICAL DEVELOPMENT,
ACTUALIZATION AND CONCERN. BECAUSE EXPERIENCES DURING THIS AGE PERIOD
ARE NOTABLY SUBJECTIVE, IT IS IMPORTANT TO RECORD HOW THIS TEENAGER SEES
EVENTS AND REPORTS FEELINGS, AND NOT ONLY HOW OTHERS MAY OBJECTIVELY
REPORT THEM TO BE. FOR COMPARATIVE PURPOSES, THESE SELF-ATTITUDES REGARDING
A WIDE RANGE OF PERSONAL, SOCIAL, FAMILIAL AND SCHOLASTIC MATTERS ARE
CONTRASTED WITH THOSE EXPRESSED BY A BROAD CROSS-SECTION OF TEENAGERS
OF THE SAME SEX AND AGE.

AS IS TYPICAL OF THE EARLY TEEN YEARS, THIS YOUNG GIRL HAS JUST BEGUN TO
DEVELOP SOME CLARITY AS TO HER FUTURE GOALS AND DESIRES. ALTHOUGH STILL UNSURE
OF HERSELF, SHE HAS AN INCREASINGLY REALISTIC SENSE OF SELF AND HAS BEGUN TO
FORM A COHERENT SET OF VALUES.

THIS YOUNGSTER COMMUNICATES A NOTABLE LEVEL OF SELF-DISSATISFACTION,
REVEALING CONSIDERABLE DISTRESS WITH REGARD TO HER SELF-WORTH. NOT ONLY DOES
SHE EXPERIENCE MINIMAL ACCEPTANCE OF HERSELF BY OTHERS, BUT SHE FEELS BOTH
PERSONALLY UNFULFILLED AND FAR FROM BEING THE PERSON SHE WISHES SHE WERE.

ALTHOUGH GENERALLY PLEASED WITH BOTH THE PROGRESS AND OUTCOME OF HER
PHYSICAL DEVELOPMENT, THIS YOUNG GIRL VOICES SOME DISSATISFACTION ABOUT CERTAIN
COMPONENTS OF HER TOTAL APPEARANCE AND DEVELOPMENT.

SEXUAL THOUGHTS ARE EXPERIENCED BY THIS YOUNG GIRL AS NOTABLY DISCORDANT
AND/OR DISAGREEABLE. THERE ARE PERIODS OF INTENSE TENSION, CONFUSION AND
DISPLEASURE ASSOCIATED WITH THE FEELINGS, IMPULSES AND HETEROSEXUAL ROLES SHE
FEELS SHE IS EXPECTED TO FILL.

psychware **383**

RECENTLY ENTERING ADOLESCENCE, THIS YOUNG GIRL HAS BEGUN THE PROCESS OF
IDENTFICATION WITH HER PEER GROUP. ALTHOUGH SHE HAS BEGUN TO ESTABLISH A
SATISFYING PEER NETWORK, SHE DOES EXPERIENCE SOME DIFFICULTIES AND CONCERNS IN
THIS REGARD.

THIS YOUNG GIRL CONSISTENTLY CHOOSES TO MAINTAIN A COOL, IMPERSONAL
DISTANCE FROM OTHERS. RATHER THAN RESPOND WITH HELP FOR OTHERS IN NEED, SHE IS
LIKELY TO BE HARSH OR JUDGMENTAL, INCLINED TO BE CRITICAL AND PLACE BLAME ON
THOSE WHO ARE WEAK OR VICTIMIZED.

THIS FAMILY SETTING IS PERCEIVED AS QUITE TROUBLING BY THIS YOUNG GIRL. AS
A POSSIBLE FOCUS OF CONFLICT HERSELF, SHE REPORTS A LACK OF COMMUNICATION AND
SEES NEITHER PARENTS NOR SIBLINGS AS A SOURCE OF WARMTH.

THIS YOUNGSTER ACKNOWLEDGES SUBSTANTIAL DIFFICULTY OVER HER INADEQUATE
LEVEL OF SCHOLASTIC PERFORMANCE. SHE IS QUITE TROUBLED ABOUT THE QUALITY OF HER
GRADES AND IS RATHER PESSIMISTIC ABOUT HER FUTURE EDUCATIONAL PROGRESS.

BEHAVIORAL CORRELATES

THE SCALES COMPRISING THIS SECTION FOCUS ON PROBLEMS THAT FREQUENTLY
COME TO THE ATTENTION OF SCHOOL COUNSELORS, FAMILY AND OTHER AGENCIES,
AS WELL AS THERAPEUTIC CLINICIANS. IT SHOULD BE NOTED THAT THESE SCALES
DO NOT PROVIDE DIRECT EVIDENCE THAT THE YOUNGSTER HAS OR IS LIKELY TO
EXHIBIT THE DIFFICULTIES REFERRED TO. RATHER, THEY GAUGE THE EXTENT TO
WHICH THE RESPONSES OF THIS TEENAGER ARE SIMILAR TO THOSE WHO HAVE BEEN
IDENTIFIED BY COUNSELORS AND CLINICIANS AS EVIDENCING TROUBLESOME
BEHAVIORS SUCH AS IMPULSIVITY, SOCIAL NONCOMPLIANCE, UNDERACHIEVEMENT AND
NONATTENDENCE.

ALTHOUGH THIS YOUNG GIRL USUALLY MAINTAINS CONTROL OVER HER BEHAVIOR,
RARELY GIVING WAY TO IMPULSES, HER MAPI RESPONSES DO SUGGEST A TENDENCY AT TIMES
TO SHOW HER FEELINGS SOMEWHAT RAPIDLY AND EXPRESSIVELY.

HER RESPONSES TO THE MAPI ARE VERY MUCH LIKE TEENAGERS WHO ARE LIKELY TO
RESPOND TO SOCIETAL REGULATIONS AND DEMANDS WITH NONCONFORMING AND EVEN OVERTLY
REBELLIOUS BEHAVIORS.

ALTHOUGH THIS YOUNGSTER WILL GENERALLY ACHIEVE ACADEMICALLY ON PAR WITH HER
ABILITIES, HER MAPI RESPONSES INDICATE THAT HER PERFORMANCE MAY BE LESS THAN
MAXIMAL AT TIMES.

THERE IS A MINOR SUGGESTION IN THE MAPI THAT THIS YOUNG GIRL MAY BE ABSENT
FROM SCHOOL MORE FREQUENTLY THAN THE AVERAGE YOUNGSTERS ARE FOR REASONS OF A
PSYCHOSOMATIC OR OTHER HEALTH-RELATED REASONS.

PUBLISHED BY INTERPRETIVE SCORING SYSTEMS,
A DIVISION OF NATIONAL COMPUTER SYSTEMS INC.
P.O. BOX 1294, MINNEAPOLIS, MN 55440

NAME: Millon Behavioral Health Inventory

SUPPLIER: NCS/Professional Assessment Services
P.O. Box 1416
Minneapolis, MN 55440
(800) 328-6759

PRODUCT CATEGORY

Personality

PRIMARY APPLICATIONS

Behavioral Medicine

SALE RESTRICTIONS American Psychological Association Guidelines

SERVICE TYPE/COST	Type	Available	Cost	Discount
	Mail-In	Yes	$16.50	Yes
	Teleprocessing	Yes	$16.50	Yes
	Local	Yes	$11.30	Yes

PRODUCT DESCRIPTION

The MILLON BEHAVIORAL HEALTH INVENTORY presents a detailed narrative interpretation regarding a patient's perception of life stresses and somatic ailments, as well as possible psychological complications associated with many diseases and their treatment. The 4-5 page report includes a plotted score profile.

The test itself is a 150 item true-false inventory requiring an 8th-grade reading level and about 20 minutes to complete. The report includes eight Coping Style scales (e.g., Cooperative), six Psychogenic Attitude scales (e.g., Somatic Anxiety), three Psychosomatic Correlate scales (e.g., Pain Treatment Responsivity), and a validity indicator.

Two systems are available for local processing of test results. MICRO-TEST Assessment Software from National Computer Systems, used with a Sentry 3000 tabletop scanner (purchase price approximately $4000) and microcomputer system ($2000-$3000 purchase price), allows tests to be administered off-line. Answer sheets are then scanned and scored automatically, one at a time or in a batch. The software also permits on-line administration of the test via microcomputer. In either case, the same report is provided. The cost for local scoring refers to the cost-per-test when diskettes are purchased in units of 20 administrations (minimum purchase).

MILLON BEHAVIORAL HEALTH INVENTORY
CONFIDENTIAL INFORMATION FOR PROFESSIONAL USE ONLY

REPORT FOR: FEMALE SAMPLE   SEX: FEMALE   AGE: 30

ID NUMBER: 222222222   DATE: 29-MAR-84

CODE: 2 **6 8 * - + 5 4 1 3 7 "   //- **E * //MM**NNOO* //PP**QQRR* //

```
*************************************************************************
 SCALES    * SCORE *        PROFILE OF BR SCORES           *
           *RAW  BR*   35  60       75        85       100  DIMENSIONS
********+**+***+***+-----+-------+---------+---------+****************
        1   14  27 XXXXX                                   INTROVERSIVE
       +--+---+---+-----+-------+---------+---------+------+---------
        2   23 105 XXXXXXXXXXXXXXXXXXXXXXXXXXXXXXXXXXXXXXXX INHIBITED
       +--+---+---+-----+-------+---------+---------+------+---------
 BASIC  3   16  13 XXX                                     COOPERATIVE
       +--+---+---+-----+-------+---------+---------+------+---------
 PERSNLTY 4 22  29 XXXXX                                   SOCIABLE
       +--+---+---+-----+-------+---------+---------+------+---------
 STYLE  5   17  31 XXXXXX                                  CONFIDENT
       +--+---+---+-----+-------+---------+---------+------+---------
        6   19  80 XXXXXXXXXXXXXXXXXXXXXXXX                 FORCEFUL
       +--+---+---+-----+-------+---------+---------+------+---------
        7   19  12 XXX                                     RESPECTFUL
       +--+---+---+-----+-------+---------+---------+------+---------
        8   21  79 XXXXXXXXXXXXXXXXXXXXXXXX                 SENSITIVE
********+**+***+***+-----+-------+---------+---------+****************
        A   16  61 XXXXXXXXXXX                             CHRONIC TENSION
       +--+---+---+-----+-------+---------+---------+------+---------
 PSYCHO- B  10  62 XXXXXXXXXXXX                            RECENT STRESS
       +--+---+---+-----+-------+---------+---------+------+---------
 GENIC  C   18  65 XXXXXXXXXXXXXX                          PREMORB PESSIMISM
       +--+---+---+-----+-------+---------+---------+------+---------
 ATTI-  D   18  69 XXXXXXXXXXXXXXXX                        FUTURE DESPAIR
       +--+---+---+-----+-------+---------+---------+------+---------
 TUDES  E   16  75 XXXXXXXXXXXXXXXXXXXXX                    SOCIAL ALIENATION
       +--+---+---+-----+-------+---------+---------+------+---------
        F   13  54 XXXXXXXXXX                              SOMATIC ANXIETY
********+**+***+***+-----+-------+---------+---------+****************
 PSYCHO- MM 18  85 XXXXXXXXXXXXXXXXXXXXXXXXXXXXXXXXXX       ALLERGIC INCLIN
       +--+---+---+-----+-------+---------+---------+------+---------
 SOMATIC NN 13  81 XXXXXXXXXXXXXXXXXXXXXXXXXXXXX            GASTRO SUSCEPTBL
       +--+---+---+-----+-------+---------+---------+------+---------
        OO  19  80 XXXXXXXXXXXXXXXXXXXXXXXXXXXX             CARDIO TENDENCY
********+**+***+***+-----+-------+---------+---------+****************
 PROG-  PP  17  85 XXXXXXXXXXXXXXXXXXXXXXXXXXXXXXXXXX       PAIN TREAT RESPON
       +--+---+---+-----+-------+---------+---------+------+---------
 NOSTIC QQ  19  83 XXXXXXXXXXXXXXXXXXXXXXXXXXXXXXXX         LIFE-THREAT REACT
       +--+---+---+-----+-------+---------+---------+------+---------
        RR   7  79 XXXXXXXXXXXXXXXXXXXXXXXXXXXX             EMOTIONALT VULNER
********+**+***+***+-----+-------+---------+---------+****************
```

This report assumes that the MBHI answer form was completed by a person undergoing professional medical evaluation or treatment. It should be noted that MBHI data and analyses do not provide physical diagnoses. Rather, the instrument supplements such diagnoses by identifying and appraising the potential role of psychogenic and psychosomatic factors in medical disease. The statements printed below are derived from cumulative research data and theory. As such, they must be considered as suggestive or probabilistic inferences, rather than definitive judgments, and should be evaluated in that light by clinicians. The specific statements contained in the report are of a personal nature and are for confidential professional use only. They should be handled with great discretion and not be shown to patients or their relatives.

COPING STYLE

The following paragraphs pertain to those longstanding traits of the patient that have characterized most personal, social and work relationships. In addition to summarizing these more general features of psychological functioning, this section will briefly review the manner in which the patient is likely to relate to health personnel, services and regimens.

386 *psychware*

The behavior of the patient is typified by a persistent undercurrent of sadness and tension with occasional periods of moodiness, anxiety and irritable outbursts of temper. She reports feeling misunderstood and unappreciated by others. In addition, she is hypersensitive to what others think and is frequently quite ill-at-ease socially, withdrawing to avoid painful social experiences. She expects that when things go well they will not last and that most events in life will turn for the worse because of the actions of others. There is an inclination to react to events in a somewhat unpredictable manner. Anger and disappointment may be expressed one time, followed by contrition, followed by blaming those around her. This angry emotionality and mood change is both physically and psychologically upsetting, and may dispose her to psychosomatic discomforts and ailments, as well as troubling social isolation.

A patient showing this profile on the MBHI will vary in the manner in which she deals with her ailments and how she relates to health professionals. At times she acts in an almost exhibitionistic manner when describing her symptoms, complaining excessively about a wide variety of physical discomforts, appearing to enjoy the role of being ill and in distress. Getting the attention of doctors and of friends and relatives who may feel sorry for her is an important compensation for the reality of her physical discomforts. However, such a patient tends to be erratic in her relations with doctors, alternately engaging and distancing to their exasperation. She may be inclined to collect doctors and medications, leaving one after another in the belief that they are not doing the right thing, or serving her best interests, shopping about, rarely satisfied with the results of any treatment regimen and combining a variety of treatments and medications without supervision.

At other times this patient will act in a totally opposite manner, being fearful and ashamed of her symptoms and inclined to conceal them. This is generally seen most clearly when emotional problems complicate the picture, or when she fears a serious illness. Expecting the worst, anticipating further pain and suffering, she is disposed to protect herself and, thereby, be hesitant about exploring her ailments and resistant to efforts to help her. Moreover, because of her fears and preoccupations, she may be too confused and anxious to understand or follow medical advice and, therefore, may not adequately comply with treatment regimens.

Both patterns of behavior may be experienced by a busy physician as demanding and time-consuming often requiring considerable patience and tact. Sensitive to exasperation or negative suggestions, she will be easily frightened, angered and upset. Expressions of genuine attention and sympathy, especially if conveyed with an air of calm competence may help moderate her unjustified or hypochondriacal concern. Although firm time limits should be set in the event that she demands excessive attention, it is important to counter her expectancy to be rejected and to find doctors disinterested in her ailments. Should there be an illness requiring long-term management, it would be advisable to have ancillary health personnel develop a continuing and personal relationship with her. Investing time in complex medical explanations, however, will only increase her anxiety and her inclination to find fault. Sympathetic listening, mixed with resolute assurances, is likely to work best.

PSYCHOGENIC ATTITUDES

The scales comprising this section compare the feelings and perceptions expressed by the patient to those of a cross section of both healthy and ill adults of the same sex. The results of these scales are summarized here since they may be associated with an increase in the probability of psychosomatic pathogenesis, or with tendencies to aggravate the course of an established disease, or with attitudes that may impede the effectiveness of medical or surgical treatment.

The patient sees daily demands of family or work as average and within manageable proportions. Some pressures do exist, but they are either periodic or at levels easily tolerated. As a consequence, the patient experiences periods of freedom from self or externally imposed demands. The perception of a modest degree of daily stress indicates a reasonably low likelihood of tension-related illness. However, this would not prevent the patient, given the personality style described above, from periodically complaining about such pressures and demands.

The events of the past year are reported as unremarkable and typical in character for the lifestyle of this patient. Prone to view events as troublesome, this modest evaluation of recent life difficulties suggests the patient has experienced a more comfortable period than usual. There is no indication, therefore, that an increased probability of a major illness will occur this coming year as a consequence of perceived life stresses.

In spite of a characteristically pessimistic outlook on life, the patient recounts both the past and the present as good sometimes, and not good at others. The inclination to interpret events in a reasonably balanced manner indicates that the patient is likely to react to an illness experience in an unexceptional manner.

Although usually expecting the worst, the patient shows only an average degree of concern regarding future prospects. Assuming that the outlook will unfold in an unexceptional manner, the patient is likely to manage future or current physical problems with less emotional upheaval than might otherwise be expected.

Consistent with lifelong expectations, the patient reports far less emotional support from friends and family than is typical. Upset by the fear that one cannot call upon these individuals if help is required, the patient feels alone and set apart. This sense of distance and lack of caring on their part does not bode well for the course of an illness or its treatment.

Regardless of other difficulties, the patient expresses no untoward anxieties regarding health and illness. Although unlikely to overreact to illness itself, the management aspects of a therapeutic program are still likely to be colored and complicated by the characteristically negative expectations of the patient.

PSYCHOSOMATIC CORRELATES

The scales comprising this section are designed for use only with patients who have previously been diagnosed by physicians as suffering one of a number of specific disease entities or syndromes, e.g., hypertension, colitis, allergy. Note that these scales do not provide data confirming such medical diagnoses, nor do they include statements which may be construed as supporting them. Rather, the primary intent of this section is to gauge the extent to which the patient is similar to comparably diagnosed patients whose illness has been judged to be substantially psychosomatic, or whose course has been judged to be complicated by emotional or social factors.

Typically quick to react emotionally, if the patient has a diagnosed allergic disorder, e.g., pruritis, urticaria, dermatitis, asthma, the evidence strongly suggests that the disorder is primarily psychosomatic in origin and readily exacerbated by any aggravation and tension.

If the patient has a history of chronic gastrointestinal disorder, e.g., peptic ulcer, colitis, dyspepsia, irritable colon, it is evident from the MBHI scores that the constant emotional upheaval experienced by the patient contributes significantly to both the frequency and intensity of the medical complaints of the patient.

Consonant with the troubled view of life of the patient, if the patient has been medically diagnosed as manifesting the symptoms of certain cardiovascular disorders, notably hypertension or angina pectoris, it would appear that the physical discomforts felt by the patient are substantially influenced by stress.

PROGNOSTIC INDICES

The scales comprising this section have been empirically constructed to assist clinicians in appraising the impact of psychosocial factors which can complicate the usual prognostic course of patients who have a history of either a chronic or life-threatening illness, or who are under review for a life-sustaining surgical or medical procedure.

If there has been a medical history of a periodic or persistent pain disorder, e.g., low back pain, headache, TMJ, it is highly likely that the patient will not respond favorably to traditional outpatient treatment. Numerous complications are likely to arise during the course of treatment as a function of emotional responses to both the disorder and the treatment program. A conservative pharmacologic and surgical course is recommended. Serious consideration should be given to the option of behavioral modification programs and those utilizing other psychological treatment components.

If the patient is suffering from a chronic and progressive life-threatening illness, e.g., metastatic carcinoma, renal failure, congestive heart disease, it is probable that there will be some unexpected difficulties in the course of the illness. It is possible that the patient may fare less well than might be anticipated, in part as a result of a sense that needed emotional support is not available. Counseling and self-help groups might prove beneficial in countering these negative attitudes and minimize problems in treatment.

If faced with major surgery or a candidate for ongoing life-dependent treatment programs, e.g., open heart procedures, hemodialysis, cancer chemotherapy, it is possible, although not probable, that the patient will suffer disorientation, a major depression or a psychotic episode. Counseling sessions both prior to and during treatment should minimize these possibilities.

NOTEWORTHY RESPONSES

The following statements were answered by the patient in the direction noted in the parenthesis. These items suggest specific problem areas that may deserve further inquiry on the part of the clinician.

POTENTIAL NONCOMPLIANCE
(Suggests a disinclination to follow medical advice)

21. I have a lot of faith that doctors can cure any sickness.   (F)
46. All doctors care about is my money, not me.   (T)

73. Doctors have always been helpful to me.   (F)

130. I would rather be in pain than take any medicines. (T)

HEALTH PREOCCUPATIONS
(Denotes an excessive attention to physical ailments)

41. I almost never worry about my health.   (F)

68. I worry a lot about my health.   (T)

140. I often think that I have a serious illness.   (T)

ILLNESS OVERREACTION
(Signifies tendencies to magnify illness consequences)

7. If I were very sick, I'm sure that everything would work out well.   (F)
57. Even if I were very sick, I'd keep fighting and never give up.   (F)

DEPRESSIVE FEELINGS
(Indicates dejection and/or dysphoric mood)

38. I have had more than my share of troubles in the past year.   (T)
50. I feel pretty upset about most things in my life. (T)
92. Even when things seem to be going well, I expect that they'll soon get worse.   (T)
134. Life has never gone well for me.   (T)

PSYCHIATRIC POSSIBILITY
(Provides indices of a potential mental disturbance)

12. I am ready to attack anyone who tries to say terrible things about me.   (T)

14. All my life I have to "blow up" every now and then. (T)
40. Many people have been spying into my private life for years.   (T)
58. I sometimes feel I am in this world all alone.   (T)

86. I often feel so angry that I want to throw and break things.   (T)
98. Ever since I was a child, I have been losing touch with the real world.   (T)

CAPSULE SUMMARY

This patient often feels misunderstood, tense and depressed. Sensitive to her physical problems she frequently overresponds, displaying irritability and anger. She may have been erratic in relating to doctors and chronically dissatisfied with plans for her treatment. Calm expressions of genuine interest and attention may help moderate her discomfort and frequent hypochondriacal concerns.

PUBLISHED BY INTERPRETIVE SCORING SYSTEMS,
A DIVISION OF NATIONAL COMPUTER SYSTEMS INC.
P.O. BOX 1294, MINNEAPOLIS, MN 55440

NAME: FEMALE SAMPLE   662 0003

NAME: Millon Clinical Multiaxial Inventory

SUPPLIER: NCS/Professional Assessment Services
P.O. Box 1416
Minneapolis, MN 55440
(800) 328-6759

PRODUCT CATEGORY

Personality

PRIMARY APPLICATIONS

Clinical Assessment/Diagnosis
Personal/Marriage/Family Counseling

SALE RESTRICTIONS American Psychological Association Guidelines

SERVICE TYPE/COST	Type	Available	Cost	Discount
	Mail-In	Yes	$17.75	Yes
	Teleprocessing	Yes	$17.75	Yes
	Local	Yes	$12.50	Yes

PRODUCT DESCRIPTION

The MILLON CLINICAL MULTIAXIAL INVENTORY presents a detailed narrative regarding patient personality patterns and clinical syndromes, as well as a listing of noteworthy responses signifying problem areas deserving further evaluation. DSM-III compatibility ensures clear communication between health professionals and third-party payers. The 4-5 page report includes a plotted score profile.

The test itself has 175 true-false items that take about 25 minutes to complete. An 8th-grade reading level is required. The test is theory-based and fully coordinated with DSM-III. It measures both relatively enduring personality characteristics (DSM-III, Axis II) and acute clinical disorders (DSM-III, Axis I). The report also includes two validity indicators. A scores only report (Profile Report) is also available at approximately 40% of costs shown here for the complete report.

Two systems are available for local processing of test results. MICRO-TEST Assessment Software from National Computer Systems, used with a Sentry 3000 tabletop scanner (purchase price approximately $4000) and microcomputer system ($2000-$3000 purchase price), allows tests to be administered off-line. Answer sheets are then scanned and scored automatically, one at a time or in a batch. The software also permits on-line administration of the test via microcomputer. In either case, the same report is provided. The cost for local scoring refers to the cost-per-test when diskettes are purchased in units of 20 administrations (minimum purchase).

```
MILLON CLINICAL MULTIAXIAL INVENTORY *DSM-III REPORT* FOR PROFESSIONAL USE ONLY

NAME=SAMPLE     TM     M              VALID REPORT  WT. FAC.= -2 30-SEP-83
CODE=2 3 1 8 **- * 7 + - " 6 4 5   //S **C * //A D H **// - //
                                                              004 0005
*********************************************************************************
SCALES     * SCORE *       PROFILE OF BR SCORES        *   DSM-III (MILLON)
           *RAW  BR*    35   60      75        85     100    PARALLELS
*********+**+***+***+---+----+----+----+-------+--------+---*********************
        [1 [ 25[100[XXXXXXXXXXXXXXXXXXXXXXXXXXXXXXXXXXXXXXXX SCHIZOID (ASOCIAL)
           +--+----+----+----+----+-------+--------+------------+
        [2 [ 31[111[XXXXXXXXXXXXXXXXXXXXXXXXXXXXXXXXXXXXXXXXXX AVOIDANT
           +--+----+----+----+----+-------+--------+------------+
BASIC   [3 [ 26[110[XXXXXXXXXXXXXXXXXXXXXXXXXXXXXXXXXXXXXXXXX DEPENDENT (SUBMIS)
           +--+----+----+----+----+-------+--------+------------+
PERSNLTY[4 [  3[  3[    !    !        !         !         ! HISTRIONIC (GREGAR)
           +--+----+----+----+----+-------+--------+------------+
PATTERN [5 [  4[  3[    !    !        !         !         ! NARCISSISTIC
           +--+----+----+----+----+-------+--------+------------+
        [6 [  3[  3[    !    !        !         !         ! ANTISOCIAL (AGGRES)
           +--+----+----+----+----+-------+--------+------------+
        [7 [ 25[ 62[XXXXXXXXXXX       !         !         ! COMPULSIVE (CONFOR)
           +--+----+----+----+----+-------+--------+------------+
        [8 [ 18[ 88[XXXXXXXXXXXXXXXXXXXXXXXXXXXXXXXXX         ! P. AGGRESS. (NEGAT)
*********+**+***+***+---+----+----+----+-------+--------+---*********************
PATHLGCL[S [ 37[104[XXXXXXXXXXXXXXXXXXXXXXXXXXXXXXXXXXXXXXXXXX SCHIZOTYPAL (SCHIZ)
           +--+----+----+----+----+-------+--------+------------+
PERSNLTY[C [ 28[ 78[XXXXXXXXXXXXXXXXXXXXXXXX     !         ! BORDERLINE (CYCL)
           +--+----+----+----+----+-------+--------+------------+
DISORDER[P [  8[ 36[XXXXXX   !        !         !         ! PARANOID
*********+**+***+***+---+----+----+----+-------+--------+---*********************
        [A [ 28[110[XXXXXXXXXXXXXXXXXXXXXXXXXXXXXXXXXXXXXXXXX ANXIETY
           +--+----+----+----+----+-------+--------+------------+
        [H [ 27[ 88[XXXXXXXXXXXXXXXXXXXXXXXXXXXXXXXXX         ! SOMATOFORM
           +--+----+----+----+----+-------+--------+------------+
        [N [  5[ -2[    !    !        !         !         ! HYPOMANIA
           +--+----+----+----+----+-------+--------+------------+
CLINICAL[D [ 29[105[XXXXXXXXXXXXXXXXXXXXXXXXXXXXXXXXXXXXXXXXXX DYSTHYMIA
           +--+----+----+----+----+-------+--------+------------+
SYNDROME[B [ 10[ 60[XXXXXXXXXXX       !         !         ! ALCOHOL ABUSE
           +--+----+----+----+----+-------+--------+------------+
        [T [  9[ 23[XXXX !    !        !         !         ! DRUG ABUSE
           +--+----+----+----+----+-------+--------+------------+
        [SS[ 17[ 71[XXXXXXXXXXXXXXXXX  !         !         ! PSYCHOTIC THINKING
           +--+----+----+----+----+-------+--------+------------+
        [CC[ 15[ 71[XXXXXXXXXXXXXXXXX  !         !         ! PSYCHOT. DEPRESSION
           +--+----+----+----+----+-------+--------+------------+
        [PP[  7[ 64[XXXXXXXXXXXX       !         !         ! PSYCHOTIC DELUSION
*********+**+***+***+---+----+----+----+-------+--------+---*********************
```

        MCMI NARRATIVES HAVE BEEN NORMED ON PATIENTS EXPERIENCING EITHER GENUINE
EMOTIONAL DISCOMFORTS OR SOCIAL DIFFICULTIES AND ARE APPLICABLE PRIMARILY DURING
THE EARLY PHASES OF ASSESSMENT OR PSYCHOTHERAPY. DISTORTIONS SUCH AS GREATER
SEVERITY MAY OCCUR AMONG RESPONDENTS WHO HAVE INAPPROPRIATELY TAKEN THE MCMI FOR
ESSENTIALLY EDUCATIONAL OR SELF-EXPLORATORY PURPOSES. INFERENTIAL AND
PROBABILISTIC, THIS REPORT MUST BE VIEWED AS ONLY ONE ASPECT OF A THOROUGH
DIAGNOSTIC STUDY. FOR THESE REASONS, IT SHOULD NOT BE SHOWN TO PATIENTS OR
THEIR RELATIVES.

        THIS MALE PATIENT MAY HAVE BEEN OVERLY SELF-CRITICAL AND SELF-DEPRECIATING
IN RESPONDING TO THE TEST ITEMS. WHILE READING THE FOLLOWING, CLINICIANS SHOULD
BE AWARE THAT HE MAY HAVE ADMITTED TO MORE PSYCHOLOGICAL SYMPTOMS THAN
OBJECTIVELY EXIST IN HIS LIFE.

                        AXIS II: PERSONALITY PATTERNS

        THE FOLLOWING PERTAINS TO THOSE ENDURING AND PERVASIVE CHARACTEROLOGICAL
TRAITS THAT UNDERLIE THE PERSONAL AND INTERPERSONAL DIFFICULTIES OF THIS MAN.
RATHER THAN FOCUS ON HIS MORE MARKED BUT ESSENTIALLY TRANSITORY SYMPTOMS, THIS
SECTION CONCENTRATES ON HIS HABITUAL, MALADAPTIVE METHODS OF RELATING, BEHAVING,
THINKING AND FEELING.

        THERE IS EVIDENCE OF A MODERATE LEVEL OF PATHOLOGY IN THE OVERALL
PERSONALITY STRUCTURE OF THIS MAN. HE IS LIKELY TO HAVE A CHECKERED HISTORY OF
DISAPPOINTMENTS IN HIS PERSONAL AND FAMILY RELATIONSHIPS. DEFICITS IN HIS

SOCIAL ATTAINMENTS MAY BE NOTABLE, AS IS A TENDENCY ON HIS PART TO PRECIPITATE
SELF-DEFEATING VICIOUS CIRCLES. EARLIER HOPES FOR HIMSELF MAY HAVE MET WITH
FRUSTRATING SETBACKS, AND EFFORTS TO ACHIEVE A CONSISTENT NICHE IN LIFE MAY HAVE
FAILED. ALTHOUGH HE IS FREQUENTLY ABLE TO FUNCTION ON A SATISFACTORY AMBULATORY
BASIS, HE MAY EVIDENCE A PERSISTENT EMOTIONAL DYSCONTROL WITH PERIODIC PSYCHOTIC
EPISODES.

THE BEHAVIOR OF THIS MAN IS TYPIFIED BY AN INTENSELY APPREHENSIVE MISTRUST
OF OTHERS, A TENDENCY TO WITHDRAW FROM SOCIAL ENCOUNTERS THAT IS COMBINED WITH
STRONG DEPENDENCY NEEDS AND AN INABILITY TO FUNCTION WELL ON HIS OWN.
BEHAVIORAL ECCENTRICITIES, AUTISTIC THINKING, AND DEPERSONALIZATION ANXIETIES
ARE ALSO OCCASIONALLY EVIDENT. HE MAY HAVE BECOME A DETACHED OBSERVER OF THE
PASSING SCENE, LEAVING TO OTHERS MOST RESPONSIBILITIES FOR OVERSEEING HIS LIFE.
HIS NEED FOR SUPPORT AND CARE FROM OTHERS IS PASSIVELY ACCEPTED. MOREOVER, HE
HAS LEARNED TO AVOID AS MANY SOCIAL AND PERSONAL OBLIGATIONS AS POSSIBLE BECAUSE
COMMITMENTS TO OTHERS CONSTITUTE A POTENTIAL THREAT TO HIS SECURITY. FEAR OF
LOSING SUPPORT AND FEAR OF GETTING TOO CLOSE TO OTHERS LEADS HIM TO EXPERIENCE
RECURRENT ANXIETIES AND A PERVASIVE DISHARMONY OF MOOD. THE EXTENDED PERIODS OF
SOLITUDE IN HIS LIFE ARE SOMETIMES PAINFUL TO HIM AND PRODUCE FEELINGS OF
EMPTINESS AND DEPERSONALIZATION. HIS OVERCONCERN WITH SOCIAL REBUFF IS OFTEN
INTENSIFIED BY A TENDENCY TO ANTICIPATE AND ELICIT REJECTION. NOT INFREQUENTLY,
HE FEELS PERSECUTED, HUMILIATED, AND DISPARAGED BY OTHERS.
THE LACK OF INITIATIVE, SELF-DEPRECIATON OF APTITUDES, AND AVOIDANCE OF
INDEPENDENT AND ASSERTIVE BEHAVIORS BY THIS MAN, LEADS HIM TO A PASSIVELY
DEPENDENT STATE. CONCILIATORY SUBMISSION TO OTHERS IS ALSO EVIDENT, AS IS A
SEARCH FOR DEPENDABLE PERSONS OR SUPPORTIVE INSTITUTIONS. AS NOTED, DESPITE A
STRONG NEED TO DEPEND ON OTHERS, HE MAY AVOID SUCH RELATIONSHIPS AND MAINTAIN A
SAFE MEASURE OF INTERPERSONAL DISTANCE. AT OTHER TIMES, HE WILL ASSUME A
PASSIVE AND ACQUIESCENT ROLE AND WILLINGLY SUBMIT TO THE DEMANDS AND
EXPECTATIONS OF OTHERS JUST TO BE ABLE TO MEET HIS DEPENDENCY NEEDS. ALTHOUGH
HE WILL BE DEPENDENT ON SUCH NURTURANT PERSONS OR INSTITUTIONS, HE IS LIKELY NOT
TO ASSUME SELF-RESPONSIBILITY, PREFERRING TO WITHDRAW INTO INCREASINGLY
PERIPHERAL SOCIAL AND VOCATIONAL ROLES, AND FOLLOWING A MEANINGLESS,
INEFFECTUAL, AND IDLE LIFE PATTERN.
AS JUST NOTED, HIS SELF-IMAGE OF WEAKNESS, FRAGILITY, AND INEFFECTUALITY
MAY MAKE THE ORDINARY STRESSES AND RESPONSIBILITIES OF LIFE SEEM EXCESSIVELY
DEMANDING TO HIM. QUITE POSSIBLY, HIS PASSIVE DEPENDENT STYLE MAY STEM FROM AN
INTRINSIC APATHY, EASE OF FATIGABILITY AND LOW ENERGY LEVEL. HIS SLUGGISH
EXTERIOR AND AFFECTIVE BLANDNESS MAY AT TIMES SERVE TO RESTRAIN AN UNDERLYING
ANGER, ANXIETY, AND DEPRESSION.
THIS MAN MAY FREQUENTLY APPEAR SELF-ABSORBED, LOST IN DAYDREAMS THAT
OCCASIONALLY BLUR FANTASY WITH REALITY. PERSONAL IRRELEVANCIES AND TANGENTIAL
ASIDES MAY BE COMMON WHEN HE SEEKS TO CONVEY HIS IDEAS OR TO ENGAGE IN EVEN

ORDINARY SOCIAL COMMUNICATIONS. ALSO NOTABLE IS HIS EFFORT TO AVOID EMOTIONAL
EXPERIENCES, AND TO SUPPRESS EVENTS THAT MAY STIR DISTURBING MEMORIES AND
FEELINGS. OF COURSE, THESE DEFENSIVE EFFORTS WILL PRECLUDE REWARDING SOCIAL
EXPERIENCES AND, TOGETHER WITH HIS CHARACTERISTIC AFFECTIVE UNRESPONSIVENESS,
BIZARRENESS AND WITHDRAWAL BEHAVIOR, MAY LEAD OTHERS TO SPEAK OF HIM AS A
SOCIALLY PECULIAR AND DISCONNECTED PERSON. HIS OCCASIONAL AUTISTIC AND MAGICAL
THINKING WILL ONLY FURTHER ALIENATE OTHERS. ALL OF THESE FACTORS CONTRIBUTE TO
THE MAINTENANCE OF HIS DETACHED, SOCIALLY ANXIOUS AND DEPENDENTLY INEFFECTUAL
LIFE PATTERN.

AXIS I: CLINICAL SYNDROMES

THE FOLLOWING DISTINCTIVE CLINICAL DISORDERS ARE NOTABLE. THEY MAY BE OF
BRIEF DURATION, ARISE IN RESPONSE TO EXTERNAL PRECIPITANTS, AND ACCENTUATE THE
MORE PERSISTENT FEATURES OF HIS BASIC PERSONALITY.

THIS MAN FEELS APPREHENSIVE AND RESTLESS AND MAY COMPLAIN OF TENSION,
RECURRENT INDECISIVENESS OVER PICAYUNE MATTERS AND ACUTE PHYSICAL DISCOMFORTS,
SUCH AS GASTROINTESTINAL PROBLEMS, INSOMNIA, MUSCULAR TIGHTNESS, HEADACHES, AND
COLD SWEATING.

THIS PATIENT EXPRESSES DEJECTION AND DISCOURAGEMENT ABOUT HIS CURRENT LIFE
SITUATION AND MAINTAINS A PESSIMISTIC VIEW OF THE FUTURE. A LOSS OF EFFICIENCY
AND SELF-CONFIDENCE, DIMINISHED PLEASURE IN PREVIOUSLY REWARDING ACTIVITIES,
PREOCCUPATION WITH MATTERS OF PERSONAL INADEQUACY AND FEELINGS OF WORTHLESSNESS
OR GUILT ARE ALSO NOTABLE.

THE MEDICAL HISTORY OF THIS MAN MAY BE CHARACTERIZED BY CHRONIC COMPLAINTS OF FATIGUE AND IRRITABILITY, AND AN OVERCONCERN WITH VARIABLE AND ESSENTIALLY VAGUE PAINS AND PHYSICAL SYMPTOMS.

THESE SYMPTOMS ARISE AS A CONSEQUENCE OF RECENT SOCIAL DEROGATION AND HUMILIATION. HIS MARKED DISTRUST OF AND ANGER TOWARD OTHERS HAVE BEEN EXPRESSED HESITANTLY LEST THEY ELICIT FURTHER REJECTION. AS A RESULT, HIS TENSION MOUNTS, AS EVIDENT IN A VARIETY OF HIS SYMPTOMS. HE MAY ALSO BE EMPLOYING PERSONAL DISTRESS AS A MEANS OF AVOIDING CRITICAL RESPONSES FROM OTHERS, AS WELL AS TO AVOID BOTH RESPONSIBILITIES AND AUTONOMY.

NOTEWORTHY RESPONSES

THE FOLLOWING STATEMENTS WERE ANSWERED BY THE PATIENT IN THE DIRECTION NOTED IN THE PARENTHESIS. THESE ITEMS SUGGEST SPECIFIC PROBLEM AREAS THAT MAY DESERVE FURTHER INQUIRY ON THE PART OF THE CLINICIAN.

HEALTH PREOCCUPATION
18. LATELY, I GET BUTTERFLIES IN MY STOMACH AND BREAK OUT IN COLD SWEATS (T).
33. I FEEL WEAK AND TIRED MUCH OF THE TIME (T).
44. I HAVE ALWAYS FELT A PAIN SOMEWHERE IN MY BODY (T).
72. LATELY, I CANNOT SEEM TO SLEEP AND WAKE UP JUST AS TIRED AS WHEN I WENT TO BED (T).
73. I HAVE A VERY TIGHT FEELING IN THE PIT OF MY STOMACH EVERY FEW DAYS OR SO (T).
112. THOUGH MY BODY PAINS AND PROBLEMS ARE REAL, NOBODY SEEMS TO UNDERSTAND THEM (T).

INTERPERSONAL ALIENATION
37. I HAVE ALWAYS AVOIDED GETTING INVOLVED WITH PEOPLE SOCIALLY (T).
47. I AM SO QUIET AND WITHDRAWN, MOST PEOPLE DO NOT EVEN KNOW I EXIST (T).
49. I AM A QUIET AND FEARFUL PERSON (T).
55. I HATE TO TALK, EVEN TO PEOPLE I KNOW (T).
83. A LONG TIME AGO, I DECIDED THAT IT IS BEST TO HAVE LITTLE TO DO WITH PEOPLE (T).
101. I HAVE ALWAYS GONE FOR LONG PERIODS WHEN I HARDLY TALK TO ANYONE (T).
141. I AM VERY ILL-AT-EASE WITH MEMBERS OF THE OPPOSITE SEX (T).
150. I HAVE ALMOST NO CLOSE TIES WITH OTHER PEOPLE (T).

EMOTIONAL DYSCONTROL
5. IN THE LAST FEW WEEKS I BEGIN TO CRY EVEN WHEN THE SLIGHTEST OF THINGS GOES WRONG (T).
26. I TEND TO BURST OUT IN TEARS OR IN ANGER FOR UNKNOWN REASONS (T).
36. LATELY, I FIND MYSELF CRYING WITHOUT ANY REASON (T).
67. LATELY, I FEEL JUMPY AND UNDER TERRIBLE STRAIN, BUT I DO NOT KNOW WHY (T).
167. LATELY, I HAVE GONE ALL TO PIECES (T).

SELF-DESTRUCTIVE POTENTIAL
54. I HAVE BEGUN TO FEEL LIKE A FAILURE IN RECENT WEEKS (T).
108. I JUST DO NOT HAVE THE STRENGTH LATELY TO FIGHT BACK (T).
120. MOST PEOPLE THINK THAT I AM A WORTHLESS NOTHING (T).

PARALLEL DSM-III MULTIAXIAL DIAGNOSES

ALTHOUGH THE DIAGNOSTIC CRITERIA UTILIZED IN THE MCMI DIFFER SOMEWHAT FROM THOSE IN THE DSM-III, THERE ARE SUFFICIENT PARALLELS TO RECOMMEND CONSIDERATION OF THE FOLLOWING ASSIGNMENTS. MORE DEFINITIVE JUDGMENTS SHOULD DRAW UPON BIOGRAPHIC, OBSERVATION AND INTERVIEW DATA, IN ADDITION TO SELF-REPORT INVENTORIES SUCH AS THE MCMI.

AXIS I: CLINICAL SYNDROME: THE MAJOR COMPLAINTS AND BEHAVIORS OF THE PATIENT PARALLEL THE FOLLOWING AXIS I DIAGNOSES, LISTED IN ORDER OF THEIR CLINICAL SIGNIFICANCE AND SALIENCE.

300.02 GENERALIZED ANXIETY DISORDER.

300.40 DYSTHYMIC DISORDER.

300.81 SOMATIZATION DISORDER; PROMINENT HYPOCHONDRIACAL FEATURES.

AXIS II: PERSONALITY DISORDER: A DEEPLY INGRAINED AND PERVASIVE PATTERN OF
MALADAPTIVE FUNCTIONING UNDERLIES THE AXIS I CLINICAL SYNDROMAL PICTURE. THE
FOLLOWING PERSONALITY DIAGNOSES PARALLEL THE MOST SALIENT FEATURES THAT
CHARACTERIZE THE INDIVIDUAL.

301.22 SCHIZOTYPAL PERSONALITY; PROMINENT AVOIDANT TRAITS (PROVISIONAL; RULE
       OUT 301.82 AVOIDANT PERSONALITY, PROMINENT SCHIZOTYPAL TRAITS).

COURSE: THE MAJOR PERSONALITY FEATURES DESCRIBED PREVIOUSLY REFLECT LONG TERM
OR CHRONIC TRAITS THAT ARE LIKELY TO HAVE PERSISTED FOR SEVERAL YEARS PRIOR TO
THE PRESENT ASSESSMENT.
THE CLINICAL SYNDROMES DESCRIBED PREVIOUSLY TEND TO BE RELATIVELY TRANSIENT,
WAXING AND WANING IN THEIR PROMINENCE AND INTENSITY DEPENDING ON THE PRESENCE OF
ENVIRONMENTAL STRESS.

AXIS IV: PSYCHOSOCIAL STRESSORS: THE REPORT ON PERSONALITY TRAITS AND CURRENT
SYMPTOMATOLOGY SUGGEST THE FOLLOWING COMPLICATING FACTORS WHICH MAY BE
EXACERBATING THE PRESENT EMOTIONAL STATE. THEY ARE LISTED IN ORDER OF PROBABLE
APPLICABILITY. THE LISTINGS SHOULD BE VIEWED AS A GUIDE FOR FURTHER
INVESTIGATION BY THE CLINICIAN AND SHOULD NOT BE ASSUMED TO BE DEFINITE FACTORS
IN THE CASE:
RECENT LIFE CHANGES
SOCIAL INADEQUACIES; WORK UPSETS; FAMILY TENSIONS

SEVERITY OF DISTURBANCE: ON THE BASIS OF THE TEST DATA IT MAY BE ASSUMED THAT
THE PATIENT IS EXPERIENCING A SEVERE MENTAL DISORDER. FURTHER PROFESSIONAL
OBSERVATION AND CARE ARE APPROPRIATE.

     THERAPEUTIC IMPLICATIONS -- THE FOLLOWING CONSIDERATIONS ARE LIKELY TO BE
OF GREATER UTILITY AND ACCURACY DURING EARLY TREATMENT PLANNING THAN IN LATER
MANAGEMENT PHASES.
     BECAUSE OF INTENSE DEPENDENCY CONFLICTS AND A GROWING MISTRUST OF OTHERS,
THIS MAN IS UNLIKELY TO SUSTAIN A THERAPEUTIC RELATIONSHIP. IF HE IS AGREEABLE
TO INTERPERSONAL TREATMENT, IT IS LIKELY TO FOLLOW AN INCONSISTENT COURSE, WITH
FREQUENT MANEUVERS TO TEST THE SINCERITY AND MOTIVES OF THE THERAPIST.
TREATMENT MAY BE TERMINATED BY THIS PATIENT LONG BEFORE SUBSTANTIAL REMEDIAL
IMPROVEMENT HAS OCCURRED. THE WITHDRAWAL STEMS, IN PART, FROM HIS UNWILLINGNESS
TO FACE THE HUMILIATION OF CONFRONTING PAINFUL MEMORIES AND FEELINGS. ALSO, HE
MAY BE UNWILLING TO REEXPERIENCE THE FALSE HOPES AND DISAPPOINTMENTS USUALLY
AWAKENED BY EXPLORATORY THERAPY. THE THERAPIST SHOULD BE CAREFUL NOT TO SET
GOALS TOO HIGH OR TO PRESS CHANGES TOO FAST SINCE THIS MAN CANNOT TOLERATE
DEMANDS OR EXPECTANCIES WELL. EFFORTS SHOULD BE MADE TO BUILD TRUST, DIRECT HIS
ATTENTION TO POSITIVE TRAITS, AND ENHANCE HIS CONFIDENCE AND SELF-ESTEEM.

NAME =SAMPLE   TM   30-SEP-83   004 0005

NAME: Minnesota Child Development Inventory

SUPPLIER: PSYCH Systems, Inc.
600 Reisterstown Road
Baltimore, MD 21208
(800) 368-3366

PRODUCT CATEGORY

Personality

PRIMARY APPLICATIONS

Clinical Assessment/Diagnosis
Personal/Marriage/Family Counseling
Educational Evaluation/Planning

SALE RESTRICTIONS Qualified Professional

SERVICE TYPE/COST	Type	Available	Cost	Discount
	Mail-In	No		
	Teleprocessing	No		
	Local	Yes	See Below	

PRODUCT DESCRIPTION

The MINNESOTA CHILD DEVELOPMENT INVENTORY provides a standard inventory format for obtaining and interpreting parents' or guardians' reports of their children's development. It is appropriate for children one to six years of age and older children functioning at a developmental level less than six years.

This program administers and scores the 320 items in the test. The interpretive report that follows provides a description of the child's current developmental status in narrative form and in profile form. When utilized in the context of other medical, psychological, and social history information about the child and family, the MINNESOTA CHILD DEVELOPMENT INVENTORY results contribute to diagnosis and to recommendations for treatment and for education.

Psych Systems programs operate on the IBM PC-XT, COMPAQ Plus, Dec Professional 350, and most DEC PDP-11 systems. Various hardware/ software configurations are available directly from Psych Systems, with single-user systems starting at approximately $12,000. A per test fee also applies.

```
-------------------------------------------------------
|          |                                          |
|  MCDI    |  Minnesota Child Development Inventory    |
|          |                                          |
-------------------------------------------------------
```

          Child: Jayne Doe
      Informant: Jonathan Doe

This clinical report is designed to aid in psychological evaluation.
It was produced by a computerized analysis of the responses provided
by the informant listed above. The report provides important developmental
information about the above-named child. This report is to be used
in conjunction with professional evaluation. No decision should
be based solely upon the contents of this report.

The computer program generating this report was designed by Psych
Systems, Inc. , Baltimore, Maryland 21208.   Copyright (C) 1984
by Psych Systems, Inc.   The interpretive analysis utilized in
the interpretation was designed by Harold R. Ireton, Ph. D.   Copyright
(C) 1981 by Harold R. Ireton.   The Minnesota Child Development
Inventory is reproduced by permission, Copyright (C) 1968, 1970,
1972 by Harold R. Ireton and Edward J. Thwing.   Published by
Behavior Science Systems, Inc. , P. O. Box 1108, Minneapolis, Minnesota
55440.   All rights reserved.

Description

This 5 year and 6 month old girl was described by her father during the
administration of the MCDI. Someone other than the child's mother
has completed the MCDI inventory. To the extent that the informant
is not intimately familiar with the child's development, the interpretation
is subject to error and should be used with due caution. She
is reported to be free of any handicaps or special problems.

Current Developmental Status

General Development

According to the informant's report, this child has a serious developmental
problem. The child's overall development is well below age expectations,
less than the development of children half this age.

Motor Development

The child's gross motor development is in the seriously delayed
range, indicating a major gross motor problem. Fine Motor skills
are seriously delayed. Eye-hand coordination is at a level less
than that of children half this age.

Language Development

This child's expressive language development is well below age
expectations, over fifty percent below the child's age level.
The child's language comprehension is significantly below age
level. A delay on the language comprehension scale is a strong
indicator of a developmental problem. A low score on this scale
could be related to a hearing or language problem, or to limited
intellectual ability.

Adaptive Comprehension

The child's comprehension of situations by primarily non-verbal
means is seriously delayed, over fifty percent below age level.
Self-Help skills are seriously delayed. Functioning is less than
that of a child half this age. This delay could reflect a major
intellectual, motor or social problem.

Personal-Social Maturity

Personal-Social Maturity is well below age level, which may indicate
a major developmental or behavioral problem.

Intellectual Status

The child's MCDI profile suggests below average intellectual development.
Note: The MCDI measures current developmental functioning from
which inferences about intellectual functioning can be made. However,
this should not be used as a substitute for an individual intellectual
assessment.

Summary

Scores on all of the developmental scales fall in the delayed range.
Intellectual status is probably below average. These MCDI results
suggest the need for further evaluation. Consideration should
be given to comprehensive medical and psychological assessment.

Scale Name	Raw Scores	Category
General Development Scale:	72	Seriously Delayed
Gross Motor Scale:	21	Seriously Delayed
Fine Motor Scale:	28	Seriously Delayed
Expressive Language Scale:	33	Seriously Delayed
Language Comprehension Scale:	40	Delayed
Situation Comprehension Scale:	25	Seriously Delayed
Self Help Scale:	19	Seriously Delayed
Personal/Social Scale:	21	Seriously Delayed

222-22-2222 Jonathan Doe   32 yr old white male 17-Feb-84

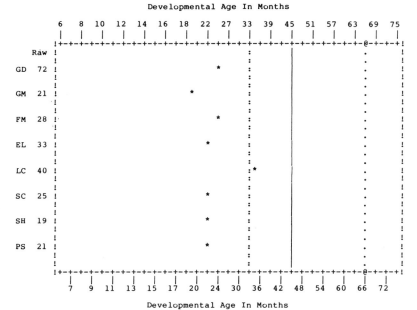

Developmental Age In Months

```
              6   8  10  12  14  16  18  22  27  33  39  45  51  57  63  69  75
              |   |   |   |   |   |   |   |   |   |   |   |   |   |   |   |   |
          !+-+-+-+-+-+-+-+-+-+-+-+-+-+-+-+-+-+-+-+-+-+-+-+-+-+-+-@-+-+-+!
      Raw !                                  :                         .        !
          !                                  :                         .        !
GD   72   !                            *     :                         .        !
          !                                  :                         .        !
GM   21   !                   *              :                         .        !
          !                                  :                         .        !
FM   28   !                            *     :                         .        !
          !                                  :                         .        !
EL   33   !                         *        :                         .        !
          !                                  :                         .        !
LC   40   !                                  :*                        .        !
          !                                  :                         .        !
SC   25   !                         *        :                         .        !
          !                                  :                         .        !
SH   19   !                         *        :                         .        !
          !                                  :                         .        !
PS   21   !                         *        :                         .        !
          !                                  :                         .        !
          !                                  :                         .        !
          !+-+-+-+-+-+-+-+-+-+-+-+-+-+-+-+-+-+-+-+-+-+-+-+-+-+-+-@-+-+-+!
              |   |   |   |   |   |   |   |   |   |   |   |   |   |   |   |
              7   9  11  13  15  17  20  24  30  36  42  48  54  60  66  72
```

Developmental Age In Months

	GD	General Development Scale	Percentage Lines
	GM	Gross Motor Scale	
	FM	Fine Motor Scale	: -> 50% below age
Graph	EL	Expressive Language Scale	
Key	LC	Language Comprehension Scale	| -> 30% below age
	SC	Situation Comprehension Scale	
	SH	Self Help Scale	+ -> 30% above age
	PS	Personal/Social Scale	

Chronological Age Line   @........@ -> 66 months

NOTE: Graphic representations are based on empirically generated values

psychware **399**

NAME: Minnesota Multiphasic Personality Inventory

SUPPLIER: Western Psychological Services
12031 Wilshire Blvd.
Los Angeles, CA 90025
(213) 478-2061

PRODUCT CATEGORY

Personality

PRIMARY APPLICATIONS

Clinical Assessment/Diagnosis

SALE RESTRICTIONS American Psychological Association Guidelines

SERVICE TYPE/COST	Type	Available	Cost	Discount
	Mail-In	Yes	$14.50	Yes
	Teleprocessing	No		
	Local	No		

PRODUCT DESCRIPTION

The WPS TEST REPORT for the MMPI features client anonymity, profile code, critical items, validated decision rules, complete adolescent and adult norms, statement references, and response frequencies. All answer sheets are processed within 8 hours of being received at WPS.

*****1
Client: Not Provided
Answer Sheet: SEND TO: #
Age: 36 Years   6 Months
Sex: Female
Race: White
Education: 17 Years
Marital Status: Single

Western Psychological Services • 12031 Wilshire Boulevard • Los Angeles, California 90025

******
Date Processed 03/30/84

*** MMPI CLINICAL PROFILE INTERPRETATION ***

The following MMPI interpretation should be viewed as a series of
hypotheses which may require further investigation. This report is a
professional consultation and should not be shared with the client.

Norms used: Adult K-Corrected

Code: 8***6**2*734''190'5: L:F***K#

     The validity scale configuration suggests that great care should be
taken in evaluating this client's test results. It is likely that a
standard interpretation of these data would result in an inaccurate
description of this client's current status. This invalidity may have
resulted from several causes:

     This client may be acutely disturbed and currently unable to
correctly complete this task. If this explanation is accurate, a
subsequent Inventory administration will be necessary after some
clinical improvement is observed.

     This client may be consciously exaggerating problems or malingering
in an attempt to obtain some goal. If this is so, another Inventory
administration following a discussion with the client of response set,
validity scale interpretation, and the listed Critical Items may lead to
a more accurate self-description.

     Other possible reasons for these results include exaggeration of
complaints as a "Cry for Help," lack of cooperation, some atypical
response set, or test error.

     Possible interpretations of the clinical profile and supplemental
scale scores are not generated due to this possible invalidity. A
qualified psychologist may be able to make a finer discrimination and
interpret those protocols judged to be valid.[1]

NOTE: The numbers following these interpretive statements refer to the
basic rules that govern the construction of this narrative
interpretation. These rules, and the data that describe statement
frequency and rated accuracy, are described in "The MMPI: Clinical
Assessment and Automated Interpretation" (1974). This monograph is
available from Western Psychological Services (W-134A). Documentation
of the following critical item set and supplemental scale
interpretations may be found in the WPS TEST REPORT MMPI User's Manual.

**** LACHAR-WROBEL CRITICAL ITEMS ****

The following statements were made by this client in the direction
indicated and may suggest topics of inquiry. Although care should be

psychware **401**

taken in the interpretation of a response to an individual Inventory statement, each Critical Item has been selected by consensual judgment and has demonstrated by its relation to independent clinical criteria potential diagnostic utility.

The following endorsed Critical Items are presented even though this protocol is of doubtful validity. A careful evaluation of item content during an interview with this client, or in light of case material, may assist in the determination of the cause for this invalidity.

Relative frequency of item endorsement in adult white female normative and psychiatric samples is indicated at the end of each statement by this notation: [normative % / psychiatric %].

---ANXIETY AND TENSION---

13. I work under a great deal of tension.(T) [23%/57%]
186. I frequently notice my hand shakes when I try to do something.(T) [27%/42%]
238. I have periods of such great restlessness that I cannot sit long in in a chair.(T) [33%/58%]
242. I believe I am no more nervous than most others.(F) [25%/65%]
287. I have very few fears compared to my friends.(F) [26%/71%]
335. I cannot keep my mind on one thing.(T) [23%/50%]
337. I feel anxiety about something or someone almost all the time.(T) [37%/63%]
352. I have been afraid of things or people that I knew could not hurt me.(T) [22%/42%]

---DEPRESSION AND WORRY---

3. I wake up fresh and rested most mornings.(F) [25%/66%]
9. I am about as able to work as I ever was.(F) [14%/50%]
76. Most of the time I feel blue.(T) [10%/65%]
86. I am certainly lacking in self-confidence.(T) [34%/75%]
139. Sometimes I feel as if I must injure myself or someone else.(T) [5%/35%]
142. I certainly feel useless at times.(T) [51%/79%]
168. There is something wrong with my mind.(T) [3%/45%]
178. My memory seems to be all right.(F) [8%/37%]
301. Life is a strain for me much of the time.(T) [18%/62%]
339. Most of the time I wish I were dead.(T) [3%/28%]
397. I have sometimes felt that difficulties were piling up so high that I could not overcome them.(T) [55%/81%]
418. At times I think I am no good at all.(T) [43%/69%]
431. I worry quite a bit over possible misfortunes.(T) [--%/67%]

---SLEEP DISTURBANCE---

5. I am easily awakened by noise.(T) [59%/55%]
43. My sleep is fitful and disturbed.(T) [16%/50%]
152. Most nights I go to sleep without thoughts or ideas bothering me.(F) [26%/63%]
359. Sometimes some unimportant thought will run through my mind and bother me for days.(T) [43%/55%]
559. I have often been frightened in the middle of the night.(T) [--%/44%]

---DEVIANT BELIEFS---

110. Someone has it in for me.(T) [11%/18%]

Western Psychological Services · 12031 Wilshire Boulevard · Los Angeles, California 90025

WPS TEST REPORT

119. My speech is the same as always (not faster or slower, or slurring; no hoarseness).(F) [15%/37%]
121. I believe I am being plotted against.(T) [2%/14%]
123. I believe I am being followed.(T) [2%/10%]
197. Someone has been trying to rob me.(T) [2%/6%]
275. Someone has control over my mind.(T) [3%/11%]
284. I am sure I am being talked about.(T) [22%/43%]
291. At one or more times in my life I felt that someone was making me do things by hypnotizing me.(T) [3%/9%]
293. Someone has been trying to influence my mind.(T) [8%/19%]
331. If people had not had it in for me I would have been more successful.(T) [7%/13%]
347. I have no enemies who really wish to harm me.(F) [14%/27%]
364. People say insulting and vulgar things about me.(T) [7%/19%]
551. Sometimes I am sure that other people can tell what I am thinking.(T) [33%/50%]

---DEVIANT THINKING AND EXPERIENCE---

33. I have had very peculiar and strange experiences.(T) [22%/46%]
48. When I am with people I am bothered by hearing very queer things.(T) [3%/14%]
134. At times my thoughts have raced ahead faster than I could speak them.(T) [60%/74%]
184. I commonly hear voices without knowing where they come from.(T) [2%/9%]
334. Peculiar odors come to me at times.(T) [17%/20%]
341. At times I hear so well it bothers me.(T) [9%/23%]
349. I have strange and peculiar thoughts.(T) [10%/37%]
350. I hear strange things when I am alone.(T) [11%/17%]
420. I have had some very unusual religious experiences.(T) [13%/17%]
464. I have never seen a vision.(F) [32%/30]

---SUBSTANCE ABUSE---

156. I have had periods in which I carried on activities without knowing later what I had been doing.(T) [7%/27%]
466. Except by a doctor's orders I never take drugs or sleeping powders.(F) [14%/40%]

---ANTISOCIAL ATTITUDE---

205. At times it has been impossible for me to keep from stealing or shoplifting something.(T) [2%/9%]
250. I don't blame anyone for trying to grab everything he can get in this world.(T) [31%/38%]
269. I can easily make other people afraid of me, and sometimes do it for the fun of it.(T) [3%/9%]
280. Most people make friends because friends are likely to be useful to them.(T) [38%/32%]

---FAMILY CONFLICT---

21. At times I have very much wanted to leave home.(T) [30%/72%]
137. I believe that my home life is as pleasant as that of most people I know.(F) [5%/56%]
245. My parents and family find more fault with me than they should.(T) [11%/38%]

---PROBLEMATIC ANGER---

Western Psychological Services • 12031 Wilshire Boulevard • Los Angeles, California 90025

97. At times I have a strong urge to do something harmful or shocking.(T) [14%/43%]
145. At times I feel like picking a fist fight with someone.(T) [17%/28%]
234. I get mad easily and then get over it soon.(T) [58%/50%]

---SEXUAL CONCERN AND DEVIATION---

20. My sex life is satisfactory.(F) [10%/63%]
37. I have never been in trouble because of my sex behavior.(F) [15%/35%]
74. I have often wished I were a girl.(T) (or if you are a girl) I have never been sorry that I am a girl.(F) [--%/42%]
133. I have never indulged in any unusual sex practices.(F) [18%/30%]
179. I am worried about sex matters.(T) [8%/53%]
297. I wish I were not bothered by thoughts about sex.(T) [11%/35%]
519. There is something wrong with my sex organs.(T) [25%/13%]

---SOMATIC SYMPTOMS---

36. I seldom worry about my health.(F) [28%/58%]
44. Much of the time my head seems to hurt all over.(T) [4%/31%]
47. Once a week or oftener I feel suddenly hot all over, without apparent cause.(T) [14%/31%]
55. I am almost never bothered by pains over the heart or in my chest.(F) [30%/45%]
62. Parts of my body often have feelings like burning, tingling, crawling, or like "going to sleep."(T) [35%/51%]
68. I hardly ever feel pain in the back of the neck.(F) [27%/50%]
174. I have never had a fainting spell.(F) [54%/56%]
175. I seldom or never have dizzy spells.(F) [28%/45%]
189. I feel weak all over much of the time.(T) [11%/40%]
194. I have had attacks in which I could not control my movements or speech but in which I knew what was going on around me.(T) [8%/22%]
243. I have few or no pains.(F) [23%/44%]
251. I have had blank spells in which my activities were interrupted and I did not know what was going on around me.(T) [8%/27%]
330. I have never been paralyzed or had any unusual weakness of any of my muscles.(F) [23%/34%]
544. I feel tired a good deal of the time.(T) [--%/72%]

Western Psychological Services • 12031 Wilshire Boulevard • Los Angeles, California 90025

WPS TEST REPORT

MMPI   PROFILE

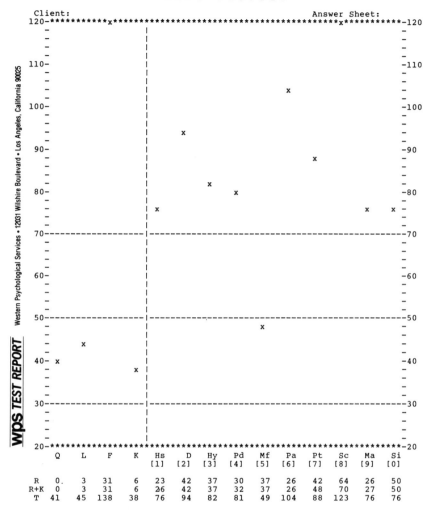

*** SUPPLEMENTAL SCALE INFORMATION ***

Obvious - Subtle Scales

	D-O	D-S	Hy-O	Hy-S	Pd-O	Pd-S	Pa-O	Pa-S	Ma-O	Ma-S
Raw Scores	33	9	28	9	22	8	19	7	17	9
T-Scores	97	43	95	40	98	47	115	57	89	50

Experimental Scales

	A	R	ES	Ca	MAH	Lb	O-H	Ps
Raw Scores	37	17	25	28	21	7	11	41
T-Scores	76	48	26	80	60	41	44	83

Wiggins Content Scales

	ORG	HEA	DEP	MOR	SOC	HOS	FAM	AUT	FEM	PHO	PSY	HYP	REL
Raw Scores	24	15	24	21	21	19	12	14	23	19	36	19	7
T-Scores	87	75	80	75	72	75	82	66	59	74	108	65	49

*** SUPPLEMENTAL SCALE INTERPRETATION ***

Hypotheses that reflect supplemental scale elevations are not presented, due to possible test protocol invalidity.

Item responses for client no.   Answer sheet no.

```
  1(F)    11(T)    21(T)    31(F)    41(T)    51(F)    61(T)    71(T)    81(F)    91(F)
  2(T)    12(F)    22(T)    32(T)    42(T)    52(T)    62(T)    72(F)    82(T)    92(F)
  3(F)    13(T)    23(T)    33(T)    43(T)    53(F)    63(F)    73(F)    83(F)    93(T)
  4(F)    14(F)    24(T)    34(F)    44(T)    54(F)    64(T)    74(F)    84(T)    94(T)
  5(T)    15(T)    25(T)    35(T)    45(T)    55(F)    65(F)    75(T)    85(F)    95(T)
  6(F)    16(F)    26(F)    36(F)    46(F)    56(F)    66(F)    76(F)    86(T)    96(T)
  7(F)    17(F)    27(T)    37(F)    47(T)    57(F)    67(F)    77(T)    87(T)    97(T)
  8(F)    18(F)    28(F)    38(F)    48(T)    58(T)    68(F)    78(T)    88(T)    98(F)
  9(F)    19(F)    29(F)    39(T)    49(T)    59(F)    69(F)    79(T)    89(T)    99(F)
 10(F)    20(F)    30(T)    40(T)    50(T)    60(T)    70(F)    80(F)    90(T)   100(T)

101(T)   111(F)   121(T)   131(F)   141(T)   151(F)   161(T)   171(T)   181(T)   191(T)
102(T)   112(F)   122(F)   132(T)   142(T)   152(F)   162(T)   172(T)   182(T)   192(F)
103(F)   113(T)   123(T)   133(F)   143(F)   153(F)   163(F)   173(T)   183(T)   193(T)
104(T)   114(F)   124(T)   134(T)   144(F)   154(T)   164(T)   174(F)   184(T)   194(T)
105(T)   115(T)   125(T)   135(F)   145(T)   155(F)   165(T)   175(F)   185(T)   195(T)
106(T)   116(T)   126(T)   136(T)   146(F)   156(T)   166(T)   176(F)   186(T)   196(F)
107(T)   117(T)   127(F)   137(F)   147(T)   157(T)   167(F)   177(T)   187(T)   197(T)
108(T)   118(F)   128(F)   138(F)   148(T)   158(T)   168(T)   178(F)   188(F)   198(T)
109(T)   119(F)   129(T)   139(T)   149(T)   159(F)   169(T)   179(F)   189(T)   199(T)
110(T)   120(T)   130(T)   140(T)   150(T)   160(F)   170(F)   180(T)   190(T)   200(F)

201(T)   211(F)   221(T)   231(T)   241(T)   251(T)   261(T)   271(F)   281(T)   291(T)
202(T)   212(T)   222(F)   232(F)   242(F)   252(F)   262(F)   272(T)   282(T)   292(T)
203(F)   213(F)   223(F)   233(T)   243(F)   253(T)   263(F)   273(F)   283(F)   293(T)
204(F)   214(F)   224(T)   234(T)   244(T)   254(F)   264(F)   274(F)   284(T)   294(T)
205(T)   215(F)   225(T)   235(F)   245(T)   255(T)   265(T)   275(T)   285(F)   295(T)
206(F)   216(F)   226(T)   236(T)   246(F)   256(F)   266(T)   276(T)   286(F)   296(T)
207(F)   217(T)   227(T)   237(F)   247(T)   257(T)   267(T)   277(T)   287(T)   297(T)
208(F)   218(F)   228(F)   238(F)   248(T)   258(F)   268(T)   278(T)   288(F)   298(T)
209(F)   219(F)   229(T)   239(T)   249(T)   259(T)   269(T)   279(F)   289(T)   299(T)
210(F)   220(T)   230(F)   240(F)   250(T)   260(F)   270(F)   280(T)   290(T)   300(F)

301(T)   311(F)   321(T)   331(T)   341(T)   351(F)   361(T)   371(F)   381(F)   391(T)
302(F)   312(T)   322(T)   332(T)   342(F)   352(T)   362(T)   372(T)   382(T)   392(T)
303(F)   313(F)   323(T)   333(T)   343(T)   353(F)   363(T)   373(F)   383(T)   393(F)
304(F)   314(T)   324(F)   334(T)   344(F)   354(F)   364(T)   374(T)   384(T)   394(T)
305(T)   315(F)   325(T)   335(T)   345(T)   355(T)   365(T)   375(T)   385(T)   395(T)
306(F)   316(T)   326(T)   336(T)   346(F)   356(T)   366(T)   376(T)   386(T)*  396(T)
307(T)   317(T)   327(T)   337(T)   347(F)   357(T)   367(F)   377(T)   387(T)   397(T)
308(T)   318(T)   328(T)   338(T)   348(T)   358(T)   368(T)   378(T)   388(F)   398(T)
309(T)   319(T)   329(F)   339(T)   349(T)   359(T)   369(F)   379(F)   389(T)   399(T)
310(F)   320(F)   330(F)   340(T)   350(T)   360(F)   370(T)   380(T)   390(T)   400(F)

401(T)   411(T)   421(T)   431(T)   441(F)   451(T)   461(F)   471(F)   481(F)   491(F)
402(T)   412(F)   422(F)   432(F)   442(T)   452(F)   462(F)   472(T)   482(F)   492(T)
403(F)   413(T)   423(F)   433(F)   443(T)   453(T)   463(F)   473(F)   483(F)   493(F)
404(F)   414(T)   424(T)   434(F)   444(F)   454(F)   464(F)   474(F)   484(T)   494(F)
405(T)   415(F)   425(T)   435(T)   445(T)   455(T)   465(F)   475(T)   485(T)   495(T)
406(T)   416(T)   426(T)   436(T)   446(F)   456(T)   466(F)   476(T)   486(T)   496(T)
407(T)   417(F)   427(T)   437(F)   447(F)   457(F)   467(F)   477(T)   487(T)   497(T)
408(T)   418(F)   428(T)   438(T)   448(T)   458(T)   468(T)   478(F)   488(F)   498(F)
409(T)   419(F)   429(T)   439(T)   449(T)   459(T)   469(T)   479(F)   489(F)   499(T)
410(T)   420(T)   430(T)   440(F)   450(T)   460(T)   470(F)   480(T)   490(F)   500(T)

501(F)   511(T)   521(F)   531(T)   541(F)   551(T)   561(F)
502(T)   512(F)   522(F)   532(T)   542(F)   552(T)   562(T)
503(T)   513(T)   523(T)   533(T)   543(F)   553(F)   563(F)
504(F)   514(F)   524(T)   534(T)   544(T)   554(T)   564(T)
505(T)   515(T)   525(T)   535(T)   545(T)   555(T)   565(F)
506(T)   516(T)   526(F)   536(T)   546(F)   556(F)   566(T)
507(T)   517(F)   527(T)   537(F)   547(T)   557(T)
508(T)   518(T)   528(F)   538(F)   548(F)   558(T)
509(T)   519(T)   529(T)   539(F)   549(T)   559(T)
510(T)   520(T)   530(T)   540(T)   550(F)   560(T)
```

[* indicates a double response]
[( ) indicates blank or light mark]

Western Psychological Services • 12031 Wilshire Boulevard • Los Angeles, California 90025

WPS TEST REPORT

NAME: Minnesota Multiphasic Personality Inventory

SUPPLIER: Integrated Professional Systems
5211 Mahoning Avenue Suite 135
Youngstown, OH 44515
(216) 799-3282

PRODUCT CATEGORY

Personality

PRIMARY APPLICATIONS

Clinical Assessment/Diagnosis
Personal/Marriage/Family Counseling
Personnel Selection/Evaluation

SALE RESTRICTIONS Qualified Professional

SERVICE TYPE/COST	Type	Available	Cost	Discount
	Mail-In	No		
	Teleprocessing	No		
	Local	Yes	See Below	

PRODUCT DESCRIPTION

This product provides an interpretive report of up to 10 pages and evaluates as many as 106 MMPI scales in doing so. Adult and adolescent profiles are presented for the standard validity and clinical scales. Configural patterns are examined and age- appropriate description for individuals with similar profiles are printed. Common diagnoses, prognoses, and suggested treatment approaches are presented, when available. Interpretive statements are also presented for the Clinical scales, the Harris & Lingoes, Obvious/Subtle, Wiggins Content, Tryon, Stein & Chu, and 30 other experimental/research scales. A list of critical items and the subject's item responses are provided at the end of the report.

An operating software package, priced from $200-$850 depending on the complexity of the package, is required for program use, plus an additional fee of $5.00 per use.

JOHN DOE is a 16 year old white male with 10 years of education. He was
tested on June 12, 1983.

This is a confidential report for use by professional staff only. The
words used in the interpretation are technically defined and have
specific meaning for clinical patients. The program which generates
this profile considers many types of decision rules and the results
need to be interpreted in light of the limitations of the instrument.
Statements are based on analyses which should be considered as
hypotheses for further consideration in combination with the patient's
verbal admissions and other clinical factors.

Profile interpretation
Subscale analyses of the clinical scales and of the Tryon Stein and Chu
scales are presented in descending order of scale elevation. Asterisks
indicate the number of standard deviations above the mean.   Hyphens are
used to indicate the number of standard deviations below the mean.
Experimental scale names are followed by a letter to indicate the scale
author's name where:
A = McAndrews   M = Mayo Experimental
E = Edwards   O = Megargee O-H Scale
F = Finney   P = Pepper & Strong
G = Gough   W = Wiggins Content
L = Welsh

psychware **409**

```
                              ADOLESCENT PROFILE
     T    L    F    K         1    2    3    4    5    6    7    8    9    0  T
     100                 +                                                    100
     -                   +                                                    -
     -                   +                                                    -
     -                   +                                                    -
     -                   +                                                    -
     90                  +                                                    90
     -                   +                                                    -
     -                   +                                                    -
     -                   +                                                    -
     -                   +                                                    -
     80                  +                                                    80
     -                   +                                                    -
     -                   +                                                    -
     -                   +                                                    -
     -                   +                                                    -
     70 - - - - - - - -  + - - - - - - - - - - - - - - - - - - - - - - - - -70
     -                   +                                                    -
     -    *         *    +                                                    -
     -                   +              *                                     -
     -                   +                 *                                  -
     60                  +                                                    60
     -                   +                                                    -
     -                   +                    *                               -
     -                   +                                                    -
     -                   +                                                    -
     50 - - - - - - - -  + - - - - - -*- - - - - - - - - - - - - - - - - - -50
     -                   +                          *                        -
     -                   +                                          *         -
     -         *         +                                                    -
     -              -    +    *                                               -
     40                  +                                    *    *          40
     -                   +                                              *     -
     -                   +                                                    -
     -                   +                                                    -
     -                   +                                                    -
     30 - - - - - - - -  + - - - - - - - - - - - - - - - - - - - - - - - - -30

     /#                      1    2    3    4    5    6    7    8    9    0
     SCL   L    F    K       HS   D    HY   PD   MF   PA   PT   SC   MA   SI
     RAW   8    5   21       3   19   24   24   23   11    7    9   17   20
     TSC  67   44   67      42   51   63   62   55   49   39   41   47   37

     RANKING      SCALE      3    4    5    2    6    9    1    8    7    0
                T SCORE     63   62   55   51   49   47   42   41   39   37
```

This person answered 566 items and the validity configuration indicates a
valid profile in subject who tends to present self in positive light. May
reflect good ego or resistance. Marked evasiveness is present in a
neurotic pattern of repression and denial. Subject lacks insight.
Configural Analysis : There are no significant elevations, no
configuration available.

410 *psychware*

```
                         ADULT PROFILE
T    L    F    K         1    2    3    4    5    6    7    8    9    0  T
100            +                                                        100
 -             +                                                         -
 -             +                                                         -
 -             +                                                         -
 -             +                                                         -
90             +                                                        90
 -             +                                                         -
 -             +                                                         -
 -             +                                                         -
 -             +                        *                                -
80             +                                                        80
 -             +                                                         -
 -             +                                                         -
 -             +                                                         -
 -             +                                                         -
70  - - - - - -- - - - - - - - - - - - - - - - - - - - - - - - - - . -70
 -             +                                                         -
 -        *    +                                                         -
 -    *        +              *                        *                 -
 -             +                                  *                      -
60             +                             *                    *     60
 -             +    *                                                    -
 -             +         *              *                                -
 -        *    +                                                         -
 -             +                                                         -
50  - - - - - -+ - - - - - - - - - - - - - - - - - - - - - - - - - - -50
 -             +                                                         -
 -             +                                                   *    -
 -             +                                                         -
 -             +                                                         -
40             +                                                        40
 -             +                                                         -
 -             +                                                         -
 -             +                                                         -
 -             +                                                         -
30  - - - - - -+ - - - - - - - - - - - - - - - - - - - - - - - - - - -30


   /#                    1    2    3    4    5    6    7    8    9    0
   SCL   L    F    K    HS    D   HY   PD   MF   PA   PT   SC   MA   SI
   RAW   8    5   21    14   19   24   32   23   11   28   30   21   20
   TSC  63   54   66    57   56   64   81   55   59   61   65   60   45

   RANKING    SCALE      4    8    3    7    9    6    1    2    5    0
              T SCORE   81   65   64   61   60   59   57   56   55   45
```

This person answered 566 items and the validity configuration indicates a
valid profile in subject who tends to present self in positive light. May
reflect good ego or resistance. Configural analysis of the patient's
responses and studies of people with similar response patterns suggests
that these individuals are angry, rebellious and unconventional.
Impulsiveness, poor social judgement, & limited frustration tolerance are
characteristics. They are typically extroverted and energetic, but often
lack definite goals and have superficial relationships with other people.
Marital difficulties, a poor work history, substance abuse, ad sexual
acting-out are common problems. Common diagnoses : conduct disorder. These
individuals lack insight and generally disregard the consequences of their
behavior. Their behavior patterns are resistant to change and they
generally do not profit from experience (including psychotherapy). The
prognosis for significant improvement is good. Goldberg sign = psychosis.

```
Clinical, O/S, and Harris & Lingoes Analysis        Scale          Raw T / T
-----------------------------------------------------------------------------
Expect anti-social behavior,  often involving  *** PSYCH DEVIANCY    32  81
authority conflicts.  Psychopathic  features.
Evidence of a  behavior disorder  is present.        Ob/Sub T-scores     56/ 78
Patient is aware of and may be minimizing it.
Expresses discontent with family relations.   **     Family Discord   6  74
```

psychware **411**

Description		Scale	Raw	T	/ T
Describes family as unsupportive, unpleasant. Normally accepts authority figures without resentment and accepts parental restrictions.		Authority Prob	5	55	
Does not experience any unusual discomfort in social situations. Able to talk with others.		Soc Imperturb	9	55	
Feels accepted and understood by others, sees them as supportive. Has feeling of belonging.		Soc Alienation	1	35	
Depicts self as generally happy and does not express undue regret or guilt about the past.		Self Alienation	2	43	
Probably alienated from others, prefers abstract interests & fantasy to personal contact.	*	SCHIZOPHRENIA	30	65	
Reports having adequate emotional involvement with others, does not resent family members.		Soc Alienation	2	44	
Feels that life is worthwhile. Denies feeling depressed/ despairing, denies sadistic needs.		Emotional Alien	1	39	
Describes some difficulties in concentration and memory. May experience strange thoughts.	*	-Ego Mastery Cog	4	66	
Does not find daily life rewarding & tends to be pessimistic about future. Feels strained.	*	-Ego Mastery Con	4	62	
Feels in control of emotions & impulses. Not unusually restless, irritable or hyperactive.		Defect Inhibit	0	41	
Has not experienced body changes, feelings of depersonalization, or psychomotor problems.		Sensory Exper	2	48	
Hysteroid personality traits present. Often exhibits somatic symptoms when under stress.	*	HYSTERIA	24	64	
Hysterical personality traits are present. Expect symptoms to be genuine but controlled.		Ob/Sub T-scores		49/	66
Able to admit to social inadequacies when it is appropriate. Usually comfortable socially.		Deny Soc Anxiety	5	58	
Probably too trusting, sees others as honest. Needs affection & will avoid confrontations.	*	Need Affection	8	63	
Usually feels comfortable and in good health. Feels rested unless fatigued by some illness.		Lassitude	3	53	
Does not report multiple somatic symptoms. If any are present, they are probably realistic.		Somatic Probs	2	47	
Somewhat sensitive, avoids aggressive content in own verbalizations, newspapers, and books.	*	Inhibit Aggress	5	68	
Perfectionistic & self-critical attitudes can be expected. Exhibits excessive worry/anxiety	*	PSYCHASTHENIA	28	61	
Expect an energetic, enthusiastic orientation with optimistic feelings. Has wide interests.	*	HYPOMANIA	21	60	
High energy level probably reflects a personality characteristic rather than disturbance.		Ob/Sub T-scores		47/	60
Does not view self or others as selfish/ dishonest and is not manipulative or exploitive.		Amorality	2	52	
Has a normal need for change, but able to adjust to routine when necessary. Not restless.		Psymotor Accel	4	52	
Denies anxiety in social situations. Is irritable and insensitive to others' opinions.	**	Imperturbability	7	71	
Realistically evaluates own self-worth & may be overly self-critical. accepting of demands		Ego Inflation	0	34	
Has a flexible, adaptable approach to interpersonal contacts. Cooperative with others.		PARANOIA	11	59	
This person does not appear to experience any significant problem with suspicious thinking.		Ob/Sub T-scores		44/	68
Respondent has an appropriate amount of trust in others. Is not overly suspicious or angry.		Persecute Ideas	0	41	
Does not describe self as any more sensitive than other people. Usually feels understood.		Poignancy	1	42	
Has naive, optimistic attitudes about people. Sees others as honest, altruistic, generous.	**	Naivete	8	71	
Has realistic concern about body functions. A few specific somatic symptoms may be present.		HYPOCHONDRIASIS	14	57	
Has balanced optimism and realism. Good level of energy and enthusiasm for life & projects.		DEPRESSION	19	56	
Depression does not appear to represent a significant problem for the person at this time.		Ob/Sub T-scores		51/	52
Client has normal level of satisfaction with life situation and self. Is generally happy.		Subjective Dep	4	42	
Describes self as having an average level of energy & endurance. Has variety of interests.		Psymotor Retard	5	48	
Feels physically healthy and denies psychosomatic complaints such as fatigue and nausea.		Phy Malfunction	1	35	

412 *psychware*

Tends to have difficulties in concentration, * Mental Dullness   4 61
poor memory & judgement. May feel inadequate.
Feels happy most of the time. Generally feels   Brooding   1 44
competent to deal with normal stress in life.

Prefers action to intellectual pursuits, with MASCULINITY   23 55
interests typical of avg. middle class male.
The person usually feels confident & does not   Sensitivity (P)   3 43
admit to unusual concerns about sex matters.
Responses suggest that The person has an ap-   Sexual Id. (P)   0 39
propriate sexual identification at this time.

This person is able to relate to others on a SOC INTROVERSION   20 45
comfortable manner. Socially competent/adept.

Wiggins, Mayo, and other scales	Scale	A	Raw	T

These scales concern organic problems.
Has a realistic concern about physical health — Poor Health   W   1 40
& may report some gastrointestinal symptoms.
Did not report symptoms which would suggest   Organic Symptoms   W   4 47
presence of an organic/neurological disorder.
If low back pain is present, it is likely ** Low Back Pain   M 14 70
to be psychosomatic in a passive individual.
Responses do not show definite trend towards — Caudality   M   4 40
either frontal or parietal lobe dysfunction.

Problems with self control are as follows:
Does not admit to Psychotic symptoms such as — Psychoticism   W   2 39
disorientation, hallucinations, or paranoia.
Depicts self as having limited drive and low — Hypomania   W   5 34
energy level. Probably reliable & persistent.
Presents self as happy & satisfied with life — Depression   W   1 38
situation. Optimistic and denies depression.
Denies having multiple fears, although a few   Phobias   W   2 41
specific fears may be present. Comfortable.
Does not exhibit hostile or retaliatory tend- — Manifest Hostility W 3 37
encies toward other people. Is not sadistic.
May have some conflict between expression of   Over-con Hostile   O 15 58
aggression and inhibition of these impulses.
Tends to be stable, self-confident. Adaptable * Ego-Strength   M 55 67
when under stress. Responds well in therapy.
A relatively sophisticated individual with an   Control   M 24 47
average amount of self-control & restraint.
Self-sufficient person with a preference for — Dependency   M   9 39
solving own problems. Socially independent.
Exhibits appropriate sensitivity toward other   Impotence   F   3 44
people. Feels comfortable in own sexual role.

Following are areas of social functioning:
Depicts self as confident and optimistic. Not — Poor Morale   W   1 36
socially suggestible and may be insensitive.
Is able to relate to other people without un-   Soc. Maladjustment W   4 41
due self-consciousness and can be assertive.
Has some interests which are traditionally   Feminine Interests W 10 52
feminine but does not have strong preference.
Denies having an unpleasant childhood home &   Family Problems   W   5 56
generally feels family life was supportive.
Has a trusting attitude & sees others as hon- — Authority Conflict W 4 36
est. Respects the law and authority figures.
Does not have delinquency orientation. Denies   Delinquency   G   4 56
school misconduct, problems with authorities.

Exhibits a normal ability to accept responsi-   Soc. Responsibility M 23 57
bility for actions, act in dependable manner.
Does not exhibit high number of traits which — Alcoholism   A 16 40
are often present in alcoholic individuals.
Person has an average level of dominance and   Dominance   M 17 57
assertiveness. Handles problems adequately.
Usually seen by others as relaxed & satisfied — Worried Breadwinner M 5 39
with self. Tends to be somewhat opinionated.
Is socially poised, ambitious, and confident. * Status   M 25 65
Characteristics similar to upper social class

Social desirability tendencies are below.
Doesn't subscribe to fundamentalist religious — Religious Fundament W 1 32
beliefs, tends to be tolerant of differences.
Person is flexible in thinking, open-minded & — Prejudice   M   1 31
non-prejudiced. Can accept other viewpoints.
Positive self-description may reflect a good * Soc. Desirability   E 34 62
self-concept or an attempt at faking good.

	Scale	A	Raw	T
Interpretation of the two main factors are: The person exhibits average levels of anxiety — and indecisiveness. Usually feels competent.	Anxiety	L	4	40
Internalizes and tends to be emotionally un- * stable and cautious. May react with violence.	Repression	L	23	66
Response pattern of hospitalized patients: Tends to be self-centered with many somatic complaints. May exhibit mild anxiety, tension but usually not depressed. Pain in head & ex- tremities is likely. Profits from reassurance	A/R Ratio			

Tryon, Stein, and Chu factors (1968 norms)

	Scale	Raw	T
Denies feelings of unreality, excessive day- dreaming or unusual thoughts. Is able to con- centrate & to focus attention. Usually feels calm & does not exhibit problems with memory.	Autism/Disrup Thoughts	4	48
Generally friendly towards others and comfor- table in social settings. Has normal level of self-confidence & interpersonal sensitivity. Can stand up for own beliefs when necessary.	Introversion	4	47
Feels self-confident, comfortable, & optimis- tic about the future most of the time. Gener- ally finds daily life interesting and reward- ing. Can cope with problems in realistic way.	Depression & Apathy	2	45
Person denies presence of anger or aggressive impulses towards other people. Is generally self-confident & decisive. When own anger has been expressed, client does not feel guilty.	Resentment & Aggress	2	44
Exhibits average level of concern with bodily functions and somatic problems. May have some mild complaints about pains in head or chest, nausea, etc. which reflect minor ailments.	Body Symptoms	1	43
Respondent usually feels understood by others with average level of trust. Can defend own opinions and rights when this is appropriate. Denies feelings of hostility or aggression.	Suspicion & Mistrust	3	42
Client exhibits few fears. Usually is calm & free of unnecessary anxiety. Denies major dis turbances of sleep or concentration. Specific fears such as fear of small places are absent	Anxiety Worry & Fear	1	40

Revised Fowler Modification of Grayson Critical Items

```
---   Peculiar thoughts and experiences   ---
33    I have had very peculiar and strange experiences.  (true)
---   Suspicion and ideas of reference   ---
---   Suicidal ideation   ---
---   Depression and guilt   ---
---   Health and somatic concerns   ---
163   I do not tire quickly.  (true)
---   Sexual difficulties   ---
---   Family conflict   ---
21    At times I very much wanted to leave home.  (true)
96    I have very few quarrels with members of my family.  (false)
216   There is very little love in my family as compared to other homes.  (true)
237   My relatives are nearly all in sympathy with me.  (false)
---   Socialization problems   ---
118   In School I was sometimes sent to the principal for cutting up.  (true)
294   I have never been in trouble with the law.  (false)
---   Substance Abuse   ---
466   Except by doctor's orders I never take drugs or sleeping powders.  (false)
Items are in form G format
1 = True              2 = False              3 = Don't Know
          1234567890 1234567890 1234567890 1234567890 1234567890
  1 -  50 1122221122 2222221121 1122112221 2112211212 1122212222
 51 - 100 1221121222 2212122122 1222122112 2212222111 2222222212
101 - 150 1212221221 2112222122 2122222121 1212121222 1222222221
151 - 200 2111122221 2111222212 2211112222 2222121221 2122112212
201 - 250 2222221122 2221212221 1122212121 2222222221 2112222222
251 - 300 2212211222 2121222122 2121222222 1222122222 2222222121
301 - 350 2122212111 2222222122 2212222121 2222222222 2222221222
351 - 400 2222212222 2222221222 1222212212 2222222222 2222221212
401 - 450 1212121222 2122222222 2222222221 2222222222 2221122221
451 - 500 1222222221 2121222222 2221222112 1122212222 2222212222
501 - 550 2111222122 2212111222 1111221112 2112222211 2122221222
551 - 566 2122222222 2222222
          1234567890 1234567890 1234567890 1234567890 1234567890
```

414 *psychware*

End of MMPI interpretation

NAME: Minnesota Multiphasic Personality Inventory

SUPPLIER: Behaviordyne, Inc.
599 College Ave. Suite 1
Palo Alto, CA 94306
(415) 857-0111

PRODUCT CATEGORY

Personality
Career/Vocational

PRIMARY APPLICATIONS

Clinical Assessment/Diagnosis
Personal/Marriage/Family Counseling
Vocational Guidance/Counseling

SALE RESTRICTIONS   American Psychological Association Guidelines

SERVICE TYPE/COST	Type	Available	Cost	Discount
	Mail-In	Yes	See Below	
	Teleprocessing	No		
	Local	No		

PRODUCT DESCRIPTION

Behaviordyne's computer reports for the MINNESOTA MULTIPHASIC PERSONALITY INVENTORY provide a variety of options to the test user. Specific report types include a comprehensive clinical, diagnostic, physician's, correctional, counseling, personnel, and profile report. Each report can also be obtained in a brief form.

Prices for reports range from $40.00 for the comprehensive clinical report to $8.00 for the profile report, with most other reports at $16.00. Brief reports range in price from $10.00 to $18.00.

NAME: Minnesota Multiphasic Personality Inventory

SUPPLIER: PSYCH Systems, Inc.
600 Reisterstown Road
Baltimore, MD 21208
(800) 368-3366

PRODUCT CATEGORY

Personality

PRIMARY APPLICATIONS

Clinical Assessment/Diagnosis
Personal/Marriage/Family Counseling

SALE RESTRICTIONS Qualified Professional

SERVICE TYPE/COST	Type	Available	Cost	Discount
	Mail-In	No		
	Teleprocessing	No		
	Local	Yes	See Below	

PRODUCT DESCRIPTION

This program presents the 566 true/false items in the Group Booklet Form of the MMPI. Over 100 special scales are then scored and a complicated interpretive system uses five different schemes and extensive branching logic to produce the narrative report. A special profile is generated that uses adolescent norms for those under 19 years of age.

Psych Systems programs operate on the IBM PC-XT, COMPAQ Plus, Dec Professional 350, and most DEC PDP-11 systems. Various hardware/ software configurations are available directly from Psych Systems, with single-user systems starting at approximately $12,000. A per test fee also applies.

```
-------------------------------------------------------------
|         |                                                 |
|  MMPI   |   Minnesota Multiphasic Personality Inventory   |
|         |                                                 |
-------------------------------------------------------------
```

This clinical report is designed to assist in psychodiagnostic
evaluation. It is available only to qualified professionals.
This report was produced by a computerized analysis of the data
given by the client listed above. The techniques utilized in the
analysis of the data and in generation of this report were designed
by several psychologists, psychiatrists, and other professionals
utilizing highly validated clinical research. However, this report
is to be used in conjunction with professional evaluation. No
decision should be based solely upon the contents of this report.

The computer program generating this report was designed by Psych
Systems, Inc., Baltimore, Maryland 21208. Copyright (C) 1984 by
Psych Systems, Inc. Portions of this report may have been
reproduced or derived from the MINNESOTA MULTIPHASIC PERSONALITY
INVENTORY (MMPI), such being done by permission of and under
copyrights held by THE UNIVERSITY OF MINNESOTA dated 1943, renewed
1970. All rights reserved.

psychware **417**

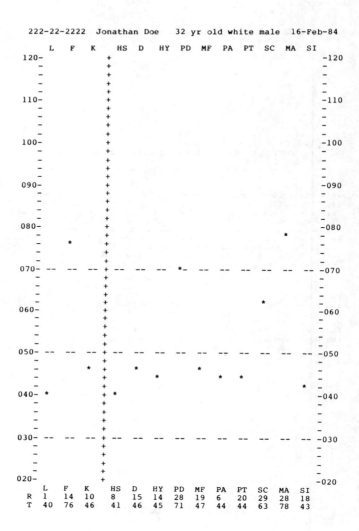

```
        222-22-2222  Jonathan Doe    32 yr old white male  16-Feb-84

            L    F    K    HS   D   HY   PD   MF  PA   PT   SC   MA   SI
    120-              +                                                     -120
      -               +                                                     -
      -               +                                                     -
      -               +                                                     -
      -               +                                                     -
    110-              +                                                     -110
      -               +                                                     -
      -               +                                                     -
      -               +                                                     -
      -               +                                                     -
    100-              +                                                     -100
      -               +                                                     -
      -               +                                                     -
      -               +                                                     -
      -               +                                                     -
    090-              +                                                     -090
      -               +                                                     -
      -               +                                                     -
      -               +                                                     -
      -               +                                                     -
    080-              +                                      *              -080
      -        *      +                                                     -
      -               +                                                     -
      -               +                                                     -
      -               +                                                     -
    070- --  --  --   + --  --   --  *-  --   --   --   --   --  -- -070
      -               +                                                     -
      -               +                                                     -
      -               +                                                     -
      -               +                                *                    -
    060-              +                                                     -060
      -               +                                                     -
      -               +                                                     -
      -               +                                                     -
      -               +                                                     -
    050- --  --  --   + --  --   --  --   --   --   --   --   --  -- -050
      -          *    +      *                                              -
      -               +                   *                                 -
      -               +          *               *    *                     -
      -               +                                           *         -
    040- *            + *                                                   -040
      -               +                                                     -
      -               +                                                     -
      -               +                                                     -
      -               +                                                     -
    030- --  --  --   + --  --   --  --   --   --   --   --   --  -- -030
      -               +                                                     -
      -               +                                                     -
      -               +                                                     -
      -               +                                                     -
    020-              +                                                     -020
            L    F    K    HS   D   HY   PD   MF  PA   PT   SC   MA   SI
          R 1   14   10    8   15  14   28   19   6   20   29   28   18
          T 40  76   46   41   46  45   71   47  44   44   63   78   43
```

418   *psychware*

222-22-2222 Jonathan Doe   32 yr old white male   16-Feb-84

                    -Current Clinical Status-

This is a valid profile.

This profile type is more frequently found in a correctional rather
than psychiatric population. Presentation in a psychiatric setting
is often associated with or secondary to legal difficulties. The
profile suggests a classic sociopathic orientation, as described by
Cleckly.

These individuals are energetic, active, and outgoing. They become
restless and easily bored with the routine or mundane pursuits of
everyday life. Such persons appear to have a strong need to program
stimulation and excitement in their lives, and choice of friends and
activities are often based on these needs. Being impulsive and
risk-taking, they are accident prone. Alcohol/Drug abuse is one
method commonly used by such persons to meet their needs for stimulus
change.

Individuals like this are egocentric, selfish and demanding of others
in a narcissistic manner. However, they lack empathy and concern for
the rights and needs of others. There is a lack of adequate
conscience development and these persons are free of inhibiting
guilt, anxiety, or remorse. Thus, they can violate social norms with
relative personal impunity. Non-conforming, antisocial, and illegal
behavior is common. However, having good social skills and being
able to "read" people well, such persons are often able to impress
others, at least on initial meeting. Relationships are maintained at
a superficial level and often with manipulative intent. Longer term
observation will reveal a pattern of behavior reflecting impulsivity,
irresponsibility, and untrustworthiness.

Judgement is typically poor. These individuals do not seem to learn
from past experience and repeatedly make the same mistakes. Their
inability to postpone gratification, low frustration tolerance, and
poor planning ability lead to difficulty in any enterprise requiring
sustained effort. A high percentage of these individuals have
extremely poor marital adjustments. They do not maintain personal
loyalty, become bored, and often seek extra-marital involvement.

This pattern of behavior often diminishes with increasing age. As
they approach middle age, these persons may reflect upon lost
relationships and opportunities, and realize that their lives are not
going well. Concomitantly, they may experience increased emotional
distress. However, these persons often are unable to translate this
into positive life changes.

Treatment considerations: Most persons with this profile have an
extremely poor prognosis for change with any type of psychotherapy.
Their motivation is poor and they tend to discontinue therapy
impulsively. Often therapeutic involvement is under duress, for
example, spouse or the courts. If in legal difficulty, correctional
supervision can have a salutory impact. These persons seem to

respond best to the presence of clearcut guidelines and immediate
consequences.

DIAGNOSTIC IMPRESSION

Although a formal diagnosis must be based on demographic, interview
and case history data, psychological test results can sometimes be of
assistance to the clinician in making the diagnostic decision. The
DSM-III diagnostic categories most frequently associated with various
MMPI profile types were identified and subsequently confirmed by a
panel of experienced clinicians. The following, while not presented
as a diagnosis, is a diagnostic possibility based on that consensus.

Impression: Axis I   V71.09 None

                Axis II 301.70 Antisocial Personality Disorder

                - Extended Personality Trait Information -

This person tends to be impulsive, self-indulgent, poorly controlled,
and easily frustrated. He is willing to manipulate others to gratify
his needs, perhaps to the point of conscious deceit. His behavior
tends to be unpredictable, and his mood is prone to rapid
fluctuations.

This person is likely to be verbally fluent and relatively at ease in
social interactions. Others see him as usually cheerful,
good-humored, and not overly difficult to approach. He is able to
deal with adverse circumstances without exaggerated discomfort.

Whatever problems this person is currently experiencing, he is
generally not overly pessimistic about life. His self-esteem is
relatively intact and he is not overly apprehensive about the long
term future. Depending on his current situation, this may be
inappropriate. He portrays himself as self-confident and competent
and not easily influenced by the opinions of others.

He is basically mistrustful of people and feels they are motivated
primarily by relentless self-interest. He tends to view an
interpersonal relationship as a condition of mutual exploitation.

He has an adequate reservoir of energy and can mobilize his resources
to meet everyday problems.

He suffers from tendencies toward excessive demandingness, cynicism
and resentment for real or imagined harms. Preferred defense
mechanisms are intellectualization, projection and regression.

                - Special Medical Symptoms -

Results suggest that this individual is not excessively concerned
about health and physical functioning. He may be prone to substance
abuse and addictive behavior. He is likely to show faster recovery
from physical illness, injury or surgery than most people.

                - Attitudes Toward Work -

Although this person appears to have normal ambition, he may
demonstrate poor work adjustment secondary to emotional or
characterological difficulties. He is probably seen as dominant by
others. Interpersonally, he will appear strong and not readily
intimidated by other people. This person will be realistic and
task-oriented in his work. He tends to have innovative ideas about
his job. He is likely to make important decisions impulsively and
without sufficient deliberation. Generally, he does not have trust
and confidence in his capacity to perform his own work successfully.
He is typically a self-sufficient individual. This person may be
cynical about others around him. He can easily become resentful
about situations and people. Such individuals tend to have average
work attitudes but may lack sufficient self-control for effective job
performance. He enjoys working in groups but empathizes poorly with
his co-workers. He is likely to have difficulty accepting directives
from work supervisors.

This individual's responses to the following items may be useful in
subsequent interviewing.

420   *psychware*

** Reality testing **
I have had blank spells in which my activities were interrupted and I
did not know what was going on around me (t)
I have strange and peculiar thoughts (t)

** Sexual complaints **
My sex life is satisfactory (f)
I have never indulged in any unusual sex practices (f)
I am worried about sex matters (t)
I wish I were not bothered by thoughts about sex (t)

** Self-harm **
Sometimes I feel as if I must injure either myself or someone else (t)

** Self-esteem **
No one cares much what happens to you (t)
At times I think I am no good at all (t)

** Behavior problems **
I have never done anything dangerous for the thrill of it (f)
In school I was sometimes sent to the principal for cutting up (t)
At times it has been impossible for me to keep from stealing or
shoplifting something (t)
I have used alcohol excessively (t)
I can easily make other people afraid of me, and sometimes do for the
fun of it (t)
I have never been in trouble with the law (f)

Welsh Code: 94'8-/5236701 F'-/KL

                     Research Scales   Standard Scores

Item Factors
(Tryon, Stein & Chu)   R   T
--------------------   -   -
TSC-I Social introversion 1   41 . | * | .   .   .
TSC-II Bodily concern   5   56 . | * | .   .   .
TSC-III Suspicion   20   71 . | *|.   .   .   .
TSC-IV Depression   9   64 . | * | .   .   .   .
TSC-V Resentment   12   70 . | *| .   .   .   .
TSC-VI Autism   11   69 . | * |.   .   .   .
TSC-VII Tension   11   61 . | * | .   .   .
                              20   30   40   50   60   70   80   90   100

Content Scales (Wiggins)

Social maladjustment   2   36 . | * | .   .   .
Depression   8   52 . | * | .   .   .
Feminine interests   5   39 . | * | .   .   .
Poor morale   5   44 . | * | .   .   .
Religious fundamentalism   4   42 . | * | .   .   .
Authority conflict   20   76 . | *|.   .   .   .
Psychoticism   10   53 . | * | .   .   .
Organic symptoms   2   42 . | * | .   .   .
Family problems   9   73 . | |*.   .   .   .
Manifest hostility   21   73 . | *|.   .   .   .
Phobias   2   40 . | * | .   .   .
Hypomania   15   57 . | * | .   .   .
Poor health   4   48 . | * | .   .   .
                              20   30   40   50   60   70   80   90   100

Special Scales

A   First Factor   13   51 . | * | .   .   .
R   Second Factor   7   32 . | * | .   .   .
Ego strength (Barron)   51   61 . | * | .   .   .
Caudality (Williams)   13   56 . | * | .   .   .
Social status (Gough)   21   58 . | * | .   .   .
Dominance (Gough)   20   65 . | * | .   .   .
Social resp (Gough)   12   30 . |* | .   .   .
Manifest anxiety (Taylor) 10   44 . | * | .   .   .
Dependency (Navran)   16   46 . | * | .   .   .
Prejudice (Gough)   19   63 . | * | .   .   .
Control (Cuadra)   33   71 . | *| .   .   .
Alcoholism (MacAndrew)   30   ** . | |*.   .   .   .
                              20   30   40   50   60   70   80   90   100
** - High Addiction Proneness

                                                        psychware **421**

222-22-2222 Jonathan Doe   32 yr old white male   16-Feb-84

Factor Scales (Johnson, Butcher, Null & Johnson)

Scale	Code	R	T
Neuroticism-General Anxiety & Worry	(N)	29	43
Psychotism-Peculiar Thinking	(P)	3	47
Cynicism-Normal Paranoia	(C)	19	66
Denial of Somatic Problems	(DSP)	21	60
Social Extroversion	(SE)	18	66
Stereotypic Feminity	(SF)	4	36
Psychotic Paranoia	(PP)	1	41
Delinquency	(DL)	8	66
Stereotypic Masculinity	(SM)	9	59
Neurasthenic Somatization	(NS)	0	41
Phobias	(PH)	1	36
Family Attachment	(FA)	5	36
Intellectual Interests	(II)	8	59
Religious Fundamentalism	(RF)	3	36

Plot columns: T values scaled across 30 40 50 60 70

Harris & Lingoes SubScales

Scale	Code	R	T
Subjective Depression	(D1)	9	56
Psychomotor Retardation	(D2)	2	32
Physical Malfunctioning	(D3)	3	49
Mental Dullness	(D4)	0	40
Brooding	(D5)	3	54
Denial of Social Anxiety	(Hy1)	5	59
Need for Affection	(Hy2)	1	34
Lassitude-malaise	(Hy3)	3	53
Somatic Complaints	(Hy4)	0	39
Inhibition of Aggression	(Hy5)	2	46
Familial Discord	(Pd1)	6	74
Authority Problems	(Pd2)	6	61
Social Imperturbability	(Pd3)	11	64
Social Alienation	(Pd4A)	9	63
Self-Alienation	(Pd4B)	5	54
Persecutory Ideas	(Pa1)	2	50
Poignancy	(Pa2)	3	55
Naivete	(Pa3)	0	31
Social Alienation	(SclA)	6	60
Emotional Alienation	(SclB)	2	48
Lack of Ego Mastery, Cognitive	(Sc2A)	2	53
Lack of Ego Mastery, Conative	(Sc2B)	0	39
Lack of Ego Mastery, Defect. Inhib.	(Sc2C)	3	60
Bizarre Sensory Experiences	(Sc3)	3	52
Amorality	(Ma1)	5	74
Psychomotor Acceleration	(Ma2)	6	66
Imperturbability	(Ma3)	4	53
Ego Inflation	(Ma4)	6	71

Plot columns: T values scaled across 30 40 50 60 70

Standard scores are based on statistics derived according to the
procedures described in Dahlstrom, W.G., Welsh, G.S., & Dahlstrom, L.E. An
MMPI Handbook, Vol. II. Minneapolis, University of Minnesota Press, 1975.

NAME: MMPI/Basic Profile Report

SUPPLIER: NCS/Professional Assessment Services
P.O. Box 1416
Minneapolis, MN 55440
(800) 328-6759

PRODUCT CATEGORY	PRIMARY APPLICATIONS
Personality	Clinical Assessment/Diagnosis Personal/Marriage/Family Counseling

SALE RESTRICTIONS American Psychological Association Guidelines

SERVICE TYPE/COST	Type	Available	Cost	Discount
	Mail-In	Yes	$4.75	Yes
	Teleprocessing	Yes	$4.75	Yes
	Local	Yes	$3.10	Yes

PRODUCT DESCRIPTION

The Minnesota Multiphasic Personality Inventory provides information regarding psychiatric symptomology and personality dynamics for normal adults and adolescents as well as individuals with psychological or psychiatric difficulties. The MMPI/BASIC PROFILE REPORT presents scores on four validity, ten clinical, and twelve special research scales in a single-page format.

Two systems are available for local processing of test results. MICRO-TEST Assessment Software from National Computer Systems, used with a Sentry 3000 tabletop scanner (purchase price approximately $4000) and microcomputer system ($2000-$3000 purchase price), allows tests to be administered off-line. Answer sheets are then scanned and scored automatically, one at a time or in a batch. The software also permits on-line administration of the test via microcomputer. In either case, the same report is provided. The cost for local scoring refers to the cost-per-test when diskettes are purchased in units of 20 administrations (minimum purchase).

```
                                                     TM*        742 0002
                        MINNESOTA MULTIPHASIC PERSONALITY INVENTORY

                        BY STARKE R. HATHAWAY AND J. CHARNLEY MCKINLEY

        NAME: SAMPLE      MALE          GENDER: MALE      AGE: 21    DATE: 11-AUG-83

    T    K    RAW
  SCORE COR. SCORE          30   40   50   60   70   80   90  100  110  120
  +----+----+----+----+----+----+----+----+----+----+----+----+----+---
  : 41 :    :  0 : ?                  *                                  ?
  +----+----+----+----:        :         :         :              :----
  : 53 :    :  5 : L                    *         :              :    L
  +----+----+----+----:        :         :         :              :----
  :110 :    : 32 : F                  :         :         :    *       F
  +----+----+----+----:        :         :         :              :----
  : 61 :    : 18 : K                  :         :   *                   K
  -------------------------------------------------------------------
  : 85 : 9  : 16 : HS       :         :         :         *          1
  +----+----+----+----:        :         :         :     *        :----
  : 87 :    : 32 : D        :         :         :         *          2
  +----+----+----+----:        :         :         :              :----
  : 71 :    : 28 : HY       :         :         :   *                 3
  +----+----+----+----:        :         :         :              :----
  : 67 : 7  : 19 : PD       :         :         *                     4
  +----+----+----+----:        :         :         :              :----
  : 71 :    : 31 : MF       :         :         :   *                 5
  +----+----+----+----:        :         :         :              :----
  : 88 :    : 21 : PA       :         :         :         *          6
  +----+----+----+----:        :         :         :              :----
  : 87 : 18 : 23 : PT       :         :         :         *          7
  +----+----+----+----:        :         :         :              :----
  :117 : 18 : 39 : SC       :         :         :              *    8
  +----+----+----+----:        :         :         :              :----
  : 73 : 4  : 22 : MA       :         :         :       *            9
  +----+----+----+----:        :         :         :              :----
  : 53 :    : 28 : SI       :         *         :                    0
  +----+----+----+----+----+----+----+----+----+----+----+----+----+----
                            30   40   50   60   70   80   90  100  110  120
```

	A	R	ES	MAC	LB	CA	DY	DO	RE	PR	ST	CN
RAW SCORE	22	20	38	26	14	19	29	16	17	21	22	26
T SCORE	62	59	40	61	70	68	61	53	42	67	60	53

INTERPRETIVE SCORING SYSTEMS, A DIVISION OF NATIONAL COMPUTER SYSTEMS, INC.
P.O. BOX 1294, MPLS, MN 55440

NAME: MMPI: Computer Version 2.0

SUPPLIER: Psychological Assessment Resources
P.O. Box 98
Odessa, FL 33556
(813) 977-3395

PRODUCT CATEGORY	PRIMARY APPLICATIONS
Personality	Clinical Assessment/Diagnosis Personal/Marriage/Family Counseling

SALE RESTRICTIONS   American Psychological Association Guidelines

SERVICE TYPE/COST	Type	Available	Cost	Discount
	Mail-In	No		
	Teleprocessing	No		
	Local	Yes	$5.00	

PRODUCT DESCRIPTION

This program administers the test items, calculates raw scores and T-scores for up to 100 scales, and prints a summary of the raw scores and T-scores for all scales, a 7-category critical item summary, and a summary of the patient's response to each test item. The MMPI: COMPUTER VERSION 2.0 is entirely menu driven and allows input of answers directly by the client or clinician. A significant redesign of the operator-entry option allows input of responses on a standard Form R answer sheet into a visual grid system which greatly enhances this mode of use.

The price shown above is the per-test fee when diskettes are purchased in quantities of 25 units (minimum purchase). Operation of the program requires a one-time purchase of PAR-DOS ($100.00), an operating system for psychological test software. Versions of the program are available for the Apple IIe, II +, and IBM PC computer systems. The program requires 64K and 2 disk drives.

P.O. Box 98 / Odessa, Florida 33556

Telephone: (813) 977-3395

THE MMPI:COMPUTER VERSION 2.0

Developed By

PSYCHOLOGICAL ASSESSMENT RESOURCES, INC.
P.O. Box 98
Odessa, Florida 33556

Demographic Information
=========================

Client	. . .	JONES
File Name	. .	1001-22
Age	. . . .	37
Sex	. . . .	MALE
Marital Status	.	M
Education	. -.	20
Date of Birth	.	15-FEB-45
Prepared for .	.	TEST
Date .	. . .	17-JUL-82

```
14 STANDARD VALIDITY AND CLINICAL SCALES
============================================
```

Scales	Raw	K-Raw	T	Miss
CANNOT SAY (?)	1	1	41	1
VALIDITY (L)	1	1	40	0
VALIDITY (F)	8	8	62	0
VALIDITY (K)	13	13	51	0
HYPOCHONDRIASIS (HS-1) . . .	3	10	47	0
DEPRESSION (D-2)	25	25	70 *	0
HYSTERIA (HY-3)	18	18	53	0
PSYCHOPATHIC DEVIATE (PD-4) . .	24	29	74 *	0
MASCULINITY - FEMININITY (MF(M)-5)	24	24	57	1
PARANOIA (PA-6)	14	14	67	0
PSYCHASTHENIA (PT-7)	18	31	66	0
SCHIZOPHRENIA (SC-8)	19	32	69	0
HYPOMANIA (MA-9)	16	19	55	0
SOCIAL INTROVERSION (SI-0) . .	43	43	70 *	0

MMPI Profile for Validity and Clinical Scales

```
            ?   L   F   K   Hs   D   Hy  Pd  Mf  Pa  Pt  Sc  Ma  Si
  110  - --  -- -- -- + -- -- -- -- -- -- -- -- -- -         110
       -                +                                    -
       -                +                                    -
       -                +                                    -
       -                +                                    -
  100  -                +                                    -  100
       -                +                                    -
       -                +                                    -
       -                +                                    -
       -                +                                    -
   90  -                +                                    -   90
       -                +                                    -
       -                +                                    -
       -                +                                    -
       -                +                                    -
   80  -                +                                    -   80
       -                +                                    -
       -                +                                    -
       -                +              *                     -
       -                +                                    -
   70  - -- -- -- -- + -- -* -- -- -- -- -- -* -- -* -       70
       -                +                              *     -
       -                +                        *  *        -
       -           *    +                                    -
   60  -                +                                    -   60
       -                +                                    -
       -                +                    *               -
       -                +                              *     -
       -                +              *                     -
   50  - -- -- -- -* + -- -- -- -- -- -- -- -- --          -   50
       -                + *                                  -
       -                +*                                   -
       -                +                                    -
   40  - *   *          +                                    -   40
       -                +                                    -
       -                +                                    -
       -                +                                    -
   30  - -- -- -- -- + -- -- -- -- -- -- -- -- --          -   30
       -                +                                    -
       -                +                                    -
       -                +                                    -
       -                +                                    -
   20  - -- -- -- -- + -- -- -- -- -- -- -- -- --          -   20
                        1   2   3   4   5   6   7   8   9   0
            ?   L   F   K   Hs  D   Hy  Pd  Mf  Pa  Pt  Sc  Ma  Si
Raw Score   1   1   8  13   10  25  18  29  24  14  31  32  19  43
  T-Score  41  40  62  51   47  70  53  74  57  67  66  69  55  70
```

428 *psychware*

```
                         16 RESEARCH SCALES
                         ===================
              Scales                            Raw      T     Miss
              ------                            ---      -     ----
   ANXIETY (A)    .    .    .    .    .    .     18      57      0
   REPRESSION (R)    .    .    .    .    .       20      59      1
   MANIFEST ANXIETY (MAS)    .    .    .         24      63      0
   EGO STRENGTH (ES).    .    .    .    .        50      59      0
   LOW BACK PAIN (LB)    .    .    .    .         8      45      0
   CAUDALITY (CA)    .    .    .    .    .       12      55      0
   DEPENDENCY (DY)    .    .    .    .    .      28      59      0
   DOMINANCE (DO)    .    .    .    .    .       16      53      0
   SOCIAL RESPONSIBILITY (RE)    .    .    .     20      50      0
   PREJUDICE (PR)    .    .    .    .    .       17      60      0
   SOCIAL STATUS (ST)    .    .    .    .        18      51      0
   CONTROL (CN) .    .    .    .    .    .       30      63      0
   COLLEGE MALADJUSTMENT (CM)    .    .    .     16      54      0
   ALCOHOLISM (MACANDREWS)    .    .    .        15      34      0
   OVERCONTROLLED HOSTILITY (OH).    .    .       9      36      1
   REPRESSION-SENSITIZATION (RS).    .    .      47      55      0
```

The following supplementary scales are printed out in the same format as listed above:

```
                     13 WIGGINS CONTENT SCALES
                     =========================
                     7 TRYON-STEIN-CHU-SCALES
                     =========================
                     28 HARRIS-LINGOES SCALES
                     =========================
                     10 SUBTLE-OBVIOUS SCALES
                     =========================
                     12 SERKOWNEK SCALES
                     ===================
```

                KOSS-BUTCHER CRITICAL ITEMS SUMMARY
                ===================================

The following items were endorsed by this individual in the direction indicated and may suggest leads for inquiry but are not authenticated fact. They should not be used to determine the client's level of adjustment and should only be interpreted in light of relevant clinical history and other MMPI information.

                         Acute Anxiety State

```
3.    I WAKE UP FRESH AND RESTED MOST MORNINGS.              FALSE
5.    I AM EASILY AWAKENED BY NOISE.                         TRUE
290.  I WORK UNDER A GREAT DEAL OF TENSION.                  TRUE
337.  I FEEL ANXIETY ABOUT SOMETHING OR SOMEONE ALMOST ALL  TRUE
      THE TIME.
506.  I AM A HIGH-STRUNG PERSON.                            TRUE
543.  SEVERAL TIMES A WEEK I FEEL AS IF SOMETHING DREADFUL IS TRUE
      ABOUT TO HAPPEN.
555.  I SOMETIMES FEEL THAT I AM ABOUT TO GO TO PIECES.     TRUE
```
                     Depressed Suicidal Ideation

                        Threatened Assault

                         Mental Confusion

                         Persecutory Ideas

A listing of responses - (T)rue or (F)alse - for each question is also printed out.

NAME: MMPI Interpretation

SUPPLIER: Applied Innovations, Inc.
South Kingstown Office Park, Suite A-1
Wakefield, RI 02879
(800) 272-2250

PRODUCT CATEGORY

Personality

PRIMARY APPLICATIONS

Clinical Assessment/Diagnosis
Personal/Marriage/Family Counseling

SALE RESTRICTIONS American Psychological Association Guidelines

SERVICE TYPE/COST	Type	Available	Cost	Discount
	Mail-In	No		
	Teleprocessing	No		
	Local	Yes	$425.00	

PRODUCT DESCRIPTION

This computer-generated MMPI interpretation has four major sections: general profile interpretation, interpretation based on single scale elevation, chemical abuse profile, and treatment plan. The key feature of this report is the general profile interpretation which addresses test validity, personality dynamics, defense mechanisms, somatic complaints, prognosis, treatment approach, diagnosis, and more.

This program prints a five- to six-page narrative-style report based on the client's sex and 14 T-scores which are typed into the computer. The program is easy to use and comes with a fully documented manual. The software operates on most available personal computers including IBM, Apple, Digital, and Kaypro.

NAME/ID: "Harry S. Clark"   AGE: 33

COMPUTER GENERATED MMPI INTERPRETATION

COPYRIGHT 1981

Bruce Duthie, Ph.D.
&
Ernest G. Allen

APPLIED INNOVATIONS, INC.
SOUTH KINGSTOWN OFFICE PARK, SUITE A-1
WAKEFIELD, RHODE ISLAND 02879
(800) 272-2250


```
? SCALE =   0
L SCALE =  56
F SCALE =  55
K SCALE =  42

HS (1) =  57
D  (2) =  87
HY (3) =  64
PD (4) =  67
MF (5) =  67

PA (6) =  67
PT (7) =  79
SC (8) =  73
MA (9) =  75
SI (0) =  72
```

GENERAL PROFILE INTERPRETATION

VALIDITY SCALES CONFIGURATION

INTRAPERSONAL

HE GENERALLY HAS A GREAT DEAL OF AMBITION AND HE EXPECTS A HIGH
LEVEL OF SUCCESS FOR HIMSELF, BUT LACKS CLEAR-CUT GOALS.
FEELINGS OF SELF-WORTH ARE DEPENDENT, IN PART, UPON ACHIEVEMENT.
HE IS BASICALLY PASSIVE AND HAS STRONG DEPENDENCY NEEDS.
HE TENDS TO BE ANXIOUS AND NERVOUS. PERFECTIONISM AND
COMPULSIVITY ARE OFTEN PRESENT. HE TENDS TO BE IRRITABLE,
DEPRESSED, AND SHY. HE TENDS TO WORRY A LOT. SEVERE DEPRESSION
WITH ANXIETY AND AGITATION ARE INDICATED. A DEEPLY INGRAINED,
CHRONIC, BUT MILD DEPRESSION IS SUGGESTED. REGRESSION IS A
PROMINENT DEFENSE MECHANISM EMPLOYED. HIS JUDGEMENT IS IMPAIRED
AND HE FAILS TO LEARN FROM EXPERIENCE. RESENTFULNESS,
HOSTILITY, AND AGGRESSIVENESS MAY BE PRESENT. DISSOCIATION AND
MEMORY BLACKOUTS MAY OCCUR. FANTASY AND REALITY ARE OFTEN SEEN
AS THE SAME. HE MAY ENGAGE IN PERSONAL FANTASY AND DAYDREAMING.
PARANOID DELUSIONS MAY BE EVIDENT. A DELUSIONAL SYSTEM WITH
ACCOMPANYING HALLUCINATIONS ARE POSSIBLE. DIFFICULTY THINKING
AND CONCENTRATING ARE INDICATED. HE SEEMS TO LACK ADEQUATE EGO
CONTROL AND DEFENSE MECHANISMS.

INTERPERSONAL

GUILT CENTERED AROUND SEXUAL MATTERS IS INDICATED.
SEXUAL DIFFICULTIES AND A POOR MARITAL ADJUSTMENT ARE INDICATED.
DEPERSONALIZATION AS AN ATTEMPT TO WITHDRAW FROM OTHERS IS
INDICATED. HE IS WITHDRAWN. HE TENDS TO FEEL REMOTE FROM
OTHERS AND TO FEEL SOCIALLY INADEQUATE. LACK OF HETEROSEXUAL
DATING SKILLS IS OFTEN PROMINENT. FEELINGS OF INADEQUACY IN
SOCIAL SITUATIONS AND A MARKED LACK OF SOCIAL SKILLS ARE
EVIDENT. HE IS SUSPICIOUS AND TYPICALLY REACTS TO OTHERS WITH
HOSTILITY. SUICIDAL RUMINATION IS PROBABLE. POOR JOB
PERFORMANCE IS INDICATED. SPEECH IS SOMETIMES RAPID AND
INCOHERENT.

SOMATIC COMPLAINTS

HE MAY EXPRESS CONCERN OVER SOMATIC COMPLAINTS.
UPPER G.I. SYMPTOMS ARE INDICATED. PAIN, FATIGUE, AND ANXIETY
ARE OFTEN MANIFEST. NEUROLOGICAL TRAUMA AND O.B.S. ARE
POSSIBLE. SOMATIC DELUSIONS ARE COMMON. HE IS EXPERIENCING
ACUTE STRESS, IS TENSE, RESTLESS, AND FRUSTRATED.
HE DOES NOT SEEM TO BE CONCERNED WITH SOMATIC PROBLEMS. A
PSYCHOSOMATIC ILLNESS IS NOT INDICATED.

ALCOHOL AND DRUG ABUSE

HE MAY HAVE A DRINKING PROBLEM. ESCAPE DRINKING MAY BE USED TO
COPE WITH PROBLEMS AND CONCERNS.

PSYCHOTHERAPY CONCERNS

PROGNOSIS IS UNCERTAIN. HE OFTEN FORMS PASSIVE-DEPENDENT
RELATIONSHIPS WITH THE THERAPIST. PROGNOSIS IS FAVORABLE IF
ALCOHOLISM IS NOT MANIFEST, AND IF ORGANICITY CAN BE RULED OUT.
HE READILY ADMITS TO PSYCHOLOGICAL PROBLEMS AND OFTEN SEEKS HELP
FOR THEM. RESISTANCE TO CHANGE AND PSYCHOLOGICAL INTERPRETATION
OF PROBLEMS IS EVIDENT. IF STRESS IS ACUTE AND HISTORICALLY NOT
OF LONG DURATION, PROGNOSIS IS MORE FAVORABLE.

DIAGNOSTIC POSSIBILITIES

1   SCHIZOID
2   PSYCHOTIC
3   SCHIZO-AFFECTIVE
4   MANIC-DEPRESSIVE, MANIC PHASE
5   CATATONIC STATE
6   AGITATED DEPRESSION
7   ANXIETY DEPRESSION
8   ALCOHOLISM
9   ORGANIC BRAIN SYNDROME

INTERPRETATION BASED ON SINGLE SCALE ELEVATION

? SCALE

L SCALE

INDIVIDUALS WITH THIS PROFILE TYPE TEND TO SEE THEMSELVES AS
VIRTUOUS, CONFORMING, AND SELF-CONTROLLED. THEY HAVE A
SIGNIFICANT NEED TO PRESENT THEMSELVES IN A FAVORABLE LIGHT AND
ARE VERY CONCERNED ABOUT WHAT OTHERS THINK OF THEM.
F SCALE

HE TENDS TO BE A SINCERE, CALM, DEPENDABLE PERSON. A
CONVENTIONAL, NARROW RANGE OF INTERESTS IS SUGGESTED.
K SCALE

THIS PERSON IS PROBABLY EXPERIENCING DIFFICULTIES IN SEVERAL
MAJOR AREAS. A LOW SELF-ESTEEM AND LITTLE EGO-STRENGTH ARE
SUGGESTED. INADEQUATE EGO DEFENSES AND A HIGHLY CRITICAL
ATTITUDE TOWARD SELF ARE INDICATED.
HS (1) SCALE

HE HAS A REALISTIC CONCERN ABOUT HIS BODILY FUNCTIONS. FEW
PHYSICAL SYMPTOMS ARE SUGGESTED.
D (2) SCALE

A PROFILE IN THIS RANGE SUGGESTS A CLINICAL DEPRESSION.
EXCESSIVE WORRY AND PESSIMISM EXIST. SUICIDAL IDEATION AND
TENDENCIES MAY EXIST. A PERVASIVE SADNESS IS LIKELY TO BE
MANIFEST. SOCIAL WITHDRAWAL, EXTREME PESSIMISM, AND SLEEP
DISTURBANCE ARE INDICATED. FEELINGS OF INADEQUACY AND
SELF-DEPRECATION MAY REACH DELUSIONAL PROPORTION.

HY (3) SCALE

HE IS OPTIMISTIC IN A NAIVE, SHALLOW WAY. LACK OF INTERPERSONAL
INSIGHT IS INDICATED. HE MAY SOMATICIZE IN TIMES OF STRESS.
PD (4) SCALE

HE MAY SHOW CONCERN OVER THE SOCIAL PROBLEMS OF THE WORLD.
PEOPLE FROM THE HELPING PROFESSIONS OFTEN HAVE A SIMILAR SCALE
SCORE. IN SOME INDIVIDUALS, THIS MAY INDICATE A SITUATIONAL
CRISIS OR MARITAL DISCORD.
MF (5) SCALE

AN AESTHETIC INTEREST PATTERN REFLECTING IMAGINATION AND
SENSITIVITY IS INDICATED. COLLEGE EDUCATED MALES TYPICALLY FALL
INTO THIS RANGE.

PA (6) SCALE

OVER-SENSITIVITY AND RIGIDITY ARE INDICATED. SUSPICIOUSNESS, DISTRUST, AND RESENTMENT OVER REAL OR IMAGINED ISSUES ARE INDICATED. MORAL SELF-RIGHTEOUSNESS IS PROBABLE.

PT (7) SCALE

PUNCTUALITY IS INDICATED. HE TENDS TO PLAN AHEAD AND TO MEET DEADLINES. HE TENDS TO BE PERFECTIONISTIC, ORDERLY, AND SELF-CRITICAL. HE MAY WORRY OVER MINOR PROBLEMS. RATIONALIZATION AND INTELLECTUALIZATION ARE OFTEN USED DEFENSE MECHANISMS. HE TENDS TO BE RELIGIOUS, MORALISTIC, APPREHENSIVE, RIGID AND METICULOUS. HE IS DISSATISFIED WITH HIS LIFE AND DOES POORLY IN SOCIAL RELATIONSHIPS. SEVERE LEVELS OF ANXIETY ARE INDICATED. ANXIETY MAY PSYCHOLOGICALLY CRIPPLE FUNCTIONING. AGITATION IS INDICATED.

SC (8) SCALE

HE APPEARS TO OTHERS TO BE UNCONVENTIONAL AND ECCENTRIC. A SCHIZOID ADJUSTMENT PATTERN IS INDICATED. HE RELATES POORLY TO OTHERS AND IS SOCIALLY INTROVERTED. CONSIDER THE POSSIBILITY OF A THOUGHT DISORDER. HE IS LIKELY TO BE VERY INEPT IN SOCIAL SITUATIONS. ASSOCIATIONS MAY BE LOOSE AND HARD TO FOLLOW.

MA (9) SCALE

HE TENDS TO BE PLEASANT, ENERGETIC, ENTHUSIASTIC, AND SOCIABLE. A PLEASANT, OUTGOING PERSONALITY AND A BROAD RANGE OF INTERESTS IS LIKELY. HE TENDS TO BE HAPPY WITH LIFE. HE TENDS TO BE OPTIMISTIC, INDEPENDENT, AND SELF-CONFIDENT. A PLANFUL, PRODUCTIVE PERSON IS INDICATED.

SI (0) SCALE

HE IS LIKELY TO BE RESERVED IN SOCIAL SITUATIONS. HE MAY BE HARD TO GET TO KNOW. HE MAY BE TIMID, SHY AND RETIRING. HE PREFERS TO BE ALONE OR WITH A FEW GOOD FRIENDS. HE IS LIKELY TO BE ACTIVELY WITHDRAWING FROM OTHERS BECAUSE OF PERSONAL PROBLEMS. HE IS LIKELY TO BE SOCIALLY INEPT. SOCIAL INTERACTIONS ARE LIKELY TO MAKE HIM ANXIOUS AND TENSE. LACK OF SELF-CONFIDENCE IS INDICATED.

CHEMICAL ABUSE PROFILE

THE RESEARCH UPON WHICH THIS PROFILE IS BASED WAS CONDUCTED ON DRUG AND ALCOHOL ABUSING POPULATIONS. THIS PROFILE INTERPRETATION IS PROBABLY INVALID UNLESS DRUG AND/OR ALCOHOL ABUSE IS STRONGLY SUSPECTED OR THE CLIENT IS KNOWN TO BE A CHEMICAL ABUSER.

ALCOHOL ABUSE

IN A CHEMICAL ABUSER, A PROFILE OF THIS TYPE TENDS TO INDICATE A
PREFERENCE FOR ALCOHOL. THIS PROFILE IS SIMILAR TO THAT OF A
TYPE III ALCOHOLIC. A LONG HISTORY OF ALCOHOLISM WITH ACUTE
BENDERS IS INDICATED. SPORADIC HOSPITALIZATIONS FOLLOWED BY
UNSUCCESSFUL ATTEMPTS AT ABSTINENCE ARE INDICATED.
THESE CLIENTS OFTEN LEAVE INPATIENT UNITS PREMATURELY.
PROGNOSIS IS POOR. THIS PROFILE IS SIMILAR TO THAT OF A TYPE IV
ALCOHOLIC. AN ALCOHOL ABUSER OF THIS TYPE MAY ALSO ABUSE OTHER
DRUGS; IN PARTICULAR, DEPRESSANTS. PERSONS WITH THIS PROFILE
TYPE CAN OFTEN 'GIVE UP' ALCOHOL RATHER READILY.
THEIR HISTORIES OFTEN SHOW LONG PERIODS OF ABSTINENCE.
OUTPATIENT COUNSELING MAY BE EFFECTIVE FOR CLIENTS WITH THIS
PROFILE TYPE. CLIENTS WITH THIS PROFILE TYPE TEND TO RESPOND TO
BEHAVIORAL TREATMENTS FOR ALCOHOL ABUSE BETTER THAN CLIENTS WITH
OTHER PROFILE TYPES.

DRUG ABUSE

DRUG ABUSERS WITH THIS PROFILE TYPE MAY ABUSE HALLUCINOGENS.
THEY TEND TO VIEW THEIR PARENTS AS PUNISHING. HE TENDS TO BE
PSYCHOLOGICALLY DISTURBED AND MAY HAVE A PREVIOUS PSYCHIATRIC
HISTORY. A POOR MARITAL STABILITY IS INDICATED.
HE TENDS NOT TO ABUSE ALCOHOL. HE IS PROBABLY AN UNDERACHIEVER.
 HIS USE OF DRUGS IS SEEN BY OTHERS AS AN EXPRESSION OF AN
UNDERLYING ANTI-SOCIAL TENDENCY. RESEARCHERS GENERALLY AGREE
THAT UNDERLYING PSYCHOPATHOLOGY MANIFESTS ITSELF IN DRUG USE.
A GENERAL TREATMENT APPROACH THAT DOES NOT ADDRESS THE
UNDERLYING PSYCHOLOGY WILL PROBABLY FAIL. HEROIN ADDICTS WITH
THIS PROFILE TYPE TEND TO DISPLAY FLATTENED AFFECT, SEVERE
THINKING DISORDERS, SOCIAL WITHDRAWAL AND SOMETIMES DELUSIONS.

TREATMENT PLAN

EVALUATE FOR DEPRESSION.
DETERMINE IF THE DEPRESSION IS REACTIVE OR CHRONIC.
IF THE DEPRESSION IS CHRONIC, CONSIDER AN ANTI-DEPRESSANT.
FOR SEVERE CHRONIC DEPRESSION, CONSIDER INPATIENT TREATMENT.
ASSESS SUICIDAL POTENTIAL.
PROVIDE SUPPORTIVE THERAPY.
FOR REACTIVE DEPRESSION, PROVIDE BRIEF GOAL-ORIENTED COUNSELING.
CONSIDER THE USE OF IMAGERY AND, POSSIBLY, SYSTEMATIC
    DESENSITIZATION FOR THE CONTROL OF ANXIETY.
CONSIDER USING THOUGHT-STOPPING FOR TREATING OBSESSIONS.
BRIEF GOAL-ORIENTED COUNSELING, FOCUSED ON DEALING
    WITH LIFE STRESSES MAY BE EFFECTIVE.
BIO-FEEDBACK MAY BE EFFECTIVE.
ANTI-ANXIETY MEDICATION COULD BE CONSIDERED.
EVALUATE FOR SCHIZOPHRENIA.
CONSIDER THE USE OF AN ANTI-PSYCHOTIC MEDICATION.
CONSIDER FAMILY THERAPY.
CONSIDER INPATIENT THERAPY.
EVALUATE FOR BI-POLAR MOOD DISORDER.
CONSIDER THE USE OF LITHIUM.
CONSIDER ISOLATION IF AGITATION BECOMES SEVERE.
CONSIDER ASSERTIVENESS TRAINING.
WORK TOWARD BUILDING SOCIAL SKILLS.

NAME: MMPI-Morris-Tomlinson Report

SUPPLIER: Psych Lab
1714 Tenth Street
Wichita Falls, TX 76301
(817) 723-0012

PRODUCT CATEGORY	PRIMARY APPLICATIONS
Personality	Clinical Assessment/Diagnosis Personal/Marriage/Family Counseling

SALE RESTRICTIONS American Psychological Association Guidelines

SERVICE TYPE/COST Type	Available	Cost	Discount
Mail-In	Yes	$10.00	
Teleprocessing	No		
Local	Yes	$4.25	

PRODUCT DESCRIPTION

This program produces the Morris-Tomlinson report for the MMPI (566 item form). The software is designed for use on the Apple II+ and IIe computers. Scores must first be obtained and then entered into the computer. The resulting printout provides patient identifying data, a graphical presentation of the scores, and a verbal interpretation of the data.

The cost for local service refers to the cost-per-test when diskettes are purchased in units of 20 administrations (minimum purchase).

NAME: MMPI Report

SUPPLIER: Psychologistics, Inc.
P.O. Box 3896
Indialantic, FL 32903
(305) 727-7900

PRODUCT CATEGORY	PRIMARY APPLICATIONS
Personality	Clinical Assessment/Diagnosis
Motivation/Needs	Personnel Selection/Evaluation
	Personal/Marriage/Family Counseling

SALE RESTRICTIONS American Psychological Association Guidelines

SERVICE TYPE/COST	Type	Available	Cost	Discount
	Mail-In	No		
	Teleprocessing	No		
	Local	Yes	$295.00	

PRODUCT DESCRIPTION

This report generates an automatic interpretation of the MMPI. T-scores are typed in using a simple procedure which allows easy error correction. The one-to two-page narrative output is intended to supplement a clinician's own knowledge and facilitate report generation. The interpretive report is based on adult research. A profile page is automatically printed which graphically presents the T-scores.

The narrative report contains four sections. The validity paragraph assesses the probable relevance of the interpretive paragraphs and describes test-taking attitude. The next section contains an appropriate configural analysis. This analysis uses a 2-point code classification approach. The third section contains up to five additional paragraphs describing aspects of the profile not addressed in the configural analysis. The final section is a summary which presents key words based on scales that are significantly elevated.

Software versions are available for the Apple II + , IIe, III and IBM PC computer systems. The price shown includes a manual and unlimited usage of the program. This program allows the user to save the report in a text file for future word processing.

NAME: JOHN X. DOE   SEX: MALE
DATE: 2-27-84   AGE: 40

This is a valid profile. It does not seem that an unusual response
set affected the results. It is likely that this profile reflects
this individual's current psychological state.

People with similar test results are typically seen as depressed,
agitated, and restless. These individuals tend to vacillate between
acting out and experiencing marked feelings of guilt. They
frequently engage in self-defeating behavioral patterns. Inadequate
impulse control and low self-control leads to frustration.
This pattern is typically chronic. In extreme cases a psychotic
disorder can be present. Addictive state should be ruled out. Even
though these individuals frequently expressed the need for change and
the desire to change, their chronic condition is resistant to change
and their low frustration tolerance typically interferes with
successful completion of treatment. Suicide potential should be be
evaluated. A personality disorder should be ruled out.

Similar individuals are frequently seen as being very active. They
tend to become involved in many projects. Some restlessness and
impulsivity may be observed. A low frustration tolerance and
hyperactivity are possibilities. People with these scores are
frequently seen as having excessive energy. Common characteristics
include distractibility, restlessness, and rapid paced thoughts.
Difficulty completing projects and an overinvolvement in activities
are likely. Manic characteristics need to be evaluated.

These people tend to be optimistic and avoid thinking about some of
the unpleasant things in their life. They tend to use suppression,
repression, and denial to deal with some of their psychological
stressors. Functional physical problems, such as headaches and
gastrointestinal problems, can develop after periods of stress.

Similar people are typically described as distrustful, thin-skinned,
and overly sensitive. They can be rigid and may have periods of
brooding. Areas of resentment need to be evaluated.

Similar scores suggest an individual who prefers to be alone or only
with a few people. Accompanying characteristics can include shyness
and introversion.

This profile suggests manipulativeness, depression, restlessness,
histrionic traits, distrust, and the possibility of functional
physical complaints.

----

438 *psychware*

NAME: JOHN X. DOE SEX: MALE
DATE: 2-27-84 AGE: 40

```
        L)  F)  K)   HS  D.  HY  PD  MF  PA  PT  SC  MA  SI
110  -                +                                         - 110
     -                +
     -                +
     -                +
     -                +
100  -                +                                         - 100
     -                +
     -                +
     -                +
     -                +
 90  -                +                                         - 90
     -                +
     -                +
     -                +
     -                +
 80  -                +                                         - 80
     -                +              *
     -                +     *
     -                +                                    *    -
     -                +                                         -
 70  - -- -- -- + -- -- -- -- -- -- -- -- -- -- 70
     -                +         *
     -                +                 *       *              -
     -                +                                         -
     -                +                     *            *     -
 60  -                +                                         - 60
     -                +
     -                +
     -        *       +
     -                + *
 50  - -- -- -- + -- -- -- -- -- -- -- -- -- -- 50
     -             *  +
     - *              +
     -                +
     -                +              *
 40  -                +                                         - 40
     -                +
     -                +
     -                +
     -                +
 30  - -- -- -- + -- -- -- -- -- -- -- -- -- -- 30
     -                +
     -                +
     -                +
     -                +
 20  -                +                                         - 20
                      1   2   3   4   5   6   7   8   9   0
        L)  F)  K)   HS  D.  HY  PD  MF  PA  PT  SC  MA  SI
     R   3   5   11   13  31  26  31  17  14  29  31  26  35
     T  46  55  48   53  76  68  78  43  67  63  67  73  62
```

psychware **439**

NAME: MMPI Report

SUPPLIER: Precision People, Inc.
3452 North Ride Circle. S.
Jacksonville, FL 32217
(904) 262-1096

PRODUCT CATEGORY	PRIMARY APPLICATIONS
Personality	Clinical Assessment/Diagnosis Personal/Marriage/Family Counseling

SALE RESTRICTIONS American Psychological Association Guidelines

SERVICE TYPE/COST	Type	Available	Cost	Discount
	Mail-In	No		
	Teleprocessing	No		
	Local	Yes	$475.00	

PRODUCT DESCRIPTION

This computer-generated MMPI interpretation has four major sections: general profile interpretation, interpretation based on single scale elevation, chemical abuse profile, and treatment plan. The key feature of this report is the general profile interpretation which addresses test validity, personality dynamics, defense mechanisms, somatic complaints, prognosis, treatment approach, diagnosis, and more.

This program prints a five- to six-page narrative-style report based on the client's sex and 14 T-scores which are typed into the computer. The program is easy to use and comes with a fully documented manual.

The software is compatible with IBM PC, Apple, and TRS-80 (Models I, II, and III) microcomputers. A manual and sample are available for $34.00. For a sample printout of this product, see the one shown under MMPI INTERPRETATION.

NAME: MMPI Scoring

SUPPLIER: Applied Innovations, Inc.
South Kingstown Office Park, Suite A-1
Wakefield, RI 02879
(800) 272-2250

PRODUCT CATEGORY

Personality

PRIMARY APPLICATIONS

Clinical Assessment/Diagnosis
Personal/Marriage/Family Counseling

SALE RESTRICTIONS American Psychological Association Guidelines

SERVICE TYPE/COST	Type	Available	Cost	Discount
	Mail-In	No		
	Teleprocessing	No		
	Local	Yes	$225.00	

PRODUCT DESCRIPTION

This program is designed to score, but not administer, five versions of the MMPI: Form R, Group Form, Card Form, MMPI-399 and MMPI-168. Raw scores are converted into T-scores for the validity scales, clinical scales, and many research scales. It can also be integrated with an MMPI interpretive program available from the same supplier. The software operates on most available personal computers including IBM, Apple, Digital, and Kaypro.

BY ARTHUR L. AARONSON
COPYRIGHT (C) 1983 -ALL RIGHTS RESERVED-

NAME: SAMPLE PATIENT   SEX: MALE
DATE: 10/14/83   AGE: 36
TEST FORM: BOOKLET FORM   NORMS: MIN. ADULTS (K-COR)

```
        L    F    K       Hs   D   Hy   Pd   Mf   Pa   Pt   Sc   Ma   Si
110  -                 +                                                    -  110
     -                 +
     -                 +
     -                 +
100  -                 +                                                    -  100
     -                 +
     -                 +
     -                 +
90   -                 +                                                    -  90
     -                 +
     -                 +          *
     -                 +
80   -                 +                                   *                -  80
     -                 +
     -                 +
     -                 +                                          *
70   -  --   --   --   +   --  --   --   --   --   --   *  --   --   *  -   -  70
     -                 +                                  *
     -                 +         *    *    *
60   -                 +                                                    -  60
     -                 +
     -  *              +   *
     -       *         +
50   -  --   --   --   +   --  --   --   --   --   --   --   --   --  --  -   -  50
     -                 +
     -                 +
     -            *    +
40   -                 +                                                    -  40
     -                 +
     -                 +
     -                 +
30   -  --   --   --   +   --  --   --   --  --T   --   --   --   --  --  -   -  30
     -                 +
     -                 +
     -                 +
20   -                 +                                                    -  20
        1    2    3    4    5    6    7    8    9    0
        L    F    K    Hs   D   Hy   Pd   Mf   Pa   Pt   Sc   Ma   Si
RAW     6    5    8    10   32   24   23   29   14   29   26   25   45
TSCORE  56   55   42   57   87   64   67   67   67   79   73   75   72
```

442 *psychware*

-PAGE 2-

```
CANNOT SAY = 5      OR 0%
# OF TRUE RESPONSES = 290      OR 51%
# OF FALSE RESPONSE = 271      OR 47%
F MINUS K = -3
GOLDBERG INDEX = 59 PSYCHOTIC - IF INPATIENT
TR INDEX = 3
CARELESSNESS INDEX = 8
TAULBEE-SISSON SCORE = 5 SCHIZOPHRENIC
WELCH CODE = 2''7980 '4563 -1 /L /F /K :
```

CRITICAL ITEMS

33. I HAVE HAD VERY STRANGE EXPERIENCES-TRUE
114. OFTEN I FEEL IF THERE WERE A TIGHT BAND ABOUT MY HEAD-TRUE
133. I HAVE NEVER INDULGED IN ANY UNUSUAL SEX PRACTICES-FALSE
146. I HAVE THE WANDERLUST AND AM NEVER HAPPY UNLESS I AM ROAMING OR
     TRAVELING ABOUT-TRUE
156. I HAVE HAD PERIODS IN WHICH I CARRIED ON ACTIVITIES WITHOUT KNOWING
     LATER WHAT I HAD BEEN DOING-TRUE
182. I AM AFRAID OF LOSING MY MIND-TRUE
215. I HAVE USED ALCOHOL EXCESSIVELY-TRUE
251. I HAVE HAD BLANK SPELLS IN WHICH MY ACTIVITIES WERE INTERUPTED AND I
     DID NOT KNOW WHAT WAS GOING ON AROUND ME-TRUE
334. PECULIAR ODORS COME TO ME AT TIMES-TRUE
337. I FEEL ANXIETY ABOUT SOMETHING OR SOMEONE ALMOST ALL THE TIME-TRUE
339. MOST OF THE TIME I WISH I WERE DEAD-TRUE

FREQUENTLY SCORED SCALES

SCALE NAME	RAW	T-SCORE	20	30	40	50	60	70	80	90	100
A	25	66	.	:		:		* :	.	.	.
R	15	49	.	:		* :		:	.	.	.
MAS	36	80	.	:	*	:		:	*	.	.
ES	35	35	.	:	*	:		:	.	.	.
LB	7	41	.	:	*	:		:	*	.	.
CA	24	77	.	:		:		: *	.	.	.
DY	31	63	.	:		:	*	:	.	.	.
DO	10	37	.	:	*	:		:	.	.	.
RE	14	35	.	:	*	:		:	.	.	.
PR	16	58	.	:		:	*	:	.	.	.
ST	18	51	.	:		*		:	.	.	.
CN	29	61	.	:		:	*	:	.	.	.
AL	27	71	.	:		:		*	.	.	.
O-H	10	43	.	:	*	:		:	.	.	.
			20	30	40	50	60	70	80	90	100

HARRIS, LINGOES, & SERKOWNEK SUBSCALES

SCALE NAME	RAW	T-SCORE	20	30	40	50	60	70	80	90	100
D1	21	91	.	:		:		:	.	*	.
D2	8	65	.	:		:	*	:	.	.	.
D3	3	49	.	:		* :		:	.	.	.
D4	11	95	.	:		:		:	.	. *	.

psychware **443**

-PAGE 3-

SCALE NAME	RAW	T-SCORE	20	30	40	50	60	70	80	90	100
D5	8	82	.	:		:		:	.*	.	.
HY1	0	31	.	*		:		:	.	.	.
HY2	4	46	.	:	*	:		:	.	.	.
HY3	7	70	.	:		:		*	.	.	.
HY4	8	71	.	:		:		*	.	.	.
HY5	3	53	.	:		: *		:	.	.	.
PD1	3	57	.	:		: *		:	.	.	.
PD2	6	61	.	:		:	*	:	.	.	.
PD3	5	40	.	:	*	:		:	.	.	.
PD4A	10	66	.	:		:		* :	.	.	.
PD4B	13	85	.	:		:		:	. *	.	.
PA1	3	55	.	:		: *		:	.	.	.
PA2	6	75	.	:		:		:	*	.	.
PA3	2	41	.	:	*	:		:	.	.	.
SC1A	3	48	.	:		* :		:	.	.	.
SC1B	3	57	.	:		: *		:	.	.	.
SC2A	7	85	.	:		:		:	. *	.	.
SC2B	8	83	.	:		:		:	.*	.	.
SC2C	4	67	.	:		:		* :	.	.	.
SC3	9	77	.	:		:		: *	.	.	.
MA1	1	45	.	:		* :		:	.	.	.
MA2	8	80	.	:		:		:	*	.	.
MA3	3	47	.	:		* :		:	.	.	.
MA4	6	71	.	:		:		*	.	.	.
SI1	20	101	.	:		:		:	.	.	*
SI2	7	68	.	:		:		* :	.	.	.
SI3	13	72	.	:		:		: *	.	.	.
SI4	5	65	.	:		:		*	.	.	.
SI5	6	58	.	:		:	*	:	.	.	.
SI6	6	87	.	:		:		:	. *	.	.
MF1	12	89	.	:		:		:	.	* .	.
MF2	5	61	.	:		:	*	:	.	.	.
MF3	2	43	.	:	*	:		:	.	.	.
MF4	2	46	.	:	*	:		:	.	.	.
MF5	4	55	.	:		: *		:	.	.	.
MF6	4	42	.	:	*	:		:	.	.	.
			20	30	40	50	60	70	80	90	100

WIGGINS CONTENT SCALES

SCALE NAME	RAW	T-SCORE	20	30	40	50	60	70	80	90	100
SOC	21	76	.	:		:		: *	.	.	.
DEP	19	73	.	:		:		: *	.	.	.
FEM	9	50	.	:		*		:	.	.	.
MOR	17	68	.	:		:		* :	.	.	.
REL	7	52	.	:		: *		:	.	.	.
AUT	13	59	.	:		:	*	:	.	.	.
PSY	11	55	.	:		: *		:	.	.	.
ORG	17	77	.	:		:		: *	.	.	.
FAM	7	64	.	:		:	*	:	.	.	.
HOS	13	57	.	:		:	*	:	.	.	.
PHO	12	67	.	:		:		* :	.	.	.

444 *psychware*

MMPI SCORING PROGRAM

-PAGE 4-

SCALE NAME	RAW	T-SCORE	20	30	40	50	60	70	80	90	100
HYP	20	68						*			
HEA	2	42			*						

TRYON, STEIN AND CHU CLUSTER SCALES

SCALE NAME	RAW	T-SCORE	20	30	40	50	60	70	80	90	100
TSC-I	20	79							*		
TSC-II	11	76						*			
TSC-III	13	59					*				
TSC-IV	20	94								*	
TSC-V	14	75						*			
TSC-VI	10	66					*				
TSC-VII	28	96								*	

WEINER-HARMON SUBTLE-OBVIOUS SUBSCALES

SCALE NAME	RAW	T-SCORE	20	30	40	50	60	70	80	90	100
D-O	24	87								*	
D-S	8	41			*						
HY-O	14	72						*			
HY-S	9	41			*						
PD-O	15	75						*			
PD-S	8	46				*					
PA-O	7	65					*				
PA-S	7	54				*					
MA-O	16	85								*	
MA-S	9	48				*					

NAME: MMPI/The Minnesota Report: Adult Clinical System

SUPPLIER: NCS/Professional Assessment Services
P.O. Box 1416
Minneapolis, MN 55440
(800) 328-6759

PRODUCT CATEGORY

Personality

PRIMARY APPLICATIONS

Clinical Assessment/Diagnosis
Personal/Marriage/Family Counseling

SALE RESTRICTIONS American Psychological Association Guidelines

SERVICE TYPE/COST	Type	Available	Cost	Discount
	Mail-In	Yes	$20.50	Yes
	Teleprocessing	Yes	$20.50	Yes
	Local	Yes	$14.75	Yes

PRODUCT DESCRIPTION

This product employs content and well-established code-type interpretations, as well as special indexes and demographic data, to generate interpretive statements. THE MINNESOTA REPORT narrative assesses the individual's test-taking attitudes and such issues as interpersonal relationships and behavioral stability. Included are sections on DSM-III compatible diagnostic hypotheses and treatment considerations that can help the clinician in drawing appropriate conclusions about the individual case. A scores only report (Profile Report) is also available at approximately 40% of costs shown here for the complete report.

Two systems are available for local processing of test results. MICRO-TEST Assessment Software from National Computer Systems, used with a Sentry 3000 tabletop scanner (purchase price approximately $4000) and microcomputer system ($2000-$3000 purchase price), allows tests to be administered off-line. Answer sheets are then scanned and scored automatically, one at a time or in a batch. The software also permits on-line administration of the test via microcomputer. In either case, the same report is provided. The cost for local scoring refers to the cost-per-test when diskettes are purchased in units of 20 administrations (minimum purchase).

By James N. Butcher, Ph.D.

Client No. : 987654321   Gender : Female
Setting : Medical   Age : 40
Report Date : 10-NOV-83
ISS Code Number : 00003522 114 0003

PROFILE VALIDITY

This is a valid MMPI profile. The client's responses to the MMPI validity items suggest that she cooperated with the evaluation enough to provide useful interpretive information. The resulting clinical profile is an adequate indication of her present personality functioning.

SYMPTOMATIC PATTERN

Individuals with this MMPI profile tend to be chronically maladjusted. Narcissistic and rather self-indulgent, the client is somewhat dependent and demands attention from others. She appears to be rather hostile and irritable and tends to resent others.

She has great trouble showing anger and may express it in passive-agressive ways. She may have a problem with acting-out behavior and may have experienced difficulty with her sexual behavior in the past. She tends to blame her own difficulties on others and refuses to accept responsibility for her own problems.

Her response content also suggests that she may feel somewhat estranged from people--somewhat alienated and concerned over the actions of others-- and may blame others for her negative frame of mind. She views the world as a threatening place, sees herself as having been unjustly blamed for others' problems, and feels that she is getting a raw deal out of life. These characteristics are reflected in the content of her responses. The items she endorsed include content suggesting that her thinking is confused and bizarre. She feels that others do not understand her and are trying to control her . She is also tending toward withdrawal into a world of fantasy.

INTERPERSONAL RELATIONS

She is experiencing great difficulty in her social relationships, and feels that others do not understand her and do not give her enough sympathy. She is somewhat aloof, cold, non-giving, and uncompromising, and attempts to advance herself at the expense of others. Her lack of trust may prevent her from developing warm, close relationships.

BEHAVIORAL STABILITY

This profile reflects a pattern of long-standing poor adjustment. Her anger may produce periods of intense interpersonal difficulty.

DIAGNOSTIC CONSIDERATIONS

NOTE: This MMPI interpretation can serve as a useful source of hypotheses about clients. This report is based on objectively derived scale indexes and scale interpretations that have been developed in diverse groups of patients. The personality descriptions, inferences and recommendations contained herein need to be verified by other sources of clinical information since individual clients may not fully match the prototype. The information in this report should most appropriately be used by a trained, qualified test interpreter. The information contained in this report should be considered confidential.

An individual with this profile is usually viewed as having a Personality Disorder, such as a Passive-Aggressive or Paranoid Personality. The possibility of a Paranoid Disorder should be considered, however.

TREATMENT CONSIDERATIONS

Individuals with this profile tend not to seek psychological treatment on their own, and they are usually not good candidates for psychotherapy. They resist psychological interpretation, argue, and tend to rationalize and to blame others for their problems. In addition, they frequently leave therapy prematurely.

CLINICAL PROFILE

Client No. : 987654321   Gender : Female
Setting : Medical   Age : 40
Report Date : 10-NOV-83

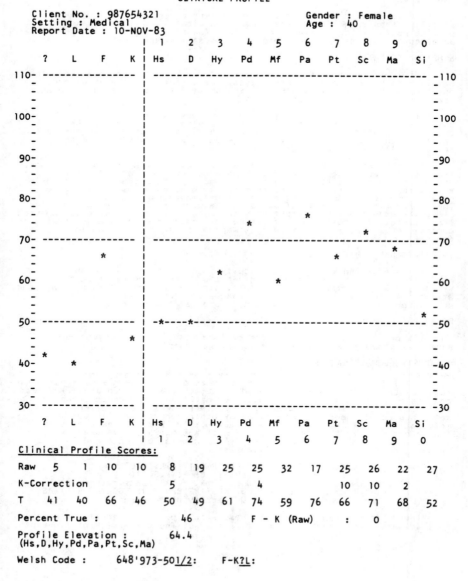

Clinical Profile Scores:

	?	L	F	K	Hs	D	Hy	Pd	Mf	Pa	Pt	Sc	Ma	Si
Raw	5	1	10	10	8	19	25	25	32	17	25	26	22	27
K-Correction					5			4			10	10	2	
T	41	40	66	46	50	49	61	74	59	76	66	71	68	52

Percent True :   46   F - K (Raw)   :   0

Profile Elevation :   64.4
(Hs,D,Hy,Pd,Pa,Pt,Sc,Ma)

Welsh Code :   648'973-501/2:   F-K?L:

448 *psychware*

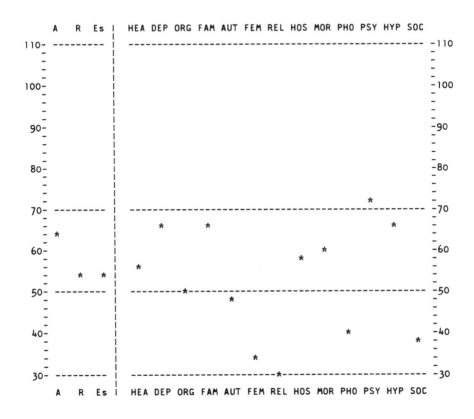

Supplemental Profile Scores:

	A	R	Es		HEA	DEP	ORG	FAM	AUT	FEM	REL	HOS	MOR	PHO	PSY	HYP	SOC
Raw	26	19	43		8	17	7	8	7	14	1	12	15	4	19	19	4
T	63	53	54		55	66	50	66	47	33	27	57	60	39	72	66	38

The Minnesota Multiphasic Personality Inventory
EXTENDED SCORE REPORT

Client No. : 987654321   Report Date : 10-NOV-83   Page   5

Supplementary Scales: Raw Score   T Score

	Raw Score	T Score
Dependency (Dy)	31	57
Dominance (Do)	19	62
Responsibility (Re)	19	43
Control (Cn)	31	64
College Maladjustment (Mt)	24	63
Overcontrolled Hostility (O-H)	10	37
Prejudice (Pr)	13	52
Manifest Anxiety (MAS)	22	60
MacAndrew Addiction (MAC)	20	51
Social Status (St)	23	62

Depression Subscales (Harris-Lingoes):

Subjective Depression (D1)	8	49
Psychomotor Retardation (D2)	4	40
Physical Malfunctioning (D3)	4	55
Mental Dullness (D4)	6	68
Brooding (D5)	3	50

Hysteria Subscales (Harris-Lingoes):

Denial of Social Anxiety (Hy1)	5	59
Need for Affection (Hy2)	4	47
Lassitude-Malaise (Hy3)	7	67
Somatic Complaints (Hy4)	2	43
Inhibition of Aggression (Hy5)	4	54

Psychopathic Deviate Subscales (Harris-Lingoes):

Familial Discord (Pd1)	3	57
Authority Problems (Pd2)	7	76
Social Imperturbability (Pd3)	6	68
Social Alienation (Pd4a)	15	85
Self Alienation (Pd4b)	10	74

Masculinity-Femininity Subscales (Serkownek):

Narcissism-Hypersensitivity (Mf1)	11	75
Stereotypic Feminine Interests (Mf2)	4	24
Denial of Stereo. Masculine Interests (Mf3)	7	58
Heterosexual Discomfort-Passivity (Mf4)	1	23
Introspective-Critical (Mf5)	4	55
Socially Retiring (Mf6)	4	44

Paranoia Subscales (Harris-Lingoes):

Persecutory Ideas (Pa1)	7	75
Poignancy (Pa2)	5	69
Naivete (Pa3)	3	47

Schizophrenia Subscales (Harris-Lingoes):

Social Alienation (Sc1a)	7	64
Emotional Alienation (Sc1b)	2	50
Lack of Ego Mastery, Cognitive (Sc2a)	4	66
Lack of Ego Mastery, Conative (Sc2b)	4	59
Lack of Ego Mastery, Def. Inhib. (Sc2c)	3	58
Bizarre Sensory Experiences (Sc3)	4	55

Hypomania Subscales (Harris-Lingoes):

Amorality (Ma1)	1	47
Psychomotor Acceleration (Ma2)	10	92
Imperturbability (Ma3)	3	51
Ego Inflation (Ma4)	5	64

Social Introversion Subscales (Serkownek):

Inferiority-Personal Discomfort (Si1)	11	59
Discomfort with Others (Si2)	2	35
Staid-Personal Rigidity (Si3)	7	59
Hypersensitivity (Si4)	3	42
Distrust (Si5)	3	66
Physical-Somatic Concerns (Si6)	3	60

450   *psychware*

The following Critical Items have been found to have possible significance in analyzing a client's problem situation. Although these items may serve as a source of hypotheses for further investigation, caution should be taken in interpreting individual items because they may have been inadvertently checked. Critical item numbers refer to The Group Form test booklet. Corresponding item numbers for Form R (only items 367-566 differ) can be found in the MMPI "Manual" or Volume I of "An MMPI Handbook." Corresponding item numbers for the Roche Testbook can be found in "The Clinical Use of the Automated MMPI."

ACUTE ANXIETY STATE   (Koss-Butcher Critical Items)

3.   I wake up fresh and rested most mornings. (F)
13. I work under a great deal of tension. (T)
72. I am troubled by discomfort in the pit of my stomach every few days or oftener. (T)
238. I have periods of such great restlessness that I cannot sit long in a chair. (T)
337. I feel anxiety about something or someone almost all the time. (T)
543. Several times a week I feel that something dreadful is about to happen. (T)
555. I sometimes feel that I am about to go to pieces. (T)

DEPRESSED SUICIDAL IDEATION   (Koss-Butcher Critical Items)

41. I have had periods of days, weeks, or months when I couldn't take care of things because I couldn't "get going". (T)
76. Most of the time I feel blue. (T)
84. These days I find it hard not to give up hope of amounting to something. (T)
107. I am happy most of the time. (F)
259. I have difficulty in starting to do things. (T)
301. Life is a strain for me much of the time. (T)
379. I very seldom have spells of the blues. (F)
526. The future seems hopeless to me. (T)

THREATENED ASSAULT   (Koss-Butcher Critical Items)

39. At times I feel like smashing things. (T)
97. At times I have a strong urge to do something harmful or shocking. (T)
145. At times I feel like picking a fist fight with someone. (T)
234. I get mad easily and then get over it soon. (T)
381. I am often said to be hotheaded. (T)

MENTAL CONFUSION   (Koss-Butcher Critical Items)

33. I have had very peculiar and strange experiences. (T)
50. My soul sometimes leaves my body. (T)
66. I see things or animals or people around me that others do not see. (T)
345. I often feel as if things were not real. (T)

PERSECUTORY IDEAS   (Koss-Butcher Critical Items)

16. I am sure I get a raw deal from life. (T)
35. If people had not had it in for me I would have been much more successful. (T)
110. Someone has it in for me. (T)
121. I believe I am being plotted against. (T)
278. I have often felt that strangers were looking at me critically. (T)
284. I am sure I am being talked about. (T)

CHARACTEROLOGICAL ADJUSTMENT -- ANTISOCIAL ATTITUDE
(Lachar-Wrobel Critical Items)

38. During one period when I was a youngster, I engaged in petty thievery. (T)
118. In school I was sometimes sent to the principal for cutting up. (T)

CHARACTEROLOGICAL ADJUSTMENT -- FAMILY CONFLICT
(Lachar-Wrobel Critical Items)

21. At times I have very much wanted to leave home. (T)

SEXUAL CONCERN AND DEVIATION   (Lachar-Wrobel Critical Items)

37. I have never been in trouble because of my sex behavior. (F)
74. I have often wished I were a girl.(Or if you are a girl) I have never been sorry that I am a girl. (T-Males, F-Females)
133. I have never indulged in any unusual sex practices. (F)
179. I am worried about sex matters. (T)

SOMATIC SYMPTOMS   (Lachar-Wrobel Critical Items)

55. I am almost never bothered by pains over the heart or in my chest. (F)
62. Parts of my body often have feelings like burning, tingling, crawling, or like "going to sleep." (T)
72. I am troubled by discomfort in the pit of my stomach every few days or oftener. (T)
281. I do not often notice my ears ringing or buzzing. (F)
330. I have never been paralyzed or had any unusual weakness of any of my muscles. (F)
544. I feel tired a good deal of the time. (T)

NCS Interpretive Scoring Systems P.O. Box 1416, Mpls, MN 55440

MINNESOTA MULTIPHASIC PERSONALITY INVENTORY
Copyright THE UNIVERSITY OF MINNESOTA
1943, Renewed 1970. This Report 1982. All rights reserved.
Scored and Distributed Exclusively by NCS INTERPRETIVE SCORING SYSTEMS
Under License From The University of Minnesota

NAME: MMPI/The Minnesota Report: Personnel Selection System

SUPPLIER: NCS/Professional Assessment Services
P.O. Box 1416
Minneapolis, MN 55440
(800) 328-6759

PRODUCT CATEGORY	PRIMARY APPLICATIONS
Personality	Personnel Selection/Evaluation
	Vocational Guidance/Counseling

SALE RESTRICTIONS American Psychological Association Guidelines

SERVICE TYPE/COST Type	Available	Cost	Discount
Mail-In	Yes	$22.50	Yes
Teleprocessing	Yes	$22.50	Yes
Local	Yes	$17.20	Yes

PRODUCT DESCRIPTION

The MINNESOTA PERSONNEL REPORTS provide objective, pre- employment appraisals of individuals seeking occupations that involve a high degree of public trust. They are particularly well-suited for use with those jobs that not only involve responsibility, but a high degree of stress. The reports are based on the empirical literature on the use of the MMPI with normals (including personnel selection) and the author's practical experience using the MMPI for personnel selection in several settings.

Two types of reports are available. The Screening Report has five parts. Part 1 provides ratings along five dimensions that detect key potential problem areas: openness to evaluation, social facility, addiction potential, stress tolerance, and overall adjustment. Brief interpretive statements are also included when applicable. The remaining parts of the report present a standard MMPI clinical profile, raw and T-scores for MMPI scales A, R, Es and the Wiggins content scales, an extended score report for a number of special scales, and a section that considers significant content themes. The Personnel Interpretive Report includes everything in the Screening Report except the ratings which are replaced with a detailed narrative summarizing the applicant's approach to taking the MMPI, personal adjustment, interpersonal relations, personal stability, and possible employment problems. Prices shown here are for the Interpretive Report. Costs for the Screening Report are approximately 60% lower.

Two systems are available for local processing of test results. MICROTEST Assessment Software from National Computer Systems, used with a Sentry 3000 tabletop scanner (purchase price approximately $4000) and microcomputer system ($2000-$3000 purchase price), allows tests to be administered off-line. Answer sheets are then scanned and scored automatically, one at a time or in a batch. The software also permits on-line administration of the test via microcomputer. In either case, the same report is provided. The cost for local scoring refers to the cost-per-test when diskettes are purchased in units of 20 administrations (minimum purchase).

for the Minnesota Multiphasic Personality Inventory

By James N. Butcher, Ph.D.

Client No. :   SAMPLE   Gender : Male
Report Date : 20-MAR-84   Age : 30
ISS Code Number : 00000991 114 0002
Occupation : Air Traffic Controller

PROFILE VALIDITY

    This is a valid MMPI profile. However, the applicant approached the
items in a cautious manner as many job applicants do. He was somewhat
unwilling to admit to many personal faults. Individuals with similar
profiles are not interested in discussing their problems openly.

PERSONAL ADJUSTMENT

    This applicant's MMPI profile is within normal limits. He reported
very few psychological problems and clearly feels that his adjustment to
present circumstances is quite good. Individuals with this profile tend to
view their lives as happy and their personality functioning as effective.
Individuals with this profile are typically assertive and independent.
They usually show some willingness to take risks in life.

    He may experience some conflicts concerning his sex-role identity. He
seems somewhat insecure in masculine roles, showing a generally feminine
pattern of interests. He may be somewhat uncomfortable in relationships
with women.

INTERPERSONAL RELATIONS

    He appears to be quite comfortable in social relationships. He shows
no social anxiety and tends to view himself as outgoing and sociable.

    The content of this applicant's MMPI responses suggests the following
additional information concerning his interpersonal relations. He tends to
be interpersonally dominant, asserting a high degree of self-confidence and
forcefulness. He willingly expresses strong opinions. He reports that his
family relationships are good and that his home life is pleasant. He does
not view himself as being overly competitive or aggressive toward others.

BEHAVIORAL STABILITY

    His normal-range MMPI performance suggests generally stable personality
functioning. He is not likely to engage in erratic or abnormal behaviors.

POSSIBLE EMPLOYMENT PROBLEMS

    His MMPI profile does not suggest possible employment problems related
to his personality functioning. He seems to be generally well-adjusted and
would probably be able to adapt to a wide range of employment settings.

NOTE: This MMPI interpretation can serve as a useful source of hypotheses
about clients applying for positions in which stable pysychological
adjustment has been determined to be essential for success on the job.
The MMPI was not originally developed for use in personnel selection,
however, and contains a number of items that some people believe to be
irrelevant or inappropriate for that purpose. This report is based upon
empirical descriptions derived largely from clinical populations. Caution
should be taken in applying these interpretations in a pre-employment
screening situation. The MMPI should NOT be used as the SOLE means of
determining a candidate's suitability for employment. The information
in this report should be used by qualified test interpretation specialists
ONLY.

for the Minnesota Multiphasic Personality Inventory

By James N. Butcher, Ph.D.

CLINICAL PROFILE

Client No. :   SAMPLE   Gender : Male
Report Date : 20-MAR-84   Age :   30
Occupation : Air Traffic Controller

Clinical Profile Scores:

	?	L	F	K	Hs	D	Hy	Pd	Mf	Pa	Pt	Sc	Ma	Si
Raw	11	2	1	22	1	17	22	15	32	10	3	5	11	20
K-Correction					11				9			22	22	4	
T	44	44	46	68	52	51	60	62	73	56	54	59	45	45

Percentage True :   32   F - K (Raw) :   -21

Average Profile Elevation :   54.9   Disturbance Index (DsI) :   451
(Hs,D,Hy,Pd,Pa,Pt,Sc,Ma)

     Welsh Code :   5'43-86712/ 90:   K-F?L:

psychware   **455**

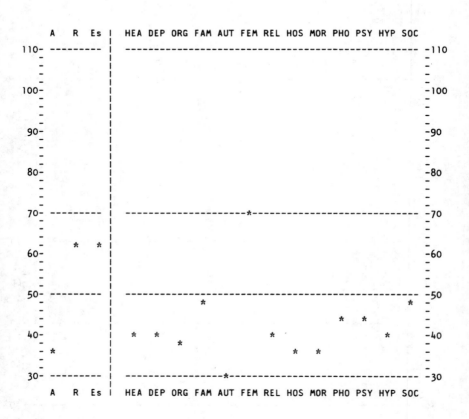

Supplemental Profile Scores:

Raw	1	21	51		1	2	0	3	1	16	3	2	1	3	4	7	7
T	36	61	61		40	40	37	47	29	69	39	35	36	43	43	39	47

456 *psychware*

EXTENDED SCORE REPORT

Client No. :   SAMPLE   Report Date : 20-MAR-84   Page 4

Supplementary Scales:	Raw Score	T Score
Dependency (Dy)	7	36
Dominance (Do)	22	70
Responsibility (Re)	28	69
College Maladjustment (Mt)	3	39
Overcontrolled Hostility (O-H)	13	52
Prejudice (Pr)	3	34
Manifest Anxiety (MAS)	6	38
MacAndrew Addiction (MAC)	15	30
Cynicism (CYN)	1	28
Social Status (St)	24	64
Favorable Impression (Fi)	21	83

Depression Subscales (Harris-Lingoes):

Subjective Depression (D1)	4	41
Psychomotor Retardation (D2)	7	59
Physical Malfunctioning (D3)	4	56
Mental Dullness (D4)	0	40
Brooding (D5)	0	38

Hysteria Subscales (Harris-Lingoes):

Denial of Social Anxiety (Hy1)	5	59
Need for Affection (Hy2)	11	75
Lassitude-Malaise (Hy3)	1	45
Somatic Complaints (Hy4)	0	39
Inhibition of Aggression (Hy5)	3	53

Psychopathic Deviate Subscales (Harris-Lingoes):

Familial Discord (Pd1)	1	45
Authority Problems (Pd2)	2	37
Social Imperturbability (Pd3)	9	56
Social Alienation (Pd4a)	2	38
Self Alienation (Pd4b)	2	43

Masculinity-Femininity Subscales (Serkownek):

Narcissism-Hypersensitivity (Mf1)	4	45
Stereotypic Feminine Interests (Mf2)	5	61
Denial of Stereo. Masculine Interests (Mf3)	6	73
Heterosexual Discomfort-Passivity (Mf4)	3	58
Introspective-Critical (Mf5)	3	46
Socially Retiring (Mf6)	8	70

Paranoia Subscales (Harris-Lingoes):

Persecutory Ideas (Pa1)	1	46
Poignancy (Pa2)	2	49
Naivete (Pa3)	6	61

Schizophrenia Subscales (Harris-Lingoes):

Social Alienation (Sc1a)	3	48
Emotional Alienation (Sc1b)	0	31
Lack of Ego Mastery, Cognitive (Sc2a)	0	41
Lack of Ego Mastery, Conative (Sc2b)	0	39
Lack of Ego Mastery, Def. Inhib. (Sc2c)	0	41
Bizarre Sensory Experiences (Sc3)	0	40

Hypomania Subscales (Harris-Lingoes):

Amorality (Ma1)	1	45
Psychomotor Acceleration (Ma2)	1	31
Imperturbability (Ma3)	4	53
Ego Inflation (Ma4)	2	46

psychware   **457**

Social Introversion Subscales (Serkownek):

Inferiority-Personal Discomfort (Si1)	1	18
Discomfort with Others (Si2)	2	36
Staid-Personal Rigidity (Si3)	12	66
Hypersensitivity (Si4)	1	35
Distrust (Si5)	1	26
Physical-Somatic Concerns (Si6)	1	44

CONTENT THEMES

The following Content Themes may serve as a source of hypotheses for further investigation. These content themes summarize similar item responses that appear with greater frequency with this applicant than with most people.

No significant Content Themes are apparent in this applicant's MMPI.

NCS Interpretive Scoring Systems P.O. Box 1416, Mpls, MN 55440

MINNESOTA MULTIPHASIC PERSONALITY INVENTORY
Copyright THE UNIVERSITY OF MINNESOTA
1943, Renewed 1970. This Report 1983. All rights reserved.
Scored and Distributed Exclusively by NCS INTERPRETIVE SCORING SYSTEMS
Under License From The University of Minnesota

*   "The Minnesota Personnel Interpretive Report," "MMPI," and "Minnesota Multiphasic Personality Inventory" are trademarks owned by the University Press of the University of Minnesota.

NAME: Motivation Analysis Test Narrative Report

SUPPLIER: Institute for Personality and Ability Testing, Inc.
P.O. Box 188
Champaign, IL 61820
(217) 352-4739

PRODUCT CATEGORY	PRIMARY APPLICATIONS
Motivation/Needs	Personnel Selection/Evaluation Personal/Marriage/Family Counseling

SALE RESTRICTIONS American Psychological Association Guidelines

SERVICE TYPE/COST	Type	Available	Cost	Discount
	Mail-In	Yes	$16.00	Yes
	Teleprocessing	No		
	Local	No		

PRODUCT DESCRIPTION

The Motivation Analysis Test measures 10 important comfort, social, and achievment needs. Five are basic drives---Caution, Sex, Self-Assertion, Aggressiveness, and Self-Indulgence. Five are interests that develop and mature through learning experiences---Career, Affection, Dependency, Responsibility, and Self-Fulfillment.

The test uses objective devices (paper-and-pencil format) which are less susceptible to deliberate faking or distortion than questionnaires or checklists. For each of the 10 interest areas, scores measure drive or need level, satisfaction level, degree of conflict, and total motivation strength.

The MOTIVATION ANALYSIS TEST NARRATIVE REPORT provides a multipage report for each individual, identifying their dynamic factors of importance.

THE INSTITUTE FOR PERSONALITY AND ABILITY TESTING
P. O. BOX 188   CHAMPAIGN, ILLINOIS 61820
MOTIVATION ANALYSIS TEST REPORT

-NOTE-

MOTIVATION SCORES ARE INHERENTLY LESS STABLE THAN PERSONALITY OR ABILITY
SCORES.   THIS IS PARTICULARLY TRUE IN YOUNGER INDIVIDUALS WHOSE GOALS AND
INTERESTS MAY NOT YET BE WELL DEFINED.   AVOID CONSIDERING THESE SCORES AS
UNCHANGING OR FIXED CHARACTERISTICS OF THE INDIVIDUAL. INSTEAD, THEY MUST
BE UNDERSTOOD IN LIGHT OF THE INDIVIDUAL'S PRESENT LIFE SITUATION, RECOG-
NIZING THAT THEY WILL CHANGE IN RESPONSE TO STIMULI AND OPPORTUNITIES, AS
THE INDIVIDUAL ADAPTS.
NAME-SMITH   JOHN J
 AGE-25
 SEX-M

BROAD DYNAMIC PATTERNS

	LOW	1 2 3 4 5 6 7 8 9 10		HIGH
TOTAL INTEREST		*	TOTAL INTEREST	
EXPECTATION		*	EXPECTATION	
FULFILLMENT		*	FULFILLMENT	
FRUSTRATION		*	FRUSTRATION	

THE TOTAL AMOUNT OF INTEREST WHICH HE SHOWS IN THE AREAS TAPPED BY
 THIS TEST IS TYPICAL OF PEOPLE IN GENERAL.

HE TENDS TO BE OBJECTIVE IN HIS EVALUATION OF SITUATIONS, NEITHER
 OVERLY OPTIMISTIC NOR OVERLY PESSIMISTIC.

HE HAS NOT BEEN EXCEPTIONALLY SUCCESSFUL OR UNSUCCESSFUL IN
 ORGANIZING HIS ENERGIES TOWARDS THE ATTAINMENT OF REALISTIC,
 WELL-INTEGRATED GOALS.

HE SHOWS NO EVIDENCE OF HAVING BEEN PARTICULARLY FRUSTRATED IN THE
 REALIZATION OF HIS AMBITIONS NOR OF HAVING BEEN PARTICULARLY SUCCESSFUL.

UNINTEGRATED MOTIVE STRENGTH

THE FOLLOWING SCORES AND OBSERVATIONS REFLECT UNSATISFIED
NEED LEVELS AND ASPIRATION LEVELS IN EACH OF THE TEN DYNAMIC AREAS
MEASURED BY THIS TEST

STEN SCORE	LOW INTEREST	STEN SCORE 1 2 3 4 5 6 7 8 9 10	HIGH INTEREST	CENTILE
7	CAREER	*	CAREER	77
6	HOME	*	HOME	60
3	SECURITY	*	SECURITY	11
7	SELF-INDULGENCE	*	SELF-INDULGENCE	77
5	ETHICAL VALUES	*	ETHICAL VALUES	40
6	SELF-SENTIMENT	*	SELF-SENTIMENT	60
5	HETEROSEXUALITY	*	HETEROSEXUALITY	40
2	HOSTILITY	*	HOSTILITY	4
6	SELF-ASSERTION	*	SELF-ASSERTION	60
4	MATE	*	MATE	23

STRENGTHS OF INTEGRATED INTEREST

THE FOLLOWING SCORES AND OBSERVATIONS REFLECT THE PORTION OF
TOTAL DYNAMIC ENERGY THAT HAS ARISEN FROM SUCCESSFUL FULFILLMENT OF
NEEDS IN EACH PARTICULAR AREA OF EXPRESSION.   THESE SCORES DESCRIBE
LEVELS OF EXPERIENTIAL, REALITY-TESTED EXPRESSION AND MOST CLOSELY
INDICATE THE RELATIVE STRENGTH OF CURRENT MOTIVATIONAL OUTLETS.

STEN SCORE	LOW INTEREST	1	2	3	4	5	6	7	8	9	10	HIGH INTEREST	CENTILE
6	CAREER						*					CAREER	60
5	HOME					*						HOME	40
3	SECURITY			*								SECURITY	11
9	SELF-INDULGENCE									*		SELF-INDULGENCE	96
5	ETHICAL VALUES					*						ETHICAL VALUES	40
7	SELF-SENTIMENT							*				SELF-SENTIMENT	77
6	HETEROSEXUALITY						*					HETEROSEXUALITY	60
7	HOSTILITY							*				HOSTILITY	77
3	SELF-ASSERTION			*								SELF-ASSERTION	11
3	MATE			*								MATE	11

TOTAL MOTIVATION SCORES

THE FOLLOWING SET OF SCORES REFLECTS THE TOTAL AMOUNT OF INTEREST IN EACH OF THE AREAS MEASURED BY THE TEST. THAT IS, THESE SCORES ARE A COMBINATION OF UNINTEGRATED AND INTEGRATED SCORES FOR EACH OF THE DYNAMIC AREAS.

STEN SCORE	LOW INTEREST	1	2	3	4	5	6	7	8	9	10	HIGH INTEREST	CENTILE
7	CAREER							*				CAREER	77
6	HOME						*					HOME	60
1	SECURITY	*										SECURITY	1
10	SELF-INDULGENCE									*		SELF-INDULGENCE	99
5	ETHICAL VALUES					*						ETHICAL VALUES	40
7	SELF-SENTIMENT						*					SELF-SENTIMENT	77
5	HETEROSEXUALITY					*						HETEROSEXUALITY	40
3	HOSTILITY			*								HOSTILITY	11
3	SELF-ASSERTION			*								SELF-ASSERTION	11
1	MATE	*										MATE	1

CONFLICT (FRUSTRATION) SCORES

THE EXTENT OF CONFLICT OR FRUSTRATION WHICH THE CLIENT SHOWS IS GIVEN IN THE FOLLOWING PROFILE. WHETHER THE FRUSTRATION IN ANY PARTICULAR AREA ARISES FROM HIS OWN INADEQUACY IN STRUCTURING REALISTIC GOALS OR WHETHER IT ARISES FROM SITUATIONS BEYOND HIS CONTROL WOULD BE AN APPROPRIATE TOPIC FOR EXPLORATION IN AN INTERVIEW.

STEN SCORE	LOW INTEREST	1	2	3	4	5	6	7	8	9	10	HIGH INTEREST	CENTILE
7	CAREER							*				CAREER	77
7	HOME							*				HOME	77
6	SECURITY						*					SECURITY	60
3	SELF-INDULGENCE			*								SELF-INDULGENCE	11
6	ETHICAL VALUES						*					ETHICAL VALUES	60
5	SELF-SENTIMENT					*						SELF-SENTIMENT	40
4	HETEROSEXUALITY				*							HETEROSEXUALITY	23
1	HOSTILITY	*										HOSTILITY	1
9	SELF-ASSERTION									*		SELF-ASSERTION	96
7	MATE						*					MATE	77

DYNAMIC ADJUSTMENT PATTERNS

THERE IS EVIDENCE OF POSSIBLE DISSATISFACTION OR SELF-REPROACH ARISING FROM PAST SELF-INDULGENCE.

HIS SEXUAL NEEDS HAVE BEEN SATISFACTORILY CHANNELED AND AT PRESENT ARE NOT A SOURCE OF TENSION.

NAME: Multidimensional Aptitude Battery

SUPPLIER: Research Psychologists Press
P.O. Box 984
Port Huron, MI 48061
(800) 265-1285

PRODUCT CATEGORY

Cognitive/Ability

PRIMARY APPLICATIONS

Vocational Guidance/Counseling
Clinical Assessment/Diagnosis
Personnel Selection/Evaluation

SALE RESTRICTIONS American Psychological Association Guidelines

SERVICE TYPE/COST	Type	Available	Cost	Discount
	Mail-In	Yes	$3.25	Yes
	Teleprocessing	No		
	Local	No		

PRODUCT DESCRIPTION

The MULTIDIMENSIONAL APTITUDE BATTERY assesses aptitudes and intelligence, yielding a profile of ten subtest scores, Verbal IQ, Performance IQ, and Full Scale IQ. The test was designed to assess the same factors as does the Weschler family of scales but with greater ceiling and a convenient structured format amenable to group administration and objective scoring.

The 5-page report includs a one-page professional file summary. Results can be expressed as either Standard Scores or IQs.

NAME: Multidimensional Aptitude Battery

SUPPLIER: PSYCH Systems, Inc.
600 Reisterstown Road
Baltimore, MD 21208
(800) 368-3366

PRODUCT CATEGORY

Cognitive/Ability

PRIMARY APPLICATIONS

Vocational Guidance/Counseling
Clinical Assessment/Diagnosis
Personnel Selection/Evaluation

SALE RESTRICTIONS Qualified Professional

SERVICE TYPE/COST	Type	Available	Cost	Discount
	Mail-In	No		
	Teleprocessing	No		
	Local	Yes	See Below	

PRODUCT DESCRIPTION

The MULTIDIMENSIONAL APTITUDE BATTERY is a computer-administered test that parallels the Weschler Adult Scales. The five verbal subtests and five performance subtests are designed to be administered in less that 10 minutes each. Correlations of MULTIDIMENSIONAL APTITUDE BATTERY full scale scores with WAIS full scale scores have been reported to be in the .90's. The test offers a broadly effective and comprehensive analysis of academic and practical functioning levels. It is a highly effective tool for personal counseling in academic and vocational settings.

This Psych Systems program administers and scores the test. It also provides a brief printout of test results.

Psych Systems programs operate on the IBM PC-XT, COMPAQ Plus, Dec Professional 350, and most DEC PDP-11 systems. Various hardware/ software configurations are available directly from Psych Systems, with single-user systems starting at approximately $12,000. A per test fee also applies.

```
-------------------------------------------------
|       |                                       |
| MAB   | Multidimensional Aptitude Battery     |
|       |                                       |
-------------------------------------------------
```

The computer program generating this report was designed by Psych
Systems, Inc., Baltimore, Maryland 21208. Copyright (C) 1984 by
Psych Systems, Inc. The Multi-Dimensional Aptitude Battery is
reproduced by permission. Copyright (C) 1983 by Douglas N.
Jackson. Reproduced under license from Research Psychologists
Press, Inc., Port Huron, Michigan 48060. All rights reserved.

	Raw Score	Percentile	Estimated IQ
Information	28	80	
Comprehension	24	77	
Arithmetic	23	99	
Similarities	8	7	
Vocabulary	12	15	
Digit Symbol	4	NA	
Picture Completion	2	NA	
Spatial Orientation	6	NA	
Picture Arrangement	3	NA	
Object Assembly	1	NA	
Verbal	95	43	97
Performance	16	1	52
Total	111	3	71

NOTE: Due to insufficient data on the Performance Subtest Distributions, we are unable to provide you with accurate percentile scores for these subtests at this time. Such percentile scores will be made available in a subsequent update.

The results reported in this interpretation are based on the relative standing of Jonathan Doe's performance on the Multidimensional Aptitude Battery. Jonathan Doe's performance is compared to a normative sample based on the MAB subtests.

On this administration of the MAB, Jonathan Doe obtained an overall MAB score of 111 with a verbal scale score of 95 and a performance scale score of 16. When compared to the relevant norm group, this finding indicates that Jonathan Doe's overall IQ score is better than 3% of the testees in the normative sample. With regard to his total verbal scale score, Jonathan Doe performed better than 43% of the people in the norm group. His total performance scale score corresponds to a percentile score of 1. This score suggests that Jonathan Doe is functioning intellectually at a level equal to or better than approximately 1% of his peers.

The verbal-performance pattern indicates that Jonathan Doe performed significantly better on items reflecting verbal abilities than on tasks requiring perceptual-mechanical abilities.

His performance on items tapping verbal comprehension skills reveals that psycho-educational deficits are likely in the following areas:

    Analogical reasoning
    Language development and word knowledge

Jonathan Doe displayed strengths in the following areas:

    General fund of knowledge or practical orientation
    Practical judgement and common sense
    Numerical reasoning skills

In comparison to his peers Jonathan Doe performed poorly on items requiring perceptual organization. As such, deficits are likely to be in one or more of the following areas:

    Speed of mental operations and short term visual memory
    Visual alertness, visual recognition and identification
    Nonverbal concept formation and spatial visualization
    Ability to organize visual stimuli in proper sequence
    Analysis and synthesis of visually presented material

The current evaluation should be interpreted in light of Jonathan Doe's current academic functioning, cultural and racial background, and any other relevant situational factors that may have affected his performance.

psychware **465**

NAME: Multidimensional Personality Questionnaire

SUPPLIER: NCS/Professional Assessment Services
P.O. Box 1416
Minneapolis, MN 55440
(800) 328-6759

PRODUCT CATEGORY	PRIMARY APPLICATIONS
Personality	Vocational Guidance/Counseling Personnel Selection/Evaluation Personal/Marriage/Family Counseling

SALE RESTRICTIONS American Psychological Association Guidelines

SERVICE TYPE/COST	Type	Available	Cost	Discount
	Mail-In	Yes	NA	
	Teleprocessing	Yes	NA	
	Local	Yes	NA	

PRODUCT DESCRIPTION

The MULTIDIMENSIONAL PERSONALITY QUESTIONNAIRE is a factor- analytically developed self-report instrument designed to assess normal personality. The 300 dichotomous items require an 8th-grade reading level and 35-45 minutes for completion. Scores are provided on a total of 20 scales including 11 personality characteristics (Well-Being, Social Potency, Achievement, Social Closeness, Stress Reaction, Alienation, Aggression, Control, Traditionalism, Absorption, Harm Avoidance); 3 higher-order personality traits (Positive Affectivity, Negative Affectivity, Constraint); and five validity scales. Applications of the MULTIDIMENSIONAL PERSONALITY QUESTIONNAIRE include vocational counseling, personnel selection, and career development. The test may also be a useful adjunct to clinical personality tests in counseling, psychiatric, and medical settings.

Two systems are available for local processing of test results. MICROTEST Assessment Software from National Computer Systems, used with a Sentry 3000 tabletop scanner (purchase price approximately $4000) and microcomputer system ($2000-$3000 purchase price), allows tests to be administered off-line. Answer sheets are then scanned and scored automatically, one at a time or in a batch. The software also permits on-line administration of the test via microcomputer. In either case, the same report is provided.

NAME: Myers-Briggs Type Indicator

SUPPLIER: Integrated Professional Systems
5211 Mahoning Avenue Suite 135
Youngstown, OH 44515
(216) 799-3282

PRODUCT CATEGORY	PRIMARY APPLICATIONS
Personality Interest/Attitudes	Clinical Assessment/Diagnosis Vocational Guidance/Counseling Personal/Marriage/Family Counseling Personnel Selection/Evaluation Educational Evaluation/Planning

SALE RESTRICTIONS   Qualified Professional

SERVICE TYPE/COST	Type	Available	Cost	Discount
	Mail-In	No		
	Teleprocessing	No		
	Local	Yes	See Below	

PRODUCT DESCRIPTION

The MYERS-BRIGGS TYPE INDICATOR is a measure of personality disposition based on Jung's theory. Scores are derived for four bi-polar aspects of personality: introversion-extroversion, sensing-intuition, thinking-feeling, and judging-perceptive. Individuals are classified as one of two types on each of the four scales.

This interpretive report presents narrative statements corresponding to the type (four-letter code) of the respondent. It also presents narrative statements for vocational/occupational considerations and learning styles/teaching strategies. The occupational areas in which the abilities of the respondent can be utilized are also presented.

An operating software package, priced from $200-$850 depending on the complexity of the package, is required for program use, plus an additional fee of $3.00 per use.

ALICE SMITH is a 28 year old female with 16 years of education. She was tested on February 18, 1983.

This is a confidential report for use by professional staff only. The words used in the interpretation are technically defined and have specific meaning for clinical patients. The program which generates this profile considers many types of decision rules and the results need to be interpreted in light of the limitations of the instrument. Statements are based on analyses which should be considered as hypotheses for further consideration in combination with the patient's verbal admissions and other clinical factors.


```
                              --------------------      -----------
                              REVIEWING PROFESSIONAL         DATE
```


MYERS-BRIGGS TYPE INDICATOR

```
          50   40   30   20   10   0   10   20   30   40   50
         ----!----!----!----!----!----!----!----!----!----!-------------
E EXTRAVERT .                        !                 *    . INTROVERT  I
S SENSING   .                       *!                      . INTUITIVE  N
T THINKING  .                        !              *       . FEELING    F
J JUDGING   .                        !*                     . PERCEPTIVE P
         ----!----!----!----!----!----!----!----!----!----!-------------
```

SCORE   SCALE   This subject's type is ISFP.

39   I   Has a clear preference for the inner world
                              of personal thoughts and ideas, rather than
                              the external world of people and things. Tends
                              to be reflective.

1   S   Reports a slight preference for using the
                              five senses for perception, rather   than
                              intuition. Prefers to deal with established
                              facts and tangibles than with theory.

27   F   Judgments are based more on subjective,
                              personal values than on logical analysis.
                              A clear preference for the use of feeling
                              rather than thinking processes is suggested.

1   P   Has a slight desire for flexibility and
                              spontaneity. Prefers to use energies to
                              understand events and people rather than to
                              control or organize them.

468 *psychware*

VOCATIONAL / OCCUPATIONAL CONSIDERATIONS

These people bring a variety of skills to their work setting : an ability to concentrate, thoroughness and attention to detail, accepts routine, sympathy towards other people, tactfulness, and adaptability. These people focus their attention on facts but also tend to be sympathetic and enjoy occupations that provide practical help to people. Their abilities can be successfully used in the following occupational areas :

Sales	Nursing	Education
Customer Service	Customer relations	Community Service
(If ESFP : Psychiatry)		

They tend to prefer quiet settings in which they can work alone without interruptions. These individuals like to think before they act and may have difficulties initiating projects or interacting with others. Precise work is usually done well, if it is routine. Use of skills that have already been learned is preferred over learning new skills. In a work setting, these people are sensitive to the needs and feelings of others. They like to please others and may have difficulty confronting or reprimanding fellow employees. They lack objectivity and are easily influenced by otherpeople's wishes. A need to have complete information about job expectations and ideas behind new jobs is present. These people tend to be curious and may start several projects at one time, without worrying about their completion. Unpleasant jobs may be postponed in favor of more interesting tasks. Some trouble with decision-making might be expected.

LEARNING STYLES / TEACHING STRATEGIES

These students enjoy quiet study time and prefer to work alone rather than in groups. Lectures and audio-visual aids are good teaching strategies. A step-by-step, sequential approach to learning is needed as well as direct experience and well-defined goals. These students have a need for approval and support; they want to know that their accomplishments are valued and appreciated by others. They enjoy being helpful to others and can make good tutors. They work well with friends and will try to maintain harmony and avoid disagreements in group situations. Variety, flexibility, and the opportunity for individual study are needed in the classroom. They prefer spontaneous to planned activities, are curious, and enjoy exploring topics of interest to them. IS students are good at making plans for a class project and keeping records.

TREATMENT AND THERAPY CONSIDERATIONS

Intraverted clients often need to think through their problems and goals before they act on them. They may be distrustful of behavioral therapies, and doubt that simple changes in behavior or action can make changes in their environment or feelings. A good response might be obtained from bibliotherapy in which they read relevant books between sessions and have the opportunity to think through ideas before discussing them with a therapist.

Clients with a preference for feeling have often been hurt in the past due to their emotional sensitivity. They respond best to warmth and unconditional positive regard for the therapist. They need to develop a more objective and detached point of view, and be able to think through the possible reasons for other's actions to avoid misperceptions. Assertiveness training might be used to counteract their tendencies to accept unfair treatment and to be easily influenced.

LEGEND :   0 = No answer given

```
           1234567890 1234567890 1234567890 1234567890 1234567890

  1 -  50   2120002002 2112012021 0122021110 0222222111 2222211212
 51 - 100   1211112222 2112212111 1222112121 3222021222 2121122211
101 - 126   2211111022 1122102212 213221

           1234567890 1234567890 1234567890 1234567890 1234567890
```

NAME: Myers-Briggs Type Indicator

SUPPLIER: NCS/Professional Assessment Services
P.O. Box 1416
Minneapolis, MN 55440
(800) 328-6759

PRODUCT CATEGORY

Personality

PRIMARY APPLICATIONS

Vocational Guidance/Counseling
Training/Development
Personal/Marriage/Family Counseling

SALE RESTRICTIONS American Psychological Association Guidelines

SERVICE TYPE/COST	Type	Available	Cost	Discount
	Mail-In	Yes	$4.00	Yes
	Teleprocessing	Yes	$4.00	Yes
	Local	No		

PRODUCT DESCRIPTION

The MYERS-BRIGGS TYPE INDICATOR is a measure of personality dispositions and interests based on Carl Jung's theory of types. It characterizes 16 types of people who differ in their styles of gathering information, making decisions, and in their orientation to the world around them. It has applications in career counseling, executive development programs, marriage and family counseling, and other areas.

The instrument includes eight scales that indicate four different personality dispositions including Introversion-Extraversion, Sensing-Intuition, Thinking-Feeling, and Judging-Perceptive. The single page profile records and plots all scores on clearly defined scales for easy interpretation.

REPORT FORM FOR MYERS-BRIGGS TYPE INDICATOR

Name: ENTJ   Sex: Female   Age: 28   Date Tested: 3/15/84   Date Scored: 4/30/84   Other: _____

PREFERENCE STRENGTHS

POINTS FOR		60	40	20	0	20	40	60		POINTS FOR
EXTRAVERSION	26	*							INTROVERSION	0
SENSING	9					*			iNTUITION	25
THINKING	33	*							FEELING	5
JUDGING	28	*							PERCEPTIVE	1

TYPE | E | N | T | J |

Indicator questions deal with the way you like to use your perception and judgment, that is, the way you like to look at things and the way you like to go about deciding things. The answers given reflect four separate preferences called EI, SN, TF and JP. The profile above shows your score on each preference. The four letters of your 'type' tell how you came out on all four preferences. What each preference means is shown below.

E An E for extraversion probably means you relate more easily to the outer world of people and things than to the inner world of ideas.

S An S for sensing probably means you would rather work with known facts than look for possibilities and relationships.

T A T for thinking probably means you base your judgments more on impersonal analysis and logic than on personal values.

J A J for the judging attitude probably means you like a planned, decided, orderly way of life better than a flexible, spontaneous way.

I An I for introversion probably means you relate more easily to the inner world of ideas than to the outer world of people and things.

N An N for intuition probably means you would rather look for possibilities and relationships than work with known facts.

F An F for feeling probably means you base your judgments more on personal values than on impersonal analysis and logic.

P A P for the perceptive attitude probably means you like a flexible, spontaneous way of life than a planned, decided, orderly way.

Each combination of preferences tends to be characterized by its own set of interests, values and skills. On the back of this page is a description of your type. For a more complete discussion of the types and their vocational and personal implications, see *Introduction to Type* by Isabel Briggs Myers, or consult your counselor.

NATIONAL COMPUTER SYSTEMS

Report for the Myers-Briggs Type Indicator. Copyright (c) 1983, 1984 by Consulting Psychologists Press, Inc., 577 College Avenue, Palo Alto, California 94306. Copyright (c) 1943, 1944, 1957 by Katherine C. Briggs and Isabel Briggs Myers. Copyright (c) 1962, 1976, 1977 by Isabel Briggs Myers. All rights reserved. Printed under license from Consulting Psychologists Press, Inc.

Scored by NATIONAL COMPUTER SYSTEMS, P.O. Box 1294, Minneapolis, Minnesota 55440

ENTJ

Extraverted thinkers use their thinking to run as much of the world as may be theirs to run. They organize their facts and operations well in advance, define their objectives and make a systematic drive to reach these objectives on schedule. Through reliance on thinking, they become logical, analytical, often critical, impersonal and unlikely to be convinced by anything but reasoning.

They enjoy being executives, deciding what ought to be done, and giving the necessary orders. They have little patience with confusion, inefficiency, halfway measures, or anything aimless and ineffective, and they know how to be tough when the situation calls for toughness.

They think conduct should be governed by logic, and govern their own that way as much as they can. They live according to a definite formula that embodies their basic judgments about the world. Any change in their ways requires a deliberate change in the formula.

Like other judging types, they run some risk of neglecting perception. They need to stop and listen to the other person's side of the matter, especially with people who are not in a position to talk back. They seldom find this easy, but if (repeat, if) they do not manage to do it, they may judge too hastily, without enough facts or enough regard for what other people think or feel.

Feeling is their least developed process. If they suppress or neglect it too long, it can explode in damaging ways. They need to make some conscious use of feeling, preferably in appreciation of other people's merits—an art that comes less naturally to thinkers than to feeling types. Thinkers can, if they will, "make it a rule" in their formula to mention what is well done, not merely what needs correcting. The results will be worthwhile, both in their work and in their private lives.

These people look at things with their intuition rather than with their sensing, and hence they are mainly interested in seeing the possibilities beyond what is present or obvious or known. Intuition heightens their intellectual interest, curiosity for new ideas, tolerance for theory, taste for complex problems, insight, vision, and concern for long-range consequences.

They are seldom content in jobs that make no demand on intuition. They need problems to solve and are expert at finding new solutions. Their interest is in the broad picture, not in detailed procedures or facts. They tend to choose like-minded intuitives as associates. They also tend to need sensing types to keep them from overlooking facts and important details.

Adapted by permission from Introduction to Type (3rd Ed.) by Isabel Briggs Myers. Copyright (c) 1962, 1970, 1976, 1984 by Isabel Briggs Myers. Copyright (c) 1980, 1984 Consulting Psychologists Press, Inc., 577 College Avenue, Palo Alto, CA 94306.

Scored by NATIONAL COMPUTER SYSTEMS, P.O. Box 1294, Minneapolis, Minnesota 55440

NATIONAL COMPUTER SYSTEMS

NAME: Myers-Briggs Type Indicator

SUPPLIER: Center for Applications of Psychological Type, Inc.
2720 N.W. 6th Street, Suite A
Gainesville, FL. 32601
(904) 375-0160

PRODUCT CATEGORY	PRIMARY APPLICATIONS
Personality	Personal/Marriage/Family Counseling Vocational Guidance/Counseling

SALE RESTRICTIONS American Psychological Association Guidelines

SERVICE TYPE/COST	Type	Available	Cost	Discount
	Mail-In	Yes	$6.00	Yes
	Teleprocessing	No		
	Local	No		

PRODUCT DESCRIPTION

The MYERS-BRIGGS TYPE INDICATOR is a questionnaire developed to facilitate use of that part of Jung's theory concerned with psychological types. The essence of the theory is that variations in behavior which may seem random are actually consistent and orderly when one understands differences in the ways people prefer to take in information and make decisions. Four preferences are scored and combine to generate sixteen types, each with its own characteristics and gifts, its own road to excellence, and its own pitfalls to be avoided.

The Individual Report is designed to be given to the person who completes the questionnaire. It provides a graph of the four preference scales and a narrative analysis of the meaning of those scale scores. A unique feature of this service is that users may elect (for a nominal additional charge of $4.00 per group) to have their own personalized message included in the report. A Scoring Breakdown is printed as a separate report for the counselor's file copy or for the researcher's data sheet. Also, for each group of cases submitted, a Type Table is provided that shows all members of the group under their types in standard type table order. For each type and for each of the type groupings, the number and percent are given.

NAME: Negotiation Edge

SUPPLIER: Human Edge Software, Inc.
2445 Faber Pl.
Palo Alto, CA 94303
(415) 493-1593

PRODUCT CATEGORY	PRIMARY APPLICATIONS
Interest/Attitudes	Training/Development

SALE RESTRICTIONS   None

SERVICE TYPE/COST	Type	Available	Cost	Discount
	Mail-In	No		
	Teleprocessing	No		
	Local	Yes	$250.00	

PRODUCT DESCRIPTION

The NEGOTIATION EDGE is designed to help the user develop a successful strategy for negotiating a contract. The program can be constantly updated with information on the negotiation process and can respond with modified stragegies and suggestions for change. The program can also be used as a dress rehearsal prior to actual negotiation, producing different scenarios with their likely outcomes, to help the user select the optimum course of action.

The program uses artificial intelligence techniques that allow the user to communicate with the computer in English to reach solutions to business problems.

The program is designed for use on IBM PC and PC-compatible microcomputer systems.

NAME: Occupational Interest Check List

SUPPLIER: Integrated Professional Systems
5211 Mahoning Avenue Suite 135
Youngstown, OH 44515
(216) 799-3282

PRODUCT CATEGORY	PRIMARY APPLICATIONS
Interest/Attitudes	Vocational Guidance/Counseling

SALE RESTRICTIONS American Psychological Association Guidelines

SERVICE TYPE/COST	Type	Available	Cost	Discount
	Mail-In	No		
	Teleprocessing	No		
	Local	Yes	See Below	

PRODUCT DESCRIPTION

The OCCUPATIONAL INTEREST CHECK LIST consists of 211 items that relate to work activities representing a broad range of vocations in the U.S. economy. The twelve main work areas considered are: Artistic, Scientific, Plants and Animals, Protective, Mechanical, Industrial, Business Detail, Selling, Accommodating, Humanitarian, Leading-Influencing, and Physical Performing.

This 9-page report provides descriptions of interest areas recommended for further exploration. It then provides scores for 66 different work groups. For any work group recommended for further exploration on the basis of high test scores, the progam provides a description of the general work group and a listing of specific occupations within that work group, including the D.O.T. codes for the specific occupations. The report concludes with a record of individual item responses for record-keeping purposes.

An operating software package, priced from $200-$850 depending on the complexity of the package, is required for program use, plus an additional fee per administration.

Reproduced by permission granted to

IPS Scoring Services
5211 Mahoning Avenue, Suite 135
Youngstown, OH 44515
Phone (216) 799-3282

MARY SAMPLE is a 18 year old female with 12 years of education. She
completed the questionaire on March 1, 1983.

This is a confidential report for use by professional staff only. The
program which generates this report considers many decision rules and
the results need to be interpreted in light of the limitations of the
instrument. A copy of this report may be given to the counselee provided
the counselee is capable of and is furnished with sufficient information
to properly interpret the results.

                      ---------------------------   ------------
                      REVIEWING PROFESSIONAL   DATE

          THE   OCCUPATIONAL   INTEREST   CHECK   LIST   PROFILE

Interest   Low   High Interest
  Area   0   20   40   60   80 100   Area   Code RS WS
----------------!----!----!----!----!----!------------------------------
Artistic   .   *   . Artistic   01   19 40
Scientific   .   *   . Scientific   02   13 54
Plants and Animals . *   . Plants and Animals   03   2   8
Protective   *   . Protective   04   0   0
Mechanical   . *   . Mechanical   05   2   3
Industrial   *   . Industrial   06   0   0
Business Detail .   *   . Business Detail   07   22 52
Selling   *   . Selling   08   0   0
Accommodating   .   *   . Accommodating   09   5 17
Humanitarian   .   * . Humanitarian   10   17 94
Leading-Influencing .   *   . Leading-Influencing   11   23 32
Physical Performing *   . Physical Performing   12   0   0
----------------!----!----!----!----!----!------------------------------
                0   20   40   60   80 100   Code RS WS
                Low   High

        Code : Two-digit code identifying the Interest Area
        RS : Raw Score   WS : Weighted Score
        +++
        +   Like   Uncertain Dislike   +
        + Number of Responses   36   31   131   +
        +++

Descriptions of Interest Areas Recommended for Further Exploration :
----

10   HUMANITARIAN   (WS = 94)

Interest in helping others with their mental, spiritual, social, physical, or
vocational needs.

476 *psychware*

Code	Work Group	RS	WS

---

10   HUMANITARIAN

Code	Work Group	RS	WS
10.01	Social Services	6	100
10.02	Nursing, Therapy and Specialized Teaching Services	6	100
10.03	Child & Adult Care	5	83

02   SCIENTIFIC

Code	Work Group	RS	WS
02.03	Medical Science	6	100
02.02	Life Sciences	3	50
02.04	Laboratory Technology	3	50
02.01	Physical Sciences	1	17

07   BUSINESS DETAIL

Code	Work Group	RS	WS
07.06	Clerical Machine Operation	5	83
07.02	Mathematical Detail	4	67
07.03	Financial Detail	4	67
07.05	Records Processing	3	50
07.07	Clerical Handling	3	50
07.04	Oral Communications	2	33
07.01	Administrative Detail	1	17

01   ARTISTIC

Code	Work Group	RS	WS
01.01	Literary Arts	4	67
01.02	Visual Arts	4	67
01.04	Performing Arts: Music	4	67
01.06	Craft Arts	3	50
01.05	Performing Arts: Dance	2	33
01.03	Performing Arts: Drama	1	17
01.08	Modeling	1	17
01.07	Elemental Arts	0	0

11   LEADING-INFLUENCING

Code	Work Group	RS	WS
11.02	Educational & Library Services	6	100
11.07	Services Administration	6	100
11.03	Social Research	4	67
11.01	Mathematics & Statistics	2	33
11.09	Promotion	2	33
11.05	Business Administration	1	17
11.06	Finance	1	17
11.08	Communications	1	17
11.04	Law	0	0
11.10	Regulations Enforcement	0	0
11.11	Business Management	0	0
11.12	Contracts & Claims	0	0

09   ACCOMMODATING

Code	Work Group	RS	WS
09.02	Barber & Beauty Services	2	33
09.01	Hospitality Services	1	17
09.04	Customer Services	1	17
09.05	Attendant Services	1	17
09.03	Passenger Services	0	0

03   PLANTS AND ANIMALS

Code	Work Group	RS	WS
03.03	Animal Training & Services	2	33
03.01	Managerial Works: Plants & Animals	0	0
03.02	General Supervision: Plants & Animals	0	0
03.04	Elemental Work: Plants & Animals	0	0

---

05   MECHANICAL

		RS	WS
05.09	Materials Control	2	33
05.01	Engineering	0	0
05.02	Managerial Work: Mechanical	0	0
05.03	Engineering Technology	0	0
05.04	Air & Water Vehicle Operation	0	0
05.05	Craft Technology	0	0
05.06	Systems Operation	0	0
05.07	Quality Control	0	0
05.08	Land & Water Vehicle Operation	0	0
05.10	Crafts	0	0
05.11	Equipment Operation	0	0
05.12	Elemental Work: Mechanical	0	0

04   PROTECTIVE

04.01	Safety & Law Enforcement	0	0
04.02	Security Services	0	0

06   INDUSTRIAL

06.01	Production Technology	0	0
06.02	Production Work	0	0
06.03	Quality Control	0	0
06.04	Elemental Work: Industrial	0	0

08   SELLING

08.01	Sales Technology	0	0
08.02	General Sales	0	0
08.03	Vending	0	0

12   PHYSICAL PERFORMING

12.01	Sports	0	0
12.02	Physical Feats	0	0

Descriptions of Work Groups Recommended for Further Explorations :

10.01 SOCIAL SERVICES (WS = 100)

Workers in this group help people deal with their problems. They may work with one person at a time or with groups of people. Workers sometimes specialize in problems that are personal, social, vocational, physical, educational, or spiritual in nature. Schools, rehabilitation centers, mental health clinics, guidance centers, and churches employ these workers. Jobs are also found in public and private welfare and employment services, juvenile courts, and vocational rehabilitation programs.

Occupations in this Work Group include (the numbers are D.O.T. codes):

195.367-010 Case Aide
129.107-014 Christian Science
            Practitioner
045.107-018 Director of Counseling
094.227-010 Educational Therapist
195.164-010 Group Worker
195.167-034 Probation Officer
045.107-026 Psychologist, Counseling
045.107-038 Residence Counselor
195.107-026 Social Worker,
            Delinquency Prevention
195.107-030 Social Worker, Medical
094.227-014 Teacher, Blind
094.227-018 Teacher, handicapped
            Students
187.167-108 Veterans Contact
            Representative

195.107-010 Caseworker
120.007-010 Clergy Member
045.107-010 Counselor
129.107-018 Director of Religious
            Activities
195.167-030 Parole Officer
045.107-022 Psychologist, Clinical
045.107-034 Psychologist, School
195.107-022 Social Group Worker
195.107-034 Social Worker,
            Psychiatric
195.107-038 Social Worker, School
094.224-010 Teacher, Deaf
094.227-022 Teacher, Mentally
            Retarded
045.107-042 Vocational-
            Rehabilitation
            Counselor

10.02 NURSING, THERAPY AND SPECIALIZED TEACHING SERVICES (WS = 100)

Workers in this group care for, treat, or train people to improve their
physical and emotional well being. Most workers in this group deal with sick,
injured, or handicapped people. Some workers are involved in health education
and sickness prevention. Hospitals, nursing homes, and rehabilitation centers
hire workers in this group, as do schools, industrial plants, doctors'
offices, and private homes. Some sports also have a need for workers in this
group.

Occupations in this Work Group include (the numbers are D.O.T. codes):

076.127-010 Art Therapist	078.361-010 Dental Hygienist
079.374-010 Emergency Medical	079.157-010 Hypnotherapist
Technician	076.167-010 Industrial Therapist
076.127-014 Music Therapist	075.371-010 Nurse Anesthetist
075.374-010 Nurse, General Duty	075.127-018 Nurse, Head
075.121-010 Nurse, Instructor	079.374-014 Nurse, Licensed
075.374-014 Nurse, Office	Practical
075.374-018 Nurse, Private Duty	075.124-010 Nurse, School
075.124-014 Nurse, Staff, Community	075.374-022 Nurse, Staff,
Health	Occupational Health
075.127-022 Nurse, Supervisor	Nursing
076.121-010 Occupational Therapist	076.364-010 Occupational Therapy
079.371-014 Orthoptist	Assistant
076.121-014 Physical Therapist	076.224-010 Physical Therapist
079.364-018 Physician Assistant	Assistant
079.374-018 Podiatric Assistant	195.227-010 Program Aide, Group
078.362-026 Radiologic Technologist	Work
076.124-014 Recreational Therapist	079.361-010 Respiratory Therapist
092.227-014 Teacher, Kindergarten	092.227-018 Teacher, Preschool

02.03 MEDICAL SCIENCE (WS = 100)

Workers in this group are involved in the prevention, diagnosis, and treatment
of human and animal diseases, disorders, or injuries. It is common to
specialize in specific kinds of illnesses, or special areas or organs of the
body. Workers who prefer to be more general may become general practitioners,
family practitioners, or may learn to deal with groups of related medical
problems. A wide variety of work environments is available to medical workers
ranging from large city hospitals and clinics, to home offices in rural areas,
to field clinics in the military or in underdeveloped countries.

Occupations in this Work Group include (the numbers are D.O.T. codes):

070.101-010 Anesthesiologist	076.101-010 Audiologist
079.101-010 Chiropractor	072.101-010 Dentist
070.101-018 Dermatologist	070.101-022 General Practitioner
070.101-034 Gynecologist	070.101-038 Intern
070.101-042 Internist	070.101-046 Medical Officer
070.101-054 Obstetrician	070.101-058 Ophthalmologist
079.101-018 Optometrist	072.061-010 Oral Pathologist
072.101-018 Oral Surgeon	072.101-022 Orthodontist
071.101-010 Osteopathic Physician	070.101-066 Pediatrician
072.101-026 Pedodontist	072.101-030 Periodontist
070.101-070 Physiatrist	070.101-074 Physician, Head
070.101-078 Physician, Occupational	079.101-022 Podiatrist
072.101-034 Prosthodontist	070.107-014 Psychiatrist
070.101-090 Radiologist	076.107-010 Speech Pathologist
070.101-094 Surgeon 1	070.101-098 Urologist
073.101-010 Veterinarian	073.264-010 Veterinary Meat-
073.261-010 Veterinary Virus-	Inspector
Serum Inspector	

11.02 EDUCATIONAL & LIBRARY SERVICES (WS = 100)

Workers in this group do general and specialized teaching, vocational
training, advising in agriculture and home economics, and library work of
various kinds. Jobs are found in schools, colleges, libraries, and other
educational facilities.

Occupations in this Work Group include (the numbers are D.O.T. codes):

Descriptions of Work Groups Recommended for Further Explorations :

100.267-010 Acquisition Librarian
100.167-014 Bookmobile Librarian
100.387-010 Catalog Librarian
100.167-018 Children's Librarian
077.127-010 Community Dietitian
096.127-010 County-Agricultural Agent
090.117-010 Dean of Students 1
091.107-010 Dean of Students 2
129.107-022 Director, Religious
            Education
222.367-026 Film-or-Tape Librarian
096.127-022 Four-H Club Agent
309.354-010 Homemaker
090.227-018 Instructor, Extension
            Work
097.227-014 Instructor, Vocational
            Training
100.267-014 Librarian, Special
            Collections
249.367-046 Library Assistant
100.367-022 Music Librarian
099.277-030 Teacher, Adult Education
092.227-010 Teacher, Elementary
            School
166.227-010 Training Representative
100.167-034 Young-Adult Librarian

100.367-010 Bibliographer
249.367-014 Career-Guidance
            Technician
100.367-014 Classifier
045.107-010 Counselor
096.121-010 County Home
            Demonstration Agent
077.127-022 Dietitian, Teaching
090.227-010 Faculty Member,
            College or University
295.367-018 Film Rental Clerk
096.121-014 Home Economist
099.227-014 Instructor,
            Correspondence School
099.224-010 Instructor, Physical
            Education
100.127-014 Librarian
100.167-026 Librarian, Special
            Library
100.167-030 Media Specialist, School
            Library
099.327-010 Teacher Aide 1
091.221-010 Teacher, Industrial Arts
091.227-010 Teacher, Secondary School
099.227-034 Tutor

11.07 SERVICES ADMINISTRATION (WS = 100)

Workers in this group manage programs and projects in agencies that provide
people with services in such areas as health, education, welfare, and
recreation. They are in charge of program planning, policy making, and other
managerial activities. The jobs are found in welfare and rehabilitation
agencies and organizations, hospitals, schools, churches, libraries, and
museums.

Occupations in this Work Group include (the numbers are D.O.T. codes):

090.117-010 Academic Dean
195.117-010 Administrator, Social
            Welfare
195.167-010 Community Organization
            Worker
090.117-022 Director, Athletic
187.117-014 Director, Community
            Organization
187.117-018 Director, Institution
075.117-022 Director, Nursing
            Service
094.117-014 Director, Special
            Education
099.167-022 Educational Specialist
189.267-010 Field Representative

187.117-010 Administrator, Hospital
188.117-014 Business-Enterprise
            Officer
102.017-010 Curator
090.167-010 Department Head, College
            or University
099.117-010 Director, Educational
            Program
099.167-018 Director, Instructional
            Material
090.167-014 Director of Admissions
096.161-010 District Extension
            Service Agent
096.127-014 Extension Service
            Specialist

Descriptions of Work Groups Recommended for Further Explorations :

100.117-010 Library Director
079.167-014 Medical-Record
            Administrator
090.117-034 President, Educational
      .   Institution
187.117-054 Superintendent,
            Recreation
188.117-126 Welfare Director

166.167-026 Manager, Education
            and Training
049.127-010 Park Naturalist
099.117-018 Principal
079.117-014 Public Health Educator
099.117-022 Superintendent, Schools
099.117-026 Supervisor, Education

10.03 CHILD & ADULT CARE (WS = 83)

Workers in this group are concerned with the physical needs and the welfare of
others. They assist professionals in treating the sick or injured. They care
for the elderly, the very young, or the handicapped. Frequently these workers
help people do the things they cannot do for themselves. Jobs are found in
hospitals, clinics, day care centers, nurseries, schools, private homes, and
centers for helping the handicapped.

Occupations in this Work Group include (the numbers are D.O.T. codes):

355.374-010 Ambulance Attendant
354.377-010 Birth Attendant
355.674-010 Child-Care Attendant,
            School
309.677-010 Companion
078.362-018 Electrocardiograph
            Technician
309.677-014 Foster Parent
354.377-014 Home Attendant
355.674-014 Nurse Aide
359.677-018 Nursery School Attendant
355.674-018 Orderly
355.354-010 Physical Therapy Aide
355.377-014 Psychiatric Aide

359.677-010 Attendant, Children's
            Institution
301.677-010 Child Monitor
099.277-010 Children's Tutor
079.371-010 Dental Assistant
078.362-022 Electroencephalographic
            Technologist
371.567-010 Guard, School-Crossing
079.367-010 Medical Assistant
354.374-010 Nurse, Practical
355.377-010 Occupational Therapy
            Aide
359.677-026 Playroom Attendant
079.374-022 Surgical Technician

07.06 CLERICAL MACHINE OPERATION (WS = 83)

Workers in this group use business machines to record or process data. They
operate machines that type, print, sort, compute, send, or receive
imformation. Their jobs are found in businesses, industries, government
agencies, or wherever large amounts of data are processed, sent, or received.

Occupations in this Work Group include (the numbers are D.O.T. codes):

216.482-014 Adding-Machine Operator
203.362-010 Clerk-Typist
213.382-010 Computer-Peripheral-
            Equipment Operator
203.582-030 Keypunch Operator
203.582-034 Magnetic-Tape-
            Typewriter Operator
650.582-022 Phototypesetter Operator

214.482-010 Billing-Machine Operator
213.362-010 Computer Operator
203.582-022 Data Typist
211.482-014 Food Checker
650.582-010 Linotype Operator
650.582-014 Monotype-Keyboard
            Operator
217.382-010 Proof-Machine Operator

psychware **481**

Descriptions of Work Groups Recommended for Further Explorations :

213.682-010 Tabulating-Machine   203.582-050 Telegraphic-Typewriter
            Operator   Operator
203.582-058 Transcribing-Machine   217.382-014 Transit Clerk
            Operator   203.582-062 Typesetter-Perforator
203.582-066 Typist   Operator
203.382-026 Varitype Operator   203.582-070 Verifier Operator

RAW DATA :   1 = like   2 = uncertain   3 = dislike

             1234567890 1234567890 1234567890 1234567890 1234567890

  1 - 50   1323133223 2323323333 2331333313 3331333233 1313333113
 51 - 100   1333331331 2333313331 3333323233 3313313323 3313333131
101 - 150   3333313233 1313321333 3233333333 3313233333 1333113123
151 - 198   3211313223 2213323323 3133332322 2333311333 33132232

             1234567890 1234567890 1234567890 1234567890 1234567890

End of OICL Report

NAME: Ohio Vocational Interest Survey-II

SUPPLIER: Psychological Corporation
7500 Old Oak Blvd.
Cleveland, OH 44130
(216) 234-5300

PRODUCT CATEGORY	PRIMARY APPLICATIONS
Career/Vocational	Vocational Guidance/Counseling Personal/Marriage/Family Counseling

SALE RESTRICTIONS American Psychological Association Guidelines

SERVICE TYPE/COST	Type	Available	Cost	Discount
	Mail-In	Yes	$1.30	
	Teleprocessing	No		
	Local	No		

PRODUCT DESCRIPTION

This second edition of the OHIO VOCATIONAL INTEREST SURVEY (OVIS II) is designed to assist students from Grade 7 through college and adults with their educational and vocational plans. OVIS II combines an interest inventory with an optional Career Planning Questionnaire and Local Survey to provide the student and counselor with background data for interpreting interest scores and to provide the school with summary data for planning guidance services and curriculum changes. The new OVIS II also includes career information and decision-making components, orientation and interpretive aids, and improved scoring and reporting options.

OVIS II can be administered during one regular class period. Two full-color, sound filmstrips assist in administering and interpreting OVIS II. Because of its linkage to the Fourth Edition of the DOT and the new Guide for Occupational Exploration, OVIS II can be used as an entry into most occupational information systems and career planning programs.

Student Report for: PETER A. SMITH   Grade: 12
        School: MEMORIAL HIGH SCHOOL   Sex: male
        Counselor: MS. YATES   Test date: 11/17/83

Interest Scales	D-P-T Codes	IS	IS Profile low	average	high	SCI	Weighted Responses	Natl PR M	F
3 Machine Operation	L-L-A	46			*	H	45354555433	94	99
7 Crafts and Precise Operations	A-L-H	41			*	H	45443353334	88	99
14 Visual Arts	H-L-H	38		*		H	44343334334	85	72
15 Agriculture and Life Sciences	H-L-H	38		*		H	44244433433	81	86
16 Engineering and Physical Sciences	H-L-H	37		*		F	43444443232	74	93
9 Sports and Recreation	A-A-L	35		*		F	53344433114	61	52
11 Regulations Enforcement	H-L-L	35		*		F	25434322343	70	74
4 Quality Control	A-L-L	34		*		F	33442432333	81	95
18 Performing Arts	H-A-L	30		*		F	44233232322	62	38
21 Management	H-H-L	26	*			H	23231323223	38	31
17 Music	H-A-L	25	*			H	32323222222	45	29
23 Medical Services	H-H-L	23	*			H	32222222222	48	42
6 Health Services	A-L-L	22	*			H	22222222222	40	25
10 Customer Services	A-A-L	21	*			H	32112331212	35	17
8 Skilled Personal Services	A-L-H	19	*			H	12222222121	32	15
12 Communications	H-L-L	19	*			H	22312211221	16	11
19 Marketing	H-A-L	19	*			H	22221222112	20	13
22 Education and Social Work	H-H-L	18	*			H	11212221222	19	5
2 Basic Services	L-L-L	17	*			H	22121141111	17	5
13 Numerical	H-L-L	15	*			H	11211131121	14	20
1 Manual Work	L-L-L	14	*			H	22111111211	13	20
20 Legal Services	H-H-L	14	*			H	11211211211	8	5
5 Clerical	A-L-L	12	*			H	12111111111	6	3

Legend:
  D-P-T = Data-People-Things
  IS = Interest Scores   SCI = Scale Clarity Indexes
  Natl PR = National Percentile Rank, grades 10 to 12

In addition to your interest in the activities that make up Scales 3 and 7, you have shown a preference for a number of other activities. Your Work Characteristic Analysis and Summary are based on the 46 activities to which you responded "Like" or "Like Very Much". The characteristics associated with those activities are described below.

484 *psychware*

Student Report for: PETER A. SMITH   Grade: 12
        School: MEMORIAL HIGH SCHOOL   Sex: male
        Counselor: MS. YATES   Test date: 11/17/83

Your Responses to the   Work Characteristic Summary
Career Planning Questionnaire

A What school subjects do you like best?   H *Data*
                                                  L *People*
                                                    Things
  1st choice: Industrial Arts

                                                    Vocational Preparation
  2nd choice: Art   Up to three months
                                                      Three months to one year
B What high school program are you   *   One to four years
  taking now or planning to take?   More than four years

  Vocational or Technical   *Aptitudes*
                                                  *   General Ability
C What type of education or training do   Verbal
  you plan to take after leaving high   Numerical
  school?   *   Spatial
                                                      Form Perception
  Vocational or Technical School   Clerical Perception
                                                      Motor Coordination
D If business or vocational programs   Finger Dexterity
  were offered as part of your high   Manual Dexterity
  school curriculum, would you take one?
                                                    Work Preferences
  I am already enrolled in one.   Objects
                                                      Ideas
E If you answered yes to question D,   Business
  what programs would you take?   Scientific
                                                      Organization
  1st choice: Innovation
   Trade and Industrial - Commercial   Service
   Art, Photography   *   Technology
                                                      Prestige
  2nd choice: Product
   Trade and Industrial - Auto/Diesel
   Mechanics   *Work Environments*
                                                      Variety
F What kinds of work would you most like   Repetition
  to do?   Supervision
                                                      Personal Contact
  1st choice: Influence
   Machine Operation   Stress
                                                  *   Judgment
  2nd choice: *   Standards
   Visual Arts   Creativity
                                                  *   Detail

                                                    Physical Demands
                                                      Light
                                                      Medium or Heavy

                                                    Work Settings
                                                      Indoor
                                                      Outdoor

psychware **485**

Student Report for: PETER A. SMITH   Grade: 12
                School: MEMORIAL HIGH SCHOOL   Sex: male
                Counselor: MS. YATES   Test date: 11/17/83

Work Characteristic Analysis

Data, people, and things levels provide clues about the complexity of work and the amount of ability and education required. In general, the higher the level, the more preparation is required. The following levels are associated with the job activities you liked. The greater the number of activities you liked that are associated with a particular level, the stronger the association.
   Data (information such as ideas, concepts, words, numbers, or other symbols)
      Strongly associated: high involvement
   People (human beings and animals dealt with as individuals)
      Very strongly associated: low involvement
   Things (machines, tools, materials, and products)
      Moderately associated: high involvement

Vocational preparation is the time it takes to learn how to do a job. This includes time for related education, on-the-job training, and experience in other jobs. The activities you liked are associated with the following preparation times.
   Strongly associated:
      One to four years

Aptitudes are special talents or abilities. They make it easier for you to learn some things than others. The following aptitudes are associated with the activities you liked. The greater the number of activities you liked that are associated with an aptitude, the stronger the association.
   Very strongly associated:
      General Ability (reasoning)
   Strongly associated:
      Spatial (visualizing in three dimensions)
   Moderately associated:
      Verbal (using language)
      Numerical (doing arithmetic)
      Form Perception (seeing small differences in figures and lines)
      Manual Dexterity (using hands skillfully to place and turn objects)

There are many ways of describing interests. The OVIS II scales provide one way. Another is to look at *work preferences*. The following work preferences are common to many of the activities you liked.
   Strongly associated:
      Technology (dealing with machines)
   Moderately associated:
      Objects (dealing with things)
      Ideas (communicating ideas to people)
      Product (producing tangible products)

Work environments are situations to which workers must adjust. The following work environments are associated with many of the activities you liked.
   Strongly associated:
      Judgment (basing decisions on judgment)
      Standards (basing decisions on facts)
      Detail (working precisely)
   Moderately associated:
      Variety (variety and change)
      Supervision (directing and planning work)
      Personal Contact (dealing with people)

Most of the activities you liked are associated with *light physical demands*; however, at least one-third of them require heavier physical work. If you have the strength to handle objects up to 100 pounds and you do not mind a lot of standing and walking, you may wish to expand your job search beyond jobs with light physical demands.

The activities you liked are almost equally divided between *inside and outside work settings*. This could mean that the setting is not important to you, or it could mean that you prefer activities that involve both work settings.

486 *psychware*

NAME: Perfil de Desarrollo Personal

SUPPLIER: Consultores Psico-Sociales, S.A.
Apartado 7211
Zona 5, REPUBLIC OF PANAMA
(507) 69-5568

PRODUCT CATEGORY

Personality

PRIMARY APPLICATIONS

Vocational Guidance/Counseling
Personnel Selection/Evaluation

SALE RESTRICTIONS   Qualified Professional

SERVICE TYPE/COST	Type	Available	Cost	Discount
	Mail-In	Yes	NA	
	Teleprocessing	No		
	Local	No		

PRODUCT DESCRIPTION

This two-page report, in Spanish, provides a computer-based interpretation of Cattell's 16 Personality Factor Questionnaire. Primary scores are plotted graphically. Significant primary characteristics are discussed verbally. Then broad patterns that have implications for career planning, vocational guidance, and personal counseling are presented in a concise, verbal form.

For a sample printout of this product (in English), see the one shown under the 16 PF NARRATIVE SCORING REPORT.

NAME: Personal Career Development Profile

SUPPLIER: Institute for Personality and Ability Testing, Inc.
P.O. Box 188
Champaign, IL 61820
(217) 352-4739

PRODUCT CATEGORY

Career/Vocational

PRIMARY APPLICATIONS

Vocational Guidance/Counseling
Personal/Marriage/Family Counseling
Educational Evaluation/Planning
Personnel Selection/Evaluation

SALE RESTRICTIONS   American Psychological Association Guidelines

SERVICE TYPE/COST	Type	Available	Cost	Discount
	Mail-In	Yes	$16.00	Yes
	Teleprocessing	Yes	$17.00	Yes
	Local	No		

PRODUCT DESCRIPTION

PERSONAL CAREER DEVELOPMENT PROFILES offer a professionally developed computer interpretation of the 16 PF for career exploration and personal development purposes. The reports organize relevant information about individual strengths, behavioral attributes, and gratifications to accomplish personal career development objectives. The report helps individuals achieve deeper insights about their strengths and needs and provides administrators with a powerful tool for identifying hidden employee talent. PERSONAL CAREER DEVELOPMENT PROFILES are also available in Spanish.

PERSONAL-CAREER DEVELOPMENT PROFILE

John   Sample   ID Number CUPC-78-003
Sex M   Age 42   4/20/1984

ORIENTATION TO THE 16PF QUESTIONNAIRE

Mr Sample appears to have answered most of the questions in the
inventory realistically. He seems to have wanted to describe
himself as accurately as possible. Even so, the information that
follows in this report should be read in light of what is actually
known about his personal career life-style patterns.

PROBLEM-SOLVING PATTERNS

Mr Sample functions quite comfortably with problems which involve
abstract reasoning and conceptual thinking. He is quite able to
integrate detail and specifics into meaningful, logical wholes. He
is very alert mentally. He sees quickly how ideas fit together and
is likely to be a fast learner. If Mr Sample feels like doing it,
he shows about average interest in the kind of controlled learning
activities which formal university training offers.

Mr Sample's approach to tasks is usually balanced between getting
things done efficiently and having an awareness of the often hidden
steps and outcomes that are part of the process of getting things
done. Mr Sample is sometimes so sure that he can easily handle most
any problem that comes up that he may not do enough planning and
preparing for thoroughness. He is prone to act on the spur-of-the-
moment without taking the needed time to prepare himself to decide
and act on important issues. As a result, his decisions and actions
tend to be rather risk-seeking and with the expectation that somehow
luck will intervene. He sticks mostly to practical methods as he
deals with life and its problems. He usually pays attention to the
everyday aspects and requirements of situations.

PATTERNS FOR COPING WITH STRESSFUL CONDITIONS

For the most part, Mr Sample seems to be well-adjusted. He does
not usually show signs of tension and worry, even when he is under a
lot of pressure. He tries to be calm and even-tempered most of the
time. He rarely allows his emotional needs to get in the way of what
he does or tries to do in situations or relationships. He seems to
be quite casual in the way he reacts to most circumstances and
situations. He usually follows his own urges and feelings. He
seldom gives much attention to controlling his behavior and sometimes
finds it hard to consciously discipline himself. He feels confident
in himself, and he has little need to explain his actions to himself
or to other people. At the present time, he presents himself as a
person who is relaxed and composed. He does not seem to be worried
or frustrated. As a result, he probably does not really wish to
change himself in any major way. He may come across to other people,
though, as being too complacent and self-accepting. Generally, when
Mr Sample is faced with conflict or disagreement from others, he
likes to challenge those who differ with him and to clearly state
his views on the subject. However, if pushed far enough, he is
likely to either give in or to break off the conversation --
whichever seems to be best for him.

PATTERNS OF INTERPERSONAL INTERACTION

Most of the time, Mr Sample tends to pay rather close attention
to people around him and to their concerns and problems. He seldom
spends a lot of effort and time being overly concerned about himself
or his own problems. He likes to put forth a feeling of warmth and
easygoingness when interacting with others. He is a good natured
person and one who generally prefers participation in group
activities. He is generally very forward and bold when meeting and
talking with others. Mr Sample may sometimes want to get others to
do something so much that he may try too hard, and as a result, he

psychware **489**

could run the risk of coming across as overly pushy and demanding in such instances. Nevertheless, he appears to relate to most people with ease and comfort. He is normally inclined to state his desires and needs clearly and quite forcefully. He likes to have things his way most of the time and prefers freedom from other people's influence. Although Mr Sample usually likes to be free from other people's influence, he can easily adjust his manner and he can be thoughtful of other people and their concerns or needs when it is important to do so. He normally feels closest to people who are competitive and who understand the importance of being in firm control of their lives and what they do to reach their goals. Sometimes, Mr Sample may be in such a hurry to get things done that he tends to forget how others may be affected by his actions and how others may feel about matters that are important to them.

Mr Sample seems to have a sharp sense of what is socially necessary, and he is usually aware of the right thing to say and do in social get togethers with others. For the most part, he tries to be friendly and helpful to people since he tends to be trusting and accepting of himself and what he does in his life. Mr Sample tends to gain his greatest satisfaction in life from being involved in activities that have chances for personal achievement while competing with others. When things are going well between himself and others, he likes to have influence over other people as he faces and meets difficult challenges.

ORGANIZATIONAL ROLE AND WORK-SETTING PATTERNS

Mr Sample tends to experience considerable satisfaction when he is given the chance to be in a position of leadership in organizational settings. He likes to be in charge of others, particularly a group of friends or co-workers. He usually feels comfortable in situations which require him to provide direction over others. His group members, too, are likely to respond favorably to his leadership patterns. Mr Sample generally attempts to influence others by directing, persuading and challenging them to get things done. He seems to truly enjoy talking and interacting with people to get them to agree with his points-of-view when it's important to him. If he were to take on a leadership role with others, he would probably strive to administer duties by focusing attention on the conditions which foster or hinder the performance of subordinates rather than on personnel problems which may be present. Being more solution-seeking than blame oriented, he strives to remove personality and power struggles from the work situation.

Mr Sample generally prefers to build feelings of mutual respect and interdependence among people. He usually likes to share with others whatever power may be necessary to accomplish assignments. He appears to value objective working relationships between superiors and subordinates.

Mr Sample is likely to feel most at home when working in relaxed and flexible settings that are not boring or routine in nature. If some structure would be necessary, he likes to design it himself rather than having someone else impose it on him. He is basically quite flexible. He does not usually feel the need to follow rigid or long-established practices. He should enjoy and do a good job on trouble-shooting-type assignments in which he has chances to tackle and solve difficult problems. Mr Sample seems to be a person who fits well into jobs which demand correct and quick decisions.

PATTERNS FOR CAREER ACTIVITY INTERESTS

Mr Sample's profile suggests that he is likely to enjoy career-oriented and/or avocational activities which entail:

* working out ways for accomplishing and doing things by convincing, directing or persuading others to attain organizational goals and/or economic gain — an activity pattern similar to people who express interest for one or more of the following career fields: administration, business management, consulting, law/politics, marketing, merchandising or sales.

490 *psychware*

* the use of verbal and numerical skills to organize information according to prescribed plans and well-established
  procedures required in administrative, data processing and
  office practice systems - an activity pattern similar to
  people who express interest in one or more of the following
  career fields: business data processing, clerking, finance or
  office practices.

* opportunity to be near or at the center of group endeavors
  and solving problems through discussions with others or by
  encouraging relationships between people so as to enlighten,
  serve or train them - an activity pattern similar to people
  who express interest for one or more of the following career
  fields: counseling, education, health care, religion, social
  service or training.

Mr Sample's strongest interest themes are similar to those of
people employed in some of the following occupations. In reviewing
this list, he may find support for past or present career choices.
Alternatively, he may find it helpful to review his interests,
skills, and experience with respect to occupations he may not have
considered. There are indications he may find it relatively easy to
identify with and relate to people who are successfully pursuing
careers in some of these occupations: Administrative Manager, Claim
Manager, Credit Manager, Industrial Relations Manager, Insurance
Manager, Wholesaler. Additional occupations Mr Sample may wish to
consider include: Administrative Services Director, Chamber of
Commerce Executive, Community Service Director, Compensation-Benefits
Director, Consultant, Customer Service Manager, Food Service Manager,
Public Relations Director, Retail Store Manager Salesperson, and
Advertising Account Manager, Art Center Director, Attorney,
Buyer, Journalist/Reporter, Public Relations Specialist.

The occupational information reported here is based on career
preferences suggested by Mr Sample's general personality orientation.
The occupational listings should not be treated as specific job
suggestions. Some may not appeal to him. Others may not relate well
to his training and experience. However, each represents an option
open to Mr Sample in his personal growth and career planning at this
point in time. A careful review may bring to mind other alternatives
that represent even more appealing career paths.

PERSONAL CAREER LIFE-STYLE EFFECTIVENESS CONSIDERATIONS

Mr Sample's life style is typical of people who value self-
directedness and independence. He generally strives to achieve
control of and freedom of choice in his personal life and work-
related situations. He shows a marked preference for activities and
work which involves meeting and interacting with people. He
generally gains much satisfaction when he is in a position of
leadership and is able to direct the actions of others. He likes to
be in charge of projects, to take on challenges, to accomplish things
and to work in a business-like manner.

In terms of Mr Sample's needs for performance effectiveness and
self-growth, he could be urged to guard against: (*) his tendency, at
times, to act with so much eagerness, energy and optimisim that he
may overlook important details; fail to prepare himself enough for
what he undertakes; or sufficiently anticipate consequences of what
he does; (*) the tendency to make spur of the moment decisions,
rather than preparing himself enough before making decisions and
taking action or giving thoughtful consideration of possible
consequences of such actions; (*) being overly confident about his
ability to handle most any problems or situations that come up when
more accurate thinking and more realistic planning may be required to
accomplish what he most desires to do; (*) showing too much of his
emotions or feelings in tense or stressful situations; (*) being in
such a hurry to get things done that he does not see how others may
feel about things that are important to them; (*) tendencies to avoid

or to get out of his responsibilities because of his need to build more effective work habits than he seems to have at this time; (*) urges to change from one career field or job to another or to not stay with one organization long enough to feel as if he belongs there; and (*) taking on activities or assignments which involve ordinary, routine tasks without much creative thought or tasks which may not fully challenge Mr Sample's intelligence or curiosity.

In conclusion, Mr Sample seems to place importance on making an honest and sincere impression when he presents himself to others. Mr Sample's career and life-style appears to be well integrated and progressing with overall personal effectiveness.

This page of career activity interest theme, career field and occupational scores is intended for use by qualified professionals only. Any review of the scores for career planning should be used for explorative counsel only.

OCCUPATIONAL TITLE	SCORE*	OCCUPATIONAL TITLE	SCORE
VENTUROUS-INFLUENTIAL (V) OCCUPATIONS	9.8	NURTURING-ALTRUISTIC (N) OCCUPATIONS	7.1
Administrators:Mid-Level	8.9	Employment Counselors	5.6
Airline Pilots	8.7	Psychologists	7.9
Business Executives	4.8	School Superintendents	7.3
Real Estate Agents	9.7	Social Worker	10.0
Sales:Wholesale	7.8	Teaching:General	5.6
CREATIVE-SELF EXPRESSIVE (C) OCCUPATIONS	6.7	PROCEDURAL-SYSTEMATIC (P) OCCUPATIONS	7.2
Artists	5.3	Accountants	6.5
Elementary School Teachers	5.2	Bank Managers	8.7
High School Teachers	3.1	Credit Union Managers	8.4
School Counselors	9.3	Department Store Managers	1.9
University Administrators	7.2	Personnel Managers	10.0
Writers	6.7	Sales Managers/Supervisors	8.5
ANALYTIC-SCIENTIFIC (A) OCCUPATIONS	5.8	MECHANICAL-OPERATIVE (M) OCCUPATIONS	5.6
Biologists	6.1	Firefighters	10.0
Chemists	7.0	Plant Forepersons	7.3
Computer Programmers	9.9	Production Managers	9.1
Engineers	3.0	Service Station Dealers	4.6
Geologists	6.3	Urban Police Officers	10.0
Physicians	2.2		
Physicists	5.9		
University Professors	1.7		

* Scores range from 1 through 10. Scores of 1-3 are considered very low. Scores of 8-10 are considered very high. Scores of 4-7 are average.

Sex M   Age 42   ID Number CUPC-78-003

This page of 16PF scores is intended for use by qualified professionals only. Data on this page should be treated with utmost confidentiality.

16PF PROFILE

		Low Meaning	1 2 3 4 5 6 7 8 9 10	High Meaning
A	8	Autonomous-Reserved	*	Participating-Warm
B	9	Concrete Thinking	*	Conceptual Thinking
C	9	Affected by Feelings	*	Calm-Unruffled
E	10	Considerate-Humble	*	Assertive-Competitive
F	7	Reflective-Serious	*	Talkative-Impulsive
G	4	Changeable-Expedient	*	Persistent-Conforming
H	8	Cautious-Shy	*	Socially Bold
I	5	Tough-Minded	*	Tender-Minded-Sensitive
L	3	Accepting-Trusting	*	Mistrusting-Oppositional
M	6	Conventional-Practical	*	Imaginative
N	8	Forthright-Unpretentious	*	Sophisticated-Shrewd
O	3	Confident-Self-Assured	*	Apprehensive-Concerned
Q1	5	Conservative-Traditional	*	Experimenting-Liberal
Q2	6	Group-Oriented	*	Self-Sufficient
Q3	3	Lax-Uncontrolled	*	Disciplined-Compulsive
Q4	3	Composed-Relaxed	*	Tense-Driven

BROAD PATTERNS

Extraversion is high (7.8).
Tough Poise is above average (6.8).
Independence is high (7.9).
Preference for structured situations is extremely low (1.0).
Preference for work with a definite/predictable future is extremely low (1.0).
Potential to learn from on-the-job experience is average (4.8).
Potential to profit from formal academic training is above average (6.8).
Creativity and inventiveness are estimated to be average (6.1).
Preference for a dominant leadership role is extremely high (10.0).
Potential for attaining an elected leadership role is high (7.6).
Similarity to persons attaining career-life integration is very high (9.0).

COUNSELING CONSIDERATIONS

Accident-Error proneness is predicted to be average (5.7).
Adequacy of adjustment is very high (9.2).
Level of anxiety is very low (2.4).
Effectiveness of behavior controls is average (5.1).
Acting-out behavior tendencies are high (7.8).
Perseverance and stamina in face of difficulties is below average (4.2).
The personality profile pattern code is 3123.
Tendency to fake good (motivational distortion) is average (6.0).
Tendency to fake bad is high (8.0).

REPORT PROCESSED USING MALE, ADULT (GP) NORMS FOR FORM A, 67-68 EDITION

THE RAW SCORES FOR THIS REPORT ARE:

A	B	C	E	F	G	H	I	L	M	N	O	Q1	Q2	Q3	Q4	FG	FB	RM
14	11	21	21	17	10	21	7	3	13	12	5	8	10	9	6	6	6	3

PROCESS COMPLETION CODE: 2.2 5.3 2.5 2.6 4.3 3.1 (SNFE) /

NAME: Personal and Career Development Profiles

SUPPLIER: Independent Assessment & Research Centre, Ltd.
47 Marylebone High Street
London W1M 3AE ENGLAND
(011) 441 486 6106

PRODUCT CATEGORY	PRIMARY APPLICATIONS
Personality	Vocational Guidance/Counseling
	Personnel Selection/Evaluation

SALE RESTRICTIONS   Qualified Professional

SERVICE TYPE/COST	Type	Available	Cost	Discount
	Mail-In	Yes	$18.85	Yes
	Teleprocessing	No		
	Local	No		

PRODUCT DESCRIPTION

This report provides an objective, professionally developed computer interpretation of Cattell's 16 Personality Factor Questionnaire which provides a
unique supplement to career guidance/planning and personal development
counseling. The report brings together relevant information about individual
characteristics, styles of behavior and potential in order to point to steps that
could be taken toward personal and career development.

This report is an anglicization of the Personal Career Development Profile,
available in the United Kingdom. For a sample printout of this product, see the
one shown under PERSONAL CAREER DEVELOPMENT PROFILE.

NAME: Personality Inventory for Children

SUPPLIER: Western Psychological Services
12031 Wilshire Blvd.
Los Angeles, CA 90025
(213) 478-2061

PRODUCT CATEGORY	PRIMARY APPLICATIONS
Personality	Clinical Assessment/Diagnosis Personal/Marriage/Family Counseling

SALE RESTRICTIONS American Psychological Association Guidelines

SERVICE TYPE/COST — Type	Available	Cost	Discount
Mail-In	Yes	$10.90	Yes
Teleprocessing	No		
Local	Yes	$10.90	Yes

PRODUCT DESCRIPTION

The PERSONALITY INVENTORY FOR CHILDREN was developed over a 20 year period, is based on the Minnesota Multiphasic Personality Inventory test construction model, and was standardized on nearly 2,400 normal boys and girls aged 6-16 years and nearly 200 boys and girls aged 3-5 years.

The WPS TEST REPORT program for this instrument features narrative paragraphs which reflect comprehensive actuarial studies of behaviorally disturbed children, with content based on correlates of both individual elevations and multiple scale patterns. The interpretations summarize and integrate the salient content of 700 correlates that are descriptive of all children including sex- and age-specific correlates.

The microcomputer, disk-operated version allows for local administration, scoring, and interpretation of results. Items can be administered on the computer display or off-line. A complete WPS TEST REPORT is generated.

Client: 000000001   Date Processed: 04/04/84
Answer Sheet: 000000245   SEND TO: Dr John Smith, PhD #0000003631
Sex: Male   Race: White   89 W 89th Street
Age: 10 Years 7 Months   Seattle, WA 98199
School Grade: 4 th
Informant: Mother

* * * * * PIC INTERPRETATION * * * * *

Form: IV (Factor, Full-Length and Research Scales)

This PIC interpretation is based on the systematic analysis of data obtained in the evaluation of behaviorally disturbed children and adolescents. This report consists of a series of hypotheses that may serve to guide further investigation.

GENERAL ADJUSTMENT AND INFORMANT RESPONSE STYLE:

Inventory responses do not suggest that this informant attempted to minimize or deny any problems that this child may have.

The description of this child's behavior suggests that a psychological/psychiatric evaluation may assist in the remediation of current problems.

COGNITIVE DEVELOPMENT AND ACADEMIC PERFORMANCE:

Parents and teachers are likely to be concerned about this child's limited academic achievement. Classroom performance may reflect poor study skills, distractibility, or difficulty in completion of classroom assignments. Retarded achievement may be demonstrated in reading, mathematics, spelling, handwriting, or verbal expression. School history may include retention in grade to promote skill acquisition. A psychological/psychiatric evaluation may result in specific recommendations to school personnel.

PERSONALITY AND FAMILY EVALUATION:

This child is likely to have difficulty making and keeping friends. Similar children may not initiate relationships with peers and are often unskilled at the mutual give-and-take of play. Social isolation or conflict may result.

This child's behavior is likely to reflect the presence of sadness and unhappiness. Presenting complaints may include problems with sleeping and eating, emotional lability, distrust of others, multiple fears, isolation, or excessive worry, self-blame, or self-criticism. Among adolescents, these symptoms may be associated with suicidal thought and behavior.

A disregard for rules and societal expectations is likely to be evidenced by behavior displayed at both home and school. Similar children may express a dislike for school and demonstrate a hostile, defiant response to school personnel. Current behavior is likely to reflect impulsivity, poor judgment, or unmodulated hostility. An antisocial adjustment may be suggested by symptoms such as lying, theft, or association with similarly troubled children, or by an established tendency to blame others for current problems.

Current child behavior may reflect a poor social and academic adjustment

496 *psychware*

that is associated with overactivity, distractibility, or provocation of peers.
Similar children are frequently described as restless, fidgety, and inattentive
in the classroom. They are excessively social in school and may require adult
intervention to limit impulsive, disruptive, and annoying behaviors.
Demonstrating limited frustration tolerance, such children frequently fight
with and pick on other children, break things, displace anger, distrust others,
or are described as poor losers. Poor gross-motor coordination or accident
proneness may be present.

The home is likely to reflect the impact of divorce or separation and may
be characterized by instability and conflict. Parental inconsistency in
setting limits is suggested. The resulting parent-child interaction may
contribute to the development of child behavior problems.

NOTE: The studies that form the foundation for this PIC REPORT are
presented in three publications published by Western Psychological Services:
"Multidimensional Description of Child Personality: A Manual for the Personality
Inventory for Children" (Catalog No. W-152G), "Actuarial Assessment of Child
and Adolescent Personality: An Interpretive Guide for the Personality Inventory
for Children Profile" (W-305), and "Personality Inventory for Children Revised
Format Manual Supplement" (W-152GS).

* * * * CRITICAL ITEMS * * * *

These Inventory items were answered by the informant in the direction
indicated. Although too much interpretive value should not be placed on
individual responses, they may suggest areas for further inquiry.

Relative frequency of item endorsement in male normative and clinic
samples is indicated at the end of each statement by this notation:
[normative % / clinic %].

--- DEPRESSION AND POOR SELF-CONCEPT ---

2. My child hardly ever smiles. (T) [4%/11%]
13. My child has little self-confidence. (T) [18%/54%]
132. My child tends to pity himself. (T) [26%/38%]
185. Several times my child has threatened to kill himself. (T) [2%/6%]
274. My child speaks of himself as stupid or dumb. (T) [7%/22%]

--- WORRY AND ANXIETY ---

4. My child worries about things that usually only adults worry about. (T)
   [15%/21%]
21. My child often asks if I love him. (T) [10%/19%]
169. Often my child goes about wringing his hands. (T) [1%/9%]

--- REALITY DISTORTION ---

244. Often my child will wander about aimlessly. (T) [5%/27%]

--- PEER RELATIONS ---

47. My child really has no real friend. (T) [6%/29%]
158. Most of my child's friends are younger than he is. (T) [8%/29%]
160. My child never takes the lead in things. (T) [13%/32%]
199. I do not approve of most of my child's friends. (T) [3%/17%]
215. My child would rather be with adults than with children his own age. (T)
   [7%/23%]
284. If my child can't run things, he won't play. (T) [5%/14%]
401. Hardly a day goes by when my child doesn't get into a fight. (T) [3%/15%]

Western Psychological Services • 12031 Wilshire Boulevard • Los Angeles, California 90025

--- UNSOCIALIZED AGGRESSION ---

17. My child seems to enjoy destroying things. (T) [4%/21%]
104. Many times my child has become violent. (T) [8%/30%]
276. Several times my child has threatened to kill others. (T) [2%/11%]
340. Often my child smashes things when angry. (T) [8%/30%]
404. My child has a terrible temper. (T) [12%/35%]

--- CONSCIENCE DEVELOPMENT ---

56. My child often disobeys me. (T) [17%/50%]
122. Spanking doesn't seem to affect my child. (T) [5%/41%]
360. Several times my child took money from home without permission. (T) [9%/28%]

--- POOR JUDGMENT ---

87. My child will do anything on a dare. (T) [7%/26%]
344. Playing with matches is a problem with my child. (T) [6%/18%]
365. I have a problem stopping my child from eating everything. (T) [9%/14%]

--- DISTRACTIBILITY, ACTIVITY LEVEL, AND COORDINATION ---

71. My child can't seem to wait for things like other children do. (T) [17%/49%]
193. My child can't seem to keep attention on anything. (T) [7%/36%]
356. Five minutes or less is about all my child will ever sit at one time. (T) [6%/22%]
390. When talking my child often jumps from one topic to another. (T) [10%/23%]

--- SOMATIC COMPLAINTS/CURRENT HEALTH ---

25. My child frequently complains of being hot even on cold days. (T) [6%/12%]
92. My child often has headaches. (T) [6%/17%]
134. Several times my child had complaints, but the doctor could find nothing wrong. (T) [6%/12%]
365. My child often vomits when getting a headache. (T) [2%/6%]

--- SCHOOL ADJUSTMENT ---

20. The school says my child needs help in getting along with other children. (T) [5%/36%]
61. Reading has been a problem for my child. (T) [23%/53%]
79. School teachers complain that my child can't sit still. (T) [9%/41%]
198. My child can't sit still in school because of nervousness. (T) [5%/40%]
204. My child has never failed a grade in school. (F) [12%/44%]

--- FAMILY DISCORD ---

188. My child seems unhappy about our home life. (T) [7%/27%]
226. The child's parents disagree a lot about rearing the child. (T) [10%/27%]
245. Several times my child has threatened to run away. (T) [10%/28%]
275. There is a lot of tension in our home. (T) [17%/39%]
335. We often argue about who is the boss at our house. (T) [6%/12%]
345. The child's mother frequently has crying spells. (T) [7%/14%]

--- OTHER ---

154. I am afraid my child might be going insane. (T) [1%/6%]

```
                                            T SCORES
                   SCORES      20   30   40   50   60   70   80   90  100  110  120
                   T   RAW     |++++|++++|++++|++++|++++|++++|++++|++++|++++|++++|
   Factor Scales               |                   |         |                    |
      I        38  (23)        |                   |         |      X             |
      II       70  (14)        |                   |        X|                    |
      III      76  (10)        |                   |         |  X                 |
      IV       57  ( 4)        |              X    |         |                    |
   Validity Scales             |====|====|====|====|====|====|====|====|====|====|
      L        30  ( 0)        |    X              |         |                    |
      F        58  ( 5)        |              X    |         |                    |
      DEF      37  ( 9)        |         X         |         |                    |
      ADJ     109  (54)        |                   |         |               X    |
   Standard Clinical Scales    |====|====|====|====|====|====|====|====|====|====|
      ACH      72  (19)        |                   |        |X                    |
      IS       54  (13)        |              X    |         |                    |
      DVL      65  (11)        |                   |    X    |                    |
      SOM      61  ( 9)        |                   |   X     |                    |
      D        85  (25)        |                   |         |   X                |
      FAM      67  (15)        |                   |     X   |                    |
      DLQ      96  (26)        |                   |         |       X            |
      WDL      54  ( 5)        |              X    |         |                    |
      ANX      75  (14)        |                   |         |  X                 |
      PSY      76  (10)        |                   |         |  X                 |
      HPR      69  (21)        |                   |        X|                    |
      SSK      76  (21)        |                   |         |  X                 |
                   T   RAW     |++++|++++|++++|++++|++++|++++|++++|++++|++++|++++|
                   SCORES      20   30   40   50   60   70   80   90  100  110  120
                                            T SCORES
```

* * * SCALES FOR RESEARCH APPLICATIONS * * *

	AGM	AGN	ASO	CDY	DP	ES	EXC	EXT	INF	INT	I-E	K	LDP	RDS	SR	SD	SM
RAW	37	12	16	26	25	43	10	28	0	14	17	12	35	8	8	16	11
T	97	89	78	53	50	87	70	91	45	70	39	26	75	69	13	23	57

134c

psychware **499**

Western Psychological Services • 12031 Wilshire Boulevard • Los Angeles, California 90025

WPS TEST REPORT

NOTE: Abbreviations on the PIC profile refer to the following scales:

Factor I: Undisciplined/Poor Self-Control
Factor II: Social Incompetence
Factor III: Internalization/Somatic Symptoms
Factor IV: Cognitive Development

L: Lie
F: F
DEF: Defensiveness
ADJ: Adjustment

ACH: Achievement
IS: Intellectual Screening
DVL: Development
SOM: Somatic Concern
D: Depression
FAM: Family Relations
DLQ: Delinquency
WDL: Withdrawal
ANX: Anxiety
PSY: Psychosis
HPR: Hyperactivity
SSK: Social Skills

AGM: Adolescent Maladjustment
AGN: Aggression
ASO: Asocial Behavior
CDY: Cerebral Dysfunction
DP: Delinquency Prediction
ES: Ego Strength
EXC: Excitement
EXT: Externaltization
INF: Infrequency
INT: Internalizaation
I-E: Introversion-Extroversion
K: K
LDP: Learning Disability Prediction
RDS: Reality Distortion
SR: Sex Role
SD: Social Desirability
SM: Somatization

Western Psychological Services • 12031 Wilshire Boulevard • Los Angeles, California 90025

Item responses for client no. 000000001   Answer sheet no. 00000245

```
  1(T)    11(F)    21(T)    31(F)    41(T)    51(T)    61(T)    71(T)    81(F)    91(F)
  2(T)    12(F)    22(F)    32(F)    42(T)    52(T)    62(F)    72(F)    82(F)    92(T)
  3(T)    13(T)    23(T)    33(F)    43(F)    53(F)    63(T)    73(F)    83(F)    93(T)
  4(T)    14(F)    24(T)    34(T)    44(T)    54(T)    64(F)    74(T)    84(T)    94(T)
  5(F)    15(T)    25(T)    35(T)    45(F)    55(F)    65(F)    75(F)    85(T)    95(F)
  6(T)    16(F)    26(T)    36(F)    46(T)    56(T)    66(T)    76(F)    86(F)    96(F)
  7(T)    17(T)    27(F)    37(F)    47(T)    57(T)    67(F)    77(F)    87(T)    97(F)
  8(T)    18(F)    28(F)    38(F)    48(F)    58(F)    68(T)    78(T)    88(T)    98(T)
  9(F)    19(F)    29(T)    39(T)    49(F)    59(F)    69(T)    79(T)    89(F)    99(F)
 10(F)    20(T)    30(F)    40(F)    50(T)    60(T)    70(T)    80(T)    90(T)   100(F)

101(T)   111(F)   121(F)   131(F)   141(T)   151(F)   161(F)   171(T)   181(F)   191(T)
102(T)   112(F)   122(T)   132(T)   142(F)   152(F)   162(F)   172(T)   182(T)   192(T)
103(T)   113(T)   123(F)   133(F)   143(F)   153(F)   163(T)   173(F)   183(F)   193(T)
104(T)   114(F)   124(F)   134(T)   144(T)   154(T)   164(T)   174(T)   184(F)   194(T)
105(T)   115(F)   125(F)   135(F)   145(T)   155(F)   165(F)   175(F)   185(T)   195(F)
106(F)   116(T)   126(F)   136(F)   146(T)   156(T)   166(F)   176(T)   186(F)   196(T)
107(F)   117(F)   127(F)   137(T)   147(T)   157(F)   167(T)   177(F)   187(T)   197(F)
108(T)   118(T)   128(T)   138(F)   148(F)   158(T)   168(F)   178(T)   188(T)   198(T)
109(F)   119(F)   129(F)   139(T)   149(T)   159(T)   169(T)   179(F)   189(T)   199(T)
110(T)   120(T)   130(F)   140(T)   150(T)   160(T)   170(F)   180(F)   190(T)   200(T)

201(T)   211(T)   221(T)   231(F)   241(T)   251(F)   261(F)   271(F)   281(F)   291(F)
202(F)   212(T)   222(F)   232(F)   242(T)   252(F)   262(T)   272(F)   282(T)   292(T)
203(F)   213(F)   223(T)   233(T)   243(T)   253(F)   263(F)   273(F)   283(F)   293(F)
204(F)   214(T)   224(F)   234(F)   244(T)   254(T)   264(T)   274(T)   284(T)   294(F)
205(F)   215(T)   225(F)   235(T)   245(T)   255(F)   265(T)   275(T)   285(F)   295(F)
206(F)   216(T)   226(T)   236(F)   246(F)   256(T)   266(F)   276(T)   286(F)   296(F)
207(T)   217(F)   227(F)   237(F)   247(T)   257(T)   267(F)   277(T)   287(F)   297(F)
208(T)   218(F)   228(F)   238(T)   248(T)   258(F)   268(T)   278(T)   288(F)   298(T)
209(F)   219(F)   229(F)   239(F)   249(F)   259(T)   269(T)   279(T)   289(F)   299(F)
210(F)   220(T)   230(F)   240(T)   250(T)   260(F)   270(F)   280(F)   290(T)   300(T)

301(F)   311(F)   321(T)   331(T)   341(T)   351(T)   361(F)   371(F)   381(F)   391(T)
302(F)   312(F)   322(F)   332(F)   342(T)   352(T)   362(T)   372(T)   382(F)   392(T)
303(F)   313(F)   323(F)   333(F)   343(F)   353(F)   363(F)   373(F)   383(T)   393(T)
304(T)   314(F)   324(T)   334(T)   344(T)   354(T)   364(T)   374(T)   384(F)   394(T)
305(F)   315(F)   325(F)   335(T)   345(T)   355(F)   365(T)   375(F)   385(T)   395(T)
306(T)   316(T)   326(F)   336(T)   346(T)   356(T)   366(F)   376(F)   386(F)   396(F)
307(F)   317(F)   327(T)   337(F)   347(F)   357(T)   367(T)   377(T)   387(T)   397(T)
308(F)   318(F)   328(F)   338(F)   348(T)   358(T)   368(F)   378(F)   388(F)   398(T)
309(F)   319(F)   329(F)   339(T)   349(F)   359(F)   369(T)   379(F)   389(F)   399(F)
310(T)   320(F)   330(F)   340(T)   350(F)   360(T)   370(F)   380(T)   390(T)   400(T)

401(F)   411(T)   421(T)   431(F)   441(F)   451(F)   461(T)   471(F)   481(F)   491(F)
402(F)   412(F)   422(T)   432(F)   442(T)   452(F)   462(T)   472(T)   482(F)   492(F)
403(F)   413(F)   423(F)   433(F)   443(F)   453(F)   463(T)   473(T)   483(F)   493(F)
404(T)   414(F)   424(F)   434(T)   444(T)   454(T)   464(F)   474(T)   484(T)   494(F)
405(F)   415(T)   425(F)   435(F)   445(F)   455(F)   465(T)   475(F)   485(T)   495(T)
406(F)   416(F)   426(T)   436(T)   446(T)   456(T)   466(F)   476(F)   486(F)   496(T)
407(F)   417(F)   427(F)   437(T)   447(T)   457(F)   467(F)   477(T)   487(T)   497(T)
408(F)   418(F)   428(F)   438(T)   448(F)   458(T)   468(T)   478(F)   488(F)   498(T)
409(F)   419(F)   429(F)   439(F)   449(T)   459(F)   469(T)   479(T)   489(F)   499(F)
410(F)   420(T)   430(F)   440(T)   450(T)   460(F)   470(F)   480(F)   490(F)   500(T)

501(T)   511(F)   521(F)   531(T)   541(F)   551(F)   561(F)   571(T)   581(T)   591(F)
502(T)   512(T)   522(F)   532(F)   542(T)   552(F)   562(T)   572(T)   582(T)   592(T)
503(T)   513(F)   523(F)   533(F)   543(F)   553(F)   563(F)   573(F)   583(T)   593(T)
504(F)   514(F)   524(F)   534(F)   544(T)   554(F)   564(F)   574(F)   584(T)   594(F)
505(F)   515(F)   525(T)   535(T)   545(F)   555(F)   565(T)   575(T)   585(F)   595(F)
506(F)   516(F)   526(T)   536(F)   546(F)   556(T)   566(F)   576(T)   586(F)   596(F)
507(T)   517(F)   527(T)   537(T)   547(F)   557(T)   567(F)   577(T)   587(T)   597(T)
508(F)   518(F)   528(F)   538(F)   548(T)   558(F)   568(F)   578(F)   588(T)   598(F)
509(F)   519(F)   529(T)   539(F)   549(F)   559(F)   569(F)   579(T)   589(F)   599(F)
510(T)   520(F)   530(F)   540(T)   550(T)   560(T)   570(T)   580(T)   590(T)   600(T)
```

[* indicates a double response]
[( ) indicates blank or light mark]

NAME: Personality Inventory for Children

SUPPLIER: PSYCH Systems, Inc.
600 Reisterstown Road
Baltimore, MD 21208
(800) 368-3366

PRODUCT CATEGORY	PRIMARY APPLICATIONS
Personality	Clinical Assessment/Diagnosis
	Personal/Marriage/Family Counseling

SALE RESTRICTIONS Qualified Professional

SERVICE TYPE/COST	Type	Available	Cost	Discount
	Mail-In	No		
	Teleprocessing	No		
	Local	Yes	See Below	

PRODUCT DESCRIPTION

The PERSONALITY INVENTORY FOR CHILDREN provides a detailed picture of the child's personality programming based on the answers of one or both parents to 600 true-false items. The primary scales which are presented graphically in the report are titled Adjustment, Achievement, Intellectual Screening, Development, Somatic Concern, Depression, Family Relations, Delinquency, Withdrawal, Anxiety, Psychosis, Hyperactivity, and Social Skills. Three validity scales are scored as well as 24 other experimental scales.

This report also includes a 3-page narrative analysis of the test scores. Topics covered include Family Context, Parental Attitudes, Present Problem Areas, Child's Adjustment, Cognitive Integrity, and a detailed personality description. The report also includes a listing of critical items classified in terms of Depression, Anxiety, Reality Distortion, Peer Relations, Unsocialized Aggression, Conscience Development, Poor Judgment, Atypical Development, Distractibility, Speech and Language, Somatic Complaints, School Adjustment, and Family Discord.

Psych Systems programs operate on the IBM PC-XT, COMPAQ Plus, Dec Professional 350, and most DEC PDP-11 systems. Various hardware/software configurations are available directly from Psych Systems, with single-user systems starting at approximately $12,000. A per test fee also applies.

222-22-2222 John Doe   32 yr old white male   23-Feb-84


```
-------------------------------------------------
                |
      PIC       | Personality Inventory for Children
                |
-------------------------------------------------
```


Child: Doe, Jayne

Informant: John Doe

This clinical report is designed to aid in psychodiagnostic
evaluation. It is available only to trained professionals.
This report was produced by a computerized analysis of the
responses provided by the informant listed above. The report
is to be used in conjunction with professional evaluation. No
decision should be based solely upon the contents of this report.

The computer program generating this report was designed by Psych
Systems, Inc., Baltimore, Maryland 21208. Copyright (C) 1984 by
Psych Systems, Inc. The interpretive logic utilized in this
report was designed by James K. Klinedinst, Ph. D. Copyright (C)
1980 by James K. Klinedinst. All rights reserved.

This is a valid protocol.

Demography

This 10 year old white school-age girl has been described by her
father. She has lived in two residences within the past five year
period.

Family Context

The information in this section was reported by the father during
administration of the PIC, and may contain information which has not
been shared with the girl. The family consists of a divorced father
and one child. This child is an only child. The parental
relationship into which this child was born is reported to be no
longer intact. According to the father this child was planned. The
child's parents were unable to maintain family harmony and stability.
Poor cooperation among family members and general discouragement with
family relationships is being described. Much anger is being openly
expressed in this family. Only six of one hundred non-clinic
families show angry behavior to this degree.

Parental Attitudes/Adjustment

Sometimes this test result indicates a tendency to exaggerate
difficulty as a means of attracting involvement by others. The
profile suggests that the parent is currently very distressed.
Feelings of ineffectiveness, uncertainty and frustration are being
expressed, and at times render this parent incapable of performing
capably. The relationship between this father and child is too
distant, too disengaged. The father's emotional adjustment may be
unstable. The protocol suggests that he gets drunk and mean.
Further inquiry is necessary to determine the extent of these
behaviors.

Present Problem Areas

The primary forms of dysfunctional behavior presented by this child
are disordered conduct and subjective distress. Areas of behavior
clearly suggested for further psychological observation are:
managing angry feelings, handling practical matters, social
participation and health maintenance anxiety.

Child's Adjustment Status

Most clinicians would agree that this child is showing clear signs of
emotional disturbance and recommend some 'outpatient' form of
psychological intervention. Both home and school performance are
impaired by this condition.

General Ability/Cognitive Integrity

This girl is quite likely to be at least average in functional
intelligence, though this estimate should not be considered as a
substitute for individual intellectual assessment. Given her level
of intellectual functioning, she achieves about as well as is to be
expected.

Personality Description

This girl often (characteristically) is overtly, impulsively, and inappropriately angry at others. Generally weak restraint in expression of emotional states can be expected.

This protocol contains a pattern observed in mental health settings, but not usually outside of such settings. (Nor is the pattern of recent onset. The pattern suggests a combination of avoidance, irresponsible behavior, and impaired communication and empathy.).

Her current interests and attitudes favor active play and physical skill development. She is likely to be seen as uninhibited and active, perhaps becoming a behavior problem at times. The child is also highly prone to teasing from other children with physically aggressive behavior. Being involved in fights is likely to be a significant problem behavior. This child is experiencing health problems which may be stress-related. The respondent is concerned with the child's somatic functioning. Over involvement will extend beyond concern with health into other areas of functioning. The respondent is not allowing the child sufficient room for independent thought and social activity.

The adequacy of this child's general abilities and skills is being called into question by the respondent. The clinician should be alert for disturbances in attentional processes. An increased likelihood of encountering distractibility, too much daydreaming, inability to manage complexity, and poor schoolwork is associated with this test pattern.

Consider the possibility that she maintains a sense of security through preoccupation with fantasy, leading to periodic lapses in relatedness to external events. Obvious internal discomfort and unhappiness are present. The respondent is too closely identified with the child's fears and worries, pessimistic mood and low self-esteem to promote growth-producing activities. The child's

behavior is being fostered by the high level of sympathetic or grudging recognition given it by the respondent.

Insufficiently controlled motor activity is being reported. In clinical settings children with similarly elevated profiles are descriptively overactive. The mother may report any of a variety of specific excited behaviors such as 'showing off', talking too much, acting without thinking, performing silly actions, being loud, boisterous, restless, or overactive.

A pattern of anti-social behavior is likely in this childs' history. The child is likely to dislike participation in school activities. Often parents show concern or complain about the undesirable group of 'friends' chosen by children with these profile patterns.

Critical Items

-- DEPRESSION & POOR SELF-CONCEPT --

                    Question # 6   (T)
                    Question # 9   (T)
                    Question # 158 (T)
                    Question # 371 (T)
                    Question # 532 (T)

```
        -- WORRY & ANXIETY --

                              Question #  17  (T)
                              Question #  71  (T)
                              Question #  84  (T)
                              Question #  92  (T)
                              Question # 151  (T)
                              Question # 175  (T)
                              Question # 228  (T)
                              Question # 246  (T)
                              Question # 298  (T)
                              Question # 373  (T)
                              Question # 399  (T)
                              Question # 505  (T)
                              Question # 511  (T)

        -- REALITY DISTORTION --

                              Question #  26  (T)
                              Question #  43  (T)
                              Question # 101  (T)
                              Question # 161  (T)
                              Question # 176  (T)
                              Question # 379  (T)
                              Question # 397  (T)
                              Question # 475  (T)
                              Question # 550  (T)

        -- PEER RELATIONS --

                              Question #  69  (T)
                              Question #  85  (T)
                              Question #  90  (T)
                              Question #  91  (T)
                              Question # 164  (T)
                              Question # 195  (T)
                              Question # 208  (T)
                              Question # 262  (T)
                              Question # 289  (T)
                              Question # 340  (T)
                              Question # 410  (T)
                              Question # 515  (T)

        -- UNSOCIALIZED AGGRESSION --

                              Question # 116  (T)
                              Question # 152  (T)
                              Question # 465  (T)
                              Question # 537  (T)

        -- CONSCIENCE DEVELOPMENT --

                              Question # 284  (T)
                              Question # 299  (T)
                              Question # 565  (T)

        -- POOR JUDGEMENT --

                              Question # 238  (T)
                              Question # 339  (T)
                              Question # 395  (T)
                              Question # 467  (T)
                              Question # 186  (F)

        -- ATYPICAL DEVELOPMENT --

                              Question #   3  (T)
                              Question #  18  (T)
                              Question #  65  (T)
```

```
                              Question # 79   (T)
                              Question # 131  (T)
                              Question # 182  (T)
                              Question # 355  (T)
                              Question # 448  (T)
                              Question # 460  (T)
                              Question # 579  (T)
                              Question # 593  (T)
                              Question # 597  (T)
                              Question # 215  (F)
                              Question # 351  (F)

-- DISTRACTIBILITY, ACTIVITY LEVEL & COORDINATION --

                              Question # 33   (T)
                              Question # 167  (T)
                              Question # 234  (T)
                              Question # 248  (T)
                              Question # 272  (T)

-- SPEECH & LANGUAGE --

                              Question # 47   (T)
                              Question # 406  (T)
                              Question # 485  (T)
                              Question # 569  (T)
                              Question # 366  (F)

-- SOMATIC COMPLAINTS/CURRENT HEALTH --

                              Question # 12   (T)
                              Question # 104  (T)
                              Question # 108  (T)
                              Question # 117  (T)
                              Question # 334  (T)
                              Question # 400  (T)
                              Question # 420  (T)
                              Question # 434  (T)
                              Question # 473  (T)
                              Question # 507  (T)
                              Question # 534  (T)
                              Question # 564  (T)
                              Question # 566  (T)

-- SCHOOL ADJUSTMENT --

                              Question # 11   (T)
                              Question # 81   (T)
                              Question # 260  (T)
                              Question # 487  (T)
                              Question # 441  (F)

-- FAMILY DISCORD --

                              Question # 119  (T)
                              Question # 204  (T)
                              Question # 214  (T)
                              Question # 240  (T)
                              Question # 369  (T)
                              Question # 535  (T)
                              Question # 583  (T)

-- MISCELLANEOUS ITEMS OF NOTE --

                              Question # 172  (T)
                              Question # 479  (T)
```

psychware **507**

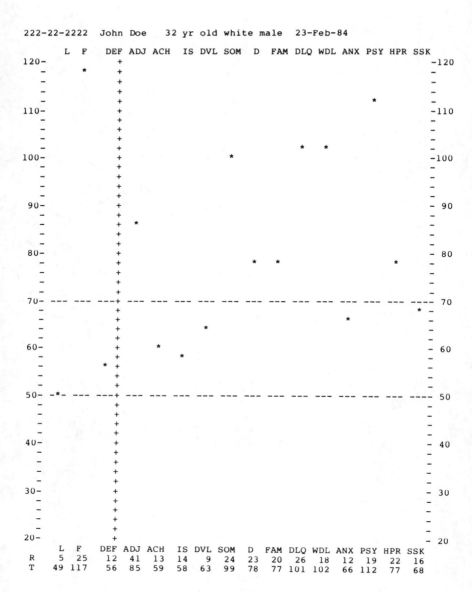

222-22-2222 John Doe   32 yr old white male   23-Feb-84

```
            L   F    DEF ADJ ACH   IS  DVL SOM   D  FAM DLQ WDL ANX PSY HPR SSK
120-                  +                                                          -120
  -         *         +                                                           -
  -                   +                                                           -
  -                   +                                                           -
  -                   +                                               *          -
110-                  +                                                          -110
  -                   +                                                           -
  -                   +                                                           -
  -                   +                                     *   *                 -
100-                  +                      *                                   -100
  -                   +                                                           -
  -                   +                                                           -
  -                   +                                                           -
90-                   +                                                          - 90
  -                   +   *                                                        -
  -                   +                                                            -
  -                   +                                                            -
80-                   +                                                          - 80
  -                   +                          *   *                      *     -
  -                   +                                                            -
  -                   +                                                            -
  -                   +                                                            -
70- --- --- ---+ --- --- --- --- --- --- --- --- --- --- --- --- ---- 70
  -                   +                                                  *  -
  -                   +                                         *                 -
  -                   +                  *                                         -
60-                   +   *                                                       - 60
  -                 * +        *                                                   -
  -                   +                                                            -
  -                   +                                                            -
50- -*- --- ---+ --- --- --- --- --- --- --- --- --- --- --- --- ---- 50
  -                   +                                                            -
  -                   +                                                            -
  -                   +                                                            -
40-                   +                                                           - 40
  -                   +                                                            -
  -                   +                                                            -
  -                   +                                                            -
30-                   +                                                           - 30
  -                   +                                                            -
  -                   +                                                            -
  -                   +                                                            -
20-                   +                                                           - 20
            L   F    DEF ADJ ACH   IS  DVL SOM   D  FAM DLQ WDL ANX PSY HPR SSK
      R     5   25    12  41  13   14   9   24  23  20  26  18  12  19  22  16
      T    49  117    56  85  59   58  63   99  78  77 101 102  66 112  77  68
```

508 *psychware*

Supplementary Scales

Respondent Description Scales

```
         R    T 0   10   20   30   40   50   60   70   80   90  100
DSM     49   92 !                        !         !          *  !
K       16   32 !              *         !         !             !
```

Prediction Scales

```
         R    T 0   10   20   30   40   50   60   70   80   90  100
LDP     31   67 !                        !       * !       *     !
DP      36   83 !                        !         !     *       !
```

Empirical Personality Scales

```
         R    T 0   10   20   30   40   50   60   70   80   90  100
ES      32   66 !                        !      *  !             !
SR      21   66 !                        !      *  !             !
I-E     24   52 !                        !*        !             !
```

Auxilliary Scales

```
         R    T 0   10   20   30   40   50   60   70   80   90  100
CDY     21   36 !                  *     !         !             !
INF      8  106 !                        !         !             *
SD      30   38 !                  *     !         !             !
SM      17   70 !                        !       *!              !
AGM     28   81 !                        !         !     *       !
```

222-22-2222   John Doe   32 yr old white male   23-Feb-84

```
           SOM  FAM  ASO  AGN  DVL  WDL  ANX  RDS    EXC  SSK  INT  EXT
     120-                                             +                      -120
       -                                              +                       -
       -                                              +                       -
       -                        *                     +              *        -
     110-                                             +                      -110
       -                                              +                       -
       -                                        *     +                       -
       -                              *               +                       -
     100-  *                                          +                      -100
       -                                              +                       -
       -                                              +                       -
       -                                              +                       -
      90-                                             +                       - 90
       -                                              +                       -
       -                                              +                     *  -
      80-                                             +                      - 80
       -        *                                     +                       -
       -             *                                +                       -
      70- ---  ---  ---  ---  ---  ---  ---  ---  ---  + --- --- --- --- - 70
       -                                              + *                     -
       -                        *         *           +                       -
      60-                                     *        +                     - 60
       -                                              +                       -
       -                                              +                       -
      50- ---  ---  ---  ---  ---  ---  ---  ---  ---  + --- --- --- --- - 50
       -                                              +                       -
       -                                              +                       -
       -                                              +                       -
      40-                                             +                      - 40
       -                                              +                       -
       -                                              +                       -
       -                                              +                       -
      30-                                             +                      - 30
       -                                              +                       -
       -                                              +                       -
       -                                              +                       -
      20-                                             +                      - 20
           SOM  FAM  ASO  AGN  DVL  WDL  ANX  RDS    EXC  SSK  INT  EXT
       R    24   20   12   12    9   18   12   18     7   16   35   18
       T    99   77   74  109   63  102   66  105    61   68  110   81
```

510 *psychware*

NAME: Personality Research Form E

SUPPLIER: PSYCH Systems, Inc.
600 Reisterstown Road
Baltimore, MD 21208
(800) 368-3366

PRODUCT CATEGORY	PRIMARY APPLICATIONS
Personality	Personal/Marriage/Family Counseling Clinical Assessment/Diagnosis

SALE RESTRICTIONS Qualified Professional

SERVICE TYPE/COST	Type	Available	Cost	Discount
	Mail-In	No		
	Teleprocessing	No		
	Local	Yes	See Below	

PRODUCT DESCRIPTION

The PERSONALITY RESEARCH FORM E is used to assess normal personality functioning. Computer administration allows Form E to be administered in a shorter time and to a wider range of the population than all four of its predecessor forms. It has a broad normative base, including students in grades seven through all university levels, unselected adults, and adult psychiatric patients.

Because the PERSONALITY RESEARCH FORM E focuses on areas of normal functioning rather than on psychopathology, it is a useful tool in indicating individual vocational preference and ability assessment, job counseling, and vocational rehabilitation.

In addition to presenting and scoring the test, this program also provides a brief printout of test results.

Psych Systems programs operate on the IBM PC-XT, COMPAQ Plus, Dec Professional 350, and most DEC PDP-11 systems. Various hardware/ software configurations are available directly from Psych Systems, with single-user systems starting at approximately $12,000. A per test fee also applies.

222-22-2222 Jonathan Doe   32 yr old white male 16-Feb-84

```
-------------------------------------------------------
|         |                                           |
|  PRF-E  |  Personality Research Form - Extended     |
|         |                                           |
-------------------------------------------------------
```

This report is designed to assist in the evaluation of the client's
personality and vocational preferences. It is available to qualified
professionals. This report was produced by a computerized analysis of
the data given by the client listed above, and is to be used in conjunction
with professional evaluation. No decision should be based solely upon
the contents of this report.

512 *psychware*

The PRF-E assesses normal personality functioning. The scales measure the needs which everyone experiences to a greater or lesser degree.

The first part of this report presents the definition of each of the 20 scales and the scores obtained by the subject on each scale. HIGH scores (T=60+) on a scale suggest that this is an area in which the subject's needs are strong relative to his other needs. LOW scores suggest an area of relatively low need while MEDIUM scores suggest an average level of need. Descriptive statements may be developed by referring to the description for HIGH scorers.

The report which follows gives the definition of each scale as it would apply to a person with a HIGH score and the actual score obtained by the subject of this test.

RESPONSE STYLE

There is evidence that some questions were not carefully answered. These results may therefore not be reliable.

PRF-E Scale Definitions for HIGH Scorers

ABASEMENT (AB)

HIGH scorers show a HIGH degree of humility. They accept blame and criticism even when not deserved. They often expose themselves to situations which put them subordinate to others.

Standard score obtained by this client 47   Range MEDIUM

ACHIEVEMENT (AC)

HIGH scorers aspire to accomplish difficult tasks. As such they work purposefully toward distant goals. These resourceful individuals respond positively to competition and challenges.

Standard score obtained by this client 46   Range MEDIUM

AFFILIATION (AF)

HIGH scorers accept people readily and need to be close to others. They put forth the effort to win friendships and will work to maintain associations with people.

Standard score obtained by this client 53   Range MEDIUM

AGGRESSION (AG)

HIGH scorers may hurt others to get their way or to get even. They enjoy combat and argument.

Standard score obtained by this client 48   Range MEDIUM

AUTONOMY (AU)

These individuals try to break away from restraints. When faced with restraints, however, they may become rebellious.

Standard score obtained by this client 57   Range MEDIUM

CHANGE (CH)

HIGH scorers prefer new and different experiences while avoiding routine, regular work. These individuals may readily change opinions or values in different circumstances.

Standard score obtained by this client 49   Range MEDIUM

COGNITIVE STRUCTURE (CS)

HIGH scorers avoid ambiguous problems or situations. They want questions answered completely and desire to make decisions based on definite knowledge.

Standard score obtained by this client 45   Range MEDIUM

DEFENDENCE (DE)

HIGH scorers suspect that people mean to harm them. They defend themselves at all times. These self-protective individuals do not accept criticism readily.

Standard score obtained by this client 50   Range MEDIUM

DOMINANCE (DO)

HIGH scorers seek to control their environment and to direct the activity of others. They expresss their views forcefully and persuasively. They enjoy the role of leader and may assume it spontaneously.

Standard score obtained by this client 55   Range MEDIUM

ENDURANCE (EN)

HIGH scorers seldom give up quickly on a problem. These durable, energetic individuals persevere. They see themselves as patient and unrelenting in their work habits.

Standard score obtained by this client 45   Range MEDIUM

EXHIBITION (EX)

HIGH scorers enjoy entertaining others. As such they engage in behavior which wins the notice of others. They may be at times pretentious and immodest.

Standard score obtained by this client 63   Range HIGH

HARMAVOIDANCE (HA)

HIGH scorers withdraw from adventurous, exciting activities, especially if danger is involved. These cautious individuals avoid risks and seek to maximize their personal safety.

Standard score obtained by this client 53   Range MEDIUM

IMPULSIVITY (IM)

HIGH scorers frequently act on the spur of the moment and without deliberation. They speak freely and spontaneously. These quick-thinking individuals may be volatile in emotional expression.

Standard score obtained by this client 55   Range MEDIUM

NURTURANCE (NU)

HIGH scorers offer a helping hand to those in need. They are caring individuals who give unselfishly of themselves.

Standard score obtained by this client 42   Range MEDIUM

ORDER (OR)

HIGH scorers like to keep materials methodically organized.

Standard score obtained by this client 61   Range HIGH

PLAY (PL)

HIGH scorers maintain a lighthearted, easy going attitude toward life. Such individuals do may things "just for fun."

Standard score obtained by this client 64   Range HIGH

SENTIENCE (SE)

HIGH scorers are perceptive, sensitive people who maintain a rather aesthetic view of life. They enjoy physical sensation and believe these feelings to be an important part of life.

Standard score obtained by this client 80   Range HIGH

SOCIAL RECOGNITION (SR)

HIGH scorers seek approval and recognition from others. They are well-behaved, socially proper individuals who desire to be held in HIGH esteem by acquaintances.

Standard score obtained by this client 50   Range MEDIUM

SUCCORANCE (SU)

HIGH scorers seek support and reassurance of other people. These individuals appeal to others for advice and help.

Standard score obtained by this client 40   Range LOW

UNDERSTANDING (UN)

HIGH scorers are curious reflective people who want to understand many areas of knowledge. They value the synthesis of ideas.

Standard score obtained by this client 62   Range HIGH

T-Scores

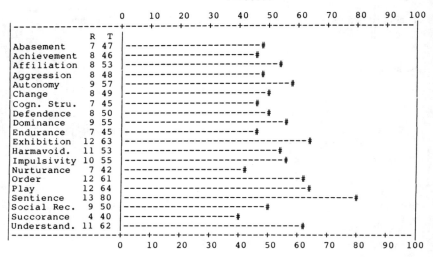

```
                        0    10   20   30   40   50   60   70   80   90  100
------------------------+----+----+----+----+----+----+----+----+----+----|
                 R   T
Abasement        7  47  |-----------------------#
Achievement      8  46  |-----------------------#
Affiliation      8  53  |--------------------------#
Aggression       8  48  |-----------------------#
Autonomy         9  57  |----------------------------#
Change           8  49  |------------------------#
Cogn. Stru.      7  45  |----------------------#
Defendence       8  50  |------------------------#
Dominance        9  55  |---------------------------#
Endurance        7  45  |----------------------#
Exhibition      12  63  |-------------------------------#
Harmavoid.      11  53  |--------------------------#
Impulsivity     10  55  |---------------------------#
Nurturance       7  42  |---------------------#
Order           12  61  |------------------------------#
Play            12  64  |-------------------------------#
Sentience       13  80  |----------------------------------------#
Social Rec.      9  50  |------------------------#
Succorance       4  40  |--------------------#
Understand.     11  62  |------------------------------#
------------------------+----+----+----+----+----+----+----+----+----+----|
                        0    10   20   30   40   50   60   70   80   90  100
```

PERSONALITY RESEARCH FORM (E)
PART 2: VOCATIONAL PREFERENCE SCALE DEFINITIONS

In this part of the report, the PRF scales are grouped to yield
empirically derived vocational preference information. These
statements may be useful in evaluating a client's career
possibilities. They should be used in conjunction with the results
of other tests, interview data and aptitude measures.

TECHNICALLY-ORIENTED ACHIEVEMENT

These individuals enjoy working with things rather than people. They
are resourceful, aspiring people whose work interests are directed
toward distant, even abstract goals. Their willingness to invest
time and energy to achieve future goals suggest that they are driven
by the challenge of the task. HIGH scorers seldom undertake a task
for the purpose of gaining social recognition or approval of others.
These independent, self-assured persons are intellectually curious
and are often well-versed on many different matters. They prefer
vocations in technical areas such as engineering, chemistry, physics,
or production management. These individuals are steadfast in their
viewpoints. As such, HIGH scorers seldom waver in their stance for
the sake of obliging others.

Composite score obtained by this client 45   Range MEDIUM

HUMAN RELATIONS MANAGEMENT

HIGH scorers desire to help others. Their helpful behavior seldom
places them in a position in which they are subservient to others.
They are characteristically at ease and often are quite adroit in
dealing with other people. Their willingness to help others may at
times reflect their needs to behave in a socially desirable manner.
They receive a sense of satisfaction from organizing and directing
the activities of others. Although power and control are sought,
HIGH scorers are perceived by other people as good-natured

individuals who tend to express themselves in a rather colorful, entertaining way. The personality of HIGH scorers makes them well-suited for jobs in areas such as public administration, personnel management, education, counseling, and ministry. These gregarious individuals take charge and seek dominance over others in social situations.

Composite score obtained by this client 43   Range MEDIUM

VERBAL EXPRESSION

HIGH scorers prefer a structured, well-regulated environment. They prefer to be well informed of the rules and policies of their environment and typically use such information to govern their actions. They approach tasks in a methodical, deliberate manner. They seek to avoid ambiguity and uncertainty. HIGH scorers make decisions after gathering, in a precise, organized fashion, relevant information. Because of their need for precision and order, these individuals are quite predictable in their behavior. Imaginative, creative thinking is also less common among individuals with HIGH scores on this dimension. The productivity and job satisfaction of these individuals will depend on whether job tasks and duties are well-structured and defined. HIGH scorers tend to be modest and non-conspicuous in the assessment of their accomplishments. These are patient, unhurried individuals who prefer a consistent, unchanging environment. They are likely to find employment in job areas such as accounting, bookkeeping, and office work.

Composite score obtained by this client 59   Range MEDIUM

PRACTICAL

HIGH scorers prefer activities which involve work or mastery over concrete, practical aspects of the environment. HIGH scorers avoid situations in which they are the focus of attention. Although they seldom seek attention, they are rarely viewed as fearful, timorous persons. Most individuals HIGH on this dimension enjoy activities involving a degree of risk. The are decisive and quite practical in their thinking and problem solving approach. Still these uncomplicated individuals prefer to accept things the way they are. They are likely to find satisfaction in occupations that allow them to work outdoors.

Composite score obtained by this client 14   Range LOW

AGGRESSIVE LEADERSHIP

HIGH scoring individuals are expected to fulfill a role involving leadership. HIGH scorers are viewed as forceful, persuasive individuals. They are disinclined to be self-critical or apologetic in their relationships with other people. When attacked, HIGH scorers retaliate. These fearless, adventurous people are more comfortable on the offensive rather than on the defensive. HIGH scorers seldom see their mistakes as weighty or significant. They minimize the importance of their ineptitude or errors. These individuals want control and supervisory
responsibilities. They are usually willing to take risks to obtain such power. HIGH scorers are likely to find the work of a military officer or an industrial relation expert satisfying.

Composite score obtained by this client 39   Range LOW

AESTHETIC/INTELLECTUAL INTERESTS

These are perceptive, responsive individuals who seek enjoyment and pleasure from the environment. Such pleasure-seeking tendencies do not need to be of a self-indulgent variety. HIGH scorers tend to be analytical and curious people. They are very adaptable and flexible individuals. Their flexiblity may at times reflect their unpredictable nature especially when it comes to making decisions. HIGH scorers are inclined to enjoy jobs in areas such as physical education, architecture, and music.

Composite score obtained by this client 37   Range LOW

SOCIAL CONTACT

Individuals scoring HIGH on this dimension tend to find contact with other people pleasant and enjoyable. Such individuals are described by others as "happy-go-lucky." For some individuals with HIGH scores, the upbeat, engaging appearance is superficial and shallow. For the most part, however, these individuals seek genuine contact with others. HIGH scorers possess an easy-going orientation toward others and are thus perceived by others as warm and lighthearted. They are less inclined to be achievers. Equally important they are viewed by others as non-ambitious and non-competitive individuals. Their carefree, gleeful personal style is usually accompanied by a tendency to be only marginally inquisitive and curious about their social surroundings.

Composite score obtained by this client 33   Range LOW

VOCATIONAL PREFERENCE PROFILE

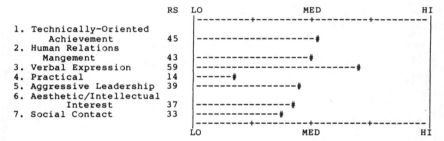

```
                              RS  LO              MED              HI
                                  |---------+---------+---------+---------|
1. Technically-Oriented
     Achievement             45   |--------------------#
2. Human Relations
     Mangement               43   |-------------------#
3. Verbal Expression         59   |---------------------------#
4. Practical                 14   |------#
5. Aggressive Leadership     39   |-----------------#
6. Aesthetic/Intellectual
     Interest                37   |----------------#
7. Social Contact            33   |--------------#
                                  |---------+---------+---------+---------|
                                  LO              MED              HI
```

RS = Raw Score

```
      **************
      *            *
      *   NOTE     *
      *            *
      **************
```

The PRF-E is best suited for measuring normal personality functioning. In this report the PRF scale descriptions are constructed to yield vocational preference information. These descriptions should add to the assessment of one's vocational interests.

This report is likely to be most useful when it is considered along with information gathered from other measures. The information obtained from this report should not be used to choose a career. Interest inventories and personality instruments are different from ability measures. A complete evaluation of a client's career possibilities should include an ability assessment.

NAME: Personnel Behavior Report

SUPPLIER: Institute for Personality and Ability Testing, Inc.
P.O. Box 188
Champaign, IL 61820
(217) 352-4739

PRODUCT CATEGORY

Personality
Interest/Attitudes
Motivation/Needs

PRIMARY APPLICATIONS

Personnel Selection/Evaluation
Clinical Assessment/Diagnosis

SALE RESTRICTIONS American Psychological Association Guidelines

SERVICE TYPE/COST	Type	Available	Cost	Discount
	Mail-In	Yes	$75.00	Yes
	Teleprocessing	No		
	Local	No		

PRODUCT DESCRIPTION

The PERSONNEL BEHAVIOR REPORT is primarily intended to assess critical personnel for the nuclear power industry, using a validated and documented screening model directed specifically to the NRC guidelines for unescorted access. The PERSONNEL BEHAVIOR REPORT narrative discusses available validity indicators, provides a security summary, and discusses the person's emotional profile and degree of responsibility. Also included is information on the candidate's interpersonal style, cognitive factors, and motivation.

PERSONNEL BEHAVIORAL REPORT

NAME... Mr Sample
SEX.... M
AGE.... NA
DATE... 4/20/1984

VALIDITY INDICATORS

Indications are that Mr Sample's answers to the surveys used were made without excessive attention paid to the "social desirability" of the various alternatives. As a consequence, the following report is likely to represent a fair analysis of his attitudes, interests, and personality makeup. While there is no reason to doubt the accuracy of the report it must be integrated with other information that is known about him. In this respect, the report will be most useful as a tool to suggest areas for further exploration and inquiry.

SECURITY SUMMARY

In terms of Mr Sample's emotional makeup, responsibility, and degree of behavioral control, the available psychometric data provide no indications of factors or combinations of factors that would make him a high risk for security placement. He is an acceptable candidate for jobs involving unescorted access to security areas.

EMOTIONAL PROFILE

The qualities described in this section of the report deal with his ability to act appropriately and calmly in stressful situations. At the present time Mr Sample sees himself as less anxious than most people. He approaches problems with calm emotional stability and realism. At the present time he feels he has been considerably obstructed in the realization of his goals and this has led to much personal conflict. Overall, his ability to react appropriately and effectively in high stress situations is average.

RESPONSIBILITY AND CONTROL

His ability to control his impulses and handle inner conflicts in a responsible way is high. His reported regard for rules and group standards is average. As far as accidents and errors are concerned he is no more susceptible than the average person. Overall, Mr Sample's life style balances a need to control the environment with a willingness to adapt to what is available.

Mr Sample   -2-   4/20/1984

RELATING TO OTHERS

In general, Mr Sample shows about equal preference for situations that involve working alone and those that involve working with others. He tends to be somewhat self-sufficient, but not strongly so.

COGNITIVE FACTORS

Mr Sample tends to arrive at decisions by evaluating a good balance of intellectual and emotional factors. Before making any decision he is likely to evaluate both the factual evidence at hand as well as any impact it might have on others. In general, his capacity for abstract verbal skills is about average; however, he tends to take a rather creative approach to problem-solving.

MOTIVATION

In comparison with others, Mr Sample's career interests appear to be high. However, he appears to be experiencing a marked degree of frustration and conflict in his career development. He has strong achievement needs that have not been met. Competitiveness and achievement needs are below average. He indicates that he has extremely low tendencies toward security and caution. He does not appear to hold rigidly to traditional societal standards and his behavior may be distinctly unconventional on occasion.

NAME: Personnel Reliability Evaluation Program

SUPPLIER: Institute for Personality and Ability Testing, Inc.
P.O. Box 188
Champaign, IL 61820
(217) 352-4739

PRODUCT CATEGORY	PRIMARY APPLICATIONS
Personality	Clinical Assessment/Diagnosis Personnel Selection/Evaluation

SALE RESTRICTIONS American Psychological Association Guidelines

SERVICE TYPE/COST	Type	Available	Cost	Discount
	Mail-In	Yes	$25.00	
	Teleprocessing	No		
	Local	No		

PRODUCT DESCRIPTION

The PERSONNEL RELIABILITY EVALUATION PROGRAM has its primary application in security screening of job applicants. It uses previously validated and documented models relevant to the issue of personnel reliability and yields a bottom-line statement about an individual's suitability for critical job placements.

Feedback of results is provided in a nontechnical report format that has had extensive field use and testing. Reports are normally returned within a 24 hour period after receipt of test materials. The supplier also offers training on the evaluation concepts to key administrative personnel.

PREP REPORT

NAME...Mr Sample
SEX....M
AGE....NA
DATE... 4/20/1984

VALIDITY INDICATORS

Indications are that Mr Sample's answers to the surveys used were made without excessive attention paid to the "social desirability" of the various alternatives. As a consequence, the following report is likely to represent a fair analysis of his attitudes, interests, and personality makeup. While there is no reason to doubt the accuracy of the report it must be integrated with other information that is known about him. In this respect, the report will be most useful as a tool to suggest areas for further exploration and inquiry.

RISK STATUS

In terms of Mr Sample's emotional makeup, responsibility, and degree of behavioral control, the available psychometric data provide no indications of factors or combinations of factors that would make him a high risk for critical placement. He is an acceptable candidate for jobs requiring crisis response capability.

EMOTIONAL PROFILE

The qualities described in this section of the report deal with his ability to act appropriately and calmly in stressful situations. At the present time Mr Sample sees himself as less anxious than most people. He approaches problems with calm emotional stability and realism. Overall, his ability to react appropriately and effectively in high stress situations is average.

RESPONSIBILITY AND CONTROL

His ability to control his impulses and handle inner conflicts in a responsible way is high. His reported regard for rules and group standards is average. As far as accidents and errors are concerned he is no more susceptible than the average person. Overall, Mr Sample's life style balances a need to control the environment with a willingness to adapt to what is available.

RELATING TO OTHERS

In general, Mr Sample shows about equal preference for situations that involve working alone and those that involve working with others. He tends to be somewhat self-sufficient, but not strongly so.

COGNITIVE FACTORS

Mr Sample tends to arrive at decisions by evaluating a good balance of intellectual and emotional factors. Before making any decision he is likely to evaluate both the factual evidence at hand as well as any impact it might have on others. In general, his capacity for abstract verbal skills is about average, however, he tends to take a rather creative approach to problem-solving.

NAME: PIAT-80 Diagnostic Report

SUPPLIER: Precision People, Inc.
3452 North Ride Circle. S.
Jacksonville, FL 32217
(904) 262-1096

PRODUCT CATEGORY	PRIMARY APPLICATIONS
Cognitive/Ability	Educational Evaluation/Planning Clinical Assessment/Diagnosis

SALE RESTRICTIONS American Psychological Association Guidelines

SERVICE TYPE/COST	Type	Available	Cost	Discount
	Mail-In	No		
	Teleprocessing	No		
	Local	Yes	$149.00	

PRODUCT DESCRIPTION

PIAT-80 DIAGNOSTICS is a computerized program for the Peabody Individual Achievement Test. This program translates results of the Peabody into meaningful educational strategies. This program produces a 6-page report in less than five minutes. PIAT-80 DIAGNOSTICS converts raw scores to grade equivalents for all subtests. By entering items missed on the math subtest, the following are also produced: (1) an error matrix which organizes Peabody items; (2) behavioral objectives for each student's incorrect items; and (3) correct and incorrect items and percent correct.

The software is compatible with the IBM PC, Apple, and TRS-80 (Models I, II, and III) microcomputers. A manual and sample printout are available for $34.00.

```
                    WELCOME TO

               PIAT 80 - APPLE

      A DIAGNOSTIC MATHEMATICS PROGRAM BY
            JOHN J. TRIFILETTI, PH.D.

           ROBERT ALGOZZINE, PH.D.

             ALFRED H. TRACY III
            COPYRIGHT  (C) 1980

   NAME           (1)   ALICE SOMMES
   AGE            (2)   10-0
   SEX            (3)   FEMALE
   PARENT         (4)   GLADYS SOMMES
   SCHOOL         (5)   CLEARWATER ELEMENTARY
   GRADE          (6)   SIX
   REFERRED BY (7)      DR. HOLMES

   REASON FOR REFERRAL        (8)   SUPERIOR
      MATH ABILITY           IMPULSIVITY

   OTHER TESTS ADMINISTERED (9)   NONE

   EXAM DATE (MM/DD/YY)      (10)   10/15/81


   ****************************************
            PIAT ITEMS MISSED
   ****************************************

    25     63    64    65    66    67

   ****************************************
     PERFORMANCE SUMMARY - FOUNDATIONS
   ****************************************

   NUM. DISCRIMINATION 1C   2C   3C   4C   12C
      15C   17C   25E   33C   89%

   SIZE DISCRIMINATION 5C   6C   100%

   SHAPE DISCRIMINATION11C   22C   41C   100%
```

GENERAL INFORMATION 19C 21C 28C 35C
    40C 53C 69 100%

****
    PERFORMANCE SUMMARY - BASIC FACTS
****

ADDITION   7C   9C   10C 23C
  26E 80%
SUBTRACTION   8C   14C 24C 27C
  100%

MONEY   16C 18C 29C 42C
  43C 100%
MULTIPLICATION   30C 34C 36C 46C
  100%

DIVISION   31C 32C 38C 39C
  52C 100%
****
    PERFORMANCE SUMMARY - APPLICATIONS
****

FRACTIONS   13C 20C 47C 55C
  100%

NUM. RELATIONSHIPS 37C 44C 48C 51C
    54C 60C 62C 65E 72   88%

WORD PROBLEMS   45C 49C 50C 58C
    59C 61C 63E 66E 78   75%

GEOMETRY   56C 57C 64E 68
    73   74   76   79   81   84   67%

ALGEBRA   67E 70   71   75
    77   80   82   83   0%
****
    INDIVIDUALIZED EDUCATIONAL PLAN
****
ITEM: 25
GIVEN A SET OF NUMBERS; THE CHILD CAN
IDENTIFY THE ONE THAT COMES JUST BEFORE
100 (NUMBERS; JUST BEFORE; 100).

```
******************************************
     INDIVIDUALIZED EDUCATIONAL PLAN
******************************************

ITEM: 63

BEGINNING WITH A SINGLE DIGIT NUMBER;
THE CHILD CAN IDENTIFY THE NUMBER WHICH
WOULD END A SEQUENCE INVOLVING ADDITION
OF EACH CONSECUTIVE NUMBER BEGINNING
WITH ONE AND ENDING WITH FIVE (TREE; 4;
INCHES; TALL; PLANTED; ONE YEAR; 5; TWO
YEARS; 7; THREE YEARS; 10; FOUR YEARS;
14; HOW MANY; AFTER; FIVE YEARS).

******************************************
     INDIVIDUALIZED EDUCATIONAL PLAN
******************************************

ITEM: 64

GIVEN A DESCRIPTION OF A TYPE OF
TRIANGLE AND FOUR WRITTEN CHOICES;
THE CHILD CAN IDENTIFY AN ISOSCELES
TRIANGLE (TRIANGLE; TWO; THREE; SIDES;
EQUAL; LENGTH; TYPE; EQUILATERAL;
OBTUSE; ISOSCELES; ACUTE).

******************************************
     INDIVIDUALIZED EDUCATIONAL PLAN
******************************************

ITEM: 65

GIVEN A MULTIPLICATION PROBLEM; THE
CHILD CAN DROP TWO ZEROS FROM THE
MULTIPLIER AND IDENTIFY THE PRODUCT AS
A FRACTION OF THE ORIGINAL PRODUCT
(EFFECT; PRODUCT; DROPPING; TWO ZEROS;
MULTIPLIER; STATEMENT; AS GREAT; THE
SAME; TIMES).

******************************************
     INDIVIDUALIZED EDUCATIONAL PLAN
******************************************
```

ITEM: 66

GIVEN AN AMOUNT OF MONEY; THE CHILD
COMPLETES A PERCENTAGE OF THE AMOUNT
(25%); SUBTRACTS THAT PRODUCT AND
IDENTIFIES RESULT (MAN; EARNED; $60.00;
PER; WEEK; 25; PERCENT; WITHHELD;
TAXES; HOW MUCH; MONEY; TAKE; HOME;
$35.00; $45.00; $48.00; $25.00).

****
        INDIVIDUALIZED EDUCATIONAL PLAN
****

ITEM: 67

GIVEN AN ALGEBRAIC EQUATION INVOLVING
AN UNKNOWN NUMBER AND ITS SQUARE; THE
CHILD CAN IDENTIFY THE FACTORS OF THE
EXPRESSION (FACTORS; EXPRESSION).

****
          SINGLE SKILL SUMMARY
****

GEOMETRY   56C   57C   64E   68
    73   74   76   79   81   84   67%

****
          GRADE EQUIVALENT SCORES
****

MATHEMATICS GRADE   9.9

READING RECOGNITION GRADE   5.2

READING COMPREHENSION GRADE   3.4

SPELLING GRADE   ---

GENERAL INFORMATION GRADE   10.1

NAME: Picture Identification Test

SUPPLIER: Center for Psychological Services
College of William and Mary
Williamsburg, VA 23185

PRODUCT CATEGORY

Personality

PRIMARY APPLICATIONS

Clinical Assessment/Diagnosis

SALE RESTRICTIONS Qualified Professional

SERVICE TYPE/COST	Type	Available	Cost	Discount
	Mail-In	Yes	$3.00	
	Teleprocessing	No		
	Local	No		

PRODUCT DESCRIPTION

The PICTURE IDENTIFICATION TEST measures a person's effectiveness in dealing with combative, personal, and competitive motivations. The individual is presented with 12 photographs representing a variety of facial expressions. In Part I of the test, the individual rates the person's expression in each picture on a five-point scale from very positive to very negative. In Part II, the individual is given a list of 22 needs based on Murray's system and three time dimension items. The individual rates each of the 12 pictures for the 25 items on a five-point scale expressing the degree to which each picture expresses the motives or needs defined in the test items. A multidimensional scale analysis yields scores on three dimensions: Combative, Personal, and Competitive. Specific attitude scores are also computed for each of the 22 needs. These attitude scores are correlated with target dimension need locations to provide an attitude score for each dimension. This test is used for personality analysis and research in psychotherapy.

TABLE 1: POSITION OF NEEDS ON DIMENSION SCALES FOR

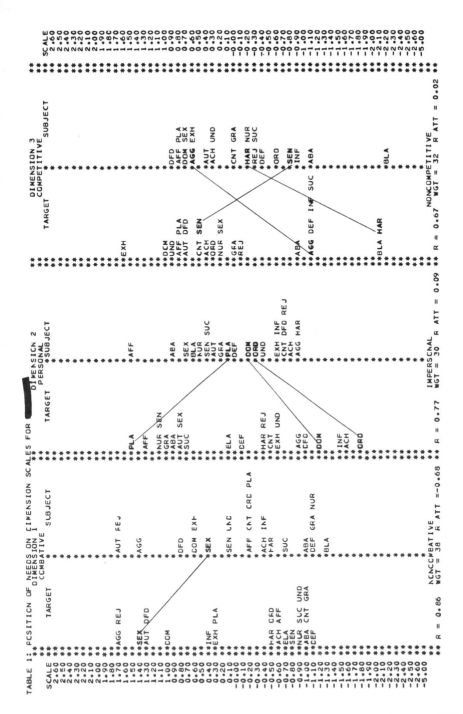

psychware **529**

TABLE 1 PRESENTS A MULTI-DIMENSIONAL SCALING ANALYSIS OF YOUR PIT NEED RATINGS. YOUR LOCATIONS OF THE 22 PIT NEEDS IN EACH OF THREE DIMENSIONS CAN BE COMPARED WITH THE NEED LOCATIONS PROVIDED BY THE TARGET MODEL WHICH ARE ALSO PRESENTED IN TABLE 1.

NEED ABBREVIATIONS ARE PRINTED IN BOLD TYPE IN CASES WHERE YOUR LOCATION DIFFERS SIGNIFICANTLY FROM THE TARGET LOCATION. STATEMENTS OF GENERAL INFORMATION ARE PRINTED WITH IN THE INTERPRETATION WHICH FOLLOWS. STATEMENTS OF GENERAL INFORMATION ARE PRINTED WITH NORMAL TYPE; STATEMENTS ABOUT YOUR INDIVIDUAL RESULTS ARE PRINTED IN BOLD TYPE.

PICTURE IDENTIFICATION TEST NEED DEFINITIONS

(ABA) ABASEMENT: THE NEED TO ADMIT FAULTS AND WEAKNESSES.

(ACH) ACHIEVEMENT: THE NEED TO WORK HARD TO ATTAIN GOALS.

(AFF) AFFILIATION: THE NEED TO BE FRIENDLY AND SOCIABLE.

(AGG) AGGRESSION: THE NEED TO BE FORCEFUL AND CRITICIZE OR ATTACK OTHERS.

(ALT) AUTONOMY: THE NEED TO BE FREE, INDEPENDENT, AND UNINHIBITED.

(BLA) BLAME AVOIDANCE: THE NEED TO AVOID DOING THINGS WHICH MIGHT AROUSE CRITICISM OR DISAPPROVAL.

(CNT) COUNTERACTION: THE NEED TO IMPROVE ONESELF AND CORRECT MISTAKES AND SHORTCOMINGS.

(DFD) DEFENDANCE: THE NEED TO STAND UP FOR ONE'S RIGHTS AND DEFEND ONESELF

(DEF) DEFERENCE: THE NEED TO FOLLOW THE ADVICE AND GUIDANCE OF THOSE WITH EXPERIENCE AND AUTHORITY.

(DOM) DOMINANCE: THE NEED TO ASSERT LEADERSHIP AND ACT IN A COMMANDING AND PERSUASIVE WAY.

(EXH) EXHIBITION: THE NEED TO EXPRESS IDEAS AND EXHIBIT ONE'S TALENTS AND ABILITIES.

(GRA) GRATITUDE: THE NEED TO BE APPRECIATIVE, THANKFUL, AND GRATEFUL.

(HAR) HARM AVOIDANCE: THE NEED TO AVOID HARM AND DANGER.

(INF) INFERIORITY AVOIDANCE: THE NEED TO AVOID FAILURE, INADEQUACY, AND INFERIORITY.

(NUR) NURTURANCE: THE NEED TO GIVE AID AND COMFORT TO OTHERS.

(ORD) ORDER; THE NEED TO SYSTEMATIZE, ORGANIZE, AND PUT THINGS IN ORDER.

(PLA) PLAY: THE NEED TO PLAY, HAVE FUN, AND ENJOY ONESELF.

(REJ) REJECTION: THE NEED TO RESIST PRESSURES TO DO THINGS ONE DOES NOT WISH TO DO.

(SEN) SENTIENCE: THE NEED TO APPRECIATE THE BEAUTY AND HARMONY OF ONE'S SURROUNDINGS.

(SEX) SEX: THE NEED TO SATISFY SEXUAL DESIRES.

(SUC) SUCCORANCE: THE NEED TO RECEIVE HELP, SUPPORT, AND ASSISTANCE.

(UND) UNDERSTANDING: THE NEED TO LEARN, UNDERSTAND, AND FIND THE MEANING OF THINGS.

TABLE 2: DIMENSION DATA

NEED DIFFERENTIATION SUM = 41.26

	DIM 1 COMBATIVE	DIM 2 PERSONAL	DIM 3 COMPETITIVE
WEIGHT PERCENT SCORE	38%	30%	32%
DIMENSION SCALE R	0.86	0.77	0.67
DIMENSION ATTITUDE R	-0.68	0.05	0.02

INTER-DIMENSION CONFUSION SCORES

COMBATIVE-PERSONAL		0.32
PERSONAL-COMBATIVE		0.42
	AVE	0.37
PERSONAL-COMPETITIVE		0.18
COMPETITIVE-PERSONAL		0.22
	AVE	0.20
COMBATIVE-COMPETITIVE		0.47
COMPETITIVE-COMBATIVE		0.54
	AVE	0.51

PICTURE IDENTIFICATION TEST INTERPRETATION

SOME OF YOUR PICTURE IDENTIFICATION TEST RESULTS ARE PRESENTED IN TABLE 1 UNDER THE HEADING: POSITION OF NEEDS ON DIMENSION SCALES FOR TARGET AND SUBJECT NO. 11111, SEX = 1.

THE TABLE SHOWS HOW YOU (THE SUBJECT) ORGANIZED THE 22 MURRAY NEEDS IN THREE DIMENSIONS. YOU CAN COMPARE YOUR ORGANIZATION WITH A TARGET WHICH PRO- VIDES A GENERAL MODEL APPROPRIATE FOR MOST ADULTS. YOUR ORGANIZATION OF THE NEEDS IN A THREE DIMENSIONAL SYSTEM WAS CALCULATED BY A COMPUTER ON THE BASIS OF HOW YOUR NEED RATINGS OF THE 12 PICTURES VARY IN RELATION TO EACH OTHER. BE- CAUSE OF LIMITED SPACE, THE NEEDS PRINTED IN THE TABLE ARE ABBREVIATED. THE ABBREVIATIONS, THE NEED NAMES, AND THE NEED DEFINITIONS ARE PRINTED ON ANOTHER PAGE.

THE THREE DIMENSIONS ARE CALLED THE COMBATIVE, THE PERSONAL, AND THE COM- PETITIVE DIMENSIONS. ALTHOUGH ALL THREE DIMENSIONS ARE ACTIVE TO SOME EXTENT IN MOST SITUATIONS, SOME SITUATIONS EMPHASIZE THE COMBATIVE DIMENSION, SOME THE PERSONAL DIMENSION, AND SOME THE COMPETITIVE DIMENSION. WHEN A PARTICULAR DIM- ENSION IS EMPHASIZED, IT STANDS OUT AS THE FIGURE IN OUR AWARENESS AND THE OTHER

DIMENSIONS RECEDE INTO THE BACKGROUND. THIS IS ANALAGOUS TO OUR ATTENTION TO SPATIAL DIMENSIONS WHEN TRYING TO FIND A ROOM IN A HOTEL. WHEN WE GET IN THE HOTEL ELEVATOR WE ARE MOST CONCERNED WITH WHICH FLOOR LEVEL (VERTICAL DIMENSION) WE ARE ON WHEN WE ARRIVE AT OUR FLOOR, WE SWITCH OUR ATTENTION TO THE FRONT-BACK OR THE LEFT-RIGHT DIMENSION IN SEEKING THE ROOM.

THE SCALE FOR ALL THREE DIMENSIONS IS PRINTED AT EACH SIDE OF THE TABLE. THE TARGET DISTRIBUTION OF THE NEEDS ON THIS SCALE IS A MODEL OF HOW THE NEEDS CAN BE ORGANIZED IN EACH DIMENSION TO PROVIDE A BUILT-IN SET OF SUPPORTS, CHECKS, AND BALANCES FOR EXAMPLE, THE TARGET HAS NEEDS IN THE UPPER PART OF THE COMBATIVE DIMENSION WHICH MUTUALLY REINFORCE AND SUPPORT EACH OTHER TO INI-TIATE COMBATIVE ACTION. THE NEEDS IN THE LOWER PART OF THE DIMENSION COMBINE TO OPPOSE-CHECK-LIMIT, AND INHIBIT COMBATIVE ACTION. THUS, THE TARGET PROVIDES US WITH DISTINCT ALTERNATIVE MOTIVATION CHOICES FOR EACH DIMENSION: THESE AL-TERNATIVES HELP US AVOID CONFUSION, AMBIVALENCE, AND INEFFECTIVENESS IN RESPOND-ING TO SITUATIONS.

IT WOULD BE VERY UNUSUAL IF YOU LOCATED ALL OF THE NEEDS IN EACH DIMENSION IN THE SAME ORDER AS THE TARGET MODEL. SOME DIFFERENCES BETWEEN YOUR ORDER AND LOCA-TION ARE TO BE EXPECTED. HOWEVER, LARGE DIFFERENCES BETWEEN YOUR ORDER AND NEEDS AND THE TARGET MAY PROVIDE CLUES TO UNUSUAL BELIEFS OR CONCEPTS YOU HAVE ABOUT YOUR NEEDS. SUCH BELIEFS MAY BE RELATED TO PROBLEMS OF OVERREACTIVE, UNDERREAC-TIVE, CONFUSED, INEFFECTIVE, OR MISDIRECTED ATTEMPTS TO SATISFY YOUR NEEDS.

THE COMBATIVE DIMENSION

THE COMBATIVE DIMENSION IS EMPHASIZED IN SITUATIONS WHERE THERE IS A STRUGGLE FOR POSSESSION, CONTROL, OR INFLUENCE OVER PEOPLE AND THINGS. WE AS-SERT THE NEEDS AT THE TOP END OF THE SCALE WHEN WE WISH TO IMPOSE OUR WILL ON THE WORLD AND WE EXPRESS THE NEEDS AT THE LOWER END WHEN WE MAY CHOOSE TO SUBMIT TO EXTERNAL CONTROL. COMBATIVE CONFLICTS CAN VARY ALL THE WAY FROM SLIGHT ARGU-MENTS AND DISAGREEMENTS TO VIOLENT PHYSICAL ASSAULTS. NON-VERBAL COMBATIVE BE-HAVIOR CAN BE CONVEYED BY THREATENING GESTURES OR BODY ATTITUDES OR EVEN BY BE-HOSTILE SILENCE. A COMBATIVE CONFLICT CAN END IN VICTORY, DEFEAT, TRUCE, STALE-MATE, OR A DRAW. THE ANTAGONISTS DECIDE THE OUTCOME AMONG THEMSELVES, INSOFAR AS OPPONENTS SUBMIT THEIR ISSUES TO ARBITRATION OR OBJECTIVE EVALUATION, THE SITUATION BECOMES LESS COMBATIVE.

THE PERSONAL DIMENSION

THE PERSONAL DIMENSION IS EMPHASIZED IN SITUATIONS WHERE WE WISH TO ESTAB-LISH OR MAINTAIN A CERTAIN DEGREE OF EMOTICAL CLOSENESS OR DISTANCE IN OUR RE-LATIONSHIPS WITH PEOPLE. THE NEEDS AT THE TOP OF THE DIMENSION ARE SELECTED WHEN WE RELATE TO PEOPLE WITH WARMTH, INTIMACY, AND CLOSENESS. THE NEEDS AT THE LOWER END OF THE DIMENSION ARE EXPRESSED WHEN A SITUATION CALLS FOR DISTANT, OB-JECTIVE, IMPERSONAL INTERACTION WITH OTHERS. FAMILY MEMBERS, LOVERS, AND FRIENDS USUALLY RELATE TO EACH OTHER IN PERSONAL WAYS. WE TEND TO BECOME IMPER-SONAL IN OUR ACTIONS (EVEN TOWARD THOSE WITH WHOM WE ARE OTHERWISE PERSONALLY INVOLVED) WHEN WE TRANSACT BUSINESS, MAKE OR CARRY OUT PLANS, OR COMMUNICATE OR RECEIVE NECESSARY INFORMATION.

THE COMPETITIVE DIMENSION

THE COMPETITIVE DIMENSION IS EMPHASIZED IN SITUATIONS WHERE WE WISH TO DE-VELOP COMPETENCE, SKILL, KNOWLEDGE, AND ABILITY OR WHEN WE WISH TO TEST OUR ABILITY AGAINST OUR OWN PERFORMANCE OR THE PERFORMANCE OF OTHERS. NEEDS AT THE UPPER END OF THE DIMENSION ARE ACTIVE WHEN WE ARE WORKING, LEARNING, AND COMPET-ING. NEEDS AT THE LOWER END OF THE SCALE INHIBIT US FROM ATTEMPTING TASKS OR PURSUING GOALS WHEN WE DO NOT FEEL CONFIDENT OF OUR ABILITY TO SUCCEED. TO BE

TRULY COMPETITIVE, PERFORMANCE MUST BE EVALUATED BY OBJECTIVE MEASURES OR BY THE JUDGMENT OF THOSE CONSIDERED COMPETENT TO MAKE OBJECTIVE EVALUATIONS. UNLIKE COMBATIVE STRUGGLES, WHICH USUALLY CENTER AROUND THE CONTROL OF MATERIAL WEALTH, COMPETITIVE STRIVING IS REWARDED BY SYMBOLS SUCH AS GRADES, TITLES, AND MEDALS. AND BY RESPECT AND ADMIRATION. STATUS OR RECOGNITION OBTAINED BY INTIMIDATION, FORCE OR MANIPULATION REPRESENTS COMBATIVE POWER RATHER THAN COMPETITIVE ABIL-ITY.

THERE ARE TWO IMPORTANT POINTS TO REMEMBER ABOUT YOUR PICTURE IDENTIFICA-TION TEST RESULTS AND THE INTERPRETATIONS OF YOUR RESULTS: 1) YOUR RESULTS CAN CHANGE JUST AS YOUR MOTIVATION SYSTEM CAN CHANGE. THUS, NOT ALL THE RESULTS ARE RELIABLE INDICATORS OF THE WAY YOUR MOTIVATION SYSTEM USUALLY OPERATES.

WAYS 2) IN A SYSTEM, THE SAME RESULT CAN HAVE DIFFERENT CAUSES. SO THERE ARE AL-OTHER POSSIBLE MEANINGS AND INTERPRETATIONS FOR A RESULT. IT IS BEST TO THINK OF YOUR RESULTS AS CLUES TO THE WAY YOUR MOTIVATION SYSTEM WORKS AND TO MAKE YOUR OWN INTERPRETATIONS AFTER YOU HAVE GAINED SOME UNDERSTANDING OF THE SYSTEM.

******* PART I: DIMENSION DATA *******

NEED DIFFERENTIATION SUM

YOUR NEED DIFFERENTIATION SUM, PRINTED AT THE TOP OF YOUR DIMENSION DATA, IS COMPUTED BY ADDING THE ABSOLUTE SCALE LOCATIONS (DISTANCES FROM ZERO) OF ALL 22 NEEDS IN ALL THREE DIMENSIONS. THE LARGER YOUR SCORE, THE MORE "SPACE" YOUR NEED DISTRIBUTION TAKES UP IN THE THREE DIMENSIONS.

A HIGH NEED DIFFERENTIATION SUM INDICATES SENSITIVITY TO DIFFERENCES BE-TWEEN NEEDS AND AN ABILITY TO PERCEIVE THESE DIFFERENCES IN FACIAL EXPRESSIONS. IT ALSO MEANS THAT YOUR NEED CONCEPTS ARE ORGANIZED IN A SYSTEMATIC WAY. THUS, A HIGH NEED DIFFERENTIATION SUM INDICATES AN ABILITY TO ANALYZE AND ORGANIZE MO-TIVES TO PROMOTE NEED SATISFACTION.

A LOW NEED DIFFERENTIATION SUM CAN RESULT FROM DIFFICULTY IN PERCEIVING DIFFERENCES BETWEEN NEEDS DIFFICULTY IN PERCEIVING NEEDS IN FACIAL EXPRESSIONS, AN UNUSUAL DIMENSIONAL STRUCTURE, OR A RANDOM OR CARELESS ASSIGNMENT OF NEED RATINGS.

YOUR NEED DIFFERENTIATION SUM IS 41.26 WHICH FALLS IN THE HIGH RANGE. AC-CORDING TO THIS SCORE YOU CAN ANALYZE AND DIFFERENTIATE YOUR MOTIVES VERY WELL AND YOU ARE ABLE TO ORGANIZE NEED CONCEPTS INTO THE COMMONLY SHARED THREE DIMEN-SIONAL STRUCTURE PRESENTED IN TABLE 1. THESE ABILITIES CAN HELP YOU ADAPT EF-FECTIVELY TO CHANGE AND CAN ENABLE YOU TO STRUCTURE SITUATIONS SO YOU WILL BEST SATISFY YOUR NEEDS.

DIMENSION WEIGHTS

THE NEED DIFFERENTIATION SCORES OF ALL THREE DIMENSIONS ARE ADDED TO COM-PUTE YOUR NEED DIFFERENTIATION SUM. FOR MOST PEOPLE, THE COMBATIVE DIMENSION PROVIDES APPROXIMATELY 40% OF THIS SUM. THE PERSONAL AND COMPETITIVE DIMENSIONS EACH CONTRIBUTE APPROXIMATELY 30%. THESE AVERAGE PROPORTIONS PROVIDE THE MODEL FOR A WELL BALANCED ACTIVATION STRUCTURE.

THE PERCENTAGES CONTRIBUTED BY THE THREE DIMENSIONS TO THE NEED DIFFERENTI-ATION SUM ARE CALLED THE DIMENSION WEIGHTS. FOR SOME PEOPLE THE DIMENSION WEIGHTS DIFFER FROM THE MODEL PERCENTAGES LISTED ABOVE. OVERWEIGHTED OR UNDER-WEIGHTED DIMENSIONS MAY CREATE IMBALANCES IN THE MOTIVATION SYSTEM WHICH CAN CAUSE PERSONALITY PROBLEMS. A HIGHER THAN AVERAGE DIMENSION WEIGHT REFLECTS AN

OVEREMPHASIS ON THE DIMENSION WHEREAS A LOWER THAN AVERAGE DIMENSION WEIGHT REFLECTS AN UNDEREMPHASIS ON THE DIMENSION.

YOUR DIMENSION WEIGHTS, PRINTED IN TABLE 2, INDICATE A BALANCED STRUCTURE SIMILAR TO THE MODEL. THIS STRUCTURE HELPS PREVENT OVEREMPHASIS ON ONE DIMENSION AT THE EXPENSE OF THE OTHERS. IT ALSO PROVIDES YOU WITH STRONG ALTERNATIVES FOR MEETING THE OPPORTUNITIES AND REQUIREMENTS OF SITUATIONS.

DIMENSION SCALE CORRELATIONS

TABLE 1 SHOWS THE ORDER OF THE NEEDS FOR EACH DIMENSION FOR THE TARGET MODEL AND FOR YOUR PIT RESULTS. CORRELATION COEFFICIENTS HAVE BEEN COMPUTED BETWEEN THE TARGET AND YOUR SCALE LOCATIONS OF THE NEEDS FOR EACH DIMENSION. THE CORRELATION FOR EACH DIMENSION IS PRINTED IN TABLE 2 ON THE LINE WHICH READS "DIMENSION SCALE R". THE CLOSER YOUR CORRELATION IS TO 1.00 FOR A DIMENSION, THE BETTER YOUR AGREEMENT WITH THE TARGET. IN GENERAL, HIGH AGREEMENT WITH THE TARGET FOR A DIMENSION MEANS THAT YOU HAVE YOUR NEEDS ORGANIZED IN A WAY WHICH PROMOTES EFFECTIVENESS AND SATISFACTION WHEN YOU ARE OPERATING IN THAT DIMENSION.

YOUR DIMENSION SCALE CORRELATIONS ARE 0.86 FOR THE COMBATIVE DIMENSION, 0.77 FOR THE PERSONAL DIMENSION, AND 0.67 FOR THE COMPETITIVE DIMENSION. THESE COEFFICIENTS INDICATE CLOSE CORRESPONDENCE BETWEEN YOUR DIMENSIONAL STRUCTURE AND THE TARGET MODEL. ALTHOUGH THERE MAY BE SOME SPECIFIC NEEDS OUT OF ORDER IN EACH DIMENSION, YOUR OVERALL STRUCTURE INDICATES THAT YOU GENERALLY KNOW HOW TO FUNCTION EFFECTIVELY IN EACH OF THE THREE DIMENSIONS.

DIMENSION ATTITUDE CORRELATIONS

THE BELIEFS WHICH MOST STRONGLY AFFECT YOUR PIT RESULTS ARE OF TWO TYPES. BELIEFS OF ONE TYPE ARE CALLED ASSOCIATION BELIEFS AND BELIEFS OF THE OTHER TYPE ARE CALLED ATTITUDE OF VALUE BELIEFS. ASSOCIATION BELIEFS HAVE TO DO WITH THE INTERACTION BETWEEN NEEDS. ASSOCIATION BELIEFS DETERMINE YOUR DIMENSION LOCATION OF THE NEEDS. ATTITUDE BELIEFS HAVE TO DO WITH WHETHER YOU CONSIDER THE EXPRESSION OF A NEED TO BE GENERALLY RIGHT OR WRONG, GOOD OR BAD. YOUR ATTITUDE TOWARD A NEED EXERTS A STRONG INFLUENCE ON WHETHER OR NOT YOU EXPRESS THE NEED. A POSITIVE ATTITUDE ENCOURAGES YOU TO EXPRESS THE NEED; A NEGATIVE ATTITUDE INHIBITS YOUR EXPRESSION OF THE NEED.

AN ATTITUDE SCORE IS COMPUTED FOR EACH NEED. YOUR NEED ATTITUDE SCORE IS BASED ON THE RELATIONSHIPS BETWEEN YOUR PART I RATINGS (POSITIVE-NEGATIVE QUALITIES IN THE RELATIONS) AND YOUR PART II RATINGS (STRENGTH OF EXPRESSION OF THE NEEDS). A POSITIVE RELATIONSHIP BETWEEN PART I AND PART II RATINGS PRODUCES A POSITIVE ATTITUDE SCORE FOR A NEED. AN OPPOSITE RELATIONSHIP BETWEEN PART I AND PART II RATINGS PRODUCES A NEGATIVE ATTITUDE SCORE FOR A NEED.

YOUR ATTITUDE SCORES FOR THE 22 NEEDS WERE CORRELATED WITH THE TARGET NEED LOCATIONS FOR EACH DIMENSION. THESE RESULTS ARE PRINTED IN TABLE 2 (SEE DIMENSION ATTITUDE R). BRIEF INTERPRETATIONS OF YOUR DIMENSION ATTITUDE CORRELATIONS ARE PRESENTED BELOW.

YOUR COMBATIVE DIMENSION ATTITUDE CORRELATION IS -0.68 WHICH FALLS WITHIN THE RANGE OF THE COMBATIVE DIMENSION ATTITUDE CORRELATIONS HELD BY MOST PEOPLE. TECHNICALLY, YOUR CORRELATION MEANS THAT YOUR VALUES TEND TO BE NEGATIVE TOWARD THE NEEDS AT THE TOP PART OF THE RANGE MODEL COMBATIVE DIMENSION AND POSITIVE TOWARD MOST OF THE NEEDS IN THE BOTTOM PART. MOST PEOPLE FEEL THAT IT IS GENERALLY UNDESIRABLE TO BE COMBATIVE BUT THEIR ATTITUDE IS NOT ABSOLUTE OR EXTREMELY NEGATIVE THEY SOMETIMES FEEL IT IS JUSTIFIED OR EVEN GOOD TO ASSERT THEIR WILL AND TO SEEK SATISFACTION OF THEIR OWN INTERESTS. YOUR RESULTS AGREE WITH THIS

MODERATELY NEGATIVE ATTITUDE TOWARD COMBATIVE ASSERTIVENESS.

YOUR PERSONAL DIMENSION ATTITUDE CORRELATION IS 0.09 WHICH IS LOWER THAN THE MODERATELY POSITIVE CORRELATIONS HELD BY MOST PEOPLE. TECHNICALLY, YOU TEND TO HAVE NEUTRAL OR MIXED ATTITUDES TOWARD THE NEEDS AT EITHER END OF THE TARGET MODEL PERSONAL DIMENSION. ACCORDING TO THIS RESULT, YOU DO NOT VALUE CLOSE PERSONAL TIES AS STRONGLY AS OTHERS.

YOUR COMPETITIVE DIMENSION ATTITUDE CORRELATION IS 0.02 WHICH FALLS IN THE NEUTRAL ATTITUDE CORRELATION RANGE. TECHNICALLY, YOUR CORRELATION MEANS THAT YOU HAVE NEUTRAL OR MIXED VALUES WITH REGARD TO THE NEEDS AT EITHER END OF THE TARGET MODEL COMPETITIVE DIMENSION. MOST PEOPLE HAVE A LOW BUT POSITIVE COMPETITIVE DIMENSION ATTITUDE CORRELATION. YOUR CORRELATION SUGGESTS THAT YOU HAVE SOME POSITIVE AND SOME NEGATIVE FEELINGS ABOUT IMPROVING YOUR KNOWLEDGE, SKILLS, ABILITIES, AND ACCEPTING COMPETITIVE CHALLENGES.

INTER-DIMENSION CONFUSION SCORES

EACH OF THE THREE TARGET MODEL DIMENSIONS HAVE INDEPENDENT STRUCTURES. THIS MEANS THAT THEY ARE NEITHER SIMILAR NOR OPPOSITE TO EACH OTHER AND THUS THE CORRELATIONS BETWEEN THEM ARE CLOSE TO ZERO. THE INDEPENDENCE OF THE THREE TARGET DIMENSIONS MEANS THAT THEY PROVIDE THREE DISTINCT ALTERNATIVE MODES OF ACTION FOR MEETING OUR NEEDS. THESE DIMENSIONAL MODES REPRESENT THE WAY MOST PEOPLE ORGANIZE THEIR MOTIVATION SYSTEMS.

THE CONFUSION SCORES FOR A DIMENSION DEPEND ON THE DIMENSION SCALE CORRELATIONS (SEE ABOVE AND TABLE 2). AN EXTREMELY HIGH DIMENSION SCALE CORRELATION (R GREATER THAN .90) PRECLUDES A HIGH CONFUSION SCORE FOR THAT DIMENSION. IN SUCH CASES, THE HIGH SIMILARITY TO THE INDEPENDENT TARGET MODEL LIMITS POSSIBLE CONFUSION WITH OTHER DIMENSIONS. A LOW DIMENSION SCALE CORRELATION (R LESS THAN .50) ALSO DECREASES THE POSSIBILITY OF HIGH CONFUSION SCORES. IN SUCH CASES, THE DIMENSION DOES NOT HAVE SUFFICIENT SIMILARITY TO THE TARGET MODEL TO PRODUCE CONFUSION WITH ANOTHER DIMENSION.

INDIVIDUALS DO NOT ALWAYS HAVE DIMENSION STRUCTURES WHICH ARE AS INDEPENDENT AS THE TARGET MODEL. SOMETIMES A PERSON HAS A DIMENSION WHICH IS ORGANIZED SO THAT IT IS A MIXTURE OF TWO TARGET DIMENSIONS. FOR EXAMPLE, A SUBJECT MAY HAVE A DIMENSION WHICH IS MOST LIKE THE TARGET COMBATIVE DIMENSION BUT WHICH IS ALSO SIMILAR TO THE TARGET COMPETITIVE DIMENSION. SUCH A MIXTURE OR BLEND OF DIMENSIONS IS CALLED INTER-DIMENSION CONFUSION. CONFUSION SCORES HAVE BEEN COMPUTED FOR EACH OF YOUR DIMENSIONS (SEE TABLE 2). THESE SCORES INDICATE THE DEGREE OF CONFUSION FOR EACH DIMENSION IN RELATION TO EACH OF THE OTHER TWO DIMENSIONS. A CONFUSION SCORE OF .40 OR HIGHER IS CONSIDERED SIGNIFICANT. IN CASES WHERE THERE IS A LOW DIMENSION SCALE CORRELATION, THE DIMENSION SCALE CORRELATION IS OF PRIMARY CONCERN RATHER THAN THE DIMENSION CONFUSION SCORES. IT IS DESIRABLE TO HAVE HIGH DIMENSION SCALE CORRELATIONS AND LOW INTER-DIMENSION CONFUSION SCORES.

HIGH PERSONAL-COMBATIVE CONFUSION SCORE

YOUR PERSONAL-COMBATIVE CONFUSION SCORE IS HIGH. THE HIGH SCORE IS CAUSED BY A NEGATIVE CORRELATION BETWEEN YOUR PERSONAL DIMENSION AND THE TARGET COMBATIVE DIMENSION. THE CORRELATION IS NEGATIVE WHEN THE TOP AND BOTTOM PARTS, RESPECTIVELY, OF YOUR PERSONAL DIMENSION ARE SIMILAR TO THE BOTTOM AND TOP PARTS, RESPECTIVELY, OF THE TARGET COMBATIVE DIMENSION.

THE SIMILARITY BETWEEN THE TOP PART OF YOUR PERSONAL DIMENSION AND THE BOTTOM PART OF THE TARGET COMBATIVE DIMENSION MAY CAUSE YOU TO MIX OR CONFUSE THESE TWO MODES OF INTERACTING. THE TOP PART OF THE PERSONAL DIMENSION (SEE TARGET

MODEL) IS ORGANIZED TO PROMOTE WARM, CLOSE, TRUSTING FEELINGS AND PLEASURE AND ENJOYMENT IN PERSONAL RELATIONSHIPS. THE BOTTOM PART OF THE COMBATIVE DIMENSION IS DESIGNED TO PROMOTE SUBMISSION, COMPLIANCE AND DEFERENCE TOWARD THE COMBATIVE DIMENSION SUPERIOR POWER AND AUTHORITY. THE MIXTURE OF THESE TWO MODES OF ACTION MAY CAUSE YOU TO FEEL SQUELCHED, DOMINATED, AND CONTROLLED BY THOSE WITH WHOM YOU DEVELOP CLOSE TIES. SUCH MIXED FEELINGS MAY CAUSE FEELINGS OF RESENTMENT AND REBELLION AGAINST YOUR FRIENDS, FAMILY, AND COMPANIONS.

THE SIMILARITY BETWEEN THE BOTTOM PART OF YOUR PERSONAL DIMENSION AND THE TOP PART OF THE TARGET COMBATIVE DIMENSION MAY CAUSE YOU TO BECOME ACTIVELY COMBATIVE WHEN YOU AND THOSE CLOSE TO YOU ARE CONFRONTED WITH PROBLEMS AND FRUSTRATIONS. THE LOWER PART OF THE PERSONAL DIMENSION IS DESIGNED TO HELP US RESPOND EFFECTIVELY TO SITUATIONS INVOLVING INTERPERSONAL TRANSACTIONS WHERE PEOPLE NEED TO WORK OUT THEIR DIFFERENCES AND DISAGREEMENTS IN RATIONAL, REASONABLE, ORDERLY, AND IMPERSONAL WAYS. THE UPPER PART OF THE COMBATIVE DIMENSION MOVES US TO ACT IN FORCEFUL, SELF-ASSERTIVE WAYS TO IMPOSE OUR WILL WITHOUT REGARD TO REASON OR CONCERN FOR OTHERS. IF CONFUSION OF YOUR PERSONAL AND COMBATIVE DIMENSIONS CAUSES YOU TO BECOME COMBATIVE RATHER THAN IMPERSONAL IN HANDLING YOUR DIFFERENCES WITH FAMILY, FRIENDS, AND COMPANIONS, YOUR PERSONAL RELATIONSHIPS MAY SUFFER. IT COULD ALSO MEAN THAT YOU FEEL THAT COMBATIVE FEELINGS ARE SO EXTREME AND OUT OF PLACE IN A PERSONAL RELATIONSHIP THAT YOU FIND IT DIFFICULT TO ASSERT YOUR WILL IN AN IMPERSONAL WAY AROUND THOSE CLOSE TO YOU.

HIGH COMBATIVE-COMPETITIVE CONFUSION SCORE

YOUR COMBATIVE-COMPETITIVE CONFUSION SCORE IS HIGH. THE HIGH SCORE IS CAUSED BY A POSITIVE CORRELATION BETWEEN YOUR COMBATIVE DIMENSION AND THE TARGET COMPETITIVE DIMENSION. ALTHOUGH YOUR COMBATIVE DIMENSION IS MOST LIKE THE TARGET COMBATIVE DIMENSION, IT ALSO HAS SOME SIMILARITY TO THE TARGET COMPETITIVE DIMENSION.

THE UPPER PART OF THE COMBATIVE DIMENSION (SEE TARGET MODEL) HOLDS ALL OF THE SIX EGO NEEDS. THE EGO NEEDS MOBILIZE US FOR FORCEFUL, ASSERTIVE ACTIONS AIMED AT ASSERTING OUR WILL AND EXECUTING OUR DECISIONS. TO EFFECTIVELY ASSERT OUR WILL AGAINST STRONG OPPOSITION WE MUST BE BOLD, TOUGH, HARD, DETERMINED, RESOLUTE, COURAGEOUS, AND UNDAUNTED BY RESISTANCE. ONCE WE ARE COMMITTED TO COMBATIVE ACTION WE CANNOT AFFORD TO BE DOUBTFUL, TIMID, CAUTIOUS, SENSITIVE, TENDERHEARTED, OR REFLECTIVE.

THE UPPER PART OF THE COMPETITIVE DIMENSION MOTIVATES US TO LEARN AND TO DEMONSTRATE OUR KNOWLEDGE, SKILLS, AND ABILITIES. OUR COMPETITIVE SUCCESSES ARE ATTAINED WHEN OBJECTIVE DATA OR IMPARTIAL JUDGMENT INDICATES OUR EXCELLENCE AND SUPERIORITY. COMPETITIVE SUCCESS CANNOT BE ATTAINED BY COMBATIVE THREATS AND INTIMIDATION. MUCH OF OUR COMPETITIVE ACTIVITY IS COLLABORATIVE, COOPERATIVE, BASED ON RATIONAL ANALYSIS, FEEDBACK, AND SENSITIVITY TO STYLE AND BEAUTY AS WELL AS TO EFFICIENCY.

YOUR CONFUSION OF THE COMPETITIVE DIMENSION WITH YOUR COMBATIVE DIMENSION MAY HAVE ADVERSE EFFECTS ON YOUR ABILITY TO EXECUTE DECISIONS, ASSERT YOUR WILL, AND MAINTAIN YOUR AUTONOMY. ATTEMPTING TO BE RATIONAL AND CONSIDERATE IN THE FACE OF HOSTILE ANTAGONISM MAY GIVE OPPONENTS AN ADVANTAGE AND DISTRACT YOU FROM DEFENDING YOUR OWN INTERESTS. A COMPETITIVE APPEAL TO REASON, FACTS, AND OBJECTIVE ANALYSIS IS PERCEIVED AS IRRELEVANT BY THOSE IN A COMBATIVE MOOD. IT MAY BE DESIRABLE FOR YOU TO MAKE CLEARER DISTINCTIONS BETWEEN SITUATIONS WHERE PROBLEMS CAN BE COMPETITIVELY RESOLVED BY KNOWLEDGE, WORK, AND ABILITY, AND COMBATIVE SITUATIONS WHERE STRENGTH OF RESOLVE AND USE OF POWER ARE THE PRIMARY REQUIREMENTS FOR ATTAINING YOUR GOALS.

THE LOWER PART OF THE COMBATIVE DIMENSION HOLDS A VARIETY OF NEEDS. ALL OF

WHICH SERVE TO LIMIT, CONTROL, AND INHIBIT COMBATIVE ASSERTIVENESS. THESE NEEDS PROVIDE NON-COMBATIVE ALTERNATIVES TO COMBATIVE ACTION. FEAR OF BLAME AND HARM, NEED FOR FURTHER KNOWLEDGE AND UNDERSTANDING, NEED TO ORGANIZE RESOURCES, CONCERN FOR THE WELL-BEING OF OTHERS, RESPECT FOR AUTHORITY, AND AWARENESS OF WEAKNESS AND DEPENDENCY, DESIRES TO WORK CONSTRUCTIVELY, AND NEED FOR SELF-IMPROVEMENT ARE SOME OF THE MOTIVES FOR NOT BEING COMBATIVE WHICH ARE LOCATED IN THE LOWER PART OF THE COMBATIVE DIMENSION.

THE CONTROLS AND ALTERNATIVES FOR COMPETITIVE STRIVING ARE SIMPLER AND LESS VARIED THAN THE CONTROLS FOR COMBATIVE ASSERTION. THE NEEDS IN THE LOWER PART OF THE COMPETITIVE DIMENSION MOVE US AWAY FROM COMPETITION WHEN THERE IS REASON TO FEAR FAILURE, BLAME, HARM, AND WHEN WE ARE AWARE OF OUR WEAKNESSES. MOVES US (ACCESS) GUIDANCE, BLAME HELP RATHER THAN RELY ON OUR OWN SKILLS AND ABILITIES. THE AGGRESSION NEED IS ALSO LOCATED IN THE LOWER PART OF THE COMPETITIVE DIMENSION (AGGRESSION IS AT THE TOP OF THE COMBATIVE DIMENSION). AGGRESSION IS TOO HIGHLY COMBATIVE AND DESTRUCTIVE TO COMBINE WITH THE RATIONAL, CREATIVE, LEARNING NEEDS WHICH MOTIVATE COMPETITIVE STRIVING.

YOUR CONFUSION OF THE COMBATIVE AND COMPETITIVE DIMENSION MAY HAVE ADVERSE EFFECTS ON YOUR ABILITY TO ACT EFFECTIVELY AND APPROPRIATELY WHEN YOU WISH TO OPERATE FROM THE LOWER PART OF THE COMBATIVE DIMENSION AND AVOID COMBATIVE IN-VOLVEMENT. BECAUSE COMBATIVE ACTIONS CAN HAVE SUCH SERIOUS CONSEQUENCES (FOR OTHERS AS WELL AS OURSELVES) WE NEED A GREATER VARIETY OF CONTROLS AND ALTERNA-TIVES FOR COMBATIVE MOTIVES THAN WE NEED FOR COMPETITIVE MOTIVES. SOME OF THE COMBATIVE CONTROLS WHICH MAY BE LOST OR WEAKENED BY COMBATIVE-COMPETITIVE CON-FUSION ARE NEEDS FOR RATIONAL ANALYSIS OF SITUATIONS, NEED TO ORGANIZE OUR RE-SOURCES, FEELINGS OF FRIENDLINESS AND CONCERN FOR OTHERS, DESIRES FOR HARMONY, AND NEED FOR SELF-IMPROVEMENT. BETTER DIFFERENTIATION OF YOUR COMBATIVE AND COMPETITIVE DIMENSIONS CAN HELP YOU STRENGTHEN YOUR ALTERNATIVES TO COMBATIVE INVOLVEMENT.

HIGH COMPETITIVE-COMBATIVE CONFUSION SCORE

YOUR COMPETITIVE-COMBATIVE CONFUSION SCORE IS HIGH. THE HIGH SCORE IS CAUSED BY A POSITIVE CORRELATION BETWEEN YOUR COMPETITIVE DIMENSION AND THE TAR-GET COMBATIVE DIMENSION. ALTHOUGH YOUR COMPETITIVE DIMENSION IS MOST LIKE THE TARGET COMPETITIVE DIMENSION, IT ALSO HAS SOME SIMILARITY TO THE TARGET COMBA-TIVE DIMENSION.

IN THE FIRST STAGES OF COMPETITIVE DEVELOPMENT (SEE TARGET MODEL) WE ORGAN-IZE OUR RESOURCES AND WORK TO LEARN AND ACQUIRE KNOWLEDGE AND SKILL. OUR PROG-RESS IS USUALLY ENHANCED IF THERE IS PERSONAL INVOLVEMENT WITH OUR INSTRUCTORS AND FELLOW LEARNERS. COLLABORATION, COOPERATION, AND PLAYFUL COMPETITION PRO-MOTE LEARNING. A CERTAIN AMOUNT OF EGO-INVOLVEMENT IS ALSO IMPORTANT TO INSURE COMMITMENT TO COMPETITIVE GOALS BUT ANTAGONISTIC EGO NEEDS SUCH AS AGGRESSION AND REJECTION ARE NOT A PART OF COMPETITIVE EGO-INVOLVEMENT. COMPETITIVE DEVEL-OPMENT CULMINATES IN THE EXPRESSION OF THE NEEDS AT THE TOP OF THE COMPETITIVE DIMENSION WHICH MOTIVATE US TO ASSERT LEADERSHIP AND SEEK RECOGNITION FOR OUR KNOWLEDGE AND ABILITIES.

THE UPPER PART OF THE COMBATIVE DIMENSION HAS A SIMPLE STRUCTURE AS COM-PARED TO THE UPPER PART OF THE COMPETITIVE DIMENSION. ALL SIX OF THE EGO NEEDS ARE CLUSTERED IN THE TOP PART OF THE COMBATIVE DIMENSION. THESE NEEDS COMBINE TO MOBILIZE OUR WILL POWER AND DETERMINATION. TOWARD THE MIDDLE OF THE COMBA-TIVE DIMENSION ARE NEEDS (INFERIORITY AVOIDANCE, EXHIBITION, AND PLAY) WHICH MODERATE BUT DO NOT INHIBIT COMBATIVE ASSERTION. THUS, COMBATIVENESS DIFFERS FROM COMPETITIVENESS IN THAT IT IS MORE MILITANT AND IT LACKS THE PERSONAL AND RATIONAL CONCERNS OF THE COMPETITIVE MODE. IN COMPETITION WE CAN BE CONCERNED WITH REASONABLENESS AND COOPERATION AS WELL AS ACCOMPLISHMENT.

MAY HAVE ADVERSE EFFECTS ON YOUR ABILITY TO FUNCTION EFFECTIVELY WHEN YOU ARE
BEING TESTED OR ATTEMPTING TO LEARN, PERFORM, OR WORK. YOU MAY "ATTACK" WORK
WITH TOO MUCH OF A COMBATIVE ATTITUDE. YOU MAY BE IMPATIENT AND TOO READY TO
USE FORCE INSTEAD OF CAREFUL ANALYSIS AND PERSEVERANCE WHEN YOU ENCOUNTER FRUS-
TRATION IN YOUR COMPETITIVE EFFORTS. YOU MAY BE MORE EGO-ORIENTED THAN TASK-
ORIENTED IN YOUR WORK. YOU MAY HAVE LOST SOME OF YOUR CONCERN FOR OTHERS IN
YOUR DESIRES TO ATTAIN SUCCESS. IT MAY HELP YOU IN YOUR COMPETITIVE ENDEAVORS
TO BECOME MORE AWARE OF THE DIFFERENCES BETWEEN THE COMBATIVE USE OF FORCE TO
ASSERT YOUR WILL AND THE COMPETITIVE DEVELOPMENT OF SKILL AND KNOWLEDGE TO A-
CHIEVE A GOAL.

THE LOWER PART OF THE COMBATIVE DIMENSION IS MORE COMPLEX THAN THE LOWER
PART OF THE COMPETITIVE DIMENSION. THERE ARE MORE REASONS FOR CHOOSING NOT TO
ACT COMBATIVELY THAN FOR WITHDRAWING FROM COMPETITIVE CHALLENGES. NON-COMBATIVE
MOTIVES INCLUDE MOST OF THE NON-COMPETITIVE MOTIVES PLUS THE RATIONAL NEEDS
(NEEDS TO STOP AND THINK, PLAN, AND ORGANIZE BEFORE TAKING COMBATIVE ACTION).

YOUR CONFUSION OF THE COMBATIVE DIMENSION WITH THE COMPETITIVE DIMENSION
MAY CAUSE YOU TO BE UNNECESSARILY INHIBITED WITH REGARD TO TAKING COMPETITIVE
RISKS. THE MAJOR REASONS FOR REJECTING A COMPETITIVE CHALLENGE ARE: PREDIC-
TABLE FAILURE WITH SERIOUS NEGATIVE CONSEQUENCES; NEED FOR HELP AND GUIDANCE BE-
FORE ATTEMPTING A GOAL, AND SHORTCOMINGS AND DEFICIENCIES WHICH RULE OUT THE
POSSIBILITY OF SUCCESS. IF ADDITIONAL INHIBITORS FROM THE COMBATIVE DIMENSION
BECOME CONFUSED WITH YOUR COMPETITIVE INHIBITORS, YOU MAY BE TOO CAUTIOUS ABOUT
UNDERTAKING COMPETITIVE CHALLENGES.

****** PART II: NEED DATA ******

THE FIRST PART OF YOUR PIT INTERPRETATION IS BASED ON A MULTIDIMENSIONAL
SCALING ANALYSIS. THIS DIMENSION DATA PROVIDES AN OVERALL VIEW OF HOW YOUR
NEEDS OPERATE IN A THREE DIMENSION SYSTEM. PART II OF YOUR INTERPRETATION IS
BASED ON MORE SPECIFIC ANALYSES OF EACH OF THE 22 NEEDS TO SEE HOW EFFECTIVELY
EACH NEED IS FUNCTIONING IN YOUR MOTIVATION SYSTEM.

EACH NEED RECEIVE FOUR SCORES. THE FOUR SCORES ARE CALLED: 1) THE CENTRAL
-PERIPHERAL SCORE, 2) THE EGO SCORE, 3) THE ASSOCIATION DEVIATION SCORE, AND 4)
THE JUDGMENT SCORE. THESE SCORES ARE NOT ENTIRELY INDEPENDENT OF EACH OTHER BUT
THEY ARE SUFFICIENTLY DIFFERENT TO MAKE IT WORTHWHILE TO REPORT YOUR RESULTS FOR
EACH ONE. ALL FOUR SCORES ARE COMBINED TO PRODUCE A FIFTH SCORE CALLED THE
PROBLEM NEED SCORE. THE PROBLEM NEED SCORE IS AN OVERALL MEASURE WHICH INDI-
CATES NEEDS THAT MIGHT BE SOURCES OF FRUSTRATION AND CONFLICT FOR YOU.

THE CENTRAL-PERIPHERAL (CENTER) SCORE

IT IS POSSIBLE TO MAKE A THREE DIMENSION SPATIAL MODEL OF YOUR NEED SYSTEM
FROM THE DATA PRESENTED IN TABLE I. THIS THREE DIMENSIONAL SPATIAL MODEL MAY
BE THOUGHT OF AS A "CONSTELLATION" OF NEEDS. IF CONSTRUCTED, SUCH A CONSTEL-
LATION WOULD VISUALLY SHOW WHICH NEEDS ARE LOCATED IN THE CENTER AND WHICH ARE
AT THE EDGES OR PERIPHERY OF THE CONSTELLATION.

IN A CONSTELLATION PROVIDED BY THE TARGET MODEL, EACH NEED HAS ITS OWN
SPECIAL LOCATION. THE CENTER SCORE INDICATES WHICH, IF ANY, OF YOUR NEEDS ARE
LOCATED DIFFERENTLY FROM THIS TARGET MODEL IN TERMS OF BEING CLOSER TO THE CEN-
TER OR FURTHER OUT IN THE PERIPHERY.

NEEDS WHICH ARE TOO CENTRAL

CENTRALLY LOCATED NEEDS ARE MORE CLOSELY ASSOCIATED WITH OTHER NEEDS, ON THE AVERAGE THAN NEEDS AT THE PERIPHERY. AS A RESULT, CENTRAL NEEDS ARE ACTIVATED AND EXPERIENCED MORE FREQUENTLY THAN PERIPHERAL NEEDS. THEY ARE "IN THE CENTER OF OF THINGS".

WHEN A NEED WHICH IS NOT CENTRALLY LOCATED IN THE TARGET MODEL, BECOMES CENTRALIZED IN AN INDIVIDUAL'S MOTIVATION SYSTEM, THERE ARE USUALLY TWO CONSEQUENCES. ONE CONSEQUENCE IS THAT THE NEED BECOMES MORE FREQUENTLY ACTIVATED AND EXPERIENCED. THE SECOND CONSEQUENCE IS THAT PROBLEMS WITH THE NEED MAY DEVELOP BECAUSE OF UNUSUAL NEED ASSOCIATIONS WHICH MAY BE FORMED AS A RESULT OF THE UNUSUAL LOCATION OF THE NEED.

TO COPE WITH THESE CONSEQUENCES, PEOPLE SOMETIMES ATTEMPT TO SUPPRESS AN OVERLY CENTRALIZED NEED BY COVERING OR CONCEALING IT WITH OTHER MOTIVES. THEY MAY ALSO DEVELOP DISGUISED OR CONCEALED WAYS OF EXPRESSING THE NEED. BECAUSE IT IS SO FREQUENTLY ACTIVATED, PEOPLE SOMETIMES GET USED TO AN OVERLY CENTRALIZED NEED AND LOSE AWARENESS OF IT.

IT WILL BE HELPFUL FOR YOU TO BECOME MORE AWARE OF YOUR OVERLY CENTRALIZED NEEDS. THIS WILL ENABLE YOU TO MOVE THEM BACK TO THEIR LESS CENTRAL NATURAL LOCATIONS (SEE TARGET MODEL, TABLE 1) WHICH WILL PREVENT THEM FROM INTRUDING INTO MANY SITUATIONS WHERE THEY ARE NOT APPROPRIATE.

BELOW IS A LIST OF NEEDS YOU HAVE LOCATED MORE CENTRALLY THAN MOST PEOPLE:

(UND) UNDERSTANDING: THE NEED TO LEARN, UNDERSTAND, AND FIND THE MEANING OF THINGS.
(ORD) ORDER: THE NEED TO SYSTEMATIZE, ORGANIZE, AND PUT THINGS IN ORDER.

NEEDS WHICH ARE TOO PERIPHERAL

PERIPHERAL NEEDS ARE MORE DISTANTLY ASSOCIATED WITH OTHER NEEDS, ON THE AVERAGE, THAN CENTRAL NEEDS. THEY ARE THUS PERCEIVED AS EXTREME AND SOMEWHAT ALIEN MOTIVES WHICH DO NOT ASSOCIATE OR COMBINE WELL WITH MOST OTHER NEEDS. THEY ARE CONSIDERED TO BE APPROPRIATE FOR EXPRESSION ONLY ON RARE AND UNUSUAL OCCASIONS. THEY ARE ALSO SOMETIMES PERCEIVED AS REQUIRING EXTREME OR UNUSUAL BEHAVIORAL EXPRESSION.

INHIBITIVE NEEDS (E.G. HARM AVOIDANCE, BLAME AVOIDANCE, DEFERENCE) WHICH ARE TOO PERIPHERAL CAN HAVE DIFFERENT KINDS OF NEGATIVE EFFECTS ON OUR MOTIVATION SYSTEM. MUCH OF THE TIME THEY ARE INACTIVE AND INEFFECTIVE AS INHIBITORS BECAUSE THEY ARE EXTREMELY DISTANT. HOWEVER, WHEN THEY DO BECOME ACTIVATED THEY EXERT AN EXTREME INHIBITIVE EFFECT SINCE THEY DRAW MOTIVATION SO FAR AWAY FROM OTHER NEEDS.

IF YOU HAVE LOCATED A NEED FURTHER OUT TOWARD THE PERIPHERY THAN ITS TARGET MODEL LOCATION, IT MAY BE A SIGN THAT YOU HAVE PROBLEMS WITH THE NEED AND WOULD LIKE TO DO AWAY WITH THE PROBLEMS BY REMOVING THE NEED. UNFORTUNATELY, THIS OUT-OF-SIGHT OUT-OF-MIND STRATEGY CAN HAVE NEGATIVE CONSEQUENCES. UNFORTUNATELY THIS ALIENATE A NEED WHICH SHOULD BE READILY AVAILABLE TO YOU. YOU LOSE THE MOTIVATION NECESSARY TO COPE WITH SITUATIONS WHERE THE NEED IS APPROPRIATE.

CAN EVEN NEEDS WHICH ARE PERIPHERALLY LOCATED IN THE TARGET MODEL CONSTELLATION CAN BE MOVED EVEN FURTHER OUT SO THAT THE NEEDS BECOME TOO DETACHED AND ALIENATED FROM THE REST OF YOUR MOTIVATION SYSTEM TO BE USEFUL. IT WILL BE HELPFUL FOR YOU, WHEN CORRECTING FOR A NEED WHICH HAS BECOME TOO PERIPHERAL, TO DEVELOP LESS EXTREME WAYS TO EXPRESS THE NEED SO IT CAN BECOME AVAILABLE TO YOU IN SITUATIONS WHICH CALL FOR MODERATE EXPRESSION OF THE NEED.

(BLA) BLAME AVOIDANCE: THE NEED TO AVOID DOING THINGS WHICH MIGHT AROUSE CRITICISM OR DISAPPROVAL.
(AFF) AFFILIATION: THE NEED TO BE FRIENDLY AND SOCIABLE.
(ABA) ABASEMENT: THE NEED TO ADMIT FAULTS AND WEAKNESSES.

THE EGO SCORES

IN MOTIVATION TERMS, THE EGO CAN BE DEFINED AS A SET OF NEEDS WHICH HAS THE PRIMARY FUNCTION OF MOTIVATING US TO ASSERT OUR WILL, PROTECT AND ENHANCE OUR BASIC INTERESTS, AND EXECUTE THE CHOICES OF OUR DECIDER. IN THE COMBATIVE DIMENSION, THE EGO NEEDS ARE LOCATED ON A DISTINCT CLUSTER IN THE UPPER PART OF THE DIMENSION (SEE TARGET MODEL, TABLE I). THEY FUNCTION LESS AS A UNIT AND ARE MORE DISPERSED IN THE PERSONAL AND COMPETITIVE DIMENSIONS. THE EGO NEEDS ARE: AUTONOMY, AGGRESSION, DEFENDANCE, REJECTION, DOMINANCE, AND SEX. THESE SIX NEEDS COMBINE TO HELP US ASSERT OUR WILL OVER OTHERS AND OVER OUR ENVIRONMENT. THEY PROVIDE US WITH "WILL POWER".

MOST OF THE NON-EGO NEEDS CAN ACT AS CHECKS, CONTROLS, AND ALTERNATIVES TO THE EGO NEEDS. ATTITUDES AND VALUES ALSO HELP CONTROL THE EGO. PEOPLE TEND TO HOLD NEGATIVE ATTITUDES TOWARD THE EGO NEEDS WHICH HELP INHIBIT EGO IMPULSES. WELL AROUSED PEOPLE HAVE STRONG EGOS BUT THEY ALSO HAVE STRONG CONTROLS TO KEEP THEM FROM BECOMING EGOCENTRIC.

AS IS TRUE FOR ALL THE NEEDS IN THE MOTIVATION SYSTEM, THE EGO NEEDS HAVE AN OPTIMAL DEGREE OF ASSOCIATION AND DIFFERENTIATION. THE EGO NEEDS ARE MORE CLOSELY ASSOCIATED THAN MOST OTHER NEEDS BUT IF THEY BECOME TOO CLOSELY ASSOCIATED THEY BECOME TOO SIMILAR TO MAKE INDIVIDUAL CONTRIBUTIONS TO EGO FUNCTIONS. AN UNDIFFERENTIATED SET OF EGO NEEDS TENDS TO PRODUCE PRIMITIVE, CHILDISH, IRRESPONSIBLE, IRRITABLE, STUBBORN, SELF-CENTERED, WILLFUL BEHAVIOR. IN EXTREME CASES, BEHAVIOR BECOMES ANTISOCIAL.

WHEN THE EGO NEEDS ARE TOO DISTANTLY ASSOCIATED THEY BECOME ISOLATED FROM EACH OTHER AND CANNOT PROVIDE THE MUTUAL SUPPORT NECESSARY TO MAINTAIN EFFECTIVE FUNCTIONING. WHEN THIS DEVELOPS IN PEOPLE THEY BECOME VAGUE, UNDIRECTED, IN- CONSISTENT, CONFUSED, AND SUGGESTIBLE. SUCH "SPREAD OUT" EGO NEEDS CAN ALSO CAUSE PEOPLE TO BECOME TOO EGO-INVOLVED IN TOO MANY THINGS.

YOUR ASSOCIATIONS BETWEEN ALL SIX OF THE EGO NEEDS FALL WITHIN THE BOUND- ARIES SET BY THE TARGET MODEL. THIS INDICATES THAT YOUR EGO NEEDS ARE WELL IN- TEGRATED BY MUTUALLY SUPPORTIVE. THEY CAN THEREFORE FUNCTION EFFECTIVELY AS A UNIT TO HELP YOU ASSERT YOUR WILL AND PROTECT YOUR VITAL INTERESTS.

INTERACTION BETWEEN EGO AND NON-EGO NEEDS

EACH OF THE NON-EGO NEEDS HAS A SPECIAL RELATIONSHIP WITH THE SET OF EGO NEEDS. IN MOST CASES, THE RELATIONSHIP IS ONE OF DISTANT ASSOCIATION WHICH MEANS THAT THE NON-EGO NEEDS PROVIDE US WITH MOTIVES WHICH MAY BE USED AS ALTER- NATIVES TO EGO ASSERTION. IF WE CHOOSE EGO ASSERTION IN A SITUATION, THE NON- EGO NEEDS ARE SUPPRESSED. IF WE CHOOSE EGO ASSERTION IN A SITUATION, THE NON- SION IS INHIBITED. WHEN NON-EGO NEEDS BECOME TOO CLOSELY ASSOCIATED, EGO EXPRES- NEEDS, AN ATTACHMENT IS FORMED WHICH DOES NOT ALLOW FREE EXPRESSION OF EITHER SET OF NEEDS. THIS LACK OF PROPER DIFFERENTIATION ALSO LIMITS USE OF OUR JUDG- MENT IN MAKING DECISIONS.

BELOW ARE LISTED DEFINITIONS AND INTERPRETATIONS OF THE NON-EGO NEEDS FOR WHICH YOU DO NOT HAVE THE OPTIMAL ASSOCIATION DISTANCES TO THE EGO NEEDS. IN MOST CASES THESE NEEDS ARE TOO CLOSELY ASSOCIATED WITH THE EGO NEEDS. IN SOME

CASES THE INTERPRETATIONS ARE FOR NEEDS WHICH YOU HAVE ASSOCIATED TOO DISTANTLY FROM THE EGO NEEDS.

** COUNTERACTION (THE NEED TO IMPROVE ONESELF AND CORRECT MISTAKES AND SHORTCOMINGS)

THE COUNTERACTION NEED IS AIMED AT CORRECTING NEGATIVE CHARACTERISTICS IN OURSELVES. THIS AIM RUNS COUNTER TO THE EGO NEEDS WHICH MOVE US TO MAKE CHANGES IN OUR EXTERNAL WORLD AND ENVIRONMENT. THE TIME TO WORK ON SELF IMPROVEMENT IS NOT THE TIME TO BATTLE WITH THE WORLD. IF THE COUNTERACTION NEED IS TOO CLOSELY ASSOCIATED WITH THE EGO NEEDS, CONFLICTS BETWEEN THESE OPPOSING NEEDS MAY INTERFERE WITH EFFECTIVE EGO ASSERTION. LACK OF DIFFERENTIATION BETWEEN THE COUNTERACTION AND EGO NEEDS MAY ALSO LEAD TO HARSH, PUNITIVE ATTEMPTS AT SELF IMPROVEMENT. THIS COMBINATION CAN CAUSE RESENTMENT AGAINST OURSELVES, LOWERED SELF ESTEEM, AND DISCOURAGEMENT.

**UNDERSTANDING (THE NEED TO LEARN, UNDERSTAND, AND FIND THE MEANING OF THINGS)

WHEN WE SEEK UNDERSTANDING WE ARE OCCUPIED WITH RECEIVING INFORMATION AND ANALYZING EVENTS AND DATA. EGO ASSERTION, OR THE EXECUTION OF DECISIONS, SHOULD FOLLOW ANALYSIS OF A SITUATION. THERE IS A TIME TO THINK AND PLAN AND A TIME TO DECIDE AND ACT. THUS, A LACK OF DIFFERENTIATION BETWEEN THE UNDERSTANDING AND THE EGO NEEDS CAN CREATE CONFUSION, INDECISION, OBSESSIVE DOUBTING AND COMBATIVE FANTASIES.

THE ASSOCIATION DEVIATION SCORE

IN THE TARGET MODEL, EACH NEED HAS A CERTAIN ASSOCIATION DISTANCE FROM EACH OF THE 21 OTHER NEEDS. THE DIFFERENCES BETWEEN YOUR ASSOCIATION DISTANCES FOR A NEED AND THE CORRESPONDING TARGET DISTANCES ARE SUMMED TO PRODUCE AN ASSOCIATION DEVIATION SCORE FOR EACH NEED. IN GENERAL, NEEDS WITH HIGH-ASSOCIATION DEVIATION SCORES ARE APT TO BE SOURCES OF CONFLICT AND FRUSTRATION.

BELOW ARE LISTED NEEDS WHICH HAVE SIGNIFICANTLY HIGH ASSOCIATION DEVIATION SCORES AS COMPUTED FROM YOUR PIT RESULTS:

(BLA) BLAME AVOIDANCE: THE NEED TO AVOID DOING THINGS WHICH MIGHT AROUSE CRITICISM OR DISAPPROVAL.
(AFF) AFFILIATION: THE NEED TO BE FRIENDLY AND SOCIABLE.

THE NEEC JUDGMENT SCORE

IN PART II OF THE PIT YOU RATED EACH NEED AS TO HOW STRONGLY YOU FELT IT WAS EXPRESSED IN EACH OF THE 12 PICTURES. YOUR RATING HAVE BEEN CORRELATED WITH THE AVERAGED RATINGS OF THE TARGET GROUPS TO SEE HOW YOUR PERCEPTUALS JUDGMENT OF THE EXPRESSION OF EACH NEED AGREES WITH THE JUDGMENT OF OTHERS. A JUDGMENT CORRELATION OF .70 OR HIGHER SHOWS VERY GOOD AGREEMENT OF THE FS. TARGET. CORRELATION BETWEEN .50 AND .70 SHOW GOOD AGREEMENT. CORRELATIONS BETWEEN .50 AND .30 SHOW FAIR TO POOR AGREEMENT AND CORRELATIONS BELOW .30 SHOW LITTLE OR NO AGREEMENT.

IN GENERAL, PEOPLE WITH HIGH JUDGMENT CORRELATIONS FOR NEEDS SATISFY THEIR NEEDS MORE EFFECTIVELY THAN DO PEOPLE WITH LOW CORRELATIONS. A HIGH JUDGMENT CORRELATION FOR A NEED MEANS THAT YOU INTERPRET EXTERNAL CUES FOR THE NEED IN MUCH THE SAME WAY OTHERS DO, AND SO YOU ARE GENERALLY IN AGREEMENT WITH OTHERS AS TO WHEN THE NEED IS APPROPRIATE AND WHEN IT IS NOT. A LOW JUDGMENT CORRELATION FOR A NEED MEANS THAT YOU INTERPRET THE WORDS USED TO DEFINE THE NEED DIFFERENTLY FROM OTHERS OR THAT YOU PERCEIVE THE FACIAL EXPRESSIONS DIFFERENTLY FROM OTHERS WITH REFERENCE TO THE NEED. PEOPLE CAN USUALLY SHARPEN THEIR PERCEPTUAL JUDGMENTS PERTAINING TO A NEED BY MAKING A CONSCIOUS EFFORT TO BECOME

MORE AWARE OF SITUATIONAL FACTORS WHICH ELICIT OR INHIBIT THE NEED.

BELOW ARE LISTED THE THREE NEEDS WHICH RECEIVED YOUR HIGHEST JUDGMENT COR-
RELATIONS AND THE THREE WHICH RECEIVED YOUR LOWEST JUDGMENT CORRELATIONS.

NEEDS WITH HIGHEST JUDGMENT SCORES

JUDGMENT R	NEED
0.82	(ACH) ACHIEVEMENT: THE NEED TO WORK HARD TO ATTAIN GOALS.
0.81	(AUT) AUTONOMY: THE NEED TO BE FREE, INDEPENDENT, AND UNINHIBITED.
0.79	(DFD) DEFENDANCE: THE NEED TO STAND UP FOR ONE'S RIGHTS AND DEFEND ONESELF

NEEDS WITH LOWEST JUDGMENT SCORES

JUDGMENT R	NEED
0.29	(UND) UNDERSTANDING: THE NEED TO LEARN, UNDERSTAND, AND FIND THE MEANING OF THINGS.
0.35	(INF) INFERIORITY AVOIDANCE: THE NEED TO AVOID FAILURE, INADEQUACY, AND INFERIORITY.
0.32	(SEN) SENTIENCE: THE NEED TO APPRECIATE THE BEAUTY AND HARMONY OF ONE'S SURROUNDINGS.

PROBLEM NEED SCORES

A PROBLEM SCORE IS COMPUTED FOR EACH NEED. THE PROBLEM SCORE IS MADE UP OF
WEIGHTED CONTRIBUTIONS FROM THE SUPER-EGO, ASSOCIATION DEVIATION, AND JUDGMENT
SCORES. THE PROBLEM SCORE IS THE BEST INDICATOR OF HOW WELL EACH NEED FITS INTO
THE OVERALL PATTERN OF YOUR MOTIVATION SYSTEM. THE HIGHER THE PROBLEM SCORE FOR
A NEED, THE GREATER THE POSSIBILITY OF CONFLICTS AND FRUSTRATIONS RELATED TO THE
NEED.

PROBLEM SCORES OF 2.00 OR HIGHER ARE CONSIDERED SIGNIFICANT SCORES WHICH
INDICATE POSSIBLE PROBLEMS. ALL 22 NEED HAVE BEEN ORDERED FROM THE NEED WITH
THE LARGEST PROBLEM SCORE TO THE NEED WITH THE SMALLEST. THIS ORDERED LIST IS
PRINTED BELOW.

A CLIENT READING PAPER IS AVAILABLE FOR EACH OF THE 22 NEEDS. IT MAY BE
HELPFUL TO YOU TO READ THE PAPERS ABOUT NEEDS WHICH HAVE A PROBLEM NEED SCORE
OF 2.00 OR HIGHER.

PROBLEM SCORE	NEED
4.47	(BLA) BLAME AVOIDANCE: THE NEED TO AVOID DOING THINGS WHICH MIGHT AROUSE CRITICISM OR DISAPPROVAL.
3.51	(AFF) AFFILIATION: THE NEED TO BE FRIENDLY AND SOCIABLE.
2.97	(UND) UNDERSTANDING: THE NEED TO LEARN, UNDERSTAND, AND FIND THE MEANING OF THINGS.
2.02	(ABA) ABASEMENT: THE NEED TO ADMIT FAULT AND WEAKNESSES.
1.68	(HAR) HARM AVOIDANCE: THE NEED TO AVOID HARM AND DANGER.
1.63	(ORD) ORDER: THE NEED TO SYSTEMATIZE, ORGANIZE, AND PUT THINGS IN ORDER.
1.62	(CNT) COUNTERACTION: THE NEED TO IMPROVE AND CORRECT MISTAKES AND SHORTCOMINGS.
1.37	(INF) INFERIORITY AVOIDANCE: THE NEED TO AVOID FAILURE, INADEQUACY, AND INFERIORITY.
1.28	(SEN) SENTIENCE: THE NEED TO APPRECIATE THE BEAUTY AND HARMONY OF ONE'S SURROUNDINGS.
1.24	(SUC) SUCCORANCE: THE NEED TO RECEIVE HELP, SUPPORT, AND ASSISTANCE.
1.20	(AGG) AGGRESSION: THE NEED TO BE FORCEFUL AND CRITICIZE OR ATTACK OTHERS.
1.02	(DOM) DOMINANCE: THE NEED TO ASSERT LEADERSHIP AND ACT IN A COMMANDING AND PERSUASIVE WAY.
0.96	(SEX) SEX: THE NEED TO SATISFY SEXUAL DESIRES.
0.93	(AUT) AUTONOMY: THE NEED TO BE FREE, INDEPENDENT, AND UNINHIBITED.
0.75	(PLA) PLAY: THE NEED TO PLAY, HAVE FUN, AND ENJOY ONESELF.
0.74	(EXH) EXHIBITION: THE NEED TO EXPRESS IDEAS AND EXHIBIT ONE'S TALENTS AND ABILITIES.

```
0.71   (GRA)  GRATITUDE: THE NEED TO BE APPRECIATIVE, THANKFUL, AND GRATEFUL.
0.65   (DEF)  DEFERENCE: THE NEED TO FOLLOW THE ADVICE AND GUIDANCE OF THOSE WITH EXPERIENCE AND AUTHORITY.
0.49   (NUR)  NURTURANCE: THE NEED TO GIVE AID AND COMFORT TO OTHERS.
0.43   (REJ)  REJECTION: THE NEED TO RESIST PRESSURES TO DO THINGS ONE DOES NOT WISH TO DO.
0.24   (DFD)  DEFENDANCE: THE NEED TO STAND UP FOR ONE'S RIGHTS AND DEFEND ONESELF
       (ACH)  ACHIEVEMENT: THE NEED TO WORK HARD TO ATTAIN GOALS.
```

SUMMARY

YOUR MOST IMPORTANT NEGATIVE RESULTS ARE SUMMARIZED BELOW. YOU MAY REFER BACK TO THE INTERPRETATIONS OF THESE RESULTS TO FURTHER YOUR AWARENESS AND UNDERSTANDING OF POSSIBLE PROBLEM AREAS THEY MAY REPRESENT.

YOUR PERSONAL-COMBATIVE CONFUSION SCORE IS HIGH.
YOUR COMBATIVE-COMPETITIVE CONFUSION SCORE IS HIGH.
YOUR COMPETITIVE-COMBATIVE CONFUSION SCORE IS HIGH.

THE THREE NEEDS WHICH RECEIVED YOUR HIGHEST PROBLEM NEED SCORES ARE LISTED BELOW. CHECK BACK IN PART II OF YOUR INTERPRETATION FOR STATEMENTS ABOUT THE CENTER, EGO, ASSOCIATION DEVIATION, OR JUDGEMENT SCORES WHICH MAY HAVE CONTRI- BUTED TO THESE PROBLEM NEED SCORES.

(BLA) BLAME AVOIDANCE: THE NEED TO AVOID DOING THINGS WHICH MIGHT AROUSE CRITICISM OR DISAPPROVAL.
(AFF) AFFILIATION: THE NEED TO BE FRIENDLY AND SOCIABLE.
(UND) UNDERSTANDING: THE NEED TO LEARN, UNDERSTAND, AND FIND THE MEANING OF THINGS.

POSITIVE FINDINGS

IT IS JUST AS IMPORTANT TO CULTIVATE YOUR POSITIVE QUALITIES AS TO CORRECT NEGATIVE ASPECTS OF YOUR PERSONALITY. YOUR MOST IMPORTANT POSITIVE RESULTS ARE SUMMARIZED BELOW :

YOUR NEED DIFFERENTIATION SUM IS HIGH.
YOUR COMBATIVE DIMENSION SCALE CORRELATION IS HIGH.
YOUR PERSONAL DIMENSION SCALE CORRELATION IS HIGH.
YOUR COMPETITIVE DIMENSION SCALE CORRELATION IS HIGH.
YOUR DIMENSION WEIGHT PERCENT SCORES SHOW A BALANCED DISTRIBUTION.
YOUR COMBATIVE-PERSONAL CONFUSION SCORE IS LOW.
YOUR PERSONAL-COMPETITIVE CONFUSION SCORE IS LOW.
YOUR COMPETITIVE-PERSONAL CONFUSION SCORE IS LOW.

THE THREE NEEDS WHICH RECEIVED YOUR LOWEST PROBLEM NEED SCORES ARE LISTED BELOW. THESE ARE THE NEEDS WHICH YOU SATISFY MOST EFFECTIVELY, ACCORDING TO YOUR PIT RESULTS.

(ACH) ACHIEVEMENT: THE NEED TO WORK HARD TO ATTAIN GOALS.
(DFD) DEFENDANCE: THE NEED TO STAND UP FOR ONE'S RIGHTS AND DEFEND ONESELF
(REJ) REJECTION: THE NEED TO RESIST PRESSURES TO DO THINGS ONE DOES NOT WISH TO DO.

NAME: Piers-Harris Children's Self-Concept Scale

SUPPLIER: Western Psychological Services
12031 Wilshire Blvd.
Los Angeles, CA 90025
(213) 478-2061

PRODUCT CATEGORY

Personality

PRIMARY APPLICATIONS

Clinical Assessment/Diagnosis
Educational Evaluation/Planning

SALE RESTRICTIONS American Psychological Association Guidelines

SERVICE TYPE/COST	Type	Available	Cost	Discount
	Mail-In	Yes	$7.90	Yes
	Teleprocessing	No		
	Local	No		

PRODUCT DESCRIPTION

This instrument is a widely-used measure of self-concept for children from grades 4-12. The 80 questions are written at a third-grade reading level and can be self- or group-administered in 15-20 minutes.

The computer report provides both a brief School Summary (1-2 pages) and an extended Individual Report (10 pages). The latter is organized into five parts: (1) an assessment of validity considerations, if any; (2) a narrative report describing the child's general self-concept and self-evaluative attitudes and feelings in six major areas; (3) a summary table of empirical test results; (4) a table analyzing the variability in this child's expresed self-concepts in different areas; and (5) item responses.

Among the areas considered in the narrative report are Behavior, Intellectual and School Status, Physical Appearance and Attributes, Anxiety, Popularity, and Happiness.

PIERS-HARRIS CHILDREN'S SELF-CONCEPT SCALE
("The Way I Feel About Myself")

A WPS TEST REPORT by Western Psychological Services
12031 Wilshire Boulevard
Los Angeles, California 90025
Copyright (c) 1983 by Western Psychological Services

STUDENT ID: 581   AGE: 15
GRADE: 8   ETHNIC BACKGROUND: Hispanic
SEX: Female   DATE OF REPORT: August 27, 1983

*****PIERS-HARRIS INDIVIDUAL REPORT*****

This summary is based on a systematic analysis of this
adolescent's responses in conjunction with the currently available
research on the Piers-Harris Children's Self-Concept Scale. These
results may be useful in assessing children's reported self-concepts
as an aid to individual assessment or clinical research, and for the
purpose of identifying children or adolescents who might benefit from
a referral for further psychological evaluation. However, the
relative elevation of the Total Self-Concept Score is only one factor
in interpreting the Piers-Harris. Information on the pattern of
perceived strengths and weaknesses, as reported by the child, along
with the child's responses to individual items may provide useful
clues about the nature of his or her self-concept. In assessing
individual children, the user should keep in mind that the
Piers-Harris is intended primarily as a brief, screening instrument.
The hypotheses suggested by the scale should be corroborated by other
methods, including clinical interviews, behavioral observations, a
detailed history, and other diagnostic procedures.

As an aid to clinical interpretation, this report is organized
into six parts: (1) an assessment of validity considerations,
if any; (2) a narrative report describing the child's general self-
concept and self-evaluative attitudes and feelings in six major areas;
(3) a summary table of empirical test results; (4) a table analyzing
the variability in this child's expressed self-concepts in different
areas; (5) individual item responses; and (6) a brief school report
which can be detached and given to a teacher or other school official
as part of a broader effort to give feedback.

Studies underlying this WPS TEST REPORT are discussed in the
Manual for the Piers-Harris Children's Self-Concept Scale (WPS Catalog
Number W-180C) and in the accompanying Research Monograph (W-180D).
Appropriate use of the Piers-Harris assumes a familiarity with these
reference materials and with the relevant research literature. In
addition, potential users should also become familiar with and conform
to the ethical and professional standards for the use of tests, as
prescribed by the American Psychological Association.

1

VALIDITY CONSIDERATIONS

The pattern of responses and background information provided by
this adolescent suggest the following specific validity
considerations.

The Total Self-Concept score is extremely high (98th percentile),
indicating an unusually positive self-evaluation. While this may
represent a true assessment of how this girl feels about herself, it
may also reflect a need to appear supremely self-confident or a lack
of critical self-evaluation. Thus, the remainder of this report
should be interpreted cautiously.

The True/False (T/F) Ratio is within the normal limits for an
eighth-grade student. This ratio indicates the degree to which this
adolescent responded independently to the individual items, or was
swayed by the need to agree or disagree with the items as written.

This adolescent's age places her about one year behind in school.
If this lower grade placement is due to learning difficulties, she may
have had difficulty reading and understanding some of the items on the
Piers-Harris. However, the fact that the pattern of responses differs
significantly from random responses suggests that she was able to
understand most of the items.

The current normative data may be less appropriate for this girl
since her cultural background differs from those of the standardization
sample. Although a number of research studies have been conducted on
Hispanic children and adolescents, these studies involved youngsters
from very different cultural and geographical backgrounds. Thus, these
studies provide only a limited basis for generalizing to individual
children. In interpreting the present results, the user should keep in
mind that responses to the Piers-Harris may be influenced by a number of
factors including reading difficulties associated with bilingualism,
cultural differences in what are considered desirable or acceptable
responses, and lack of cooperation due to mistrust about how the test
results might be used.

TEST RESULTS AND INTERPRETATION

General Self-Concept

The responses given by this adolescent suggest that her
overall level of self-concept is very much above average compared
with a United States sample of public school children. Given
normal measurement variability, she would be expected to score
in the above average to very much above average range on self-

2

Western Psychological Services • 12031 Wilshire Boulevard • Los Angeles, California 90025

Western Psychological Services • 12031 Wilshire Boulevard • Los Angeles, California 90025

concept if retested with the Piers-Harris within 2-3 months.
Based on her self-report, she generally would be expected to feel
very competent and self-assured across a wide range of cognitive
and interpersonal situations.

Cluster Scales

Behavior (BEH)

This adolescent's feelings about her typical behaviors and
responsibility for her actions suggest that, more than most
teenagers, she has a very high regard for herself in this area. In
general, she seemed to feel positive about herself as a person and
about her ability to get along interpersonally both at home and in
school. However, she did express some concern about her inability to
live up to her parents' expectations.

Intellectual and School Status (INT)

This pattern of responses suggests that this adolescent feels
very positive about herself with regard to her performance on
intellectual and academic tasks. In general, she reports feeling
intellectually equal or superior to her peers. She sees herself
as being an important member of her class and as being well respected
for her ideas and ability to learn.

Physical Appearance and Attributes (PHY)

Based on this adolescent's self-report, she seems to feel
generally positive about her physical appearance and strength. While
she did express some more negative self-attitudes in certain areas,
these attitudes may be related more to sex role stereotypes than to
negative self-concept per se.

Anxiety (ANX)

This scale contains a number of items related to dysphoric mood
and anxiety. According to her self-report, this adolescent generally
feels pretty content with herself and with the way she feels. There
are no major signs of emotional problems which would suggest the need
for further psychological evaluation in this area, although this may
reflect a desire to conceal or deny uncomfortable feelings.

Popularity (POP)

In general, this adolescent reports feeling fairly positive about
herself in peer relationships. Her responses suggest that she
generally feels included in sports and other organized activities,
makes friends fairly easily, and does not feel picked on or made fun
of by peers.

Happiness and Satisfaction (HAP)

This adolescent's responses also suggest that she generally feels
satisfied with herself as a person, views herself as cheerful and
easy to get along with, and does not feel any strong desire to change.
Her score on this scale indicates a high level of general satisfaction
relative to other children, although this may be influenced in part by
a desire to appear self-confident and worthwhile.

psychware **547**

STUDENT ID: 591   DATE OF REPORT: August 27, 1983
ANSWER SHEET: 000010

                         SUMMARY OF TEST RESULTS

Western Psychological Services • 12031 Wilshire Boulevard • Los Angeles, California 90025

```
SCALES         SCORES                    PERCENTILE SCORES
                              1   2    5  10 15 25  40 50 60  75 85 90 95   98 99
               RAW  STANINE  %ile  I++I+++I++I++I++I+++I++I++I+++I++I++I++I+++I++I
                              I          :       :        :            I
                              JJJJJJJJJJJJJJJJJJJJJJJJJJJJJJJJJJJJJJJJJ        I
 BEH    (15)      8     95    JJJJJJJJJJJJJJJJJJJJJJJJJJJJJJJJJJJJJJJJJ        I
                              JJJJJJJJJJJJJJJJJJJJJJJJJJJJJJJJJJJJJJJJJ        I
                              I          :       :        :            I
                              JJJJJJJJJJJJJJJJJJJJJJJJJJJJJJJJJJJJJJJJJJJJ     I
 INT    (17)      9     98    JJJJJJJJJJJJJJJJJJJJJJJJJJJJJJJJJJJJJJJJJJJJJ     I
                              JJJJJJJJJJJJJJJJJJJJJJJJJJJJJJJJJJJJJJJJJJJJJ     I
                              I          :       :        :            I
                              JJJJJJJJJJJJJJJJJJJJJJJJJJJJJJJJJJJJ           I
 PHY    (11)      7     84    JJJJJJJJJJJJJJJJJJJJJJJJJJJJJJJJJJJJ           I
                              JJJJJJJJJJJJJJJJJJJJJJJJJJJJJJJJJJJJ           I
                              I          :       :        :            I
                              JJJJJJJJJJJJJJJJJJJJJJJJJJJJJJJJJJJJJJJJJJ     I
 ANX    (14)      9     97    JJJJJJJJJJJJJJJJJJJJJJJJJJJJJJJJJJJJJJJJJJJJJ   I
                              JJJJJJJJJJJJJJJJJJJJJJJJJJJJJJJJJJJJJJJJJJJJ   I
                              I          :       :        :            I
                              JJJJJJJJJJJJJJJJJJJJJJJJJJJJJJJJJJJ          I
 POP    (10)      7     79    JJJJJJJJJJJJJJJJJJJJJJJJJJJJJJJJJJJ          I
                              JJJJJJJJJJJJJJJJJJJJJJJJJJJJJJJJJJ          I
                              I          :       :        :            I
                              JJJJJJJJJJJJJJJJJJJJJJJJJJJJJJJJJJJJJJJJ     I
 HAP    (10)      8     90    JJJJJJJJJJJJJJJJJJJJJJJJJJJJJJJJJJJJJJJJ     I
                              JJJJJJJJJJJJJJJJJJJJJJJJJJJJJJJJJJJJJJJJ     I
                              I--------------------------------------------I
                              I          :       :        :            I
                              JJJJJJJJJJJJJJJJJJJJJJJJJJJJJJJJJJJJJJJJJJJJJJJ I
 TOTAL  (74)      9     98    JJJJJJJJJJJJJJJJJJJJJJJJJJJJJJJJJJJJJJJJJJJJJJJ I
                              JJJJJJJJJJJJJJJJJJJJJJJJJJJJJJJJJJJJJJJJJJJJJJJ I
               RAW  STANINE  %ile  I++I+++I++I++I++I+++I++I++I+++I++I++I++I+++I++I
                              1   2    5  10 15 25  40 50 60  75 85 90 95   98 99
                                             PERCENTILE SCORES
```

WPS TEST REPORT

     NOTE. All scales are scored in the direction of positive
self-concept. Thus, higher scores reflect higher reported self-concept,
whereas lower scores are associated with lower reported self-concept.
Cluster scores do not necessarily sum to the Total score (see Manual).

Western Psychological Services • 12031 Wilshire Boulevard • Los Angeles, California 90025

```
                    ***ANALYSIS OF CLUSTER SCORES***

                ****************************************
                *       Mean Stanine Score: 8.00       *
                *                                      *
                *Response Bias: 34/46 Inconsistency: 7*
                ****************************************

                            LOW SELF-CONCEPT <-----> HIGH SELF-CONCEPT
                DIFFERENCE
                  FROM                  DIFFERENCES FROM MEAN STANINE SCORE
       SCALE      MEAN     SEM    -4   -3   -2   -1    0    1    2    3    4
                               I++++I++++I++++I++++I++++I++++I++++I++++I
       BEH        .00      .75   I              ----X----                 I
                               I                   :                     I
       INT       1.00     1.09   I                   -----X-----          I
                               I                   :                     I
       PHY      -1.00     1.07   I         -----X-----:                   I
                               I                   :                     I
       ANX       1.00      .91   I                   -----X-----          I
                               I                   :                     I
       POP        .00      .97   I              -----X-----               I
                               I                   :                     I
       HAP       1.00     1.12   I                   ------X------        I
                               I                   :                     I
                               I++++I++++I++++I++++I++++I++++I++++I++++I
                                -4   -3   -2   -1    0    1    2    3    4
```

* P<.10.   ** P<.05.   *** P<.01.

    NOTE. Approximately 68% of children with a "true" score, X,
would be expected to score in the interval bounded by plus or minus
one standard error of measurement (SEM), expressed here in stanine
score units.

    This table shows the amount of variability in this adolescent's
self-concept, as assessed by the various cluster scale scores. This
information may be useful in determining areas of relative strength or
vulnerability, given this girl's overall level of self-concept. The
significance of the deviation of a stanine score for a particular
cluster scale from this individual's mean stanine score across all the
scales is given by p, the probability that a deviation of this size
could have occurred by chance.

WPS TEST REPORT

6

In this case, none of the cluster scales deviated significantly
from this adolescent's mean stanine score of 8.00. The fact that her
scores did not vary significantly suggests that her self-evaluative
attitudes and feelings are highly consistent across a number of
different areas.   This lack of variability combined with her very high
Total Self-Concept score suggests that she is very confident in her
abilities and satisfied with herself as a person. However, as stated
previously, it may also reflect an uncritical self-evaluation or a
need to deny having any self-doubts or concerns.

INDIVIDUAL ITEM RESPONSES

The individual items were answered by this adolescent in the
directions shown. Items which were responded to in a negative
direction, indicating low self-concept, are marked by an asterisk (*).

The relative frequency of item endorsement in general school
and clinic samples of children is indicated at the end of each
statement, using the following notation: (normative %/clinic %).   In
each case, the percentages represent the proportion of children in
each sample who responded in the same direction as this girl.

```
*************************************************************************
*                                                                       *
*                             IMPORTANT                                 *
*                                                                       *
*       In interpreting the results, the user should be careful not     *
*   to place too much interpretive value on any of the individual       *
*   responses.   While they may be useful in gaining a more complete    *
*   understanding of the empirical pattern of scores and in suggest-    *
*   ing areas for further inquiry, they should never be interpreted     *
*   out of context. For this reason, individual item resposes should    *
*   generally not be given to parents, teachers, or other individuals   *
*   who may not have a sufficient background to interpret them appro-    *
*   priately.  The School Reports are provided for this purpose.        *
*                                                                       *
*************************************************************************
```

7

550 *psychware*

Western Psychological Services • 12031 Wilshire Boulevard • Los Angeles, California 90025

WPS TEST REPORT

Western Psychological Services • 12031 Wilshire Boulevard • Los Angeles, California 90025

WPS TEST REPORT

--- BEHAVIOR ---

12. I am well behaved in school. (Y) [74%/78%]
13. It is usually my fault when something goes wrong. (N) [78%/71%]
14. I cause trouble to my family. (N) [81%/69%]
21. I am good in my schoolwork. (Y) [80%/59%]
22. I do many bad things. (N) [76%/80%]
25. I behave badly at home. (N) [85%/76%]
34. I often get into trouble. (N) [73%/66%]
35. I am obedient at home. (Y). [75%/70%]
* 38. My parents expect too much of me. (Y) [24%/27%]
45. I hate school. (N) [62%/67%]
48. I am often mean to other people. (N) [79%/87%]
56. I get into a lot of fights. (N) [76%/61%]
59. My family is disappointed in me. (N) [88%/70%]
62. I am picked on at home. (N) [71%/69%]
78. I think bad thoughts. (N) [69%/84%]
80. I am a good person. (Y) [91%/88%]

---INTELLECTUAL AND SCHOOL STATUS---

5. I am smart. (Y) [71%/58%]
7. I get nervous when the teacher calls on me. (N) [59%/55%]
9. When I grow up, I will be an important person. (Y) [57%/59%]
12. I am well behaved in school. (Y) [74%/78%]
16. I have good ideas. (Y) [82%/80%]
17. I am an important member of my family. (Y) [82%/64%]
21. I am good in my schoolwork. (Y) [80%/59%]
26. I am slow in finishing my schoolwork. (N) [75%/48%]
27. I am an important member of my class. (Y) [42%/36%]
30. I can give a good report in front of my class. (Y) [55%/57%]
31. In school I am a dreamer. (N) [68%/58%]
33. My friends like my ideas. (Y) [71%/66%]
42. I often volunteer in school. (Y) [56%/72%]
49. My classmates in school think I have good ideas. (Y) [62%/59%]
53. I am dumb about most things. (N) [84%/77%]
66. I forget what I learn. (N) [72%/66%]
70. I am a good reader. (Y) [70%/68%]

8

psychware **551**

Western Psychological Services • 12031 Wilshire Boulevard • Los Angeles, California 90025

---PHYSICAL APPEARANCE AND ATTRIBUTES---

```
  5. I am smart. (Y) [71%/58%]
  8. My looks bother me. (N) [73%/71%]
* 15. I am strong. (N) [39%/37%]
 29. I have pretty eyes. (Y) [66%/57%]
 33. My friends like my ideas. (Y) [71%/66%]
 41. I have nice hair. (Y) [71%/66%]
 49. My classmates in school think I have good ideas. (Y) [62%/59%]
 54. I am good looking. (Y) [62%/59%]
 57. I am popular with boys. (Y) [62%/41%]
 60. I have a pleasant face. (Y) [72%/67%]
* 63. I am a leader in games and sports. (N) [60%/73%]
 69. I am popular with girls. (Y) [64%/44%]
 73. I have a good figure. (Y) [56%/76%]
```

---ANXIETY---

```
  4. I am often sad. (N) [70%/56%]
  6. I am shy. (N) [63%/65%]
  7. I get nervous when the teacher calls on me. (N) [59%/55%]
  8. My looks bother me. (N) [73%/71%]
 10. I get worried when we have tests in school. (N) [43%/45%]
 20. I give up easily. (N) [82%/81%]
 28. I am nervous. (N) [69%/56%]
 37. I worry a lot. (N) [53%/45%]
 39. I like being the way I am. (Y) [83%/68%]
 40. I feel left out of things. (N) [59%/60%]
 43. I wish I were different. (N) [72%/56%]
 50. I am unhappy. (N) [86%/77%]
 74. I am often afraid. (N) [83%/69%]
 79. I cry easily. (N) [87%/77%]
```

---POPULARITY---

```
  1. My classmates make fun of me. (N) [80%/66%]
  3. It is hard for me to make friends. (N) [82%/67%]
  6. I am shy. (N) [63%/65%]
 11. I am unpopular. (N) [73%/54%]
 40. I feel left out of things. (N) [59%/60%]
 46. I am among the last to be chosen for games. (N) [70%/55%]
 49. My classmates in school think I have good ideas. (Y) [62%/59%]
 51. I have many friends. (Y) [83%/69%]
 58. People pick on me. (N) [72%/55%]
 65. In games and sports I watch instead of play. (N) [81%/60%]
* 77. I am different from other people. (Y) [62%/55%]
```

9

WPS TEST REPORT

552 *psychware*

Western Psychological Services • 12031 Wilshire Boulevard • Los Angeles, California 90025

---HAPPINESS AND SATISFACTION---

    2. I am a happy person. (Y) [93%/84%]
    8. My looks bother me. (N) [73%/71%]
   36. I am lucky. (Y) [59%/65%]
   39. I like being the way I am. (Y) [88%/68%]
   43. I wish I were different. (N) [71%/56%]
   50. I am unhappy. (N) [91%/77%]
   52. I am cheerful. (Y) [89%/77%]
   60. I have a pleasant face. (Y) [72%/67%]
   67. I am easy to get along with. (Y) [81%/72%]
   80. I am a good person. (Y) [91%/88%]

---OTHER ITEM RESPONSES---

 * 18. I usually want my own way. (Y) [57%/40%]
   19. I am good at making things with my hands. (Y) [61%/76%]
   23. I can draw well. (Y) [53%/59%]
   24. I am good in music. (Y) [72%/66%]
   32. I pick on my brother(s) and sister(s). (N) [40%/56%]
   44. I sleep well at night. (Y) [73%/80%]
   47. I am sick a lot. (N) [82%/78%]
   55. I have lots of pep. (Y) [82%/74%]
   61. When I try to make something everything seems to go wrong. (N) [53%/6
   64. I am clumsy. (N) [75%/78%]
   68. I lose my temper easily. (N) [59%/57%]
 * 71. I would rather work alone than with a group. (Y) [37%/52%]
   72. I like my brother (sister). (Y) [84%/84%]
   75. I am always dropping or breaking things. (N) [74%/81%]
   76. I can be trusted. (Y) [91%/85%]

SUMMARY OF PIERS-HARRIS ITEM RESPONSES

1(N)	11(N)	21(N)	31(Y)	41(Y)	51(N)	61(N)	71(Y)
2(Y)	12(Y)	22(N)	32(N)	42(N)	52(N)	62(Y)	72(Y)
3(N)	13(N)	23(N)	33(Y)	43(N)	53(N)	63(N)	73(N)
4(N)	14(N)	24(Y)	34(N)	44(Y)	54(Y)	64(N)	74(N)
5(Y)	15(Y)	25(N)	35(Y)	45(Y)	55(Y)	65(N)	75(N)
6(N)	16(Y)	26(Y)	36(Y)	46(N)	56(N)	66(Y)	76(Y)
7(Y)	17(Y)	27(N)	37(N)	47(N)	57(Y)	67(Y)	77(Y)
8(N)	18(N)	28(N)	38(Y)	48(N)	58(N)	68(N)	78(N)
9(Y)	19(Y)	29(Y)	39(Y)	49(N)	59(Y)	69(N)	79(N)
10(Y)	20(Y)	30(N)	40(N)	50(N)	60(Y)	70(N)	80(Y)

10

WPS TEST REPORT

A WPS TEST REPORT by Western Psychological Services
12031 Wilshire Boulevard
Los Angeles, California   90025
Copyright (c) 1983 by Western Psychological Services

STUDENT ID: 581   AGE: 15
DATE OF REPORT: August 27, 1983   SEX: Female
ANSWER SHEET: 000010   GRADE: 8

#####PIERS-HARRIS SCHOOL REPORT#####

This summary is based on an analysis of this adolescent's self-
decription using the 80-item Piers-Harris Children's Self-Concept
Scale ("The Way I Feel About Myself"), a standardized and widely used
measure of self-concept in children and adolescents. The scale
presents a number of statements about the way some children feel about
themselves, for example "I am a happy person" or "It is hard for me to
make friends." Children are asked to read each statement and decide
whether or not it describes the way they feel about themselves.

     This is not a test that has any right or wrong answers. It is
simply one way of trying to find out how individual children say they
feel about themselves. Because some children may not want to say
anything bad about themselves, they may respond not as they feel but
as they want others to think they feel. Other children may be made
anxious by this task or may not want to share their feelings about
themselves. Consequently, they may respond randomly or even not at
all to some of the statements. For these reasons, it is important to
view the statements presented below with caution, and to see if they
make sense given your personal experience with this girl and other
information you may have about her background. If you have any
questions, you should consult the psychologist or other professional
person who gave you this report.

     This girl's pattern of responses suggests that her overall level
level of self-concept is very much above average compared to other
adolescents her age. In general, her responses indicate that she
feels very good about herself in a number of areas, including general
behavior, school and academic performance, physical appearance and
sports, general emotional adjustment, happiness and satisfaction with
things as they are, and interpersonal relationships. This positive
self-image was consistent across all areas.

     Although this pattern of responses may reflect a very positive self-
concept, it may also indicate a lack of critical self-evaluation or a
need to deny having any self-doubts or concerns. In addition, the fact

that her cultural background differs from that of the normative sample
raises some questions about the appropriateness of using the normative
data to interpret her results. Because of these concerns, this report,
and the scores on which it is based, should be regarded as tentative.

Western Psychological Services • 12031 Wilshire Boulevard • Los Angeles, California 90025

WPS TEST REPORT

554   *psychware*

NAME: Problem-Solving Rehabilitation I

SUPPLIER: Robert J. Sbordone, Ph.D., Inc.
8840 Warner Ave. Suite 301
Fountain Valley, CA 92708
(714) 841-6293

PRODUCT CATEGORY	PRIMARY APPLICATIONS
Cognitive/Ability	Training/Development

SALE RESTRICTIONS American Psychological Association Guidelines

SERVICE TYPE/COST	Type	Available	Cost	Discount
	Mail-In	No		
	Teleprocessing	No		
	Local	Yes	$150.00	

PRODUCT DESCRIPTION

The PROBLEM-SOLVING REHABILITATION I program provides computer-based training in visual-spatial problem-solving skills for patients with impaired cognitive functioning. The program carefully monitors responsivity and determines when rest periods are needed and when a particular training session should be terminated. It automatically increases task complexity as the patient's performance improves and offers a wide variety of tasks. The program also maintains patient performance data over training sessions and provides a comprehensive analysis of these data on request. A speech synthesizer option produces a voice accompaniment to the program's visual display.

The program operates on the Apple II +, IIe, III, or Apple-compatible hardware and on the IBM PC-100 microcomputer system. No special computer knowledge is needed. The software comes with an instruction manual.

NAME: Problem-Solving Rehabilitation II

SUPPLIER: Robert J. Sbordone, Ph.D., Inc.
8840 Warner Ave. Suite 301
Fountain Valley, CA 92708
(714) 841-6293

PRODUCT CATEGORY

Cognitive/Ability

PRIMARY APPLICATIONS

Training/Development

SALE RESTRICTIONS American Psychological Association Guidelines

SERVICE TYPE/COST	Type	Available	Cost	Discount
	Mail-In	No		
	Teleprocessing	No		
	Local	Yes	$150.00	

PRODUCT DESCRIPTION

The **PROBLEM-SOLVING REHABILITATION II** program improves planning skills to facilitate effective problem-solving behavior and train the patient to plan and evaluate the consequences of future behavior. The program carefully monitors patient responses and determines when rest period are needed. It automatically increases task complexity as the patient's performance improves and offers a wide variety of tasks to maintain interest. The program also maintains patient performance data over training sessions and provides a comprehensive analysis of these data on request. A speech synthesizer option produces voice accompaniment to the program's visual display.

The program operates on the Apple II + , IIe, III, or Apple-compatible hardware and on the IBM PC-100 microcomputer system. No special computer knowledge is needed. The software comes with an instruction manual.

NAME: Profile Analysis Decision Support System

SUPPLIER: Computer Diversified Services, Inc.
7207 Regency Square Blvd.
Suite 210
Houston, TX 77036

PRODUCT CATEGORY	PRIMARY APPLICATIONS
Personality	Personnel Selection/Evaluation
Career/Vocational	Personal/Marriage/Family Counseling
	Clinical Assessment/Diagnosis
	Vocational Guidance/Counseling

SALE RESTRICTIONS Authorized/Certified Representatives

SERVICE TYPE/COST	Type	Available	Cost	Discount
	Mail-In	Yes	$55.00	Yes
	Teleprocessing	No		
	Local	Yes	$55.00	Yes

PRODUCT DESCRIPTION

Computer Diversified Services offers various personality-based description narratives regarding selecting, training, and developing managers, sales personnel, life insurance agents, and other employees. Two forms (C and D) of the Sixteen Personality Factor Questionnaire are used as the basis for all computer- generated printouts. Statistical analyses and in-company validation are available for companies wishing specific user norms. Supplemental and interpretive materials are available. Local service is provided via a software lease arrangement.

NAME: Projective Drawing Analysis

SUPPLIER: Joseph M. Eisenberg, Ph.D.
204 E. Joppa Road Suite #10
Towson, MD 21204
(301) 321-9101

PRODUCT CATEGORY

Personality

PRIMARY APPLICATIONS

Clinical Assessment/Diagnosis

SALE RESTRICTIONS American Psychological Association Guidelines

SERVICE TYPE/COST	Type	Available	Cost	Discount
	Mail-In	Yes	NA	
	Teleprocessing	No		
	Local	Yes	$300.00	

PRODUCT DESCRIPTION

The PROJECTIVE DRAWING ANALYSIS is designed to facilitate the scoring and analysis of the House-Tree-Person Drawing Test and/or the Human Figure Drawing Test. The thirteen areas covered in the interpretive report are: Interpersonal Relationships, Psychosexual Development, Coping Mechanisms, Conflict Areas, Psychopathology, Normality/Health, Reality Contact, Affect/Attitudes, Personality, Intellectual Development, Organicity/Psychosomatic, Family/Home, and Environment. The clinician has two options by which data can be entered into the comptuer. The first is through a selection of scoring criteria from a hard copy of the protocol. Alternatively, the clinician can use an online procedure by which scoring criteria are selected and entered through the keyboard. After the data have been entered, the program selects various interpretive statements and groups them according to those categories outlined above. The clinician can include the interpretive statements in a report or restructure the interpretive statements according to individual style. The program is designed to execute on Apple, IBM PC, and compatible systems. A manual is provided that lists all sources from which interpretive statements were drawn.

NAME: Psychological Resources Reports

SUPPLIER: Psychological Resources, Inc.
74 14th Street, N.W.
Atlanta, GA 30309
(404) 892-3000

PRODUCT CATEGORY

Personality
Career/Vocational
Interest/Attitudes
Cognitive/Ability

PRIMARY APPLICATIONS

Clinical Assessment/Diagnosis
Personnel Selection/Evaluation
Vocational Guidance/Counseling

SALE RESTRICTIONS American Psychological Association Guidelines

SERVICE TYPE/COST Type	Available	Cost	Discount
Mail-In	Yes	$40.00	Yes
Teleprocessing	Yes	$40.00	Yes
Local	Yes	$40.00	Yes

PRODUCT DESCRIPTION

PSYCHOLOGICAL RESOURCES REPORTS is a system of integrated psychological reports, each report oriented toward specific referral issues. REPORTS are in wide use throughout several state correctional systems and have important applications in the selection of public safety candidates and assessment of psychological factors in health risk.

Large-volume users may have special custom-built reports based, if desired, on local research data.

NAME: Psychosocial History Report

SUPPLIER: Psychologistics, Inc.
P.O. Box 3896
Indialantic, FL 32903
(305) 727-7900

PRODUCT CATEGORY	PRIMARY APPLICATIONS
Structured Interview	Clinical Assessment/Diagnosis
	Personnel Selection/Evaluation
	Personal/Marriage/Family Counseling
	Vocational Guidance/Counseling
	Educational Evaluation/Planning

SALE RESTRICTIONS American Psychological Association Guidelines

SERVICE TYPE/COST	Type	Available	Cost	Discount
	Mail-In	No		
	Teleprocessing	No		
	Local	Yes	$295.00	

PRODUCT DESCRIPTION

The PSYCHOLOGICAL/SOCIAL HISTORY REPORT presents an automated structured interview which gathers basic information and generates a written narrative. Areas covered are those most relevant for a psychological report: Presenting Problem, Family/Developmental History, Education, Financial History and Status, Employment History, Military Service, Alcohol and Drug History, Medical History, Marital and Family Life, Diet and Exercise, and Psychological and Social Stressors.

In addition to the narrative report, a section is printed which highlights important responses. Two categories of answers, and their corresponding questions, are printed in one list. One category consists of clinically significant answers. The second category consists of answers that the client indicated a desire to discuss in more detail.

The PSYCHOLOGICAL/SOCIAL HISTORY REPORT can be administered by computer or in a pencil-and-paper format. The questionnaire takes 30-45 minutes. Software versions are provided for the Apple II + , IIe, III and IBM PC computer systems. The price shown is for unlimited usage of the program. This program also allows the user to save the report in a text file for additional word processing.

PSYCHOLOGICAL/SOCIAL REPORT

CLIENT'S NAME: JOHN X. DOE
AGE: 38   DATE: 2-27-84
RACE: CAUCASIAN   OCCUPATION: WELDER

PRESENTING PROBLEM   The primary problem is related to alcohol use.
The onset of this difficulty was more than ten years ago. This
problem has had a significant effect on every day life. This problem
occurs several times a year. In addition to the primary problem, Mr.
Doe is also plagued by difficulties associated with marriage, family,
physical state, and work.

FAMILY/DEVELOPMENTAL HISTORY   Mr. Doe was raised primarily by his
natural parents. In retrospect he describes his childhood as being
happy and regimented. Mother was characterized as warm, over
protective, understanding, and affectionate. He describes his father
as distant, strict, and domineering. Characteristics of his parents'
relationship were given as follows: ambivalent and
domineering/submissive. There were three other children in the
family. He was the middle child. As a child, Mr. Doe was
characteristically outgoing, active, happy, and rebellious. The
following problems occurred during childhood: father, teachers, and
academic. Parents argued about money and discipline of children. As
a child Mr. Doe's father worked primarily in military service and his
mother worked primarily as a homemaker. Mother's method of
discipline is described as lenient and father's as strict. Childhood
fears included: none. Sexual experiences are reported to have been
pleasant.

EDUCATION   Mr. Doe reports that he graduated high school. The self
rating of intellectual ability is Average. He has never repeated a
grade. Grades were generally C's. He recalls occasionally getting
into trouble while in school. Learning to read was not a problem.
In learning math he encountered no problems. Compared to other
children, Mr. Doe feels that he was more often the brunt of teasing
and ridicule than were other children.

FINANCIAL HISTORY AND STATUS   Economic status during childhood and
adolescence is rated within the Working Class. The major source of
family income came from father. In deciding on how the family's
money was to be spent, there was disagreement at times between
parents. Finances were occasionally a source of family problems.
Currently Mr. Doe's household is supported by an income of
$20,000-$30,000. He reports no change in income during the last two
years. Family income is derived primarily from personal earnings.
Providing enough income is an important stressor.

EMPLOYMENT HISTORY   He is currently employed. The present
occupation has been pursued for 3 to 5 years. Hours worked per week
averages 30 to 45. Mr. Doe feels neutral about work. He has never
been dismissed by an employer. Mr. Doe did lose work when laid off
by an employer. The greatest length of employment in one position
was for a period of 3 to 5 years. Since beginning work on a full
time basis he has gone unemployed at the most for one to six months.
At this time he is not experiencing problems at work. The following
vocations have been pursued in the past: a skilled laborer and an
unskilled worker.

MILITARY SERVICE   Mr. Doe has been a member of the armed forces. Service in the Army occurred for a period of 2 to 4 years. The following problems were reported as occurring while in the military: military life and drugs. Duty in a combat zone was not part of the military experience. The highest rank attained was as an enlisted person. Mr. Doe advises that he received an honorable discharge from military service. When questioned as to whether a psychologist or psychiatrist has been seen while in the military, Mr. Doe reported that he did but had only been evaluated. He affirms having no disability connected to military service.

ALCOHOL AND DRUG HISTORY   Regarding past drug use, the following was reported: cocaine and marijuana. A report of using alcohol to excess on several occasions was acquired. Mr. Doe says that he uses alcohol several times a week, and uses illegal drugs once or twice a year. Past involvement in a treatment program for alcoholism or drug abuse was denied. While growing up Mr. Doe's father had a drinking problem. Regarding the use of tobacco, Mr. Doe reports that he smokes a pack of cigarettes a day.

MEDICAL HISTORY   The following family members have experienced mental illness: neither immediate nor distant relatives are known to have had disturbed mental faculties. Mr. Doe remembers that he did not have serious illnesses as a child. During the past three years Mr. Doe has been involved in at least one accident and has not had any major illness. General level of health is rated as good. Currently Mr. Doe is under the care of a physician. The following medications are being taken at this time: no medications.

MARITAL AND FAMILY LIFE   In regards to marital status, Mr. Doe is married. He has been involved in this relationship for more than ten years. Divorce has occurred. Mr. Doe is a parent of two children. Behavioral problems are reported to be an issue in child rearing. Mr. Doe describes his partner as enjoyable, faultfinding, and tense. The frequency of sex is not seen as a problem. At present Mr. Doe has completed mortgage payment obligations and resides in this home. Arguments with his partner are alleged to occur about once a week. The current relationship has been threatened by a self-initiated affair. Shared interests in this relationship include children, movies, television, and hunting/fishing. The partner is evaluated as fulfilling her role fairly well.

DIET AND EXERCISE   In regards to eating habits, Mr. Doe eats a balanced diet. A regular exercise program is not a part of daily routine. Mr. Doe is currently about average weight.

PSYCHOLOGICAL AND SOCIAL STRESSORS   In the past two years Mr. Doe has experienced the following stressful events and circumstances: change in number of arguments with partner. The following stressful events and circumstances also occurred during this same period: personal injury or illness. Regarding legal involvement, he has never been implicated in civil matters or arrested. Current ability to cope with existing stressors is rated as good. The following characteristics were chosen as being self descriptive: outgoing, active, self-confident, easygoing, and impatient. The descriptors selected to portray current mental state are as follows: worried, confused, and regretful.

EAR-MARKED AND CLINICALLY SIGNIFICANT ANSWERS
(EAR-MARK = EM & CLINICALLY SIGNIFICANT = CS)

CS 3. WHICH DESCRIPTOR(S) CHARACTERIZE YOUR MOTHER (MATERNAL CARETAKER)?
warm, over protective, understanding, and affectionate
CS 5. HOW WOULD YOU DESCRIBE YOUR PARENTS' (OR PARENT SUBSTITUTES') RELATIONSHIP?
ambivalent and domineering/submissive
CS 9. WHAT WERE PROBLEMS FOR YOU AS A CHILD?
father, teachers, and academic
CS 10. WHAT DID YOUR PARENTS (PARENTAL CARETAKERS) ARGUE ABOUT?
money and discipline of children
CS 14. HOW WOULD YOU DESCRIBE YOUR FATHER'S METHOD OF DISCIPLINE?
strict
CS 24. DID YOUR PEERS RIDICULE, TEASE OR MAKE FUN OF YOU MORE THAN OTHER KIDS?
was more often
CS 27. DID YOUR PARENTS AGREE ON HOW MONEY SHOULD BE SPENT?
disagreement at times
CS 32. IS PROVIDING ENOUGH INCOME FOR YOUR FAMILY A BIG STRESS IN YOUR LIFE?
is
CS 38. HAVE YOU EVER BEEN LAID OFF?
did lose work when laid off by an employer
CS 46. WHAT KINDS OF PROBLEMS DID YOU EXPERIENCE WHILE IN THE MILITARY?
military life and drugs
CS 50. DID YOU EVER SEE A PSYCHOLOGIST OR PSYCHIATRIST WHILE IN THE MILITARY?
did but had only been evaluated
CS 52. WHICH OF THE FOLLOWING HAVE YOU USED?
cocaine and marijuana
CS 53. HAVE YOU EVER FELT THERE WAS A TIME YOU DRANK TOO MUCH ALCOHOL?
using alcohol to excess on several occasions
CS 57. DID YOUR PARENTS HAVE A PROBLEM WITH ALCOHOL WHEN YOU WERE A CHILD?
father had
CS 58. DO YOU SMOKE CIGARETTES?
smokes a pack of cigarettes a day
CS 61. HAVE YOU HAD ANY ACCIDENTS IN THE PAST THREE YEARS?
has been involved in at least one accident
CS 64. ARE YOU CURRENTLY UNDER THE CARE OF A PHYSICIAN?
is
CS 70. HOW WOULD YOU DESCRIBE YOUR PARTNER?
enjoyable, faultfinding, and tense
CS 71. ARE YOU HAVING PROBLEMS WITH YOUR CHILD(REN)'S BEHAVIOR?
are
CS 74. HOW OFTEN DO YOU AND YOUR PARTNER ARGUE?
to occur about once a week
CS 75. HAS YOUR RELATIONSHIP EVER BEEN THREATENED BY AN AFFAIR?
has been threatened by a self-initiated affair
CS 79. DO YOU PARTICIPATE IN A REGULAR EXERCISE PROGRAM?
is not
CS 81. WHICH OF THE FOLLOWING HAVE YOU EXPERIENCED IN THE PAST TWO YEARS?
personal injury or illness
CS 84. HOW WOULD YOU DESCRIBE YOURSELF?
outgoing, active, self-confident, easygoing, and impatient
CS 85. HOW WOULD YOU DESCRIBE YOUR MENTAL STATE?
worried, confused, and regretful

NAME: Rorschach Comprehensive System-Exner Report

SUPPLIER: NCS/Professional Assessment Services
P.O. Box 1416
Minneapolis, MN 55440
(800) 328-6759

PRODUCT CATEGORY	PRIMARY APPLICATIONS
Personality	Clinical Assessment/Diagnosis Personal/Marriage/Family Counseling

SALE RESTRICTIONS American Psychological Association Guidelines

SERVICE TYPE/COST	Type	Available	Cost	Discount
	Mail-In	No		
	Teleprocessing	Yes	$15.00	Yes
	Local	No		

PRODUCT DESCRIPTION

The EXNER REPORT FOR THE RORSCHACH COMPREHENSIVE SYSTEM provides immediate calculations and interpretive results for the Rorschach Test. The report automatically calculates and reproduces the test's Structural Summary and then scans all of the structural data included in the test, ensuring that none of the data are neglected and that all variables are considered in relation to others. Thirty-one critical clusters, derived from 352 scores and derivations of scores, are considered in the report. After scanning the clusters, interpretive statements describing both normal and psycho-pathological personality characteristics are presented. Each interpretive statement in the report establishes a working hypothesis about the client's personality structure and/or behavioral tendencies. The clinician can use these hypotheses to better understand the individual and to integrate Rorschach results with information obtained from other assessment procedures.

The typical printout has from 18-23 interpretive paragraphs. The length of each paragraph varies from 1-2 lines to 15-25 lines.

DATE: 23-DEC-83 -- PRINTED FOR: Sample Examiner
SUBJECT: 12-23-83- Sample -- 29 YEAR OLD WHITE FEMALE.
  MARRIED, SES 7 (UPPER - LOWER CLASS INCOME), 12 YEARS COMPLETED EDUCATION.
  HISTORY OF DRUG ABUSE INVOLVING AMPHETAMINES, AND PCP (ANGEL DUST).
  HISTORY OF ALCOHOLISM. SEATING WAS SIDE-TO-SIDE. COOPERATION WAS GOOD.

SEQUENCE OF SCORES

CARD NO.	LOC. #	DETERMINANT(S)	(2)	CONTENT(S)	POP	Z	SPECIAL SCORES
I	1:Do	2:Fo		:A	:P		
	2:Do	4:Mpo		:H	:P		
	3:Wo	1:Fo		:A	:P	:1.0:	
II	4:Do	3:FCo		:A,Fd			
	5:DSo	5:FC'o		:Id			
	6:Dv	2:C		:Bl			
III	7:D+	1:Ma.FC'o	:2	:H	:P	:3.0:	
	8:Do	3:Fo		:Cg			
	9:Dv	2:FC-	:2	:An			:ALOG
	10:Dv	7:F-		:Ad			
IV	11:Wo	1:FTo		:Ad	:P	:2.0:	
	12:Wv	1:C'		:Ab			
	13:Do	1:Fo		:Ad			
	14:Do	7:Fo	:2	:Cg	:P		
V	15:Wo	1:FMpo		:A	:P	:1.0:	
	16:Ddo	29:Fo	:2	:Bt			
	17:Wv	1:F-		:Bt		:1.0:	:DV
	18:W+	1:Ma+		:H		:2.5:	
	19:Do	7:Fo		:(H)			:INC
VI	20:Do	2:Mao		:Sx			
	21:Do	9:FMao		:A			
	22:Dd+	30:FMpo	:2	:A,Id		:2.5:	
	23:Dv	12:VF.YFo		:Ls			
VII	24:Do	4:Fo		:Ad			:PSV
	25:Do	3:Fo	:2	:Ad			
	26:Wv	1:TFo		:Fd		:2.5:	
	27:W+	1:Ma+	:2	:H		:3.0:	
VIII	28:W+	1:FMa.FC.Fro		:A,Ls	:P	:4.5:	
	29:Wv	1:CFo		:An		:4.5:	
	30:Do	5:Fo	:2	:Id			
IX	31:D+	1:Ma+		:H		:2.5:	
	32:W+	1:FC+		:Bt		:5.5:	
	33:D+	3:Ma.FCo	:2	:(H)		:4.5:	
	34:DdSv	30:FC'-		:Sx			:ALOG
X	35:Do	1:FCo	:2	:A	:P		:INC
	36:Do	7:FMao	:2	:A			
	37:D+	11:FMao	:2	:A		:4.0:	:FAB

ABBREVIATIONS USED ABOVE:
  FOR DQ: "/" = "v/+"; FOR CONTENTS: "Id" = "IDIO" (IDIOGRAPHIC CONTENT)
  SPECIAL SCORES: "INC" = "INCOM", "FAB" = "FABCOM", "CON" = "CONTAM"

DATE: 23-DEC-83 -- PRINTED FOR: Sample Examiner
SUBJECT: 12-23-83- Sample -- 29 YEAR OLD WHITE FEMALE.

SEQUENCE OF SCORES

CARD NO.	LOC. #	DETERMINANT(S)	(2)	CONTENT(S)	POP	Z	SPECIAL SCORES
	38:Do	3:Mp.FCo		:Bt			
	39:Wv	1:CFo		:Id		:5.5:	
	40:Dv	13:C		:Fd			:ALOG

ABBREVIATIONS USED ABOVE:
  FOR DQ: "/" = "v/+"; FOR CONTENTS: "Id" = "IDIO" (IDIOGRAPHIC CONTENT)
  SPECIAL SCORES: "INC" = "INCOM", "FAB" = "FABCOM", "CON" = "CONTAM"

STRUCTURAL SUMMARY

```
=================================================================================
     R = 40          Zf = 16        ZSum = 49.5        P = 8         (2) = 12
```

LOCATION FEATURES	DETERMINANTS BLENDS	SINGLE	CONTENTS	S-CONSTELLATION (ADULT)
			H = 5, 0	
W = 12	M.FC'	M = 5	(H) = 2, 0	NO..FV+VF+V+FD>2
D = 25	VF.YF	FM = 5	Hd = 0, 0	NO..Col-Shd Bl>0
Dd = 3	FM.FC.Fr	m = 0	(Hd)= 0, 0	NO..3r+(2)/R<.30
S = 2	M.FC	C = 2	A = 10, 0	NO..Zd > +- 3.5
	M.FC	Cn = 0	(A) = 0, 0	NO..ep > EA
		CF = 2	Ad = 5, 0	NO..CF+C+Cn > FC
		FC = 4	(Ad)= 0, 0	NO..X+ < .70
DQ		C' = 1	Ab = 1, 0	NO..S > 3
.........(FQ-)		C'F= 0	Al = 0, 0	NO..P < 3 or > 8
		FC'= 2	An = 2, 0	NO..Pure H < 2
+ = 9 (0)		T = 0	Art = 0, 0	NO..R < 17
v/+ = 0 (0)		TF = 1	Ay = 0, 0	0.....TOTAL
o = 20 (0)		FT = 1	Bl = 1, 0	
v = 11 (4)		V = 0	Bt = 4, 0	SPECIAL SCORINGS
		VF = 0	Cg = 2, 0	
		FV = 0	Cl = 0, 0	DV = 1
		Y = 0	Ex = 0, 0	INCOM = 2
		YF = 0	Fi = 0, 0	FABCOM = 1
FORM QUALITY		FY = 0	Fd = 2, 1	ALOG = 3
		rF = 0	Ge = 0, 0	CONTAM = 0
		Fr = 0	Hh = 0, 0	--- WSUM5 =24
		FD = 0	Ls = 1, 1	AG = 0

	FQx		FQf		M Qual.			
						F = 12	Na = 0, 0	CP = 0
+ =	4	+ =	0	+ =	3		Sc = 0, 0	MOR = 0
o =	29	o =	10	o =	5		Sx = 2, 0	PER = 0
w =	0	w =	0	w =	0		Xy = 0, 0	PSV = 1
- =	4	- =	2	- =	0		Idio= 3, 1	= 0
none=	3			none=	0			

```
=================================================================================
```

RATIOS, PERCENTAGES, AND DERIVATIONS

```
ZSum-Zest = 49.5 - 52.5        FC:CF+C  =  7: 4      W:M       = 12: 8
                                  (Pure C =  2)
Zd        = -3.0                                     W:D       = 12:25
                               Afr      = 0.48
---------------------------.                         A%        = 0.38
:EB =  8: 8.5   EA = 16.5:     3r+(2)/R = 0.38
:                   >D=  0                           Cont:R    = 11:40
:eb =  6: 8     ep = 14  :     L        = 0.43
'---------------------------'                        Isolate:R =  6:40
(FM= 6 " C'= 4 T= 2) (Adj D=  0)  Blends:R = 5:40
(m = 0 " V = 1 Y= 1)                                 H+Hd:A+Ad =  7:15
                               X+%      = 0.82
a:p       = 10: 4              (F+%     = 0.83) (H+Hd):(A+Ad)=  2: 0

Ma:Mp     =  6: 2                                    H+A:Hd+Ad = 17: 5
--------------------------------------------------------------------------------
D TOT;(Adj)=  0;(  0)       SCZI = 3<4>     DEPI = 2<4>      S-CON = 0<8>
=================================================================================
```

DATE: 23-DEC-83 -- PRINTED FOR: Sample Examiner
SUBJECT: 12-23-83- Sample -- 29 YEAR OLD WHITE FEMALE.

SEMANTIC INTERPRETATION OF THE RORSCHACH
PROTOCOL UTILIZING THE COMPREHENSIVE SYSTEM
(COPYRIGHT 1983, JOHN E EXNER, JR.)

THE FOLLOWING COMPUTER-BASED INTERPRETATION IS DERIVED ** EXCLUSIVELY **
FROM THE STRUCTURAL DATA OF THE RECORD AND DOES NOT INCLUDE CONSIDERATION OF
THE SEQUENCE OF SCORES OR THE VERBAL MATERIAL. IT IS INTENDED AS A GUIDE FROM
WHICH THE INTERPRETER OF THE TOTAL PROTOCOL CAN PROCEED TO STUDY AND REFINE
THE HYPOTHESES GENERATED FROM THESE ACTUARIAL FINDINGS.

* * * * *

1. DUE TO THE LARGE NUMBER OF RESPONSES, CAUTION SHOULD BE EXERCISED IN
    THE USE OF SOME NORMATIVE DATA. THIS IS ESPECIALLY TRUE FOR THOSE
    VARIABLES HAVING VERY LOW MEANS AND/OR STANDARD DEVIATIONS.
    PROPORTIONAL ESTIMATES MAY BE MORE USEFUL TO ASCERTAIN IF THOSE
    VARIABLES ARE TRULY DEVIANT IN THIS RECORD.

2. THIS PROTOCOL INDICATES A POSSIBILITY OF SCHIZOPHRENIA.

3. THERE IS CLEAR EVIDENCE OF SIGNIFICANT COGNITIVE SLIPPAGE. THIS
    USUALLY INDICATES THE PRESENCE OF DISORDERED THINKING.

4. THIS IS THE TYPE OF PERSON WHO DOES NOT HAVE A WELL ESTABLISHED
    COPING STYLE. INSTEAD, THERE IS A TENDENCY TO VACILLATE BETWEEN
    "THINKING THROUGH" AND TRIAL-AND-ERROR BEHAVIORS. NEITHER FORMAT HAS
    BEEN VERY WELL DEVELOPED. THUS, SUCH PEOPLE TEND TO BE LESS
    PREDICTABLE AND LESS EFFICIENT THAN THOSE WITH MORE WELL ESTABLISHED
    RESPONSE STYLES.

5. THIS SUBJECT USUALLY HAS ENOUGH RESOURCES TO FORM AND GIVE SOME
    DIRECTION TO RESPONSES PROMPTED BY STIMULUS DEMANDS. HOWEVER, THEY
    HAVE A MORE LIMITED TOLERANCE FOR STRESS THAN MIGHT BE DESIRABLE.
    CONSEQUENTLY, THEY ARE SUBJECT TO "STIMULUS OVERLOAD" MORE FREQUENTLY
    BY UNUSUAL OR UNEXPECTED SITUATIONS.

6. THERE IS EVIDENCE INDICATING THE PRESENCE OF CONSIDERABLE DISTRESS.

7. THIS SUBJECT TENDS TO INTERNALIZE FEELINGS MUCH MORE THAN IS
    CUSTOMARY AND THIS OFTEN RESULTS IN SUBSTANTIAL DISCOMFORT THAT CAN
    TAKE THE FORM OF TENSION AND/OR ANXIETY.

8. THIS PERSON IS EXPERIENCING CONSIDERABLE MENTAL ACTIVITY THAT IS
    BEING PROMOTED BY UNMET NEED STATES. SUCH MENTAL ACTIVITY USUALLY
    INTERFERES WITH ATTENTION AND/OR CONCENTRATION AND INCREASES
    DISTRACTIBILITY.

9. THIS TYPE OF PERSON IS NOT VERY FLEXIBLE IN THINKING, VALUES OR
    ATTITUDES. IN EFFECT, PEOPLE SUCH AS THIS HAVE SOME DIFFICULTY IN
    VIEWING THINGS DIFFERENTLY.

10. THE SUBJECT IS CAPABLE OF MODULATING EMOTIONAL DISPLAYS ABOUT AS WELL
    AS MOST ADULTS.

11. ALTHOUGH THE SUBJECT USUALLY EXERTS ADEQUATE CONTROL OVER THE
    DISPLAY OF EMOTIONS, A CLEAR POTENTIAL EXISTS FOR LOSS OF THIS
    CONTROL MORE OFTEN THAN SHOULD BE THE CASE.

12. THIS IS A PERSON WHO IS PROBABLY LESS AT EASE IN PROCESSING AND/OR
    RESPONDING TO EMOTIONALLY TONED SITUATIONS THAN MIGHT BE EXPECTED FOR
    MOST ADULTS. CONSEQUENTLY, THERE IS A TENDENCY TO AVOID THOSE
    SITUATIONS IN WHICH THOSE REQUIREMENTS APPEAR TO BE PRESENT. THIS
    MAY BE AN INDICATION OF SOME AWARENESS OF PROBLEMS IN EMOTION CONTROL
    AND REFLECTIVE OF AN EFFORT TO AVOID BEING DISRUPTED BY THOSE
    PROBLEMS. THIS KIND OF PERSON TENDS TO OVERGLORIFY THEIR PERSONAL
    WORTH AND PROBABLY HARBORS MANY OF THE FEATURES THAT WOULD BE
    CONSIDERED "NARCISSISSTIC." THIS FEATURE OFTEN BECOMES A MAJOR
    OBSTACLE TO FORMS OF TREATMENT THAT INVOLVE UNCOVERING OR
    RECONSTRUCTIVE EFFORTS.

psychware **567**

==

13.   THE SUBJECT APPEARS TO DEMONSTRATE A LEVEL OF PERCEPTUAL ACCURACY
      COMMENSURATE WITH MOST NON-PATIENTS.

14.   THESE KINDS OF PEOPLE OFTEN STRIVE TO INVOLVE THEMSELVES MORE THAN
      IS NECESSARY IN A STIMULUS FIELD. PEOPLE LIKE THIS OFTEN EXPEND MUCH
      MORE ENERGY THAN IS REQUIRED IN PROCESSING INFORMATION AND FORMING
      RESPONSES.

15.   THIS PERSON IS SOMEWHAT CONSERVATIVE IN SETTING GOALS. USUALLY
      PEOPLE LIKE THIS WANT TO COMMIT THEMSELVES ONLY TO OBJECTIVES WHICH
      OFFER A SIGNIFICANT PROBABILITY OF SUCCESS.

16.   THIS PERSON USUALLY SEEKS AN ECONOMICAL APPROACH TO PROBLEM SOLVING
      OR COPING. THIS IS TYPICAL OF MANY PEOPLE AND CAN BE AN ASSET.
      HOWEVER, IT CAN ALSO BECOME A LIABILITY IN MORE COMPLEX AND DEMANDING
      SITUATIONS THAT REQUIRE HIGHER LEVELS OF MOTIVATION AND EFFORT TO
      ACHIEVE EFFECTIVE RESULTS.

17.   MUCH OF THE COGNITIVE ACTIVITY OF THIS SUBJECT IS LESS SOPHISTICATED
      OR LESS MATURE THAN IS EXPECTED. THIS MAY BE A FUNCTION OF A
      DEVELOPMENTAL LAG, DISORGANIZATION, OR MAY SIMPLY REFLECT A
      RELUCTANCE TO COMMIT RESOURCES TO A TASK.

18.   THIS PERSON IS EXPERIENCING CONSIDERABLE EMOTIONAL IRRITATION
      BECAUSE OF STRONG, UNMET NEEDS FOR CLOSENESS THAT ARE USUALLY
      MANIFEST AS SOME EXPERIENCE OF LONELINESS. THIS IS MADE MORE
      IRRITATING BECAUSE SOME DATA SUGGEST A PREFERENCE FOR DEPENDENCY ON
      OTHERS.

19.   WHEN THIS PERSON ENGAGES IN SELF EXAMINATION A TENDENCY EXISTS TO
      FOCUS UPON NEGATIVE FEATURES PERCEIVED TO EXIST IN THE SELF IMAGE,
      AND THIS RESULTS IN CONSIDERABLE INTERNAL PAIN. THIS PROCESS IS
      OFTEN A PRECURSOR TO FEELINGS OF SADNESS, PESSIMISSIM OR EVEN
      DEPRESSION.

20.   THIS PERSON IS MORE PRONE TO INTERPERSONAL ISOLATION THAN MOST
      PEOPLE.

21.   THIS SUBJECT APPEARS TO HAVE A MARKED SEXUAL PREOCCUPATION.

22.   END OF REPORT***

NAME: Rorschach Interpretive System

SUPPLIER: PSYCH Systems, Inc.
600 Reisterstown Road
Baltimore, MD 21208
(800) 368-3366

PRODUCT CATEGORY

Personality

PRIMARY APPLICATIONS

Clinical Assessment/Diagnosis
Personal/Marriage/Family Counseling

SALE RESTRICTIONS Qualified Professional

SERVICE TYPE/COST	Type	Available	Cost	Discount
	Mail-In	No		
	Teleprocessing	No		
	Local	Yes	See Below	

PRODUCT DESCRIPTION

This on-line instrument allows for the input of raw Rorschach parameters into the computer. The raw scores are then interpreted using Exner's scoring system to output a comprehensive narrative report. The system also outputs the raw data to allow the clinician to reinterpret the scores in light of any other scoring system that may be preferred. Validation studies show the narrative reports to be strong in describing psychological states, trait characteristics, and defense mechanisms used by the patient.

Psych Systems programs operate on the IBM PC-XT, COMPAQ Plus, Dec Professional 350, and most DEC PDP-11 systems. Various hardware/ software configurations are available directly from Psych Systems, with single-user systems starting at approximately $12,000. A per test fee also applies.

NAME: RSCORE: Version 2.0

SUPPLIER: Psychological Assessment Resources
P.O. Box 98
Odessa, FL 33556
(813) 977-3395

PRODUCT CATEGORY

Personality

PRIMARY APPLICATIONS

Clinical Assessment/Diagnosis
Personal/Marriage/Family Counseling

SALE RESTRICTIONS American Psychological Association Guidelines

SERVICE TYPE/COST	Type	Available	Cost	Discount
	Mail-In	No		
	Teleprocessing	No		
	Local	Yes	$100.00	

PRODUCT DESCRIPTION

RSCORE: VERSION 2.0 is a computer program designed to handle data generated from the Rorschach Test according to Exner's Comprehensive System. It saves much of the time and effort involved in recopying Rorschach raw scores and computing frequencies, ratios, and percentages. The clinician simply enters the raw scores. The program then performs all operations necessary to list the sequence of scores and produce the structural summary.

Software versions of the program are available for TRS-80 Models II and III and Apple II+ and IIe microcomputers. The price shown is for unlimited usage of the program.

```
SUBJECT'S NAME:SAM PSYCHE                              RSCORE #536-CP
SUBJECT'S DATE OF BIRTH:5/2/52                                537-CP
DATE TEST ADMINISTERED:4/23/82                                538-CP
SEX:M
EXAMINER:MICHAEL GORDON
                          SEQUENCE OF SCORES
```

CARD	RT	NO	LOC	DETERMINANTS	CONTENT	POP	ZSCR	SPECIAL
1	38	1	W+	MA.FR.MA+	A,KEY	P	1	ALOG
		2	D-	FMA-	XY			MOR,ALOG
2	67	3	DDSV	CF.MA.FMAO	BAZOOKA			PSV
		4	WS-	MA- (2)	HD,AD,KEY	P	4.5	
3	50	5	WO	FC.FMA.MAW	HH,(AD)		5.5	FABCOM
		6	DO	FO (2)	A			
4	44	7	WSO	FTO	H		2	
		8	DD-	F-	GUITAR			ALOG,PER
5	16	9	DO	FMA+ (2)	A,AN			
6	13	10	WO	FO (2)	SPEAR		2.5	
7	45	11	DV	C	FI			
8	34	12	WO	FY.FC'O	FD		4.5	CP
9	47	13	DDO	FO (2)	A	P		
10	11	14	DO	FMAO	A	P		FABCOM

```
                          STRUCTURAL SUMMARY
```

```
R = 14        Zf = 6   ZSUM = 20    P = 4    (P) = 0    (2) = 5
Locations     Determinants              Contents        Contents
                                                        (Idiographic)
W   = 6                            H   = 1   Bl  =      KEY = 2
           MA.FR.MA = 1            (H) =     Bt  =      BAZOOKA = 1
D   = 5    CF.MA.FMA = 1           Hd  = 1   Cg  =      GUITAR = 1
           FC.FMA.MA = 1           (Hd)=     Cl  =      SPEAR = 1
Dd  = 3    FY.FC' = -1             A   = 5   Ex  =
                                   (A) =     Fi  = 1
S   = 3                            Ad  = 1   Fd  = 1
                                   (A) = 1   Ge  =
DW  = 0                            Ab  =     Hh  = 1
                        M   = 1    Al  =     Ls  =
           DQ  M Quality FM  = 3   An  = 1   Na  =
                        M'  =      Art =     Sx  =
                        C   = 1    Ay  =     Xy  = 1
+  =  1      + = 2      Cn  =
                        CF  =                        Special Scorings
O  =  8      O = 1      FC  =
                        C'  =      S-Constellation (Adult)    DV   =
V  =  2      W = 1      C'F =
                        FC' =      .....FV+VF+V+FD > 2        INCOM =
-  =  3      - = 1      T   =      .....Col-Shd Bl > 0
                        TF  =      .....3R+(2)/R < .30        FABCOM = 2
Form Quality            FT  = 1    .....ZD > +/- 3.5
                        V   =      .....ep > EA               ALOG  = 3
FQx      FQf            VF  =      ..*..CF + C >FC
                        FV  =      ..*..X+% < .70             CONTAM =
+  =  2      + =        Y   =      .....S > 3
                        YF  =      .....P < 3 OR > 8          CP    = 1
O  =  7      O = 3      FY  =      ..*..H < 2
                        RF  =      ..*..R < 17                MOR   = 1
W  =  1      W =        FR  =      . 4 .....Total
                        FD  =                                 PER   = 1
-  =  3      - = 1      F   = 4
                                                             PSV   = 1
```

```
                    RATIOS, PERCENTAGES, AND DERIVATIONS
```

```
ZSum:Zest  = 20 : 17        FC:CF+C = 1 : 2      Afr       = .27

Zd         = 3              W:M     = 6 : 5      3r+(2)/R  = .57

EB         = 5 : 3   EA = 8  W:D    = 6 : 5      CONT:R    = 11 : 14

eb         = 5 : 3   ep = 8  L      = .4         H+Hd:A+Ad = 2 : 7

(FM= 5 M'= 0 T= 1 C'= 1 V= 0 Y= 1 )

Blends:R   = 4 : 14          F+%     = 75 %       H+A:Hd+Ad = 6 : 3

a:p        = 10 : 0          X+%     = 64.29 %    XRT Achrom =

Ma:Mp      = 5 : 0           A%      = 50 %       XRT Chrom  = 96
```

Format Reproduced with Permission of Rorschach Workshops   *psychware* **571**

NAME: Sacks Sentence Completion Test-K

SUPPLIER: Psychological Assessment Resources
P.O. Box 98
Odessa, FL 33556
(813) 977-3395

PRODUCT CATEGORY	PRIMARY APPLICATIONS
Personality	Clinical Assessment/Diagnosis
Structured Interview	

SALE RESTRICTIONS American Psychological Association Guidelines

SERVICE TYPE/COST	Type	Available	Cost	Discount
	Mail-In	No		
	Teleprocessing	No		
	Local	Yes	$105.00	

PRODUCT DESCRIPTION

The SACKS SENTENCE COMPLETION TEST-K is a revised, computer-assisted version of the Sacks Sentence Completion Test. The computer inputs completions for each of 60 sentence stems, in addition to accepting the client's demographic information. The completions may be typed in directly by the client, entered from handwritten forms, or the test can be administered verbally while being entered by the examiner. Administration time is 15-20 minutes for faster typists and about 40 minutes for slower test takers. The test is excellent for pre-therapy screening, as a structured interview aid, or for gathering primary assessment data.

To assist scoring, the computer rearranges the completed sentences, grouping them into 15 content areas, which are, in turn, organized under four major areas of adjustment: Family, Interpersonal Relations, Sex, and Self-Concept. This reorganization greatly assists interpretation by making client conflict areas more apparent and by organizing the scoring and evaluation.

NAME: Sales Edge

SUPPLIER: Human Edge Software, Inc.
2445 Faber Pl.
Palo Alto, CA 94303
(415) 493-1593

PRODUCT CATEGORY	PRIMARY APPLICATIONS
Interest/Attitudes	Training/Development

SALE RESTRICTIONS None

SERVICE TYPE/COST	Type	Available	Cost	Discount
	Mail-In	No		
	Teleprocessing	No		
	Local	Yes	$250.00	

PRODUCT DESCRIPTION

The SALES EDGE is designed to give salespeople a detailed strategy for managing sales through a matching-up of the psychological characteristics of both parties. Users respond to 80 statements dealing with personal attitudes and characteristics. They then evaluate the intended customer with respect to a series of 50 descriptive adjectives. The resulting report, ranging in length from 8-10 pages, presents specific suggestions for opening, presentation, and closing strategies based on rated personal characteristics of each party.

The program is designed for the IBM PC microcomputer system.

NAME: Sales Preference Questionnaire*Plus

SUPPLIER: Behavioral Science Research Press
695 Villa Creek Suite 180
Dallas, TX 75234
(214) 243-8543

PRODUCT CATEGORY

Motivation/Needs

PRIMARY APPLICATIONS

Personnel Selection/Evaluation
Training/Development

SALE RESTRICTIONS   None

SERVICE TYPE/COST	Type	Available	Cost	Discount
	Mail-In	No		
	Teleprocessing	No		
	Local	Yes	See Below	

PRODUCT DESCRIPTION

The SALES PREFERENCE QUESTIONNAIRE*PLUS is designed to provide objective measurement of the fear of prospecting in direct sales personnel. It measures 9 areas of call reluctance (Threat-Sensitivity, Over-Preparation, Excuse-Making, Group Presentations, Calling on Personal Friends, Pride in Sales Career, Intrusion-Sensitivity, Up-Market Resistance, Calling on Relatives) and provides scores on two addition scales: Emotional Energy Spent Resisting Making Calls and Emotional Freedom to Initiate Prospecting Calls with Prospective Buyers. The 45 items in the questionnaire require approximately 15-20 minutes to complete without assistance.

Software versions of the program are compatible with IBM PC, TRS 80, and other microcomputer systems. Several different types of software licenses are available at varying costs. Special security access codes allow clerical access to the questionnaire, but not to the confidential scores.

The report begins with a graphic presentation of the basic scales followed by an analysis of various critical items. The last section of the output provides a narrative discussion of those areas in which reluctance is significantly elevated for both selection and training purposes.

Call Reluctance Scale for JOHN W SMITH

	RAW SCORES	CONTRAST NORMS*	GEN'L NORMS

Presence / Severity

```
==== BRAKE =========== XXXXXXXXXXXXXXX          56        38        45
==== ACCELERATOR ===== XXXXXXXXXX               34        52        45
```

Type(s) or Predisposition(s)
```
                       --1--2--3--4--5--6--7--8--9-10
THREAT SENSITIVITY . . XXXXXXXXXXXXXXX            5         4         5
DESURGENCY . . . . . . XXXXXXXXXXXXXXX            5         4         5
PROTENSION . . . . . . XXXXXXXXXXXXXXXXXX         6         5         5
GROUP  . . . . . . . . XXXXXXXXXXXX              4         4         5
FRIENDS  . . . . . . . XXX                        1         5         5
ROLE . . . . . . . . . XXXXXXXXXXXXXXXXXXXXX      7         4         5
DISRUPTION SENSITIVITY XXXXXXXXXXXXXXXXXXXXXXXXXXXXXX  10    5         5
SOCIAL DIFFERENTIAL  . XXXXXXXXXXXXXXXXXXXXXX     8         2         5
FAMILY . . . . . . . . XXXXXXXXXXXXXXXXXXXXXXXXXXXXXX  10    5         5
                       --1--2--3--4--5--6--7--8--9-10
```
* Contrast Norms are for Inexperienced prospective Life Insurance Agents

Critical Items Listing
10 critical question/answer combinations were observed.

I prefer a professional sales training program that :
Does not require salespersons to telephone or visit prospects who do not wish
to be contacted.

I prefer a sales training program that encourages salesmen and women to be
non-intrusive as opposed to training programs that encourage salespeople to
make EVERY possible sale.
True.

Some people believe that success in sales requires rather pushy individuals.
What is your opinion ?
(D) False. Worthwhile products and services rarely require aggressive
presentations because they are able to sell themselves.

Most professional sales people should be trained to avoid using relatives as
sales prospects.
True.

I personally don't like being intruded on by salespeople, and would
appreciate a professional sales training program that recognized when people
say "No" to a salesperson, they generally mean "No".
True.

I tend to be somewhat sceptical, and prefer a sales training program that
will allow me to use my critical perceptiveness by questioning assumptions,
disputing unconvincing "facts", and making alternative suggestions.
True. I tend to be this way, and most people respect my judgement and have,
at times, even hinted that I might know as much about some of the subjects as
my instructor.

psychware **575**

Some people do not think very highly of sales people. Without disputing the validity of their position, estimate how many people probably hold this view. One out of three adults.

Salespeople, in my opinion, should be cautious about approaching members of their own family as sales prospects, and should do so - if at all - only as a LAST resort.
I strongly agree.

I really don't feel comfortable with aggressive salespeople myself, and would prefer training that is based upon the quality of service and not the quantity of sales.
Very true.

OVERVIEW
========
This candidate's answers to SPQ questions indicate considerably more than usual hesitation to initiate self-promotional contact in a variety of situations. This could translate into job-related emotional distress, and an insufficient number of contacts to sustain personal or career objectives.

Disruption-Sensitivity
=========================
Individuals scoring high in this area fear the possibility that they might interrupt someone and be accused of being intrusive, rude or pushy. They tend to assume that whatever the prospect is doing at the time they want to call is probably more important and they procrastinate until they FEEL they are SURE they will not be interrupting the prospect. Therefore, few calls are made because the salesperson can never be ABSOLUTELY sure that a prospect will be receptive when he or she calls on him. This type of call-reluctance is easy to predict and diagnose and difficult to prevent and correct.

Social Differential
=====================
Individuals scoring high in this area are afraid to call upon professionals, such as accountants, attorneys, doctors, or anyone who they perceive to be socio-economically better off than they are. Typically, they will call on anyone but these individuals and can be quite successful until it becomes necessary that they upgrade their business contacts. This type of call-reluctance is difficult to predict, moderately easy to prevent, and easy to diagnose and correct.

Family
======
Individuals falling into this category find it extremely difficult if not impossible to call on personal relatives. They fear that they would be jeopardizing their family by mixing business with their personal lives. This type of call-reluctance is difficult to predict and prevent, and moderately difficult to diagnose and correct.

* * *   END OF REPORT   * * *

NAME: Sbordone-Hall Memory Battery

SUPPLIER: Robert J. Sbordone, Ph.D., Inc.
8840 Warner Ave. Suite 301
Fountain Valley, CA 92708
(714) 841-6293

PRODUCT CATEGORY

Cognitive/Ability

PRIMARY APPLICATIONS

Behavioral Medicine
Clinical Assessment/Diagnosis

SALE RESTRICTIONS American Psychological Association Guidelines

SERVICE TYPE/COST	Type	Available	Cost	Discount
	Mail-In	No		
	Teleprocessing	No		
	Local	Yes	$175.00	

PRODUCT DESCRIPTION

The SBORDONE-HALL MEMORY BATTERY provides fully automatic serial testing of 18 discrete memory functions utilizing computer-generated test stimuli. The program is intended to be used with normal, brain-injured, or cognitively-impaired patients for clinical assessment, cognitive rehabilitation, or research.

The program provides user-friendly, on-line testing that is understandable by all levels of users with little or no supervision required. The resulting report reflects a comprehensive quantitative and qualitative analysis of the patient's performance in comparison with normative data.

The program operates on the Apple II + , IIe, III, or Apple-compatible hardware and on the IBM PC-100 microcomputer system. No special computer knowledge is needed. The software comes with an instruction manual.

NAME: SCL-90-R

SUPPLIER: Applied Innovations, Inc.
South Kingstown Office Park, Suite A-1
Wakefield, RI 02879
(800) 272-2250

PRODUCT CATEGORY	PRIMARY APPLICATIONS
Personality	Clinical Assessment/Diagnosis

SALE RESTRICTIONS American Psychological Association Guidelines

SERVICE TYPE/COST	Type	Available	Cost	Discount
	Mail-In	No		
	Teleprocessing	No		
	Local	Yes	$125.00	

PRODUCT DESCRIPTION

This self-report symptom checklist consists of 90 items designed to aid in the identification of psychiatric disability. Psychological symptomatic distress is measured in terms of nine dimensions (Somatization, Obsessive-Compulsive, Interpersonal Sensitivity, Depression, Anxiety, Hostility, Phobic Anxiety, Paranoid Ideation, Psychoticism) and three global indices of distress (Global Severity Index, Positive Symptom Index, Positive Symptom Total). The checklist is used primarily for psychological screening and treatment planning and evaluation in mental health settings.

This program provides for rapid input of the 90 item scores, generally in less than two minutes. Once the scores have been entered, the program calculates T-scores, adjusts for norms, and reports in three areas: pathological behavior, probable symptoms, and similar patient groups. The software operates on most available personal computers including IBM, Apple, Digital, and Kaypro.

Name: HARRY S. CLARK   Sex: Male   Age: 33   Date: 3/21/84

SCL-90-R COMPUTERIZED SCORING AND INTERPRETATION

Copyright 1983

by

Bruce Duthie, Ph.D

APPLIED INNOVATIONS INC.
SOUTH KINGSTOWN OFFICE PARK, SUITE A-1
WAKEFIELD, RHODE ISLAND 02879
(800) 272-2250

1-0	19-0	37-1	55-2	73-2
2-1	20-2	38-0	56-0	74-0
3-2	21-1	39-2	57-2	75-1
4-3	22-0	40-1	58-0	76-0
5-0	23-2	41-2	59-1	77-2
6-2	24-3	42-0	60-0	78-3
7-1	25-1	43-2	61-2	79-0
8-0	26-0	44-0	62-3	80-2
9-2	27-2	45-0	63-4	81-0
10-1	28-3	46-2	64-0	82-3
11-0	29-0	47-3	65-2	83-0
12-2	30-2	48-1	66-3	84-0
13-3	31-0	49-0	67-2	85-2
14-1	32-2	50-2	68-0	86-0
15-0	33-1	51-1	69-2	87-2
16-2	34-0	52-2	70-0	88-0
17-1	35-2	53-0	71-1	89-2
18-4	36-3	54-2	72-0	90-0

This is a computer-generated psychological interpretation of the SCL-90-R. The
results are confidential and should be considered as a professional-to-profes-
sional consultation. All interpretations should be considered as working hypotheses to be further investigated by a qualified mental health professional.

psychware **579**

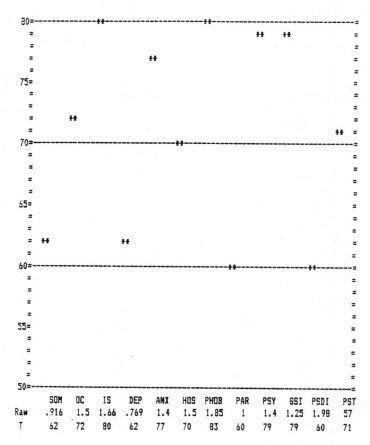

	SOM	OC	IS	DEP	ANX	HOS	PHOB	PAR	PSY	GSI	PSDI	PST
Raw	.916	1.5	1.66	.769	1.4	1.5	1.85	1	1.4	1.25	1.98	57
T	62	72	80	62	77	70	83	60	79	79	60	71

Moderate Somatization (T-Score greater than or equal to 60 but less than 65)

This individual may feel that his body is not functioning properly. Cardio-vascular, gastrointestinal, and respiratory complaints are evident. This individual may also complain of headaches, generalized pain, or muscle pain. The symptoms this patient endorsed are generally considered functional symptoms, although organic disease cannot be ruled out on the basis of this scale. These individuals tend to repress psychological conflict which leaks out in vague, generalized somatic symptoms.

The following symptoms may be endorsed by individuals scoring high on this scale: headaches, dizziness, chest pain, lower back pain, nausea, muscle soreness, breathing difficulty, hot spells, cold spells, numbness, bodily weakness, and extremity heaviness.

This scale is often elevated in psychiatric inpatients, depressives, alcoholics, cancer patients, and obese individuals. Individuals with chronic pain often have this scale extremely elevated and it is often one of the highest scales on their profile.

Clinical Obsessive-Compulsive (T-Score greater than or equal to 70 but less than 75)

These individuals ruminate obsessively. They have thoughts, impulses, and

behavioral patterns that repeat themselves incessantly and that are experienced
as out of the patient's control. At less severe elevations these individuals
tend to be perfectionistic, logical, somewhat argumentative, and very conventional.

Individuals scoring high on this scale may endorse the following symptoms:
repeat unpleasant thoughts, memory problems, excessive worries, difficulty with
decisions, and trouble concentrating.

Psychiatric patients, obese women, alcoholics, individuals with sexual dysfunction, and cancer patients often have this scale elevated. Individuals suffering from depression may have this scale as one of their highest.

Severe Clinical Interpersonal Sensitivity (T-score greater than or equal to 75)

Individuals with this profile type often feel inadequate and inferior. They
have a poor self concept and often lack ego strength. They are often anxious
when around others and generally do not like parties and crowds. They are
usually socially introverted and may have depressive symptoms. They generally
lack social skills and they are extremely uneasy in dating situations.

Individuals scoring high on this scale often admit to the following symptoms:
feeling critical, feeling shy, being easily hurt, feeling misunderstood, feel-
ing disliked, feeling inferior, feeling self-conscious, and feeling uncomfortable while eating in public.

Psychiatric patients, alcoholics, chronic pain patients, cancer patients,
individuals with sexual dysfunction and depressives often score moderately high
on this scale. This scale is often one of the highest scales elevated on
individuals who are obese or transexual.

Moderate Depression (T-Score greater than or equal to 60 but less than 65)

Individuals scoring high on this scale are probably experiencing many depressive symptoms. They tend to exhibit a clinically depressed mood, psychomotor
retardation, biological depressive symptoms, or a neurosthenic symptom pattern.
They often experience suicidal ideation and can be suicide risks.

Specific symptoms they endorse include loss of sexual interest, low energy,
suicidal ideation, crying, feeling trapped, self blame, feeling lonely and blue,
excessive worry, loss of interest, feeling hopeless, and feeling worthless.

Most psychiatric inpatients generally have elevated depressive scale scores.
Individuals who are diagnosed as having depression often have this scale as the
highest scale on their profile. Patients with sexual dysfunction, cancer, cardiac problems, obesity, alcohol abuse, or chronic pain often have this scale
markedly elevated and as one of their highest scales.

Severe Clinical Anxiety (T-score greater than or equal to 75)

Individuals scoring high on this scale often show overt clinical signs of
anxiety. They are often nervous, tense, frustrated individuals who are prone to
have panic attacks. Individuals scoring high on this scale may often be significantly depressed as well as anxious. They may have some obsessive-compulsive
tendencies and often harbor resentful feelings toward others.

Specific symptoms individuals scoring high on this scale often endorse are:
nervousness, shakiness, trembling, feeling suddenly scared, feeling fearful,
feeling tense, terror, panic, feeling restless, and having frightening thoughts
and images.

Obese women, patients with sexual dysfunctions, transexuals, and anxiety
neurotics often have elevated anxiety scales. Depressives, cancer patients,
psychiatric inpatients, alcoholics, and chronic pain patients often have this
scale markedly elevated and as one of their highest scales.

Clinical Hostility (T-Score greater than or equal to 70 but less than 75)

Individuals scoring high on this scale tend to be angry and hostile. They

are resentful, aggressive, and easily irritated. They may act out their hostility unexpectedly and in some cases could become assaultive. These individuals
are often suspicious, mistrust others and appear to be somewhat depressed or
agitated.

Specific symptoms they endorse include feeling annoyed, feeling irritated,
getting into arguments, having uncontrollable temper outbursts, having urges to
injure others, and having urges to break things.

Psychiatric inpatients, obese women, cancer patients, individuals with sexual
dysfunction, often have an elevated hostility scale. People with antisocial
personality patterns, or borderline personality patterns, often have this scale
markedly elevated and as one of their highest scoring scales.

Severe Clinical Phobic Anxiety (T-score greater than or equal to 75)

Individuals scoring high on this scale often have phobic fears. They cope
with these fears by avoiding the object or person they are afraid of. These
individuals often tend to be obsessive-compulsive and manifest the plethora of
anxiety symptoms. They are also prone to depression. Specific symptoms they
often endorse include many different kinds of fears, avoidant behavior, avoidance of social situations, and feelings of abandonment.

Psychiatric inpatients, cardiac and cancer patients, obese individuals, and
depressives often have this scale elevated. Anxiety neurotics, alcoholics, and
transexuals often have this scale markedly elevated and as one of their highest
scales.

Moderate Paranoid Ideation (T-Score greater than or equal to 60 but less than
65)

Individuals scoring high on this scale are often paranoid. Lower scores may
suggest hostility, suspiciousness, irritability and cantankerousness. At higher
elevations ideas of reference, grandiosity, and delusional systems may be
apparent.

Specific items that individuals with this profile often endorse include blaming others for their troubles, distrustfullness, feeling watched or talked
about, having unusual beliefs or ideas, and feeling that others will take advantage of them.

Psychiatric inpatients, alcoholics, cancer patients, and depressives often
score high on this scale.

Severe Clinical Psychoticism (T-score greater than or equal to 75)

Individuals scoring high on this scale tend to be withdrawn, isolated, and
seclusive. They may also have schizophrenic symptoms such as hallucinations
and bizarre sensory experiences. These individuals also may be somewhat suspicious, anxious, and have unconventional moral and value symptoms.

Depressives, alcoholics, cancer and cardiac patients, transexuals and obese
women may have this scale somewhat elevated. Individuals with anxiety neurosis,
sexual dysfunction, or psychiatric inpatients often have this scale as one of
their highest elevated scales.

NAME: Self-Description Inventory

SUPPLIER: NCS/Professional Assessment Services
P.O. Box 1416
Minneapolis, MN 55440
(800) 328-6759

PRODUCT CATEGORY	PRIMARY APPLICATIONS
Interest/Attitudes	Vocational Guidance/Counseling
Personality	Personal/Marriage/Family Counseling
	Personnel Selection/Evaluation

SALE RESTRICTIONS None

SERVICE TYPE/COST	Type	Available	Cost	Discount
	Mail-In	Yes	$4.25	Yes
	Teleprocessing	No		
	Local	No		

PRODUCT DESCRIPTION

The SELF-DESCRIPTION INVENTORY measures 11 personality and six vocationally-oriented dimensions. The latter correspond to Holland's RIASEC classification. It complements vocational interest inventories and ability tests used in career counseling.

The SELF-DESCRIPTION INVENTORY is intended for students in grade 9 or higher and adults. It features 200 self-descriptive adjectives with three response choices. An 8th-grade reading level and 15-20 minutes are required to complete the inventory. Personality scales included are: Adventurous, Analytical, Relaxed, Confident, Imaginative, Patient, Altruistic, Outgoing, Forceful, Industrious, and Orderly.

CLINICAL INTERPRETIVE ANALYSIS

OF THE

SELF-DESCRIPTION INVENTORY

CASE NO. 111111

TEST DATE: 1/13/84

This computer-generated report is based on the Self-Description
Inventory. Its purpose is to assist qualified professionals in
the evaluation of personality and vocational orientation.
Decisions should not be based solely on this report or any
other single source.

REVIEWING PROFESSIONAL

ADMINISTRATIVE INDICES
```
/-------------------------------------------------------\
:Yes % = 37  :? % = 38 :No % = 24  :Response check: 21 :
                Total Responses: 200
\-------------------------------------------------------/
```
PERSONAL DESCRIPTION SCALES

```
DESCRIPTION  SS   30        40        50        60        70 DESCRIPTION
/----------------:---------:---------:---------:---------:---------------\
:            : :      :::::::::::::::              :             :
:  Cautious   :52:            *                    :Adventurous:
:            : :      ===============              :             :
:------------------:---------:---------:---------:---------:---------------:
:            : :      :::::::::::::::              :             :
:Nonscientific:50:          *                      :Analytical :
:            : :      ==============               :             :
\------------------:---------:---------:---------:---------:---------------/
:            : :      ::::::::::::::::             :             :
:   Tense     :41:    *                            :  Relaxed   :
:            : :      ================             :             :
\------------------:---------:---------:---------:---------:---------------/
:            : :      ::::::::::::::::             :             :
:  Insecure   :56:                  *              :  Confident :
:            : :      ===============              :             :
\------------------:---------:---------:---------:---------:---------------/
:            : :      ::::::::::::::::             :             :
:Conventional :52:            *                    :Imaginative:
:            : :      ==============               :             :
\------------------:---------:---------:---------:---------:---------------/
:            : :      :::::::::::::::::            :             :
:  Impatient  :53:            *                    :  Patient   :
:            : :      ================             :             :
:------------------:---------:---------:---------:---------:---------------:
:            : :      ::::::::::::::               :             :
: Unconcerned :59:                       *         :Altruistic :
:            : :      ================             :             :
\------------------:---------:---------:---------:---------:---------------/
:            : :      ::::::::::::::::             :             :
:  Reserved   :55:                 *               :  Outgoing  :
:            : :      ================             :             :
\------------------:---------:---------:---------:---------:---------------/
:            : :      ::::::::::::::::             :             :
: Soft-spoken :40:    *                            :  Forceful  :
:            : :      ==============               :             :
\------------------:---------:---------:---------:---------:---------------/
:            : :      ::::::::::::::               :             :
:Lackadaisical:56:                 *               :Industrious:
:            : :      ===============              :             :
\------------------:---------:---------:---------:---------:---------------/
:            : :      ::::::::::::::::             :             :
: Unorganized :30: *                               :  Orderly   :
:            : :      ===============              :             :
\------------------:---------:---------:---------:---------:---------------/
               30        40        50        60        70
                [:] Average range for females
                [=] Average range for males
```

584   *psychware*

VOCATIONALLY-ORIENTED SCALES

```
   DESCRIPTION   SS      30        40        50        60        70
   /-------------------|---------|---------|---------|---------|---\
   :              : :          ::::::::::::::            :
   :R-realistic   :49:              *                    :
   :              : :          ===============           :
   \-------------------|---------|---------|---------|---------|---/
   :              : :          ::::::::::::::            :
   :I-investigative:45:          *                       :
   :              : :          ===============           :
   \-------------------|---------|---------|---------|---------|---/
   :              : :          :::::::::::::::           :
   :A-artistic    :58:                      *            :
   :              : :          ===============           :
   \-------------------|---------|---------|---------|---------|---/
   :              : :          :::::::::::::::           :
   :S-social      :55:                  *                :
   :              : :          ================          :
   \-------------------|---------|---------|---------|---------|---/
   :              : :          :::::::::::::::           :
   :E-enterprising:43:          *                        :
   :              : :          ===============           :
   \-------------------|---------|---------|---------|---------|---/
   :              : :          :::::::::::::::           :
   :C-conventional:27: *                                 :
   :              : :          ==============            :
   \-------------------|---------|---------|---------|---------|---/
                        30        40        50        60        70
```

[:] Average range for females
[=] Average range for males

TABLE OF RESPONSES

	1	2	3	4	5	6	7	8	9	10
0+	S	S	T	S	T	F	T	T	F	F
10+	T	T	T	S	T	S	T	T	S	T
20+	S	T	T	S	T	S	T	T	S	S
30+	F	S	T	S	T	S	S	S	T	F
40+	T	T	S	S	T	T	S	T	S	F
50+	T	T	T	T	T	F	S	S	F	S
60+	S	T	S	S	S	T	S	F	T	S
70+	F	S	F	F	S	S	T	F	S	F
80+	S	T	S	T	T	F	F	T	T	T
90+	T	S	S	S	T	T	F	S	S	F
100+	F	T	S	F	S	S	F	S	S	S
110+	T	S	S	T	S	S	F	T	S	S
120+	F	S	T	T	T	T	T	F	F	S
130+	T	T	S	F	S	T	S	T	S	T
140+	T	S	S	F	T	S	F	F	S	F
150+	F	S	S	T	F	S	F	T	S	F
160+	S	F	F	F	F	S	T	S	S	T
170+	T	T	T	F	F	S	T	S	S	F
180+	F	S	F	T	S	F	F	T	F	T
190+	F	T	T	S	F	S	F	T	T	T

T: True responses
S: Uncertain responses
F: False responses

```
                    ADMINISTRATIVE INDICES
         /----------------------------------------------------\
         :Yes % = 37  :? % = 38 :No % = 24  :Response check: 21 :
         :                Total Responses: 200                 :
         \----------------------------------------------------/
                    PERSONAL DESCRIPTION SCALES

  DESCRIPTION  SS   30        40        50        60       70 DESCRIPTION
/-------------------:---------:---------:---------:---------:-------------\
:             :  :  :         ::::::::::::::::::    :                      :
:   Cautious  :52:  :                   *          :            :Adventurous:
:             :  :  :               ===============:                      :
\-------------------:---------:---------:---------:---------:-------------/
:             :  :  :          :::::::::::::::::   :                      :
:Nonscientific:50:  :                  *           :            :Analytical :
:             :  :  :              ==============  :                      :
\-------------------:---------:---------:---------:---------:-------------/
:             :  :  :          ::::::::::::::::    :                      :
:   Tense     :41:  :          *                   :            : Relaxed  :
:             :  :  :          ===============     :                      :
\-------------------:---------:---------:---------:---------:-------------/
:             :  :  :          ::::::::::::::::    :                      :
:  Insecure   :56:  :                       *      :            : Confident :
:             :  :  :              ============    :                      :
\-------------------:---------:---------:---------:---------:-------------/
:             :  :  :          ::::::::::::::::    :                      :
:Conventional :52:  :                  *           :            :Imaginative:
:             :  :  :              ============    :                      :
\-------------------:---------:---------:---------:---------:-------------/
:             :  :  :          :::::::::::::::::   :                      :
:  Impatient  :53:  :                  *           :            : Patient  :
:             :  :  :              ================:                      :
\-------------------:---------:---------:---------:---------:-------------/
:             :  :  :         ::::::::::::::::     :                      :
: Unconcerned :59:  :                        *     :            :Altruistic :
:             :  :  :            ================  :                      :
\-------------------:---------:---------:---------:---------:-------------/
:             :  :  :         ::::::::::::::::     :                      :
:  Reserved   :55:  :                     *        :            : Outgoing :
:             :  :  :             ==============   :                      :
\-------------------:---------:---------:---------:---------:-------------/
:             :  :  :          ::::::::::::::::    :                      :
: Soft-spoken :40:  :          *                   :            : Forceful :
:             :  :  :              ============    :                      :
\-------------------:---------:---------:---------:---------:-------------/
:             :  :  :         ::::::::::::::::     :                      :
:Lackadaisical:56:  :                     *        :            :Industrious:
:             :  :  :             ===============  :                      :
\-------------------:---------:---------:---------:---------:-------------/
: Unorganized :30:  *         ::::::::::::::::::    :            : Orderly  :
:             :  :  :             ==============   :                      :
\-------------------:---------:---------:---------:---------:-------------/
                   30        40        50        60       70
              [:] Average range for females
              [=] Average range for males



                   VOCATIONALLY-ORIENTED SCALES

   DESCRIPTION  SS     30        40        50        60       70
/-----------------------:---------:---------:---------:---------:---\
:              :  :  :            ::::::::::::::::::    :             :
:R-realistic   :49:  :                     *           :             :
:              :  :  :                 ===============  :            :
\-----------------------:---------:---------:---------:---------:---/
:              :  :  :            :::::::::::::::::     :             :
:I-investigative:45: :                 *                :            :
:              :  :  :             ================     :            :
\-----------------------:---------:---------:---------:---------:---/
:              :  :  :            :::::::::::::::::     :             :
:A-artistic    :58:  :                         *        :            :
:              :  :  :                 ===============  :            :
\-----------------------:---------:---------:---------:---------:---/
:              :  :  :            ::::::::::::::::      :             :
:S-social      :55:  :                        *         :            :
:              :  :  :               ================   :            :
\-----------------------:---------:---------:---------:---------:---/
:              :  :  :            :::::::::::::::::     :             :
:E-enterprising:43:  :                *                 :            :
:              :  :  :                ================  :            :
\-----------------------:---------:---------:---------:---------:---/
:              :  :  :            :::::::::::::::::     :             :
:C-conventional:27:  *                                  :            :
:              :  :  :                ===============   :            :
\-----------------------:---------:---------:---------:---------:---/
                       30        40        50        60       70


               [:] Average range for females
               [=] Average range for males
```

586   *psychware*

UNDERSTANDING YOUR RESULTS

The results on this profile are based on your answers to the
Self-Description Inventory. They can give you useful
information by (1) making you aware of how you compare with
other people, and (2) helping you understand how your self-
descriptions fit with some major career areas.

Your Total Responses should be close to 200, the number of
items on the inventory. At the top of the profile is an
Administrative Indices section. The Yes % shows the percentage
of items that you indicated were "true" for you, the ? % shows
the percentage that you answered "uncertain", and the No %
shows the percentage that you answered "not true" for you.
The Response Check value generally is greater than 5 for most
people; a value of 5 or below indicates that you may not have
understood the instructions clearly or that you tended to be
very critical in your self-evaluation.

Your scores are printed in the Score column and plotted with
asterisks on the graph. The basis of your scores is a
comparison of how you described yourself with how individuals
in a general population described themselves. The average range
of scores for a group of females and males in a general
population is between 43 and 57 for each scale. The top bar
for each scale is the average range of scores for females,
and the bottom bar is the average range of scores for males.

THE PERSONAL DESCRIPTION SCALES - These eleven scales represent
basic descriptive dimensions on the inventory. For each scale,
a score of 50 is the overall average for a general population.
Scores above 50 indicate that the right-hand adjective is
more descriptive of your answers, scores less than 50 indicate
that the left-hand adjective is more descriptive.

CAUTIOUS - ADVENTUROUS: Scores toward the cautious end
indicate a tendency to "play it safe", and to be wary and
nonrugged; scores toward the adventurous end indicate more of
an aggressive nature that can be described as daring, bold,
rough, and courageous.

NONSCIENTIFIC - ANALYTICAL: Scores toward the nonscientific
end indicate a tendency to respond negatively to investigative
and scientific types of descriptions; scores toward the
analytical end are related to descriptions of being inventive,
scientific, curious, logical, and resourceful.

TENSE - RELAXED: Scores toward the tense end indicate
restless, anxious, high-strung, nervous, and tense feelings;
scores toward the relaxed end indicate more calm and easygoing
feelings.

INSECURE - CONFIDENT: Scores toward the insecure end indicate
feelings of uncertainty, pessimism, loneliness, and fear;
scores toward the confident end indicate feelings of self-
assurance, optimism, and stability.

CONVENTIONAL - IMAGINATIVE: Scores toward the conventional end
indicate feelings of being traditional, conforming, and
restrained; scores toward the imaginative end indicate more of
a tendency to be witty, funny, creative, humorous, and
unconventional.

IMPATIENT - PATIENT: Scores toward the impatient end indicate
a tendency to be short-tempered, demanding, hasty, impulsive,
picky, and unreasonable; scores toward the patient end indicate
a tendency to be tactful, calm, tolerant, and agreeable.

UNCONCERNED - ALTRUISTIC: Scores toward the unconcerned end
indicate a noninvolvement in social/religious concerns or an
indifference to them; scores toward the altruistic end indicate
feelings of being religious, gentle, unselfish, moral,
generous, and giving.

RESERVED - OUTGOING: Scores toward the reserved end are
related to being shy, withdrawn, quiet, and bashful; scores
toward the outgoing end are related to being sociable,
talkative, entertaining, expressive, and enthusiastic.

SOFT-SPOKEN - FORCEFUL: Scores toward the soft-spoken end are
related to being quiet, moderate, and gentle-voiced; scores
toward the forceful end are related more to being outspoken,
frank, persuasive, argumentative, and blunt.

LACKADAISICAL - INDUSTRIOUS: Scores toward the lackadaisical
end are related to descriptions of being slower-paced; scores
toward the industrious end are related to being energetic,
enterprising, hardworking, achieving, and progressive.

UNORGANIZED - ORDERLY: Scores toward the unorganized end are
related to being forgetful, careless, and absentminded; scores
toward the orderly end are related to being neat, organized,
thorough, tidy, and perfectionistic.

THE VOCATIONALLY-ORIENTED SCALES: Your scores on these scales may help you to get a better feeling for how you relate to six general career areas. Research indicates that descriptive adjectives can be used to help identify these six basic career areas: R-I-A-S-E-C. Since each description below describes a group of people, all the characteristics may not fit any one person. Generally, the higher your score, the more likely these descriptions will be true for you.

R - realistic: People who have high scores on the realistic scale prefer working with machines rather than with people, like to work outside, and prefer working alone or with only one or two people. Mechanic, skilled tradesperson, farmer, military officer, and forester are some of the occupations preferred by these people.

I - investigative: This type like activities and occupations that are related to science and mathematics. They enjoy working with ideas and words to find their own solutions, especially in scientific areas. They prefer scientific occupations such as laboratory research worker, medical technician, and computer programmer.

A - artistic: People of this type have artistic tendencies. Generally, high scores are related to interests in writing, poetry, or drawing and sketching. Occupational choices include those of artist, author, cartoonist, singer, poet, actor/actress, and other artistically-oriented vocations.

S - social: People with high scores on this scale generally tend to have a very strong concern for other people and to like solving problems. They prefer to solve problems by talking things out, and they get along well with many types of people. There are many social types of occupations in the world of work, among which are social worker, recreational leader, teacher, nurse, and camp counselor.

E - enterprising: People of this type generally are good at talking with people and at using words to persuade people. Often they are in sales work, and they are clever at thinking up new ways to lead and convince people. Related occupations are buyer/merchandiser, real estate sales, hotel manager, and other kinds of sales jobs.

C - conventional: This type usually prefers activities and jobs in which they know exactly what is expected of them and what they are supposed to do. They like activities such as book-keeping, typing, filing, and general business types of work. They prefer jobs in the business world such as bookkeeper, accountant, secretary, and computer operator.

Remember, your scores measure how you answered the inventory and how your answers compare to the responses of a general population. Use them to better understand yourself and how your preferences fit with various personal and work-related settings. However, do not expect miracles from this or any inventory. Each individual is unique and no inventory can predict perfectly all the differences among people. For additional information, consult a professional counselor.

SELF-DESCRIPTION INVENTORY
33 YEAR OLD FEMALE

CASE NO. 111111   1/13/84

TABLE OF RESPONSES

	1	2	3	4	5	6	7	8	9	10
0+	S	S	T	S	T	F	T	T	F	F
10+	T	T	T	S	T	S	T	T	S	T
20+	S	T	T	S	T	S	T	T	S	S
30+	F	S	T	S	T	S	S	S	T	F
40+	T	T	S	S	T	T	S	T	S	F
50+	T	T	T	T	T	F	S	S	F	S
60+	S	T	S	S	S	T	S	F	T	S
70+	F	S	F	F	S	S	T	F	S	F
80+	S	T	S	T	T	F	F	T	T	T
90+	T	S	S	S	T	T	F	S	S	F
100+	F	T	S	F	S	S	F	S	S	S
110+	T	S	S	T	S	S	F	T	S	S
120+	F	S	T	T	T	T	T	F	F	S
130+	T	T	S	F	S	T	S	T	S	T
140+	T	S	S	F	T	S	F	F	S	F
150+	F	S	S	T	F	S	F	T	S	F
160+	S	F	F	F	F	S	T	S	S	T
170+	T	T	T	F	F	S	T	S	S	F
180+	F	S	F	T	S	F	F	T	F	T
190+	F	T	T	S	F	S	F	T	T	T

T: True responses
S: Uncertain responses
F: False responses

psychware **589**

NAME: Self-Directed Search

SUPPLIER: Integrated Professional Systems
5211 Mahoning Avenue Suite 135
Youngstown, OH 44515
(216) 799-3282

PRODUCT CATEGORY

Career/Vocational
Interest/Attitudes

PRIMARY APPLICATIONS

Vocational Guidance/Counseling
Educational Evaluation/Planning
Personnel Selection/Evaluation

SALE RESTRICTIONS   Qualified Professional

SERVICE TYPE/COST	Type	Available	Cost	Discount
	Mail-In	No		
	Teleprocessing	No		
	Local	Yes	See Below	

PRODUCT DESCRIPTION

The SELF DIRECTED SEARCH is a widely-used instrument for career counseling and vocational guidance. Six types of vocational interests are assessed: realistic, investigative, artistic, social, enterprising, and conventional. Responses to questions in these six areas are used to identify appropriate vocational options.

The report produced by this program includes graphs illustrating the various profiles of the respondent. Narrative statements, as well as occupations listed in the Occupational Finder that match the vocational code type, are presented.

An operating software package, priced from $200-$850 depending on the complexity of the package, is required for program use, plus an additional fee of $3.00 per use.

NAME: Self-Directed Search

SUPPLIER: PSYCH Systems, Inc.
600 Reisterstown Road
Baltimore, MD 21208
(800) 368-3366

PRODUCT CATEGORY	PRIMARY APPLICATIONS
Career/Vocational	Vocational Guidance/Counseling Personal/Marriage/Family Counseling Educational Evaluation/Planning

SALE RESTRICTIONS Qualified Professional

SERVICE TYPE/COST	Type	Available	Cost	Discount
	Mail-In	No		
	Teleprocessing	No		
	Local	Yes	See Below	

PRODUCT DESCRIPTION

Developed for career planning and vocational exploration by the examiner, this diagnostic tool is based on Holland's personality-vocational typology. It is intended to be self- interpreting and to aid the client in understanding vocational alternatives and the decision-making process itself.

The SELF-DIRECTED SEARCH has four separate sections: activities, competencies, occupations, and self-estimates. Each section is scored for the six Holland types: Realistic, Investigative, Artistic, Social, Enterprising, and Conventional. Based on an analysis of these theme scores, the program presents possible occupational choices to the individual. Two reports are printed, one for the client and a summary report for the counselor.

Psych Systems programs operate on the IBM PC-XT, COMPAQ Plus, Dec Professional 350, and most DEC PDP-11 systems. Various hardware/ software configurations are available directly from Psych Systems, with single-user systems starting at approximately $12,000. A per test fee also applies.

222-22-2222   Jonathan Doe   32 yr old white male   16-Feb-84

```
-----------------------------------
|       |                           |
|  SDS  |   Self-Directed Search    |
|       |                           |
-----------------------------------
```

The SDS is designed to assist in vocational decision-making. This
report was reproduced by a computerized analysis of the responses
provided by the client listed above. There are two sections : a
summary for the counselor and a vocational planning report for the
client.

The computer program generating this report was designed by Psych
Systems, Inc., Baltimore, Maryland 21208. Copyright (C) 1984 by Psych
Systems, Inc. The Self Directed Search is reproduced by permission.
Copyright (C) 1974, 1979, 1982 by Consulting Psychologists Press,
Incorporated, 577 College Avenue, Palo Alto, California 94306. No
portion of the SDS may be reproduced by any process without prior
written permission of the publisher. All rights reserved.

Self-Directed Search
Counselor's Summary

Jonathan Doe is 32 years of age. He attends high school and works full time. He reports being somewhat dissatisfied with his current occupation. This person reports no specific expectations about the outcome of testing.

Results of the SDS indicate this person has conventional, enterprising and realistic interests. Thus, the Holland Occupational Code (HOC) is CER. Although consistent, his vocational interests are not well-defined.

The next part of this report will present occupations congruent with this person's interests as measured by the SDS. Because this person has poorly defined interests, he should be cautioned that his occupational code, CER, and thus possible vocational choices, are subject to change. If these occupations are incongruent with his expectations or plans, then further vocational counseling may be necessary. On occasion, only occupational experience and increased vocational maturity can substantially clarify the vocational decision-making process.

The following occupations are congruent with this person's HOC and have been considered as possible career choices. They are most likely to represent enduring and satisfying career choices. Also printed will be the Dictionary of Occupational Titles (DOT) code for each occupation.

HOC	Occupation	DOT Code
CEI	Financial Analyst	020.167-014
CES	Accountant	160.167-010
ECI	Bank President	186.117-054
ECS	Credit Analyst	241.267-022

The following occupations are most consistent with this person's vocational interests and educational level (or expressed educational goals), but have not been considered previously as possible career choices.

Occupation	DOT Code
HOC : CES	
Credit Manager	168.167-054
HOC : ECS	
Insurance Underwriter	169.167-058
Grain Buyer	162.167-010
Real Estate Appraiser	191.267-010
HOC : CSE	
Business (Commercial) Teacher	091.227-010

These occupations are congruent with the client's vocational interests, but do not match his educational level or educational goals.

Occupation	DOT Code
HOC : CER	
Data Processing Worker	see note
Mail Clerk	209.587-026
HOC : CES	
Clerk, General	209.562-010
Court Reporter	202.362-010
Stenographer	202.362-014
HOC : REC	
Supervisor, Natural-Gas Plant	542.130-010

```
                         HOC : RCE
Crane Operator                                           921.663-010
Lumber Inspector                                         669.587-010
Tractor Operator                                         929.683-014
Tractor-Trailer-Truck Driver                             904.383-010
Truck Driver, Light                                      906.683-022
Fork-Lift Truck Operator                                 921.683-050
                         HOC : ERC
Postmaster                                               188.167-066
                         HOC : CRE
Electric-Motor Assembler                                 721.684-022
Sewing Machine Operator                                  787.682-046
                         HOC : ECS
Buyer (Purchasing Agent)                                 162.157-018
Customer Services Manager                                187.167-082
Florist (Retailer)                                       185.167-046
Furniture Buyer                                          162.157-018
Manager, Procurement Services                            162.167-022
Real Estate Sales Agent                                  250.357-018
Sales Representative, Farm Equipment                     272.357-014
Supervisor, Ticket Sales                                 238.137-022
Bill Collector                                           241.367-010
                         HOC : CRI
Timekeeper                                               215.367-022
Linotype Operator                                        650.582-010
Biller                                                   214.482-010
Key Punch Operator                                       203.582-030
Tabulating-Machine Operator                              213.682-010
Duplicating-Machine Operator                             207.682-010
                         HOC : CRS
File Clerk                                               206.367-014
                         HOC : CIE
Office Worker                                            see note
Payroll Clerk                                            215.482-010
Proofreader                                              209.387-030
                         HOC : CIR
Adding Machine Operator                                  216.482-014
Telegraphic-Typewriter Operator                          203.582-050
                         HOC : CSE
Personnel Clerk                                          209.362-026
Sales Correspondent                                      221.367-062
Travel Clerk                                             237.367-018
Receptionist                                             237.367-038
Typist                                                   203.582-066
Telephone Operator                                       235.662-022
Teller                                                   211.362-018
                         HOC : CSR
Reservations Agent                                       238.367-018
Traffic Checker                                          205.367-058
Messenger, Office                                        239.567-010
```

Note - For D.O.T. numbers, look under a more specific job title.

The client is expressing the following vocationally-related concerns:
    -Believes he lacks the special talents to follow his career choice.
    -Doesn't have the money to follow a preferred career.
    -An influential person does not approve of his career choice.

The client is expressing a need for the following:
    -Information about employment opportunities.
    -Information about his major strengths and weaknesses.

```
          R       I       A       S       E       C
      ------------------------------------------------
 50 +  -       -       -       -       -       -     + 50
    -                                                -
    -                                                -
    -                                                -
 40 +  -       -       -       -       -       -     + 40
    -                                                -
    -                                          *     -
    -                                   *            -
 30 +  *       -       *       -       -       -     + 30
    -                           *                    -
    -                                                -
    -                                                -
    -          *                                     -
 20 +  -       -       -       -       -       -     + 20
    -                                                -
    -                                                -
    -                                                -
 10 +  -       -       -       -       -       -     + 10
    -                                                -
    -                                                -
    -                                                -
      ------------------------------------------------
          R       I       A       S       E       C
```

	R	I	A	S	E	C
Raw Score	30	22	29	28	31	33
T Score	55	49	64	55	63	74
Percentile	71	47	91	71	90	99

Differentiation = 6th percentile   Consistency = High

Note : The HOC is determined by using raw scores as recommended by
Holland. Standard T-score and percentile transformations are presented
as a supplementary counseling tool. This information may be useful in
helping the client compare his interests with a reference group of the
same sex and similar educational background.

Self-Directed Search
Vocational Planning Report

The Self-Directed Search (SDS) is a tool for educational and vocational
planning. It was developed by Dr. John Holland and is based on his
theory of how people choose careers. He identifies six personality
types or dimensions. These are the Realistic, Investigative, Artistic,
Social, Enterprising, and Conventional types.

The Realistic (R) type likes realistic jobs such as aircraft
controller, surveyor, mechanic, and electrician. This type has
mechanical abilities.

The Investigative type (I) likes investigative jobs such as biologist,
chemist, and medical technologist. This type has mathematical and
scientific abilities.

The Artistic type (A) likes artistic jobs such as musician, writer,
actor/actress, and interior decorator. This type has esthetic
interests and artistic abilities.

The Social type (S) likes social jobs such as teacher, counselor,
psychologist, speech therapist, and social worker. This type has
social interests and abilities.

The Enterprising (E) type likes enterprising jobs such as manager, salesperson, business executive, and retail buyer. This type has leadership and speaking abilities.

The Conventional (C) type likes conventional jobs such as bookkeeper, stenographer, financial analyst, and banker. This type has clerical and arithmetical abilities.

Each type results from the interaction of personal experiences and social forces such as parents, friends, social class, and school involvement. Job environments can be classified according to the same six types. Each work environment is dominated by a similar personality type. For example, social environments are dominated by social types. People seek environments that allow them to use their abilities and skills, express their attitudes and values, and assume agreeable roles. Enterprising types seek enterprising environments, realistic types seek realistic environments, and so forth. Thus, people and jobs can be classified and matched by using the six personality types.

The SDS estimates how you resemble each of these types. Later in this report, profiles will be presented that will show the scores you obtained on each of the SDS scales which measure these types. The scores are placed in order, from high to low. The highest three scores are used to determine your Holland Occupational Code (HOC). The first letter of your code shows the type you resemble most, the next letter shows the type you resemble somewhat less, and the third letter indicates the type you resemble still less. The types that are not in your three letter code are the types you resemble least or not at all.

Your summary Holland Occupational Code is obtained by adding the scores from the four parts of the SDS. These four sections are scored on the same six dimensions: realistic, investigative, artistic, social, enterprising, and conventional. Before discussing your summary HOC, we will first look at your response to these four sections. This can provide useful information about your interests and how you view your abilities.

The first section of the SDS asked you to report whether you liked or disliked a wide range of activities. The following profile graphically shows your evaluation. Below the profile is presented the raw score for each of the six scales.

```
                     Activity Profile

             R       I       A       S       E       C
        ----------------------------------------------------------
         -                                                    -
         -                                                    -
   12 +   -       -       -       -       -       -    + 12
         -                                                    -
         -                                                    -
         -                       *                            -
    8 +   -       -       -       -       -       -    + 8
         -       *               *               *    -
         -                                                    -
         -               *               *                    -
    4 +   -       -       -       -       -       -    + 4
         -                                                    -
         -                                                    -
         -                                                    -
        ----------------------------------------------------------
             R       I       A       S       E       C
Raw Score    7       5       9       7       5       7
```

The next section asked you to evaluate your competency across a wide range of tasks and skills. The following profile presents your perception of competencies. Please remember that these are self-estimates of competency and you should not view them as objective measures of your ability.

Competencies Profile

```
           R       I       A       S       E       C
      ------------------------------------------------------
        -                                                -
        -                                                -
  12 +  -       -       -       -       -       -      + 12
        -                                                -
        -  *                                             -
   8 +  -       -       -       -       -       -      + 8
        -                                       *      -  *
        -       *       *               *              -
        -                       *                      -
   4 +  -       -       -       -       -       -      + 4
        -                                                -
        -                                                -
        -                                                -
      ------------------------------------------------------
           R       I       A       S       E       C
Raw Score  9       6       6       5       7       7
```

The third section of the SDS asked you to evaluate a number of occupations along a dimension of personal appeal to you. Occupations can be categorized along the same six dimensions of Holland's model. The following profile graphically portrays your preferences along the six personality dimensions.

Occupations Profile

```
           R       I       A       S       E       C
      ------------------------------------------------------
        -                                                -
        -                                                -
  12 +  -       -       -       -       -       -      + 12
        -                                                -
        -                               *                -
   8 +  *       -       -       *       -       *      + 8
        -               -  *                           -
        -       *                                      -
        -                                                -
   4 +  -       -       -       -       -       -      + 4
        -                                                -
        -                                                -
        -                                                -
      ------------------------------------------------------
           R       I       A       S       E       C
Raw Score  8       6       7       8       9       8
```

The final section of the SDS asked you to rate yourself on different dimensions of ability, for example, mechanical, sales, and math. These self-ratings can also be evaluated in terms of Holland's six personality-vocational dimensions and are presented in the following section.

Self-Estimates Profile

```
            R        I        A        S        E        C
      ----------------------------------------------------------
        -                                                    -
        -                                                    -
   12 +  -        -        -        -        -        -    + 12
        -                                            *       -
        -                                   *                -
        -                                                    -
    8 +  -        -        -        *        -        -    + 8
        -                  *                                 -
        -    *                                               -
        -             *                                      -
    4 +  -        -        -        -        -        -    + 4
        -                                                    -
        -                                                    -
        -                                                    -
      ----------------------------------------------------------
            R        I        A        S        E        C
Raw Score   6        5        7        8       10       11
```

While each section of the test provides useful information, possible vocational and career choices can be recommended most accurately by considering all four sections as a whole. Thus, we add the scores for each of the four sections together to obtain your summary Holland Occupational Code (HOC). The HOC is a simple way of organizing information about people and jobs. It may be used to learn how your special pattern of interests, self-estimates, and skills resemble the patterns of interests and skills that many common occupations demand. Thus, we can use your HOC to select suitable groups of occupations for you to consider. The next profile shows your summary scores on all six scales. The first row of numbers below the profile presents your raw score for each scale. The second row of numbers presents your percentile score. This allows you to compare your score to that obtained by other people. For example, on the Realistic scale, you obtained a raw score of 30. This corresponds to a percentile score of 71. Thus, your score equals or exceeds that of 71 percent of those who take this test. You can make this same comparison for the remaining scores on this profile.

Summary Profile

```
            R        I        A        S        E        C
      ----------------------------------------------------------
        -                                                    -
        -                                                    -
   48 +  -        -        -        -        -        -    + 48
        -                                                    -
        -                                                    -
        -                                                    -
   32 +  *        -        -        -        *        *    + 32
        -                  *        *                        -
        -             *                                      -
   16 +  -        -        -        -        -        -    + 16
        -                                                    -
        -                                                    -
        -                                                    -
      ----------------------------------------------------------
            R        I        A        S        E        C
Raw Score   30       22       29       28       31       33
Percentile  71       47       91       71       90       99
```

You obtained your highest scores on the conventional, enterprising and realistic scales. Thus, your Holland Occupational Code (HOC) is CER.

In order to use your HOC to assist in selecting possible occupations, you must consider other aspects of your SDS scores. How closely you will resemble these types depends on several factors.

Generally speaking, the higher the score for a particular scale, the stronger your interests are in that area. Currently, you appear to have moderately strong realistic, artistic, social , enterprising and conventional interests.

Looking at your profile, you may see that you resemble several types rather than just one. If you have only one or two high scores or if there are relatively large differences between the high and low scores, then you have a well-differentiated profile.

A hexagon is used to show the similarities and differences among the types and between people and jobs. Look at the hexagon below. Each letter designates one of the six scales: realistic (R), investigative (I), artistic (A), social (S), enterprising (E), and conventional (C).

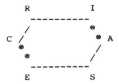

If the letters of your summary HOC are next to each other on the hexagon, then you have more consistent or compatible interests. The further apart the letters are, the less compatible are your interests. For example, realistic and investigative are consistent types, while investigative and enterprising are inconsistent types. People with consistent codes are less likely to change career fields. Your vocational preferences, though not well-defined, are consistent. This may help to explain your uncertainty or confusion about choosing a career and why no occupation strongly appeals to you at the present time .

Jobs and work environments can be categorized along the same six dimensions. Thus, the hexagon can be used to estimate the degree of fit between a person and a job. For example, an investigative person in an investigative occupation fits the job well. An investigative person in a realistic occupation is not as close a fit. An investigative person in an enterprising occupation is in the most incompatible job possible. The following part of this report will present to you occupations that are, in varying degrees, compatible with your summary code of CER.

The following occupations are consistent with your HOC and have been considered by you as possible career choices. Vocational research indicates these are most likely to represent enduring and satisfying career choices. Also printed will be the Dictionary of Occupational Titles (DOT) code for each occupation.

HOC	Occupation	DOT Code
CEI	Financial Analyst	020.167-014
CES	Accountant	160.167-010
ECI	Bank President	186.117-054
ECS	Credit Analyst	241.267-022

The following occupations are most consistent with your vocational interests and educational level (or educational goals). However, you did not indicate these were previously considered as possible occupational choices.

Occupation	DOT Code
HOC : CES	
Credit Manager	168.167-054
HOC : ECS	
Insurance Underwriter	169.167-058
Grain Buyer	162.167-010
Real Estate Appraiser	191.267-010
HOC : CSE	
Business (Commercial) Teacher	091.227-010

These occupations are consistent with your vocational interests, but do not match your educational level or your educational goals.

Occupation	DOT Code
HOC : CER	
Data Processing Worker	see note
Mail Clerk	209.587-026
HOC : CES	
Clerk, General	209.562-010
Court Reporter	202.362-010
Stenographer	202.362-014
HOC : REC	
Supervisor, Natural-Gas Plant	542.130-010
HOC : RCE	
Crane Operator	921.663-010
Lumber Inspector	669.587-010
Tractor Operator	929.683-014
Tractor-Trailer-Truck Driver	904.383-010
Truck Driver, Light	906.683-022
Fork-Lift Truck Operator	921.683-050
HOC : ERC	
Postmaster	188.167-066
HOC : CRE	
Electric-Motor Assembler	721.684-022
Sewing Machine Operator	787.682-046
HOC : ECS	
Buyer (Purchasing Agent)	162.157-018
Customer Services Manager	187.167-082
Florist (Retailer)	185.167-046
Furniture Buyer	162.157-018
Manager, Procurement Services	162.167-022
Real Estate Sales Agent	250.357-018
Sales Representative, Farm Equipment	272.357-014
Supervisor, Ticket Sales	238.137-022
Bill Collector	241.367-010
HOC : CRI	
Timekeeper	215.367-022
Linotype Operator	650.582-010
Biller	214.482-010
Key Punch Operator	203.582-030
Tabulating-Machine Operator	213.682-010
Duplicating-Machine Operator	207.682-010
HOC : CRS	
File Clerk	206.367-014
HOC : CIE	
Office Worker	see note
Payroll Clerk	215.482-010
Proofreader	209.387-030
HOC : CIR	
Adding Machine Operator	216.482-014
Telegraphic-Typewriter Operator	203.582-050
HOC : CSE	
Personnel Clerk	209.362-026
Sales Correspondent	221.367-062
Travel Clerk	237.367-018
Receptionist	237.367-038
Typist	203.582-066

Telephone Operator	235.662-022
Teller	211.362-018

HOC : CSR

Reservations Agent	238.367-018
Traffic Checker	205.367-058
Messenger, Office	239.567-010

Note - For D.O.T. numbers, look under a more specific job title.

Although providing coverage for 95% of the labor force, this report does not catalogue all the occupations contained in the Dictionary of Occupational Titles (DOT). If you wish to search for all the DOT occupations that correspond to your SDS summary code, please use the following conversion list. The DOT is printed by the Department of Labor and should be available at your library or counselor's office.

Conventional

CRI	207,208,229
CRS	206,236
CRE	221
CIS	203,213,214,215,217,219
CIE	209
CIR	216
CSE	205,211,235,237,238,241
CSR	230
CSI	210
CSA	201,243,245,247,248,249
CER	
CEI	
CES	160,161,202

We hope the SDS has been helpful in your vocational and career planning. The SDS, or any vocational interest inventory, is most useful when it reassures you about your vocational choice or reveals new possibilities worthy of consideration. If it fails to support a choice you have tentatively made, don't automatically change your plans. Instead, do some investigation to make sure you really understand the career you have chosen and the occupations suggested by the SDS. Then make a decision.

Keep in mind that your SDS results are affected by many factors in your background - your sex, your age, your parents' occupations, ethnic or social influences, etc. For example, because society often encourages men and women to aspire to different vocations, women as a group tend to receive more S, A, and C codes than men, while men tend, as a group to obtain more I, R, and E codes. Yet we know that almost all jobs can be successfully performed by members of either sex. If your codes differ from occupational goals or dreams you had prior to testing, keep these influences in mind; they may account for the differences and you may decide to stick with these already established goals or dreams.

Now that you have some occupational possibilities for exploration, here are some additional things you can do.

1. Seek more information about these occupations from local counseling centers, school counselors, libraries, labor unions, employment services, and occupationsl information files (usually found in counseling offices).

2. Talk to people employed in the occupations in which you are especially interested. Most people enjoy talking about their work. Remember, however, that they may have personal biases, either positive or negative.

3. Try to obtain part-time work experience that is similar to the activities in the occupations you are considering, even if you must give your time without pay.

4. Consider any health or physical limitations that might affect your choice.

5. Investigate the educational requirements for the occupations that interest you. Where could you obtain the required training? Is it financially possible? Is it reasonable in terms of your learning ability, age, family situation, etc.?

6. Read articles and books that describe occupations or attempt to explain current scientific knowledge about the choice of an occupation.

If you want more information about Holland's theory, which forms the basis for the SDS, then the following book would be helpful to you.

Holland, J.L., Making Vocational Choices: A Theory of Careers. Englewood Cliffs, N.J. Prentice-Hall, 1973. This book provides further interpretive material about each personality type in the SDS Codes.

In order to learn more about employment opportunities, the following may be helpful.

The Occupational Outlook Handbook, U.S. Department of Labor, Bureau of Labor Statistics. This handbook is published every two years and is the best single source for information about occupations. It is available at your library, counselor's office, or order from the Superintendent of Documents, U.S. Government Printing Office, Washington, D.C. 20402.

Best, F. (Ed.), The Future of Work, Englewood Cliffs, N.J. Prentice-Hall. This book offers readings about the changes to expect in work during the coming years - the growth and decline in different kinds of jobs.

Remember: no one can make your vocational decision for you. Our current knowledge of vocational decision-making does not permit us to provide you with an exact choice, but we hope the SDS has helped you to focus on some of the most likely possibilities.

The final section of the SDS asked you to rate yourself on different dimensions of ability, for example, mechanical, sales, and math. These self-ratings can also be evaluated in terms of Holland's six personality-vocational dimensions and are presented in the following section.

```
                   Self-Estimates Profile
            R       I       A       S       E       C
        ---------------------------------------------------------
            -                                               -
            -                                               -
    12 +    -       -       -       -       -       -     + 12
            -                                       *       -
            -                               *               -
            -                                               -
     8 +    -       -       -       *       -       -     + 8
            -               *                               -
            -       *                                       -
            -               *                               -
     4 +    -       -       -       -       -       -     + 4
            -                                               -
            -                                               -
            -                                               -
        ---------------------------------------------------------
            R       I       A       S       E       C
Raw Score   6       5       7       8      10      11
```

While each section of the test provides useful information, possible vocational and career choices can be recommended most accurately by considering all four sections as a whole. Thus, we add the scores for each of the four sections together to obtain your summary Holland Occupational Code (HOC). The HOC is a simple way of organizing information about people and jobs. It may be used to learn how your special pattern of interests, self-estimates, and skills resemble the patterns of interests and skills that many common occupations demand. Thus, we can use your HOC to select suitable groups of occupations for you to consider. The next profile shows your summary scores on all six scales. The first row of numbers below the profile presents your raw score for each scale. The second row of numbers presents your percentile score. This allows you to compare your score to that obtained by other people. For example, on the Realistic scale, you obtained a raw score of 30. This corresponds to a percentile score of 71. Thus, your score equals or exceeds that of 71 percent of those who take this test. You can make this same comparison for the remaining scores on this profile.

NAME: Self-Directed Search: Computer Version

SUPPLIER: Psychological Assessment Resources
P.O. Box 98
Odessa, FL 33556
(813) 977-3395

PRODUCT CATEGORY

Career/Vocational

PRIMARY APPLICATIONS

Vocational Guidance/Counseling
Personal/Marriage/Family Counseling
Educational Evaluation/Planning

SALE RESTRICTIONS American Psychological Association Guidelines

SERVICE TYPE/COST	Type	Available	Cost	Discount
	Mail-In	No		
	Teleprocessing	No		
	Local	Yes	NA	

PRODUCT DESCRIPTION

The SELF-DIRECTED SEARCH: COMPUTER VERSION is an administration, scoring, and interpretive program for the Self-Directed Search. The design of the program and the interpretive report were developed by Dr. Robert Reardon and staff of Psychological Assessment Resources in consultation with the test author, Dr. John Holland.

The program allows the user to take the Self-Directed Search by computer, then calculates all scores and summary codes and provides the user with his or her summary code. The program next provides an interpretive report which includes information related to perceived barriers to finding a job, vocational aspirations, the meaning of the user's summary code, possible occupations based upon all permutations of the user's summary code, and the similarity of the user's current vocational aspirations to his or her obtained Holland summary code. Finally the program provides additional scores and information for the vocational counselor.

The program is designed for use on Apple II, IBM PC, and compatible microcomputer systems.

NAME: Self-Motivated Career Planning

SUPPLIER: Institute for Personality and Ability Testing, Inc.
P.O. Box 188
Champaign, IL 61820
(217) 352-4739

PRODUCT CATEGORY

Career/Vocational

PRIMARY APPLICATIONS

Vocational Guidance/Counseling
Personnel Selection/Evaluation

SALE RESTRICTIONS American Psychological Association Guidelines

SERVICE TYPE/COST	Type	Available	Cost	Discount
	Mail-In	Yes	$22.40	Yes
	Teleprocessing	No		
	Local	No		

PRODUCT DESCRIPTION

The SELF-MOTIVATED CAREER PLANNING approach has been professionally developed by psychologists from extensive experience in a variety of business and organizational settings. This clear and interesting workbook includes exercises that take the participant through a tested step-by-step examination of career-relevant experiences, goals, and ambitions.

By incorporating psychometric instruments and a comprehensive computer interpretation of one of them—Cattell's 16 PF—into the process, SELF-MOTIVATED CAREER PLANNING provides an important reality test of people's perceptions of themselves, their strengths, behavioral attributes, and sources of gratifications that permits them to chart a course toward accomplishment of personal career development objectives. The exercises culminate in the preparation of a Personal Development Summary. This document is designed to facilitate communication between the individual and a psychologist or career counselor.

For a sample printout of the computer report contained in this product, see the one shown under PERSONAL CAREER DEVELOPMENT PROFILE.

NAME: Sequential Organization of Needs

SUPPLIER: Center for Psychological Services
College of William and Mary
Williamsburg, VA 23185

PRODUCT CATEGORY

Motivation/Needs

PRIMARY APPLICATIONS

Personal/Marriage/Family Counseling
Clinical Assessment/Diagnosis

SALE RESTRICTIONS American Psychological Association Guidelines

SERVICE TYPE/COST	Type	Available	Cost	Discount
	Mail-In	Yes	$3.00	
	Teleprocessing	No		
	Local	No		

PRODUCT DESCRIPTION

The SEQUENTIAL ORGANIZATION OF NEEDS test was designed to assess the ways a subject organizes and relates needs to each other in a temporal sequence. It is intended to provide quantitative analysis about the motivational system of the examinee.

Each of 22 Murray-based needs is represented by a single statement. The subject's task is to select from the remaining 21 statements that which is most likely to have preceded the present situation and one that is most likely to follow the present situation.

The computer report provides a detailed analysis of the need sequences in terms of Starts, Stops, and Loops. Starts are the number of times a need was used as the starting step in a path and reflect the most frequent initiators of a person's actions. Stops are the number of times a need was described as the last step in a path and are interpreted as terminal or end needs in various courses of actions. In some cases these may be interpreted as goals which complete and satisfy a purposeful series of actions.

The number of times a need ends a path but loops back or joins a preceding path is called Loops. Theoretically, a high frequency of loops indicates a need which generates repetitive sequences of actions for the subject, especially if the loop returns to the same path.

SEQUENTIAL ORGANIZATION OF NEEDS FOR

BASE NEED	PATH	NEED STEPS

1. ABASEMENT
    1. AGG-ABA-CNT-BLA-ORD-DCM-ELA-DFD-EXH-
       STOP

2. ACHIEVEMENT
    1. DEF-ACH-ORD-DCM-BLA-CFD-EXH-
       STOP

3. AFFILIATION
    1. NUR-AFF-PLA-SEN-UND-DEF-ACH-EXH-AFF-NUR-EXH-
       STOP
    2. PLA-SEX-SEN-UND-EXH-
       STOP
    3. UND-ORD-ACH-
       LOOP TO PATH 1 STEP 8
    4. AFF-PLA-SEN-
       LOOP TO PATH 2 STEP 4

    BRANCH FROM PATH 1,STEP 3
    BRANCH FROM PATH 1,STEP 5
    BRANCH FROM PATH 1,STEP 9

4. AGGRESSION
    1. DFD-AGG-CCM-
       STOP

5. AUTONOMY
    1. REJ-AUT-CCM-
       STOP

6. BLAME AVOIDANCE
    1. CNT-BLA-CRD-DCM-BLA-CFD-EXH-
       STOP

7. COUNTERACTION
    1. DEF-CNT-ORD-DCM-BLA-CFD-EXH-
       STOP

8. DEFENDANCE
    1. ELA-DFD-EXH-STOP

9. DEFERENCE
    1. UND-DEF-ACH-EXH-AFF-NUR-EXH-
       STOP
    2. AFF-PLA-SEN-UND-EXH-
       STOP

    BRANCH FROM PATH 1,STEP 5

10. DOMINANCE
    1. CRD-DCM-ELA-CFD-EXH-
       STOP

11. EXHIBITION
    1. ACH-EXH-AFF-NUR-EXH-
       STOP
    2. AFF-PLA-SEN-UND-EXH-
       STOP

    BRANCH FROM PATH 1,STEP 3

12. GRATITUDE
    1. CEF-GRA-AFF-NUR-EXH-
       STOP

```
          BRANCH FROM PATH 1,STEP 3    2.  AFF-PLA-SEN-UND-EXH-
                                           STOP

13. HARM AVOIDANCE                     1.  REJ-HAR-INF-REJ-ELA-CFD-EXH-
                                           STOP

14. INFER. AVOIDANCE                   1.  REJ-INF-CRD-DCM-ELA-CFD-EXH-
                                           STOP

15. NURTURANCE                         1.  AFF-NUR-EXH-
                                           STOP

16. ORDER                              1.  UND-ORD-ACH-EXH-AFF-NUR-EXH-
                                           STOP
          BRANCH FROM PATH 1,STEP 5    2.  AFF-PLA-SEN-UND-EXH-
                                           STOP

17. PLAY                               1.  AFF-PLA-SEN-UND-EXH-
                                           STOP

18. REJECTION                          1.  INF-REJ-ELA-DFD-EXH-
                                           STOP

19. SENTIENCE                          1.  PLA-SEN-UND-DEF-ACH-EXH-AFF-NUR-EXH-
                                           STOP
          BRANCH FROM PATH 1,STEP 3    2.  UND-ORD-ACH-   LCOP TO PATH 1 STEP 6
          BRANCH FROM PATH 1,STEP 7    3.  AFF-PLA-SEN-UND-EXH-
                                           STOP

20. SEX                                1.  PLA-SEX-SEN-UND-EXH-
                                           STOP

21. SUCCORANCE                         1.  ABA-SUC-DEF-ACH-ORD-DCM-ELA-DFD-EXH-
                                           STOP
          BRANCH FROM PATH 1,STEP 3    2.  DEF-CNT-CRD-   LCOP TO PATH 1 STEP 6
          BRANCH FROM PATH 1,STEP 3    3.  DEF-GRA-AFF-NUR-EXH-
                                           STOP
          BRANCH FROM PATH 3,STEP 3    4.  AFF-PLA-SEN-UND-EXH-
                                           STOP

22. UNDERSTANDING                      1.  SEN-UND-EXH-
                                           STOP
```

SEQUENTIAL ORGANIZATION OF NEEDS FOR ▬▬▬

BASE NEED	STEP FREQ.	STARTS	STOPS	LOOPS	BEFORE COUNT	AFTER COUNT
1. ABASEMENT	2 1%	1 3%	0 0%	0 0%	1	0
2. ACHIEVEMENT	9 5%	1 3%	0 0%	2 50%	1	2
3. AFFILIATION	17 9%	9 26%	0 0%	0 0%	2	2
4. AGGRESSION	2 1%	1 3%	0 0%	0 0%	1	0
5. AUTONOMY	1 1%	0 0%	0 0%	0 0%	0	0
6. BLAME AVOIDANCE	12 7%	1 3%	0 0%	0 0%	1	2
7. COUNTERACTION	4 2%	1 3%	0 0%	0 0%	1	1
8. DEFENDANCE	11 6%	1 3%	0 0%	0 0%	1	0
9. DEFERENCE	9 5%	5 15%	0 0%	0 0%	3	1
10. DOMINANCE	9 5%	0 0%	0 0%	0 0%	0	2
11. EXHIBITION	33 18%	0 0%	28 93%	0 0%	0	3
12. GRATITUDE	2 1%	0 0%	0 0%	0 0%	0	0
13. HARM AVOIDANCE	1 1%	0 0%	0 0%	0 0%	0	0
14. INFER. AVOIDANCE	3 2%	1 3%	0 0%	0 0%	1	1
15. NURTURANCE	9 5%	1 3%	0 0%	0 0%	1	0
16. ORDER	11 6%	1 3%	0 0%	1 25%	1	4
17. PLAY	12 7%	3 9%	0 0%	0 0%	2	1
18. REJECTION	5 3%	3 9%	0 0%	0 0%	3	0
19. SENTIENCE	13 7%	1 3%	0 0%	1 25%	1	2
20. SEX	2 1%	0 0%	0 0%	0 0%	0	0
21. SUCCORANCE	1 1%	0 0%	0 0%	0 0%	0	0
22. UNDERSTANDING	16 9%	4 12%	0 0%	0 0%	2	1
TOTAL	184	34	30	4	22	22

NAME: Shipley Institute of Living Scale

SUPPLIER: Integrated Professional Systems
5211 Mahoning Avenue Suite 135
Youngstown, OH 44515
(216) 799-3282

PRODUCT CATEGORY

Cognitive/Ability

PRIMARY APPLICATIONS

Clinical Assessment/Diagnosis
Vocational Guidance/Counseling
Personal/Marriage/Family Counseling
Educational Evaluation/Planning
Personnel Selection/Evaluation

SALE RESTRICTIONS Qualified Professional

SERVICE TYPE/COST	Type	Available	Cost	Discount
	Mail-In	No		
	Teleprocessing	No		
	Local	Yes	See Below	

PRODUCT DESCRIPTION

This product administers and scores two subtests: Vocabulary and Abstractions. Vocabulary level is measured by presenting a series of 40 words on the screen in multiple choice format. Abstract Reasoning is assessed by a 20-item test in which the subject must grasp the relationship involved in a progressive series of items and respond by completing the final missing member of the series. Both subtests have a 10-minute time limit.

Mental age norms for Vocabulary, Abstractions, and Total Functional Level are presented. Intellectual impairment is expressed by a Conceptual Quotient or C.Q. based on the difference between the two subtest scores. Overall WAIS IQ is predicted from equations developed by Paulson and Linn for subjects 16 years and older.

An operating software package, priced from $200-$850 depending on the complexity of the package, is required for program use, plus an additional fee of $2.00 per use.

NAME: Sixteen Personality Factor Questionnaire

SUPPLIER: Integrated Professional Systems
5211 Mahoning Avenue Suite 135
Youngstown, OH 44515
(216) 799-3282

PRODUCT CATEGORY	PRIMARY APPLICATIONS
Personality	Clinical Assessment/Diagnosis Personnel Selection/Evaluation Personal/Marriage/Family Counseling Vocational Guidance/Counseling Educational Evaluation/Planning

SALE RESTRICTIONS   Qualified Professional

SERVICE TYPE/COST	Type	Available	Cost	Discount
	Mail-In	No		
	Teleprocessing	No		
	Local	Yes	See Below	

PRODUCT DESCRIPTION

This 16 PF report program provides a graphical presentation of the primary sten scores and a narrative report that includes validity interpretation, clinical hypotheses, and vocational observations.

In the clinical section, second-order factor interpretations are presented together with the factor interpretations that contribute most to the second order factor. The profile code type is determined based on elevations of the second-order factors Extraversion, Anxiety, Tough Poise, and Independence. The DI/AN formula is used to identify patients who will more likely benefit from desipramine/imipramine or from amitriptyline/nortriptyline if anti-depressant medication is indicated.

An operating software package, priced from $200-$850 depending on the complexity of the package, is required for program use, plus an additional fee of $2.00 per use.

JOHN SMITH is a 40 year old male with 16 years of education. He was
tested on May 25, 1983. The College Norm is used.

This is a confidential report for use by professional staff only. The
words used in the interpretation are technically defined and have
specific meanings. The program which generates this profile considers
many decision rules and the results need to be interpreted in light of
the limitations of the instrument. Statements are based on analyses
which should be considered as hypotheses for further clarification.


```
       -------------------------       ------------
          REVIEWING PROFESSIONAL            DATE
```

psychware **611**

THE SIXTEEN PERSONALITY FACTORS PROFILE

```
-------------------------------------------------------------------------------
LOW                        AVERAGE                HIGH
          1    2    3    4    5    6    7    8    9    10                 F  RAW S
----------!----!----!----!---!------!----!----!----!----!----------------------
Reserved   .                 !    *!              .Warm             A  10   6
Dull       .                 !    !         *     .Bright           B  11   8
Weak Ego   .                 !*   !               .Strong Ego       C  15   5
Submissive .            *    !    !               .Dominant         E  11   4
Serious    .                 !*   !               .Impulsive        F  16   5
Superego - .                 !    !         *     .Superego +       G  16   8
Shy        .                 !*   !               .Bold             H  11   5
Tough Minded .          *    !    !               .Sensitive        I   6   4
Trusting   .            *    !    !               .Suspicious       L   6   4
Practical  .                 !    !    *          .Imaginative      M  15   7
Naive      .            *    !    !               .Shrewd           N   6   4
Untroubled .                 !*   !               .Guilt Prone      O   8   5
Conservative .          *    !    !               .Liberal          O1  8   4
G Dependent .                 !    !         *    .Independent      O2 17   9
Uncontrolled .                !    *!             .Controlled       O3 12   6
Relaxed    .                 !    !         *     .Tense            O4 18   8
----------!----!----!----!---!------!----!----!----!----!----------------------
          1    2    3    4    5    6    7    8    9    10                 F  RAW S
LOW                        AVERAGE                HIGH
-------------------------------------------------------------------------------
```

Interpretation		Scale Name	Raw	S
RESPONSE STYLES				
Response pattern suggests that no attempt has been made to give favorable self-presentation	-	FG Faking Good	5	5
Response pattern suggests that the respondent did not attempt to present self unfavorably	-	FB Faking Bad	0	5
The respondent answered items in an alert and conscientious manner. Adequate understanding	-	RA Random	3	
INTELLECTUAL PERFORMANCE				
High general mental capacity, good ability to solve abstract problems suggested as compared to own normative group. Person understood the instructions, was conscientious & organized.	*	B Intelligence	11	8

PROFILE CODE TYPE =   2222

DI / AN formula indicates that if an anti - depressant medication is needed then amitripyline or nortriptyline should be used.

```
**   Very high score,            --  Very low score
 *       high score,             -   low score
 F   Factor                      S   Sten score
```

Interpretation	Scale Name	Raw	S
This person has an average need for interpersonal contacts. Is capable of relating easily	## EXTRAVERSION ##		4.9
Average tendencies toward introspection and spontaneity are present. Can be cautious and dependable, but is able to act quickly in an emergency. Normal sociability, energy levels.	F Impulsivity	16	5
Average score reflects normal level of responsiveness to the world and other people. Can be adventurous but is able to foresee danger & be cautious. Relates well to opposite sex.	H Boldness	11	5
Person shows a normal balance of objectivity and warmth towards others. Can be cooperative but also skeptical when this is appropriate. Has an average amount of trust/ adaptability.	A Warmth	10	6

Normal amounts of anxiety & guilt appear when appropriate. Can cope with stress adequately.

ANXIETY ## 6.3

Person reported relatively high level of free * floating anxiety. Tends to be tense, frustra- ted, driven. Often is fretful, over-reacts to unrealistic fears/worries. Neurotic symptoms.

O4 Anxiety 18 8

Normal amounts of security & apprehensiveness indicated. May exhibit feelings of anxiety, worry, & guilt when this is appropriate, but is not unduly troubled. No phobic symptoms.

O Guilt Proneness 8 5

This person exhibits a relatively high level * of moral awareness. Tends to be responsible, conscientious, & able to discipline self. Is typically orderly and concerned about rules.

G Conformity 16 8

Individual tends to be aloof, tough-minded & * not prone to fantasy. Rational/mentally alert

TOUGH POISE ## 6.7

Person tends to be tough-minded & practical. - Has few artistic interests, is unsentimental & acts on tne basis of logical evidence. Will tend to be self-reliant and business-like.

I Sensitivity 6 4

VOCATIONAL INTERPRETATION
Statements are provided where the subject is somewhat different from others.

Interpretation		Scale Name	Raw	S
Will be alert and attentive when working on complex or abstract tasks. Is conscientious .	*	B Intelligence	11	8
Accomodates reality to requests, may be pass- ive. Tactful and / or timid with associates.	-	E Dominance	11	4
Usually is a self-exacting and conscientious worker. Will accept responsibility readily.	*	G Conformity	16	8
Seen by others as poised, logical & business- like. Is often depended upon by associates.	-	I Sensitivity	6	4
Generally is considerate, helpful to others, and non-competitive. Works well with a team.	-	L Suspiciousness	6	4
Is individualistic, creative & self-motivated May be rejected by more practical associates.	*	M Imagination	15	7
tends to be socially awkward. Is uncritical and easily pleased in most work settings.	-	N Shrewdness	6	4
Usually is opposed to innovation and does not like to change established rules or orders.	-	Q1 Rebelliousness	8	4
Is seclusive & may find group decision-making to be a waste of time. Prefers to act alone.	**	Q2 Self Sufficiency	17	9
In a work setting, stressful events or dead- lines may lead to irritability or undue worry	*	Q4 Free Anxiety	18	8

RAW DATA :   1 = a   2 = b   3 = c

```
                1234567890 1234567890 1234567890 1234567890 1234567890

  1 -  50       1111312333 1123113311 2313311232 3133112311 1113131211
 51 - 100       1122211331 3211133132 1123332212 3313113113 1131333111
101 - 150       1221313323 2333333331 3323333233 3311111333 3331331213
151 - 187       1133311112 1132213133 2311111131 3111111

                1234567890 1234567890 1234567890 1234567890 1234567890
```

End of IPS 16PF Interpretation

Interpretation		Scale Name	Raw	S
Can be somewhat clumsy in social relation-ships, may be too direct and forthright. Has simple tastes & trusts others without trying to analyze their motives. Lacks self-insight.	-	N Shrewdness	6	4
This individual is highly self-sufficient and resourceful. Tends to reject help and is not suggestible or influenced by others. Prefers to make own decisions and find own solutions.	**	Q2 Self Sufficiency	17	9
Average emotional stability, maturity & endurance are indicated. Client accepts responsibility & has an adequate adjustment to life. Undue worries & neurotic symptoms are absent.		C Ego Strength	15	5
Person has an average level of independence. Can be self-sufficient but accepts direction.	##	INDEPENDENCE ##		5.2
Conforming, obedient orientation is present. Person tends to be quiet & often submissive. Accepts authority readily and is dependent on others for direction. Tactful and expressive.	-	E Dominance	11	4
Person tends to be unconventional & imaginative. Interested in art & theory, can easily be influenced by creative thoughts. Aware of practical matters but is absorbed by ideas.	*	M Imagination	15	7
Person exhibits low level of rebelliousness. Has conservative attitudes and temperament, and is tolerant of normal societal problems. Respects established ideas/authority figures.	-	Q1 Rebelliousness	8	4
The client has a trusting, accepting attitude with relatively high levels of understanding/tolerance. Tends to avoid confrontations with others. Complies with requests/is permissive.	-	L Suspiciousness	6	4
A normal ability to inhibit unnecessary feelings of anxiety is suggested. Individual will be concerned about things when appropriate, but is neither compulsive nor uncontrolled.		Q3 Inhibited Anxiety	12	6

NAME: 16 Personality Factor Questionnaire

SUPPLIER: NCS/Professional Assessment Services
P.O. Box 1416
Minneapolis, MN 55440
(800) 328-6759

PRODUCT CATEGORY	PRIMARY APPLICATIONS
Personality	Clinical Assessment/Diagnosis Personal/Marriage/Family Counseling Personnel Selection/Evaluation

SALE RESTRICTIONS American Psychological Association Guidelines

SERVICE TYPE/COST	Type	Available	Cost	Discount
	Mail-In	Yes	$16.25	Yes
	Teleprocessing	Yes	$16.25	Yes
	Local	Yes	$6.65	Yes

PRODUCT DESCRIPTION

This 16 PF report provides a scale-by-scale analysis of significant primary personality characteristics and a graphical presentation of those scores. Segments relevant to clinical and vocational decision-making are also included.

Two systems are available for local processing of test results. MICRO-TEST Assessment Software from National Computer Systems, used with a Sentry 3000 tabletop scanner (purchase price approximately $4000) and microcomputer system ($2000-$3000 purchase price), allows tests to be administered off-line. Answer sheets are then scanned and scored automatically, one at a time or in a batch. The software also permits on-line administration of the test via microcomputer. In either case, the same report is provided. The cost for local scoring refers to the cost-per-test when diskettes are purchased in units of 20 administrations (minimum purchase).

For a sample printout of this product, see the one shown under 16 PF NARRATIVE SCORING REPORT.

NAME: 16 Personality Factor Test—Computer Version

SUPPLIER: Psychological Assessment Resources
P.O. Box 98
Odessa, FL 33556
(813) 977-3395

PRODUCT CATEGORY	PRIMARY APPLICATIONS
Personality	Clinical Assessment/Diagnosis Personal/Marriage/Family Counseling Personnel Selection/Evaluation

SALE RESTRICTIONS American Psychological Association Guidelines

SERVICE TYPE/COST Type	Available	Cost	Discount
Mail-In	No		
Teleprocessing	No		
Local	Yes	$15.00	Yes

PRODUCT DESCRIPTION

This is an administration, scoring, and interpretive program for the 16 Personality Factor Test. The interpretive report provided is the widely used and highly respected 16 PF Clinical Report developed by Samuel Karson, Ph.D.

Features of the 16 PF: COMPUTER VERSION include both narrative and charted display of scores. The concise narrative provides a complete overview of the personality and clinical patterns. Charts are provided for five significant areas: primary traits, clinical signs, personality patterns, cognitive features, and need patterns.

The price shown above is the per-test fee when diskettes are purchased in quantities of 10 uses (minimum purchase). Operation of the program requires a one-time purchase of PAR-DOS ($100.00), an operating system for psychological test software. Versions of this program are available for the Apple IIe, II +, and IBM PC computer systems. The program requires 64K and 2 disk drives for execution. For a sample printout of this product, see the one shown under KARSON CLINICAL REPORT.

NAME: 16 PF/CL

SUPPLIER: Precision People, Inc.
3452 North Ride Circle. S.
Jacksonville, FL 32217
(904) 262-1096

PRODUCT CATEGORY	PRIMARY APPLICATIONS
Personality	Clinical Assessment/Diagnosis Personal/Marriage/Family Counseling

SALE RESTRICTIONS American Psychological Association Guidelines

SERVICE TYPE/COST	Type	Available	Cost	Discount
	Mail-In	No		
	Teleprocessing	No		
	Local	Yes	$475.00	

PRODUCT DESCRIPTION

The 16 PF/CL clinical interpretation has several report sections. The clinical section addresses personality dynamics, psychopathology, prognosis, and more. The personality profile describes the client based on 16 bipolar scales. Ego Strength, Dominance, Level of Abstraction, Introversion-Extroversion, Social Sophistication, Rebelliousness, and Tension are a few of the dimensions this program evaluates and reports on. The diagnostic section compares the client's profile to the profiles of known diagnostic groups and includes in the report those that are similar. The client's profile is also compared to known profiles of various occupational categories and those categories the profile is similar to are listed. Medical concerns are also reported in a separate section.

The software is compatible with IBM PC, Apple, and TRS-80 (Models I, II, and III) microcomputers. A manual and sample are available for $34.00. For a sample printout of this product, see the one shown under the listing for 16 PF/CL CLINICAL INTERPRETATION.

psychware **617**

NAME: 16 PF/CL Clinical Interpretation

SUPPLIER: Applied Innovations, Inc.
South Kingstown Office Park, Suite A-1
Wakefield, RI 02879
(800) 272-2250

PRODUCT CATEGORY	**PRIMARY APPLICATIONS**
Personality	Clinical Assessment/Diagnosis Personal/Marriage/Family Counseling

SALE RESTRICTIONS   American Psychological Association Guidelines

SERVICE TYPE/COST	Type	Available	Cost	Discount
	Mail-In	No		
	Teleprocessing	No		
	Local	Yes	$375.00	

PRODUCT DESCRIPTION

The 16 PF/CL clinical interpretation has several report sections. The clinical section addresses personality dynamics, psychopathology, prognosis, and more. The personality profile describes the client based on 16 bipolar scales. Ego Strength, Dominance, Level of Abstraction, Introversion-Extraversion, Social Sophistication, Rebelliousness, and Tension are a few of the dimensions this program evaluates and reports on. The diagnostic section compares the client's profile to the profiles of known diagnostic groups and includes in the report those that are similar. The client's profile is also compared to known profiles of various occupational categories and those categories the profile is similar to are listed. Medical concerns are also reported in a separate section.

The software operates on most available personal computers including IBM, Apple, Digital, and Kaypro.

NAME/ID: Harry S. Clark   AGE: 33   DATE: 3/23/84

16 PF CLINICAL INTERPRETATION

COPYRIGHT 1982

BY

Bruce Duthie, Ph.D
&
Ernest G. Allen

APPLIED INNOVATIONS INC.
SOUTH KINGSTOWN OFFICE PARK
WAKEFIELD R.I. 02879

A = 1
B = 2
C = 2
E = 3

F = 3
G = 3
H = 4
I = 4

L = 4
M = 5
N = 5
O = 5

Q1 = 1
Q2 = 2
Q3 = 2
Q4 = 1

MD = 1
FB = 3

** CLINICAL PROFILE INTERPRETATION **

THIS CLIENT SEEMS TO HAVE ANSWERED THE QUESTIONS HONESTLY, NEITHER
EXAGGERATING NOR MINIMIZING PSYCHOLOGICAL CONFLICT AND SYMPTOMS.
THIS PROFILE INDICATES THE POSSIBILITY OF SEVERE PSYCHOPATHOLOGY. MULTIPLE
PSYCHOPATHOLOGICAL SYMPTOMS ARE OFTEN PRESENT. SCHIZOID TENDENCIES IN TIMES
OF STRESS ARE INDICATED. THIS PERSON IS EXPERIENCING ACUTE STRESS. HE MAY
HAVE TROUBLE SEPARATING HIS IDENTITY FROM THAT OF OTHERS. PERSONS WITH THIS
PROFILE TYPE EXHIBIT A GROSS INABLILITY TO COPE WITH HOSTILITY. WHEN FACED
WITH HOSTILE ACTS THEY WITHDRAW PHYSICALLY AND PSYCHOLOGICALLY.

** GENERAL PROFILE INTERPRETATION **

- INTRAPERSONAL -

A RIGID, INFLEXIBLE COGNITIVE STYLE IS INDICATED. HIS ABILITY TO HANDLE
ABSTRACT PROBLEMS MAY BE LIMITED. ORGANIZATION MAY BE A PROBLEM.
HE IS EASILY FRUSTRATED AND OFTEN BECOMES EMOTIONAL. HE TENDS TO WORRY A LOT.
HE IS HUMBLE. HE IS A SILENT, RATHER INTROSPECTIVE PERSON. HE IS A
CONCERNED, REFLECTIVE PERSON; SOBER AND SERIOUS. HE IS A RATHER SLACK,
INDOLENT PERSON.

- INTERPERSONAL -

HE IS SOMEWHAT CRITICAL OF OTHERS. HE HAS GREAT FAITH IN HIS OWN IDEAS AND
JUDGEMENT AND MAY HAVE A TENDENCY TO BE STUBBORN. A COOL, ALOOF, SOMEWHAT
DETACHED ATTITUDE TOWARD OTHERS CAN BE EXPECTED. A DISTRUSTFUL, SKEPTICAL
STYLE OF RELATING CAN BE HYPOTHESIZED. HE IS PRONE TO SULK WHEN GOALS ARE
BLOCKED OR WHEN CONTROLLED. HE IS SUBMISSIVE AND EASILY DOMINATED BY OTHERS.
HE IS A DEPENDENT PERSON. HE NEEDS ANOTHER PERSON TO LIKE AND CARE ABOUT HIM
BEFORE HE CAN FEEL GOOD ABOUT HIMSELF. HE IS CONVENTIONAL AND CONFORMING TO
THE WISHES OF OTHERS AND OF SOCIETY. HE IS SOMETIMES UPSET BY AUTHORITY
FIGURES. HE IS SELF-INDULGENT, HEDONISTIC, AND MAY DISREGARD THE WISHES OF
OTHERS WHEN THEY GET IN THE WAY. HE MAY DISREGARD HIS OBLIGATIONS TO OTHERS
AND TO SOCIETY. HE TENDS TO BE GROUP ORIENTED AND WOULD MAKE A GOOD FOLLOWER.
HE IS UNCONTROLLED AND LAX, FOLLOWS HIS URGES AND IS CARELESS ABOUT FOLLOWING
SOCIAL RULES.

- BEHAVIOR -

HE HAS A LOWERED MORALE, QUITTING TASKS WHEN THEY BECOME DIFFICULT.
HE IS CHANGEABLE IN INTERESTS AND ATTITUDES, OFTEN TRYING NEW THINGS AND
QUICKLY DROPPING THEM. HE IS EVASIVE OF RESPONSIBILITIES AND TENDS TO GIVE UP
EASILY. HE IS CONSERVATIVE - TRADITIONAL IDEAS ARE RESPECTED AND TRADITIONAL
WAYS ARE TOLERATED IF NOT FOLLOWED.

** PSYCHODIAGNOSTIC PROFILE **

THE FOLLOWING ANALYSIS COMPARES THIS PROFILE CONFIGURATION TO STANDARD
DIAGNOSTIC PROFILES AND LISTS THE DIAGNOSTIC GROUPS THIS PROFILE IS MOST
SIMILAR TO.

** OCCUPATIONAL PROFILE **

THE FOLLOWING ANALYSIS COMPARES THIS PROFILE CONFIGURATION TO STANDARD
OCCUPATIONAL PROFILES AND LISTS THE OCCUPATIONAL GROUPS THIS PROFILE IS MOST
SIMILAR TO.

** MEDICAL PROFILE **

HE IS LIKELY TO DISREGARD THE PHYSICIAN'S ADVICE AND WILL HAVE TROUBLE
COMPLYING WITH TREATMENT.

NAME: 16 PF Narrative Scoring Report

SUPPLIER: Institute for Personality and Ability Testing, Inc.
P.O. Box 188
Champaign, IL 61820
(217) 352-4739

PRODUCT CATEGORY

Personality

PRIMARY APPLICATIONS

Educational Evaluation/Planning
Personnel Selection/Evaluation
Vocational Guidance/Counseling
Clinical Assessment/Diagnosis

SALE RESTRICTIONS American Psychological Association Guidelines

SERVICE TYPE/COST	Type	Available	Cost	Discount
	Mail-In	Yes	$16.00	Yes
	Teleprocessing	No		
	Local	No		

PRODUCT DESCRIPTION

A general, all-purpose type of report that is very economical, the 16 PF NARRATIVE SCORING REPORT provides a complete report for each individual, including descriptions of all personality characteristics of significance as well as vocational and occupational comparisons of importance in counseling.

The 16 PF is a 105-187 item paper-and-pencil inventory measuring 16 primary personality traits: Warmth, Intelligence, Emotional Stability, Dominance, Impulsivity, Conformity, Boldness, Sensitivity, Suspiciousness, Imagination, Shrewdness, Insecurity, Radicalism, Self-suficiency, Self-discipline, and Tension. The test requires a 6th-7th-grade reading level and 45-60 minutes completion time.

THE INSTITUTE FOR PERSONALITY AND ABILITY TESTING
P. O. BOX 188   CHAMPAIGN, ILLINOIS 61820

THIS COMPUTER INTERPRETATION OF THE 16 PF IS INTENDED ONLY FOR PROPERLY
QUALIFIED PROFESSIONALS AND SHOULD BE TREATED AS A CONFIDENTIAL REPORT.

4/20/1984

NAME-JOHN SAMPLE   AGE-29
ID NUMBER-   SEX-M


```
*  * * * * * * * *   V A L I D I T Y    S C A L E S   * * * * * * * * * * *
*                                                                         *
* THERE IS REASON TO SUSPECT SOME DISTORTION IN HIS TEST RESPONSES.       *
* THIS IS SOMETHING THAT SHOULD BE EXPLORED FURTHER.                      *
*    FAKING GOOD/MD (STEN) SCORE IS VERY LOW (2.0).                       *
*    FAKING BAD (STEN) SCORE IS HIGH (8.0).                               *
*                                                                         *
* * * * * * * * * * * * * * * * * * * * * * * * * * * * * * * * * * * * * *
```

16 PF
PERSONALITY PROFILE

SCORES				LOW MEANING	1 2 3 4 5 6 7 8 9 10	HIGH MEANING	%
R	U	C					
8	4	4	A	COOL, RESERVED	<---	WARM, EASYGOING	23
10	8	8	B	CONCRETE THINKING	----->	ABSTRACT THINKING	89
10	2	3	C	EASILY UPSET	<-----	CALM, STABLE	11
22	10	10	E	NOT ASSERTIVE	--------->	DOMINANT	99
21	9	9	F	SOBER, SERIOUS	------->	HAPPY-GO-LUCKY	96
11	4	4	G	EXPEDIENT	<---	CONSCIENTIOUS	23
19	7	7	H	SHY, TIMID	--->	VENTURESOME	77
9	6	6	I	TOUGH-MINDED	->	TENDER-MINDED	60
11	8	8	L	TRUSTING	----->	SUSPICIOUS	89
16	7	7	M	PRACTICAL	--->	IMAGINATIVE	77
4	2	2	N	FORTHRIGHT	<-------	SHREWD	4
15	8	7	O	SELF-ASSURED	--->	APPREHENSIVE	77
15	9	9	Q1	CONSERVATIVE	------->	EXPERIMENTING	96
14	8	8	Q2	GROUP-ORIENTED	----->	SELF-SUFFICIENT	89
12	5	5	Q3	UNDISCIPLINED	<-	SELF-DISCIPLINED	40
14	7	6	Q4	RELAXED	->	TENSE, DRIVEN	60

NOTE: "R" DESIGNATES RAW SCORES, "U" DESIGNATES (UNCORRECTED) STEN SCORES,
      AND "C" DESIGNATES STEN SCORES CORRECTED FOR DISTORTION (IF APPROP-
      RIATE). THE INTERPRETATION WILL PROCEED ON THE BASIS OF CORRECTED
      SCORES.

PERSONAL COUNSELING OBSERVATIONS

ADEQUACY OF ADJUSTMENT IS ABOVE AVERAGE (6.5).
ACTING-OUT BEHAVIOR TENDENCIES ARE HIGH (7.9).
EFFECTIVENESS OF BEHAVIOR CONTROLS IS LOW (3.3).

INTERVENTION CONSIDERATIONS

THE INFLUENCE OF A CONTROLLED ENVIRONMENT MAY HELP. SUGGESTIONS INCLUDE-
      A GRADED SERIES OF SUCCESS EXPERIENCES TO IMPROVE SELF-CONFIDENCE

PRIMARY PERSONALITY CHARACTERISTICS OF SIGNIFICANCE

CAPACITY FOR ABSTRACT SKILLS IS HIGH.
INVOLVEMENT IN PROBLEMS MAY EVOKE SOME EMOTIONAL UPSET AND INSTABILITY.
IN INTERPERSONAL RELATIONSHIPS HE LEADS, DOMINATES, OR IS STUBBORN.
HIS STYLE OF EXPRESSION IS OFTEN LIVELY, OPTIMISTIC, AND ENTHUSIASTIC.
HE TENDS TO PROJECT INNER TENSION BY BLAMING OTHERS, AND BECOMES JEALOUS
      OR SUSPICIOUS EASILY.
IN HIS DEALINGS WITH OTHERS, HE IS EMOTIONALLY NATURAL AND UNPRE-
      TENTIOUS, THOUGH SOMEWHAT NAIVE.
HE IS EXPERIMENTING, HAS AN INQUIRING MIND, LIKES NEW IDEAS, AND TENDS
      TO DISPARAGE TRADITIONAL SOLUTIONS TO PROBLEMS.
BEING SELF-SUFFICIENT, HE PREFERS TACKLING THINGS RESOURCEFULLY, ALONE.

BROAD INFLUENCE PATTERNS

HIS PERSONALITY ORIENTATION IS EXTRAVERTED. THAT IS, HIS ATTENTION IS DIR-
ECTED OUT INTO THE ENVIRONMENT. THIS TENDENCY IS ABOVE AVERAGE (7.5).
AT THE PRESENT TIME, HE SEES HIMSELF AS SOMEWHAT MORE ANXIOUS THAN
MOST PEOPLE. HIS ANXIETY SCORE IS ABOVE AVERAGE (6.6).
TASKS AND PROBLEMS ARE APPROACHED WITH EMPHASIS UPON RATIONALITY AND
GETTING THINGS DONE. LESS ATTENTION IS PAID TO EMOTIONAL RELATIONSHIPS.
THIS TENDENCY IS HIGH (8.1).
HIS LIFE STYLE IS INDEPENDENT AND SELF-DIRECTED LEADING TO ACTIVE ATTEMPTS
TO ACHIEVE CONTROL OF THE ENVIRONMENT. IN THIS RESPECT, HE
IS EXTREMELY HIGH (10.0).

VOCATIONAL OBSERVATIONS

AT CLIENT'S OWN LEVEL OF ABILITIES, POTENTIAL FOR CREATIVE FUNCTIONING IS
VERY HIGH (9.0).
POTENTIAL FOR BENEFIT FROM FORMAL ACADEMIC TRAINING, AT CLIENT'S OWN LEVEL
OF ABILITIES, IS HIGH (7.6).
IN A GROUP OF PEERS, POTENTIAL FOR LEADERSHIP IS AVERAGE (5.6).
CONDITIONS OF INTERPERSONAL CONTACT OR ISOLATION ARE IRRELEVANT, BUT
EXTREMES SHOULD BE AVOIDED.
NEED FOR WORK THAT TOLERATES SOME UNDEPENDABILITY AND INCONSISTENT HABITS
IS VERY HIGH (9.0).
POTENTIAL FOR GROWTH TO MEET INCREASING JOB DEMANDS IS BELOW AVERAGE (4.1).
THE EXTENT TO WHICH THE CLIENT IS ACCIDENT PRONE IS HIGH (8.3).

OCCUPATIONAL FITNESS PROJECTIONS

IN THIS SEGMENT OF THE REPORT HIS 16 PF RESULTS ARE COMPARED WITH VARIOUS
OCCUPATIONAL PROFILES. ALL PROJECTIONS SHOULD BE CONSIDERED WITH RESPECT
TO OTHER INFORMATION ABOUT HIM, PARTICULARLY HIS INTERESTS AND ABILITIES.

1. ARTISTIC PROFESSIONS

ARTIST	ABOVE AVERAGE (7.1).
MUSICIAN	EXTREMELY HIGH (10.0).
WRITER	VERY HIGH (8.9).

2. COMMUNITY AND SOCIAL SERVICE

EMPLOYMENT COUNSELOR	AVERAGE (5.7).
FIREFIGHTER	BELOW AVERAGE (3.8).
NURSE	AVERAGE (4.9).
PHYSICIAN	HIGH (8.1).
POLICE OFFICER	BELOW AVERAGE (3.8).
PRIEST (R.C.)	LOW (3.3).
SERVICE STATION DEALER	VERY LOW (2.4).
SOCIAL WORKER	BELOW AVERAGE (3.6).

3. SCIENTIFIC PROFESSIONS

BIOLOGIST	ABOVE AVERAGE (6.9).
CHEMIST	ABOVE AVERAGE (6.8).
ENGINEER	BELOW AVERAGE (4.3).
GEOLOGIST	HIGH (7.9).
PHYSICIST	AVERAGE (6.3).
PSYCHOLOGIST	HIGH (7.7).

4. TECHNICAL PERSONNEL

ACCOUNTANT	ABOVE AVERAGE (7.5).
AIRLINE FLIGHT ATTENDANT	ABOVE AVERAGE (7.0).
AIRLINE PILOT	VERY HIGH (8.7).
COMPUTER PROGRAMMER	VERY HIGH (8.7).
EDITORIAL WORKER	AVERAGE (6.0).
ELECTRICIAN	EXTREMELY LOW (1.4).
MECHANIC	BELOW AVERAGE (3.7).
PSYCHIATRIC TECHNICIAN	AVERAGE (5.1).
TIME/MOTION STUDY ANALYST	AVERAGE (6.4).

5. INDUSTRIAL/CLERICAL PERSONNEL

        JANITOR   LOW (2.9).
        KITCHEN WORKER   EXTREMELY LOW (1.2).
        MACHINE OPERATOR   LOW (2.9).
        SECRETARY-CLERK   AVERAGE (5.0).
        TRUCK DRIVER   VERY LOW (1.6).

6. SALES PERSONNEL

        REAL ESTATE AGENT   ABOVE AVERAGE (7.2)
        RETAIL COUNTER CLERK   HIGH (8.1).

7. ADMINISTRATIVE AND SUPERVISORY PERSONNEL

        BANK MANAGER   HIGH (7.6).
        BUSINESS EXECUTIVE   VERY HIGH (9.1).
        CREDIT UNION MANAGER   AVERAGE (5.1).
        MIDDLE LEVEL MANAGER   AVERAGE (4.8).
        PERSONNEL MANAGER   HIGH (8.4).
        PRODUCTION MANAGER   EXTREMELY HIGH (10.0).
        PLANT FOREMAN   AVERAGE (4.6).
        SALES SUPERVISOR   AVERAGE (5.8).
        STORE MANAGER   LOW (2.8).

8. ACADEMIC PROFESSIONS

        TEACHER-ELEMENTARY LEVEL AVERAGE (5.6).
        TEACHER-JUNIOR HIGH LEVEL VERY HIGH (8.6).
        TEACHER-SENIOR HIGH LEVEL VERY HIGH (9.1).
        UNIVERSITY PROFESSOR   AVERAGE (6.0).
        SCHOOL COUNSELOR   ABOVE AVERAGE (6.6).
        SCHOOL SUPERINTENDENT   AVERAGE (5.1).
        UNIVERSITY ADMINISTRATOR AVERAGE (6.1).

THIS PROFILE SHOWS THE 3233 PATTERN TYPE. FOR ADDITIONAL INTERPRETIVE
INFORMATION REGARDING THIS PATTERN, SEE "INTERPRETING 16PF PROFILE
PATTERNS" BY DR. SAMUEL KRUG. THIS PUBLICATION IS AVAILABLE THROUGH IPAT.

NAME: 16 PF Report

SUPPLIER: Psychologistics, Inc.
P.O. Box 3896
Indialantic, FL 32903
(305) 727-7900

PRODUCT CATEGORY

Personality

PRIMARY APPLICATIONS

Clinical Assessment/Diagnosis
Personal/Marriage/Family Counseling

SALE RESTRICTIONS American Psychological Association Guidelines

SERVICE TYPE/COST	Type	Available	Cost	Discount
	Mail-In	No		
	Teleprocessing	No		
	Local	Yes	$149.00	

PRODUCT DESCRIPTION

The 16 PF REPORT generates an automated interpretation of the Sixteen Personality Factor Questionnaire. A self-contained narrative report is printed, along with a test profile which graphically displays the 16 PF standard scores entered through the console.

The report is suitable for use as a written summary of the results of the evaluation. It consists of a scale-by-scale interpretation of the test data. A validity paragraph evaluates the probable relevance of the interpretive statements.

The report serves several functions for the clinician. It saves professional staff time, enables rapid feedback, evaluates all test data in a consistent and rule-based manner, and provides a variety of interpretive hypotheses. The report may also be used to document services rendered to third party carriers. The program does not provide scoring of the test. As a consequence, there are no additional use charges.

The program is compatible with Apple II + , IIe and IBM PC microcomputer systems.

```
                        16PF REPORT PROFILE

        NAME: JOHN X. DOE
        DATE: 2-27-84
                                  FG STEN SCORE = 6
                                  FB STEN SCORE = 6

    F                                                              S
    A                                                              T
    C                                                              E
    T                                                              N
    O
    R

                   1   2   3   4   5   6   7   8   9  10

    A  RESERVED      -       * :               :         - OUTGOING       3

    B  LESS INTELL.  -         :               :       * - MORE INTELL.   9

    C  EMOT. LABILE  -         : *             :         - EMOT. STABLE   4

    E  HUMBLE        -       * :               :         - ASSERTIVE      3

    F  SOBER         -         :     *         :         - ENTHUSIASTIC   5

    G  EXPEDIENT     -         :             * :         - CONSCIENTIOUS  7

    H  SHY           -     *   :               :         - VENTURESOME    2

    I  REALISTIC     -         :             : *         - SENSITIVE      8

    L  TRUSTING      -         :         *     :         - SUSPICIOUS     6

    M  PRACTICAL     -         :             * :         - IMAGINATIVE    7

    N  FORTHRIGHT    -         :     *         :         - ASTUTE         5

    O  SELF-ASSURED  -         :             * :         - APPREHENSIVE   7

    Q1 CONSERVATIVE  -         :     *         :         - EXPERIMENTING  5

    Q2 GRP-DEPENDENT -         :         *     :         - SELF-SUFFIC.   6

    Q3 UNDISCIPLINED -         :             * :         - CONTROLLED     7

    Q4 RELAXED       -         :             * :         - TENSE          7

                   1   2   3   4   5   6   7   8   9  10


              16PF COPYRIGHT (C) 1978 IPAT, INC.

          AUTOMATED 16PF PROGRAM COPYRIGHT (C) 1983
        BY THOMAS H. HARRELL, PH.D. & GILES D. RAINWATER, PH.D.
```

626 *psychware*

16PF REPORT

NAME: JOHN X. DOE   SEX: MALE
DATE: 2-27-84   AGE: 25

The following statements should be considered as interpretive
hypotheses. They suggest possible personality characteristics
and behavioral dispositions. Caution should be used in applying
these interpretive statements to a specific individual. Patterns
of behavior suggested by this report should be validated before
they are accepted.

The validity configuration indicates that this individual responded
truthfully and realistically. There is no evidence of a response
tendency to either minimize or exaggerate specific characteristics.

OUTGOINGNESS Individuals who score like this appear to be somewhat
distant and cold. These individuals may tend to avoid others, and
be perceived by others as aloof and distant. Similar individuals
experience difficulty in expressing their thoughts and feelings, but
are often perceptive and quite aware of others feelings.

INTELLIGENCE Similar scores suggest the presence of high general
mental capacity. Associated characteristics include insightfulness,
quick mastery of tasks, critical thinking, and intellectual
adaptability.

STABLITY Similar scores suggest an average degree of emotional
stability. These individuals are typically not seen as being overly
affected by feelings nor are they seen as being especially
emotionally stable. They typically face situations with an average
amount of maturity and calmness.

ASSERTIVENESS Similar individuals demonstrate characteristics
consistent with submissiveness. They tend to be obedient, mild
mannered, easily led, docile, and accommodating. In addition to
exhibiting dependency, they can also exhibit consideration and
diplomacy. Conventional and conforming behavior can be expected.
Conflict with authority often produces emotional distress.

ENTHUSIASM These individuals are typically balanced between
impulsive action and over-control. They are not seen as
particularly sober or enthusiastic. Similar individuals tend to act
appropriately on impulses after consideration of likely outcomes and
consequences.

CONSCIENTIOUSNESS An approach to life which is balanced in the area
of conformity can be expected. Similar people tend to have a
reasonable regard for rules. They demonstrate an average degree of
responsibility, emotional discipline, dependability, and morality.

SHYNESS These individuals are often shy, restrained, timid, and
emotionally cautious. An inhibited attitude may be associated with
restrained affect and limited interests. A careful, cautious
outlook leads them to over identify potential problems and may be
associated with behavioral withdrawal and concern over social and
personal adequacy.

TENDER-MINDEDNESS These test results describe a sensitive
individual. Appropriate descriptors include tender-minded,
dependent, over-protected, and kind. Expectations of affection and

psychware **627**

attention, as well as help- seeking are typical. These individuals can be emotionally dramatic and are often seen by others as impractical or overly sentimental.

SUSPICIOUSNESS This person is neither particularly trusting nor particularly suspicious. While generally accepting of others, their trust is tempered by realistic caution. They are typically seen by others as reasonably conciliatory and not prone to irritability or jealousy.

IMAGINATIVENESS These test results indicate an individual who is neither excessively practical nor exceptionally imaginative. A blend of pragmatism and creative thinking can be expected in problem solving and performance.

ASTUTENESS This score depicts a person who is neither socially inept nor socially polished. An average amount of warmth and spontaneity is likely to be expressed in interpersonal relationships. Similar individuals are most comfortable in familiar social situations and are likely to avoid novel situations. Their insight into others and their own interpersonal impact is typically average.

APPREHENSIVENESS This person is probably in the mid-range between being self-assured and apprehensive. Similar individuals are usually not seen as particularly cheerful nor as particularly anxious/depressed. They are not typically perceived by others as being particularly secure and complacent nor as being especially insecure or troubled

CONSERVATIVENESS This individual is probably neither particularly conservative nor particularly liberal. Similar individuals typically demonstrate a blend of traditional ideas with a guarded acceptance of new approaches. Such people are usually able to get along well with both more conservative and liberal individuals and often serve to moderate the views of others.

SELF-SUFFICIENCY Individuals with similar scores are neither seen as particularly group dependent nor especially self-sufficient. They tend to be average regarding independent resourcefulness, preference for own decisions, and social group dependency.

WILL-POWER These people tend to be average regarding their control over impulses. A typical amount of willpower can be expected. Neither carelessness nor compulsive behavior is expected regarding social behavior.

TENSENESS A balance between a relaxed versus a tense posture is expected. Similar scores typically do not correlate with either a tranquil or a fretful attitude. It is unlikely that this individual would be seen as characteristically composed or characteristically overwrought.

EXAMINER

NAME: Slosson Intelligence Test-Computer Report

SUPPLIER: Psychological Assessment Resources
P.O. Box 98
Odessa, FL 33556
(813) 977-3395

PRODUCT CATEGORY

Cognitive/Ability

PRIMARY APPLICATIONS

Clinical Assessment/Diagnosis
Educational Evaluation/Planning
Personal/Marriage/Family Counseling

SALE RESTRICTIONS American Psychological Association Guidelines

SERVICE TYPE/COST

Type	Available	Cost	Discount
Mail-In	No		
Teleprocessing	No		
Local	Yes	$275.00	

PRODUCT DESCRIPTION

The SLOSSON INTELLIGENCE TEST-COMPUTER REPORT is designed to aid the psychologist and educator in making decisions regarding whether or not to evaluate further, determining expected achievement levels, finding levels of ability, and identifying basic areas of weakness. In addition to identification data about the client, the report provides a comparison of achievement with ability using both grade equivalent and standard scores. The degree of scatter is also provided. Results are analyzed according to a classification scheme using the following categories: General Information, Comprehension, Arithmetic, Similarities and Differences, Vocabulary, Digit Span, and Visual Motor. Recommendations are provided for improvement in areas of weakness. This program provides educators with excellent guidelines for educational and programmatic decision making.

The software is compatible with the TRS-80 III, IV, Apple II + and IIe microcomputer systems.

NAME: Social History

SUPPLIER: PSYCH Systems, Inc.
600 Reisterstown Road
Baltimore, MD 21208
(800) 368-3366

PRODUCT CATEGORY

Structured Interview
Personality

PRIMARY APPLICATIONS

Clinical Assessment/Diagnosis
Personal/Marriage/Family Counseling

SALE RESTRICTIONS Qualified Professional

SERVICE TYPE/COST	Type	Available	Cost	Discount
	Mail-In	No		
	Teleprocessing	No		
	Local	Yes	See Below	

PRODUCT DESCRIPTION

This instrument was developed for use with adults to gather information in the areas of genetic and childhood history, adolescent adjustment, vocational adjustment, marital adjustment, quality of life, and recent stressful events. A branching strategy is employed by the program to insure that the client doesn't encounter items that are inappropriate and to speed up the information gathering process. All questions are either multiple-choice or true-false. The total number of items is dependent upon the response pattern and will usually vary between 50 and 200.

When the administration phase is complete, this program provides an interpretive report of questionnaire results. Psych Systems programs operate on the IBM PC-XT, COMPAQ Plus, Dec Professional 350, and most DEC PDP-11 systems. Various hardware/software configurations are available directly from Psych Systems, with single-user systems starting at approximately $12,000. A per test fee also applies.

222-22-2222 Jonathan Doe   32 yr old white male   16-Feb-84

```
    ----------------------------
   |          |                 |
   |   SHX    |  Social History |
   |          |                 |
    ----------------------------
```

The computer program generating this report was designed by Psych
Systems, Inc., Baltimore, Maryland 21208. Copyright (C) 1984 by
Psych Systems, Inc. All rights reserved.

Jonathan Doe is a 32 year old white divorced father of 1 child.
He attended business school or partial college. Currently he is a
part-time student and employed full time in sales. Monthly income
for his household is $1000-$2000 derived primarily from his job. He
has no trouble with the law. He has had no psychiatric hospitalization but
has had outpatient therapy. He currently resides in a house which is
owned. He lives alone.

FAMILY HISTORY

The respondent was raised primarily by both natural parents. He has 3
siblings. His natural mother has died from an illness. The
respondent reports the presence of obvious psychopathology and
physical health problems in immediate blood relatives as follows:

father : severe nervous troubles, alcohol problems, stomach trouble,
severe headaches and numerous physical complaints before age 40.

mother : nervous breakdown, psychiatric hospitalization, suic.ial
behavior, alcohol problems, extreme moodiness and numerous physical
complaints before age 40.

siblings: severe nervous troubles, severe depression, suicidal
behavior, stomach trouble, severe headaches and numerous physical
complaints before age 40.

He reports that his mother and father would physically attack each
other and would frequently lose their tempers. His mother is viewed
as having been domineering and cruel. His father is seen as having
been brutal and unfaithful. He complains of generally impaired
relationships with them manifested by exclusion from conversation,
frequent disagreements, running away from home and severe restrictions.

CHILDHOOD AND ADOLESCENCE

He admits to childhood difficulties with overt aggression (temper
tantrums and quick to anger), hyperactivity (always on the go) and
emotional lability (frequent crying). He reports engaging in lying,
thievery and fire-setting at an early age. In school he was slow in
learning to read. He received failing grades and was not promoted
normally. He admits to having trouble with school authorities. As an
adolescent he states that he was generally happy. He had friends but
did not date.

LIFE STRESS AND ROLE IMPAIRMENT

He reports experiencing several stressful events during the past year.
These were in the area of social participation (church activities
family get-togethers) and work situation (change in working
conditions, change in responsibilities and being fired). He indicated
some financial difficulties. His financial problems include a poor
credit rating. He reports problems with his child. These include
getting easily frustrated, feeling his care is inadequate and noticing
the child seems to be having more problems. At work, he indicates
that he has been increasingly absent. The respondent admits to
having used narcotics but not marijuana, amphetamines, cocaine,
barbiturates and hallucinogens.

NAME: Social History Questionnaire

SUPPLIER: Integrated Professional Systems
5211 Mahoning Avenue Suite 135
Youngstown, OH 44515
(216) 799-3282

PRODUCT CATEGORY	PRIMARY APPLICATIONS
Structured Interview Personality	Clinical Assessment/Diagnosis Personal/Marriage/Family Counseling Vocational Guidance/Counseling Personnel Selection/Evaluation Educational Evaluation/Planning

SALE RESTRICTIONS   Qualified Professional

SERVICE TYPE/COST	Type	Available	Cost	Discount
	Mail-In	No		
	Teleprocessing	No		
	Local	Yes	See Below	

PRODUCT DESCRIPTION

This program presents a series of questions on the computer screen and the respondent answers by pressing numbers on the keyboard. The questions are easy to understand and take approximately 15 minutes to complete. A narrative report can be produced immediately, which can then be used as a guide during subsequent personal interview or to identify topics which need to be further explored.

This report presents information concerning the respondent's current status as well as childhood, educational, military, criminal, and substance abuse history. Personal relations with friends and family members are described and a series of self-descriptive adjectives are reported. Major problem areas and psychological/medical history information are also presented. The instrument is designed primarily for use as a self-report device for adults.

An operating software package, priced from $200-$850 depending on the complexity of the package, is required for program use, plus an additional fee of $2.00 per use.

Reproduced by permission granted to

IPS Scoring Services
5211 Mahoning Avenue, Suite 135
Youngstown, OH 44515
Phone (216) 799-3282

This is a confidential report for use by professional staff only. IPS
Social History is designed for use as a self-report device for adults.
Statements are based solely on information supplied by the patient, and
should be considered as hypotheses for further considerations.

CURRENT STATUS

ALICE DOE is a 35 year old white female who lists her religious
affiliation as Catholic. She is presently married and has two children.
ALICE resides in a house and has lived at this location for two to five
years with three other people. The economic status of the neighborhood
is described as middle income. ALICE is currently employed 40 hours per
week and classifies her occupation as unskilled. She earns $100.00 to
$199.00 per week and is somewhat dissatisfied with her current
occupation. In addition, ALICE feels that her employer is reasonably
pleased with the quality of her work.

FAMILY HISTORY

Ms. DOE was raised by natural parents in a middle income home with three
siblings. She states her relationships with family members were as
follows: Mother was a lenient disciplinarian and a reasonably
affectionate person who was often excitable in frustrating situations.
The client's mother had problems in the following areas: emotional
distress, financial difficulties, expression of anger, serious physical
illness and marital conflicts. Father was described as a very strict,
reasonably nurturing person who was a very calm authority figure. The
client's father experienced problems with alcohol consumption, financial
difficulties and marital discord. Ms. DOE's relationship with her
siblings was poor. ALICE's siblings had problems in the following areas:
emotional, learning, alcohol and drug abuse. During childhood Ms. DOE
had difficulties with fears, nail biting, stammering, unhappy childhood,
alcohol abuse, drug abuse, emotional problems and learning. During
adolescence ALICE was a reasonably happy person. She describes herself
as an affectionate teenager with several friends.

EDUCATIONAL HISTORY

Ms. DOE has completed 12 years of school and has obtained a high school
diploma. The respondent did fail at least one grade in school and was
not placed in special education classes. During her school years the
respondent got along with teachers fairly well and was not active in
extra curricular activities.

634 *psychware*

MILITARY SERVICE

ALICE DOE was not in the military service.

CRIMINAL HISTORY

During adolescence the respondent was arrested two times for status and
drug offenses. ALICE has never been subject to official action for prior
offenses. After the age of 17 the respondent has been arrested one time
for a driving offense. The respondent has not been subjected to official
court proceedings. Ms. DOE is not on parole or probation at this time.

ALCOHOL AND DRUG USE HISTORY

The respondent reports alcohol problems and notes that she began
drinking at age 16. Her most serious problem seems to be with beer.   The
respondent reported these symptoms of alcohol abuse: memory loss,
missing work or school, loss of job, financial difficulties and sexual
maladjustment. Ms. DOE began using illicit substances at age 16. Her
drug usage is restricted to marijuana. ALICE has reported problems with
missing work or school, lost jobs and financial management.

PERSONAL RELATION / SELF DESCRIPTION

At the present time ALICE gets along with her spouse reasonably well.
She notes that the spouse is a warm person who is somewhat conservative
in his thinking. Marital problems include arguments, poor sexual
relations, financial difficulties, unable to confide and sexual affairs.
Ms. DOE's relations with her children are quite good and she feels that
she is taking care of the children as she should. The children present
problems in the area of disobedience and school adjustment. The
respondent describes herself as unhealthy, anxious, misunderstood,
unhappy, nervous, lonely, emotional, guilty, useless, moody, unloved,
stubborn, rebellious, suspicious, angry, tense, determined, generous,
kind, considerate, sensitive, helpful, sentimental, easy going,
imaginative and understanding. Ms. DOE is experiencing the following
problems: stomach trouble, fatigue or weakness, headaches, poor
concentration, memory recall, insomnia, difficulty getting up in the
morning, anger, depression, tension and worry, feelings of regret,
difficulty with decisions, feelings of hopelessness, unhappy home life,
few friends, financial troubles, job difficulties, sexual maladjustment
and arguments with others.

PSYCHOLOGICAL / MEDICAL HISTORY

Ms. DOE states that she is currently seeing a mental health therapist.
She has not been hospitalized for emotional problems and is not taking
psychoactive medication at this time. The respondent is satisfied with
the quality of prior mental health care and is a little concerned about
her emotional well being at this time. She has seen a medical doctor
less than six months ago. The respondent has not been hospitalized in
the last two years and is not taking medication for a physical ailment
at this time. Ms. DOE is not satisfied with the quality of prior health
care. At the present time she is a little concerned about physical
health matters.

DATE TAKEN : 8/10/83

NAME: SOI Careers and Vocations Test

SUPPLIER: SOI Institute
343 Richmond Street
El Segundo, CA 90245
(213) 322-5532

PRODUCT CATEGORY

Cognitive/Ability

PRIMARY APPLICATIONS

Vocational Guidance/Counseling
Clinical Assessment/Diagnosis
Educational Evaluation/Planning

SALE RESTRICTIONS American Psychological Association Guidelines

SERVICE TYPE/COST

	Type	Available	Cost	Discount
	Mail-In	Yes	$40.00	
	Teleprocessing	No		
	Local	No		

PRODUCT DESCRIPTION

The SOI CAREERS AND VOCATIONS TEST contains 24 different tests of intellectual abilities based on the Structure of Intellect model developed by Guilford and his associates. Three main areas are tapped: figural/spatial abilities, symbolic abilities, and semantic/verbal abilities.

The report, which may run as long as 40 pages, begins with a graphical report of scores. This is followed by an evaluation of 14 general intellectual abilities which are composites of the individual tests. These general areas include the ability to comprehend, remember, make judgments, solve problems, be creative, classify, work with consequences, and seven others. A narrative, clinical interpretation of each of the 14 general ability areas follows. Recommendations are made when the scores fall within a high or low range (e.g., Ask her parents to help her make collections of rocks, shells, stamps, and leaves to develop Classifications.)

Next, the report compares the individual's skill levels with those of successful two- and four-year college graduates. An indication is given as to whether each ability falls at satisfactory or unsatisfactory levels in comparison with the normative group.

The final section of the report provides occupational analyses based on the obtained test scores. The user may request specific analyses. If none have been selected for evaluation, the report will provide appropriate selections and indicate which abilities need to be improved in order to qualify for the various jobs and careers analyzed.

The sample printout shown here is a condensed form of the complete report.

```
                        Part I: TEST RESULTS

ANNE was administered the SOI Careers and Vocations Test.
It contains many different tests of intellectual abilities.  Below
are:  a definition of each test, the letters designating the test and the
scores that ANNE achieved (in terms of raw scores and percent correct).
These are the results of the testing; the interpretations will follow.

                                        LETTER                 PERCENT
                                     DESIGNATION    SCORE      CORRECT
FIGURAL (spatial) abilities:

   Visual closure.............................(CFU).....  16 ....... 100
   Visual conceptualization...................(CFC).....   9 ....... 100
   Comprehension of spatial systems...........(CFS).....  26 ....... 100
   Comprehension of spatial perspectives......(CFT).....  13 .......  50
   Visual memory for details..................(MFU).....  20 .......  71
   Visual discrimination......................(EFU).....  19 .......  73
   Judging similarity of concepts.............(EFC).....  14 .......  82
   Psycho-motor coordination..................(NFU).....  33 ....... 100
   Creative ideas and fluency with shapes.....(DFU).....  42 .......  75

SYMBOLIC (notational) abilities:

   Comprehension of abstract relations........(CSR).....   5 .......  63
   Comprehension of basic numerical facts.....(CSS).....   8 ....... 100
   Auditory attending and concentration.......(MSU).....  18 ....... 100
   Auditory sequencing........................(MSS).....  18 ....... 100
   Conceptualizing arithmetic processes.......(ESC).....  27 ....... 100
   Selecting correctness of numerical processes....(ESS).....  6 .......  75
   Application of numerical facts.............(NSS).....   7 .......  88
   Speed of word recognition..................(NST).....  166 .......  83
   Form reasoning and logic...................(NSI).....  21 ....... 100
   Mathematical creativity....................(DSR).....  58 .......  31

SEMANTIC (verbal) abilities:

   Vocabulary.................................(CMU).....  26 .......  87
   Comprehension of verbal relations..........(CMR).....  24 .......  96
   Comprehending extended verbal information..(CMS).....  15 .......  71
   Memory for abstract verbal inferences......(MMI).....  18 ....... 100
   Verbal creativity..........................(DMU).....  110 .......  79

   N/A = Not Administered
                                                         Page 1


        Part II:  PERSONAL INTELLECTUAL PROFILE -- SPECIFIC ABILITIES
This is a report for ANNE ADULT.  The following graph shows
ANNE's personal pattern of intellectual abilities; in this evaluation
no comparison is being made with others; this is a personal profile.

                                          Personal      Personal      Personal
                                          Low           Average       High

   Creative ideas and fluency with shapes......-------------------X
   Verbal creativity...........................------------------------X
   Visual closure..............................--------------------------X
   Vocabulary..................................------------------------X
   Comprehension of spatial systems............----------------------------X
   Comprehension of spatial perspectives.......--------X
   Comprehension of verbal relations...........----------------------X
   Comprehending extended verbal information....--------------------X
   Mathematical creativity.....................--X
   Comprehension of abstract relations.........----------------X
   Auditory attending and concentration........----------------------------X
   Auditory sequencing.........................----------------------------X
   Visual discrimination.......................--------------------X
   Visual conceptualization....................----------------------------X
   Judging similarity of concepts..............--------------------------X
   Conceptualizing arithmetic processes........----------------------------X
   Comprehension of basic numerical facts......----------------------------X
   Selecting correctness of numerical processes----------------------X
   Application of numerical facts..............------------------------X
   Speed of word recognition...................----------------------------X
   Form reasoning and logic....................----------------------------X
   Visual memory for details...................-----------------------X
   Psycho-motor coordination...................----------------------------X
   Memory for abstract verbal inferences.......----------------------------X

                                                         Page 2
```

psychware **637**

Part III: PERSONAL INTELLECTUAL PROFILE -- GENERAL ABILITIES

This is a report for ANNE ADULT. The following graph shows
ANNE's personal pattern of intellectual abilities; in this evaluation
no comparison is being made with others; this is a personal profile.

GENERAL INTELLECTUAL ABILITIES

	Personal Low	Personal Average	Personal High
Comprehending--learning new info............	----------------------X		
Memory--recalling information...............	-----------------------------X		
Planning--practical decisions...............	-----------------X		
Solving problems/following instructions.....	------------------------X		
Creative problem solving....................	--X		

INFORMATION PROCESSING ABILITIES *

	Personal Low	Personal Average	Personal High
Spatial/figural info--forms, shapes.........	---------------------X		
Symbolic info--numbers and notations........	----------------------X		
Semantic info--words, ideas.................	----------------------X		

    * This profile of abilities indicates that ANNE would be most
      comfortable working with WORDS, IDEAS, and PEOPLE and next with DATA
      and next with THINGS.

COMPLEXITY HANDLING ABILITIES

	Personal Low	Personal Average	Personal High
Units--informational details................	---------------------X		
Classes--organizing and classifying.........	-------------------------------X		
Relations--associative info.................	--X		
Systems--sets of relations..................	----------------------------X		
Transformations--perspectives...............	---X		
Implications--consequences, outcomes........	-------------------------------X		

                                                                    Page 3

Part VII: CLINICAL ANALYSIS -- EDUCATION

Content Considerations from SOI-LA Test

     One way that intellectual abilities can be examined is by
dividing them into categories which we call "content areas."
There are three content areas:
        1) Figural   2) Symbolic   3) Semantic

     FIGURAL intelligence is the ability to work with shapes,
objects, and spatial relationships.

     SYMBOLIC intelligence is the ability to work with numbers,
letters, and musical notes.

     SEMANTIC intelligence is the ability to work with words and
ideas.

     When considering the content abilities, we are concerned with
the levels of each ability, as well as the "spread" of abilities, that is, whether some abilities are higher or lower than
others, and how much difference there is among them.

     ANNE shows a pattern of content abilities which is
very high and relatively cohesive. She is facile with all
three kinds of information--figural, symbolic, and semantic.

638 *psychware*

In ANNE's case, since she is very high in all three
content areas, she is well prepared intellectually to deal
successfully with school material. She may want to look outside of the school for an activity which will given her an
opprotunity to take full advantage of her figural abilities.

Figural intelligence, while often unappreciated in school, is
very valuable in everyday life. People like ANNE who are
high-figural, tend to be very mechanically inclined. She
should be provided with the opportunity to make household re-
pairs. Fixing things is a good way to get positive feedback for
the figural abilities which are often ignored.

The graphic arts is another area where figural intelligence
proves invaluable--painting, sculpting, photography, and
mechanical drawing all require figural/spatial skills and
could provide ANNE with a very rewarding outlet for
her capabilities.

Finally, ANNE might find sports to be a good field
in which to demonstrate her figural ability. The marshall
arts, especially, require acute spatial perception. Sports help
people who already have the necessary intellectual capabilites
to develop the corresponding figural-motor capabilities.

High symbolic intelligence often manifests itself in the
ability to work with numerical concepts and abstract ideas.
ANNE should do well in arithmetic and math. She will
also probably have an affinity for computers. If possible, try
to find a way for ANNE to work with computers, either
through school or community classes, or on a home computer.

Computers are the way of the future, and ANNE's high
symbolic ability makes her especially well suited to success
in this area.

People with high symbolic ability are often very musical.
Regardless of whether or not ANNE can carry a tune,
she will probably be able to move into the world of music very
easily. This ability should be nurtured.

Highly semantic people are often articulate and well spoken.
They are the people most often recognized as bright. A high-
semantic thinker may be very poor in figural and symbolic intelligence, and yet she speaks so well that she just sounds
"smart."

ANNE is very forturnate in that high verbal people
tend to score well on achievement tests--though not necessarily
in arithmetic or math--and on tests of verbal aptitude, such
as standard IQ tests and college entrance exams.

Certainly ANNE will tend to be more successful and
happy in any work or activity where communication skills are at
a premium.

Cognitive Style Considerations from SOI-LA Test

COGNITION

ANNE may sometimes feel that she is psychic, because
she is so gifted in comprehension that she can take in information and process it more quickly than most people. Those
decisions she makes on what she calls intuition are probably

decisions and judgments which are being made from her quick-
ness at sizing up situations. If she has not learned to scan
reading material, a speed reading course will increase even
more her present gifted ability to understand her
environment. She may be at a disadvantage if she must work
for or with people who cannot understand or take in as much
information as quickly as she does. If she finds herself
impatient with them, the impatience needs to be tempered with
her knowing that they really cannot take in all the clues and
process them to the extent that she can. She really should
not get bogged down with too many details or such precise,
detailed work that she cannot put her gifted comprehension
and understanding to work. She needs varied and stimulating
activities to keep her from job hopping.

MEMORY

No one has to tell ANNE that she is like a walking
encyclopedia, she is so gifted in memory of all kinds. She
will do well in jobs which depend heavily upon gifted memory
such as her. She wants to be sure that she does not 'slay'
others with all she can recall. Few people have such well
developed ability to recall information as ANNE
does.

ANNE should be aware that she has a superior memory.
She should be well aware that her concentration is superb--
even more so when she is interested. Not many people can
process information as well as she does and retain unrelated
sequences in mind at the same time. She can improve her
memory even more by working with the Memory Handbooks I and II,
and the SOI Training Modules that train memory.

CREATIVITY

ANNE shows high creative ability--a fluency with
ideas and an ability to break sets and get outside the bounds
of the conventional. We do not know if she has the talent to
go with her creativity, but her potential for being creative
needs maintaining and enriching. Inquire about the Creativity
Modules and the Higher Thinking Skill packets from the SOI
Institute.

EVALUATION

ANNE's ability to evaluate and make decisions is very
high. This kind of intelligence is extremely valuable in everyday life. ANNE's decision-making ability will show up in
social and leadership skills.
Decision-making skill is necessary for any kind of job in
management or where initiative is important. ANNE would
do well in a position of authority and responsibility.

    Information-handling Considerations from SOI-LA Test

Since ANNE's problem solving abilities are also high,
she has the ability to handle very large problems--she sees
the big picture and has problem solving abilities.

ANNE would be great at organizing parties, games,
tours, cruises, etc., if she has the desire to do so.

ANNE is so flexible that she is able to see many ways
to solve problems and to change solutions. Being flexible often
leads to creative responses. For example, does she pun easily?
Laugh quickly at humor? See the funny side of things when
others don't ? Or before they do? If others see her as mer-
curial, it is because she can appreciate many other facts
others don't even perceive. She needs to find people who are
compatible and as flexible in their thinking, too. It may be a
long search.

ANNE has a great ability to work with details.
She will pay close attention to details and prefer to work with
one thing at a time. Other people who are not so detail minded
as she may have a hard time appreciating how competent she
is. She may need to be understanding of their lack of interest
in details if they tell her that she is too picky.
She can vent her love for details by getting into
hobbies which depend on awareness of details such as stamp collecting, antique studying, archaeology, gemology, or art.

Specific Learning Ability Considerations from SOI-LA Test

The different subtests in the SOI-LA Basic test were selected
from the Structure of Intellect model because each is known to
have a significant relationship to some aspect of school learning. Specifically, some of the subtests are related to reading
(basic), others to reading (advanced), others to arithmetic and
mathematics, and others to creativity.

We can also interpret test scores in terms of basic academic
learning abilities.

With regard to BASIC READING skills:

With regard to ADVANCED READING:

ANNE's score in CMU and CMR would indicate no difficulty with vocabulary acquisition and verbal relations--but a
low score on CMS would indicate difficulty with processing these
concepts sequentially. Does ANNE seem to have difficulty
following instrustuctions and/or long lectures, directions or
sequences of visual presentations? Work with CMS tasks to build
her processing ability.

With regard to ARITHMETIC skills:

ANNE's scores on the arithmetic-related abilities
are all in the average or above range. If she has any
difficulty with arithmetic, look at her low-average scores
in either CSS, ESS, NSS, MSS-auditory, MSU-auditory, or ESC
for specific remediation.

With regard to MATHEMATICS skills:

Four of the tests--CFS, CFT, CSR, and NSI--are necessary
abilities for mathematics. Since ANNE's scores are
average or above for all of these tests, we would expect no
difficulty with non-verbal aspects of mathematics. Some of
these abilities are in the low-average range; you may want to
pay attention to those before ANNE enters mathematics.

        A COMPARISON OF YOUR SKILLS ON THE SOI WITH THOSE OF SUCCESSFUL COLLEGE
                GRADUATES (TWO-YEAR AND FOUR-YEAR COLLEGES)

(This is provided as a supplement to your career analysis: those careers
requiring college diploma include the evaluation below)

These are EXIT skills, not entry skills. A difference of less than -15% is not
significant but will require more effort, more development or compensation.

                                                       Do your
Required abilities.........Ability is: %-Required scores match?   %-Obtained

  Comprehending...............ESSENTIAL........ 78 .... YES--STRONG.......... 85
  Remembering.................ESSENTIAL........ 75 .... YES--EXCELLENT....... 93
  Judging and planning........Suggested........ 63 .... Yes--Excellent....... 83
  Solving problems............ESSENTIAL........ 74 .... YES--EXCELLENT....... 93
  Symbolic information........Suggested........ 70 .... Yes--Strong.......... 84
  Verbal information..........ESSENTIAL........ 79 .... YES--STRONG.......... 87
  Details.....................ESSENTIAL........ 70 .... YES--EXCELLENT....... 86
  Classifications.............Suggested........ 63 .... Yes--Excellent....... 94
  Relations...................ESSENTIAL........ 60 .... YES--ADEQUATE........ 63
  Systems.....................Suggested........ 81 .... Yes--Strong.......... 89
  Consequences................Suggested........ 62 .... Yes--Excellent....... 100

        A COMPARISON OF YOUR SCORES WITH SUCCESSFUL GRADUATES WHO HAVE ADVANCED DEGREES
                (MASTER'S, DOCTORATES OR PROFESSIONAL)
                                                       Do your
Required abilities.........Ability is: %-Required scores match?   %-Obtained

  Comprehending...............ESSENTIAL........ 80 .... YES--STRONG.......... 85
  Remembering.................ESSENTIAL........ 80 .... YES--STRONG.......... 93
  Judging and planning........ESSENTIAL........ 79 .... YES--ADEQUATE........ 83
  Solving problems............ESSENTIAL........ 89 .... YES--ADEQUATE........ 93
  Symbolic information........Suggested........ 78 .... Yes--Strong.......... 84
  Verbal information..........ESSENTIAL........ 80 .... YES--STRONG.......... 87
  Details.....................ESSENTIAL........ 75 .... YES--STRONG.......... 86
  Classifications.............Suggested........ 63 .... Yes--Excellent....... 94
  Relations...................ESSENTIAL........ 65 .... YES--ADEQUATE........ 63
  Systems.....................Suggested........ 89 .... Yes--Adequate........ 89
  Consequences................Suggested........ 75 .... Yes--Excellent....... 100

Career titles followed by any of these initials require a
degree in the corresponding field:

        A = Social Science   E = Specialty
        B = Business   T = Special talents
        C = Humanitites   V = Vocational training
        D = Natural Science   and/or advanced degree

                    Part IX: JOB ANALYSIS REPORT

        ==
                        COMPUTER MATCHES
            The following jobs have been selected by the
            computer on the basis of how well your pattern
            of abilities matches the job pattern. Some of
            them may not be your choice--if so, discount
            the ones you are not interested in and consider
            the others.
        ==

MICROBIOLOGY

Based on the SOI-LA test we would say that there is a mixed match--some good aspects and some poor aspects--between you profile of abilities and those required for MICROBIOLOGY.

Abilities needing improvement:

Systems

MICROBIOLOGY would require you to make judgements on a superb level. Your ability to make judgements is excellent. This is adequate for the requirements of the job. To maintain this match you should take care to maintain this ability.

In order to work in MICROBIOLOGY, you will need an outstanding ability to work with spatial and figural. Your ability to work with spatial and figural is outstanding. So, the match between your profile and the job requirements in this report is good.

In order to work in MICROBIOLOGY, you will need an outstanding ability to work with symbols and numbers. Your ability to work with symbols and numbers is outstanding. So, the match between your profile and the job requirements in this report is good.

MICROBIOLOGY would require you to work with individual details on a superb level. Your ability to work with individual details is outstanding. So, the match between your profile and the job requirements in this report is good.

Being successful in MICROBIOLOGY means that you must frequently classify and sort. Your ability to classify and sort is outstanding. This is a very positive match with the established job requirements indicating that you are already very well prepared in this regard.

A career in MICROBIOLOGY requires a superb ability to work with interrelated systems. Your ability to work with interrelated systems is high average. This is below the requirement, so unless you improve this ability you will have difficulty in this field.

A career in MICROBIOLOGY requires a superb ability to work with consequences. Your ability to work with consequences is outstanding. So, the match between your profile and the job requirements in this report is good.

MICROBIOLOGY would require you to comprehend and perform visual closure on an outstanding level. Your ability to comprehend and perform visual closure is outstanding. So, the match between your profile and the job requirements in this report is good.

Working in MICROBIOLOGY requires you to frequently discriminate detailed information. Your ability to discriminate detailed information is average. You will be at a disadvantage unless you work hard to improve this weakness; in other words this is a limiting ability with regard to this career.

Being successful in MICROBIOLOGY means that you must frequently code, identify and transform symbolic information. Your ability to code, identify and transform symbolic information is excellent. However, even this is inadequate for the requirements of the job, so you will need to improve this ability.

COMPARISON PROFILE OF ABILITIES
(In this section we are interpreting ANNE's abilities
in comparison with other people)

General Thinking Abilities:

One of ANNE's strengths is her ability to do
on-line learning; in other words, she has a better than average
ability to learn newly presented material. We would expect
her to do well in jobs that have changing directions, instructions or procedures.

ANNE's overall ability to recall and remember information indicates that she will do well at taking instructions
on the spot and being able to use the information accurately.

ANNE's ability to make practical judgments is a
strong ability for her. She should do well in jobs where
she must make decisions about the material at hand, or make
judgments about actions to be taken. This is a critical
ingredient in taking on a supervisory or leadership role.

ANNE has the ability to stay on task as well as an
ability to trouble-shoot and/or solve problems.

Information Processing:

ANNE can handle plans and charts well; her ability
to deal with figural content should qualify her for jobs that
require spatial information.

ANNE works well with information which is symbolic
or notational such as numbers, codes, or other abstractions of
material. We do not know about her ability to handle calculations and other symbolic manipulations, but she should be
comfortable with notational content.

ANNE does well working with verbal material; she
can handle words and ideas well so she should do well in jobs
that require communication and verbal interaction.

Informational Complexity:

ANNE has the ability to work with information at the
units level--working with things one at a time. We would expect her to do well in jobs demanding attention to detail.

ANNE has the ability to work with grouped infor-
mation--information that is organized into sets or classes.
We would expect her to do well jobs that require classification or cataloguing.

ANNE has the ability to draw out the implications
or consequences from presented material. This is an important
ability in jobs that require skill in trouble-shooting, plan-
ing, or text interpretation.

PERSONAL PROFILE OF ABILITIES
(In this section we are interpreting ANNE's own pattern
of strengths for occupations.)

ANNE's ability to remember material that she has
learned is a personal intellectual strength.

In handling information, one of ANNE's strengths is
in the figural area--reading diagrams, plans, maps, etc.

With respect to handling different kinds of information,

NAME: Stanton Survey

SUPPLIER: PSYCH Systems, Inc.
600 Reisterstown Road
Baltimore, MD 21208
(800) 368-3366

PRODUCT CATEGORY	PRIMARY APPLICATIONS
Interest/Attitudes	Personnel Selection/Evaluation

SALE RESTRICTIONS Qualified Professional

SERVICE TYPE/COST	Type	Available	Cost	Discount
	Mail-In	No		
	Teleprocessing	No		
	Local	Yes	See Below	

PRODUCT DESCRIPTION

The STANTON SURVEY is a pre-employment screening test that measures the honesty of the job applicant. To do so, applicants' attitudes toward theft and their admissions of thefts are combined to form an overall risk index. The logic of the test is that the more a person thinks like a dishonest person, the more likely the person is to be dishonest, and the more admissions of past dishonesty the person makes the more likely will be the future occurrence of dishonest behavior.

This Psych Systems product administers, scores, and provides a 4-page printout of test results. In addition to an analysis of the attitude, admission, and overall index scores, the program also provides a listing of critical items.

Psych Systems programs operate on the IBM PC-XT, COMPAQ Plus, Dec Professional 350, and most DEC PDP-11 systems. Various hardware/ software configurations are available directly from Psych Systems, with single-user systems starting at approximately $12,000. A per test fee also applies.

222-22-2222   Jonathan Doe   32 yr old white male   16-Feb-84


```
     ------------------------------
    |          |                   |
    |   STAN   |   Stanton Survey  |
    |          |                   |
     ------------------------------
```


The Stanton Survey should be used ONLY for Pre-Employment Screening.
It is recommended that the screening process entail a personal interview,
biodata information, and other job-related materials. Decisions to hire
should not rest solely with the Stanton Survey results or the contents of
this report. To avoid the misuse of the Stanton Survey, it should never
be administered to current employees. Other instruments are more suited
for assessing attitudes toward honest behavior of incumbents.

STANTON SURVEY

The STANTON SURVEY is a Pre-Employment Screening test that measures
the honesty of the job applicant. To measure honesty, the job
applicant's attitude toward theft and his admissions of thefts are
combined to form a risk index. The job applicant's attitude toward
theft is captured by his Numerical Base score. Actual Admissions of
theft which are differentially weighted yield an Admission Score.
These two scale scores are combined to form the Survey Score.

NUMERICAL BASE (NB)

The NB score refers to the number of times the applicant has agreed
with the thinking of proven, dishonest persons. The higher the NB
score, the more the applicant thinks like a dishonest person. The
more the person thinks like a dishonest person, the more likely the
person is a dishonest person.

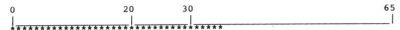

```
0               20        30                                   65
|               |         |                                    |
|***************************************************
```

The applicant's NB score is 35. This score falls in the negative
attitude toward honesty range.

                    20 >   NORMAL
                    20 <= BORDERLINE <= 30
                    30 <   NEGATIVE

ADMISSIONS SCORE (AS)

The AS score assesses the quantity and quality of the applicant's
admissions of previous dishonesty. As such, honest people believe
dishonest behavior is abnormal (even they, too, have done some of it)
and make few or no admissions. Dishonest people believe stealing is
normal and admit it but do not make a total disclosure. Admissions
made (none,some,many) are accurate back-up measures of the
applicant's dishonesty. However, admissions should not be taken as
total disclosures but only as a measure of what the applicant
considers to be NORMAL behavior.

```
0    18   34                                   200
|    |    |                                      |
|*********************
```

The applicant's AS score is 75. His score falls in the range that
suggests serious admissions of past behavior.

                    18 >   PETTY
                    18 <= SIGNIFICANT <= 34
                    34 <   SERIOUS

SURVEY SCORE (SS)

The SS is a composite score of the applicant's attitude toward
honesty and the seriousness of previous dishonesty, if any. This
applicant's score is 110 which falls in the HIGH Risk range.

The HIGH Risk applicants generally believe in dishonesty as a way of
life. When they steal something, it is considered excusable because
the owner did not protect his property. There is no recognition of
the moral wrongness of theft; the wrongness is in getting caught, IF
one is caught.

HIGH Risk applicants are exceedingly dangerous to a company, not only because they steal, but because their thefts are planned (which increases in value with each additional successful theft) and they recruit other employees to assist them, reducing the number of people who could possibly report them.

```
0    30   55                                             265
|____|____|_____|
**********************
```

The applicant's SS score places him in the high risk range.

```
                    30 >  LOW
                    30 <= MARGINAL <= 55
                    55 <  HIGH
```

The following admissions and opinions were expressed by this applicant:

Someone tried to get applicant to steal something by showing him how to do it.

Admits previous theft of unknown item. Such thefts are usually petty and occur during childhood.

Admits walking out of a store with merchandise that wasn't paid for because he couldn't find a clerk.

Thinks it is human nature to look for ways to beat the system.

Applicant has been asked to steal something, but refused.

Doesn't believe unauthorized discounting is wrong.

Admits teenage shoplifting.

Admits recent shoplifting in the last three years.

Admits theft of merchandise from job. Estimated dollar value of theft is $1.

Admits theft of money from job. Estimated dollar value of theft is $1.

```
++++++++++++++++++++++++++++++++++++++++++++++++++++++++++++++++++++++++
```
Information contained in this report is based exclusively on the work of Carl S. Klump and the Stanton Corporation.
```
++++++++++++++++++++++++++++++++++++++++++++++++++++++++++++++++++++++++
```

NAME: State-Trait Anxiety Inventory

SUPPLIER: PSYCH Systems, Inc.
600 Reisterstown Road
Baltimore, MD 21208
(800) 368-3366

PRODUCT CATEGORY	PRIMARY APPLICATIONS
Personality	Clinical Assessment/Diagnosis Personal/Marriage/Family Counseling

SALE RESTRICTIONS Qualified Professional

SERVICE TYPE/COST Type	Available	Cost	Discount
Mail-In	No		
Teleprocessing	No		
Local	Yes	See Below	

PRODUCT DESCRIPTION

This instrument contains items designed to measure how an individual is responding to stress at the present time. A separate set of 20 items measures the individual's typical response to stress and serves as an indicator of clinical anxiety. The instrument has been found to be sensitive to changes in transitory anxiety experienced by clients in counseling. It has also been used to assess the level of anxiety induced by real-life stressors, such as imminent surgery, dental treatment, employment interviews, or important school tests. The trait scale has been shown to reliably differentiate neurotic and depressed patients from normal adults.

This program presents and scores the inventory. It then provides a brief printout of test results.

Psych Systems programs operate on the IBM PC-XT, COMPAQ Plus, Dec Professional 350, and most DEC PDP-11 systems. Various hardware/ software configurations are available directly from Psych Systems, with single-user systems starting at approximately $12,000. A per test fee also applies.

222-22-2222 Jonathan Doe   32 yr old white male   16-Feb-84

```
+-------------------------------------------------------+
|          |                                            |
|   STAI   |      State-Trait Anxiety Inventory         |
|          |                                            |
+-------------------------------------------------------+
```

The State-Trait Anxiety Inventory (STAI) has been added to Fasttest
for use by qualified professionals. The STAI should be administered
as part of a test battery. Since the STAI, like most self-report
instruments, is susceptible to response bias, it is highly recommended
that the test battery includes a validity measure such as the
MMPI Lie Scale.

The Fasttest version of the STAI requires the administration of both
sections for a report to be generated.

The computer program generating this report was designed by Psych
Systems, Inc., Baltimore, Maryland 21208. Copyright (C) 1984 by
Psych Systems, Inc. The State-Trait Anxiety Inventory is
reproduced by permission. Copyright (C) 1968, 1977, 1983 by Consulting
Psychologists Press, Incorporated, 577 College Avenue, Palo Alto,
California 94306. No portion of the STAI-Y may be reproduced by
any process without prior written permission of the publisher.
All rights reserved.

650 *psychware*

The State-Trait Anxiety Inventory (STAI) contains two related but
different measures of anxiety. The S-Anxiety Scale assesses how one
feels RIGHT NOW. This scale provides information on one's feelings of
apprehension, tension, and nervousness at the present time. The
T-Anxiety Scale is an index of ANXIETY PRONENESS. The T-Anxiety scale
score reflects the person's tendency to experience anxiety in stressful
situations. A person with a high T-Anxiety score is more inclined to
experience S-Anxiety elevations than a low T-Anxiety person. This is
manifested in the high T-Anxiety person's tendency to view his/her
surroundings as dangerous and threatening.

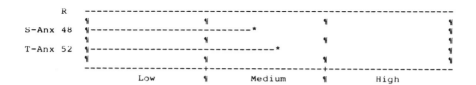

```
        R    --------------------------------------------------------------
             ¶                         ¶                 ¶                 ¶
S-Anx 48     ¶---------------------------*               ¶                 ¶
             ¶                         ¶                 ¶                 ¶
T-Anx 52     ¶-------------------------------*           ¶                 ¶
             ¶                         ¶                 ¶                 ¶
             --------------------+------------------+--------------------
                 Low             ¶     Medium       ¶     High
```

Raw scores on the S-Anxiety and the T-Anxiety scales range from a minimum
of 20 to a maximum of 80. S-Anxiety and T-Anxiety raw scores greater
than 60 fall in the high anxiety range, whereas scores less than 40 are
in the low anxiety range.

Abnormally high or low STAI scores should be carefully reviewed when
devising treatment plans.

                         Raw Data

               1234567890 1234567890 1234567890

       1- 30 3222222122 2113322112 2223333344
      31- 40 3333322322

psychware **651**

NAME: Strong-Campbell Interest Inventory: Interpretive Report

SUPPLIER: NCS/Professional Assessment Services
P.O. Box 1416
Minneapolis, MN 55440
(800) 328-6759

PRODUCT CATEGORY

Career/Vocational
Interest/Attitudes

PRIMARY APPLICATIONS

Vocational Guidance/Counseling

SALE RESTRICTIONS   None

SERVICE TYPE/COST	Type	Available	Cost	Discount
	Mail-In	No		
	Teleprocessing	Yes	$10.00	Yes
	Local	Yes	$7.50	Yes

PRODUCT DESCRIPTION

This product consists of an individualized narrative, ranging from 20-22 pages. The narrative report contains scale descriptions, score interpretation and comparisons, plus additional reference information followed by a 4-page detachable summary. A scores only report (Profile Report) is also available at approximately 40% of costs shown here for the complete report.

The test itself is comprised of 325 trichotomous items requiring an 8th-grade reading level and 30-40 minutes to complete. Designed to aid in career development by assessing vocational interests of those planning to obtain a 4-year college degree or advanced technical training, the STRONG-CAMP-BELL INTEREST INVENTORY has 162 Occupational scales, 23 Basic Interest scales, 6 General Occupational Themes (corresponding to Holland's RIASEC scheme), and 11 Non-occupational scales and Administrative indexes.

Two systems are available for local processing of test results. MICRO-TEST Assessment Software from National Computer Systems, used with a Sentry 3000 tabletop scanner (purchase price approximately $4000) and microcomputer system ($2000-$3000 purchase price), allows tests to be administered off-line. Answer sheets are then scanned and scored automatically, one at a time or in a batch. The software also permits on-line administration of the test via microcomputer. In either case, the same report is provided. The cost for local scoring refers to the cost-per-test when diskettes are purchased in units of 20 administrations (minimum purchase).

PREPARED BY--
NCS/INTERPRETIVE SCORING SYSTEMS
P.O. BOX 1294
MINNEAPOLIS, MN 55440
22-SEP-83

002 0009

STRONG-CAMPBELL INTEREST INVENTORY

INTERPRETIVE REPORT FOR

****
SAMPLE   S   MALE
****

THE IMPORTANT PROCESS OF CHOOSING A CAREER REQUIRES THAT SEVERAL THINGS BE CONSIDERED. YOUR ABILITIES ARE VERY IMPORTANT IN DECIDING UPON A JOB, BUT YOUR INTERESTS, PERSONAL PREFERENCES, AND LIFE EXPERIENCES ALSO PLAY AN IMPORTANT PART IN HELPING YOU DECIDE ON AN OCCUPATION WHERE YOU WILL BE SATISFIED. RESEARCH HAS SHOWN THAT INDIVIDUALS HAVE A BETTER CHANCE OF BEING SATIS- FIED IN AN OCCUPATION IF THEIR INTERESTS ARE SIMILAR TO THOSE OF PEOPLE ALREADY EMPLOYED IN THAT OCCUPATION. THE RESULTS BELOW ARE BASED ON YOUR LIKE AND DISLIKE ANSWERS TO THE ITEMS ON THE STRONG-CAMPBELL INTEREST INVENTORY. THESE RESULTS WILL POINT OUT AREAS WHERE YOUR INTERESTS DO AND DO NOT MATCH THOSE OF PEOPLE WHO ARE WORKING IN DIFFERENT OCCUPATIONS. THE RESULTS CAN HELP YOU UNDERSTAND BETTER HOW YOUR PREFERENCES FIT INTO THE WORLD OF WORK.

IMPORTANTLY, THESE RESULTS ARE MEASURES OF ONLY YOUR INTERESTS AND NOT OF YOUR ABILITIES OR APTITUDES. FOR EXAMPLE, YOUR RESULTS MAY INDICATE THAT YOU WOULD LIKE THE DAILY ROUTINE OF ART- ISTS AND THAT YOU LIKE ARTISTIC ACTIVITIES, BUT THE RESULTS WILL NOT TELL YOU IF YOU HAVE THE TALENT TO BE AN ARTIST.

THESE RESULTS CAN GIVE YOU SOME USEFUL INFORMATION ABOUT YOURSELF, BUT DO NOT EXPECT MIRA- CLES. WHILE YOU MAY FEEL THAT THE SCORES TELL YOU NOTHING MORE THAN YOU ALREADY KNOW ABOUT YOURSELF, THEY WILL PERMIT YOU TO SEE HOW THE STRENGTHS OF YOUR INTERESTS COMPARE TO THE AVERAGE INTERESTS OF OTHER PEOPLE. THESE RESULTS ARE DESIGNED TO BE AN AID TO HELP YOU REACH A CAREER DECISION THAT WILL BE MOST SATISFYING TO YOU.

* *

THREE MAIN SETS OF SCORES ARE PRESENTED ON THE FOLLOWING PAGES. FIRST ARE YOUR RESULTS ON SIX GENERAL OCCUPATIONAL THEMES--THEY GIVE YOU A GENERAL OVERALL VIEW OF YOUR INTERESTS. SECOND ARE YOUR RESULTS ON THE BASIC INTEREST SCALES--THESE SCORES TELL YOU ABOUT THE STRENGTH OF YOUR INTERESTS IN MORE SPECIFIC AREAS SUCH AS SALES, WRITING, AND MECHANICAL ACTIVITIES. THIRD ARE THE OCCUPATIONAL SCALES--THEY TELL YOU HOW SIMILAR OR DISSIMILAR YOUR INTERESTS ARE TO PEOPLE IN DIFFERENT OCCUPATIONS SUCH AS POLICE OFFICER, INTERIOR DECORATOR, MATHEMATICIAN, AND SO FORTH.

* *

GENERAL OCCUPATIONAL THEMES

RESEARCH HAS SHOWN THAT INTERESTS CAN BE GROUPED INTO SIX CATEGORIES AND THAT EACH OF THESE GROUPINGS CAN BE DESCRIBED BY A GENERAL THEME. BELOW ARE YOUR SCORES ON THE SIX GENERAL THEME SCALES AND A GRAPH TO VIEW YOUR RESULTS BETTER. THE ABBREVIATED THEME NAMES ARE LISTED IN THE SCALE COLUMN WITH THE COMPLETE NAMES LISTED TO THE RIGHT OF THE GRAPH. MOST PEOPLE HAVE SCORES BETWEEN 43 AND 57 ON THESE SCALES, SO THIS RANGE, 43-57, IS CALLED THE AVERAGE RANGE OF SCORES. SCORES BELOW 43 GENERALLY ARE CONSIDERED AS LOW INTEREST IN THAT THEME. SCORES ABOVE 57 GENER- ALLY ARE CONSIDERED AS HIGH INTEREST IN THAT THEME. ALSO, IF YOU INDICATED YOUR SEX ON THE IN- VENTORY, THERE IS A RANGE OF DOTS FOR EACH SCALE SHOWING THE AVERAGE SCORE RANGE FOR YOUR SEX.

SCALE	YOUR SCORE	3	4	5	6	7		MIN-MAX
C-THEME	59				.... *		(CONVENTIONAL)	23-79
R-THEME	59				............*....		(REALISTIC)	27-75
I-THEME	56				.........*...		(INVESTIGATIVE)	20-69
A-THEME	45			.*........			(ARTISTIC)	24-67
E-THEME	44			.*......			(ENTERPRISING)	30-77
S-THEME	34		*				(SOCIAL)	19-73

DESCRIPTIONS ARE GIVEN BELOW FOR EACH OF THE THEMES. THESE ARE IDEAL DESCRIPTIONS OF THE INTERESTS AND CHARACTERISTICS RELATED TO EACH THEME, SO ALL THE DESCRIPTIONS MAY NOT EXACTLY FIT ANY ONE PERSON. FEW PEOPLE HAVE HIGH SCORES ON JUST ONE THEME AND LOW SCORES ON THE OTHERS. MOST PEOPLE SCORE HIGH ON TWO OR EVEN THREE THEMES AND THUS THEY SHARE SOME OF THE DESCRIPTIONS WITH MORE THAN ONE THEME. SOME PEOPLE SCORE LOW ON ALL THEMES WHICH WOULD INDICATE THAT STRONG PATTERNS OF INTERESTS, AS MEASURED BY THESE THEMES, HAVE NOT BEEN FORMED YET--THIS IS PARTICU- LARLY TRUE FOR YOUNG PEOPLE. GENERALLY, THE HIGHER YOUR SCORE, THE MORE CHARACTERISTICS YOU SHARE WITH THAT PARTICULAR THEME.

C   C-THEME--HIGH SCORERS ON THIS THEME LIKE JOBS WHERE THEY KNOW EXACTLY WHAT IS EXPECTED OF
C   THEM.   PROBLEMS USING VERBAL AND NUMERICAL SKILLS ARE PREFERRED TO THOSE REQUIRING PHYSICAL
C   SKILLS.   C-THEME PEOPLE FIT WELL INTO LARGE ORGANIZATIONS AND RESPOND TO AUTHORITY, BUT THEY DO
C   NOT SEEK LEADERSHIP. THEY HAVE LITTLE INTEREST IN INTENSE RELATIONSHIPS WITH OTHERS, BUT VALUE
C   MATERIAL POSSESSIONS AND STATUS.   SUCH PEOPLE DESCRIBE THEMSELVES AS CONVENTIONAL, STABLE, WELL-
C   CONTROLLED, AND DEPENDABLE.   VOCATIONAL PREFERENCES ARE MOSTLY WITHIN THE BUSINESS WORLD AND IN-
C   CLUDE BANK EXAMINER, BANK TELLER, BOOKKEEPER, FINANCIAL ANALYST, COMPUTER OPERATOR, INVENTORY
C   CONTROLLER, TAX EXPERT, STATISTICIAN, TRAFFIC MANAGER, AND SOME ACCOUNTING JOBS. ALTHOUGH ONE
C   WORD CANNOT ADEQUATELY REPRESENT THE ENTIRE THEME, THE WORD CONVENTIONAL SUMMARIZES THIS PAT-
C   TERN, THUS C-THEME.
C   YOUR SCORE OF 59 ON C-THEME INDICATES THAT PROBABLY MANY OF THE ABOVE PHRASES ARE TRUE FOR
C   YOU AND YOU POSSIBLY WOULD ENJOY CLERICAL TYPES OF WORK SUCH AS TYPING OR CHECKING NUMBERS.

R-THEME---R-THEME PEOPLE TEND TO BE RUGGED, PRACTICAL, AND PHYSICALLY STRONG. THEY ENJOY CREATING THINGS WITH THEIR HANDS AND WOULD RATHER WORK WITH OBJECTS, SUCH AS TOOLS OR LARGE MACHINES, THAN WITH IDEAS OR PEOPLE. THEY LIKE TO WORK OUTDOORS AND PREFER OCCUPATIONS SUCH AS MECHANIC, CONSTRUCTION WORKER, FISH AND WILDLIFE MANAGER, LABORATORY TECHNICIAN, SOME ENGINEERING SPECIALTIES, SOME MILITARY JOBS, AGRICULTURE, OR THE SKILLED TRADES. TO CAPTURE THE BROAD MEANING OF THIS THEME, THE WORD REALISTIC HAS BEEN USED, THUS R-THEME.

YOUR SCORE OF 59 ON THE R-THEME SCALE INDICATES THAT VERY LIKELY MANY OF THE ABOVE DESCRIPTIONS ARE TRUE FOR YOU AND YOU MIGHT ENJOY ACTIVITIES THAT ALLOW YOU TO WORK WITH YOUR HANDS.

I-THEME---THIS THEME TENDS TO CENTER AROUND SCIENTIFIC ACTIVITIES. HIGH SCORERS ON THIS THEME WOULD RATHER WORK ALONE THAN WITH PEOPLE. THEY HAVE QUESTIONING MINDS AND LIKE LOOSELY DEFINED PROBLEMS WHICH THEY CAN SOLVE BY WORKING WITH IDEAS, WORDS, AND SYMBOLS. THEY DO NOT LIKE SITUATIONS IN WHICH THEY HAVE TO FOLLOW MANY RULES. FREQUENTLY, THEY ARE ORIGINAL AND CREATIVE, ESPECIALLY IN SCIENTIFIC AREAS. OCCUPATIONS PREFERRED BY SUCH PEOPLE INCLUDE BIOLOGIST, MATHEMATICIAN, PSYCHOLOGIST, RESEARCH LABORATORY WORKER, PHYSICIST, PHYSICIAN, DESIGN ENGINEER, TECHNICAL WRITER, OR METEOROLOGIST. THE WORD INVESTIGATIVE HAS BEEN USED TO SUMMARIZE THIS PATTERN, HENCE, I-THEME.

YOUR SCORE OF 56 ON THE I-THEME SCALE INDICATES THAT SOME OF THE ABOVE PHRASES ARE PROBABLY TRUE FOR YOU, WHILE SOME OF THE OTHER PHRASES DO NOT DESCRIBE YOU AS WELL.

A-THEME---PEOPLE SCORING HIGH ON THIS THEME ARE ARTISTICALLY INCLINED AND PREFER TO WORK ALONE IN SETTINGS THAT ALLOW THEM TO EXPRESS THEMSELVES CREATIVELY. THEY DO NOT LIKE SITUATIONS THAT REQUIRE THEM TO USE PHYSICAL STRENGTH, AND THEY DESCRIBE THEMSELVES AS INDEPENDENT, UNCONVENTIONAL, ORIGINAL, AND TENSE. THEY USUALLY SCORE HIGHER ON MEASURES OF ORIGINALITY THAN DO ANY OF THE OTHER TYPES. VOCATIONAL CHOICES INCLUDE ARTIST, AUTHOR, CARTOONIST, SINGER, COMPOSER, DRAMATIC COACH, POET, ACTOR/ACTRESS, AND SYMPHONY CONDUCTOR. THIS IS THE ARTISTIC THEME, OR A-THEME.

YOUR SCORE OF 45 ON THE A-THEME SCALE INDICATES THAT SOME OF THE ABOVE PHRASES MAY BE TRUE FOR YOU, WHILE SOME OF THE OTHERS DO NOT DESCRIBE YOU AS WELL.

E-THEME---E-THEME PEOPLE ARE FREQUENTLY IN SALES WORK BECAUSE THEY ARE GOOD AT LEADING AND CONVINCING PEOPLE. ENTHUSIASTIC, SELF-CONFIDENT, AND DOMINANT, THEY THINK UP NEW WAYS OF DOING THINGS, ARE FULL OF ENERGY, AND LIKE ADVENTURE. THEY ARE IMPATIENT WITH WORK INVOLVING MANY DETAILS, OR LONG PERIODS OF INTELLECTUAL EFFORT OR CONCENTRATION. THEY PREFER SOCIAL SITUATIONS WHERE THEY CAN LEAD AND DIRECT OTHERS. THEY LIKE POWER, STATUS, AND MATERIAL WEALTH, AND ENJOY WORKING IN EXPENSIVE SETTINGS. VOCATIONAL PREFERENCES INCLUDE BUSINESS EXECUTIVE, MERCHANDISE BUYER, HOTEL MANAGER, INDUSTRIAL RELATIONS CONSULTANT, POLITICAL CAMPAIGNER, REALTOR, SPORTS PROMOTER, TELEVISION PRODUCER, AND MANY KINDS OF SALES WORK. THE WORD ENTERPRISING SUMMARIZES THIS PATTERN OF INTEREST, THUS E-THEME.

YOUR SCORE OF 44 ON THE E-THEME SCALE INDICATES THAT SOME OF THE ABOVE PHRASES ARE MORE TRUE FOR YOU THAN OTHERS. YOU MAY FIND SOME BUSINESS OR SELLING ACTIVITIES SOMEWHAT SATISFYING.

S S—THEME---PEOPLE WHO FIT THIS THEME DESCRIBE THEMSELVES AS CHEERFUL, POPULAR, SOCIABLE, RE-
S SPONSIBLE, AND CONCERNED WITH THE WELFARE OF OTHERS. THEY SEE THEMSELVES AS ACHIEVERS AND GOOD
S LEADERS. USUALLY ABLE TO EXPRESS THEMSELVES WELL WITH WORDS, THEY GET ALONG WELL WITH OTHERS
S AND ENJOY BEING THE CENTER OF ATTENTION IN A GROUP. THEY PREFER SOLVING PROBLEMS THROUGH DIS-
S CUSSIONS OR BY ARRANGING OR REARRANGING RELATIONSHIPS BETWEEN OTHERS. THEY HAVE LITTLE INTEREST
S IN SITUATIONS REQUIRING PHYSICAL ACTIVITY OR WORKING WITH MACHINERY. THEY PREFER OCCUPATIONS
S SUCH AS SCHOOL SUPERINTENDENT, CLINICAL PSYCHOLOGIST, HIGH SCHOOL TEACHER, MARRIAGE COUNSELOR,
S PLAYGROUND DIRECTOR, SPEECH THERAPIST, OR VOCATIONAL COUNSELOR. THIS IS THE SOCIAL THEME, OR
S S—THEME.
S   YOUR SCORE OF 34 ON S—THEME INDICATES THAT PROBABLY NONE OF THE ABOVE DESCRIPTIONS ARE TRUE
S FOR YOU AND YOU WOULD NOT ENJOY WORKING WITH PEOPLE OR HELPING THEM SOLVE THEIR PROBLEMS.

* *

    AN EXCELLENT BOOK THAT DISCUSSES THE SIX GENERAL OCCUPATIONAL THEME SCALES AND MAKING A
CAREER CHOICE IS --- IF YOU DO NOT KNOW WHERE YOU ARE GOING YOU WILL PROBABLY END UP SOMEWHERE
ELSE --- BY DR. DAVID P. CAMPBELL. THIS MAY BE AVAILABLE IN YOUR LOCAL BOOKSTORE OR IT MAY BE
PURCHASED FROM NCS/INTERPRETIVE SCORING SYSTEMS, P.O. BOX 1416, MINNEAPOLIS, MINNESOTA 55440.
SEND A CHECK ($2.95) PAYABLE TO NCS/INTERPRETIVE SCORING SYSTEMS.

    THE PRECEDING GENERAL OCCUPATIONAL THEME SCORES PROVIDE YOU WITH A BROAD, GENERAL OVERVIEW
OF YOUR INTERESTS. THE NEXT SECTION PRESENTS YOUR RESULTS ON TWENTY-THREE BASIC INTEREST SCALES
THAT ARE MORE SPECIFIC MEASURES OF YOUR INTERESTS IN AREAS SUCH AS MECHANICAL ACTIVITIES, ART,
SCIENCE, SALES, TEACHING, AND SO FORTH.

* *

BASIC INTEREST SCALES

BELOW ARE YOUR RESULTS ON 23 BASIC INTEREST SCALES. THEY SHOW THE STRENGTH OF YOUR INTEREST IN A VARIETY OF PURE TYPES OF AREAS. THESE SCORES WILL SHOW AREAS WHERE YOU WILL FIND SATISFACTION OR DISSATISFACTION. THEY CAN BE IMPORTANT IN MAKING CAREER CHOICES OR IN DECIDING ON LEISURE-TIME ACTIVITIES. AN AVERAGE INTEREST FALLS BETWEEN 43 AND 57 ON EACH SCALE. ON SOME OF THE SCALES, FEMALES AND MALES RESPOND SOMEWHAT DIFFERENTLY AND, IF YOU INDICATED YOUR SEX ON THE INVENTORY, A SERIES OF DOTS APPEAR FOR EACH SCALE SHOWING THE AVERAGE RANGE OF SCORES FOR YOUR SEX. ALSO, THE MINIMUM (MIN) AND MAXIMUM (MAX) POSSIBLE SCORES ARE LISTED TO THE RIGHT.

BASIC INTEREST SCALES	YOUR SCORE	MIN-MAX
VERY HIGH INTEREST(66+)		
MECHANICAL ACTIVITIES	67	30-72
HIGH INTEREST (65-58)		
SCIENCE	62	28-69
MATHEMATICS	61	31-67
OFFICE PRACTICES	60	36-79
AVERAGE INTEREST (57-43)		
LAW/POLITICS	54	30-69
DOMESTIC ARTS	53	27-75
ART	52	26-68
PUBLIC SPEAKING	51	31-71
BUSINESS MANAGEMENT	49	29-72
WRITING	48	26-66
TEACHING	47	23-67
MEDICAL SERVICE	45	33-76
SOCIAL SERVICE	45	24-69
LOW INTEREST (42-35)		
MUSIC/DRAMATICS	42	26-73
ADVENTURE	42	30-71
MERCHANDISING	42	31-72
NATURE	42	17-67
MILITARY ACTIVITIES	41	41-76
MEDICAL SCIENCE	41	29-68
SALES	39	37-81
RELIGIOUS ACTIVITIES	37	31-68
AGRICULTURE	36	30-68
VERY LOW INTEREST (34-)		
ATHLETICS	32	24-70

psychware 657

YOUR HIGHEST SCORES IN THE BASIC INTEREST AREAS ARE LISTED BELOW WITH A DESCRIPTION OF THE KINDS OF ACTIVITIES AND OCCUPATIONS RELATED TO EACH OF THE AREAS. THE HIGHER YOUR SCORE, THE MORE YOU LIKE THE ACTIVITIES THAT ARE A PART OF THAT SCALE. IN GENERAL, THESE AREAS PROBABLY CAN BE SOURCES OF SATISFACTION IN YOUR LIFE. ALTHOUGH THEY MAY OR MAY NOT BE PART OF THE OCCUPATION THAT YOU CHOOSE, THEY WILL BE AREAS OF LEISURE-TIME SATISFACTION. IF YOU CAN CHOOSE A CAREER THAT IS RELATED TO YOUR HIGHEST SCORES, YOU PROBABLY WILL FIND IT MORE REWARDING.

ALSO LISTED ARE PAGE REFERENCES FOR THE OCCUPATIONAL OUTLOOK HANDBOOK (OOH), BULLETIN NO. 2075. THIS BOOK CAN BE FOUND IN YOUR LOCAL LIBRARY AND PROVIDES INFORMATION ABOUT RECENT TRENDS IN EMPLOYMENT OPPORTUNITIES AND EDUCATIONAL REQUIREMENTS FOR VARIOUS OCCUPATIONS THAT ARE RELATED DIRECTLY TO YOUR HIGHEST INTEREST AREAS.

67 MECHANICAL ACTVS.----ACTIVITIES THAT INVOLVE WORKING WITH YOUR HANDS, OPERATING MACHINERY, AND USING TOOLS TO REPAIR OR BUILD SOMETHING ARE OF HIGH INTEREST IN THIS AREA. AUTO MECHANICS, CARPENTERS, MACHINISTS, AND TOOLMAKERS FALL INTO THIS AREA.

    OOH 320-359

62 SCIENCE------------PEOPLE WHO ENJOY SCIENTIFIC ACTIVITIES, SUCH AS DOING RESEARCH WORK AND PERFORMING EXPERIMENTS, SCORE HIGH ON THIS SCALE. GEOLOGISTS, BIOLOGISTS, CHEMISTS, AND METEOROLOGISTS ARE EXAMPLES OF SCIENCE-MINDED PEOPLE.

    OOH 75-96

61 MATHEMATICS---------PEOPLE INTERESTED IN THE OPERATIONS WHICH CAN BE PERFORMED WITH NUMBERS SCORE HIGH IN THIS AREA AND LIKE TO STUDY ARITHMETIC, ALGEBRA, CALCULUS, AND STATISTICS. SUCH PEOPLE MAY BE ENGINEERS, MATHEMATICIANS, OR STATISTICIANS.

    OOH 67-74

THE PRECEDING TWO SECTIONS HAVE ANALYZED YOUR RESULTS IN TERMS OF GENERAL THEME SCALES AND THE MORE SPECIFIC BASIC INTEREST SCALES. AGAIN, YOU SHOULD TRY TO LOCATE THE OCCUPATIONAL OUTLOOK HANDBOOK IN YOUR LOCAL LIBRARY OR COUNSELING CENTER AND READ FURTHER ABOUT THE VARIOUS CAREERS THAT ARE RELATED TO YOUR HIGH INTERESTS.

* * * * * * * * * * * * * * * * * * * *

THE FOLLOWING STARTS THE NEXT SECTION OF ANALYSIS, THE OCCUPATIONAL SCALES. THESE RESULTS ARE STILL MORE SPECIFIC. THEY COMPARE YOUR ANSWERS TO THOSE OF PEOPLE IN A VARIETY OF OCCUPATIONS. SINCE FEMALES AND MALES IN THE SAME OCCUPATION RESPOND SOMEWHAT DIFFERENTLY TO SOME OF THE ITEMS ON THIS INVENTORY, OCCUPATIONAL SCALES HAVE BEEN DEVELOPED SEPARATELY FOR EACH SEX. SO AS TO NOT LIMIT YOUR CONSIDERATION OF A CAREER NOT PRESENTLY REPRESENTED BY YOUR SEX, YOUR SCORES ON BOTH FEMALE AND MALE SCALES ARE PRESENTED BELOW. ALTHOUGH OCCUPATIONAL SCALES BASED ON THE SEX CORRESPONDING TO YOURS ARE MORE LIKELY TO BE BETTER PREDICTORS FOR YOU THAN SCALES BASED ON THE OTHER SEX, ALL SCORES ARE PRESENTED AS ADDITIONAL INFORMATION FOR YOU.

OCCUPATIONAL SCALES

THE OCCUPATIONAL SCALES INDICATE THE DEGREE OF SIMILARITY BETWEEN YOUR INTERESTS AND THOSE OF EMPLOYED PEOPLE IN VARIOUS OCCUPATIONS. IF YOU REPORTED THE SAME LIKES AND DISLIKES AS THEY DO, YOUR SCORE WILL BE HIGH AND YOU WOULD PROBABLY ENJOY WORKING IN THAT OCCUPATION OR A CLOSELY RELATED ONE -- MEMBERS OF AN OCCUPATION SCORE ABOUT 50 ON THEIR OWN SCALE. IF YOUR LIKES AND DISLIKES ARE DIFFERENT FROM THOSE OF PEOPLE IN THE OCCUPATION, YOUR SCORE WILL BE LOW AND YOU WOULD PROBABLY NOT BE HAPPY IN THAT KIND OF WORK. IF YOUR SCORE IS IN THE MID-RANGE, BETWEEN 28 AND 39, YOU HAVE RESPONDED IN THE WAY PEOPLE-IN-GENERAL DO.

RESEARCH HAS INDICATED THAT PEOPLE WHO ENTER AN OCCUPATION WHERE THEY HAVE SIMILAR SCORES TEND TO REMAIN IN THAT OCCUPATION AND ARE MORE SATISFIED THAN IF THEY ENTER AN OCCUPATION WHERE THEY HAVE DISSIMILAR SCORES. FURTHERMORE, THESE SCORES MAY INDICATE INTEREST IN AN OCCUPATION THAT YOU MAY NOT HAVE CONSIDERED BEFORE AND THEY CAN HELP YOU THINK ABOUT VARIOUS CAREERS. THE FOLLOWING SCORES INDICATE HOW YOUR INTERESTS MATCH THOSE OF MALES IN VARIOUS OCCUPATIONS.

VERY SIMILAR 55+	SIMILAR 54-46	MODERATELY SIMILAR 45-40	MID-RANGE 39-28
60 SYSTEMS ANALYST	50 ENGINEER	44 PHYSICIST	39 FORESTER
56 COMPUTER PROGR.	48 COLLEGE PROF.	43 BIOLOGIST	38 GEOLOGIST
	48 CHEMIST	43 MATH-SCI. TCHR.	37 MUSICIAN
	47 SOCIOLOGIST	42 IRS AGENT	37 ARCHITECT
	47 GEOGRAPHER	41 LIBRARIAN	37 PSYCHOLOGIST
	46 MATHEMATICIAN	40 ACCOUNTANT	35 FOR. LANG. TCHR.
			35 SKILLED CRAFTS
			34 MEDICAL TECH.
			33 DIETITIAN
			33 X-RAY TECHNICIAN
			33 FARMER
			32 OPTOMETRIST
			32 BANKER
			32 INVEST. FUND MGR
			31 EXEC HOUSEKEEPER
			31 AIR FORCE OFF.
			31 SPEECH PATHOL.
			31 PHOTOGRAPHER
			30 CHIROPRACTOR
			30 CREDIT MANAGER
			30 PURCHASING AGENT
			29 NAVY OFFICER
			29 PHYSICIAN
			29 ELEM. TEACHER
			28 BUSINESS ED. TCH
			28 LIC. PRAC. NURSE

MODERATELY DISSIMILAR 27-22	DISSIMILAR 21-13	VERY DISSIMILAR 12-
27 PUBLIC ADMINIST.	21 PHARMACIST	11 YMCA DIRECTOR
27 DENTIST	20 VOC AGRIC. TCHR.	10 ART TEACHER
26 PERSONNEL DIR.	20 MINISTER	10 POLICE OFFICER
26 BEAUTICIAN	20 SPECIAL ED. TCHR	9 CHAM. OF COMM.
26 FLIGHT ATTENDANT	20 ELECT. PUBL. OFF	9 PHYS. ED. TCHR.
25 OCCUP. THERAPIST	19 RESTAURANT MGR.	7 ADVERTISING EXEC
25 LAWYER	19 MARKETING EXEC.	6 PUBLIC REL. DIR.
25 SCHOOL ADMINIST.	18 GUIDANCE COUNS.	6 LIFE INS. AGENT
25 ARMY OFFICER	18 INT. DECORATOR	
	18 SOCIAL WORKER	
	18 DEPT. STORE MGR.	
	17 VETERINARIAN	
	17 ENGLISH TEACHER	
	17 REGISTERED NURSE	
	16 REPORTER	
	16 AGRIBUS. MANAGER	
	15 RECREAT. LEADER	
	15 PHYS. THERAPIST	
	14 FINE ARTIST	
	14 REALTOR	
	13 SOCIAL SCI. TCHR	
	13 NURS. HOME ADM.	
	13 BUYER	
	13 COMMERCIAL ART.	

* * * * * * * * * *

YOUR HIGHEST SCORES APPEARED ON THE FOLLOWING SCALES AND INDICATE THE GREATEST DEGREE OF SIMILARITY BETWEEN YOUR ANSWERS AND THOSE OF MALES IN THESE OCCUPATIONS. AS BEFORE, REFERENCES ARE GIVEN FOR THE OCCUPATIONAL OUTLOOK HANDBOOK (OOH) WHICH GIVES ADDITIONAL INFORMATION ON EMPLOYMENT OPPORTUNITIES AND RELEVANT WORK SITUATIONS. ALSO, REFERENCES ARE LISTED FOR THE DICTIONARY OF OCCUPATIONAL TITLES (DOT), FOURTH EDITION. THE DOT GIVES DETAILED JOB DESCRIPTIONS OF THE DUTIES AND FUNCTIONS OF EACH OCCUPATION AND SHOULD BE AVAILABLE IN YOUR LOCAL LIBRARY OR LOCAL COUNSELING OFFICE. THE FIRST DOT REFERENCE IS FOR PAGE NUMBER AND THE SECOND DOT REFERENCE IS FOR THE DOT CODE FOR THAT OCCUPATION.

YOUR HIGHEST SCORES APPEARED ON THE FOLLOWING SCALES AND INDICATE THE GREATEST DEGREE OF SIMILARITY BETWEEN YOUR ANSWERS AND THOSE OF MALES IN THESE OCCUPATIONS---

60 SYSTEMS ANALYST————SYSTEMS ANALYSTS SOLVE DATA PROCESSING PROBLEMS BY ANALYZING THE TYPE OF DATA THAT IS REQUIRED AND FINDING THE MOST EFFICIENT WAY OF PROVIDING IT. A FOUR-YEAR COLLEGE DEGREE, ESPECIALLY IN A COMPUTER-RELATED FIELD, IS DESIRABLE FOR MOST POSITIONS. SYSTEMS ANALYSTS MUST BE GOOD AT WORKING WITH DETAILS, BE ABLE TO THINK LOGICALLY, AND LIKE WORKING WITH IDEAS. RELATED OCCUPATIONS IN-CLUDE COMPUTER PROGRAMMER AND MATHEMATICIAN. EMPLOYMENT FOR THIS OCCUPATION IS EXPECTED TO GROW FASTER THAN THE AVERAGE FOR ALL OCCUPATIONS THROUGH THE 1980S.

OOH 72-74
DOT 29
DOT 012.167

56 COMPUTER PROGRAMMER————COMPUTER PROGRAMMERS ANALYZE PROBLEMS AND CONVERT THEM TO A FORM SUITABLE FOR SOLUTION BY A COMPUTER. TRAINING FOR THIS FIELD RANGES FROM SOME DATA PROCESSING TRAINING TO A FOUR-YEAR COLLEGE DEGREE, DEPENDING UPON THE TYPE OF PROGRAMMING IN WHICH A PERSON IS INTERESTED. LOGICAL THINKING, PATIENCE, PERSISTENCE, ACCURA-CY, AND INGENUITY ARE NECESSARY TRAITS FOR THIS FIELD. RELATED FIELDS ARE SYSTEMS ANALYST AND COMPUTER OPERATOR. EMPLOYMENT OF COMPUTER PROGRAMMERS IS EXPECTED TO GROW FASTER THAN THE AVERAGE FOR ALL OCCUPATIONS THROUGH THE 1980S.

OOH 230-232
DOT 38-39
DOT 020.162-.187

50 ENGINEER————ENGINEERS WORK IN RESEARCH AND DEVELOPMENT, DESIGN PRODUCTION, CONSULTING, TECHNICAL WRITING, AND TECHNICAL SALES. AT LEAST FOUR YEARS OF COLLEGE TRAINING ARE REQUIRED. ENGINEERS MUST BE CREATIVE AND ANALYTICAL, ABLE TO WORK AS PART OF A TEAM, AND WILLING TO CONTINUE THEIR EDUCATION THROUGHOUT THEIR CAREER. ENGINEERING SPECIALTIES INCLUDE AERONAUTICAL, CHEMICAL, CIVIL, ELECTRICAL, MECHANICAL, AND METALLURGICAL. EMPLOYMENT OPPORTUNI-TIES ARE EXPECTED TO BE GOOD THROUGH THE 1980S.

OOH 57-66
DOT 15-31
DOT 002.061-015.061

* * * * * * * * * *

THE U.S. GOVERNMENT PRINTING OFFICE ALSO HAS A REPRINT SERIES THAT WILL PROVIDE YOU WITH ADDITIONAL INFORMATION ON EMPLOYMENT, WORKING CONDITIONS, AND THE SALARY FOR MANY JOBS. THESE REPRINT BULLETINS ARE SECTIONS OF THE OOH IN PAMPHLET FORM. LISTED BELOW IS THE BULLETIN NUMBER AND COST FOR EACH REPRINT THAT WOULD BE IMPORTANT FOR YOU IF THE OOH IS NOT READILY AVAILABLE. THESE PAMPHLETS CAN BE ORDERED FROM THE GOVERNMENT PRINTING OFFICE .

BULLETIN NO.	COST	TITLE
2075- 22	$1.25	MATHEMATICS AND RELATED OCCUPATIONS
2075- 6	$1.25	OFFICE MACHINE AND COMPUTER OCCUPATIONS
2075- 20	$1.25	ENGINEERING AND RELATED OCCUPATIONS

TO LEARN MORE ABOUT THE DAILY ROUTINE OF PEOPLE IN OCCUPATIONS WHERE YOU HAVE HIGH SCORES, YOU MAY WISH TO CONSIDER READING THE FOLLOWING--

--COMPUTER CAREERS--PLANNING, PREREQUISITES, POTENTIAL. BY MANIOTES + QUASNEY. HAYDEN BOOK, 1974
--YOUR CAREER IN COMPUTER-RELATED OCCUPATIONS. BY WILLIAM KOLLER. ARCO PUBLISHING, 1979.
--YOUR FUTURE IN ENGINEERING CAREERS. BY OTIS PETERSON. ROSEN PRESS, 1975.

* * * * * * * * * * * * * * * *

YOU SHOULD PAY PARTICULAR ATTENTION TO THOSE OCCUPATIONS WHERE YOUR SCORES INDICATE THAT YOU HAVE THE MOST SIMILAR INTERESTS. YOU WILL HAVE THE BEST CHANCE OF FINDING SATISFACTION IF YOU DECIDE ON AN OCCUPATION WHERE YOUR INTERESTS ARE SIMILAR WITH YOUR CO-WORKERS AND LESS OF A CHANCE WHERE YOUR INTERESTS ARE DISSIMILAR. IF YOU RECORDED THE SAME LIKES AND DISLIKES AS THE WORKERS, YOUR SCORE WILL BE HIGH FOR THAT OCCUPATION. IF YOUR LIKE AND DISLIKE RESPONSES WERE DIFFERENT FROM THOSE IN THE OCCUPATION, YOUR SCORE WILL BE LOW AND YOU WOULD NOT LIKELY BE SATISFIED.

THE FOLLOWING ARE YOUR SCORES BASED ON FEMALES IN VARIOUS OCCUPATIONS. SCORES ON ALL THE SCALES AVAILABLE ARE PRESENTED SO AS TO GIVE YOU ADDITIONAL INFORMATION ABOUT A WIDER RANGE OF CAREERS. AGAIN, THE BEST PREDICTORS FOR YOU WILL BE THOSE SCALES CORRESPONDING TO YOUR SEX. THE FOLLOWING SCORES INDICATE HOW YOUR INTERESTS MATCH THOSE OF FEMALES IN VARIOUS OCCUPATIONS.

VERY SIMILAR 55+	SIMILAR 54-46	MODERATELY SIMILAR 45-40	MID-RANGE 39-28
59 COMPUTER PROGR.	54 LIBRARIAN	44 GEOLOGIST	39 MARKETING EXEC.
59 SYSTEMS ANALYST	54 GEOGRAPHER	43 AIR FORCE OFF.	39 SOCIOLOGIST
58 COLLEGE PROF.	53 MATH-SCI. TCHR.	43 PHYSICIAN	38 PHOTOGRAPHER
57 ACCOUNTANT	53 OPTOMETRIST	42 ARCHITECT	37 FORESTER
56 ENGINEER	52 NAVY OFFICER	42 DENTIST	35 PUBLIC ADMINST.
55 MATHEMATICIAN	52 CHEMIST	41 DIETITIAN	35 PSYCHOLOGIST
55 PHYSICIST	49 BIOLOGIST	40 CREDIT MANAGER	35 VETERINARIAN
	48 IRS AGENT	40 FARMER	34 X-RAY TECHNICIAN
	47 BANKER		34 SOCIAL SCI. TCHR
	47 PHARMACIST		34 LAWYER
	47 ARMY OFFICER		33 PERSONNEL DIR.
	47 MEDICAL TECH.		33 GUIDANCE COUNS.
			32 MUSICIAN
			31 PURCHASING AGENT
			31 RESTAURANT MGR.
			31 CHIROPRACTOR
			29 ADVERTISING EXEC
			29 YWCA DIRECTOR

MODERATELY DISSIMILAR 27-22	DISSIMILAR 21-13	VERY DISSIMILAR 12-
27 OCCUP. THERAPIST	21 LIC. PRAC. NURSE	12 REALTOR

27	DEPT. STORE MGR.	21	DENTAL HYGIENIST	11	INT. DECORATOR
26	FOR. LANG. TCHR.	20	DENTAL ASSISTANT	10	REGISTERED NURSE
26	ELECT. PUBL. OFF	20	COMMERCIAL ART.	8	ART TEACHER
26	BEAUTICIAN	20	PUBLIC REL. DIR.		
26	SCHOOL ADMINIST.	20	PHYS. ED. TCHR.		
25	SECRETARY	20	LIFE INS. AGENT		
25	BUSINESS ED. TCH	19	HOME ECON. TCHR.		
25	FINE ARTIST	19	ELEM. TEACHER		
24	SOCIAL WORKER	18	REPORTER		
23	POLICE OFFICER	18	SPEECH PATHOL.		
23	SPECIAL ED. TCHR	18	MINISTER		
22	EXEC HOUSEKEEPER	17	RECREAT. LEADER		
22	PHYS. THERAPIST	17	NURS. HOME ADM.		
22	CHAM. OF COMM.	15	BUYER		
		14	FLIGHT ATTENDANT		
		14	ENGLISH TEACHER		

* * * * * * * * * * * * * * * * * *

59 COMPUTER PROGRAMMER--------COMPUTER PROGRAMMERS ANALYZE PROBLEMS AND CONVERT THEM TO A FORM
SUITABLE FOR SOLUTION BY A COMPUTER. TRAINING FOR THIS FIELD
RANGES FROM SOME DATA PROCESSING TRAINING TO A FOUR-YEAR COLLEGE
DEGREE, DEPENDING UPON THE TYPE OF PROGRAMMING IN WHICH A PERSON
IS INTERESTED. LOGICAL THINKING, PATIENCE, PERSISTENCE, ACCURA-
CY, AND INGENUITY ARE NECESSARY TRAITS FOR THIS FIELD. RELATED
FIELDS ARE SYSTEMS ANALYST AND COMPUTER OPERATOR. EMPLOYMENT OF
COMPUTER PROGRAMMERS IS EXPECTED TO GROW FASTER THAN THE AVERAGE
FOR ALL OCCUPATIONS THROUGH THE 1980S.

OOH 230-232
DOT 38-39
DOT 020.162-.187

59 SYSTEMS ANALYST----------SYSTEMS ANALYSTS SOLVE DATA PROCESSING PROBLEMS BY ANALYZING THE
TYPE OF DATA THAT IS REQUIRED AND FINDING THE MOST EFFICIENT WAY
OF PROVIDING IT. A FOUR-YEAR COLLEGE DEGREE, ESPECIALLY IN A
COMPUTER-RELATED FIELD, IS DESIRABLE FOR MOST POSITIONS. SYSTEMS
ANALYSTS MUST BE GOOD AT WORKING WITH DETAILS, BE ABLE TO THINK
LOGICALLY, AND LIKE WORKING WITH IDEAS. RELATED OCCUPATIONS IN-
CLUDE COMPUTER PROGRAMMER AND MATHEMATICIAN. EMPLOYMENT FOR THIS
OCCUPATION IS EXPECTED TO GROW FASTER THAN THE AVERAGE FOR ALL
OCCUPATIONS THROUGH THE 1980S.

OOH 72-74
DOT 29
DOT 012.167

58 COLLEGE PROFESSOR---------COLLEGE PROFESSORS PREPARE AND DELIVER LECTURES, CONDUCT RE-
SEARCH, WRITE RESEARCH ARTICLES, AND ADVISE STUDENTS. A MASTERS
DEGREE OR A PH.D. IS REQUIRED. PEOPLE IN THIS FIELD MUST KEEP
INFORMED OF CURRENT ADVANCEMENTS IN THEIR FIELDS AND BE ABLE TO
MOTIVATE STUDENTS TO LEARN. RELATED OCCUPATIONS INCLUDE RE-
SEARCHER, LECTURER, AND WRITER. CANDIDATES FOR COLLEGE TEACHING
ARE EXPECTED TO FACE KEEN COMPETITION THROUGH THE 1980S.

OOH 131-133
DOT 67
DOT 090.227

YOU SHOULD PAY ATTENTION TO YOUR HIGH AND LOW SCORES ON ALL THREE SETS OF SCALES THAT HAVE BEEN PROVIDED --- THE 6 GENERAL THEME SCALES, THE 23 BASIC INTEREST AREAS, AND THE OCCUPATIONAL SCALES. YOU MAY FIND THAT EVEN THOUGH YOU HAVE A HIGH SCORE IN ONE OF THE BASIC AREAS, SUCH AS SALES, YOUR RESPONSES MAY HAVE INDICATED THAT YOU WOULD NOT LIKE THE ROUTINE AND LIFE SITUATIONS OF AN INSURANCE AGENT AND YOU HAD A LOW SCORE ON THE INSURANCE AGENT SCALE. SUCH COMPARISONS CAN HELP YOU BETTER EVALUATE THE TYPES OF WORK SITUATIONS THAT MATCH YOUR INTERESTS.

SUMMARIZED BELOW ARE YOUR SCORES ON EACH THEME SCALE, RELATED BASIC INTEREST AREA SCALES, AND OCCUPATIONAL SCALES WITHIN EACH THEME AREA. AFTER EACH OCCUPATIONAL SCALE IS F OR M WHICH INDICATES THE SEX (FEMALE, MALE) OF THE GROUP USED FOR THE DEVELOPMENT OF THAT SCALE. IN THE GENERAL POPULATION THE AVERAGE SCORES FOR ADULTS ARE IN THE 43-57 RANGE ON EACH OF THE 6 THEME SCALES AND EACH OF THE 23 BASIC INTEREST AREA SCALES. HOWEVER, FOR THE OCCUPATIONAL SCALES, SCORES OF 46 AND HIGHER INDICATE SIMILARITY WITH WORKERS IN THE OCCUPATION AND LOWER SCORES INDICATE MORE DISSIMILARITY.

I.   59 C-THEME ----- (CONVENTIONAL) -----

BASIC AREA SCALES	CODE	OCCUP. SCALES	
60 OFFICE PRACTICES	57 C	ACCOUNTANT	F
	48 CE	IRS AGENT	F
	47 CE	BANKER	F
	42 CE	IRS AGENT	M
	40 C	ACCOUNTANT	M
	40 CE	CREDIT MANAGER	F
	32 CE	BANKER	M
	31 CER	EXEC HOUSEKEEPER	M
	30 CE	CREDIT MANAGER	M
	28 CES	BUSINESS ED. TCH	M
	27 CA	PUBLIC ADMINIST.	M
	25 C	SECRETARY	F
	25 CES	BUSINESS ED. TCH	F
	22 CER	EXEC HOUSEKEEPER	F
	20 C	DENTAL ASSISTANT	F

II.   59 R-THEME ----- (REALISTIC) -----

BASIC AREA SCALES	CODE	OCCUP. SCALES	
67 MECHANICAL ACT.	56 RI	ENGINEER	F
42 ADVENTURE	52 R	NAVY OFFICER	F
42 NATURE	50 RI	ENGINEER	M
41 MILITARY ACTVS.	47 RC	ARMY OFFICER	F
36 AGRICULTURE	43 RC	AIR FORCE OFF.	F
	40 RC	FARMER	F
	39 R	FORESTER	M
	37 RI	FORESTER	F
	35 R	SKILLED CRAFTS	M
	34 R	X-RAY TECHNICIAN	F
	33 RI	X-RAY TECHNICIAN	M
	33 R	FARMER	M
	31 RC	AIR FORCE OFF.	M
	29 RC	NAVY OFFICER	M
	27 RAS	OCCUP. THERAPIST	F
	25 RAS	OCCUP. THERAPIST	M
	25 RC	ARMY OFFICER	M
	23 RE	POLICE OFFICER	F
	21 RIC	LIC. PRAC. NURSE	F
	20 RCE	VOC AGRIC. TCHR.	M
	17 RI	VETERINARIAN	M
	10 RE	POLICE OFFICER	M

III. 56 I-THEME ----- (INVESTIGATIVE)-----

BASIC AREA SCALES		CODE	OCCUP. SCALES	
62	SCIENCE	60	IRC SYSTEMS ANALYST	M
61	MATHEMATICS	59	IRC COMPUTER PROGR.	F
45	MEDICAL SERVICE	59	IRC SYSTEMS ANALYST	F
41	MEDICAL SCIENCE	58	IA COLLEGE PROF.	F
		56	IRC COMPUTER PROGR.	M
		55	IR PHYSICIST	F
		55	I MATHEMATICIAN	F
		54	I GEOGRAPHER	F
		53	IRC MATH-SCI. TCHR.	F
		53	IR OPTOMETRIST	F
		52	IR CHEMIST	F
		49	I BIOLOGIST	F
		48	IA COLLEGE PROF.	M
		48	IR CHEMIST	M
		47	IA SOCIOLOGIST	M
		47	I GEOGRAPHER	M
		47	IR MEDICAL TECH.	F
		47	I PHARMACIST	F
		46	I MATHEMATICIAN	M
		44	IR GEOLOGIST	F
		44	IR PHYSICIST	M
		43	IRS MATH-SCI. TCHR.	M
		43	IR PHYSICIAN	M
		43	I BIOLOGIST	M
		42	IR DENTIST	F
		39	IA SOCIOLOGIST	F
		38	IR GEOLOGIST	M
		37	IAS PSYCHOLOGIST	M
		35	IAS PSYCHOLOGIST	F
		35	IR VETERINARIAN	F
		34	IR MEDICAL TECH.	M
		32	IR OPTOMETRIST	F
		31	IRC CHIROPRACTOR	M
		30	IRC CHIROPRACTOR	F
		29	IR PHYSICIAN	M
		27	IR DENTIST	M
		22	IR PHYS. THERAPIST	F
		21	IE PHARMACIST	M
		21	IR DENTAL HYGIENIST	F
		17	IRS REGISTERED NURSE	M
		15	IR PHYS. THERAPIST	M

IV. 45 A-THEME ----- (ARTISTIC) -----

BASIC AREA SCALES		CODE	OCCUP. SCALES	
52	ART	54	A LIBRARIAN	F
48	WRITING	42	AIR ARCHITECT	F
42	MUSIC/DRAMATICS	41	A LIBRARIAN	M
		38	A PHOTOGRAPHER	F
		37	AIR ARCHITECT	M
		37	A MUSICIAN	M
		35	A FOR. LANG. TCHR.	M
		34	AI LAWYER	F
		32	A MUSICIAN	F
		31	A PHOTOGRAPHER	M
		29	AE ADVERTISING EXEC	F
		26	A FOR. LANG. TCHR.	F
		25	AI LAWYER	M
		25	A FINE ARTIST	F
		20	AE PUBLIC REL. DIR.	F
		20	A COMMERCIAL ART.	F
		18	AE REPORTER	F
		18	AE INT. DECORATOR	M
		17	AS ENGLISH TEACHER	M
		16	A REPORTER	M
		14	A FINE ARTIST	M
		14	A ENGLISH TEACHER	F
		13	A COMMERCIAL ART.	M
		11	AE INT. DECORATOR	F
		10	A ART TEACHER	M
		8	A ART TEACHER	F
		7	AE ADVERTISING EXEC	M
		6	AE PUBLIC REL. DIR.	M

V. 44 E-THEME ----- (ENTERPRISING) -----

BASIC AREA SCALES	CODE	OCCUP. SCALES	
54 LAW/POLITICS	41 EC	DIETITIAN	F
51 PUBLIC SPEAKING	39 EI	MARKETING EXEC.	F
49 BUS. MANAGEMENT	35 E	PUBLIC ADMINST.	F
42 MERCHANDISING	33 ECR	DIETITIAN	M
39 SALES	33 E	PERSONNEL DIR.	F
	32 EI	INVEST. FUND MGR	M
	31 EC	PURCHASING AGENT	F
	31 EC	RESTAURANT MGR.	F
	30 EC	PURCHASING AGENT	M
	27 E	DEPT. STORE MGR.	F
	26 E	BEAUTICIAN	F
	26 E	ELECT. PUBL. OFF	F
	26 EA	PERSONNEL DIR.	M
	26 E	BEAUTICIAN	M
	26 EA	FLIGHT ATTENDANT	M
	22 EC	CHAM. OF COMM.	F
	20 E	ELECT. PUBL. OFF	M
	20 E	LIFE INS. AGENT	F
	19 ES	HOME ECON. TCHR.	F
	19 EI	MARKETING EXEC.	M
	19 E	RESTAURANT MGR.	M
	18 E	DEPT. STORE MGR.	M
	17 EC	NURS. HOME ADM.	M
	16 ERC	AGRIBUS. MANAGER	M
	15 EC	BUYER	F
	14 EA	FLIGHT ATTENDANT	F
	14 E	REALTOR	M
	13 EC	BUYER	M
	13 ECS	NURS. HOME ADM.	F
	12 E	REALTOR	F
	9 E	CHAM. OF COMM.	M
	6 E	LIFE INS. AGENT	M

VI. 34 S-THEME ----- (SOCIAL) -----

BASIC AREA SCALES	CODE	OCCUP. SCALES	
53 DOMESTIC ARTS	34 SEC	SOCIAL SCI. TCHR	F
47 TEACHING	33 SEC	GUIDANCE COUNS.	F
45 SOCIAL SERVICE	31 SA	SPEECH PATHOL.	M
37 RELIGIOUS ACTVS.	29 SE	YWCA DIRECTOR	F
32 ATHLETICS	29 S	ELEM. TEACHER	F
	28 S	LIC. PRAC. NURSE	M
	26 SE	SCHOOL ADMINIST.	F
	25 SE	SCHOOL ADMINIST.	M
	24 SA	SOCIAL WORKER	F
	23 S	SPECIAL ED. TCHR	F
	20 S	SPECIAL ED. TCHR	M
	20 SIE	MINISTER	F
	20 SR	PHYS. ED. TCHR.	F
	19 S	ELEM. TEACHER	M
	18 SA	SPEECH PATHOL.	F
	18 SCE	GUIDANCE COUNS.	M
	18 SA	MINISTER	F
	18 SA	SOCIAL WORKER	M
	17 SRE	RECREAT. LEADER	F
	15 SRE	RECREAT. LEADER	M
	13 SEC	SOCIAL SCI. TCHR	M
	11 SE	YMCA DIRECTOR	M
	10 SI	REGISTERED NURSE	F
	9 SR	PHYS. ED. TCHR.	M

ADMINISTRATIVE INDEXES

THE FOLLOWING ARE THE ADMINISTRATIVE INDICES AND SPECIAL SCALES. DATA FOR I-VII INDICATE YOUR RESPONSE PERCENTAGES -- LIKE - INDIFFERENT - DISLIKE -- TO THE SEVEN SECTIONS OF THE INVENTORY THAT YOU ANSWERED. ALL PARTS INDICATE YOUR AVERAGE ON THE SEVEN PARTS OF THE INVENTORY. TOTAL RESPONSES INDICATE THE TOTAL NUMBER OF ITEMS YOU ANSWERED ON THE INVENTORY. DESCRIPTIONS OF THE OTHER SCORES ARE GIVEN BELOW.

	RESPONSE PERCENTAGES		
	LP	IP	DP
I. OCCUPATIONS	24	43	33
II. SCHOOL SUBJECTS	47	39	14
III. ACTIVITIES	25	49	25
IV. AMUSEMENTS	26	44	31
V. TYPES OF PEOPLE	4	67	29
VI. PREFERENCES	43	23	33
VII. CHARACTERISTICS	29	57	14
ALL PARTS	27	44	28

TOTAL RESPONSES = 324

INFREQUENT RESPONSES = 11

ACADEMIC COMFORT = 54

INTROVERSION-EXTROVERSION = 60

YOUR HIGH SCORE ON THE ACADEMIC COMFORT SCALE INDICATES THAT YOUR INTEREST PREFERENCES ARE SIMILAR TO INDIVIDUALS WHO GRADUATE FROM A LIBERAL ARTS COLLEGE WITH A BACCALAUREATE OR ADVANCED DEGREE. THESE INDIVIDUALS HAVE A STRONG LIKING FOR MANY CREATIVE, AESTHETIC, MATHEMATIC, AND SCIENTIFIC ACTIVITIES AND ENJOY COURSE WORK IN THEIR STUDIES.

YOUR SCORE ON THE INTROVERSION-EXTROVERSION SCALE INDICATES THAT YOU WOULD PREFER WORKING WITH THINGS MORE THAN WITH GROUPS OF PEOPLE. SKILLED TRADES WORKERS, RESEARCH WORKERS, AND TECHNICIANS TEND TO HAVE HIGH SCORES ON THIS SCALE, WHILE SALES AND SOCIAL-SERVICE OCCUPATIONS TEND TO HAVE LOW SCORES.

CLOSING COMMENTS

YOUR ANSWERS TO THE STRONG-CAMPBELL INTEREST INVENTORY HAVE PRODUCED YOUR INTEREST SCORES ON A WIDE RANGE OF GENERAL INTERESTS AND SPECIFIC OCCUPATIONAL SCALES. YOU SHOULD NOT BE SET TOTALLY ON A SINGLE OCCUPATION WHERE YOUR SCORE IS HIGH, AT LEAST NOT AT AN EARLY AGE. IN THE WORLD OF WORK THERE ARE HUNDREDS OF SPECIALTIES AND RELATED CAREERS, AND YOU SHOULD USE THE IN-FORMATION IN THIS REPORT AS A GUIDE FOR FURTHER CAREER EXPLORATION AND THINKING.

RESEARCH WITH INVENTORIES SUCH AS THE STRONG-CAMPBELL INTEREST INVENTORY HAS SHOWN THAT THESE TYPES OF SCORES ARE VERY STABLE. ADULTS WILL SHOW VERY LITTLE CHANGE IN THEIR SCORES OVER THE YEARS. HIGH SCHOOL STUDENTS AND YOUNG ADULTS WILL SHOW SOME CHANGE AFTER TWO OR THREE YEARS AND MORE CHANGE AFTER TEN OR FIFTEEN YEARS. GENERALLY, SCORES ON INTEREST INVENTORIES ARE VERY STABLE AND OVERALL, YOU WOULD FIND YOUR SCORES TO BE VERY SIMILAR IF YOU ANSWERED THE INVENTORY AGAIN DURING THE NEXT SIX MONTHS TO A YEAR.

EACH PERSON IS UNIQUE AND NO INVENTORY CAN PREDICT WITH PERFECT ACCURACY ALL THE DIVERSITY AMONG VARIOUS INDIVIDUALS. THUS, THE RESULTS PRESENTED TO YOU SHOULD BE USED AS GUIDELINES IN HELPING YOU TO UNDERSTAND BETTER YOUR CAREER AND VOCATIONAL INTERESTS AND SHOULD BE CONSIDERED TOGETHER WITH OTHER RELEVANT INFORMATION IN MAKING ANY CAREER DECISION.

FOR ADDITIONAL INFORMATION, THE FOLLOWING SOURCES ARE RECOMMENDED--
--CONSULT A PROFESSIONALLY TRAINED GUIDANCE COUNSELOR.
--THE MANUAL FOR THE STRONG-CAMPBELL INTEREST INVENTORY ($11.00). WRITE NCS/INTERPRETIVE SCORING SYSTEMS, P.O. BOX 1416, MINNEAPOLIS, MINNESOTA 55440.
--WHAT COLOR IS YOUR PARACHUTE -- BY RICHARD BOLES ($7.95). WRITE NCS/INTERPRETIVE SCORING SYSTEMS.
--THE DICTIONARY OF OCCUPATIONAL TITLES (DOT) FOURTH EDITION, 1977, WRITE THE US GOV. PRINTING OFFICE, WASHINGTON D.C. 20402.
--THE OCCUPATIONAL OUTLOOK HANDBOOK (OOH), BULLETIN NO. 2075 WRITE THE US GOV. PRINTING OFFICE, WASHINGTON, D.C. 20402.

INTERPRETIVE NARRATIVE REPORT FOR THE STRONG-CAMPBELL INTEREST INVENTORY--COPYRIGHT 1981 DR. CHARLES B. JOHANSSON, NCS/INTERPRETIVE SCORING SYSTEMS, P.O. BOX 1416, MINNEAPOLIS, MINNESOTA 55440.

STRONG-CAMPBELL INTEREST INVENTORY OF THE STRONG VOCATIONAL INTEREST BLANK, FORM T325. COPYRIGHT 1933, 1938, 1945, 1966, 1968, 1974, 1981 BY THE BOARD OF TRUSTEES OF THE LELAND STAN-FORD JUNIOR UNIVERSITY. ALL RIGHTS RESERVED. PRINTED UNDER LICENSE FROM STANFORD UNIVERSITY PRESS, STANFORD, CALIFORNIA 94305.

***** END OF REPORT FOR SAMPLE S MALE 22-SEP-83 002 0009 *****

PREPARED BY
NCS INTERPRETIVE SCORING SYSTEMS
P.O. BOX 1294
MINNEAPOLIS, MN. 55440
22-SEP-83

STRONG-CAMPBELL INTEREST INVENTORY

REPORTS FOR SAMPLE   S   MALE

SECTION A. ADMINISTRATIVE INDEXES AND SPECIAL SCALES

THE FOLLOWING ARE THE ADMINISTRATIVE INDICES AND SPECIAL SCALES.
DATA FOR I-VII INDICATE THE RESPONSE PERCENTAGES -- LIKE - INDIFFERENT -
DISLIKE -- TO THE SEVEN SECTIONS OF THE INVENTORY. DATA FOR INTERPRE-
TATION OF THE OTHER SCALES CAN BE FOUND IN THE MANUAL FOR THE SCII.

TOTAL RESPONSES = 324

INFREQUENT RESPONSES = 11

ACADEMIC COMFORT = 54

INTROVERSION-EXTROVERSION = 60

RESPONSE PERCENTAGES

		LP	IP	DP
I.	OCCUPATIONS	24	43	33
II.	SCHOOL SUBJECTS	47	39	14
III.	ACTIVITIES	25	49	25
IV.	AMUSEMENTS	26	44	31
V.	TYPES OF PEOPLE	4	67	29
VI.	PREFERENCES	43	23	33
VII.	CHARACTERISTICS	29	57	14
	ALL PARTS	27	44	28

SECTION B. GENERAL OCCUPATIONAL THEME SCORES AND PROFILE

IF SEX OF THE INDIVIDUAL WAS INDICATED ON THE INVENTORY, THEN THE
PROFILE CONTAINS A SERIES OF DOTS INDICATING THE AVERAGE RANGE OF SCORES
RELATIVE TO THE SEX OF THE INDIVIDUAL.

	YOUR			
SCALE	SCORE	....0.........0.........0.........0.........0.....		MIN-MAX
		3 4 5 6 7		
C-THEME	59		(CONVENTIONAL)	23-79
R-THEME	59		(REALISTIC)	27-75
I-THEME	56		(INVESTIGATIVE)	20-69
A-THEME	45		(ARTISTIC)	24-67
E-THEME	44		(ENTERPRISING)	30-77
S-THEME	34		(SOCIAL)	19-73

SECTION C. BASIC INTEREST SCALE SCORES AND PROFILE

IF SEX OF THE INDIVIDUAL WAS INDICATED ON THE INVENTORY, THEN THE
PROFILE CONTAINS A SERIES OF DOTS INDICATING THE AVERAGE RANGE OF SCORES
RELATIVE TO THE SEX OF THE INDIVIDUAL. MINIMUM (MIN) AND MAXIMUM (MAX)
POSSIBLE VALUES ARE LISTED FOR EACH SCALE.

BASIC INTEREST SCALES	YOUR SCORE	MIN-MAX
VERY HIGH INTEREST(66+)		
MECHANICAL ACTIVITIES	67	30-72
HIGH INTEREST (65-58)		
SCIENCE	62	28-69
MATHEMATICS	61	31-67
OFFICE PRACTICES	60	36-79
AVERAGE INTEREST (57-43)		
LAW/POLITICS	54	30-69
DOMESTIC ARTS	53	27-75
ART	52	26-68
PUBLIC SPEAKING	51	31-71
BUSINESS MANAGEMENT	49	29-72
WRITING	48	26-66
TEACHING	47	23-67
MEDICAL SERVICE	45	33-76
SOCIAL SERVICE	45	24-69
LOW INTEREST (42-35)		
MUSIC/DRAMATICS	42	26-73
ADVENTURE	42	30-71
MERCHANDISING	42	31-72
NATURE	42	17-67
MILITARY ACTIVITIES	41	41-76
MEDICAL SCIENCE	41	29-68
SALES	39	37-81
RELIGIOUS ACTIVITIES	37	31-68
AGRICULTURE	36	30-68
VERY LOW INTEREST (34-)		
ATHLETICS	32	24-70

SECTION D. OCCUPATIONAL SCALES AND BASIC INTEREST SCALES WITHIN THEME AREA

THE CODES IN FRONT OF EACH OCCUPATION ARE THE ONE TO THREE LETTERS INDICATING THE GEN-
ERAL THEME CHARACTERISTICS OF THAT OCCUPATION. AFTER EACH OCCUPATIONAL SCALE IS F OR M
INDICATING THE SEX (FEMALE, MALE) OF THE GROUP USED FOR DEVELOPMENT OF THAT SCALE.

I. 59 C-THEME ----- (CONVENTIONAL) -----

BASIC AREA SCALES	CODE	OCCUP. SCALES	
60 OFFICE PRACTICES	57 C	ACCOUNTANT	F
	48 CE	IRS AGENT	F
	47 CE	BANKER	F
	42 CE	IRS AGENT	M
	40 C	ACCOUNTANT	M
	40 CE	CREDIT MANAGER	F
	32 CE	BANKER	M
	31 CER	EXEC HOUSEKEEPER	M
	30 CE	CREDIT MANAGER	M
	28 CES	BUSINESS ED. TCH	M
	27 CA	PUBLIC ADMINIST.	M
	25 C	SECRETARY	F
	25 CES	BUSINESS ED. TCH	F
	22 CER	EXEC HOUSEKEEPER	F
	20 C	DENTAL ASSISTANT	F

II. 59 R-THEME ----- (REALISTIC) -----

BASIC AREA SCALES	CODE	OCCUP. SCALES	
67 MECHANICAL ACT.	56 RI	ENGINEER	F
42 ADVENTURE	52 R	NAVY OFFICER	F
42 NATURE	50 RI	ENGINEER	M
41 MILITARY ACTVS.	47 RC	ARMY OFFICER	F
36 AGRICULTURE	43 RC	AIR FORCE OFF.	F
	40 RC	FARMER	F
	39 R	FORESTER	M
	37 RI	FORESTER	F
	35 R	SKILLED CRAFTS	M
	34 R	X-RAY TECHNICIAN	F
	33 RI	X-RAY TECHNICIAN	M
	33 R	FARMER	M
	31 RC	AIR FORCE OFF.	M
	29 RC	NAVY OFFICER	M
	27 RAS	OCCUP. THERAPIST	F
	25 RAS	OCCUP. THERAPIST	M
	25 RC	ARMY OFFICER	M
	23 RE	POLICE OFFICER	F
	21 RIC	LIC. PRAC. NURSE	F
	20 RCE	VOC AGRIC. TCHR.	M
	17 RI	VETERINARIAN	M
	10 RE	POLICE OFFICER	M

III. 56 I-THEME ----- (INVESTIGATIVE)-----

BASIC AREA SCALES	CODE	OCCUP. SCALES	
62 SCIENCE	60 IRC	SYSTEMS ANALYST	M
61 MATHEMATICS	59 IRC	COMPUTER PROGR.	F
45 MEDICAL SERVICE	59 IRC	SYSTEMS ANALYST	F
41 MEDICAL SCIENCE	58 IA	COLLEGE PROF.	F
	56 IRC	COMPUTER PROGR.	M
	55 IR	PHYSICIST	F
	55 I	MATHEMATICIAN	F
	54 I	GEOGRAPHER	F
	53 IRC	MATH-SCI. TCHR.	F

IV. 45 A-THEME ----- (ARTISTIC) -----

BASIC AREA SCALES	CODE	OCCUP. SCALES	
52 ART	54 A	LIBRARIAN	F
48 WRITING	42 AIR	ARCHITECT	F
42 MUSIC/DRAMATICS	41 A	LIBRARIAN	M
	38 A	PHOTOGRAPHER	F
	37 AIR	ARCHITECT	M
	37 A	MUSICIAN	M
	35 A	FOR. LANG. TCHR.	M
	34 AI	LAWYER	F
	32 A	MUSICIAN	F

CODE	OCCUP. SCALES	M/F
31 A	PHOTOGRAPHER	M
29 AE	ADVERTISING EXEC	F
26 A	FOR. LANG. TCHR.	M
25 AI	LAWYER	F
25 A	FINE ARTIST	F
20 AE	PUBLIC REL. DIR.	F
20 A	COMMERCIAL ART.	F
18 A	REPORTER	F
18 AE	INT. DECORATOR	M
17 AS	ENGLISH TEACHER	M
16 A	REPORTER	M
14 A	FINE ARTIST	F
14 A	ENGLISH TEACHER	F
13 A	COMMERCIAL ART.	M
11 AE	INT. DECORATOR	F
10 A	ART TEACHER	M
8 A	ART TEACHER	F
7 AE	ADVERTISING EXEC	M
6 AE	PUBLIC REL. DIR.	M

CODE	OCCUP. SCALES	M/F
53 IR	OPTOMETRIST	F
52 I	CHEMIST	F
49 I	BIOLOGIST	F
48 IA	COLLEGE PROF.	M
48 IR	CHEMIST	M
47 IA	SOCIOLOGIST	M
47 I	GEOGRAPHER	F
47 IR	MEDICAL TECH.	F
47 I	PHARMACIST	M
46 I	MATHEMATICIAN	F
44 IR	GEOLOGIST	M
44 IR	PHYSICIST	M
43 IRS	MATH-SCI. TCHR.	M
43 I	PHYSICIAN	F
43 I	BIOLOGIST	M
42 IR	DENTIST	F
39 IA	SOCIOLOGIST	F
38 IA	GEOLOGIST	M
37 IAS	PSYCHOLOGIST	M
35 IAS	PSYCHOLOGIST	F
35 IR	VETERINARIAN	F
34 IR	MEDICAL TECH.	M
32 IR	OPTOMETRIST	M
31 IRC	CHIROPRACTOR	F
30 IRC	CHIROPRACTOR	M
29 IR	PHYSICIAN	M
27 IR	DENTIST	M
22 IR	PHYS. THERAPIST	F
21 IE	PHARMACIST	M
21 IR	DENTAL HYGIENIST	F
17 IRS	REGISTERED NURSE	M
15 IR	PHYS. THERAPIST	M

V. 44 E-THEME ----- (ENTERPRISING) -----

BASIC AREA SCALES	CODE	OCCUP. SCALES	M/F
54 LAW/POLITICS	41 EC	DIETITIAN	F
51 PUBLIC SPEAKING	39 EI	MARKETING EXEC.	F
49 BUS. MANAGEMENT	35 E	PUBLIC ADMINST.	F
42 MERCHANDISING	33 ECR	DIETITIAN	M
39 SALES	33 E	PERSONNEL DIR.	F
	32 EI	INVEST. FUND MGR	M
	31 EC	PURCHASING AGENT	M
	31 EC	RESTAURANT MGR.	F

VI. 34 S-THEME ----- (SOCIAL) -----

BASIC AREA SCALES	CODE	OCCUP. SCALES	M/F
53 DOMESTIC ARTS	34 SEC	SOCIAL SCI. TCHR	F
47 TEACHING	33 SEC	GUIDANCE COUNS.	F
45 SOCIAL SERVICE	31 SA	SPEECH PATHOL.	M
37 RELIGIOUS ACTVS.	29 SE	YWCA DIRECTOR	F
32 ATHLETICS	29 S	ELEM. TEACHER	M
	28 S	LIC. PRAC. NURSE	M
	26 SE	SCHOOL ADMINIST.	F
	25 SE	SCHOOL ADMINIST.	M

24	SA	SOCIAL WORKER	F
23	S	SPECIAL ED. TCHR	F
20	S	SPECIAL ED. TCHR	M
20	SIE	MINISTER	M
20	SR	PHYS. ED. TCHR.	F
19	S	ELEM. TEACHER	F
18	SA	SPEECH PATHOL.	M
18	SCE	GUIDANCE COUNS.	F
18	SA	MINISTER	M
18	SA	SOCIAL WORKER	M
17	SRE	RECREAT. LEADER	F
15	SRE	RECREAT. LEADER	M
13	SEC	SOCIAL SCI. TCHR	M
11	SE	YMCA DIRECTOR	M
10	SI	REGISTERED NURSE	F
9	SR	PHYS. ED. TCHR.	M

30	EC	PURCHASING AGENT	M
27	E	DEPT. STORE MGR.	F
26	E	BEAUTICIAN	F
26	E	ELECT. PUBL. OFF	F
26	EA	PERSONNEL DIR.	M
26	EA	BEAUTICIAN	M
22	EC	FLIGHT ATTENDANT	M
20	E	CHAM. OF COMM.	F
20	E	ELECT. PUBL. OFF	M
19	ES	LIFE INS. AGENT	F
19	EI	HOME ECON. TCHR.	F
19	E	MARKETING EXEC.	M
18	E	RESTAURANT MGR.	M
17	EC	DEPT. STORE MGR.	M
16	ERC	NURS. HOME ADM.	F
15	EC	AGRIBUS. MANAGER	M
14	EC	BUYER	M
14	EA	FLIGHT ATTENDANT	F
13	EC	REALTOR	M
13	ECS	BUYER	M
12	E	NURS. HOME ADM.	F
9	E	REALTOR	M
6	E	CHAM. OF COMM.	M
		LIFE INS. AGENT	M

NAME: Symptom Check List

SUPPLIER: PSYCH Systems, Inc.
600 Reisterstown Road
Baltimore, MD 21208
(800) 368-3366

PRODUCT CATEGORY	PRIMARY APPLICATIONS
Structured Interview Personality	Clinical Assessment/Diagnosis Personal/Marriage/Family Counseling

SALE RESTRICTIONS   Qualified Professional

SERVICE TYPE/COST	Type	Available	Cost	Discount
	Mail-In	No		
	Teleprocessing	No		
	Local	Yes	See Below	

PRODUCT DESCRIPTION

This multidimensional, self-report inventory consists of 90 items derived from the Hopkins Symptom Checklist. The SCL-90 functions effectively as a screening instrument in psychiatric, medical, and non-patient populations to detect psychopathology. The scales are designed to measure fluctuating emotional states experienced by the individual. It is an effective assessment tool when employed as a brief measure of therapy progress prior to, during, and at the conclusion of therapy.

This Psych Systems program presents and scores the test items. It then produces a brief printout of test results.

Psych Systems programs operate on the IBM PC-XT, COMPAQ Plus, Dec Professional 350, and most DEC PDP-11 systems. Various hardware/ software configurations are available directly from Psych Systems, with single-user systems starting at approximately $12,000. A per test fee also applies.

222-22-2222 Jonathan Doe   32 yr old white male   16-Feb-84

```
--------------------------------------------------
|                    |                              |
|    SCL90-R         |   Symptom Checklist 90 Revised |
|                    |                              |
--------------------------------------------------
```

This clinical report is designed to assist in psychodiagnostic
evaluation. It is available to qualified professionals. This
report was produced by a computerized analysis of the data given
by the client listed above, and is to be used in conjunction
with professional evaluation. No decision should be based solely
upon the contents of this report.

The computer program generating this report was designed by Psych
Systems, Inc., Baltimore, Maryland 21208. Copyright (C) 1984 by
Psych Systems, Inc. The Symptom Checklist-90-Revised is
reproduced by permission of the author. Copyright (C) 1975,
Leonard R. Derogatis, Ph.D., Towson, Maryland 21204. All rights
reserved.

psychware **675**

```
222-22-2222   Jonathan Doe    32 yr old white male    16-Feb-84
T-Score                                                              % Rank
75- --- --- --- --- --- --- --- --- --- + --- --- --- -99
  -                                       +                    -
  -                                       +                    -
  -                                       +                    -
  -                                       +                    -
70-                                       +                    -98
  -                                       +                    -
  -   *                                   +                    -
  -                                       +                    -
65-                                       +                    -93
  -                                       +                    -
  -                           *     *     +                    -
  -                                   *   +                *   -
60-                                       +                    -84
  -                                       +                    -
  -                                       + *                  -
  -                       *               +                    -
55-       *                               +                    -70
  -                                       +                    -
  -           *       *                   +                    -
  -                                       +            *       -
50- --- --- --- --- --- --- --- --- --- + --- --- --- -50
  -                   *                   +                    -
  -                                       +                    -
  -                                       +                    -
45-                                       +                    -30
  -                                       +                    -
  -                                       +                    -
  -                                       +                    -
40-                                       +                    -16
  -                                       +                    -
  -                                       +                    -
  -                                       +                    -
35-                                       +                    - 7
  -                                       +                    -
  -                                       +                    -
  -                                       +                    -
30- --- --- --- --- --- --- --- --- --- + --- --- --- - 2
     SOM  O-C  I-S  DEP  ANX  HOS PHOB  PAR  PSY   GSI PSDI  PST
R=  2.00 1.80 1.56 1.31 1.40 1.33 1.71 2.33 1.60  1.52 2.04 67.0
T=   67   55   53   48   53   56   63   63   61    57   52   61
              Scale Scores (outpatients)
              _____

       SOM  O-C  I-S  DEP  ANX  HOS PHOB  PAR  PSY   GSI PSDI  PST
        67   55   53   48   53   56   63   63   61    57   52   61


            Global Scores:
            --------------

            Grand Total: 137.00

            GSI:    1.52

            PST:   67.00

            PSDI:   2.04
```

676 *psychware*

```
                     Items of Note:
                     ----------------
 1 The idea that someone else can control your thoughts.:  1
 2 Feelings that others are to blame for most of your troubles.:  2
 3 Thoughts of ending your life.:  1
 4 Hearing voices that other people do not hear.:  1
 5 Poor appetite.:  1
 6 Blaming yourself for things.:  2
 7 Other people being aware of your private thoughts.:  1
 8 Feeling inferior to others.:  2
 9 Trouble falling asleep.:  1
10 Feeling afraid to travel on buses, subways, or trains.:  1
11 Feeling hopeless about the future.:  1
12 Trouble concentrating.:  1
13 Thoughts of death or dying.:  3
14 Overeating.:  1
15 Having thoughts that are not your own.:  4
16 Feeling of guilt.:  4
```

```
                     Symptoms of Note:
                     -----------------
```

The individual obtained scores equal to or higher than those found
by Derogatis (1979) for outpatients on the following dimensions:

SOMATIZATION: This dimension reflects distress arising from
perceptions of bodily dysfunction. Complaints focused on
cardiovascular, gastrointestinal, respiratory, and other systems
with strong autonomic mediation included. Headaches, pain and
discomfort of the gross musculature and additional somatic equivalents
of anxiety are components of the definition. These symptoms and signs
have all been demonstrated to have high prevalence in disorders
demonstrated to have a functional etiology, although all may be
reflections of true physical disease.

PHOBIC ANXIETY: This is defined as a persistent fear response to a
specific person, place, object or situation which is characterized as
being irrational and disproportionate to the stimulus, and which leads
to avoidance or escape behavior. The items of the present dimension
focus on the more pathognomic and disruptive manifestations of phobic
behavior. The actual structure of the dimension is in close agreement
with the definition of "Agoraphobia" (Marks 1969), also termed
"Phobic Anxiety Depersonalization Syndrome" by Roth (1959).

PARANOID IDEATION: This dimension represents paranoid behavior
fundamentally as a disorder of thinking. The cardinal characteristics
of projective thought, hostility, suspiciousness, grandiosity,
centrality, fear of loss of autonomy, and delusions are viewed as
primary reflections of this disorder, and item selection was oriented
toward representing this conceptualization.

PSYCHOTICISM: This scale was designed in a fashion to represent the
construct as a continuous dimension of human experience. Items indicative
of a withdrawn, isolated, schizoid life style were included, as were
first-rank symptoms of schizophrenia, such as hallucinations and
thought-broadcasting. This scale provides a graduated continuum from
mild interpersonal alienation to dramatic evidence of psychosis. In this
respect the present definition owes much to the work of Eysenck (1968).

NAME: Symptom Check List-90-Revised

SUPPLIER: NCS/Professional Assessment Services
P.O. Box 1416
Minneapolis, MN 55440
(800) 328-6759

PRODUCT CATEGORY

Structured Interview
Personality

PRIMARY APPLICATIONS

Clinical Assessment/Diagnosis
Personal/Marriage/Family Counseling

SALE RESTRICTIONS American Psychological Association Guidelines

SERVICE TYPE/COST	Type	Available	Cost	Discount
	Mail-In	Yes	$8.50	Yes
	Teleprocessing	Yes	$8.50	Yes
	Local	Yes	$7.00	Yes

PRODUCT DESCRIPTION

The SCL-90-R measures psychological symptom patterns of psychiatric and medical patients. It is intended to aid in the identification of psychiatric symptomatology and personality dynamics, screening for psychopathology among individuals entering dangerous occupations such as police work, assessing psychological components of medical illness, treatment planning and evaluation in mental health settings. The 90 self-report items rated on a 5-point scale of distress require about 30 minutes for completion.

The report provides a summary of patient responses along nine primary symptom dimensions (Somatization, Obsessive-Compulsive, Interpersonal Sensitivity, Depression, Anxiety, Hostility, Phobic Anxiety, Paranoid Ideation, Psychoticism) and three global indexes.

Two systems are available for local processing of test results. MICRO-TEST Assessment Software from National Computer Systems, used with a Sentry 3000 tabletop scanner (purchase price approximately $4000) and microcomputer system ($2000-$3000 purchase price), allows tests to be administered off-line. Answer sheets are then scanned and scored automatically, one at a time or in a batch. The software also permits on-line administration of the test via microcomputer. In either case, the same report is provided. The cost for local scoring refers to the cost-per-test when diskettes are purchased in units of 20 administrations (minimum purchase).

NAME: Temperament and Values Inventory

SUPPLIER: NCS/Professional Assessment Services
P.O. Box 1416
Minneapolis, MN 55440
(800) 328-6759

PRODUCT CATEGORY	PRIMARY APPLICATIONS
Personality	Vocational Guidance/Counseling
Motivation/Needs	Personnel Selection/Evaluation

SALE RESTRICTIONS None

SERVICE TYPE/COST Type	Available	Cost	Discount
Mail-In	Yes	$10.00	Yes
Teleprocessing	Yes	$4.25	Yes
Local	No		

PRODUCT DESCRIPTION

This 10-page individualized narrative contains scale descriptions and score interpretation and comparisons followed by a two-page detachable summary. A scores only report (Profile Report) is also available at approximately 40% of costs shown here for the complete report.

The test itself has 230 items that require an 8th-grade reading level. It takes 20-30 minutes to complete. The test has seven temperament scales that measure constructs such as Consistent/Changeable and seven reward values scales such as Social Recognition. Four administrative indexes are also provided.

A scores only report is available by teleprocessing. The complete report described here is available only by mail-in service. NCS is the publisher and exclusive distributor of the Temperament and Values Inventory.

TEMPERAMENT AND VALUES INVENTORY

RESULTS FOR SAMPLE   S   FEMALE   30-SEP-83

THE RESULTS BELOW ARE BASED ON YOUR ANSWERS TO THE TEMPERAMENT AND VALUES INVENTORY. THESE
RESULTS CAN GIVE YOU SOME USEFUL INFORMATION ABOUT YOURSELF BY (1) MAKING YOU AWARE OF HOW YOU
COMPARE WITH OTHER PEOPLE, AND (2) LEADING TO GREATER SELF-UNDERSTANDING BY HELPING EXPLAIN WHY
YOU ENJOY SOME SITUATIONS AND ACTIVITIES AND DO NOT ENJOY OTHERS.   WHEN USED WITH MEASURES OF
ABILITY AND VOCATIONAL INTERESTS, THESE RESULTS CAN HELP YOU FIND WORK-RELATED ACTIVITIES THAT
FIT YOUR PERSONAL CHARACTERISTICS AND VALUES.   HOPEFULLY, A GREATER AWARENESS OF YOUR PERSONAL
BEHAVIOR STYLE WILL HELP YOU TO FIND SITUATIONS AND SETTINGS THAT YOU MAY ENJOY AND POINT OUT
SITUATIONS AND SETTINGS THAT YOU MAY NOT ENJOY.

THESE RESULTS REPRESENT HOW YOU DESCRIBED YOURSELF IN VARIOUS SITUATIONS AND WHAT YOU INDI-
CATED WAS IMPORTANT TO YOU.   SINCE EVERYONE HAS SOME FEEL FOR WHO THEY ARE, RESULTS LIKE THESE
OFTEN APPEAR TO BE ADDING LITTLE TO YOUR SELF-UNDERSTANDING. ACTUALLY, SEEING AND THINKING ABOUT
YOUR SCORES SHOULD HELP ADD TO YOUR SELF-KNOWLEDGE AND MAKE IT EASIER FOR YOU TO PUT INTO WORDS
WHAT YOU DO KNOW ABOUT YOURSELF.   IN ADDITION, THESE SCORES ALLOW YOU TO COMPARE YOURSELF TO
OTHER INDIVIDUALS.   FOR EXAMPLE, YOU MAY FEEL THAT YOU ARE AS ACTIVE AS MOST PEOPLE, BUT YOUR
SCORE ON THE QUIET-ACTIVE SCALE MAY INDICATE THAT YOU MAY BE MORE TOWARD THE QUIET END THAN MOST
PEOPLE IN A GENERAL POPULATION.   YOU SHOULD NOT EXPECT MIRACLES FROM THESE RESULTS OR FROM ANY
OTHER INVENTORY -- EACH INDIVIDUAL IS UNIQUE AND NO INVENTORY CAN PREDICT WITH PERFECT ACCURACY
ALL THE DIFFERENCES AMONG PEOPLE.

YOUR SCORES ON ALL SCALES ARE REPORTED BELOW.   THEY HAVE BEEN DIVIDED INTO TWO SECTIONS --
(1) PERSONAL CHARACTERISTICS (HOW YOU HAVE DESCRIBED YOURSELF IN VARIOUS SITUATIONS), AND (2)
REWARD VALUES (WHAT YOU FELT WAS IMPORTANT TO YOU).   ALSO, DESCRIPTIONS ARE GIVEN FOR EACH SCALE
TO HELP YOU BETTER UNDERSTAND THE VARIOUS ASPECTS OF EACH AREA.   THE BASIS OF YOUR SCORES IS A
COMPARISON OF HOW YOU ANSWERED THE QUESTIONS ON THE INVENTORY TO HOW INDIVIDUALS IN A GENERAL
POPULATION ANSWERED.   THE AVERAGE RANGE OF SCORES FOR A GROUP OF FEMALES AND MALES IN A GENERAL
POPULATION IS BETWEEN 43 AND 57 FOR EACH SCALE.

* *

```
* * * * * * * * * * * * * * * * * * * *
* * * * * *                    * * * * *
* * * * *     PERSONAL CHARACTERISTICS    * * * * *
* * * * *                    * * * *
* * * * * * * * * * * * * * * * * * * *
```

SCALES GROUPED UNDER THIS HEADING OF PERSONAL CHARACTERISTICS REPRESENT WAYS THAT YOU HAVE DESCRIBED YOURSELF IN VARIOUS ACTIVITIES AND SITUATIONS. IMMEDIATELY BELOW ARE YOUR SCORES -- LISTED FROM HIGH TO LOW -- ON THESE SEVEN SCALES. THE IMPORTANT THING TO REMEMBER WHEN LOOKING AT YOUR SCORES IS THAT THERE ARE NO GOOD OR BAD SCORES. THE SCORES REPORTED BELOW ARE BASED ON A COMPARISON OF YOUR ANSWERS TO THE ANSWERS OF GROUPS OF FEMALES AND MALES IN A GENERAL POPULATION. FOR SOME SCALES, FEMALES AND MALES RESPOND SOMEWHAT DIFFERENTLY, AS DO DIFFERENT AGE GROUPS. FOR EACH SCALE, THERE IS A RANGE OF DOTS ON THE PROFILE BELOW WHICH SHOWS THE AVERAGE RANGE OF SCORES OF INDIVIDUALS IN A GENERAL POPULATION.

ADJECTIVE DESCRIPTION	YOUR SCORE	3	4	5	6	7	ADJECTIVE DESCRIPTION
		....0.........0.........0.........0.........0.....					
RETICENT	63					*	PERSUASIVE
SERIOUS	54			.........*...			CHEERFUL
RESERVED	53			.......*....			SOCIABLE
ROUTINE	50			.....*.....			FLEXIBLE
ATTENTIVE	47			...*......			DISTRACTIBLE
CONSISTENT	35		*				CHANGEABLE
QUIET	29	*					ACTIVE

FOR EACH SCALE, A SCORE OF 50 IS THE OVERALL AVERAGE FOR A SAMPLE OF FEMALES AND MALES IN A GENERAL POPULATION. SCORES ABOVE 50 INDICATE THAT THE ADJECTIVE AT THE RIGHT SIDE IS MORE DESCRIPTIVE OF YOUR ANSWERS, WHILE SCORES LESS THAN 50 INDICATE THAT THE ADJECTIVE AT THE LEFT IS MORE DESCRIPTIVE. FOR EXAMPLE, IF YOUR SCORE WAS 49 OR LOWER ON THE QUIET-ACTIVE SCALE, YOU TENDED TO DESCRIBE YOURSELF MORE AS A QUIET INDIVIDUAL, WHEN COMPARED WITH A GENERAL POPULATION SAMPLE, OR IF YOUR SCORE WAS 51 OR HIGHER ON THIS SCALE, YOU ARE MORE IN THE ACTIVE RANGE. THE CLOSER THE ASTERISK IS TO THE RIGHT-HAND SIDE OF THE GRAPH, THE MORE TRUE IS THE RIGHT-HAND ADJECTIVE FOR THAT SCALE. THE CLOSER THE ASTERISK IS TO THE LEFT-HAND SIDE OF THE GRAPH, THE MORE TRUE IS THE LEFT-HAND ADJECTIVE.

BELOW ARE YOUR SCORES ON EACH OF THE SEVEN SCALES AND DESCRIPTIONS WHICH WILL HELP YOU TO UNDERSTAND BETTER WHAT EACH SCALE MEASURES. THESE DESCRIPTIONS ARE BASED ON RESEARCH STUDIES AND WHILE ALL THE DESCRIPTIONS MAY NOT EXACTLY FIT ANY SINGLE INDIVIDUAL, THEY DO POINT OUT THE TRENDS THAT ARE RELATED TO YOUR SCORES.

63 RETICENT-PERSUASIVE-------------COMPARED TO FEMALES AND MALES IN A GENERAL POPULATION, YOUR SCORE IS A VERY HIGH SCORE AND TOWARD THE PERSUASIVE END OF THE SCALE. INDIVIDUALS WITH SCORES SIMILAR TO YOURS INDICATE THAT THEY LIKE TO INFLUENCE OTHERS BY DEBATING WITH THEM OR JUST PLAIN TRYING TO OUT-TALK THEM. THEY ENJOY A GOOD ARGUMENT, DESCRIBE THEMSELVES AS FORCEFUL, AND ENJOY DISCUSSIONS AND TAKING PART IN GROUP DECISIONS. MANY OF THESE CHARACTERISTICS ARE RELATED TO INTERESTS IN BUSINESS TYPES OF OCCUPATIONS, SUCH AS SALES WORK, ADMINISTRATIVE WORK, AND THE CAREERS OF A TRIAL LAWYER OR POLITICIAN. IN CONTRAST, INDIVIDUALS WITH VERY LOW SCORES ARE MUCH MORE RETICENT (RESERVED, QUIET, OR SILENT) WHEN IT COMES TO GROUP DISCUSSIONS AND GROUP DECISIONS OR WHEN TRYING TO PERSUADE SOMEONE -- THEY WOULD TEND TO BE MORE INCLINED TO GO ALONG WITH SOMETHING RATHER THAN ARGUE AGAINST IT.

54 SERIOUS-CHEERFUL-------------COMPARED TO FEMALES AND MALES IN A GENERAL POPULATION, YOUR SCORE FALLS WITHIN THE RANGE OBTAINED BY MOST PEOPLE, ALTHOUGH SLIGHTLY TOWARD THE CHEERFUL END. PEOPLE WITH SCORES SIMILAR TO YOURS, INDICATE A GENERAL POSITIVE OUTLOOK ON LIFE -- THEY ARE OPTIMISTIC MUCH OF THE TIME AND ENJOY BEING WITH AND WORKING WITH PEOPLE. GENERALLY, YOU PROBABLY FEEL GOOD ABOUT YOURSELF AND ARE MORE OFTEN HAPPY THAN UNHAPPY. RELATED TO HIGH SCORES ON THIS SCALE ARE DESCRIPTIONS SUCH AS HAPPY, CALM, RELAXED, AND CONFIDENT. IN CONTRAST, DESCRIPTIONS RELATED TO VERY LOW SCORES, TOWARD THE SERIOUS END, ARE FEELINGS SUCH AS NERVOUS, TENSE, TOUCHY, INSECURE, AND ANXIOUS. IN GENERAL, MOST PEOPLE DESCRIBE THEMSELVES AS MORE CHEERFUL THAN SERIOUS ON THIS SCALE, AND YOUR SCORE INDICATES A SIMILARITY OF YOUR FEELINGS WITH THOSE OF MOST PEOPLE.

53 RESERVED-SOCIABLE-------------COMPARED TO FEMALES AND MALES IN A GENERAL POPULATION, YOUR SCORE IS IN THE UPPER AVERAGE RANGE, TOWARD THE SOCIABLE END. INDIVIDUALS WITH SCORES IN THIS RANGE TEND TO BE INVOLVED IN GROUPS, LIKE TO ATTEND SOCIAL EVENTS AND PARTIES, AND ENJOY BEING WITH OTHER PEOPLE. VERY HIGH SCORES ARE RELATED TO DESCRIPTIONS SUCH AS LIKABLE, POPULAR, OUTGOING, SOCIABLE, AND ENTERTAINING. IN CONTRAST, INDIVIDUALS WITH VERY LOW SCORES, TOWARD THE RESERVED END, TEND TO BE MORE CAUTIOUS AND RESERVED ABOUT NEW SITUATIONS AND MEETING NEW PEOPLE, AND ARE MORE LIKELY TO PREFER WORKING ALONE RATHER THAN WITH GROUPS. YOUR SCORE INDICATES THAT YOU PROBABLY WOULD LIKE TO BE IN SETTINGS THAT INVOLVE PEOPLE, SUCH AS TEACHING, SELLING, BUSINESS, NURSING, AND SO FORTH. HOWEVER, YOU MAY BE SOMEWHAT MORE HESITANT ABOUT SEEKING OUT NEW SITUATIONS OR TALKING WITH STRANGERS THAN ARE PEOPLE WHO HAVE VERY HIGH SCORES ON THIS SCALE.

50 ROUTINE-FLEXIBLE-------------COMPARED TO FEMALES AND MALES IN A GENERAL POPULATION, YOUR SCORE IS IN THE AVERAGE RANGE OF SCORES, ALTHOUGH SLIGHTLY MORE TOWARD THE FLEXIBLE END OF THE SCALE. PEOPLE WITH VERY HIGH SCORES, THAT IS, TOWARD THE FLEXIBLE END, INDICATE THAT THEY CAN ADAPT FAIRLY EASILY TO CHANGES IN THEIR DAILY LIVES. FOR EXAMPLE, THEY DO NOT HAVE SET ROUTINES OR FEEL THAT A SCHEDULE IS NECESSARY TO COMPLETE TASKS SUCH AS HOUSEHOLD OR YARD CHORES. THEY FEEL THERE IS NOT NECESSARILY AN ORDER IN WHICH TASKS MUST BE DONE. IN CONTRAST, PEOPLE WITH VERY LOW SCORES, THAT IS, TOWARD THE ROUTINE END, TEND TO PREFER MORE STRUCTURE IN ARRANGING THEIR PERSONAL LIVES -- THERE IS MORE OF AN ATTEMPT AT ESTABLISHING A SCHEDULE OR ROUTINE FOR DOING CHORES OR TASKS SO AS TO FINISH ONE THING BEFORE STARTING ANOTHER. YOUR SCORE INDICATES MORE OF A LEANING TOWARD THE FLEXIBLE SIDE. ALTHOUGH YOU MAY FIND THAT YOU DO SET SCHEDULES FOR YOURSELF, YOU ARE PROBABLY SLIGHTLY MORE FLEXIBLE THAN THE AVERAGE IN KEEPING THOSE SCHEDULES.

47 ATTENTIVE-DISTRACTIBLE---------COMPARED TO FEMALES AND MALES IN A GENERAL POPULATION, YOUR SCORE IS IN THE AVERAGE RANGE, ALTHOUGH SLIGHTLY MORE TOWARD THE ATTENTIVE END. PEOPLE WHO HAVE VERY LOW SCORES ON THIS SCALE INDICATE THAT IT IS EASY FOR THEM TO CONCENTRATE OR PAY ATTENTION TO WHAT THEY ARE DOING EVEN WHEN THERE IS NOT COMPLETE SILENCE. IN CONTRAST, PEOPLE WITH VERY HIGH SCORES, TOWARD THE DISTRACTIBLE END, FEEL THAT PEOPLE TALKING AROUND THEM MAKE IT DIFFICULT TO GET WORK DONE, OR, IF TRYING TO CONCENTRATE, A RADIO OR TELEVISION WILL BE QUITE DISTRACTING AND INTERFERING. YOU PROBABLY WILL FIND THAT YOU GET LESS TENSE OR ANXIOUS THAN DO MOST PEOPLE IF THERE ARE DISTRACTIONS AROUND YOU WHILE YOU ARE TRYING TO CONCENTRATE. HOWEVER, YOU MAY ALSO FIND THAT YOU CAN DO YOUR BEST WORK IF YOU CAN FIND A QUIET PLACE TO WORK. IN GENERAL, HIGH SCHOOL STUDENTS TEND TO HAVE SCORES MORE TOWARD THE DISTRACTIBLE END THAN DO OLDER ADULTS, BUT THERE ARE WIDE INDIVIDUAL DIFFERENCES AT EACH AGE.

35 CONSISTENT-CHANGEABLE---------COMPARED TO FEMALES AND MALES IN A GENERAL POPULATION, YOUR SCORE IS CONSIDERABLY MORE TOWARD THE CONSISTENT END. INDIVIDUALS WITH VERY LOW SCORES TEND TO SEE THEMSELVES AS LEVEL-HEADED, CALM, RELAXED, AND CONSISTENT IN THEIR FEELINGS FROM ONE DAY TO THE NEXT. IN CONTRAST, PEOPLE WITH VERY HIGH SCORES INDICATE MORE OF A TEMPERAMENTAL NATURE -- THEY DESCRIBE THEMSELVES AS BECOMING DEFENSIVE OR IRRITABLE IF CRITICIZED, BEING SHORT-TEMPERED, BEING UPSET QUITE EASILY, FLUCTUATING FROM A GOOD MOOD TO A BAD MOOD, AND LOSING THEIR TEMPER FREQUENTLY. YOUR SCORE PLACES YOU MUCH MORE TOWARD THE CONSISTENT, EVEN-TEMPERED END, AND WHILE YOU MAY BECOME UPSET OR ANGRY, THESE FEELINGS PROBABLY ARE LESS INTENSE OR FREQUENT THAN FOR PEOPLE WHO HAVE HIGH SCORES. GENERALLY, OLDER ADULTS TEND TO HAVE SCORES MORE TOWARD THE CON- SISTENT END THAN DO HIGH SCHOOL STUDENTS, AND MALES TEND TO DESCRIBE THEMSELVES AS MORE CONSIS- TENT THAN DO FEMALES. HOWEVER, THESE ARE GENERAL TRENDS AND THERE ARE DIFFERENCES AT EACH AGE.

29 QUIET-ACTIVE---------COMPARED TO FEMALES AND MALES IN A GENERAL POPULATION, YOUR SCORE PLACES YOU MUCH MORE TOWARD THE QUIET END OF THE SCALE. YOUR ANSWERS INDICATED THAT YOU CAN SIT AND RELAX WITHOUT FEELING UNCOMFORTABLE THAT YOU ARE NOT ON-THE-GO. SCORES TOWARD THE QUIET END ARE RELATED TO PREFERENCES FOR LESS VIGOROUS ACTIVITIES, SUCH AS READING, BUILDING MODELS, OR SITTING AND TALKING WITH FRIENDS ON A FREE WEEKEND. IN CONTRAST, PEOPLE WITH VERY HIGH SCORES ON THIS SCALE INDICATE MORE OF A LIKING FOR BEING A PARTICIPANT IN ACTIVE SPORTS RATHER THAN A SPECTATOR, OR BEING ACTIVE ON A VACATION RATHER THAN RESTING AND RELAXING. YOU PROBABLY WOULD NOT MIND WORKING AT A DESK FOR LONG PERIODS OF TIME OR A HOBBY THAT REQUIRES A GREAT DEAL OF SITTING STILL. GENERALLY, HIGHER SCORES TEND TO OCCUR FOR HIGH SCHOOL STUDENTS AND LOWER SCORES FOR ADULTS, BUT THERE IS A WIDE RANGE OF INDIVIDUAL DIFFERENCES FOR EACH AGE.

```
* * * * * * * * * * * * * * * *
* * * * * * * * * * * * *
* * * *           * * * *
* * * *  REWARD VALUES  * * * *
* * * *           * * * *
* * * * * * * * * * * * *
* * * * * * * * * * * * * * * *
```

THE SCALES GROUPED UNDER THIS HEADING OF REWARD VALUES MEASURE WHAT ASPECTS OF A JOB OR CAREER YOU WILL FIND REWARDING, THAT IS, WHAT ACTIVITIES OR SITUATIONS YOU ENJOY OR FEEL ARE IMPORTANT. IMMEDIATELY BELOW ARE YOUR SCORES -- LISTED FROM HIGH TO LOW -- ON THE SEVEN REWARD VALUE SCALES. AS BEFORE, THERE ARE NO GOOD OR BAD SCORES. YOUR SCORES ARE BASED ON COMPARING YOUR ANSWERS TO THE ANSWERS OF GROUPS OF FEMALES AND MALES IN A GENERAL POPULATION. FOR SOME SCALES, FEMALES AND MALES RESPOND SOMEWHAT DIFFERENTLY, AS DO DIFFERENT AGE GROUPS. FOR EACH OF THE SEVEN SCALES THERE IS A RANGE OF DOTS ON THE PROFILE BELOW WHICH SHOWS THE AVERAGE RANGE OF SCORES OF INDIVIDUALS IN A GENERAL POPULATION.

SCALE	YOUR SCORE	3	4	5	6	7
		....0.........0.........0.........0.........0.....				
LEADERSHIP	75					*
MANAGERIAL/SALES BENEFITS	60				*	
SOCIAL RECOGNITION	56			.*.		
WORK INDEPENDENCE	49			.*.		
PHILOSOPHICAL CURIOSITY	48			*.		
TASK SPECIFICITY	40		*			
SOCIAL SERVICE	23	*				

FOR EACH SCALE, A SCORE OF 50 IS THE OVERALL AVERAGE FOR A GROUP OF FEMALES AND MALES IN A GENERAL POPULATION. SCORES GREATER THAN 50 INDICATE THAT, BASED ON YOUR RESPONSES TO THE INVENTORY, YOU PLACE MORE IMPORTANCE ON THAT PARTICULAR AREA THAN MOST PEOPLE. SCORES LESS THAN 50 INDICATE THAT YOU PLACE LESS IMPORTANCE ON THAT AREA THAN MOST PEOPLE. GENERALLY, MOST INDIVIDUALS WILL HAVE A HIGH SCORE ON ONE, TWO, OR EVEN THREE AREAS. OCCASIONALLY, SOME INDIVIDUALS WILL FIND NONE OF THE SEVEN AREAS PARTICULARLY IMPORTANT TO THEM AND THEY SCORE LOW ON ALL SEVEN SCALES, WHILE OTHER INDIVIDUALS WILL FIND ALL AREAS REWARDING AND WILL SCORE HIGH ON ALL SCALES.

BELOW ARE YOUR SCORES ON EACH OF THE SEVEN SCALES AND DESCRIPTIONS WHICH WILL HELP YOU TO UNDERSTAND BETTER WHAT EACH SCALE MEASURES. THESE DESCRIPTIONS ARE BASED ON RESEARCH STUDIES AND WHILE ALL THE DESCRIPTIONS MAY NOT EXACTLY FIT ANY SINGLE INDIVIDUAL, THEY DO POINT OUT THE TRENDS THAT ARE RELATED TO YOUR SCORES.

75 LEADERSHIP----------------------COMPARED TO FEMALES AND MALES IN A GENERAL POPULATION, YOUR SCORE ON THE LEADERSHIP SCALE IS A VERY HIGH SCORE. YOUR SCORE INDICATES THAT DIRECTING AND LEADING PEOPLE, BEING RESPONSIBLE FOR HIRING AND FIRING PEOPLE, BEING RESPONSIBLE FOR MAKING MAJOR DECISIONS, AND BEING AN AUTHORITY IN YOUR FIELD ARE ALL QUITE IMPORTANT TO YOU. RELATED TO HIGH SCORES ARE INTERESTS IN PUBLIC SPEAKING, BUSINESS MANAGEMENT ACTIVITIES, AND MANAGERIAL-SUPERVISORY TYPES OF OCCUPATIONS SUCH AS CREDIT MANAGER, PERSONNEL DIRECTOR, STORE MANAGER, INN-KEEPER, SCHOOL SUPERINTENDENT, AND MILITARY OFFICER. HIGH SCORES ARE RELATED TO DESCRIPTIONS SUCH AS PERSUASIVE, FORCEFUL, COMPETITIVE, AND FRANK. IN GENERAL, MALES TEND TO HAVE HIGHER SCORES IN THIS AREA THAN DO FEMALES, AND OLDER ADULTS PLACE MORE IMPORTANCE ON THIS AREA THAN DO YOUNGER ADULTS -- HOWEVER, THERE ARE WIDE INDIVIDUAL DIFFERENCES FOR EACH GROUP.

60 MANAGERIAL/SALES BENEFITS------COMPARED TO FEMALES AND MALES IN A GENERAL POPULATION, YOUR SCORE INDICATES THAT YOU PLACE A HIGH VALUE ON FRINGE BENEFITS -- THE TYPES OF REWARDS THAT ARE ASSOCIATED WITH MANAGERIAL, SALES, AND EXECUTIVE TYPES OF POSITIONS. FOR EXAMPLE, YOUR SCORE INDICATES THAT SPENDING MONEY FREELY, HAVING BUSINESS LUNCHEONS SEVERAL TIMES A WEEK, A LARGE YEARLY PAY BONUS, A JOB WITH SHORT WORKING HOURS, AND A JOB WITH MANY EXTRA FRINGE BENEFITS ARE ALL QUITE IMPORTANT TO YOU. THESE TYPES OF VALUES ARE RELATED TO INTERESTS IN OCCUPATIONS THAT ARE SALES-ORIENTED, SUCH AS BUYER OR REALTOR, OR BUSINESS-ORIENTED, SUCH AS SALES MANAGER, HOTEL MANAGER, OR TRAVEL BUREAU AGENT. IN CONTRAST, LOW SCORES INDICATE THAT THESE TYPES OF JOB BENE-FITS ARE NOT AS IMPORTANT. FREQUENTLY, LOW SCORES ARE RELATED TO INTERESTS IN SKILLED TRADES WORK, MECHANICAL ACTIVITIES, MILITARY OCCUPATIONS, OR SCIENTIFIC-LABORATORY RESEARCH WORK WHERE MANAGERIAL/SALES BENEFITS OCCUR INFREQUENTLY, AND THUS ARE LESS OF A CONCERN.

56 SOCIAL RECOGNITION-------------COMPARED TO FEMALES AND MALES IN A GENERAL POPULATION, YOUR SCORE IS IN THE HIGH AVERAGE RANGE. THIS INDICATES THAT YOU ARE SENSITIVE TO WHAT OTHER PEOPLE SAY AND THINK ABOUT YOU, AND IT IS IMPORTANT TO YOU TO BE LIKED AND BE RESPECTED. FOR EXAMPLE, YOU PROBABLY LIKE OTHER PEOPLE TO ASK FOR YOUR ADVICE, TO BE FRIENDLY TOWARD YOU, TO DEPEND UPON YOU, AND TO HAVE RESPECT FOR YOU. OTHER CHARACTERISTICS OF PEOPLE WHO HAVE VERY HIGH SCORES ARE TO ASSOCIATE WITH FAMOUS PEOPLE, TO BE ADMIRED BY PEOPLE, TO BE SPOKEN WELL OF IN THE COMMUNITY, TO MEET FRIENDS SEVERAL TIMES A WEEK FOR LUNCH, AND TO KNOW A LARGE NUMBER OF PEOPLE. THESE ARE TYPES OF NEEDS ASSOCIATED WITH INTEREST IN ENTERPRISING/BUSINESS OCCUPATIONS, SUCH AS SALES, SCHOOL SUPERINTENDENT, PUBLIC ADMINISTRATOR, AND SO FORTH. MOST PEOPLE LIKE SOME SORT OF SOCIAL RECOGNITION, AND YOUR SCORE SUGGESTS THAT THIS IS QUITE IMPORTANT TO YOU.

49 WORK INDEPENDENCE-------------COMPARED TO FEMALES AND MALES IN A GENERAL POPULATION, YOUR SCORE IS IN THE AVERAGE RANGE. THIS SCALE COVERS SUCH THINGS AS BEING YOUR OWN BOSS, ESTABLISH-ING YOUR OWN SCHEDULE FOR DOING TASKS, WORKING WITH LITTLE SUPERVISION, HAVING FREEDOM TO COME AND GO AS YOU PLEASE, BEING ABLE TO DECIDE WHICH PARTS OF A JOB SHOULD BE GIVEN THE MOST TIME, AND GENERALLY, TO DO THE JOB AS YOU FEEL IT SHOULD BE DONE. YOUR SCORE INDICATES THAT, OVERALL, YOU PLACE SOME IMPORTANCE ON HAVING INDEPENDENCE IN YOUR WORK, BUT IT IS NOT AS IMPORTANT TO YOU AS IT IS FOR SOMEONE WHO SCORES VERY HIGH ON THIS SCALE. USUALLY THIS AREA TENDS TO BE MORE IM-PORTANT FOR OLDER ADULTS THAN FOR HIGH SCHOOL STUDENTS AND YOUNG ADULTS WHO ARE ESTABLISHING A CAREER. YOUR SCORE INDICATES THAT YOU PLACE SOME IMPORTANCE ON WORK INDEPENDENCE, BUT YOU PROB-ABLY COULD ADJUST TO OTHER SCHEDULES AND ROUTINES WITHOUT FEELING UNCOMFORTABLE ABOUT IT.

48 PHILOSOPHICAL CURIOSITY------COMPARED TO FEMALES AND MALES IN A GENERAL POPULATION, YOUR SCORE INDICATES THAT YOU PLACE SOME IMPORTANCE ON THIS AREA, BUT NOT AS MUCH AS MOST PEOPLE DO. THIS WIDE AREA COVERS SUCH THINGS AS TRYING TO UNDERSTAND THE LAWS OF NATURE, BEING A CREATIVE PERSON, READING BOOKS ABOUT THE MEANING OF LIFE, ADDING TO YOUR CULTURAL HERITAGE, PRODUCING A WORK OF ART, MAKING A SCIENTIFIC DISCOVERY, AND QUESTIONING THE BELIEFS OF SOCIETY -- YOUR SCORE INDICATES THAT SOME OF THESE AREAS PROBABLY ARE MORE IMPORTANT TO YOU THAN OTHER AREAS. HIGH SCORES TEND TO BE RELATED TO INTEREST IN CULTURAL OCCUPATIONS, SUCH AS LIBRARIAN, TO SCIENTIFIC-SERVICE OCCUPATIONS, SUCH AS DIETITIAN AND SPEECH PATHOLOGIST, AND TO SOCIAL-SERVICE OCCUPATIONS SUCH AS PRIEST, MINISTER, SOCIAL WORKER, AND GUIDANCE COUNSELOR. IN CONTRAST, LOW SCORES TEND TO BE RELATED MORE TO INTERESTS IN OCCUPATIONS NOT DIRECTLY INVOLVED WITH CULTURAL CONCERNS, SUCH AS VETERINARIAN, FARMER, OR SKILLED TRADES.

40 TASK SPECIFICITY------COMPARED TO FEMALES AND MALES IN A GENERAL POPULATION, YOUR SCORE INDICATES THAT YOU DO NOT PLACE AS MUCH IMPORTANCE ON THE TASK SPECIFICITY AREA AS DO MOST PEOPLE. THIS AREA COVERS SUCH THINGS AS WORKING ON A PROBLEM THAT HAS A CORRECT SOLUTION, BEING ABLE TO CHECK YOUR WORK IN DETAIL, KNOWING EXACTLY WHAT IS EXPECTED OF YOU BY YOUR SUPERVISOR, AND WORKING AT A JOB WHERE YOU CAN SEE WHAT YOU HAVE DONE AT THE END OF THE DAY, SUCH AS NUMBER OF LETTERS TYPED, OR MACHINES FIXED, OR PEOPLE SEEN. OVERALL, YOUR SCORE INDICATES THAT WHILE SOME OF THESE AREAS MAY BE IMPORTANT TO YOU, YOU PROBABLY WOULD PREFER MORE FLEXIBILITY OR FREE-DOM IN THE WAY YOU DO A TASK. FOR EXAMPLE, YOU MAY LIKE TO WORK PROBLEMS WHICH DO NOT HAVE A CORRECT SOLUTION, AND SOLVING THEM IN YOUR OWN WAY WOULD BE IMPORTANT. SCORES SIMILAR TO YOURS FREQUENTLY ARE RELATED TO SCIENTIFIC, INVESTIGATIVE INTERESTS SUCH AS RESEARCH.

23 SOCIAL SERVICE------COMPARED TO FEMALES AND MALES IN A GENERAL POPULATION, YOUR SCORE IS IN THE LOW RANGE OF SCORES. YOUR SCORE IS SIMILAR TO INDIVIDUALS WHO FEEL THAT SOCIAL SERVICE TYPES OF ACTIVITIES ARE NOT VERY REWARDING TO THEM. IT DOES NOT SAY ANYTHING ABOUT YOUR WILLINGNESS TO GIVE HELP WHEN NEEDED, BUT RATHER WHETHER IT IS A MAJOR DAY-TO-DAY CONCERN IN YOUR LIFE. INDIVIDUALS WHO VALUE THIS AREA VERY HIGHLY TEND TO HAVE INTERESTS IN SOCIAL AND MEDICAL TYPES OF ACTIVITIES AND OCCUPATIONS, SUCH AS TEACHER, NURSE, OR SOCIAL WORKER. IN GEN-ERAL, HIGH SCHOOL STUDENTS FEEL THAT THIS AREA IS SLIGHTLY MORE REWARDING TO THEM THAN ADULTS DO, AND FEMALES TEND TO HAVE CONSIDERABLY HIGHER SCORES ON THIS SCALE THAN MALES DO -- HOWEVER, THERE ARE WIDE INDIVIDUAL DIFFERENCES FOR EACH GROUP.

NAME: SAMPLE   S   ID: DATE: 30-SEP-83   PAGE: 8

THE TABLE BELOW INDICATES RESPONSE PERCENTAGES FOR EACH OF THE THREE SECTIONS OF THE INVEN-
TORY. THE FIRST SECTION OF THE INVENTORY LISTED VARIOUS ACTIVITIES AND IDEAS AND YOU WERE TO
INDICATE WHICH YOU FELT WERE VERY IMPORTANT (VI), IMPORTANT (I), NEUTRAL (N), UNIMPORTANT (U),
OR VERY UNIMPORTANT (VU) TO YOU. FOR EXAMPLE, THE VI NUMBER INDICATES THE PERCENTAGE OF ITEMS
YOU FOUND TO BE VERY IMPORTANT TO YOU. IN SECTION TWO, THE FORMAT WAS SIMILAR, BUT YOU WERE TO
INDICATE VERY PLEASANT (VP), PLEASANT (P), NEUTRAL (N), UNPLEASANT (U), OR VERY UNPLEASANT (VU).
SECTION THREE LISTED ACTIVITIES AND CHARACTERISTICS AND YOU WERE TO INDICATE WHICH WERE TRUE (T)
AND WHICH WERE NOT TRUE, FALSE (F), FOR YOU.

THE TOTAL RESPONSES INDEX SHOWS HOW MANY ANSWERS THE COMPUTER READ FROM YOUR INVENTORY.
SINCE THERE ARE 230 ITEMS ON THE INVENTORY, THIS NUMBER SHOULD BE CLOSE TO 230. UP TO 10 ITEMS
CAN BE OMITTED WITHOUT SIGNIFICANTLY AFFECTING THE RESULTS.

---- RESPONSE PERCENTAGES ----

	VI	I	N	U	VU
SECTION I	20	34	27	17	2

	VP	P	N	U	VU
SECTION II	19	29	16	13	23

	T	F
SECTION III	44	56

TOTAL RESPONSES= 228

* *

YOUR SCORES HAVE BEEN EVALUATED OVER A WIDE RANGE OF SELF-DESCRIPTIONS AND GENERAL VALUES.
REMEMBER, THESE ARE MEASURES OF HOW YOU ANSWERED THE INVENTORY AND HOW YOUR ANSWERS COMPARED TO
THE AVERAGE RESPONSES OF FEMALES AND MALES IN A GENERAL POPULATION. YOU SHOULD USE THEM TO HELP
YOU BETTER UNDERSTAND YOURSELF AND HOW YOUR PREFERENCES FIT WITH VARIOUS CAREERS AND SETTINGS.
FOR ADDITIONAL INFORMATION, YOU SHOULD CONSULT A PROFESSIONALLY TRAINED COUNSELOR.

*****END OF REPORT FOR SAMPLE   S   FEMALE   30-SEP-83   002 0039

NAME: SAMPLE   S   ID: DATE: 30-SEP-83   PAGE: 9

************SUMMARY COPY OF RESULTS**********

TEMPERAMENT AND VALUES INVENTORY   002 0039

RESULTS FOR SAMPLE   S   FEMALE

SECTION A. ADMINISTRATIVE INDICES.

---- RESPONSE PERCENTAGES ----

	VI	I	N	U	VU		T	F
SECTION I	20	34	27	17	2	SECTION III	44	56

	VP	P	N	U	VU	
SECTION II	19	29	16	13	23	TOTAL RESPONSES= 228

* *
SECTION B. PERSONAL CHARACTERISTICS SCORES AND PROFILE.

ADJECTIVE DESCRIPTION	YOUR SCORE	3.....0.....4.....0.....5.....0.....6.....0.....7.....0.....	ADJECTIVE DESCRIPTION
RETICENT	63	PERSUASIVE
SERIOUS	54	CHEERFUL
RESERVED	53	SOCIABLE
ROUTINE	50	FLEXIBLE
ATTENTIVE	47	DISTRACTIBLE
CONSISTENT	35	CHANGEABLE
QUIET	29	ACTIVE

THE RANGE OF DOTS FOR EACH SCALE ABOVE INDICATE THE AVERAGE RANGE
OF SCORES IN THE GENERAL POPULATION.

SECTION C.   REWARD VALUES SCORES AND PROFILE.

```
                                  3         4         5         6         7
                         ....0.........0.........0.........0.........0.....
                  YOUR
SCALE             SCORE
LEADERSHIP         75                                                      *
MANAGERIAL/SALES BENEFITS  60                               :::::::::  *
SOCIAL RECOGNITION 56                               ::::::::*
WORK INDEPENDENCE  49                          :::::*:::
PHILOSOPHICAL CURIOSITY  48                          ::::*::::
TASK SPECIFICITY   40                     *    :::::::::
SOCIAL SERVICE     23           *
```

THE RANGE OF DOTS FOR EACH SCALE ABOVE INDICATE THE AVERAGE RANGE
OF SCORES IN THE GENERAL POPULATION.

******END OF SUMMARY REPORT FOR SAMPLE   S   FEMALE   30-SEP-83   002 0039

TEMPERAMENT AND VALUES INVENTORY
BY
DR. CHARLES B. JOHANSSON AND DR. PATRICIA L. WEBBER
NATIONAL COMPUTER SYSTEMS
4401 W. 76TH STREET
MINNEAPOLIS, MN. 55435

NAME: Timeline—Customized Time Management

SUPPLIER: Institute for Personality and Ability Testing, Inc.
P.O. Box 188
Champaign, IL 61820
(217) 352-4739

PRODUCT CATEGORY	PRIMARY APPLICATIONS
Interest/Attitudes	Training/Development

SALE RESTRICTIONS Authorized/Certified Representatives

SERVICE TYPE/COST	Type	Available	Cost	Discount
	Mail-In	Yes	$30.00	
	Teleprocessing	No		
	Local	No		

PRODUCT DESCRIPTION

TIMELINE for Personal Productivity offers a novel approach to personal time management skills. Designed for use in on-the-job settings, it can be administered by specialists from the human resources, personnel, or staff development areas as a part of ongoing training and development programs. TIMELINE can also be integrated with organizational team-building activities.

TIMELINE values the idea that people should be in control of their own situation. The program injects a ʹpersonal uniquenessʹ perspective into standard time management training modes. Using a combination of personal insights and sound step-by-step exercises, participants learn how to improve their time management skills effectively.

The workbook format of the program is individually developed for each participant. This is made possible through computerized analysis of the 16 PF and a Skills Assessment Inventory. The TIMELINE trainer's manual explains how to adapt the individual's learning process into group discussion format.

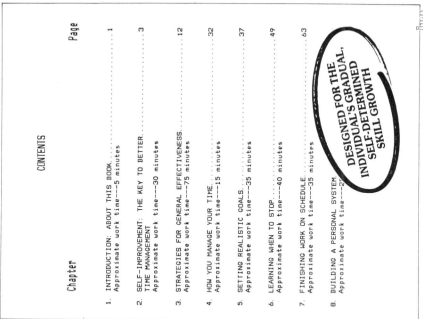

CONTENTS

Chapter   Page

DESIGNED FOR THE INDIVIDUAL'S GRADUAL, SELF-DETERMINED SKILL GROWTH

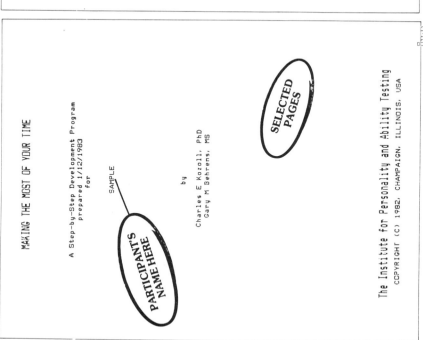

MAKING THE MOST OF YOUR TIME

A Step-by-Step Development Program
prepared 1/12/1983
for

SAMPLE

PARTICIPANT'S NAME HERE

by

Charles E Kozoll, PhD
Gary M Behrens, MS

SELECTED PAGES

The Institute for Personality and Ability Testing

1. INTRODUCTION: ABOUT THIS BOOK

SUMMARIZES CHAPTER CONTENT

This book promises you something that no other book or course about time management can match. It will help you improve your use of time in a way that is of most benefit to you alone. By that we mean the way which best fits your own special needs and objectives.

No one else has a book quite like the one you're holding now. It was prepared just for you from information you provided when you answered the questionnaire earlier. We have taken what you said about yourself and used it to create a unique workbook, one that will work best for you.

* In Chapter 2, you'll learn more about what's involved in successfully improving upon your ability to manage time.

* In Chapter 3, you'll discover some simple, but effective, general techniques that you can use every day to manage your time more effectively.

* In Chapter 4, you'll find out where you stand in terms of your current time management skills.

EASY-TO-FOLLOW STEPS TO BETTER CONCENTRATION AND DISTRESS CONTROL

3. STRATEGIES FOR GENERAL EFFECTIVENESS

In the last chapter, you learned something about the requirements for successful growth and change. Now you have a chance to find out how the TimeLine program works in practice. This chapter directs your attention to a couple of areas that seem to give everybody problems.

One of these has to do with conscious efforts at concentration. At nearly every seminar on time management, someone complains about the inability to concentrate. This is actually a very common problem and is one shared by individuals at all levels of organization and across occupations as well.

Most people can tell what it is that prevents them from giving a single task their full and undivided attention. Few understand how to achieve intense concentration in spite of distractions. So, the first part of this chapter suggests a routine that can make concentration a habit that is easily employed.

Handling stress associated with the pace of each day is another concern that seminar participants regularly express. As pressure builds, productivity declines and normally competent, self-confident individuals may feel powerless to control the drift of events.

Everyone experiences such a stressful reaction from time to time. By learning to deal with it, the negative effects can be minimized. The second part in the chapter shows you how to relieve some of the pressure and thus preserve control.

Actual Proficiency in Five Areas
Of Time Management

       10   20   30   40   50   60   70   80   90   100%

Setting Goals

Completing Tasks

Handling Demands

Planning Routines

Recognizing Limits

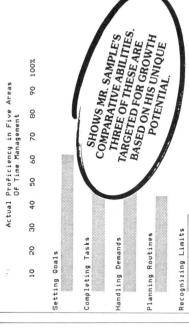

SHOWS MR. SAMPLE'S COMPARATIVE ABILITIES. THREE OF THESE ARE TARGETED FOR GROWTH BASED ON HIS UNIQUE POTENTIAL.

Right now it appears that your top strength is in the area of setting goals. You tend to utilize this skill at about 63% of maximum proficiency. Your next best strength, completing tasks falls at around a 54% proficiency level. For your remaining strengths, the approximate ratings are 54%, 45%, and 36%, in order of proficiency.

WHERE TO TARGET YOUR ATTENTION

As you learned in the previous section, you have a range of existing time management strengths. Some of these are more susceptible to improvement than others. Remember, however, that successful self-improvement depends on realistic, controlled development of new and better habits.

Your total strength profile suggests that you might profit from efforts to upgrade those skills that are pretty much established, but perhaps not yet refined enough to balance the picture completely. In your case, that means putting energy into advanced skills for completing tasks and handling demands.

To help you do this, we've grouped together a few step-by-step techniques that offer you the best chance of making significant strides in your management of time. The next few chapters of this book contain these techniques. They are titled:

---

4. HOW YOU MANAGE YOUR TIME

EXPLAINS MEASURED CONCEPTS AND PROVIDES PERSONAL RESULTS

INTRODUCTION

Effective time management is really just a set of skills. These skills can be developed through practicing certain techniques, just like learning to dance or ride a bicycle. With enough practice, the techniques eventually become habits——unconscious behavior patterns that guide us through the necessary motions of some activity.

Typically, time management skills are not taught to us by anyone as part of our growing up experiences or formal education. Rather, each person just picks up the habits along the way and adapts them to a personal style of managing time. Since the skills have not been carefully explained and coached, some undesirable habits are bound to emerge. Even so, everyone has at least some degree of skill and perhaps other special assets that make better time management possible.

The aim of this program is to help you build from identified strengths so that you can increase your personal effectiveness further. A little later you will learn about techniques that can enable you to meet specific challenges you may face. But first,

Before you begin Chapter 5, let's briefly review some of the answers you gave to the questionnaire items in order to establish a personal data base for building up your time management ability. As the graph on page 35 showed, goal setting is one out of the five areas in which you've already made important gains. Let's see what you said.

You tend to keep routine matters in perspective and not let them obscure the importance of other efforts that may have greater long term impact.

Unlike many people, you're generally able to find enough challenge in your daily activities to sustain your enthusiasm.

You typically put your main concerns foremost and don't allow your attention to wander very far from them.

You actively seek out opportunities to pursue well-defined developmental goals.

For the most part you're open to suggestions for improving upon current methods or results.

Think of these 5 items as resources, or personal growth assets, that could act as springboards for the techniques we'll explain in this chapter. When you've studied the material on the next 10 pages, you might want to come back to this page and see whether defining closer targets, for example, like those we discuss on page 44 might not be exactly the sort of thing you could effectively apply in capitalizing upon these personal resources.

PERSONAL FEEDBACK HELPS MR. SAMPLE ASSESS UTILITY OF TECHNIQUES, SUPPORTIVE OR CHALLENGING IN TONE AS MERITED BY EACH CASE.

5. GIVING WORK PROPER EMPHASIS

WHAT THIS CHAPTER IS ABOUT

This chapter covers techniques for control. If you often get that, "What next?" feeling, they may be a start in the right direction. Using one or more of the techniques will help you put a damper on reflex actions.

To that end, a method is presented that can help you sort out your priorities. To go along with this activity are a couple techniques that show you how to better regulate demands and turn down unimportant requests.

With these and other techniques at your fingertips, you can be in command of events rather than letting events command you.

CHAPTERS 5 TO 7 CONTAIN STEP-BY-STEP TECHNIQUES THAT ADDRESS MR. SAMPLE'S SPECIFIC TIME MANAGEMENT NEEDS.

double and triple "A's" are cut out. An ability to judge
levels of importance and place emphasis where needed grows.
So as you complete the steps in this chapter, think about
these tangible benefits they can offer you.

ACTION PLAN #1   ASSIGN TRUE PRIORITIES

     "Everything is on 'A' for right now" is a complaint
heard much too often. Those who work for or provide support to several managers can speak volumes about how much
tasks compete for attention. "I have three supervisors
for my different projects," an analyst, for example, com-
plained. "Each one maintains that his or hers is the most
important. So they all want theirs done first."

     Th~~~   ~listic. Only one task at a
t   ~now what to do first?
                          ~e at all identified?
                          ~ of the conflicts and
                          s produce?

                          shortly involves a com-
                          , and firmly. You will
                          ~g items and identify
                          ~ddition to benefiting you
                          you make others more sensitive
sugg~~~ ~ ~~~~ ~~~~peting priorities create. You can
suggest a more honest evaluation on their part of the
attention that each task deserves.

          <Step 1>   Examine your job description once again to
                     to be certain about your primary responsi-
                     bilities. As the beginning step to the days
                     on which this procedure will be used, list
                     the tasks you feel should be done in the
                     space below. The emphasis is on what should
                     be done!

                     a. _____
                     b. _____
                     c. _____
                     d. _____
                     e. _____

MR. SAMPLE CAN CHOOSE TO ADAPT ONE OR MORE OF THE TECHNIQUES TO FIT HIS OWN STYLE.

NAME: TRACK

SUPPLIER: TRACOM Corporation
200 Fillmore Street
Denver, CO 80206
(303) 388-5451

PRODUCT CATEGORY	PRIMARY APPLICATIONS
Career/Vocational	Personnel Selection/Evaluation Training/Development

SALE RESTRICTIONS   None

SERVICE TYPE/COST Type	Available	Cost	Discount
Mail-In	No		
Teleprocessing	No		
Local	Yes	See Below	

PRODUCT DESCRIPTION

TRACK has been designed as a total career performance system. It begins with a job candidate at the recruiting stage and follows the person throughout the selection process. Once the person is hired, TRACK continues in a monitoring mode through performance feedback reports.

TRACK takes advantage of a handheld computer that provides immediate recording/scoring of recruiting, testing, referencing, and interviewing information. The small computer provides portability and convenience for the recruiter. Its information can then be transferred to a mainframe to accumulate the data base over time and to provide a series of management reports. The complete TRACK system also provides videotapes for interview training, instructional guidebooks for training documentation, and other support services and products.

To date, this supplier has concentrated on making this system available to the life insurance industry. Because each company tends to have unique needs, consultation is normally required to customize the system for that company. The cost of the program is dependent upon the amount of customization required.

NAME: Training/Development Report for Direct Sales Personnel

SUPPLIER: Behavioral Science Research Press
695 Villa Creek Suite 180
Dallas, TX 75234
(214) 243-8543

PRODUCT CATEGORY	PRIMARY APPLICATIONS
Career/Vocational	Vocational Guidance/Counseling
Interest/Attitudes	Personnel Selection/Evaluation
Motivation/Needs	Training/Development

SALE RESTRICTIONS None

SERVICE TYPE/COST	Type	Available	Cost	Discount
	Mail-In	Yes	$50.00	Yes
	Teleprocessing	No		
	Local	No		

PRODUCT DESCRIPTION

The TRAINING/DEVELOPMENT REPORT FOR DIRECT SALES PERSONNEL is designed to provide rapid access to practical information derived from formal 16 PF instrumentation. Contents are based on more than ten years of data collection from rational and empirical sources. Printouts are not static. Improvements, reflecting successful research projects or new information from other sources, are integrated into the program as they become available.

Only topics important to managing direct sales people are reported. Presently, there are 23 areas including Time Management, Management of Frustration, Ability to Emotionally Manage a Commision Based Income, Learning, Selling Style, Sales Motivation, Optimum Teaching Strategies, Clientele-Building, and Attitude Toward the Test. Potential problems in critical areas such as Call Reluctance` and Close-Reluctance` are also reported when appropriate.

PERSONAL & CONFIDENTIAL

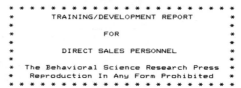

```
* * * * * * * * * * * * * * * * * * * * *
*                                         *
*       TRAINING/DEVELOPMENT REPORT       *
*                                         *
*                 FOR                     *
*                                         *
*         DIRECT SALES PERSONNEL          *
*                                         *
*   The Behavioral Science Research Press *
*    Reproduction In Any Form Prohibited  *
* * * * * * * * * * * * * * * * * * * * *
```

        The contents of this report is based upon information gathered over a
ten-year period from three sources: 1)The informal observations of practicing
sales managers, 2)The formal observations of professionally trained behavioral
scientists, and, 3)Formal statistical studies conducted according to generally
accepted methodologies for empirical research.

                    ++++++++++++++++++++++++++

==>> All measurements are inexact. Errors are made by the most technically
advanced measurement instruments. Formally constructed, rigorously developed
personality tests are technically sophisticated measurement devices, and, as
such, are also subject to error. The test upon which THE TRAINING/DEVELOPMENT
REPORT is based is no exception. Although it represents a very long and
distinguished tradition of research and development, it still remains
vulnerable to error. Therefore, well-intended managers will learn to use the
results wisely...as training and development hypotheses, and not as
hard-and-fast impersonal conclusions to be imposed upon the lives and careers
of other people.

                    ++++++++++++++++++++++++++

==>>This report is intended to be confidential. Access to, or discussions
about test-derived information should be restricted to the individual who
completed the test and other members of the management staff who have a
genuine "need-to-know".

Sample

----

698 *psychware*

This sales person's scores do not indicate unusually high or low impression-management behavior. The actual amount detected falls within the typical range for most direct salespeople. This indicates that the test was administered properly, and that the salesperson's attitude towards taking the test was sufficiently cooperative. Therefore, the training and development considerations that follow can be assumed to be acceptably accurate representations of this individual's probable sales behaviors. Each individual section should be sensitively reviewed with the salesperson, however, to help determine the areas where the information is most accurate (in his or her opinion), and where it can be put to the most immediate use.

SECTION I.   ATTITUDE TOWARDS THE MANAGEMENT OF PERSONAL FINANCES

Test scores indicate that this individual can be expected to apply a satisfactory amount of attention to the management of personal finances. "Impulse-control" problems, which create financial difficulties for some sales people, does NOT appear to be a problem in this individual at the present time.

This should not be taken to mean that personal money management could NEVER become a problem. It does mean that personal money management does not appear to require PRIORITY training attention at the present time. You should be free, therefore, to concentrate training attention and resources on more immediately pressing areas (see other sections).

SECTION II.   MANAGEMENT OF A COMMISSION-BASED INCOME

No training problems directly related to the management of a commission-based income are indicated at this time. However, the absence of negatives does not necessarily imply the presence of clear-cut strengths. Therefore, the manager should carefully examine non-test sources such as appropriate financial records to assure himself that this is not a vulnerable area.

SECTION III.   CLIENTELE-BUILDLING

This individual could find prospecting and related clientele-building or business-promotion activities among the LEAST enjoyable aspects of the career. As a consequence, considerable amounts of self-discipline may be required to "force" initiating contact with prospective buyers. There may be some question as to whether the financial return is worth the EMOTIONAL investment.

Call-Reluctance, frequent episodes of career burn out, and production plateaus are three by-products of this problem when it occurs. FAST, NON-SUPERFICIAL, INTERVENTION IS IMPERATIVE IF THE PROBLEM EXISTS NOW, OR DEVELOPS INTO AN ACTIVITY-LIMITING PROBLEM IN THE FUTURE.
....
Action Plan...

1. Try using "Interpersonal Skills Training" procedures to increase social self-confidence. Several good commercial programs are available from sources such as Xerox Learning Systems, Wilson Learning, Style Awareness Training (Tracom), and Consultative Selling skills (Systema).

psychware **699**

2. Role-playing demonstrations and simulations, where you can observe
and provide support, may help this individual enlarge the interpersonal
"reach" of his sales presentations. This should help to increase
self-confidence, product knowledge, and social poise. But, be careful.
For this to work, you must introduce the role-playing simulations GRADUALLY,
according to a well-thought out plan of action. (Role-playing, and other forms
of learning based upon interpersonal simulations, may NOT have automatic
credibility or acceptance to this individual. So, provide enough "warm-up"
time for these learning experiences to be seen as positive, worthwhile, and
non-threatening.)

3. Try professionally developed intervention formats such as P-E-P
(Prospecting Enhancement Program). It was derived from The Call-Reluctance
Clinic format which was specifically designed to help managers
prevent or correct sales activity-limiting problems and can be easily
integrated into the regular sales training curriculum. (P-E-P and
Call-Relucance Clinics are available from Dynamis Corporation.)

This individual may tend to spend excessive time PREPARING to make sales
presentations. He, or she, may arrive at the office earliest, and stay latest.
But, you should not confuse OVER-ACTIVITY with productivity. Compulsive
over-preparation, when it is observed, can signal the onset of
call-reluctance and other problems related to poor field-self-confidence.

It is critical for you to be able to discuss the possibilities of such a
problem existing now, or developing in the near future, with your sales
person. If true, you must be able to establish a means to deal with it
quickly. TIMING IS CRITICAL.

(Remember, in this case, PREVENTION before the fact is easier, cheaper, and
generally more effective than trying to correct the problem once it has taken
hold.)
....

NOTE: The above holds true only for those cases where technical sales training
HAS BEEN PROVIDED. If sufficient technical training has not been provided in
the product or the sales process, then hesitation and preparation are
appropriate, non-call-reluctant reactions.

===>>>Carefully observe this individual's contact-initiation behaviors for
evidence of call-reluctance.

Some common indicators include, but are not limited to...

1. Evidence of low number of seen calls.
2. Evidence of low number of phone calls.
3. Excessive in-office time.
4. Frequent absenteeism during scheduled prospecting activities.
5. Failure of motivational techniques to improve frequency of contacts.
6. Too much prospecting time wasted listening to "inspirational" tapes.
7. Limiting prospects to low-probability, big-payoff, accounts.
8. Failure to call on certain important and accessible market segments.

If you detect one or more of the above indicators, a quick and effective
training intervention may be called for.

Look for a tendency towards over-preparation and excuse-making in lieu of
results relative to ability. If present, these behaviors could suggest that
your sales person may be experiencing difficulty admitting to the existence
of a career-limiting problem. The problem could be call-reluctance, poor
technical preparation, or unrealistic, self-imposed expectations for
accomplishment.
....

Action Plan....

1. You should encourage your sales person to begin the process of
self-improvement by first admitting to the presence of a career-limiting
problem. THIS IS VERY IMPORTANT. If you don't do this, it's YOUR problem,
not his. Personal responsibility for performance, or lack of it, is the
foundation for ANY successful career or training intervention.

2. You should insist upon weekly minimum production requirements, IN
WRITING, for the duration of a performance problem. Explain why this is
important to your sales person. Emphasize that it is remedial, not
punitive. It is intended to help improve the alignment of performance to
ability.

700 *psychware*

3. PARTICIPATIVELY establish performance objectives. Don't impose them and
then expect cooperation.

4. Consider providing additional training to help develop more confidence
in technical skill areas such as The Approach, Getting Sales Appointments,
Fact-Finding Interviews, Closing Strategies, and Meeting Sales Objectives.
One example of a competency-building program for sales people is Consultative
Selling which is available from SYSTEMA (312-984-5000).

SECTION IV.   TIME MANAGEMENT

Test scores indicate considerable emphasis upon self-management and personal
organization. Goal-setting, and time management disciplines appear to be
higher than usual for most direct sales people.

This does not mean that problems in this area could never occur. It does mean
that management can direct immediate training/developmental attention and
resources to other, more pressing, needs (see other areas).

SECTION V.   INFORMATION MANAGEMENT

SECTION V.1:   LEARNING STYLE AND PACE

This person tends to learn very quickly. Information to be learned will be
SCANNED until INSIGHT is developed into how the various parts fit together.
Insight-oriented, discovery-based learning is the preferred approach to
learning, and you can expect some amount of rebelliousness at efforts to
require rote, mechanical, memorization of material---including sales scripts.

This individual does NOT CONSIDER MEMORIZATION TO BE LEARNING. (Learning is
equated with understanding, not verbatIm recitations.) Sales management
should provide opportunities for accelerated early learning-if possible- but
insist upon accountability for a working knowledge of the material.

Rapid-abstract learners, such as this one, tend to become quickly bored if
the manager progresses too slowly through training material. Boredom may
be coped with by daydreaming, not paying attention, and in general,
developing bad attention habits which may carry over into other areas of the
career.

What to Do...

Be careful not to bore this individual out of the business! Consider early
specialization a possible EARNED reward for willingness to memorize essential
information.

SECTION V.2:   PREPARATION FOR THE SALE

No immediate, performance-imparing problems (related to technical preparation
for the sale) are indicated at the present time. You should confirm this
through discussions, assessments of technical competence, and direct
observation in actual or simulated sales situations.

SECTION V.3:   CONTINUED SELF-DIRECTED EDUCATIONAL GROWTH

Test scores indicate that this individual appears to appreciate the need

for continued professional growth through learning. This inclination is
supported with evidence of willingness to invest sufficient amounts of effort
in continuous, self-directed, career-educational activities.

You should try to confirm this, however, by discussion and direct observation.

This individual may have a strong emotional need for professional
specialization, and an emotional need to be identified with highly
professionalized organizations. Training efforts should recognize this need
and try to be as accomodating as possible. Training materials should
be clearly distinguishable from your competitors in terms of depth and
quality. They should contain thorough and objective information about your
competitors and their products or services. It is important for this
individual to feel associated with an organization which has an
intelligent, professional, "class" image.

If educational background, ability to learn, and willingness to learn support
the desire for specialization, you should direct his or her attention to more
advanced products and markets as soon as technically feasible.

SECTION V.4:   ATTITUDE TOWARDS INSTRUCTION

Scores indicate that this individual may have the tendency to critically
reject efforts to teach and train. This rejection, if it occurs, can take
several forms...none of which, may appear on the surface, to be a simple
rejection of training. Some of the more common forms are:

1.   Excessive questions..often over trivial matters
2.   Defensive reaction to advice...as if it were criticism.
3.   Content control by adding to, subtracting from, or modifying almost every
point you try to make.

This behavior often times in new salesmen is an attempt to hide a fear of
"being average". Consequently, the individual may try to punctuate what you
know (and are trying to teach) by criticism and modification which implies
that he also knows...and that he knows the information so well that he can
amend what you are trying to teach.

You should recognize that the problem is not with the validity of the CONTENT
of the material, but with the emotional AUTHORITY for the teacher to teach.

Try to defer to the individual's need to be seen as knowing much more than the
"average" salesperson. Remember, he will probably not tolerate being dealt
with as if he were "average". Ask for his opinion and do not use categorical
statements when you teach such as "you must do it this way..." Instead, use
conditional statements that leave room for his judgement, such as, "in my
opinion, this is an important method to consider using..." Ask for his
opinion publicly in front of other new salesmen, but never, never criticize
this individual, his judgement, knowledge, or behavior in front of anyone
else.

SECTION V.5:   RECOMMENDED TEACHING STRATEGY(S)

The approach to this individual's early training should emphasize "hands-on"
practical applications. Avoid the over-use of conceptual training because
more value is placed upon knowing what works and how it works than why it
works.

Do not confuse this dimension with the "style of learning" dimension. Style
of learning deals with the PACE of learning, whereas this measure deals with
the preferred METHOD of learning...which in this case, is experience-based.
Trial-and-error learning with immediate feedback and appropriate
reinforcement should help to optimize this individual's learning in the
shortest time possible.

This individual prefers things to be reasonably organized. Training should be
well structured and proceed according to some defined plan. Avoid poorly
organized materials. Some pre-packaged modularly-designed products which are
commercially available may be especially suitable training for this
particular salesperson.

702 *psychware*

LECTURE

ONE-ON-ONE TUTORIALS

PARTICIPATORY EDUCATIONAL PLANNING

SIMULATIONS OF ACTUAL IN-FIELD PROBLEM SITUATIONS

THEORETICAL, DISCOVERY-ORIENTED, DISCUSSIONS OF PROBLEMS AND ISSUES

FREE-FORM, QUESTION AND ANSWER SUMMARIZATIONS AND REVIEW

HIGHLY PERSONALIZED LEARNING PLAN

WELL-STRUCTURED, HIGHLY ORGANIZED CIRRICULA

Sufficient on-the-job training

SECTION V.7:   RECOMMENDED INSTRUCTIONAL SUPPORTS

FREQUENT EXAMPLES

AUDIO/VISUAL SUPPORTS

CHARTS AND GRAPHS

SECTION VI.   SELLING STYLE(S)

This salesperson's selling style will feature patterns of behavior associated
with "PRODUCT-ORIENTED" Selling ("P-O-S").

Sales presentations are likely to emphasize features of the PRODUCT.
Presentation TONE will be educative or INSTRUCTIONAL. The approach will
concentrate most heavily upon "fact-finding" and other information-exchanging
sales interview procedures.

Selling, to this individual, is approached primarily as a prospective BUSINESS
TRANSACTION. Informational content and product features are emphasized.
Typically, there is little reliance upon, or use of emotionalism,
sensationalism, or aggressive-persuasive tactics. The tendency to center the
presentation around product knowledge, may be accompanied by rejecting some
subtle, but important, interpersonal dimensions. Interpersonal,
"rapport-oriented", strategies, may be discounted as inappropriate or
unnecessary.
. . . .

Sales training suggestions...

1. You should provide this sales person frequent, non-threatening,
opportunities to observe alternative selling methods in practice.

psychware   **703**

2. The use of audio/video-based "experiential" training programs are NOT RECOMMENDED for use with this sales person. Adequate preliminary "ground work" must precede their use. "Tough-minded Realism", a benchmark characteristic of this selling style, may incline this individual to DOUBT that these "packaged" programs have any real value or relevancy. Such an attitude, if present, would effectivly neutralize any positive contribution the programs could make.

3. You should explain WHY improving interpersonal skills could be important to goals that are important TO YOUR SALES PERSON. Structured, non-threatening, performance reviews are recommended settings for this discussion.

This individual's selling behavior features a concentration of initiative upon "merchandising" and "packaging" a professional self-image. Personal efforts concentrate on developing professional presentations and acquiring high-level presentation supports. This style is called Image-Oriented Selling ("I-O-S") because the behavioral emphasis is placed upon the management of a professional image.
....

Typically, presentations will feature references to authority figures, "third-party" authoritative sources of information (such as journals), or recognized community leaders. Technical jargon tends to be used more for effect than for instruction.

Personal appearance tends to be carefully orchestrated to reflect a professional image of refined taste, intellectual power, and internal strength of character. This may include wearing designer clothes (The "Dress For Success" Syndrome), prominently displaying professional certificates or awards, or investing in "simple, but elegant", business cards which are easily d istinquishable from competitors.
....

NEVER belittle or ridicule your sales person's efforts to "stand out". Heavy financial and emotional investments may have been made in the symbols used to merchandise the image of ability and accomplishment.
....

==>>SPECIAL NOTE: NEVER, EVER, ADVISE, CRITICIZE, OR CORRECT THIS INDIVIDUAL IN FRONT OF OTHER PEOPLE. Always do so only when it is necessary, and always ONE-ON-ONE, in a closed office.

Remember, this individual's selling style centers around the maintenance of a professional IMAGE (as opposed to Close-Centered, Product-Centered, or Relationship-Centered Selling Styles).

SPECIAL NOTE: To the untrained eye, this style is often mistaken for high dominance, which it is not. Image-Oriented sales people MAY also be highly dominant, but not necessarily so. High dominance and Image-Orientation are two distinct behavioral systems.

This individual's Selling Style is rational-instructive. It is focused upon identifying PROBLEMS which, then, can be solved through using the product or service being promoted. Selling consists of teaching the prospective buyer how using the product (or service) reduces or eliminates the problem. This method, like Product-Oriented Selling ("P-O-S"), is explanation-bound. The explanation is directed towards the identification of needs and the solution of problems. ("P-O-S" is product/specification-bound). This style is called "Needs-Oriented Selling" ("N-O-S").

Typically, Needs-Oriented Salespeople ASSUME that REASONABLE (rational) people will ACT on the INFORMATION which has been provided. Highly interpersonal, or emotional, or manipulative approaches may not be considered worthy, necessary, or professional by this individual. "Good products, intelligently presented, to reasonable people", are presumed to be able to "sell themselves".
....

Your sales person may be most effective using this strategy one-on-one.

You should be prepared to discuss the strengths and weaknesses of this approach to sales with your salesperson. Discuss openly how this philosophy could be career-limiting (people do not always do what is reasonable).

Point out that it can be as inflexible as some of the more promotional alternative styles if it fails to meet the needs of those consumers who WANT more than product knowledge.

Test scores indicate the presence of the following motivational themes:

Individuality

Need to be treated with dignity and respect

Need for orderliness and predictable routine

Competition

To be alert to danger

Worst-case preparation against harm

To establish empathetic warm regard

Pragmatic incomplexity

Continuity with tradition

Acceptance and Belonging

Esteem

Recognition for accomplishment

Security

SECTION VII. PRIMARY MOTIVATION(S) TO SELL

This sales person is motivated by a strong sense of personal values and the
need to be of SERVICE to other people. You can expect intense, active,
involvement with the things which your sales person is most convicted about
and COMMITTED to. Work-related activities, to be optimized, must be CONSISTENT
with your sales person's PERSONAL VALUE SYSTEM.

The sense of personal INTEGRITY is very important. The sales mission is
approached with a sense of moral obligation and fueled by evangelistic zeal
when your sales person is CONVINCED OF THE VALUE of the products and services
represented to the buying public.
....

You should consider the following suggestions...

1. This sales person respects people who demonstrate high principles and
moral character. It is important for the sales management team to conduct
themselves accordingly around this sales person.

2. Your sales person may be a deeply religious individual. You should avoid
becoming unnecessarily offensive due to the reckless use of bad language, or
inappropriate humor.

3. This sales person may approach work with a sense of moral obligation- if
there is belief in the products to be sold, or the service to be represented.
Therefore, you are advised to spend enough time early in the training, when
introducing new products, to insure that your sales person does understand
the product, and is persuaded about its inherent value to consumers.

Test scores indicate that this individual's primary sales motivation is
security- oriented. Fear of not being able to provide for himself, or his
family, plays a major role in motivating this sales person to produce.

psychware **705**

In this case, fear is not necessarily a negative motivator. It can be a positive motivator FOR THIS PARTICULAR INDIVIDUAL.

CAUTION: Sales management may be inclined to see, at times, this sales person's pre-disposition towards PRECAUTION as a "negative attitude". While a negative attitude might be present for other reasons, it is not necessarily associated with the inclination towards precautionary vigilance. This individual is motivated to POSITIVE action by the fear of NOT having a secure, predictable future.

Don't interpret this as a problem if the sales person does not. See it as the means by which this sales person propels himself towards goals which are important to him.

SECTION VIII.   RELATIONS WITH SALES MANAGEMENT

Test scores do not portray any clear-cut attitudes which might enhance or impair this individual's relationship with sales management. Other sources of information must be consulted, therefore, such as background or references, past employers, and perhaps, Social Rating Scales like Merrill"s "SOCIAL STYLE QUESTIONNAIRE".
....

     NOTE: Do not mistakenly interpret the absence of clear-cut strengths as the presence of negatives, or interpersonal "RED FLAGS"! This individual should respond cooperatively to management's direction, especially if your efforts are based upon an awareness of, and respect for, the ways that individual sales people differ from one another in terms of needs and temperament.

SECTION IX.   FRUSTRATION-TOLERANCE AND CONFLICT-CAPABILITY

Test scores suggest that this individual should be able to handle work-related stress satisfactorily. It is probable that some stressful career-related episodes will be experienced. But, this sales person's reactions to NORMAL stress-provoking situations are not expected to be excessive, in terms of severity or duration.

SECTION X.   PROXIMITY

Test scores suggest that this individual could function satisfactorily in a "detached" setting, but that CONSIDERABLE CONTACT would be required to prevent him from feeling excluded or isolated. Frequent phone calls, written correspondence, and in-person visits by management will be particularly helpful if this individual must be housed some distance from the office.

This individual does appear to have the necessary self-discipline and initiative to work autonomously, but needs to feel INVOLVED in company activities, part of the sales "team", and close to management support.

Vulnerability to competitive recruiters is a genuine possibility if this individual is left distant and unattended from the office for extended periods of time.

SECTION XI.   ADDITIONAL TRAINING/DEVELOPMENT CONSIDERATIONS...

CAREER SATISFACTION DEPENDENT UPON HOW MUCH SOCIAL STATUS OTHER PEOPLE ASSOCIATE WITH THE CAREER ROLE. PRESTIGE IS VERY IMPORTANT. FEELINGS MAY BE EASILY HURT.

===>>> POSSIBILITY OF ONE, OR MORE, FORMS OF CALL-RELUCTANCE PRESENT.

                         E N D   O F   R E P O R T
PROCESS COMPLETION DATA:

706 *psychware*

NAME: Vineland Adaptive Behavior Scales-ASSIST

SUPPLIER: American Guidance Service
Publisher's Building
Circle Pines, MN 55014
(800) 328-2560

PRODUCT CATEGORY

Structured Interview

PRIMARY APPLICATIONS

Clinical Assessment/Diagnosis
Personal/Marriage/Family Counseling
Educational Evaluation/Planning

SALE RESTRICTIONS American Psychological Association Guidelines

SERVICE TYPE/COST	Type	Available	Cost	Discount
	Mail-In	No		
	Teleprocessing	No		
	Local	Yes	$87.50	

PRODUCT DESCRIPTION

The VINELAND ADAPATIVE BEHAVIOR SCALES are designed to measure the personal and social sufficiency of mentally retarded and handicapped individuals from birth to adulthood. The inventory assesses adaptive behavior in the following four domains: communication (receptive, expressive, written); daily living skills (personal, domestic, community); socialization (interpersonal relationships, play and leisure time, coping skills); and motor skills (gross, fine). The four domains are combined to form the Adaptive Behavior Composite. Two editions, the Interview Edition, Survey Form (297 items) and the Interview Edition, Expanded Form (577 items), are administered to parents or care-givers in a semi-structured interview. The Classroom Edition (244 items) is administered in a paper-and-pencil form to classroom teachers. This test is the 1984 revision of the Vineland Social Maturity Scale.

ASSIST (Automated System for Scoring and Interpreting Standardized Tests) software programs offer quick score conversion and profiling and convenient record management. They are designed to execute on Apple II + or IIe computers operating under DOS 3.3. The software package includes two diskettes and a manual.

NAME: Vocational Information Profile

SUPPLIER: NCS/Professional Assessment Services
P.O. Box 1416
Minneapolis, MN 55440
(800) 328-6759

PRODUCT CATEGORY	PRIMARY APPLICATIONS
Career/Vocational	Vocational Guidance/Counseling

SALE RESTRICTIONS Authorized/Certified Representatives

SERVICE TYPE/COST	Type	Available	Cost	Discount
	Mail-In	Yes	NA	
	Teleprocessing	No		
	Local	Yes	$1.65	Yes

PRODUCT DESCRIPTION

This narrative report combines information from the General Aptitude Test Battery and the USES Interest Inventory. Interest level is determined in 12 interest areas. Aptitude for 66 work groups is rated as high, medium, or low. The profile and narrative integrate the information from both aptitudes and interests in order to help the individual explore various career areas.

Local Service: MICROTEST Assessment Software from National Computer Systems, used with a Sentry 3000 tabletop scanner (purchase price approximately $4000) and microcomputer system ($2000-$3000 purchase price), allows tests to be administered off-line. Answer sheets are then scanned and scored automatically, one at a time or in a batch. Complete test reports are then automatically generated and printed. The cost for local scoring refers to the cost-per-test when diskettes are purchased in units of 20 administrations (minimum purchase).

NAME: Vocational Interest Inventory

SUPPLIER: Western Psychological Services
12031 Wilshire Blvd.
Los Angeles, CA 90025
(213) 478-2061

PRODUCT CATEGORY	PRIMARY APPLICATIONS
Career/Vocational Interest/Attitudes	Vocational Guidance/Counseling Educational Evaluation/Planning

SALE RESTRICTIONS   American Psychological Association Guidelines

SERVICE TYPE/COST	Type	Available	Cost	Discount
	Mail-In	Yes	$6.95	Yes
	Teleprocessing	No		
	Local	No		

PRODUCT DESCRIPTION

The VOCATIONAL INTEREST INVENTORY measures interest strength in the eight areas of occupational interest devised by Anne Roe. Developed at the University of Washington over twelve years and standardized on more than 26,000 high school students, the VOCATIONAL INTEREST INVENTORY has become a part of Washington's state-wide testing program.

The instrument is in a forced-choice format and can be either individually or group administered in approximately 20 minutes. It controls for sex bias at the item level and encourages exploration of nontraditional careers for both sexes. The VOCATIONAL INTEREST INVENTORY must be computer scored by WPS TEST REPORT which provides a profile of scores, a score summary giving percentiles and T-scores for each scale, and a college majors profile comparing the examinee's scores with those of graduate students who took the test when in high school and then relating the scores to the major fields of study chosen by those college students. The VOCATIONAL INTEREST INVENTORY is unique in being specifically designed and validated to predict the interest patterns of students in 2-year and 4-year college majors.

NAME: AGE: 23
SEX: Female   ANSWER SHEET SERIAL NO.:
HIGHEST GRADE COMPLETED: 12   STATED EDUCATIONAL GOAL: Doctorate

INTERPRETING YOUR RESULTS ON THE VOCATIONAL INTEREST INVENTORY

The Vocational Interest Inventory (VII) is a guidance instrument to
help people make post-high-school educational and vocational decisions.
Your scores are compared to those of over 25,000 high school juniors who
have taken the VII.

The VII measures how much interest you have in eight occupational
areas which cover the entire world of work. Throughout the inventory
you were asked to choose between certain occupations or activities. Now
you will be able to see what your strongest interests are, as a result
of the choices you made on each VII question.

The VII is easy to interpret. However, career counselors can help
you to get more out of the VII. They can give you some ideas to help
you make decisions about what to study in school or what kind of work
is likely to be most satisfying to you.

This report is going to give you two kinds of information. First,
it provides a profile of your eight VII scores with their percentile
equivalents (Profile of Scores). High scores are those above the 75th
percentile. Consider exploring those areas in which you have indicated
the highest interest.

Second, the report gives you a profile that shows you which college
graduates you are most similar to in interests (College Majors Profile).
It displays the four dimensions that have been found to underlie the
eight occupational interests and shows your position on each of these
dimensions. This profile also shows you the average positions on each
dimension of people who graduated from college in various college majors
based on their VII results collected when they were in high school. This
may help you in selecting among possible college majors.

You will also be encouraged to explore any occupational areas that are
nontraditional for your sex if you have a score between the 50th and 75th
percentiles on any nontraditional scale.

YOUR PROFILE OF SCORES

On the next page is your Profile of Scores. Identify your high
scores (those above the 75th percentile) and then read the interpretation provided for you on the page following the profile. Each of
the eight scores is defined in the VII Guide to Interpretation, a
printed booklet that should be available with this report.

Western Psychological Services • 12031 Wilshire Boulevard • Los Angeles, California 90025

WPS TEST REPORT

VOCATIONAL INTEREST INVENTORY PROFILE OF SCORES

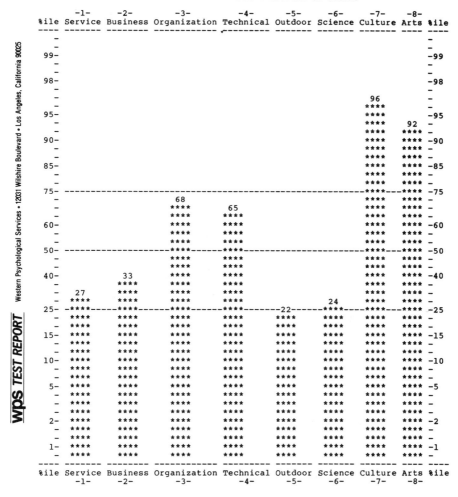

```
          -1-      -2-        -3-        -4-       -5-     -6-      -7-     -8-
%ile  Service Business Organization Technical Outdoor Science Culture Arts  %ile
----  ------- -------- ------------- --------- ------- ------- ------- ----  ----
       -                                                                    -
       -                                                                    -
 99-                                                                        -99
       -                                                                    -
 98-                                                                        -98
       -                                                                    -
       -                                                          96        -
       -                                                        ****        -
 95-                                                            ****        -95
       -                                                        ****     92 -
       -                                                        ****   ****  -
 90-                                                            ****   **** -90
       -                                                        ****   ****  -
       -                                                        ****   ****  -
 85-                                                            ****   **** -85
       -                                                        ****   ****  -
       -                                                        ****   ****  -
 75- -------------------------------------------------------****---**** -75
       -                        68                              ****   ****  -
       -                       ****            65               ****   ****  -
 60-                           ****           ****              ****   **** -60
       -                       ****           ****              ****   ****  -
       -                       ****           ****              ****   ****  -
 50- -------------------------****---------****---------------------****---**** -50
       -                       ****           ****              ****   ****  -
       -                       ****           ****              ****   ****  -
 40-             33            ****           ****              ****   **** -40
       -        ****           ****           ****              ****   ****  -
       -   27   ****           ****           ****              ****   ****  -
       - ****   ****           ****           ****       24     ****   ****  -
 25- -****------****-----------****----------****-------22------****----****---**** -25
       - ****   ****           ****           ****    ****   ****     ****   ****  -
 15-   - ****   ****           ****           ****    ****   ****     ****   **** -15
       - ****   ****           ****           ****    ****   ****     ****   ****  -
 10-   - ****   ****           ****           ****    ****   ****     ****   **** -10
       - ****   ****           ****           ****    ****   ****     ****   ****  -
  5-   - ****   ****           ****           ****    ****   ****     ****   **** -5
       - ****   ****           ****           ****    ****   ****     ****   ****  -
       - ****   ****           ****           ****    ****   ****     ****   ****  -
  2-   - ****   ****           ****           ****    ****   ****     ****   **** -2
       - ****   ****           ****           ****    ****   ****     ****   ****  -
  1-   - ****   ****           ****           ****    ****   ****     ****   **** -1
       - ****   ****           ****           ****    ****   ****     ****   ****  -
----  ------- -------- ------------- --------- ------- ------- ------- ----  ----
%ile  Service Business Organization Technical Outdoor Science Culture Arts  %ile
          -1-      -2-        -3-        -4-       -5-     -6-      -7-     -8-
```

psychware **711**

SCORE SUMMARY

	Service	Business	Organization	Technical	Outdoor	Science	Culture	Arts
Percentile	27	33	68	65	22	24	96	92
T Scores	44	46	55	54	42	43	67	64

INTERPRETING YOUR PROFILE OF SCORES

The heights of the bars in the Profile of Scores on the previous page
show how you compare with high school students in the relative amount of
interest you have in eight basic occupational areas. The percentile
number on the top of each bar tells you the percentage of students with
less interest than you in that occupational area. Scores at the 75th
percentile are higher than 3/4 of the other students' scores. Scores at
the 25th percentile are low, since only 1/4 of the students scored lower.
You may wish to explore jobs in your high interest areas. Study the
descriptions of the eight occupational areas given in the VII Guide to
Interpretation, a printed booklet that should be available with this
report. If you were planning to go into an area for which your interest
score was low, you might want to discuss this with a career counselor.

YOU HAD 2 SCORES AT OR ABOVE THE 75TH PERCENTILE

Your two highest scores at or above the 75th percentile were General
Cultural and Arts and Entertainment. These areas are closely related so
this combination of high scores is common. General Cultural people are
interested in preserving and passing on our cultural and social heritage.
They like using words and communicating with others. People with high
interest in Arts and Entertainment are drawn to music, dancing, entertainment, professional athletics, and painting. With some talent they can
express this interest through their work. Typical jobs that include
both General Cultural and Arts and Entertainment interests at the high
school diploma level are teacher aide in art or music, arts and entertainment reporter for a weekly newspaper, display manager for a bookstore, and
assistant to a dramatic coach. With a bachelor's degree in English you
could write dramatic works--plays or television and motion picture
scripts. The jobs of art critic, television news director, music librarian, radio announcer, film editor, and story editor from the radio and
television broadcasting industry also combine these two interest areas at
the highest level.

YOUR COLLEGE MAJORS PROFILE

On the next page is the College Majors Profile that shows how close
you come in your interests to groups of college majors. Underlying
VII interests are four dimensions. There is a Service versus Technical
dimension, a Business Contact versus Science dimension, an Organization
versus Outdoor dimension, and an Arts versus Detailed Work dimension.
People who score high at one end of each dimension tend to score low at
the other end. For example, people with high Service scores tend to have
low Technical scores; people with high Science scores tend to have low
Business Contact scores. The position of each college major group
is shown along with your position on each dimension. You will want
to pay particular attention to those dimensions where your position
is toward the top of the profile, indicating a high dimension score.
Also, read the interpretations on the page following the profile.

VOCATIONAL INTEREST INVENTORY COLLEGE MAJORS PROFILE

-1- TECHNICAL	-2- BUSINESS	-3- ORGANIZATION	-4- ARTS

```
-                                                                         -
-                                                                         -
-                                                                         -
-                                                                         -
-                                                                         -
-                                                                         -
-                                                                         -
-                                                                         -
-  Engineering                                                            -
-                                                     ******YOU*******     -
-                                 ******YOU*******      Art                -
-                                                                         -
-                                   Accounting                             -
-  ******YOU*******                                                       -
-                    Political Sci                                         -
-  Urban Planning                   Political Sci      Languages           -
-  Fishery/Forest                   Economics          Urban Planning      -
-  Accounting        Communications Engineering        Home Economics      -
-  Economics                        Urban Planning     History             -
-  Biological Sci    ******YOU*******                                      -
-  Art               Economics      Social Service     Communications      -
-                    Accounting     Home Economics     Health Science      -
-  --------------    --------------                    --------------      -
-                    Social Service  Nursing           Biological Sci      -
-  Communications    Urban Planning  Health Science    Political Sci       -
-                    Art             Languages         Fishery/Forest      -
-  History           Home Economics  History           Accounting          -
-  Languages         .Languages      Biological Sci    Engineering         -
-  Home Economics                                                          -
-  Health Science                   Art                                    -
-  Nursing           Health Science                                        -
-  Social Service                                                          -
-                                                                         -
-                    Engineering                                           -
-                    Fishery/Forest                                        -
-                                   Fishery/Forest                         -
-                                                                         -
-                    Nursing                                               -
-                    Biological Sci                                        -
-                                                                         -
-                                                                         -
-                                                                         -
-                                                                         -
-                                                                         -
-                                                                         -
```

SERVICE -1-	SCIENCE -2-	OUTDOOR -3-	DETAILED WORK -4-

Western Psychological Services • 12031 Wilshire Boulevard • Los Angeles, California 90025

WPS TEST REPORT

psychware **713**

INTERPRETING YOUR COLLEGE MAJORS PROFILE

Do your positions on the College Majors Profile make sense to you?
Do they correspond to what you think you would like to do? If the
results seem puzzling, look back at your Profile of Scores. High scores,
those above the 75th percentile, will be your best guide.

SERVICE VS. TECHNICAL

Your profile position is more toward the Technical end of this dimension. This means that when your interest in helping others is compared to
your interest in working with tools, the Technical side is the stronger.
You are thus more like engineering and urban planning majors than social
service majors on this dimension, preferring to work with technical issues
rather than to provide direct services to people.

BUSINESS VS. SCIENCE

You are in the middle range on this interest dimension, meaning
that your interest in persuading people or promoting business activities
is not significantly stronger than your interest in research or scientific
activities.

ORGANIZATION VS. OUTDOOR

Your profile position is more toward the Organization end of this
interest dimension, meaning that when your interest in outdoor activities
is compared to your interest in inside, organizational activities, your
interest in planning, managing, and keeping business affairs in order is
stronger. You are thus more like college graduates in accounting, political science, and economics than majors in art or fisheries/forestry, preferring office work to less organized activities in the outdoors.

ART VS. DETAILED WORK

You had a high score on Arts and Entertainment that placed you toward
the Arts end of this interest dimension. This means that your interest in
creative arts, entertainment, or sports is very strong, as strong as that
of people who graduated with an Arts and Entertainment major in college.
The majority of college majors have an average interest in artistic activities and have no real preference for either working in a highly flexible,
unstructured way or working in an orderly, detailed, and systematic way.
They like to work somewhere between these extremes. But you are more like
graduates in art, preferring flexible, even unconventional activities to
detailed work.

Western Psychological Services • 12031 Wilshire Boulevard • Los Angeles, California 90025

WPS TEST REPORT

INTERPRETING YOUR GENERAL CULTURAL SCORE

You had a high score on General Cultural that was not shown on the College Majors Profile. People who score high in General Cultural usually like going to school, learning, using words, and exercising their verbal skills. High General Cultural scores are more likely to be obtained by graduates in the humanities such as languages, history, communications, and philosophy than by graduates in such majors as engineering or forestry.

INTERPRETING NONTRADITIONAL SCORES

Interest areas in which women have traditionally scored lower than men include Business Contact, Technical, and Outdoor. Because these are nontraditional interests for women, they are worth exploring if your score was between the 50th and 75th percentiles on any of these scales. You had a nontraditional score at least at the 50th percentile, Technical. Women are in demand in all technical areas. People with high Technical interest value working with objects, tools, and machines. They like to use their hands in assembling and operating equipment. With a high school diploma you could be a bus driver, service station attendant, warehouse worker, or assembly line worker. With technical school training you could be a meat cutter, drafter, small appliance repairer, architectural engineering technician, blueprint reader, computer programmer, locksmith, paperhanger, broadcast technician, welder, carpenter, or auto mechanic. A bachelor's degree in the particular technical area is required to be an engineer, building contractor, or industrial designer.

Item responses for client   Answer sheet no.

1(B)	11(A)	21(B)	31(A)	41(A)	51(B)	61(A)	71(B)	81(B)	91(A)	101(A)
2(B)	12(A)	22(B)	32(B)	42(A)	52(A)	62(A)	72(A)	82(B)	92(A)	102(A)
3(B)	13(B)	23(A)	33(B)	43(B)	53(A)	63(B)	73(A)	83(B)	93(A)	103(A)
4(B)	14(B)	24(A)	34(B)	44(A)	54(A)	64(B)	74(B)	84(A)	94(A)	104(A)
5(B)	15(A)	25(B)	35(A)	45(B)	55(B)	65(A)	75(B)	85(A)	95(A)	105(B)
6(A)	16(B)	26(A)	36(B)	46(B)	56(A)	66(B)	76(B)	86(A)	96(A)	106(A)
7(B)	17(A)	27(A)	37(A)	47(A)	57(A)	67(A)	77(A)	87(A)	97(A)	107(A)
8(B)	18(B)	28(A)	38(B)	48(A)	58(B)	68(B)	78(A)	88(A)	98(A)	108(B)
9(B)	19(A)	29(A)	39(B)	49(A)	59(B)	69(A)	79(B)	89(A)	99(B)	109(B)
10(B)	20(A)	30(B)	40(B)	50(A)	60(B)	70(A)	80(B)	90(B)	100(B)	110(A)

111(A)
112(B)

[* indicates a double response]
[( ) indicates a blank or light mark]

Western Psychological Services • 12031 Wilshire Boulevard • Los Angeles, California 90025

WPS TEST REPORT

NAME: Vocational Interest Profile Report

SUPPLIER: Psychologistics, Inc.
P.O. Box 3896
Indialantic, FL 32903
(305) 727-7900

PRODUCT CATEGORY	PRIMARY APPLICATIONS
Career/Vocational Interest/Attitudes	Vocational Guidance/Counseling Personnel Selection/Evaluation Educational Evaluation/Planning

SALE RESTRICTIONS American Psychological Association Guidelines

SERVICE TYPE/COST	Type	Available	Cost	Discount
	Mail-In	No		
	Teleprocessing	No		
	Local	Yes	$195.00	

PRODUCT DESCRIPTION

The VOCATIONAL INTEREST PROFILE REPORT administers, scores, and interprets the Interest Check List, which was developed by the United States Department of Labor. This inventory can be administered using a pencil-and-paper format or by computer and requires about 20 minutes to complete.

This inventory consists of 211 items which relate to work activities. These activities represent a broad range of vocations in the U.S. economy. All items were selected to reflect a sampling of jobs found in twelve work categories: Artistic, Scientific, Plants and Animals, Protective, Mechanical, Industrial, Business, Detail, Selling, Accomodating, Humanitarian, Leading-Influencing, and Physical Performing.

The inventory and report are designed to be used with the USES Guide for Occupational Exploration. The Guide contains all 4th edition Dictionary of Occupational Titles listings, except for military occupations. All occupations are organized according to an interest-oriented structure developed specifically for use in vocational counseling. The program is compatible with Apple II +, IIe, and IBM PC microcomputer systems. This program also enables the user to save the report in a text file for additional text editing.

VOCATIONAL INTEREST PROFILE REPORT

NAME: JOHN X. DOE   PAGE 1
AGE: 18
EDUCATION: 12
SEX: MALE
DATE: FEBRUARY 27
REFERRED BY: JOHN Q. SMITH

This inventory is designed to help counselees learn more about their
occupational interests and how those interests relate to work. Each
of the answers on the 210 job activities has been divided into one of
12 interest scales. Consideration would best be given to the
occupations with the highest scores. All relevant jobs need to be
considered.

The interest categories are ranked below. To the right of the
category is the weighted score. The percentile represents the
weighted score divided by the total possible weighted score for
that category. You strongest interests are probably in the
categories with the three highest percentiles.

        CATEGORIES BY RANK   WEIGHTED SCORE   PERCENTILE

        PLANTS AND ANIMALS   12   1
        PHYSICAL PERFORMING   6   1
        MECHANICAL   24   .57
        SCIENTIFIC   7   .54
        INDUSTRIAL   6   .33
        ARTISTIC   7   .27
        LEADING-INFLUENCING   8   .22
        ACCOMMODATING   3   .2
        PROTECTIVE   1   .17
        SELLING   2   .17
        HUMANITARIAN   2   .17
        BUSINESS DETAIL   1   .05

                       ANSWER SHEET
DDDDDDDLLD DDDDD?DDLL LDDLL?DLLD DLDDLLLLLL LLLLLLLLDD
DDDLL?L??L LDDDLLLLLL DDDLD?DL?? LLLLDDDDL? LLL?DD?DDL
LDDD?DD?LD ?DDLDDDDDD DDDDDDDDLD DDDDDDDLDD ?DDDLDDDDD
L?DDDDDD?D ?DDLDDDDDD DLLDDDDLLL DDDDDDDLDD DDDDDD?LDD
DD?DLLLLLL

DESCRIPTIVE PARAGRAPHS

                    PLANTS AND ANIMALS

Your score within the Plants and Animals area indicates an
interest in activities to do with plants and animals, usually in an
outdoor setting.

You can satisfy this interest by working in farming, forestry,
fishing, and related fields. You may like doing physical work
outdoors, such as working on a farm. You may enjoy animals. Perhaps
training or taking care of animals would appeal to you. You may have

management ability. You could own, operate, or manage farms or
related business or services.

Four separate work groups comprise the Plants and Animals interest
area. These include occupations within Managerial Work: Plants and
Animals, General Supervision: Plants and Animals, Animal Training and
Service, and Elemental Work: Plants and Animals.

Managerial Work: Plants and Animals:

Within the Managerial Work: Plants and Animals group, workers operate
or manage farming,fishing, forestry, and horticultural service
businesses of many kinds. Some of them breed specialty plants and
animals. Others provide services to increase production or beautify
land areas. Many of them work in rural or woodland areas, on farms,
ranches, and forest preserves. Others find employment with
commercial nurseries, landscaping firms, business services, or
government agencies located in large and small communities all over
the country. Many are self-employed, operating their own large or
small businesses. The following are examples of jobs in this area.

Camp Tender	410.137-010	Farmer, Vegetable	402.161-010
Manager, Dairy Farm	180.167-026	Poultry Breeder	411.161-014
Superintendent, Prod.	180.167-058	Animal Breeder	410.161-010
Worm Grower	413.161-018	Tree Surgeon	408.181-010
Landscape Contractor	182.167-014	Forester	040.061-034

Within the General Supervision: Plants and Animals group, workers
supervise others, and often work right along with them, on farms or
ranches, fish hatcheries or forests, plant nurseries or parks. Most
of them work in rural or forest locations, but some jobs are located
in city or suburban areas. Some of these workers travel throughout
an area to inspect or treat croplands for insects or disease, or
supervise workers performing agricultural or lawn care services.
The following are examples of jobs in this area.

Field Supervisor Seed	180.167-014	Supervisor Veg.Farm.	402.131-010
Supervisor, X-Mas Tree	451.137-014	Forester Aide forest	452.364-010
Supervisor, Logging	459.133-010	Woods Boss logging	459.137-010
Supervisor, Spray, Lawn		Artificial-Breeding	
& Tree Service	408.131-010	Technician	418.384-014
Field Insp., Disease &			
Insect Control	408.687-010	Barn Boss	410.131-010

Animal Training and Service:

With the Animal Training and Service group, workers take care of
animals of many kinds, and train them for a variety of purposes.
They work in pet shops, testing laboratories, animal shelters, and
veterinarians offices. Some are employed by zoos, aquariums,
circuses, and at other places where animals are exhibited or used in
entertainment acts. Others work for animal training or obedience
schools, or in stables or kennels maintained by individuals or such
facilities as race tracks or riding academies. These workers are not
employed on farms, ranches, or other places where animals are raised

as crops. The following are examples of jobs in this area.

Horse Trainer	419.224-010	Animal-Ride Manager	349.224-010
Exerciser Horse	153.674-010	Horseshoer	418.381-010
Animal Keeper	412.674-010	Aquarist	449.674-010
Hoof and Shoe Inspect.	153.287-010	Animal Caretaker	410.674-010
Stable Attendant	410,674-022	Dog Groomer	418.674-010

Elemental Work: Plants and Animals

Within Elemental Work: Plants and Animals group, workers perform active physical tasks, usually in an outdoor, non-industrial setting. They work with their hands, use various kinds of tools and equipment, or operate machinery. They find employment on farms or ranches, at logging camps or fish hatcheries, in forests or game preserves, or with commercial fishing businesses where they may work on shore or in fishing boats. In urban areas, they work in parks, gardens, or nurseries, or for businesses that provide horticultural or agricultural services. The following are examples of jobs in this area.

Cowpuncher	410.674-014	Farm-Machine Operat.	409.683-010
Goat Herder	410.687-014	Supervisor,Pick Crew	409.131-010
Chainsaw Operator	454.687-010	Trapper, Animal	461.684-014
Laborer, Landscape	408.687-014	Groundskeeper	406.687-010
Artificial Inseminator	418.384-010	Dog Catcher	379.673-010

Additional information about the Plants and Animals interest area is found in the Guide for Occupational Exploration on pages 50-63 and the Occupations Outlook Handbook. These two references, along with the Dictionary of Occupational Titles are published by the U. S. Department of Labor and are found within the reserve section of any local public library.

PHYSICAL PERFORMING

Your score within the Physical Performing area indicates an interest in physical activities performed before an audience. You can satisfy this interest through jobs in athletics, sports, and the performance of physical feats. Perhaps a job as a professional player or official would appeal to you. You may wish to develop and perform special acts such as acrobatics or wire walking.

Two separate work groups comprise the Physical Performing interest area. These include occupations within Sports and Physical Feats.

Sports:

Within the Sports group, workers compete in professional athletic or sporting events, coach players, and officiate at games. They also give individual and group instruction, recruit players, and regulate various aspects of sporting events. Jobs in this group are found in all types of professional sports, such as football, baseball, basketball, hockey, golf, tennis and horse racing. Some jobs are also available with private recreational facilities, including ski

resorts, skating rinks, athletic clubs, and gymnasiums. The
following are examples of jobs in this area.

Head Coach	153.117-010	Sports Instructor	153.227.018
Sports Scout	153.117.018	Pit Steward	153.167.014
Dude Wrangler	353.364.010	Umpire	153.267.018
Golf Course Ranger	379.667-010	Auto Racer	153.243-010
Jockey-Room Custodian	346.667.010	Pro. Athletic	153.341-010

Physical Feats:

Within the Physical Feats group, workers perform unusual or daring
acts of physical strength or skill to entertain people. They may
perform alone or with others. Circuses, carnivals, theaters, and
amusement parks hire these workers. The following are examples of
jobs in this area.

Acrobat	159-247-010	Rodeo Performer	159.344.014
Aerialist	159-247-014	Show Horse Driver	159.344-018
Aquatic Performer	159-347-014	Stunt Performer	159.341-014
Equestrian	159.347-010	Thrill Performer	159.347-018
Juggler	159.341-010	Wire Walker	159.347-022

Additional information about the Physical Performing interest area is
found in the Guide for Occupational Exploration on pages (316-322)
and the Occupations Outlook Handbook. These two references, along
with the Dictionary of Occupational Titles are published by the U. S.
Department of Labor and are found within the reserve section of any
local public library.

MECHANICAL

Your score within the Mechanical area indicates an interest in
applying mechanical principles to practical situations using
machines, hand tools, or techniques. You can satisfy this interest
in a variety of jobs ranging from routine to complex professional
positions. You may enjoy working with ideas about things (objects).
You could seek a job in engineering or in a related technical field.
You may prefer to deal directly with things. You could find a job in
the crafts or trades, building, making or repairing objects. You may
like to drive or to operate vehicles and special equipment. You may
prefer routine or physical work in settings other than factories.
Perhaps work in mining or construction would appeal to you.

Twelve separate work groups comprise the Mechanical interest area.
These include occupations within Engineering, Managerial Work:
Mechanical, Engineering Technology, Air and Water Vehicle Operation,
Craft Technology, Systems Operation, Quality Control, Land and Water
Vehicle Operation, Materials Control, Crafts, Equipment Operation and
Elemental Work: Mechanical.

Engineering:

Within the Engineering group, workers plan, design, and direct the
construction or development of buildings, bridges, roads, airports,

dams, sewage systems, air-conditioning systems, mining machinery, and
other structures and equipment. They also develop processes and/or
techniques for generating and transmitting electrical power,
manufacturing chemicals, extracting metals from ore, and controlling
the quality of products being made. Workers specialize in one or
more kinds of engineering, such as civil, electrical, mechanical,
mining, and safety. Some are hired by individual plants, petroleum
and mining companies, research laboratories, and construction
companies. Others find employment with Federal, State and local
governments. Some have their own engineering firms, and accept work
from various individuals. The following are examples of jobs in
this area.

Welding Technician	011.261.014	Sanitary Engineer	005.061-030
Stress Analyst	002.061-030	Meteorologist	012.067-010
Sales Engineer	007.151-010	Tool Planner	007.167-074
Configuration Mgm.Anal.	012.167-010	Production Planner	012.167-050

Managerial Work: Mechanical

Within the Managerial Work: Mechanical group, workers manage
industrial plants or systems where technical work is being performed.
Jobs are found in oil fields, power plants, transportation
companies, radio and television networks, and telephone and related
communications systems. The following are examples of jobs in this
area.

Maintenance Supervisor	891.137-010	Railroad-Const.Dirt.	182.167-018
Brewing Director	183.167-010	Mgr.,Flight Control	184.167-066
Pit Supervisor	939.137-014	Property Coordinator	962.167-018
Rep., Personal Service	236.252-010	Manager, Bulk Plant	181.117-010

Engineering Technology:

Within the Engineering Technology group, workers collect, record and
coordinate technical information in such activities as surveying,
drafting, petroleum production, communications control, and materials
scheduling. Workers find jobs in construction, factories,
engineering and architectural firms, airports, and research
laboratories. The following are examples of jobs in this area.

Navigator	196.167-014	Surveyor, Geo.Prosp.	018.167-042
Drafter, Auto Design	017.281-022	Estimator	160.267-018
Air-Traf-Ctrl.Special.	193.162-014	Material Scheduler	012.187-010
Flight Engineer	621.261-018	Test Technician	019.261-022

Air and Water Vehicle Operation:

Within the Air and Water Vehicle Operation group, workers pilot
airplanes or ships, or supervise others who do. Some instruct other
persons in flying. Most of these workers are hired by shipping
companies and commercial airlines. Some find jobs piloting planes or
ships for private companies or for individuals. The following are
examples of jobs in this area.

Controller	196.263-026	Test Pilot	196.263-042
Helicopter Pilot	196.263-038	Instructor, Flying	097.227-010
Pilot, Submersible	029.383-010	Captain,Fish Vessel	197.133-010

Craft Technology:

Within the Craft Technology group, workers perform highly skilled
hand and/or machine work requiring special techniques, training, and
experience. Work occurs in a variety of nonfactory settings. Some
workers own their own shops. The following are examples of jobs in
this area.

Bricklayer	861.381-014	Carpenter, Mainten.	860.281-010
Electrician	824.261-010	Aircraft Body Repair	807.261-010
Accordion Repairer	730.281-014	Job Printer	973.381-018
Diamond Cleaver	770.381-014	Dressmaker	785.361-010

Systems Operation:

Within the Systems Operation group, workers operate and maintain
equipment in an overall system, or a section of a system, for such
purposes as generating and distributing electricity; treating and
providing water to customers; pumping oil from oilfields to storage
tanks; making ice in an ice plant; and providing telephone service to
users. These jobs are found in utility companies, refineries,
construction projects, large apartment houses and industrial
establishments, and with city and county governments. The
following are examples of jobs in this area.

Switchboard Operator	952.362-038	Auxiliary-Equip. Oper.	952.362-010
Refrigerating Engineer	950.362-014	Firer, Marine	951.685-018
Gas-Pumping Sta. Oper.	953.382-010	Ditch Rider(waterworks)	954.362-010

Quality Control:

Within the Quality Control group, workers inspect and/or test
materials and products to be sure they meet standards. The work is
carried out in a non-factory setting, and includes such activities as
grading logs at a lumber yard, inspecting bridges to be sure they are
safe; inspecting gas lines for leaks, and grading gravel for use in
building roads. Jobs may be found with construction companies,
sawmills, petroleum refineries, and utility companies. The
following are examples of jobs in this area.

Gas-Meter Checker	953.367-014	Bridge Inspector	869.287-010
Auto-Repr.-Ser.-Estimt.	620.261-018	Inspect., Heat.&Ref.	168.167-046
Elevator-Exam.-Adjust.	825.261-014	Water-Quality Tester	539.367-014
Petroleum-Insp.Super.	222.137-026	Log Grader	455.367-010

Land and Water Vehicle Operation:

Within the Land and Water Vehicle Operation, workers drive large or
small trucks, delivery vans, or locomotives, to move materials or
deliver products. Some drive ambulances; others operate small boats.
Most of these jobs are found with trucking companies, railroads and

water transportation companies. Wholesale and retail companies hire
delivery drivers; ambulance drivers are hired by hospitals, fire
departments, and other establishments concerned with moving the sick
or injured. The following are examples of jobs in this area.

Tractor-Trailer Driv. 904.383-010   Milk Driver   905.483-010
Coin Collector   292.483-010   Ambulance Driver   913.683-010
Chauffeur, Funeral Car 359.673-014   Newspaper-Deliv. Dr.292.363-010
Dock Hand   911.687-022

Material Control:

Within the Material Control group, workers receive, store, and/or
ship materials and products. Some estimate and order the quantities
and kinds of materials needed. Others regulate and control the flow
of materials to places in the plant where they are to be used. Most
have to keep records. Jobs are found in institutions, industrial
plants, and Government agencies. The following are examples of
jobs in this area.

Cargo Agent   248.367-018   Custodian, Athletic Eq.969.367-010
Complaint Clerk   221.387-014   Rug Measurer   369.367-014
Dispatcher Ready-Mix 849.137-014 Checker-in (boot-shoe) 221.587-014

Craft:

Within the Craft group, workers use hands and handtools skillfully to
fabricate, process, install, and/or repair materials, products,
and/or structural parts. They follow established procedures and
techniques. The jobs are not found in factories, but are in repair
shops, garages, wholesale and retail stores, and hotels. Some are
found on construction projects, and others with utilities, such as
telephone and power systems. The following are examples of jobs in
this area.

Net Repairer (fish) 449.664-010   Carpet Cutter   929.381-010
Automatic-Door Mech. 829.281-010 Airport Attendant   912.364-010
Dyer, supervisor   582.131-014   Cook   315.361-010
Exterminator   389.684-010

Equipment Operation:

Within the Equipment Operation group, workers operate heavy machines
and equipment to dig, drill, dredge, hoist, or move substances and
materials. They also operate machines to pave roads. These jobs are
found at mining, logging and construction sites, docks, receiving and
shipping areas of industrial plants, and large storage buildings and
warehouses. The following are examples of jobs in this area.

Bulldozer Operator   850.683-010   Snow-Removing Supt. 955.137-010
Railway-Equip.Operat. 859.683-018   Miner   939.281-010
Perforator Oper.Oil   931.382-010   Yard Worker   929.583-010
Marine Railway Operat.921.662-022   Stevedore   911.663-014

Elemental Work: Mechanical

Within the Elemental Work: Mechanical, workers perform a variety of
unskilled tasks, such as moving materials, cleaning work areas,
operating simple machines or helping skilled workers. These jobs are
found in a variety of non-factory settings. The following are
examples of jobs in this area.

Tile Setter	861.684-018	Kettle Tender	869.685-010
Laborer,Airport Maint.	899.687-014	Key Cutter	709.684-050
Test-Dept. Helper	729.664-010	Baker helper	313.684-010
Steward/Stewardess	310.137-018	Golf-Range Attendant	341.683-010

Additional information about the Mechanical interest Area is found in
the Guide for Occupational Exploration on pages 70-135 and the
Occupations Outlook Handbook. These two references, along with the
Dictionary of Occupational Titles are published by the U. S.
Department of Labor and are found within the reserve section of any
local public library.

EXAMINER

NAME: Vocational Preference Inventory

SUPPLIER: Integrated Professional Systems
5211 Mahoning Avenue Suite 135
Youngstown, OH 44515
(216) 799-3282

PRODUCT CATEGORY	PRIMARY APPLICATIONS
Interest/Attitudes Career/Vocational	Clinical Assessment/Diagnosis Vocational Guidance/Counseling Educational Evaluation/Planning Personnel Selection/Evaluation

SALE RESTRICTIONS Qualified Professional

SERVICE TYPE/COST	Type	Available	Cost	Discount
	Mail-In	No		
	Teleprocessing	No		
	Local	Yes	See Below	

PRODUCT DESCRIPTION

The VOCATIONAL PREFERENCE INVENTORY is a personality test that uses occupational item content. It is used to assess vocational and occupational interests based on the theory that occupations can be described in terms of personality characteristics. The 160 test items measure 11 dimensions related to a person's interpersonal relationships, interests, and values. The dimensions include: Realistic, Intellectual, Social, Conventional, Enterprising, Artistic, Self-Control, Masculinity, Status, Infrequency, and Acquiescence. Test items are all occupational titles and the examinees indicate which occupations they like or dislike.

This program scores all 11 scales and presents a graph showing the profile of the respondent. Validity interpretation and descriptions of the personality characteristics of the respondent follow. The vocational code type is shown together with a description of the three highest personality types. A list of occupations which match the vocational code type is presented.

An operating software package, priced from $200-$850 depending on the complexity of the package, is required for program use, plus an additional fee of $3.00 per use.

NAME: Vocational Preference Inventory

SUPPLIER: PSYCH Systems, Inc.
600 Reisterstown Road
Baltimore, MD 21208
(800) 368-3366

PRODUCT CATEGORY	PRIMARY APPLICATIONS
Career/Vocational	Vocational Guidance/Counseling Personal/Marriage/Family Counseling

SALE RESTRICTIONS   Qualified Professional

SERVICE TYPE/COST	Type	Available	Cost	Discount
	Mail-In	No		
	Teleprocessing	No		
	Local	Yes	See Below	

PRODUCT DESCRIPTION

This instruments is based on Holland's typological theory of careers. The examinee is asked to indicate like/dislike for each of 160 occupations. Responses are then scored on 11 scales. Six measure the personality-vocational types. Two others serve as validity indicators. The VPI is best used as a brief screening inventory for high school students, college students, and employed adults who are concerned about vocational interests.

This program presents and scores the test items. It then provides a narrative report of test results.

Psych Systems programs operate on the IBM PC-XT, COMPAQ Plus, Dec Professional 350, and most DEC PDP-11 systems. Various hardware/ software configurations are available directly from Psych Systems, with single-user systems starting at approximately $12,000. A per test fee also applies.

222-22-2222 Jonathan Doe   32 yr old white male 16-Feb-84

```
    --------------------------------------------------
   |           |                                      |
   |   VPI     |   Vocational Preference Inventory    |
   |           |                                      |
    --------------------------------------------------
```

The computer program generating this report was designed by Psych
Systems, Inc., Baltimore, Maryland 21208. Copyright (C) 1984 by Psych
Systems, Inc. The Vocational Preference Inventory is reproduced by
permission. Copyright (C) 1953, 1965, 1975, 1978 by Consulting
Psychologists Press, Incorporated, 577 College Avenue, Palo Alto,
California 94306. No portion of the VPI may be reproduced by any
process without prior written permission of the publisher. All rights
reserved.

Background Information
---------- -----------

Jonathan Doe is 32 years of age. He attends high school and works full
time. He reports being somewhat dissatisfied with his current
occupation. This person reports no specific expectations about the
outcome of testing.

Test Validity
---- --------

This person appears to have responded to the test items with
appropriate understanding and care. Thus, the results appear valid and
interpretable.

Personality Description
----------- -----------

The VPI can provide a description of certain personality
characteristics important in vocational choice and job performance.
These characteristics are presented in this section.

This person has adequate self-esteem and normal desires for status and
prestige. However, he may be comfortable with his current life
situation. Thus, improving his social standing may not be a primary
motivating factor in the choice of an occupation.

He is open to careers that are not traditionally associated with men.
This role flexibility may be an asset in making a vocational choice.

He clearly lacks self-discipline. Insufficient self-control and
impulsiveness may contribute to job difficulties.

Persons obtaining this profile are described as conventional,
conforming, stable, and genuine. They prefer activities that involve
manipulation of objects and the use of tools. These individuals often
have substantial mechanical or athletic ability. They tend to be
materiallistic and value tangible resources such as money.

A realistic, pratical orientation is consistent with their mechanical
interests. Interpersonally, they often appear frank, natural, and
self-effacing.

Vocational Preferences
---------- -----------

Results of the VPI indicate this person has realistic, enterprising,
and social interests. He has strong vocational preferences.

The profile suggests an ambitious, energetic person who may have
multiple talents and interests. However, his interests are not
well-differentiated. This can result in vocational conflict and
confusion as to career choice. Further vocational assessment and
counseling may be helpful.

This person's Holland Occupational Code (HOC) obtained from the VPI is
RES.

The following occupations are most congruent with this person's
vocational interests and educational level (or expressed educational
aspirations).

Occupation	DOT Code
----------	--------
HOC : RES	
Fish and Game Warden	379.167-010
HOC : SER	
Claim Adjuster	241.217-010

728 *psychware*

```
                          HOC : SRE
Athletic Coach                                    099.224-010
Building Superintendent                           187.167-190
Physical Instructor                               153.227-018
                          HOC : ERS
Warehouse Supervisor                              929.137-022
                          HOC : ERI
Industrial Engineer                               012.167-030
                          HOC : RIS
Range Manager                                     040.061-046
Commercial Engineer                               003.187-014
Forester                                          040.061-034
Industrial Arts Teacher                           091.221-010
                          HOC : RIE
Automotive Engineer                               007.061-010
Mechanical Engineer                               007.061-014
Petroleum Engineer                                010.061-018
Airline Radio Operator                            193.262-010
Building Inspector                                168.267-010
Industrial Engineer Technician                    012.267-010
Mechanical-Engineering Technician                 007.161-026
Mining Engineer                                   010.061-014
                          HOC : RSI
Vocational Agriculture Teacher                    091.227-010
```

These occupations are consistent with this person's vocational
interests, but fail to match his educational level and/or expressed
educational aspirations.

```
Occupation                                        DOT Code
----------                                        --------

                          HOC : RES
Cattle Rancher                                    410.161-018
Locomotive Engineer                               910.363-014
Crater                                            920.484-010
Braker, Passenger Train                           910.364-010
Construction Worker                               869.664-014
Fisher                                            442.684-010
Track Layer                                       869.687-026
                          HOC : REC
Supervisor, Natural-Gas Plant                     542.130-010
                          HOC : REI
Ship Pilot                                        197.133-026
Shop Supervisor                                   638.131-026
Supervisor, Paper Machine                         539.132-010
                          HOC : RSE
Blacksmith                                        610.381-010
Experimental Molder                               518.361-010
Locomotive Firer                                  910.363-010
Pipefitter                                        862.381-018
Railroad Conductor                                198.167-010
Taxi Driver                                       913.463-018
Butcher                                           316.684-022
Coal Equipment Operator                           921.683-022
Chauffeur                                         913.663-010
Fire Fighter                                      373.364-010
Streetcar Operator                                913.463-014
Waiter/Waitress                                   311.677-010
Parking-Lot Attendant                             915.473-010
Soda Clerk                                        319.474-010
Warehouse Worker                                  922.687-058
                          HOC : SRE
Children's Tutor (Governess)                      099.227-010
Driving Instructor                                099.223-010
Housekeeper                                       321.137-010
Occupational Therapist                            076.121-010
Detective                                         376.367-014
Houseparent                                       359.677-010
Professional Athlete                              153.341-010
Police Officer                                    375.263-014
```

psychware **729**

Automobile Salesperson	273.353-010
Sales Representative, Sporting Goods	277.357-026
Route Driver	292.353-010

HOC : ERI

Contractor	182.167-010
Farm Manager	180.167-018

HOC : ERC

Postmaster	188.167-066

HOC : RIS

Electrician	824.261-010
Glazier (Glass Setter)	865.381-010
Jeweler	700.281-010
Loom Fixer	683.260-018
Miller Supervisor	521.130-010
Powerhouse Mechanic	631.261-014
Power-Plant Operator	952.382-018
Tool and Die Maker	601.280-046
Baker	526.381-010
Cook	315.361-010
Filling Station Attendant	915.467-010
Heat Treater	504.682-018
Optician	716.280-014
Welder	819.384-010
Offset-Press Operator	651.685-018

HOC : RIE

Air Conditioning Mechanic	637.261-014
Air Traffic Controller	193.162-018
Aircraft Mechanic	862.381-010
Automobile Mechanic	620.261-010
Automobile-Repair-Service Estimator	620.261-018
Boilermaker	805.261-014
Diesel Mechanic	625.281-010
Drafter, Detail	017.261-030
Electronic Technician	726.281-014
Electroplater	500.380-010
Farm Equipment Mechanic	624.281-010
Farmer	421.161-010
Field Engineer	828.261-014
Flight Engineer	621.261-018
Garage Supervisor	620.131-014
Line Installer-Repairer	822.381-014
Loom Changer	683.360-010
Machinist	600.280-042
Machine Repairer	600.280-042
Mechanic/Repair Worker	see note
Millwright	638.281-018
Plumber	862.381-030
Radio Repairer	720.281-010
Sheet Metal Worker	804.281-010
Shipfitter	806.381-046
Watch Repairer	715.281-010
Automobile-Body Repairer	807.381-010
Compressor-House Operator	953.382-010
Engraver, Machine	704.682-010
Forging-Press Opeator	611.685-010
Furniture Upholsterer	780.381-018
Heavy Equipment Operator	859.683-010
Roofer	866.381-010
Logger	454.684.018
Machine Operator	616.360-018
Tool Crib Attendant	222.367-062

HOC : RSC

Exterminator	389.684-010
Elevator Operator	388.663-010
Stock Clerk	222.387-058
Kitchen Helper	318.687-010

HOC : RSI

Appliance Repairer	637.261-018
Weaver	683.682-038

```
                          HOC : RCE
      Crane Operator                             921.663-010
      Lumber Inspector                           669.587-010
      Tractor Operator                           929.683-014
      Tractor-Trailer-Truck Driver               904.383-010
      Truck Driver, Light                        906.683-022
      Fork-Lift Truck Operator                   921.683-050

      Note - For D.O.T. numbers, look under a more specific job title.

                              VPI Profile
            Real Int  Soc Conv Ent  Art        Co   Mf   St   Inf  Ac
           -----------------------------------  -------------------------
     15 +   -    -    -    -    -    -    +¶    ¶+   -    -    -    -    -   + 80
            -    *         *         *         ¶    ¶                        -
            -    *         *         *         ¶    ¶                   *    -
            -                                  ¶    ¶                        -
            -                                  ¶    ¶+   -    -    -    -    -   + 70
            -                                  ¶    ¶                        -
            -                                  ¶    ¶                        -
            -    *         *         *         ¶    ¶                        -
                                               ¶    ¶                   *    -
     10 +   -    -    -    -    -    -    +¶    ¶+   -    -    -    -    -   + 60
            -                                  ¶    ¶                        -
            -                                  ¶    ¶                        -
            -                                  ¶    ¶+------------*---------------+ 50
            -                                  ¶    ¶                        -
            -                                  ¶    ¶                        -
            -                                  ¶    ¶                        -
     05 +   -    -    -    -    -    -    +¶    ¶+   -    -    -    -    -   + 40
            -                                  ¶    ¶                        -
            -                                  ¶    ¶         *              -
            -                                  ¶    ¶+   *    -    -    -    -   + 30
            -                                  ¶    ¶                        -
            -                                  ¶    ¶                        -
           -----------------------------------  -------------------------
            Real Int  Soc Conv Ent  Art        Co   Mf   St   Inf  Ac
      R     14   11   14   11   14   11         0    6    6    10   19
      T     77   67   76   72   77   70         30   33   49   62   73
      P%    99   95   99   99   99   98         3    4    44   88   99
                              Profile Key
```

Interest Scales (Raw score profile)   Other Scales (T score profile)

   Real : Realistic   Co : Self-control

   Int : Intellectual   Mf : Masculinity-femininity
   Soc : Social   St : Status

   Conv : Conventional   Inf : Infrequency
   Ent : Enterprising   Ac : Acquiescence
   Art : Artistic

R = Raw score
T = T score
P% = Percentile

Raw Data

```
              1234567890 1234567890 1234567890

     1- 30    TTFTTFFFTT TTTTTTTFTF TFTFTFTFTF
     31- 60   TFTFTFTFTF TFTFTFTTTT TTTTTTTTTT
     61- 90   TTTTTTTTTT TTTTTTTTTT TTTTTTTTTT
     91-120   TTTTTTTTTT TTTTTTTTTT TTTTTTTTTT
     121-150  TTTTTTTTTT TTTTTTTTTT TTTTTTTTTT
     151-160  TTTTTTTTTT
```

psychware **731**

NAME: WAIS-R Report

SUPPLIER: Psychologistics, Inc.
P.O. Box 3896
Indialantic, FL 32903
(305) 727-7900

PRODUCT CATEGORY

Cognitive/Ability

PRIMARY APPLICATIONS

Educational Evaluation/Planning
Clinical Assessment/Diagnosis
Vocational Guidance/Counseling
Personnel Selection/Evaluation
Personal/Marriage/Family Counseling

SALE RESTRICTIONS American Psychological Association Guidelines

SERVICE TYPE/COST	Type	Available	Cost	Discount
	Mail-In	No		
	Teleprocessing	No		
	Local	Yes	$295.00	

PRODUCT DESCRIPTION

The WAIS-R REPORT provides automated interpretation of the Wechsler Adult Intelligence Scale-Revised. The printed report summarizes the demographic information and the subtest scaled scores. The classification range for each score is presented as well as the average Verbal and Performance subtest scores. The Full Scale IQ score, Verbal IQ score, and the Performance IQ score are listed. Major factor quotients are also printed and factor differences are evaluated for significance. Scale score differences are provided with associated significance levels.

The narrative section of the printed report consists of seven parts. The behavioral observations are presented in the first two paragraphs. The IQ paragraph describes the significance of the full scale IQ and the individual's relative verbal and performance abilities. A scale-by-scale analysis is done comparing the individual to peers. An interscale comparison focuses on intrapersonal strengths and weaknesses. The last three sections give the neuropsychological, academic, and vocational implications of the test results.

Software versions are available for the Apple II+, IIe, III and IBM PC computer systems. The price shown includes unlimited usage of the program.

```
Name:  John X. Doe              Date of test:   02-27-84
Sex:   male                     Date of birth:  02-09-44
Race:  caucasian                Age:  40 yrs., 0 mos.
Occupation: teamster            Education:  12
Marital Status: married
```

Reason for Referral: memory problems
Examiner: John Q. Smith PH.D.

The scores listed below were used for computations in this report. These age-corrected Scaled Scores should be checked carefully for errors. If discrepencies are found the entire report should be reprocessed.

Age Corrected Scaled Scores:

Information	9	Picture Completion	11
Digit Span	7	Picture Arrangement	12
Vocabulary	13	Block Design	12
Arithmetic	6	Object Assembly	13
Comprehension	12	Digit Symbol	8
Similarities	13		

RESULTS SUMMARY

Verbal Subtests:	Age Corrected Scaled Score	Range
Information	9	Average
Digit Span	7	Below Average
Vocabulary	13	Above Average
Arithmetic	6	Below Average
Comprehension	12	Above Average
Similarities	13	Above Average

Average Corrected Verbal= 10

Performance Subtests:	Age Corrected Scaled Score	Range
Picture Completion	11	Average
Picture Arrangement	12	Above Average
Block Design	12	Above Average
Object Assembly	13	Above Average
Digit Symbol	8	Average

Average Corrected Performance= 11.19

****

```
          Verbal Scale IQ Score          98    45%tile
          Performance Scale IQ Score     106   66%tile
          Full Scale IQ Score            101   53%tile
```

****

   95% Confidence Interval for Full Scale IQ Score = 97 TO 105

****

       Verbal IQ Score - Performance IQ Score = -8   (NS)

****

psychware **733**

```
Subtest Differences:
-------------------------------------------------------------------
Age-Corrected Subtest Score
minus mean Verbal Score:
----------------------------
Information                        -1.00     NS
Digit Span                         -3.00     (P<.05)
Vocabulary                          3.00     (P<.01)
Arithmetic                         -4.00     (P<.01)
Comprehension                       2.00     NS
Similarities                        3.00     (P<.05)

Age-Corrected Subtest Score
minus mean Performance Score:
----------------------------
Picture Completion                 -0.21     NS
Picture Arrangement                 0.80     NS
Block Design                        0.80     NS
Object Assembly                     1.79     NS
Digit Symbol                       -3.20     (P<.05)

                    Age Corrected
                Subtest Scaled Scores:
    Information        9      Picture Completion    11
    Digit Span         7      Picture Arrangement   12
    Vocabulary        13      Block Design          12
    Arithmetic         6      Object Assembly       13
    Comprehension     12      Digit Symbol           8
    Similarities      13

        Verbal Scale IQ Score         98
        Performance Scale IQ Score   106
        Full Scale IQ Score          101    (53%tile)
```

John Doe is a 40 year old caucasian male who was referred because of memory problems. He is a brown haired, brown eyed person of above average height and muscular body build. At the time of testing, Mr. Doe presented an overall neat appearance. Dress was appropriate and he was generally adequately groomed.

Mr. Doe's performance on the tasks indicates he is right hand dominant. During the session, no speech problems, no obvious sensory visual difficulty, and no obvious sensory hearing difficulty were observed. He exhibited appropriate skill with gross motor movements and age-appropriate skill with fine motor movements. Activity level was generally task appropriate.

Rapport with Mr. Doe was easily established. He was socially confident and comfortable in his interactions and talked to the examiner freely. Mr. Doe frequently asked to have instructions repeated. He exhibited an overall appropriate attitude towards the evaluation and maintained good interest and effort. His approach to assessment tasks was methodical and orderly and he exhibited no change in approach to difficult items. Concentration was erratic and he was appropriately persistent. Praise appeared to stimulate performance and he responded to errors/failures with apprehension and undue anxiety. No unusual or bizarre behaviors were observed during the session. In general this is believed to be an accurate estimate of Mr. Doe's current level of intellectual functioning.

On this administration of the Wechsler Adult Intelligence Scale Mr. Doe obtained a Verbal Scale IQ Score of 98 and a Performance Scale IQ Score of 106. This results in a Full Scale IQ Score of 101 which falls within the Average Range of intellectual abilities. The

Full Scale IQ Score corresponds to the 53%tile which suggests Mr. Doe
is functioning intellectually at a level equal to or better than
approximately 53% of his peers. Overall, he performed equally as
well on items reflecting verbal abilities as he did on tasks
requiring perceptual-motor abilities.

In comparison to other individuals the same age, Mr. Doe
exhibited significant strengths on subtests measuring:
  **Language development and word knowledge
  **Logical abstractive (catagorical) thinking
  **Ability to benefit from sensory-motor feedback;
    constructive ability in absence of external model;
    flexibility
Significant weaknesses in comparison to peers were exhibited on
subtests tapping:
  **Immediate auditory memory
  **Computational skills
Relative to his own level of performance on verbal and
perceptual-motor tasks, respectively, Mr. Doe exhibited significant
relative strength on subtests tapping:
  **Language development and word knowledge
  **Logical abstractive (catagorical) thinking
Significant relative weaknesses were evidenced on subtests
reflecting:
  **Immediate auditory memory
  **Computational skills
  **Speed of mental operation and short-term visual memory;
    ability to learn a new visual-motor task
If indications of possible neuropsychological problems exist,
then the following comments should be considered. The Performance IQ
is 8 points greater than the Verbal IQ. Similar differences are not
generally considered clinically significant. The Hold versus Don't
Hold analysis suggested by W. L. Hunt does not indicate a significant
difference. The results of L. R. Hewson's Ratios are within normal
limits.
IMPLICATIONS:
The following hypotheses concerning academic/vocational
performance and need for further evaluation are suggested by the
present results. These hypotheses should be evaluated in light of
the client's academic/vocational history, cultural and racial
background, and situational factors that may have affected
performance.
Present evaluation results indicate functioning in the Average
Range of intellectual abilities. This level of intellectual
functioning suggests that Mr. Doe should be able to perform and learn
cognitive/intellectual tasks at a level about the same as that of
same aged peers. Overall, Mr. Doe should be able to perform
activities involving verbal skills at about the same level as he can
tasks which involve visual-motor abilities.
Individuals of similar intellectual ability exhibit academic
attainment about the same as that of same aged peers. If history
indicates significantly lower school attainment/performance then
further evaluation of motivational, health, personality, and
family/personal factors should be obtained. When learning new
academic and other tasks, Mr. Doe probably learns material presented
verbally at about the same level as he does information presented
through visual means.
Individuals of similar abilities are usually intellectually
capable of performing skilled occupations. Independent job
functioning is probable.

NAME: WAIS-R/Holliman Report

SUPPLIER: Psych Lab
1714 Tenth Street
Wichita Falls, TX 76301
(817) 723-0012

PRODUCT CATEGORY

Cognitive/Ability

PRIMARY APPLICATIONS

Clinical Assessment/Diagnosis
Vocational Guidance/Counseling

SALE RESTRICTIONS American Psychological Association Guidelines

SERVICE TYPE/COST	Type	Available	Cost	Discount
	Mail-In	Yes	$10.00	
	Teleprocessing	No		
	Local	Yes	$6.00	

PRODUCT DESCRIPTION

This program produces the Holliman report for the Weschler Adult Intelligence Test-Revised. The software is designed for use on the Apple II + and IIe computers. Scores must first be calculated and then entered into the computer. The resulting printout provides patient identifying data, a graphical presentation of the scores, and a verbal interpretation of the data.

The cost for local service refers to the cost-per-test when diskettes are purchsed in units of 20 administrations (minimum purchase).

NAME: Wechsler Interpretation System

SUPPLIER: Applied Innovations, Inc.
South Kingstown Office Park, Suite A-1
Wakefield, RI 02879
(800) 272-2250

PRODUCT CATEGORY	PRIMARY APPLICATIONS
Cognitive/Ability	Clinical Assessment/Diagnosis
	Personal/Marriage/Family Counseling
	Personnel Selection/Evaluation

SALE RESTRICTIONS American Psychological Association Guidelines

SERVICE TYPE/COST	Type	Available	Cost	Discount
	Mail-In	No		
	Teleprocessing	No		
	Local	Yes	$425.00	

PRODUCT DESCRIPTION

The WESCHLER INTERPRETATION SYSTEM consists of a collection of computer programs which reduces the amount of time required to produce WISC-R and WAIS-R reports and evaluations. It takes approximately 10 minutes to create a report using this program after the test has been administered and scored. The software operates on most available personal computers including IBM, Apple, Digital, and Kaypro.

The Weschler Intelligence Scale for Children-Revised (WISC-R) and the Weschler Adult Intelligence Scale-Revised (WAIS-R) are both widely-used tests of general mental ability. WISC-R is used with children ages 5-15 years. WAIS-R is intended for use with those over the age of 16. Both tests consist of two sections: verbal and performance (non-verbal). Scores obtained from the two tests include a verbal IQ, a performance IQ, and a full scale IQ. WISC-R consists of six verbal and six performance subtests. WAIS-R consists of six verbal subtests and five performance subtests. Further analysis of test performance is based on interpretation of the various subtest scores within each of the tests.

The WESCHLER INTERPRETATION SYSTEM produces two types of reports, a clinical report for use by mental health professionals and a parent report suitable for clients and parents or guardians of clients. The programs are menu driven. Screen prompts guide the user through the various operational stages of the program. These reports are narrative in style and can be printed.

Name - JANE DOE
Age - 13
Sex - FEMALE
Marital Status - SINGLE
Ethnicity - WHITE
Referral Source - SCHOOL REFERRAL

Referral Question - INTELLECTUAL ASSESSMENT

Impressions: JANE is a female adolescent, 13 years old.
She has brown hair and brown eyes, is of average height and
has a medium build. Her attire was appropriate and she
was well groomed. Her dominant hand was her right hand.
No speech problems were evident. She did not seem to have
hearing impairment. She did not have obvious visual
difficulties with the test materials. Her gross motor
movements seemed age appropriate. Her fine motor skills
were age appropriate. In general, her activity level was
appropriate.
Her attitude toward the examiner was neutral and she was
cooperative with the testing procedures. Rapport was
good. She appeared to have understood the instructions
given to her and could change tasks as the testing
situation required.
She did not seem distractible. She approached the test in
an orderly manner. She seemed interested in the test
items and often became discouraged. Moderate anxiety was
observed during the testing situation. Signs of
depression were evident.
Her test performance does represent an optimal sample of
her intellectual functioning.
WISC-R: Her Full Scale IQ as measured by the WISC-R is 106,
her Verbal score is 98, and her Performance score is 115.
The full scale IQ is in the average range of intellectual
functioning and the verbal and performance scores are in
the average and bright normal ranges respectively. Scaled
scores are: Information, 9; Similarities, 12; Arithmetic,
9; Vocabulary, 9; Comprehension, 10; Digit Span, 9;
Picture Completion, 11; Picture Arrangement, 13; Block
Design, 11; Object Assembly, 15; Coding, 11.

There is a significant difference between the Verbal and
Performance scores. This individual expresses her
intelligence manipulatively. Reliance on the right
hemisphere and a greater aptitude for processing
visual-spatial stimuli is suggested. If organicity is
suspected then consider the possibility of left hemisphere
involvement. Psycholinguistic deficits may be evident.
If she is bilingual, bicultural or black, the
verbal-performance IQ differences may be normal. She may
exhibit a field-independent cognitive style; such people
are flexible in problem-solving situations. They impose
structure when it is lacking and tend to be abstract and
theoretical as opposed to people-oriented. Other reasons
for a significantly lowered verbal IQ are early
environmental deprivation and impulsivity with the
potential to act-out.

Her general intelligence, Factor G, is average. Her level
of cognitive functioning is average. Use of the 'right
brain' (holistic processing) for problems is indicated.
She can organize diverse data into a clear, concise idea or
concept. She may be creative. She tends to be
adaptable, and adjusts readily to new learning situations.
Her perceptual processes seem to be intact. She readily
perceives meaningful stimuli. She readily distinguishes
essential from non-essential detail. Her general memory
functions are adequate. Long-term memory is grossly
intact. Short-term memory is grossly intact.

The ability to anticipate the consequences of her behavior
is indicated.

===
Information = 9
Similarities = 12
Arithmetic = 9
Vocabulary = 9
Comprehension = 10
Digit Span = 9
Picture Completion = 11
Picture Arrangement = 13
Block Design = 11
Object Assembly = 15
Coding = 11
Verbal IQ = 98
Performance IQ = 115
Full scale IQ = 106
- Factors that may have affected test results -
Distractibility (Lower scores mean higher distractibility) = 9.67
Adaptability to new situations = 13.00   Test anxiety = 9.67
Attention span = 9.00   Concentration = 10.00
Extent of reading = 10.00   Richness of early environment = 9.00
School learning = 9.00   Working under time pressure = 11.67
- Scholastic Abilities -
Scholastic aptitude = 9.00   General intelligence (Factor G) = 10.20
Facility with numbers = 10.33   Learning ability = 10.00
Verbal comprehension = 10.00   Acquired knowledge = 9.00
Fund of information = 9.50   Verbal expression = 10.33
- Cognitive Processing -
Conceptual ability = 10.50   Verbal conceptualization = 10.33
General cognition = 11.17   Sequencing = 10.50
Reasoning = 11.00   Convergent production = 12.00
Synthesis = 13.00   Integrated brain functioning = 11.67
Spatial = 12.33   Associative thinking = 10.50
Creativity = 13.00
Holistic processing (right brain) = 13.00
- Perception -
Distinguishing essential from non-essential = 12.00
Perceptual organization = 12.50
Visual organization = 13.00
Visual perception of abstract stimuli = 11.00
Visual perception of meaningful stimuli = 13.00
Perceptual-motor coordination = 12.33

- Distractibility and Concentration -
Freedom from distractibility = 9.67   Mental alertness = 9.00
Attention = 11.00   Verbal concentration = 9.00
Visual concentration = 11.00

- Memory -
General memory = 9.80   Long term memory = 9.00
Short term memory = 10.00   Remote memory = 10.50
Visual memory = 11.00   Verbal memory = 9.00

- Social Skill and Judgment -
Common sense = 11.50   Social judgment = 11.50

- Vocational Abilities -
Numerical = 9.00   Spatial = 12.33
Form perception = 13.00   Clerical perception = 11.00
Motor coordination = 12.33   Finger dexterity = 12.33
Visual perception = 12.20   Mechanical = 13.00
Psycho-motor coordination = 12.33

- Ratios -
A score less than 1.0 suggests a tendency in the direction of that scale,
a score greater than 1.0 suggests an opposite tendency. These ratios
should be interpreted with extreme caution.

Male ratio = .93   Female ratio = .98
Depression ratio = 1.30   Schizophrenia ratio = 1.16
Neurosis ratio = 1.05   Organic ratio = .93

WECHSLER INTERPRETATION

APPLIED INNOVATIONS, INC.
(800) 272 2250

Name - JANE DOE
Age - 13
Sex - FEMALE
Marital Status - SINGLE
Ethnicity - WHITE

Referral Source - SCHOOL REFERRAL

Referral Question - INTELLECTUAL ASSESSMENT

Parent Report: JANE DOE has a level of intellectual
functioning, as measured by the WISC-R, in the average
range. Individuals in the average range can do most
things if they are motivated and study hard. The majority
of people function at this level. She expresses her
intelligence manipulatively. A greater aptitude for
processing visual-spatial stimuli is suggested.   She
tends to approach problem-solving with a flexible
orientation. She is abstract and theoretical and may not
be very interested in other people.

The following information gives the levels of functioning
in several areas for JANE DOE.   Each area will be rated
as high, average, or low.

Range of knowledge and general alertness: average.

Practical common sense and capacity to evaluate past
experience: average.

Mental alertness and ability to do arithmetic: average.

Capacity to perceive common elements and bring them
together under a single concept: average.

Capacity to comprehend and size up a total situation and
social intelligence: high.

Capacity to differentiate essential from non-essential
details and familiarity with culture: average.

General intelligence, organizing of problem-solving
approaches; capacity to analyze, synthesize a whole into
its component parts; and perception of patterns: average.

Associate learning involving visual acuity, motor
coordination, and speed; persistent effort or mental
efficiency: low.

Capacity to put parts into a familiar configuration;
thinking and working habits; rapid recognition; trial and
error thinking and reaction to mistakes: high.

General intelligence, verbal information: average.

        Dr. Michael Nover

740 *psychware*

NAME: Weschler Adult Intelligence Scale-Revised

SUPPLIER: PSYCH Systems, Inc.
600 Reisterstown Road
Baltimore, MD 21208
(800) 368-3366

PRODUCT CATEGORY	PRIMARY APPLICATIONS
Cognitive/Ability	Clinical Assessment/Diagnosis Educational Evaluation/Planning Vocational Guidance/Counseling Personnel Selection/Evaluation

SALE RESTRICTIONS   Qualified Professional

SERVICE TYPE/COST	Type	Available	Cost	Discount
	Mail-In	No		
	Teleprocessing	No		
	Local	Yes	See Below	

PRODUCT DESCRIPTION

The WAIS-R measures intellectual functioning levels of adults. It contributes significantly to personality assessment, clinical evaluation, treatment determination, and basic research on the mental capacities of adults. Test results are useful indicators of neuropsychological deficiencies.

This program provides a narrative report only. Administration and test scoring must be done off-line. The narrative report summarizes the obtained scores, prints a detailed description of the client, and provides an in-depth narrative evaluation of the client's intellectual functioning.

Psych Systems programs operate on the IBM PC-XT, COMPAQ Plus, Dec Professional 350, and most DEC PDP-11 systems. Various hardware/software configurations are available directly from Psych Systems, with single-user systems starting at approximately $12,000. A per test fee also applies.

```
-----------------------------------------------------------
|                |                                         |
|   WAIS-R       |   Wechsler Adult Intelligence Scale-Revised  |
|                |                                         |
-----------------------------------------------------------
```

This clinical report is designed to assist in psychodiagnostic
evaluation. It is available only to qualified professionals. This
report was produced by a computer analysis of the scores obtained by
the client listed above. The techniques utilized in the analysis of
the data and in generation of this report were designed by qualified
behavioral scientists utilizing well validated clinical research.
However this report is to be used in conjunction with professional
evaluation. No decision should be based solely upon the contents
of this report.

The computer program generating this report was designed by Psych
Systems, Inc., Baltimore, Maryland 21208. Copyright (C) 1984 by
Psych Systems, Inc. The interpretive logic utilized in the
generation of the report was designed by L. Michael Honaker, Ph.D.
and Giles Rainwater, Ph.D. Copyright (C) 1982 by L. Michael
Honaker and Giles Rainwater. Reproduced by permission and under
license from Psychologistics, Inc., Indiatlantic, Florida 32903.
All rights reserved.

```
         Name: Jonathan Doe              Date of Test: 28-Feb-1984
          Sex: Male                     Date of Birth: 2-Jan-1952
         Race: White                              Age: 32
   Occupation: Salesman                    Education: 13 Years
Marital Status: Divorced
        Reason For Referral: Emotional Problems
              Examiner: Dr. F. Test
```

The Age-Corrected Scaled Scores listed below were for computations
in this report. These scores should be checked carefully for errors.
If discrepancies are found, the entire report should be reprocessed.

Age Corrected Scaled Scores

```
        Information     10          Picture Completion     6
        Digit Span      15          Picture Arrangement    8
        Vocabulary       8          Block Design          14
        Arithmetic      10          Object Assembly       12
        Comprehension    9          Digit Symbol          10
        Similarities    11
```

                      RESULTS SUMMARY


```
Verbal              Scaled
Subtests:           Score         Range
------------------------------------------------------------------
Information           10    Average          |---------*
Digit Span            15    Superior         |--------------*
Vocabulary             8    Low Average      |-------*
Arithmetic            10    Average          |---------*
Comprehension          9    Average          |--------*
Similarities          11    Average          |----------*

            Average Verbal    10.50          |
------------------------------------------------|--------|--------|
                                              0       10      19

Performance         Scaled
Subtests:           Score         Range
------------------------------------------------------------------
Picture Completion     6    Borderline       |-----*
Picture Arrangement    8    Low Average      |-------*
Block Design          14    Superior         |-------------*
Object Assembly       12    High Average     |-----------*
Digit Symbol          10    Average          |---------*

          Average Performance   10.00        |
------------------------------------------------|--------|--------|
                                              0       10      19
```
****
```
        Verbal Scale IQ Score        105   63th Percentile
        Performance Scale IQ Score   110   75th Percentile
        Full Scale IQ Score          105   63th Percentile
```
****
   95% Confidence Interval for Full Scale IQ Score = 101 TO 109

****
        Verbal IQ Score - Performance IQ Score = -5   (NS)

****
                        Factor Scores

```
        Verbal Comprehension (VCQ)          = 97
        Perceptual Organization (POQ)       = 104
        Freedom From Distractability (FDQ)  = 114
```

                      Factor Differences

```
              VCQ - POQ =  -7      (NS)
              VCQ - FDQ = -17      (p < .01)
              POQ - FDQ = -10      (NS)
```

```
-------------------------------------------------------------------------
                    Subtest Differences
-------------------------------------------------------------------------
          Age-Corrected Subtest Score minus Mean Verbal Score
-------------------------------------------------------------------------
Information                          -0.50      (NS)
Digit Span                           4.50       (p < .01)
Vocabulary                           -2.50      (p < .01)
Arithmetic                           -0.50      (NS)
Comprehension                        -1.50      (NS)
Similarities                         0.50       (NS)
-------------------------------------------------------------------------
Age-Corrected Subtest Score minus Mean Performance Score
-------------------------------------------------------------------------
Picture Completion                   -4.00      (p < .01)
Picture Arrangement                  -2.00      (NS)
Block Design                         4.00       (p < .01)
Object Assembly                      2.00       (NS)
Digit Symbol                         0.00       (NS)
-------------------------------------------------------------------------
Age Corrected Scaled Scores

        Information     10        Picture Completion     6
        Digit Span      15        Picture Arrangement    8
        Vocabulary      8         Block Design          14
        Arithmetic      10        Object Assembly       12
        Comprehension   9         Digit Symbol          10
        Similarities    11

        Verbal Scale IQ Score          105    63th Percentile
        Performance Scale IQ Score     110    75th Percentile
        Full Scale IQ Score            105    63th Percentile
```

Jonathan Doe is a 32 year old white male who was referred because of
emotional problems. He is a brown haired, brown eyed person of above
average height and muscular body build. At the time of testing,
Jonathan Doe presented an overall neat appearance. Dress was
appropriate and he was generally adequately groomed.

Jonathan Doe's performance on the tasks indicates he is right hand
dominant. During the session, no speech problems, no obvious sensory
visual difficulty, and no obvious sensory hearing difficulty were
observed. He exhibited appropriate skill with gross motor movements
and age-appropriate skills with fine motor movements. Activity level
was erratic.

Rapport with Jonathan Doe was easily established. He was shy,
reserved, reticent and uncomfortable in his interactions and
initially reserved but became more spontaneous. Jonathan Doe
generally understood intructions readily. He exhibited an overall
appropriate attitude towards the evaluation and maintained good
interest and effort. His approach to assessment tasks was methodical
and/or orderly. He was challenged by difficult items. Concentration
was good. Praise had no observable effect on the client's behavior.
He responded to errors/failures with apprehension or undue anxiety.
No unusual or bizarre behaviors were observed during the session. In
general this is believed to be an accurate estimate of Jonathan Doe's
current level of intellectual functioning.

On this administration of the Wechsler Adult Intelligence
Scale-Revised, Mr. Jonathan Doe obtained a Verbal Scale IQ score of
105 and a Performance Scale IQ score of 110. This results in a Full
Scale IQ score of 105 which falls within the average range of
intellectual abilities. The chances are 95 out of a hundred that
Jonathan Doe's true IQ score falls between 101 and 109. The current
Full Scale IQ score corresponds to the 63 percentile which indicates
that Jonathan Doe is functioning intellectually at a level equal to
or better than approximately 63 percent of adults the same age.
Overall, performance on items tapping verbal comprehension skills was
about the same as that shown on tasks reflecting
perceptual-organization abilities.

Overall performance on subtests tapping verbal comprehension
abilities falls in the average range and corresponds to the 63
percentile. Performance was inconsistent across the different
subtests and ranged from the low average to superior levels.
Significant strength relative to overall verbal functioning was
exhibited on subtests reflecting:
- Short term auditory memory and the ability to remember the order of
symbolic material

Significant relative weaknesses were shown on subtests tapping:

- Language development and word knowledge
General performance on perceptual-organization tasks falls in the
high average range and corresponds to the 75 percentile. There was
much variability across the different subtests and performance ranged
between the superior to borderline levels.
Relative to overall functioning on perceptual-organization tasks,
significant strength was exhibited on subtests requiring:
- Analysis and synthesis of visually presented material; nonverbal
concept formation and spatial visualization

Significant relative weaknesses were shown in performance on subtests
reflecting:

- Visual alertness, visual recognition and identification (long term
visual memory)

If indications of possible neuropsychological problems exist, then
the following comments should be considered. The performance IQ is 5
points greater than the verbal IQ. Similar differences are not
generally considered clinically significant.

Other possible causes of these results include English not being the
client's primary language or a background that emphasized performance
skills (e.g., engineering, drafting, mechanics). The Hold versus
Don't Hold analysis suggested by W. L. Hunt does not indicate a
significant difference. The results of L. R. Hewson's Ratios suggest
the possibility of a Brain Dysfunction.
IMPLICATIONS:
The following hypotheses concerning treatment and need for further
evaluation are suggested by the present results. These hypotheses
should be evaluated in light of Jonathan Doe's academic/vocational
history, cultural and racial background, and situational factors that
may have affected performance.

Present evaluation results indicate functioning in the average range
of intellectual abilities. This level of intellectual functioning
suggests that Jonathan Doe should be able to perform and learn
cognitive/intellectual tasks at a level about the same as that of
same aged peers. Overall, Jonathan Doe should be able to perform
activities involving Verbal skills at about the same level as he can
perform tasks which involve Visual-Motor abilities.

Individuals of similar intellectual ability exhibit academic
attainment about the same as that of same aged peers. If history
indicates significantly lower school attainment/performance then
further evaluation of motivational, health, personality and
family/personal factors should be obtained. When learning new
academic and other tasks, Jonathan Doe probably learns material
presented verbally at about the same level as information presented
through visual means.

Individuals of similar abilities are usually intellectually capable
of performing skilled occupations. Independent job functioning is
probable.

There are aspects of the present performance which may be suggestive
of neurological impairment. If there is other evidence of Brain
Dysfunction observed in behavior, history, or other evaluation
results then a neurological evaluation should be considered.

NAME: Weschler Intelligence Scale for Children-Revised

SUPPLIER: PSYCH Systems, Inc.
600 Reisterstown Road
Baltimore, MD 21208
(800) 368-3366

PRODUCT CATEGORY

Cognitive/Ability

PRIMARY APPLICATIONS

Educational Evaluation/Planning
Clinical Assessment/Diagnosis
Vocational Guidance/Counseling

SALE RESTRICTIONS Qualified Professional

SERVICE TYPE/COST	Type	Available	Cost	Discount
	Mail-In	No		
	Teleprocessing	No		
	Local	Yes	See Below	

PRODUCT DESCRIPTION

The WISC-R assesses the intellectual abilities of children. This program provides a narrative report of scores that have been obtained by off-line testing. The report generates a profile analysis based on the computed differences between scores on the Verbal and Performance subtests, from which hypotheses about intellectual strengths and weaknesses can be developed by the clinician. The narrative report can be particularly useful in pinpointing individuals with psycho-educational deficits.

Psych Systems programs operate on the IBM PC-XT, COMPAQ Plus, Dec Professional 350, and most DEC PDP-11 systems. Various hardware/ software configurations are available directly from Psych Systems, with single-user systems starting at approximately $12,000. A per test fee also applies.

222-22-2222 Jonathan Doe Jr.   6 yr old white male   28-Feb-84

```
 ----------------------------------------------------------------
|           |                                                    |
|  WISC-R   |  Wechsler Intelligence Scale for Children-Revised  |
|           |                                                    |
 ----------------------------------------------------------------
```

This clinical report is designed to assist in psychodiagnostic evaluation.
It is available only to qualified professionals. This report was produced
by a computerized analysiis of the scores obtained by the client listed above.
The techniques utilized in the analysis of the data and in generation of
this report were designed by qualified behavioral scientists utilizing
highly validated clinical research. However, this report is to be used in
conjunction with professional evaluation. No decision should be based
solely upon the contents of this report.

The computer program generating this report was designed by Psych
Systems, Inc., Baltimore, Maryland 21208. Copyright (C) 1984 by
Psych Systems, Inc. The interpretive logic utilized in the
generation of the report was designed by L. Michael Honaker, Ph.D.
Copyright (C) 1982 by L. Michael Honaker. Reproduced by
permission and under license from Psychologistics, Inc.,
Indiatlantic, Florida 32903. All rights reserved.

psychware **747**

```
        Name: Jonathan Doe Jr.              Date of Test: 02-28-84
         Sex: Male                         Date of Birth: 07-07-77
      School: East Elementary School               Race: White
       Grade:  1
                          Examiner: Dr. F. Test

                      Current Placement: Regular
                   Reason for Referral: Emotional Problems
```

The scores listed below were used for computations in this report. These
age-corrected scaled scores should be checked carefully for errors. If
discrepencies are found, the entire report should be reprocessed.

```
-----------------------------------------------------------------------------
                      Age Corrected Scaled Scores
-----------------------------------------------------------------------------
         Information        8         Picture Completion    10
         Similarities      10         Picture Arrangement    8
         Arithmetic        14         Block Design           5
         Vocabulary         7         Object Assembly       12
         Comprehension     10         Coding                13
         Digit Span        10         Mazes                 14
-----------------------------------------------------------------------------
      *** Jonathan Doe Jr.'s test age is 6 years, 7 months, 21 days ***
-----------------------------------------------------------------------------
      Verbal           Scaled
      Subtests:        Score         Range
-----------------------------------------------------------------------------
      Information          8     Low Average      |-------*
      Similarities        10     Average          |---------*
      Arithmetic          14     Superior         |-------------*
      Vocabulary           7     Low Average      |------*
      Comprehension       10     Average          |---------*
      Digit Span          10     Average          |---------*

                   Average Verbal      9.83
-------------------------------------------------- |--------|--------|----
                                                   0       10       19

      Performance      Scaled
      Subtests:        Score         Range
-----------------------------------------------------------------------------
      Picture Completion   10     Average          |---------*
      Picture Arrangement   8     Low Average      |-------*
      Block Design          5     Borderline       |----*
      Object Assembly      12     High Average     |-----------*
      Coding               13     High Average     |-----------*
      Mazes                14     Superior         |------------*

                   Average Performance    10.33
--------------------------------------------------|--------|--------|----
                                                  0       10       19
-----------------------------------------------------------------------------

         Verbal Scale IQ Score           100  50 Percentile
         Performance Scale IQ Score      100  50 Percentile
         Full Scale IQ Score             100  50 Percentile
-----------------------------------------------------------------------------

      95% Confidence interval for Full Scale IQ Score =  93 to 107
-----------------------------------------------------------------------------

         Verbal IQ Score - Performance IQ Score =   0  (NS)
-----------------------------------------------------------------------------
                         Factor Scores:
-----------------------------------------------------------------------------

      Verbal Comprehension          (VCQ)   92  30 Percentile
      Perceptual Organization       (POQ)   99  47 Percentile
      Freedom from Distractibility  (FDQ)  109  73 Percentile
```

```
-------------------------------------------------------------------------
                        Factor Differences:
-------------------------------------------------------------------------

                    VCQ - POQ =    -7  (NS)
                    VCQ - FDQ =   -17  p<.05
                    POQ - FDQ =   -10  (NS)

-------------------------------------------------------------------------
                        Subtest Differences:
-------------------------------------------------------------------------
                Subtest Score Minus Mean Verbal Score
                -------------------------------------
            Information               -1.83       (NS)
            Similarities               0.17       (NS)
            Arithmetic                 4.17       p<.01
            Vocabulary                -2.83       (NS)
            Comprehension              0.17       (NS)
            Digit Span                 0.17       (NS)


                Subtest Score Minus Mean Performance Score
                ------------------------------------------
            Picture Completion        -0.33       (NS)
            Picture Arrangement       -2.33       (NS)
            Block Design              -5.33       p<.01
            Object Assembly            1.67       (NS)
            Coding                     2.67       (NS)
            Mazes                      3.67       (NS)

-------------------------------------------------------------------------
                    Age Corrected Scaled Scores
-------------------------------------------------------------------------
        Information      8         Picture Completion    10
        Similarities    10         Picture Arrangement    8
        Arithmetic      14         Block Design           5
        Vocabulary       7         Object Assembly       12
        Comprehension   10         Coding                13
        Digit Span      10         Mazes                 14
-------------------------------------------------------------------------
```

Jonathan Doe Jr. is a 6 year old white male who was referred because
of emotional problems. He is a blonde haired, green eyed person of
below average height and underweight body build. At the time of
testing, Jonathan Doe Jr. presented an overall neat appearance.
Dress was appropriate, and he was generally adequately groomed.

Jonathan Doe Jr.'s performance on the tasks indicates he is neither
left nor right hand dominant. During the session, no speech
problems, no obvious sensory visual difficulty, no obvious sensory
hearing difficulty were observed. He exhibited age-appropriate skill
with gross motor movements, and age-appropriate skill with fine motor
movements. Activity level was age and task appropriate.

Rapport with Jonathan Doe Jr. was easily established. He was
shy/reserved/reticent and uncomfortable in his interactions and was
reserved initially but became more spontaneous. Jonathan Doe Jr.
generally understood instructions readily. He exhibited an overall
appropriate attitude towards the evaluation and motivation was
variable across tasks. His approach to assessment tasks was
methodical and/or orderly. He was challenged by difficult items.
Concentration was erratic or variable. He was appropriately
persistent. Praise had no observable effect on Jonathan Doe Jr.'s
behavior. He responded to errors/failures with apprehension or undue
anxiety. No unusual or bizarre behaviors were observed during the
testing session. Jonathan Doe Jr.'s performance was optimal. This
is believed to be an accurate estimate of Jonathan Doe Jr.'s current
level of intellectual functioning.

On this administration of the Wechsler Intelligence Scale for
Children, Jonathan Doe Jr. obtained a Verbal Scale IQ score of 100
and a Performance Scale IQ score of 100. This results in a Full
Scale IQ score of 100 which falls within the average range of
intellectual abilities. The chances are 95 out of 100 that Jonathan
Doe Jr.'s true IQ score falls between 93 and 107. The current Full
Scale IQ score corresponds to the 50 percentile which indicates that
Jonathan Doe Jr. is functioning intellectually at a level equal to or
better than approximately 50 percent of children the same age.
Overall, performance on items tapping verbal comprehension skills was
about the same as that shown on tasks reflecting
perceptual-organization abilities.

Examination of Jonathan Doe Jr.'s pattern of performance across the different subtests suggests relative strengths were exhibited on:
- Tasks requiring attention to and manipulation of numerical stimuli
- Items reflecting mental alertness and short term memory of numerical stimuli.

No pattern of relative weakness was evidenced.

Overall performance on subtests tapping verbal comprehension abilities falls in the average range and corresponds to the 50 percentile. Performance was inconsistent across the different subtests and ranged from the low average to superior levels. Significant strengths relative to overall verbal functioning was exhibited on subtests reflecting:
- Computational skills.

Significant relative weaknesses were not shown on any of the subtests.

General performance on perceptual-organization tasks falls in the average range and corresponds to the 50 percentile. There was much variability across the different subtests and performance ranged between the borderline and superior levels. Relative to overall functioning on perceptual organization tasks, no significant strengths were exhibited.

Significant relative weakness was shown in performance on subtests reflecting:
- Analysis and synthesis of visually presented material; nonverbal concept formation and spatial visualization.

Implications

The following hypotheses concerning treatment and need for further evaluation are suggested by the present results. These hypotheses should be evaluated in

light of Jonathan Doe Jr.'s current academic functioning, cultural and racial background, and situational factors that may have influenced performance.

Present evaluation results suggest that Jonathan Doe Jr. should be able to perform academically at a level consistent with same-aged peers. If academic difficulties are evidenced, further psychological evaluation is warranted.

Dr. F. Test
Examiner

NAME: Weschler Pre-School and Primary Scale of Intelligence

SUPPLIER: PSYCH Systems, Inc.
600 Reisterstown Road
Baltimore, MD 21208
(800) 368-3366

PRODUCT CATEGORY	PRIMARY APPLICATIONS
Cognitive/Ability	Educational Evaluation/Planning
	Clinical Assessment/Diagnosis
	Vocational Guidance/Counseling

SALE RESTRICTIONS Qualified Professional

SERVICE TYPE/COST Type	Available	Cost	Discount
Mail-In	No		
Teleprocessing	No		
Local	Yes	See Below	

PRODUCT DESCRIPTION

The WESCHLER PRE-SCHOOL AND PRIMARY SCALE OF INTEL-LIGENCE assesses the intellectual abilities of young children. This program provides a narrative report of scores that have been obtained by off-line testing. The report discusses overall performance on the verbal and perform-ance subsections and identifies significant relative strengths and significant relative weaknesses on subtests in each area. The report concludes with a listing of hypotheses concerning treatment and need for further evaluation.

Two pages of charted results are also provided. This section also provides statistical tests of differences in performance on subtests within the battery to help identify psychoeducational deficits.

Psych Systems programs operate on the IBM PC-XT, COMPAQ Plus, Dec Professional 350, and most DEC PDP-11 systems. Various hardware/ software configurations are available directly from Psych Systems, with single-user systems starting at approximately $12,000. A per test fee also applies.

222-22-2222 Jonathan Doe Jr.   4 yr old white male   29-Feb-84

```
-------------------------------------------------------------------
|            |                                                    |
|   WPPSI    |   Wechsler Pre-School Primary Scale of Intelligence |
|            |                                                    |
-------------------------------------------------------------------
```

This clinical report is designed to assist in psychodiagnostic
evaluation. It is available only to qualified professionals. This
report was produced by a computerized analysis of the scores obtained
by the client listed above. The techniques utilized in the analysis
of the data and in generation of this report were designed by
qualified behavioral scientists utilizing well validated clinical
research. However, this report is to be used in conjunction with
professional evaluation. No decision should be based solely upon the
contents of this report.

The computer program generating this report was designed by Psych
Systems, Inc., Baltimore, Maryland 21208. Copyright (C) 1984 by
Psych Systems, Inc. The interpretive logic utilized in the
generation of the report was designed by L. Michael Honaker, Ph.D.
Copyright (C) 1982 by L. Michael Honaker. Reproduced by permission
and under license from Psychologistics, Inc., Indiatlantic, Florida
32903. All rights reserved.

WPPSI REPORT

Name: Jonathan Doe Jr.   Date of Test : 29-Feb-84
Sex: Male   Date of Birth: 10-Aug-79
School: Mother Goose Nursery   Race: White

          Examiner: Dr. F. Test

          Reason for Referral: Behavioral Problems

The scores listed below were used for computations in this report.
These scaled scores should be checked carefully to be sure the
correct scores were entered. If discrepancies are found, the entire
report should be reprocessed.

                          Scaled Scores

     Information   4   Animal House   9
     Vocabulary   5   Picture Completion   6
     Arithmetic   8   Mazes   4
     Similarities   10   Geometric Design   4
     Comprehension   4   Block Design   10
     Sentences   6   Animal House Retest

   *** Jonathan Doe Jr.'s test age is 4 years, 6 months, and 18 days ***

Verbal   Scaled
Subtests: Score   Range   0   10   19
---|---------|--------|
Information   4   Mental Retardation |---*
Vocabulary   5   Borderline |----*
Arithmetic   8   Low Average |-------*
Similarities   10   Average |---------*
Comprehension   4   Mental Retardation |---*
Sentences   6   Borderline |-----*

Average Verbal   6.17

Performance   Scaled
Subtests: Score   Range   0   10   19
---|---------|--------|
Animal House   9   Average |--------*
Picture Completion   6   Borderline |-----*
Mazes   4   Mental Retardation |---*
Geometric Design   4   Mental Retardation |---*
Block Design   10   Average |---------*

Average Performance 6.60

****

     Verbal Scale IQ Score   95   37%tile
     Performance Scale IQ Score   90   25%tile
     Full Scale IQ Score   92   30%tile

****

   95% Confidence Interval for Full Scale IQ = 86 to 98

****

psychware **753**

Verbal IQ Score Minus Performance IQ Score = 5   Not Significant (NS)

****

Subtest Differences:

Subtest Score Minus
Mean Verbal Score

Information   -2.17   (NS)
Vocabulary   -1.17   (NS)
Arithmetic   1.83   (NS)
Similarities   3.83   p < .01
Comprehension   -2.17   (NS)
Sentences   -0.17   (NS)

Subtest Score Minus
Mean Performance Score

Animal House   2.83   (NS)
Picture Completion   -0.17   (NS)
Mazes   -2.17   (NS)
Geometric Design   -2.17   (NS)
Block Design   3.83   p < .01

                      Subtests Scaled Scores

         Information   4   Animal House   9
         Vocabulary   5   Picture Completion   6
         Arithmetic   8   Mazes   4
         Similarities   10   Geometric Design   4
         Comprehension   4   Block Design   10
         Sentences   6   Animal House Retest

            Verbal Scale IQ Score   95
            Performance Scale IQ Score   90
            Full Scale IQ Score   92   (30%tile)

On this administration of the Wechsler Preschool and Primary Scale of
Intelligence, Jonathan Doe Jr. obtained a Verbal Scale IQ score of 95
and a Performance Scale IQ of 90. This results in a Full Scale IQ
score of 92 which falls within the average range of intellectual
abilities. The chances are 95 out of a hundred that Jonathan Doe
Jr.'s true IQ score falls between 86 and 98. The current Full Scale
IQ score corresponds to the 30%tile which indicates that Jonathan Doe
Jr. is functioning intellectually at a level equal to or better than
approximately 30% of children the same age. Overall, performance on
items tapping verbal comprehension skills was about the same as that
shown on tasks reflecting perceptual-organization abilities.

Overall performance on subtests tapping verbal comprehension
abilities falls in the average range and corresponds to the 37%tile.
Performance was inconsistent across the different subtests and ranged
from the mental retardation to average levels. Significant strength
relative to overall verbal functioning was exhibited on subtests
reflecting:

-- logical or abstractive (categorical) thinking
Significant relative weaknesses were not shown on any of the
subtests.

754 *psychware*

General performance on perceptual-organization tasks falls in the average range and corresponds to the 25%tile. There was not much variability across the different subtests and ranged between the mental retardation and average levels. Relative to overall functioning on perceptual-organization tasks, significant strength was exhibited on subtests requiring:

-- analysis and synthesis of visually presented material; nonverbal concept formation and spatial visualization
No significant relative weaknesses were shown.

The following hypotheses concerning treatment and need for further evaluation are suggested by the present results. These hypotheses should be evaluated in the light of Jonathan Doe Jr.'s current academic functioning, cultural and racial background, and situational factors that may have influenced performance.

Present evaluation results suggest that Jonathan Doe Jr. should be able to perform academically at a level consistent with same-aged peers. If academic difficulties are evidenced, further psychological evaluation is warranted.

_____

Dr. F. Test

NAME: WISC-R Compilation: Computer Edition

SUPPLIER: Psychological Assessment Resources
P.O. Box 98
Odessa, FL 33556
(813) 977-3395

PRODUCT CATEGORY	PRIMARY APPLICATIONS
Cognitive/Ability	Educational Evaluation/Planning Clinical Assessment/Diagnosis Vocational Guidance/Counseling Personal/Marriage/Family Counseling

SALE RESTRICTIONS American Psychological Association Guidelines

SERVICE TYPE/COST	Type	Available	Cost	Discount
	Mail-In	No		
	Teleprocessing	No		
	Local	Yes	$65.00	

PRODUCT DESCRIPTION

The WISC-R COMPILATION: COMPUTER EDITION is a computerized version of the popular WISC-R Compilation by Whitworth and Sutton that has been used in text form by thousands of psychologists and clinicians to identify practical objectives and remedial activities based on WISCR-R subtest scores.

The WISC-R COMPILATION program provides a printout of age appropriate goals and objectives for each deficiency identified. The objectives and activities are keyed to each of the 12 subtests and to four instructional levels (K-3, 4-6, 7-9, and 10-12) within each subtest, giving a resource of nearly 1000 different objectives.

Software versions are available for the Apple II + , IIe, TRS-80 Models III and IV computers.

P.O. Box 98 / Odessa, Florida 33556

Telephone: (813) 977-3395

WISC-R COMPILATION: COMPUTER EDITION   Apple   593-CP
                          Sample Printout   TRS-80   595-CP

Objective Report for JOHN SMITH   10/03/83
Weschler Intelligence Scale for Children - Revised (c)
Whitworth & Sutton Compilation (c)

--- -----------

Based on JOHN's performance on the WISC-R,
the following instructional plan is suggested. These goals and
objectives are for grade 2 .

Information

JOHN obtained a below average score of 6 scaled score points.

Long Range Goal:

JOHN will be able to remember particular
facts from prior learning experiences.

Short-Term Objectives:

1.   Participate in "Show and Tell" activities.

2.   State on demand full name; address and telephone number.

3.   Identify body parts as to names; locations and functions.

4.   Draw pictures of self; family and environment.

5.   Record on a chart the date and his/her height at periodic
.intervals.

6.   Recreate a bedroom or family seating arrangement at the dinner
table; etc.; using small toys and/or doll house furniture.

7.   Discuss and/or describe trips made by the student's family to
specified locations (e.g.; grocery store; post office; etc.).

8.   Draw pictures or verbally describe field trips; films; etc.; to
community agencies.

Similarities

JOHN obtained an average score of 9 scaled score points.

psychware   **757**

Sample Printout

Score does not indicate a deficiency in this area.

Arithmetic

JOHN obtained a low score of 5 scaled score points.

Long Range Goal:.

JOHN will be able to solve arithmetic
computations involving the major operations.

Short-Term Objectives:

1. Identify geometric shapes (e.g.; lines; squares; circles;
triangles; etc.).

2. Walk on a large number line placed on the floor and say the
numbers as they are stepped on.

3. Count from 1 to 10 using number line techniques.

4. Count up to 10 objects selecting specified numbers of objects in
random order. (Expand to include the numbers 1 to 50.)

5. Demonstrate comprehension of 'oneness' and 'twoness;' etc.; using
blocks; sticks and members of the class; etc.

6. Identify each numeral as it is presented using plastic numerals
and cards with numerals 1 to 50 on them.

7. Demonstrate comprehension of the vocabulary basic to math through
the manipulation of objects and audio-visual aids.

8. Play games that involve counting from 1 to 100.

Vocabulary

JOHN obtained an average score of 8 scaled score points.

Score does not indicate a deficiency in this area.

Comprehension

JOHN obtained a below average score of 7 scaled score points.

Long Range Goal:

Sample Printout

JOHN will to evaluate and respond
to real-life situations.

Short-Term Objectives:

1.   Execute simple commands (e.g.; "jump;" "bend over;" "sit down;";
etc.) gradually increasing complexity.

2.   Perform specific body movements in games (e.g.; "Simon Says;"
"Mother May I;" "Do What Chad Did;" etc.).

3.   Demonstrate comprehension of basic concepts of up; down; before;
first; last; etc.; utilizing manipulative objects.

4.   Answer specific 'why' questions (e.g. 'Why do we have houses ?'
etc.)

5. Supply missing details or invent the next thing happening in a
story told with frequent pauses by the teacher.

6.   Discuss the logical and/or illogical happenings in fables and
folklore.

7.   Discuss problems or social situations presented in pictures or
filmstrips.

8.   Discuss social situations and state consequences for one's own
behavior.

Digit Span

JOHN obtained a low score of 5 scaled score points.

Long Range Goal:

JOHN will recall and repeat auditorially
received information in correct sequence and detail.

Short-Term Objectives:

1.   Repeat simple letter and number sequences beginning with a
combination of two letters or numerals.

2.   Color a sheet of simple abstract designs following oral
directions (e.g.; "Color the circle; square; etc.").

3.   Color a sheet of simple abstract designs a specified color (e.g.;
"Color the circle red; blue; etc.").

4. Follow one or more simple directions (e.g.; "Put the pencil on the table; under the chair; etc.").

5. Repeat a sequence of two or more unrelated words.

6. Repeat a sequence of two or more nonsense syllables.

7. Repeat a sequence of numerals in reverse order.

8. Repeat a sequence of names of objects and arrange pictures of the objects in the same order.

Picture Completion

JOHN obtained an average score of 11 scaled score points.

Score does not indicate a deficiency in this area.

Picture Arrangement

JOHN obtained an average score of 8 scaled score points.

Score does not indicate a deficiency in this area.

Block Design

JOHN obtained an above average score of 14 scaled score points.

Score does not indicate a deficiency in this area.

Object Assembly

JOHN obtained a high score of 16 scaled score points.

Score does not indicate a deficiency in this area.

Coding

JOHN obtained an average score of 12 scaled score points.

Score does not indicate a deficiency in this area.

Mazes

JOHN obtained an above average score of 13 scaled score points.

Score does not indicate a deficiency in this area.

NAME: WISC-R Report

SUPPLIER: Psychologistics, Inc.
P.O. Box 3896
Indialantic, FL 32903
(305) 727-7900

PRODUCT CATEGORY	PRIMARY APPLICATIONS
Cognitive/Ability	Educational Evaluation/Planning Clinical Assessment/Diagnosis Vocational Guidance/Counseling Personal/Marriage/Family Counseling

SALE RESTRICTIONS American Psychological Association Guidelines

SERVICE TYPE/COST	Type	Available	Cost	Discount
	Mail-In	No		
	Teleprocessing	No		
	Local	Yes	$295.00	

PRODUCT DESCRIPTION

The WISC-R REPORT provides automated interpretation of the Weschler Intelligence Scale for Children-Revised. The interpretive logic used is similar in principle to that of Kaufman (1979) and Sattler (1982).

The printed report summarizes the demographic information and the subtest scaled scores. The classification range for each score is presented as well as the average Verbal and Performance subtest scores. The Full Scale IQ score, Verbal IQ score, and the Performance IQ score are listed. Major factor quotients are also printed and factor differences are tested for significance. Scale score differences are provided with associated significance levels.

The narrative section consists of four parts. First, demographic and score information is summarized. The child and his/her test behaviors are described. A successive level analysis examines the meaning of the IQ scores, areas of strength and weakness and performance variability. The final part summarizes the implications of the findings.

Software versions are available for the Apple II +, IIe, III and IBM PC computer systems. The price shown includes unlimited usage of the program.

```
                          WISC-REPORT
                      PSYCHOLOGISTICS INC.

NAME:   JOHN X. DOE JR.              DATE OF TEST:   02-27-84
SEX:    MALE                         DATE OF BIRTH:  11-01-75
SCHOOL: ANYTOWN SCHOOL               RACE:  CAUCASIAN
GRADE:  3                            EXAMINER:  JOHN Q. SMITH PH.D.


          CURRENT PLACEMENT:   REGULAR
          REASON FOR REFERRAL: BEHAVIORAL PROBLEMS


THE SCORES LISTED BELOW WERE USED FOR COMPUTATIONS IN THIS REPORT. THESE
AGE-CORRECTED SCALED SCORES SHOULD BE CHECKED CAREFULLY FOR ERRORS.   IF
DISCREPENCIES ARE FOUND, THE ENTIRE REPORT SHOULD BE REPROCESSED.


---------------------------------------------------------------------
AGE CORRECTED SCALED SCORES:
---------------------------------------------------------------------
        INFORMATION      12         PICTURE COMPLETION    13
        SIMILARITIES      8         PICTURE ARRANGEMENT   14
        ARITHMETIC       12         BLOCK DESIGN          14
        VOCABULARY        9         OBJECT ASSEMBLY       16
        COMPREHENSION    15         CODING                 9
        DIGIT SPAN       11         MAZES


---------------------------------------------------------------------

   *** JOHN'S TEST AGE IS 8 YEARS, 3 MONTHS, AND 26 DAYS ***

---------------------------------------------------------------------
VERBAL              SCALED
SUBTESTS:           SCORE      RANGE
---------------------------------------------------------------------
INFORMATION          12        ABOVE AVERAGE    ============*
SIMILARITIES          8        BELOW AVERAGE    ========*
ARITHMETIC           12        ABOVE AVERAGE    ============*
VOCABULARY            9        AVERAGE          =========*
COMPREHENSION        15        SUPERIOR         ===============*
DIGIT SPAN           11        AVERAGE          ===========*

AVERAGE VERBAL     11.16
---------------------------------------------------------------------
PERFORMANCE         SCALED
SUBTESTS:           SCORE      RANGE
---------------------------------------------------------------------
PICTURE COMPLETION   13        ABOVE AVERAGE    =============*
PICTURE ARRANGEMENT  14        SUPERIOR         =============*
BLOCK DESIGN         14        SUPERIOR         =============*
OBJECT ASSEMBLY      16        VERY SUPERIOR    ===============*
CODING                9        AVERAGE          ========*


AVERAGE PERFORMANCE                 13.19


     WISC-R COPYRIGHT (C) 1974 BY THE PSYCHOLOGICAL CORPORATION.
       WISC-REPORT COPYRIGHT (C) 1982 BY L. MICHAEL HONAKER.
                     ALL RIGHTS RESERVED.
```

762 *psychware*

```
**************************************************************************

             VERBAL SCALE IQ SCORE      107  68%TILE

             PERFORMANCE SCALE IQ SCORE 123  94%TILE

             FULL SCALE IQ SCORE        116  86%TILE

**************************************************************************

   95% CONFIDENCE INTERVAL FOR FULL SCALE IQ SCORE = 110 TO 122

**************************************************************************

        VERBAL IQ SCORE - PERFORMANCE IQ SCORE = -16  P<.01

**************************************************************************


FACTOR SCORES:
--------------------------------------------------------------------------

   VERBAL COMPREHENSION          (VCQ) 106  66%TILE
   PERCEPTUAL ORGANIZATION       (POQ) 127  96%TILE
   FREEDOM FROM DISTRACTIBILITY  (FDQ) 104  61%TILE

FACTOR DIFFERENCES:
--------------------------------------------------------------------------

              VCQ - POQ =  -21  P<.01
              VCQ - FDQ =    2  (NS)
              POQ - FDQ =   23  P<.01
--------------------------------------------------------------------------

SUBTEST DIFFERENCES:
--------------------------------------------------------------------------
SUBTEST SCORE MINUS
MEAN VERBAL SCORE
------------------------
INFORMATION                      0.83        (NS)
SIMILARITIES                    -3.16        (NS)
ARITHMETIC                       0.83        (NS)
VOCABULARY                      -2.16        (NS)
COMPREHENSION                    3.83        P<.05
DIGIT SPAN                      -0.17        (NS)

SUBTEST SCORE MINUS
MEAN PERFORMANCE SCORE
------------------------
PICTURE COMPLETION              -0.21        (NS)
PICTURE ARRANGEMENT             0.80         (NS)
BLOCK DESIGN                    0.80         (NS)
OBJECT ASSEMBLY                 2.79         (NS)
CODING                         -4.19         P<.05
```

psychware **763**

```
                         WISC-REPORT
                      PSYCHOLOGISTICS INC.


NAME:    JOHN X. DOE JR.          DATE OF TEST:   02-27-84
SEX:     MALE                     DATE OF BIRTH:  11-01-75
SCHOOL:  ANYTOWN SCHOOL           RACE:  CAUCASIAN
GRADE:   3                        EXAMINER:  JOHN Q. SMITH PH.D.

              CURRENT PLACEMENT:    REGULAR
              REASON FOR REFERRAL: BEHAVIORAL PROBLEMS


                    SUBTEST SCALED SCORES


        INFORMATION     12      PICTURE COMPLETION     13
        SIMILARITIES     8      PICTURE ARRANGEMENT    14
        ARITHMETIC      12      BLOCK DESIGN           14
        VOCABULARY       9      OBJECT ASSEMBLY        16
        COMPREHENSION   15      CODING                  9
        DIGIT SPAN      11      MAZES


              VERBAL SCALE IQ SCORE       107
              PERFORMANCE SCALE IQ SCORE  123
              FULL SCALE IQ SCORE         116   (86%TILE)
```

JOHN DOE JR. IS A 8 YEAR OLD CAUCASIAN MALE WHO WAS REFERRED
BECAUSE OF BEHAVIORAL PROBLEMS. HE IS A BLONDE HAIRED, GREEN EYED
PERSON OF AVERAGE HEIGHT AND AVERAGE BODY BUILD. AT THE TIME OF
TESTING, JOHN PRESENTED AN OVERALL NEAT APPEARANCE. DRESS WAS
APPROPRIATE AND HE WAS GENERALLY WELL GROOMED.

JOHN'S PERFORMANCE ON THE TASKS INDICATES HE IS LEFT HAND
DOMINANT. DURING THE SESSION, SOME SPEECH PROBLEMS, NO OBVIOUS
SENSORY VISUAL DIFFICULTY, AND NO OBVIOUS SENSORY HEARING DIFFICULTY
WERE OBSERVED. HE EXHIBITED APPROPRIATE SKILL WITH GROSS MOTOR
MOVEMENTS AND AGE-APPROPRIATE SKILL WITH FINE MOTOR MOVEMENTS.
ACTIVITY LEVEL WAS GENERALLY OVERLY ACTIVE.

RAPPORT WITH JOHN WAS EASILY ESTABLISHED. HE WAS SOCIALLY
CONFIDENT AND COMFORTABLE IN HIS INTERACTIONS AND TALKED TO THE
EXAMINER FREELY. JOHN GENERALLY UNDERSTOOD INSTRUCTIONS READILY. HE
EXHIBITED AN OVERALL INDIFFERENT ATTITUDE TOWARDS THE EVALUATION AND
MOTIVATION WAS VARIABLE ACROSS TASKS. HIS APPROACH TO ASSESSMENT
TASKS WAS IMPULSIVE AND POORLY PLANNED. HE PREFERRED ONLY EASY ITEMS.
   CONCENTRATION WAS ERRATIC.HE GAVE UP TOO QUICKLY. PRAISE HAD NO
OBSERVABLE EFFECT. HE OVERRACTED TO ERRORS/FAILURES AND BECAME
SELF-CRITICAL OR ANGRY. NO UNUSUAL OR BIZARRE BEHAVIORS WERE
OBSERVED DURING THE SESSION. IN GENERAL THIS IS BELIEVED TO BE AN
ACCURATE ESTIMATE OF JOHN'S CURRENT LEVEL OF INTELLECTUAL FUNCTIONING.

764 *psychware*

ON THIS ADMINISTRATION OF THE WECHSLER INTELLIGENCE SCALE FOR CHILDREN-REVISED, JOHN OBTAINED A VERBAL SCALE IQ SCORE OF 107 AND A PERFORMANCE SCALE IQ SCORE OF 123. THIS RESULTS IN A FULL SCALE IQ SCORE OF 116 WHICH FALLS WITHIN THE HIGH AVERAGE (BRIGHT) RANGE OF INTELLECTUAL ABILITIES. THE FULL SCALE IQ SCORE CORRESPONDS TO THE 86%TILE WHICH INDICATES HE IS FUNCTIONING INTELLECTUALLY AT A LEVEL EQUAL TO OR BETTER THAN APPROXIMATELY 86% OF THE CHILDREN THE SAME AGE. OVERALL, JOHN PERFORMED SIGNIFICANTLY POORER ON ITEMS TAPPING VERBAL COMPREHENSION SKILLS THAN HE DID ON TASKS REQUIRING PERCEPTUAL ORGANIZATION. THE ABILITY TO ATTEND TO, CONCENTRATE ON, AND MANIPULATE NUMERICAL MATERIAL, MAY INTERFERE WITH OPTIMAL PERFORMANCE AND IS SIGNIFICANTLY BELOW PERCEPTUAL ORGANIZATION SKILLS.

EXAMINATION OF JOHN'S PERFORMANCE ACROSS THE DIFFERENT SUBTESTS INDICATES HE EXHIBITED A PATTERN OF STRENGTH ON SUBTESTS TAPPING SOCIAL JUDGMENT. A PARTICULAR PATTERN OF WEAKNESS WAS EXHIBITED ON SUBTESTS THAT TEND TO TAP LEARNING ABILITY AND ON TASKS TAPPING VISUAL MEMORY.

IN COMPARISON TO JOHN'S OVERALL PERFORMANCE ON VERBAL COMPREHENSION ITEMS, HE EXHIBITED RELATIVE STRENGTH ON SUBTEST MEASURING:
** JUDGEMENT AND COMMON SENSE; PRACTICAL INFORMATION PLUS ABILITY TO EVALUATE AND USE PAST EXPERIENCE

SIGNIFICANT RELATIVE WEAKNESSES ON THE VERBAL ITEMS WERE NOT EXHIBITED.

PERFORMANCE ON PERCEPTUAL ORGANIZATION SUBTESTS DOES NOT INDICATE ANY SIGNIFICANT RELATIVE STRENGTHS.

SIGNIFICANT RELATIVE WEAKNESSES WERE EXHIBITED ON PERCEPTUAL ORGANIZATION SUBTESTS REFLECTING:
** SPEED OF MENTAL OPERATION AND SHORT TERM VISUAL MEMORY; ABILITY TO LEARN A NEW VISUAL-MOTOR TASK QUICKLY

IN COMPARISON TO OTHER CHILDREN JOHN'S AGE, HE EXHIBITED SIGNIFICANT STRENGTHS ON SUBTESTS MEASURING:
** JUDGEMENT AND COMMON SENSE; PRACTICAL INFORMATION PLUS ABILITY TO EVALUATE AND USE PAST EXPERIENCE
** VISUAL ALERTNESS, VISUAL RECOGNITION AND IDENTIFICATION (LONG TERM VISUAL MEMORY)
** ANTICIPATION OF CONSEQUENCES AND TEMPORAL SEQUENCING; INTERPRETATION OF SOCIAL SITUATIONS AND NONVERBAL REASONING
** ANALYSIS AND SYNTHESIS OF VISUALLY PRESENTED MATERIAL; NONVERBAL CONCEPT FORMATION AND SPATIAL VISUALIZATION
** ABILITY TO BENEFIT FROM SENSORY-MOTOR FEEDBACK; CONSTRUCTIVE ABILITY IN ABSENCE OF EXTERNAL MODEL

SIGNIFICANT WEAKNESSES RELATIVE TO HIS AGE GROUP WERE NOT SHOWN ON ANY OF THE SUBTESTS.

IMPLICATIONS:

THE FOLLOWING HYPOTHESES CONCERNING TREATMENT AND NEED FOR

FURTHER EVALUATION ARE SUGGESTED BY THE PRESENT RESULTS. THESE
HYPOTHESES SHOULD BE EVALUATED IN LIGHT OF JOHN'S CURRENT ACADEMIC
FUNCTIONING, CULTURAL AND RACIAL BACKGROUND, AND SITUATIONAL FACTORS
THAT MAY HAVE AFFECTED PERFORMANCE.

     PRESENT EVALUATION RESULTS SUGGEST THAT JOHN IS CAPABLE OF
FUNCTIONING ACADEMICALLY AT A LEVEL SOMEWHAT ABOVE THAT OF SAME-AGED
PEERS. SOME ACADEMIC ENRICHMENT EXPERIENCES MAY PROVE USEFUL IN
MAINTAINING MAXIMUM INTEREST IN CLASSROOM ACTIVITIES. IF JOHN IS
CURRENTLY EXHIBITING DIFFICULTIES THEN FURTHER PSYCHOLOGICAL
EVALUATION WOULD BE APPROPRIATE.

     TEST RESULTS INDICATE THAT GENERALLY JOHN PERFORMED
SIGNIFICANTLY BETTER ON TASKS REQUIRING PERCEPTUAL ORGANIZATION THAN
ON ITEMS REFLECTING VERBAL COMPREHENSION SKILLS. VERBAL
DEFICITS/DYSFUNCTIONS MAY BE INTERFERING WITH OPTIMAL FUNCTIONING.
FURTHER EVALUATION TO ASCERTAIN THE PRESENCE AND EXTENT OF ANY VERBAL
RECEPTIVE/EXPRESSIVE DIFFICULTIES IS RECOMMENDED. IN THE CLASSROOM,
IT MAY PROVE HELPFUL TO PRESENT MATERIAL THROUGH VISUAL MEANS RATHER
THAN VERBAL MEANS, PARTICULARLY IN SUBJECTS WHERE JOHN IS LEARNING
NEW MATERIAL OR IN AREAS WHERE REMEDIATION IS NEEDED.

                         JOHN Q. SMITH PH.D.
                         EXAMINER

NAME: WISC-R/Holliman Report

SUPPLIER: Psych Lab
1714 Tenth Street
Wichita Falls, TX 76301
(817) 723-0012

PRODUCT CATEGORY	PRIMARY APPLICATIONS
Cognitive/Ability	Clinical Assessment/Diagnosis Vocational Guidance/Counseling

SALE RESTRICTIONS American Psychological Association Guidelines

SERVICE TYPE/COST Type	Available	Cost	Discount
Mail-In	Yes	$10.00	
Teleprocessing	No		
Local	Yes	$6.00	

PRODUCT DESCRIPTION

This program produces the Holliman report for the Weschler Intelligence Scale for Children-Revised. The software is designed for use on the Apple II + and IIe computers. Scores must first be calculated and then entered into the computer. The resulting printout provides patient identifying data, a graphical presentation of the scores, and a verbal interpretation of the data.

The cost for local service refers to the cost-per-test when diskettes are purchsed in units of 20 administrations (minimum purchase).

NAME: Woodcock Reading Mastery Tests-ASSIST

SUPPLIER: American Guidance Service
Publisher's Building
Circle Pines, MN 55014
(800) 328-2560

PRODUCT CATEGORY	PRIMARY APPLICATIONS
Cognitive/Ability	Educational Evaluation/Planning Clinical Assessment/Diagnosis

SALE RESTRICTIONS American Psychological Association Guidelines

SERVICE TYPE/COST	Type	Available	Cost	Discount
	Mail-In	Yes	$0.70	
	Teleprocessing	No		
	Local	Yes	$31.50	

PRODUCT DESCRIPTION

The WOODCOCK READING MASTERY TESTS provide educational diagnosticians, reading and Title I specialists, school psychologists and learning disabilities specialists with a highly precise measure of individual reading achievement. These multipurpose tests are used to help detect reading problems, to group students for instruction, and to evaluate school reading programs. The battery is particularly valuable for both clinical and research purposes because of its broad content, age range, array of normative data, and availability in two parallel forms.

ASSIST (Automated System for Scoring and Interpreting Standardized Tests) software converts Woodcock raw test scores to derived scores instantaneously and greatly facilitates the test interpretation process. It is designed for use with an Apple II+ or IIe microcomputer operating under DOS 3.2.1 or DOS 3.3. The program gets reading grade levels, relative mastery scores, percentile ranks, and NCEs for Title I. The diskette contains storage space for pre- and post-test scores of up to 50 students.

On mail-in service, there is a minimum charge of $10.00 per order.

ASSIST FOR THE WOODCOCK READING MASTERY TESTS

STUDENT REPORT

NAME: PRACTICE RUN   TEST: PRE
TEST DATE: 5/4/82   GRADE: 2.8
FORM: A   REPORT DATE: 6/29/84

TEST	EASY READING LEVEL	READING GRADE SCORE	FAILURE READING LEVEL	RELATIVE MASTERY SCORE	PERCENTILE RANK	NORMAL CURVE EQUIVALENT
LETTER IDENTIFICATION RAW SCORE = 38	2.5	2.9	3.4	92	55	49
WORD IDENTIFICATION RAW SCORE = 81	2.6	2.9	3.3	93	56	55
WORD ATTACK RAW SCORE = 30	2.9	3.9	5.8	97	70	59
WORD COMPREHENSION RAW SCORE = 25	2.6	3.3	4.6	95	61	62
PASSAGE COMPREHENSION RAW SCORE = 34	2.8	3.5	4.6	97	71	65
TOTAL READING	2.8	3.2	4.0	96	70	58

NA = NOT AVAILABLE

ASSIST IS A TRADEMARK OF AMERICAN GUIDANCE SERVICE, INC.

NAME: Word and Number Assessment Inventory

SUPPLIER: NCS/Professional Assessment Services
P.O. Box 1416
Minneapolis, MN 55440
(800) 328-6759

PRODUCT CATEGORY

Cognitive/Ability

PRIMARY APPLICATIONS

Educational Evaluation/Planning
Vocational Guidance/Counseling

SALE RESTRICTIONS   None

SERVICE TYPE/COST	Type	Available	Cost	Discount
	Mail-In	Yes	$10.00	Yes
	Teleprocessing	No		
	Local	No		

PRODUCT DESCRIPTION

This 11-17 page narrative compares the individual's scores to those obtained by several educational and occupational groups, provides correct answers and solutions, and references self- improvement materials.

The test itself is comprised of 50 vocabulary and 30 math items in a multiple-choice format and requires an 8th-grade reading level. It takes about an hour to complete, but is untimed.

WORD AND NUMBER ASSESSMENT INVENTORY

RESULTS FOR SAMPLE   S   1   MALE   28-DEC-83

    These results are based on your answers to the Word and Number Assessment Inventory. The inventory consists of two parts -- (1) a fifty-item word section which measures your skill at knowing and defining words of varying difficulty, and (2) a thirty-item number section which measures your mathematical reasoning and computation skills for number problems of varying difficulty.

    The report of your results which appears on the following pages is divided into four parts. The first part of the report shows how many items you answered correctly for the word portion and number portion of the inventory and how your totals compare to the averages of people with different educational backgrounds. The second part of the report presents information about how your scores compare to individuals in various occupations. The third part of the report provides you with information on how you answered the items -- (1) for the word section, each of the items is listed with the correct answer and how you answered, (2) for the number section, a detailed description is given for each item that you answered incorrectly with a step-by-step solution to the problem. The fourth part provides you with additional references to help you improve your word and number skills if you so desire.

    The purpose of these results is to give you an idea of how your word and number skills, as measured by this inventory, compare to those of other groups of people. These results can help you see what areas you may need to improve if your scores are lower than the averages for an occupation you may be considering as a career, or if you are considering additional educational training. You should not be overly concerned if your scores are lower than you thought they would be. Generally, word scores will tend to increase with age as a result of daily use, while number scores will tend to decrease with age as a result of disuse. For example, unless a person works with numbers consistently, a large amount of math knowledge tends to be forgotten over the years. A low score may simply mean that you have not had the necessary educational training or that you have allowed your skills to become rusty. However, if you desire, these skills can be improved through practice.

            *

NAME: SAMPLE   S   ID: 1   DATE: 28-DEC-83   PAGE: 2

          *
          *
               PART I-A WORD SECTION SCORE
            EDUCATIONAL BACKGROUND SECTION
          *
          *

    Below is a graph showing how your word score compares with average word scores of people with varying educational backgrounds. Your score is plotted by asterisks, while the average range of scores for people with various educational backgrounds is shown by a series of dots. For example, the average range of word scores for students in college is 22-30, as indicated by the dots. By comparing your score with the range of scores for college students you can see if your word score is higher, lower, or about the same as the average range for people in college. Likewise, you can compare your score with other educational groups.

```
                                  *******
    EDUCATIONAL          AVERAGE  *YOUR *      1        2        3        4        5
    BACKGROUND            SCORE   *SCORE*  0........0........0.........0........0.........0
                          RANGE   * 25  *
                                  *******

STUDENTS IN HIGH SCHOOL   17-23                       ....... *

STUDENTS IN COLLEGE       22-30                      ...*...

ADULTS WITH NO
COLLEGE EDUCATION         27-36                    *  .......

ADULTS WITH SOME BUSINESS
OR TECHNICAL EDUCATION    29-37                     *  .......

ADULTS WITH SOME
COLLEGE EDUCATION         30-37                      *  .......

ADULTS WITH FOUR OR
MORE YEARS OF COLLEGE     35-41                       *     .......

                                           1        2        3        4        5
                                  0........0........0.........0........0.........0
```

       *
    The next page of the report, part I-B, presents the same type of information for your score on the number section.

```
* * * * * * * * * * * * * * * * * * * * * * * *
  * * * * * * * * * * * * * * * * * * * * * * * *
            PART I-B  NUMBER SECTION SCORE
            EDUCATIONAL BACKGROUND SECTION
  * * * * * * * * * * * * * * * * * * * * * * * *
* * * * * * * * * * * * * * * * * * * * * * * *
```

Below is a graph showing how your number score compares with the average number scores of people with varying educational backgrounds. Your score is plotted by asterisks, while the average range of number scores for people with various educational backgrounds is indicated by a series of dots. For example, the average range of scores for students in college is 19-24, as indicated by the dots. By comparing your score with the range of scores for college students you can see if your number score is higher, lower, or about the same as the average range for people in college. Likewise, you can compare your score with other educational groups.

```
                                    *******
EDUCATIONAL                 AVERAGE *YOUR *            1         2         3
BACKGROUND                   SCORE  *SCORE*     0.........0.........0.........0
                             RANGE  * 19  *
                                    *******

STUDENTS IN HIGH SCHOOL      16-22                            ...*...

STUDENTS IN COLLEGE          19-24                               *.....

ADULTS WITH NO
COLLEGE EDUCATION            16-21                            ...*..

ADULTS WITH SOME BUSINESS
OR TECHNICAL EDUCATION       17-23                           ..*....

ADULTS WITH SOME
COLLEGE EDUCATION            18-23                            .*....

ADULTS WITH FOUR OR
MORE YEARS OF COLLEGE        20-25                               *......

                                                  1         2         3
                                           0.........0.........0.........0
```

```
* * * * * * * * * * * * * * * * * * * * * * * *
          PART II-A  WORD SECTION
        OCCUPATIONAL GROUP COMPARISON
* * * * * * * * * * * * * * * * * * * * * * * *
```

The average word section scores of people in several different occupations have been split into four groups below. By comparing your word score with these four groupings, you can see to which group your skill at defining the fifty word items is most comparable.

WORD SCORE AVERAGE	OCCUPATIONAL EXAMPLES
- 29	Lab. technician, veterinarian assistant, waiter/waitress, printer, truck driver, machinist, nurse-licensed practical, police officer, drafter, janitor, physical therapy assistant, beautician, barber, letter carrier, plumber, hardware store owner, painter, cafeteria worker, computer oper.
30 - 34	Firefighter, automobile mechanic, security guard, food service manager, dental assistant, keypunch operator, airline reservation agent, florist, aircraft mechanic, department store sales clerk, travel agent, operating room technician, nurse-registered, emergency medical technician, executive housekeeper, radiological technician, tool and die maker, bus driver, bookkeeper, flight attendant, optician, photographer, gardener, buyer/merchandiser, surveyor
35 - 39	Conservation officer, park/forest ranger, veterinarian, chiropractor, computer programmer, purchasing agent, secretary, personnel director, child care assistant, interior designer, nurse aide, math-sci. teacher, realtor, insurance agent, court reporter, hotel manager, accountant, advertising executive, newspaper reporter, elementary teacher
40 +	Dental hygienist, legal assistant, author/writer, librarian, biologist, chemist, physicist, mathematician, exec. secretary, engineer, architect

Your word section score of 25 indicates that your skill at defining words is most similar to those adults who are in careers where there is a minimal need for written or verbal skills. While adults in these careers may work alone or be involved with the public, this public contact is often on an informal or conversational level. For example, people in service-types of occupations (such as barbers, beauticians, or police officers), skilled trades people, or drafters do not have to prepare extensive written reports or be involved in the creative or persuasive use of the language to the same degree that a secretary, author, librarian, court reporter, or salesperson does. If you are interested in a career that requires more extensive use of word skills, you may wish to consider ways of improving those skills. The better your word skills, the better you will be prepared for those occupations that deal extensively with the written and spoken word.

* *
PART II-B NUMBER SECTION
OCCUPATIONAL GROUP COMPARISON
* *

The average number section scores of people in several different occupations have been divided into four groups below. By comparing your number score with these four groupings, you can
see to which group your skill at solving the thirty number problems is most comparable.

NUMBER SCORE AVERAGE	OCCUPATIONAL EXAMPLES
- 15	Truck driver, janitor, security guard, sheet metal worker, beautician, barber, painter
16 - 18	Police officer, plumber, machinist, printer, author/writer, operating room technician, legal assistant, travel agent, child care assistant, keypunch operator, dental assistant, chiropractor, cafeteria worker, gardener
19 - 22	Veterinarian assistant, firefighter, waiter/waitress, aircraft mechanic, executive housekeeper, newspaper reporter, dental hygienist, bus driver, computer operator, laboratory technician, radiological technician, optician, hardware store owner, insurance agent, realtor, emergency medical technician, interior designer, photographer, florist, nurse-registered, nurse-licensed practical, nurse aide, physical therapy assis-tant, flight attendant, airline reservation agent, department store sales clerk, hotel manager, purchasing agent, secretary, court reporter, book-keeper, letter carrier
23 +	Drafter, auto mechanic, conserv. officer, park/forest ranger, computer programmer, physicist, surveyor, engineer, adver. exec., tool/die maker, librarian, buyer, architect, exec. secretary, accountant, psychologist, personnel director, mathematician, chemist, math-sci. teacher, biologist

Your number section score of 19 indicates that your number skills are most similar to those
of people in occupations that require them to perform some mathematical operations. They have
to take accurate measurements, plan a budget, determine the cost of products or services, or be
responsible for handling money transactions. People in these types of careers generally require
a thorough skill in basic arithmetic operations. Usually a thorough understanding of more advanced mathematics is not required. Scores in this range are slightly lower than those of individuals in occupations that depend almost exclusively on the use of math for performing various
job functions. If you are considering a career such as computer programmer, accountant, or re-
iearch scientist, you may wish to consider ways of improving your number skills.

* *
* *
PART III-A DEFINITION OF WORDS
* *
* *

Part I of the inventory presented a list of 50 words. For each of the 50 words you were
asked to choose from five possibilities another word which you believed was the closest in meaning or the best definition. Below are listed the 50 words that appeared in part I, the best answer that matched each word, and your answer. For some of the words none of the choices were
correct, and thus the correct answer was none. If you did not answer an item, then **missing**
is printed in the column for your answer. An asterisk appears beside each of the words where
your answer matched the best answer.

	WORD	BEST ANSWER	YOUR ANSWER		WORD	BEST ANSWER	YOUR ANSWER
* 1	ASTOUNDING	AMAZING	AMAZING	26	MOMENTOUS	IMPORTANT	PERIODIC
* 2	UNSAVORY	UNPLEASANT	UNPLEASANT	27	PRODIGIOUS	ENORMOUS	COMPLICATED
* 3	PROFICIENCY	SKILL	SKILL	*28	GROVEL	CRAWL	CRAWL
* 4	IMMACULATE	SPOTLESS	SPOTLESS	*29	INDOLENT	LAZY	LAZY
* 5	TOLERATE	ENDURE	ENDURE	*30	DIFFIDENT	TIMID	TIMID
6	SQUALID	FILTHY	NONE OF THESE	31	MORTIFICATION	SHAME	NONE OF THESE
7	PRUDENT	CAUTIOUS	NONE OF THESE	32	INTERIM	NONE OF THESE	FINAL
8	SOJOURN	TEMPORARY STAY	SORROW	*33	INERT	INACTIVE	INACTIVE
9	SUPPLICATE	BEG	PROVIDE	*34	SUCCINCT	CONCISE	CONCISE
*10	SIMULATE	IMITATE	IMITATE	35	REMUNERATION	PAYMENT	NOSTALGIA
*11	ABATE	LESSEN	LESSEN	36	CORROBORATE	CONFIRM	ASSOCIATE
12	GREGARIOUS	SOCIABLE	SENILE	*37	TORRENTIAL	VIOLENT	VIOLENT
13	QUIP	WISECRACK	SCANT	*38	INCESSANT	CONTINUAL	CONTINUAL
*14	INTERMINABLE	ENDLESS	ENDLESS	39	IMMINENT	NONE OF THESE	CONSPICUOUS
15	MOLLIFY	CALM	ANNOY	40	TACITURN	SILENT	DISAPPROVING
*16	SUPERFLUOUS	EXCESSIVE	EXCESSIVE	*41	ABDICATE	RENOUNCE	RENOUNCE
17	IMPLACABLE	UNALTERABLE	NONE OF THESE	*42	TENACIOUS	PERSISTENT	PERSISTENT
*18	BEMUSED	BEWILDERED	BEWILDERED	*43	SAGACIOUS	SHREWD	SHREWD
19	CITE	QUOTE	COMPUTE	44	NEFARIOUS	EVIL	UNRELIABLE
20	VACILLATE	WAVER	INOCULATE	45	LASSITUDE	WEARINESS	DEVOTION
*21	INSIPID	DULL	DULL	46	OBSEQUIOUS	SERVILE	OBVIOUS
22	CONFLAGRATION	FIRE	COOPERATION	*47	QUIESCENT	INACTIVE	INACTIVE
*23	PRECIPITOUS	STEEP	STEEP	*48	PERUSE	EXAMINE	EXAMINE
*24	TANTAMOUNT	EQUIVALENT	EQUIVALENT	49	EMULATE	IMITATE	SPEW
25	CONJECTURE	GUESS	PLAN	50	SALUTARY	REMEDIAL	RESPECTFUL

THE NUMBER OF CORRECT ANSWERS
THAT YOU GAVE = 25
WHICH IS 50 PERCENT CORRECT

```
* * * * * * * * * * * * * * * * *
* * * * * * * * * * * * * * * * *
*       PART III-B  NUMBER PROBLEMS       *
* * * * * * * * * * * * * * * * *
* * * * * * * * * * * * * * * * *
```

Part II of the inventory consisted of 30 number problems. For each of the 30 problems you were asked to choose the correct answer from several possibilities. Below are listed the number problems which you answered incorrectly. Your answer and the correct answer for each problem are shown, and the solution (SOLN.) for each problem is written out.

3. 5/9 divided by 2/3   SOLN. When dividing fractions you invert the divisor, which in this problem is 2/3, and then multiply. The problem becomes 5/9 x 3/2 which equals 15/18. This fraction reduces to 5/6, which is the correct answer.

ANS. = 5/6
YOUR ANS. = none of the choices

5.   1 1/3   SOLN. 1 1/3 is the same as 4/3 and 2 5/8 is the same as 21/8.
      x 2 5/8   4/3 x 21/8 = 84/24. 84/24 is the same as 3 12/24, which re-
      -------   duces to the correct answer of 3 1/2.
ANS. = 3 1/2
YOUR ANS. = 2 5/24

6.   2/W   SOLN. When adding fractions, find the common denominator (the bot-
      + 1/Z   tom of a fraction). In this case you first multiply W by Z
      -----   to get the common denominator (WZ). When finding a common
                           denominator, anything you do to the denominator of a frac-
                           tion must also be done to the numerator (the top of a frac-
                           tion). So, 2/W x Z/Z = 2Z/WZ and 1/Z x W/W = 1W/WZ. Now
                           the problem can be written as 2Z/WZ + 1W/WZ, which is the
                           same as (2Z + 1W)/WZ. This answer was not one of the
                           choices given, so the correct answer is none of the choices.
ANS. = none of the choices
YOUR ANS. = 3/W+Z

7. If a race car is traveling 104 miles per hour, how many miles per minute is it traveling?

SOLN. 104 miles/hour divided by 60 minutes/hour = 1 11/15 miles per minute. This choice was not given, so the correct ans-wer is none of the choices.
ANS. = none of the choices
YOUR ANS. = 1 2/3

9. A box of Crunchie Rice cereal contains 7/10 of a pound of cereal. A box of Chewey Wheat cereal contains 10.5 ounces of cereal. Both cereals have the same food value and cost the same amount. Which is the better buy?

  SOLN. Since both cereals have the same food value and cost the same amount, the brand which gives you more cereal for your money will be the better buy. There are 16 ounces in a pound. 7/10 pound X 16 ounces equals 11 1/5 ounces, which makes the Crunchie Rice cereal a better buy than the 10.5 ounce box of Chewey Wheat.

  ANS.= Crunchie Rice
YOUR ANS.= chewey wheat

10. Slim ate 1/3 of a pie. Later Tubby ate 3/4 of the remainder. What part of the total pie did Tubby eat?

  SOLN. After Slim ate 1/3, there was 2/3 left. Tubby then ate 3/4 of the 2/3 remaining, thus he ate 2/3 x 3/4 = 6/12 of the total pie. 6/12 reduces to 1/2, the correct answer.

  ANS.= 1/2
YOUR ANS.= 5/12

12. If you answer 63 problems correctly on an 87 question test, what percent correct do you have, taken to the nearest percent?

  SOLN. To find out what percent 63 is of 87, divide 63 by 87. This equals .7241 which, to the nearest percent, equals the correct answer of 72 percent.

  ANS.= 72 percent
YOUR ANS.= 75 percent

15. Shoppers will pay the lowest price per ounce for macaroni if they buy it at the store which offers--

  A) 8 ounces for $.89
  B) 12 ounces for $1.31
  C) 1 1/2 pounds for $1.88
  D) 2 pounds for $2.56
  E) all are equally good buys

  SOLN. This equals $.11125 per ounce ($.89 divided by 8 ounces)
         This equals $.10917 per ounce ($1.31 divided by 12 ounces)
         This equals $.07833 per ounce ($1.88 divided by 24 ounces)
         This equals $.08000 per ounce ($2.56 divided by 32 ounces)

  ANS.= C
YOUR ANS.= D

17. If 1/Y + 1/Y + 1/Y + 1/Y = 1/4, then Y =

  SOLN. 1/Y + 1/Y + 1/Y + 1/Y is the same as 4/Y. If 4/Y = 1/4, then y must equal 16, since 4/16 = 1/4.

  ANS.= 16
YOUR ANS.= 1/16

psychware   **775**

27. A track star wishes to run a certain distance in 20 percent less time than it usually takes. By what percent must the overall average speed be increased?

SOLN. Assume 200 yards can be run in 10 seconds (this would be 20 yards per one second). To run 200 yards 20 percent faster, it must be run 2 seconds faster or run in 8 seconds. If 200 yards are run in 8 seconds, this would be 25 yards per one second. Thus, the track star is running 5 yards per second faster than the 20 yards per second previously run. This is an increase of 25 percent in the average speed.

ANS.= 25 percent
YOUR ANS.= 20 percent

30. $(-2/3 \times -2/3)/(1 + 2/3) + 2/3 =$

SOLN. $-2/3 \times -2/3$ equals 4/9, since a negative number multiplied by a negative number equals a positive number. 4/9 divided by 1 2/3 is the same as 4/9 divided by 5/3, which equals 4/15. Thus 4/15 + 2/3 is the same as 4/15 + 10/15, which equals 14/15, the correct answer.

ANS.= 14/15
YOUR ANS.= 2 1/3

* * * * * * * * * * * * * * *
* * * * * * * * * * * * * * *
*   CLOSING COMMENTS   *
* * * * * * * * * * * * * * *
* * * * * * * * * * * * * * *

Your scores on the Word and Number Assessment Inventory have been compared with the scores of people having varying educational backgrounds and the scores of people employed in various occupations. In using the information provided by this report, keep in mind that the comparisons are based solely on the word and number skills measured by this one inventory.

If you would like to improve your word and number skills you may wish to consult some of the self-help books listed below. Usually, these books can be found in your local library, your local bookstore or can be obtained by writing the publisher.

--ARCO ARITHMETIC Q AND A REVIEW. By David R. Turner. Arco Publishing, 1973.
  Two thousand questions and answers taken from actual previous exams provide intensive practice for all tests which stress arithmetic.

--GOOD ENGLISH WITH EASE. By Samuel Beckoff, PH.D. Arco Publishing, 1972.
  Over two thousand tips for correct usage, grammar, spelling, punctuation, pronunciation and vocabulary, with hundreds of practice questions and answers.

--MATHEMATICS, SIMPLIFIED AND SELF-TAUGHT. Arco Publishing, 1968.
  Explains simply and clearly all the basic mathematics usually encountered on civil service, license, scholarship, and college entrance tests.

--SCHOLASTIC APTITUDE TEST. Simon And Schuster, 1975.
   Complete test preparation - including verbal and math practice, a 1000 word vocabulary
   test, and five full length SAT-type practice tests to help students prepare for the S.A.T.

--SCORING HIGH ON COLLEGE ENTRANCE TESTS. By David R. Turner. Arco Publishing, 1975.
   A complete study manual to prepare students for every type of college entrace exam -- including full-length professionally constructed exams and eleven specimen achievement tests.

--2300 STEPS TO WORD POWER. Arco Publishing.
   A programmed book prepared in small sequential steps to help anyone increase their
   speaking, reading, and writing knowledge of the English language.

--VOCABULARY BUILDER AND GUIDE TO VERBAL TESTS. Arco Publishing, 1973.
   Thousands of questions and answers from tests on word origins, vocabulary, verbal ability,
   analogies, antonyms, synonyms, spelling, and grammar are included in this book.

--VOCABULARY, SPELLING, AND GRAMMAR. Arco Publishing, 1975.
   A complete, intensive review course of the three subjects which occur most often on
   civil service, military, scholastic, employment, and scholarship exams.

--Cross-word puzzles in your local newspaper can be an excellent means for practicing and
   expanding your word skills.

--Many local bookstores frequently have mathematical games and puzzles in paperback form
   which can be used to refresh and expand your number skills.

01/18/80 COPYRIGHT 1980. Jean C. Johansson and Charles B. Johansson. All rights reserved.
NATIONAL COMPUTER SYSTEMS, 4401 West 76th Street, Minneapolis, Minnesota 55435.

***** END OF REPORT FOR SAMPLE   S   1   MALE 28-DEC-83 ***** 001 0012

```
* * * * * * * * * * * * * * * * * * * *
  * * * * * * * * * * * * * * * * * *
    * * SUMMARY COPY OF RESULTS * *
  * * * * * * * * * * * * * * * * * *
* * * * * * * * * * * * * * * * * * * *
```

WORD AND NUMBER ASSESSMENT INVENTORY

SECTION A.   ADMINISTRATIVE INDICES

     Total responses listed below are the number of items the individual answered on the Word
section and the Number section of the inventory. Also listed are the number of items the individual answered correctly in each section and the corresponding percent correct.

	NUMBER OF ITEMS IN THE SECTION	TOTAL RESPONSES	NUMBER CORRECT	PERCENT CORRECT
I. WORD SECTION	50	50	25	50
II. NUMBER SECTION	30	30	19	63
III. TOTAL	80	80	44	55

SECTION B. GRAPHIC REPRESENTATION

     The graphs below show how the Word and Number section raw scores of the individual compare
with the average Word and Number section scores of people with varying educational backgrounds.
The raw scores of the individual are indicated by asterisks, while the average ranges are indicated by a series of dots.

WORD SECTION SCORE
EDUCATIONAL BACKGROUND COMPARISON

```
EDUCATIONAL        AVERAGE  *******              1         2         3         4         5
BACKGROUND         SCORE    *SCORE*  0.........0.........0.........0.........0.........0
                   RANGE    * 25  *
                            *******

STUDENTS IN HIGH SCHOOL    17-23                        .......*

STUDENTS IN COLLEGE        22-30                      ...*...

ADULTS WITH NO
COLLEGE EDUCATION          27-36                              *  .......

ADULTS WITH SOME
COLLEGE EDUCATION          30-37                              *    .......

ADULTS WITH FOUR OR
MORE YEARS OF COLLEGE      35-41                              *        .......
```

NUMBER SECTION SCORE
EDUCATIONAL BACKGROUND COMPARISON

```
EDUCATIONAL        AVERAGE  *******              1         2         3
BACKGROUND         SCORE    *SCORE*  0.........0.........0.........0
                   RANGE    * 19  *
                            *******

STUDENTS IN HIGH SCHOOL    16-22                        ...*...

STUDENTS IN COLLEGE        19-24                          *.....

ADULTS WITH NO
COLLEGE EDUCATION          16-21                        ...*..

ADULTS WITH SOME
COLLEGE EDUCATION          18-23                         .*....

ADULTS WITH FOUR OR
MORE YEARS OF COLLEGE      20-25                          *......
```

SECTION C. INTERPRETATION OF SCORES

Printed below are interpretive statements based on how the word and number scores of the individual compared to the averages of individuals in various occupations.

WORD SCORE = 25

This word score indicates that the word skills of the individual are similar to those adults who are in careers where there is a minimal need for written or verbal skills. While adults in these careers may work alone or be involved with the public, this public contact is often on an informal or conversational level. For example, people in service-types of careers (such as beauticians, barbers, or police officers), skilled trades people, or drafters do not have to prepare written reports or be involved in the creative or persuasive use of the language to the same degree that a secretary, author, librarian, court reporter or salesperson does. If the individual is interested in a career that requires more sophisticated word skills, consideration should be given to improving relevant word skills. This word score does not mean that the individual would not be successful in one of those careers -- however, people in those occupations deal extensively with the written and spoken language. Generally, the better the word skills, the better will be the preparation for those careers.

NUMBER SCORE = 19

This number score indicates that the number skills of the individual are similar to those of people in occupations that require them to perform some mathematical operations. They have to take accurate measurements, plan a budget, determine the cost of products or services, or be responsible for the handling of money transactions. People in these careers generally need a thorough skill in basic arithmetic operations. Usually a thorough understanding of more advanced mathematics is not required. Scores in this range are slightly lower than those of people in occupations that depend exclusively on the use of math for performing job functions such as a research scientist or computer programmer.

NAME: WPPSI Report

SUPPLIER: Psychologistics, Inc.
P.O. Box 3896
Indialantic, FL 32903
(305) 727-7900

PRODUCT CATEGORY

Cognitive/Ability

PRIMARY APPLICATIONS

Educational Evaluation/Planning
Clinical Assessment/Diagnosis

SALE RESTRICTIONS American Psychological Association Guidelines

SERVICE TYPE/COST	Type	Available	Cost	Discount
	Mail-In	No		
	Teleprocessing	No		
	Local	Yes	$295.00	

PRODUCT DESCRIPTION

The WPPSI REPORT provides automated interpretation of the Weschsler Preschool and Primary Scale of Intelligence. The test is a battery of 10 subtests which measures the intelligence level of children ages 4-6 years. The subtests are divided into two major sections, yielding a verbal IQ, a performance (non-verbal) IQ, and a full scale IQ. The verbal section consists of the following subtests: information, vocabulary, arithmetic, similarities, and comprehension. The performance section includes: animal house, picture completion, mazes, geometric design, and block design.

The program provides for the entry of relevant demographic data, scaled scores, and behavioral observations (optional). An extensive behavioral checklist is provided to facilitate collecting behavioral observations of the child during assessment. The interpretive logic is similar in principle to that of Kaufman and Satler.

The narrative section of the printed report consists of four sections: (1) a demographic summary; (2) a description of the child and relevant test behaviors from the behavioral observation checklist; (3) a discussion of the child's significant strengths and weaknesses; and (4) interpretive implications for academic performance. The program operates on the Apple II +, IIe, and III computer systems. The price shown is for unlimited usage of the program.

```
                          WPPSI REPORT
                      PSYCHOLOGISTICS INC.

NAME:    JOHN X. DOE                DATE OF TEST:    02-27-84
SEX:     MALE                       DATE OF BIRTH:   03-26-77
SCHOOL:  ANYTOWN SCHOOL             RACE:  CAUCASIAN

              EXAMINER:  JOHN Q. SMITH PH.D.

              REASON FOR REFERRAL: EMOTIONAL PROBLEMS


THE SCORES LISTED BELOW WERE USED FOR COMPUTATIONS IN THIS REPORT.
THESE SCALED SCORES SHOULD BE CHECKED CAREFULLY FOR ERRORS.  IF
DISCREPENCIES ARE FOUND, THE ENTIRE REPORT SHOULD BE REPROCESSED.

---------------------------------------------------------------------
SCALED SCORES:
---------------------------------------------------------------------
      INFORMATION      11         ANIMAL HOUSE           7
      VOCABULARY       12         PICTURE COMPLETION     6
      ARITHMETIC        6         MAZES                  6
      SIMILARITIES      6         GEOMETRIC DESIGN      12
      COMPREHENSION    10         BLOCK DESIGN          11
      SENTENCES        10         ANIMAL HOUSE RETEST

---------------------------------------------------------------------


    *** JOHN'S TEST AGE IS 6 YEARS, 11 MONTHS, AND 1 DAY ***


---------------------------------------------------------------------
VERBAL            SCALED
SUBTESTS:         SCORE       RANGE
---------------------------------------------------------------------
INFORMATION         11     AVERAGE          ==========*
VOCABULARY          12     ABOVE AVERAGE    ===========*
ARITHMETIC           6     BELOW AVERAGE    =====*
SIMILARITIES         6     BELOW AVERAGE    =====*
COMPREHENSION       10     AVERAGE          =========*
SENTENCES           10     AVERAGE          =========*

AVERAGE VERBAL      9.16
---------------------------------------------------------------------
PERFORMANCE       SCALED
SUBTESTS:         SCORE       RANGE
---------------------------------------------------------------------
ANIMAL HOUSE         7     BELOW AVERAGE    ======*
PICTURE COMPLETION   6     BELOW AVERAGE    =====*
MAZES                6     BELOW AVERAGE    =====*
GEOMETRIC DESIGN    12     ABOVE AVERAGE    ===========*
BLOCK DESIGN        11     AVERAGE          ==========*


AVERAGE PERFORMANCE                8.40
```

780 *psychware*

```
************************************************************************

            VERBAL SCALE IQ SCORE        94   34%TILE

            PERFORMANCE SCALE IQ SCORE   89   23%TILE

            FULL SCALE IQ SCORE          91   27%TILE

************************************************************************

    95% CONFIDENCE INTERVAL FOR FULL SCALE IQ SCORE = 85 TO 97

************************************************************************

        VERBAL IQ SCORE - PERFORMANCE IQ SCORE = 5  (NS)

************************************************************************
```

SUBTEST DIFFERENCES:
```
------------------------------------------------------------------------
SUBTEST SCORE MINUS
MEAN VERBAL SCORE
------------------------
INFORMATION                     1.83        (NS)
VOCABULARY                      2.83        (NS)
ARITHMETIC                     -3.16        P<.05
SIMILARITIES                   -3.16        P<.05
COMPREHENSION                   0.83        (NS)
SENTENCES                       0.83        (NS)

SUBTEST SCORE MINUS
MEAN PERFORMANCE SCORE
------------------------
ANIMAL HOUSE                   -1.40        (NS)
PICTURE COMPLETION             -2.40        (NS)
MAZES                          -2.40        (NS)
GEOMETRIC DESIGN                3.60        P<.01
BLOCK DESIGN                    2.60        (NS)

                    SUBTEST SCALED SCORES

        INFORMATION     11          ANIMAL HOUSE          7
        VOCABULARY      12          PICTURE COMPLETION    6
        ARITHMETIC       6          MAZES                 6
        SIMILARITIES     6          GEOMETRIC DESIGN     12
        COMPREHENSION   10          BLOCK DESIGN         11
        SENTENCES       10          ANIMAL HOUSE RETEST


            VERBAL SCALE IQ SCORE        94
            PERFORMANCE SCALE IQ SCORE   89
            FULL SCALE IQ SCORE          91   (27%TILE)
```

    JOHN DOE IS A 6 YEAR OLD CAUCASIAN MALE WHO WAS REFERRED BECAUSE
OF EMOTIONAL PROBLEMS. HE IS A BROWN HAIRED, BLUE EYED PERSON OF
ABOVE AVERAGE HEIGHT AND AVERAGE BODY BUILD. AT THE TIME OF TESTING,
JOHN PRESENTED AN OVERALL NEAT APPEARANCE. DRESS WAS APPROPRIATE AND
HE WAS GENERALLY WELL GROOMED.

JOHN'S PERFORMANCE ON THE TASKS INDICATES HE IS RIGHT HAND
DOMINANT. DURING THE SESSION, NO SPEECH PROBLEMS, NO OBVIOUS SENSORY
VISUAL DIFFICULTY, AND NO OBVIOUS SENSORY HEARING DIFFICULTY WERE
OBSERVED. HE EXHIBITED APPROPRIATE SKILL WITH GROSS MOTOR MOVEMENTS
AND AWKWARDNESS IN FINE MOTOR MOVEMENTS. ACTIVITY LEVEL WAS
GENERALLY ERRATIC.

RAPPORT WITH JOHN WAS EASILY ESTABLISHED. HE WAS SOCIALLY
CONFIDENT AND COMFORTABLE IN HIS INTERACTIONS AND TALKED TO THE
EXAMINER FREELY. JOHN FREQUENTLY ASKED TO HAVE INSTRUCTIONS
REPEATED. HE EXHIBITED AN OVERALL APPROPRIATE ATTITUDE TOWARD THE
EVALUATION AND MOTIVATION WAS VARIABLE ACROSS TASKS. HIS APPROACH TO
ASSESSMENT TASKS WAS IMPULSIVE AND POORLY PLANNED. HE EXHIBITED NO
CHANGE IN APPROACH TO DIFFICULT ITEMS. CONCENTRATION WAS ERRATIC.
HE GAVE UP TOO QUICKLY. PRAISE HAD NO OBSERVABLE EFFECT. HE DID NOT
RECOGNIZE ERRORS/FAILURES. NO UNUSUAL OR BIZARRE BEHAVIORS WERE
OBSERVED DURING THE SESSION. IN GENERAL THIS IS BELIEVED TO BE AN
ACCURATE ESTIMATE OF JOHN'S CURRENT LEVEL OF INTELLECTUAL FUNCTIONING.

ON THIS ADMINISTRATION OF THE WECHSLER PRESCHOOL AND PRIMARY
SCALE OF INTELLIGENCE, JOHN OBTAINED A VERBAL SCALE IQ SCORE OF 94
AND A PERFORMANCE SCALE IQ SCORE OF 89. THIS RESULTS IN A FULL SCALE
IQ SCORE OF 91 WHICH FALLS WITHIN THE AVERAGE RANGE OF INTELLECTUAL
ABILITIES. THE FULL SCALE IQ SCORE CORRESPONDS TO THE 27%TILE WHICH
INDICATES HE IS FUNCTIONING INTELLECTUALLY AT A LEVEL EQUAL TO OR
BETTER THAN APPROXIMATELY 27% OF THE CHILDREN THE SAME AGE. OVERALL,
JOHN PERFORMED ABOUT AS WELL ON ITEMS TAPPING VERBAL COMPREHENSION
SKILLS AS HE DID ON TASKS REQUIRING PERCEPTUAL ORGANIZATION.

IN COMPARISON TO JOHN'S OVERALL PERFORMANCE ON VERBAL
COMPREHENSION ITEMS, HE DID NOT EXHIBIT SPECIFIC RELATIVE STRENGTHS
ON ANY SUBTEST.

SIGNIFICANT RELATIVE WEAKNESSES ON THE VERBAL ITEMS WERE
EVIDENCED ON SUBTESTS TAPPING:
** COMPUTATIONAL SKILLS AND ABILITY TO WORK WITH QUANTITATIVE
CONCEPTS
** LOGICAL OR ABSTRACTIVE (CATEGORICAL) THINKING

PERFORMANCE ON PERCEPTUAL ORGANIZATION SUBTESTS INDICATES
RELATIVE STRENGTH ON TASKS MEASURING:
** DEVELOPMENT OF PERCEPTUAL AND VISUAL-MOTOR ORGANIZATION SKILLS

SIGNIFICANT RELATIVE WEAKNESSES WERE NOT EXHIBITED ON ANY OF THE
PERCEPTUAL ORGANIZATION SUBTESTS.

IN COMPARISON TO OTHER CHILDREN JOHN'S AGE, HE DID NOT EXHIBIT
ANY SPECIFIC STRENGTHS ON THE DIFFERENT SUBTESTS.

SIGNIFICANT WEAKNESSES RELATIVE TO HIS AGE GROUP WERE EXHIBITED
ON SUBTESTS REFLECTING:
** COMPUTATIONAL SKILLS AND ABILITY TO WORK WITH QUANTITATIVE
CONCEPTS
** LOGICAL OR ABSTRACTIVE (CATEGORICAL) THINKING
** LEARNING ABILITY; ATTENTION SPAN; MANUAL DEXTERITY
** VISUAL ALERTNESS, VISUAL RECOGNITION AND IDENTIFICATION (LONG
TERM VISUAL MEMORY)
** PLANNING ABILITY AND PERCEPTUAL ORGANIZATION AND VISUAL MOTOR
CONTROL

IMPLICATIONS:

THE FOLLOWING HYPOTHESES CONCERNING TREATMENT AND NEED FOR
FURTHER EVALUATION ARE SUGGESTED BY THE PRESENT RESULTS. THESE
HYPOTHESES SHOULD BE EVALUATED IN LIGHT OF JOHN'S CURRENT ACADEMIC
FUNCTIONING, CULTURAL AND RACIAL BACKGROUND, AND SITUATIONAL FACTORS
THAT MAY HAVE AFFECTED PERFORMANCE.

PRESENT EVALUATION RESULTS SUGGEST THAT JOHN SHOULD BE ABLE TO
PERFORM ACADEMICALLY AT A LEVEL CONSISTENT WITH SAME-AGED PEERS. IF
ACADEMIC DIFFICULTIES ARE BEING EVIDENCED, FURTHER PSYCHOLOGICAL
EVALUATION IS WARRANTED.

COMPARED TO PERFORMANCE ON OTHER VERBAL COMPREHENSION ITEMS, JOHN
PERFORMED RELATIVELY POORLY ON ITEMS MEASURING NUMERICAL REASONING
ABILITY. LACK OF EXPOSURE TO QUANTITATIVE/ARITHMETIC CONCEPTS, POOR
CONCENTRATION/ATTENTION, LOW ACHIEVEMENT ORIENTATION, AND/OR SPECIFIC
ANXIETIES ABOUT MATH MAY BE INTERFERING WITH OPTIMAL FUNCTIONING.
BEHAVIORAL OBSERVATIONS SUGGEST THAT DIFFICULTY IN
CONCENTRATION/ATTENTION IS A POSSIBLE EXPLANATION AND SHOULD BE
EVALUATED FURTHER.

RELATIVE TO PERFORMANCE ON OTHER VERBAL COMPREHENSION TASKS JOHN
PERFORMED POORLY ON ITEMS REQUIRING LOGICAL THINKING AND VERBAL
CONCEPTFORMATION. INADEQUATE CULTURAL OPPORTUNITIES, AN OVERLY
CONCRETE APPROACH TO VERBAL TASKS, POOR CONCEPTUAL ABILITY, AND/OR
NEGATIVISM MAY ACCOUNT FOR THIS PERFORMANCE. IF BEHAVIORAL AND
CULTURAL FACTORS CAN BE RULED OUT, FURTHER EVALUATION OF VERBAL
ABSTRACTION ABILITIES IS WARRANTED.

JOHN Q. SMITH PH.D.
EXAMINER

NAME: WRI Assessment and Development Program

SUPPLIER: Winslow Research Institute
951 Mariners Island Blvd.
San Mateo, CA 94404
(415) 571-1100

PRODUCT CATEGORY	PRIMARY APPLICATIONS
Career/Vocational	Personnel Selection/Evaluation

SALE RESTRICTIONS None

SERVICE TYPE/COST	Type	Available	Cost	Discount
	Mail-In	Yes	$175.00	Yes
	Teleprocessing	No		
	Local	No		

PRODUCT DESCRIPTION

WRI's ASSESSMENT AND DEVELOPMENT PROGRAM is intended to assist in staff development efforts by objectively assessing the behavior and attitudes of employees. The ASSESSMENT AND DEVELOPMENT program is an integrated system of easy-to-understand and use components that meet the specific developmental needs of each organization. These components aid in guiding the growth and development of participants to their full potential. The people-oriented reports and overlays provide how to advice and hands-on information to help personnel plan for growth and develop profit building behavior and attitudes.

The system includes 30-40 page reports for each employee, a condensed report on each participant for that participant's manager, and an executive summary report for the organization.

NAME: WRI Selection and Development Program

SUPPLIER: Winslow Research Institute
951 Mariners Island Blvd.
San Mateo, CA 94404
(415) 571-1100

PRODUCT CATEGORY	PRIMARY APPLICATIONS
Career/Vocational	Personnel Selection/Evaluation

SALE RESTRICTIONS None

SERVICE TYPE/COST	Type	Available	Cost	Discount
	Mail-In	Yes	$140.00	Yes
	Teleprocessing	No		
	Local	No		

PRODUCT DESCRIPTION

WRI's SELECTION AND DEVELOPMENT PROGRAM measures 30 behavioral characteristics relevant to job success. Two reports are prepared from the assessment results. A condensed report provides management with basic results coordinated with a previously prepared Success Profile. A detailed 30-40 page report that can be used for staff development purposes is prepared for the applicant. Managers learn the individual differences of their employees and know which buttons to push to obtain top performance from their people. Employees obtain insight into their behavior and attitudes, enabling them to capitalize on their assets and minimize the influence of their liabilities.

PRODUCT INDEXES

This section contains five indexes that have been prepared to facilitate use of Psychware: Product Title; Product Category; Product Application; Service Listing; and Supplier. Within the Category, Application, and Service Listing indexes, a product is entered under as many headings as necessary. An asterisk (*) in front of a product title indicates that this entry is the primary one for that product.

PRODUCT TITLE

psychware **787**

PRODUCT CATEGORY

PRODUCT APPLICATION

SUPPLIER

800 *psychware*

ABOUT THE EDITOR

SAMUEL E. KRUG, Ph.D., a graduate of Holy Cross College (1965) and the University of Illinois (1968 and 1971), specializes in the fields of personality, motivation, and psychological and educational measurement and testing. In 1966, while serving as a research assistant and associate to Raymond B. Cattell, Ph.D., at the University of Illinois' Laboratory of Personality and Group Analysis, Dr. Krug began his affiliation with the Institute for Personality & Ability Testing (IPAT) where he has served as director of the Test Services Division since 1976. Dr. Krug is also the president of MetriTech, Inc., a company which he founded in 1982. As a speaker and educator, Dr. Krug has made extensive presentations throughout the United States, Canada, England, and South Africa and has served as a visiting professor in psychology at the University of Illinois. He has authored eight tests, thirteen books, twenty-five articles, and five chapters and has done extensive research in the use of computer analysis in psychological assessment procedures. Dr. Krug is a Fellow in both the American Psychological Association and the Society for Personality Assessment, is a member of the National Council on Measurement in Education, and serves as director of the Editorial Policy Board, Multivariate Experimental Clinical Research.